The Oxford Dictionary of

Slang

JOHN AYTO

OXFORD UNIVERSITY PRESS
1998

Oxford University Press, Great Clarendon Street, Oxford OX2 6DP

Oxford New York

Athens Auckland Bangkok Bogotá Buenos Aires Calcutta
Cape Town Chennai Dar es Salaam Delhi Florence Hong Kong Istanbul
Karachi Kuala Lumpur Madrid Melbourne Mexico City Mumbai
Nairobi Paris São Paulo Singapore Taipei Tokyo Toronto Warsaw

and associated companies in
Berlin Ibadan

Oxford is a trade mark of Oxford University Press

Published in the United States
by Oxford University Press Inc., New York

British Library Cataloguing in Publication Data
Data available

Library of Congress Cataloging in Publication Data
Data available

ISBN 0-19-863157-X

10 9 8 7 6 5 4 3 2 1

Designed by Jane Stevenson
Typeset in Swift and Univers by
Alliance Phototypesetters, Pondicherry
Printed in Great Britain
on acid-free paper by
Biddles Ltd
Guildford and King's Lynn

Contents

Preface

Our longstanding love affair with the undignified bits of our language—the unguarded vocabulary of conversation, the quirky slang of in-groups, the colourful outbursts of lexis in extremis—has assured us a continuing tradition of collecting such words together in dictionaries. From the earliest exposés of underworld cant from writers such as John Awdelay and Thomas Harman in the sixteenth century, through Francis Grose's pioneering *Classical Dictionary of the Vulgar Tongue* (1785), J. S. Farmer and W. E. Henley's seven-volume *Slang and its Analogues* (1890–1904), and Eric Partridge's influential *Dictionary of Slang and Unconventional English* (1936), to Jonathan Lighter's *Historical Dictionary of American Slang* (1994–), the development of colloquial English vocabulary has been voluminously and enthusiastically documented.

However, almost all of this documentation has been—not surprisingly—in alphabetical format: extremely convenient for looking up individual words, but not so useful if you are interested in the language of a particular area of activity, or if you want to find a word for a concept. That's the traditional role of the thesaurus. Thesauruses group words thematically, not alphabetically—so words expressing, for instance, 'anger' or 'similarity' can all be found together. What better format for looking at the history of English vocabulary topic by topic? That's where the *Oxford Dictionary of Slang* comes in: taking in turn each area of life and each aspect of the world that generates significant amounts of slang, it plots its lexical development over time, recording the arrival of each new item on the scene and building up a picture of how our off-guard speech has changed down the years. (If you need to access the book alphabetically, there is a full index at the back.)

Each entry has a date after it. This represents the earliest written record we have of the appearance of that word, or that meaning of that word, in English. It's important to remember that it does not necessarily mean that the word came into the language in that year. Indeed, as far as slang is concerned, it's more often than not the case that new usages have a lengthy currency in the spoken language before they start to appear regularly in print. Before dates, the letter *a* stands for 'before' and the letter *c* stands for 'approximately'.

Most entries also detail the origin of the word, if it is known, and any noteworthy features of its usage; particularize its meaning, if this is more specific than is indicated by the grouping of words to which it belongs; and illustrate it with an example taken in most cases from the *Oxford English Dictionary* or its files.

The contents of the book are based on the *Oxford Dictionary of Modern Slang*, but the number of entries has been considerably expanded, to cover more extensively that uncertain borderland between slang and colloquial usage. One person's slang is another's colloquialism, but the wider scope of this dictionary should ensure that few genuine candidates for 'slang' status escape its net. At the same time, its range is circumscribed by its format: areas rich in slang are included, but those which can barely scrape together a handful of slang terms are not. Do not expect to find every single piece of English slang here.

The dictionary concerns itself largely with words that have been current during the past hundred years or so, but some words and usages that died out earlier than that are included if they are important in illustrating the development of a particular semantic field.

My grateful thanks are due to John Simpson, chief editor of the *Oxford English Dictionary*, and to his staff on the *OED*, particularly Michael Proffitt, Sue Baines, Anthony Esposito, Jennie Miell, Hania Porucznik, Peter Sweasey, and Tania Young, for their invaluable help in scouring the files of the *OED* for information not reliably available elsewhere on the dating of English slang.

John Ayto
London, 1998

The Body and its Functions

1. **The Body and its Parts**

(See also under Fatness p. 12 and **Nakedness** p. 11)

Head

noddle (1509) Origin unknown ■ *Independent*: There are not many opportunities for them now to use their noddle rather than do what the FA tells them to do. (1991)

block (1635) Especially in the phrase *knock someone's block off* strike someone powerfully on the head ■ H. G. Wells: Many suggestions were made, from 'Knock his little block off', to 'Give him more love'. (1939)

nob (a1700) Probably a variant of *knob*; latterly (now dated) especially in the phrase *bob a nob*, a shilling a head, a shilling each

knob (1725) Dated ■ Richard Whiteing: They invariably . . . 'ketch it in the knob' in the form of a bilious headache. (1899)

napper (1785) British; origin unknown ■ G. M. Wilson: If anyone ever asked for an orangeade bottle on his napper, Fruity did. (1959)

pimple (1818) Dated ■ *Racing Song*: Sharp brains in my noble pimple. (a1887)

nut (1846) ■ *Swell's Night Guide*: She's getting groggy on her pins, and if you don't pipe rumbo, she'll go prat over nut (head over heels). (1846)

chump (1859) British; from earlier sense, lump of wood ■ Vladimir Nabokov: Think how unpleasant it is to have your chump lopped off. (1960)

twopenny, tuppenny (1859) Dated; from *twopenny loaf* = *loaf of bread*, rhyming slang for *head*; compare **loaf** (below) head ■ C. E. Montague: 'Into it, Jemmy,' I yelled. 'Into the sewer and tuck in your tuppenny.' (1928)

noggin (1866) Orig and mainly US; from earlier sense, small mug ■ P. G. Winslow: A rap on the back of the noggin that knocked her out. (1975)

filbert (1886) From earlier sense, hazel nut; compare **nut** (above) head

bonce (1889) British; from earlier sense, large playing-marble ■ Len Deighton: This threat . . . is going to be forever hanging over your bonce like Damocles' chopper. (1962)

bean (1905) Orig US ■ R. D. Paine: If these Dutchmen get nasty, bang their blighted beans together. (1923)

beezer (1915) Perhaps from Spanish *cabeza* head

lemon (1923) ■ *Coast to Coast*: If you had any brains in that big lemon you'd wipe me. (1952)

hat-rack (1942) ■ L. Hairston: If you spent half as much time tryin' to put something inside that worthless hat-rack as you did having your brains fryed. (1964)

Uncle Ned (1955) Rhyming slang ■ *Listener*: I have spent an hour fixing the big, loose curls on top of my Uncle Ned. (1964)

cruet (1966) Australian; origin uncertain; there may be some connection with **crumpet** (below) head, and compare Australian slang *crudget* head, recorded once, in 1941, of unknown origin ■ R. Beilby: 'Where did he get it?' 'Through the cruet.' (1977)

Head as repository of sanity and source of common sense

(See also under **Sanity** pp. 301–6)

onion (1890) Especially in the phrase *off one's onion* mad, crazy ■ H. G. Wells: He came home one day saying Tono-Bungay till I thought he was clean off his onion. (1909)

crumpet (1891) British; especially in the phrase *balmy* or *barmy on* (or *in*) *the crumpet* mad, crazy ■ R. H. Morrieson: It's Madam Drac, gone right off her crumpet at last. (1963)

pannikin (1894) Mainly Australian; from earlier sense, metal drinking- vessel; in the phrase *off one's pannikin* mad, crazy ■ C. J. Dennis: Per'aps I'm orf me pannikin wiv' sittin' in the sun. (1916)

noodle (1914) Compare earlier sense, fool ■ M. Trist: Take no notice. . . . She's off her noodle. (1945)

loaf (1925) Probably from *loaf of bread*, rhyming slang for *head*; especially in the phrase *use one's loaf* ■ *Jewish Chronicle*: Use your loaf. Didn't Sir Jack Cohen of Tesco . . . start the same way? (1973)

scone (1942) Australian & New Zealand; from earlier sense, round bun ■ D'Arcy Niland: I can just see you running a house. I'd give you a week before you went off your scone. (1957)

barnet (1969) British; from earlier sense, hair ■ George Sims: 'Use your barnet!' Domino said. (1969)

Hair

barnet (1931) British; short for *Barnet fair*, rhyming slang for 'hair', from the name of the London borough of *Barnet* ■ Frank Norman: They send you to a doss house, so that you can get lice in your barnet. (1962)

Hair colour

bluey (1918), **blue (1932)** Australian & New Zealand; a nickname for a red-haired person; origin unknown

Bald person

slaphead (1990) British

Face

phiz (1688) Archaic; shortened from *physiognomy*

mug (1708) Perhaps from the drinking mugs made with a grotesque imitation of the human face that were common in the 18th century ■ L. Cody: What! Miss a chance to get your ugly mug in the papers! (1986)

phizog (1811) Now dated or jocular; shortened from *physiognomy* ■ *Radio Times*: The phizog is definitely familiar. . . . 'I get recognized wherever I go.' (1980)

dial (1842) British; from a supposed resemblance to the dial of a clock or watch; compare **clock** (p. 2) *face* ■ L. A. G. Strong: You should have seen the solemn dials on all the Gardas and officials. (1958)

mooey, **moey**, **mooe (1859)** Dated; from Romany *mooi* mouth, face ■ Peter Wildeblood: All nylons and high-heeled shoes and paint an inch thick on their mooeys. (1955)

mush, **moosh (1859)** British; from earlier sense, soft matter, apparently with reference to the soft flesh of the face ■ T. Barling: A big grin all over his ugly mush. (1974)

chivvy, **chivy**, **chivey (1889)** British; short for *Chevy Chase*, rhyming slang for *face* ■ Angus Wilson: I can't keep this look of modest pride on my chivvy forever. (1958)

puss (1890) Mainly US; from Irish *pus* lip, mouth ■ Carson McCullers: When you looked at the picture I didn't like the look on your puss. (1961)

kisser (1892) From earlier sense, mouth ■ Damon Runyon: He is a tall skinny guy with a long, sad, mean-looking kisser, and a mournful voice. (1938)

map (1908) Dated ■ James Curtis: What d'you want to sit there staring at me for? I'm not a bloody oil-painting. You ought to know my map by now. (1936)

clock (1918) Compare **dial** p. 2 *face* ■ J. I. M. Stewart: His clock was still the affable Brigadier's, but you felt now that if you passed a sponge over it there'd be something quite different underneath. (1961)

pan (1923) Compare *dead-pan* ■ Eric Linklater: I never want to see that pan of yours again. (1931)

boat, **boat-race (1958)** British; rhyming slang ■ Robin Cook: We've seen the new boat of the proletariat, all gleaming eyes. (1962)

Eyes

lamps (1590) Dated; orig. poetical ■ F. D. Sharpe: He had his lamps on the copper. (1938)

peepers (a1700) From earlier sense, person who peeps ■ *Observer*: Or is it Liz Hurley? So hard to tell now the old Pendennis peepers have started to fail spectacularly. (1997)

gogglers (1821) Dated; from *goggle* look with wide eyes + *-ers* ■ W. M. Thackeray: Her ladyship . . . turning her own grey gogglers up to heaven. (1840)

mince-pies (1857), **minces (1937)** Rhyming slang ■ Robin Cook: A general look of dislike in the minces, which tremble a bit in their sockets. (1962)

saucers (1864) Dated; from the comparison of wide eyes with saucers, first recorded in the 14th century

Having bulging eyes

bug-eyed (1922) Orig US; from the verb *bug* bulge ■ Raymond Chandler: An angular bug-eyed man with a sad sick face. (1943)

Ear

lug (1507), **lughole (1895)** *lug* from earlier sense, flap of a cap, etc., covering the ears; perhaps of Scandinavian origin ■ Taffrail: Give 'im a clip under the lug! (1916)

listener (1821) Dated, mainly boxing slang; from earlier sense, person who listens ■ Pierce Egan: Hooper planted another hit under Wood's listener. (1827)

tab (1866) Orig dialect ■ *New Statesman*: Dad was sitting by the fire, behind his paper with one tab lifted. (1959)

earhole (1923) ■ *John O'London's*: Before you know it you'll be out on your earhole. (1962)

Ear swollen by blows

cauliflower ear (1896) From the distorted ear's shape ■ George Melly: Bouncers with cauliflower ears circling the dance-floor in evening dress. (1965)

thick ear (1909) British; especially in the phrase *give* (someone) *a thick ear*, hit someone hard (on the ear) ■ Taffrail: I sed I'd give yer a thick ear if yer went on worryin' me. (1916)

tin ear (1923) ■ Young & Willmott: A man with skill as a boxer, and a 'tin ear' (cauliflower ear) to prove it, had . . . prestige. (1962)

Nose

smeller (a1700) Dated, mainly boxing slang; from earlier sense, one who smells ■ *Nation*: He would rather not have to draw his claret and close his peepers and mash his smeller and break his breadbasket. (1894)

snitch (a1700) From earlier sense, a blow on the nose; ultimate origin unknown ■ L. Marshall: I'm not curious. I never had a long nose. . . . Peter . . . had a very long snitch. He had to push it into things that shouldn't have bothered him. (1965)

beak (1715) Jocular; from earlier sense, bird's bill ■ E. C. Clayton: A large, fat, greasy woman, with a prominent beak. (1865)

nozzle (1771) Dated; from earlier sense, small spout or mouthpiece; ultimately a diminutive of **nose** ■ J. H. Speke: But Bombey, showing his nozzle rather flatter than usual, said 'No; I got this on account of your lies'. (1863)

conk (1812) Perhaps a figurative application of *conch* type of shell ■ Tiresias: We soon become familiar with the regulars: . . . the keen young one whose hat is too big; the lugubrious one with the Cyrano de Bergerac conk. (1984)

scent-box (1826), snuff-box (1829) Dated boxing slang ■ Cuthbert Bede: There's a crack on your snuff-box. (1853)

sniffer (1858) ■ Robin Cook: They'll . . . look down their sniffers at you. (1962)

boko, (US) boke (1859) Origin unknown ■ P. G. Wodehouse: For a moment he debated within himself the advisability of dotting the speaker one on the boko, but he decided against this. (1961)

snoot (1861) Dialectal variant of *snout* ■ D. M. Davin: At first I was all for poking the bloke in the snoot. (1956)

snorer (1891) Compare earlier sense, person who snores

razzo (1899) Dated; probably an alteration of *raspberry* ■ James Curtis: If the queer fellow tried to come any acid he would get hit right on the razzo. (1936)

beezer (1908) Perhaps from *beezer* head, but this sense is not recorded until slightly later ■ P. G. Wodehouse: It is virtually impossible to write a novel of suspense without getting a certain amount of ink on the beezer. (1960)

schnozzle, schnozzola (1930) US; used especially as a nickname for the entertainer Jimmy Durante (1893–1980); pseudo-Yiddish (see **schnozz** (p. 3) nose, but compare also dated **nozzle** (p. 3) nose) ■ *Tamarack Review*: What a way to louse up this new magenta outfit—streaming eyes, a shiny schnozzola! (1959) ■ *Listener*: Hebrew amens are breathed through Yiddish schnozzles. (1977)

shonk (1938) From earlier sense, Jew; from the stereotypical view of Jews having large noses

schnozz, schnoz (1942) US; apparently Yiddish; compare German *Schnauze* snout ■ Roy Hayes: 'You remember what our boy looks like?' 'Gray hair, widow's peak, big schnozz, red ski parka and no luggage.' (1973)

honker (1948) Dated; probably from the sound made by blowing the nose ■ R. Park: It's yer own fault for having such a God-forgotten honker [*sc*. a large nose]. (1948)

hooter (1958) Probably from the sound made by blowing the nose ■ *Times*: Derek Griffiths is a young coloured comedian with a face like crushed rubber . . . and a hooter to rival Cyrano de Bergerac. (1972)

Mouth

gob (a1550) Mainly British; perhaps from Gaelic and Irish *gob* beak, mouth, or from *gab* talk

■ Julia O'Faolain: Would you be up to that? Just to try to get her to keep her gob shut? (1980)

hole (1607) I. & P. Opie: Habitual grumblers in London's East End receive the poetic injunction: 'Oo, shut yer moanin' 'ole.' (1959)

trap (1776) Especially in the phrase *shut one's trap*, keep silent; compare **potato trap** p. 3 mouth and obsolete slang *fly-trap* mouth (c1795) ■ Maureen Duffy: If Emily should open her great trap and spill the lot she could find herself deep in trouble. (1981)

potato trap (1785) Dated ■ W. M. Thackeray: And now Tom . . . delivered a rattling clinker upon the Benicia Boy's potato-trap. (1860)

clam, clam-shell (1825) US, dated

gash (1852) US, dated ■ Harriet Beecher Stowe: Ef Zeph Higgins would jest shet up his gash in town-meetin', that air school-house could be moved fast enough. (1878)

kissing-trap (1854) Dated

north and south (1858) British; rhyming slang ■ Frank Norman: Dust floating about in the air, which gets in your north and south. (1958)

mooey, moey, mooe (1859) Dated; from Romany *mooi* mouth, face

mush, moosh (1859) British; probably from *mush* face ■ Ian Jefferies: He said if anybody opened his mush, he'd kill 'em. (1959)

kisser (1860) = that which kisses, from earlier sense, one who kisses; compare earlier **kissing-trap** (p. 3) mouth ■ John Wainwright: Open that sweet little, lying little, kisser of yours, and start saying something that makes sense. (1973)

rag-box (1890) Dated ■ Rudyard Kipling: Now all you recruities what's drafted to- day, You shut up your rag-box an' 'ark to my lay. (1890)

yap (1900) US; probably from earlier verb sense, chatter ■ Howard Fast: They know that if they open their yaps, we'll close them down. (1977)

smush (1930) US, dated; alteration of *mush* mouth ■ Damon Runyon: He grabs Miss Amelia Bodkin in his arms and kisses her kerplump on the smush. (1935)

gate (1936) Mainly British ■ Bill Naughton: Shut your big ugly gate at once. (1966)

cake-hole (1943) ■ I. & P. Opie: Shut your cake-hole. (1959)

Teeth

peg (1598), toothy-peg (1828), toospeg (1921) Used especially by or to children ■ Agatha Christie: He took his elephant's trotters and his hippopotamus's toothy pegs and all the sporting rifles and what nots. (1931)

ivories (1782) Dated ■ *Tit-Bits*: His friend who gets one of his 'ivories' extracted with . . . skill by the same dentist. (1898)

Hampstead Heath, Hampsteads (1887) British; rhyming slang; from the name of a district in north London ■ Robin Cook: The rot had set in something horrible with her hampsteads and scotches. (1962)

tats, tatts (1906) Australian; applied especially to false teeth; from earlier sense, dice; ultimate origin unknown ■ R. Park: He heard her calling after him, 'Hey, you forgot yer tats! Don't you want yer teeth?' (1949)

pearlies (1914), pearly whites (1935) ■ Thomas Pynchon: Secretaries . . . shiver with the winter cold . . . their typewriter keys chattering as their pearlies. (1973)

snappers (1924) Applied especially to false teeth ■ *Listener:* Do your snappers fit snugly? (1958)

choppers (1940) Orig US; applied especially to false teeth ■ *Sun:* A set of false choppers were once found in the grounds of Buckingham Palace, after a Royal Garden Party. (1965)

Men's facial hair

face-fungus (1907), fungus (1925) Jocular ■ *Listener:* Svengali . . . with his face-fungus and rolling eyes. (1959)

door-mat (1909) British, dated ■ J. R. Ware: *Door-mat*, the name given by the people to the heavy and unaccustomed beards which the Crimean heroes brought home from Russia in 1855–56. . . . By 1882 the term came to be applied to the moustache only. (1909)

five o'clock shadow (1937) Applied to a growth of stubble which becomes visible in the late afternoon on the face of a man who has shaved earlier in the day ■ *New Yorker:* Mr. Nixon, however, was given a deep five-o'clock shadow by the Rumanian artist. (1969)

bum fluff (1961) British; applied to the incipient growth of hair on the face of an adolescent boy ■ *New Musical Express:* You must be a pretty crap Satan if you can only appeal to bumfluff-faced adolescent, social inadequates out to shock their mums. (1995)

Beard

ziff (1917) Australian & New Zealand; origin unknown ■ George Melly: 'Better get rid of that ziff,' she said pointing to his embryonic beard. (1981)

Moustache

tash, tache (1893) Abbreviation ■ Roger Simons: 'E 'ad a little tash, just under 'is nose. (1965)

mo (1894) Australian & New Zealand; abbreviation ■ K. Garvey: His mo he paused to wipe. (1981)

walrus moustache (1918) Applied to a large moustache which overhangs the lips; from its similarity to the whiskers of a walrus ■ Theodora Fitzgibbon: I remember Conan Doyle as a large man with sad thoughtful eyes and a walrus moustache. (1982)

soup-strainer (1932) Jocular; applied to a long moustache ■ Ellis Lucia: A soulfully humming male quartet in soup-strainers and sideburns. (1962)

cookie-duster (1934) US, jocular

stash (1940) US; abbreviation ■ *Time:* Sandy is a superannuated swinger, complete with stash, burns and a 17-year-old hippie on his arm. (1971)

taz (1951) Variant of *tash* moustache ■ Maureen Duffy: He was proud of his little toothbrush taz and elegant white raincoat. (1969)

mush (1967) Shortening and alteration of *moustache* ■ Kenneth Giles: He read one of those Service ads. . . . You know, a young bloke with a mush telling to troops to go plunging into the jungle. (1969)

Whiskers

sluggers, slugger whiskers (1898) Orig and mainly US; applied to ear-to-chin whiskers

Shave

ocean wave (1928) Dated; rhyming slang ■ *John O'London's:* I 'as my ocean wave an' when I've got my mince pies open I goes down the apples and pears. (1934)

Bearded person

beardie, beardy (1941) ■ *Spectator:* There were more than forty thousand of us—weirdies and beardies, colonels and conchies, Communists and Liberals. (1960)

Arm

wing (1823) ■ *Sun* (Baltimore): He came up with a bad arm during the season, and had been troubled before with it. If the big man's wing behaves this year he should be of considerable value. (1947)

Hand

paw (1605) Often jocular; from earlier sense, animal's foot ■ Ernie Money: He stuck out his paw, and said Good-bye. (1887)

mauler (1820) Often applied specifically to the fists; compare earlier sense, one who mauls; also obsolete slang *mauley* hand, probably from the verb *maul*, but perhaps connected with Shelta *malya*, said to be a transposition of Gaelic *lamh* hand ■ John Rossiter: You keep your big maulers off this. (1973)

flipper (1832), flapper (1833) Dated; compare contemporary sense, broad fin of a fish, etc. ■ W. H. Smyth: The boatswain's mate exulted in having 'taken a lord by the flipper'. (1867) ■ *Lessons of Middle Age:* Come, Frank, and extend the flapper of friendship. (1868)

mud-hook (1850) Dated

duke, dook (1859) Often applied specifically to the fists; probably short for *Duke of Yorks*, rhyming slang for *forks* fingers ■ Jessica Mitford: The funeral men are always ready with dukes up to go to the offensive. (1963)

mitt (1896) Orig US; from earlier sense, mitten ■ Raymond Chandler: 'Freeze the mitts on the bar.' The barman and I put our hands on the bar. (1940)

meat-hook (1919)

Left-handed person

molly-dook, molly-dooker, molly-duke **(1941)** Australian; probably from obsolete slang *molly* effeminate man, from the female personal name *Molly*, a pet form of *Mary* + *dook*, variant of *duke* hand; compare earlier Australian *mauldy* left-handed, *molly-hander* left-hander ■ *Northern Daily Leader* (Tamworth): Five of the top seven batsmen doing battle for Australia are left-handers. Kepler Wessels, Wayne Phillips, etc. . . . are all molly dookers. (1983)

Fingers

forks (a1700) Dated; applied especially to the fingers as used for picking pockets; from earlier sense, prongs of a fork ■ Harrison Ainsworth: No dummy hunter had forks so fly. (1834)

pinky, pinkie (1808) Mainly North American & Scottish; applied specifically to the little finger; from Dutch *pinkje*, diminutive of *pink* little finger ■ W. H. Auden: O lift your pin-kie, and touch the win-ter sky. (1962)

Breasts

titties (1746), tits (1928) *tit*, variant of *teat*; *titty*, originally a dialectal and nursery diminutive of *teat*, now as a diminutive of *tit* ■ *Oz*: Mary Anne Shelley, with the best tits off-off-Broadway. (1969) ■ *Screw*: Man, those nice firm buttocks and titties filled that bikini to overflowing. (1972)

charlies (1873) Unexplained use of the male personal name *Charlie*, diminutive of *Charles* ■ Peter Wildeblood: Carrying her famous bosom before her like the tray of an usherette she was disconcerted to hear . . . a nasal cry of: 'Coo, look at them charlies!' (1957)

bazooms (1928) Orig US; jocular alteration of *bosoms* ■ Elmore Leonard: Another case of Bio-Energetic Breast Cream ... for South Beach bazooms. (1983)

boobs (1929), boobies (1934) *boob*, probably shortened from *booby*; *booby*, probably alteration of dialectal *bubby* breast ■ *Guardian*: The characters were constantly referring to her large bosom (even descending to calling them 'big boobies'). (1968) ■ *Daily Mirror*: If people insist on talking about her boobs, she would rather they called them boobs, which is a way-out word, . . . rather than breasts. (1968)

knockers (1941) Perhaps from the notion of pendulous breasts knocking together ■ M. J. Bosse: I'm jealous. She has those big knockers, and I'm afraid you like them. (1972)

jugs (1957) Orig US; perhaps from the notion of a jug as a receptacle for milk or other liquids ■ Tom Wolfe: She must allow him the precious currency he had earned, which is youth and beauty and juicy jugs and loamy loins. (1987)

bristols (1961) British; short for *Bristol Cities*, rhyming slang for *titties*; from the name of *Bristol City* Football Club ■ Robin Cook: These slag girls used to go trotting upstairs . . . arses wagging and bristols going. (1962)

norks (1962) Australian; origin uncertain; perhaps from the name of the *Norco* Co-operative Ltd., a butter manufacturer in New South Wales ■ *Australian* (Sydney): The minimum requirement is an 'Aw, whacko, cop the norks!' followed by at least a six decibel wolf whistle. (1984)

bazookas (1963) Applied especially to large breasts; from earlier sense, portable rocket launcher, but presumably suggested mainly by *bazooms*

melons (1972) Orig US; applied especially to large breasts ■ *Pussycat*: Her full and shapely melons swung and swayed . . . as she moved. (1972)

bazongas, bazoongas, bazonkas (1972) US; probably a jocular alteration of **bazookas**

dingleberries (1980) From the earlier US sense, a cranberry, *Vaccinium erythrocarpum*, of the south-eastern US. The origin of *dingle* is uncertain ■ *British Journal of Photography*: Daddy says knockers and jugs and bazooms and dingleberries. . . . And then he laughs and goes 'wuff! wuff!' (1980)

Large-breasted

stacked, stacked up, well stacked (1942) Orig US; used as a term of male approval ■ D. Shannon: A cute little blond chick . . . really stacked. (1981)

Ribs

slats (1898) Orig and mainly US ■ John Masefield: Billy bats Some stinging short-arms in my slats. (1911)

Abdomen

victualling office (1751) Dated, mainly boxing slang; from earlier sense, office concerned with providing naval food supplies ■ *Sporting Magazine*: Spring put in a heavy claim on his opponent's victualling office. (1820)

bread-basket (1753) From earlier sense, receptacle for bread; now often used with reference to the abdomen as the target for a punch or shot ■ John Bristed: Our landlady, who was standing . . . with her mouth wide open, and her hands locked together . . . resting on her prominent breadbasket. (1803)

bingy, bingee, bingie, bingey, binjy (1832) Australian; from Aboriginal (Dharuk) *bindi* ■ *Australasian Post*: Plenty tucker here! Just look at those binjies! (1963)

tummy (1869), tum (1864), tum-tum (1869) *tummy* representing a childish alteration of *stomach*; *tum* shortened from *tummy*; *tum-tum* reduplication of *tum* ■ James Joyce: Cissy poked him out . . . of fun in his wee fat tummy. (1921) ■ *Time*: To re-establish old wisdom and simple certitudes: hot chestnuts in the hand, calories in the tum. (1977)

Derby kelly, Darby kelly, Derby kel (1906), kelly (1970) British; rhyming slang for *belly* ■ Terence Rattigan: Just that ride home. Cor, I still feel it down in the old derby kel. (1942) ■ Alfred Draper: My old kelly was rumbling and I fancied a pie and chips. (1970)

Maconochie (1919) Dated British services' slang, jocular; from earlier sense, stewed meat

amidships (1937) Used to refer to the striking of a blow in the abdomen; from earlier sense, in the middle of a ship, implying the most crucial or vulnerable part ■ *Times*: Buss hit him painfully amidships and he had to leave the field. (1961)

puku (1941) New Zealand; Maori ■ P. Grace: Your puku's getting in the way. (1978)

beer belly (1942), beer gut (1976) Used to refer to an abdomen enlarged by drinking beer ■ *Rolling Stone*: Woods pauses to tuck his shirt between a beer belly and a silver belt buckle. (1969) ■ *Los Angeles Times*: Fregosi took to wearing the jacket . . . when he began to develop a beer gut while trying to play for the Mets. (1986)

Ned Kelly (1945) Australian; rhyming slang for *belly*; from the name of *Ned Kelly* (1857–80), Australian bushranger ■ Barry Humphries: If I don't get a drop of hard stuff up me old Ned Kelly there's a good chance I might chunder in the channel. (1970)

Navel

belly button (1877) ■ J. B. Priestley: If you'd ever gone to school with your belly-button knockin' against your backbone. (1946)

Waist

middle (971) ■ George Borrow: He has got it buckled round his middle, beneath his pantaloons. (1842)

Heart

ticker (1930) Orig US; from the resemblance of the beating of the heart to the steady ticking of a clock ■ J. Cartwright: Put something at the bottom about your heart. Say, 'The ticker seems to be a little dodgy at the moment'. (1980)

Intestines

guts (a1000) Orig a standard term, but now colloquial when applied to human beings

inside (1741), insides (1840) ■ Charles Kingsley: So now away home; my inside cries cupboard. (1855)

innards (1825) Dialect pronunciation of *inwards* intestines, from noun use of *inward* internal ■ J. T. Farrell: His innards made slight noises, as they diligently furthered the process of digesting a juicy beefsteak. (1932)

shitbags (1937) Dated

comic cuts, comics (1945) Australian; rhyming slang for *guts*; from *comic cuts*, originally the name of a children's paper, later applied to strip cartoons ■ F. A. Reeder: I got a bit crook in the comic cuts and had to run for the latrine about ten times a day. (1977)

kishke, kishka, kishkeh, kishker (1959) From earlier sense, sausage made with beef intestine; from Yiddish ■ Leo Rosten: I laughed until my *kishkas* were sore. (1968)

Womb

oven (1962) Especially in expressions suggesting pregnancy, in allusion to *have a bun in the oven* be pregnant ■ David Fletcher: She's in the club, you know. Got one in the oven, eh? (1976)

Pubic hair

pubes First recorded in the late 16th century as a two-syllable word adopted from Latin *pubes* pubic hair; the slang usage, pronounced /pju:bz/, is a comparatively recent development ■ *International H & E Monthly*: If I did shave my pubes I would end up sporting lots of elastoplast in all the places where I had cut myself. (1990)

bush (c1650) ■ Anthony Powell: He insisted on taking a cutting from my bush—said he always did after having anyone for the first time. (1973)

thatch (1933) ■ C. McKay: Looking to the stand where the girls were, Tack, indicating Rita, said, 'And tha's a finer piece a beauty than thisere. Man! Man! Oh how I'd love to get under her thatch.' (1933)

Genitalia

thing (c1386) Euphemistic; applied especially to the penis ■ J. P. Donleavy: Men wagging their things at you from doorways. Disgusting. (1955)

privates (1602) Shortened from earlier *private parts*; first recorded as a pun on the sense 'intimate friends' in Shakespeare *Hamlet* 2 ii: In the middle of her favour . . . her privates, we ■ Ed McBain: The dancer . . . wiped the black man's glasses over what the Vice Squad would have called her 'privates'. (1979)

sex (1938) ■ Herbert Gold: His eyes turned to his pants, gaping open, and his sex sick as an overhandled rattler gaping through. (1956) ■ Ted Allbeury: The narrow white briefs that barely captured her sex. (1977)

Male genitals

jock (a1790) Origin unknown; perhaps from an old slang word *jockum, -am* penis ■ Ian Cross: Sprigs clattering on the floor, knees, jocks, backsides and shouting as everybody dressed. (1960)

family jewels (1916) Orig US; often applied specifically to the testicles; from the notion of a husband's genitals being precious, and vital to the fathering of a family ■ Peter O'Donnell: 'E might be in 'ospital. . . . I'm not quite sure what spirits of salts does to the old family jewels. (1965)

crown jewels (1970) Often applied specifically to the testicles; from the notion of preciousness; compare **family jewels** p. 6 in same sense ■ J. Mitchell: This one's [sc a horse] a gelding. . . . He lost his crown jewels. (1986)

lunchbox (1992) British; mainly applied to the genitals visible through tight clothing ■ *Guardian*: 'What is Linford

Christie's lunchbox?' Mr Justice Popplewell . . . asked the Olympic gold medallist in bemusement. 'They are making a reference to my genitals, your honour,' replied the agitated athlete. (1998)

Penis

weapon (a1000) ■ H. & R. Greenwald: This sexual thrill still comes over me whenever I see a horse flashing his weapon. (1972)

yard (1379) Dated; from earlier sense, rod; compare Latin *virga* rod, penis ■ John Payne: Aboulhusn . . . abode naked, with his yard and his arse exposed. (1884)

cock (c1450) Probably from the notion of the cock as the male bird ■ *Landfall*: 'She had her hand on his cock.' 'There's no need to be crude.' (1969)

tool (1553) ■ Leonard Cohen: You uncovered his nakedness!—You peeked at his tool! (1966)

prick (1592) ■ Ed McBain: Jocko had . . . a very small pecker. . . . Blood on the bulging pectorals, tiny contradictory prick. (1976)

meat (1595) See also **beat the meat** under To masturbate at **Sex** (p. 79) ■ *Black Scholar*: She was in his arms . . . and grabbing his erect meat. (1971)

needle (1638) Dated ■ Erica Jong: 'Won't ye have a Nestlecock?' cries the second Tart, '. . . a Needlewoman fer yer e'er-loving Needle?' (1980)

pego (1680) Origin unknown ■ H. R. F. Keating: There's some as likes . . . her dirty old fingers round their pego. (1974)

pudding (1719), pud (1939) From earlier sense, sausage; see also **pull one's pudding** under To masturbate at **Sex** (p. 79) ■ James Joyce: There's a lot of lecit pleasure coming bangslanging your way, Miss Pimpernelly satin. For your own good, you understand, for the man who lifts his pud to a woman is saving the way for kindness. (1939)

machine (1749) Dated ■ Philo cunnus: I then seized his stiff machine in my grasp. (c1863)

root (1846) ■ Kate Millett: It measures intelligence as 'masculinity of mind', condemns mediocre authors for 'dead-stick prose', praises good writers for setting 'virile example' and notes that since 'style is root' (penis), the best writing naturally requires 'huge loins'. (1970)

Johnson, Jim Johnson (1863) Arbitrary use of the surname *Johnson* ■ *Screw*: So I went to take my turn with the hopes of somehow getting my *Jim Johnson* wet. (1972)

John Thomas (1879), John, john (1934) Arbitrary use of a male name ■ *Times Literary Supplement*: The grotesquely coy accounts of sex, during which Tony tells us that his 'John Thomas' was 'up and raring to go'. (1972) ■ David Ballantyne: How often did the nurse find him with his old john lying limply? (1948)

dick (c1888) Pet form of the male forename *Richard*; compare earlier sense, riding whip ■ Philip Roth: You might have thought that . . . my dick would have been the last thing on my mind. (1969)

dingus (c1888) US; compare earlier sense, whatchamacallit

dong (a1900) Mainly US; origin uncertain; perhaps from *Dong*, name coined by Edward Lear (1877) for an imaginary creature with a luminous nose ■ Philip Roth: I was wholly incapable of keeping my hands off my dong. (1969)

pisser (1901) Now mainly in *pull someone's pisser* pull someone's leg; see under **To make fun of someone or something** at Ridicule (pp. 330–1).

old man (1902) ■ Brian Aldiss: She had been opening up her legs before the reprise. Those glorious mobile buttocks. . . . I felt my old man perking up again at the memory. (1971)

pecker (1902) Mainly US; perhaps from the earlier phrase *keep one's pecker up* remain brave or optimistic ■ N. Levine: Ground sunflower seeds. . . . This will make your pecker stand up to no end of punishment. (1958)

peter (1902) From the male forename ■ Joseph Wambaugh: If you look very closely you can see a gerbil's dick, but not a parakeet's peter. (1977)

rod (1902) Applied especially to the erect penis ■ Ezra Pound: His rod hath made god in my belly. (1934)

organ (1903) Euphemistic; often in the phrase *male organ* ■ M. Campbell: He had the largest organ that anyone had ever seen. It was a truncheon. (1967)

willy, willie (1905) British; from a pet form of the male forename *William* ■ P. Angadi: We used to hold each other's willies. . . . We didn't know about sex then. (1985)

micky (1922) From a pet form of the male forename *Michael* ■ James Joyce: I'll put on my best shift and drawers to let him have a good eyeful out of that to make his micky stand for him. (1922)

middle leg (1922) ■ Dylan Thomas: Men should be two tooled and a poet's middle leg is his pencil. (1935)

tube (1922) ■ James Joyce: I suppose the people gave him that nickname [*sc.* Mr de Kock] going about with his tube from one woman to another. (1922)

putz (1934) Mainly US; Yiddish, from Middle High German *putz* ornaments ■ Philip Roth: He simply cannot—*will* not—control the fires in his putz, the fevers in his brain. (1964)

whang, wang (1935), whanger, wanger (1939) Orig and mainly US; *whang* from earlier sense, thong ■ G. Hammond: Maybe you're not as ready with your whang as you were, or maybe you couldn't keep it up. (1981) ■ Milton Machlin: She didn't get the idea so fast, so he whipped the old whanger out of his union suit and laid it on the table in front of her. (1976)

pencil (1937) ■ Dick Francis: That Purple Emperor strain is as soft as an old man's pencil. (1967)

dingdong (1944) US jocular

sausage (1944) Australian; mainly in the jocular phrase *hide the sausage* have sexual intercourse ■ D. Williamson: Raylene's a hell of a nice girl but the word is she's not a great one for hiding the sausage. (1977)

plonker (1947) Not recorded in print before 1947, but reported in use around the time of World War I; origin unknown; compare dated Australian slang *plonker* explosive shell
■ *Loaded*: An appendage of some magnificence, news of his powerhouse plonker brought the groupies . . . ever-knocking at the Hendrix bedroom door. (1996)

todger, tadger (1951) Origin unknown
■ *Sunday Sport*: My todger stood to attention as she joked: 'I'm sure that it winked at me then!' (1994)

winkle (1951) From earlier sense, small mollusc; applied especially to a small boy's penis ■ Ted Hughes: O do not chop his winkle off His Mammy cried. (1970)

dork (1961) Mainly US; origin uncertain; perhaps a variant of *dirk* dagger, influenced by *dick* penis
■ *Spectator*: A man with one leg and a vermilion bladder, violet stomach and testicles and a scarlet dork is seen putting it into another amputee. (1984)

stalk (1961) Applied especially to the erect penis
■ Alan White: I had a stalk on me as long as my arm. A right handful, that one. (1976)

rig (1964) ■ Martin Amis: All weekend I cried, . . . thought of ways of committing suicide, . . . considered lopping off my rig with a razor-blade. (1973)

wee-wee (1964) From earlier sense, urination
■ *Screw*: [The] self-righteous defender of what he thought to be his threatened wee wee, could not contain his machismo. (1977)

ding (1967) US; compare **ding-a-ling** p. 8, **dingdong** p. 7, **dingus** p. 7

swipe (1967) US, Black English ■ I. Slim: Slim, pimping ain't no game of love, so prat 'em and keep your swipe outta 'em. (1967)

ding-a-ling (1968) ■ R. H. Rimmer: My damned ding-a-ling was pointing my bathrobe into a tent. (1975)

prong (1969) ■ Martin Amis: This old prong has been sutured and stitched together in a state-of-the-art cosmetics lab. (1984)

tonk (1970) Compare earlier, mainly Australian senses, fool, homosexual man ■ John Carey: Most of his boyhood was spent worrying about the size of his 'tonk' (as he disarmingly dubs it). (1980)

knob (1971) ■ *Melody Maker*: No pictures of pop stars' knobs this week due to a bit of 'Spycatcher' type censorship round these parts. (1987)

meat tool (1971) Compare **meat** p. 7 and **tool** p. 7 ■ Bernard Malamud: What do you do . . . with your meat tool? You got no girl, who do you fuck other than your hand? (1971)

shaft (1971) ■ Brian Aldiss: It was never enough merely to lower your trousers—they had to come off, . . . so that you could crouch there naked but for your shirt, frantically rubbing your shaft. (1971)

chopper (1973) ■ Jonathon Green: We all know who's got the big choppers, and there's no way you can have a big chopper and money and power. (1993)

dipstick (1973) From earlier sense, rod for measuring depth liquid, especially engine oil;

probably reinforced by *dip one's wick* (of a man) have sex ■ *Maledicta*: I overheard in a cinema once the cry 'Keep your lipstick off my dipstick'. (1980)

An erection of the penis

horn (1785) ■ *Guardian*: Dirty old goat. . . . He only bows his head to get his horn up. (1972)

cock-stand, stand (1866) ■ Angus Wilson: Marcus . . . found, as his eyes took in the young man's flirtatious glance, that he was beginning a cock-stand. (1967) ■ *Index Expurgatorius of Martial*: Maevius, who while sleeping only gets A piss-proud stand that melts away on waking. (1868)

hard-on, hard (1893) ■ *Screw*: Billy and I talked down our hardons and . . . went downstairs to load the truck. (1972)

ramrod (1902) ■ Alan Sillitoe: I'd undone my belt and zip on our way across, and fell onto her with my ramrod already out. (1979)

rise (1949) Usually in *get a rise* ■ Martin Amis: 'Have you fucked Sue? . . . What was it like?' . . . 'It was okay, except I couldn't get a proper rise.' (1973)

stiff (1980)

Testicles

stones (1154) Originally in standard use, but now slang

balls (*a*1325) From their approximately spherical shape ■ D. H. Lawrence: She . . . gathered his balls in her hand. (1928)

bollocks (1744), **ballocks** (1382) *bollock*, variant of *ballock*, from late Old English *bealluc* testicle; related to *ball* spherical object ■ *Landfall*: Fine specimen of a lad, my Monty. All bollocks and beef. (1968)

knackers (1866) From earlier sense, castanets, from *knack* make a sharp cracking noise
■ Graham Greene: I may regret him for a while tonight. His knackers were superb. (1969)

nuts (1915) ■ Roger Busby: Russell got a boot in the nuts. (1973)

cobblers (1936) British; short for *cobbler's* (or *cobblers'*) *awls*, rhyming slang for *balls* ■ James Curtis: Well, they got us by the cobblers. (1936)

goolies (1937) Apparently of Indian origin; compare Hindustani *gol** bullet, ball, pill
■ *Guardian*: To get a performance out of them [*sc* actors] . . . it is sometimes necessary to kick them in the goolies. (1971)

pills (1937) From earlier sense, ball ■ Adam Diment: I . . . wished I had followed up my elbow in the throat with a hefty boot in his peasant pills. One in the balls is worth two in the teeth—a motto of unarmed combat instructors. (1968)

rocks (1948) See also **get one's rocks off** under To have sex (with) at Sex p. 76 ■ John Braine: I'd get a swift kick in the rocks. (1975)

dingdongs (1957) US, jocular; compare **dingdong** p. 7 penis

cojones (1966) From Spanish, plural of *cojón* testicle ■ **Truman Capote**: The baseball field was mud up to your *cojones*. (1966)

Female genitals

cunt (**c1230**) Middle English *cunte*, *count(e)*, ultimately from Germanic **kuntōn* ■ **Henry Miller**: O Tania, where now is that warm cunt of yours? (1934)

hole (1592) ■ **Thomas D'Urfey**: It has a Head much like a Mole's, And yet it loves to creep in Holes: The Fairest She that e'er took Life, For love of this, became a Wife. (1719)

meat (1611) ■ **Germaine Greer**: It would be unbearable, but less so, if it were only the vagina that was belittled by terms like *meat*. (1970)

slit (1648) ■ *Rolling Stone*: What am I going to call it? Snatch, Twat? Pussy? Puss puss, nice kitty, nice little animal that's so goddam patronizing it's almost as bad as saying 'slit'. (1977)

twat, **twot(t** (1656) Origin unknown ■ **Patrick White**: This young thing with the swinging hair and partially revealed twat. (1973)

muff (1699) From the supposed resemblance between the pubic hair and a fur muff ■ **Henry Miller**: The local bookie's got Polaroids of her flashing her muff. (1973)

honey-pot (1709) ■ **Germaine Greer**: If a woman is food, her sex organ is for consumption also, in the form of *honey-pot*. (1970)

quim (1735) Of uncertain origin; perhaps related to obsolete *queme* pleasant ■ **H. R. F. Keating**: Is it worse to have it on me belly than to have it in me quim? (1974)

gash (**c1866**) From earlier sense, cut ■ *Viz*: 'Hey, I think we're in here, San!' 'Aye! I'm juicin' up already. A couple more o' these an' I'll be frothin' at the gash.' (1991)

fanny (1879) Mainly British; origin unknown ■ **James Joyce**: Two lads in scoutsch breeches went through her . . . before she had a hint of hair at her fanny to hide. (1939)

pussy (1880), **puss** (1902) Probably from the supposed resemblance between a cat's fur and the pubic hair, but compare Old Norse *púss* pocket, pouch, Low German *pūse* vulva and Old English *pusa* bag ■ **Jimmy O'Connor**: He killed about five prostitutes, cut them to pieces and stuffed various objects up their pussies. (1976)

minge (1903) Origin unknown ■ *New Direction*: They've all . . . scented and talced their minges. (1974)

snatch (1904) Perhaps from earlier obsolete sense, a brief fondle or act of sexual intercourse ■ **Philip Roth**: Know what I did when I was fifteen? Sent a lock of my snatch-hair off in an envelope to Marlon Brando. (1961)

box (1916) Mainly US; previously in use in the 17th century ■ **R. Drewe**: I've seen some great tits and some of the bushiest boxes you could imagine. (1983)

jelly roll (1927) US, mainly Black English; from earlier sense, cylindrical cake containing jelly or jam ■ **Bernard Malamud**: Irene Lost Queen I miss To be between Your Jelly Roll. (1971)

pocketbook (1942) US; from earlier sense, purse or handbag; probably either from the supposed resemblance between the labia and a closed or folded purse, or from the notion of the vagina as a receptacle (compare **box** p. 9) ■ **Maya Angelou**: Momma had drilled into my head: 'Keep your legs closed, and don't let nobody see your pocketbook.' (1969)

zatch (1950) Perhaps an alteration of *satchel* in similar slang sense ■ **Robert Dentry**: Scotsmen playing the bagpipes give me a pain in the prick. . . . Pathan tribesmen playing them is enough to make the harlot of Jerusalem snatch her zatch! (1971)

Clitoris

clit, **clitty** (**c.1866**) Abbreviation ■ *Gay Times*: Now available. . . . Set of 4 clit stimulators. (1990)

(little) man in the boat (1979)

Buttocks

arse (Old English), **ass** (1860) *arse*, Old English *ærs*; *ass* mainly US; originally in standard use, but now slang ■ *Guardian*: Bush's rhetoric has occasionally dropped to the level of schoolboy abuse: 'Saddam is going to get his arse kicked.' (1991)

tail (1303) Now mainly US; now mainly in figurative phrases, such as *work one's tail off*, or applied to a woman's buttocks and genital area regarded as an object of sexual desire ■ **William Faulkner**: This is the first time you've had your tail out of that kitchen since we got here except to chop a little wood. (1942) ■ *Transatlantic Review*: He had been after her tail for months, but Judy, being an old-fashioned girl, declined his advances. (1977)

bum (1387) Mainly British; origin unknown ■ *Looks*: Begin with a warm-up and concentrate on your bum and thighs, and work on your boobs and tum as well when you turn the poster over. (1989)

butt (**c1450**) From probable earlier sense, broader end of something; originally in standard use, but now slang, mainly US ■ **John Bartlett**: The word is used in the West in such phrases as, 'I fell on my butt,' 'He kick'd my butt'. (1860)

backside (**c1500**) From earlier sense, rear part ■ *Gentleman's Magazine*: He shall fall on his back-side. (1827)

prat (1567) Orig criminals' slang; origin unknown ■ **David Delman**: I'm a *shmo* about tennis, so if I fall on my prat a time or two you have to bear with me. (1972)

cheeks (**a1600**) Used especially with reference to the two halves of the buttocks ■ **Norman Mailer**: A car . . . is already a girl. . . . The tail-lights are cloacal, the rear is split like the cheeks of a drum majorette. (1959)

moon (1756) Dated; from the shape of the buttocks; used in the singular and the plural with the same meaning ■ **Samuel Beckett**: Placing her hands upon her moons, plump and plain. (1938)

rass (1790) Jamaican; by metathesis of *arse* ■ **A. Salkey**: You class-war rass hole, you! (1959)

rear (1796) Euphemistic ■ **N. R. Nash**: Just once is enough, Baby. (*She slaps her on the rear*) Come on—get to work. (1949)

behind (*a*1830) Euphemistic ■ George Bernard Shaw: You can say 'If I catch you doing that again I will ... smack your behind.' (1928)

duff (*c*1835) US; origin unknown

buns (1877) US; from the hemispherical shape of the buttocks ■ Elmore Leonard: She saw ... a white band below his hips, sexy, really nice buns. (1985)

jacksy, jacksie, jaxey, jaxie, jacksy-pardo, jacksy-pardy (1896) From the male personal name *Jack* + *-sy* ■ Alfred Draper: The amount of love in our house you could stick up a dog's jacksie and he wouldn't even yelp. (1970)

can (1914) Orig and mainly US ■ John McCormick: A toilet bowl in the corner with a scratched metal lid that freezes your can when you do sit on it. (1967)

tochus, tochas, tochess, tuchus, tuchas, tokus, tocus, etc. **(1914)** Mainly North American; from Yiddish *tokhes*, from Hebrew *taḥaṭ* beneath ■ W. R. Burnett: I was ... getting my tokus pinched all over the place. (1952)

fanny (1919) Orig and mainly US; origin unknown ■ Nevil Shute: I'd never be able to think of John and Jo again if we just sat tight on our fannies and did nothing. (1960)

beam (1929) From earlier sense, width of a ship; used especially with reference to the width of the hips and buttocks ■ Mrs Hicks-Beach: A cast-off of Jim's. He's grown too broad in the beam for it. (1944)

keister, keester, keyster (1931) US; origin unknown; compare earlier senses, bag, strong-box ■ *New Yorker*: Just put your keyster in the chair and shut your mouth. (1985)

bim (1935) Alteration of *bum* ■ Cecil Day Lewis: He slid gracefully down it on his bim. (1948)

slats (1935) Orig and mainly US; usually in the phrase *a kick in the slats* ■ *Business Week*: Unless we get a new kick in the slats from inflation next year, I would look for continued relative restraint in settlements. (1975)

posterior (1936) Euphemistic or jocular; the plural *posteriors* was used for 'buttocks' between the 17th and the 19th centuries ■ *Sea Spray* (New Zealand): It is soft so that a crewman winding the spinnaker sheet winch down aft can rest his posterior on it. (1976)

quoit, coit (1941) Australian; from earlier sense, rope ring, in allusion to the anus ■ John Bailey: 'I think he needs a good kick up the coit,' says Cromwell. (1972)

Khyber Pass, Khyber (1943) British; rhyming slang for *arse*; from the name of the chief pass in the Hindu Kush mountains between Afghanistan and north-west Pakistan ■ *Crescendo*: If we sit on our Khybers, we will miss out on all the things that make our lives the richer. (1968)

chuff (1945) Origin unknown ■ *Observer*: It was two hours of unmitigated boredom, that could only have been enjoyed by people too lazy to get off their chuffs and book themselves on a real tour of stately homes. (1996)

zatch (1950) Perhaps an alteration of *satchel* in similar slang sense ■ E. B. White: You are just sticking out your zatch, and many a tosspan and strutfart will run you through. (1950)

bronze, bronza, bronzo (1959) Australian; from earlier sense, anus ■ Les Ryan: Go and sit on your bronze while we give scabs your jobs. (1975)

tush, tushie, tushy (1962) Mainly North American; alteration or diminutive of *tochus* buttocks ■ *Pix* (Australia): Pretty young girls who walk around ... with their tushes out there asking for it. (1970)

acre, acher (1965) Australian, euphemistic; from *acre* measure of area, from the notion of a large expanse of buttocks; the spelling *acher* perhaps inspired by the notion of a 'pain in the arse' ■ Frank Hardy: Wiping between his toes and falling on his acre. (1971)

heinie, hiney (1982) US; perhaps from *behind*, influenced by *heinie* German (soldier) ■ *New Yorker*: I could tell how tight that girl's shorts were. I could see her heinie clear across the square. (1985)

Anus

arsehole (1400), **asshole** (1935) *asshole*, mainly US ■ Ezra Pound: Faces smeared on their rumps. ... Addressing crowds through their arse-holes. (1930)

hole (1607) ■ Leonard Cohen: Don't give me this all diamond shit, shove it up your occult hole. (1966)

shithole (1937)

ring (1949) From its annular shape ■ R. Stow: I bet I would have booted him in the ring if he hadn't run. (1965)

ort (1952) Australian; also applied more broadly to the buttocks; origin unknown ■ J. Wynnum: Take it from me, there's more ways of killin' a cat than fillin' its ort with sand. (1962)

bronze, bronza, bronzo (1953) Australian; from its colour ■ D'Arcy Niland: I know the one with an ugly face like a handful of bronzas. Who's the other? (1957)

freckle (1967) Australian; from previous sense, brown mark on the skin ■ Barry Humphries: I too believed that the sun shone out of Gough's freckle. (1978)

The rectum

back passage (1960) Euphemistic ■ P. Falconer: As she sucked, so her fingers reached his back passage. Uninvited, she positioned two fingers at the entrance of his arsehole, and crudely thrust into him. (1993)

Legs

stumps (*a*1460) Jocular; from earlier sense, remaining part of an amputated limb; now mainly in *stir one's stumps* act quickly

pins (1530) From earlier sense, peg ■ *Daily Mirror*: You look a bit wobbly on your pins, pet. (1976)

timbers (1807) From earlier sense, wooden leg ■ John Clare: Boys, miss my pegs ... and hit my legs, My timbers well can stand your gentle taps. (1821)

props (1828) Dated ■ *Sportsman*: There are those ... who assert that with such 'props' he will never successfully negotiate the Epsom gradients. (1891)

pegs (1833) Jocular; often also applied to a wooden or other artificial leg ■ Thomas Hood: The army-surgeons made him limbs: Said he,—'They're only pegs'. (a1845)

underpinnings (1848) US ■ R. B. Parker: I learned Vic's technique for developing 'sinewy and shapely under-pinnings'. (1974)

benders (1849) Orig US ■ H. W. Longfellow: Young ladies are not allowed to cross their benders in school. (1849)

Scotch peg (1857) Rhyming slang ■ Ward Muir: If he had occasion to allude to his leg he would probably have called it 'Scotch peg'. (1917)

stems (1860) ■ *Vanity Fair*: Among some of Conway's more famous expressions are: . . . 'Stems' and 'Gambs' (legs). (1927)

wheels (1927) US, orig criminals' slang ■ Ed McBain: Bid blonde job, maybe five-nine, five-ten. Blue eyes. Tits out to here. Wheels like Betty Grable. (1985)

Shortness of legs

duck's disease, ducks' disease, duck-disease (1925) Jocular ■ B. Marshall: Plinio, the barman with duck's disease, came running up. (1960)

Knees

benders (1925) Orig US ■ A. S. M. Hutchinson: They say family prayers there with the servants every night, all down on their benders. (1925)

Feet

tootsy, tootsie, tootsy-wootsy, tootsie-wootsie, etc. (1854) Jocular; alteration of *foot* + diminutive suffix *-sy* ■ Mary Wesley: You can rest your tootsies while I listen to music. (1983)

mud-hooks (1850) Dated

plates of meat (1857), plates (1896), platters of meat (1923), platters (1945) *plates/platters of meat*, rhyming slang ■ Cecil Day Lewis: 'Your clodhopping feet.' 'Plates of meat,' murmured Dick Cozzens, who is an expert in slang. (1948) ■ P. Branch: He . . . took off his shoes. 'Heaven!' he sighed. 'My plates have been quite, quite killing me.' (1951)

beetle-crushers, beetle-squashers (1860) Jocular ■ Anthony Gilbert: He looked down . . . at his own enormous beetle-crushers in bright tan Oxfords. (1958)

dogs (1913) ■ John Steinbeck: We ain't gonna walk no eight miles . . . tonight. My dogs is burned up. (1939)

Skin

hide (a1000) From earlier sense, animal's skin; originally in standard use, but now jocular, especially in metaphorical expressions ■ Lord Lytton: The poor fellow meant only to save his own hide. (1873)

Breath

puff (1827) From earlier sense, short emission of air ■ W. C. Baldwin: Sustaining three more savage charges, the last . . . far from pleasant, as my horse had all the puff taken out of him. (1863)

2. Nakedness

Naked

in one's birthday suit (1753) ■ *Guardian*: The sight of me in my bathing-suit might tip the balance in a world already veering towards collapse. Ditto, me in my birthday suit. (1992)

in the altogether (1894) From the notion of being 'altogether' or 'completely' naked ■ Nigel Balchin: *Should* I get a kick out of just seeing a girl in the altogether? (1947)

bollock-naked, ballock-naked (1922) British ■ *Viz*: Yes indeed! 'BIG' BEN is 'STARK' bollock naked! Porno action on page 19! (1990)

starkers (1923) British; from *stark* (naked) + *-ers* *Guardian*: There was no stripping. . . . The girls were starkers all the time. (1963)

starko (1923) British; from *stark* (naked) + *-o* ■ J. Pudney: Leave him in his birthday suit. Miss bloody Garth can walk back to Midsomer starko and explain to the folks that she's been a man all the time. (1961)

in the raw (1941) From earlier (mainly metaphorical) use of *the raw* to denote exposed flesh ■ Evelyn Waugh: Auberon surprised her in her bath and is thus one of the very few men who can claim to have seen his great-great-grandmother in the raw. (1944)

in the nuddy (or **nuddie**) **(1953)** Jocular, orig Australian; from *nudd-*, jocular alteration of *nude* + *-y* ■ S. Weller: Quick—ring her back—she's in the nuddy—give her a scare. (1976)

No clothing

not a stitch (1885) ■ Alan Bennett: And he will insist on not wearing a stitch. Zoe gets quite agitated. Normally, you see, they wear what I believe is called a posing pouch. (1972)

The bare skin

the buff (1654) Now mainly in the phrases *in the buff* naked and *to the buff* so as to be naked; from earlier sense, buffalo-skin (leather) ■ Vivian Jenkins: They went swimming, sunbathed, did their training stripped to the buff. (1956) ■ *Rolling Stone*: The girls call themselves the Groupies and claim they recorded their song in the buff. (1969)

To undress

peel (1785) Often followed by *off*; originally used in boxing slang, referring to contestants getting stripped ready to fight ■ *Variety*: The gals are peelin' in 23 clubs through Los Angeles County. (1950)

To go naked

skinny-dip (1966) Orig US; applied to swimming naked; from the notion of swimming only in one's skin ■ Lisa Birnbach: Once every summer, teenagers are caught skinny-dipping after dark. (1980). Hence **skinny-dipper** (1971)

streak (1973) Orig US; applied to running naked in a public place as a stunt ■ *Daily Telegraph*: The girls . . . had danced on the lawns in the nightdresses, 'streaked' to chapel and enjoyed midnight parties. (1979) Hence **streaker** (1973) ■ John Irving: A young

woman had reported that she was approached by an exhibitionist—at least, by a streaker. (1978)

Clothed

decent (1886) Used especially in asking whether someone is clothed before entering their room ■ Ruth Harvey: Sometimes, if she knew one of the actors or actresses, she would knock at a door and call 'Are you decent?' (That old theatrical phrase startled people who didn't belong to the theatre, but it simply meant 'Are you dressed?') (1949)

3. Physique

Fat

roly-poly (1820) A fanciful formation based on the verb *roll* ■ Dinah Mulock: A little roly-poly woman, with a meek, round, fair-complexioned face. (1865)

tubby (1835) From earlier sense, tub-shaped ■ Rudyard Kipling: Fat Captains and tubby Majors. (1891)

pudgy (1836), podgy (1846) Used to suggest shortness or squatness as well as fatness; apparently popularized in the writings of William Thackeray; from *pudge, podge* fat person or thing + *-y* ■ William Thackeray: Their fingers is always so very fat and pudgy. (1837)

jelly-bellied (1899) From the noun *jelly-belly*

broad in the beam (1929) Euphemistic; applied to large hips or buttocks; *beam* from earlier sense, breadth of a ship ■ Mrs Hicks-Beach: A cast-off of Jim's. He's grown too broad in the beam for it. (1944)

Fat person

fatty (1797) Often used as a derisive nickname; from the adjective *fat + -y*; compare the earlier adjective *fatty* ■ *Petticoat*: Success stories connected with slimming are few and far between, so any fatties who might be reading this—take note of this tale! (1971)

Mother Bunch (1847) Applied to a fat or untidy old woman; from the name of a noted fat woman of Elizabethan times ■ *Guardian*: She no more looks like a Mother Bunch than sounds like one . . . a fairly plump but elegant, well-dressed woman. (1964)

slob (1861) Used to associate fatness and moral delinquency; from the earlier (especially Irish) sense, mud, muddy land ■ S. Ellis: A big, fat, gutless slob. (1958)

jelly-belly (1896) ■ L. A. G. Strong: If I ever want a ginger-chinned jelly-belly's advice . . . I'll ask for it. (1935)

slump (1906) Applied to a fat, slovenly person; from earlier sense, sudden decline ■ Jeffrey Ashford: D'you reckon we'd waste good bees and honey on a slump like you for nothing? (1960)

flop (1909) Applied to a soft or flabby person ■ Frank O'Connor: She was a great flop of a woman. (1936)

slug (1931) ■ I. & P. Opie: The unfortunate fat boy . . . is known as . . . slug. (1959)

fatso (1933) Often used as a derisive nickname; probably from the adjective *fat* or the designation *Fats* ■ Len Deighton: I began to envy Fatso his sausage sandwiches. (1962)

lard-ass (1946) Mainly North American, orig nautical; often applied specifically to a large-buttocked person, or to the buttocks themselves ■ R. A. Hill: All they do is eat and sit on their lard asses around the guns. (1959)

Fatness

middle-age spread, middle-aged spread (1931) Applied to paunchiness in a middle-aged person ■ *John o' London's*: Join the happy throng who have learnt to control the 'middle-age spread' by wearing the . . . supporting belt. (1937)

puppy fat (1937) Applied to fatness in a young person, which supposedly soon disappears

flab (1958) ■ Kenneth Giles: She looks pretty good . . . no flab round the thighs yet. (1966)

spare tyre (1961) Applied to a roll of fat around the midriff

Muscular; massive

beef to the heel(s) (1867) ■ James Joyce: Transparent stockings, stretched to breaking point. Not like . . . the one in Grafton street. White. Wow! Beef to the heel. (1922)

hefty (1871) From earlier sense, weighty ■ E. F. Norton: The bucolic bumpkin with coarse features and slow brain fails no less than the hefty giant. (1925)

Thin

skinny (1605) From earlier sense, like or consisting of skin ■ *Saturday Review*: A chicken . . . sometimes skinny and often ill-kept. (1879)

spindly (1827) From earlier sense, (of plants) growing weakly ■ Bayard Taylor: Therefore I've worn, like many a spindly youth, False calves these many years upon me. (1872)

weedy (1852) Used to denote unhealthy thinness and weakness; from earlier sense, like a weed

■ *Nation*: In order to fill the ranks large numbers of weedy men have been enlisted. (1892)

Thin person or animal

beanpole (1837) Applied to a tall thin person; see at **Size** (p. 395).

weed (1869) Applied to a thin and unhealthily delicate person ■ *Times*: A girl torn between a brainy weed and a moronic body-builder. (1970)

hat-rack (1935) Applied to a scraggy animal; from the resemblance of the protruding ribs and other bones to the pegs of a hat-rack ■ Roy

Campbell: One trick is to deprive a hatrack of an old horse of water, and let him have a good lick of salt. (1957)

string-bean (1936) US; applied to a thin tall person; from earlier sense, type of narrow-podded bean ■ *New Yorker*: 'Did Germany need living space?' Hellmann asked, translating the stringbean's German word. (1977)

streak (1941) Orig Australian; applied to a thin tall person; from earlier sense, long narrow strip ■ *Listener*: That long streak of misery in a blue shirt. (1966)

Skinny Liz (1959) Applied to a thin girl or woman ■ N. Fitzgerald: She takes no interest in . . . eatin'. That's why she's such a Skinny Liz. (1961)

4. **Sight, Vision**

A look, a glance

squint (1673) ■ G. M. Fenn: Better get back to him as soon as you've had your squint round. (1894)

deck, dekh (1853) Orig Anglo-Indian, dated; from Hindustani *dekhā* sight, *dekhnā* see, look at ■ E. Milne: Crikey, have a deck at Ronald Colman! (1951)

look-see (1883) Pidgin-like formation from the noun or verb *look* + the verb *see* ■ Adam Diment: I took a long looksee through my . . . binoculars. (1968)

decko, dekko (1894) British, orig army slang; from Hindustani *dekho*, imperative of *dekhnā* to look ■ *Observer*: Once I'd grabbed hold of the script and taken a good dekko at it, my worst fears were confirmed. (1958)

double O (1913) US; applied to an intense look; from the resemblance to a pair of staring eyes ■ R. A. Heinlein: The cashier came over and leaned on my table, giving the seats on both sides of the booth a quick double-O. (1957)

squiz, squizz (1913) Australian & New Zealand; probably a blend of *squint* and *quiz* ■ K. Smith: Hey, youse blokes! Come over here and take a squiz at *this*! (1965)

gander (1914) Orig US; from the verb *gander* ■ *Scientific American*: Take a gander at the see-through door below. (1971)

geek (1919), gig (1924), gink (1945) Australian; from British dialect verb *geek* peep, look ■ Robert Close: Get a gink at that chin, mates! (1961)

Captain Cook (1932) Australian; rhyming slang for *look*; from the name of James *Cook* (1728–79), British navigator and explorer ■ D. O'Grady: Got a Captain Cook at your dossier—it's thicker than your frickin' head. (1974)

butcher's (1936) British; short for *butchers's hook*, rhyming slang for *look* ■ Kingsley Amis: Have a butcher's at the *News of the World*. (1960)

bo-peep (1941) Australian & New Zealand; extension of *peep*, after *bo-peep* nursery game ■ *Landfall*: Take a bo-peep at old Lionel. (1969)

shufti, shufty (1943) British, orig army slang; from Arabic *šufti* have you seen?, from *šāf* see ■ Richard Adams: Let's 'ave a crafty shufti round with that in mind. (1980)

To see

lay eyes on (*a*1225), clap eyes on (1838) ■ Walter Besant: I never clapped eyes on you before to my knowledge. (1887)

To look (at)

twig (1764) Dated; origin unknown ■ Charles Dickens: 'They're a twiggin' of you, sir,' whispered Mr. Weller. (1837)

pipe (1846) Origin uncertain ■ H. J. Parker: During the daytime wandering about the area, 'pipe-ing', looking over a car, became a regular practice. (1974)

gander (1887) US; from the resemblance between a goose and an inquisitive person stretching out the neck to look

get an eyeful (1899) ■ Nigel Balchin: He thought to himself this is a bit of all right and started right in to get an eye-ful, see? (1947)

eyeball (1901) Orig US; from the noun *eyeball* ■ *Listener*: This movie is so richly risible that I advise all, in John Wayne's phrase, to go down to the Warner and eyeball it. (1968)

take a lunar (1906) Dated; from earlier sense, observe the moon ■ John Guthrie: Charles took a lunar. (1950)

get (1911) Used to denote looking at or noticing especially someone who is conceited or laughable; usually used in the imperative with a pronoun as object ■ *News Chronicle*: If he is conceited the girls mutter get *yew*! (1958)

lamp (1916) Orig US; compare **lamps** p. 2 eyes ■ Roger Busby: I'd like to know how the coppers got on to us. They couldn't have lamped us on the road. (1969)

screw (1917) Orig Australian ■ J. North: From the way he was screwin' her phiz. (1922)

clock (1929) Orig US; perhaps from the notion of observing someone in order to time their actions ■ *Sunday Express Magazine*: Our waiter . . . was so busy clocking him that he spilt a precious bottle of appleade over the table cloth. (1986)

get a load of (1929) Orig US ■ Dennis Bloodworth: Get a load of that chick over there. (1972)

goggle (1938) From earlier sense, look with wide eyes ■ *Listener*: The contemporary reader . . . has better things to do than goggle into the dim past. (1965)

squiz, squizz (1941) Australian & New Zealand; from the noun *squiz* look ■ C. B. Maxwell: He only wanted to squiz at the beach from the best vantage point of all. (1949)

shufti, shufty (1943) British, dated; from the noun *shufti*

To appraise visually

give someone or something **the once-over (1915)** Orig US; *once-over* from the notion of a single rapid all-encompassing glance ■ *New Yorker*: He gave his display of perfect strawberries the once-over. (1977)

give something **the up-and-down (1923)** From the notion of 'looking something up and down' ■ P. G. Wodehouse: 'Read this letter.' He gave it the up-and-down. (1923)

eye someone **up (1982)** ■ *Sun*: Modest John likes to play down his good looks and says he gets a bit embarrassed when girls eye him up. (1992)

To keep watch, be observant

stag (1796) Dated; probably from the noun *stag* informer ■ G. Bartram: Who set ye on to watch me? . . . And at last . . . he admitted that Master John had told him to keep an eye on me and Jenny—to 'stag' us if he saw us out together—and to get a witness to what went on between us. (1897)

keep one's eyes peeled (1853) or **skinned (1833)** Orig US; from the notion of having the eyelids open ■ Richard Tate: Keep your eyes peeled for a break in the mist. (1974)

keep tabs on, keep (a) tab on (1889) Orig US; from *tab* an account, a check ■ Dorothy Sayers: The one person . . . likely to have kept tabs on Mr Perkins . . . was old Gaffer Gander. (1932)

keep nit (1903) Australian; from earlier obsolete use as a warning that someone is coming; *nit* perhaps a variant of *nix* used to warn of someone's approach ■ B. Scott: They'd pick a couple of the mob to keep nit then they'd hoe into the corn. (1977)

stake out (1942) Orig US; used to denote placing somewhere under surveillance; probably from the notion of surrounding a place as if with stakes ■ Len Deighton: When . . . the French police staked out the courier routes, they found . . . 50,000 dollars of forged signed travellers' cheques. (1962). Hence **staked out** placed so as to maintain surveillance (1951) ■ Henry Kissinger: David Bruce . . . came to the Embassy through the front door where the press was staked out. (1979)

keep yow (1942) Australian; origin unknown ■ Graham McInnes: Molly kept a look-out ('kept yow', as we used to say). (1965)

Observation

obbo, obo (1933) Abbreviation of *observation*; applied especially to police surveillance of a person, building, etc. ■ Busby & Holtham: Now I got a fix on the place I got to do some obo first. (1968)

stake-out (1942) Orig US; applied to a period of (especially police) surveillance; from the verb *stake out* ■ Raymond Chandler: Somebody stood behind that green curtain . . . as silently as only a cop on a stake-out knows how to stand. (1943)

obs (1943) Orig services' slang; abbreviation of *observation* ■ Olive Norton: Hurry up. I'm keeping obs. (1970)

To catch sight of, spot

twig (1796) Dated; from earlier sense, look at ■ FitzWilliam Pollok: I twigged the tigress creeping away in front of us. (1879)

To stare inquisitively or in astonishment

gawp (1682) Perhaps an alteration of *gape* ■ *European*: St Tropez is packed with these threadbare tourists who gawp at sights they have long only heard about—especially the topless bathers on the beaches. (1991)

gawk (1795) Orig US; perhaps from the noun *gawk* awkward person, but perhaps an iterative from the obsolete verb *gaw* stare (with suffix as in *tal-k, wal-k, lur-k*), from Old Norse *gá* heed. ■ C. D. Eby: Gawking in wonder at the falling bombs. (1965)

rubberneck (1896) Orig US; from the notion of someone with a flexible neck who looks this way and that ■ *Daily Telegraph*: Hortensio was rubbernecking like an American tourist, admiring the scenery, sniffing the breeze. (1969)

To hallucinate visually

see things (1922) ■ Douglas Rutherford: Was I seeing things or was that Sally driving your truck? (1977)

A person who looks

gongoozler (1904) Applied to a person who stares idly or protractedly at something, originally at activity on a canal; origin uncertain, but compare Lincolnshire dialect *gawn* stare vacantly or curiously, and *gooze(n)* stare aimlessly, gape ■ *New Yorker*: I stopped off in the Galeana sports park . . . to watch a game on one of the three huge outdoor screens that the city had supplied for gongoozlers like me. (1986)

Glasses

specs, specks (1807) Abbreviation of *spectacles* ■ Don Delillo: Peter, her son, . . . reddish hair, wire-frame specs. (1982)

gig-lamps (1853) Dated; from earlier sense, lamp at the side of a gig

goggles (1871) From earlier sense, spectacles for protecting the eyes

cheaters (1908) US, orig gamblers' slang
■ Raymond Chandler: The eyes behind the rimless cheaters flashed. (1949)

bins (1981) British; first recorded in print in 1981, but other evidence (e.g. obsolete Cockney rhyming slang *Errol Flynns* spectacles) suggests much earlier use; abbreviation of *binoculars*
■ John McVicar: Frank gives me the once-over and pushes the bins back tight on my eyes. If George saw my minces, he might pull the deal. (1992)

Sunglasses

shades (1958) Orig US ■ George Higgins: I looked at Emerson, hiding behind his shades and his imported-cigarette smoke. (1980)

A monocle

window-pane (1923) Dated ■ P. G. Wodehouse: Freddie no longer wore the monocle. . . . His father-in-law had happened to ask him one day would he please remove that damned window-pane from his eye. (1966)

5. Hearing

To listen, hear

get an earful (1917) ■ Frank Sargeson: I tried to get an earful when I heard somebody out on the landing-place. (1946)

earwig (1927) Often jocular; used to denote eavesdropping ■ Guardian: Anyway, apparently you sometimes get a Miss Millett 'earwigging' in a dark corner, so she was paraded towards me for a formal introduction. (1992)

get a load of (1929) Orig US; often used ironically in commenting on what someone has said

earhole (1958) Used to denote listening, and often specifically eavesdropping ■ Frank Norman: You can always shtoom up if any screws are earholeing. (1958)

To have delusions of hearing

hear things (1991) First recorded in 1991, but certainly older than that; *hear voices* = 'imagine one hears voices' dates from the late 19th century ■ Ticket: Three and a bit minutes later it's wheedled its way into your mind, where it burrows away with sitars and voices so buried in the mix you wonder whether you're hearing things. (1994)

Listening attentively

all ears (1865) Earlier *all ear* ■ Guardian: We've been

Binoculars

binocs (1943) Abbreviation

bins (1971) Abbreviation

Wearing glasses

specky (1956) Derogatory, mainly Scottish; from *spec(s* + *-y* ■ R. Jenkins: The unbraw unlovable puke married to yon specky gasping smout of a barber. (1956)

A bespectacled person

four-eyes (1873) Jocular; often used as a term of address ■ Courier-Mail (Brisbane): Aha, foureyes! You're nicked! (1988)

Visually impaired

boss-eyed (1860) Applied to someone who is cross-eyed or has only one eye; origin unknown; compare slang *boss bungle* and *boss shot* unsuccessful attempt ■ I. & P. Opie: When somebody who is boss-eyed goes by you spit on the ground. (1959)

Visibility

vis (1943) Orig military slang; abbreviation

hearing a lot about the Government having to listen, and he's all ears. (1992)

Deaf

deaf as a post (a1845) Denoting extreme deafness

Mutt and Jeff (1960) Rhyming slang; from the names of two characters called *Mutt* and *Jeff* in a popular cartoon series by H. C. Fisher (1884–1954), American cartoonist ■ Bowlers' World: They don't hear the cry 'Feet!' sometimes on account of being a bit 'Mutt and Jeff'. (1992)

cloth-eared (1965) From *cloth ears* ■ George Melly: It was more difficult for a band on the road to know what was going on than for the most cloth-eared member of a provincial jazz club. (1965)

Impaired hearing

cloth ears (1912) Often used to criticize an inattentive listener

A deaf person

dummy (1874) Applied to a deaf-mute ■ Carson McCullers: But a dummy! . . . 'Are there any other deaf-mute people here?' he asked. (1940)

cloth ears (1965) From earlier sense, impaired hearing; mainly used as a derogatory form of address to an inattentive listener ■ New Statesman: I've told you once, cloth-ears. (1965)

6. Smell

A smell

funk (1623) Applied to a strong, usually unpleasant smell, and also to an oppressively thick atmosphere, especially one full of tobacco smoke; from the obsolete verb *funk* blow smoke on, probably from northern French dialect *funkier*, from Latin **fūmicāre, fūmigāre* smoke ■ Martin Amis: The darts contest took place, not in the Foaming Quart proper (with its stained glass and heavy drapes and crepuscular funk), but in an adjoining hall. (1989)

niff (1903) British; often applied specifically to an unpleasant smell; perhaps from the noun *sniff* ■ *Draconian*: The customary Oxford autumn niff, usually readily recognisable, redolent as it is of bonfires and long grass. (1975)

hum (1906) British; applied to an unpleasant smell; from the verb *hum* smell bad ■ W. E. Collinson: An awful pong or hum. (1927)

pong (1919) Applied to an unpleasant smell; origin unknown ■ Gwen Moffat: She's burning the feathers. . . . She only does it when the wind takes the smell away from us. . . . The pong's not bothering us. (1973)

To smell unpleasantly

pen and ink, pen (1892) Rhyming slang for *stink* ■ G. F. Newman: 'I don't mind, provided he takes a bath.' 'Yeah, he does pen a bit.' (1972)

whiff (1899) ■ Rudyard Kipling: Then she'll whiff. Golly, how she'll whiff! (1899)

hum (1902) British ■ *Daily Telegraph*: When the wind drops this stuff really hums. (1970)

niff (1927) British; from the noun *niff* ■ Kenneth Giles: It smelled. . . . 'Niffs, don't it?' said one of the youths. (1967)

pong (1927) From the noun *pong* bad smell ■ Ruth Rendell: The place . . . just pongs of dirty clothes. (1979)

stink (or smell) to high heaven (1963) ■ F. Richards: I probably smell to high heaven of insect repellent. (1963)

Smelly

loud (1641) Now mainly US ■ G. B. Goode: The natives . . . prefer to have the meat tainted rather than fresh, declaring that it is most tender and toothsome when decidedly 'loud'. (1887)

funky (1784) Now only US; from *funk* bad smell + -*y* ■ James Baldwin: They knew . . . why his hair was nappy, his armpits funky. (1962)

whiffy (1849) From *whiff* impression of an (unpleasant) smell + -*y* ■ Rose Macaulay: 'A bit whiffy,' Hero said, as they passed among the cottages that encircled the muddy . . . pool. (1934)

niffy (1903) British; from *niff* (bad) smell + -*y* ■ Baron Corvo: The niffy silted-up little Rio della Croxe. (1934)

pongy (1936) From *pong* bad smell + -*y* ■ Graham McInnes: Dad . . . kept turning up . . . with loot from the Prahran market: strings of saveloys and frankfurters, pongy cheeses, . . . and huge Portuguese sardines. (1965)

on the nose (1941) Australian ■ Frank Huelin: He removed his boots and the narrow strips of rag wrapped round his feet. 'By cripes! They're a bit on the nose,' said my mate, wrinkling his nose. (1973)

7. Bodily Functions

To urinate or defecate

do it (1922) Euphemistic ■ Herbert Gold: It's so easy, boy, after you do it once. Before that it's hard. You sweat. You do it in your pants. (1956)

go (1926) Euphemistic ■ *Time*: I took off all my clothes but my drawers and-well-I had to go. (1935)

spend a penny (1945) British, euphemistic; often applied specifically to urination; from the necessity in former times of inserting a penny in a slot in the door to gain admission to a cubicle in a public lavatory ■ *People's Journal* (Inverness & Northern Counties ed.): Anyone on the Islands . . . after that time who wants to 'spend a penny' must make a 10-minute walk . . . to the public toilets. (1973)

An unintentional act of urinating or defecating

accident (1899) Euphemistic ■ *Nation*: Then a new child had, as Mabel calls it, 'an accident'. She may have been afraid of asking to go out. (1926)

To have an urgent need to urinate or defecate

be caught (or taken) short (1890) ■ *Private Eye*: Taken badly short when on his way to work, and finding that both of the public lavatories in Putney were closed, Mr. Peter Herring entered a police station and asked if he could use their convenience. (1977)

Urination

number one (1902) A children's word or euphemism; contrasted with *number two* defecation ■ Angus Wilson: This little ginger [kitten] is going to do a number one if we're not careful. (1967)

pee (1902) From the verb *pee* urinate ■ *Daily Telegraph*: If people came in just to use the lavatory, he would ask them for their address 'in case I need a pee when I'm passing your house'. (1973)

pee-wee (1907) Mainly a children's word or euphemism; reduplicated form of *pee*; see also *wee* ■ Simon Raven: Don't forget the little dears do a pee-wee before they go to bed. (1962)

piss (1916) From earlier sense, urine ■ Philip Larkin: Groping back to bed after a piss. (1974)

wet (1925) From the verb *wet* urinate ■ Jon Cleary: The children want to wet. . . . Come on, love. Have your wet. (1975)

leak (1934) From the verb *leak* urinate ■ Graham Greene: All these hours of standing without taking a leak. (1969)

piddle (1937) From earlier sense, urine ■ E. Burgess: Take the poodle for its piddle. (1959)

Jimmy Riddle, **jimmy** (1937) Rhyming slang for *piddle* ■ Douglas Clark: Mrs. D. was in there having a jimmy. (1971)

wee-wee (1937), **wee** (1968) Imitative; a child's word or euphemism ■ Jack Scott: When he needed a wee-wee he did it in a corner of the hut. (1982) ■ Philip Purser: Hurry up, I want to do a wee. (1971)

slash (1950) British; perhaps from obsolete *slash* a drink, of uncertain origin ■ N. J. Crisp: He decided to risk a quick slash, which . . . he needed. (1977)

widdle (1954) Imitative; compare *piddle* and *wee* ■ Alan Coren: Love is . . . mekkin' sure yer betrothed 'as a pensionable position wi' luncheon vouchers an' gets out of 'is bath when he wants a widdle. (1977)

run-off (1961) ■ H. W. Sutherland: What with the cold and the beer she was bursting for a run off again. . . . The nearest ladies she knew was at Pier Head. (1967)

tinkle (1965) From the verb *tinkle* urinate ■ Ernest Brawley: And went over and had a tinkle. (1974)

whizz, **whiz** (1971) From the verb *whizz* urinate ■ Douglas Clark: She could have left him alone . . . while she went for a whizz or changed her clothes. (1971)

To urinate

piss (1290) Ultimately (through French and Latin) from the sound; also in the phrase *piss oneself* wet oneself ■ J. Barnett: You've pissed yourself . . . you dirty bastard. (1978)

leak (1596) ■ Jack Kerouac: The prowl car came by and the cop got out to leak. (1957)

pluck a rose (1613) Dated, euphemistic; applied to a woman

pee (1788) Orig transitive, in the sense 'make wet by urinating'; the intransitive use emerged later (1880); from the sound of the first letter of *piss* ■ Mary McCarthy: 'My God', you yell . . . 'can't a man pee in his own house?' (1948)

pump ship (1788) Orig nautical ■ Douglas Rutherford: A couple of men had come in to pump ship at the stand-up urinals. (1973)

piddle (1796) Perhaps from *piss* + the verb *puddle* (compare *widdle*); probably not the same word as earlier *piddle* work or act in a trifling way ■ Richard Adams: I have no idea what portents he employs—possibly the bear piddles on the floor and he observes portents in the steaming what-not. (1974)

wet (1925) Also in the phrase *wet oneself* urinate involuntarily (1922) ■ Virginia Woolf: The marmoset is just about to wet on my shoulder. (1935) ■ *Times Literary Supplement*: She also sweats, weeps, vomits and wets herself. (1976)

whizz, **whiz** (1929) ■ R. B. Parker: I wondered if anyone had ever whizzed on Allan Pinkerton's shoe. (1976)

wee-wee (1930), **wee** (1934) Imitative; a children's word or euphemism ■ Danny Abse: I suddenly rushed into the sea . . . and wee-weed in the water for a joke. (1954) ■ *Daily Mail*: Our headmaster told us that any boy caught short should if absolutely necessary wee into an empty milk bottle. (1983)

tinkle (1960) Orig US ■ Ed McBain: I'm looking for the loo. . . . I really have to tinkle. (1976)

strain the potatoes (or **spuds**) (1965) Australian, jocular; used of males ■ P. Burgess: Keep Ted's chair for him. He's only gone out to strain the spuds. (1982)

syphon the python (1968) Jocular, orig Australian; used of males; from the common analogy between the penis and a snake ■ D. Ball: Brooks was struck with an overwhelming desire to piss. Syphon the python, he thought. (1978)

widdle (1968) From the noun *widdle* urination ■ W. Harriss: He headed straight for me. . . . I damn near widdled. (1983)

Urine

piss (1386) From the verb *piss* urinate ■ Nicolas Freeling: The hallway smelt. . . . Piss, cabbage, stale sweat. (1979)

piddle (1901) From the verb *piddle* urinate ■ Maureen Duffy: I envied him his ability to tie his little soft winkle into a knot at the end and blow it out like a balloon with unshed piddle. (1962)

wet (1925) From the verb *wet* urinate ■ D. H. Lawrence: But see old Leo Tolstoi wetting on the flame. As if even his wet were absolute! (1925)

wee-wee (1948) From earlier sense, urination ■ A. N. Keith: Our barrack . . . smelled of kids, pots, and wee-wee. (1948)

pee (1961) From the verb *pee* urinate ■ P. Cave: Sarcasm runs off them like pee on a plastic bedsheet. (1976)

The urinary system

waterworks (1902) British euphemistic ■ Wallace Hildick: I'd been plagued for a long time . . . by—well—let's call it waterworks trouble. (1977)

A bed-wetter

pissabed (1643) Literally 'piss in bed'; the word existed earlier as a name for the dandelion, so called after its diuretic properties ■ Roy Fuller: He beat me at the beginning of term for peeing my bed. . . Now he thinks of me as a pissabed. (1959)

Defecation

number two (1902) A children's word or euphemism; contrasted with *number one* urination ■ Mary McCarthy: When I had done Number Two, you always washed them out yourself before sending them to the diaper service. (1971)

crap (1926) From the verb *crap* defecate ■ Brendan Behan: And then, God of war, did I want a crap. (1959)

shit, shite (1928) From the verb *shit* defecate ■ Roseanne Barr: Daddy will go over and he'll turn on the TV and then he'll go take a shit, like he always does. (1989)

dump (1942) From the verb *dump* defecate ■ W. H. Auden: To start the morning With a satisfactory Dump is a good omen All our adult days. (1966)

tom-tit (1943) Rhyming slang for *shit* ■ Christopher Wood: Perhaps 'e stopped for a tomtit. (1970)

biggies (1953) British; a children's word or euphemism; contrasting the physical and psychological weight of defecation with the lesser importance of urination ■ Angus Wilson: He's a bit erratic where he does his biggies, now he's a grown up parrot. (1967)

To defecate

shit, shite (c1308) Also used transitively to mean 'defecate in' (1877) and reflexively to mean 'make oneself dirty by defecating' (1914); from Old English *scītan*, recorded in the past participle *be-sciten*

do one's business (1645) Dated euphemistic

crap (1846) Probably from the noun *crap* excrement, although this is not recorded until later ■ Alexander Baron: They'd crapped on the floor, in the same rooms they'd slept in. (1953)

poop (1903) From earlier sense, fart ■ *Cape Times*: Five-year-old eyes grow round with wonder at the memory of the elephant 'pooping' on the carpet. (1974)

dump (1929) Orig and mainly US; probably from earlier sense, deposit rubbish

do (go, make, etc.) poo-poo(s) (1976) Mainly a children's term; compare **pooh-pooh** excrement ■ *Mother & Baby*: Show her the nappy and tell her that she can do her wee-wee and poo-poo (or whatever your family words are!) in the potty instead of the nappy now that she is a big girl. (1988)

pooh, poo (1980) Euphemistic, orig a children's word; from the noun *pooh* excrement ■ Clive James: The citizens of Munich are . . . dog-crazy . . . but have somehow trained their pets not to poo. (1982)

Excrement

turd (c1000) Applied to a piece of excrement; from Old English *tord* ■ Nadine Gordimer: It was true that it was difficult to get the children to remember to bury the paper along with the turd. (1981)

dirt (a1300) Now euphemistic, but orig a standard term; now applied mainly to animal excrement; by metathesis from Middle English *drit*, probably from Old Norse *drit* excrement

shit, shite (a1585) From the verb *shit* defecate ■ Erica Jong: In general the toilets run swift here and the shit disappears long before you can leap up and turn around to admire it. (1973)

crap (1889) First recorded in 1889, but implied in the earlier adjective *crappy* (see below); compare earlier sense, *chaff*, refuse from fat-boiling; ultimately from Dutch *krappe* ■ J. D. Salinger: There didn't look like there was anything in the park except dog crap. (1951). Hence **crappy** made dirty by excrement (1846)

mess (1903) Euphemistic; applied mainly to animal excrement ■ *Woman's Own*: It's the dog. It made a mess on the carpet. (1960)

dingleberry (1938) Orig US; applied to a piece of dried faecal matter attached to the hair around the anus; from earlier US sense, a cranberry, *Vaccinium erythrocarpum*, of the south-eastern US; the origin of *dingle* is uncertain

road apples (1942) North American, euphemistic; applied to horse droppings ■ J. H. Gray: The best pucks were always those supplied by passing horses, 'road apples' we called them. (1970)

doo-doo (1948) Orig and mainly US, mainly a children's word or euphemism; reduplication of *do* excrement

poop (1948) From the verb *poop* defecate ■ *Telegraph* (Brisbane): A young woman claims a 'bird poop treatment' has cured her of a chronic dandruff. . . . She's been free of dandruff since a mynah bird relieved himself on her head during lunch one day. (1976). Hence **poopy** (1988) US; denoting being made dirty with excrement

poopy, poopie (1955) Mainly a children's word; from *poop* + *-y*

pooh, poo, pooh-pooh, poo-poo (1960) Mainly a children's word; from the exclamation *pooh* expressing disgust at an unpleasant smell ■ *Independent Magazine*: Mashed carrots today can resemble brightly coloured babies' poo (and when you contemplate some of the bottled vegetable purées people feed them with, it is little wonder). (1996)

doings (1967) British, euphemistic; from earlier more general application to something unspecified ■ Paul Beale: There's a lump of bird's doings on the windowsill. (1984)

do, doo (1972) Mainly a children's word or euphemism; first recorded in 1972, but implied by the earlier *doo-doo*, and remembered in use c1920 (private letter to the editor of the *Oxford English Dictionary*); from the verb *do* (compare *doings*) ■ *Time Out*: 'Eat crap!' barked the film director. And suddenly Divi was up to his dentures in doggy doo. (1985)

Diarrhoea

squitters (1664) From the obsolete verb *squitter* squirt, have diarrhoea, probably of imitative origin ■ Lord Harewood: We went incessantly to those over-public latrines. . . . My squitters were at their worst. (1981)

the squits (1841) British, euphemistic; from the obsolete dialectal verb *squit* squirt ■ David Lodge:

'Olive oil doesn't agree with me.' 'Gives you the squits, does it?' (1988)

the trots (1904) Euphemistic; from the notion of having to move hurriedly to the lavatory ■ **Colleen McCullough:** 'Go easy on the water at first,' he advised. 'Beer won't give you the trots.' (1977)

gippy tummy, gyppy tummy (1943) Applied especially to diarrhoea suffered by visitors to hot countries; *gippy* from *gip(sy)* + *-y*, influenced by *Egyptian* ■ **G. Egmont:** Always take . . . whatever is your favourite antidote to gippy tummy when you go abroad. (1961)

Delhi belly (1944) Applied to diarrhoea suffered by visitors to India; *Delhi* from the name of the capital of India

the shits (1947) ■ *Zigzag:* 'I've had the shits,' he cried. 'You want to avoid the food.' (1977)

Aztec hop, Aztec revenge, Aztec two-step (1953) Applied to diarrhoea suffered by visitors to Mexico; *Aztec* from the name of a former native American people of Mexico; *two-step* from the name of a type of dance ■ **Joseph Wambaugh:** So long, Puerto Vallarta! With his luck he'd die of Aztec Revenge anyway, first time he had a Bibb lettuce salad. (1978)

Montezuma's revenge (1962) Applied to diarrhoea suffered by visitors to Mexico; from the name of *Montezuma* II (1466–1520), Aztec ruler at the time of the Spanish conquest of Mexico ■ *Times:* England's World Cup football squad suffered their first casualty in Mexico on Wednesday, when 20-year-old Brian Kidd was struck down by what is known as 'Montezuma's Revenge'—a stomach complaint. (1970)

the runs (1962) Euphemistic; from the notion of having to run to the lavatory ■ **Bernard Malamud:** Sam Clemence, a witness from Harlem U.S.A., despite a bad case of the runs . . . , stands up for his friend Willie. (1971)

A lavatory

jakes (1538) Dated; origin uncertain; perhaps from the male forenames *Jacques* or *Jack* ■ **James Joyce:** He kicked open the crazy door of the jakes. (1922)

bog (*a*1789) British; short for *bog-house,* of uncertain origin ■ *New Left Review:* Toilet paper in the bogs. (1960)

shit-house (1795) ■ **P. Cave:** 'Nothing wrong with it—safe as a brick-built shithouse,' I assured her. (1976)

can (1900) US ■ **J. D. Salinger:** She kept saying . . . corny . . . things, like calling the can the 'little girls' room'. (1951)

place (1901) Euphemistic ■ **James Joyce:** They did right to put him up over a urinal. . . . Ought to be places for women. (1922)

rear (1903) Orig school and university slang; often used in the plural; perhaps from their position behind a building ■ **Bruce Marshall:** And now let's raid the rears and rout out any of the other new swine that are hiding there. (1946)

lav (1913) British; abbreviation of *lavatory* ■ **June Thomson:** Gilbert Leacock went out to the lav. . . . I heard the chain being pulled. (1973)

dyke, dike (1923) From earlier sense, ditch ■ **Jon Cleary:** I learned . . . to respect her privacy. And I don't mean just when she went to the dike. (1967)

crapper (1927) From *crap* defecate + *-er* ■ **Chester Himes:** Go to the crapper? What for? They weren't children, they didn't pee in bed. (1969)

lat (1927) Usually used in the plural; abbreviation of *latrine* ■ **J. I. M. Stewart:** Turk says that conscientious objectors have to clean out the lats in lunatic asylums. (1957)

john, johnny (1932) Mainly US; compare earlier *cuzjohn* lavatory (1735) ■ **Colin McInnes:** 'You poor old bastard,' I said to the Hoplite, as he sat there on my john. (1959) ■ **D. Conover:** Why, oh, why, do little boys (and big ones) rush to a johnny when nature provides opportunity everywhere? (1971)

dunny, dunnee (1933) Australian & New Zealand; orig applied specifically to an outdoor earth-closet; from British dialect *dunnekin* privy, of unknown origin ■ *Private Eye:* It seems a bit crook for old bazza to spend the night in the dunnee! (1970)

loo (1940) British; origin uncertain; perhaps from *Waterloo* ■ **Peter Wildeblood:** The loo's on the landing, if you want to spend a penny. (1957)

shouse, shoush, sh'touse (1941) Australian; syncopated form of *shit-house* ■ **Thomas Keneally:** I'd like some trees on it, pines and gums, so you don't have to see your neighbour's shouse first thing each morning. (1968)

recess (1950) Criminals' slang; applied to a prison lavatory; usually used in the plural ■ *Observer:* Locked in their cells *sc.* in Winson Green Prison, Birmingham at 5.30., with one opening later to go to the recesses (lavatories) and to have a hot drink. (1974)

W (1953) Abbreviation of *W.C.* ■ **E. Malpass:** A small garden of weeds, with a cinder path leading to a W. (1978)

House of Lords (1961) British, euphemistic or jocular ■ *Listener:* When you need the House of Lords, it's through there. (1967)

karzy, carsey, carsy, karsey, karzey (1961) British; alteration of Italian *casa* house ■ **T. E. B. Clarke:** You made a real thorough search? Everywhere? Outhouses, karzey, the lot? (1968)

lavvy (1961) British; from *lav* + *-y* ■ *Guardian:* A house where the lavvy is behind an arras. (1971)

toot (1965) Australian; probably from British dialect *tut* small seat or hassock ■ **J. Rowe:** Waldon added over his shoulder, 'Gobind's in the toot. He'll be right out.' (1978)

A lavatory pan or other receptacle

jerry (1859) Probably an abbreviation of *jeroboam* very large wine bottle, from the name of *Jeroboam* king of northern Israel, described in the Bible (1 Kings xi. 28) as a 'mighty man of valour'; compare W. Maginn: The naval officer . . . came into the Clarendon for a Jerry = jeroboam of punch. (1827) ■ **George Orwell:** A bed not yet made and a jerry under the bed. (1939)

po (1880) Applied to a chamber-pot; from French *pot (de chambre)* ■ *Punch:* I kneelin' by de bed . . . peein' in de smart Victorian po. (1974)

thunder-mug (1890) Applied to a chamber-pot

article (1922) British, euphemistic; applied to a chamber-pot ■ Joanna Cannan: How could he be so rude, she asked, when he said 'pot' instead of 'bedroom article'. (1958)

throne (1922) Often jocular ■ J. J. Rowlands: Our plumber . . . revealed that the water level in the 'throne' works just like the old glass water barometer. (1960)

honey-bucket (1931) North American; applied to a container for excrement ■ *Beaver* (Winnipeg, Manitoba): A woman taxi driver tells me many houses have honey-buckets, and galvanized bath tubs filled by hand. (1969)

thunder-box (1939) Applied to a portable commode, and hence to any lavatory ■ Evelyn Waugh: 'If you *must* know, it's my thunderbox.' . . . He . . . dragged out the treasure, a brass-bound, oak cube. . . . On the inside of the lid was a plaque bearing the embossed title *Connolly's Chemical Closet*. (1952)

potty (1942) Applied to a chamber-pot; from *pot + -y* ■ W. H. Auden: Lifted off the potty, Infants from their mothers Hear their first impartial Words of worldly praise. (1966)

shitter (1969) From *shit + -er* ■ *Black Scholar*: He lit a square and sat down on the shitter and tried to collect his thoughts. (1971)

pooperscooper, pooperscoop (1976) Applied to a small shovel carried to clear up (a dog's) excrement from the street, etc. ■ Joseph Wambaugh: Bring your pooper-scoopers, boys. The dogs are covering the red carpet in a sea of shit. (1977)

To vomit

spew (c897) Old English; orig a standard usage, but 'not now in polite use' (*Oxford English Dictionary*)

puke (1600) Probably imitative

whip the cat (1622), shoot the cat (1785) Dated

cat (1785) Probably from *shoot the cat*

throw up (1793) ■ A. E. Fisher: Ogy got drunk and threw up in the backyard. (1980)

turn up (1892) Used to denote making someone vomit or feel sick ■ Stella Gibbons: Turns you up, don't it, seein' ter-day's dinner come in 'anging round someone's neck? (1932)

sick up (1924) Used intransitively and transitively ■ Rudyard Kipling: I have ate grass and sicked up. (1930) ■ Charles Sweeney: On the way the reptile sicked up another hen, and half-way it regurgitated a third hen on the floor of my vehicle. (1966)

blow (1950) US; used transitively with usually a metaphorical object (e.g. *one's lunch*) denoting broadly 'vomiting'

chunder, chunda (1950) Australian; probably from rhyming slang *Chunder Loo* spew, after a cartoon character *Chunder Loo of Akin Foo* originally drawn by Norman Lindsay (1879–1969) and appearing in advertisements

for Cobra boot polish in the Sydney *Bulletin* between 1909 and 1920 ■ *Private Eye*: Many's the time we've chundered in the same bucket. (1970)

barf (1956) Orig and mainly US; not recorded until 1956, but implied in earlier rare US slang *barfer*, used as a term of abuse (1947); origin unknown; perhaps imitative ■ *Chicago Sun-Times*: If you are Princess Diana, you have to stay home and do needlepoint until all danger of barfing in public is past. (1982)

chuck (1957) Often followed by *up*; based on *throw up* ■ *Swag* (Sydney): The Pommy bird woke up and chucked all over the multi-coloured woollen blanket. (1968)

go for the big spit (1960) Australian ■ *Private Eye*: He goes for the big spit and accidentally entombs a nice old lady and her dog in tepid chuck. (1970)

upchuck (1960) US ■ Tobias Wells: Anyway, Natalie had to upchuck, it's that kind of bug. (1967)

ralph (1967) Orig and mainly US; often followed by *up*; apparently a use of the personal name, but perhaps imitative of the sound of vomiting ■ *Village Voice*: He ralphs up the downers and the quarts of beer. (1974)

Vomiting

technicolor yawn, technicolour yawn (1964) Australian ■ *Bulletin* (Sydney): The sick-making sequences will probably have less impact in this country because we've all been well initiated with Bazza McKenzie and his technicolor yawns. (1974)

chuck (1966) Australian; from the verb *chuck* vomit ■ *Kings Cross Whisper* (Sydney): He sat down in the gutter to have a bit of a chuck and flaked out. (1966)

chunder (1967) Australian; from the verb *chunder* vomit

Vomit

sick (1959) From the adjective *sick* nauseated ■ *Listener*: There's blood on the windscreen, sick on the trousers. (1977)

chunder (1960) Australian; from the verb *chunder* vomit ■ C. Kelen: Wiping the chunder from his mouth. (1980)

puke (1961) From the verb *puke* vomit ■ *New Society*: At the Black Raven, by Liverpool Street station, . . . there is a slight odour of puke and disinfectant. (1975)

barf (1974) US; first recorded in 1974, but implied in earlier metaphorical use referring to disgusting foodstuffs (1962); from the verb *barf* vomit ■ *New York Times*: Whereas the horror film was once spooky, now it is nauseating, measured by the barf, rather than the shiver. (1981)

chuck (1976) Australian; from the verb *chuck* vomit ■ McDonald & Harding: Were there chuck stains around the toilet? (1976)

A fart

raspberry tart (1892) Dated; rhyming slang

breezer (1973) Australian ■ Gerald Murname: Barry Launder has ordered every boy to write in his composition *at the picnic I let a breezer in my pants,* or else be bashed to smithereens after school. (1974)

To belch

gurk (1923) British; imitative ■ *New Statesman:* They grunted and gurked with an unconcern that amazed me. (1966). Hence **gurk** a belch (1932)

burp (1929) Orig US; imitative ■ W. R. Burnett: He belched, 'It's an old Arab custom. . . . You no like food—no burp—host insulted.' (1953). Hence **burp** a belch (1932) ■ Vladimir Nabokov: A comfortable burp told me he had a flask of brandy concealed about his warmly coated person. (1962)

To spit

gob (1872) Now mainly British; from the noun *gob* slimy lump ■ **Dylan Thomas:** And they thank God, and gob at a gull for luck. (1953)

Nasal mucus

snot (c1425) Probably from Middle Dutch, Middle Low German *snotte,* Middle High German *snuz* ■ Arthur Haley: Trying futilely to breathe through nostrils nearly plugged with snot, he gaped open his cracked lips and took a deep breath of sea air. (1976). Hence **snotty** running with or dirty with nasal mucus (1570) ■ I. M. Gaskin: A baby can seem snorty and snotty, but sometimes it sounds worse than it is. (1978)

bogy, bogey (1937) British; applied to a piece of dried nasal mucus; compare earlier sense, policeman ■ David Pinner: He . . . removed wax from ears, bogeys from nose, blackheads from chin. (1967)

Sexual secretions

come, cum (1923) Usually applied specifically to ejaculated semen; from the verb *come* have an

orgasm ■ *Miss London:* His attitude to sex is ambivalent. 'Each night I had to clean the come off the back seat of the cab,' he remarks in reasonable disgust. (1976)

love juice (1965) ■ *Pussycat:* I could feel his lovejuice so hot, trickling down into the start of my stomach. (1972)

scum (1967) Mainly US; applied specifically to semen

To ejaculate

shoot (1922) ■ H. C. Rae: I wanted him to shoot and get it over. (1972)

Menstruation

the curse (1930) Euphemistic; from the oppressive nature of menstruation ■ Graham Greene: I forgot the damn pill and I haven't had the curse for six weeks. (1969)

rag (1948) Euphemistic; applied to a sanitary towel; mainly used in various phrases denoting menstruation, such as *be on the rag, have the rag(s) on,* and *ride the rag* ■ *Maledicta:* There were several references to menstruous conditions or activities, found equally commonly in both male and female rest rooms ('Sue Ellen's on the rag' etc.). (1978)

jam-rag (a1966) Applied to a sanitary towel ■ *Viz:* The new Vispre Shadow jam rag is designed to suit *your* lifestyle, with a wrap-a-round gusset flap to keep the blood off your knicker elastic. (1992)

visitor (1980) Euphemistic; applied to a menstrual discharge; compare obsolete *visit* in the same sense ■ *New Yorker:* Girls used to say they had the curse. Or they had a visitor. (1984)

Dilatation and curettage

scrape (1968) ■ Margaret Drabble: She was having a D and C, a routine scrape. (1980)

8. **Pregnancy & Childbirth**

Pregnant

in the (or a, that) way (1742) Euphemistic ■ J. Rose: She suspected herself of being pregnant, 'in the way' as she called it. (1980)

gone (1747) Used to specify the length of pregnancy ■ Winifred Holtby: Brought her to the Home, four months gone, and won't be fifteen till next March. (1931)

in the family way (1796) Euphemistic ■ *Listener:* Wretched little dramas of scruffy girls in jeans being aborted after men with sideburns . . . had got them in the family way. (1967)

expecting (1890) Euphemistic ■ R. Longrigg: 'Make him do a Charleston.' 'Have a heart,' said Sue. 'I'm expecting.' (1957)

in pod (1890) ■ Melvin Bragg: Your working-class lad is still a bit worried if he gets his girl in pod. (1968)

in the (pudding) club (1890) Euphemistic ■ J. N. Smith: When the doctor told me I was in the club I

told him he was daft—that I'd never—well, you know. (1969) ■ Lionel Davidson: 'Was she in the pudding club?' . . . 'Probably. They aren't saying.' (1978)

in trouble (1891) Euphemistic ■ *Daily News:* She said she consented to come to London to be married to the prisoner as she believed she was in trouble. (1891)

up the pole (1922) Euphemistic; from earlier sense, in difficulty ■ Flann O'Brien: To say nothing of a lot of crooked Popes with their armies and their papal states, putting duchesses and nuns up the pole, and having all Italy littered with their bastards. (1961)

up the spout (1937) Euphemistic; from earlier sense, spoiled, ruined ■ S. Troy: Up the spout, isn't she? I thought Michel would have had more bloody savvy. (1970)

in the spud line (1937) Euphemistic ■ H. W. Sutherland: It couldn't have been himself that put Kathleen Ertall in the spud line. (1967)

preggy, preggie (1938) Euphemistic; from *preg(nant + -y* ■ *Star* (Sheffield): Final fling for noisy Parkers shows Michael and preggie June back in England. (1976)

up the duff (1941) Mainly Australian; from *duff* (pudding made of) dough, from the same notion as inspired *pudding club* and *bun in the oven* ■ Robert Dentry: 'There was a strong suspicion that one of the women was preggers.' 'Eh?' 'Up the duff, sir.' (1971)

up the stick (1941) Euphemistic ■ J. I. M. Stewart: Do you know what it's like, Cyril, to be a decent and penniless young man who isn't sure he hasn't got his girl up the stick? (1976)

preggers (1942) British; from *preg(nant + -ers* (as in *bonkers, crackers,* etc.) ■ Monica Dickens: Let anyone mention in her hearing that they felt sick, and it would be all over the hospital that they were 'preggers'. (1942)

in pig (1945) From earlier standard use, applied to a sow ■ Dorothy Halliday: Since when had her mother paid the slightest attention to anything her darling daughter said or did, except to do her level best to keep her from marrying anything less than a duke, until she had to get herself in pig. (1976)

preggo (1951) Australian; also used as a noun, denoting a pregnant woman; from *preg(nant +* the Australian suffix *-o* ■ Patrick White: 'Can't resist the bananas.' 'Yeah. They say you go for them like one thing when you're preggo.' (1965)

preg (1955) Often euphemistic; abbreviation of *pregnant* ■ *London Magazine*: A bit of news which may just interest you, I am P-R-E-G and not by Roy. (1967)

up the creek (1961) Euphemistic; from earlier sense, in difficulty ■ E. Lambert: I know a girl who thinks her bloke may have put her up the creek. (1963)

To make pregnant

knock up (1813) US ■ H. C. Rae: He screwed her, knocked her up first go and . . . married her . . . before she could even contemplate abortion. (1971)

stork (1936) US; from the noun *stork*, with reference to the nursery fiction that babies are brought by the stork ■ Rex Stout: 'Didn't she stop because she was pregnant?' . . . 'Yes,' he said. 'She was storked.' (1968)

A conceived child in the womb

a pudding in the oven (1937) Compare **in the (pudding) club** p. 21 ■ Joyce Porter: 'None of us

ever suspected that she'd got a pudding in the oven.' 'She was going to have a baby?' asked Dover. (1965)

a bun in the oven (1951) ■ Nicholas Monsarrat: 'I bet you left a bun in the oven, both of you,' said Bennett thickly. . . . Lockhart explained . . . the reference to pregnancy. (1951)

Unplanned pregnancy

afterthought (1914) Applied to the youngest child in a family, especially one born considerably later than the other children; from the supposition that the birth of such a child was not envisaged when the older children were conceived ■ Graham McInnes: Terence was the youngest child. . . . ('I'm a little afterthought.') (1965)

accident (1932) ■ Margaret Drabble: I had two, and then Gabriel was an accident. (1967)

A miscarriage

miss (1897) Abbreviation ■ Dell Shannon: She had a miss, that time, lost the baby. (1971)

A premature birth or baby

preemie, premie, premy (1927) North American; (alteration, after American pronunciation, of) *prem(ature + -ie* ■ *Time* (Canada edition): The preemie's sense of security is further heightened by the recorded sound of a pregnant mother's heartbeat piped into the artificial womb. (1975)

A Caesarian section

Caesar (1952) ■ *Guardian*: One Roman Catholic doctor . . . will awaken this convenient custodian of his conscience with the words: 'I'm doing a fourth Caesar.' (1964)

Midwifery; a midwifery case

midder (1909) From *mid(wifery + -er* ■ M. Polland: Although he . . . did his medicine in Edinburgh, he came here to the Rotunda for his midder. (1965)

Contraception

Vatican roulette (1962) Jocular; applied to the rhythm method of birth control, as permitted by the Roman Catholic Church; by analogy from *Russian roulette*; from the method's unpredictable efficacy ■ David Lodge: That's another thing against the safe method there are so many things that can affect ovulation. . . . No wonder they called it Vatican Roulette. (1965). See also Contraceptives under **Sex** (p. 79)

9. Tiredness

Tired

fagged (1780) British; often followed by *out*; from the past participle of the obsolete verb *fag* tire, of unknown origin ■ Edward Pennell-Elmhirst: I have seldom seen so many fagged faces as on Saturday. (1883)

beat (1832) From past participle of the verb *beat*; usually in the phrase *dead beat* ■ Pamela Frankau: I was too beat and hazy to take anything in. (1954)

tuckered (c.1840) US; often followed by *out*; past participle of the verb *tucker* tire ■ S. W. Baker: The old bear got regularly tuckered-out. (1890)

jiggered up (1862) Orig dialect; *jiggered* probably a euphemistic substitution for *buggered*

bushed (1870) North American; from earlier sense, lost in the bush ■ Castle & Bailey: You thought you'd reached the end then—completely bushed, with not another ounce left in you. (1958)

stove-up (1901) North American; *stove* from irregular past participle of the verb *stave* crush inwards ■ Harper Lee: Mr Avery'll be in bed for a week—he's right stove-up. He's too old to do things like that. (1960)

all in (1902) ■ Marghanita Laski: You look all in. . . . Been doing too much, that's what it is. (1952)

stonkered (1918) Mainly Australian & New Zealand; past participle of the verb *stonker* kill, defeat ■ Peter Carey: She ate heartily . . . only announcing herself stonkered after scraping clean the large monogrammed plate of steaming pudding. (1985)

whacked (1919) Mainly British; often followed by *out* ■ John Snow: I was whacked when I arrived back in England from the MCC tour. (1976)

creased (1925) Mainly US; from earlier sense, stunned, killed

shattered (1930) ■ *Listener*: I came in at tea-time, I sat down and I was absolutely shattered. (1968)

euchred (1932) Australian; from earlier US sense, outwitted, originally in the card game euchre ■ J. Morrison: This man has worked hard in Australia for forty years, but he's euchred now. . . . All he asks for is the old age pension. (1973)

pooped (1932) Orig US; past participle of the verb *poop* tire; often followed by *out* ■ J. T. Farrell: Studs took a large rocker, and carried it slowly downstairs. . . . When he set it down in the alley, he was breathless, and all pooped out. (1934)

shagged (1932) Often followed by *out*; origin uncertain; perhaps related to the verb *shag* have sex with ■ G. W. Target: The two other-rankers were now sitting in the back of the jeep, with all of 'em looking shagged out. (1975)

shot (1939) From earlier sense, worn out ■ Joseph Gores: He . . . [was] literally too tired to move. . . . Shot, utterly shot. (1972)

like death warmed up (1939) Used to denote extreme or prostrating exhaustion ■ J. Pendower: It damned near killed me. . . . I still feel like death warmed up. (1964)

whipped (1940) US; sometimes followed by *up* ■ G. Lea: 'Oh sure.' He pulled in his feet, hugged his knees, yawned. 'I'm whipped.' (1958)

rooted (1944) Australian; from past participle of the verb *root* ruin ■ J. Hibberd: Er, why don't you grab a pew, Valhalla. You must be rooted. (1982)

buggered (1947) From past participle of the verb *bugger* ruin ■ H. C. Rae: He was so utterly buggered that he had no hunger left. (1968)

knackered (1949) Past participle of the verb *knacker* tire ■ *Times*: I kept thinking I should whip up the pace and then I'd think 'I'm knackered, I'll leave it for another lap'. (1971)

wiped (1958) Orig US; usually followed by *out* ■ Margaret Atwood: 'Christ, am I wiped,' he says. 'Somebody break me out a beer.' (1972)

zonked (1972) From earlier sense, intoxicated; often followed by *out* ■ *Daily Telegraph*: 'Fairly zonked' by his non-stop 17 weeks of filming, he is recharging himself for the next stage. (1980)

wasted (1995) Compare earlier senses, drunk or under the influence of drugs ■ *Cambridge International Dictionary of English*: Man, I'm wasted! I've been on duty for 36 hours! (1995)

Tiredness

the bonk (1952) Applied to (a sudden attack of) fatigue or light-headedness sometimes experienced by especially racing cyclists; origin unknown ■ Watson & Gray: The British call this attack of nauseous weakness the 'Bonk'. (1978)

To tire, exhaust

finish (1816) Often followed by *off*

sew up (1837) From earlier sense, tire out a horse

tucker (*c*.1840) US; from the verb *tuck* put tucks in ■ *Turnover*: Set us to runnin', an' I could tucker him— (1853)

do in (1917) From earlier sense, ruin, kill ■ Edmund Hillary: For the first time I really feel a bit done in. (1955)

poop (1932) Orig US; often followed by *out*; origin unknown ■ *Time*: Pheidippides . . . was so pooped by his performance that he staggered into Athens. (1977)

knacker (1946) From earlier sense, kill, castrate, from the noun *knacker* horse-slaughterer

10. Sleep

bye-bye, bye-byes (1867) Used as a nursery word for 'sleep', and sometimes also for 'bed'; often in the phrase *go to bye-bye(s)* go to sleep or to bed; from earlier use as a sound to lull a child to sleep ■ Michael Harrison: You tucked up for bye-byes all on your little ownsome. (1939)

beddy-byes, beddy-bye (1906) Used as a nursery word for 'sleep', and sometimes also for 'bed'; often used to indicate to a child that it is time for bed; from *bed* + *-y* + *bye* (*-bye* ■ Sarah Russell: Mrs. Chalmers rolled up her knitting and said she supposed it was time for beddy-byes. (1946)

sack time (1944), sack drill, sack duty (1946) Orig US services'; also applied more broadly to time spent in bed; from *sack* bed

(A period of) sleep

kip (1893) From earlier sense, bed ■ Brian Aldiss: I had to stay with the captain . . . while the other lucky sods settled down for a brief kip. (1971)

skipper (1935) British; applied to an act of sleeping rough; esp. in the phrase *to do a skipper*; from earlier sense, sleeping place for a vagrant ■ *Observer:* There are not enough beds. Many will be turned away and have to do a 'skipper' in station, park or ruin. (1962)

nod (1942) Applied to a state of drowsiness brought on by narcotic drugs; esp. in the phrase *on the nod* ■ Kenneth Orvis: While I was on the nod. (1962)

A short sleep

snooze (1793) From the verb *snooze* ■ J. R. Rees: With a warm ejaculation on his tongue, the interrupted sleeper returns to his snooze. (1886)

forty winks (1872) ■ George Sims: I'm tired, and I want my forty winks. (1889)

caulk (1917) Nautical; from the obsolete verb *caulk* to sleep, perhaps from a comparison between closing the eyes and stopping up a ship's seams ■ H. C. Bailey: 'Having a caulk' where he sat and . . . he woke at eight. (1942)

zizz, ziz (1941) From earlier sense, buzzing sound, with reference to the sound of snoring ■ M. Tabor: Philip's having a zizz. He can't stay awake. (1979)

snore-off (1950) Mainly Australian & New Zealand; applied esp. to a nap after drinking ■ D. O'Grady: He emerged from his plonk-induced snore-off. (1968)

A rest

lie-down (1840) Applied to a rest on a bed or similar ■ M. Birmingham: I won't risk our clients to you in your concussed state. . . . Why don't you go and have a little lie-down? (1974)

sit-down (1861) Applied to a rest on a chair ■ Nicolas Freeling: The sit-down had done his leg . . . some good. (1967)

To sleep

snooze (1789) Origin unknown; applied esp. to light or brief sleeping ■ Catherine Gore: She withdrew, leaving him to snooze beside the fire. (1842)

kip (1889) From the noun *kip* ■ J. Curtis: I'm kipping here tonight and all. (1938)

pound one's ear (1899) Dated, orig US ■ M. Walsh: 'Only just awakened,' I admitted . . . and how are my comrades in misfortune?' . . . 'Still pounding their ears, no doubt.' (1926)

zizz (1942) From the noun *zizz*; applied especially to light or brief sleeping ■ D. Moore: Reckon this sector's safe. Might as well zizz. (1961)

catch (or get, bag, etc.) some z's (1963) US; from the use of *z* (usually repeated) to represent the sound of snoring ■ Alan Dundes: Got to go . . . cop me some z's. (1973)

To go to bed

turn in (1695) Orig nautical ■ Nat Gould: It's late . . . and quite time we turned in. (1891)

doss (1789) British; in earliest usage, usually spelled *dorse*; probably of the same origin as obsolete *doss* ornamental covering for a seat-back, etc., from Old French *dos*, ultimately from Latin *dorsum* back; often used with *down*; often applied specifically to sleeping rough or in cheap lodgings ■ *Daily Express:* If he wants to be on his way at daybreak, he dosses down with his face to the east. (1932)

kip down (1889) From the noun *kip* bed ■ *Weekly News* (Glasgow): A driver whose van broke down near Bristol, decided to kip down in the driver's seat. (1973)

hit the hay, hit the sack (1912) Orig US; *hay* from the notion of a bed made of hay ■ Arthur Miller: Well, I don't know about you educated people, but us ignorant folks got to hit the sack. (1961)

crash (1943) Often used with *out*; often applied specifically to sleeping for a night in an improvised bed ■ *Guardian:* The homeless one was sure that someone would always offer him a place 'to crash'. (1970)

sack out (1946) Mainly US; from the noun *sack* bed ■ *Daily Telegraph:* Many young travellers . . . are faced with the choice of curling up in a doorway or 'sacking out' in one of London's parks. (1971)

sack down (1956) From the noun *sack* bed ■ E. V. Cunningham: I lost a night's sleep. . . . How about I sack down for a few hours? (1978)

To go to sleep

drop off (1820) British ■ Charles Dickens: Whenever they saw me dropping off, [they] woke me up. (1862)

nod off (1845) ■ *New York Times:* Children merely fall asleep when they are sleepy. Within minutes of seating themselves in the car, they both nodded off. (1991)

go off (1887) British ■ *Daily News:* He . . . began inhaling, and soon 'went off' to his entire satisfaction. (1896)

zonk out (1970) From *zonk* lose consciousness ■ *New York News Magazine:* If mothers zonk out at three in the afternoon every day, they may continue that pattern after it's no longer necessary. (1984)

To snore

saw gourds (1870) US; from the sound of snoring

To waken

knock up (1663) British; used to refer to waking someone by knocking on their door or window ■ *New Scientist:* If then the police did arrive to knock him up at three o'clock in the morning, he would react with amazement and dismay to the news that they would be bringing. (1991)

Waking up

wakey-wakey, wakee-wakee, waky-waky (1941) Orig services' slang; applied to reveille, and also used as a command to wake up; often combined with the phrase *rise and shine* ■ Martin Woodhouse: 'Wakey-wakey,' he said. 'Stand by your beds.' (1968)

To get up or leave one's room in the morning

surface (1963) ■ Roger Simons: 'Has there been any sign of that damned Tebaugh woman yet?' 'Afraid not. . . . She still hasn't surfaced.' (1968)

To remain in bed late in the morning

sleep in (1888) Orig nautical

lie in (1893) ■ E. M. Clowes: On Sunday her husband and son 'lay in', as she called it, till midday, while she gave them their breakfast in bed. (1911). So the noun **lie-in** applied to a period of remaining in bed late (1867) ■ Gillian Freeman: I'm going to 'ave a bit of a lie in . . . seeing I'm on 'oliday. (1959)

sack in (1946) Orig US; from the noun *sack* bed ■ Tobias Wells: Benedict's call, at about nine o'clock, woke me up. . . . I'd planned to sack in till about eleven. (1967)

A place to sleep

doss (1744) British; applied especially to a bed in cheap lodgings; also with a suffixed adverb; from the verb *doss* ■ Enid Blyton: Only an old fellow who wants a doss-down somewhere. (1956)

letty (1846) Applied to a lodging or bed; from Italian *letto* bed ■ John Osborne: *Jean*: We can't all spend our time nailing our suitcases to the floor, and shin out of the window. *Archie*: Scarper the letty. (1957)

spike (1866) British; applied to a doss-house ■ George Orwell: D'you come out o' one o' de London spikes (casual wards), eh? (1933)

kip, kip-house, kip-shop (1883) British; from earlier sense, bed ■ *Observer*: Dossers at a London kip-house. (1962)

doss-house, dosser (1889) Orig & mainly British; applied to a cheap lodging-house, especially for vagrants ■ *Courier-Mail* (Brisbane): The State Health Department is planning a crack-down on 'glorified dosshouses' operating as hostels and exploiting residents. (1990)

dorm (1900) Abbreviation of *dormitory* ■ Aldous Huxley: It was against the school rules to go up into the dorms during the day. (1936)

flop (1910) US; also applied to a bed and to a cheap lodging-house ■ John Dos Passos: They couldn't find any-place that looked as if it would give them a flop for thirty-five cents. (1930)

flop-house (1909) Orig US; applied to a cheap lodging-house, especially for vagrants

skipper (1925) British; applied to a vagrant's sleeping place; from earlier cant sense, a barn, shed, etc. used by vagrants; perhaps from Cornish *sciber* or Welsh *ysgubor* a barn ■ *Country Life*: He had painfully to learn the rudiments of vagrant survival; to make sure of his 'skipper' or kip before dark. (1978)

crash pad (1967) From *crash* go to bed and *pad* place to sleep; applied especially to a place to sleep in an emergency or for a single night ■ *Guardian*: I have . . . lived 'underground', slept in 'crash pads' and taken my food on charity. (1970)

Bed

sack (1829) Mainly US; orig naval slang, applied to a hammock or bunk; now mainly used with reference to sexual intercourse, and in the phrase *hit the sack* go to bed ■ John Updike: Women with that superheated skin are usually fantastic in the sack. (1968)

flea-bag (1839) Also applied to a soldier's sleeping-bag ■ R. Pertwee: He snaked his feet into his flea bag. (1930)

kip (1879) From earlier sense, brothel ■ Leon Griffiths: Half of the time they're tucked up in their kip reading the *Mirror* and drinking cups of tea. (1985)

Uncle Ned, uncle (1925) Rhyming slang ■ J. Scott: You did right, shoving him back in his uncle. (1982)

mick (1929) Nautical; applied to a hammock; origin unknown

hot bed (1945) US; applied to a bed in a flop-house which is used continuously by different people throughout the day, and hence to a flop-house containing such beds

pit (1948) Orig services' slang ■ D. Tinker: In our pits at night we always get rattled around a bit. (1982)

wanking pit, wanking couch (1951) From *wank* masturbate

Sleeping soundly

like a log (1886)

well away (1927) ■ Joyce Porter: Many great men . . . [can] drop off to sleep at any time, and Chief Inspector was no exception. He was well away by the time MacGregor climbed back into the car. (1973)

Bedding

weeping willow (1880) British, dated; rhyming slang for *pillow* ■ Noel Streatfield: Time young Holly was in bed. . . . Hannah wants your head on your weeping willow, pillow to you. (1944)

nap (1892) Australian; applied to blankets or other covering used by a person sleeping in the open air; probably from *knapsack* ■ *Coast to Coast 1944*: If you carry enough nap, you goes hungry; if you carry enough tucker you sleeps cold. (1945)

Sleeping-pill

sleeper (1961) ■ Celia Dale: Take a sleeper, I would, put yourself right out. (1979)

Sleepy

dopey, dopy (1932) Orig US; from earlier sense, stupified by a drug; from *dope* + *-y* ■ E. Eager: The four children . . . went on being dopey and droopy and sleepy all afternoon when they *did* get up. (1957)

11. **Illness**

Ill

queer (1781) From earlier sense, abnormal ■ F. Parrish: Jake's off queer, wi' a rumblin' stummick. (1978)

peaky (1821) From *peak* become weak or ill, of unknown origin; used to denote slight illness or sickliness ■ E. J. Worboise: The second child has sickened, and the third is reported to be looking 'peaky'. (1881)

all-overish (1832) Dated; from the notion of a feeling affecting the whole body; used to denote an indefinite unlocalized malaise

under the weather (1850) Orig US ■ F. R. Stockton: They had been very well as a general thing, although now and then they might have been under the weather for a day or two. (1887)

seedy (1858) From earlier sense, shabby, ill-looking; probably from the notion of a plant that has run to seed ■ Jerome K. Jerome: We were all feeling seedy, and we were getting nervous about it. (1889)

off colour (1876) From earlier sense, not of the usual or proper colour; used to suggest slight indisposition ■ Anthony Fowles: 'Where's Christine?' he said. 'Over her mum's. Her mum's off colour. She's staying . . . till she picks up.' (1974)

rotten (1881) From earlier, more general sense, bad ■ Dmitri Nabokov: She was feeling rotten, was in bed with a hot-water bottle and spoke to him in a singsong through the door. (1986)

dicky, dickey (1883) British; from earlier sense, of poor quality; ultimate origin uncertain; perhaps connected with the phrase *as queer as Dick's hatband* ■ Sir John Astley: Poor 'Curly' was uncommon dicky for several days from concussion of the brain. (1894)

fragile (1883) From earlier sense, liable to break

rough (a1893) Orig dialectal ■ Joseph O'Connor: For someone about to unleash himself on the world, Eddie was looking rough. (1991)

funny (1898) From earlier sense, strange ■ *On The Edge*: My body felt a bit funny still, still a bit gibbery, but I was happier. (1995)

crook (1908) Australian & New Zealand; from earlier sense, of poor quality ■ A. J. Holt: I'm crook in the guts now. (1946)

icky-boo, icky-poo (1920), icky, ikky (1939) *icky* probably a baby-talk alteration of *sick* or *sickly* ■ Berkeley Mather: Call the airline office . . . and tell 'em you're feeling an icksy bit icky-boo and want a stopover. (1970)

lousy (1933) From earlier sense, of poor quality ■ Patricia Moyes: A brisk, pretty, coloured nurse came in. . . . 'Ah, you're awake. . . . How do you feel?' 'Lousy,' said Henry. (1973)

like death warmed up (1939) ■ J. Pendower: It damned near killed me. . . . I still feel like death warmed up. (1964)

ropy, ropey (1945) From earlier sense, of poor quality ■ *Sunday Express*: I feel a bit ropey . . . I think I've picked up some sort of virus. (1961)

green about the gills (1949), pale about the gills (1959) Often applied specifically to feeling nauseous; from the notion of a pale face as a sign of illness; compare obsolete *white* and *yellow about the gills*, current in the same sense in the 19th century ■ *New Age Journal*: [With] 110 pesticides in nonorganic raisins, 80 in the nonorganic apple, and 29 in the whole milk, . . . it's a wonder that Junior doesn't come home looking green around the gills. (1991)

peculiar (1954) From earlier sense, strange ■ R. Elliot: I admit I felt a little peculiar for a while, but whatever it was has passed and I'm absolutely fine now. (1992)

butcher's hook, butcher's (1967) Australian; rhyming slang for *crook* ill ■ Barry Humphries: Still feeling butcher's after your op, are ya? (1981)

on the sick (1976) Used to denote incapacity due to illness, and receipt of sickness benefit ■ Leslie Thomas: I took it [an allotment] on . . . but then I was on the sick for months . . . and the council . . . takes it off me. (1976)

grim (1984) First recorded in 1984, but in use earlier ■ B. Rowlands: Dora must be feeling pretty grim at the moment. Perhaps we shouldn't have left her on her own. (1993)

An illness

woofits (1918) Used to denote an unwell feeling, especially in the head, or moody depression; origin unknown ■ Nevil Shute: Getting the woofits now, because I don't sleep so well. (1958)

crud (1932) Orig army slang; used to denote any disease or illness; variant of *curd* ■ Frank Shaw et al.: *I got Bombay crud*, I am suffering from looseness of the bowels. (1966)

lurgy, lurgi (1954) British; used to denote a fictitious, highly infectious disease; usually in the phrase *the dreaded lurgy*; coined by the writers of *The Goon Show*, British radio comedy programme first broadcast in 1951 ■ Hamish MacInnes: I was beginning to feel weak and knew that I had caught the dreaded swamp lurgy. (1974)

A sick person

wreck (1795) ■ W. R. H. Trowbridge: I think I am in for influenza. I feel a perfect wreck. (1901)

martyr (1847) Applied to someone who is habitually a prey to a particular ailment ■ *Law Times*: The deceased . . . had been a martyr for years to rheumatic gout. (1892)

To suffer illness

come over (1922) Used to denote the sudden onset of symptoms ■ N. F. Simpson: There was nothing wrong with him . . . and then next day he came over funny at work. (1960)

To injure

do in (1905) ■ *Oxford Advanced Learner's Dictionary*: He did his back in lifting heavy furniture. (1995)

To cause pain to

kill (1800) Originally Irish English ■ Joyce Porter: The long cold walk . . . did nothing to lighten Dover's mood. His feet were killing him. (1965)

Bruising

mouse (1854) Applied especially to a black eye ■ S. Moody: Touched the mouse under her eye. She just hoped a *Vogue* photog wasn't going to show up. (1985)

shiner (1904) Applied to a black eye ■ G. F. Fiennes: Out shot a telescopic left, and I had the shiner of all time for weeks. (1967)

Cancer

big C (1964) Euphemistic ■ *Time*: John Wayne: . . . accepted the news with true grit. 'I've licked the big C before,' he said. (1979)

Cold

snuffles (1770), sniffles (1825) Applied to a slight cold characterized by nasal congestion and discharge ■ Thomas Bryant: The snuffles in infancy are very characteristic. (1878)

To catch a bad cold

catch one's death (1712) Short for *catch one's death of cold* ■ Graham Greene: She had walked in the rain seeking a refuge and 'catching her death' instead. (1951)

Cramp

Charley-horse, charley-horse (1888) North American; applied to cramp in the arm or leg, especially in baseball players; origin uncertain ■ *Globe & Mail* (Toronto): Rookie centre Gordon Judges departed in the second half suffering a severe charley horse in his left thigh. (1968)

Diarrhoea

See under **Bodily Functions** pp. 18–19

Dizzy

woozy, whoosy, whoozy, woozey (1897) Orig US; origin unknown ■ *Black Mask*: I got hit. It made me woozey for a minute. (1937)

slug-nutty (1933) US; applied to dizziness caused by punching; from *slug* blow with the hand ■ Ernest Hemingway: He's been beat up so much he's slug-nutty. (1950)

slap-happy (1936) Applied originally to dizziness caused by punching; from *slap* blow with the hand ■ *Detective Tales*: He was a little slap-happy from a decade of slug-festing. (1940)

A fit, a sudden feeling of illness

turn (1775) Dated or jocular ■ Edith Wharton: Her mother . . . sat in a drooping attitude, her head sunk on her breast, as she did when she had one of her 'turns'. (1913)

spazz out, spaz out (1984) US; used to denote someone suffering a spasm, losing physical control; *spazz* short for *spasm*

A haemophiliac

bleeder (1803)

A headache

thick head (1991) Often applied specifically to a headache caused by alcohol; first recorded in 1991, but in use earlier ■ P. Wilson: Should you decide to stick to sherry and branch out into the heavier oloroso you will have a thick head tomorrow and we will have an entertaining evening. (1993)

Nitrogen narcosis

the narks (1962) Used by divers, who are prone to nitrogen narcosis, which is caused by breathing air under pressure; from *narc* (short for *narcosis*) + *-s* ■ J. Palmer: It's lucky the ship lies in such shallow water. We shan't get the 'narks'. (1967)

Paralysis

Saturday night palsy (1927) Jocular; mainly US; applied to temporary local paralysis in the arm, usually as a result of sleeping on it after hard drinking; from *Saturday night*, the traditional evening for enjoying oneself ■ Elliot Paul: Berthe was suffering from what is known in the United States as Saturday-night paralysis, . . . when drunken men go to sleep in gutters, with one arm across a sharp kerbstone. (1951)

Rheumatism

screwmatics, screwmaticks (1895) Dated; humorous alteration of *rheumatics* after (presumably earlier) *screws* ■ E. V. Lucas: Wet, and rats, . . . and dirt and screwmaticks. (1916)

the screws (1897) Perhaps from the notion of a twisting pain ■ Lionel Black: Any rheumatism? An occasional touch of the screws, she admitted. (1976)

A spot, pimple

hickey, hickie (1934) US; origin unknown; compare earlier sense, gadget ■ Herbert Gold: A woman is not just soul and hickie-squeezing. (1956)

zit (1966) Mainly North American; origin unknown ■ *Courier-Mail* (Brisbane): You know playing with teenagers will give you zits. (1980)

Stomach pain

belly-ache (1552) ■ Michael Bishop: A few months back, it turned where I couldn't listen to . . . any of them 'ere comedy people 'thout coming down with a bellyache. (1992)

gripes (1601) From the notion of a 'clutching' pain; originally a standard usage ■ John Baxter:

Excess of green food, sudden exposure to cold, are . . . occasional causes of gripes. (1846)

mulligrubs (1802) Dated; from earlier sense, fit of depression; originally a fanciful coinage ■ George Colman: His Bowels; Where spasms were . . . Afflicting him with mulligrubs and colic. (1802)

collywobbles (1823) Fanciful formation based on *colic* stomach pain and *wobble*, or perhaps an alteration of *colera morbus* ■ F. T. Bullen: He laughingly excused himself on the grounds that his songs were calculated to give a white man collywobbles. (1901)

gut-rot (1979) British; compare earlier sense, unwholesome liquor or food ■ *Independent*: Next day I developed gut rot, so I can't say I gave Puerto Rico a fair chance. (1989)

Trembling

the shakes (1782) Often applied specifically to delirium tremens ■ Martin Woodhouse: It was like getting the shakes on an exposed pitch of rock. (1966) ■ *New Yorker*: Have you ever had the D.T.s? The shakes? (1977)

See also under The effects of drinking (too much) alcohol under **Alcohol** p. 154.

Tropical diseases

yellow jack (1836) Dated; applied to yellow fever

Unconscious

out like a light (1934) ■ Billie Holiday: When it came time to come out for the third curtain call I said, 'Bobby, I just can't make it no longer,' and I passed out like a light. (1956)

spark out (1936) From earlier sense, completely extinguished ■ Margery Allingham: He's spark out, only just breathin'. Bin like that two days. (1952)

To become unconscious

flake out (1942) From earlier sense, become limp; *flake* originally a variant of *flag* ■ Barry Crump: I flaked out more thoroughly than a man who is blind drunk. (1960)

Venereal diseases

pox (1503) Altered plural of *pock* spot, pustule; applied especially to syphilis ■ Jimmy O'Connor: Wally . . . strangled a prostitute for giving him a dose of the pox. (1976)

clap (1587) Old French *clapoir* venereal bubo; applied especially to gonorrhoea ■ Adam Diment: Rocky Kilmarry is about as good for you as a dose of clap. (1967)

dose (1914) Applied to a bout of venereal infection ■ Bill Turner: She's riddled with pox. I know four blokes who've copped a dose from her. (1968)

syph, siph, siff (1914) Abbreviation of *syphilis* ■ C. Willingham: Why don't you tell us about that time you got siff from your nigger maid? (1947)

load (1937) Applied to a bout of venereal infection ■ Frank Sargeson: They displayed their rubber goods, and . . . were doubly protected against finding themselves landed with either biological consequences or a load. (1965)

jack (1954) Australian; short for *jack in the box*, rhyming slang for *pox* ■ N. Medcalf: Got malaria, beri-beri, malnutrition and probably a dose of jack. (1985)

Protection against venereal disease

propho (1919) Dated; orig US; abbreviation of *prophylaxis* ■ John Dos Passos: That's one thing you guys are lucky in, don't have to worry about propho. (1921)

Wounds

Blighty, Blighty one (1916) British; from earlier sense, Britain; used in World War I to denote a wound sufficiently serious to warrant return to Britain ■ W. J. Locke: Mo says he's blistering glad you're out of it and safe in your perishing bed with a Blighty one. (1918)

strawberry (1921) North American, dated; used to denote a graze on the skin

homer (1942) Australian & New Zealand; from *home* + *-er*; used in World War II to denote a wound sufficiently serious to warrant repatriation ■ Richard Bielby: She's apples. Now you just lie back an' take it easy. Ya got a homer, mate, you arsey bastard. (1977)

road rash (1970) Used to denote cuts and grazing caused by falling off a skateboard

Disability: Lame

gammy (1879) British; dialectal derivative of *game* lame, crippled, perhaps from French *gambi* crooked ■ D. M. Davin: That gammy foot of mine. (1947)

gimp (1925) Orig US; applied to a lame person or leg; also used as a verb, in the sense 'to limp, hobble'; origin uncertain; perhaps an alteration of *gammy* ■ *New Yorker*: He'd just kick a gimp in the good leg and leave him lay. (1929) ■ P. Craig: I gimped back on deck. (1969). So the noun and adjective **gimpy** a cripple; lame, crippled. (1925)

A disabled person

wingy (1880) Applied to a one-armed person; from *wing* arm + *-y* ■ Dean Stiff: Missions are very anxious to recruit the 'wingies' and 'armies', or the one-armed hobos. (1931)

basket case (1919) Orig US military slang; applied especially to someone who has lost all four limbs; from the notion of someone who has no mobility and has to be carried around ■ Mario Puzo: 'Hunchbacks are not as good as anyone else?' I asked. . . . 'No . . . nor are guys with one eye, basket cases and . . . chickenshit guys.' (1978)

wheelie (1977) Australian; applied to someone in or confined to a wheelchair; from *wheel* + *-ie*

■ *Sunday Mail* (Brisbane): So many places and things are inaccessible to the 'wheelie'. (1978)

cabbage (1987) Applied to someone incapacitated through brain damage or brain malfunction; compare earlier sense, inactive and intellectually inert person ■ Irvine Welsh: Poor Ma, still blaming hersel fir that fucked up gene that caused ma brother Davie tae be born a cabbage. Her guilt, eftir struggling wi him fir years, at pittin him in the hoespital. (1993)

Germs

bug (1919) From earlier sense, (harmful) insect ■ Joyce Cary: May I get into your bed, Harry?—I'm freezing. I won't breathe any of my bugs on you. (1941)

wog (1941) Australian; from earlier sense, (harmful) insect ■ C. Green: A 'flu wog' struck, and several families of children were absent with . . . 'terrible hackin' coffs'. (1978)

Sick leave

sickie (1953) Australian & New Zealand; applied to a day's sick leave, especially one taken without valid medical reason; from *sick* + *-ie* ■ *Courier-Mail* (Brisbane): A part-time fireman's sense of duty cost him his job after he answered an emergency call when he was taking a 'sickie' from work. (1981)

In good health

right as a trivet (1837), right as ninepence (1890), right as rain (1909) ■ George Sanders: It had severed some ligaments or what-not that caused him to have a slight limp afterwards, but apart from that he was as right as rain. (1960) ■ Jennie Melville: He'll surface as right as ninepence in due course. (1980)

fit as a fiddle (1882) From earlier sense, in excellent condition

in the pink (1914) From earlier sense, in good condition; from the phrase *in the pink of condition* etc., from *pink* flower, hence finest ■ P. G. Wodehouse: 'Oh, hallo!' I said. 'Going strong?' 'I am in excellent health, thank you. And you?' 'In the pink. Just been over to America.' (1923)

Recovering health

on the mend (1802) ■ John Barth: Heart-scarred still, but on the mend; doing nicely, thanks. (1994)

pull round (1891) ■ *Pall Mall Magazine*: He thinks he's going to pull round again; but I'll bet on his not being alive this day week. (1896)

Medical practitioners and nurses

medico (1689) From Italian *medico* physician ■ *Nature*: The twenty thousand or so scientists, engineers, medicos and so on on the staff of British universities. (1973)

medic (1823) From Latin *medicus* medical person; in standard use in the 17th century, and revived in American college slang ■ *Evening Standard*: Dr Brian Warren, Mr Heath's personal physician, called to see him at Downing Street—but as a friend, not as a medic. (1974)

zambuk, zambuc, zambuck (1918) Australian & New Zealand; applied to a first-aider, a St. John Ambulance man or woman, especially at a sporting event; from the proprietary name of a brand of antiseptic ointment

prick-farrier (1961) Services' slang; applied to a medical officer; from *prick* penis and *farrier* horse-doctor, in allusion to the examinations for venereal disease carried out by medical officers

physio (1962) Applied to a physiotherapist, and also to physiotherapy; abbreviation ■ *Times*: I remember we didn't have a physio of our own, so we had to go to the athletics one. (1971)

Doctors

pill-peddler, pill-pusher, pill-roller, pill-shooter (1857) Also applied to chemists ■ James Curtis: He was damned if he let a lousy pill-roller know just how bad he felt. (1936)

croaker (1859) Now mainly US; applied especially to prison doctors; from *croak*, perhaps with ironic reference to the sense 'kill' + *-er*; compare also obsolete slang *crocus* quack doctor, perhaps from the Latinized surname of Dr Helkiah Crooke, a 17th-century surgeon ■ Mezzrow & Wolfe: The most he needed was some bicarbonate of soda and a physic, not a croaker. (1946)

pill (1860) Dated; also applied to (a member of) the Royal Army Medical Corps

quack (1919) Orig Australian & New Zealand; from earlier sense, an unqualified doctor, a charlatan; also applied in services' slang to a medical officer ■ John Iggulden: I'll get the quack at the Bush Hospital to have a look at it in the morning. (1960)

vet (1925) Jocular; from earlier sense, veterinary surgeon ■ Anthony Powell: Saw my vet last week. Said he'd never inspected a fitter man of my age. (1975)

right croaker (1929) Dated; applied by criminals to a doctor who will treat criminals without informing the police, or supply drugs

Surgeons

sawbones (1837) Also applied to physicians ■ Rider Haggard: I found her the affianced bride of a parish sawbones. (1898)

orthopod (1960) Applied to an orthopaedic surgeon; alteration of *orthopaedic* ■ Dick Francis: I telephoned to the orthopod who regularly patched me up after falls. (1969)

gynae (1982) Shortening of *gynaecologist* ■ Barr & York: Sloanes who aren't producing will go to their sweet gynae, who will tell them to stand on their heads afterwards. (1982)

Medicine

pick-me-up (1900) Applied to a tonic medicine; from earlier sense, any stimulating drink

jollop (1955) Applied especially to a purgative; alteration of *jalap* type of purgative obtained from a Mexican plant, ultimately from *Jalapa*, *Xalapa* name of a city in Mexico, from Aztec *Xalapan* sand by the water ■ D'Arcy Niland: He nutted out some jollop for her cough. (1955)

Hospital

in/out of dock (1785) Denoting in/out of hospital, receiving/after treatment ■ *News Chronicle*: He's just out of dock after the old appendix. (1960)

Ambulance

blood wagon (1922) ■ Stirling Moss: Out came the 'blood wagon' and to the ambulance station in the paddock I went. (1957)

meat wagon (1925) Mainly US ■ Hartley Howard: She hadn't deserved to become a parcel of broken flesh and bone in the meat wagon. (1973)

Medical examination

short-arm (1919) Orig & mainly military slang; applied to an inspection of the penis for venereal disease or other infection; from the notion of the penis as an additional (but shorter) limb ■ Mario Puzo: Before you go to bed with a guy, give him a short arm. ... You strip down his penis, you know, like you're masturbating him, and if there's a yellow fluid coming out like a drippage, you know he's infected. (1978)

Medical treatment: Surgery

op (1925) Abbreviation of *operation* ■ G. L. Cohen: The probationers agreed that minor ops gave the most trouble. (1964)

Gynaecology

gynae, gynie (1933) Shortening (and alteration) of *gynaecology* ■ G. L. Cohen: 'We didn't come across any horrors,' said Dr. Duncum ... 'unless you count adolescent girls in gynae wards.' (1964)

Injection

jab (1914) Orig US drug-users' slang ■ *Times*: The visitor must ... take precautions and submit to a variety of jabs. (1973)

Nursing

special (1961) Used of a nurse, to attend continuously to (a single patient) ■ *Nursing Times*: A nurse will have to 'special' the patient to make the necessary observations. (1967)

Autopsy

post (1942) Abbreviation of *post-mortem*; also used as a verb, in the sense 'perform an autopsy on (someone)' ■ F. Richards: She died last night. Overdose, probably. They're doing a post. (1969)

12. Death

Death

curtains (1901) Orig US; from the notion of the closing of the curtain at the end of a theatrical performance ■ Wallis & Blair: If the Party ever got on to it ... it would be curtains for Kurt. (1956)

wooden cross (1919) Services' slang; applied ironically to death in battle, from the notion of a medal awarded for merit; from earlier sense, cross of wood marking a soldier's grave ■ A. Murphy: There is no other branch of the army that offers so many chances for the Purple Heart, the Distinguished Wooden Cross, the Royal Order of the Mattress Covers. (1949)

deep-six (1929) Orig & mainly US; usually in the phrase *give someone the deep-six* kill someone; probably from the custom of burial at sea, at a depth of six fathoms ■ S. Palmer: My old lady went over the hill with my bank account before I was out of boot camp. I'd have given her the deep-six if I coulda got a furlough. (1947)

thirty (1929) US; used by journalists, printers, etc.; from earlier use of the figure 30 to mark the end of a piece of journalist's copy ■ *Sun* (Baltimore): Newsmen ... mourned today at the bier of Edward J. Neil, ... who was killed by shrapnel while covering the civil war ... in Spain. Prominent ... was a shield of white carnations with a red-flowered figure '30'—the traditional 'good night' in the lore of the fourth estate. (1938)

the big sleep (1938) Orig US; popularized by the name of the novel *The Big Sleep* (1938) by Raymond Chandler, and probably coined by Chandler himself

the chop, the chopper (1945) Orig services' slang; usually in the phrase *get the chop*, originally denoting being killed in action, specifically by being shot down, and subsequently more generally, being killed ■ Aidan Crawley: 'The chop' in Buchenwald meant execution or the gas chamber. (1956)

Dead

off the hooks (1840) Dated ■ John Galsworthy: Old Timothy; he might go off the hooks at any moment. I suppose he's made his Will. (1921)

bung (1882) Australian & New Zealand; also in the phrase *go bung* die; from Aboriginal (Jagara) ba*

napoo, na poo, napooh (1919) Dated; alteration of French (*il n'y e)n a plus* there is no more ■ Laurence Meynell: Prudence ... fell down dead in the croupier's bag. Fini. Napoo. (1973)

loaf o(f) bread (1930) British; rhyming slang ■ Auden & Isherwood: O how I cried when Alice died The day we were to have wed! We never had our Roasted Duck And now she's a Loaf of Bread. (1935)

brown bread (1973) British; rhyming slang

(To be) dead and buried

under the daisies (1866) ■ Sherrard Vines: I think she's drinking herself under the daisies, so to speak. (1928)

push up (the) daisies (a1918) ■ *Guardian*: In ten years time I think I should be pushing up daisies. (1970)

six feet under (1942) ■ J. Gerson: In Islay . . . we make sure the dead are stiff and cold and six feet under. (1979)

To die

pop off (1764) ■ Dorothy Sayers: Perhaps it's just as well he popped off when he did. He might have cut me off with a shilling. (1928)

kick the bucket (1785) Perhaps from obsolete *bucket* beam from which something may be hung (perhaps from Old French *buquet* balance), from the notion of an animal hung up for slaughter kicking in its death throes ■ Salman Rushdie: Pinkie was a widow; old Marshal Aurangzeb had kicked the bucket at last. (1983)

hop the twig (or stick) (1797) ■ Mary Bridgman: If old Campbell hops the twig. (1870)

croak (1812) From the sound of the death rattle ■ John Welcome: Your old man has croaked and left you the lot. (1961)

turn up one's toes (1851) ■ *Daily Chronicle*: It is . . . quite a commonplace remark to hear young men boast of the time when 'the old man turns up his toes', and they can 'collar the chips'. (1905)

peg out (1855) Apparently from the notion of reaching the end of a game of cribbage ■ *European*: You state that she is 'an ancestor of Fabius Maximus, five times consul of Ancient Rome'. He pegged out in 203 BC. (1991)

pass (or hand) in one's chips (1879) Orig US; from the notion of exchanging counters for money at the end of a gambling game

cash in, cash in one's chips, cash in one's checks (1884) Orig US; from the notion of exchanging counters for money at the end of a gambling game ■ Desmond Varaday: Because of the size of the dead animal, at first I thought it to be buffalo. 'Poor Bill or Phyl, cashed in?' (1966)

snuff it (1885) From the notion of extinguishing a candle ■ M. Gee: I mean, he didn't let the grass grow under his feet, it wasn't much more than a year after the first Mrs Tatlock snuffed it. (1981)

stop (1901) Denoting being hit and killed by a bullet, shell, etc.; often in the phrase *stop one* be killed in this way ■ Hugh Walpole: Maurice stood there wishing that he might 'stop one' before he had to go over the top. (1933)

hand (or pass, turn) in one's dinner-pail (1905) Jocular ■ P. G. Wodehouse: My godfather . . . recently turned in his dinner pail and went to reside with the morning stars. (1964)

pass (chuck, etc.) in one's marble (1908) Australian, dated; from *marble* small glass sphere used in games ■ Dal Stivens: I'm not going to pass in my marble just yet. (1951)

get his, hers, theirs, etc. (1909) Orig & mainly services' slang; denoting being killed ■ Norman Mailer: He was going to get his, come two three four hours. That was all right, of course, you didn't live forever. (1959)

go west (1915) Perhaps from the notion of the sun setting in the west ■ Eugene Corri: I shall once again be in the company of dear old friends now 'gone West'. (1915)

buy it (1920) Orig British, services' slang; originally and mainly applied to being killed in action, often specifically to being shot down; mainly used in past tenses ■ J. E. Morpurgo: I'm afraid we want you elsewhere. . . . Jim Barton bought it, and you'll have to take on his troop. (1944)

kick off (1921) Orig US ■ Robert Lowell: The old bitches Live into their hundreds, while I'll kick off tomorrow. (1970)

off it (1930) From earlier sense, depart

seven out (1934) US; from earlier sense, in the game of craps, throw a seven and so lose one's bet ■ Saul Bellow: 'Why do you push it, Charlie?' he said. 'At our age one short game is plenty. . . . One of these days you could seven out.' (1975)

go for a Burton (1941) British, services' slang; applied to a pilot being killed in an air crash; origin unknown; perhaps connected with *Burton* type of beer from Burton-on-Trent

kiss off (1945) US

buy the farm (1958), buy the ranch (1963) US, orig services' slang; originally denoting being killed (in action), and hence more generally dying; from earlier sense, crash in an aircraft

kark, cark (1977) Australian; often in the phrase *kark it*; perhaps from Australian *cark* caw, from the association of crows with death ■ *Sydney Morning Herald*: We talked parties, weddings, people karking it and the attendant floral arrangements. (1982)

keel over (1977) From earlier sense, fall to the ground ■ *Daily Mail*: The moment when the hero's uncle keeled over in the lobby of the Ritz Hotel with a fatal heart attack. (1991)

Doomed to die

one's number is up (1899) ■ J. Aiken: He'd got leukaemia. He knew his number was up. (1975)

Someone who has died

goner (1847) From *gone* + *-er* ■ *Boys' Magazine*: When I found the car burnt out I thought you were a 'goner'. (1933)

stiff (1859) From the effects of rigor mortis ■ Thomas Pynchon: Ten thousand stiffs humped under the snow in the Ardennes take on the sunny Disneyfied look of numbered babies under white wool blankets. (1973)

floater (1890) US; applied to a dead body found floating in water ■ Jessica Mitford: Floaters . . . are another matter; a person who has been in the Bay for a week or more . . . will decompose more rapidly. (1963)

A coffin

box (1864) ■ W. Henry: Personally, I'll believe he's dead when the box is shut and covered up. (1957)

wooden overcoat (1903), wooden kimono (1926), wooden suit (1968) ■ Mezzrow & Wolfe: I expected the man to turn up . . . with his tape measure to outfit me with a wooden kimono. (1946) ■ *Guardian*: The paratroops were edgy and the one who let me through the barricade reckoned I would come out in a wooden overcoat. (1971)

pine drape (1945) US; *drape* = curtain

A cemetery

marble orchard (1929), marble town (1945) US; from the marble used for the headstones ■ B. Broadfoot: A couple more punches and it would have been the marble orchard for him. (1973)

A hearse

meat-wagon (1942) Compare earlier sense, ambulance ■ Stephen Longstreet: The band would march out behind the meat-wagon, black plumes on the hearse horses. (1956)

To bury

plant (1855) Orig US ■ Roderic Jeffries: The funeral must be fixed up at once. Where did non-Catholics get planted? (1974)

Rigor mortis

rigmo (1966) British; used by undertakers, embalmers, etc.; shortening ■ *Observer*: Embalmers' aids like the Natural Expression Former (a plastic device which, inserted into the mouth after rigmo—as we call it in the trade—sets in, can produce a seraphic smile on the deceased face). (1975)

People and Society

1. Ethnic & National Groups

English people

tyke (a1700) British; applied to a person from Yorkshire; from earlier sense, dog, from Old Norse *tík* bitch ■ P. Ryan: The Yorkshire terrier seems fitter mate for the volatile Taffy than for the taciturn Tyke. (1967)

Limey (1888) Applied originally, mainly in Australia, New Zealand and South Africa, to a British immigrant, and subsequently (1918) in the US to a British person (originally a sailor) or ship; abbreviation of obsolete *lime-juicer*, from the former enforced consumption of lime juice as an antiscorbutic in the British Navy ■ John Steinbeck: Fights in the bar-rooms with the goddam Limeys. (1952)

Brit (1901) Now mainly US, but rare in the US before the 1970s; short for *Briton* or *Britisher* ■ Rhona Petrie: Goddam Limey! You're a Brit. (1969)

pommy, pommie, pom (1912) Mainly Australian and New Zealand; often applied specifically to an English immigrant; possibly short for obsolete *pommygrant*, a jocular blend of *pomegranate* and *immigrant* ■ John Galsworthy: They call us Pommies and treat us as if we'd took a liberty in coming to their blooming country. (1926) ■ Adelaide Lubbock: Be seein' yer soon in England. Hooray! Aroo! Good on yer, Pom. (1963)

choom (1916) Australian & New Zealand; applied especially to an English soldier; variant of *chum* friend ■ *Bulletin* (Sydney): He wasn't a choom; he came straight from Brisbane and had been born and reared in Sydney. (1935)

Woodbine (1919) Australian, dated; applied especially to an English soldier; from the proprietary name of a British brand of cigarettes ■ E. Hill: Bagtown became 'Woodbine Ave' . . . so-called for the number of English settlers in residence. (1937)

homey, homie (1927) New Zealand; applied to a British immigrant, especially one newly arrived; from *home* + *-y* ■ D. M. Davin: An English accent. How hard it was to remember that it was as natural to a homey as your own accent was to you. (1970)

Brummy, Brummie (1941) Applied to someone from Birmingham; short for *Brummagem*, a local variant of *Birmingham* ■ *New Statesman*: He proclaims proudly, in a modulated Birmingham accent that makes him sound like a well-bred Australian: 'I'm a natural born Brummie.' (1965)

pongo (1942) Australian & New Zealand; from earlier sense, soldier ■ *Private Eye*: The pongos are shooting through like streaks of *weasle piss*! (1969)

kipper (1943) Australian; applied especially to English immigrants; from a popular Australian association of kippers with the English ■ Kenneth Giles: You kippers—no guts and two faces—are only strong under the armpits. . . . What about the east of Suez caper, eh? (1967)

Scouse (1945) Used as an adjective and noun denoting 'Liverpudlian', and also applied to the dialect of English spoken in Liverpool; abbreviation of *lobscouse* ■ *Guardian*: Scouse House was the tongue-in-cheek name given to the Merseyside Development Office. (1973) ■ *Times*: A roly-poly, amiable Liverpudlian, with the Scouse's seemingly god-given gift of being able to send up an overblown . . . occasion. (1980). Hence **Scouser** a Liverpudlian (1959) ■ *Liverpool Echo*: It's pretty well established that where there's a ship there you'll find a Scouser. (1976)

loiner (1950) Applied to an inhabitant of Leeds, West Yorkshire; origin unknown ■ P. Ryan: I ran through the ranks of rumbling loiners and out into the eternal, grey twilight of Leeds. (1967)

French people

frog, Frog (1778) Applied derogatorily to a French person and (1955) to the French language; from French people's reputation for eating frogs ■ Iris Murdoch: Not that I want you to marry a frog, but she sounded quite a nice girl. (1962) ■ William Faulkner: Ask him. . . . You can speak Frog. (1955)

froggy, Froggy, froggee (1872) Applied derogatorily to a French person, and also used adjectivally; from *frog* + *-y* ■ *Guardian*: A group of stage-type Limeys spend a weekend in France where they mix with a series of stage-type Froggies. (1965) ■ Iris Murdoch: What about that froggy girl, the one you met in Singapore? (1962)

Frenchy, Frenchie (1883) Applied derogatorily to a French person or French Canadian; from earlier adjective *Frenchy* French-like, from *French* + *-y* ■ *Maclean's*: I was constantly laughed at, pointed at and corrected, as a stupid Frenchy. (1966)

Germans

sausage (1890) Dated; from the prevalence of sausages in the German diet

Dutchy, Dutchee, Dutchie (1835) Orig US; used derogatorily; from *Dutch* German (immigrant in the US) + *-y*

Hun (1902) Applied derogatorily to a German, especially a German soldier of World War I; from earlier sense, member of a warlike Asian tribe; the application was inspired by a speech delivered by Wilhelm II to German troops about to leave for China on 27 July 1900, exhorting them to be as fierce as Huns ■ *Times*: 'Supposed' statements . . . of American 'advisers' . . . simply smell of Hun propaganda. (1918)

squarehead (1903) Mainly US; applied derogatorily to a foreigner of Germanic extraction, specifically a German soldier in World War I ■ H. C. Witwer: The English call 'em 'Uns . . . we call 'em squareheads. (1918)

Heinie, Heine, Hiney (1904) North American; applied especially to a German soldier; from the German male personal name *Heinrich* ■ *Listener*: It's not the Russians we should be congratulating . . . but the Heinies. Sure, we got Von Braun, but the Russians grabbed all the rest of the German rocket guys. (1961)

Boche (1914) Applied derogatorily to a German, especially a German soldier, or to Germans collectively; from French slang *boche* rascal, applied to German soldiers in World War I ■ E. F. Davies: If the Boche wanted a rough-house he could rely on Pickering to give it to him. (1952)

Fritz (1915) Mainly derogatory; applied especially to a German soldier of World War I; from German *Fritz*, nickname for *Friedrich* ■ Jack Thomas: I gathered he was more of a *collaborateur* than anything else. He praised you Fritzes up to the skies. (1955)

Kraut (1918) Applied derogatorily to a German, specifically a German soldier; abbreviation of *sauerkraut*, from its prevalence in the German diet ■ Thomas Pynchon: Maybe . . . he should have been in a war, Japs in trees, Krauts in Tiger tanks. (1966)

Jerry (1919) British; applied to a German, specifically a German soldier or aircraft, or to Germans or German soldiers collectively; probably an alteration of *German* ■ Wynford Vaughan-Thomas: They almost felt a sympathy for the Jerries under that merciless rain of explosions. (1961)

sale Boche (1919) A French term of abuse for a German; from French *sale* dirty + *Boche* ■ Dorothy Sayers: A man . . . called him *sale Boche*—but Jean knocked him down. (1934)

Erich, Eric (1985) British; applied to a male German, usually derogatorily; from the German male forename *Erich*

Gibraltarians

scorpion (1845), scorp (1912) British services' slang; from earlier *rock scorpion* in same sense ■ W. Tute: Perks and privileges for the ruling classes. Fifteen in a room for the poor-quality 'Scorps' whose Rock it was. (1957)

Greeks

bubble and squeak, bubble (1938) British, derogatory; rhyming slang for *Greek* ■ Robin Cook: All the best Anglo-Saxon grafters come from mine [*sc.* my school], and the Bubbles and the Indians from the other. (1962)

Irish people

bog-trotter (1682) Derogatory; from the boggy nature of some Irish terrain

Paddy, paddy (1780) Often used as a nickname; often derogatory; from the common Irish male personal name *Padraig* Patrick ■ Bernard Shaw: Paddy yourself! How dar you call me Paddy? (1907)

Pat (1806) Used as a nickname; compare **Paddy** p. 34

Mick, mick (1856) Derogatory; from the supposed commonness of the male personal name *Mick* in Ireland ■ Michael Kenyon: Where's Ireland, huh? Who needs Micks? (1970)

harp (1904) US; from the harp as a symbol of Ireland ■ John Dos Passos: The foreman was a big loudmouthed harp. (1936)

Turk, turk (1914) Mainly US; applied, usually derogatorily, to a person of Irish birth or descent; perhaps from Irish *torc* boar, hog, influenced by *Turk* Turkish person, but compare *Turkey* ■ *Observer*: Their backs are to the wall in a desperate tyre-chain feudal war to protect the integrity of their declining manor against the invasion of 'bubbles and squeaks' (Greeks and Cypriots), 'turks' (Irish) and 'spades' (coloureds). (1959)

turkey (1932) US; applied to an Irish person, especially an Irish immigrant in the US

See also **Taig** at **Religion** (p. 129).

Italians

macaroni (1845) From the Italian origin of the foodstuff macaroni ■ Denys Hamson: They dropped us practically on to the Italian garrison at Karpen°si. . . . Doug was playing hidey-ho with a couple of macaronis, taking potshots round bushes at each other. (1946)

wop (1914) Orig US; applied derogatorily to an Italian and to the Italian language, and also occasionally to any southern European; origin uncertain; perhaps from Italian *guappo* bold, showy, from Spanish *guapo* dandy, from Latin *vappa* sour wine, worthless fellow ■ Ernest Hemingway: Wops, said Boyle, I can tell wops a mile off. (1924) ■ Evelyn Waugh: You'll find her full of wop prisoners. (1955) ■ A. Melville-Ross: There's a lot of chat in Wop which I doesn't understand. (1982)

Eyetie, Eyety, Eyetye, Eytie, Eyto (1925) Derogatory; from *Eyetalian*, representing a non-standard or jocular pronunciation of *Italian* ■ E. H. Clements: The Yugoslavians, the two Eyetyes, some West Germans. (1958)

ginzo, guinzo (1931) US; applied derogatorily to someone of Italian extraction; perhaps from *Guinea* Italian or Spanish immigrant ■ Wallace Markfield: I have a boss, a ginzo—though he speaks a great Jewish. (1964)

spaghetti (1931) Derogatory; from the Italian origin of the foodstuff spaghetti

spag (1967) Australian, derogatory; applied to an Italian immigrant; short for *spaghetti* ■ *Bulletin*

(Sydney): But the migration level had fallen under Labor. 'No, y'know, those coons and spags.' (1974)

Poles
Polack (1898) Mainly derogatory; ultimately from Polish *Polak* a Pole ■ **S. K. Padover:** You cowardly little sneak! It's craven pups like you that make the Polacks trample on us! If we Jews would learn to . . . kill . . . like they do, the Polacks would grovel at our feet! (1933)

Russians
Ivan (1925) Applied especially to a Russian soldier; from the Russian male personal name *Ivan*, equivalent to English *John* ■ **Berkeley Mather:** We'd knocked off quite a few of their side so far, and even dedicated Ivans could be expected to show a little exacerbation under the circumstances. (1968)

Rusky, Roosky, Russki, Ruski (1858) Also applied to the Soviets; from Russian *Russkiy* Russian ■ **Colin MacInnes:** We've got to produce our own variety, and not imitate the Americans—or the Ruskis, or anybody. (1959)

Scandinavians
squarehead (1903) Mainly US, derogatory

herring-choker (1944) US; from their supposed predilection for herrings

Scots
Jock (1788) Scottish form of the male personal name *Jack* ■ **New Statesman:** Why can't the Jocks support their team without dressing up like that? (1965)

Welsh people
Taffy (a1700), Taff (1929) Often derogatory; often used as a nickname; *Taffy* representing a supposed Welsh pronunciation of the name *Davy = David* (Welsh *Dafydd*) ■ **Brendan Behan:** 'Welsh are the most honest of the lot,' murmured Knowlesy, 'you never see a Taffy in for knocking off.' (1958) ■ **Listener:** Taffs and Geordies and Scouses who were barely intelligible. (1977)

Welshy, Welshie (1951) From *Welsh* + *-y*

Taffia, Tafia (1980) Applied jocularly to any supposed network of prominent or influential Welsh people, especially one which is strongly nationalistic; blend of *Taffy* and *Mafia* ■ **Tim Heald:** I heard murmurings from the London Welsh network (otherwise known as the 'tafia') on the subject of Sir Geoffrey's repudiation of true Welshness. (1983)

Southern Europeans; people of the western Mediterranean
dago (1832) Applied derogatorily to a Spaniard, Portuguese, or Italian, and also to the Spanish or Italian language; from the Spanish male personal name *Diego*, equivalent to English *James* ■ **Listener:** England should have won. All that stopped us was that the dagos [*sc.* Paraguayans] got more goals than us. (1968) ■ **M. Watts:** They were eternally being

enjoined to say it in French, say it in German, say it in dago! (1923)

guinea, ginny, guinny (1890) US, dated; applied derogatorily to an immigrant of Italian or Spanish origin; from earlier sense, person of mixed black, white and Indian ancestry; short for *Guinea negro* slave imported from Guinea or elsewhere on the West Coast of Africa ■ **John O'Hara:** Tony Murascho, who up to that time had been known only as a tough little guinny, was matched to fight a preliminary bout at McGovern's Hall. (1934)

grease-ball (1922) Applied derogatorily to someone of Mediterranean origin; from the association of oil with the cuisine and other cultural aspects of such countries

grill (1957) Australian, derogatory; from a perceived abundance of Greeks and other southern Europeans as proprietors of cafés

Central and Southeastern Europeans
hunk, hunkey, hunky, hunkie (1896) North American; applied derogatorily to an immigrant from central or southeastern Europe; see **bohunk** ■ **Maclean's:** I don't know if I should get mad if someone insults the Irish, or makes cracks about Polacks or Hunkies. (1971)

bohunk (1903) North American; applied derogatorily to an immigrant from central or southeastern Europe, especially one of inferior class, and often specifically to a Hungarian; apparently from *Bo(hemian)* + *-hunk*, alteration of *Hung(arian)* ■ **John Dos Passos:** Bohunk and polak kids put stones in their snowballs. (1930)

hunyak, honyock (1911) US; a synonym of *hunk*; alteration of *Hungarian* based on *Polack* ■ **Pat Frank:** She cooked a Hungarian goulash better than any he'd tasted at a hunyak table. (1957)

Egyptians
gippy, gyppie, gyppy (a1889), gippo, gypo, gyppo (1916) Usually derogatory; applied especially to a native Egyptian soldier; shortening and alteration of *Egyptian* ■ **Evelyn Waugh:** 'What's to stop him coming round the other side?' asked Tommy. 'According to plan—the Gyppos,' said the Brigadier. (1955)

Chinese
pigtail (1858) Derogatory or offensive, orig Australian, dated; from the former stereotype of a Chinese male wearing a pigtail ■ **C. MacAlister:** The fall broke the poor 'pigtail's' neck. (1907)

chow (1864) Derogatory, mainly Australian; short for *chow-chow* medley, assortment, from Pidgin English (Indian and Chinese) ■ **Patrick White:** Like one of the Chinese beans the Chow had given them at Christmas. (1970)

Chinkey, Chinkie, Chinky (1878) Derogatory or offensive; as *Chink* + *-ie* ■ **Norman Mailer:** A certain Chinkie. (1959)

Chink (1891) Derogatory or offensive; irregularly from *China* ∎ J. Durack: We used to have a couple staying with us. Chinks, they were, medical students. (1969)

Pong (1906) Australian, derogatory or offensive; probably a mixture of *pong* 'stink' with Chinese surnames such as *Wong* ∎ Berkeley Mather: I'm the only Pong I know who wouldn't say Charling Closs. (1970)

Filipinos

Flip (1931) US, often derogatory; from a casual pronunciation of the first two syllables of *Filipino*

Japanese

Jap (c1880) Mainly derogatory or offensive; abbreviation of *Japanese* ∎ G. F. Newman: Nice little tape-recorder. . . . Snazzy Jap job. (1970)

Charlie, Charley (1942) US services' slang; applied to a Japanese soldier, or to Japanese forces collectively

Nip (1942) Mainly derogatory or offensive; abbreviation of *Nipponese* Japanese ∎ John Osborne: Few little Nips popping away with cameras. (1971)

Tojo (1942) Services' slang; applied to a Japanese soldier, or to Japanese forces collectively; from the name of Hideki *Tojo*, Japanese minister of war and prime minister during World War II ∎ J. Binning: The monotone of the bombers is easing. Tojo is on his way out and now it is safe to get up. (1943)

Pakistanis

Paki (1964), Pak (1965) Derogatory or offensive; often applied specifically to an immigrant from Pakistan ∎ Michael Kelly: I don't see all this secrecy and drama. Smuggling us out like a load of Paks. (1971)

Vietnamese

Charlie, Charley (1965) US services' slang; usually applied specifically to North Vietnamese or Vietcong soldier(s); short for *Victor Charlie* ∎ New Statesman: Friendly forces have made contact with Charlie and a fire fight followed. (1966)

Victor Charlie (1966) US services' slang; usually applied specifically to North Vietnamese or Vietcong soldier(s); from the communications code-names for the initial letters of *Viet Cong* ∎ Saturday Night (Toronto): [Westmoreland's] men say they have to get them one 'Victor Charlie'. (1968)

dink (1967) US services' slang, derogatory; perhaps from earlier obsolete Australian slang *dink* East Asian person, of unknown origin ∎ Guardian: These are not people. . . . They are dinks and gooks and slant-eyed bastards. (1970)

nog (1969) Australian, derogatory; usually applied specifically to a North Vietnamese or Vietcong soldier; from *nig-)nog* black or coloured person ∎ W. Nagle: 'We suspect that there are about twenty or thirty nogs dug in. . .' 'VC or NVA?' asks Harry. (1975)

East Asians

yellow peril (1900) Applied to the military or political threat regarded as emanating from Asian peoples, especially the Chinese

slant-eye, slant-eyes (1929) Orig US, derogatory or offensive; also applied more broadly to anyone of a race with slanting eyes ∎ Times Literary Supplement: And those Jap Ph.D.'s, their questionnaires! (Replying 'Sod off, Slant-Eyes' led to friction.) (1974)

slant (1942) US, derogatory or offensive; short for *slant-eye* ∎ Milton Machlin: And the fuckin' Eskimo slants are tryin' to get the rest of it. (1976)

gook (1947) Orig and mainly US, derogatory or offensive; from earlier sense, foreigner ∎ Guardian: The Gooks [sc. Viet Cong] hit from bunkers and the Marines had to carry half the company back. (1968)

slope, slopy, slopey (1948) US, derogatory or offensive; in later use often applied specifically to Vietnamese; from Asians' stereotypically slanting eyes ∎ R. Thomas: All the Chinaman's gotta do is get into Saigon. . . . Once he's in nobody's gonna notice him, because all those slopes look alike. (1978)

moose (1953) US, services' slang; applied to a young Japanese or Korean woman, especially the wife or mistress of a serviceman stationed in Japan or Korea; from Japanese *musume* daughter, girl ∎ American Speech: Signs urging Americans . . . to meet the best mooses in Kyoto. (1954)

noggy (1954) Australian, derogatory or offensive; applied especially to an Asian immigrant to Australia; from *nig-)nog* black or coloured person + -*y* ∎ Canberra Times: I guess you blokes know why I am around. . . looking for 'noggies' and 'dapto dogs'. (1982)

slopehead (1966) US, derogatory or offensive ∎ Listener: At Can Tho, two years ago, I heard American Air Force men sing a ballad about the Vietnamese, whom they then called 'slopeheads' or 'slopes'. (1968)

Americans; the US

Yankee, (dated) Yankey, Yanky (1765) Often derogatory; in early use, applied to New Englanders or inhabitants of the northern states generally; perhaps from Dutch *Janke*, diminutive of *Jan* John

Yank (1778) Often derogatory; in early use, applied to New Englanders or inhabitants of the northern states generally; abbreviation of *Yankee* ∎ Joanna Trollope: They give me vast tips, especially the Yanks who love it that I'm titled. (1989)

Sammy (1917) British, dated; applied during World War I to a US soldier; from *Uncle Sam* personification of the US government

prune picker (1918) Dated; applied to a Californian

snow-bird (1923) US; applied to someone from the Northern states who goes to live or work in the South during the winter

septic tank (1967), **septic** (1976) Mainly Australian; *septic tank* rhyming slang for *Yank* ■ D. Stuart: Jesus, lover of my soul, if it isn't the Goddams, the Septics themselves!. . . Stick around long enough, I told myself, and . . . you'll see some real live Yanks. (1981)

Canadians

Canuck (1835) In US, sometimes derogatory; originally applied specifically to French-Canadians, and subsequently (1849) to Canadians in general; also applied to the French-Canadian patois; perhaps a variant of Hawaiian *kanaka* South Sea Islander—French-Canadians and South Sea islanders having been employed together in the Pacific Northwest fur trade—later re-analysed as *Can(adian + an* arbitrary suffix

pea-soup (1896), **pea-souper** (1942) North American, derogatory; applied to a French-Canadian, and also to the French-Canadian patois ■ *Globe & Mail* (Toronto): Our childhood forays in Ottawa between pea-soup and English-speaking gangs. (1965)

herring-choker (1899) Canadian; applied to a native or inhabitant of the Maritime Provinces; from their supposed predilection for herrings

Spud Islander (1957) Canadian; applied to a native or inhabitant of Prince Edward Island; from the island's reputation for fine potatoes

Joe (1963) Canadian; applied to a French-Canadian

Native Americans

nitchie (1850) Canadian, usually derogatory; from Ojibwa *ni:či:* friend ■ R. D. Symons: 'Quick, you fellows,' he said, 'them Nitchies are crawling up all around.' (1973)

Latin Americans

greaser (1836) US, derogatory; from the association of oil with the cuisine and other cultural aspects of Latin American countries ■ R. May & J. Rosa: Mexicans . . . and . . . Latin temperaments did not always sit well with Texans who were open in their dislike of 'greasers'. (1980)

spiggoty, **spiggity**, **spigotti**, **spigoty** (1910) US, dated, derogatory or offensive; perhaps an alteration of *spika de*, as in *no spika de English* '(I do) not speak the English', supposedly representing a common response of Spanish-Americans to questions in English ■ Rex Stout: 'He's a dirty spiggoty.' 'No, Archie, Mr Manuel Kimball is an Argentine.' (1934)

spic, **spick**, **spig**, **spik** (1913) US, derogatory or offensive; applied to a Latin American, and also to the Spanish-American language; abbreviation and alteration of *spiggoty* ■ Donald Westlake: You'd put your kid in a school with a lotta niggers and kikes and wops and spics? (1977)

wetback (1929), **wet** (1973) US; applied to an illegal immigrant from Mexico to the US, and hence to any illegal immigrant; from the

practice of swimming the Rio Grande to reach the US ■ G. Swarthout: Why doesn't this [system] detect every wet who puts a toe across the line? (1979)

grease-ball (1943) US, derogatory; from earlier sense, someone of Mediterranean origin; compare *greaser* ■ I. Wolfert: Love thy neighbor if he's not . . . a mockie or a slicked-up greaseball from the Argentine. (1943)

Argentinians

Argie (1982) British; mainly in the context of the Anglo-Argentinian conflict over sovereignty of the Falkland Islands (1982) ■ *Sunday Telegraph*: Small boys still play at Argies and Commandos. (1986)

Costa Ricans

Tico (1905) Mainly US; from American-Spanish *Tico*, apparently after the frequent use of the diminutive -*tico* in Costa Rican Spanish

Mexicans

chili-eater (1911) US, derogatory

Australians

pure merino (1826) Australian; applied to a (descendant of a) voluntary settler in Australia (as opposed to a transported convict), especially one who finds in this a basis for social pretension; from *merino* type of sheep introduced into Australia in the early years of settlement ■ *Daily Mail* (Sydney): Will pure merino progressives invade city fold? (1922)

cornstalk (1827) Australian, dated; applied originally to a native-born, non-aboriginal Australian, and subsequently specifically to someone from New South Wales ■ Sydney Hart: 'Never say that to anyone in New South Wales, or you'll be laid out flat as a pancake!' he warned me. . . . Couldn't the Cornstalks take a joke? (1957)

gumsucker (1855) Australian; applied to someone from Victoria, and more broadly to any native-born, non-aboriginal Australian; from the notion of sucking the juice of gum-trees ■ W. Lawson: Some men . . . called them 'gumsuckers', and a few other things. (1936)

tothersider (c1872) Australian; applied to someone from the eastern states of Australia; from *tother* the other + -*sider*; from these states being viewed as 'on the other side' of the continent from Western Australia ■ *Sydney Morning Herald*: Kalgoorlie was a huge seat with a big population of radical T'Othersider miners. (1983)

Bananalander (1887), **Banana-bender** (1976) Australian, jocular; applied to someone from Queensland; from the abundance of bananas grown in that state ■ K. Denton: I c'n tell a bananalander any time. I c'n pickem. You come from Queensland 'n' I *know* it! (1968)

sand-groper (1896) Australian; applied to a non-Aboriginal person, native to or resident in Western Australia

Groper (1899) Australian; applied to a Western Australian, especially a (descendant of an) early settler; short for *sand-groper*

Tassie, **Tassey**, **Tassy (1899)** Australian; applied to a Tasmanian; from earlier sense, Tasmania ▪ **S. Weller**: You know, I can always pick a Tassy. (1976)

digger (1916) Often applied specifically to an Australian or New Zealand soldier in World Wars I and II, especially a private; from earlier sense, one who digs for gold, from the high profile of such people in late 19th-century Australia ▪ **Roderick Finlayson**: Put your bag under the seat, digger. (1948)

dig (1916) Australian & New Zealand; abbreviation of *digger* ▪ **Graham McInnes**: Often they shouted at us . . . 'Howsit up in the dress circle, dig?' (1965)

ocker, **Ocker (1916)** Australian; used originally as a nickname for an Australian man, and hence (1968) for a typically rough or aggressively boorish Australian; often used adjectivally; originally a variant of names like *Oscar* and *O'Connor*, and in later use from the name of a character devised and played by Ron Frazer (1924–83) in the Australian television series 'The Mavis Bramston Show' (1965–8) ▪ *Telegraph* (Brisbane): It is no use telling Australians to wake up; it is not in the ocker character. (1976). Hence **ockerism** (1974), **ockerdom** (1975)

Aussie (1917) Used as a noun and an adjective to denote '(an) Australian'; from *Aus(tralian + -ie* ▪ **S. Hope**: Most Aussies, contrary to popular belief, are town-dwellers. (1957)

Ozzie (1918) Orig Australian; a respelling of *Aussie*, after *Oz* Australia ▪ *Nation Review* (Melbourne): Sydney Femme, 27, bored by ozzie ockers and oedipal neurotics, desires to develop dynamic dalliance with . . . male human beings. (1973)

Oz (1971) Orig Australian; applied as an adjective and noun to (an) Australian; from earlier sense, Australia ▪ *Sunday Telegraph*: These Oz intellectuals fell over themselves in a desperate parade of learning heavily-worn. (1989)

Barcoo salute (1973) Australian; applied to a gesture with which one brushes flies from one's face, considered to be typical of Australians; from *Barcoo* river and district in Queensland ▪ *Sydney Morning Herald*: The Barcoo salute . . . is also the feature of Australia most often commented on by overseas visitors. (1974)

Aboriginals

Mary (1830) Australian; applied to an Aboriginal woman or other non-white woman; from the female personal name ▪ *Coast-to-Coast 1961–2*: Some of the older marys did not remove frayed or dirty skirts. (1962)

Jacky, **Jacky-Jacky (1845)** Australian, derogatory; from the male personal name ▪ **K. J. Gilbert**: As the blacks are quick to point out, you don't get to be a councillor unless you are a good jacky who is totally under the manager's thumb. (1973)

binghi, **Binghi (1902)** Australian, derogatory; from Aboriginal (Awabakal and neighbouring languages) *biŋay* (elder) brother ▪ **M. Durack**: Before long every white family in Broome had acquired a mission educated 'binghi' couple. (1964)

abo, **Abo (1908)** Australian, now mainly derogatory; shortened from *aboriginal* ▪ *Bulletin* (Sydney): The idea of better housing for the abos. (1933)

boong (1924) Australian, derogatory; applied to an Australian aboriginal, and also to a New Guinean; from Aboriginal (Wemba Wemba dialect of Wemba) *beŋ* man, human being

New Zealanders

kiwi (1918) Orig applied specifically to New Zealand troops, and subsequently often to New Zealand sports teams; from the name of the flightless bird, thought of as symbolic of New Zealand ▪ **R. France**: Laurie was not a real Kiwi, or hard-bitten New Zealander. (1958)

Arabs and other Middle Eastern peoples

Abdul (1916) Applied to a Turkish man or Arab, often specifically a Turkish soldier, especially in World War I; from the Arabic male forename *Abdul* ▪ **G. Berrie**: I'd give a quid to be planted somewhere where I could watch some Abdul go in. (1949)

camel jockey (1965) US, derogatory; from the use of the camel as a method of transport (and allegedly as a vehicle for sexual gratification) in the Middle East ▪ *Observer*: The British papers quickly followed the American lead. Although none quite sank to the level of 'Camel jockeys killed your kids' . . . the British tabloids were not far behind. (1996)

Jews

Jew boy (1796) Derogatory or offensive; applied to a Jewish male ▪ *Observer*: Mrs Lane Fox dismisses what she calls the country set, who call their children 'the brats', talk about 'thrashing them into shape', support Enoch Powell and still refer to 'jew boys'. (1972)

sheeny, **shen(e)y**, **sheeney**, **-ie (1816)** Derogatory or offensive; origin uncertain; compare Russian *zhid*, Polish, Czech *žid* (pronounced /ʒiːd/) a Jew ▪ *Honolulu Star-Bulletin*: Hey mom, there's a couple of sheenies at our door with a turkey. (1976)

ikey, **ike**, **iky (1835)** Dated, derogatory or offensive; abbreviated form of the male personal name *Isaac*

Yid (1874) Derogatory or offensive; back-formation from *Yiddish* ▪ **Vladimir Nabokov**: Then she went and married a yid. (1963)

goose (1898) US, derogatory or offensive; perhaps from earlier sense, tailor's smoothing-iron (so called from the resemblance of the handle to a goose's neck), in allusion to the traditional Jewish occupation of tailoring

Yahudi, **Yehudi** (1900) Mainly US; also used adjectivally to denote 'Jewish'; from Arabic *yahudi*, Hebrew *yehūdī*, Jew; in earlier non-slang English use (1823–) referring to Jews in Arabic-speaking or Muslim countries ■ **Ian Jefferies:** As far as the Yehudis were concerned I knew the dirt that was being done. (1959) ■ *Washington Post:* I see the hate in your eyes, you Yahudi (Jewish) whore, and when we go to work on you, you'll be sorry. (1977)

kike (1904) Derogatory or offensive, mainly US; said to be an alteration of -*ki* (or -*ky*), a common ending of the personal names of Eastern European Jews who emigrated to the US in the late 19th and early 20th centuries ■ *Spectator.* He knocks down Stern's wife, calls her a kike. (1963)

five-to-two (1914) British, derogatory or offensive; rhyming slang ■ **Evelyn Waugh:** They respect us. Your five-to-two is a judge of quality. (1948)

shonicker, **shoniker**, **shonnicker** (1914) US, derogatory or offensive; origin uncertain; perhaps from Yiddish *shoniker* itinerant trader ■ **J. T. Farrell:** Two hooknoses . . . did come along. Andy and Johnny O'Brien . . . stopped the shonickers. (1932)

ikeymo (1922) Dated, derogatory or offensive; from *ikey* + *Mo*(*ses* ■ **Julian Symons:** I'm a Hackney Jew, Dave. At school they called us Ikeymoes and Jewboys. (1954)

mocky, **mockey**, **mockie** (1931) US, derogatory or offensive; origin uncertain; perhaps from Yiddish *makeh* a boil, sore ■ **I. Wolfert:** Love thy neighbor if he's not . . . a mockie or a slicked-up greaseball from the Argentine. (1943)

four-by-two (1936) British, derogatory or offensive; rhyming slang ■ **Edmund McGirr:** 'This Marx, was he a four by two?' demanded Quimple. 'Pardon?' 'A Jew, sir, a Jew.' (1970)

shonk (1938) Derogatory or offensive; shortened form of *shonicker* ■ **William Haggard:** 'Brighton?. . . It's full of shonks.'. . . 'Which means there are hotels with night clerks.' (1981)

yekke, **Yekke**, (anglicized) **Yekkie** (1950) Derogatory or offensive; applied to a German Jew; from Yiddish, of uncertain origin; compare German *Geck* fool, idiot ■ **H. Kemelman:** The bunch of Anglo-Saxons and Yekkies that run Hadassah and your hospital, too, you call them real Israelis? (1972)

bagel (1955) US, derogatory or offensive; from the Jewish origins of the bagel, a ring-shaped bun

God forbid, **Gawd forbid** (1960) British, derogatory or offensive; rhyming slang for *yid*

Hymie, **hymie** (1984) US, derogatory or offensive; pet-form of *Hyman*, anglicization of the popular Jewish male forename *Chaim* ■ **Tom Wolfe:** Yo, Goldberg! You, Goldberg! You, Hymie! (1987)

Red Sea pedestrian (1984) Jocular, offensive; from the crossing of the Red Sea by the children of Israel on foot after God created a passage through the water (Exodus 14:21–22)

Gentiles

yok (1923) Derogatory; Yiddish, *goy* 'Gentile' reversed with unvoicing of final consonant ■ **R. Samuel:** There were five Jewish boys in the gang— I was the only 'Yok'. (1981)

White people

white trash (1831) Applied to the poor white population of the Southern States of America, and hence, contemptuously, to white people in general ■ *Sunday Times:* He said that all the Australians were white trash. (1973)

gringo (1849) Used contemptuously by Spanish-Americans to refer to English people or Anglo-Americans; from Mexican Spanish *gringo* gibberish ■ **Aldous Huxley:** Annoying foreigners and especially white Gringoes is a national sport in Honduras. (1933)

Mary (1853) Australian; applied to a white woman, especially in the phrase *white Mary*; compare earlier sense, Aboriginal woman ■ **N. Cato:** They made their usual inquiries, saying they were investigating the death of a 'white mary' at the coast. (1974)

jeff, **Jeff Davis** (1870) US Black English, used contemptuously or dismissively; from *Jefferson Davis* (1808–89), president of the Confederate States 1861–5

white nigger (1871) Contemptuous or dismissive, orig US; applied to a white person who does menial work; compare earlier sense, a servile black

combo, **comboman** (1896) Australian; applied to a white man who lives with an Aboriginal woman; from *comb*(*ination* + -*o*

kelch, **kelt**, **-tch**, **keltz** (1912) Contemptuous or dismissive; origin unknown ■ **Chester Himes:** Then he met a high-yellah gal, a three-quarter keltz, from down Harlem way. (1938)

ofay (1925) US derogatory, mainly Black English; origin unknown, but probably African ■ **Billie Holiday:** Most of the ofays, the white people, who came to Harlem those nights were looking for atmosphere. (1956)

Miss Ann, **Miss Anne**, **Miss Annie** (1926) US Black English; applied to a white woman

Charlie, **Mr. Charlie**, **Boss Charlie** (1928) US Black English; applied contemptuously to white men considered as oppressors, and subsequently (1964) to any white man ■ *Guardian:* Stokely Carmichael was there promising 'Mr. Charlie's' doomsday. (1967)

peckerwood, **peckawood** (1929) US; applied especially to a poor white; from earlier sense, woodpecker ■ **William Faulkner:** Even a Delta peckerwood would look after even a draggle-tail better than that. (1942)

peck (1932) US Black English; abbreviation of *peckerwood* ■ **C. Brown:** A poor white peck will cuss worse'n a nigger. I am talking about white men who ain't poor like them pecks. (1969)

wonk (1938) Australian, contemptuous or dismissive; applied to a non-Aboriginal; compare earlier sense, inexperienced person ■ E. Webb: Sometimes whites would get out of cars along the road and walk over to the Camp and peer inside the humpies, or rough bough shelters, curious to see how the abos lived. . . . One of the boys nailed a board up on a tree near the road with 'wonks—keep out!' on it. (1959)

white meat (1940) Mainly US; applied to white women considered as sexual conquests or partners ■ Michael Maguire: I'm off white meat. I have a good thing going with a negro film editor. (1976)

pink toe, pink toes (1942) US Black English; applied to a young white woman ■ Chester Himes: When *Word* whispered it about that even the great Mamie Mason had lost her own black Joe to a young Pinktoe, the same panic prevailed among the black ladies of Harlem as had previously struck the white ladies downtown. (1965)

Whitey, Whitie (1942) Contemptuous or dismissive, mainly Black English; from *white* + *-y* ■ Charles Drummond: Get to hell away from me! You Whities stink! (1967)

Babylon (1943) Black English, mainly Jamaican, contemptuous or dismissive; applied to anything which represents the degenerate or oppressive state of white culture, especially the police or a policeman, (white) society or the Establishment; earlier applied to any great luxurious city (e.g. Rome or London), after the Biblical city ■ G. Slovo: My father him work as a labourer for thirty years in Babylon. (1986)

grey (1944) US Black English; also used adjectivally to denote 'white-skinned' ■ O. Harrington: The year was 1936, a bad year in most everybody's book. Ellis the cabdriver used to say that even the grays downtown were having it rough. (1965) ■ Ed Lacy: Funny thing with grey chicks. . . . They're always so sure their white skin is the sexiest ever. (1965)

pale-face (1945) US Black English, used contemptuously or dismissively

pink (1945), pinky, pinkie (1967) US Black English; from the colour of white people's skin ■ Trevanian: P'tit Noel shrugged. 'All pinks sound alike.' (1973)

Jumble (1957) Black English; alteration of *John Bull* ■ Monica Dickens: Get all you can out of the Jumbles. (1961)

the man, the Man (1963) US Black English; from earlier sense, people in authority ■ *Guardian*: Rus is not Uncle Tomming it around Harlem with 'the Man'. He has brought about a foreign visitor. (1972)

ridge-runner (1966) US Black English; from earlier sense, hillbilly

honky, honkey, honkie (1967) US Black English, contemptuous or dismissive; origin unknown ■ Bernard Malamud: Mary forcefully shoved him away. 'Split, honky, you smell.' (1971)

roundeye (1967) Applied by Asians to a European, in contrast to *slant-eye, slopehead*, etc. ■ John Le Carré: In the East a roundeye could live all his life

in the same block and never have the smallest notion of the secret tic-tac on his doorstep. (1977)

Amerika, Amerikkka (1969) Derogatory, orig US; applied to American society viewed as racist, fascist, or oppressive, especially by black consciousness; from German *Amerika* America; variant form *Amerikkka* with the initial letters of *Ku Klux Klan* ■ *Black Panther*: The political situation which exists here in Nazi Amerikkka. (1973)

Coloured people

darky, darkie (1775) Orig a neutral colloquial use, but now derogatory or offensive; from *dark* + *-y* ■ John Le Carré: Was it something about not taking the darkies on as conductors? (1983)

skepsel, schepsel (1844) South African; applied derogatorily or offensively to a Black or Coloured person; from earlier sense, creature, from Afrikaans *skepsel*, Dutch *schepsel*, from *scheppen* create

black velvet (1899) Australian & New Zealand, offensive; applied to a black or coloured woman, especially as the sexual partner of a white man ■ G. Casey: Did you see the girls, when you were out there? . . . The sort of black velvet that sometimes makes me wish I wasn't a policeman. (1958)

wog (1929) British, derogatory or offensive; often applied specifically to Arabs, but also widely used to denote blacks and other dark-skinned people; also applied to the Arabic language; origin unknown; often said to be an acronym (e.g. 'worthy Oriental gentleman'), but this is not supported by early evidence ■ J. Savarin: He hated Arabs. . . . They were all wogs to him. (1982) ■ William Haggard: 'I've picked up a few words of wog, sir.' . . . The driver spoke terrible barrack-room Arabic. (1982)

boong (1943) Australian, derogatory or offensive; from earlier sense, Aboriginal

jungle bunny (1966) Derogatory or offensive ■ *New Society*: White South Africans who wanted to gamble, buy Playboy . . . and go to bed with a 'jungle bunny'. (1974)

Black people

Sambo (1704) A nickname and, more recently, a derogatory or offensive term for a black; origin uncertain; perhaps from Spanish, person of mixed race, or from an African language (e.g. Foulah, uncle)

nigger (1786) Now mainly derogatory or offensive when used by white people, but neutral or approving in Black English; alteration of obsolete *neger* black person, from French *nègre* ■ L. Hughes: A klansman said, 'Nigger, Look me in the face—And tell me you believe in The great white race.' (1964)

nig (c1832), nig-nog (1959) Derogatory or offensive; *nig*, abbreviation of *nigger*; *nig-nog*, reduplicated abbreviation of *nigger* ■ R. Gadney: Judd read National Front puts Britain First. Someone had scribbled Nigs Out. (1974) ■ Julian Symons: He wanted to send the nig nogs and the Pakis back where they belong, in the jungle. (1975)

coon (1834) Orig US, derogatory or offensive; abbreviation of *racoon* ■ *Oz*: You might . . . deplore the way that the publicity was angled—poor old coon, he'll thank us in the end. (1969)

Jim Crow (1838) Derogatory or offensive, orig and mainly US; from the name of a black character in the early 19th-century plantation song 'Jim Crow' ■ *Saturday Review*: Jim Crow works at the depot. (1948)

sooty (1838) Derogatory or offensive, orig US ■ *Sunday Express*: I am not racialist, but I can't bear to watch the sooties any more—it's like Uncle Tom's Cabin. (1986)

dinge (1848), **dingy (1895)** US, derogatory or offensive; also used adjectivally, especially with reference to a jazz style developed by black musicians; *dinge* back-formation from the adjective *dingy* dark ■ Ernest Hemingway: That big dinge took him by surprise . . . the big black bastard. (1933) ■ V. Bellerby: The 'dinge' piano trill, deriving from the efforts of the early Negro instrumentalists to sing through their instruments, instinctively holding the rich overtones of Negro speech. (1958)

kink (1865), **kinky (1926)** US, derogatory or offensive, dated; in allusion to blacks' tightly curled hair

shine (1908) US, derogatory or offensive ■ Raymond Chandler: His voice said bitterly: 'Shines. Another shine killing. That's what I rate after eighteen years in this man's police department.' (1940)

jigaboo, **jiggabo**, **jijjiboo**, **zigabo**, etc. **(1909)** US, derogatory or offensive; origin unknown; compare *jig* and *bugaboo* ■ Lawrence Sanders: The tall one . . . was a jigaboo. (1970)

smoke (1913) US, derogatory or offensive ■ Lawrence Sanders: Five men. One's a smoke. (1970)

boogie (1923) US, derogatory or offensive; perhaps an alteration of *bogy* ■ Ernest Hemingway: I seen that big boogie there mopping it up. (1937)

jazzbo, **jasbo (1923)** US; from earlier sense, vaudeville act ■ Jack Kerouac: He dodged a mule wagon; in it sat an old Negro plodding along. . . . He slowed down the car for all of us to turn and look at the old jazzbo moaning along. (1957)

jig (1924) US, derogatory or offensive; origin unknown; compare *jigaboo* ■ Ernest Hemingway: This jig we call Othello falls in love with this girl. (1935)

spade (1928) Derogatory or offensive, orig US; from the colour of the playing-card suit ■ N. Saunders: On Saturdays try Brixton market—nearly as big, more genuine, lots of spades. (1971)

jit (1931) US, derogatory or offensive; origin unknown

peola (1942) US Black English; applied to a light-skinned Afro-American, especially a girl; origin unknown ■ Z. N. Hurston: Dat broad I seen you with wasn't no pe-ola. (1942)

pink toe(s) (1942) US Black English; applied to a light-skinned Afro-American woman

nigra, **nigrah (1944)** Mainly Southern US, now mainly derogatory or offensive; from a regional pronunciation of *Negro* ■ F. Richards: 'Pretty little thing, as nigras go, Mrs. Prender said.' ' "Nigras"? Like that, Henderson?' 'Way it sounded to me.' 'It's a Southern variant,' Heimrich said. 'Between "nigger", which they're beginning—some of them are beginning—not to use so much and "Negro", which a lot of them can't get used to.' (1969)

spook (1945) Derogatory or offensive, orig and mainly US ■ Elmore Leonard: We almost had another riot. . . . The bar-owner . . . shoots a spook in his parking lot. (1977)

munt (1948) South African, derogatory or offensive; from Bantu *umuntu* person ■ *New Statesman*: The old 'munt', as the African is still widely and insultingly termed. (1962)

boot (1954) Mainly Black English, sometimes derogatory ■ H. Simmons: A lot of paddy studs still didn't know that boots were human. (1962)

schvartze(r), **schwartze(r) (1961)** Mainly US, rather derogatory; applied especially to a black maid; from Yiddish, from *shvarts* (German *schwarz*) black: the forms in final -r should represent the masculine, but the sexual distinction is commonly confused

member (1964) US; from the notion of fellow membership of the black race ■ L. Hairston: Three more, one of 'em a member,. . . sailed over. (1964)

splib (1964) US Black English; origin unknown ■ A. Young: Nobody want no nice nigger no more. . . . They want an angry splib A furious nigrah. (1969)

pongo (1968) Derogatory or offensive; from earlier sense, anthropoid ape ■ Len Deighton: You wouldn't want no breech block blowing back and crippling some poor pongo, no matter what country he's in. (1968)

buppie (1984) Orig US; applied to a black city-dwelling professional person who is (or attempts to be) upwardly mobile; acronym formed on black urban (or upwardly mobile) professional, after *yuppie* ■ *Independent*: Derek Boland—the . . . rap singer Derek B—was present as a representative of 'buppies' (black yuppies). (1988)

A subservient black person

white nigger (1837) Orig US

Uncle Tom (1922) Orig US; applied to a servile black man; from the name of the hero of *Uncle Tom's Cabin*, a novel (1851–2) by Harriet Beecher Stowe ■ *New Yorker*: Pryor goes through his part pop-eyed, playing Uncle Tom for Uncle Toms. (1977). Hence **Uncle Tom** to act like an Uncle Tom (1947) ■ *Punch*: An obligation . . . applies constantly to all underdog groups, constantly tempted by rewards to uncle-tom, to pull the forelock. (1967)

pink chaser (1926) US; from Black English *pink* white person ■ Carl Van Vechten: Funny thing about those pink-chasers the ofays never seem to have any use for them. (1926)

tom, Tom (1959) US; short for *Uncle Tom* ■ *Publishers Weekly*: By installing 'American Nigger Toms' as the Third World élite, the U.S. has controlled the angry hunger of the poor populace. (1975). Hence **tom, tom it (up)** to behave servilely to someone of another (especially white) race (1963) ■ M. J. Bosse: Vergil just smiled, Tomming it up. (1972)

oreo (1969) US; 'the term comes from a standard commercially prepared cookie which has two disc-shaped chocolate wafers separated by sugar cream filling. An "oreo" is thus brown outside but white inside' (Alan Dundes, *Mother Wit from the Laughing Barrel* (1973))

pork chop (1970) US ■ *New York Review of Books*: This is the year of the Bionic Black, and porkchop nationalists have lost prestige. (1977)

coconut, coconut head (1988) From the notion of the coconut's brown exterior and white interior ■ *Daily Telegraph*: Mrs Boateng, former member of Lambeth council's social services committee, has been barred from Brent's Black Section for two years after being branded a 'coconut'. (1988)

Gipsies

didicoi, didakai, -kei, diddekai, diddicoy, didekei, -ki, -kie, -ky, didicoy, didikai, -koi, didycoy (1853) Romany

gippo, gypo, gyppo (1902), gippy, gyppie, gyppy (1913) From *gip(sy* + *-o/-y*, influenced by *Egyptian* ■ Dylan Thomas: Ducking under the gippo's clothespegs. (1953)

Foreigners

dago (1903) Derogatory or offensive; from earlier sense, person of Spanish or Italian extraction ■ Ngaio Marsh: 'Such indiscretion has doubtless been suitably chastised,' remarked the Russian. . . . Charles Rankin . . . slipped his arm through Nigel's. 'Not a very delicious gentleman, that dago,' he said loudly. (1934)

wog (1942) Derogatory or offensive; from earlier sense, coloured person ■ C. Hollingworth: King Zog Was always considered a bit of a Wog, Until Mussolini quite recently Behaved so indecently. (1942) ■ *Times Literary Supplement*: We have travelled some distance from the days when Wogs began at Calais. (1958)

gook (1959) US, derogatory or offensive; from earlier sense, Asian person

Johnny Foreigner (1990) British, usually derogatory; used as a personification of a foreign person, usually with ironic reference to British xenophobia; first recorded in 1990, but in use earlier ■ *Sunday Times*: When Moore was arrested on a trumped-up charge in Bogota just before the 1970 World Cup, we all knew that it was a dastardly ruse by Johnny Foreigner, and so it proved. (1993)

An immigrant

Jimmy Grant, jimmygrant (1845) Australian, New Zealand & South African; rhyming slang ■ F. Clune: More and more Crown land was taken up by the ever-arriving 'jimmygrants' who had government help and favour. (1948)

ethno (1976) Australian; from *ethn(ic* + *-o*

See also **bohunk** (p. 35), **guinea** (p. 35), **hunk** (p. 35), **kipper** (p. 33), **Paki** (p. 36), **snow-bird** (p. 36), **turkey** (p. 34), **wetback** (p. 37).

A person who wears a turban

rag-head (1921) North American, derogatory or offensive ■ *Canadian Magazine*: East Indians are called 'rag-heads' if they continue to wear the traditional turban of the Sikh religion. (1975)

towelhead (1985) Derogatory or offensive ■ *Observer*: If you did a brain scan of the British racist mentality, you find that, on the whole, we reckon the 'towelheads' have a pretty rough time of it. (1991)

A supporter of racial segregation

seg, seggie (1965) US ■ *New Yorker*: Fulbright for the first time openly appealed for black votes, because he believed that he couldn't win without them and that the 'seggies' . . . would vote against him no matter what he did. (1970)

2. People

A person

customer (1589) Usually mildly derogatory; applied to a person of the stated sort; from earlier sense, person with whom one has dealings ■ F. D. Davison: He was a mean customer, . . . a petty bureaucrat, and a smooger, to boot. (1940)

fish (1750) Mainly derogatory; applied to a person of the stated sort ■ F. Scott Fitzgerald: I'm tired of being nice to every poor fish in school. (1920) ■ *Listener*: The old man is revealed as having been a very cold fish. (1958)

what's-your-name (1757) Used in addressing a person whose name is not known or remembered ■ William Faulkner: Is that so? Look here, Mister What's-your-name. (1942)

cuss (1775) Orig US, mildly derogatory; applied to a person of the stated sort; probably an alteration of *curse* (although not recorded in that sense until later), but widely apprehended as being short for *customer* ■ *Economist*: This American computer company's successes include a profitable joint venture with Romania, an awkward cuss by any standards. (1988)

stick (1785) Often mildly derogatory; applied to a person of the stated sort ■ *Guardian*: He could easily convey the impression of being a dry old stick: but he had a heart of gold, a gentle, mocking humour and a genuine love for people of all sorts, all ages. (1992)

article (1811) Now mainly jocular derogatory; applied mainly to a person of the stated sort

■ **M. K. Joseph:** Listen, you sloppy article, who was on guard from twelve to two last night? (1957)

beggar (1833) British, often mildly derogatory; applied to a person (typically a man or boy) of the stated sort; from earlier sense, mendicant, partly as a euphemistic substitute for *bugger* ■ **Norman Stone:** In the old days, I played squash reasonably well, but gave it up on reaching age 41, when my small boy was born—it is a dangerous sport for over-weight middle-aged chaps who smoke too much, and I have a duty to see the little beggar through until his first divorce. (1992)

guy (1847) Orig US; orig and mainly applied to a man, but in modern use also employed with reference to women, especially in the plural; from earlier sense, grotesque-looking person, object of ridicule (in allusion to the effigies of Guy Fawkes burnt on 5 November) ■ *Daily Mail:* The way Alan Rickman plays villains, nice guys are lucky to come second. (1991) ■ *Washington Post:* Former LPGA winners, like Meg Mallon and Beth Daniels, invaded the interview room to kibitz. 'It's hard for me to talk with you guys around,' said Sheehan, quietly. (1993)

specimen (1854) Mainly derogatory; applied to a person of the stated sort ■ **D. H. Lawrence:** I am assiduously, admirably looked after by Mrs Bolton. She is a queer specimen. (1928)

egg (1855) Applied to a person (typically a man) of the stated sort ■ **Compton Mackenzie:** It doesn't look a hundred quid to a tanner on his blue. Bad luck. He's a very good egg. (1914) ■ **P. G. Wodehouse:** She's a tough egg. (1938)

outfit (1867) Mainly US, usually derogatory, dated ■ **C. E. Mulford:** You ain't believin' everythin' *this* outfit tells you, are you? (1924)

sort (*c*1869) Applied to a person of the stated sort ■ **Cecil Roberts:** On the whole he was not a bad sort. (1891)

duck (1871) US, usually derogatory; in modern use applied mainly to a person (typically a man) of the stated sort; from earlier sense, foolish or eccentric person ■ **W. H. Smith:** As you said, Goldsby, Slosher's a slick duck. (1904)

baby (1880) Mainly US; compare earlier use as a term of address ■ **Alan Lomax:** Some terrible environments . . . inhabited by some very tough babies. (1950)

individual (1888) Mildly derogatory; applied to a person of the stated sort; from earlier standard English sense, person ■ *Guardian:* They are almost invariably quite dull and friendless individuals who use hospital radio as a surrogate social life. (1991)

artist (1890) Applied to a person devoted to or unusually proficient in the stated (reprehensible) activity ■ **D. M. Davin:** A real artist for the booze, isn't he? (1949) ■ **M. Sayle:** Education, if he [*sc.* the Australian worker] thinks of it at all, seems to him a childish trick whereby the 'bullshit artist' seeks to curry favour with the boss and thus get a better job. (1960)

possum (1894) Australian; usually applied to a person of the stated sort, but also used as a term of address; from earlier sense, small marsupial ■ **R. Hall:** Goodness what an ugly little possum you've turned into. (1982)

perisher (1896) Usually implying contempt or pity (generally the former if not further qualified); compare earlier, obsolete sense, something extreme ■ **R. Park:** He had no name. In the thaw they buried him in the pass, and his epitaph was *Some Poor Bloody Perisher.* 1864. (1957)

babe (1898) Orig & mainly US; applied to both men and women; compare earlier *baby* in same sense ■ **Stanley Kauffman:** This Mrs. Adair . . . has such hotsy-totsy cottages. . . . Yesterday this Adair babe has an ad in the paper. (1952)

whatsit (1898) Used for referring to someone whose name is not known or remembered; often following a title; from earlier use referring to something the name of which is not known or remembered

scout (1912) Applied to a person (typically a man) of the stated sort ■ **John Le Carré:** I've got nothing against old Adrian. He's a good scout. (1965)

merchant (1914) Applied to a person devoted to or unusually proficient in the stated (reprehensible) activity; from earlier sense, fellow, chap ■ *Railway Magazine:* One wonders how many drivers, other than the confirmed speed merchants, will even attempt to run the 8.20 a.m. from Kings Cross from Hitchin to Huntingdon in 24 min. (1957) ■ **George Sims:** Sorry to be such a gloom merchant. But . . . we're broke, you see. (1971)

cookie (1917) Orig US; usually applied to a person of the stated type; apparently from earlier sense, small cake ■ **W. R. Burnett:** He's a real tough cookie and you know it. (1953)

animal (1922) Applied to a type of person; mainly in the phrase *there is no such animal* ■ *Times Review of Industry:* Computer makers would therefore have us believe that there is no such animal as a typical programmer. (1963)

type (1922) Usually applied to a person (typically a man) of the stated sort or belonging to the stated organization ■ **D. E. Westlake:** I was not alone in the room. Three army types were there . . . tall, fat, khaki-uniformed. (1971) ■ **M. Hebden:** 'Type over here. . . . He recognises it.' The 'type over here' was a man about thirty-five with long blond hair. (1981)

whosis, whoosis (1923) Used for referring to someone whose name is not known or remembered; often following a title; representing a casual pronunciation of *who is this?* ■ **Ian Fleming:** Don't forget one thing, Mister Whoosis. I rile mighty easy. (1965)

job (1927) Applied to a person (typically a pretty girl) of the stated sort ■ *Gen:* A 'ropey job' is likely as not to be a blonde who proved uncollaborative. (1942)

character (1931) Often mildly derogatory; from earlier sense, personage ■ **Joanna Cannan:** The character who owns Mab . . . leaves his gear out in her. (1962)

bod (1933) British; short for *body* ■ *Crescendo:* The show-tune formula is quite simple—I know dozens of bods who make a living using it. (1966)

bleeder (1938) British; often used in commiseration; from earlier sense, unpleasant person ■ Alexander Baron: She'll kill the poor little bleeder. (1952)

so-and-so (1943) Usually applied to a person (typically a man) of the stated sort; from earlier sense, unpleasant person ■ Ann Bridge: The Countess is a hard-baked, publicity-minded old So-and-so, with about as much consideration for other people as a sack of dried beans! (1958) ■ John Cleese: Eric wrote on his own, poor so-and-so. (1990)

face (1944) Orig US, Black English ■ John Morgan: Now this face was the ideal man for me to have a deal with. (1967)

whosit, whoosit, whozit, whoozit (1948) Used for referring to someone whose name is not known or remembered; often following a title; representing a casual pronunciation of *who is it?* ■ Josephine Tey: Someone, say, insists that Lady Whoosit never had a child. (1951)

gunk (1964) US, derogatory; compare earlier sense, viscous or liquid material ■ P. Marlowe: A couple of gunks who used to be bouncers at the 'Golden Pagoda'. (1968)

An old person
See under **Old** (p. 369).

A promiscuous person
See under **Sex** (pp. 66–8).

A severe, hard, or uncompromising person
See under **Severity**, **Oppressiveness** (p. 428).

An ugly person
See under **Beauty & Ugliness** (p. 219).

An unpleasant or despicable person
See under **Unpleasantness** (p. 223).

Oneself

one's arse, (mainly US) **one's ass (1698)** Orig used in imprecations; in modern use usually with *get* and an adverb or adverb phrase, as a synonym for *come* or *go* ■ *Language*: Get your ass in here, Harry! The party's started! (1972)

number one (1704) Often in *look after number one* and similar phrases ■ John Hale: Bennet, who always looks after number one, is wearing Scapa scanties next to the skin. Long underpants and a long-sleeved vest made of thick, oily wool. (1964)

us (1828) Used in dialectal and non-standard English in place of *me* ■ *Guardian*: You knock on three or four doors at once, out they all come. . . . It's 'Give me six Lemonade.' 'I don't want none.' 'Give us four Cola.' 'Give us six mixed.' (1991)

yours truly (1833) From its use preceding the signature at the foot of a letter ■ K. Munroe: Are you willing to work in cahoots with yours truly? (1889)

jills (1906) Used with a possessive adjective: *my jills* = I, *his jills* = he, etc.; from Shelta

ego (1913) British public schools' slang, dated; used instead of *I* in answer to the question *quis?* who?, especially when claiming an object; from Latin *ego* I

this baby (1919) Mainly US ■ Richard Gordon: Some skippers cook the log, but not this baby. (1953)

Terms of address to a person
See under Unisex at **Terms of Address** (p. 54).

A male person; a fellow

lad (a1553) British; applied to a lively (young) man, especially a highly sexed one; the 16th-century record of the usage is an isolated one, and the modern use (mainly in the phrases *a bit of a lad* and *quite a lad*) appears to be an early 20th-century creation; also used in the phrase *the lads*, denoting the men in one's team or social circle ■ Harry Carmichael: Bit of a lad is Mr. Alan Clark . . . running round fancy-free for years. (1960) ■ *Daily Mail*: I couldn't have asked for a better start. The lads have made it easy for me to settle in and it's looking good. (1991)

gent (1564) Short for *gentleman*: early examples are probably simply written abbreviations rather than representations of a spoken shortened form ■ *South China Morning Post*: 'How did they get my name?' wailed a gent who shall remain anonymous. (1992)

cove (1567) Now mainly Australian; from Romany *kova* thing, person ■ *Advertiser* (Adelaide): You Aussie coves are just a bunch of drongoes. (1969)

dog (a1618) Dated; applied to a man of the stated type ■ *Punch*: Algy . . . You lucky dog, you possess all the accomplishments I lack! *Jim* . . . Oh, nonsense! Why, you're making me out a regular *Crichton*! (1890)

what's-his-name (1697) Used as a substitute for a man's name that is not known or remembered ■ S. Wilson: *Marilyn*. What is going on? *Brian*. Same old thing: raising the whatsis-name-the Antichrist. (1979)

chap (1704) Now mainly British; from earlier sense, buyer, customer (compare the similar sense development of *customer*); ultimately short for *chapman* merchant ■ Elizabeth Oldfield: I don't suppose the poor chap can help looking like God's gift to women. (1983)

joker (1810) Mainly Australian & New Zealand; from earlier sense, one who jokes ■ G. H. Fearnside: You think us married jokers have got no lives of our own. (1965)

chappie, chappy (1821) Orig Scottish; from *chap* + *-ie* ■ P. G. Wodehouse: It was one of those jolly, peaceful mornings that make a chappie wish he'd got a soul or something. (1925)

feller (1825) Representing a colloquial pronunciation of *fellow*; in modern usage often used with the implication 'young man' (as contrasted with 'young woman', in the context of (potential) sexual contact), and sometimes specifically 'boyfriend, male lover' ■ *Petticoat:* If we did walk into a pub alone and not one feller blinked an eyelid we'd probably think there was something wrong with us. (1971)

bird (1843) ■ J. B. Priestley: He's one of them queer birds that aren't human until they're properly pickled. (1939)

Joe, joe (1846) From the male personal name *Joe* ■ *Publishers Weekly:* The average Joe probably thinks that cyclists . . . are eccentric folk. (1973)

bloke (1851) Now mainly British; sometimes applied specifically to a boyfriend or male lover; from Shelta ■ Alan Bleasdale: Do you know I followed a bloke to court one morning . . . and sat there and watched while he . . . pleaded guilty to the offences I was still following him for. (1983)

rye (1851) Dated; from Romany *rai* gentleman

bugger (1854) Applied to a man of the stated type, often in commiseration or affection; from earlier sense, unpleasant man ■ Frederic Manning: Not when there are two poor buggers dead, and five more not much better. (1929)

omee, omie (1859) Orig showmen's slang, an alteration of Italian *uomo* man

plug (1863) Derogatory, mainly US; from earlier sense, undistinguished or incompetent person

fella, (dated) fellah (1864) Representing a colloquial pronunciation of *fellow*; in modern usage often used with the implication 'young man' (as contrasted with 'young woman', in the context of (potential) sexual contact), and sometimes specifically 'boyfriend, male lover' ■ Sapper: 'An engaging fellah,' said Hugh. 'What particular form of crime does he favour?' (1920) ■ *Sun:* The only thing I think could come close to the thrill [sc. of bungee-jumping] would be to be a Page Seven Fella. (1992)

outfit (1867) Mainly US, usually derogatory

dude (1883) Orig & mainly US; from earlier sense, over-refined man, dandy ■ Martin Amis: I think my dog go bite one of them white dudes. (1984)

snoozer (1884) Orig US; from earlier sense, sleeper ■ Harry Marriott: Zim was a tough old snoozer. I know that he cut his knee open with an axe and sewed it up with some worsted yarn and his wife's darning needle. (1966)

geezer, geeser, geyser (1885) In earliest use applied only to old men; representing a dialectal pronunciation of *guiser* mummer ■ *New Statesman:* I have my hands full with his china who is a big geezer of about 14 stone. (1965)

gazebo, gazabo (1889) Orig & mainly US, often derogatory; perhaps from Spanish *gazapo* sly fellow ■ Henry Miller: But there was one thing he seldom did, queer gazabo that he was—he seldom asked questions. (1953)

josser (1890) British; usually mildly derogatory; from earlier sense, fool ■ Vance Palmer: We've no call to worry about the big jossers putting the screw on us; we've the legal titles to our leases and can get our price for them. (1948)

jasper (1896) US, derogatory; often applied specifically to a country bumpkin; from the male personal name *Jasper* ■ Mark Corrigan: If that dark jasper calls on you again, try and keep him here. (1963)

blighter (1904) British; applied to a male person of the stated type; from earlier sense, unpleasant man ■ *Guardian:* Jack Good . . . may be 60, but he's an energetic, opinionated old blighter. (1992)

gink (1906) Orig US, mainly derogatory; origin unknown ■ Alfred Draper: George wasn't the most talkative gink alive. (1970)

gunsel, gonsil, gunshel, gun(t)zel, gunzl (1910) US; applied to a (naïve) young man; from Yiddish *genzel*, from German *Gänslein* gosling

bimbo (1918) Orig US, mainly derogatory; from Italian *bimbo* little child, baby ■ Raymond Chandler: There's a thousand berries on that bimbo. A bank stick-up, ain't he? (1936)

bastard (1919) Usually applied to a male person of the stated type; from earlier sense, unpleasant man ■ Keith Weatherly: 'You're not a bad bastard, Hunter,' he said, 'in spite of your lousy cooking.' (1968)

cat (1920) Orig US, Black English ■ Colin MacInnes: The coloured cats saw I had an ally, and melted. (1959)

gee (1921) US; from the pronunciation of the initial letter of *guy* ■ Simon Challis: 'Just a minute, this ain't O'Brien.' 'No. This is some other gee.' (1968)

stud (1929) US, mainly Black English; from earlier sense, man of sexual prowess ■ Dan Burley: If you're a hipped stud, you'll latch on. (1944)

sod (1931) Applied to a male person (or animal) of the stated type, often in affection or commiseration; from earlier sense, unpleasant man ■ D. Wallace: That's a shame, the poor little dawg, but if that was moine I'd hev that put down. That can't help but make no end o' work, the poor little sod. (1969)

Joe Blow (c1941) US; applied to a hypothetical average man ■ Billie Holiday: But just let me walk out of the club one night with a young white boy of my age, whether it was John Roosevelt, the President's son, or Joe Blow. (1956)

Joe Public (1942) Orig US, theatrical slang, often mildly derogatory; applied originally to (a member of) the audience, and hence to (a typical male member of) the general public ■ Denis Norden: We've really got to provide Joe Public with some sort of ongoing visual reference-point. (1978)

Joe Doakes, Joe Dokes (1943) US; applied to a hypothetical average man ■ *Jazz Monthly:* All these items are essentially jazz-tinged versions of Joe Doakes's favourite melodies. (1968)

ou (*plural* ouens, ous) (1949) South African; from Afrikaans ■ J. Drummond: I ought to keep you locked up. The ou that shot Loder . . . he's dangerous. (1979)

son-of-a-bitch, sonofabitch, sonuvabitch, etc. (1951) Now mainly US; from earlier sense, unpleasant man ■ Arthur Hailey: Besides, the son-of-a-bitch had guts and was honest. (1979)

Joe Soap (1966) Applied to a hypothetical average man; from earlier sense, gullible person ■ *Guardian*: Socialists have become . . . over-eager to find out what Joe Soap is doing in order to tell him not to do it. (1969)

whatsisface, whatzisface (1967) Orig & mainly US; used as a substitute for a man's name that is not known or remembered; representing a casual pronunciation of *what's-his-face*, alteration of earlier *what's-his-name* ■ Joseph Wambaugh: They're having another Save Harry Whatzisface party there today. (1977)

Joe Bloggs (1969) British; applied to a hypothetical average man ■ *Daily Telegraph*: In too many cases these forms arrive on the desk of a busy executive who concludes that Joe Bloggs down the corridor must have signed the order. (1971)

pisser (1975) Orig US, derogatory; usually applied to a man of the stated type; compare earlier sense, someone or something extraordinary ■ *Melchior's Sleeper Agent*: The old pisser had not got away! (1975)

An old man

See under An old person at **Old** (p. 369).

A promiscuous man

See under **Sex** (pp. 66–7).

An unpleasant or despicable man

See under An unpleasant or despicable person at **Unpleasantness** (p. 223).

Terms of address to a man

See under Used to address a male at **Terms of address** (pp. 52–3).

Typical of a man

laddish (1841) In modern British use applied (often disapprovingly) to the behaviour of young men in groups; from *lad* + *-ish* ■ *Sunday Times*: They could talk Shakespeare and football, be sensitive then brutal. Sure, David Baddiel and Frank Skinner were laddish together, but there was never anything vulgar. (1996) Hence **laddishness** (1886) ■ *Guardian*: All three drank heroically and took a lot of drugs. But can we truly trust these occasional manifestations of laddishness when weighed against a lifetime of writing. (1992)

blokeish, blokish (1957) British; applied to positive behaviour associated with men, especially straightforwardness, bluffness, and lack of affectation; from *bloke* + *-ish* ■ *Sunday Times*: The Mayles then popped up in a restaurant in Provence, Lindsay Duncan all cutesy and John Thaw all blokeish ('When you're ready, maestro!'). (1993)

A woman

mot, (dated) **mort** (1561) Often with an implication of promiscuity; origin unknown ■ J. Blackburn: 'Look at them two mots, Fergus.' Dan pointed at two mini-skirted girls. (1969)

faggot (1591) Derogatory; applied to a woman of the stated (undesirable) sort; often in the phrase *old faggot*; compare earlier sense, bunch of sticks ■ *Daily Mirror*: 'Urry up wi' that glass o' beer, you lazy faggot! (1969)

tit (1599) Derogatory, dated; compare earlier sense, small horse; apparently an onomatopoeic formation, as a term for something small ■ E. R. Eddison: The Demons, . . . since they had a strong loathing for such ugly tits and stale old trots, would no doubt hang her up or disembowel her. (1922)

dame (1698) US, sometimes derogatory ■ Joanna Cannan: I've never set eyes on the dame. (1962)

biddy (1785) In modern use mainly derogatory except in US Black English; originally applied, especially in the US, to an Irish maid-servant; from the female personal name *Biddy*, an abbreviated form of *Bridget*; see also **biddy** under An old woman at **Old** (p. 369). ■ C. P. Snow: I believe she's the bloodiest awful specimen of a party biddy. (1960)

gal (1795) Representing a colloquial or dialectal pronunciation of *girl* ■ *Guardian*: My Mum, known as Annie but whose Hebrew name was Judith, was quite a gal and beautiful too. (1992)

buer (1807) British, orig northern dialect & tramps' slang; often with an implication of promiscuity; origin unknown ■ Graham Greene: 'Christ,' the boy said, 'won't anybody stop that buer's mouth?' (1938)

titter (1812) Dated; applied to a young woman or girl; origin uncertain; compare *tit* woman and *tits* woman's breasts ■ *Landfall* (New Zealand): Boys, she's a larky little titter. (1953)

what's-her-name (1816) Used as a substitute for a woman's name that is not known or remembered ■ Ouida: It makes one feel like What's-her-name in the 'Trovatore'. (1880)

sheila, sheelah, sheilah, shelah (1832) Now Australian & New Zealand; applied to a young woman, and sometimes specifically a girlfriend; probably from the generic use of the (originally Irish) female personal name *Sheila* ■ H. Garner: If I was to fight over every sheila I'd fucked there'd be fights from here to bloody Darwin. (1985)

heifer (1835) Derogatory; from earlier sense, young cow, female calf ■ *Black World*: That heifer that been trying to get next to my man Lucky since the year one. (1973)

bird (1838) Now mainly British; applied to a young woman, and sometimes specifically a girlfriend; a usage paralleled by (but not continuous with) Middle and early Modern English *bird* maiden, girl ■ *News Chronicle*: Hundreds more geezers were taking their birds to 'The Hostage' and 'Make me an Offer'. (1960) ■ *New Statesman*: Victor is an ex-seaman in his twenties, who deserted in South Africa and got in law trouble out there for shacking up with a coloured bird. (1961)

bint (1855) Mainly derogatory; applied to a (young) woman, especially non-Caucasian; in common use among British servicemen in Egypt and neighbouring countries during World Wars I & II; from Arabic *bint* daughter ■ Kingsley Amis: As the R.A.F. friend would have put it, you could never tell with these foreign bints. (1958)

quail (1859) US; applied to a (sexually attractive) young woman; compare 17th-century slang *quail* courtesan ■ *Time*: A less active sport is 'piping the flock', when Cal males watch Cal 'quails' preening in the sun on the steps of Wheeler Hall. (1947)

popsy, popsie (1862) Applied to a (sexually attractive) young woman, sometimes specifically a girlfriend; apparently a nursery extension of *pop* an obsolete term of endearment for a girl or woman, with the suffix *-sy* ■ Marghanita Laski: American colonels with their popsies. (1944)

girls (1863) Applied, often jocularly, to women of any age, especially as a form of address; used mainly by women; from earlier *girl* female child, young woman ■ *New York Times*: She referred to the women accompanying Mr. Smith and Patrick Kennedy earlier in the evening as 'you girls'. (1991)

femme, fem (1871) US; applied to a young woman; from French *femme* woman ■ *American Speech*: The organizer of a *Brush-off-club* 'made up of mournful soldiers who were given the hemlock cup by femmes back home'. (1944)

dona, donah (1873) British, dated; often applied specifically to a girlfriend; from Spanish *doña* or Portuguese *dona* woman ■ J. Farrell: Blokes and donahs . . . of the foulest slums. (1887)

judy (1885) Sometimes applied to a wife or girlfriend; from the female personal name; compare earlier sense, ridiculous or contemptible woman, perhaps from the name of the wife of Punch ■ *Guardian*: During a strike a man whose judy is working is obviously better off than the man with a wife and three kids about the house. (1973)

chippy, chippie (1886) Orig US, usually derogatory; applied to a young woman; often with an implication of promiscuity; compare earlier obsolete sense, youngster

totty (1890) British; applied to a young woman; often with an implication of promiscuity; from earlier sense, small child ■ Colin Watson: Showing off. Certainly, why not? There were a couple of totties just behind. (1977)

tootsy, tootsie, tootsey-wootsey, tootsie-wootsie, etc. **(1895)** Mainly US; applied to a young woman, and also specifically to a girlfriend; often used as a familiar form of address; compare earlier sense, foot ■ P. O'Connor: Two chicks. One for me. . . . One of the hot-time tootsies. (1979)

chick (1899) Orig US; applied to a (sexually attractive) young woman; compare earlier use as a term of endearment for a young child ■ *It*: Jackie, always a 'with-it chick'. (1971)

frail (1899) Mainly US; from earlier, obsolete sense, prostitute ■ Eric Linklater: Bullets whistling

through the air to . . . threaten widowhood for the ravished frail. (1931)

jane (1906) Orig US; applied to a (young) woman, sometimes specifically a girlfriend; from the female personal name *Jane* ■ Erle Stanley Gardner: 'Who was this jane? Anybody I know?' 'No one you know. . . . She had been a nurse in San Francisco.' (1967)

tom (1906) Australian, dated; applied to a (young) woman, sometimes specifically a girlfriend; short for obsolete Australian *Tom-tart*, rhyming slang for *sweetheart* ■ Norman Lindsay: Who's yer tom? She must be yer sweetheart. Why don't yer up an' kiss her? (1933)

frippet (1908) Derogatory; applied to a frivolous young woman; origin unknown ■ Elizabeth Taylor: 'Mistress!' he thought. . . . It was like the swine of a man to use such a word for what he and Edwards would have called a bit of a frippet. (1945)

broad (1911) Orig & mainly US, usually derogatory; often with an implication of promiscuity, especially in early use; compare obsolete US *broadwife* female slave separated from her husband, from *abroad + wife* ■ Eric Linklater: Slummock . . . had got into a jam with a broad; no ordinary broad, but a Coastguard's broad. (1931)

gash (1914) Derogatory; from earlier sense, vulva ■ L. Gould: I asked him if I could borrow *The Sun Also Rises*, and he said, 'I never lend books to any gash.' (1974)

muff (1914) Orig US; usually with an implication of promiscuity; from earlier sense, female genitals

tabby (1916) Applied to an (attractive) young woman; from earlier obsolete sense, (catty) older woman ■ John Wain: 'I said, is it true what Joe says that you've got yourself fitted out with a tabby?' 'My humble roof,' said Robert . . . 'is shared by a distinguished actress.' (1958)

deb, debby (1917) Orig US; applied to a débutante; first attested in *sub-deb*, and not recorded independently before 1920; abbreviation of *débutante* ■ *Sunday Dispatch*: The impossibility of parents doing any of the old kind of chaperonage in the hours kept by the present day (or night) 'debbies' during their present season. (1928) ■ John Betjeman: The debs may turn disdainful backs On Pearl's uncouth mechanic slacks. (1966)

sub-deb (1917) Dated, mainly US; applied to a girl who will soon come out as a débutante, and hence broadly to a girl in her mid-teens ■ *Time*: The season's debutantes danced their way into society while eager sub-debs looked on. (1947)

tab (1918) Australian, dated; applied to a (young) woman; compare earlier sense, old woman ■ H. Simpson: We don't need to go mackin' round with Chinks and wimmen's earnings. We pay our tabs . . . when we want 'em, and tell 'em to get to hell out of it when we don't. (1932)

number (1919) Usually applied to a woman of the stated type ■ William Gaddis: Have you seen a little blond number named Adeline? (1955)

bimbo (1920) Orig US; often with an implication of promiscuity; compare earlier sense, fellow, chap ■ *Detective Fiction Weekly*: We found Durken and Frenchy LaSeur, seated at a table . . . with a pair of blonde bimboes beside them. (1937)

wren (1920) US; applied to a (young) woman; from earlier sense, small bird ■ Arthur Conan Doyle: Scanlan has . . . married his wren in Philadelphia. (1929)

chicklet, chiclet (1922) US; applied to a (sexually attractive) young woman; from *chick* young woman + diminutive suffix *-let*, punningly after *Chiclets*, name of a brand of chewing gum

bit (1923) British, mainly derogatory; applied to a (young) woman; probably short for *bit of fluff*, *goods*, etc., woman viewed as a sex object ■ Barbara Goolden: If I want a common little bit for a best girl that's my look-out, too. (1953)

quiff (1923) Orig dialect; applied to a young woman, often with an implication of promiscuity; origin unknown ■ L. Snelling: If only there was some other quiff about I might be able to deal with her indifference. (1973)

wimp (1923) British, dated; origin uncertain; perhaps an abbreviated alteration of *woman*

twist-and-twirl (1924), **twist** (1926) Mainly US, often derogatory; applied to a young woman; *twist-and-twirl* rhyming slang for *girl* ■ Ross Macdonald: I hate to see it happen to a pretty little twist like Fern. (1953) ■ Herbert Gold: I'm just as good as any of those Pittsburgh twist-and-twirls. (1956)

bim (1925) US; applied to a young woman; often with an implication of promiscuity; short for *bimbo* ■ J. T. Farrell: Studs Lonigan copped off a bim whose old man is lousy with dough. (1935)

poule (1926) Applied to a (sexually attractive) young woman; often with an implication of promiscuity; from French *poule* hen ■ J. B. Priestley: He is probably amusing himself somewhere with that little brown poule of his. (1949)

sort (1933) Orig Australian; applied to a (young attractive) woman, sometimes specifically a girlfriend ■ Kit Denton: They'd told me, 'Don't worry about bringing anything except a bottle. The sorts are laid on.' Even after only ten months I understood this to mean that there would be feminine company. (1968)

palone, polone, polony, -i (1934) Derogatory; applied to a young woman; origin unknown ■ Graham Greene: 'Napoleon the Third used to have this room,' Mr. Colleoni said, 'and Eugenie.' 'Who was she?' 'Oh,' Mr. Colleoni said vaguely, 'one of those foreign polonies.' (1938)

bride (1935) British; applied to a (young) woman, especially a girlfriend ■ *Listener*: This load of squaddies . . . ain't got any brides with them. (1964)

quim (1935) Often used collectively with reference to women, often with an implication

of promiscuity; from earlier sense, vulva, vagina ■ *Saturday Night* (Toronto): The key to success in this contest is a flashy car; and if the car is both expensive and impressive 'you have to beat the quim off with a hockey stick'. (1974)

split (1935) North American, derogatory; probably from the notion of the vulva as a slit; compare **gash** p. 47 and **quim** p. 48 ■ *Globe & Mail* (Toronto): An announcement was posted that the force's first female officer Constable Jacqueline Hall, had been hired. 'He's gone and hired another split, as if we don't have enough whores and splits in the department already,' Mrs. Nesbitt quoted the sergeant as saying. (1975)

rye mort (1936) Dated; applied to a lady; from *rye* man + *mort* woman ■ James Curtis: Anyone taking a quick look at her might think she was on the up-and-up. She would give that impression too, to anyone who heard her talk and saw her act. Though . . . she would have to give up that rye mort touch. (1936)

toots (1936) Orig & mainly US; applied to a young woman, and also specifically to a girlfriend; often used as a familiar form of address; probably an abbreviation of *tootsy* ■ *New Yorker*: 'Hi, toots,' Ducky said in Donald's voice a few minutes later to a tiny girl. (1975)

mystery (1937) British; applied to a young woman newly arrived in a town or city, or with no fixed address ■ *Observer*: Many teddys, tearaways and mysteries (drifting girls) are put off by the typical orthodox youth club. (1960)

knitting (1943) British, naval slang; applied to a young woman or collectively to young women; from the stereotypical view of knitting as a woman's occupation

Richard, richard (1950) British; short for *Richard the Third*, rhyming slang for *bird* ■ G. F. Newman: I was just sleeping at this Richard's place during the day. . . I didn't know she was brassing. (1970)

trim (1955) US, mainly derogatory; often with an implication of promiscuity ■ Ed Lacy: The broad isn't worth it, no trim is. (1962)

potato (1957) Australian; short for *potato peeler*, rhyming slang for *sheila* ■ Germaine Greer: Terms . . . often extended to the female herself. Who likes to be called . . . a *potato*? (1970)

mole (1965) Australian, usually derogatory; perhaps a variant of *moll* female companion ■ R. D. Jones: Give us a hand you lazy mole! (1979)

chapess (1966) British, jocular; from *chap* + female suffix *-ess* ■ *Independent*: There are plenty of leisure interest groups catering for the brighter than average, from the Conan Doyle Society to the Sundial Society, from the queen's English Society to the Society for Psychical Research—all packed with bright chaps and chapesses eager to discuss matters of mutual interest with similar with a view to forming a lasting relationship. (1996)

Betty (1989) US; applied to a (young attractive) woman; from the female personal name *Betty*

A female partner or companion

moll (1823) Applied to a criminal's or gangster's female companion; compare earlier sense, prostitute ■ Ngaio Marsh: I can see you're in a fever lest slick Ben and his moll should get back . . . before you make your getaway. (1962)

tart (1864) Probably short for *raspberry tart*, rhyming slang for *sweetheart* ■ T. Ronan: Hangin' around my tart? (1977)

best girl (1887), best (1904) Orig US; applied to a girlfriend or female lover ■ *Saturday Review*: To pluck a bouquet for his best girl. (1944)

dinah (1898) British, dated; applied to a girlfriend or female lover; alteration of *dona* woman, sweetheart, probably influenced by the female forename *Dinah* ■ J. R. Ware: Is Mary your Dinah? (1909)

squarie, squarey (1917) Australian; from obsolete Australian slang *square* (of a woman) respectable + *-ie* ■ *Royal Australian Navy News*: You bloody beaut . . . we'll be back outside with our squaries! (1970)

patootie (1921) US; applied to a girlfriend or female lover; often in the phrases *hot patootie, sweet patootie*; probably an alteration of *(sweet) potato* ■ *New Yorker*: She was, successively, . . . the wife and/or sweet patootie of the quartet. (1977)

mamma, mama, momma (1926) US; applied to a girlfriend or wife; compare earlier sense, promiscuous woman

jelly (1931) Dated; applied to a girlfriend; compare earlier sense, attractive young woman ■ William Faulkner: Gowan goes to Oxford a lot. . . . He's got a jelly there. He takes her to the dances. (1931)

red-hot momma (1936) Compare earlier sense, earthy female jazz singer

queen (1944) Compare earlier sense, attractive young woman ■ P. Sillitoe: Both gangs used hatchets, swords, and sharpened bicycle chains . . . and these were conveyed to the scenes of their battles by their 'queens'. (1955)

frat (1945) Applied to a woman met by fratting; from *frat* establish friendly and especially sexual relationships with German women (used of British and American occupying troops after World War II) ■ G. Cotterell: Then, take my frat I go with, what harm did she ever do? (1949)

See also **ball and chain, dutch, her indoors, missus, Mrs, old girl, old lady, old woman**,

and **trouble and strife** under Wife at **Relations** (p. 51).

A domineering woman

battleaxe (1896) Derogatory, orig US ■ Christine Brooke-Rose: Do I look like a female novelist? I thought they were all battle-axes. (1957)

See also **ball-breaker** under A severe, hard, or uncompromising person at **Severity, Oppressiveness** (p. 428).

An old woman

See under An old person at **Old** (p. 369).

A promiscuous woman

See under **Sex** (pp. 67–8).

A stupid woman

dumb Dora (1922) Orig US; from the female personal name *Dora* ■ Graham McInnes: They [sc. hens] would then wait expectantly, heads cocked on one side with a sort of dumb-Dora inquisitive chuckle. (1965)

bimbo (1927) Orig US; applied to a young woman considered sexually attractive but of limited intelligence; compare earlier sense, woman ■ W. Allen: Sure, a guy can meet all the bimbos he wants. But the really brainy women—they're not so easy to find. (1976)

dumb blonde (1936) Orig US; applied to a conspicuously attractive but stupid blonde woman ■ M. Derby: The dumb blonde to whom all instruments and machinery were insoluble riddles. (1959)

bimbette (1982) Orig US; applied especially to an adolescent or teenage bimbo; from *bimb(o* + diminutive *-ette* ■ *Time*: Serious actresses, itching to play something more demanding than bimbette and stand-by wives, love divine masochist roles. (1982)

An ugly woman

See under An ugly person at **Beauty & Ugliness** (p. 219).

An unpleasant or despicable woman

See under An unpleasant or despicable person at **Unpleasantness** (p. 223).

Terms of address to a woman

See under Used to address a female at **Terms of Address** (pp. 53–4).

3. **Children**

kid (1690) From earlier sense, young goat ■ Lord Shaftesbury: Passed a few days happily with my wife and kids. (1841) ■ *Guardian*: The easy life suits me. I'll like just being at home with my kids and grandchildren. (1991)

weeny (1844) North American; from *weeny* small ■ *Ottawa Citizen*: Our five-year-old granddaughter keeps

asking when the trip is going to begin. Travelling with weenies is something that Mama and I have done for most of our lives. (1977)

shaver (1854) Dated; applied to a boy; mainly in the phrases *young shaver, little shaver*; from earlier sense, fellow, chap ■ *New Yorker*: Sometimes I think of your father when he was a little shaver of four or five setting solemnly off. (1970)

nipper (1859) Mainly British; compare earlier obsolete senses, a boy who assists a costermonger, carter or workman, a thief or pickpocket ■ *Times*: When I was a nipper at school in Glasgow [etc.]. (1972)

kiddy, kiddie (1889) From *kid* + *-y* ■ *Economist*: I bought the kiddies 'ome computers for Christmas and wrote them off against tax. (1988)

tyke (1894) Often (and probably orig) applied specifically to a mischievous child; often in the phrase *little tyke*; from earlier sense, boorish fellow ■ William Faulkner: 'That poor boy,' Cora says. 'The poor little tyke.' (1930)

kiddo (1896) From *kid* + *-o* ■ *John o' London's*: When it comes to choosing between the balance of power and unborn babies, I'm for the kiddos, every time. (1961)

tin lid (1905) Australian; rhyming slang for *kid* ■ B. Dickens: What are the things of light that made me bawl as a tinlid? (1981)

God forbid, Gawd forbid (1909) British; rhyming slang for *kid* ■ Margery Allingham: You take 'Er Ladyship and the Gawd-ferbid to the party. (1955)

sprout (1934) US ■ Ruth Moore: I'm going to beat the living pickle out of this goddam sprout of mine. (1950)

juvie, juvey (1941) US; applied to an older child; from *juv(enile* + *-ie* ■ P. Stadley: Just where would you take me, little juvie? To a drive-in movie? (1970)

sprog (1945) British, orig nautical; compare earlier sense, new recruit, trainee ■ Martin Amis: Here I attempted a few minutes' work, not easy because the fifty bawling sprogs had classes there in the afternoon. (1973)

kiddywink, kiddiewinkie, kiddywinkle, kiddywinky (1957) Fanciful extension of *kiddy* ■ Peter Bull: My performance . . . was pretty macabre, and must have frightened the bejesus out of the kiddy-winks. (1959) ■ *Times*: Dad Robinson . . . puts off the average incompetent father. Still, the kiddywinkles aren't to know. (1974)

squirt (1958) US; compare earlier sense, insignificant (but presumptuous) person ■ Bernard Malamud: George . . . remembered him giving him nickels . . . when he was a squirt. (1958)

saucepan lid (1961) Rhyming slang for *kid*

littley (1965) Australian; from *little* small, young + *-y* ■ K. Denton: Mum used to tell me that when I was a littley I wouldn't hold anyone's hand. (1976)

rug-rat (1968) US ■ Terry McMillan: Me, Gloria, and Savannah'll help you do everything but breast-feed the little rug rat when it's born. (1992)

ankle-biter (1981) Australian; from children's height and sporadic outbursts of violence ■ *Sydney Morning Herald*: Travelling overseas with an ankle-biter has its advantages. It keeps you out of museums, cathedrals and temples and shows you the raw side of life: playgrounds, supermarkets, laundrettes and public toilets. (1984)

A mischievous child

monkey (1819) Usually in the phrases *little monkey* and *young monkey* ■ Charles Dickens: 'Where have you been, you young monkey?' said Mrs Joe, stamping her foot. (1861)

horror (1846) Often in the phrase *little horror* ■ *Spectator*: Children adore reading about little horrors being taken down a peg. (1958)

Peck's bad boy (1883) Mainly US; applied to a mischievous boy; from the name of a fictional character created by G. W. Peck (1840–1916) ■ *Atlantic Monthly*: [Governor George] Wallace's motives— ego, a Peck's-bad-boy desire to make trouble, a yen to see just what would happen if a presidential election were thrown into the House of Representatives, or a combination of all these— do not actually matter. (1967)

perisher (1935) Usually in the phrase *little perisher*; from earlier use as a general term of contempt for someone ■ *Guardian*: I taught the whole school . . . about Palm Sunday. . . . Not one of the little perishers knew.

An illegitimate/legitimate child

illegit (1913) Abbreviation ■ C. Carnac: Somerset House . . . registers the illegits . . . as carefully as the rest. (1958)

legit (1955) Abbreviation ■ Elizabeth Bowen: Left no children—anyway, no legits. (1955)

A baby

snork (1941) Australian & New Zealand; from earlier sense, young pig, from the verb *snork* snort or grunt, probably from Middle Dutch or Middle Low German *snorken* ■ B. Pearson: It's better to knock it on the head at birth, isn't it? Like a snork you don't want. (1963)

A teenager

teeny-bopper (1966) Applied to a young teenager, typically a girl, who follows the latest fashions in clothes, pop music, etc.; from *teen* or *teen(ager* + *bopper* dancer to or fan of pop music; influenced by *teeny* small ■ *Guardian*: 'I think we should be paid for going to school.' Thus my teenybopper daughter. (1979)

weeny-bopper (1972) Largely interchangeable in meaning with *teeny-bopper*, although sometimes notionally applied to younger teenagers or pre-teens; from *weeny* small, after *teeny-bopper* ■ *Evening News*: Being a weeny-bopper can be a problem when it comes to clothes. . . . Our model, Karen, nearly 13, got her mum to take her round the stores. (1975)

A person who has a sexual affair with someone much younger

cradle-snatcher (1907), cradle-robber (1926) Derogatory, orig US ■ R. Erskine: Crispin asked me to dance. 'Cradle-snatcher,' said Miranda nastily. (1965)

baby-snatcher (1911) British, derogatory or jocular ■ Victoria Sackville-West: You don't imagine that he really cared about that baby-snatcher? Good gracious me, he was a year old when her daughter was born. (1930)

4. Relations

folks (1715) In American English often applied specifically to one's parents ■ *US Today*: While vacationing with his folks, 14-year-old Jerry Curran was hit on at a snack machine by a 16- year-old girl. (1991)

tribe (1833) Applied dismissively to a large family or group of relatives ■ *Blackwood's Magazine*: I could fancy her . . . writing lengthy epistles to a tribe of nieces. (1909)

people (1851) Dated; in British slang (orig public schools') often applied specifically to parents and other immediate family sharing the same house ■ Mrs. Dyan: I went down into Devonshire, for me to be introduced to my people-in-law, you know. (1894)

clan (1978) Jocular; from earlier sense, group of Scottish families ■ *Guardian*: This country is at war, though you would never believe it from the shenanigans of some members of Her Majesty's clan. (1991)

Father

dad (1500), daddy (1500), dada, dadda, dada (1688), da (1851) Perhaps imitative of a child's *da, da* ■ Charlotte Yonge: The child still cried for her da-da. (1866) ■ James Joyce: Waiting outside pubs to bring da home. (1922)

pappy (1763), pa (1811), pop (1838), poppa (1897), pops (1928) Variants and abbreviations of archaic *papa* (1681), from French *papa*, ultimately from Greek *papas* ■ H. E. Bates: 'Larkin, that's me,' Pop said. (1958) ■ Simon Harvester: Me a defenceless girl . . . without my Mom and Pops. (1976)

governor, guv'nor (1827) ■ Cuthbert Bede: I suppose the bills will come in some day or other, but the governor will see to them. (1853)

old man (1892), old boy (1892), old fellow (1922) ■ Lonnie Donnegan: My old man's a dustman. (1960)

Mother

mam (1500), mammy (1523) Perhaps imitative of a child's *ma, ma*

mummy (1784), mum (1823), mumsy (1876), mums (1939) Imitative of a child's pronunciation ■ Agatha Christie: Poor Mumsy, she was so devoted to Dad, you know. (1953)

ma (1823) Abbreviation of archaic *mama*

old girl (1846), old woman (1892), old lady (1932) ■ J. D. Brayshaw: He lets aht that Liz an' 'er ole gal was going ter the Crystal Palice. (1898)

momma (1884), mom (1876), mommy (1902) US variant of *mamma, mummy* ■ *New Yorker*: 'Of course we will, Mom,' I said, and I patted her hand. (1975)

Spouse

better half (1842) Orig used by Sir Philip Sidney in his *Arcadia* (1580): (Argalus to Parthenia, his wife) 'My dear, my better half (said he) I find I must now leave thee'; but latterly only in colloquial use; theoretically applied to husbands or wives, but in practice more often used of wives

Husband

hubby (1688) Abbreviation of *husband* ■ *Pall Mall Gazette*: In disputes between a hubby and his better half. (1887)

old man (1768) ■ John le Carré: She was a sight better qualified than her old man. (1974)

papa (1904) US; also applied to a woman's lover

pot and pan (1906) Rhyming slang for *old man*

old pot (1916) Mainly Australian; *pot* short for *pot and pan*

monkey man (1924) US; applied to a weak and servile husband

Wife

old woman (1775), old lady (1836), old girl (1853) ■ Jimmy O'Connor: If you went home and found someone indoors with your old woman, what would you do? (1976)

missus, missis (1833) Alteration of *mistress* ■ *Daily Mirror*: If you fancy taking the missus for a day out, you take her virtually free. (1975)

dutch (1889), duchess (1895) British; *dutch*, abbreviation of *duchess* (originally applied to costermongers' wives), which itself may be an abbreviation of obsolete *Duchess of Fife*, rhyming slang ■ Thomas Pynchon: Time for closeting, gas logs, shawls against the cold night, snug with your young lady or old dutch. (1973)

trouble and strife (1908) Rhyming slang ■ G. Fisher: It's the old trouble and strife—wife. I want to see her all right. (1977)

Mrs. (1920) ■ *Philadelphia Inquirer*: You know, when I go home, the Mrs. says to me: 'Well, what happened tonight, night clerk?' (1973)

ball and chain (1921) From the 'ball and chain' attached to a convict's leg to prevent escape, in humorous allusion to a wife's restriction of her husband's freedom ■ *Eastern Eye*: Attractive Arabian Yemeni male . . . seeking a pretty Sunni Muslim female (18–30) that is pleasing to my eyes and heart for the intention of marriage, not the traditional classic old ball and chain routine. (1996)

her indoors, 'er indoors (1979) British; applied to a wife or other live-in female partner, often with the implication of a domineering woman; popularized by the Thames TV series *Minder* (1979–88); applied by the character Arthur Daley to his wife, who never appears on screen ■ *Boardroom*: How many punters, one wonders, soften the blow to 'her indoors' concerning the purchase of a new Corniche by also bringing home a snappy little Lotus in her favourite colour! (1989)

Brother

bro (1937) Used as a written abbreviation since the mid 17th century, but as a spoken form, introduced into British public school slang in the 1930s

Sister

sis (1656) Abbreviation ■ Dulcie Gray: You'll be wearing clothes at the Private View, won't you, Sis? (1974)

skin and blister (1925) Rhyming slang
■ George Ingram: I saw your skin and blister last night. (1935)

Grandfather

grandaddy, grand-daddy (1769), grandad, grand-dad (1819), grandpa (1862), grandpop (1890), grandpappy (1919)
■ Nicholas Blake: Have a glass of port, won't you? It's rather delish. Grand-pop laid it down. (1953)

gramp, gramps (1898) Shortened from grandpapa ■ Linacre Lane: That ther kid's ther dead spit of 'is gramp. (1966)

Grandmother

granny (1663), gran (1863), grandma (1867)
■ R. Daniel: By the time she gets back to 'Mum' and 'Gran' she'll be wet through. (1960)

nana, nanna (1844), nan (1940), nan-nan (1959) Childish pronunciation ■ New Society: Jackie gets £1 a week off her grandmother, who owns a pub: 'My nan's got tons of money.' (1975)

nin (1958) A Liverpool usage, from Welsh nain grandmother ■ Peter Moloney: Every true wacker has three relations, viz. 'Me Mar, Me Nin, an me Anti-Mury.' (1966)

5. Terms of Address

Used to address a male

mate (c1450) From earlier sense, companion; orig 'used as a form of address by sailors, labourers, etc.' (OED) ■ Sydney Morning Herald: I asked a station attendant . . . if the train was the North-West Mail. 'I wouldn't have a clue, mate,' was the reply. (1974)

old boy (1601) British ■ C. H. Ward-Jackson: It's a perfect bind, old boy. (1943)

bud (1614) Recorded in British English in the 17th century, but now only used in American English, where it re-emerged in the mid 19th century; perhaps representing a childish pronunciation of brother; compare buddy ■ W. R. Burnett: Gamblers . . . would often hand him a quarter . . . and say: 'Keep it, bud.' (1953)

old cock (1639) Compare cock ■ Terence Rattigan: Good show, Count, old cock! (1942)

Aunt

auntie, aunty (1792) From aunt + -ie

A former spouse or lover

ex (1929) From earlier sense, one who formerly occupied a particular position, from the prefix ex- ■ Ladies' Home Journal: His 'ex' also got away with every stick of furniture and household equipment. (1971)

Marriage: To propose marriage

pop the question (1826), pop (1867) ■ New York Times: Now's the time to pop the question! 20% off diamond engagement rings. (1972) ■ Margery Sharp: I haven't actually . . . popped, yet. (1960)

To marry, get married

tie the knot (1717) ■ Independent: If he and Jill Morrell decide to delight the tabloid press and tie the knot, they might like to draw up a prenuptial agreement. (1991)

splice (1874) Back formation from spliced married ■ Tim Heald: If the old flapper spliced with the colonel she stood to lose a million dollars. (1981)

Married

spliced (1751) From earlier sense, (of two ropes) joined together ■ Christine Brooke-Rose: Yes, I worked in an office before I got spliced, didn't you know, solicitors in the Strand. (1968)

hitched (1857) Orig US; from earlier sense, tied ■ J. H. Fullarton: That's the fifth o the old gang to get hitched up in five months. (1944)

Relations by marriage

in-law (1894) ■ G. F. Newman: His in-laws bought the furniture for the new house. (1970)

pal (1681) Early vocative uses are difficult to distinguish from the primary sense 'friend' (see under A friend at **Friends** (pp. 62–3)); the neutral and hostile uses are a recent development ■ New York Times: Kramden's mantra, uttered whenever he was frightened or embarrassed or ashamed, is 'humenahumenahumena'. Gleason, no longer capable of being any of these things, simply said, 'Just wing it, pal'. (1992)

mister (1760) From earlier use as a title prefixed to a man's name ■ Elmore Leonard: Mister, gimme a dollar. (1987)

bo (1825) Mainly US; probably a shortening of boy ■ Judge: The man who tells the bootblack 'Keep the change, bo'. (1919)

baby (1835), babe (1906) US; used between men; common especially in the 1960s ■ Listener: The dialogue is over, baby. (1968)

cock (1837) British; compare *old cock* ▪ George Melly: Smarten yourself up a bit, cock, before we go on! (1965)

boss (1839) Orig US; from earlier sense, master ▪ Irvine Welsh: Spud! Awright boss? How ye livin?—Peachy catboy, peachy. Eh, yirsel likesay? (1993)

bub (1839) US; perhaps representing a childish pronunciation of *brother*, or from German *Bube* boy ▪ *Chicago Star*: Hey bub—can I get a squint at yer uppers? (1948)

dad (1847) Used originally to address an older man, from earlier sense, father; used from the 1920s (originally in jazz slang) to address any male ▪ *Time & Tide: Sunset Strip* is real zoolie, dad. (1960)

bubby (1848) US; from *bub* + *-y*, or from German *Bube* boy

guvner, guv'ner, guvnor, guv'nor (1852) British; used to a man of higher status; from earlier sense, boss ▪ *Listener*: You can be sure that if somebody calls you 'mister' on the railways he doesn't like you. The term of endearment is 'guv'nor'. (1968)

matey (1859) From *mate* + *-y* ▪ June Drummond: Right, matey, 'oo told you? (1973)

buster (1866) Mainly US; usually used disrespectfully; from earlier sense, riotous fellow (ultimately a dialectal variant of *burster*) ▪ A. Shepard: 'OK, Buster,' I said to myself, 'you volunteered for this thing.' (1962)

chum (1867) From earlier sense, friend ▪ William Deverell: And you're still in a car turning on sirens, chum. When you're not on job action. (1989)

doc (1869) US; now mainly in the phrase *What's up, Doc?*, popularized as the catch-phrase of the Warner Bros. cartoon character Bugs Bunny; from earlier sense, doctor

sonny, sonnie (1870) Used to a small boy or, disparagingly, to a man younger than the speaker; from *son* + *-y* ▪ Robert Louis Stevenson: 'Come here, sonny,' says he. (1870)

buddy (1885) US; from earlier sense, male friend ▪ *Daily Express*: When I went into the night nursery to get the boys up I was greeted with a shout of 'Stick 'em up, buddy'. (1937)

old man (1885) ▪ Dorothy Sayers: Just brush my bags down, will you, old man? (1927)

cocker (1888) British; from *cock* + *-er* ▪ Arnold Wesker: It was good of you to help us cocker. (1960)

guv (1890) British; used to a man of higher status; short for *guvner*

old chap (1892) British ▪ Len Deighton: Just tell me the whole story in your own words, old chap. (1962)

Sunny Jim, Sonny Jim (1911) Used mainly to a small boy; *Sunny Jim* coined in 1903 as the name of an energetic character used as the proprietary name for a US brand of breakfast cereal ▪ Angus Wilson: Does your mother know you're out, Sonny Jim? (1967)

cobber (1916) Australian & New Zealand; from earlier sense, friend ▪ *Bronze swagman book of bush verse*: Come in, old cobber, and swallow a pot. (1976)

old bean (1917) British, dated ▪ Jack Thomas: I say, old bean, let's stick together. (1955)

big boy (1918) Orig US; usually used ironically ▪ J. B. Priestley: 'Am I right, sirs?' 'You sure are, big boy.' (1939)

sport (1923) Mainly Australian ▪ H. Knorr: Don't get y' knickers in a knot, sport! (1982)

old fruit (1928) British, dated ▪ Terence Rattigan: You don't mind me asking, did you, old fruit? (1951)

sonny boy (1928) Used to a small boy or, disparagingly or threateningly, to a man younger than the speaker; inspired by the song 'Sonny Boy' (1928), sung by Al Jolson ▪ Ted Allbeury: What do you want, sonny boy?. . . I don't trust you, you English bastard. (1978)

daddy (1927), **daddy-o** (1948) Dated, orig jazz slang; compare *dad* ▪ *Time & Tide*: The walls are crazy,. . . And the scene uncool for you, Daddy-o. (1960)

chief (1935) Orig US; from earlier use for addressing one's superior

mush, moosh (1936) British; perhaps from Romany *moosh* man ▪ John Brown: Look, moosh, you'll strip off or I'll take them off you. (1972)

pop (1943) Orig US; applied to an old man ▪ Kylie Tennant: You've just told us, pop,. . . that if the cops catch up on you, you'll be lining a cell. (1943)

chummy (1948) British, police slang; applied to a person accused or detained; from earlier sense, friend ▪ Douglas Clark: We could get Chummy into the dock and pleading guilty, but we'd not get a verdict. (1969)

tosh (1954) British; origin uncertain: perhaps from Scottish *tosh* neat, agreeable, friendly ▪ M. Kenyon: 'Sortin' you out for a start, tosh!' came a voice. (1978)

squire (1959) British; used to a man of higher status ▪ *Times*: Tell you what, squire—keep the pension and I'll take the cash. (1982)

mac, mack (1962) From earlier sense, someone whose name contains the Gaelic prefix *Mac* ▪ John Wainwright: The bouncer . . . tapped him on the shoulder and said 'Hey, mac'. (1973)

sunshine (1972) British ▪ P. Cave: I turned back to the ticket man. 'OK now, sunshine?' (1976)

Used to address a female

missis, missus (1875) Alteration of *mistress*

girls (1906) Used to address a group of women of any age (and in ironic homosexual use to address men) ▪ Stephen Gray: I was subjected to more exploratory innuendo than if I'd strolled in, slung my handbag on the reception desk, said 'Well, hi girls!' and primped my crewcut. (1988)

sister (1906) ▪ R. Boyle: Come on, sister. . . . Why won't you stay and talk to me? I'm a nice guy. (1976)

ma (1932) Applied to an (older) married woman; from earlier sense, mother

duchess (1953) From earlier sense, woman ■ Larry Forrester: Start talkin', Duchess. We're gonna toss what you got into the computer . . . and see what comes out. (1967)

Unisex

sweetheart (c1325) Used as a term of endearment or (ironically) threateningly; from earlier sense, loved one ■ F. Parrish: Try harder, sweetheart, or I'll plug you in the guts. (1977)

honey (c1350) Used as a term of endearment ■ Lewis Nkosi: Men are monsters!. . . Especially black men, honey. (1964)

chuck (1588) British, now mainly dialectal; used as a term of endearment; alteration of *chick* chicken

duck (1590), duckie, ducky (1819), ducks (1936) British; usually as a term of endearment ■ Alan Sillitoe: Don't get like that, Ernie, duck. (1979) ■ Edward Hyams: I must have sounded disagreeable, because Matilda said, 'Don't be narky, ducky'. (1958) ■ Edward Hyams: Talked like you 'e did, ducks. (1958)

dearie, deary (1681) From *dear* + *-ie*; used as a term of endearment ■ Charles Dickens: Here's another ready for ye, deary. (1870)

fatty (1797) See under **Physique** (p. 12)

pet (1849) British, mainly Northern dialect; used mainly by women, or by men to women ■ John Wainwright: He . . . spoke to the policewoman on duty. . . . 'Now then, pet—can you help me?' (1975)

poppet (1849) Used as a term of endearment, especially to a child; from earlier sense, small delicate person or child ■ D. Devine: 'No, you don't eat the spoon, poppet.' She hoisted the child out of his chair and put him in the play-pen. (1978)

old thing (1864) British ■ June Drummond: Don't worry, old thing. It may not be as bad as it sounds. (1975)

four-eyes (1873) See under **Sight**, **Vision** (p. 15)

baby (1880), babe (1890) Mainly US; used as a term of (especially sexual) endearment ■ H. S.

Harrison: Bad-eyed young men who congregate . . . to smirk at the working girls. . . . 'Where you goin', baby?' (1911)

face (1890) Dated except in US Black English ■ Dodie Smith: Come on, face—don't get mopey. (1938)

kiddo (1896) From *kid* child + *-o*, but not applied only to young people ■ Nicolas Freeling: 'How long do I have to stay?' . . . 'Just as long as we thinks right, kiddo.' (1974)

honey-baby, honey-bun, honey-bunch (1904) Used as a term of endearment ■ R. Tashkent: I'm sorry, honeybun—sorry. Guess I'm a little upset. (1969)

darl (1930) Australian; abbreviation of *darling* ■ *Truckin' Life*: Newcastle to Gosford is only a short run darl. (1984)

sugar, sugar-babe, sugar-baby, sugar-pie, etc. (1930) Orig US; used as a term of endearment ■ James Curtis: When am I going to see you again, sugar? (1936)

sweetie (1932), sweetie pie (1928) Used as a term of endearment; *sweetie* from *sweet* + *-ie* ■ Ngaio Marsh: 'Sweetie,' Julia cried extravagantly, 'you *are* such heaven.' (1977)

fatso (1933) See under **Physique** (p. 12)

man (1933) Applied among blacks, jazz musicians, hippies, etc. to both men and women ■ *Black World*: Hey, only the squares, man, only the squares have it to keep. (1971)

face-ache (1937) British; used disparagingly; compare earlier sense, neuralgia

poopsie, poopsy (1942) US; used as a term of endearment for a sweetheart, baby, or small child ■ Stanley Kauffmann: Perry finished and hung up. 'Hiya, poopsie,' he called. 'Have a hotsy-totsy week-end?' (1952)

luv (1957) British; representing the affectionate use of *love* as a term of address; used by women, or by men to women ■ G. Bell: Watch that money, luv! It's not safe there. (1972)

6. Groups

A group of people

bunch (1622) ■ Dawn Powell: He liked knowing the 'Greenwich Village Bunch'. (1936)

mob (1688) Abbreviation of *mobile*, short for Latin *mobile vulgus* excitable crowd ■ Sylvia Ashton-Warner: I know one girl from another, course you do in my mob anyway. (1960)

and Co. (1757) Used to denote the rest of a group; from earlier use in the names of business companies ■ *Listener*: What Khrushchev and Co. might do is one thing. (1959)

crowd (1840) Orig US ■ *Woman*: She was going through a particularly rebellious phase and seemed to be in with a wild crowd. (1971)

lot (1879) ■ *Harper's Magazine*: The men who do this work are an interesting lot. (1883)

outfit (1883) Orig US; from earlier sense, travelling party ■ John Wainwright: Some of the modern outfits don't have brass. Just a four-piece sax line-up. (1977)

push (1884) Mainly Australian; originally applied to a gang of thieves or ruffians ■ *Nation Review* (Melbourne): He was portrayed almost as another Keynes—or, at the very least, the intellectual peer of the Friedman–Galbraith–Samuelson push. (1973)

crush (1904) Dated, orig US; applied to a group, crowd, or gang of people ■ A. J. Small: Any one of that crush would do murder for no more than that 500 dollars reward. (1924)

gang (1945) Applied to a person's group of friends or associates; from earlier sense, group of criminals ■ **Gillian Freeman:** All the gang would be there, and she'd be ever so proud of him. (1955)

team (1950) Mainly applied to a gang of criminals ■ **Peter Laurie:** We had a whisper about a team going to do a certain pay van. (1970)

rat pack (1951) Orig US; applied to a disorderly mob of youths

circus (1958) Applied to a group of people acting or performing together in some activity ■ *Observer:* The Kramer circus comes to Britain this year immediately after Wimbledon. (1959)

posse (1986) Mainly US; applied to a gang of black (especially Jamaican) youths involved in organized or violent crime, often drug-related; from earlier sense, body of men summoned by a sheriff, etc. to enforce the law ■ *Boston:* Enforcement agents blame Jamaican posses for some 500 homicides and . . . gun-running. (1987)

A group walking two by two in a long file

crocodile (*a*1870) Usually applied to schoolchildren ■ **Melvyn Bragg:** The crocodile rows of little children. (1968)

A group of things or people

Pip, Squeak, and Wilfred (1920) British; applied to a group of three things (often,

specifically, three widely awarded World War I medals, the 1914–15 Star, the War Medal, and the Victory Medal, worn together) or people; from the names of three animal characters in a *Daily Mirror* children's comic strip ■ *Times:* That goes for Messrs Pip, Squeak and Wilfred, too. (1977)

As a group

mob-handed (1934) Used to denote that someone is part of or accompanied by a large gang ■ **Allan Prior:** Mo and his brother had returned home penniless to find the police mob-handed. (1966)

To act in a group; conspire

row in (1897) ■ **Philip Allingham:** I think these boys had better row in with us. . . . We may as well stick together. (1934)

Acting as a group

in cahoots (1862) Orig US; usually used to suggest a conspiracy; from earlier *in cahoot*; ultimate origin unknown ■ **Arthur Upfield:** She was in cahoots with a doctor. (1953)

As an accompanying person or group

in tow (1896) ■ **S. Brett:** 'Come along, Paul.' And Walter Proud, with his writer in tow, hurried along to join them. (1979)

7. **Status**

Status, reputation

cred (1981) British; applied to status among one's peers; short for *credibility* ■ **Bob Geldof:** 'Cred' was achieved by your rhetorical stance and no one had more credibility than the Clash. (1986)

street cred (1981) British; applied to status among one's peers, especially in fashionable urban youth subculture ■ *International Musician:* I know that walking down main street with an oboe in hand does nothing for the street cred. (1985)

That which is important

the be-all and end-all (1854) Applied to something regarded as the most important element in something; from Shakespeare *Macbeth* I. vii 'That but this blow Might be the be all, and the end all.' (1605) ■ *Daily Mail:* He says . . . he has lasted because he has never been obsessed with his work. That, for him, showbusiness has never been his 'be all and end all'. (1991)

the business end (1878) Applied to the part of something which performs its main function ■ *Scientific American:* The business end of the coronagraph is the quartz polarizing monochromator. (1955)

the half of it (1932) Applied to the most significant or important part of something; usually in negative contexts ■ **Marian Babson:**

'How awful,' she said. . . . I nodded, without telling her she didn't know the half of it. (1971)

the nitty-gritty (1963) Orig US; applied to the most crucial or basic aspects of something; origin unknown ■ *Times:* To get down to what the American will call the 'nitty-gritty' of the matter—the heart, sir, the heart. (1968)

An important statement

mouthful (1922) Orig US ■ **P. G. Wodehouse:** 'Nice nurse?' 'Ah, there you have said a mouthful, Pickering. I have a Grade A nurse.' (1973)

When the most important point is reached

when the chips are down (1945) Orig US; applied to a crucial or decisive moment; from the notion of the irrevocability of laying chips on the table in a gambling game ■ *Spectator:* For the fact is that when the chips are down, the Right wing of the Tory Party comes up. (1959)

A high-ranking or important person

bigwig (1703) From the large wigs formerly worn by men of high rank or importance ■ **Len Deighton:** He was there to give the Cubans some advice when they purged some of the bigwigs in 1970. (1984)

tyee, tyhee (1792) North American; from Chinook jargon, chief ■ **Harry Marriott:** The agricultural tyees in both Canada and the United States have taken a wise view. (1966)

big bug (1817) Orig and mainly US, often derogatory ∎ *Evelyn Waugh*: He seems to have been quite a big bug under the Emperor. Ran the army for him. (1932)

big gun (1834) Variant of earlier *great gun* in same sense ∎ *Barbara Kimenye*: Mrs. Lutaya's set absolutely refused to accept this high-handed ruling, preferring to remain large fish in their own small pond, rather than compete with the big guns of Gumbi and Male villages. (1966)

big fish (1836) Orig US; often applied to the ringleader in an enterprise ∎ *New Scientist*: What with being a writer and a T.V. personality and a sort of know-all pundit A.L.W. was quite a big fish. (1991)

big dog (1843) US ∎ *Guardian*: 'This is now the big boys' play,' said the divisional chief of staff, Col Keith Kellogg. 'If you're going to piss on a tree, you better be a pretty big dog.' (1991)

brass (*c*1864) Orig US; applied to officers of high rank in the armed services; from the brass or gold insignia on officers' caps ∎ *A. C. Clarke*: The general was unaware of his *faux pas*. The assembled brass thought for a while. (1959)

brass-hat (1893) Orig British; applied to an officer of high rank in the armed services; from the brass or gold insignia on officers' caps ∎ *A. Maclean*: The German brass-hats in Norway may well be making a decision as to whether or not to try to stop us again. (1984)

big brass (1899), **high brass** (1941), **top brass** (1949) Orig US; applied to officers of high rank in the armed services, and hence to any group of people of high rank; from *brass* in same sense ∎ *Life*: I don't suppose that Congress and the Big Brass would ever agree to that. (1945) ∎ *Economist*: The 'high brass' of American business was also well represented at the meeting. (1951) ∎ *Patrick Ruell*: What I'm going to tell you is restricted information. That means it's only known to the Prime Minister, [and] security top brass. (1972)

big noise (1906) Orig US ∎ *J. B. Priestley*: He's rather a big noise here. Landed man really, but has a seat on our Board, and a local J.P. (1942)

big cheese (1914) Orig US; compare *main cheese* boss; ultimately from *cheese* right or excellent thing, probably from Urdu *chiz* thing ∎ *Guardian*: I remember the day that Gordon Manning, then a big cheese at CBS News, . . . called up with the good news. (1992)

big boy (1924) Orig US ∎ *Guardian*: The Derbyshire girl was right up there with the big boys, Yves Saint Laurent and Giorgio Armani. (1991)

biggie (1926) Orig US; from *big* + *-ie* ∎ *Melody Maker*: It's time for me to be a biggie. . . . My aim now is to get . . . on to the front page. (1969)

big shot (1927) Orig US; variant of earlier *great shot* in same sense ∎ *New Statesman*: On arrival I was asked to dine with Thomas Lamont, along with a number of big-shots in the American newspaper world, including . . . Henry Luce of *Time-Life*. (1960)

high-up (1929) ∎ *Physics Bulletin*: Whitten and Poppoff, both high-ups in NASA's Ames Research Center, have filled the gap admirably despite their lack of academic background. (1971)

wheel (1933) Orig and mainly US ∎ *A. Fox*: Some Pentagon wheel's flying in and Don feels he has to travel up there with him. (1980)

big wheel (1942) Orig and mainly US ∎ *Monica Dickens*: He was evidently quite a big wheel at the studio. (1958)

big daddy (1948) Orig US ∎ *Spectator*: Mr. Francis Williams, journalism's Big Daddy. (1958)

big enchilada (1973) US

The most important or highest-ranking person; the person in charge

gaffer (*a*1659) British; applied especially to one's employer or superior; from earlier sense, elderly or respected man; ultimately probably a contraction of *godfather* ∎ *Daily Mail*: Daley was geed up to a frenzy in the dressing room by his manager, Ron Atkinson. 'The gaffer has been driving home to me all week that Winterburn had a bad game against the Polish winger at Everton,' he said. (1991)

guvner, guv'ner, guvnor, guv'nor (1802) British; representing a casual pronunciation of *governor* ∎ *Observer*: Sometimes the peterman finds his own jobs and acts as guvnor of his own team. (1960)

old man (1830) Applied originally to a commanding officer or ship's captain, and hence more generally to one's employer or superior ∎ *P. B. Yuill*: Has the old man been on? He'll be wanting to ask your old mates at the Yard for help. (1974) ∎ *D. MacNeil*: The Old Man had commanded longer than most lieutenant-colonels. (1977)

skipper (1830) Applied to the captain of a sports team (originally a curling team), and hence (*services' slang*) to a commanding officer in the army or the captain of an aircraft or squadron (1906) and (*orig US*) to a police chief (1929); from earlier sense, ship's captain ∎ *Daily Mail*: Waqar Younis showed England skipper Graham Gooch that he will be just as hostile as Curtly Ambrose next summer. (1991) ∎ *R.A.F. News*: The headmaster . . . will join his wartime Whitley skipper, Gp Capt Leonard Cheshire. (1977) ∎ *Dallas Barnes*: Good piece of police work. . . . I'll fill the skipper in. I'm sure he'll be pleased. (1976)

prex, prexy (1858) Applied to the president of a college, corporation, etc.; alteration of *president* ∎ *Cleveland* (Ohio) *Plain Dealer*: While the NHL is controlled basically by the board of governors . . . the silver-haired prexy still wields a powerful stick when it comes to meting out fines and suspensions. (1974)

skull (1880) US & Australian; applied to a leader or chief, and also to an expert; compare earlier obsolete sense, the head of an Oxford college or hall ∎ *G. H. Johnston*: 'Who does he fix the deal with?' 'God knows! D'ye think the skulls tell us that?' (1948)

guv (1890) British; short for *guvner* ∎ *N. Wallington*: The Guv was seated at his desk. (1974)

the main squeeze (1896) US, dated ■ Dashiel Hammett: Vance seems to be the main squeeze. (1927)

top dog (1900) ■ *Economist*: Joint ventures often fall apart because one partner insists on being top dog. (1988)

the main cheese (1902), the head cheese (1914) US

the owner (1903) Applied to the captain of a ship, and also of an aircraft ■ G. Taylor: Scott was invariably known as The Owner, a naval term always applied to the captain of a warship. (1916)

the bloke (1914) British, naval slang; applied to the captain of a ship; from earlier sense, man, fellow ■ W. Lang: If you gets noisy and boisterous-like you sees the Bloke in the morning. (1919)

the man, the Man (1918) US; applied to the person or people in authority ■ *Guardian*: 'The Man is repressive. The Man is fascist. . . .' To the bombers and kidnappers the Man is authority. He is every policeman. He is President Nixon. He is Prime Minister Trudeau. (1970)

trump (1925) Australian & New Zealand; from earlier sense, card belonging to a suit which ranks above others ■ *Sun* (Sydney): Officers are trumps, and reinforcements reos. (1942)

king-fish (1933) US; often used as a nickname for a particular person, notably for Huey Long (1893–1935), Governor and Senator from Louisiana; from earlier sense, type of large fish ■ *Richmond* (Virginia) *Times Dispatch*: Mr. Brown . . . is sometimes referred to as the 'kingfish' of City Council. (1946)

Mr. Big (1940) ■ A. W. Sherring: Hardly the kind of district one would expect to find Mr. Big of London's underworld. (1959)

chiefy (1942) Services' slang; applied to one's superior; from *chief* in same sense + *-y* ■ M. K. Joseph: The chiefy who done him out of his stripes. (1957)

honcho (1947) Orig and mainly US; from Japanese *han'chō* group leader ■ *New Yorker*: I was the first employee who was not one of the honchos. (1973)

the pea (1969) Australian; applied to the person in authority, 'the boss'; from earlier sense, one likely to emerge as the winner ■ M. Calthorpe: 'For the time being, I'm satisfied.' 'You're the pea,' Mick said. (1969)

top banana (1974) Orig US; from earlier sense, leading comic in a burlesque entertainment ■ *Washington Post*: Clinton apparently doesn't see any problem in using a little influence with the top banana. (1993)

To raise to a higher status

kick upstairs (c1697) Denoting promotion to a senior but less important job ■ William Cooper: The plot was devastatingly simple—Dibdin was to be kicked upstairs and Albert was to take his place. (1952)

Someone unimportant

spear-carrier (1960) Applied to an unimportant participant; from earlier theatrical slang sense, actor with a walk-on part ■ *Sunday Sun-Times*

(Chicago): By the time Breakfast at Wimbledon telecasts are beamed into the United States on Fourth of July weekend, American tennis pros Davis, Dunk and Hardie will have vacated their present lodging and be long gone from the venerable tournament that they graced momentarily as spear-carriers. (1982)

A title

handle (1832) Applied to an honorific title or similar distinction attached to a personal name (e.g. *the Honourable, M.P.*, etc.); from the phrase *a handle to one's name* a title attached to one's name ■ *News of the World*: 'I get very angry if people call me Lord David.' David . . . hates the sort of questions people ask once they find out about his 'handle'. (1977)

K (1910) British; abbreviation of *knighthood* ■ *Times*: There might not have been much merit in a political knighthood, but there was no harm in it. . . . The 'K', when it came, was a boon to the Member's wife, and a blessing to the Member himself. (1973)

A titled person

lifer (1959) Applied to a life-peer; compare earlier sense, prisoner serving a life sentence ■ *Sunday Telegraph*: I will not . . . turn out for Lifers. (1969)

Service ranks

super (1857) Short for *superintendant* ■ *Guardian*: He is well supported by Trevor Cooper as a beefily nervous Super and by Lorcan Cranitch as a thuggish Inspector. (1991)

sarge (1867) Orig US; short for *sergeant*; often as a term of address ■ M. K. Joseph: Hey, sarge, there's another bugger out in the middle of the field. (1958)

buck private (1874), buck-ass private (1945), buck-ass (1965) US; applied to a private soldier, and also (in the U.S.A.F.) to a basic airman; *buck* probably from earlier sense, spirited young man ■ *Times*: From general officer to buck private. (1962)

chief (1895) Nautical; applied to the chief engineer, or lieutenant-commander, in a (war)ship ■ Gilbert Hackforth-Jones: 'Chief,' he called down the voice-pipe to the engine-room, 'Knock her up to full speed or I'll come down and stoke myself.' (1942)

loot (1898) US, military slang; applied to a lieutenant; shortened from North American pronunciation of *lieut(enant* ■ J. G. Cozzens: Don't thank the loot! (1948)

top (1898) US, military slang; short for *top sergeant* ■ T. Fredenburgh: The Top says he'll pass the word along. (1930)

top sergeant, top cutter, top kick, top kicker, top soldier (1898) US, military slang; applied to a first sergeant

snotty (1903) British, nautical; applied to a midshipman; said to be from midshipmen's use of the buttons on their sleeve for wiping their nose, from *snotty* running with nasal mucus ■ Peter Dickinson: A British Naval Party under the command of a snappily saluting little snotty. (1974)

corp (1909) Short for *corporal*; often as a term of address ■ F. D. Sharpe: 'We are going to Hendon, aren't we, corp?' The corporal replied: 'Yes.' (1938)

lance-jack (1912) British; applied to a lance-corporal or lance-bombardier; from *lance-(corporal* + obsolete *jack* chap, fellow or the male personal name *Jack* ■ Len Deighton: You're not looking too good, Colonel, if you don't mind an ex-lance-jack saying so. (1971)

Jimmy the One, **Jimmy (1916)** Nautical; applied to a first lieutenant ■ *Guardian*: Smith told Petty Officer David Lewis, 'We are going to have a sit-in and give the "Jimmy" a hard time.' (1970)

looey, looie, louie (1916) North American; applied to a lieutenant; shortened from North American pronunciation of *lieu(tenant* + *-y* ■ *Weekend Magazine* (Montreal): One scrap of the rarely-talked-about reality: after being a private 14 months, Angus was commissioned in the field as second looey. (1974)

striper (1917) Applied to an officer in the Royal Navy or the US Navy of a rank designated by the stated number of stripes on the uniform, and in the army to a lance-corporal (*one-striper*), corporal (*two-striper*) or sergeant (*three-striper*) ■ Gilbert Hackforth-Jones: It made me remember how I felt when some pompous four-striper came slumming or snooping on board my submarine. (1950) ■ Anthony Price: A two-striper like himself. (1978)

chicken colonel (1918) US; applied to a US officer of the rank of full colonel; from a colonel's insignia of a silver eagle ■ Ernest Hemingway: Maybe they treat me well because I'm a chicken colonel on the winning side. (1950)

topper (1918) US, military slang; applied to a first sergeant; from *top* first sergeant + *-er* ■ *Our Army* (US): 'I'm sure there's no Lieutenant McGonigle here,' replies the Topper. (1937)

quarter-bloke (1919) Services' slang, dated; applied to a quartermaster(-sergeant) ■ *Gen*: Nickly overstepped the mark when he suggested to the quarter-bloke . . . that he was flogging the rations. (1944)

killick (1920) British, nautical; applied to a leading seaman; from earlier sense, leading seaman's badge ■ Tackline: Been in barracks for a matter of six months. Killick then, o' course. (1945)

erk, irk (1925) British; applied (*dated*) to a naval rating and also (1928, *R.A.F. slang*) to someone of lowest rank, an aircraftman; origin unknown ■ Brennan, Hesselyn & Bateson: The erks came running up to tell us that . . . the 109 had been diving down. (1943)

buck sergeant (1934) US; applied to an ordinary sergeant of the lowest grade; based on *buck private* ■ H. Roth: He had acquired the rank of buck sergeant. (1955)

one-pipper (1937) British, services' slang; applied to a second lieutenant; based on earlier obsolete *one-pip* (1919), from the single star on a second lieutenant's uniform ■ G. M. Fraser: Keith was a mere pink-cheeked one-pipper of twenty years, whereas

I had reached the grizzled maturity of twenty-one and my second star. (1974)

P.F.C., pfc (1941) US, services' slang; abbreviation of *Private 1st Class* ■ Ed McBain: 'A man named James Harris, served with the Army.' . . . 'Rank?' 'Pfc.' (1977)

plonk (1941) R.A.F. slang, dated; applied to an aircraftman second class; origin unknown ■ J. R. Cole: I was only an A.C. plonk at the time. (1949)

snake (1941) Australian, military slang; applied to a sergeant ■ E. Lambert: Baxter reckoned the officers and snakes are pinching our beer. (1951)

wingco, winco, winko (1941) R.A.F. slang; abbreviation of *wing commander* ■ F. Parrish: There was a pub . . . taken over by a retired Wing Commander. . . . The Winco, as he liked to be called, was a ready market. (1982)

chiefy (1942) R.A.F. slang; applied to a flight sergeant; from *chief* + *-y* ■ I. Gleed: To this day I can see distinctly 'Chiefy' N., stripped naked, putting on . . . a spotless clean tunic. (1942)

groupie (1943) R.A.F. slang; applied to a group captain; from *group* + *-ie* ■ I. Lambot: Groupie's a devil for the girls. (1968)

buck general (1944) US; applied to a brigadier general; based on *buck private*, from its being the lowest grade of general

spec (1958) US; abbreviation of *specialist* enlisted man in the army employed on specialized duties ■ Ed McBain: These are designations of rank. An E-3 is a Pfc., a Spec 4 is Specialist 4th Class, a corporal. An E-5 is a three-striper, and so on. (1977)

butterbar (1973) US; applied to a second lieutenant; from *butterbars* two gold bars worn as a badge of rank by a second lieutenant, from their yellow colour (not recorded before 1983 but apparently extant in the mid 1960s)

A badge or other insignia of rank

hash-mark (1909) US; applied to a military service stripe; apparently from the notion that each stripe (representing a year's service) signifies a year's free 'hash' or food provided by the government

killick (1915) British, nautical; applied to a leading seaman's badge; from earlier sense, small anchor, from the fact that the badge of a leading seaman in the Royal Navy bears the symbol of an anchor; ultimate origin unknown

pip (1917) Applied to a star worn on an officer's epaulette ■ Peter Driscoll: The authority of the two pips shining on his shoulders. (1972)

scrambled egg (1943) Mainly services' slang; applied to the gold braid or insignia on an officer's dress uniform ■ Monica Dickens: I don't care about the scrambled egg, but it may be a bit tough at first, not being an officer. (1958)

tape (1943) British; applied to a chevron indicating rank ■ *R.A.F. Journal*: I wouldn't leave this unit for three tapes. (1944)

The upper classes

the upper crust (1843) ■ *New Statesman*: Views which are commonplace in upper-crust circles. (1957)

A member of the upper classes

royal (1774) Applied to a member of the royal family; usually used in the plural ■ *Daily Mail*: A Buckingham Palace source said no one would be able to get near the Royals. (1991)

nob (1809) British, often derogatory; applied to someone of wealth or high social position; variant of earlier Scottish *knabb, nab*; ultimate origin unknown ■ *Independent*: With Harvey Nichols sold this week for a cool £60m, there is a rustle of interest in the dwindling group of independent retailers to the nobs. (1991)

toff (1851) British; applied to an upper-class, distinguished, or well-dressed person; perhaps an alteration of *tuft* titled undergraduate at Oxford and Cambridge, from the gold tassel formerly worn on the cap ■ William Golding: The mantelpiece or overmantel as the toffs say. (1984) Hence **toff up** dress up like a toff (1914) ■ *East End Star*: Notice the perfect stillness when the 'lovely lidy all toffed up' sings. (1928)

Hooray Henry, Hooray (1936) British, derogatory; applied originally to a loud, rich, rather ineffectual or foolish young society man, and hence more specifically to a fashionable, extroverted, but conventional upper-class young man; from the interjection *hooray* + the male personal name *Henry* ■ Barr & York: Hooray Henrys are the tip of the Sloane iceberg, visible and audible for miles. (1982) ■ *Expression!*: A blanket or rug is also a good idea (tartans for hoorays; kilims for aesthetes). (1986)

upper (1955) From the adjective *upper* ■ *Economist*: The genuine uppers' genuine feeling of superiority. (1968)

Sloane Ranger, Sloane (1975) British; applied to a fashionable and conventional upper-middle-class young person (usually female), especially living in London; blend of *Sloane* Square, London, and Lone *Ranger*, a hero of western stories and films ■ Peter York: Once a Sloane marries and moves to Kennington and starts learning sociology through the Open University, she is off the rails. (1975) ■ S. Allan: She wore a cashmere sweater . . . a Sloane ranger type. (1980) Hence **Sloaney** (1983) ■ *Mail on Sunday*: Berkoff is an East Ender and doesn't normally like Sloaney girls. (1991)

Sloanie (1982) British; from *Sloan* (*Ranger* + *-ie* ■ Barr & York: 'A Sloanie has a pony' is . . . ingrained in the Sloanie mind. (1982)

Of or characteristic of the upper classes; socially superior

posh (1918) Perhaps related to the older noun *posh* money, dandy: apparently nothing to do with 'port out, starboard home', of cabins on the sea-passage between Britain and India ■ P. G. Wodehouse: Practically every posh family in the country has called him in at one time or another. (1923) Hence **posh up** smarten up, make posh (1919)

A snob

pure merino (1826) Australian; applied originally to an Australian whose descent from a free settler (as opposed to a convict) gave him or her a basis for social pretension; from *merino* type of fine-woolled sheep introduced into Australia in the early years of settlement ■ Caddie: She used to boast that her ancestors had come out as free settlers . . . and that she was entitled to mix with the Pure Merinos. (1953)

high-hat (1923) Orig US; from earlier sense, top hat, from the notion that such hats are worn by snobbish or pretentious people ■ G. B. Stern: That hot-tempered young high-hat. (1931)

toffee-nose (1943) British; back-formation from *toffee-nosed* ■ *Woman*: People thought I was a bit of a toffee-nose for the first few months because I didn't speak to them. (1958)

Snobbish, pretentious

hoity-toity (1820) From earlier sense, frolicsome, flighty ■ *Sunday Times*: On Anne Diamond: 'She wasn't the least bit hoity-toity. She was always having me back to her place for a bit of cheese on toast.' (1993)

stuck-up (1829) ■ *Daily Mirror*: The exchanges between the yobbish millionaire he plays and his stuck-up, witless wife . . . in this desperate sitcom are too weedy even for the hard-of-laughing. (1992)

la-di-da (1895) From earlier obsolete noun use, snobbish or pretentious person; imitative of a supposed typical utterance of such people ■ *Guardian*: He was . . . the American air-force sergeant with whom a duke's daughter, Anna Neagle, falls in love, his pleasant American baritone providing welcome relief from the lah-di-dah accents. (1991)

snooty (1919) From *snoot* snout, nose + *-y*; from the notion of having one's nose haughtily in the air ■ Robert Barard: You know how the English can say 'Really?'—all cold and snooty. (1980)

county (1921) British; from the notion of being typical of the country gentry (of a county) ■ Christopher Isherwood: Mummy's bringing her up to be very county. (1937)

toffee-nosed (1925) Mainly British ■ T. E. Lawrence: A premature 'life' will do more to disgust the select and superior people (the R.A.F. call them the 'toffee-nosed') than anything. (1928)

A self-important person

I am (1926) From earlier sense, Lord Jehovah, from Exodus iii.14 'And God said unto Moses, I am that I am: And he said, Thus shalt thou say unto the children of Israel, I AM hath sent me unto you' ■ Nubar Gulbenkian: Cyril Radcliffe . . . did not take the short-cut favoured by so many of his colleagues who say. . . : 'I am the great I am, Queen's Counsel.' (1965)

Self-important

uppity (1880) Orig US; from *up* + *-it-* + *-y* ■ *Sun* (Baltimore): [She] could have plenty o' friends. The trouble with her is she thinks folks too common to bother with unless they're too uppity to bother with her. (1932)

A lower-class person

pleb (1865) Short for *plebian* ■ *New Scientist*: A German visitor lost his [nerve] in the silence of a British Rail first-class compartment and uncoupled the coach as a gesture of solidarity with the plebs in the second class. (1983)

prole (1887) Short for *proletarian* ■ George Orwell: There's a lot of rot talked about the sufferings of the working class. I'm not so sorry for the proles myself. (1939)

Of or characteristic of the lower classes; ill-bred

hairy at (about, in, round) the heel(s), hairy-heeled, hairy (1890) ■ Ngaio Marsh: I

always say that when people start fussing about family and all that, it's because they're a bit hairy round the heels themselves. (1962)

plebby, plebbie (1962) From *pleb* lower-class person + -*y* ■ James McClure: Portland Bill . . . all coach parties and orange peel. . . . It does tend to be a bit plebbie. (1977)

To descend to the level of the lower classes

slum, slum it (1928) From earlier sense, visit slums (for charitable purposes, or out of curiosity) ■ *Birds*: It [*sc.* a brambling] was quite unabashed by the proximity of the feeding area to the back door and was happily 'slumming it' with the resident sparrows, chaffinches and greenfinches. (1981)

8. Social Categories

Lifestyle

empty nester (1962) Mainly US; applied to either member of a couple whose children have grown up and left home ■ *Sunday Times*: Builders . . . have ignored an increasingly important category of housebuyer—the busy, well-off executive couple who either have no children or whose children have grown up and left. Americans call them 'empty nesters'. (1980)

buppie (1984) Orig US; applied to a black city-dwelling professional person who is (or attempts to be) upwardly mobile; acronym formed on *b*lack *u*rban (or *u*pwardly mobile) *p*rofessional, after *yuppie* ■ *Independent*: Derek Boland—the . . . rap singer Derek B—was present as a representative of 'buppies' (black yuppies). (1988)

guppie (1984) Applied to a homosexual yuppie; blend of *gay* and *yuppie* ■ *New York Newsday*: On Wednesdays at midnight, Razor Sharp appears with her Go-Go Boys at this upper West Side Guppie hangout. (1989)

yump, yumpie (1984) Orig US, dated; applied to a member of a socio-economic group comprising young professional people working in cities; acronym formed from *y*oung *u*pwardly *m*obile *p*eople + -*ie*

yup (1984) Orig and mainly US; abbreviation of *yuppie* ■ *Chicago Tribune*: One group of yups asked the conference information desk: 'Where's the spouses' volleyball game?' (1990)

yuppie, yuppy (1984) Orig US; applied to a member of a socio-economic group comprising young professional people working in cities; originally an acronym formed from *y*oung *u*rban *p*rofessional; subsequently also often interpreted as *y*oung *u*pwardly mobile professional (or person, people) ■ *Guardian*: The yuppies themselves, in the 25–34 age group, supported Senator Gary Hart in the primaries. (1984)

guppie (1985) Applied to a yuppie concerned about the environment and ecological issues; blend of *green* and *yuppie* ■ *Daily Telegraph*: The magazine claims that . . . her fellow thinkers, whom it derides

as green yuppies or 'guppies', have 'delivered the green movement into the lap of the industrialist'. (1989)

dinky, dinkie (1986) Orig North American; applied to either partner of a usually professional working couple who have no children, characterized as affluent consumers with few domestic demands on their time and money; acronym formed on *d*ouble (or *d*ual) *i*ncome, *n*o *k*ids; the final *y* is sometimes interpreted as *y*et

woopie, woopy (1986) Orig North American; applied to an elderly person able to enjoy an affluent and active lifestyle in retirement; acronym formed on *w*ell-*o*ff *o*ld(er) *p*erson + -*ie*, after *yuppie*, probably reinforced by the exclamation *whoopee!* ■ *Daily Telegraph*: We are in the age of the 'woopy' . . . and it is about time we all recognised that fact, planned for our own future and helped them to enjoy theirs. (1988)

dink (1987) Orig North American; applied to either partner of a usually professional working couple who have no children, characterized as affluent consumers with few domestic demands on their time and money; acronym formed on *d*ouble (or *d*ual) *i*ncome, *n*o *k*ids ■ *Chicago Tribune*: The DINKS . . . and empty-nesters now have a greater potential to travel off-season. (1990)

oink (1987) Jocular; applied to either partner of a couple with no children, living on a single (usually large) salary; acronym formed on *o*ne *i*ncome, *n*o *k*ids, after *dink* ■ *Newsweek*: In the 1980s cable has penetrated urban areas with more upscale viewers like DINKS . . . OINKS . . . and the standard-issue Yuppies. (1987)

chuppie, chuppy (1988) Orig and mainly North American; applied to a Chinese yuppie; blend of *Chinese* and *yuppie* ■ *Guardian*: A backlash has built up in Vancouver . . . against the 'Chuppies' (Chinese urban professionals) in the long established community. (1989)

To change in lifestyle

yuppify (1984) Orig US, often derogatory; denoting changing an area, building, clothing, etc. so as to be characteristic of or suitable to yuppies; from *yuppie* + *-fy* ■ *Observer*: Their 'bashers' (shacks) will be forcibly removed by police to make way for developers who want to 'yuppify' the Charing Cross area. (1987)

Youth groups

bodgie (1950) Australian & New Zealand; applied to the Australasian equivalent of the Teddy-boy; perhaps from *bodger* inferior, worthless + *-ie* ■ *New Zealand Listener*: Every psychologist who has talked with bodgies will know that fear of an uncertain future is one of the factors in youthful misconduct. (1958)

widgie, weegie (1950) Australian & New Zealand; applied to an Australasian Teddy-girl, the female equivalent to a *bodgie*; origin unknown ■ *Times*: Gang delinquency . . . has made its mark around the world . . . in Australia the bodgies and widgies. (1977)

9. Conventionality

Conventional, conservative, respectable

starchy (1823) Orig US; applied to someone very formal, stiff, or conventional; from earlier sense, of or like starch (from its stiffening effect) ■ W. C. Hazlitt: My father . . . got into trouble by asking some rather starchy people to meet him at dinner. (1897)

corn-fed (1929) Orig US, jazz slang; applied to something banal or provincial; punningly from earlier sense, fed on corn (i.e. maize) and *corn* something hackneyed or banal ■ *Architectural Review*: Either way this is a rather negative formulation; part of the literary impedimenta of the modern movement, useful to the critic defending the Bauhaus to a cornfed audience of Ruskinians. (1954)

stick-in-the-muddish (1936) From *stick-in-the-mud* unadventurous person + *-ish* ■ A. Salkey: He's slow and easy and a little 'stick-in-the-muddish'. (1959)

square (1946) Orig US, jazz slang ■ Frederick Raphael: You know books. Those things with pages very square people still occasionally read. (1965)

straight (1960) Orig US; from earlier more specific senses, such as law-abiding and heterosexual ■ John Crosby: Few of the revolutionary youth . . . threw it all up and came back to the straight world. (1976)

way-in (1960) Based on *way-out* unconventional, eccentric ■ *New York Times Magazine*: A famous lady columnist with a way-out taste in millinery but a way-in taste in film fare. (1960)

A conventional person

stick-in-the-mud (1733) Applied to someone unprogressive, unadventurous, or lacking initiative ■ David Gervais: But if Betjeman was a 'stick-in-the-mud', like Larkin, he was an unusually exuberant one. (1993)

ted, Ted (1956) British; short for *Teddy-boy* ■ *New Scientist*: The gangs [of baboons] appeared to carry out his orders, roaming through the troupe like a bunch of leather-jacketed teds. (1968)

duck-tail (1959) South African; applied to the South African equivalent of the Teddy-boy; from earlier sense, type of hair-style favoured by Teddy-boys ■ *Guardian*: He [*sc.* Dr. Verwoerd] described South Africa's overseas critics as 'the ducktails (Teddy boys) of the political world'. (1960)

sharpie (1965) Australian; applied to a young person who adopts styles of hair, dress, etc. similar to those of the British skinhead ■ *Sunday Mail* (Brisbane): Carmel says her mother accepted her being a sharpie—even a punk—till she shaved her hair off. (1977)

skin (1970) British; short for *skinhead* ■ *Times*: 'There's good and bad skinheads,' is as far as he will go. . . . The picture is complicated: there are black skins, and there are non-violent skins. . . . Certainly, many of the skins are thugs. (1981)

mossback, mossy-back (1878) Mainly North American; from earlier sense, large old fish ■ Trevanian: The moss-backs of the National Gallery had pulled off quite a coup in securing the Marini Horse for a one-day exhibition. (1973)

square John (1934) North American ■ Kenneth Orvis: I played it even safer with those uptown Square Johns. (1962)

shellback (1943) Applied to someone with reactionary views; from earlier sense, hardened or experienced sailor ■ *Listener*: I have no doubt a lot of right-wing shell-backs are now conceding, with blimpish magnanimity, that there's really something to be said for these young fellows after all. (1963)

square (1944) Orig US, jazz slang ■ Harold Hobson: The odd fifty million citizens who don't dig them are dead-beats—squares. (1959)

cube (1957) Orig US; applied to an extremely conventional or conservative person; from the notion of being even more conventional than a 'square' ■ G. Bagby: When I sang it to him . . . he told me I was a complete fool. Daisy Bell was for the cubes. (1968)

A conventional place or institution

squaresville, squareville (1956) Orig US; also used adjectivally to denote conventionality; from *square* + the suffix *-ville* denoting a place with the stated characteristics ■ Ed McBain: This guy is from Squaresville, fellas, I'm telling you. He wouldn't know a '45 from a cement mixer. (1956) ■ *Listener*: And they went away, more than ever convinced that the war between the generations was for real. And through the window there floated a querulous, puzzled voice. 'A queer fish, real squaresville.' (1968)

auntie (1958) Used sarcastically as or before the name of an institution considered to be conservative in style or approach, specifically (*British*) the BBC or (*Australian*) the Australian Broadcasting Corporation; from the notion of an aunt as a comfortable and conventional figure ■ **J. Canaan:** I saw about Uncle Edmund in auntie *Times*. (1958) ■ *Listener*: The BBC needs to be braver and sometimes is. So let there be a faint hurrah as Auntie goes over the top. (1962)

cubesville (1959) Orig US; also used adjectively to denote conventionality; from *cube* very conventional person + the suffix *-ville* denoting a place with the stated characteristics ■ *Woman*: No need to feel cubesville (that's worse than being a square) if

10. **Friends**

A friend

mate (*c*1380) From Middle Low German *mate*, *gemate*, ultimately from a base related to *meat* (the etymological sense being 'one who shares meat (i.e. food)') ■ *Observer*: A 17-year-old boy . . . said, 'I haven't got a real mate. That's what I need.' (1966)

pal (1681) From Romany *pal* friend, brother, ultimately from Sanskrit *bhrātṛ* brother ■ **Mazo de la Roche:** I have talked to her . . . as I couldn't to anyone else. . . . Well, she's been a complete pal—if you know what I mean. (1936)

chum (1684) Originally applied to a roommate, and not recorded in the independent sense 'friend' until the mid 19th century; probably an alteration of an unrecorded *cham*, short for *chamber fellow* roommate ■ *Daily Mail*: James will see that he has a father who doesn't look like the fathers of his school chums. (1991)

buddy (1788) Orig US, Black English; alteration of *brother* ■ **Nancy Mitford:** Little Bobby Bobbin . . . is a great buddy of mine. (1932)

matey (1833) Often used as a form of address; from *mate* friend + *-y* ■ **June Drummond:** Right, matey, 'oo told you? (1973)

cobber (1893) Australian & New Zealand; perhaps from British dialect *cob* take a liking to ■ **Maurice Shadbolt:** Jack was my cobber in the timber mill. Jack and I went on the bash every Saturday. (1959)

the lads (1896) British; applied to a group of male friends ■ *Independent*: 'I wasn't one of the lads,' he said. 'I didn't mix with the sporting types and . . . I'm still not very interested in sport.' (1991)

baby (1901) Orig US; applied to a person's sweetheart; often used as a term of address ■ **Carl Sandburg:** My baby's going to have a new dress. (1918)

side-kicker (1903) US, dated; applied especially to a subordinate companion

sidekick (1906) Orig US; applied especially to a subordinate companion; back-formation from *side-kicker* ■ **J. McVean:** It was the White House. . . . And not just some little cotton-tail sidekick either, but counsel to the President. (1981)

you don't follow Kookie patter; even many Americans reckon it odd! (1961)

Unconventional, avant-garde

way out (1959) ■ **J. Dunbar:** One thing I like about Cambridge, people don't try to be too way out. At places like Oxford, or Reading, I've seen blokes going around barefoot and wearing ear-rings. (1964)

far out (1960) ■ *Science Journal*: Talking with computers, so much a far-out idea when this journal discussed IBM's work on it four years ago, now seems quite straightforward. (1970)

raggie (1912) Naval slang; applied especially to a close friend or colleague on board ship ■ *Taffrail*: Men who are friendly with each other are 'raggies', because they have the free run of each others' polishing paste and rags; but if their friendship terminates they are said to have 'parted brass-rags'. (1916)

china (1925) British; short for *china plate*, rhyming slang for *mate* ■ *New Statesman*: I have my hands full with his china who is a big geezer of about 14 stone. (1965)

palsy, palsie (1930) Orig US; from *pal* friend + *-sy* ■ **E. Wilson:** Ratoff appealed to him. 'Look, palsy,' he said, 'whawt time I wawz in your house this morning?' (1945)

OAO (1936) Services' slang, orig US; applied to someone's sweetheart; abbreviation of *one and only* ■ *Everybody's Magazine* (Australia): All would refer to a special girlfriend as their OAO—one and only. Probably, the OAO was met on skirt patrol. (1967)

palsy-walsy, palsie-walsie, palsey-walsey (1937) Orig US; often derogatory, connoting excessive or conspiratorial friendship; fanciful rhyming form based on *palsy* friend ■ **H. Smith:** There was nothing to do but I must go along with them. I even went into SRO with them. Talk about palsy-walsies! (1941)

oppo (1939) Orig services' slang; abbreviation of *opposite number* ■ **B. W. Aldiss:** He's dotty on them Wog gods, aren't you, Stubby, me old oppo? (1971)

winger (1943) British, mainly services' slang ■ *Penguin New Writing*: He had seen his 'winger', his best friend, decapitated. (1943)

buddy-buddy (1947) Orig US; reduplication of *buddy* friend ■ **Len Deighton:** This way they stopper up the information without offence to old buddy buddies. (1962)

mucker (1947) British; probably from *muck in* share tasks, etc. equally ■ **Martin Woodhouse:** 'Is that my old mucker?' said Bottle. 'None other,' I said. (1972)

goombah, goomba, gumbah (1955) US; applied to a close or trusted male friend or crony; from an Italian dialectal pronunciation of Italian *compare* godfather, male friend; popularized by the US boxer and actor Rocky Graziano on the *Martha Ray Show* ■ **L. D. Estleman:** 'I guess you two were pretty close.' 'He was my goombah. I was a long time getting over it.' (1984)

good buddy (1956) US, mainly Southern; often as a term of address

homeboy, homegirl (1967) Orig and mainly US, orig Black English; from earlier sense, person from one's home town

main man (1967) US; applied to a person's best male friend

main squeeze (1970) US; applied to a man's principal woman friend; compare earlier sense, important person

squeeze (1980) Mainly US; applied especially to a girlfriend or lover; shortened from *main squeeze* ■ R. Ford: I would love to grill him about his little seminary squeeze, but he would be indignant. (1986)

Having a friendly relationship; friendly

in with (a1677) Often in the phrases *get in with, keep in with, well in with* ■ Richmal Crompton: So far County had persistently resisted the attempts of Mrs. Bott to 'get in' with it. (1925) ■ P. M. Hubbard: We . . . go along to the Carrack for a drink . . . occasionally, but we're not really in with the people staying there. (1964) ■ Joan Fleming: She was well in with what is now called the Chelsea set. (1968)

thick (c1756) ■ Robert Louis Stevenson: He and the squire were very thick and friendly. (1883)

chummy (1884) From *chum* friend + -*y* ■ Economist: Many fear that accountants are too chummy with the managers of the companies they audit. (1987)

pally (1895) From *pal* friend + -*y* ■ Scottish Review: She joined a Whist club and got very pally with another auld maid like herself. (1976)

matey (1915) From *mate* friend + -*y* ■ Warwick Deeping: Elizabeth would . . . want to be matey with people. (1929)

buddy-buddy (1944) US; reduplication of *buddy* friend ■ Kenneth Orvis: Those two got real buddy-buddy. (1962)

palsy-walsy, palsie-walsie, palsey-walsey (1947) Orig US; often derogatory, connoting excessive or conspiratorial friendship; from the noun *palsy-walsy* friend ■ John Wainwright: He's one of those matey types. . . . Very palsy-walsy. (1977)

palsy (1962) Orig US; from *pal* friend + -*y* ■ Daily Telegraph: The New York police and I are not too palsy right now. (1969)

11. **Solitude**

On one's own

like a shag on a rock (1845) Australian; denoting the isolation or unhappiness associated with solitude; from *shag* type of cormorant ■ K. Smith: It was the voice of Godley, in high gear, raised to compete with the noise around him, but suddenly left by itself like a shag on a rock, when everyone else quietened down in response to the gong. (1965)

on one's Pat Malone, on one's pat (1908) Mainly Australian; *Pat Malone* rhyming slang for

To take a liking to someone

hit it off (1780) Compare earlier *hit it* in the same sense ■ T. S. Eliot: Mr. Kaghan is prejudiced. He's never hit it off with Lady Elizabeth. (1954)

take a shine to (1839) Orig US ■ Times Literary Supplement: If her [sc. Barbara Pym's] heroines were married, they were not unfaithful to their husbands, although they might take a shine to the curate. (1980)

cotton to (1840) ■ Rachael Praed: I object to you personally. I have never cottoned to you from the moment I set eyes upon you. (1881)

To form a friendship

take up (a1619) Usually followed by *with* ■ Daily Express: The story is of a poor but pretty girl . . . who breaks her engagement to a morose butcher . . . and takes up instead with a feckless punter. (1977)

pal (1879) Now usually followed by *up*; from *pal* friend ■ Bruce Hamilton: I got tight one night with a chap I'd palled up with. (1958)

chum (1884) Now usually followed by *up*; from *chum* friend ■ A. L. Rowse: Hicks and Callice chummed up. (1955)

click (1915) ■ Constant Lambert: Receiving the glad eye from presumably attractive girls with whom he ultimately and triumphantly 'clicks'. (1934)

cobber up (1918) Australian & New Zealand; from *cobber* friend ■ Bill Pearson: It's natural for a young chap to cobber up with chaps his own age. (1963)

buddy (1919) US; usually followed by *up*; from *buddy* friend ■ Nelson Algren: My cot was next to his, and we started buddying up. (1948)

To associate with someone as a friend

pal around (1915) From *pal* friend ■ High Times: Lenny picked up part of his *schtick* from the characters that he palled around with in New York. (1975)

An introduction to a person

knock-down (1865) US, Australian, & New Zealand ■ Sun-Herald (Sydney): That's a grouse-looking little sheila over there, Sal. Any chance of a knockdown to her later on? (1981)

own ■ Ngaio Marsh: We're dopey if we let that bloke go off on his pat. (1943)

on one's Jack Jones, on one's jack (1925) *Jack Jones* partial rhyming slang for *own* ■ Alfred Draper: You're on your Jack Jones. Ben's deserted you. (1972)

single-o (1930) US, mainly criminals' slang; often applied specifically to working without an accomplice ■ Evening Bulletin (Philadelphia): Instead of working single-o as was his custom. Ernie used an accomplice to drive the getaway car. (1948)

on one's tod (1934) British; *tod* from *Tod Sloan*, name of a US jockey (1874–1933), used as rhyming slang for *own* ■ G. Gaunt: Maybe they don't want your company. . . . Never seen you on your tod before. (1981)

on one's ownsome (1939) *ownsome* blend of *own* and *lonesome* ■ Gerald Seymour: He's been left on his ownsome, and doesn't like it. (1976)

Someone on their own

wallflower (1820) Applied to especially a woman sitting out at a dance for lack of partners; from such women sitting along the wall of the room in which dancing is taking place ■ *TV Times*: I used to go to dances when I was young but I was always the wall-flower, always the shy one. (1990)

loner (1947) Applied to someone who avoids company and prefers to be alone; from *lone* + -*er* ■ *Daily Telegraph*: On course, as in private life, he is a loner, a man of few words who finds it impossible to chat and joke with the crowds. (1970)

To act alone

paddle one's own canoe (1828) Applied to acting independently or making one's way by one's own unaided efforts ■ *Time*: They seem more interested in paddling their own canoes than shaping a strong third force that would be the best weapon against the communism they all hate. (1949)

12. **Sex**

Sexual desire

lech, letch (1796) Back-formation from *lecher* ■ *Sunday Times*: Many so-called platonic friendships . . . are merely one-way leches. (1972)

the glad eye (1911) Applied to a glance suggestive of sexual desire ■ Aldous Huxley: I *do* see her giving the glad eye to Pete. (1939). Hence the verb **glad-eye** (1935) ■ A. J. Cronin: Purves . . . 'glad-eyeing' Hetty, trying 'to get off with her'. (1935)

hot pants (1927) US; applied to strong sexual desire; usually in the phrase *have* (or *get*) *hot pants* ■ Stanley Price: You've got the hot-pants for some good-looking piece. (1961)

bedroom eyes (1947) Applied to eyes or a look suggestive of sexual desire ■ Jeremy Potter: George's wife had blue bedroom eyes. (1967)

the hots (1947) Orig US; applied to strong sexual desire; from *hot* lustful ■ *Times Literary Supplement*: It is Blodgett who has the hots for Smackenfelt's mother-in-law. (1973)

Feeling sexual desire, lustful

hot (1500) ■ William Hanley: 'I'm hot as a firecracker is what I am,' she said demurely. (1971)

randy (1847) Orig dialectal; from earlier sense, boisterous ■ Frank Sargeson: I was randy myself at your

do one's (own) thing (1841) Orig US; applied to following one's own interests or inclinations independently of others ■ Robert Barnard: A ghastly warning against . . . aiming at total self-fulfilment, doing your own thing regardless. (1981)

stag (1900) US; applied to attending a social occasion unaccompanied ■ *Lebende Sprachen*: He had planned to stag at the class dance. (1973)

Acting independently

off one's own bat (1845) From the notion of a batsman's own personal score, independent of teammates' runs and extras ■ Arthur Koestler: It seemed impossible that the editorialist of the paper had dared to write this off his own bat. (1941)

under one's own steam (1912) ■ Julian Symons: 'Would you be kind enough to . . . see Miss Cleverly home.' 'That's not necessary. . . . I can move under my own steam.' (1949)

minding one's own business (1932) Implying that one is acting on one's own and not disturbing anyone else; from *mind one's own business* attend to one's own affairs and not be intrusive ■ *Washington Post*: You're sitting in the little brick bandbox of a minor-league ballpark, minding your own business, trying to keep track of all the strikeouts and wild throws, when suddenly they're booming your name over the PA system. (1993)

age. But be careful. These native girls can put you right into hospital if you don't take care. (1965)

red-hot (1887)

horny (1889) From *horn* erect penis + -*y* ■ *Black World*: Ain't that the horny bitch that was grindin with the blind dude. (1971)

horn-mad (1893) From *horn* erect penis ■ Roy Campbell: The evil-minded and horn-mad levantine. (1951)

sexed up (1942) Applied to someone who is sexually aroused ■ *Nature*: Erickson and Zenone tested the reaction of 35 males to two groups of females. . . The males . . . showed more aggression and less courtship towards the 'sexed up' females. (1976)

randy-arsed (1968) ■ H. C. Rae: Beefy, randy-arsed wives crying out for a length. (1968)

To experience sexual desire

lech, letch (1911) Back-formation from *lecher* ■ *Guardian*: A fortyish factory worker . . . lives with . . . an obsessively nubile sister whom he obviously leches after. (1973)

To ogle

perv, perve (1941) Mainly Australian; followed by *at* or *on*; from earlier sense, behave as a pervert; ultimately short for *pervert* ■ Ian Hamilton: She's a cheap thrill machine for the boys to stare at and perve on. (1972)

Infatuated

sweet on (1740) Dated　■ John Saunders: I'm a little sweet on her maid, slap-up creature, I can tell you. (1876)

soft on (1840) ■ Theodore Dreiser: He's kinda soft on me, you know. (1925)

spoons with (or **about**, **on**) (*c*1859) Dated; from *spoon* behave amorously, woo ■ D. C. Murray: Tregarthen . . . has gone spoons on the Churchill. (1883)

cunt-struck (*c*1866) Denoting infatuation with women ■ Frank Sargeson: We were all helplessly and hopelessly c . . . struck, a vulgar but forcibly accurate expression. (1965)

shook on (1868) Australian & New Zealand ■ B. Scott: Those stories you read about in books where two blokes get shook on the same sheila. (1977)

gone on (1885) ■ Saul Bellow: I was gone on her and . . . gave her a real embrace. (1978)

stuck on (1886) Orig US ■ Alison Lurie: Sandy, who was rather pathetically stuck on her for a while, took her to hear *The Magic Flute*. (1974)

To be infatuated (with)

have a case on (1852) Dated, orig & mainly US ■ *Story-Teller*: By the end of the second year the girls were saying that Salesby had quite a case on Chips. (1931)

have got it bad(ly) (1911) ■ Webster & Ellington (*song-title*): I got it bad and that ain't good. (1941)

fall for (1914) ■ John Galsworthy: 'He's fallen for Marjorie Ferrar.' ' "Fallen for her"?' said Soames. 'What an expression!' 'Yes, dear; it's American.' (1926)

An infatuation

puppy love (1834) Applied to temporary affection between very young people; compare earlier *calf love* in same sense (1823) ■ *Black Cat*: He adored her with all the fatuous idolatry of puppy love. (1907)

spoons (1846) Dated; from *spoon* behave amorously, woo ■ Archibald Gunter: The moment he saw Ethel it became a wonderful case of 'spoons' upon his part. (1888)

crush (1895) Orig US; from earlier sense, person with whom one is infatuated ■ Victor Gollancz: It is common to make fun of schoolboy and schoolgirl 'pashes' and 'crushes'. (1952)

pash (1914) Applied particularly to a schoolgirl's infatuation; short for *passion* ■ Graham Greene: When you've got a pash for someone like I have, anybody's better than nothing. (1934)

thing (1967) Often applied to a love affair of limited duration ■ Dorothy Halliday: Janey . . . had obviously just finished a thing with Guppy Collins-Smith and was looking for new material. (1970)

A glance indicative of infatuation

sheep's eyes (1811) Earlier *sheep's eye* (*a*1529)

goo-goo eyes (1897) *goo-goo* perhaps connected with *goggle* ■ James Thurber: There was so much spooning and goo-goo eyes. (1959)

To flirt, woo, court

run after (1526) Denoting seeking someone's company with a view to a sexual relationship ■ D. H. Lawrence: I don't do any high and pure mental work, nothing but jot down a few ideas. And yet I neither marry nor run after women. (1928)

pick up (1698) Applied to forming a casual friendship with a view to sexual intercourse ■ D. Marlowe: Who was that old man? . . . He was trying to pick you up. (1976). Hence **pick-up** someone picked up for this purpose (1871) ■ Marguerite Yourcenar: She was fairly throbbing against me, and no previous feminine encounter, whether with a chance pick-up, or with an avowed prostitute, had prepared me for that sudden, terrifying sweetness. (1957)

spoon (1831) Dated; denoting (foolishly) amorous behaviour, or (in transitive use) sentimental wooing; probably from obsolete *spoon* simpleton, fool ■ Henry Williamson: It's like one of the Mecca coffee rooms in the City, where men go to spoon with the waitresses. (1957)

chat (1898) British; denoting flirtatious talking; often followed by *up* ■ *Sunday Express*: He saw a pretty girl . . . smiling at him. He smiled right back. 'I like chatting the birds,' he said. (1963) ■ Kingsley Amis: I must have spent a bit of time chatting them up. (1966)

track with (1910) Australian; applied to courting a potential sexual partner ■ D. Stuart: Maybe some married couple'll move in with a daughter for you to track with. (1978)

be all over someone **(1912)** Denoting a display of great or excessive affection ■ Agatha Christie: 'Were they friendly?' 'The lady was. . . . All over him, as you might say.' (1931)

get off with (1915) Denoting becoming acquainted with someone with a view to sexual intercourse ■ F. Lonsdale: What fun it would be if one of us could get off with him. (1925)

pirate (1927) Australian; applied to forming a casual friendship with a view to sexual intercourse ■ N. Keesing: Who but a woman would complain that a man is a 'linen lifter', or is 'trying to pirate me'. (1982)

make time (1934) North American; denoting making sexual advances; usually followed by *with* ■ William Burroughs: At another table two young men were trying to make time with some Mexican girls. (1953)

trot (1942) New Zealand; applied to courting a woman; from earlier British *trot out* escort, trot ■ *Weekly News* (Auckland): I didn't know she was going steady with you. . . . If I'd known you were trotting her [etc.]. (1964)

frat (1945) Applied (originally to Allied troops in West Germany and Austria after World War II) to a soldier establishing friendly and especially sexual relations with a woman of an occupied country; abbreviation of *fraternize* ■ M. K. Joseph:

'He was fratting, wasn't he?' 'Sure—dark piece, lives up the Ludwigstrasse.' (1957). Hence the nouns **fratter** (1949) and **fratting** (1945) ■ G. Cotterell: So he's married. . . . I bet she doesn't know what a shameless old fratter you were. (1949)

horse (1952) Denoting amorous play or philandering; usually followed by *around* ■ C. Smith: She'd be horsing around with Nicky, giving me grounds for divorce. (1956)

pull someone (1965), give someone **a pull (1976)** Applied to picking up a sexual partner ■ Boyd & Parkes: Five years ago you did the big male-menopause bit, didn't you? Skulking off to Paris to prove you could still pull the birds. (1973)

race off (1965) Australian; applied to seducing a woman ■ M. Wilding: Perhaps Peter thought he would try to race her . . . off. He relished the phrase, race off. He had not heard it in England. (1967)

groove (1967) Denoting amorous play ■ *New Yorker*: Sad Arthur put away his boots and helmet . . . to stay in Nutley and groove with the fair Lambie. (1970)

A person who flirts or courts

lady killer (1811) Applied to a man who is credited with a dangerous power of fascination over women ■ *Washington Post*: Rebecca DeMornay . . . plays a confident criminal attorney who wears tight skirts and is easily duped by a lady killer (Don Johnson). (1993)

spoon (1882) Dated; from *spoon* behave amorously, woo ■ D. H. Lawrence: Yes, his reputation as a spoon would not belie him. He had lovely lips for kissing. (*c*1921)

cock-teaser (1891) Derogatory; applied to a sexually provocative woman who evades or refuses intercourse ■ James Baldwin: What are you, anyway—just a cock-teaser? (1962)

debs' delight, debbies' delight (1934) British, mainly derogatory; applied to an elegant and attractive young man in high society ■ Ngaio Marsh: Lord Robert half suspected his nephew Donald of being a Debs' Delight. (1948)

prick-teaser (1961) Derogatory; applied to a sexually provocative woman who evades or refuses intercourse ■ Frank Norman: That Gloria's a right prick teaser. She'll con 'im somethin' rotten. (1978)

Courtship

monkey parade, monkey's parade, monkeys' parade (1910) British derogatory, dated; applied to a promenade of young men and women in search of sexual partners. Hence **monkey-parading** (1934) ■ J. B. Priestley: A Sabbatarian town of this kind, which could offer its young folk nothing on Sunday night but a choice between monkey-parading and dubious pubs. (1934)

blind date (1925) Orig US; applied to a date with an unknown person

pass (1928) Applied to an amorous advance; especially in the phrase *make a pass at* ■ Dorothy Parker: Men seldom make passes At girls who wear glasses. (1936)

skirt patrol (1941) Orig US; applied to a search for female sexual partners ■ *Everybody's Magazine* (Australia): In each war, a new vocabulary is created. Today, in Vietnam, Australians are again catching up on American Army slang. . . . All would refer to a special girlfriend as their OAO—one and only. Probably, the OAO was met on skirt patrol. (1967)

sexcapade (1965) Applied to a sexual excapade; blend of *sex* and *escapade* ■ *Honolulu Star-Bulletin*: A generally less swinging group than the lone men off on sexcapades who helped give tourism a bad name. (1976)

Looking for sexual partners

on the make (1929) Orig US ■ Anne Blaisdell: You mean he was still on the make? At his age? (1973)

on the pirate (1946) Australian; from the verb *pirate* pick up a sexual partner ■ G. Gelbin: They are on the pirate. We goes round St. Kilda and tries a few but we want three together. (1964)

on the pull (1990) From the verb *pull* pick up a sexual partner ■ *Guardian*: It's easier to pick up four grand simply by smiling when Chris asks if you and Trevor ever go out on the pull. (1996)

One who interferes with courtship

gooseberry (1837) Applied to a third person present when two lovers wish to be alone together; often in the phrase *play gooseberry*; compare obsolete *gooseberry picker* chaperon, perhaps from the notion of one who ostensibly picks gooseberries while acting as chaperon ■ Elizabeth Oldfield: She would be too busy to spend the day playing gooseberry to a pair of love-struck sixty-year-olds. (1983)

A promiscuous person

swinger (1964) Often applied specifically to someone who engages in group sex, partner-swapping, etc.; from *swing* + *-er* ■ *Time*: Some operators have converted nudist colonies into 'swinger camps', the new rural retreats for the randy. (1977)

goer (1966) From earlier sense, one who goes fast ■ Peter Willmott: 'She was a right banger,' said a 17 year old of one girl. 'A banger's a goer—a girl who'll do anything with anyone.' (1966)

swingle (1967) North American; applied to a promiscuous single person, especially one in search of a sexual partner; blend of *swinging* and *single* ■ *Chatelaine* (Canada): When she went out with her women friends for an evening, their husbands felt she was luring their wives into swingles bars and white slavery. (1978)

raver (1971) Applied to a promiscuous (young) man or especially woman

A promiscuous man

goat (1675) Applied to a lecherous (older) man; often in the phrase *old goat*; from the male goat's reputation for sexual insatiability ■ *Independent*: From naughty schoolboy to filthy old goat in the twinkling of an eye. (1991)

wolf (1847) Applied to a sexually aggressive man ■ Ellis Peters: He did not look like a wolf, but he did look like a young man with an eye for a girl. (1973)

Don Juan (1848) Applied to a man who has great sexual success with a large number of women; from the name of a legendary dissolute Spanish nobleman, popularized in Britain by Byron's poem *Don Juan* (1819–24) ■ W. H. Auden: B . . . tries to be a Don Juan seducer in an attempt to compel life to take an interest in him. (1963)

chaser (1894) US; applied to an amorous pursuer of women ■ Sam Greenlee: The women thought him an eligible bachelor, if a bit of a chaser. (1969)

poodle-faker (1902) Mainly services' slang; applied to a man who cultivates female society, especially for professional advancement; from the idea of fawning to be petted, like a poodle or lap-dog ■ Joyce Porter: There's some blooming Parisian couturier coming to see her. . . . To hear her talk you'd think a bunch of corn slicers and foreign poodle-fakers was more important than solving the crime of the century. (1977)

lounge lizard (1918) Derogatory; applied to a man who frequents fashionable parties, bars, etc. in search of a wealthy patroness ■ *Times*: The £50 a week contract which . . . lets her keep her lounge lizard husband, Queckett, in the manner to which he is accustomed, lacks conviction. (1973)

ram (1935) Applied to a virile or sexually aggressive man ■ *Penguin New Writing*: 'Yes, it's the Chalk all right,' Willie said. 'The old ram!' he added, happily. (1946)

skirt-chaser (1942) Applied to an amorous pursuer of women ■ L. Peters: He had always despised . . . the indiscriminate skirt-chaser. (1962). Hence **skirt-chasing** (1943) ■ Stephen Ransome: I always told you you'd regret your skirt-chasing. . . . A man should stick with his wife and family. (1950)

lech, letch (1943) Back-formation from *lecher* ■ *Guardian*: A rich man can have a beautiful young wife even if he is a gropy old letch! (1970)

lover boy, lover man (1952) Orig US; applied to a woman-chaser ■ Charles Williams: He's a Lover Boy, one of those big, flashy, conceited types that has to . . . give all the girls a break. (1959)

A promiscuous woman

The distinction between words applied to professional female prostitutes and those applied insultingly to women considered sexually promiscuous is not always clearly drawn, and many can cross and re-cross the border-line. See further under Prostitutes at **Prostitution** (pp. 84–5).

chippy, chippie (1886) Derogatory, orig US, dated ■ Grace Metalious: Running out every night to go see that little chippy. (1956)

tart (1887) Derogatory; from earlier neutral sense, (young) woman ■ E. J. Howard: People don't . . . call other people tarts because they go to bed with people without marrying them. (1965)

scrub (1900) Derogatory; compare earlier obsolete sense, insignificant or contemptible person ■ *New Statesman*: A 'scrub' is a Rocker girl; that is, someone not fond of washing, according to the Mods, and a bit of a tart. (1964)

floozie, floosie, floozy (1902) Derogatory; compare *flossy* fancy, showy, and dialect *floosy* fluffy ■ Len Deighton: Stinnes had reached that dangerous age when a man was only susceptible to an innocent cutie or to an experienced floozy. (1984)

man-eater (1906) Applied to a sexually voracious woman ■ D. Gray: 'She's pretty, you said?'. . . 'Very, sir.' 'And a man-eater?' 'I'd say so, yes, sir.' (1968)

vamp (*a*1911) Dated; applied to a woman who intentionally attracts and exploits men (often as a stock character in plays and films); abbreviation of *vampire* ■ *Times*: Exotic red flowers like the lips of vamps. (1973)

tramp (1922) Orig US, derogatory; from earlier sense, vagrant ■ John Welcome: You can usually tell . . . the nice girls from the tramps. (1959)

mamma, mama, momma (1925) Orig & mainly US; compare *red-hot momma* earthy female jazz singer ■ *Times*: She denied ever being present at an impromptu or organized gathering where there was a 'mama' present, someone available to the whole group for sexual intercourse. (1980)

alley cat (1926) US; applied to an immoral frequenter of city streets, especially a prostitute; from the reputation of stray cats for promiscuity

round heels (1926) Derogatory, mainly US; from the notion of being unsteady on the feet, and hence readily agreeing to lie down for sexual intercourse ■ Raymond Chandler: You'd think . . . I'd . . . pick me a change in types at least. But little roundheels over there ain't even that. (1944)

roach (1930) US, derogatory; compare earlier sense, cockroach ■ T. Morrison: They watched her far more closely than they watched any other roach or bitch in the town. (1974)

nympho (1935) Applied to a sexually voracious woman; short for *nymphomaniac* ■ D. Schwartz: Some girls at school said that Phoebe was a nympho. (1954)

low-heel (1939) Australian, derogatory; perhaps, like *round heels*, from the notion of being unsteady on the feet, and hence readily agreeing to lie down for sexual intercourse

bike (1945) Derogatory, orig Australian; from the notion of being ridden, as in the act of sexual intercourse ■ Barbara Pepworth: Juicy Lucy is the school bike, everyone's ridden her. (1980)

lowie, lowey (1953) Australian, derogatory; from *low*(*-hell* + *-ie* ■ *Sydney Morning Herald*: Harkins points out the 'rev heads' (fast driving teenage yobos) and the 'loweys' (equally fast young girls) he knows lolling about outside the Commercial Hotel. (1979)

slag (1958) Derogatory; compare earlier sense, contemptible or objectionable person

■ *Observer*: 'Ulrika Jonsson? Bloody slag.' 'Slag? Why?' 'Well—the way she just goes on holiday and flashes her arse all over the place.' (1996)

punch-board (1963) Derogatory; from the comparison between sexual penetration and punching holes, designs, etc.; compare earlier sense, gambling board with holes containing slips of punched paper ■ **Germaine Greer:** Girls who pride themselves on their monogamous instincts . . . speak of the 'campus punchboard'. (1970)

hot pants (1966) US; applied to a highly sexed (young) woman; compare earlier sense, fashion shorts worn by young women ■ **Kingsley Amis:** It would help to hold off little hot-pants, and might distract him from the thought of what he was so very soon going to be doing to her. (1968)

groupie, groupy (1967) Applied to a young female fan of a pop group who follows them on tour and tries to have sex with them; from *group* + *-ie* ■ *Times*: His defence described the sisters as 'groupies', girls who deliberately provoke sexual relations with pop stars. (1970)

puta (1967) Derogatory; from Spanish *puta* whore

scupper (1970) Derogatory; from earlier sense, prostitute

slapper (1992) British, derogatory; compare earlier, obsolete dialect sense, large or strapping person, especially female ■ *Private Eye*: Paula . . . is no run-of-the-mill slapper. (1996)

See also **bim**, **bimbo**, **broad**, **buer**, **mot**, **muff**, **poule**, **quiff**, **quim**, **totty**, and **trim** under A woman (pp. 46–8) at **People**.

To behave promiscuously

cruise (1674) Not in general use until the second half of the 19th century, when it was mainly applied to prostitutes soliciting for customers while walking the streets; latterly applied to walking or driving around the streets in search of a sexual (especially homosexual) partner ■ *Times Literary Supplement*: Male metropolitan homosexuals . . . who cruise compulsively. (1984)

tom-cat (1927) US; applied to a man pursuing women promiscuously for the sake of sexual gratification; often followed by *around*; from the reputation of male cats for sexual voraciousness ■ **G. Thompson:** A man who's been tom-catting around with three women all day long. (1980)

sleep around (1928) Orig US ■ **Marghanita Laski:** I don't think for a minute she's been sleeping around . . . but you know what gossip is. (1952)

fool around (1937) Orig US; applied to having a casual (and often adulterous) sexual relationship ■ **G. Paley:** I'd never fool around with a Spanish guy. They all have tough ladies back in the barrio. (1985)

hawk one's **mutton (1937)** Applied disparagingly to a woman seeking a lover; from

obsolete slang *mutton* female genitals ■ **James Patrick:** They're aw cows hawkin' their mutton. (1973)

screw around (1939) Orig US ■ **Tim Heald:** I've been sort of screwing around a little. . . . I don't want to upset my husband, but a girl only has one life. (1981)

put out (1947) US; applied to a woman who offers herself for sexual intercourse; often followed by *for* ■ **David Lodge:** If she won't put out the men will accuse her of being bourgeois and uptight. (1975)

swing (1964) Often applied specifically to engaging in group sex, partner-swapping, etc. ■ **E. M. Brecher:** If only one-tenth of one percent of married couples (one couple in a thousand) swing, however, the total still adds up to some 45,000 swinging American couples. (1970). Hence **swinging** promiscuous (1964) ■ *Bulletin* (Sydney): 'Swinging couples' are no longer addicted to square dancing but to the less innocuous pastime of wife-swapping. (1978)

pull a train (1965) Denoting sexual intercourse with a succession of partners ■ **H. L. Foster:** Trains are pulled everywhere. . . . Selby . . . described Tralala pulling endless trains in Brooklyn. (1974)

A city characterized by licentiousness and vice

sin city (1973) Often jocular ■ **A. Thackeray:** What's going to happen in Chicago? . . . All you want to do is run amok in 'Sin City'. (1975)

Sex appeal

it (1904) Dated ■ **L. P. Bachmann:** She really had 'It', as it was called. (1972)

S.A., s.a. (1926) Abbreviation ■ **Edmund McGirr:** I saw you and the dame go into her apartment. . . . I expected you to take longer. Losing the old s.a., Piron? (1974)

oomph (1937) Dated; imitative of energy and verve ■ *Guardian*: A Lhasa belle, complete with high heels, lipstick, and 'oomph'. (1960)

A sexually attractive person

peach (1754) Usually applied to a female; from the association of the peach with lusciousness ■ **Richmal Crompton:** Now would you think that a peach like her would fall for a fat-headed chump like that? (1930)

ripper (1846) Now mainly Australian; usually applied to a female; from earlier, more general sense, excellent person or thing ■ *Bulletin* (Sydney): The woman . . . will be Cynthia Morisey, a little ripper from Perth. . . . Miss Morisey, from every aspect, is almost derangingly beautiful. (1976)

stunner (1848) *Daily Telegraph*: The bride, of course, was a stunner—all demure in white broderie anglaise with a sweetheart neckline. (1981)

scorcher (1881) ■ **P. G. Wodehouse:** When I'd had a look at the young lady next door and seen what a scorcher she is. (1935)

a (little) bit of all right (1898) From (probable) earlier, more general sense, something satisfactory ■ **Monica Dickens:** 'What's she like?' . . . 'The daughter? Bit of all right, from her pictures.' (1956)

hot stuff (1899) Usually also implying promiscuity ■ M. Paneth: The men say of her, 'Joan is hot stuff.' (1944)

peacherino, peacherine, peacheroo (1900) Mainly US; from (probable) earlier, more general sense, excellent person or thing ■ C. Rougvie: When I was his age, they were hauling them out from under me. . . . And all young peacherinos, too. (1967)

cutie, cutey (a1904) Orig US; applied especially to women; from *cute + -ie* ■ James Barbican: He goes about with a high-stepping cutie who's ace-high on the face and figure. (1927)

corker (1909) From earlier, more general sense, excellent person or thing ■ R. D. Abrahams: My girl's a corker. (1969)

looker (1909) Orig US; applied especially to beautiful women; from earlier *good looker* ■ Roger Parkes: Bit of a looker. . . . Otherwise . . . a ranking detective on a priority case, would hardly have bothered driving her home. (1971)

cracker (1914) British; from (probable) earlier, more general sense, excellent person or thing ■ *Mizz*: Matt . . . also likes 'girls, drinking, reading the NME and Goth clothes. I'd also like to pull a real cracker—I don't have any special preferences looks-wise, I'd just like someone really special.' (1992)

babe (1915) Orig US: applied originally to women and latterly (since the 1970s) also to men; from earlier sense, baby ■ *Observer*: With her big eyes, handsome embonpoint and handspan waist, Margaret Rose was a bit of a babe in her day, but this wasn't enough to stop her being . . . 'on the shelf' at 29. (1997)

dish (1921) From the idea of an attractive or tasty dish of food ■ Angus Wilson: That man I've been talking to is rather a dish, but I'm sure he's a bottom-pincher. (1958)

heart-throb (1928) Orig US; applied especially to a male entertainer with whom many women fall in love; from earlier sense, thrill as if caused by a fast-beating heart ■ *Wall Street Journal*: Robert Redford may be a heartthrob in Hollywood, but in this town he gives his neighbors heartburn. (1989)

sweetie-pie (1928) Applied to a lovable (and attractive) person ■ Edward Hyams: 'I think they're all perfect sweetie-pies,' Barbara said. (1957)

eyeful (1934) Applied especially to a strikingly beautiful woman; compare earlier sense, long steady look at something remarkable or beautiful ■ P. G. Wodehouse: Unquestionably an eyeful, Pauline Stoker had the grave defect of being one of those girls who want you to come and swim a mile before breakfast. (1934)

cutie-pie (1941) Orig US; applied especially to women ■ G. Donaldson: He could see a flicker in the eyes of the local cutie-pies. (1993)

dream-boat (1947) Orig US ■ Terence Rattigan: I thought you'd be quite old and staid and ordinary and, my God, look at you, a positive dream boat. (1951)

smasher (1948) Mainly British; from earlier sense, something unusually excellent ■ Angus Wilson: When the jeunes filles met Rodney, Jackie . . . put her head on one side and said, 'I say, isn't he a smasher!' (1957)

glamour puss (1952) ■ Colin MacInnes: 'Now listen, glamour puss,' I said, flicking his bottom with my towel. (1959)

sexpot (1957) Applied especially to women ■ *London Magazine*: Tough Games Mistress. Rebellious sexpot pupil (pregnant again). (1981)

sexboat (1962) US; applied especially to women ■ Ed Lacy: I don't buy the bit that every mademoiselle is automatically a sexboat because she's French. (1962)

sex-bomb (1963) Applied especially to women ■ P. Cave: Sex-bomb, Sonya Stelling might be. Oscar contender she was not. (1976)

spunk (1978) Australian; applied especially to a man; usually in the phrase *young spunk*; compare earlier senses, courage, spirit, semen ■ *Sunday Mail* (Brisbane): No matter how skittish she might feel, old girls of 59 mustn't even flutter an eyelash at a young spunk. (1986)

A sexually attractive man

stud (1895) Applied to a man of (reputedly) great sexual prowess; from earlier sense, horse kept for breeding ■ Salman Rushdie: A notorious seducer; a ladies'-man; a cuckolder of the rich; in short, a stud. (1981)

beefcake (1949) Orig US; applied to (a display of) sturdy masculine physique; and hence to an individual muscular man; based jocularly on *cheesecake* ■ *Guardian*: The other poster . . . shows Albert Finney in a beefcake pose with his shirt slit to the navel. (1963)

God's gift (1953) Mainly ironic; applied to a man irresistible to women; from earlier more general sense, godsend ■ Hugh Clevely: It may do him a bit of good to find out he isn't God's gift to women walking the earth. (1953)

hunk (1968) Orig US; from earlier sense, very large person ■ *Mandy*: I'm not losing my chance with a hunk like Douglas, for any boring old vow. (1989)

A sexually attractive woman

doll (1840) Orig US; often used as a form of address; from earlier sense, model of a human figure used as a toy ■ *Scope* (South Africa): You don't have to do it, doll. (1971)

jelly (1889) Dated; apparently from the wobbliness associated with buxom women ■ William Faulkner: Don't think I spent last night with a couple of your barber-shop jellies for nothing. (1931)

queen (1900) Dated ■ J. T. Farrell: Wouldn't it be luck if a ritzy queen fell for him! (1937)

cutie, cutey (a1904) Orig US; from *cute + -ie* ■ James Barbican: He goes about with a high-stepping cutie who's ace-high on the face and figure. (1927)

dolly (1906) ■ *Daily Mirror*: He is very gone on girls, is always falling wildly in and out of love with dishy dollies. (1968)

cookie (1920) Orig US; compare earlier sense, person

snuggle-pup, **snuggle-pupper**, **snuggle-puppy (1922)** US, dated; applied to an attractive young girl ■ *Forum & Century* (New York): I glimmed him with a snuggle-puppy. (1933)

patootie (1923) US; usually in such phrases as *sweet patootie*, *hot patootie*; from earlier sense, girlfriend, sweetheart ■ Peter De Vries: You like to shake a leg with a hot patootie now and then, do you? (1958)

Ruby Queen (1925) Dated services' slang; applied to an attractive young female nurse ■ Edmund Blunden: With Ruby Queens We once crowned feeds of pork and beans. (1934)

tomato (1929) Orig US ■ Howard Fast: This tomato is twenty-three years old and she's a virgin. (1977)

cheesecake (1934) Orig US; applied to a display of sexually attractive females, especially in photographs, and hence to an individual attractive woman ■ John Wain: She had a sexy slouch like a Hollywood cheesecake queen. (1958)

package (1945) US

nymphet (1955) Applied to a sexually attractive young girl; compare earlier sense, young nymph; first used in this sense by Vladimir Nabokov in *Lolita* ■ Joseph Di Mona: Most of the 'sales executives' had turned out to be eighteen- and nineteen-year-old nymphets. (1973)

gorgeous Gussie (1956) Applied to a glamorous and beautiful young woman; from the nickname of Gertrude ('Gussie') Moran, US tennis player, so called because of the frilly panties she wore on court ■ *People*: Put a Gorgeous Gussie among a group of Plain Janes . . . and a whole office or factory routine can be upset. (1956)

sex kitten (1958) Applied to a young woman who asserts her sex appeal ■ *Guardian*: Brigitte Bardot . . . the original sex kitten with the French charm. (1966)

fox (1961) US, orig Black English; back-formation from *foxy* sexually attractive ■ L. Hairston: Daddy, she was a real fox! (1964)

dolly-bird (1964) Mainly British ■ Robert Crawford: You'll have to take . . . that dolly-bird you hide in Romford with you. (1971)

See also **bimbette**, **bimbo** under A stupid woman at **People** (p. 49).

A sexually attractive thing or person

turn-on (1969) From *turn on* attract or stimulate sexually ■ Judith Krantz: Masturbation isn't a great big turn-on in my life. (1978)

Sexually attractive

stunning (1856) Usually applied to a female ■ *Listener*: Yvonne Brathwaite Burke . . . the stunning and extremely saucy 'Vice-Chairperson'. (1972)

husky (1869) Orig US; applied to a man who is big, vigorous and muscular; from earlier sense,

like a corn-husk, from the toughness and strength of corn-husks

foxy (1895) US, mainly Black English; usually applied to a female; from earlier sense, amorous ■ *Easyriders*: W/f [white female] . . . 21 years old and foxy, would like to hear from a gorgeous man with a terrific body. (1983)

tasty (1899) From earlier, more general sense, attractive ■ R. Thomas: One of the women, a new actress with hopes of a plum part, turned to the other. 'Tasty guy, wouldn't you say, Dinah?' (1984)

peachy (1926) From earlier sense, like a peach, from the lusciousness associated with peaches ■ William Trevor: Your mum has a touch of style, Kate. I heard that remarked in a vegetable shop. I'd call her an eyeful, Kate. Peachy. (1976)

sexational, **sexsational (1928)** Orig US; applied to someone or something sexually sensational; blend of *sex* and *sensational* ■ *Time*: Sexational, robustious Cinemactress Mae West appeared on a commercial broadcast for the first time in four years. (1937) ■ *West Lancs. Evening Gazette*: 1st Blackpool showing of the Sexsational *Highway through the Bedroom* (X). (1976)

dreamy (1941) Orig US; usually applied to a male ■ Monica Dickens: She said she had a date with a dreamy boy. (1953)

dishy (1961) From *dish* attractive person + *-y* ■ John Gardner: 'Mm, is *that* him?' said the girl, all velvet. 'He's dishy.' (1964)

glam (1963) Short for *glamorous* ■ Celia Dale: She was . . . wearing eye-shadow and a great deal of lipstick. 'You're looking very glam,' he said. (1964)

spunky (1975) Australian; from *spunk* attractive person + *-y* ■ *Sydney Morning Herald*: Gynaecologists in Sydney have been known to leave their wives for younger, spunkier patients. (1984)

hunky (1978) Orig US; applied to a man who is ruggedly handsome and sexually attractive; from *hunk* attractive man + *-y* ■ *Sun*: Sheer escapism for all the family with hunky Harrison Ford. (1986)

babelicious (1992) US; blend of *babe* sexually attractive person and *delicious*; popularized in the film *Wayne's World* (1992) ■ *Sun*: Party down to Wayne and Garth and a babelicious celebrity guest in their basement studios in beautiful downtown Aurora, Illinois. (1992)

To attract or stimulate sexually

turn on (1966) Orig US ■ J. I. M. Stewart: It's a funny thing . . . how quite sure I was she wasn't going to turn me on. (1975)

A person considered as an object of sexual desire or availablity

crumpet (1936) British; used collectively, originally of women but latterly also of men; often in the phrase *bit* (or *piece*) *of crumpet* ■ D. Lambert: Ansell . . . watched the couples wistfully. 'Plenty of crumpet here, you know. Why don't you chance your arm?' (1969) ■ *Observer*: His performance as a trendy and hung-up LA painter in 'Heart-breakers' made him the thinking woman's West Coast crumpet. (1987)

make (1942) Orig US; applied to a sexual conquest, especially an easily seduced woman ■ *Landfall:* 'A widow's an easy make,' He said, 'you pedal and let her steer.' (1951)

homework (1945) Usually applied to a woman; usually in the phrase *bit (or piece) of homework* ■ **Julian Symons:** He produced a dog-eared snap of a girl in a bikini. 'How's that for a piece of homework?' (1968)

talent (1947) Used collectively, especially in the phrase *local talent* ■ *Sunday Times:* You can take a turn on the [sea-]front and see what the talent is like. (1963)

A female sex object

cunt (1674) Often applied collectively to women; from earlier sense, female genitals

bit of fluff (goods, muslin, mutton, skirt, stuff, etc.) **(1847), bit (1923)** ■ **Warwick Deeping:** Got a little party on, you know, two bits of fashionable fluff. (1919) ■ **Barbara Goolden:** If I want a common little bit for a best girl that's my look-out, too. (1953) ■ **B. W. Aldiss:** The infantry myth that one spent one's whole leave yanking it up some willing bit of stuff in a pub yard. (1971) ■ **J. I. M. Stewart:** They mustn't quarrel over a bit of skirt. (1977)

skirt (1914) Applied to a woman or collectively to women; often in the phrase *bit of skirt* ■ **Kate Millett:** The two patriarchs, never tired of chasing twenty-year-old skirts in their old age. (1974)

ass (1916) Orig US; applied to a woman or collectively to women; from earlier sense, woman's buttocks and genital area, regarded as an object of sexual desire ■ **John Updike:** Then he comes back from the Army and all he cares about is chasing ass. (1960)

tail (1933) Applied collectively to women, often in the phrase *piece* (or *bit*) *of tail;* from earlier sense, woman's buttocks and genital area, regarded as an object of sexual desire ■ **Jeremy Potter:** Where's all the tail today? No Hermione, no Bunty, no Christabel. (1967)

quim (1935) Often applied collectively to women; from earlier sense, female genitals ■ *Saturday Night* (Toronto): The key to success in this contest is a flashy car; and if the car is both expensive and impressive 'you have to beat the quim off with a hockey stick'. (1974)

brush (1941) Australian & New Zealand; applied collectively to women; perhaps from the female pubic hair ■ *Sun-Herald* (Sydney): He [was] intrigued by the younger men's comments about the beautiful 'brush' (women) eager to be entertained by visiting trainers. (1984)

piece of ass (tail, etc.)**, piece (1942)** Mainly US ■ **G. V. Higgins:** Him and four buddies want a little dough to get a high class piece of tail. (1972) ■ **Judith Krantz:** He . . . thought she was a flaming, fabulous piece of ass. (1978)

crackling (1947) British; applied collectively to women, and in the phrase *piece of crackling;* from earlier sense, crisp skin of roast pork ■ **Peter Dickinson:** 'You know her?' 'I do, sir. Nice bit of crackling, she is.' (1968)

poontang (1947) Sometimes applied collectively to women, and in the phrase *piece of poontang;* from earlier sense, sexual intercourse ■ *Listener.* Massa gonna smack yo black ass, nigger. You can't go chasing white poontang all night long. (1972)

pussy (1959) Applied collectively to women; from earlier sense, female genitals ■ *Guardian:* This new Bugis Street, not old one; it government one, no girls, no good. You want pussy? Come, I take you there. (1992)

grumble (1962) British; applied collectively to women; shortened from *grumble and grunt,* rhyming slang for *cunt* ■ *Melody Maker.* American visitors are invariably delighted by references to birds, scrubbers, grumble. (1966)

bit of lumber (1966) Scottish; related to the verb *lumber* make sexual advances to, grope

beaver (1968) US; from earlier sense, female genitals or pubic area

spare (1969) Applied to an unattached woman, especially one available for casual sex; usually used collectively in the phrase *bit of spare* ■ **Roger Busby:** I . . . got the impression Maurice was . . . on the look-out for a bit of spare. . . . Some of the girls we get in here . . . don't leave much to the imagination. (1978)

A sexual partner or partner in sexual intercourse

fancy man (1811) Derogatory; applied to a woman's lover, often adulterous ■ **Bill Naughton:** You won't get one husband in ten feels any thanks to the wife's fancy man for the happiness he brings to the marriage. (1966)

cliner, clinah (1895) Australian, dated; applied to a girlfriend or female lover; probably from German *kleine* small ■ **A. W. Upfield:** I 'elped to get 'is clinah out of quod for what she and 'im did for me. (1928)

papa (1904) US; applied to a husband or male lover

patootie (1921) US; applied to a sweetheart or girlfriend, or to a pretty girl; probably an alteration of *potato* ■ *New Yorker.* She was, successively, . . . the wife and/or sweet patootie of the quartet. (1977)

trick (1925) Orig & mainly US; applied to a casual sexual partner, often specifically a prostitute's client; from earlier sense, act of sexual intercourse ■ **Bill Turner:** I doubt there's one trick in twenty who isn't a married man. (1968)

mamma, mama, momma (1926), red-hot mamma (1936) US; applied to a girlfriend or female lover; compare earlier sense, promiscuous woman

easy rider (1927) US, Black English; applied to a sexually satisfying lover

sweetback, sweetback man (1929) US; applied to a woman's lover or to a ladies' man

OAO (1936) Services' slang, orig US; applied to someone's sweetheart; abbreviation of *one and only* ■ *Everybody's Magazine* (Australia): In each war, a new vocabulary is created. Today, in Vietnam, Australians are again catching up on American Army slang. . . . All would refer to a special girlfriend as their OAO—one and only. Probably, the OAO was met on skirt patrol. (1967)

sweet man (1942) US; applied to a woman's lover or to a ladies' man

shack-job (1946) US; applied to a (temporary) sexual partner; from *shack (up* cohabit + *job* ■ William Gaddis: Look, rabbit, I'm looking for a shack-job, see? (1955)

lover boy, lover man (1952) Orig US ■ Len Deighton: 'There's no hurry, loverman,' she said. (1968)

pull (1969) Applied to a woman picked up as a sexual partner; from the verb *pull* pick up as a sexual partner ■ Martin Amis: It was so obviously me and my pull and Geoffrey and his pull getting together to plan a spotty removal to someone's house. (1973)

shack-up (1969) Mainly US; applied to a (temporary) sexual partner; from *shack up* cohabit ■ Joseph Gores: He didn't even know if the guy was married or single. He might have a shack-up there for the night. (1972)

main squeeze (1970) US; applied to a man's principal woman friend; compare earlier sense, important person

squeeze (1980) Mainly US; applied to a close friend, especially a girlfriend or lover; shortened from *main squeeze* ■ R. Ford: I would love to grill him about his little seminary squeeze, but he would be indignant. (1986)

A person considered solely as a partner in sexual intercourse

fuck (1874) From earlier sense, act of sexual intercourse ■ John Morris: She was a good fuck. . . . She was great in bed. (1969)

lay (1932) Orig US; from the verb *lay* have sex with ■ William Gaddis: She's the girl you used to go around with in college? She's a good lay. (1955)

screw (1937) From earlier sense, act of sexual intercourse ■ Milton Machlin: As a matter of fact, he's not such a great screw, but at least he isn't a nag, the way you are. (1976)

root (1961) Australian; applied to a woman; from earlier sense, act of sexual intercourse ■ D. Ireland: Johnny Bickel . . . thought she'd be an easy root and began to take notice of her. (1976)

poke (1968) From earlier sense, act of sexual intercourse ■ H. C. Rae: 'Caroline', said Derek . . . 'wouldn't make a good poke for a blind hunchback.' (1968)

hump (1969) From earlier sense, act of sexual intercourse ■ Philip Roth: Now you want to treat me like I'm nothing but some hump. (1969)

An older sexual partner

cradle-snatcher (1907), cradle-robber (1926) Jocular, orig US; applied to someone who enters into a sexual relationship with a much younger person ■ R. Erskine: Crispin asked me to dance. 'Cradle-snatcher,' said Miranda nastily. (1965). Hence the verb **cradle-snatch** (1938)

daddy (1909) US; applied to an older male lover

baby-snatcher (1911) Jocular; applied to someone who enters into a sexual relationship with a much younger person ■ Vita Sackville-West: You don't imagine that he really cared about that baby-snatcher? Good gracious me, he was a year old when her daughter was born. (1930). Hence the verb **baby-snatch** (1933)

dirty old man (1932) Applied to a lecherous older man ■ Douglas Clark: A man of my age on the look out for a lovely young lass puts me into the dirty-old-man class. (1971)

DOM (1959) Abbreviation of *dirty old man* ■ Bruce Rodgers: DOMs should know better than to come to the tubs and fuck it up for the rest of us. (1972)

See also **nonce** at Someone with unconventional sexual tastes (p. 78)

A younger sexual partner

jail-bait (1934) Orig US; applied to a girl who is too young to have sex with legally; from the fact that sexual intercourse with such a girl may result in imprisonment ■ John Braine: I'm not interested in little girls. Particularly not in jail-bait like that one. (1957)

toy boy (1981) Applied to a woman's much younger male lover ■ *News of the World:* At 48 she is like a teenage girl again—raving it up with four different lovers including a toyboy of 27! (1987)

A kiss

smack (1604) Applied to a loud kiss ■ John Gay: Come, noble captain, take one hearty smack upon her lips, and then steer off. (1729)

smacker (1775) Applied to a loud kiss ■ *Sun:* William Crawford, QC, planted a smacker on each cheek and put his hands on the busty blonde's waist. (1992)

peck (1893) Applied to a brief or perfunctory kiss ■ *Daily Mail:* The wayward star . . . showed the gentle touch yesterday with a peck on the cheek and a bouquet for his opponent. (1991). Hence the verb **peck** kiss in this way (1969) ■ Colleen McCullough: Meggie leaned over to peck her brothers on their cheeks self-consciously. (1977)

banger (1898) Applied especially to a violent kiss ■ Hank Hobson: 'Here—give us a banger first.' Honeypuss . . . obediently offered him her lips. (1959)

smoush (1963) Australian; a variant of *smooch* ■ D. Ireland: Reminds me of a widow I knew at Richmond. Whenever I visited her and a plane went over she'd drop whatever she was doing and rush over for a smoush. (1971)

A love-bite

hickey, hickie (1956) US; compare earlier sense, a pimple ■ *Good Housekeeping:* A recent letter . . . reports a case of catching herpes from a love bite or, as it's known in the USA, a hickey. (1987)

Caressing, foreplay

grope (c1250) Applied to fondling or attempting to fondle a person's genitals or a woman's breasts ■ Gerald Maclean: When he starts to grope another woman in church, she takes out a set of pins 'to prick me if I should touch her again'. (1994). Hence the noun **grope** applied to an instance of groping someone, and hence to foreplay involving manual genital stimulation (1946) ■ *Guardian*: If everyone agrees that pushing girls around, looking up their skirts, taking a quick grope and talking in sexual innuendos is just boys being boys, then no one will take a stand. (1991) ■ *Independent*: The great British tradition of puerile smut: 'Played cards with my girlfriend the other night.' 'Poker?' 'No, we just had a bit of a grope.' (1991)

neck (1825) Applied to kissing and caressing ■ John O'Hara: I was even surprised I could neck her at all. (1940) ■ John Le Carré: A loving couple necking in the back of a Rover. (1974)

bill and coo (1854) Applied to caressing and making other displays of affection; from the bonding behaviour of a pair of doves (*bill* from earlier sense, stroke each other's beaks, from *bill* beak)

canoodle (1859) Orig US, now mainly jocular; applied to kissing and cuddling; origin unknown ■ Hugh Walpole: She's in there. . . . I'm off on some business of my own for an hour or two, so you can canoodle as much as you damned well please. (1921)

lallygag, lollygag (1868) US, dated; applied to amorous cuddling; from earlier sense, fool around

touch up (1903) Applied to fondling someone's genitals ■ Clive Egleton: Good-looking tart. . . . I wouldn't have minded her touching me up. (1973)

clinch (1901) Orig US; applied to an embrace; from earlier sense, close-quarter grappling in a fight ■ John Osborne: The 'King' and 'Queen' go into a clinch. (1959). So the verb **clinch** embrace (1899) ■ *Punch*: They . . . sit like lovers about to clinch. (1953)

footie, footy (1921), footsie, footsy (1944) Orig US; also used in reduplicated forms; applied to amorous play with the feet; jocular diminutive of *foot* ■ G. Fowler: I played footsie with her during Don José's first seduction by Carmen. (1944) ■ James Thurber: In [a drawing] . . . showing a man and his wife and another woman at a table . . . the designing minx was playing footy-footy with the husband. (1959)

slap and tickle (1928) British; denoting light-hearted kissing, caressing, etc. ■ Colleen McCullough: He'd woo her the way she obviously wanted, flowers and attention and not too much slap-and-tickle. (1977)

feel (1930) Applied to fondling someone's genitals; usually followed by *up* ■ Mordecai Richler: He literally bumped into Ziggy feeling up the prettiest girl at the party in a dark damp corner. (1968). Hence the noun **feel** (1932) ■ *Zeno*: I gave her a feel, and she pulled away. (1970)

smooch (1932) Orig US; applied to kissing and caressing, especially while dancing to slow romantic music; variant of obsolete *smouch* kiss, related to German dialect *schmutzen* kiss, smile ■ Lewis Nkosi: Mary and Gama are sharing a studio couch on which they are smooching quietly. (1964). Hence the noun

smooch applied to a fondling embrace or caress, and also to slow close dancing (1942) ■ *Time*: Ethel Merman and Fernando Lamas . . . found that their nightly onstage smooch grated too harshly on their star-crossed sensibilities. (1957)

mush (1939) Applied to kissing and caressing; from *mush* mouth ■ Saul Bellow: There's plenty of honest kids to choose from, the kind who'd never let you stick around till one a.m. mushing with them on the steps. (1953)

snog (1945) British; applied to kissing and caressing; perhaps related to *snug* ■ Anthony Sampson: The cinema has lost its hold—except among unmarried teenagers, two-thirds of whom go at least once a week, perhaps to snog in the doubles. (1962) ■ *Private Eye*: *Mirror* cartoonist Griffin even put the hapless Parsons in last Friday's cartoon: a line of 'nutters' queuing for a turn to snog the Princess of Wales—an unshaven 'Chucky' at the tail end. (1995). Hence the noun **snog** a period or session of snogging (1959) ■ Martin Amis: They were enjoying a kiss—well, more of a snog really. (1973)

love-up (1953) Applied to an act of caressing, hugging, etc. ■ M. Allwright: He looked so beaten by the world that I wanted to gather him in my arms on the spot and give him a good love-up. (1968)

lumber (1960) Scottish; used of a man making (physical) sexual advances; origin uncertain; perhaps related to the noun *lumber* useless odds and ends and the verb *lumber* encumber ■ Alasdair Gray: 'Last Friday I saw her being lumbered by a hardman up a close near the Denistoun Palais.' 'Lumbered?' 'Groped. Felt.' (1981)

reef (1962) Applied to feeling a person's genitals; compare earlier sense, pick someone's pocket ■ Parker & Allerton: I enjoyed reefing girls much more than lessons. The girls enjoyed it too. (1962)

Sexual activity, sexual intercourse

it (1611) Euphemistic; applied to sexual intercourse ■ Francis Warner: He doesn't even know I'm overdue. And he hasn't had it for a week. (1972)

fuck (1680) Applied to an act of sexual intercourse; from the verb *fuck* copulate ■ E. J. Howard: Eat well, don't smoke, and a fuck was equal to a five-mile walk. (1965)

that there (1819) British, euphemistic; applied to sexual activity, especially in the catch-phrase *you can't do that there 'ere*; the catch-phrase derives from a popular song by Squiers and Wark, published in *Feldman's 41st Song and Dance Album* (1933) ■ *Evening News*: The British Government gives vent to a 'John-Bullism', and says, after the abduction of a Hindu girl from within the border, 'You can't do that there 'ere!' (1937)

the other thing (1846) Dated, euphemistic; applied to sexual activity ■ James Joyce: Besides there was absolution so long as you didn't do the other thing before being married. (1922)

frig (c1888) Applied to an act of sexual intercourse; from the verb *frig* copulate

greens (1888) Perhaps from the notion that sexual intercourse is as beneficial as eating one's greens (i.e. cabbages and other green vegetables) ■ **Graham Greene:** Why not go after the girl? . . . She's not getting what I believe is vulgarly called her greens. (1967)

knee-trembler (1896) Applied to an act of sexual intercourse between people standing up ■ **B. W. Aldiss:** They would be going to the pub for a pint and afterwards Nelson would get her against our back wall for a knee-trembler. . . . He claimed that knee-tremblers were the most exhausting way of having sex. (1971)

poke (1902) Applied to an act of sexual intercourse; from the verb *poke* have sex with ■ **Laurence Meynell:** Landladies can nearly always be paid in kind. Services in lieu of rent. A poke a night. (1970)

tumble (1903) Applied to an act of sexual intercourse, especially in the phrase *give a tumble*; from the verb *tumble* have sex with ■ **J. Trench:** He was . . . giving la Vitrey a tumble somewhere. (1954)

ass (c1910) Orig US; applied to male sexual gratification; from earlier sense, woman's buttocks and genital area, regarded as an object of sexual desire ■ **R. D. Abrahams:** When we got upstairs I threw her on the floor I was anxious to get some ass off that frantic whore. (1970)

zig-zig (1918) US military slang; variant of *jig-a-jig* ■ **W. Robinson:** 'Allo, baybee! Comment alley vooz-zigzig? (1962)

the other (1922) Euphemistic; applied to sexual activity or intercourse, or occasionally to homosexual activities; short for *the other thing* ■ *Spectator.* I've got to be noticed by any guy who's on the prowl away from home and looking for a bit of the other. (1974)

oats (1923) Applied to male sexual gratification; usually in such phrases as *have* or *get one's oats*; perhaps from *sow one's wild oats* commit youthful indiscretions ■ **John Wainwright:** This wife he was lumbered with. Okay—he loved her. . . . But, even *he* wanted his oats, occasionally. He was human. (1978)

jazz (1924), jazzing (1958) Orig Southern US Black English; applied to sexual intercourse ■ **Alan Lomax:** Winding Boy is a bit on the vulgar side. Let's see—how could I put it—means a fellow that makes good jazz with the women. (1950) ■ **Murtagh & Harris:** She asked if I wanted to do a little jazzing. . . . I said, 'How much?' 'Two dollars,' she said. (1958)

trick (1926) Orig & mainly US; applied to an act of sexual intercourse, especially a prostitute's session with a client

jelly roll (1927) US, mainly Black English; applied to sexual intercourse; compare contemporary sense, female genitals ■ **Thomas Wolfe:** 'What yo' want?' she asked softly. 'Jelly roll?' (1929)

nooky, nookie (1928) Applied to sexual intercourse; perhaps from *nook* secluded corner + *-y* ■ **Anthony West:** Still nooky was nooky he told himself, and who cared what the woman was like if the lay was good. (1960)

poontang (1929) US; applied to sexual intercourse; probably from French *putain*

prostitute ■ *Honolulu Star-Bulletin:* The other girls majored in home ec. . . . but Debby majored in Poon-tang. (1976)

screw (1929) Applied to an act of (casual or hasty) sexual intercourse; from the verb *screw* have sex (with) ■ **P. L. Cave:** Five or six Angel birds sat around over cold cups of coffee waiting for a fast ride or a quick screw. (1971)

bang (1931) Applied to an act of sexual intercourse; from earlier sense, a pelvic thrust during intercourse ■ **John Updike:** I bet she even gives him a bang now and then. (1968)

hump (1931) Applied to an act of sexual intercourse; from the verb *hump* have sex

jig-a-jig, jig-jig (1932) Applied to sexual intercourse; from earlier sense, jerking movement; of imitative origin ■ **Alexander Baron:** He put his hand on her knee. 'You like jig-a-jig?' (1953)

jump (1934) Applied to an act of sexual intercourse ■ **Germaine Greer:** A wank was as good as a jump in those days. (1970)

lay (1936) Applied to an act of sexual intercourse; from *lay* have sex with ■ **Bernard Malamud:** Tonight an unexpected party, possibly a lay with a little luck. (1971)

shag (1937) Applied to an act of sexual intercourse; from *shag* have sex (with) ■ **B. W. Aldiss:** It was not just a good shag I needed. It was romance. (1971)

hanky-panky (1938) Applied to surreptitious sexual activity; compare earlier sense, dishonest dealing ■ *New Yorker.* They were still 'courting', still occupying separate quarters in Dr. Round's boarding house . . . where, according to Lunt, no 'hanky-panky' was permitted. (1986)

yum-yum (1939) Applied to sexual activity; from earlier sense, pleasurable activity ■ **Samuel Beckett:** Come, ducky, it's time for yum-yum. (1967)

tail (1951) Applied to male sexual gratification; from earlier sense, woman's buttocks and genital area, regarded as an object of sexual desire ■ **Richard Gordon:** Even if it was deciding whether to go out on the booze at night or have a bit of tail off of the wife. (1976)

naughty (1959) Mainly Australian & New Zealand; applied to (an act of) (illicit or surreptitious) sexual intercourse ■ **R. Beilby:** It was also the opinion of the platoon, privately expressed, that Peppie had enjoyed more thoughties than naughties. (1977)

root (1959) Australian; applied to an act of sexual intercourse; from the verb *root* have sex (with) ■ **P. Kenna:** Have you ever gone all the way with a girl? . . . You know what I mean. Have you ever had a real root? (1974)

trim (1961) US; applied to sexual intercourse; from earlier sense, woman ■ **H. L. Foster:** Female student: 'Somebody always askin for some trim and haven't even got anything.' (1974)

one-night stand (1963) Applied to a brief sexual liaison or affair; from earlier sense, single theatrical performance

a length (1968) Applied to female sexual gratification; from earlier sense, an (erect) penis ■ **H. C. Rae**: Beefy, randy-arsed wives crying out for a length. (1968)

wham, bam (or **bang**), **thank you ma'am (1971)** Used with reference to sexual intercourse done quickly and without tenderness ■ *Playgirl*: Not all men are 'wham bam thank you ma'am' types. (1977)

zipless (1973) Used to denote a sexual encounter that is brief and passionate; coined by Erica Jong, 'because when you came together, zippers fell away like petals' ■ **Gore Vidal**: Girls who feared flying tended to race blindly through zipless fucks. (1978)

patha patha, phata phata (1977) South African; applied to sexual intercourse; from earlier sense, type of sensuous dance; ultimately from Xhosa and Zulu *phatha phatha*, literally 'touch-touch' ■ **A. P. Brink**: 'Others looking for phata-phata'—illustrated by pushing his thumb through two fingers in the immemorial sign. (1979)

pussy (1978) Applied to sexual intercourse; from earlier sense, female genitals ■ *Maclean's Magazine*: As one blonde in a black leather coat bluntly replied, 'I sell pussy, not opinions.' (1979)

zatch (1980) Applied to an act of sexual intercourse, often in the phrase *give a zatch*; from earlier senses, buttocks, female genitals ■ **Judith Krantz**: You're going to take her home and give her a zatch. (1980)

how's your father (1983) British, jocular euphemism; applied to sexual intercourse; from earlier more general use as a word for something unnamed or whose name has been forgotten ■ *Q*: 'The Princess and The Pea Brain', as one paper 'dubbed' them, usurped Hugh Grant and Divine Brown as the premier concern of the nation's gossipmongers. Naturally, both parties strenuously denied any how's-your-father. (1996)

bonk (1984) British; applied to an act of sexual intercourse; from the verb *bonk* copulate ■ *Sun*: All they want is a quick bonk. (1993)

rumpy-pumpy, rumpty-tumpty, rumpo (1986) British; applied to (surreptitious) sexual intercourse; probably elaborated from *rump* buttocks, or a derivative ■ *Guardian*: One is . . . an untimid bank manager (Richard Griffiths in fine form) in extra-marital pursuit of what he dubs a bit of rumpy-pumpy. (1992)

Simulated sexual intercourse

dry fuck (1938) US; applied to a simulated act of sexual intercourse, without penetration, or to an unsatisfactory or anticlimactic act of intercourse. So the verb **dry-fuck** (*c*1937), **dry-hump** (1964)

To have sex (with), copulate (with)

fuck (*c*1500) Used transitively and intransitively; origin unknown ■ *Ink*: I don't want to fuck anyone, and I don't want to be fucked either. (1971)

ride (1520) Used transitively; formerly also used intransitively, since the Middle Ages ■ **S. Allen**: She mounted him and rode him . . . until they climaxed together. (1978)

bed (1548) In original use, mainly in the context of marrying a woman and taking her to bed on the wedding night ■ *Sun*: Albert—dubbed Dirty Bertie because of the 120 women he is said to have bedded—thinks Claudia is 'fantastic'. (1992)

frig (1598) Mainly euphemistic; used transitively and intransitively; original sense, move restlessly; perhaps an onomatopoeic alteration of obsolete *frike* dance, move briskly ■ **Mezzrow & Wolfe**: *High-pressure romancing* (find 'em, fool 'em, frig 'em and forget 'em). (1946)

have (1594) Used transitively ■ *Private Eye*: He's had more sheilahs than you've had spaghetti breakfasts. (1970)

knock (1598) British; used transitively, of a male ■ **David Pinner**: I've knocked some girls in my time but I've never had such a rabbiter as you. The cruder it is, the more you like it. (1967)

tumble (1602) Used transitively ■ **Roy Lewis**: Tommy Elias had tumbled the schoolgirl in the ferns. (1976)

do (*c*1650) Used transitively, and also in the phrase *do it* have sex ■ **Victor Canning**: Some service-man . . . did your mother in Cyprus . . . and then . . . made an honest woman of her. (1967)

bang (1698) Used transitively and intransitively ■ **Jack Kerouac**: He rushes from Marylou to Camille . . . and bangs her once. (1957)

roger, rodger (1711) Used transitively, of a male; apparently a metaphorical use of the male personal name; the noun *roger* penis is now obsolete (1700–1863) ■ **Angus Wilson**: I'm not at all sure about the Empress Theodora. I fancy she was rogered by an ape more than once in her circus acts. (1961)

screw (1725) Used transitively and intransitively ■ **Thomas Pynchon**: Santa's bag is filled with all your dreams come true: Nickel beers that sparkle like champagne, Barmaids who all love to screw. (1963)

pump (1730) Used transitively and intransitively ■ **James Patrick**: Skidmarks had come by her name through the boys' practice of kicking her naked behind after they had 'pumped' her. (1973)

tail (1778) Used transitively, of a male ■ **John Wainwright**: So, I tailed his wife. . . . So what? (1973)

hump (1785) Used transitively and intransitively ■ **Malcolm Bradbury**: Story is he humped the faculty wives in alphabetical order. (1965)

shag (1788) Used transitively and intransitively; origin uncertain; perhaps from obsolete *shag* shake, waggle ■ **Richard Adams**: 'He's never absent.' And the corporal next to Jack muttered, 'Well, I 'ope 'e ain't 'angin' around when I'm shaggin' my missus.' (1980)

poke (1868) Used transitively, of a male ■ **John Braine**: I wanted to poke Lucy so I poked her. (1962)

diddle (1870) Now mainly US; used transitively and intransitively; from earlier sense, move jerkily from side to side ■ **William Faulkner**: 'I'll find all three of them. I'll—' 'What for? Just out of curiosity to find out for certain just which of them was and wasn't diddling her?' (1940)

do over (1873) Used transitively, often with the implication of violent seduction ■ *John o' London's*: A truly Moravian rape-scene in a ruined church, with Cesira and Rosetta both done over by a screeching pack of Moroccan *goums*. (1961)

goose (1879) Dated; sometimes denoting specifically anal intercourse; compare obsolete *goose and duck* act of copulating, rhyming slang for *fuck* ■ F. Griffin: It's the commonest thing possible in the army. As soon as . . . I had learned the goose-step, I had learned to be goosed. (1881)

get into (*c*1888) Used transitively, of a man ■ Jack Kerouac: I've just got to get into her sister Mary tonight. (1957)

get some (1889) Euphemistic, orig US; applied especially to having sex on a regular basis, or to succeeding in finding a sexual partner ■ Judith Krantz: Since his last visit she was getting some, somewhere, he'd bet his life on it. (1978)

plug (1901) Used transitively, of a male ■ *American Speech*: I plugged her last night. (1977)

take (1915) Used transitively, of a male ■ Ted Allbeury: She lay with her eyes open as he took her. (1978)

go all the way (or **the whole way**) (1924) Euphemistic; applied to having sexual intercourse, as opposed to engaging only in kissing or foreplay ■ W. J. Burley: The things we found in her room! I mean it was obvious she was going all the way and her not fifteen! (1970)

make (1926) Orig US; used transitively, often denoting success in persuading someone to have sex; from earlier sense, make (successful) sexual advances to ■ E. Goffman: James Bond makes the acquaintance of an unattainable girl and then rapidly makes the girl. (1969)

jazz (1927) Used transitively and intransitively; from *jazz* sexual intercourse ■ H. MacLennan: My sister was being jazzed by half the neighbourhood cats by the time she was fifteen. (1948)

mollock (1932) Used intransitively; apparently invented by Stella Gibbons (*Cold Comfort Farm*), and perhaps influenced by *moll* prostitute, female companion ■ W. Bawden: And yet, here they were, not more than a foot away, bedhead to bedhead, merrily mollocking. (1983)

lay (1934) Orig US; used transitively, or (of a woman) intransitively, denoting having or willingness to have sex ■ Philip Roth: All I know is I got laid, *twice*. (1969) ■ John Updike: You've laid for Harrison, haven't you? (1960)

boff (1937) Usually used transitively; from earlier sense, hit hard ■ *Observer*: They're the only two decent-looking people on *Brookside*: who on earth else would they want to boff? (1996)

have it off (or **away**) (**with**) (1937) British ■ George Melly: I derived iconoclastic pleasure from having it off in the public parks where fifteen years before my brother

and I . . . accompanied our nurse on sunny afternoons. (1965) ■ R. Perry: No one would dream of having it away with his mistress. (1972)

make out (1939) Orig US; often stressing success in achieving sexual intercourse with a woman; usually followed by *with* ■ *Times*: The detailed accounts of how he 'made out' sexually and emotionally with some sixteen different girls. (1961)

tear it off a bit (or **piece**) (1941) Orig Australian; applied to a man having sex with a woman ■ *Custom Car*: Italian wives must sit and suffer if the men tear off a bit on the sly. (1977)

get one's **rocks off** (1948) Orig US; applied to a man obtaining sexual release by copulation and ejaculation; from *rocks* testicles

slip someone **a length** (1949) Used of a man; from *length* (erect) penis ■ Christopher Wood: Come on, Suggy, you're 'is batman, 'e's never slipped you a crafty length 'as 'e? (1970)

knock off (1952) British; used transitively, of a male ■ *Times Literary Supplement*: Knocking off his best friend's busty wife during boozy sprees on leave in Soho. (1974)

ball (*c*1953) Orig US; used transitively and intransitively, especially of a man; perhaps an extension of *ball* enjoy oneself, influenced by *balls* testicles ■ Gore Vidal: And you can tell the world all about those chicks that you ball. (1978)

make it (1957) Usually followed by *with*; from earlier sense, be successful ■ *Times Literary Supplement*: He finally makes it with long-desired Rachel. (1973)

dip one's **wick** (1958) Used of a man; from the notion of inserting the penis ■ Robert Barnard: None of your barmaids or local peasant wenches for Pete. He's very calculating where he dips his wick. (1981)

root (1958) Australian; used transitively and intransitively, especially of a man; also in the phrase *root like a rattlesnake* (i.e. vigorously); compare *root* penis ■ K. Cook: We found this bloody little poofter down on the beach fiddling with a bird. . . . Couldn't even root her. (1974)

nail (1960) US; used transitively, usually of a man, often with the implication of aggression ■ R. Grossbach: Who would you rather marry, then—the publishing cupcake in the Florsheims who nailed you on the couch and then fired you? (1979)

score (1960) Used intransitively or transitively, of a male; usually used to imply success in persuading a woman to have sexual intercourse ■ Germaine Greer: The boys used to go to the local dance halls and stand around . . . until the . . . sexual urge prompted them to *score a chick*. (1970) ■ David Craig: They talk about 'taking' a woman. . . . Or, 'Did you score last night?'—like some great goal, scheming and forcing. (1976)

stuff (1960) Used transitively, of a male ■ *Sunday Times*: He was sacked from Eton for stuffing the boys' maids. (1983)

naughty (1961) Mainly Australian & New Zealand; used transitively; from the noun *naughty* (act of) sexual intercourse ■ C. Klein: He didn't want to dob the hard word on her, last thing he had on his mind was to try and naughty her. (1977)

saw a chunk (etc.) **off** (1961) ■ John Wainwright: The act is . . . known, in polite circles, as 'copulation'. Known, in less polite circles, as . . . 'sawing a length off'. (1977)

make time (1962) North American; often used to denote success in persuading someone to have sex; usually followed by *with*; from earlier sense, make (successful) sexual advances to ■ Dell Shannon: Frankly, he'd have liked to make time with that girl, but she'd turned up her nose at him. (1971)

trick (1965) US; used intransitively; applied to having casual sex, especially for money; usually followed by *with*; from the noun *trick* sexual intercourse (with a prostitute) ■ Joseph Wambaugh: He tricked with a whore the night before in the Orchid Hotel. (1973)

sex (1966) Used intransitively ■ J. Barnett: Maybe we sex together at yo' place. (1980)

lay pipe (1967) US; used of a man, implying vigorous copulation ■ Arthur Hailey: It made him horny just to look at her, and he laid pipe, sometimes three times a night. (1971)

shtup (1969) Used transitively and intransitively; from earlier sense, push; from Yiddish; compare German *stupfen* nudge, jog ■ Donald Westlake: He'd go on home . . . shtup the wife . . . then shlep on back here. (1974) ■ *Custom Car*: Italian men can actually murder their wives if they find 'em shtupping around. (1977)

get one's **nuts off** (1970) Orig US; applied to a man obtaining sexual release by copulation and ejaculation; from *nuts* testicles

shaft (1970) Used transitively, of a male; compare *shaft* penis ■ B. W. Aldiss: How sinful he looked, squatting there by the water while his wife was being shafted by some dirty big Mendip only a few feet away! (1971)

tup (1970) Used transitively, of a man; from earlier sense, of a ram, to copulate with (a ewe) ■ Roderic Jeffries: You wouldn't tup her? . . . Neither of us cut out for adultery. (1976)

bonk (1975) British; used transitively and intransitively; from earlier sense, hit resoundingly or with a thud ■ *Daily Telegraph*: Fiona . . . has become so frustrated that she has been bonking the chairman of the neighbouring constituency's Conservative association. (1986)

get (or **have**) one's **end away** (1975) British; usually used of a man ■ *Guardian*: They called him Grandad, asked him how his girlfriends were. 'Are you getting it?' they kept repeating. 'Getting your end away?' (1995)

get (**have**, etc.) one's **leg over** (1975) Used of a man; compare 18th-century *lift a leg over* (someone) in same sense ■ D. Kartun: Daft spending like that on a tart like her. Half the garrison have had their leg over. (1987)

Having sex

up (1937) Applied to a man having sex with (someone) ■ James Patrick: We've aw been up her. (1973)

on the job (1966) Applied to someone engaged in sexual intercourse ■ *Daily Telegraph*: 'Why the hell did you play Eric Clapton's Easy Now? . . . Didn't you realise it was all about some guy on the job?' And I said, 'Yeah. How many songs aren't?' (1972)

To achieve orgasm

come (*c*1600) Sometimes followed by *off* ■ D. H. Lawrence: And when I'd come and really finished, then she'd start on her own account. (1928)

spend (1662) ■ R. L. Duncan: He felt himself spending at the very moment she contracted around him. (1980)

go off (*c*1866) ■ Henry Miller: Bango! I went off like a whale. (1949)

get off on (1973) Denoting experiencing orgasm by means of something ■ Newton Thornburg: And the shrink getting off on it all, sitting there with one hand stuck in his fly. (1976)

Multiple sex

daisy chain (a1927) Applied to sexual activity involving three or more people ■ Saul Bellow: You have to do more than take a little gas, or slash the wrists. Pot? Zero! Daisy chains? Nothing! Debauchery? A museum word. (1964)

gang-shag (1927) US; applied to an act of or occasion for multiple intercourse, especially one in which several men in succession have sex with the same woman

gang-bang (1945) Orig US; applied to an act of or occasion for multiple intercourse, especially one in which several men in succession have sex with the same woman ■ Bill Turner: What's the next arrangement to be? A gang-bang for the whole Vice Squad? (1968). Hence the verb **gang-bang** (1949) ■ *Guardian*: A pretty 18-year-old girl . . . used to 'stuff' herself with heroin and let herself be 'gang-banged' all the time. (1969)

To perform oral sex (on)

gamahuche, gamaruche (1865) Dated; from French slang *gamahucher* in the same sense ■ P. Perret: My dear, do you know, this is my only ambition! To gamahuche a lady of fashion! (1888)

eat (1916) Orig US ■ Lisa Alther: '*Eat me*,' he said, seizing my head with his hands and fitting my mouth around his cock and moving my head back and forth. (1975)

go down (1916) Orig US; usually followed by *on* ■ Kate Millett: I do not want her body. Do not want to see it, caress it, go down on it. (1974)

French (1923) From the noun *French* oral sex ■ Wayland Young: In England . . . we call . . . cunt-licking Frenching. (1965)

suck (1928) Used intransitively or (usually followed by *off*) transitively ■ *Guardian*: One American GI is forcing a Vietnamese woman to suck him off. (1971) ■ E. Hannon: White chicks dig suckin, that's a fact. That's cause suckin's sophisticated. (1975)

plate (1961) ■ Fabian & Byrne: I wondered whether I should plate him. I hadn't done much of that, but I knew guys on the scene liked it because Nigel had told me so. (1969)

give head (1967) Orig US ■ *Independent*: A scene in which Wesley Snipes refuses to accept that cunnilingus can be a fulfilling alternative to intercourse has raised many eyebrows, not least for including the line, 'Black guys don't give head'. (1992)

Oral sex

sixty-nine, **69** (1888) Applied to mutual oral stimulation of the genitals; literal translation of French *soixante-neuf* in same sense ■ D. Lang: We spent many hours lying on her bed, more or less in the classical 69 position, but motionless. (1973)

soixante-neuf (1888) Applied to mutual oral stimulation of the genitals; French, literally sixty-nine; from the position of the couple ■ Martin Amis: The other couple were writhing about still, now seemingly poised for a session of fully robed soixante-neuf. (1973)

French (1916) From the supposed predilection of the French for oral sex ■ Tony Parker: There's two things I won't let her do though, that's French and sadism. (1969)

To perform cunnilingus

eat pussy (*c*1938) Orig US; also used more generally to denote sexual intercourse ■ M. McClure: When we talk about eating pussy we make it sound as dirty and vulgar as possible. (1967)

A cunnilinguist

muff-diver (1935) ■ Julie Burchill: A Designer Dyke isn't just any old muff-diver; oh goshi, no. (1986)

To fellate

blow (*c*1930) Orig US; from an analogy with playing a musical wind instrument ■ Philip Roth: 'I want you to come in my mouth,' and so she blew me. (1969)

nosh (1965) From earlier sense, eat

Fellatio

blow job (1942) Orig US ■ P. Booth: Turning the other cheek was for girls who hadn't had to give blow jobs to tramps in exchange for a few pieces of candy. (1986)

A fellator or fellatrix

prick-sucker (1868) ■ *New Direction*: From then onward she became an ardent Prick-sucker. (1974)

cock-sucker (1891) ■ *Playboy*: I know one women's lib leader who, friends tell me, is a great cock-sucker. (1971)

Someone with unconventional sexual tastes

perv, **perve** (1944) Orig Australian; short for *pervert* ■ E. Lambert: He was a perv. Special attention given to small boys. (1959). Hence **pervy** (1944) ■ G. F. Newman: Twenty maximum security, the lights never out, pervy screws watching every movement. (1970)

secko (1949) Australian; applied to a sexual deviant or sex offender; from *sex* + *-o* ■ W. Dick: You look like you'd be the sorta bloke who'd take little kids down a lane and give 'em two bob, yuh bloody secko. (1969)

kinky (1959), **kink** (1965) Ultimately from *kink* twist, abnormality ■ Adam Diment: Porny photos, various drugs and birds for kinkies at Oxford. (1967) ■ J. Ripley: I have known queers. I have known kinks. (1972). So the adjective **kinky** (1959) ■ Francis Warner: Kinky sex makes them feel inadequate. (1972)

nonce (1975) British, prisoners' slang; applied to someone convicted of a sexual offence, especially child-molesting; origin uncertain; perhaps from *nancy* male homosexual, but compare British dialect *nonce* good-for-nothing fellow ■ *Sunday Telegraph*: As what prisoners call a 'nonce', he now faces years of solitary confinement and regular assaults from fellow inmates. (1986)

Sado-masochism

fladge, **fladj**, **flage** (1958) Applied to flagellation as a means of sexual gratification, and also to pornographic literature concentrating on flagellation; shortened from *flagellation* ■ J. I. M. Stewart: I have some damned odd fantasies when it comes to quiet half-hours with sex. Flage, and all that. (1975)

Anal sex

postilion, **postillion** (1888) Denoting stimulating a sexual partner anally with the finger

ream (1942) US; denoting having anal sex with someone; from earlier sense, widen a hole ■ Tom Wolfe: The man reams him so hard the pain brings him to his knees. (1979)

rim (1959) US; denoting licking the anus, especially before sexual intercourse; probably a variant of *ream* ■ Martin Amis: Skip'd rim a snake so long as someone held its head. (1975)

fist-fuck (*a*1972) Orig US; used as a noun and a verb to denote the insertion of the hand into the rectum as a means of sexual gratification. Hence the nouns **fist-fucking** (*a*1972), **fisting** (1981)

To expose one's genitals as a means of sexual gratification

flash (1846) Used of a man; from the brevity of the exposure ■ Gore Vidal: Men stared at me. Some leered. None, thank God, flashed. (1978). Hence **flasher** a man who does this (1962) ■ Anthony Powell: He was apparently a 'flasher', who had just exposed himself. (1976)

Autoeroticism

scarfing (1994) British; applied to the practice of auto-asphyxiation for sexual stimulation

To masturbate

rub up (1656) In earliest use transitive; not recorded intransitively until the 20th century ■ Compton Mackenzie: Just as I was going down the steps into our area B—asked me if I ever rubbed up. . . . In bed that night I tried the experiment recommended by B—. (1963)

frig (1680) From earlier sense, have sex (with) ■ *My Secret Life*: I have frigged myself in the streets before entering my house, sooner than fuck her. (*c*1888)

toss off (1879) ■ D. Kavanagh: Would you like me to toss you off? . . . It's ten if you're worried about the price. (1981)

pull off (1922) ■ Leonard Cohen: Can an old scholar find love at last and stop having to pull himself off every night so he can get to sleep? (1966)

diddle (1934) From earlier sense, have sex (with) ■ Kate Millett: Paraphernalia with the scarf. . . . Supposed to diddle herself with it. Male fantasy of lonely chick masturbating in sad need of him. (1974)

jerk off (1937) ■ Bernard Malamud: The mother . . . dies unattended, of malnutrition, as Herbert jerks off in the hall toilet. (1971)

pull one's **pudding** (or **wire**) **(1944)** ■ Wilbur Smith: Jesus. . . . That was ugly. I felt like a peeping tom, watching someone, you know, pulling his pudding. (1970) ■ John Osborne: Remember what I said about sex. Keep away from the maids and pretty boys. As for pulling your wire, that's no occupation for a gentleman. (1970)

wank (1950) Often followed by *off*; origin unknown ■ William McIlvanney: You've been wankin'. . . . That's no' nice in public places. (1977) ■ Julian Barnes: I saw a monkey in the street jump on a donkey and try to wank him off. (1984). Hence **wanker** (1950) ■ B. W. Aldiss: Failed fucker, failed wanker was an inglorious double billing. (1971)

jack off (1959) ■ R. A. Carter: You miserable little queer. . . . You can jack off in Llewellyn's best hat for all I care. (1971)

beat the (or one's) **meat (1967)** Orig US; from *meat* penis ■ Julia O'Faolain: What did people do in a place like this? Beat their meat probably. (1980)

whack off (1969) US ■ *Transatlantic Review*: 'What-in-hell you do for sex anyway?' he asked the boy one night. 'Whack off into the tin pot where they keep the mashed potatoes?' (1977)

Masturbation

pocket billiards (1940) Orig schoolboys' slang; applied to playing with the testicles with one's hands in one's trouser pockets, for masturbatory stimulation; often in the phrase *play pocket billiards*

wank (1948) Applied to an act of (male) masturbation; origin unknown ■ *Sniffin' Glue*: Behind that bog door are you thinkin', readin' or just havin' a wank? (1977)

hand-job (1969) ■ D. Leavitt: First he had been satisfied with the films alone; then a quick hand-job in the back row. (1986)

Contraceptives

French letter, french letter (c1856), Frenchy, frenchy, Frenchie (1953) Mainly British; applied to a condom; *letter* perhaps = hinderer, from *let* hinder ■ J. R. Ackerley: My elder brother Peter was the accident. 'Your father happened to have

run out of french letters that day.' (1968) ■ Tom Sharpe: You can't feel a thing with a Frenchie. You get more thrill with the pill. (1976)

safe (1897) Applied to a condom ■ E. Koch: Just in time he remembered his safe. He took it out of his pants pocket. (1979)

rubber (1947) Applied to a condom ■ William Gaddis: What are you reading? . . . Malthus, for Christ sake. . . . The next thing, you'll be peddling rubbers in the street. (1955)

frog, froggie (1952) Australian; applied to a condom; from *frog* French (person), in allusion to *French letter* condom ■ A. Buzo: 'Jees I forgot the frog,' he said. . . . I was disgusted. I put my pants back on and told him to take me home immediately. (1969)

skin (1960) Orig US; applied to a condom ■ Tom Sharpe: 'You got those rubbers you use?' he asked suddenly. . . . 'I want those skins.' (1976)

johnny (1965) British; applied to a condom; from the male personal name ■ *Times Educational Supplement*: [A mark of] 100 . . . , my informant wrote, 'is rightly reserved for full intercourse without a johnny'. (1970)

scumbag (1967) Mainly US; applied to a condom; from *scum* semen + *bag* ■ *Time Out*: Young blades carried their sheaths or condoms or . . . 'scumbags' in their wallets. (1974)

rubber johnny (1980) Applied to a condom ■ *Guardian*: Can't be easy for a bishop to buy rubber johnnies in the Irish Republic. (1992)

Pornographic, erotic

naughty (1882) Euphemistic ■ *Guardian*: A News of the World reporter had approached her first husband . . . asking if he had any 'naughty photographs' of her. (1991)

hot (1892) ■ J. T. Farrell: A burlesque show. The hottest ones were south of Van Buren. (1935)

sexational, sexsational (1928) Orig US; blend of *sex* and *sensational* ■ *West Lancs. Evening Gazette*: 1st Blackpool showing of the Sexsational *Highway through the Bedroom* (X). (1976)

feelthy (1933) Jocular imitation of a foreign pronunciation of *filthy* ■ B. S. Johnson: Maurie has a great collection of feelthy books down here—including a first edition of Cleland's *Fanny Hill, or the Memoirs of a Woman of Pleasure*. (1963)

jerk-off (c1957) From *jerk off* masturbate; from the notion of such material as a stimulus to masturbation

adult (1958) Euphemistic, orig US; from the unsuitability of such material for children ■ *Tampa (Florida) Tribune*: Rentals for adult videos outstrip purchases by 12 to 1. (1984)

porny (1961) From *porn(ographic* + *-y* ■ J. Wilson: You make it sound like one of those porny books—'His hand caressed her silken knee' and all that rubbish. (1973)

beaver (1967) Applied to photographs, films, etc. that feature the female genitals and pubic area; from the noun *beaver* female genitals or pubic area ■ M. Gee: He hadn't been very intelligent . . . showing him the skin flick picture of Moira. . . . It was probably too dirty, they can't use beaver shots. (1981)

raunchy (1967) Applied to something sexually suggestive, salacious, or bawdy; from earlier sense, disreputable, grubby ■ D. Anthony: If you mean *Couplings*, I liked it. . . . I happen to like raunchy films. (1977)

steamy (1970) ■ R. McInerny: It was a moral outlook, one that had never . . . been disturbed by the steamy fiction that was her steady diet. (1980)

split beaver (1972) Applied to photographs of the female genitals that show the inner labia

tit(s) and ass (or **arse**), **tits and bums (1972)** Denoting the crude display of female sexuality on stage, in films, newspapers, magazines, etc. ■ *Sunday Times*: Ugly George, America's prime TV porn artist (who invites women to undress for his video camera), with his 'tit n' ass' cable channel. (1982)

Pornography

leg art (1940) Orig US; applied to portrayals of scantily clad or naked women

pornie (1966) Applied to a pornographic film; from *porn(ographic + -ie* ■ *Publishers Weekly*: A nice California kid until she was conned into filming pornies to pay off her lover's addict brother's connection. (1975)

schmutz, shmutz (1968) Mainly US; from earlier sense, dirt, filth, from Yiddish or German *schmutz* ■ Mordecai Richler: 'Of my son's ability there is no question.' '—and, em, the contents of your son's novel. You see—' '*Shmutz*,' Daniels shouted at Katansky. 'Pardon?' 'Filth. Today nothing sells like filth.' (1968)

See also **beefcake** at Sexually attractive man (p. 69); **cheesecake** at Sexually attractive woman (p. 70).

To make more sexy

sex up (1942) ■ *Observer*: Reads rather like an old-time boy's book sexed up and sadistified for the 1950s. (1959)

Virginity

cherry (1918) Orig US; often in the phrase *lose one's cherry*; also applied to a virgin (1935); from the red colour of the vagina or of the blood from the ruptured hymen ■ R. H. Rimmer: The day I lost my cherry didn't amount to much, anyway. (1975) ■ Mordecai Richler: Gin excites them. Horseback riding gives them hot pants too. Cherries are trouble, but married ones miss it something terrible. (1959)

Virility

lead in one's **pencil (1941)** Often in the phrase *put lead in one's pencil* enable one to have an erection ■ Dan Lees: The couscous is supposed to put lead in your pencil but with Daria I needed neither a talking point nor an aphrodisiac. (1972)

Relationships

old flame (1840) Applied to a former lover; from earlier more general use of *flame* for 'lover' ■ *Sun*: You walk into a pub or a party and see an old flame standing there with someone new. (1992)

bach, batch (1855) North American, Australian, & New Zealand; abbreviation of *bachelor*. Hence the verb **bach, batch** live alone and do one's own cooking and housekeeping (1862) ■ D. Ireland: How are you getting on, batching? Are you going to get married again? (1971)

split up (1903) Denoting ending a relationship ■ W. Corlett: 'He thought his parents were . . . splitting up?' 'Divorce? . . . he thought it was on the cards.' (1976)

sleeping dictionary (1928) Applied to a foreign woman with whom a man has a sexual relationship and from whom he learns the rudiments of her language

seven-year itch (1936) Applied jocularly to an urge to infidelity after seven years of marriage ■ Patricia Moyes: There's something called the seven-year itch . . . middle-aged men quite suddenly cutting loose. (1980)

item (1970) Orig US; applied to a pair of lovers regarded (especially socially acknowledged) as a couple ■ Kurt Vonnegut: I hadn't realized that he and she had been an item when they were both at Tarkington, but I guess they were. (1990)

To have a sexual relationship (with)

carry on (1856) Often followed by *with* ■ W. S. Maugham: It was impossible that she could be 'carrying on' with Lord George. (1930)

go with (1892) ■ H. K. Fink: I was going with girls . . . and I didn't feel the urge to play with myself. (1954)

go steady (1905) Orig US; denoting having a regular boyfriend or girlfriend ■ Fay Weldon: I'm going steady with one of the young doctors. (1978)

shack up, be shacked up (1935) Applied to people who cohabit, especially as lovers; usually followed by *with* or *together* ■ David Lodge: Philip Swallow is shacked up with Melanie at that address. (1975)

have something going (1971) Denoting having a close (sexual) relationship; often followed by *with* ■ *Philadelphia Inquirer*: Is it true that Sammy Davis Jr. has something going with Linda Lovelace? (1973)

An expert on sexual matters

sexpert (1924) Orig US; blend of *sex* and *expert* ■ *Radio Times*: Every other interviewed sexpert seemed to come from California where . . . you can graduate in any old spurious subject. (1979)

13. **Sexual Orientation**

Homosexual
....

queer (1922) Mainly derogatory; also in the phrase *as queer as a coot* ■ Alan White: 'I say, Peter, you're not turning *queer* by any chance, are you?' The thought that I might be queer had haunted me. (1976)

so (1937) Dated, orig euphemistic ■ J. R. Ackerley: A young 'so' man, picked up by Arthur in a Hyde Park urinal. (1968)

bent (1959) Derogatory; from earlier sense, out of order ■ Frederick Raphael: 'Great thing about gay people. . . .' 'Gay?' Tessa said. 'Bent, queer, you know. Homosexual.' (1960)

that way (a1960) Euphemistic ■ J. R. Ackerley: I divined that he was homosexual, or as we put it, 'one of us,' 'that way', 'so', or 'queer'. (a1967)

A homosexual
....

homo (1929) Mainly derogatory; also used as an adjective; abbreviation ■ *Listener*: Sally's breathless confession to Dr Dale about hubby being a homo must have caused many a benighted bigot's heart to stop. (1967)

one of those, one of them (1933), one of us (1961) Euphemistic ■ J. R Ackerley: I divined that he was homosexual, or as we put it, 'one of us'. (a1967) ■ *Gay News*: Her husband . . . probably fits none of the stereotypes whereby she would normally identify 'one of those'. (1977)

queer (1935), queerie (1938) Mainly derogatory; applied especially to male homosexuals; from the adjective *queer* ■ Angus Wilson: I quite like queers if it comes to that, so long as they're not on the make. (1952) ■ Bruce Rodgers: That little "queerie" is the only one I know who shoots Sal Hepatica. (1972)

ginger-beer, ginger (1959) Also used as an adjective; rhyming slang for *queer* ■ A. Williams: 'Unless you prefer ginger.' 'Ginger?' 'Beer, dear.' . . . 'You ever meet an Aussie who was queer?' (1968)

A male homosexual
....

sod (c1855) Derogatory; abbreviation of *sodomite* ■ Percy Wyndham Lewis: When you come to write your book, its scene our day to day life, I should put in the sods. Sartre has shown what a superb figure of comedy a homo can be. (1949)

poof, pouf, pouff, poove (1860) Derogatory; also applied more broadly to an effeminate man; probably an alteration of *puff* braggart ■ A. Richards: A young man . . . had been heard in the showers to refer to Elgar as 'a bit of a pouf'. (1976). Hence the verb *poof*, etc. denoting behaving effeminately or like a male homosexual (1971)

Mary Ann, Mary (1880) Derogatory; from the female personal name(s

wife (1883) Applied to the passive member of a homosexual partnership ■ Joseph Hyams: The group's leader [a homosexual] . . . made his 'wife' head of production. (1978)

pretty-boy (1885) Mainly derogatory; also applied more broadly to an effeminate man

fairy (1895) Derogatory; applied to an effeminate male homosexual; from earlier sense, woman ■ Evelyn Waugh: Two girls stopped near our table and looked at us curiously. 'Come on,' said one to the other, 'we're wasting our time. They're only fairies.' (1945)

fruit (1900) Derogatory, orig US ■ *Guardian*: He is a fruit, which means . . . that he is a queer. (1970)

puff (1902) Derogatory; also applied more broadly to an effeminate man; compare *pouf* ■ H. W. Sutherland: He'd be a puff boy, this Magnie, and God knows what entertainment he laid on for Arthur. (1967)

poofter, pooftah, poofteroo (1903) Derogatory, mainly Australian; extension of *poof* ■ Ian Fleming: 'You pommy poofter.' . . . Bond said mildly, 'What's a poofter?' 'What you'd call a pansy.' (1964)

nancy, nancy-boy (1904) Derogatory; also applied more broadly to an effeminate man; from obsolete slang *Miss Nancy* effeminate man, from pet-form of the female forename *Ann* ■ Lawrence Durrell: I can't stand that Toto fellow. He's an open nancy-boy. (1958). Hence **nancified (1937)** ■ Kenneth Giles: Beautiful smooth dark rum, not like that nancified white stuff you poms put in your cokes. (1967)

punk (1904) Mainly US; applied to a passive male homosexual, or to a tramp's young male companion

lizzie, lizzie boy (1905) Applied to an effeminate young man; abbreviation of the female forename *Elizabeth* ■ N. L. McClung: She's married to a no-good Englishman, a real lizzie-boy. (1912)

faggot (1914) Orig and mainly US, derogatory; from earlier derogatory application to a woman ■ Harry Kane: Duffy was no queen, no platinum-dyed freak, no screaming faggot. (1962). Hence **faggoty (1927)** ■ A. Binkley: Albie in his faggoty silk pajamas. (1968)

wolf (1917) Orig US; applied to a male homosexual seducer or one who adopts an active role with a partner ■ K. J. Dover: In prisons the 'wolf' is the active homosexual, and does not reverse roles with his partners. (1978)

gunsel, gonsil, gunshel, gun(t)zel (1918) US; applied to tramp's young male companion or lover, and hence to any homosexual youth; from earlier sense, a naïve youth

fag (1921) US, derogatory; abbreviation of *faggot* ■ Lesley Egan: You can't tell the fags from outside looks. (1964). Hence **faggy (1951)** ■ John Le Carré: 'I had such a good time,' says Grant, with his quaint, rather faggy indignation. (1986)

nance (1924) Derogatory; short for *nancy* ■ Frederick Forsyth: We're looking for a fellow who screwed the arse off a Baroness . . . not a couple of raving nances. (1971)

queen (1924) Applied especially to a passive or effeminate homosexual; compare *quean* ■ Evelyn

Waugh: 'Now what may you want, my Italian queen?' said Lottie as the waiter came in with a tray. (1930). Hence **queeny** (1936) ■ Graham McInnes: Thereafter he said he'd rather play football with the other fellows: reading aloud was a bit 'queeny'. (1966)

bum-boy (1929) Derogatory; applied to a young male homosexual, especially a prostitute; from *bum* buttocks ■ Dylan Thomas: A ringed and dainty gesture copied from some famous cosmopolitan bumboy. (1938)

moffie, mophy (1929) Mainly South African; perhaps a shortening and alteration of *hermaphrodite*; compare Afrikaans *moffiedaai*, dialectal variant of *hermafrodiet* ■ *Post* (South Africa): The life of Edward Shadi—described as a beautiful, sexy moffie with a sweet soprano voice—was a strange affair. (1971)

pansy, pansy-boy (1929) Derogatory; *pansy* also used as an adjective ■ John Betjeman: There Bignose plays the organ And the pansies all sing flat. (1960) ■ Edmund Crispin: I'd want her to be walking out with a decent lad, not a pansy little foreign gramophone-record. (1951). Hence **pansy** (**up**) (1946) used to denote dressing or adorning affectedly or effeminately ■ John Wainwright: Originally, his hair had been mousy brown. He'd tried to pansy himself up—and failed. (1966)

ponce (1932) British, derogatory; also applied more broadly to an effeminate man; from earlier sense, pimp ■ Nik Cohn: Mods thought that Rockers were yobs, Rockers thought that Mods were ponces. (1969). Hence **ponce about** (1954) denoting behaving in an effeminate way

poncey, poncy (1964) ■ Martin Amis: You haven't half got poncy mates. (1973)

queenie, queeny (1933) Applied to effeminate male homosexuals, often as a term of address; from *queen* + *-ie* ■ James Curtis: 'You're not a man. You're a pouf.' . . . 'I'll show you who's a pouf.' 'Call yourself a man do you this morning, Queenie? Well you wasn't one last night, see. You gets into bed and goes straight off to kip.' (1936)

flit (1935) US, derogatory; perhaps from the notion of light fluttering effeminate movements ■ J. D. Salinger: Sometimes it was hard to believe, the people he said were flits and lesbians. (1951)

jocker (1935) North American; from earlier sense, tramp with a young homosexual companion

quean (1935) Applied to an effeminate male homosexual; the original sense of *quean* is 'woman', and it was generally used as a term of abuse, 'strumpet, harlot, etc.'; it is not clear whether *queen* represents the older form (it is certainly the commoner spelling), and whether *quean* is just a purist's respelling ■ J. R. Ackerley: I did not want him to think me 'queer' and himself a part of homosexuality, a term I disliked since it included prostitutes, pansies, pouffs and queans. (1968)

tart (1935) Applied to the young homosexual companion of an older man, or loosely to a male prostitute ■ *Times Literary Supplement*: The boys that

Isherwood and his friends picked up were not professional tarts only out for what they could get. (1977)

trade (1935) Applied to someone picked up for homosexual activity, or to such people collectively; especially in the phrase *rough trade* a rough or especially lower-class person (or people) engaged in homosexual prostitution ■ *Jeremy*: These are men who because they are too old, or unattractive, cannot pick up free 'trade'. (1969) ■ *Playboy*: The gay boys call us 'rough trade'! We're the ones they date. . . . We're the ones they buy presents for. (1965)

iron (1936) Derogatory; short for *iron hoof*, rhyming slang for *poof* ■ Eric Partridge: Gorblimey, 'e's an iron, did'n yeh know? (1961)

sister (1941) Orig US; applied to a fellow homosexual, or to a homosexual who is a friend rather than a lover

swish (1941) US, derogatory; also applied more broadly to an effeminate man ■ J. F. Burke: [He] dresses mod, and he talks like some kind of a swish. (1975). Hence **swishy** (1941) ■ Christopher Isherwood: You thought it meant a swishy little boy with peroxided hair, dressed in a picture hat and a feather boa, pretending to be Marlene Dietrich? Yes, in queer circles, they call that camping. (1954)

pussy (1942) Also applied more broadly to an effeminate man or boy; from earlier sense, woman ■ Lawrence Durrell: 'I first met Henry James in a brothel in Algiers. He had a naked houri on each knee.' 'Henry James was a pussy, I think.' (1958)

tonk (1943) Mainly Australian; compare earlier sense, fool ■ *TV Times* (Australia): There was also a homosexual (who was referred to as a 'tonk'—thereby dating Mr Porter rather badly). (1970)

wonk (1945) Australian, derogatory; also applied more broadly to an effeminate man; from earlier sense, white man ■ Patrick White: I'd have to have a chauffeur to drive me about—with a good body—just for show, though. I wouldn't mind if the chauffeur was a wonk. (1970)

white-shoe (1957) Derogatory, mainly US; used as an adjective to denote effeminacy

jessie, jessy (1958) Derogatory; from earlier sense, cowardly or ineffectual man ■ Kingsley Amis: Darling, you really don't have to convince me that you're not a jessie. (1958)

steamer (1958) Applied especially to a homosexual who seeks passive partners; perhaps from earlier sense, gullible person ■ *Times Literary Supplement*: Terry . . . spending his time . . . among the young homosexuals and their 'steamers'. (1958)

arse bandit (1961) Derogatory; applied especially to homosexual sodomists ■ *Private Eye*: The Chief Rabbi . . . is very sound in . . . things like cracking down on the arsebandits. (1989)

twinkie, twinky, twink (1963) US, derogatory; also applied more broadly to an effeminate man; probably related to the verbs *twink* 'twinkle' and *twinkle*, though popularly associated with the proprietary *Twinkie*, a brand of cupcake with a creamy filling

weeny (1963) US, derogatory; applied to an effeminate man; from earlier sense, girl

shirtlifter (1966) Australian, derogatory ■ Barry Humphries: When I first seen them photos of him in his 'Riverina Rig' I took him for an out-of-work ballet dancer or some kind of shirtlifter. (1974)

palone, polone, polony (1969) Derogatory; applied to an effeminate man; from earlier sense, young woman

nelly, nellie (1970) Applied especially to an ostentatious homosexual; from earlier senses, silly person, effeminate man ■ C. Wittman: There is a tendency among 'homophile' groups to deplore gays who play visible roles—the queens and the nellies. (1973)

woofter, wooftah (1977) Derogatory; fanciful alteration of *poofter* ■ *Observer:* A figure straight out of a P. G. Wodehouse story who . . . would be happy to give you his considered view that the BBC is run by a bunch of woofters in the pay of Moscow. (1996)

bufu (1982) US; probably from *butt-fucker*

she-male (1983) Applied to a passive male homosexual; from earlier US colloquial sense, woman

guppie (1984) Jocular or derogatory; applied to a homosexual yuppie; blend of *gay* and *yuppie*

friend of Dorothy (1988) From the name, *Dorothy*, of the heroine of L. Frank Baum's *Wizard of Oz* (1900). Judy Garland's performance in the role in the film version (1939) subsequently achieved cult status among gays ■ *Private Eye:* Just because you don't go on holiday with her doesn't mean you're a friend of Dorothy. (1990)

A female homosexual

bull-dyke(r), bull-dike(r) (1925) Derogatory; applied to a lesbian with masculine tendencies ■ J. Rechy: On the dance-floor, too, lesbians—the masculine ones, the bulldikes—dance with hugely effeminate queens. (1964)

les, les(s)ie, lessy, lez(z), lezzy (1929) Mainly derogatory; abbreviation of *lesbian* ■ *New Society:* I reckon she's a les you know. (1972)

dyke, dike (1931) Mainly derogatory; often applied specifically to a lesbian with masculine tendencies; perhaps from *morphadike*, a dialectal variant of *hermaphrodite* ■ Ed McBain: 'Was your wife a dyke?' 'No.' 'Are you a homosexual?' 'No.' (1965). Hence **dykey, dikey (1964)** ■ John Morris: Helen's gone dikey in her old age. (1969)

bulldagger (1938) US, mainly Black English, derogatory; applied to a lesbian with masculine tendencies; variant of *bull-dyker* (an intermediate form was *bull-digger* (a1929))

lesbo, lesbie (1940) Mainly derogatory; from *lesb(ian + -o* ■ Chester Himes: 'One was a man; a good-looking man at that.' 'Man my ass, they were lesbos.' (1969)

leso, lezo, lezzo (1945) Australian, mainly derogatory; from *les(bian + -o* ■ *National Times*

(Sydney): And *Gay!* What an insult to the poofs and lezzos who made this country what it is today! (1983)

lizzie (1949) Mainly derogatory; probably an alteration of *lesbian*, assimilated to the female personal name *Lizzie* ■ Julian Symons: You'd never have thought I was a lizzie, would you? And butch at that. (1970)

butch (1954) Orig US; applied to a lesbian with masculine tendencies; also used adjectivally; from earlier sense, tough young man ■ *New Statesman:* One of the femmes, secure in the loving protection of her butch. (1966)

femme (1957) Applied to a lesbian who adopts a passive, feminine role; from French *femme* woman ■ W. Brown: A step upward on the social ladder are the female transvestites and their '*femmes*' who congregate in the 'gay' bars of Greenwich Village. (1961)

diesel, diesel dyke (1958) Orig US; applied to a lesbian with aggressively masculine tendencies; from the stereotypically male associations of *diesel* engines, vehicles, etc.

Places of homosexual assignation

cottage (1932) British; applied to a public lavatory or urinal used by male homosexuals for assignations ■ *Guardian:* Wakefield's answer to Danny La Rue trips out of a little hutch at the side of the stage labelled 'Ye Olde Camp Cottage'. (1968)

tea room (1970) US; applied to a public lavatory used by homosexuals for assignations

Concealment and revelation

come out (1941), come out of the closet (1971) Orig US; used to denote open admission of one's homosexuality ■ *Literary Review:* Old Cheever, crowding seventy, has gone Gay. Old Cheever has come out of the closet. (1985)

closet queen (1959) Applied to a secret male homosexual ■ *Mail on Sunday:* His colleagues' retort is that Jimmy is a closet queen because he doesn't live with a woman. (1984)

out (1979) Used to denote open acknowledgement of one's homosexuality; from the notion of being '*out* of the closet' ■ *Venue:* Homosexuals find it easier to be 'out' than bisexuals. (1987). Hence the verb **out** reveal someone's homosexuality (1990) ■ *Los Angeles Times:* Instead of . . . outing this congressman, I . . . called to his attention the hypocrisy that he had been legislating against gays. (1990)

A homosexual's pimp

poofter rorter (1945) Australian; from *poofter* male homosexual + *rorter* fraudster

A woman who habitually consorts with homosexual men

fag hag (1969) Derogatory, orig and mainly US; rhyming formation on *fag* male homosexual + *hag* woman; compare earlier US *fag hag* woman who chain-smokes ■ Armistead Maupin: Do you think

I'm a fag hag? . . . Look at the symptoms. I hardly know any straight men anymore. (1978)

Assault on homosexuals

queer-bashing (1970) ■ *Times*: Four of 12 youths said to have taken part in a 'queer bashing' expedition on Wimbledon Common on September 25 were found Guilty of murder. (1970). Also **queer-basher** (1970) ■ *New Wave Magazine*: To fight the National Front, the queer-bashers and any other diseases. (1977)

(A) heterosexual

straight (1941) Orig US ■ *San Francisco Examiner*: A lot of us have 'straight' friends. (1965) ■ *Gay News*: It was a campaign shared and supported by a number of gays—even straights. (1977)

(A) bisexual

ambisextrous (1926) Jocular; blend of *ambidextrous* and *sex* ■ *Spectator*: She avoids ever producing her ambi-sextrous young publisher. (1960)

AC/DC, AC-DC (1954) Euphemistic, orig US; from the abbreviations *A.C.* 'alternating current' and *D.C.* 'direct current', suggesting contrasting options ■ Kate Millett: You can also tell *Time* Magazine you're bisexual, be AC-DC in the international edition. (1974)

bi (1956) Abbreviation of *bisexual* ■ *Listener*: Some were gay, many apparently bi, and a few were so hard that they would be given a wide berth in a Gorbals pub. (1983)

versatile (1959) Euphemistic ■ Muriel Spark: Dougal was probably pansy. 'I don't think so. . . . He's got a girl somewhere.' 'Might be versatile.' (1960)

switch-hitter (1960) US, euphemistic; from earlier sense, ambidextrous baseball batter ■ *Pussycat*: The buddy would shove cock to me. I can still remember the first switch-hitter. (1972)

ambidextrous (1966) Euphemistic, orig US; from earlier sense, able to use right and left hands equally well

bi-guy (1973) Applied to a bisexual male ■ *Gay News*: Good looking bi-guy, 30s . . . wants friendship with similar couple. (1977)

gender-bender, gender-blender (1980) Applied to someone, especially a pop singer or follower of a pop cult, who deliberately affects an androgynous appearance by wearing sexually ambiguous clothing, make-up, etc. Hence **gender-bending, gender-blending**

To be bisexual

swing both ways (1972) ■ J. G. Vermandel: As for the mystery that still surrounded Robin Aseltine's death, the police had picked up and questioned several former girl and boy friends, Robin having been found to swing both ways. (1972)

A transexual

shim (1975). Also applied to an effeminate or passive male homosexual and to a transvestite; a blend of *she* and *him*

A transvestite

drag queen (1941) Applied to a male homosexual transvestite; from *drag* women's clothing worn by men + *queen* male homosexual ■ *Listener*: He met . . . the prototype for Terri Dennis—the real-life drag queen being an altogether less arch, more interesting individual. (1984)

TV (1965) Orig and mainly North American; abbreviation of *transvestite* ■ *The Magazine*: We get a lot of TVs in and a few of the leather boys of course. (1983)

she-male (1983) From earlier colloquial US sense, woman

trannie (1983) From *tran(svestite + -ie* ■ *Gay Times*: By 11pm they seem drunkenly immune to the influx of trannies, trendies, and other creatures of the night. (1990)

14. **Prostitution**

Prostitutes

The distinction between the terminology applied to professional female prostitutes and sexually promiscuous women is very fine. Words denoting the former tend to be applied insultingly to women perceived as the latter, and words originally denoting the latter are frequently extended to the former. The same considerations apply to the terminology of male prostitutes and promiscuous homosexuals. See further under A promiscuous woman at **Sex** (pp. 67–8).

moll (1604) Dated; pet form of the female personal name *Mary*

hooker (1845) Mainly US; from the notion of 'hooking' clients ■ John Dos Passos: Ain't you got the sense to tell a good girl from a hooker? (1932)

frail (1846) Dated; short for *frail sister*, obsolete euphemism for *prostitute*

chromo (1883) Australian; abbreviation of *chromolithograph* picture lithographed in colours, with reference to the 'painted' face of the prostitute ■ John Iggulden: Some rotten poxy bitch of a chromo dubbed them in. (1960)

chippy, chippie (1886) Orig US, dated; from earlier sense, (sexually promiscuous) young woman ■ *Times Literary Supplement*: Opal and other 'chippies' at Moll's 'sporting house'. (1938)

tart (1894) From earlier sense, (sexually promiscuous) woman ■ Graham Greene: A woman policeman kept an eye on the tarts at the corner. (1936)

broad (1914) Orig and mainly US; from earlier sense, woman ■ *John o' London's*: Prostitutes are variously termed *tarts, toms, broads*. (1962)

gash (1914) From earlier sense, woman

muff (1914) Orig US; from earlier sense, (sexually promiscuous) woman ■ Louis Jackson & C. R. Hellyer: 'The muffs are cruising on the drag tonight', i.e. soliciting on the street. (1914)

hustler (1924) From earlier sense, person who lives by dishonest or immoral means ■ John Steinbeck: They would think she was just a buzzed old hustler. (1952)

lady of the night (or **evening**) (1925) Euphemistic ■ *Gainesville* (Florida) *Sun*: Around Subic Bay in the Philippines, the U.S. military men outnumber the licensed ladies of the night by 20,000 to 8,000. (1984)

prosty, prostie (1930) US; abbreviation of *prostitute* ■ J. Hayes: If she was a prostie, he couldn't afford her fee. (1976)

quiff (1931) Compare earlier dialectal sense, young woman, and the obsolete slang verb *quiff* copulate, of obscure origin

brass (1934) British; short for *brass nail*, rhyming slang for *tail* ■ Frank Norman: His old woman who was a brass on the game. (1958)

scupper (1935) From earlier sense, hole in a ship's side to carry away water

pro (1937) Abbreviation of (*professional*) *prostitute* ■ Ed McBain: Benny already had himself two girls . . . experienced pros who were bringing in enough cash each week to keep him living pretty good. (1976)

pross, pros (1937) Abbreviation of *prostitute* ■ J. Seabrook: She's been hanging round the Cherry Tree— that's the pub where all the old prosses go—and she's been going down there since she was thirteen. (1973)

bimbo (1937) From earlier sense, (sexually promiscuous) woman ■ Stanley Kauffmann: Not that you were just a bimbo to me. . . . I've discovered that I'm a little in love with you too. (1952)

mystery (1937) Applied to a young or inexperienced prostitute; from earlier sense, girl newly arrived in a town or city ■ G. F. Newman: Instead of calling a couple of mysteries, he called a cab. (1974)

prossy, prossie, prozzy (1941) Orig Australian; from *pross* + *-y* ■ Frederick Raphael: A shipmate of mine had this gag. . . . 'What's in a prossie's telegram?' Answer, 'Come at once.' (1971)

tom (1941) British; from earlier Australian sense, woman or girlfriend ■ Macdonald Hastings: I'll bet she's holding out on us. We know these toms, sir. (1955)

pusher (1944) From earlier sense, young woman ■ Alan Wykes: A pusher for me. I'm off the beer, but I could use a judy. (1944)

poule-de-luxe (1946) French, 'luxury hen' ■ *Times Literary Supplement*: Returns to France to find that his wife has remarried and that his daughter is in business as a *poule de luxe* and doing very well. (1976)

crow, cro (1950) Australian; probably an abbreviation of *chromo* prostitute ■ B. Herbert: What are you, anyway? A Kings Cross crow. Every Yank in town's been rootin' you. (1980)

twopenny upright (1958) From the charge made for an act of sexual intercourse standing up out of doors ■ *Maledicta*: At the turn of the century, an Iowa woman was awarded $200 for being called a 'whore', while in England, at about the same time, a woman was denied any award for being called a 'two-penny upright'. (1978)

scrubber (1959) Perhaps from earlier Australian sense, animal that runs wild in 'scrub' country, or (from the related sense, slovenly woman) from the notion of one who 'scrubs' hard to clean ■ Robin Cook: This aged scrubber, Mrs. Marengo . . . she was so old, forty. (1962)

slack (1959) ■ Wayland Young: The slack is afraid of disease, and afraid of the sex maniac who thinks it'd be fun to strangle her. (1965)

yum-yum girl, yum-yum tart (1960) Euphemistic; from *yum-yum* sexual activity ■ Art Buchwald: Don't let her kid you. All her girls are really yum-yum girls from the dance halls. (1962)

working girl (1968) Euphemistic, orig US ■ *Chicago Sun-Times*: U.S. Prostitutes has estimated that thousands of 'working girls' will travel to San Francisco for business generated by the convention. (1984)

slag (1970) From earlier sense, promiscuous woman ■ David Craig: Does anyone care what happens to a slag? (1970)

pavement princess (1976) Citizens' band; applied to a prostitute who touts for business over the radio network

Male prostitutes

renter (1893) ■ Oscar Wilde: I would sooner be blackmailed by every renter in London, than have you bitter, unjust, hating. (1893)

bum-boy (1929) From *bum* buttocks

rough trade (1935) Applied to male homosexual prostitute practices, or to someone picked up for these; from earlier sense, the tough or sadistic element among male homosexuals ■ Cecil Beaton: He made friends too easily with the 'rough trade'. (1978)

trade (1935) Also used as a collective term for male prostitutes ■ Jeremy: These are men who because they are too old, or unattractive, cannot pick up free 'trade'. (1969)

pimp (1942) US; from earlier sense, procurer

rent (1967) Used adjectivally to denote a male prostitute ■ *Gay News*: A word of warning about the Strand Bar in Hope Street. . . . It's rough and some of the people there are rent. (1977)

rent-boy (1969) ■ Deakin & Willis: Between the ages of fifteen and twenty he had been a rent boy, a boy prostitute living and working in the West End. (1976)

chicken (1988) Applied to a young inexperienced male prostitute; compare earlier services' slang sense, young male companion ■ *Guardian*: The chickens . . . these days are much wiser. They don't hang around Euston Station, they come straight to the places they have read about where they know they can do business. (1988)

Working as a prostitute

on the turf (1860) ■ J. O'Donoghue: 'I might have been one of Ma Dolma's brasses for all you know.' . . . 'Come off it. You've never been on the turf.' (1984)

on the game (1898) Mainly British; compare 'Set them down for sluttish spoils of opportunity, and daughters of the game', Shakespeare, *Troilus and Cressida* (1606) ■ Tony Parker: Betty's on the game, isn't she? Has she got you at it too. (1969)

on the bash (1936) British ■ *Streetwalker* [Anon.]: From the hours you keep . . . I'd say you were on the bash. (1959)

on the knock (1969) *knock* from earlier sense, copulation ■ Desmond Bagley: Maybe she was on the knock. (1969)

To work as a prostitute

hustle (1930) Orig US; probably a back-formation from *hustler* ■ *Listener*: She . . . revolted in revenge against her family, 'hustled' in Piccadilly, hated men as clients, took a ponce. (1959)

hawk one's mutton (1937) From obsolete slang *mutton* female genitals ■ James Patrick: They're aw cows hawkin' their mutton. (1973)

hook (1959) Back-formation from *hooker* ■ Disch & Sladek: Bessie's girls didn't have to go out hooking in hotel lobbies or honkytonks, no indeedy. (1969)

tom (1964) From the noun *tom* prostitute ■ Z. Progl: They were perfectly willing to go 'tomming' on the streets to earn a few quid, but I never could. (1964)

Prostitution

the trade (1680) ■ Eric Partridge: *The trade* is prostitution: late C. 18–19. (1937) ■ K. A. Porter: Two inordinately dressed-up young Cuban women, frankly ladies of trade, had been playing cards together in the bar for an hour before the ship sailed. (1962)

An assignation with a prostitute

trick (1926) Orig & mainly US; from earlier sense, a robbery; especially in the phrase *turn a trick* (of a prostitute) have a session with a client ■ *Time*: Some of the young prostitutes live at home and turn tricks merely for pocket money. (1977)

short time (1937) Used to denote a brief visit to a prostitute, or a brief stay in a hotel for sexual purposes ■ *Guardian*: Miles of girlie bars, short time hotels. (1971)

business (1983) ■ John Ayto: Prostitutes' use of *business* both to designate their occupation and as a shorthand euphemism for their services—as in 'You want business, love?' (1993)

A prostitute's client

short-timer (1923) Applied to someone who visits a prostitute or stays briefly at a hotel for

sexual purposes ■ Graham Greene: The shabby hotel to which 'short timers' come. (1939)

trick (1925) From earlier sense, assignation with a prostitute ■ Bill Turner: I doubt there's one trick in twenty who isn't a married man. (1968)

sugar daddy (1926) Orig US; applied to an elderly man who lavishes gifts on a young woman (in return for sex) ■ *Times*: Norma Levy, a prostitute, had a 'sugar daddy' called Bunny who paid her rent and gave her a Mercedes car. (1973)

john, John (1928) Orig US; from the male personal name *John* ■ *New York*: Many working girls, when they are new in the city, spend at least a few months with a madam to meet the better johns. (1972)

score (1961) ■ George Baxt: I got my hot tail out of there. I heard the score yelling. (1972)

Brothels

kip, kip-house, kip-shop (1766) British, dated; compare Danish *kippe* mean hut, low alehouse; *horekippe* brothel

crib, crib-house, crib-joint (*c*1857) Mainly US; from obsolete slang *crib* house, pub, etc. ■ Peter Gammond et al.: Forced into dives and crib-joints of the red-light district of New Orleans. (1958)

drum (1859) Mainly US; from earlier sense, place where someone lives ■ Criena Rohan: Each one of these houses was that dreariest, dullest, loneliest and ugliest institution in the whole history of harlotry—the one-woman drum. (1963)

knocking-shop (1860) From *knock* have sex with ■ Ludovic Kennedy: Yes, it seems that some of the girls are running a knocking-shop on the side. (1969)

parlour-house (1872) Mainly US; applied to an expensive type of brothel

hook-shop (1889) From *hooker* prostitute ■ John Steinbeck: This kid could be pure murder in a hook-shop. (1954)

meat-house (1896) From obsolete slang *meat* prostitute

meat-market (1896), meat rack (1972) Applied to a place or area where prostitutes ply their trade, and to a place frequented by people (heterosexuals or homosexuals) in search of sexual partners; from obsolete slang *meat* prostitute ■ John Osborne: Every tart and pansy boy in the district are in that place. . . . It's just a meat-market. (1957)

creep-house (1913), creep joint (1921) US; applied especially to a brothel or other place where prostitutes rob their clients ■ Alan Lomax: Creep joints where they'd put the feelers on a guy's clothes. (1950)

slaughter-house (1928) Applied to a cheap brothel ■ William Faulkner: Both of you get to hell back to that slaughterhouse. (1962)

cat-house (1931) Compare obsolete slang *cat* prostitute ■ George Orwell: He's took her abroad an' sold her to one o' dem flash cat-houses in Parrus. (1935)

notch-house (1931) *notch* perhaps an alteration of *nautch* dancing (girl), from Urdu *nāch* ■ Herbert Gold: Nancy ran a notch-house for travelers who loved to see things. (1956)

peg-house (1931) US; from earlier sense, public house; also applied to a meeting-place for male homosexuals

juke, jook, jouk, juke-house, juke-joint (1935) Orig US; also applied more generally to an establishment providing food and drink and music for dancing ■ Stephen Longstreet: *Juke* from juke box came from juke house—which was once a whorehouse. (1956)

whore-shop (1938) ■ Angus MacVicar: I hate the Golden Venus. . . . It's just a whoreshop. (1972)

joy-house (1940) ■ Berkeley Mather: All right—so you're a sailor in a joy-house with a sore foot. (1970)

rib-joint (1943) US ■ C. Colter: Forty-third Street, . . . the street of rib joints and taverns. (1965)

chicken ranch (1973) US; claimed to be from the name of an actual brothel in La Grange, Texas, which was the subject of the musical *The Best Little Whorehouse in Texas* ■ Stephen King: Someone finally found a way to clean up the dope in Boston's Combat Zone and the chicken-ranch business in Times Square. (1990)

Pimps

ponce (1872) British; perhaps from *pounce* spring upon someone ■ Germaine Greer: The role of the ponce . . . is too established for us to suppose that prostitutes have found a self-regulating lifestyle. (1970)

mack, mac (1887) Short for obsolete *mackerel* pimp, from Old French *maquerel* pimp, of

uncertain origin ■ *Washington Post*: Now comes 'The Mack', a movie about the rise and fall of a sweet pimp named Goldie. (1973)

bludger (1898) Shortened from *bludgeoner* someone armed with a bludgeon ■ *Observer*: They are strikingly different to the white prostitutes who ply their trade for coloured bludgers. (1960)

daddy (1924) US; from earlier sense, male lover, boyfriend

sweetback, sweetback man (1929) US ■ Blesh & Janis: The dapper, foppish 'macks' or 'sweet-back men' . . . got their gambling stakes from the girls. (1950)

jelly bean (1935) US; from earlier sense, unpleasant person

To act as a pimp

pimp (1636) From the noun *pimp* ■ *New Yorker*: I also especially enjoyed Roscoe Onman as Pretty Eddie, the 'happy dust' addict who pimps for his girl. (1976)

bludge (1947) Back-formation from *bludger*

A group of prostitutes working for the same person or organization

string (1913) US; from earlier sense, set of horses kept together ■ L. Block: She wants out of my string of girls. (1982)

stable (1937) From earlier sense, set of horses kept together ■ J. Crad: He . . . now runs a 'stable' of white women for coloured seamen in Cardiff. (1940)

The vice squad

pussy posse (1963) From *pussy* female genitals

15. Crime

Dishonest, corrupt

crooked (1859) ■ *Guardian*: The resident Molina and Bird went . . . undercover, posing as tourists to trap a crooked hotel manager. (1991)

dodgy (1861) Mainly British; applied to one thought likely to be dishonest ■ *Guardian*: Why live in slummy parts of cities and get ripped off by dodgy landlords when you could do this? (1992)

shady (1862) Applied to one thought likely to be dishonest; from earlier sense, unreliable ■ Evelyn Waugh: Five Scots people . . . were caught by a very shady guide who took them up to the Kasbar in a taxi-cab. (1930)

wide (1879) British; applied to someone engaged in or skilled in sharp practice ■ F. D. Sharpe: Underworld men and women . . . refer to themselves as 'wide people' or 'one of us'. They're a colourful, rascally lot these 'wide 'uns'. (1938)

cronk (1889) Australian; originally applied specifically to fraudulently run horseraces;

probably from British dialect *crank* infirm, sick ■ Jack Lindsay: Not that I believe in anything cronk. (1958)

crook (1898) Australian & New Zealand; shortened from *crooked* ■ M. Neville: Accused him of some crook dealings. (1954)

bent (1914) Orig US ■ *Sunday Pictorial*: A 'bent screw' . . . a crooked warder who is prepared to traffic with a prisoner. (1948)

Dishonestly or illegally acquired or produced

sly (1828) Mainly Australian ■ *Bulletin* (Sydney): The Board of Works has actually asked people to dob in their neighbours for sly watering. (1973)

crooked (1864) ■ *Daily Chronicle*: In the event of his being found . . . to be dealing in 'crooked' things, or refusing to give information as to where he got his stuff. (1902)

shonky, shonkie (1970) Australian; perhaps from *shonk* Jew or from British dialect *shonk* smart + *-y* ■ *Australian*: The woman . . . was forthright about the cut-price air fares. . . . 'We call these tickets shonky,' she said. (1981)

hooky (1985) British; applied to something stolen or counterfeit; probably from *hook* (from the notion of not being straight— compare *bent*, *crooked*) + -*y*; compare obsolete *hooky-crooky* dishonest ■ *Guardian*: Does a fake Renoir matter any more than a hooky Rolex? (1996)

See also **bent**, **hot**, and **kinky** under Stolen (p. 96).

Not illegal

legit (1908) Abbreviation of *legitimate*; also in the phrase *on the legit* within the law ■ Hartley Howard: This dough isn't strictly legit. (1973)

Dishonest or corrupt activity

hanky-panky (1841) An arbitrary formation, probably related to *hocus pocus*; compare obsolete sense, sleight of hand, jugglery ■ *Economist*: Several of the lists of signatures required to enable a candidate to run in Texas appear to have forged names on them—Mr Dole, Mr Haig and Mr du Pont. This does not mean hanky-panky in the Dole campaign, since the task of collecting the signatures had been contracted out. (1988)

shenanigan, shenanigin(g), shennan-, etc. **(1855)** Orig US; now usually used in the plural; origin unknown ■ *Ridge Citizen* (Johnston, South Carolina): We don't condone whatever wrongdoing or shenanigans that may have taken place at Watergate or elsewhere. (1974)

graft (1865) Orig US; from *graft* act dishonestly ■ *Daily Telegraph*: Victims in a wave of graft, corruption and fear were making regular payments for protection. (1970)

funny business (1891) Applied to illegal, underhand, or deceitful dealings; from earlier sense, jesting, nonsense ■ Olivia Manning: Our permits . . . are issued on the understanding that we do not get mixed up in any funny business. (1960)

lurk (1891) Australian & New Zealand; applied to a profitable stratagem of questionable honesty; from earlier obsolete slang sense, method of fraud ■ Barbara Cooper: She was a very rich girl indeed, and Hilary, with considerable influence over her, might well be on to a very good 'lurk'. (1966)

jiggery-pokery (1893) British; applied to deceitful or dishonest dealing; compare Scottish *joukery-pawkery* clever trickery, from *jouk* dodge, skulk ■ Gladys Mitchell: Business reasons could make any alliance respectable . . . so long as there was no jiggery-pokery. (1973)

grift (1914) US; perhaps an alteration of *graft* ■ Raymond Chandler: Hell, I thought he sold reefers. With the right protection behind him. But hell, that's a small-time racket. A peanut grift. (1940)

jobs for the boys (1950) Derogatory; applied to appointments given preferentially to one's own associates or supporters ■ Michael Gilbert: 'It wasn't exactly a popular appointment, was it?' 'It certainly wasn't,' said the General. . . . 'Jobs for the Boys.' (1955)

mumping (1970) British; applied to the acceptance by the police of small gifts or bribes from tradespeople; from obsolete *mump* beg

To act dishonestly or corruptly

graft (1859) Orig US; from British dialect sense, dig ■ John Morgan: They used to graft together . . . they pulled one or two big capers. (1967)

grift (1915) US; denoting small-time dishonest or criminal undertakings; from *grift* dishonest activity ■ Herbert Gold: How long you been grifting? (1956)

rort (1919) Australian; denoting engaging in corrupt practices; from *rorty* boisterous ■ *Sunday Mail* (Brisbane): Overseas tax havens and 'rorting' claimed. $3,000 m. a year in tax dodges. (1980)

spiv (1947) British; denoting making one's living as a spiv; from the noun *spiv* ■ *Times*: Instead of that brave new Britain all they had left was a land fit for bookies to spiv in. (1947)

To put to a dishonest or corrupt use; to induce to behave corruptly

nobble (1856) British; often denoting specifically inducing a jury to return a corrupt verdict; from earlier sense, drug or lame a racehorse to prevent its winning ■ Michael Underwood: What about the rest of the delegation? . . . No chance of nobbling one of them? (1973)

bend (1864) ■ *Observer*: There are honest landladies in districts like Victoria who let a flat to someone they think is an ordinary girl, who then proceeds to 'bend' it: uses it for prostitution. (1958)

A criminal undertaking

job (1722) Often applied specifically to a robbery ■ *Daily Express*: Bird asked Edwards: 'Can you do a job on my old woman?' Edwards is said to have replied: 'No sweat'. The trial continues. (1984) ■ *Cosmopolitan*: Sadie, the barmaid, was saying: 'Hey, Bob, that bank job was a bit cheeky, wasn't it?' (1990)

caper (1867) From earlier more general sense, course of action, undertaking ■ Jack Black: If anything had gone wrong with this caper and we had to take a pinch. (1926)

frame-up (1900), frame (1911) Orig US; applied to a (criminal) conspiracy or plot ■ A. L. Rowse: Their signatures were very cleverly forged. Coming at such a moment it looks like a frame-up. (1956)

inside job (1908) Applied to a crime committed by or with the connivance of someone living or working in the place where it happened ■ Dorothy Sayers: You seem convinced that the murder of Victor Dean was an inside job. (1933)

outside job (1925) Applied to a crime committed by someone not otherwise associated with the place where it happened ■ Agatha Christie: The police are quite certain that this is not what they call an 'outside job'—I mean, it wasn't a burglar. The broken open window was faked. (1931)

single-o (1930) US; applied to a crime committed without an accomplice

tickle (1938) Applied to a successful crime or illegal deal ■ D. Webb: If there is a good tickle, say for as much as £10,000, which is as much as anyone got from any job, it soon goes to the birds, . . . the bookmakers, the hangers-on. (1955)

A dishonest or corrupt person

shyster (1844) Orig & mainly US; applied to someone who uses unscrupulous methods; origin unknown

grafter (1896) Orig US; often applied specifically to a politician, official, etc. who uses his or her position in order to obtain dishonest gain or advantage; compare earlier sense, small-time criminal ■ A. J. Cronin: They've always been a set of grafters down there; local government has been one long sweet laugh. (1935)

spiv (1934) British; applied to a man, often flashily dressed, who makes a living by illicit or unscrupulous dealings; origin uncertain; perhaps from *spiff* smarten up, *spiffy* smart, handsome ■ *Cornish Guardian*: Metrication will be an open invitation for every spiv and racketeer to cheat the British public. (1978)

lurkman (1945) Australian; applied to someone who lives by sharp practice; from *lurk* scheme, dodge + *man* ■ L. Horsphol: I felt strangely sorry for the old man. Lurkman he might have been. (1978)

See also **crook** under A criminal (p.89).

A criminal

hustler (1825) Applied to someone who lives by stealing or other dishonest means ■ William Burroughs: *Pop corn*, someone with a legitimate job, as opposed to a 'hustler' or thief. (1953)

grafter (1866) US, dated; applied to a small-time criminal, such as a pickpocket or thief ■ Josiah Flynt: *Grafter*, a pickpocket. (1899)

crook (1877) Orig US; originally applied to a dishonest or corrupt person, and hence to a professional criminal ■ Michael Innes: 'The fact is that a gang of crooks—' 'I beg your pardon?' Miss Candleshoe is wholly at sea. 'The fact is that a band of robbers is prowling about outside this house now.' (1953)

talent (1879) Australian; applied collectively to (members of) the criminal underworld ■ Dymphna Cusack: He'd learn responsibility quicker married than he would knocking about the ports with the rest of the talent. (1953)

punter (1891) Applied to any of various types of criminal, especially one who assists as a confederate; compare earlier sense, gambler ■ S. J. Baker: We [in New Zealand] have also acquired [this century] some underworld slang of our own: . . . punter, an assistant of a pickpocket who diverts the victim's attention while robbery is committed. (1941)

streetman (1908) US; applied to a petty criminal who works on the city streets, especially as a pickpocket or drug pedlar ■ *Publishers Weekly*: He is playing partner to the pusher whose street man is keeping the girl hooked. (1974)

crim (1909) US & Australian; abbreviation of *criminal* ■ *Telegraph* (Brisbane) (*headline*): Crims 'in turmoil'. (1970)

kink (1914) US

grifter (1915) US; applied to a small-time criminal; from *grift* act dishonestly + *-er* ■ R. O'Connor: He lived off the horoscope trade until the World Fair of 1893 suggested a move to Chicago, as it did to thousands of other . . . grifters. (1965)

punk (1917) Mainly US; applied to a young hooligan or petty criminal; compare earlier senses, rotten wood, something worthless ■ C. R. Cooper: 'The punks', as youthful offenders are often called. (1939)

urger (1919) Australian; applied to someone who obtains money illegally or by deceit, especially as a tipster at a racecourse ■ *Bulletin* (Sydney): He was a tout or an urger, I gathered. 'Mixed up in racecourses,' was the way she put it. (1934)

inside man (1935) US; applied to someone involved in any of various special roles in a confidence trick or robbery ■ F. D. Sharpe: When the 'mug's' name is announced in the restaurant by the page, he is followed to the telephone by the 'inside man' and identified. (1938)

wheelman (1935) Orig US; applied to the driver of a criminals' getaway vehicle ■ Kenneth Orvis: Later on, . . . he began driving a cab. Also being a wheel-man for the mobs. (1962)

baddy (1937) Orig US; applied especially to a villain in a play, film, etc.; usually used in the plural; from *bad* + *-y* ■ *European*: His thin legs seem to shuffle at the sight of a linebacker, as if they were Tintin's running away from the baddies. (1991)

juvie, juvey (1941) US; applied to a juvenile delinquent; abbreviation of *juvenile* ■ *Time*: Los Angeles County police went after the 'juvies' (minors under 18), began carting them off by the busload. (1966)

ram (1941) Orig & mainly Australian; applied to an accomplice in petty crime; origin uncertain; perhaps simply a transferred use of *ram* male sheep ■ S. J. Baker: The ram would say, 'Give the old boy a fair go; he's nearly too old to spin them!' (1966)

chummy (1948) British, police slang; applied to someone suspected or accused of or charged with a crime; from earlier sense, friend ■ Douglas Clark: We could get Chummy into the dock and pleading guilty, but we'd not get a verdict. (1969)

slag (1955) Applied to a petty criminal, or to such people collectively ■ Peter Laurie: I could get them up the nick and take their prints with ink, but that's really for slag. (1970)

villain (1960) British; from earlier sense, wicked person, wrongdoer ■ *Sunday Telegraph*: A flying squad officer said: 'As far as we know these are no ordinary villains. We believe they are Irish IRA.' (1975)

scammer, skammer (1972) Orig US; applied usually to a petty criminal; from *scam* swindle + *-er* ■ *Rolling Stone*: Trader Red was a dope smuggler, or skammer as he preferred to be called. (1974)

perp (1981) US; applied to the perpetrator of a crime; abbreviation of *perpetrator* ■ T. N. Murari: Yolande had testified. The perp got twenty-five to life. (1984)

A rogue, ne'er-do-well

skeezicks, -sicks, -zacks, -zecks (1850) US, dated; probably a fanciful coinage ■ P. A. Rollins: Eb Hawkins, that ol' skeezicks you met on th' railway train an' liked, is th' feller that's acted as th' owners' agent in sellin' rights to your uncle. (1939)

chancer (1884) British; applied to someone who does outrageous or dishonest things at high risk of discovery; from the verb *chance* + *-er* ■ J. Milne: If you're a detective where's your warrant card? I don't think you're a detective at all. You're just a chancer. (1986)

wide boy (1937) British ■ Val Gielgud: Blackmailed—for the murder? Not even the widest of the local wide-boys could have got on to it. (1960)

Jack the Lad (1981) British; applied to a (brash) young male rogue or villain; apparently the nickname of Jack Sheppard, a celebrated 18th-century thief ■ *Interview*: The East End urchin Tony, later a Jack-the-lad and Jack-of-all-trades. (1991)

scally (1986) Liverpool and Manchester slang; shortened from *scallywag* ■ *Independent*: I think McCartney has the philosophy that he was one of four scallys who did it all with no assistance. (1990)

A member of a criminal gang

moll (1823) Applied to a gangster's or other criminal's female companion; compare earlier sense, prostitute ■ Ngaio Marsh: I can see you're in a fever lest slick Ben and his moll should get back . . . before you make your getaway. (1962)

mug (1890) US; applied to a thug; compare earlier sense, fool

mobster (1917) Orig US; from *mob* criminal gang, often specifically the Mafia + *-ster* ■ D. E. Westlake: I was afraid to think about Vigano and his mobsters. (1972)

minder (1924) Applied to a bodyguard hired to protect a criminal ■ Edmund McGirr: Comes of a whole family of wrong 'uns. . . . A high class 'minder' around the big gambling set. (1973)

hood (1930) US; abbreviation of *hoodlum* ■ P. G. Wodehouse: The hood was beating the tar out of me. (1966)

goombah, goomba, gumbah (1969) US; applied to a member of a gang of organized criminals, often specifically a mafioso, and also to a gangland boss; from an Italian dialectal pronunciation of Italian *compare* godfather, male friend, accomplice ■ *Washington Post*: My father was the boss, and in those days, your father got to pick your goomba (godfather). (1978)

made (1969) Orig & mainly US; applied as an adjective to someone who has been initiated into the Mafia ■ C. Sifakis: Jack Dragma . . . presided over the Weasel's initiation as a made man in the Los Angeles crime family. (1987)

yardie (1986) Applied to a member of any of a number of West Indian, and especially Jamaican, gangs engaged in usually drug-related organized crime; from West Indian *yard* dwelling, home + *-e* ■ *Financial Times*: The so-called Godfather of Britain's Yardie gangs . . . was deported to Jamaica, for questioning about murders. (1988)

A criminal gang

mob (1927) US; applied to an organization of violent criminals, often specifically the Mafia; from earlier sense, (unruly) group of people ■ *Guardian*: The Mob from its Chicago headquarters runs the subcontinent. (1969)

An armed criminal

gun moll (1908) US; applied to an armed female thief or other criminal, and also to the female companion of a male gunman or gangster ■ Arthur Koestler: Fierce-looking Yemenite gun-molls, Sephardi beauties. (1949)

gun-slinger (1928) Mainly US; often applied specifically to a western gunfighter ■ *Boston Sunday Herald*: The gunslinger . . . comes to town, cigar between teeth, his prowess with a gun for sale. (1967)

rodman (1929) Mainly US; applied to a gunman; from *rod* gun + *man* ■ *John o'London's*: Robert is victim number two of this assassination, the only witness who could identify the rod-man. (1962)

torpedo (1929) US; applied to a professional gunman ■ Raymond Chandler: There's yellow cops and there's yellow torpedoes. (1940)

gunsel, gunshel, gun(t)zel, gunzl (1943) US; applied to a gunman or armed thug; from earlier sense, young man, influenced by *gun*, *gunslinger*, etc. and apparently also by its use in the film *The Maltese Falcon* (1941) (e.g. 'Let's give them the gunsel. He actually did shoot Thursby and Jacoby, didn't he?') applied to a young male armed criminal ■ Wallace Markfield: After all, didn't Ben Gurion himself hand her a blank cheque, she should have what to hire a couple gunsels? (1964)

A criminal's equipment

dub (a1700) Dated; applied to a key used by a burglar; from the verb *dub* open, probably an alteration of obsolete *dup* open, from *do up*

twirl (1879), **twirler** (1921) Applied to a skeleton key ■ P. Kinsley: She scarcely heard him open the old lock . . . with the set of 'twirls'. (1980) ■ Jeffrey Ashford: Weir, who was an expert with the twirlers, forced the lock in six seconds. (1974)

squeeze (1882) Applied to an impression of an object made for criminal purposes ■ G. D. H. & M. Cole: Where did the dummy keys . . . come from?. . . If they were forgeries it would be simpler, for Sir Hiram might remember if anyone had handled his keys long enough to take a squeeze. (1930)

ripper (1889) Applied to a tool for opening safes, etc.

can-opener (1912) Applied to a tool for opening safes, etc.; from earlier sense, tin-opener ■ R. I. McDavid: The use of *stew* is declining, modern *heavy gees* preferring to use a *stick*, *ripper* or *can opener* on laminated safes. (1963)

iron (1941) Applied to a jemmy used in housebreaking

loid, 'loid (1958) Applied to a celluloid or plastic strip used by thieves to force locks; shortened from *celluloid* ■ Bill Turner: 'Have you got keys to all Creedy's places?' 'Beatty has. I use a loid myself.' He showed a tapered wedge of blank celluloid. (1968)

shim (1968) Mainly US; applied to a plastic strip used by thieves to force locks; from earlier sense, thin slip used to fill up or adjust the space between parts; ultimate origin unknown ■ Lesley Egan: Denny and I went to Nonie's place, and he used a shim to get us in. (1977)

To reconnoitre with a view to committing a robbery or other crime

case (1914) Orig US; perhaps from gamblers' slang *keep cases on* watch closely ■ M. Gair: What he was doing was casing the gaff; or, in police terms, 'loitering with intent to commit a felony'. (1957)

prowl (1914) US ■ Raymond Chandler: I went back to the kitchen and prowled the open shelves above and behind the sink. (1943)

drum (1933) British; denoting ringing or knocking on the door of a house to see if it is unoccupied before attempting a robbery, and hence more generally, reconnoitring with a view to robbery; probably from earlier sense, knock

A criminals' look-out or sentinel

cockatoo (1934) Australian ■ *Telegraph* (Brisbane): They watched Foster (the 'cockatoo' or spy) point out our punters who had laid a large bet. (1966)

An area frequented by criminals

tenderloin (1887) US; applied to a district of a city where vice and corruption are rife; from earlier sense, undercut of a sirloin steak; originally applied specifically to a district of New York City, from the notion that the proceeds from corruption made it a 'juicy' morsel for the local police

Costa del Crime (1984) British, jocular; applied to the south-east coast of Spain, as used by several British criminals as a bolt-hole to escape British justice; *Costa* from Spanish, coast, with reference to the names of various holiday coastlines in Spain, e.g. *Costa Brava*

A victim of crime

fly-flat (1864) British, dated; applied to someone taken in by confidence tricksters; from *fly* knowing, alert + obsolete *flat* gullible person ■ Joyce Cary: 'I don't see why we should consider the

speculators.' 'A lot of fly-flats who thought they could beat us at the game.' (1938)

mark (1883) Orig US; applied to the intended victim of confidence tricksters; often in the phrase *a soft* (or *easy*) *mark* ■ Edmund McGirr: In the twenties it was the Yanks who was the suckers, but now . . . it's us who are the marks. (1973)

package (1933) Mainly US; applied to a kidnap victim ■ *Sun* (Baltimore): The 'package', as the kidnapped victim is called, is rushed across the State line and delivered to the 'keepers'. (1933)

A getaway after committing a crime

stoppo (1935) British; now mainly used attributively with reference to a quick getaway by car from the scene of a crime ■ Michael Kenyon: Walk, then, to the stoppo car. . . . And wait. . . . Till Slicker comes. (1975)

Stealing, theft

hoist (*a*1790), hoisting (1936) Applied to shoplifting; *hoist* often in the phrase *on the hoist* engaged in shoplifting; compare *lift* steal ■ Frank Norman: My old woman's still out on the hoist now. (1958) ■ *New Statesman*: You know Annie Ward, well she's on the hoisting racket. (1966)

on the game (1739) Dated, mainly British; applied to someone actively engaged in burglary

dragging (1812) Dated; applied to stealing from a vehicle ■ James Curtis: I'm a screwsman and not on the dragging lark. (1936)

bust (1859) Applied to a burglary ■ *Science News*: The back of a pub where you and a 'screwer' . . . had decided to 'do a bust'. (1947)

dip (1859) Applied to pocket-picking; usually in the phrase *on the dip* picking pockets

trick (1865) US; especially in the phrase *turn a trick* commit a successful robbery ■ Donald MacKenzie: Campbell's claim was that he hadn't turned a trick in a year but the money had to be coming in from somewhere. (1979)

blag (1885) British; applied to an act of robbery (with violence); origin unknown ■ *Observer*: The top screwing teams, the ones who went in for the really big blags, violent robberies. (1960)

stick-up (1887) Orig Australian, now mainly US; applied to an armed robbery; from *stick up* rob at gunpoint, knifepoint, etc. ■ *Sun* (Baltimore): The bank manager told police that the bandit . . . drew a gun and said: 'This is a stickup.' (1944)

roadwork (1925) Dated; applied to the work of a travelling thief ■ *Publications of the American Dialect Society*: Because of the stresses and strains of road work, he is usually a sharp, alert thief. (1955)

whizz, whiz (1925) Orig & mainly US; applied to the practice of picking pockets; mainly in the phrase *on the whizz* engaged in picking pockets; perhaps from the swift movement involved in removing the contents of pockets ■ James Curtis: They might pinch him for being on the whizz. (1936)

creep (1928) Orig US; applied to stealthy robbery; mainly in *at* (or *on*) *the creep* engaged in such robbery; from *creep* stealthy robber ■ F. D. Sharpe: Billy's at 'the Creep' means that Billy earns his living stealing by stealth from tills whilst a shop is momentarily unwatched, or from a warehouse. (1938)

pick-up (1928) From *pick up* steal, rob ■ F. D. Sharpe: He had been persuaded to try his hand at 'the pick up' (stealing from unattended motor cars). (1938)

heist (1930) US; applied to a robbery or hold-up; representing a local US pronunciation of *hoist* ■ Elleston Trevor: A heist was when you took a motor with the idea of doing a repaint and flogging it with a bent log-book you'd got from a breaker. (1968)

sting (1930) Mainly US; applied to a burglary or other act of theft, fraud, etc., especially a complex and meticulously planned one carried out quickly ■ *Courier-Mail* (Brisbane): A transaction between a jewellery salesman and a professed buyer with $230,000 in his pocket was intercepted yesterday by a cab driver who made off with the cash. Investigators believe the theft was a set-up 'sting'. (1975)

knock-off (1936) Applied to a robbery; also in the phrase *on the knock-off*, denoting someone engaged in stealing; from *knock off* steal, rob ■ James Curtis: They [*sc.* gloves] . . . gave away the fact that he was still on the knock-off. (1936) ■ John Gardner: The really profitable knock-offs, like the Train Robbery. (1969)

five-finger discount (1966) US, euphemistic, mainly CB users' slang; applied to the activity or proceeds of stealing or shoplifting ■ Lieberman & Rhodes: The perfect 'gift' for the 'midnight shopper' looking for a 'five-finger discount'. (1976)

fingers in the till (1974) Applied to stealing money from one's place of work or money for which one is responsible ■ *Sunday Times*: Occasionally, a cabinet minister will be caught with his fingers in the till. (1993)

steaming (1987) British; applied to a gang rushing through a public place, train, etc. robbing bystanders or passengers by force of numbers; probably from the notion of a train proceeding 'at full steam' ■ *Independent*: Hard policing is sought to deal with 'steaming' attacks, Yardies, cocaine, the Notting Hill Carnival or to combat no-go areas. (1991)

wilding (1989) US; applied to rampaging by a gang of youths through a public place, attacking or mugging people along the way; originally associated with an incident in New York City's Central Park in April 1989; probably from the adjective *wild* + *-ing* ■ *New York Times*: There has been little response by the city government to the widespread concern over wilding in general. (1990)

ram-raiding (1991) British; applied to smash-and-grab raiding in which access to the goods is obtained by ramming a vehicle into the shopfront ■ *Daily Telegraph*: The ram-raiding started about five years ago, they say, going first for soft targets like tobacconists and off-licences, then later for television shops and jewellers. (1991)

To steal; to rob

thieve (*a*901) Old English *þēofian*, from *þēof* thief; originally a standard usage; not recorded between the 10th century and the 16th century, when it was again a standard usage; it apparently came to be regarded as slang in the 19th century ■ *Pall Mall Gazette*: The prisoner . . . said it was the first time he had 'thieved' anything. (1867) ■ *Independent*: When I started thieving on my own, my stepdad would slip me £25 and take what I'd pinched off my hands. (1991)

lift (1526) Denoting stealing and in modern use (1892) also, more specifically, plagiarizing ■ John Wainwright: Lift a bleedin' gun from somewhere. (1973) ■ A. Cross: Fran has lifted the perfect phrase for the occasion from a recent Iris Murdoch novel: *Sic biscuitus disintegrat*: that's how the cookie crumbles. (1981)

nip (*c*1560) Now US; denoting stealing or snatching ■ *Columbus Dispatch*: A business man . . . from whom he nipped a $250 shirt stud. (1894)

stall (1592) Dated; denoting surrounding, decoying, jostling, or distracting someone whose pocket is being picked; from obsolete *stall* decoy-bird

pinch (1656) Denoting stealing and also (formerly) robbing ■ *Daily News*: Brown was . . . alleged, in sporting phrase, to have 'pinched' the defendant out of £6 10s. (1869) ■ *Listener*: 'This was by car I take it—was there petrol?' 'Well, we somehow managed to pick it up.' 'You mean pinch it?' (1969)

cabbage (1712) British, dated; originally applied specifically to a tailor stealing some of the cloth provided for him to make up into a garment; from the noun *cabbage* off-cuts of cloth appropriated by a tailor, perhaps from Old French *cabas* theft

walk off with (1727) Often implying appropriating to oneself something lent or entrusted to one by another ■ *Economist*: The department stood by while sharp men at Lloyd's of London walked off with millions. (1988)

knock (1767) Denoting robbing especially a safe or till ■ *Times*: The appellant had been asked if he had told someone in the 'Norfolk' that he got the money by safe breaking. The appellant had replied: 'Aye but you will never prove that I got it by knocking a safe.' (1963)

pick up (1770) Dated; denoting stealing or robbing ■ *Detective Fiction Weekly*: Gentleman George . . . would mark down his traveler, knowing him to be in possession of jewelry or other valuables, and tirelessly follow him until the opportunity arose to 'pick-up' his all-important bag. (1928)

do (1774) Denoting burgling or robbing a place ■ H. R. F. Keating: My Billy noticed the set in a shop-window. . . . He did the place that very night. (1968)

snavel, snavvel (*a*1790) Now mainly Australian; denoting stealing or grabbing; perhaps a variant of obsolete slang *snabble* plunder, mug or *snaffle* seize ■ Vance Palmer: They're booming the notion o' a new township and snavelling all the land within a mile o' it. (1948)

shake (1811) Now Australian; denoting stealing or robbing; compare earlier obsolete *shake someone out of something* rob someone (15th & 16th centuries) ■ **Ted Schurmann:** 'You're not going to take his pliers!' 'Heck, I'm only borrowing them, not shaking them.' (1979)

stick up (1846) Orig Australian; denoting robbing a place (or in early use also a person) at gunpoint, knifepoint, etc. ■ **S. Brill:** They had served time for sticking up a variety store in Akron, Ohio. (1978)

knock down (*a*1854) US; denoting stealing or embezzling especially passengers' fares ■ **J. Evans:** Some . . . clerk who was knocking down on the till. (1949)

bust (1859) Denoting breaking into and robbing a place ■ **Edgar Wallace:** There's a little house just outside of Thatcham . . . me and Harry . . . thought we might 'bust' it and get a few warm clothes. (1927)

duff (1859) Australian; denoting stealing cattle, sheep, etc., often altering their brands; probably a back-formation from *duffer* such a thief ■ **H. C. Baker:** Complaining to the police that his stock was being duffed. (1978)

whip (1859) British; denoting stealing or taking roughly or without permission ■ **M. K. Joseph:** 'Where's your hat, Barnett?' . . . 'Dunno, Someone musta whipped it.' (1958)

go through (1861) Orig US; denoting searching and robbing a person or place ■ **R. W. Service:** The girls were 'going through' a drunken sailor. (1945)

mug (1864) Denoting attacking and robbing someone; from earlier obsolete boxing slang sense, hit in the face, from the noun *mug* face ■ **Daily Telegraph:** Judge Hines, Q.C., jailed three youths for three years for 'mugging' a middle-aged man and stealing £7 from his wallet. (1972)

nick (1869) Denoting stealing; from earlier more general sense, take ■ **Courier Mail** (Brisbane): Nicking toys from chain stores. (1973)

roll (1873) Denoting robbing someone, especially someone who is asleep, drunk, or otherwise incapacitated ■ **Raymond Chandler:** Here we are with a guy who . . . has fifteen grand in his pants. . . . Somebody rolls him for it and rolls him too hard, so they have to take him out in the desert and plant him among the cactuses. (1939)

crook (1882) US; denoting stealing

swipe (1889) Denoting stealing or taking roughly or without permission; apparently from earlier sense, hit ■ **T. Roethke:** That beautiful Greek anthology you sent me some student swiped. (1970)

attract (1891) Euphemistic; denoting stealing ■ **E. Cambridge:** He 'attracted' some timber and built a boat house. (1933)

glom (1897) US; denoting stealing; variant of Scottish *glaum* snatch, from Gaelic *glam* grab ■ **G. H. Mullin:** I learnt that stealing clothes from a clothes-line is expressed in Hoboland by the hilarious phrase, 'Glomming the grape-vine'. (1926)

reef (1903) Denoting pulling up a pocket-lining to steal the contents, or to steal from a pocket, or more broadly to steal or obtain dishonestly ■ **Times:** As the talent suckers chummy, the wire reefs his leather. . . . A slick pickpocket team has a private language for its dirty work. (1977)

rip (1904) Denoting stealing ■ **Telegraph** (Brisbane): They believe some have ripped millions of dollars from Medibank since it began. (1976)

snitch (1904) Denoting stealing; compare earlier sense, inform on someone ■ **Milton Machlin:** How about that guy who snitched a whole D-9 tractor, brand-new? (1976)

snipe (1909) Mainly North American; denoting stealing or taking without (official) permission; often used in the context of gold prospecting ■ **New Yorker:** He 'sniped' a lot of his gold—just took it from likely spots without settling down to the formalities of a claim. (1977)

hot-stuff (1914) Dated services' slang; denoting stealing or scrounging; probably from *hot stuff* stolen goods (compare *hot* stolen) ■ **H. Rosher:** I at once hot-stuffed one of his inlet valves and set the men to work changing it. (1914)

knock something off (1919) Denoting stealing or robbing ■ **Observer:** The boys either knocked off a hut where they knew gelly was kept or straightened a quarry man. (1960) ■ **Alan Hunter:** Just met a bloke . . . in the nick. . . . Him what was in there for knocking-off cars. (1973)

rat (1919) Mainly Australian & New Zealand; denoting searching someone, their belongings, etc. for something to steal, or more broadly to robbing or pilfering surreptitiously ■ **Kylie Tennant:** Some thieving (*adjective*) robber was 'ratting' his tucker-box. (1941)

souvenir (1919) Euphemistic, orig services' slang; denoting taking something as a 'souvenir', and hence pilfering or stealing ■ **Frank Clune:** I dug up his body, souvenired his false teeth and diaries, and reburied him in whiteman fashion. (1944)

drum (1925) British; denoting stealing from an unoccupied house, room, etc.; probably from earlier sense (not recorded till later), find out if anyone is at home before attempting a robbery

half-inch (1925) British; denoting stealing; rhyming slang for *pinch* steal ■ **Times:** If people are going to go around half-inching planets the situation is pretty serious. (1972)

kick something in (1926) US; denoting breaking into a building, room, safe, etc. ■ **Detective Fiction Weekly:** Harold G. Slater's big jewelry store safe had been 'kicked in' and robbed of twelve thousand dollars. (1931)

take (1926) Denoting robbing ■ **Damon Runyon:** Someone takes a jewellery store in the town. (1930)

knock something over (1928) Denoting robbing or burgling a place ■ **Illustrated London News:** The job looks easy enough—a big hotel at Tropico Springs that any fool could 'knock over'. (1940)

work the tubs (1929) Denoting picking pockets on buses or at bus-stops; from *tub* bus

heist (1931) Orig US; denoting stealing, robbing, or holding up; representing a local US pronunciation of *hoist* steal ■ *Punch*: Six years ago Jim Tempest was one of a bunch of tearaways heisting cars round the North Circular. (1965)

hoist (1931) Orig US; denoting stealing or robbing; compare *lift* steal; there is no documentary evidence of any connection with the much earlier *hoist, hoisting* shoplifting or with the obsolete 18th-century slang *hoist* break into and steal from a house (said to be from the notion of hoisting an accomplice up to a window left open) ■ *Coast to Coast 1961–62*: 'I know where we can hoist a car,' Mick said. 'We'll carry the stuff in it.' (1962)

blag (1933) British; denoting robbing (with violence) or stealing; from *blag* robbery ■ F. D. Sharpe: 'Johnny blagged the till'—Johnny took the till. (1938)

score (1942) Orig US; denoting stealing; from earlier sense, make dishonest gain ■ Donald MacKenzie: 'Where did you get it [*sc.* a newspaper]?' . . . 'Nicked it. . . . It was too early to score any milk.' (1977)

rabbit (1943) Australian nautical slang, dated; denoting scrounging or stealing; compare earlier *rabbit* something smuggled or stolen ■ Kylie Tennant: Why were Australian Navy men better at 'rabbiting' little valuable articles than Americans? (1953)

liberate (1944) Euphemistic or jocular; applied to looting or stealing ■ George Melly: He . . . wore a sombrero liberated, I suspect, from the wardrobe of some Latin American group he had worked with in the past. (1965)

tickle (1945) Mainly Australian & New Zealand; denoting robbing or burgling; often in the phrase *tickle the peter* rob a till or cash box ■ F. Greenland: Get a Portuguese villain to tickle the place. (1976)

peter (1962) Denoting blowing open a safe in order to steal from it; from the noun *peter* safe ■ Bill Knox: The Dolman boys are going to peter a pawnshop safe tonight. (1962)

dodge (1965) Australian; denoting stealing an animal; from earlier sense, drive sheep or cattle ■ Tom Ronan: For every poddy that's up in the Coronet breakaways there's a dozen blokes trying to dodge it off. (1965)

hot-wire (1966) Orig North American; denoting stealing a vehicle by bypassing its ignition system

loid, 'loid (1968) Denoting breaking open a lock or letting oneself in using a loid; from *loid* celluloid or plastic strip for forcing locks ■ *Observer*: Mortice deadlocks with five or more levers, difficult to pick and impossible to loid. (1968)

take someone or something **off** (1970) US, Black English; denoting robbing someone or burgling or holding up a place ■ *Black World*: He and Cecil B were to take off a supermarket in San Jose. (1973)

wog (1971) Denoting stealing; origin unknown ■ P. Ferguson: A new acquisition, no less, and one smuggled out of the shop under the assistant's very nose; one snaffled, pocketed, pinched, wogged, nicked. (1985)

shim (1972) Mainly US; denoting breaking open a lock using a shim; from *shim* plastic strip for forcing locks ■ Joseph Wambaugh: The burglar . . . would shim doors which isn't too hard to do in any hotel. (1972)

steam (1987) British; denoting rushing in a gang through a public place, train, etc. robbing anyone in one's path; probably a back-formation from *steaming* robbery of this sort ■ *Times*: Several members of a mob of young robbers who 'steamed' through crowds at the Notting Hill Carnival in 1987 were jailed yesterday. (1989)

A thief

hooker (1567) Dated; applied originally to any thief or pilferer, and subsequently to a pickpocket, often specifically a stealer of pocket-watches; from obsolete *hook* steal (stealthily) (from the notion of snatching an article with a hook) + *-er* ■ *Tit Bits*: The hooker, having . . . got a hold of the desired prize, detaches it from the chain by breaking the ring and passes it to number two. (1888)

hoister (1790) Applied to a shoplifter or pickpocket ■ F. D. Sharpe: Gangs of women shop-lifters or 'Hoisters' are to be found in Hoxton. (1938)

cracksman (1812) Dated; applied to a housebreaker; from obsolete slang *crack* housebreaking + *man* ■ Joseph Conrad: 'Give it up—whatever it is,' he said in an admonishing tone, but not so kindly as if he were condescending to give good advice to a cracksman of repute. (1907)

screwsman (1812) Applied to a thief or housebreaker; from obsolete slang *screw* false key + *man* ■ J. Prescot: What does our imaginary screwsman do? He gets his hands on the keys . . . to take impressions. (1963)

staller (1812) Dated; applied to a pickpocket's accomplice; from *stall* distract someone whose pocket is being picked + *-er*

duffer (1844) Australian; applied to someone who steals stock, often altering their brands; perhaps from earlier sense, one who sells trashy goods as valuables, under false pretences ■ *Age* (Melbourne): Some time during the night of 7–8 May a group of duffers drove their truck on to Mr Wheelhouse's 50-hectare farm at Mooroopna . . . and stole 28 Hereford steers worth about $13,000. (1984)

drummer (1856) British; in recent use applied especially to a thief who robs an unoccupied house ■ *Observer*: Nobody wanted to know the drummers, those squalid daytime operators who turn over empty semi-detached villas while the housewives are out shopping. (1960)

dip (1859) Applied to a pickpocket ■ *Daily Telegraph*: New Yorkers who have had their pockets picked or handbags rifled on the city's Underground in recent years learned yesterday that the person responsible was probably a professional 'dip'. (1970)

rampsman (1859) Applied to someone who commits robbery with violence; from *ramp* swindle + *man* ■ Michael Crichton: Barlow was a reformed buzzer turned rampsman—a pickpocket who had degenerated to plain mugging. (1975)

buzzer (1862) Applied to a pickpocket; from obsolete *buzz* pick someone's pocket (of unknown origin) + *-er*

hook (1863) Applied to a thief or pickpocket; originally denoting specifically someone who stole from a pocket while the victim's attention was distracted by someone else; compare obsolete *hook* steal (stealthily) ■ G. J. Barrett: We've nothing on him. But then we've nothing on half the hooks in Eastport. (1968)

dancer (1864) Dated; applied to a thief who gains entry through upper-storey windows ■ Edgar Wallace: There were active young men who called themselves dancers, and whose graft was to get into first-floor flats and get out quickly with such overcoats, wraps, and movables as could be whisked away in half a minute. (1930)

mugger (1865) Applied to someone who commits robbery with violence in a public place; from *mug* rob in this way + *-er* ■ *Sun*: Muggers attacked detective. (1973)

second-stor(e)y man (1886) North American; applied to a cat-burglar ■ Malcolm X: Hustlers . . . sold 'reefers', or had just come out of prison, or were 'second-story men'. (1965)

waddy, waddie (1897) US; applied to a cattle rustler; origin unknown

parlour-jumper (1898) Applied to a house-breaker

pennyweighter (1899) US; applied to a jewellery thief; from *pennyweight* unit in the Troy system of weight measurement + *-er* ■ *Daily News*: In the American description of her she was said to be a 'penny weighter'. . . . That is, one who goes into a jeweller's shop, inspects jewellery, and by means of some sticky substance on the fingers, manages to palm an article, and deposits it beneath the counter for a confederate to pick up. (1905)

peterman (1900) Applied to a safe-breaker; from *peter* safe + *man* ■ Bruce Graeme: The wall safe . . . would [not] have presented much difficulty to an expert peterman. (1973)

prop-getter, prop-man (1901) Dated; applied to a pickpocket; from *prop* diamond or valuable piece of jewellery

tea-leaf (1903) British; rhyming slang for *thief* ■ Douglas Clark: A tea-leaf wouldn't find the key on your person if he broke in. (1977)

houseman (1904) US, dated; applied to a burglar

creeper (1906), creep (1914) Orig US; applied to a stealthy robber, or to a sneak thief, especially a prostitute who steals from her clients while they are asleep or unconscious ■ *Observer*: A creep is a highly expert thief. . . . He is so quiet that he can move about a house for hours without waking anybody. (1960)

prat-digger (1908) US, dated; applied to a pickpocket; from *prat* hip-pocket

pete-man (1911) Applied to a safe-breaker; from *pete* safe + *man*

heel (1916) US derogatory criminals' slang, dated; applied to a sneak-thief or pickpocket

finger (1925) Applied to a pickpocket ■ K. Hopkins: He's a finger, works in Fulham mostly. Small profits, quick returns. (1960)

whizzer (1925), whizz, whiz, whizz boy (1931), whizz man (1932) Orig US; applied to a pickpocket; from *whiz(z)* pocket picking ■ *Listener*: The quick-fingered craft of those whom the Elizabethans called nips and we call whizz boys. (1959) ■ Tom Tullett: The pickpocket, known in the underworld as the 'whiz' . . . is always a specialist. (1963) ■ R. Edwards: It was also a right place for 'whizzers'—pick-pockets. (1974)

heister (1927) US; in earliest use applied to a shoplifter, subsequently to a robber; from *heist* steal, rob + *-er* ■ Stephen Ransome: Any heister . . . would face a bit of a problem in moving his loot. (1953)

pick-up man (1928) Applied especially to someone who steals luggage

whizz-mob (1929) Applied to a gang of pickpockets ■ D. Webb: Provincial police forces looked to him for help when they wanted their towns cleared of the 'whiz mob', as English pickpockets are known in the underworld. (1955)

screwer (1932) Applied to a thief or housebreaker; probably from *screw(sman* thief, housebreaker + *-er* ■ *Science News*: The back of a pub where you and a 'screwer' . . . had decided to 'do a bust'. (1947)

reefer (1935) Applied to a pickpocket or pickpocket's accomplice; from *reef* pick pockets + *-er*

blagger (1938) British; from *blag* rob + *-er* ■ D. W. Smith: Reluctant though I am to say so, the blaggers have pretty well stuffed us on this one. . . . We've done a lot of bloody good police work for sweet Fanny Adams. (1986)

tool-man (1949) Applied to a lock-picker or (US) a safe-breaker ■ Kyril Bonfiglioli: Every sound, professional team of thieves has . . . a 'toolman' who knows how to neutralize burglar-alarm systems and to open locks. (1979)

moll (1955) US; applied to a female pickpocket or thief; from earlier sense, gangster's female companion

stair dancer (1958) Applied to a thief who steals from open buildings ■ Edmund Crispin: Since he was a stair dancer, a walk-in thief, judges had been inclined to be lenient until the last occasion, when his offence had been said . . . to have been aggravated by his having broken a window to 'effect an entrance'. (1977)

klepto (1958) Abbreviation of *kleptomaniac* ■ E. V. Cunningham: You got it . . . right out of Helen Sarbine's purse. . . . What are you—some kind of nut or klepto? (1964)

steamer (1987) British; applied to a member of a gang engaged in steaming ■ *Sunday Times*: Last November, steamers . . . hit crowds outside a rock concert at Hammersmith Odeon. (1988)

ram-raider (1991) British; applied to a perpetrator of ram-raiding

Inclined to steal

light-fingered (1547) Euphemistic ■ *Washington Post*: They maintain Bodie in a state of 'arrested decay', an oxymoron that means fending off vandals and light-fingered tourists. (1993)

thieving (1598) Originally a standard usage ■ *Evening Standard*: It is filled with . . . constant collisions between pregnant daughters, thieving accountants, snotty bankers, dumb sidekicks, hysterical wives, saucy maids. . . . (1991)

sticky-fingered (1890) ■ *Daily Telegraph*: Mr Steel announced menacingly that a list of sticky fingered policemen had been made available. (1982)

Stolen

hot (1925) Applied especially to stolen articles that are easily identifiable and therefore difficult to dispose of ■ **H. L. Lawrence**: You come here, in a hot car. . . . And the police know. (1960)

bent (1930) Orig US; from earlier sense, dishonest ■ **Peter Wildeblood**: He had got a short sentence for receiving stolen goods, which he swore he had not known to be 'bent'. (1955)

kinky (1927) Orig US ■ *Collier's*: 'Why, you can't tell me that you didn't know those five big cars were kinky.' 'Kinky?' . . . 'Those cars were bent.' (1927)

Stolen property

swag (1794) ■ **J. Fenton**: And there were villains enough, but none of them slipped away with the swag. (1982)

take (1888) Mainly US; applied to money acquired by theft or fraud ■ **C. F. Coe**: After the stick-up . . . Carrots . . . can watch the take till I send the porter over after it. (1927)

score (1914) Applied to the proceeds of a robbery ■ *New Yorker*: A million dollars from a computer crime is considered a respectable but not an extraordinary score. (1977)

kinky (1927) Orig US; from *kinky* dishonestly obtained, stolen ■ *American Mercury*: The titles of every car Joe sold could be searched clear back to the factory. . . . Yet the cars were strictly kinkies. (1941)

the goods (1900) Applied especially to stolen articles as evidence of guilt ■ **R. D. Paine**: You have caught me with the goods, Wyman. It was my way of getting a slant on you. (1923)

rabbit (1929) Naval slang & Australian; applied to something smuggled or stolen ■ **F. H. Burgess**: *Rabbit*, an article unlawfully obtained and smuggled ashore. (1961)

knock-off (1963) From *knock off* steal ■ *Australian T.V. Times*: Knock-off, loot or illegally found goods. (1963)

A hiding-place for stolen goods

lumber (1753) British, dated; applied to a house or room where stolen goods are hidden; from earlier sense, pawnbroking establishment; ultimately a variant of obsolete *Lombard* pawnbroking establishment, bank, etc., from the traditional role of natives of Lombardy as bankers and pawnbrokers

trap (1930) US ■ *Time*: Other mobsters keep their escape money in bank safe-deposit boxes or hiding-places called 'traps'. (1977)

drop (1931) ■ *American Mercury*: The immediate problem after a trucking theft is to unload the merchandise and abandon the empty truck. For this purpose the gang must have a 'drop' where the loot can be stored until the fence can arrange for its sale and distribution. (1947)

run-in (1959) ■ **D. Warner**: Sapper Neal and a bunch of the Sparrow boys been seen cruising around this manor in a car like they was looking for something. Is the run-in round here? (1962)

To handle or sell stolen goods

fence (1610) ■ **Saul Bellow**: After stealing your ring, he didn't even know how to fence it. (1989)

A dealer in stolen goods

fence (a1700) From *fence* deal in stolen goods ■ **B. Reid**: She'd had a fence living in while I was away, and she'd flogged my expensive wedding presents. (1984)

drop (1915) ■ **Kenneth Orvis**: You say you buy expensive jewels. You say you pay better prices than ordinary drops do. (1962)

placer (1969) British ■ **Peter Laurie**: There are thieves and dealers—we call them placers. (1970)

Possession of stolen or illicit goods

possession (1970) Orig US; often applied specifically to the possession of illegal drugs ■ **R. L. Simon**: What's a few years in the cooler for possession? (1973)

Extortion

shake-down (1902) Orig & mainly US; applied to an instance of extortion; from *shake down* extort money from ■ **S. Brill**: While the shakedown was proved, it was never shown that the money went to Presser personally. (1978)

bagman (1928) Orig & mainly US; applied to someone who collects or administers the collection of money obtained by racketeering and other dishonest means; from the bag supposedly carried to hold the money collected; compare earlier sense, commercial traveller ■ *National Times* (Australia): The money is always paid in cash, by personal contact in a pub or a car. The police 'bag man' will call once a month to collect. (1973)

racket (1928) Orig US; applied to a criminal scheme for extorting money, etc., especially in organized crime; from earlier sense, plan, scheme ■ *Times*: Ulster by the middle of 1974 was suffering from rackets and violent crime on a scale equal to some of Europe's most notorious cities. (1977)

juice (1935) US; applied to protection money ■ **Estes Kefauver**: When the combine's books finally were seized, examination disclosed recorded payments totalling $108,000 for the service known as 'juice', which is the

California gambling profession's euphemism (in Florida the term is 'ice') for 'protection' money. (1951)

ice (1948) US; applied to protection money ■ *Economist*: Gross . . . who had confessed to paying this sum in 'ice' for the protection that made it possible for him to earn $100,000 a year. (1951)

See also **hustle**, **ramp**, and **scam** under Deception, swindling, fraud at **Deception**, **Cheating** (pp. 282–3).

To extort money from

shake someone **down (1872)** Orig & mainly US ■ Jonathan Ross: Sickert had been shaken down for protection money. (1976)

sting someone **for (1903)** Orig US ■ Ngaio Marsh: We hope to sting Uncle G. for two thousand [pounds]. (1940)

To blackmail

put the black on (1924) ■ J. B. Priestley: Got a lovely pub . . . and yet wants to start putting the black on people! (1951)

black (1928) ■ George Sims: He . . . took naughty photos of them and then blacked them. (1964)

Rape and sexual assault

date rape (1983) Orig US; applied to the rape by a man of his partner on a date

A sex offender

nonce (1975) British, prisoners' slang; applied especially to a child-molester; origin uncertain; perhaps from *nancy* effeminate man, but compare British dialect *nonce* good-for-nothing fellow ■ *Sunday Telegraph*: As what prisoners call a 'nonce', he now faces years of solitary confinement and regular assaults from fellow inmates. (1986)

beast (1989) Prisoners' slang ■ *Daily Telegraph*: The arrival of a police van at a prison might often be accompanied by comments such as 'a couple of beasts for you', with the result that the prisoners are immediately identified. (1989)

Illegal falsification or misrepresentation: Counterfeit

queer (1740) From earlier sense, odd ■ Raymond Chandler: If it was discovered to be queer money, as you say, it would be very difficult to trace the source of it. (1941)

flash (1812) Dated; compare earlier sense, gaudy, showy ■ Thomas Hood: 'A note', says he . . . 'thou'st took a flash 'un.' (1837)

snide (1859) Dated; origin unknown

duff (1889) British; from the noun *duff* something worthless or spurious ■ *Sessions Paper*: I rang it [sc. a coin] on the counter; he said 'Break it up—it is duff.' (1910)

dud (1903) From the noun *dud* a counterfeit ■ *Economist*: Mr Giancarlo Parretti, who once spent a month in an Italian jail for passing a dud cheque. (1987)

Counterfeit money, cheques, etc.

queer (1812) Applied to counterfeit money, and also (*US*) to forged banknotes or bonds; from *queer* counterfeit ■ Emma Lathen: Nobody's laying off any queer on the Sloan [Bank]. (1981)

shice, **shise (1877)** Dated; compare earlier sense, nothing, no payment; ultimately from German *Scheiss* shit ■ *Five Years of Prison Life*: Seeing how the fellow was acting he sent him two 'shise' notes, which gave him a dose that 'corked him'. (*c*1890)

snide (1885) Dated; applied to counterfeit jewellery or money; from *snide* counterfeit

stumer, **stumor (1890)** Applied to a counterfeit coin or banknote or to a worthless cheque; from earlier, more general sense, something worthless ■ *Daily News*: I did pass a bad florin, guv'nor, but I did it innocent. I didn't know it was a stumer. (1912)

tweedle (1890) Dated; applied to a counterfeit ring used in a swindling racket; probably from the verb *tweedle*, a variant of *twiddle* twist, twirl

schlenter (1892) South African; applied especially to a fake diamond; from Afrikaans, Dutch *slenter* trick ■ J. M. White: The best Schlenters in South West are made from the marbles in the necks of the lemonade or mineral-water bottles that can be found in dozens at the old German diggings. (1969)

duff (1895) British; from earlier sense, something worthless or spurious

dud (1897) Applied to a counterfeit coin, banknote, etc.; perhaps from earlier *dud* ragged garment

wooden nickel, **wooden money (1915)** US; applied to a counterfeit or worthless coin or money

slush (1924) Dated; applied to counterfeit banknotes ■ D. Hume: We've been handling slush lately—ten bobs and quids. Where they were printed doesn't matter to you. (1933)

funny money (1938) Orig US

A fraudulent substitute

ringer (1890) Orig US; applied originally to a horse, player, etc. fraudulently substituted in a competition to boost the chances of winning, and in recent use (1962) to a false registration plate on a stolen vehicle; from *ring* substitute fraudulently + *-er* ■ E. Parr: The car is now driven to a hideaway, where ringers (false number-plates) are substituted. (1964) ■ *Times*: The Crown claimed that the horse had been switched and that the winner was in fact a 'ringer', a more successful stablemate called Cobblers March. (1980)

A fraudulent substitution

ring-in (1918) Australian; applied especially to a fraudulent substitution in a race

switch (1938) ■ William Gaddis: Somebody pulled the old twenty-dollar-bill switch on her, Ellery said looking up from his magazine. (1955)

To counterfeit, forge

scratch (1859) US, dated; denoting forging banknotes and other papers ■ *Flynn's Magazine*: Well, scratch th' note an' we'll blow. (1926)

phoney something **up (1942)** Mainly US; from *phoney* spurious ■ *Daily Telegraph*: Furs are often not clearly labelled. Cat skins could be passed off as 'bunny'. You can phoney anything up. (1977)

To pass counterfeit money, cheques, etc.

drop (1926) ■ Lionel Black: The known value of counterfeit fivers dropped is more than double that. (1968)

To substitute fraudulently

ring (1812) In recent use (1967) denoting specifically the fraudulent changing of the identity of a car; from *ring* sound of a bell ■ Alan Hunter: The Parry brothers . . . copped three apiece for ringing cars. (1977)

To misrepresent or fraudulently alter

cook (1636) Denoting surreptitious or fraudulent alteration or falsification; in modern use often in the phrase *cook the books* falsify financial accounts ■ *Daily Telegraph*: When the spending got out of hand and the money was not coming in, 'the only thing to do was to cook the books'. (1991)

fix (1790) Orig US; denoting influencing by illegal means, especially bribery ■ *Daily Telegraph*: He was told that a [driving] test could be 'fixed' for £10. (1959)

salt (1852) Denoting originally the misrepresenting of the value of a mine by introducing ore from elsewhere, and hence (1882) misrepresenting the contents of an account by adding ghost entries, falsifying details, etc.; from the notion of adding salt to a dish

launder (a1961) Denoting changing something illegally to make it acceptable or legitimate, and hence (from the use of the word in connection with the Watergate inquiry in the United States in 1973–4) transferring funds, especially to a foreign bank account, in order to conceal a dubious or illegal origin; from earlier sense, wash linen ■ *Globe & Mail* (Toronto): Kerr concedes U.S. criminals 'launder' money in Ontario. (1974) ■ *New York Times*: Unscrupulous dealers . . . 'launder' the mileage of cars. (1976)

skim (1966) US; denoting concealing or diverting some of one's earnings or takings, especially from gambling, to avoid paying tax on them ■ Mario Puzo: Gronevelt felt that hotel owners who skimmed money in the casino counting room were jerks, that the FBI would catch up with them sooner or later. (1978). Hence **skimmer** (1970) ■ S. Brill: The cash was being split, some to be counted for taxes and the rest to go to the skimmers. (1978)

fiddle (1970) From earlier sense, swindle ■ *Guardian*: They have come to get the key to the exam-cupboard so that they can fiddle the maths results. (1991)

rort (1980) Australian; denoting manipulating a ballot, records, etc. fraudulently; from earlier sense, engage in corrupt practices ■ *Bulletin* (Sydney): A plan to rort the roll could involve isolating the names of members who are listed under out-of-date addresses. (1985)

To contrive fraudulently

frame something **up (1899)** US, dated ■ R. D. Paine: All I need is a little work with your catcher, to frame up signals and so on. (1923)

A counterfeiter, forger

scratcher (1859) Orig US, dated ■ V. Davis: The actual forger, known by such names as 'the scratcher', 'the scribe', 'the penman', may consider himself extremely fortunate if his period of office exceeds two years. (1941)

penman (1865) ■ Hugh McLeave: You'll need a passport. . . . I've got a penman who can doctor it. (1974)

ringer (1970) Applied to someone who fraudulently changes the identity of a car; from *ring* + *-er* ■ *Drive*: When the professionals—the car 'ringers'—get to work, the profit on a skilfully doctored vehicle can be more than £500. (1971)

Someone who passes counterfeit money, cheques, etc.

shover (1859) US, dated ■ *Harper's Weekly*: Eight persons, mostly 'shovers' or passers, were arrested in Russo's gang. (1889)

passer (1889) ■ William Gaddis: I'm going out to meet a passer, to hand this stuff over to him. It's all arranged and paid for. (1955)

paper-hanger (1914) Orig US; applied to someone who passes forged or fraudulent cheques ■ J. G. Brandon: 'Paper-hanger,' McCarthy echoed. 'That's a new one on me, William.' 'Passin' the snide, sir,' Withers informed him. 'Passing flash paper. Bank of Elegance stuff.' (1941)

dropper (1938) British ■ Cyril Hare: The functionary whose mission it is to put forged currency into circulation is known technically as a dropper. (1959)

A smuggler

runner (1930) Mainly US; applied to someone who traffics in illicit liquor, drugs, etc.; from earlier standard sense, smuggler of contraband, guns, etc. ■ Tom Tullett: Members of the gang, known as 'runners', were sent to Paris, or Marseilles, to pick up the drug. (1963)

mule (1935) Orig US; applied to someone employed as a courier to smuggle illegal drugs into a country and often to pass them on to a buyer; from the role of the mule as a beast of burden ■ Ed McBain: I bought from him a coupla times. He was a mule, Dad. That means he pushed to other kids. (1959)

Arson

torch (1931) Orig US; denoting deliberately setting fire to something, especially in order to claim insurance money ■ *Time*: Griffith relied on an arsonist turned informant . . . who worked as a 'broker' for landlords eager to torch their property. (1977)

An arsonist

torch (1938) US ■ *Reader's Digest*: The torch is now serving a 20-year sentence. (1938)

Joyriding

hotting (1991) British; applied to joyriding in stolen high-performance cars, especially dangerously and for show; from *hot* stolen, perhaps reinforced by *hot-wire* steal a car by bypassing the ignition system ■ *Observer*: What started as a campaign against 'hotting'—displays of high-speed handbrake turns in stolen cars—has turned into a dispute over territory. (1991). Hence **hotter** someone who does this (1991)

To incriminate

plant (1865) Denoting hiding stolen goods, etc. in order to incriminate the person in whose possession they are found; used from 1601 with no sense of ulterior incriminating motive ■ *Times Literary Supplement*: The nephew . . . sought to clinch the available, and misleading, evidence by planting the victim's dental plate on the spot. (1930)

fit (1882) Orig Australian; denoting (attempting to) incriminate someone, especially by planting false evidence; often followed by *up*; from obsolete British *fit* punish in a fitting manner ■ G. F. Newman: Danny James might have fitted him, Sneed thought, but immediately questioned how. (1970) ■ *Observer*: He says he was fitted up by the police, who used false evidence to get a conviction. (1974)

job (1903) Orig US; denoting incriminating someone ■ Jack Black: I was in the district attorney's office . . . and I know you got 'jobbed'. I'll take your case for nothing. (1926)

frame (1915) Orig US; denoting (attempting to) incriminate someone, especially by planting false evidence; from earlier *frame up* pre-arrange fraudulently ■ Russell Braddon: If they were prepared to lie about Marseille then obviously they intended to frame her. (1956)

put someone **in (1922)** ■ D'Arcy Niland: Don't put me in. Don't try to hang anything on me. (1958)

set someone **up (1956)** Denoting pre-arranging things or leading someone on in order to incriminate the person ■ Saul Bellow: Of course he understood that Tennie was setting him up, and that he was a sucker for just the sort of appeal she made. (1964)

verbal (1963) Orig & mainly British; denoting attributing an incriminating statement to an arrested or suspected person; often followed by *up*; from *verbal* such a statement ■ C. Ross: 'He's made no statement yet either.' 'But you verballed him?' . . . The police officer said nothing. (1981)

stitch someone **up (1970)** British; denoting causing someone to be wrongfully arrested, convicted, etc. by informing, fabricating evidence, etc. ■ *New Society*: Both Sheila and Gary

have many stories of being 'stitched up' by the police or fleeced. Gary says the Dip Squad—the special police patrol looking for pickpockets—are 'a bunch of wankers'. (1977)

An act of unjust incrimination

frame-up (1908), **frame (1929)** Orig US; from earlier sense, (criminal) conspiracy ■ *It*: While serving a six month sentence . . . Ian learned a lot about frame ups, about prison conditions. (1971) ■ J. Evans: He . . . wasn't a killer but just the victim of a frame. (1948)

set-up (1968) Orig US; applied to a scheme or trick by which an innocent person is incriminated; from *set up* incriminate ■ John Gardner: Arthur's clean. . . . It was a set-up. . . . I had him checked like you'd check a dodgy engine. (1978)

bag job (1971) US; applied to an illegal search of a suspect's property by agents of the Federal Bureau of Investigation for the purpose of copying or stealing incriminating documents

stitch-up (1984) British; applied to an act of unjustly transferring blame to someone else; from *stitch up* incriminate ■ *Guardian*: There's obviously been a stitch-up and it leaves Calcutt with egg on his face. (1992)

fit-up (1985) From *fit (up)* incriminate ■ Roger Busby: We was fitted, you ratbag! . . . Nothing but a lousy fit-up! (1985)

Something incriminating

plant (1926) Applied to something hidden in a person's clothing, among their possessions, etc. in order to incriminate them; from *plant* hide in such a way ■ G. Vaughan: 'Heroin!' the detective shouted. . . . Yardley had never seen the package before. . . . He said: 'That stuff's a plant.' (1978)

verbal (1963) Orig & mainly British; applied to an incriminating statement attributed to an arrested or suspected person; from *verbal* spoken ■ Michael Underwood: 'Have a look through the police evidence.' . . . 'At least, they haven't put in any verbals.' (1974)

A scapegoat for a crime or misdemeanour

fall guy (1904) Orig US ■ *Spectator*: Ward began to hear from friends that he was being cast for the part of fall guy (I know of no equivalent expression here) by Profumo's friends. (1963)

To suspect of a crime

suss, sus (1953) British; abbreviation of *suspect* ■ D. Webb: He turned to Hodge and said, 'Who's sussed for this job?' (1953)

Suspicion of having committed a crime

sus, suss (1936) British; often in the phrase *on sus*; abbreviation of *suspicion* or *suspicious* ■ G. F. Newman: Chance nickings in the street, from anything on sus, to indecent exposure. (1970)

Someone suspected of a crime

sus, suss (1936) British; abbreviation of *suspect* ■ Kenneth Giles: Sorry, old man, they found your chief sus. with his neck broken. (1967)

To raid; to search

turn something or someone **over (1859)**
Denoting ransacking a place, usually in order to
commit robbery, or searching a person
■ Laurence Meynell: What about that girl's bedroom that got
turned over? (1981)

shake something or someone **down (1915)**
Orig & mainly US; applied especially to the
police searching a place or person ■ Desmond
Bagley: Once Mayberry had been shaken down the guards
were taken from Penny and Gillian. (1977)

bust (1971) Applied to the police searching a
place for drugs, stolen property, etc.; from
earlier noun sense, police raid

A (police) raid; a search

shake-down (1914) Orig & mainly US ■ Landfall:
But about nine o'clock, without any warning, there was a
shake-down [of prisoners]. (1958)

bust (1938) Orig US ■ It: At the moment, there are over a
hundred of our kids in nick as a result of the busts at 144
Piccadilly & Endell Street. (1969)

To follow

tail (1907) Orig US; denoting following a
criminal, suspect, etc. secretly ■ S. Brill: I'm not
gonna let you tail me like some kinda cop. (1978)

Arrest and charging

dead to rights (1859) British; applied to a
criminal who is caught red-handed ■ A. A. Fair:
We've got her this time dead-to-rights. (1947)

collar (1871) Orig US; applied to an arrest; from
the notion of seizing someone by the collar
■ New York Review of Books: The only guys that want to
make a collar today are the guys who are looking for the
overtime. (1977)

hot beef (1879) British, dated; rhyming slang for
stop, thief! ■ Gwendoline Butler: 'Hot beef, hot beef,'
cried the schoolboys. 'Catch him. . .' (1973)

bang to rights (1904) British; applied to a
criminal who is caught red-handed ■ Frank
Norman: One night a screw looked through his spy hole and
captured him bang to rights. (1958)

bum rap (1926) Mainly US; applied to a false
charge

hummer (1932) Mainly US; applied to false or
mistaken arrest

bust (c1953) Orig & mainly US; from earlier
sense, police raid

lay-down (1938) British; applied to a remand in
custody

sting (1976) Mainly US; applied to a police
undercover operation to catch criminals
■ Observer: His second reaction was to inform the American
authorities and get their approval for an elaborate and costly
'sting'. (1983)

To arrest

nab (1686) Origin uncertain; compare obsolete
slang nap seize, preserved in kidnap ■ Boston
Sunday Herald: Town marshall is slain and a former lawman
nabs the killer. (1967)

have someone **up (1749)** Originally denoting
bringing someone before a court to answer a
charge ■ Mrs Humphrey Ward: The man who had let
them the rooms ought to be 'had up'. (1892)

do (1784) British; denoting arresting or charging
someone ■ Guardian: 'This is a murder charge. There is
no certainty that you will be done for murder.' . . . He did not
say that Kelly would only be 'done' for robbery and not murder.
(1963)

have the law on (or (dated) **of**) someone
(1800) Denoting reporting someone to the
police ■ Anne Barton: When the gentlemen . . . steal his
best silver-gilt goblet, Candido has the law on them. (1993)

nick (1806) From earlier sense, catch, take
unawares ■ John Wainwright: I am talking to you,
copper . . . either nick me . . . or close that bloody door. (1973)

pull (1811) ■ G. F. Newman: They . . . pulled drunks and
bathed tramps, saw children across the road and directed
traffic. (1970)

pull someone **up (1812)** Dated

pinch (1837) ■ H. L. Foster: A traffic policeman had
stopped us. But not to pinch us for speeding. (1925)

book (1841) Denoting the official recording of
the name of someone who has committed an
offence; from the notion of writing the name
down in a book ■ P. Barry: If you hadn't been a learner
driver . . . I'd have booked you for that! (1961)

cop (1844) From earlier sense, catch, lay hold of
■ Pall Mall Gazette: Prisoner said, 'Yes, I am the man. I am
glad you have copped me.' (1888)

lag (1847) Dated; from earlier sense, imprison
■ Augustus Mayhew: They tell him adventures of how they
were nearly 'lagged by the constables'. (1858)

fully (1849) Dated; denoting commiting someone
for trial; from the adverb fully, in the phrase fully
committed for trial ■ James Curtis: They'll fully me to
the Old Bailey, I reckon. (1936)

cuff (1851) Denoting handcuffing someone; from
cuffs handcuffs; previously used in the 17th
century to denote restraining someone with
wrist-fetters ■ Wall Street Journal: It's very, very rare
that you would arrest anyone, cuff them in public and take
them from their offices. (1989)

collar (1853) Dated; from earlier sense, take hold
of (as if) by the collar

run someone **in (1859)** ■ New Yorker: 'Am I going to
have to run you in?' the policeman asked. (1951)

haul someone **up (1865)** Denoting bringing
someone before a judge or other person in
authority in order to answer a charge, and
hence arresting or charging someone ■ Daily
Mail: Loui Micalleff took his go-kart for a spin in his

neighbourhood cul-de-sac, and was hauled up by the local police for driving an uninsured, unregistered vehicle. (1991)

put the collar on someone **(1865)** US

pick someone **up (1871)** Orig US ■ J. T. Farrell: He gazed around the church to see if any of the boys were present. Seeing none of them, he guessed that they must all have been picked up, and were enjoying Christmas Day in the can. (1934)

fall (1873) Denoting being arrested or convicted

nail (1889) From earlier sense, succeed in catching or getting hold of ■ C. F. Burke: The cops . . . nail Ben for havin' the cup. (1969)

pull someone **in (1893)** ■ Dorothy Sayers: We could pull him in any day, but he's not the real big noise. (1933)

blister (1909) British; denoting arresting or summonsing someone; from the noun *blister* summons ■ Herbert Hodge: When the policeman puts his notebook away again, we've usually been 'blistered'. During recent years, policemen have been blistering us over three thousand times in a twelvemonth. (1939)

drag (1924) British, dated ■ Edgar Wallace: If you particularly want him dragged, you'll tell me what I can drag him on. (1928)

knock someone **off (1926)** ■ R. V. Beste: You're the sort who'd knock off his mother because she hadn't got a lamp on her bike five minutes after lighting up time. (1969)

put the sleeve on someone **(1930)** US ■ Damon Runyon: These coppers . . . know who he is very well indeed and will take great pleasure in putting the old sleeve on him if they only have a few charges against him, which they do not. (1930)

lumber (1931) British; from earlier sense, imprison ■ Barry Crump: We were sneaking into the church to bunk down last night when the johns lumbered us. (1961)

bust (1940) Orig & mainly US ■ *Landfall*: The little man came out of his cell. . . . 'This your first time busted?' (1958)

take someone **in (1942)** ■ Janwillem van de Wetering: You're not taking me in, sheriff. (1979)

feel someone's **collar (1950)** British ■ *Daily Telegraph*: Will old-timers be able to play dominoes or cribbage without the risk of having their collars felt? (1985)

Arrested

popped (1960) US; sometimes applied to someone caught with illegal drugs in their possession

Liable to arrest; wanted

hot (1931) Compare earlier sense, stolen ■ Patricia Moyes: Griselda was 'hot'. Griselda had to disappear. (1973)

A summons

blister (1903) British ■ Frank Sargeson: He'd been paying off a few bob every time he had a few to spare. . . . And then he gets a blister! (1947)

bluey (1909) Australian & New Zealand; from the colour of the document ■ *N.Z.E.F. Times*: That speed cop, who gave me my last bluey on point duty. (1942)

Handcuffs

bracelets (1816) Previously applied in the 17th century to iron wrist-fetters ■ Frederick Forsyth: Letting him run sticks in my craw. He should be on a flight Stateside—in bracelets. (1989)

nippers (1821) ■ *Fortune*: At 2145 one of the detectives put nippers on the prisoner's wrist. (1939)

cuffs (1861) Previously applied in the 17th century to iron wrist-fetters

mittens (1880) From earlier sense, type of glove

snaps (1895) ■ Maurice Procter: Sergeant, we'd better have the snaps on these three. (1967)

An identification parade

show-up (1929) US ■ *Sun* (Baltimore): Lyman Brown . . . picked Graham out of a 'showup' of seven jail inmates. (1955)

stand-up (1935) US ■ *Philadelphia Evening Bulletin*: Jackson was brought to City Hall last night to take a look at Norman in a police standup, but he could not positively identify the prisoner. (1949)

A criminal record

pedigree (1911) ■ Dell Shannon: Dorothy had a little pedigree for shoplifting. (1964)

previous (1935) British; short for *previous (criminal) convictions* ■ G. F. Newman: 'Neither has any previous, Terry,' Burgess said. 'I thought perhaps the fella might have had a little bit,' he shrugged. (1970)

mug shot (1950) Orig US; applied to a police photograph of a criminal; from *mug* face

form (1958) British; from horse-racing use, a horse's past performance as a race-guide ■ Michael Underwood: He has form for false pretences, mostly small stuff. (1960)

mug book (1958) Applied to a book kept by the police containing photographs of criminals; from *mug* face

sheet (1958) US; applied to a police record of convictions ■ Carolyn Weston: Somebody scared him into it. Let's take a look at his sheet, I want to know who. (1976)

rap sheet (1960) Mainly US; applied to a police record of convictions; from *rap* criminal accusation or charge ■ G. V. Higgins: He was convicted. . . . Two charges . . . were dismissed, but remained on his rap sheet as having been brought. (1976)

prior (1978) US; short for *prior conviction*; usually used in the plural ■ Joseph Wambaugh: Burglary . . . rarely drew a state prison term, unless you had a lot of priors. (1978)

Having a criminal record

tasty (1975) British ■ *Daily Mail*: A 'tasty villain' (a known criminal). (1980)

Judges, magistrates, lawyers, etc.

beak (1838) British, dated; applied to a magistrate or justice of the peace; probably from thieves' cant, though derivation from *beak* bird's bill cannot be entirely discounted ■ D. W. Smith: Just tell me what I want to know and we'll tell the beak you were a good boy. Keep on like this and it's porridge for life. (1986)

shyster (1844) Orig and mainly US; applied to an unscrupulous lawyer; origin uncertain; perhaps related to German *Scheisser* worthless person, from *Scheisse* excrement ■ John Wainwright: The shyster lawyers . . . swear blind the client's been manhandled while in police custody. (1981)

mouthpiece (1857) Applied to a barrister, solicitor, etc.; from the lawyer's speaking in court for the accused ■ P. B. Yuill: The Abreys would get legal aid. The state would fix them up with a good mouthpiece. (1974)

stipe, stip (1860) Applied to a stipendiary magistrate; abbreviation of *stipendiary* ■ *New Society*: Roberts devoted the remainder of his . . . speech to

remembering odd little incidents in the early career of the senior 'stip'. (1978)

lip (1929) US, dated; applied to a lawyer, especially a criminal lawyer; from the lawyer's speaking in court for the accused ■ H. E. Goldin: The lip took a hundred skins (dollars) and never showed (appeared) in court. (1950)

brief (1977) British; applied to an accused person's solicitor or barrister; from earlier sense, legal case given to a barrister to argue in court ■ Peter Whalley: Fair sang your praises he did. Said I could tell you things I wouldn't tell my own brief. (1986)

Criminal evidence

dabs (1926) British; applied to fingerprints ■ K. Farrer: You'll get his photo and dabs by airmail today. (1957)

make (1950) Orig US; applied to an identification of, or information about, a person or thing from police records, fingerprints, etc. ■ R. K. Smith: We got a make on the Chevvy. . . . Stolen last week. (1972)

16. **Killing**

To kill deliberately

brain (1382) Originally used in standard English to denote literally killing someone by smashing their brain, but latterly in slang use denoting more broadly killing someone by hitting them on the head ■ *Guardian*: Not for him the behaviour of his grandfather, of whom it is told that he brained a serving boy while drunk in a tavern near London. (1992)

top (1718) Originally denoting execution by hanging (perhaps from an earlier notion of beheading, i.e. removing someone's *top*), but subsequently used more broadly for killing; often used reflexively to denote committing suicide ■ *Listener*: I have to try and get a key to it all, otherwise I'll just top myself. (1983) ■ M. Litchfield: That shooter . . . wasn't used to top Frost. (1984)

croak (1823) Compare earlier sense, die ■ L. A. G. Strong: Who croaked Enameline? (1945)

pop off (1824), pop (1940) Compare earlier *pop off* die ■ Edgar Wallace: You might have been 'popped off' yourself if you'd only got within range of a bullet. (1922) ■ G. S. Gordon: I have joined the Defence Volunteers, and hope to pop a parachutist before the business ends. (1940)

rub out (1848) Orig US ■ Alan Lomax: The gangsters . . . had promised to rub him out if he didn't stop trying to hire away their star New Orleans side-men. (1950)

out (1900) From earlier sense, knock unconscious ■ Edgar Wallace: I've heard fellers in Dartmoor say that if ever they got the chance they'd 'out' him. (1927)

guzzle (1901) Dated; from earlier sense, seize by the throat, throttle; compare obsolete *guzzle* throat ■ Damon Runyon: He will be safe from being guzzled by some of Black Mike's or Benny's guys. (1931)

stretch (1902) ■ Michael Gilbert: Once . . . Annie had a husband. She got tired of him, so she 'stretched him with a bottle'. (1953)

do in (1905) ■ *Listener*: These were professional killers who 'did in' John Regan. (1963)

bump off, bump (1907) Orig US ■ Evelyn Waugh: They had two shots at bumping me off yesterday. (1932) ■ Peter Cheyney: You didn't want him . . . to know you had bumped Clemensky. (1943)

blow away (1913) Orig Southern US dialect, but given wider currency during the Vietnam War; usually applied to killing by shooting or explosion ■ *Guardian*: A gunman smiled as he shot dead a young policeman after being jilted by his girlfriend, the Old Bailey was told yesterday. 'I blew your copper away because my girlfriend blew me away,' Mark Gaynor . . . told officers later. (1991)

crease (1913) Mainly US ■ D. Warner: Christ . . . you creased him. . . . It's a topping job. (1962)

napoo, na poo, napooh (1915) British, dated; alteration of French (*il n'y e)n a plus* there is no more ■ Norman Venner: If you haven't got a job to do, you're a washout. You might as well be napood right off. (1925)

stonker (1917) Mainly Australian & New Zealand; probably from *stonk* artillery bombardment + *-er* ■ *Bulletin* (Sydney): Then one [shell from a gun] comes in and stonkers 'Iggins and the Company Sergeant-Major. (1928)

huff (1919) British, services' slang, dated

knock off (1919) Orig US; compare earlier sense, dispatch, dispose of ■ Hank Hobson: One of my boys

. . . got knocked off—an' nobody does a damn' thing about who knocked him off. (1959)

cool (1920) US ■ John Morris: He wasn't killed in any private fight. . . . He was cooled by a Chinese agent. (1969)

tip off (1920) Dated; compare obsolete dialect *tip off* die ■ *Evening News*: Jake's sort o' done me a good turn, getting himself tipped off. (1928)

do away with (1927) From earlier sense, get rid of; often used reflexively to denote committing suicide ■ *Guardian*: Jeremy Irons led the way . . . as Best Actor for his performance as Klaus von Bulow, accused of doing away with his rich wife in real life as well as in Reversal Of Fortune. (1991)

take someone **for a ride (1927)** Orig US; denoting taking someone in a car to murder them ■ Erle Stanley Gardner: These persons whispered that some day Carr would mysteriously disappear, and no one would ever know whether he had quietly faded into voluntary oblivion or had been 'taken for a ride'. (1944)

scrag (1930) US; from earlier sense, hang, garotte ■ *Reader's Digest*: If they aim at me they will overshoot or undershoot and scrag some scared civilian. (1950)

set over (1931) US ■ W. R. Burnett: I've been trying to find you ever since you set Doc over. (1944)

snuff out (1932), snuff (1973) Compare earlier *snuff* it die ■ E. Behr: If I cause too much embarrassment, they'll just snuff me out. (1980) ■ Thomas Gifford: We should have snuffed this little shit when we had the chance. (1978)

smear (1935) Mainly Australian ■ *American Speech*: He [*sc.* S. J. Baker] gives examples of Australian argot, of which several follow: . . . *smear*, to murder, [etc.]. (1944)

take out (1939) Orig US ■ J. M. Fox: 'He took out two people who could have involved him'. . . . 'Took out? You mean he killed them?' (1967)

dust off (1940), dust (1972) Orig US; compare earlier sense, hit, thrash

wash (1941) US; sometimes followed by *away* ■ Ed McBain: 'This Alfredo kid, he not such a bad guy.' 'He's getting washed and that's it.' (1960)

zap (1942) Orig US; often applied specifically to killing with a gun; from earlier use representing the sound of a bullet, ray gun, etc. ■ Nicolas Freeling: Unbureaucratically, any bugger who shoots, you zap. (1982)

hit (1955) Orig US ■ *Publishers Weekly*: A professional killer who has 'hit' 38 victims. (1973)

waste (1964) Orig & mainly US ■ Carolyn Weston: They wasted Barrett because he blew their deal. (1975)

off (1968) Mainly US, Black English ■ R. B. Parker: There were various recommendations about pigs [*sc.* police officers] being offed scrawled on the sidewalk. (1974)

wax (1968) US, orig services' slang; from earlier sense, beat, thrash ■ L. Block: A whole family gets

waxed because somebody burned somebody else in a coke deal. (1982)

wipe (1968) Often followed by *out* ■ James McClure: Someone tried to wipe Bradshaw. . . . The shot caught him here in the collar-bone. (1980)

gun down (1969) Denoting killing with a gun ■ W. Nelson: The spot where Sinn Feiners gunned down a British Field-Marshall, Sir Henry Wilson, in 1922, on the doorstep of his home. (1979)

ice (1969) US ■ *Guardian*: A would-be assassin who considers it his mission to 'ice the fascist pig police'. (1973)

frag (1970) US, services' slang; denoting killing (or wounding) an officer on one's own side, especially one considered too eager for combat, with a hand grenade; from *frag*, abbreviation of *fragmentation* (*grenade*)

terminate (dismiss, etc.**) with extreme prejudice (1972)** US; used in espionage slang to denote assassinating someone

nut (1974) Usually passive; sometimes followed by *off* ■ E. Fairweather: He's hated so much he knows he'd be nutted straight away. (1984)

stiff (1974) Probably from *stiff* corpse ■ Clive Egleton: Did she blow their cover too? Is that how they got stiffed in Prague? (1978)

To commit suicide

do a (or **the**) **Dutch** (**act**) **(1902)** Orig US; compare earlier sense, run away, desert ■ M. A. de Ford: You can't face it . . . so you're doing the Dutch and leaving a confession. (1958)

Killing, murder

rub-out (1927) Orig US; applied especially to an assassination in gang warfare; from *rub out* kill ■ *Washington Post*: Two hoodlums were gunned to death on Chicago's West Side today and police said at least one of the executions was probably a crime syndicate 'rubout'. (1959)

wipe-out (1968) Orig US; applied especially to an assassination in gang warfare; from *wipe* (*out*) kill ■ M. Hebden: Think it was a gang wipe-out, Patron? (1984)

murder one (1971) US; applied to (a charge of) first-degree murder

A professional killer

hatchet man (1880) Originally applied specifically to a hired Chinese assassin in the US ■ Pat Frank: He was a hatchet man for the NKVD. . . . He may have delivered Beria over to Malenkov and Krushchev. (1957)

hit-man (1970) ■ *Daily Telegraph*: Bryant is alleged to have been a 'hit man' (assassin) for drug traffickers and to have carried out a 'contract' to kill Finley. (1973)

mechanic (1973) ■ John Gardner: Bernie Brazier was Britain's top mechanic. (1986)

An arrangement to kill someone professionally

contract (1940) Orig US; often in the phrase *put a contract (out) on* someone, arrange for someone to be killed by a hired assassin ■ *Maclean's Magazine*: Some policemen believe that a West End mobster named 'Lucky' has put a contract out for Savard. (1976)

To arrange for someone to be killed

put someone **on the spot (1929)** US ■ *Punch*: You get rid of inconvenient subordinates . . . by 'putting them on the spot'—that is deliberately sending them to their death. (1930)

A list of people to be killed

hit list (1976) ■ *Time*: One intelligence official . . . bitterly labeled *Counterspy*'s roster of CIA agents as nothing more or less than 'a hit list'. (1976)

Portraying the actual killing of a person

snuff (1975) Applied to a pornographic film, photograph, etc.; compare *snuff it* die, *snuff out* kill ■ Sidney Sheldon: For the last several years we have been hearing increasing rumors of snuff films, pornographic films in which at the end of the sexual act the victim is murdered on camera. (1978)

To execute or be executed

swing (1542) Denoting being killed by hanging ■ Arthur Conan Doyle: Yes, I am Bob Carruthers and I'll see this woman righted if I have to swing for it! (1905)

stretch (1595) Dated; denoting killing by hanging ■ *Irish Song*: The night before Larry was stretch'd The boys they all paid him a visit. (c1800)

string up (1810) Denoting killing by hanging ■ *Sunday Telegraph*: She gives the impression she'd like to string them up from the nearest lamppost. (1991)

fry (1928) US; denoting executing or being executed in the electric chair ■ John Wyndham: You'll hang or you'll fry, every one of you. (1956)

(Methods of) execution

the rope (1670) Applied to execution by hanging, and hence sometimes more generally to capital punishment

necktie party (1882) Orig and mainly US; applied to a lynching or hanging; from the notion of putting a rope round someone's neck like a tie ■ *Listener*: A drunk or a loud-mouth could wind up like a rustler—the victim of a neck-tie party. (1973)

the chair (1900) US; short for *electric chair* ■ J. J. Farnol: I've left papers—proofs, 'n' it'ud be the chair for yours—savvy? (1917)

Old Sparky (1923) US; applied to the electric chair; the alternative *Old Smokey* was also formerly used ■ *New York Times*: Speed Graphic portrayals of an uncontrollable crime wave of mad-dog felons fairly begged Old Sparky denouements, if only in the interests of popular entertainment. (1994)

the hot seat, the hot chair, the hot squat (1925) US; applied to the electric chair ■ Raymond Chandler: That scene at the end where the girl visits him in the condemned cell a few hours before he gets the hot squat! (1952)

ride the lightning (1935) US; denoting being executed in the electric chair

17. **Reprimanding & Punishing**

A reprimand or instance of reprimanding

rap (1777) From earlier sense, sharp hit; often in the phrases *a rap on the knuckles, a rap over the knuckles* (1897) ■ *Cumberland News*: A top Carlisle haulage firm got a council room rap yesterday for jumping the gun over planning. (1976) ■ *Times*: Elsewhere all praise—and a rap on the knuckles for all those Stravinskyites who stayed at home. (1961)

wigging (1813) From obsolete slang *wig* a rebuke (perhaps as administered by a *bigwig*) + *-ing* ■ *Guardian*: Ministerial expressions of dismay spilled out. The ambassador was summoned for a wigging. (1992)

going-over (1872) Orig US ■ Edward Blishen: Sir, don't give me a going over—but this desk's too small for me. Honest! (1969)

what for (1873) ■ Jacqueline Wilson: She deserves to have her bottom smacked . . . and I shall give young Alice what for too. (1972)

pi-jaw (1891) Dated; applied to a long sanctimonious moral lecture, as delivered by a school-teacher or parent; from *pi* sanctimonious + *jaw* talk

bawl-out, ball-out (1915) US; from the verb *bawl out* reprimand ■ Jack Black: I . . . don't want to . . . give myself a bawl-out in front of the woman. (1926)

razz (1919) Orig US; often in the phrase *get the razz* be reprimanded; abbreviation of *raspberry* ■ *Times Literary Supplement*: Even the peppiest, most two-fisted and up-and-coming borough librarian would get the razz for buying it. (1977)

raspberry (1920), razzberry (1922) From earlier sense, contemptuous noise ■ Muriel Spark: The security officer mutters all the way to the compound about what a raspberry the police are going to get because of this, a raspberry in these days being already an outdated expression meaning a reprimand. A man less set in his limited ways . . . would call it a rocket in this English spring of 1944. (1973)

office hours (1922) US, services' slang; applied to a disciplinary session ■ A. Dubus: He committed an offense, he was brought in to office hours. (1967)

rollicking (1932) British; probably a euphemistic substitution of *rollicking* (earlier sense 'boisterous play') for *bollocking* ■ M. K. Joseph: Someone's dropped a clanger. Someone's going to get a rollicking. (1958)

bollocking, ballocking (1938) British; from the verb *bollock* reprimand ■ *Times Literary Supplement*: Sir John French, CIGS, came down for open day at 'The Shop', gave everyone a bollocking for slackness and indiscipline, and shortly afterwards retired the Commandant. (1978)

bottle (1938) British, naval slang ■ G. H. Jones: Others came in to see me over-anxious to please, full of 'yes, sirs' expecting always to be given what is called a 'bottle'. (1950)

rocket (1941) Orig military slang ■ Iris Murdoch: Demoyte had pondered the outrage . . . made a mental note to give Mor a rocket when he next saw him, . . . and felt immensely better. (1957)

earful (1945) Applied to a strong and often lengthy reprimand; from earlier sense, as much as one can hear ■ *Times*: I used to put a bottle on the seat and if it rolled off when the pupil let his clutch out, he got an earful. (1964)

To reprimand

blow someone **up (1712)** ■ Balcarres Ramsay: He began to blow me up for not having provided quarters for his men and horses. (1882)

rap someone **over the knuckles, rap the knuckles of** someone **(1759)** ■ Pierre Berton: Dr. A. J. Sparling felt the need to rap the knuckles of certain men of the cloth who, he said, were spending more time in the real estate offices than in visiting the homes of their congregations. (1973)

haul someone **over the coals (1795)** From earlier *fetch over the coals*; from the former treatment of heretics ■ Frederick Marryat: Lest he should be 'hauled over the coals' by the Admiralty. (1832)

give it to someone **(hot/hot and strong) (1831)** ■ James Cowan: I wish you'd give it to them hot and strong about the blasted 'kuris' worrying my sheep. (1930)

pull someone **up (1836)** ■ John Hall: It is difficult . . . before the company, to 'pull up' a boy, or to lecture a girl. (1884)

carpet (1840) Compare *on the carpet* being reprimanded ■ J. Kelman: It was a while since he had been carpeted. (1989)

give someone **a piece of one's mind (1861)** ■ Erle Stanley Gardner: He said I could wear what I had on, no matter where I went. And I certainly gave him a piece of my mind about that. (1946)

jump down someone's **throat (1879)** ■ Nicholas Blake: There's no need to jump down my throat. I was only trying to be helpful. (1940)

come down on someone **(1888)** Often in the phrase *come down on someone like a ton of bricks* ■ Graham Greene: If there's any fighting I shall come down like a ton of bricks on both of you. (1938)

pi-jaw (1891) British, dated; from the noun *pi-jaw* ■ A. S. M. Hutchinson: You . . . get me here to pijaw me about my duty to my pretty young wife. (1922)

give someone **gyp, give** someone **gip (1893)** *gyp* probably from *gee-up*

bawl someone **out, ball** someone **out (1899)** Orig US ■ L. A. G. Strong: He bawled him out. Gave him such a tongue lashing as the louse will remember to his dying day. (1942)

tell someone **where** they **get** (or **to get**) **off (1900)** Orig US ■ J. Trench: I'm sure you knew how to deal with the police. Told them where they got off, I expect. (1953)

larn (1902) Used as a threat of punishment; from earlier sense, teach, from a dialect form of *learn* ■ C. Blackstock: That'll larn you, you so-and-sos. (1956)

give (1906) Used in threats of reprimanding or punishing someone with reference back to what the person has just said or done ■ D. H. Lawrence: Hark at her clicking the flower-pots, shifting the plants. He'd give her shift the plants! He'd show her! (*a*1930)

rap (1906) Orig US; from the noun *rap* reprimand ■ *Trinidad & Tobago Overseas Express* (headline): Bar body raps Sir Hugh for attack. (1973)

take someone **(in)to the woodshed (1907)** North American; from the former practice of spanking a child in the woodshed, i.e. not in the presence of others ■ *Chicago Sun-Times*: Assuming the Fed is traditionally pliant, why does not Reagan simply take Volcker to the woodshed and tell him to ease up? (1983)

scrub (1911) Services' slang, mainly naval, dated

tick someone **off (1915)** Orig services' slang ■ *Listener*: 'Ticked off' by one of the boys for leaving his car unlocked and complete with ignition key. (1957)

roar someone **up (1917)** Mainly Australian ■ N. Lindsay: Bill was able to roar him up, anyway, for having the blinkin' cheek to come shoving his nose into Bill's affairs. (1947)

tell someone **off (1919)** ■ G. Arthur: 'It required a very great man,' said F. E. when he emerged from his interview, 'to resist the temptation to tell me off.' (1938)

go someone **scone-hot (1927)** Australian ■ Kylie Tennant: When my big brother Jim come home from work, he went Dad scone hot. (1967)

give someone **curry (1936)** Australian ■ *National Times* (Sydney): He used to play football, until he was sent down for giving curry to the ref. (1984)

ruck (1936) Variant of earlier *rux* reprimand (recorded once in 1899), of uncertain origin; perhaps related to *ruction* ■ Peter Willmott: The governor of my place is horrible. . . . He rucks you if you take more than ten minutes for a quarter of an hour's job. (1966)

chew someone **out (1937)** US, orig services' slang ■ *Guardian*: Gen Schwarzkopf also has a small personal office he sometimes uses for private discussions. It has also been used to chew out officers whose performance does not please him. (1991)

bollock, ballock (1938) British; from *bollocks* testicles ■ Peter Wright: I got ballocked left, right and centre. (1974)

tear a strip off someone, **tear** someone **off a strip (1940)** Orig R.A.F. slang ■ L. P. Hartley: If my wife saw me wearing one, she would tear me off a strip. (1957)

sort someone **out** (1941)

brass someone **off** (1943) British, orig services' slang ■ Victor Canning: After I'd brassed you off for pinching my parking space. (1964)

word (1945) Australian; from earlier sense, speak to ■ J. Murray: The 'donahs' would grimace and giggle, and the boys would 'word' 'em. (1973)

bottle (1946) British, naval slang; from the noun *bottle* reprimand

chew someone's **ass** (1946) US ■ *Black Panther*: Maybe if he saw it, some pig might . . . get his ass chewed. (1973)

mat (1948) British; compare *on the mat* being reprimanded ■ William Haggard: The interviewer had been matted and now he was uncertain. (1969)

rocket (1948) Orig military slang; from the noun *rocket* reprimand ■ John Wainwright: The assistant chief constable was still rocketing Sergeant Sykes. (1971)

ream (1950) US; usually followed by *out*; compare earlier slang senses, cheat, have anal sex with ■ Arthur Hailey: A half-wit in my department has been sitting on the thing all morning. I'll ream her out later. (1979)

knock/bang people's **heads together** (1957) Used to denote reprimanding a group of people, often in order to get them to cooperate ■ Dennis Bloodworth: Provoking desperate people into believing that they can only bring about unity among men by knocking their moronic heads together. (1975)

rub someone's **nose in it** (1963) Used to denote reprimanding someone by reminding them humiliatingly of their error ■ P. M. Hubbard: I'm sorry. I've said I'm sorry. . . . Don't rub my nose in it. (1963)

kick ass (1976) Orig and mainly US; used to denote aggressively assertive behaviour, including the reprimanding of subordinates or opponents ■ *Guardian*: A friend . . . is wrongly implicated in the crime. Thus our hero is obliged to kick some ass as well as bust some heads. (1992)

Being reprimanded

on the carpet (1900) Orig US; probably from the notion of an employee, etc. standing on the carpet in front of a superior's desk when being reprimanded ■ *Sketch*: His manager had just had him on the carpet, pointing out that his work had been getting steadily bad for the last few months. (1936)

on the peg (1904) Services' slang; applied to someone who is on a charge

in the rattle (1914) British, naval slang; denoting being on the commander's report of defaulters, and hence more broadly in confinement or in trouble ■ John Hale: The Andrew, that had taken him round the world a few times, given him his good conduct stripes and removed them when he'd been in the rattle. (1964)

on the mat (1917) Orig military slang ■ J. R. Cole: Then I was on the mat again. Now it seems a wonder I kept out of trouble as long as I did. (1949)

on the pan (1923) US

Punishment

rap (1903) Orig & mainly US; applied to a criminal conviction; often in such phrases as *bum rap* undeserved punishment (1926), *beat the rap* escape punishment, especially a prison sentence (1927), *take the rap* accept responsibility and punishment, especially for a crime (1930) ■ William Burroughs: At the time, he was out on bail, but expected to beat the rap on the grounds of illegal seizure. (1953)

the book (1908) Orig US; denoting the maximum penalty: in such phrases as (US) *get* or *do the book* suffer the maximum penalty (1927) and *throw the book at* impose the maximum penalty on (1932); from the notion of a complete book detailing all possible penalties ■ Bruce Graeme: They'll dig out some old act that hasn't been repealed . . . and then they'll throw the book at him. (1962)

See also **fizzer** and **jankers** under Discipline at **Military, Maritime, & Airforce** (p. 123).

Corporal punishment

toco, toko (1823) Dated; from Hindi *ṭhōko*, imperative of *ṭhoknā* beat, thrash ■ Joyce Cary: You'd better tell people how I took your trousers down last time and gave you toko. (1941)

swishing (1860) Used especially at Eton College; applied to a beating with a cane, etc.; from the sound of the cane ■ *Athenaeum*: Had not our young friend enjoyed better luck than he deserved, his visits to the 'swishing-room' would have been even more frequent. (1901)

six of the best (1912), **sixer** (1927) British; applied to six strokes of the cane as a school punishment; from *six + -er* ■ P. G. Wodehouse: He was . . . an officious little devil who needed six of the best with a fives-bat. (1929) ■ Colleen McCullough: They all got sixers, but Meggie was terribly upset because she thought she ought to have been the only one punished. (1977)

cuts (1915) Australian & New Zealand; applied to corporal punishment, especially of schoolchildren ■ D. Adsett: If anyone was careless enough to use the wrong peg, their coat, hat and bag could be thrown to the floor without fear of getting the cuts. (1963)

Capital punishment

See under To execute at **Killing** (p. 104).

To punish

weigh someone **off** (1925) Orig services' slang; mainly applied to sentencing someone to punishment ■ T. & P. Morris: One young man . . . commented that he had been 'weighed off at X Assizes by some old geezer togged up like Father Christmas'. (1963)

To punish by hitting

box someone's **ears** (1601) ■ William Black: I've a good mind to box your ears. (1876)

tan someone's **hide, tan** someone's **arse**

(**backside**, etc.), **tan** someone (*c*1670)
Denoting hitting someone with a cane, etc.,
especially on the buttocks, as a punishment
■ **Maggie Gee**: If you lock this door I'll tan your bum.
(1985)

swish (1856) British school slang, dated;
denoting beating someone with a cane, etc.;
from the sound of the cane ■ **Charles
Reynardson**: How he [*sc.* Dr. Keate] used to 'swish' a fellow if
he caught him up at barracks! (1875)

See also **baste, belt, clip, clout, do, dust,
larrup, lather, leathe, wallop, whack**,
under To hit and To hit repeatedly at **Violence**
(pp. 259–62).

18. **The Police**

A police officer

trap (1705) Now only Australian ■ **K. Garvey**:
Muldoon heads for town and gets the traps. (1978)

horny, horney (1753) Dated; compare earlier
sense, devil ■ **James Joyce**: Can't blame them after all
with the job they have especially the young hornies. (1922)

pig (1811) Apparently not in use in the early 20th
century, and the modern usage may be a recoinage ■ **David Lodge**: Any pig roughs you up, make sure
you get his number. (1975)

nab (1813) From the verb *nab* arrest ■ **John
Wainwright**: All the nabs in the world were in the downstairs
front. (1971)

peeler (1817) British, dated; now only used
jocularly; applied originally to a member of the
Irish constabulary, and hence to any police
officer; from the name of Robert Peel, who
founded the Irish constabulary ■ *Observer*. The
stately Conservative 'Sir' Gerald Nabarro (who, if memory
serves, had a stupid handlebar moustache and was once
apprehended by the Peelers driving a car the wrong way round
a roundabout . . .). (1997)

bobby (1844) British; from *Bobby*, a pet form of
Bob, itself a familiar form of the male personal
name *Robert*, probably in allusion to Robert Peel
who, as Home Secretary, founded the
Metropolitan Police in 1828 ■ *Washington Post*.
Some guards have always been armed, unlike traditional
English bobbies. (1993)

copper (1846) Probably from *cop* arrest + *-er*
■ **John Wainwright**: And yet he was still Lennox; the man-
hunter; the thief-taker; one of that very rare breed of men who
are born coppers. (1980)

Johnny, Johnnie (*a*1852) Dated; probably from
the male personal name (compare *John*
policeman), but compare *johndarm* policeman

johndarm (1858) Dated; from French *gendarme*
policeman ■ **Herbert Hodge**: A policeman is the usual
cockney 'Grass'. . . . Or sometimes 'Johndarm'—thus proving
we know French. (1939)

To undergo punishment

face the music (1850) Applied usually to
accepting or facing up to the unpleasant
consequences of one's own actions ■ **J. Byrom**: So
the old bitch did recognize me! Mrs Kernan and I were pretty
sure she had. That's why we did a bunk so hastily, leaving
Byron to face the bill and the music. (1958)

To avoid punishment

walk (1958) US; denoting escaping legal custody
as a result of being released from suspicion or
from a charge ■ **F. Kellerman**: They plea bargained him
down to the lesser charge . . . in exchange for the names of his
friends. Old Cory's going to walk. (1986)

cop (1859) Probably short for *copper* ■ **Len
Deighton**: A police car with two cops in it cruised past very
slowly. (1983)

slop (1859) British, dated; modification of *ecilop*,
back-slang for *police* ■ **H. G. Wells**: 'Here's a slop. Don't
let on I ran you down. Haven't a lamp, you know. Might be a bit
awkward, for *me*.' Kipps looked up towards the advancing
policeman. (1905)

scuffer, scufter (1860) Mainly Northern; origin
uncertain; perhaps from the noun *scuff* scruff of
the neck (seized for lifting, etc.) or the verb *scuff*
strike ■ **Peter Moloney**: Scuffer! Scuffer! on the beat,
With thy elephantine feet, You can't see the way to go Cos yer
'at comes down too low. (1966)

nailer (*c*1863) Dated; from *nail* arrest + *-er*

flatty, flattie (1866) Orig US; often applied
specifically to uniformed officers, as opposed to
detectives; probably from *flat-foot* police officer
(although not recorded until later) ■ **P. G.
Wodehouse**: 'You know Dobbs?' 'The flatty?' 'Our village
constable, yes.' (1949)

shoo-fly (1877) US; applied to a policeman,
usually in plain clothes, whose job is to watch
and report on other police officers; from the
interjection *shoo!* + *fly*, originally popularized by
the song 'Shoo! fly! don't bother me!' ■ **Ed
McBain**: 'You want a beer? . . . Officially I'm still on duty, but
fuck it.' 'Shooflies are heavy around the holidays.' (1980)

demon (1889) Australian; from earlier sense,
person of more than human energy, speed, skill,
etc. ■ **Kenneth Giles**: 'Tell the truth, Bert,' said the
Australian, 'always help a demon in distress.' (1967)

jack (1889) Compare *john* policeman

split (1891) From earlier sense, informer
■ **George Orwell**: He would . . . exclaim 'Fucking toe-rag!' . . .
meaning the 'split' who had arrested him. (1932)

bull (1893) US ■ **Jack London**: I noticed the bull, a
strapping policeman in a grey suit. . . . I never dreamed that
bull was after me. (1909)

grasshopper (1893) British, dated; rhyming slang for *copper* ■ *Daily Chronicle*: The criminal classes always speak of policemen as 'grasshoppers'. (1907)

rozzer (1893) Origin unknown ■ *Observer*: Horribly posh little monsters who are forever poking their noses into other people's business and turning common-as-muck smugglers over to the rozzers. (1996)

sparrow cop (1896) US; applied to a police officer assigned low-grade duties such as patrolling parks

john, John (1898) Abbreviation of *johndarm*; latterly in Australia, New Zealand, and US perhaps shortened directly from *John Hop* and *John Law* ■ R. Hall: He took possession of the book. . . . The johns'll get it if we leave it here. (1982)

harness bull, harness cop (1903) US; denoting a uniformed officer of low rank, often as opposed to a detective ■ J. Godey: The cops. From the chief on down to the harness bulls. (1972)

John Hop (1905) Australian & New Zealand; rhyming slang for *cop* ■ G. Cross: A couple of John-Hops arrived to investigate the accident. (1981)

gendarme (1906) From French *gendarme* (French) policeman ■ Hart Crane: I am to sail to *Mexico* (damn the gendarmes!) next Saturday. (1931)

John Law (1907) US; used as a personification of the police; compare *john* policeman ■ Jack London: A lot of my brother hoboes had been gathered in by John Law. (1907)

dick (1908) Dated, mainly US; compare contemporaneous sense, detective ■ *American Speech*: 'Dick' and 'bull' and 'John Law' have become established as names for the police. (1924)

flat-foot (1912) Orig US; often applied specifically to uniformed officers, as opposed to detectives; from the alleged flatness of policemen's feet ■ Cecil Day Lewis: Suppose the flatfeet got to hear of it? (1948)

Fed (1916) US; applied to an FBI agent; from more general sense, federal official; ultimately an abbreviation of *federal* ■ *Publications of the American Dialect Society*: Anyway, the Feds got the letter where I sent him $400. (1955)

Hop (1916) Australian; short for *John Hop* ■ *Bulletin* (Sydney): The Hops were taking the shattered body out of the water. (1933)

bogy, bogey (1924) British; compare earlier sense, object of dread ■ James Curtis: One of the bogies from Vine Street reckernizes me. (1936)

speed cop (1924) Applied to a traffic police officer, especially a motorcycle patrolman ■ *American Speech*: His Grace, on being stopped, demanded 'Are you a speed-cop?' The patriotic magistrates fined him £10. 10s. and suspended his license for three months. (1933)

shamus, sharmus, shommus (1925) US, dated; origin uncertain; perhaps from *shamas* Jewish beadle or sexton (from Yiddish *shames*) or from the Irish male personal name *Seamus*

■ J. O'Connor: Every Shommus on the beat knew we were going South with the stuff, but they couldn't prove it. (1928)

town clown (1927) US; applied to a police officer working in a village or small town

polis, polisman (1928) Mainly Irish and Scottish; from earlier sense, police ■ Henry Calvin: 'But I'll have to get on to the police,' I protested, and Jumbo . . . pointed to Eddie Bone and said: 'He's a polis. Get on to him.' (1967)

skipper (1929) Orig US; applied to a police captain or sergeant, or to a police chief; from earlier senses, captain, commanding officer ■ Dallas Barnes: Good piece of police work. . . . I'll fill the skipper in. I'm sure he'll be pleased. (1976)

fuzz (1930) Orig US; from earlier sense, the police ■ Damon Runyon: A race-track fuzz catches up with him. (1938)

roach (1932) US; probably from earlier sense, despicable person

statie (1934) US; applied to a state trooper or police officer; from *state* (*trooper*, etc.) + *-ie* ■ R. Banks: Study at the trooper academy down in Concord and become a statie. (1989)

Keystone (1935) From the '*Keystone* Cops', policemen featured in a series of US slapstick comedy films produced by the Keystone film company, formed by 'Mack Sennett' in 1912 ■ Alan Hunter: The local Keystones move in demanding alibis. (1971)

gangbuster (1936) Orig and mainly US; applied to an officer of a law-enforcement agency noted for its successful (and often aggressive) methods in dealing with organized crime; from *gang* + *-buster*, popularized by the long-running US radio serial *Gang Busters* (1936–57) ■ *Washington Post*: In his floppy banana trench coat and fabulous matching fedora, Warren Beatty looks more like the fashion police than a gangbuster. (1990)

jonnop (1938) Australian; contraction of *John Hop* policeman ■ Adelaide Lubbock: He's not a bad sort for a jonnop. (1963)

pounder (1938) US; perhaps from the notion of 'pounding' the beat

grass (1939) British, dated; short for dated *grasshopper* police officer

law (1944) US; applied to a police officer, sheriff, or other representative of the law ■ William Burroughs: We were in the third precinct about three hours and then the laws put us in the wagon and took us to Parish Prison. (1953)

walloper (1945) Australian; from *wallop* hit + *-er* ■ D. O'Grady: Roebourne boasted one pub, one police station with two wallopers in it, . . . and a hospital. (1968)

cozzer, kozzer (1950) British; probably an alteration of *copper*, but compare also Hebrew *chazar* pig, pork ■ *Guardian*: I grin at the picture of Frank opening the door . . . to a couple of kozzers asking him the name of the jibber who rang him on the day in question from the Cavendish Hotel. (1992)

brown bomber (1953) Australian; applied in New South Wales to a traffic warden or 'parking cop'; from the colour of their uniforms until 1975

Old Bill (1958) British; origin uncertain; perhaps from the cartoon character *Old Bill*, created by Bruce Bairnsfather (1888–1959), and portrayed as a grumbling old soldier with a large moustache ■ *Guardian*: He observed a couple of men supping nearby who looked suspiciously like plainclothes men. Coulson asked the landlord. 'Oh no,' he said, 'they're drinking pints. Old Bills only drink halves.' (1967)

cozzpot (1962) British; probably from the first syllable of *cozzer* police officer + *pot* person of importance ■ **Jeffrey Ashford**: The cozzpots ain't givin' me a chance. (1969)

roller (1964) US ■ **C. & R. Milner**: Look, for a roller (policeman) to come to this door—he's insane, he's gotta be a nut. (1973)

woolly (1965) British; applied to a uniformed police officer; compare *wolly* ■ *Private Eye*: A small army of 'Woollies'—CID slang for uniformed officers—were summoned. (1984)

narc, nark, narco (1967) US; applied to a member of a federal, state, or local drug squad; abbreviation of *narcotics agent* (+ *-o*) ■ *New Yorker*: Bo, a rookie detective . . . is so confused by the Department's manipulations that he doesn't guess that she is an undercover narc. (1975)

wolly, wally (1970) British; applied to a uniformed police officer, especially a constable; origin uncertain; perhaps the same word as *wally* fool ■ **J. B. Hilton**: These traffic Wollies make sure it all goes down, once they've licked their pencils. (1983)

roz (1971) Abbreviation of *rozzer* police officer ■ **John Wainwright**: The roz has removed his helmet. (1977)

Smokey Bear, Smoky Bear, Smok(e)y the Bear, Smok(e)y (1974) US; applied to a state police officer, and sometimes also collectively to the state police; from the name of an animal character used in US fire-prevention advertising ■ **O. McNab**: That Smoky looking at us? (1979)

bear (1975) Orig and mainly US; applied mainly to a highway patrol officer or state trooper; usually used in the plural; short for *Smokey Bear* ■ *Daily Province* (Victoria, British Columbia): The Bear in the Air will be staying up there. (1977)

sky bear (1975) North American; applied to an officer in a police helicopter

plod, P.C. Plod (1977) British; in allusion to Mr Plod the Policeman in Enid Blyton's *Noddy* stories for children ■ *Mail on Sunday*: I might well have pulled out the big hammer at the thought of that distinguished plod, John Stalker, leading a team consisting of Loyd Grossman, Fred Housego and Peter Stringfellow in the investigation of dodgy customer practices. (1991)

noddy (1980) Applied to a motor-cycle police officer; from *noddy* (bike police motor-cycle

woodentop (1981) British; applied to a uniformed police officer; from the notion that uniformed police officers have 'wooden tops' (i.e. are slow-witted), in contrast with the mental acuteness of detectives; probably a re-application of *Woodentops*, the name of a BBC television children's puppet programme first broadcast in 1955 ■ **John Wainwright**: I'm a copper. An ordinary flatfoot. . . . A real old woodentop. That's me. (1981)

A female police officer

Dickless Tracy (1963) Jocular, orig US; punningly from *dick* penis and the name of *Dick Tracy* US comic-strip detective introduced in 1931 by Chester Gould

A detective

D (1879) Abbreviation ■ **F. D. Sharpe**: They [*sc.* crooks] very often know that a man is a 'D', as they call us, without being aware of his identity, because of the fact that he happens to be on the lookout. (1938)

tec, 'tec (1879) Abbreviation ■ *Daily Mirror*: Porn tec admits bribe plot. (1977)

dee (1882) The first letter of *detective* ■ **Erik De Mauny**: You've got to look out, if the dees come. (1949)

jack (1899) From earlier sense, police officer ■ **John Wainwright**: These county coppers . . . couldn't get their minds unhooked from the words 'New Scotland Yard'—as if every jack in the Metropolitan Police District worked from there. (1971)

demon (1900) Australian; from earlier sense, police officer ■ *Sunday Mail Magazine* (Brisbane): To the Australian criminal a demon is a . . . detective. (1967)

eye (1900) US; used originally in the phrase *the Eye* to denote the Pinkerton Detective Agency (from the Pinkerton trademark, an all-seeing eye), and hence applied to a Pinkerton detective or armed guard and more generally to any detective, especially a private one

busy (1904) British; from the adjective *busy* ■ **Margery Allingham**: I don't know 'ow long we've got before the busies come trampin' in. (1948)

Pink (1904) US; applied to a member of the Pinkerton detective agency; abbreviation of *Pinkerton*

gumshoe (1906) US; from the notion of someone who walks around stealthily wearing 'gumshoes' or galoshes: *gumshoe* from *gum* rubbery material + *shoe* ■ **Dashiel Hammett**: He . . . looked me up and down, growled: 'So you're a lousy gum-shoe.' (1927)

dick (1908) Perhaps an arbitrary contraction of *detective*; perhaps a back-formation from Irish gypsy slang *dicked* being watched, from Romany *dik* look, see, from Hindi *dekhnā* look (compare *dekko*) ■ **Edgar Wallace**: They'd persuaded a couple of dicks—detectives—to watch the barriers. (1928)

Richard, richard (1914) Mainly US; punningly from *dick* detective (also a familiar form of the name *Richard*) ■ **Edmund McGirr**: A surprisingly high proportion of well-to-do murderers hire private richards to delve into the demise of the victim. (1974)

fink (1925)

shamus, sharmus, shommus (1925) US; origin uncertain; see **shamus** under A police officer (p. 108) ■ *New Yorker*: I think my wife is having me tailed by a private shamus. (1977)

op (1926) Applied to a (private) detective; short for *operative*

The police

the boys (or **gentlemen, men) in blue (1851)** From the colour of police officers' uniforms ■ *Sun*: But BOLA, the bookie-funded flunkies, have called in 'the boys in blue'. (1992)

the polis (*c*1874) Mainly Irish and Scottish; representing a regional pronunciation of *police* ■ John Buchan: Ye'll get a good turn-out at your meeting . . . but they're sayin' that the polis will interfere. (1919)

the fuzz (1929) Orig US; origin unknown ■ P. G. Wodehouse: If the fuzz search my room, I'm sunk. (1971)

the law (1929) Orig US ■ *Times*: I inquired of the Law where I might cash a cheque, and was directed to the nearest travel agency. (1972)

the Sweeney, the Sweeny (1936) British; applied to the flying squad; short for *Sweeney Todd*, rhyming slang for *flying squad*; from the name of a London barber who murdered his customers, the central character of a play by George Dibdin Pitt (1799–1855) ■ *Guardian Weekly*: Was designed—as they say in The Sweeney—to put the frighteners on Labour knockers. (1977)

heat (1937) Orig US; also in early use applied to an individual police officer; usually preceded by *the*; from earlier sense, intensive pursuit (by the police) ■ *New Yorker*: Out the door comes this great big porcine member of the heat, all belts and bullets and pistols and keys. (1969)

the man, the Man (1962) US; from earlier sense, people in authority

the filth (1967) British ■ John Wainwright: He's a big wheel in the filth, Mr Nolan. Y' know . . . assistant chief constable and all that. (1979)

the bill (1969) British; short for *Old Bill* ■ *British Journal of Photography*: There wasn't going to be no questions asked in the House about some working-class kid getting hisself duffed up by the Bill if said Bill got his old man too chicken-shit to say a dicky-bird about it. (1979)

Old Bill (1970) British; from earlier sense, a policeman ■ *New Statesman*: If they were caught at it when the Old Bill . . . staged one of their frequent raids then we would all be up on a charge of 'maintaining a disorderly house'. (1976)

bacon (1974) US; suggested by *pig* police officer

the plod (1986) British; from *plod* police officer ■ Lloyd Bradley: So far so good Miami Vice . . . until the plod learns that the cartel's Mr. Big now enjoys US government approval and is therefore untouchable. (1993)

A police station

factory (1891) ■ Roger Busby: Detectives relieved the tedium of observation duties by using the facilities of the local police stations, the 'factory' in the area they happened to be working. (1987)

cop-shop (1941) ■ Maureen Duffy: The blue light above the cop-shop door for once meant safety. (1962)

nick (1957) British; compare earlier sense, prison ■ Joan Lock: Back at the nick the station officer was very cross. (1968)

A police district

manor (1924) British ■ Robin Cook: 'Then they whipped him down to the nick on the hurry-up.' 'Which manor?' 'The local nick.' (1962)

A police vehicle

pie-wagon (1898) US; applied to a police van or black Maria

paddy wagon (1930) US; applied to a police van or car ■ *Chicago Tribune*: He was informed by the pink faced lockup keeper that all Chicago's 'paddy waggons' are motor driven. (1932)

meat wagon (1954) Applied to a police van or black Maria ■ *Listener*: The bogeys . . . bundle us into the back of a meat-wagon. (1964)

squadrol (1961) US; applied to a small police van; from *squad* + *pat(rol*

noddy bike, noddy (1964) Applied to a lightweight police motor-cycle; perhaps in allusion to *Noddy* small elf-like boy in children's stories by Enid Blyton (1897–1968), from the toy-like characteristics of the motor-cycle (although said to be due to the rider's inability to salute safely, which necessitates nodding to acknowledge a superior officer) ■ *Police Review*: Making its debut appearance yesterday was the probable successor to the Noddy. (1972)

squad (1974) US; applied to a police car; short for *squad car* ■ Dell Shannon: Bill Moss, riding a squad on night watch, . . . picked up a man lying against the curb in the street. (1984)

sky bear (1975) North American; applied to a police helicopter

jam sandwich (1987) British; applied to a police car; from the car's colour: white bodywork with a horizontal red stripe ■ B. Whitehead: 'Look, there's a jam sandwich,' said Ann. . . . 'Jam sandwich. Police car painted white and red. Don't they teach you colloquial English at your Swedish schools?' (1992)

A police bell

gong (1938) Dated; applied to a warning bell on a police car. Hence the verb **bell** denoting getting a driver to stop by sounding this bell (1934) ■ Tom Wisdom: He will then have to 'gong' you into the side on a busy trunk road. (1966)

Police action

squeal (1949) Applied to a call for police assistance or investigation ■ Ed McBain: Parker's on the prowl, Hernandez is answering a squeal. (1960)

Police surveillance

obbo, obo (1933) From *ob(servation + -o* ■ Bruce Graeme: We're keeping a man, suspected of robbery . . . under obbo. (1972)

Police information

reader (1920) US, criminals' slang, dated; applied to a circular notifying police officers of a suspected criminal to be arrested

19. **Prisons**

Prison

quod (1700) Often in the phrase *in quod* in prison; origin unknown ■ Listener: Now, one of this chap's maternal uncles . . . has got to pay a 50 quid debt or go to quod. (1968)

(the) clink (1785) From the name of a former prison in Southwark, London ■ Kylie Tennant: They'll only dock my pay or shove me in clink. (1946)

factory (1806) Australian, dated; applied to a women's prison

(the) jug (1815) Orig US; short for obsolete slang *stone-jug* prison, often applied specifically to Newgate, former prison in the City of London ■ Economist: Incarceration is incarceration; those in jug will care little whether they are said to have been punished or regulated. (1987)

mill (1851) Dated; from earlier sense, treadmill ■ J. Jones: 'You were here when one of the old ones was in the mill, weren't you, Jack?' 'Two,' Malloy said. 'Both of them during my first stretch.' (1951)

the booby hatch (1859), the booby (1929) US; compare earlier sense, hatch on a boat which lifts off in one piece

the cooler (1872) Orig US; often also applied specifically to a solitary-confinement cell ■ C. Dickson: I am not at a time of life when one enjoys being chucked in the cooler for telling truths. (1943)

choky, chokey (1873) British; originally Anglo-Indian, from Hindi *caukī* shed ■ F. Donaldson: I'll buck you up when I get home . . . that's to say if I'm not arrested and shoved in chokey. (1982)

nick (1882) From *nick* arrest ■ It: At the moment, there are over a hundred of our kids in nick as a result of the busts at 144 Piccadilly & Endell Street. (1969)

pen (1884) US; abbreviation of *penitentiary* ■ High Times: Right now I'm in east Tennessee facing a five-to-15 year term in the state pen for something I haven't done—mainly for selling a schedule-one drug to a narc. (1975)

rock pile (1888) US; applied metaphorically to a prison, from the convicts' task of breaking

Police insignia

potsy (1932) Northeastern US; applied to a police officer's badge; from (the name of a squashed tin thrown instead of a stone in) a game similar to hopscotch ■ New York Herald Tribune: This boniface has been wearing his potsy as house dick for only a brief time. (1952)

tin (1949) US; applied to a police officer's badge or shield ■ S. Marlowe: Mason Reed flashed the tin. 'Police officer. March right out of here.' (1975)

Military police

See under **Military, Maritime & Airforce** (p. 122).

stones ■ K. Eubank: We were . . . given 30 days on the rock pile or the privilege of leaving town on the first rattler out, which took us into Memphis. (1927)

peter (1890) Orig Australian; applied to a prison cell, a cell in a police station, etc. ■ Guardian: 'Hurry up and slop out'—'Get back in your f— Peter'. (1965)

the boob (1908) Orig US; short for *booby-hatch* ■ Coast to Coast 1941: Seeing Don get chucked out of the Ballarat and carted off to the boob. (1941)

(the) hoosegow (1911) US; from American Spanish *juzgao*, Spanish *juzgado* tribunal, from Latin *judicatum*, neuter past participle of *judicare* judge ■ Diana Ramsay: I'm not going to answer any questions. . . . Okay. Off we go to the hoosegow. (1973)

the can (1912) Orig US ■ 20th Century: I'll stand by my man Though he's in the can. (1961)

the tank (1912) US; applied to a large cell in a police station, specifically (in the phrase *drunk tank*) one in which drunks are held ■ P. G. Wodehouse: It gets boring after a while being thrown into the tank, always with that nervous feeling that this time the old man won't come through with the necessary bail. (1964) ■ Len Deighton: And then tossed into the drunk tank like a common criminal. (1981)

the big house (1916) Orig US; compare earlier British sense, workhouse ■ D. Hume: You'll land yourself in the big house for fourteen years. (1942)

mush, moosh (1917) Dated, services' slang; applied to a guardroom or cell, or to a military prison; perhaps from obsolete dialect *mush* crush ■ Athenaeum: When a man was 'run in' the guardroom he was in 'clink' or in 'moosh'. (1919)

the pokey (1919) Mainly US; alteration of *pogey* hostel, poor-house, perhaps influenced by *poky* cramped, confined ■ National Observer (US): Were it possible to prosecute an actor for stealing scenes, The Missouri Breaks (United Artists) would land Marlon Brando in the pokey for life. (1976)

flowery (1925) British; applied to a prison cell; short for *flowery dell*, rhyming slang for *cell* ■ T. Clayton: Found aht on the Moor, . . . that if you have a new play to read weekends in the flowery . . . you can kid yourself you're having a Saturday night aht. (1970)

the glass-house (1925) British; applied to a military prison; from the name given to the detention barracks of the Aldershot Command at Woking, which had a glass roof; compare earlier sense, building with glass walls and roof ■ James Bertram: Someone with a lengthy 'crime sheet'—perhaps . . . a notorious frequenter of the glasshouse. (1947)

the dummy (1936) New Zealand; applied to the punishment cell in a prison ■ O. Burton: The aggressor in this case was promptly led off and incarcerated in the 'dummy'. (1945)

the slammer, the slammers (1952) Orig US; perhaps from the slamming shut of cell doors ■ Desmond Bagley: This one's not for the slammer. He'll go to Broadmoor for sure. (1977)

the slam (1960) US; perhaps an abbreviation of *slammer* prison ■ Joseph Gores: You're going to the slam for fifteen. (1978)

juvie, juvey (1967) Applied to a detention centre for juvenile delinquents; abbreviation of *juvenile*

In prison

in lumber (1812) British; compare earlier dated slang *lumber* house used by criminals ■ J. Prescot: My poor old dad was in and out of lumber all his life. (1963)

in stir (1851) Origin uncertain; perhaps from Romany *sturbin* gaol ■ Edmund Crispin: You get better conditions than that in stir. (1977)

in hock (1860) From Dutch *hok* hutch, prison

inside (1888) ■ Charles Drummond: Over the years she had been convicted three times, spending in all four years 'inside'. (1972)

up the river (1891) Euphemistic, orig US; originally applied specifically to Sing Sing prison, situated up the Hudson River from the city of New York, and hence to any prison ■ P. G. Wodehouse: A member of the jury which three years before had sent him up the river for what the Press of New York was unanimous in describing as a well-earned sentence. (1951)

upstate (1934) US, euphemistic; from earlier sense, remote from centres of population, from the placement of prisons in areas remote from large cities ■ Ed McBain: She got married while I was upstate doing time. (1977)

behind bars (1951) ■ *Borneo Bulletin*: Now Hassan . . . , who got $50 out of the deal, is behind bars for six months. (1977)

Imprisonment; a prison sentence

lag (1821) Dated; applied to a term of imprisonment or transportation; compare earlier sense, convict

stretch (1821) Sometimes used with a numeral denoting imprisonment for the stated number of years; also applied specifically to twelve months' imprisonment ■ P. Branch: He's in Joe Gurr

again. He got nicked in Cardiff on a snout gaff. . . . It's only a two stretch and a lot of the Boys had their collars felt. (1951)

moon (1830) Applied to a month's imprisonment ■ Kylie Tennant: I got a twelve moon. (1953)

time (1837) Especially in the phrase *do time* serve a prison sentence ■ E. St. Johnston: The Queen was much interested and amused for I don't expect she often lunches with someone who has 'done time'. (1978)

sixer (1849) Applied to six months' imprisonment or hard labour; from *six* + *-er* ■ D. W. Maurer: Maybe he will get off with a *bit* . . . or a *sixer*, which is six months in jail. (1955)

solitary (1854) Short for *solitary confinement* ■ W. M. Raine: 'He's been in solitary for a week,' explained the warden. (1924)

bird-lime (1857) British, dated; rhyming slang for *time* prison sentence ■ *Radio Times*: In the past Charley's done his 'birdlime' but he was given time off for good behaviour. (1962)

bit (1866) ■ J. H. Smyth: The only question was how much of a bit Lucky would get. (1951)

a trey, a tray (1887) Applied to three years' imprisonment; from earlier more general sense, set of three; ultimately from Old French and Anglo-Norman *treis, trei* three (modern French *trois*) ■ Anthony Burgess: 'I know all about you. You did a tray on the moor.' . . . 'It wasn't a tray . . . it was only a stretch.' (1960)

hard (1890) British; short for *hard labour* ■ John Braine: 'Oh my,' Roy said, 'strap me to the mast, said Ulysses. Almost worth ten years hard, isn't she?' (1957)

a neves, a nevis (1901) Applied to seven years' hard labour; back-slang for *seven* ■ Frank Norman: You're f—ing lucky, I'm doing a bleeding neves. (1958)

spot (1901) US; often used with a numeral to denote a sentence of the stated number of years ■ M. Brewer: He was serving a three spot for cunning. . . . He got into a row with one of the warders. (1966)

a carpet (1903) British; applied to three months' imprisonment; short for *carpet-bag*, rhyming slang for obsolete slang *drag* three months' imprisonment ■ James Curtis: Long enough to've been in Wandsworth and done a carpet. (1936)

life (1903) Applied to imprisonment for life ■ Edgar Wallace: He shot a copper and got life. (1924)

Kathleen Mavourneen (1910) Australian & New Zealand; applied to a prison sentence of indeterminate length; in allusion to the song 'Kathleen Mavourneen', in which the refrain runs 'It may be for years, it may be for ever' ■ H. C. Baker: The judge declared him an 'habitual criminal' and gave him a 'Kathleen Mavourneen'. (1978)

a sleep (1911) Orig US; usually applied to a comparatively short sentence ■ J. Phelan: I wasn't interested myself [in escaping]. Three years was nothing—just a sleep, as you chaps put it. (1938)

jolt (1912) Orig US ■ **D. Hume:** They are only too ready to turn King's evidence. . . . You'd take a very stiff jolt. (1936)

Paddy Doyle (1919) British services' slang, dated; usually in the phrase *do a Paddy Doyle* serve a term of confinement

bird (1924) British; often in the phrase *do (one's) bird* serve a prison sentence; short for *bird-lime* ■ **Listener:** Having done his bird, as imprisonment is called in the best circles. (1953)

sawbuck (1925) US; applied to ten years' imprisonment; from earlier sense, ten-dollar bill

newspaper (1926) Dated; applied to thirty days' imprisonment; from the time supposedly taken by a convict to read a newspaper

rap (1927) Mainly US ■ **Ellery Queen:** You're in a tough spot. Do you know what the rap for blackmail is in this State? (1935)

double sawbuck, double saw (1930) US; applied to twenty years' imprisonment; from earlier sense, twenty-dollar bill

a handful (1930) Applied to five years' imprisonment; from the five fingers of the hand ■ **Michael Gilbert:** He's had a two-stretch. . . . He'll collect a handful next time. (1953)

a taxi (1930) US; applied to between five and fifteen years' imprisonment; from the fares (in cents) displayed in New York taxis ■ **Dell Shannon:** Whalen had done a five-to-fifteen year stretch—that's a taxi. (1962)

stage (1932) Applied to a period of imprisonment during which privileges are allowed ■ **Frank Norman:** My punishment was three days bread and water . . . and twenty eight days stage. (1958)

fall (1933) US ■ **R. Novak:** Did a fall for armed robbery. (1974)

trick (1933) US ■ **Joseph Gores:** He got caught . . . and did a little trick at Quentin. (1975)

the clock (1950) Australian; applied to twelve months' imprisonment; from the number of hours on a clock face ■ **J. Alard:** Anyhow I'd better stall; if I get picked up I'll at least get the clock. (1968)

a pontoon (1950) British; applied to twenty-one months' imprisonment; from the name of the card game *pontoon* or vingt-et-un (French for 'twenty-one') ■ **Edmund Crispin:** He had been put away three times . . . the third for a pontoon. (1977)

a rouf, a rofe (1950) British; applied to four years' imprisonment; back-slang for *four* ■ **Frank Norman:** I tried to tell them that it had been a business deal, but you know what it's like talking to a moronic cozzer, so that was it I got a rouf. (1958)

porridge (1954) British; perhaps influenced by earlier *stir* prison, imprisonment, and by conventional prison food ■ **John Wainwright:** D'you think I'd forget the frigging jack 'ut sent me down for two years' porridge? (1968)

seg (1974) Mainly US; applied to an isolation unit for difficult prisoners; abbreviation of *segregation* (*unit*) ■ **New Society:** He went straight into the segregation unit [at Wormwood Scrubs]. . . . He continued his [hunger] strike simply in order to prevent an early return to 'seg'. (1977)

To send or be sent to prison

dub up (1753) Applied to locking someone up in a cell; from obsolete *dub* key ■ **Frank Norman:** Everybody in the nick had already been dubbed up for the night. (1958)

lag (1812) Dated; denoting sending someone to prison or transporting them; compare the noun *lag* prisoner

send down (1840) Orig US ■ **P. B. Yuill:** 'Is there any chance he *could* go to gaol?' 'You'd like him sent down, would you?' (1976)

slough (1848) Dated; from *slough* soft muddy ground ■ **Jack Black:** They'll . . . haul us over to Martinez . . . an' slough us in the county jail. (1926)

send up (1852) Now US; denoting sending someone to prison

put away (1872) ■ **W. M. Duncan:** He was an inspector then. He put me away. (1973)

settle (1899) US ■ **D. W. Maurer:** Maybe he will get *settled*, or sent to prison. (1955)

go down (1906) ■ **Margery Allingham:** He went down for eighteen months and is now in Italy pulling his weight, I believe. He's a crook, but not a traitor. (1945)

bang up (1950) British; probably from the slamming shut of a cell door (compare *slammer* prison) ■ **Guardian:** Stefan Kiszko, who was banged up for 16 years for a child murder he did not, in fact, commit. (1992)

A prisoner

jail-bird, gaol-bird (1618) Applied especially to someone who has been in prison a long time or is often sent to prison; from the notion of a caged bird ■ **Guardian:** One new prison rule would have appalled the most hardened jailbird. (1992)

lag (1812) Especially in the phrase *old lag* ex-convict or habitual convict; origin unknown; compare obsolete *lag* carry off, steal ■ **Sunday Mail Magazine** (Brisbane): The old lags inhabiting Queensland's prisons in 1885 must have been disappointed when the colony's official flogger, John Hutton, retired. (1989)

lifer (1830) Applied to a prisoner serving a life sentence (or earlier, someone sentenced to transportation for life); from *life* + *-er* ■ **D. A. Dye:** The swagger, clearly visible chevrons and pissed-off set to the man's jaw all spelled 'Lifer'. (1986)

con (1888) Abbreviation of *convict* ■ **Frank Norman:** I had three really good friends among the cons. (1958)

star (1903) British; applied to a convict serving a first prison sentence; from the star-shaped badge formerly worn by first-offenders in prison ■ **A. Miller:** Several . . . said that if that was what one-time Stars became, they were cured of returning. (1976)

ex-con (1906) Abbreviation of *ex-convict* ■ Jack
London: I have known ex-cons who became dead for peeping.
(1911)

loser (1912) US; often used with a numeral to
denote someone who has been to prison the
stated number of times ■ *Houston* (Texas)
Chronicle: Bob, a three-time loser with a long line of busts
and drug abuse . . . was sick of his life. (1973)

red band (1950) Applied to a privileged prisoner,
allowed to carry out special duties

yardbird (1956) US; compare earlier services'
slang sense, new recruit or one assigned to
menial duties

tobacco baron (1964) Applied to a prisoner
who controls the supply of cigarettes to other
prisoners, and so dominates them

passman (1965) Applied to a prisoner allowed
to leave his cell in order to enjoy certain
privileges

A prisoner-of-war

kriegie (1944) Applied to an Allied prisoner-of-
war in Germany during World War II;
abbreviation of German *Kriegsgefangener*
prisoner-of-war ■ D. M. Davin: But there I was, a bloody
kriegie for the rest of the war. (1956)

Prison staff

screw (1812) Applied to a prison warder; from
earlier sense, (skeleton) key, from warders'
locking and unlocking of cell doors (compare
standard English *turnkey* gaoler) ■ G. F. Newman:
The lights never out, pervy screws watching every movement.
(1970)

twirl (1891) Applied to a prison warder; from
earlier sense, (skeleton) key, from warders'
locking and unlocking of cell doors ■ *John o'
London's*: Prison officers . . . are sometimes referred to as
twirls. (1962)

ham and beef (1941) Dated; applied to the
chief warder of a prison; rhyming slang for *chief*

goon (1945) Applied by British and US prisoners-
of-war to their German guards during World
War II; from earlier sense, thug ■ *Times*: 'Goon-
baiting', which was the favourite occupation of the prisoners.
(1962)

Prison uniform

stripes (1887) US; from the stripes patterning
such uniforms ■ Preston Sturges: He's going to be in
jail, Trudy, for a long time. He can't do you any good in stripes,
honey. (1943)

patch (1958) British; applied to any of a number
of cloth pieces sewn on to a uniform in order to
identify a prisoner as an escapee ■ S. McConville:
He would be put on the E(scape) *list* and compelled to wear an
easily identifiable uniform; this is known as *being in patches*.
(1980)

Prison discipline

dry bath (1933) Applied to a search of a prisoner
who has been stripped naked ■ *New Statesman*:
Two or three times a week the Heavy Mob rushed into our cells
and gave us a 'dry bath', which adequately describes the
search of a man who is standing 'starkers' in the middle of his
cell. (1965)

Communication inside prison

kite (1923) Applied to a letter or message
smuggled into or out of prison; from earlier,
more general sense, letter. Hence the verb **kite**
smuggle a letter or message into or out of
prison (1925) ■ *Detective Fiction Weekly*: A letter
which I had 'kited' out of the prison. (1936)

floater (1933) British; applied to a book,
newspaper, etc. passed surreptitiously from cell
to cell ■ Frank Norman: It's [*sc.* a book] a floater so you
can sling it if you think you are going to get a turn over. (1958)

Parole

violate (1971) US; denoting accusing or finding a
prisoner on parole guilty of violating the
conditions of parole ■ H. B. Franklin: Living outside
Los Angeles, with life going reasonably well, Brady suddenly
found himself with a zealous new parole officer, who
threatened to violate him for driving a car, for having a woman
spend the night in his apartment, or for writing anything he
disapproved of. (1978)

To leave prison

spring (1900) Orig US; used both transitively and
intransitively, to denote release and escape
■ *Daily Telegraph*: Miss Mary Tyler, the English school-
teacher who has spent more than four years in Indian jails
awaiting trial, is to be returned to a high security prison this
week in case militant Maoists try to 'spring' her. (1974)
■ Kenneth Orvis: When I sprung . . . Moss was standing by
the prison door. (1962)

hit the bricks (1931) US; denoting being set
free

have it away (1958) British; denoting escaping
from prison or custody ■ Tony Parker: After I'd had it
away three times, they decided it was no use bothering with
me in these open places. (1969)

Leaving prison

spring (1901) Orig US; applied to a release or an
escape; from the verb *spring* release, escape
■ F. Ross: Springing some bugger from the Scrubs—O.K. Not
easy. . . . You can't pull a spring like that without help on the
inside. (1977)

Out of prison

on the grass (1885) Australian

Escaped from prison

over the wall (1935) Often in the phrase *go over
the wall* escape from prison ■ *Times*: He knew it was
an unwritten law that an escape extinguished such a debt, and
so he decided to 'go over the wall'. He gave himself up at

Clacton-on-Sea. (1963) ■ G. Beare: He's out. Over the wall. (1973)

The world out of prison

the outside (1903) *outside* also used adverbially to denote 'out of prison' ■ Charles Drummond: Kath

hasn't been having it so good, what with a couple of worthless sons who haven't the sense to keep on the outside. (1972)
■ *Research Studies* (Washington State College, Pullman): A boy entering this institution [*sc.* a reformatory] learns more bad habits than he would ever think of learning outside. (1937)

20. **Vagrancy**

A vagrant, tramp, etc.

mumper (1673) From obsolete *mump* beg + *-er*
■ *Countryman*: Besides the gypsies there are many other pickers—tramps, mumpers, all sorts. (1972)

pikey (1847) Dated; applied to a gypsy or traveller; from *pike* turnpike ■ Peter Wildeblood: My family's all Pikeys, but we ain't on the road no more! (1955)

bum (1864) Orig and mainly US; probably short for obsolete *bummer* idler, loafer ■ *Punch*: The bums in the dosshouse have reached bottom. (1958)

dosser (1866) British; from *doss* sleep rough + *-er*
■ *Police Review*: The tipple of the down-and-out itinerant, the 'dosser' or 'scat'. (1984)

vag (1868) Australian & North American; abbreviation of *vagrant* ■ M. Rutherford: The vag waited but the policeman just walked past him to a car. (1979)

whaler, waler (1878) Australian; applied originally to a tramp whose route followed the course of a river; from their catching 'whales' (a type of freshwater fish) in the rivers they lived by ■ Charles Barrett: I've been a whaler . . . since I was a nipper, mostly on the Murray. (1941)

toe-ragger (1891) Australian; from obsolete slang *toe-rag* tramp, from the rags wound round a tramp's foot in place of a sock

jocker (1893) North American; applied to a tramp who is accompanied by a youth who begs for him or is his homosexual partner; from *jock* male genitals + *-er*

prushun (1893) US, dated; applied to a tramp's boy; origin unknown ■ *Dialect Notes*: The tramp lives in idleness while the boy goes about begging food for both. Many continue as *prushuns* until middle life, and when their master dies are left helpless. (1927)

swamper (1894) Australian; applied to a tramp who travels on foot but has his swag carried on a wagon, and hence to one who obtains a lift; from earlier sense, assistant to the driver of horses, mules, etc. ■ T. Ronan: My . . . fellow swamper tossed his swag off [the mailman's truck] here; he was home. (1966)

gay-cat (1897) US; applied to a young or inexperienced tramp, especially one who has a homosexual relationship with an older tramp

drummer (1898) Australian & New Zealand, dated; partly from earlier sense, commercial traveller, partly from *drum* swagman's pack

stiff (1899) Applied especially to a migratory worker ■ Edmund Ward: The driver . . . reached out to pull

Burnett into the dusty cab. Construction stiff. A wandering freemasonry. (1976)

bindle man, bindle stiff (1900) North American; from *bindle* tramp's bedding-roll

stew-bum (1902) US, dated; applied especially to a tramp who is habitually drunk; compare *stewed* drunk ■ B. Harwin: How come you to be a drunk damn' stew-bum when I found you? (1952)

dingbat (1918) US; origin uncertain ■ Jack Black: If you was some kind of a rank dingbat you wouldn't have been invited down here. (1926)

dyno, dino (1918) US; apparently shortened from obsolete vagrants' slang *dynamiter* sponger

skipper (1925) British; from earlier sense, sleeping place for a vagrant ■ *Guardian*: It was the night of the big Government census of the 'skippers'—the people who sleep rough. (1965)

ring-tail (1927) US

saddle tramp (1942) North American; applied to a vagrant who travels on horseback ■ *Radio Times*: Kirk Douglas back on the range for King Vidor, in the one about the saddle tramp up against the barbed wire. (1979)

slag (1955) From earlier sense, objectionable person

road kid (1970) Applied to a young tramp

bag lady (1972) Orig US; applied to a homeless woman who carries her possessions in shopping bags ■ Martin Amis: They even had a couple of black-clad bagladies sitting silently on straight chairs by the door. (1984)

skell (1982) US; applied in New York City to a homeless person or derelict, especially one who sleeps in the subway system; perhaps shortened from *skeleton*

scat (1984) British; often applied specifically to a vagrant seeking work in a London market; first recorded in 1984, but in use earlier; origin unknown ■ C. H. Rolph: One of the regular market fish-porters . . . would need an extra hand on the barrow, and he took the first comer from among the 'scats' who were waiting to pounce. (1987)

Vagrants collectively

profesh (1901) Applied to the community of professional tramps; abbreviation of *profession*

Vagrancy

vag (1859) Australian & North American; abbreviation; often in the phrase *on the vag* on a charge of vagrancy ■ K. S. Prichard: Was you on the game, love? Or did they get you on the vag? (1959)

A vagrant's possessions, equipment, etc.

drum (1866) Australian & New Zealand; applied to a swagman's pack ■ *Bulletin* (Sydney): I sees a bloke comin' along the road from Winton with 'is drum up. (1933)

bluey (1891) Australian; applied to a blanket as used by travellers in the bush; from its colour ■ S. Campion: To bed they went, wrapped as before in their blueys on the rain-loud verandah. (1941)

Matilda, matilda (1892) Australian; applied to a vagrant's pack; from the female personal name *Matilda*; the reason for the application is unknown ■ Marshall & Drysdale: We unrolled our Matildas between the dunes. (1962)

nap (1892) Australian; applied to blankets or other covering used by someone sleeping rough; probably from *knapsack* ■ *Coast to Coast 1944*: If you carry enough nap, you goes hungry; if you carry enough tucker you sleeps cold. (1945)

shiralee, shirallee (1892) Australian; applied to a traveller's bundle of blankets and personal belongings; origin unknown ■ *Sunday Sun* (Brisbane): The fences, the barns, the houses—they're all gone and I'm out on the road with my shiralee. (1974)

turkey (1893) North American & Australian; applied to a bundle or holdall carried by itinerant workers, vagrants, etc. ■ R. D. Symons: The cowboys' 'turkeys'—as they call their bedrolls, in which were wrapped their personal possessions such as tobacco—when the outfit was on the move. (1963)

bindle (1900) North American; applied to a vagrant's bedding-roll; probably an alteration of *bundle*, but compare Scottish *bindle* cord or rope that binds something ■ John Steinbeck: George unslung his bindle and dropped it gently on the bank. (1937)

Wagga, Wagga blanket, Wagga rug (1900) Australian; applied to an improvised covering, especially of sacking; abbreviation of *Wagga*

Wagga, name of a town in New South Wales ■ L. Hadow: 'Take your wagga, then.' 'No, it's too heavy.' (1969)

lump (1912) US; applied to a parcel of food given to a tramp ■ Kenneth Allsop: I met a husky burly taking of his rest And he flagged me with a big lump and a can. (1967)

To travel as a vagrant, carrying one's possessions

hump one's **swag** (**bluey, drum, knot, Matilda**) **(1851)** Australian ■ Barry Norman: He was unable to get a lift home so he decided to hump his bluey the sixty miles to the mission. (1976)

waltz Matilda (1893) Australian ■ Jean Devanny: Nowadays they waltz Matilda on bikes. (1945)

A place frequented by vagrants

jungle (1914) Orig US; applied to a camp for vagrants ■ *Islander* (Victoria, British Columbia): During the depression of the 1930s gangs of youths ranged across the country, riding the rails and sleeping in jungles, and caused us concern. (1971)

stem (1914) US; applied to a street frequented by vagrants ■ Dean Stiff: The hobo also damns the hash houses along the stem. (1931)

skid row (1931) Mainly North American; applied to a part of a town frequented by vagrants, alcoholics, etc.; alteration of *skid road* in same sense, from earlier sense, part of town frequented by loggers (original sense, track formed by skids along which logs are rolled)

derry (1968) Applied to a derelict building; from *derelict* + *-y* ■ *Guardian*: Mary . . . lives with her husband, two Belgian boys, three girls, and a young Frenchman in a 'derry'—a deserted house—in Chelsea. (1969)

A place where vagrants sleep

See **doss, doss-house, flop-house, kip, kip-house, kip-shop, skipper, spike** at Place to sleep and **hot bed** at Bed, both under **Sleep** (p. 25).

21. **Politics**

Politicians and political activists

politico (1630) Usually derogatory; from Italian or Spanish *politico* politician ■ *Guardian*: The press is here . . . and surprisingly important politicoes in ineffective disguises. (1960)

red (1851) Derogatory; applied to an anarchist or republican, a Russian Bolshevik, or a Communist or extreme socialist; often in the phrase *reds under the bed*; from the association of the colour red with left-of-centre radicals ■ Dorothy Sayers: I'm a Tory, if anything. I'm certainly not a Red. Why should I help to snatch the good gold from the Primrose Leaguers and hand it over to the Third International? (1928) ■ John Le Carré: There's a story that you people had

some local Russian embassy link. . . . Any Reds under your bed . . . if I may ask? (1977)

straddle-bug (1872) US, dated; applied to a politician who is non-committal or who equivocates; from earlier sense, name of a type of beetle; from the notion of 'straddling' or being equivocal about an issue ■ *Saturday Evening Post*: I will not support either a conservative or a straddlebug. (1948)

high-binder (1890) US; applied to a fraudulent politician; from earlier, more general sense, swindler ■ A. H. Lewis: He's goin' to take copies of th' accounts that show what th' Chief an' them other high-binders at the top o' Tammany have been doin'. (1903)

snollygoster (1895) US; applied to a shrewd unprincipled politician; from earlier, more general sense, shrewd unprincipled person; ultimate origin uncertain; perhaps connected with *snallygaster*, name of a monster supposedly found in Maryland, from German *schnelle Geister* quick spirits ■ *Columbus* (Ohio) *Dispatch*: A Georgia editor kindly explains that 'a snollygoster is a fellow who wants office, regardless of party, platform or principles, and who, whenever he wins, gets there by the sheer force of monumental talknophical assumnacy'. (1895)

red-ragger (1916) Australian, derogatory; applied to a Communist or socialist; from the red flag that symbolizes the Communist movement ■ N. Medcalf: Bluey was considered a bit of a red-ragger. (1985)

Shinner (1921) Applied to a member or supporter of Sinn Fein; from *Shinn-* representing the pronunciation of *Sinn + -er* ■ Jennifer Johnston: I thought I'd heard it about that you were with the Shinners. (1974)

pink (1927) Derogatory; applied to someone who holds left-of-centre (but not far-left) views; also used as an adjective; from earlier sense, pale red, from the notion of red symbolizing Communism ■ R. Cassilis: One of those old-fashioned egalitarians, like the pompous Pinks who had once been the backbone of the ... Labour Party. (1978)

parlour pink (1929) Derogatory; applied to someone whose professed left-wing principles are insincere or not matched by their lifestyle; from *parlour* used to characterize people of comfortable or prosperous circumstances who profess support, usually non-participatory, for radical, extreme, or revolutionary political movements + *pink* liberal socialist ■ *News Chronicle*: A wonderfully reactionary view of country life. It makes John Buchan look a 'parlour pink'. (1960)

Colonel Blimp, Blimp, blimp (1934) Derogatory; applied to someone with reactionary views; from *Colonel Blimp* character invented by David Low (1891–1963), cartoonist and caricaturist, pictured as a rotund pompous ex-officer voicing a rooted hatred of new ideas ■ *Daily Telegraph*: His usual comic character of pub pundit or cockney blimp. (1968). Hence **blimpish (1938)** ■ *Sunday Times*: The few homosexuals attracted by the career prospects there (broadly, alternate bullying and rape by the brute soldiery, while blimpish colonels fear troop massacre by AIDS). (1993)

lefty, leftie (1935) Usually derogatory; applied to a left-winger; also used as an adjective; from *left + -y* ■ Kingsley Amis: I mean the kind of person who ... buys unexamined the abortion–divorce–homosexuality–censorship–racialism–marijuana package; in a word, the Lefty. (1970)

pinko (1936) Derogatory; applied to someone who holds left-of-centre or mildly Communist views; also used as an adjective; from *pink* liberal socialist + *-o* ■ *Spectator*: The statement 'we are all guilty' ... is enough in itself to identify the speaker as a trendy pinko. (1976) ■ *Transatlantic Review*: It's the number

three song in China, sir. Saw it in one of those magazines my pinko parents subscribe to. (1977)

Commie (1939) Often derogatory; from *Comm(unist + -ie*; used as a noun and an adjective ■ Muriel Spark: After all, one might speak in that manner of the Wogs or the Commies. (1965)

Commo (1941) Australian, New Zealand & US, often derogatory; from *Comm(unist + -o* ■ Jon Cleary: I've been reading how the Commos have eliminated all the flies in China. (1959)

pol (1942) North American; abbreviation of *politician* ■ James Carroll: What had he become? A two-bit pol, flashing about other people's corridors, waiting for his break? (1978)

polly (1942) US & Australian; from *pol* politician + *-y* ■ *Sunday Sun* (Brisbane): The eight pollies are members of an all-Party Parliamentary delegation led by Industry Minister Norm Lee. (1978)

shellback (1943) Applied to someone with reactionary views; from earlier sense, person (especially a sailor) with long experience ■ *Listener*: I have no doubt a lot of right-wing shell-backs are now conceding, with blimpish magnanimity, that there's really something to be said for these young fellows after all. (1963)

prog (1958) Applied to someone who is progressive in their political or social views; abbreviation of *progressive* ■ *Guardian Weekly*: Liberal-minded South Africans cheered their favoured Progressive Federal Party. ... Much applause for the gains of the 'progs', as they are locally termed. (1977)

redneck (1960) Orig US; applied to a reactionary; from earlier sense, Southern rural white ■ *Daily Telegraph*: Was it because they might think his [*sc.* Governor George Wallace's] reputation as a Right-wing 'red neck' a political embarrassment? (1975)

Trot (1962) Mainly derogatory; abbreviation of *Trotskyite*; also used as an adjective ■ Germaine Greer: The most telling criticisms will come from my sisters of the left, the Maoists, the Trots. (1970)

libber (1971) Applied to an advocate of liberation; often in the phrase *women's libber*, and sometimes used elliptically for *women's libber*; from *lib* liberation + *-er* ■ *Daily Telegraph*: The ... debate set things off by producing a truly appalling female whose anti-male views were so extreme and so crudely expressed that orthodox Libbers in the audience showed dismay. (1977)

Stickie, Sticky (1972), Stick (1978) Applied to a member of the official I.R.A. or Sinn Fein; from the verb *stick + -ie*; perhaps from the use of an adhesive Easter Lily badge by the official I.R.A., in contrast to the pin used by the Provisionals ■ D. Murphy: Her son ... was 'executed' last year as a punishment for deserting from the Stickies. (1978) ■ *An Phoblacht*: In a typical pro-British statement ... the Sticks' chairman in South Antrim, Kevin Smyth, accused the IRA of 'gross sectarianism' in bombing the Lisburn premises. (1979)

pinky, pinkie (1973) Derogatory; applied to someone who holds left-of-centre or mildly

Communist views; from *pink* liberal socialist + *-y* ■ **Robert Barnard:** He was always a drawing-room pinkie. . . . As far as contact with the working-class movement was concerned, he hadn't any. (1978)

wet (1980) British, derogatory; applied to a Conservative politician with liberal or middle-of-the-road views (often applied to those opposed to the monetarist policies of Margaret Thatcher); also used as an adjective ■ *Listener:* In considering the promotion of wet (or wettish) Ministers, she will tell herself that Pope was right. (1982) ■ *Economist:* In September 1981, she sacked three 'wets' and banished their leader, Mr James Prior, to Northern Ireland. (1987)

fundi, fundie, fundy (1982) Applied to a fundamentalist politician, specifically a member of the radical left wing of the German Green Party; from *fund(amentalist* + *-i(e), -y* ■ *Daily Telegraph:* The fundies are the purists who believe the only way to save the Earth is to dismantle industry. (1989)

dry (1983) British, derogatory; applied to a Conservative politician who advocates individual responsibility, free trade, and economic stringency, and opposes high government spending; also used as an adjective ■ *Sunday Telegraph:* For ten years the Tory party has been split between Wets and Dries. (1987)

tanky, tankie (1985) Applied to a member of the former British Communist Party who supported hardline (especially interventionist) Soviet policies; usually used in the plural; from *tank* + *-y*, from the use of Soviet tanks to put down uprisings ■ *Guardian:* The New Communist Party of Britain . . . has issued this guidance to the world's press. 'Please do not describe the NCP as "Stalinists" or "Tankies".' (1988)

Politically progressive

right-on (1970) Orig US; used approvingly to denote someone of politically progressive views; from *right on* an exclamation of solidarity and agreement ■ *Guardian:* It is safe to say that Doris's prune-faced PA, right-on toy-boy, gentleman-accountant and scumbag future editor may not be all they seem. (1991)

Administrators

lame duck (1910) US; applied to an office-holder who has not been, or cannot be, re-elected; from earlier, more general sense, disabled person or thing ■ *Economist:* Johnson was a lame-duck president; his power over Congress had waned. (1988)

veep (1949) US; applied to a vice-president; shortened from the pronunciation of the initial letters *V.P.* ■ *Fortune:* His Makati business club constituents would be happy to nominate E.Z. for veep. (1983)

Whitehall warrior (1973) British; applied to a civil servant; from *Whitehall* name of a street in London where several principal government offices are situated ■ **Kenneth Giles:** I'm Quarles, a battered old Whitehall Warrior. (1973)

Campaigning

on the stump (1891) Orig US; from the notion of standing on the stump of a large felled tree to address a crowd ■ *Economist:* What he is really good at, even after 16 hours on the stump, is pressing the flesh, complete with trilingual small-talk. (1987)

press the flesh (1926) Orig and mainly US; applied to greeting potential supporters by shaking their hands ■ *National Observer* (US): After the assassination of John Kennedy, some said no future President would be able to 'press the flesh'. But both Lyndon Johnson and Gerald Ford felt that personal appearances were integral to campaigning. (1977)

demo (1936) Abbreviation of *demonstration* ■ *Guardian:* She was fined £1 for obstruction in an anti-nuclear 'demo' this spring. (1961)

lib (1970) Applied to a campaign for political or social enfranchisement; usually with a modifier identifying the group of people involved; abbreviation of *liberation* ■ *Listener:* With Scots Lib, as with Women's Lib, it's no good the oppressors expecting the past to be forgotten when convenient. (1974)

Elections

shoo-in (1948) US; applied to a candidate considered certain to win; from earlier sense, horse considered certain to win a race ■ *Economist:* Governor Rockefeller became the Republicans' leading presidential hopeful for 1964. The press thought him a shoo-in for the nomination. (1968)

Political corruption

graft (1865) Orig US; applied to (practices, especially bribery, used to secure) illicit political advantage; from the verb *graft* make money dishonestly ■ *Daily Chronicle:* During the hearing of the latest 'graft' scandal here [*sc.* in Pittsburgh] evidence was given that sixty members of the City Council received 45,000 dollars as bribe money. (1908). Hence **grafter** a politician who uses his or her position to obtain dishonest gain or advantage (1896) ■ **A. J. Cronin:** They've always been a set of grafters down there; local government has been one long sweet laugh. (1935)

sleaze (1983) Orig US; applied especially to the payment of money to politicians in return for political influence; from the earlier more general sense, squalor, sordidness. Ultimately a back-formation from *sleazy* ■ *Daily Telegraph:* Although Tory disunity and uncertainty about Britain's economic prospects are undoubtedly the main reasons underlying voter discontent with the Government, the 'sleaze factor' is almost certainly making an independent contribution. (1995)

See also **pork barrel, slush fund** at **Money** (p. 182).

Displaced persons

reffo (1941) Australian; applied to a European refugee, especially one who left Germany or German-occupied Europe before World War II; from *ref(ugee* + *-o* ■ **Patrick White:** He was . . . a blasted foreigner, and bloody reffo, and should have been glad he was allowed to exist at all. (1961)

22. **Military, Maritime, & Airforce**

Personnel

See also Service ranks at **Status** (pp. 57–8), and see **brass, brass-hat**, and **top brass** at A high-ranking or important person (p. 56), and **the bloke, old man**, and **skipper** at The most important or highest-ranking person (pp. 56–7), both at **Status**.

mustang (1847) Applied to an officer in the US forces who has been promoted from the ranks ■ *New York Times Magazine*: The most decorated enlisted man in the Korean War—the mustang everybody thought was the perfect combat commander. (1971)

pipes (1856) Naval slang; used as a nickname or form of address for a boatswain; from the boatswain's whistle ■ *Penguin New Writing*: When Pipes went for supper he had a side-parting and looked quite different. (1942)

pill (1860) Applied to a medical officer or orderly in the services; often used in the plural as a facetious title or form of address; from earlier sense, small ball of medicine ■ Bartimeus: They seized the Young Doctor, who was a small man, and deposited him on the deck. 'Couldn't you see I was asleep, Pills?' demanded the other. (1915)

lamps (1866) Naval slang, dated; used as a nickname for a sailor responsible for looking after the lamps on board ship ■ Eugene O'Neill: Fetch a light, Lamps, that's a good boy. (1919)

Pay (1878) British, orig & mainly naval slang; used as a form of address for the paymaster ■ Taffrail: Cashley, the fleet pay-master, was vainly endeavouring to get up a four at auction bridge. . . . 'Going to take a hand?' . . . 'Bridge, . . . not to-night, Pay; thanks, all the same.' (1916)

red legs (1900) US; applied to an artilleryman ■ S. N. Spetz: Anyway, you'll get a chance to cool it down there, just guarding a bunch of Red Legs. (1969)

jaunty, jaundy, jonty (1902) British; applied to the master-at-arms on board ship; apparently from a nautical pronunciation of *gendarme* ■ *Weekly Dispatch*: The sailor spun a yarn that would make the hardest-hearted jonty (master-at-arms) weep. (1928)

plank-owner (1901) Naval slang, mainly US; applied to a member of the original crew of a ship, or to a long-serving marine ■ M. Dibner: He became her first gunnery officer as a 'plank owner' . . . at her commissioning. (1967)

Jack Shalloo, Jack Shilloo (1904) Applied to an (excessively) easy-going naval officer; apparently an alteration of *Jack Chellew*, the name of such an officer in the Royal Navy

terrier (1908) British; applied to a Territorial; from *terrier* small dog, punning on the resemblance to *Territorial* ■ *Times*: More Terriers. The strength of the Territorial Army on December 31 last year was just under 62,000. (1980)

tanky, tankie (1909) British, naval slang; applied to the navigator's assistant, or to the

captain of the hold; from *tank* + *-y*; apparently from the care of the freshwater tanks, which was part of the tanky's duties ■ H. Tunstall-Behrens: The sharp-witted Amigo had the job of Mate's Tanky. (1956)

salt horse (1914) British, naval slang; applied to an officer with general duties; compare earlier sense, salted beef ■ D. Macintyre: Here was a simple 'salt-horse', indeed, and such were not often selected, in time of peace, for the higher ranks of the Service. (1957)

dug-out (1915) British; applied to a superannuated officer, etc. recalled for temporary military service; from earlier sense, person of old-fashioned appearance or ideas ■ W. J. Locke: The Colonel was immensely proud of them and sang their praises to any fellow dug-out who would listen to him. (1918)

guns (1916) British, naval slang; applied to a gunnery officer

paybob (1916) British, naval slang; applied to the paymaster ■ *Navy News*: The paybob and his chum never batted an eyelid as I signed my chit and I often wonder if they paid the difference. (1978)

red hat (1916) British; applied to an army staff officer; from the red cap-bands of senior officers in the British army ■ Auberon Waugh: A number of very high-ranking officers were invited. . . . The visiting red hats were not impressed. (1978)

Saturday night soldier (1917) Applied to a volunteer soldier or a Territorial

kiwi (1918) Applied to a non-flying member of an airforce; from the kiwi's flightlessness

penguin (1918) R.A.F. slang; applied to a non-flying member of an airforce, such as a member of a ground crew or (often specifically in early use) a member of the Women's Royal Air Force; from penguins' flightlessness ■ Guy Gibson: In the average Bomber Officers' Mess, . . . while penguins sing loudly in the mornings as they get up to shave, it was rather hard for the boys who had been up all night to get a good day's rest. (1944)

Wren, wren (1918) Applied to a member of the Women's Royal Naval Service, the women's service of the Royal Navy; from three of the initial letters of the service's name, assimilated to *wren* small bird

shoey (1919) British; applied to a shoeing smith in a cavalry regiment; from *shoe* + *-y* ■ S. Mays: Shoey. . . . Slap some shoes on my new horse. (1969)

Wraf (1921) Applied to a member of the Women's Royal Air Force, the women's corps of the Royal Air Force; pronounced /ræf/; from the initial letters of the corps' name

erk, irk (1925) British; applied originally to a naval rating (now obsolete in this sense), and subsequently to a person of lowest rank in the R.A.F. (1928); origin unknown ■ Paul Brennan: The erks came running up to tell us that . . . the 109 had been diving down. (1943)

orderly buff (1925) British, dated; applied to an orderly sergeant, the sergeant acting as officer of the day

orderly dog (1925) British, dated; applied to an orderly corporal, a corporal attending an officer to carry orders or messages ■ V. M. Yeates: Grey . . . was censoring the men's letters, being orderly dog for the day. (1934)

ack emma (1930) R.A.F. slang, dated; applied to an air mechanic; from the former military communications code-names for the letters *a* and *m*

odds and sods (1930) Applied to service personnel assigned to miscellaneous tasks or not regularly classified ■ Evelyn Waugh: They left me behind with the other odds and sods. (1955)

ATS, **Ats** (1941) Applied collectively to members of the Auxiliary Territorial Service, a British army corps consisting of women (1938–48); pronounced /æts/; singular forms *AT*, *At*; acronym from *A.T.S.*, abbreviation of *Auxiliary Territorial Service* ■ John Betjeman: As beefy ATS Without their hats Come shooting through the bridge. (1958)

plumber (1941) British; applied to an armourer or engineering officer ■ *Flight.* I am not an engineer (or 'plumber', as the Royal Air Force equivalent is unofficially called). (1962)

retread (1941) Mainly US, Australian, & New Zealand; applied to a retired soldier recalled for service; from earlier sense, refurbished tyre ■ *American Legion Magazine*: Retreads will reune: Retreads, men who served in both World Wars . . . will hold their first reunion . . . at Miami. (1948)

snake (1941) Australian; applied to a sergeant; probably from *snake pit* sergeants' mess ■ Eric Lambert: Baxter reckoned the officers and snakes are pinching our beer. (1951)

tail-end charlie (1941) R.A.F. slang; applied to a rear-gunner in an aircraft ■ *Daily Mail*: The average lifespan of a 'Tail-end Charlie' was reckoned as ten 'ops.' (1976)

pin-party (1942) Naval slang, dated; applied to a gang of flight-deck workers on an aircraft-carrier who prepare aircraft for take-off

orderly pig (1943) British, dated; applied to an orderly officer, the officer of the day

pongo (1943) British; applied to an army officer; compare earlier sense, soldier ■ Olivia Manning: What were you doing walking about holding on to that bloody little pongo? (1965)

paddlefoot (1946) US; applied originally to an infantry soldier, and subsequently (1948) to an airforce ground-crew member ■ *Life*: Murray was a paddlefoot in Europe. (1950)

ping, **pinger**, **ping-man** (1946) Naval slang, dated; applied to an Asdic (= Anti-Submarine Detection Investigation Committee) officer or rating; *ping* from the sound made by the Asdic signal

staff wallah (1951) British, derogatory; applied to a noncombatant army officer

straight leg (1951) US; applied to a member of the ground staff in an airforce, as opposed to one of the flying personnel ■ *Everybody's Magazine* (Australia): Today, in Vietnam, Australians are again catching up on American Army slang. . . . An airborne soldier is called a Trooper, and he knows his counter-part on the ground as a Straight-leg. (1967)

white hat (1956) US, naval slang; applied to an enlisted man

Wrac (1956) Applied to a member of the Women's Royal Army Corps, the women's corps of the British Army; pronounced /ræk/; from the initial letters of the corps' name

Whitehall Warrior (1973) British; applied to an officer in the armed forces employed in administration rather than on active service; from *Whitehall*, name of a street in London in which several principal government offices (including the Ministry of Defence) are situated ■ W. White: I didn't want anybody to think I was a chairbound officer, a Whitehall Warrior. (1976)

An inexperienced serviceman or -woman; a recruit

See **boot, Hun, ninety-day wonder, poodle-faker, poop-ornament, quirk, red-arse, rocky, rookie, shavetail, sprog, war baby, wart, wonk,** and **yardbird** under Inexperienced person at **Experience & Inexperience** (pp. 365–6).

Soldiers

doughboy (1847) US; applied to a US infantryman, especially in World War I; perhaps from *doughboy* boiled flour dumpling, from a supposed resemblance to the large round buttons on US infantry uniforms in the Civil War ■ Anita Loos: During World War I, she dressed as a doughboy in olive drab. (1966)

Tommy (1884) Dated; applied to a British private soldier; short for *Tommy Atkins*, familiar form of *Thomas Atkins*, a name used in specimens of completed official forms

gravel-crusher (1889), **gravel-grinder** (1890), **gravel agitator** (1898) Derogatory; applied to an infantry soldier, and also to a drill instructor; from the effect of service boots on parade-ground gravel

leather-neck (1890) Naval slang, dated; from the leather neck-piece formerly worn by soldiers

poilu (1914) Applied to a French soldier, especially in World War I; from French, literally 'hairy, virile' ■ John Dos Passos: The Boche . . . scattered a few salvoes of artillery . . . just to keep the poilus on their toes. (1966)

P.B.I. (1916) Abbreviation of *poor bloody infantry(man)* ■ *Guardian*: In the trenches the PBI . . . await the order to go over the top. (1972)

pongo (1917) British, naval slang; from earlier sense, anthropoid ape ■ *Daily Mail*: Fourteen youths . . . went out looking for soldiers to beat up. . . . Favourite expressions of the gang were 'squaddy bashing' and 'pongo bashing'. (1977)

old sweat (1919) Applied to an old soldier

dogface (1932) US; applied to a soldier, especially an ordinary infantryman, in the US army; compare earlier sense, ugly person ■ *Newsweek*: No dogface who dug one [*sc.* a foxhole] will ever forget his blistered hands and aching back. (1958)

squaddie, squaddy (1933) British; applied especially to a private soldier; from *squad* + *-ie*, perhaps influenced by obsolete slang *swaddy* soldier ■ Ian Jefferies: I had a motley but effective army of luckless squaddies who had been selected by orderly sergeants. (1959)

brown job (1943) Orig R.A.F. slang; applied to a soldier, and hence collectively to the army; from the British Army's khaki uniforms ■ *Economist*: General Delacombe was a pretty undiplomatic brown-job. (1963)

choco, chocko (1943) Australian; applied to a militiaman or conscripted soldier; short for *chocolate soldier* soldier unwilling to fight (the Australian militia did not serve outside Australia and its territories in World War II) ■ Geoffrey Dutton: You are all volunteers. Your country called you and you came. Not A chocko amongst you. (1968)

doughfoot (1943) US; applied to a soldier, especially an ordinary infantryman, in the US army; suggested by *doughboy*

grunt (1962) North American; applied to an infantry soldier, especially in the Vietnam war; from earlier sense, unskilled or menial worker ■ Ian Kemp: The sound of . . . engines, among the most welcome of all music to the average infantryman—or 'grunt', as we were impolitely called—in Vietnam. (1969)

merc (1967) Applied to a mercenary soldier; abbreviation of *mercenary* ■ Ted Willis: I'm a merc, a hired gunman. . . . If I'm paid, I'm convinced. (1977)

See also **Boche, Charlie, choom, dig, digger, Fritz, Heinie, Hun, Jerry, kiwi, Kraut, Sammy, squarehead, Tojo, Victor Charlie**, and **Woodbine** at **Ethnic & National Groups** (pp. 33–42).

Sailors

tar (1676) Probably short for obsolete slang *tarpaulin* sailor ■ Erica Jong: Whereupon Lancelot started for the Deck with Horatio and his Black Pyrates trailing him, after which the Officers and Tars of the *Hopewell* also followed with great Whoops of Delight. (1980)

Jack-tar (1781) See *tar* ■ Hart Crane: My old jack tar friend . . . was back from his long trip . . . so I just piked in and saw him. (1927)

salt (1840) Applied especially to an experienced sailor; often in the phrase *old salt*; from the saltiness of the sea ■ *Daily Telegraph*: Cowes Week for the keen yachtswoman is not all grit and no glitz. The trick

. . . is how quickly you can make the switch from 'old salt' to svelte swinger. (1992)

soldier (1840) Orig & mainly US; applied to a worthless seaman; often in the phrase *old soldier* ■ Bruce Hamilton: He's a bit of an old soldier, but a first-rate seaman, and a hundred per cent reliable at sea. (1958)

shellback (1853) Jocular; applied especially to a hardened or experienced sailor

farmer (1886) Applied to a sailor who has no duties at the wheel or on watch during the night ■ P. A. Eaddy: I was a 'farmer' that night, . . . not having any wheel or look-out. (1933)

gobby (1890) Dated; applied to an American sailor, or to a coastguard; perhaps from *gob* lump of slimy matter, from the notion of a typically pipe-smoking, spitting sailor

peggy (1902) Naval slang; applied to a sailor assigned to menial tasks, or to a mess-steward; from the female forename *Peggy* ■ Stanley Waters: I was initiated into the mysteries of acting as 'Peggy'. As the name implies this menial does all the domestic chores. (1967)

matelot, matlow, matlo (1903) British; from French *matelot* sailor ■ *Listener*: Our screen matelots . . . should be as reticent as . . . *Captain Horatio Hornblower*. (1974)

gob (1915) Orig US; applied to an American sailor or ordinary seaman; compare *gobby* ■ Terence Rattigan: Can you beat that—an earl being a gob. (1944)

old ship (1927) Naval slang, dated; applied to an old shipmate

Paddy Wester (1927) British, naval slang, dated; applied to an inefficient or novice seaman; supposedly from the name of a notorious Liverpool boarding-house keeper who betrayed his guests to the press-gangs for payment ■ W. E. Dexter: They had a pack of fake seamen sailing on dead men's discharges—a crew of 'Paddy Westers'. (1938)

oily wad (1929) British, naval slang, dated; applied to a seaman with no special skill; from the amount of time they have to spend cleaning brass-work with oily wads

fowl (1937) Naval slang; applied to a troublesome or undisciplined sailor ■ Giraldus: I was a 'fowl' of the first water. I was always getting 'run-in', always in trouble and had no zeal for the Navy whatsoever. (1938)

stripey (1942) British, naval slang; applied to a long-service able seaman, especially one with good-conduct stripes; from *stripe* + *-y* ■ Tackline: Stripey was a small, middle-aged A.B. (1945)

The Navy

the Andrew (1867) Applied to the Royal Navy; short for earlier *Andrew Millar* or *Miller*, reputedly a notorious member of a press-gang ■ Gillian Freeman: That's 'ow it is in the Andrew. . . . That's what we call the navy. (1955)

the Wavy Navy (1918) Applied to the Royal
Naval Volunteer Reserve; from the wavy braid
worn by officers on their sleeves before 1956

the red duster (1925) Applied to the red
ensign, the flag of the British merchant navy;
red from its colour + British naval slang *duster*
flag (1904), from earlier sense, cloth for wiping
dust ■ *Daily Express*: His papers have not yet come
through allowing him to fly the White Ensign, so, meanwhile,
the Vita sails under the 'red duster'. (1928)

Marines

jolly (1829) British, dated; from the adjective *jolly*
■ Rudyard Kipling: I'm a Jolly—'Er Majesty's Jolly-Soldier
and Sailor too. (1896)

leather-neck (1914) US; compare earlier sense,
soldier ■ Richard West: The U.S. Marine Corps. These
legendary troops, nick~named 'leathernecks'. (1968)

pongo (1917) British, naval slang, dated; from
earlier sense, soldier

Airmen

modoc, modock (1936) US, derogatory, dated;
applied to a man who becomes a pilot for the
sake of pilots' glamorous image; origin
unknown

fly boy (1937) US; applied to a member of an
airforce, especially a pilot ■ *Life*: The generals are no
full-throttle 'fly-boys'. (1948)

glamour boy (1941) British, dated; applied to a
member of the R.A.F.; from the glamorous
reputation of R.A.F. pilots in World War II

Military police

jack (1919) Mainly Australian; from earlier sense,
police officer ■ *Bulletin* (Sydney): Blue . . . looked up
and saw two Jacks waiting. 'Where are you going?' demanded
one M.P. (1930)

red cap (1919) British; from the colour of their
caps ■ Jimmy O'Connor: She used to take me to nightclubs tucked away which no officers or redcaps knew about.
(1976)

provo (1943) Australian; from *prov(ost-marshal*
officer in charge of military police + *-o*
■ J. McNeil: Our favourite provo, a bastard named Hunter.
(1972)

snowdrop (1944) Applied to an American
military policeman, and hence to any military
policeman; from the white helmets of American
military policemen

Batmen and other assistants

dog-robber (1863) Orig US; applied to a navy or
army officer's orderly; from earlier sense,
scavenger, scrounger

doggy, doggie (1909) Applied to an officer's
servant or assistant ■ Arthur Grimble: My function
would be to act as doggie—that is, clerical assistant and odd-
job man—to . . . the District Officer. (1952)

Jack Dusty (c1931) Applied to a ship's steward's
assistant

Units

crush (1916) Dated; applied to a body of troops
or a unit of a regiment; from earlier, more
general sense, crowd, group ■ *Observer*: The best
recruiter is the man who is pleased with his 'crush'. (1927)

mob (1916) Applied to a military unit; from
earlier, more general sense, group of people
■ Marshall Pugh: You must have heard of Sharjah and the
Trucial Oman Scouts. This mob is modelled on them. (1972)

outfit (1916) Applied to a regiment or other
military unit ■ F. A. Pottle: The bowlegged officer flew
into a disciplinary rage and addressed the boy as follows:
'What outfit do you belong to? How long have you been in the
army?' (1930)

To join the services

re-up (1906) US; denoting re-enlisting for service;
from *re-* again + *up* (apparently from the notion
of the recruit holding 'up' a hand when
swearing the oath) ■ *Black Panther*: I was told to talk
to a recruiter on base about re-enlisting. . . . He told me that if
I re-up for the four-year reserve commitment he would fix it
up so that I had a job waiting for me. (1974). Hence the
noun **re-up** someone who re-enlists in this way
(1955)

Conscription

nasho (1962) Australian; applied to compulsory
military training; from *nati(onal* (as in *national
service)* + *-o* ■ Q. Wild: One of the worst things . . . was
something that happened in nasho . . . before there was any
fighting or anything. (1981)

A conscript

zombie (1943) Canadian; applied derisively to a
man conscripted for home defence in World
War II; from earlier sense, slow-witted person

nasho (1962) Australian; from *nasho* conscription
■ *Bulletin* (Sydney): The bulk of the Nashos—how the Army
loathes that term—have little time for the 'protests'. (1966)

Leave of absence

leaf, leef (1846) Variant of *leave* ■ John Irving: A
sailor goes 'on leaf' and never on furlough. (1946)

Discharge

vet (1848) North American; applied to a former
member of the armed forces; abbreviation of
veteran ■ *Listener*: The scene is New York, . . . the
academic 'host' is Columbia University, where a number of
young Second World War vets . . . are making gestures at
working for degrees. (1968)

short-timer (1906) US; applied to someone
nearing the end of their military service
■ M. Russ: Being what is known as a short-timer . . . I'm at
peace with service life. (1952)

Section Eight (1943) US; applied to discharge
from the army under section eight of US Army

Regulations 615–360 on the grounds of insanity or inability to adjust to army life. Hence the verb **section-eight** to discharge on such grounds (1945) ■ **Ernest Hemingway:** You stay in until you are hit badly or killed or go crazy and get section-eighted. (1950)

Marching and drill

'shun (1888) Used as a military command to come to attention; shortened form of *attention* ■ **William Faulkner:** 'Bridesman,' he said but at that moment the major said "Shun!' (1955)

square-bashing (1943) British; from *square* military parade ground ■ **Gavin Black:** Attached to a Malay regiment, supervising weapon training and square bashing. (1975)

tab (1982) British, used especially in the Parachute Regiment; denoting marching with heavy equipment over difficult terrain; origin unknown ■ **McGowan & Hands:** Paras referred to a forced march at speed in fighting order as 'tabbing'. The Marines instead went 'yomping'. (1983)

yomp (1982) British, used especially by the Royal Marines; denoting marching with heavy equipment over difficult terrain; origin unknown ■ *Sunday Times:* So the sweaty soldier yomping into battle ends up with blisters and a pool of water inside the boot. (1984)

Discipline

jankers (1916) British, services' slang; applied to punishment for a defaulter; origin unknown ■ **Joyce Porter:** I pulled her leg about it a bit, you know, said something about having her put on jankers if she was late again. (1965)

AWOL (1920) Orig US; acronym formed from *absent without leave* ■ **P. G. Wodehouse:** Nothing sticks the gaff into your chatelaine more than a guest being constantly A.W.O.L. (1949)

A.W.O. Loose (1920) US; denoting absence without leave; adapted from *AWOL*

bullshit (1930), bull (1941) British; applied to unnecessary or routine tasks or ceremonial, or to excessive discipline or spit-and-polish; from earlier sense, nonsense, trivial matters ■ **Alexander Baron:** Them turning out the guard for us, us marching past eyes right, all that sort of bull. (1953) ■ **Richard Hoggart:** The world of special parades in the Services, of 'blanco and bullshit'. (1957)

fizzer (a1935) British; applied to a charge-sheet; especially in the phrase *on a* (or *the) fizzer* ■ *New Society:* Feeling I was on a fizzer (army talk for a disciplinary charge). (1966)

See also **glass-house** and **mush** at Prison (pp. 111, 112), **on the peg** and **in the rattle** under Being reprimanded at **Reprimanding & Punishing** (p. 106).

Navigation

iron mike (1926) Applied to the automatic steering device of a ship

ham-bone (1938) Naval; applied to a sextant; from its shape ■ **F. A. Worsley:** What altitude have you got on that hambone, Stringer? (1938)

angels (1943) R.A.F. slang, especially in World War II; applied to altitude, and specifically to a height of 1000 feet; originally a radio communications code, perhaps based on the notion of the altitude at which angels live ■ **Paul Brennan:** We climbed into sun, Woody advising us to get as much angels as possible. (1943)

pipsqueak (1943) British, dated; applied to a radio transmitter used to establish an aircraft's position; from earlier sense, short, high-pitched sound

Bradshaw (1946) R.A.F. slang, dated; denoting following a railway line in flying; from the name of *Bradshaw's Railway Guide*, former British railway timetable originally issued by George Bradshaw (1801–53), printer and engraver ■ **A. Phelps:** Bradshawing can sometimes lead into trouble. . . . I dislike following a railway except in extreme emergency when forced to fly low. (1946)

nav (1961) Mainly R.A.F. slang; applied to a navigator; abbreviation ■ *Aviation News:* Before long, the student 'nav' could attempt to identify ground features using fine scale maps. (1986)

Training

bull-ring (1899) Applied to a military training ground; from earlier sense, bullfight arena, with reference to *bull* excessive discipline or spit-and-polish ■ **Erik de Mauny:** Drawing equipment at the Q.M., drilling on the bull-ring. (1949)

the Shop (1899) Used as a nickname for the Royal Military Academy, Woolwich ■ **George M. Fraser:** We treated each other decently, and weren't one jot more incompetent than this Sandhurst-and-Shop crowd. (1978)

boot camp (1916) US; applied to a centre for the initial training of US naval or Marine recruits

quirk (1917) R.A.F. slang, dated; applied to a type of slow, steady aeroplane used to train pilots; from earlier sense, inexperienced airman

mad minute (1942) Applied to a minute of frenzied bayonet-practice; compare earlier sense, minute of rapid fire ■ **Brophy & Partridge:** *Mad minute* . . . was also applied to the frenzied minute spent charging down the assault course, bayoneting straw-filled dummies, representing enemy soldiers. (1965)

TEWT, tewt (1942) British; an acronym formed from the initial letters of *t*actical *e*xercise *w*ithout *t*roops, an exercise used in the training of junior officers ■ **Evelyn Waugh:** Leonard improvised 'No more TEWTS and no more drill, No night ops to cause a chill.' (1952)

boot (1944) US; applied to basic training received in a boot camp

perisher (1948) Applied to a qualifying course for submarine commanders; from earlier sense, periscope ■ **D. Reeman:** We did our *Perisher* together, and even when I got *Tristram* he was given *Tryphon*. (1973)

Uniform

giggle (1940) Australian; applied to often badly fitting items of clothing of the type issued to Australian service personnel during World War II; from their supposedly amusing appearance ■ **S. O'Leary:** Chrysalis soldiers in their ill-fitting giggle suits and floppy cloth hats. (1975)

square rig (1951) Applied to the uniform of a naval rating; from earlier sense, rig in which sails are suspended from horizontal yards ■ **Noel Coward:** Attired as they were in the usual 'Square-Rig' of British Ordinary Seamen, they caused a mild sensation. (1951)

Identity discs

dog tag (1918) US ■ *Penguin New Writing:* If I should die to-morrow, I suppose this is where my bones, if not my dog-tag, would lie for ever. (1947)

meat ticket (1919) From the notion of an identifying label tied to a carcass of meat, with reference to the use of the identity disc in identifying dead service personnel

Gas masks

nose-bag (1915) British, dated; from earlier sense, eating bag suspended round a horse's head ■ *Everybody's Weekly:* Londoners call their masks 'Dicky-birds', 'Canaries' and 'Nose-bags'. (1940)

Decorations

come up with (or **be given**) **the rations** (1925) British, derogatory; applied to a service or other medal not awarded for gallantry ■ **John Braine:** Lampton has no decorations apart from those which all servicemen who served his length of time are given, as they say, with the rations. (1957)

gong (1925) British; applied to a medal or other decoration; from its shape ■ **Monica Dickens:** Other people came out of the war with Mentions and worthwhile gongs that tacked letters after their names. (1958)

rooty gong (1925) British, dated; applied to a medal formerly awarded to members of the British Army in India; from *rooty* bread + *gong* medal ■ **Frank Richards:** The Good Conduct medal or 'Rooty Gong' . . . was so called because it was a regular ration-issue, like bread or meat or boots. (1936)

Mutt and Jeff (1937) British, dated; applied to a particular pair of medals worn together, especially the War Medal and the Victory Medal awarded to British service personnel who took part in World War I; from the name of two characters called *Mutt* and *Jeff* in a popular cartoon series by H. C. Fisher (1884–1954), American cartoonist

Pip, Squeak, and Wilfred (1937) British, dated; applied collectively to the 1914–15 Star, War Medal, and Victory Medal, three medals awarded to British service personnel who took

part in World War I; from the names of three animal characters in a *Daily Mirror* children's comic strip

fruit salad (1943) Applied to a (copious or ostentatious) display of medals, ribbons, or other decorations; from the array of colours presented by an array of medal ribbons ■ **Nevil Shute:** A red-faced old gentleman with . . . a fruit salad of medal ribbons on his chest. (1955)

ruptured duck (1945) US; applied to a button given on discharge from the services; from its eagle design ■ **William Faulkner:** The ex-soldier or -sailor or -marine with his ruptured duck pushing the perambulator with one hand. (1959)

Spam medal (1945) Applied to a medal awarded to all members of a force, especially (*British*) the 1939–45 Star, awarded to British service personnel who took part in World War II; from the ubiquitousness of Spam as a foodstuff during World War II, and in the case of the 1939–45 Star perhaps also from the resemblance of the colours of the ribbon to those of the armbands of waitresses in NAAFI canteens, where Spam was a staple item

screaming eagle (1946) US; applied to a button given on discharge from the services; from its eagle design

Armaments: Bombs

pill (1921) From earlier sense, shell, bullet; sometimes used (in the phrase *the pill*) to refer to nuclear weapons ■ **P. G. Hart:** When I got over the town I let my pills go. (1939)

bread-basket (1940) British, dated; applied to a large bomb containing smaller bombs

screamer (1942) Dated; applied to a type of bomb that makes a screaming sound as it falls

doodlebug, doodle (1944) Applied to a German V-1 flying bomb; compare earlier sense, tiger beetle, or the larva of this or various other insects ■ **Tony Parker:** I left school in 1944, just after the doodle-bugs finished. (1969)

nuke, (US) **nook (1959)** Orig US; applied to a nuclear bomb, missile, etc.; abbreviation of *nuclear* ■ **Publishers' Weekly:** They hijack a liner at sea and sink it with a baby nuke. . . . He is given the job of detonating the big nuke. (1973)

lazy dog (1965) US; applied to a type of fragmentation bomb designed to explode in mid air and scatter steel pellets at high velocity over the target area

Bombing equipment

Mickey Mouse (1941) Dated; applied to a type of electrical bomb release; from the name of a mouse-like cartoon character created by Walt Disney (1901–66), US cartoonist (apparently in allusion to the complicated machinery portrayed in Disney's cartoons)

Mickey (1944) US; applied to a type of radar-assisted bombsight; from *Mickey Mouse*

Mortars, grenades, etc.

sausage (1915) Dated; applied to a type of German trench-mortar bomb; from its shape

pineapple, pineapple bomb (1916) Applied to a hand-grenade or light trench-mortar; from its shape ■ James Quartermain: 'You . . . don't want that old-time pineapple lobbed through your store window. You know what a pineapple is, Raven?' 'A hand grenade.' 'Right.' (1972)

rum-jar (1916) Dated; applied to a type of German trench-mortar bomb

toc emma, tock emma, toch emma (1916) Dated; applied to a trench-mortar; from *toc* and *emma*, the communications code-words for *t* and *m*, representing *T.M.*, abbreviation of *trench-mortar* ■ R. C. Sherriff: Can't have men out there while the toch-emmas are blowing holes in the Boche wire. (1928)

Minnie, minnie, minny (1917) Applied to a German trench-mortar, or the bomb discharged by it; abbreviation of German *Minenwerfer* trench-mortar

oil can (1917) Applied to a German trench-mortar bomb in World War I ■ E. A. Mackintosh: 'Look out, sir, . . . oil can coming over.' Instantly self-preservation reasserted itself. (1917)

pill (1919) Applied to a hand-grenade; from earlier sense, shell, bullet ■ *American Legion Weekly*: Damn the Boche that threw the pill. (1921)

plum-pudding (1925) Dated; applied to a type of trench-mortar bomb

moaning minnie, moaning Minnie, Moaning Minnie (1941) Applied to a German trench-mortar, or the bomb discharged by it; *moaning* alluding to the sound made by the projectile in flight ■ G. Wilson: That bloody moaning Minnie. . . . It's a hell of a weapon. (1950)

red devil (1944) Applied to a type of Italian hand-grenade

Depth charges

pill (1917) From earlier sense, shell, bullet ■ P. S. Allen: The submarine proceeded to lie on the bottom. .but one day they realized they were spotted. 'Pills' kept dropping close to them, and sending the water a-swish all round. (1917)

ash-can (1918) US; from its shape, like that of a dustbin (US *ash-can*) ■ Geoffrey Jenkins: 'I give it five minutes before the ash-cans come.' . . . Waiting for a depth-charge attack is probably as bad as the attack itself. (1959)

Ammunition

pill (c1626) Applied to a bullet, shell, or, in early use, cannon ball; used collectively in the plural to denote ammunition; from earlier sense, ball

ammo (1911) Applied especially to ammunition for small arms; from *amm*(*unition* + *-o* ■ Roy

Campbell: And we'll hand in our Ammo and Guns As we handed them in once before. (1946)

woolly bear (1915) Dated; applied to a type of German high-explosive shell

pipsqueak (1916) Dated; applied to a small high-velocity shell; from earlier sense, someone small or insignificant ■ E. Thompson: The Turkish guns suddenly sent over a couple of pipsqueaks. (1927)

G.I. can (1918) US, dated; applied to a German artillery shell in World War I; from earlier sense, galvanized-iron can (= a dustbin), in allusion to its shape

plonker (1918) Australian, dated; applied to an explosive shell; from earlier dialect sense, something large or substantial of its type

Torpedoes

mouldy (1916) British, dated; origin unknown ■ *Flight*: At the same time, no doubt, the A.A. gunners on board are gleefully telling all and sundry how they simply riddled the 'Horsleys' with shells before ever a mouldy was dropped. (1932)

tin fish (1925), fish (1928) ■ *Penguin New Writing*: The air seemed full of falling bombs, and tinfish like carelessly dropped cigarettes splashed among the crowded ships. (1943) ■ Bill Knox: The Navy didn't like losing a torpedo. . . . Each 'fish' represented some £3,000 in cash. (1967)

torp (1929) Abbreviation ■ Bill Knox: If anyone does find a stray torp, then they'll make damn' sure it stays lost. (1967)

kipper (1953) ■ Geoffrey Jenkins: I evaluate its firing power at eighteen torpedoes—I think kipper is a distressing piece of naval slang—in thirty minutes. (1959)

Anti-aircraft fire

flaming onions (1917) Dated; applied to a projectile consisting of about ten incendiary shells shot upwards in quick succession; from its resemblance to a string of onions

triple-A (1983) Orig US; from earlier *AAA*, abbreviation of *anti-aircraft artillery* ■ *Times*: With triple A coming at you, it concentrates the mind wonderfully. It was the longest minute of my life. (1991)

Weapon emplacements and defensive structures

elephant, elephant dug-out (1917) British, dated; applied to a dug-out with a semi-circular corrugated-iron lining

dustbin (1934) British; applied to the gun-turret of an aircraft, especially one beneath the fuselage; from its shape

asparagus-bed, asparagus (1939) British; applied to an anti-tank obstacle consisting of an array of strong metal bars set in concrete at an angle of 45 degrees; from the resemblance of the bars to asparagus growing thickly in a bed

An attack

hate (1915) British, dated; applied to an artillery bombardment; from the German 'Hymn of

Hate', which was ridiculed in *Punch* 24 February 1915 in the caption of a cartoon, 'Study of a Prussian household having its morning hate' ■ D. Reeman: I'm going to turn in, Sub. I want a couple of hours before the night's 'hate' gets going. (1968)

mad minute (1917) Applied to a minute of rapid rifle-fire ■ C. H. B. Pridham: By 1914, many men in each regiment could exceed even twenty rounds in the 'mad minute'. (1945)

op (1925) Applied to a military operation; often used in the plural; abbreviation of *operation* ■ Adam Hall: They'd been forced to set up the op. . . . The decision-making had been at Prime Minister level. (1973)

scramble (1940) Applied to a (rapid) operational take-off by a group of aircraft ■ *Times*: The royal visitors watched a 'scramble' of four R.A.F. Vulcan bombers of the quick-reaction alert force. (1963)

party (1942) Applied to a military engagement ■ B. J. Ellan: I just fired when something came into my sights and then turned like hell as something fired at me! What a party! (1942)

rhubarb (1943) Dated; applied to a low-level strafing raid ■ J. E. Johnson: Usually our Rhubarb efforts yielded little more than a staff car. (1956)

stonk (1944) Applied to a concentrated artillery bombardment; from earlier sense, (stake in) a game of marbles ■ D. M. Davin: I wasn't so crackers I wasn't still listening for that bloody stonk to come screaming down on us. (1947)

prang (1945) Dated, orig R.A.F. slang; applied to a bombing raid; from the verb *prang* bomb

To attack

plaster (1915) Denoting bombing or shelling heavily ■ Evelyn Waugh: The bombers were not aiming at any particular target; they were plastering the ground in front of their cars. (1942)

spike-bozzle, spike-boozle (1915) Dated; denoting rendering an enemy aircraft, etc. unserviceable; from **spike** render a gun unserviceable + perhaps *bam)boozle*

lay an egg (1918) Denoting dropping a bomb from an aircraft

smear (1935) Denoting destroying a place by bombing ■ Peter Bryant: The report on the . . . Russian I.C.B.M. site had removed his . . . doubt . . . whether his bombers could smear it before the missiles were fired off. (1958)

shoot someone or something **up (1937)** R.A.F. slang; denoting diving over a person or place as if or in order to attack ■ L. M. Boston: A squadron would roar over the house from which one plane swooped down to shoot us up. (1973)

scramble (1940) Denoting making a (rapid) operational take-off; also used transitively, meaning 'cause to make such a take-off'; from the noun *scramble* such a take-off ■ Brennan & Hesselyn: The signal to scramble came at about eleven o'clock. . . . We rushed to our aircraft and in less than two minutes were off the ground. (1942) ■ *Daily Telegraph*: The

final decision to scramble fighters or launch nuclear missiles is . . . made by . . . highly trained officers. (1971)

prang (1942) Dated, orig R.A.F. slang; denoting bombing a target successfully from the air; compare earlier sense, crash-land ■ Miles Tripp: The Lancs broke off sharply at the last moment to prang Neuss. (1952)

stonk (1944) Denoting bombarding with concentrated artillery fire; from the noun *stonk* such artillery fire ■ Ralph Allen: Moaning Minnie . . . was the name they gave to the German multiple mortars that stonked their positions, wherever they were, a minimum of twice and a maximum of several dozen times in each twenty-four hours. (1946)

attrit, attrite (1956) Orig US; denoting wearing down or eroding resources, morale, etc. by unrelenting attack; back-formation from *attrition* ■ *Newsweek*: His defense was designed to attrit us. . . . Every American you kill, it's another family protesting the war. (1991)

jap (1957) US, dated; denoting making a sneak attack on someone; from the noun *Jap*, abbreviation of *Japanese*; apparently with reference to the Japanese surprise attack on Pearl Harbor, 1941 ■ H. E. Salisbury: An uncertain area where one side or another may at any sudden moment 'jap' an unwary alien. (1958)

nuke, (US) nook (1967) Denoting bombing or destroying with nuclear weapons; from *nuke* nuclear weapon ■ *Japan Times Weekly*: I asked how he could be sure that the Soviet Union would nuke us if we nuked China. (1972)

Parachuting: A parachute

chute (1920) Abbreviation ■ *Times*: Less than an hour later the big ship touches ground, the 32-foot-diameter chute billowing astern to brake it. (1958)

silk (1933) Mainly US; especially in the phrase *take to* or *hit the silk* bale out by parachute; from the use of silk for making parachutes ■ Ngaio Marsh: Over Germany . . . we got clobbered and I hit the silk. (1956)

umbrella (1933) US ■ J. Ditton: It takes ages to come down on an umbrella. . . . Then you have to get rid of the chute. (1980)

brolly (1934) British; from earlier sense, umbrella ■ J. M. B. Beard: I was floating still and peacefully with my 'brolly' canopy billowing above my head. (1940)

A paratrooper

skyman (1952) Journalistic ■ *Sunday Telegraph*: Skymen hit the target. (1964)

para (1958) Usually used in the plural; abbreviation ■ J. Cartwright: Right, paras get ready to jump. (1977)

A parachute accident

Roman Candle (1943) Applied to a parachute jump in which the parachute fails to open

■ Evelyn Waugh: The first thing the commandant asked when I reported Crouchback's accident. 'A Roman Candle?' he asked. (1961)

cigarette roll (1962) US; applied to a parachute jump in which the parachute fails to open

To jump using a parachute

step out (1942) R.A.F. slang; denoting parachuting out of a (disabled) aircraft

Accommodation and catering

bivvy, bivy (1916) Applied to a small tent or any temporary shelter for troops; short for *bivouac* ■ D. M. Davin: Snow and me were sitting outside the bivvy. (1947)

stone frigate (1917) British; applied to a naval shore establishment or barracks ■ *Mariner's Mirror*: H.M.S. *Thunderer* (our title as a 'stone frigate') has since prospered. . . . It is planned amongst other things to produce a book on the history of the college. (1979)

Naffy (1937) British; a representation of the usual pronunciation of *NAAFI*, abbreviation of *Navy, Army, and Air Force Institution*, an organization providing canteens, shops, etc. for British forces personnel

snake-pit, snake-pen (1941) Australian; applied to a sergeants' mess

Wrennery (1943) British, jocular; applied to a building used to accommodate Wrens; from *Wren + -ery*, after *rookery*, etc. ■ *Navy News*: The work included . . . the building of a Wrennery to accommodate 200 Wrens. (1964)

Terrorists

terr (1976) Applied in Rhodesia (now Zimbabwe) before independence to a guerrilla fighting to overthrow the White minority government; abbreviation of *terrorist* ■ *Times*: Infiltration over the Zambesi River by 'terrs'—or terrorists/freedom fighters, depending on your politics. (1980)

Civilians

civvy (1915) Applied to a civilian, and also used adjectivally to denote non-military items; from *civ(ilian + -y* ■ *Daily Express*: Civvy cigarettes are dearer now. (1945)

P.F.C., pfc (1947) US; abbreviation of *poor foolish (forlorn, fucking,* etc.) *civilian*, modelled on earlier *P.F.C.*, abbreviation of *Private 1st Class* ■ Thomas Pynchon: 'I would like to sing you a little song.' 'To celebrate your becoming a PFC' said Ploy. . . . 'Pore Forlorn Civilian, We're goin to miss you so.' (1963)

Civilian life

outside (1903) ■ W. Lang: You *got* to 'ave some bloody religion in the Navy. Now, wot church did you go to outside? (1919)

Civvy Street (1943) ■ John Braine: Dick was in splendid shape, sampling every delight Civvy Street had to offer. (1959)

Civilian clothes

civvies (1889) From *civ(ilian + -ies* ■ *Daily Telegraph*: Young men exchange their uniforms for 'civvies'. (1946)

dog-robbers (1898) Applied to civilian clothes worn by a naval officer on shore leave ■ Monica Dickens: Then he . . . changed into dog robbers and went into the town to get drunk. (1958)

Pacifism

conchy, conchie, conshy (1917) Derogatory; applied to a conscientious objector; from *consc(ientious + -y* ■ *Landfall*: The deal that is going on here is worse than the one the Conchies got. (1951)

Cuthbert (1917) British, derogatory, dated; applied to a man who deliberately avoids military service, especially (in World War I) one who did so by getting a job in a government office or the civil service; from the male personal name *Cuthbert*, used in a cartoon by 'Poy' in the London *Evening News* ■ Joyce Cary: All you Cuthberts are fit for is to dodge responsibility at the cost of other people's lives. (1933)

23. Espionage

A spy

spook (1942) Orig and mainly US; from earlier sense, ghost ■ L. Pryor: 'My training was also in espionage at the CIA farm.' . . . 'A spook,' I said in wonder. (1979). Hence the adjective **spooky (1975)** ■ Jennie Melville: Somebody on the spooky side of the Embassy might have a view. (1980)

sleeper (1955) Applied to a spy or saboteur who remains inactive for a long time before starting his or her work ■ *Daily Mail*: They had been responsible for a year-long campaign of bombings in the city. . . . When police cleaned up the cell, the IRA activated a reserve unit of 'sleepers'. (1975)

undercover (1962) Applied to an undercover agent ■ James Mills: She was a very good detective. She was a narcotics undercover. (1972)

cut-out (1963) Applied to someone acting as a middle-man in espionage ■ Eric Ambler: Through our cut-out I have made an offer for the shares. (1969)

plumber (1972) Mainly US; applied to a member of a White House special unit during the administration of Richard Nixon which investigated leaks of government secrets, and which was found to have been guilty of illegal practices, including bugging with concealed microphones

swallow (1972) Applied to a woman employed by the Soviet intelligence service to seduce men for the purposes of espionage ■ M. Barak: I need a swallow in America. One . . . who is sexually skilled and expert in obtaining information. (1976)

mole (1974) Applied to a person who works undercover within an organization and passes information about it to others; there is some previous evidence of the use of *mole* to denote a traitor working secretly, dating back to the 17th century, but its specific modern application was popularized by John Le Carré ■ *Times*: Clearly therefore, we suggest, this points to a 'mole' within British Telecom Prestel headquarters. (1984)

Spy organizations

the Circus (1963) Applied to the British secret service; from its address at Cambridge Circus, London ■ John Le Carré: In your day the Circus ran itself by regions. . . . Control sat in heaven and held the strings. (1974)

the trade (1966) Applied to the secret service ■ J. Gardner: Heather had that smart plummy voice which spoke of a cut-glass background. The kind of girl the trade enjoyed using: the kind they called a *lady*. (1977)

the Company (1967) US; applied to the Central Intelligence Agency ■ *Listener*: The Americans working (presumably) for 'the Company', as the CIA is universally known, are privately scathing about the failure of positive vetters. (1982)

Communication

post office (1919) Applied to a secret place where documents, etc. can be left or passed on by a spy ■ D. Williams: It became evident in 1911 that the hairdresser's shop of Karl Gustav Ernst was being used as a 'post office' or clearing-house for German espionage agents in this country. (1965)

drop (1959) Applied to a secret place where documents, etc. can be left or passed on by a

spy; from earlier sense, hiding-place for stolen goods ■ Ian Fleming: They had arranged an emergency meeting place and a postal 'drop'. (1965)

treff (1963) Orig US; applied to a secret rendezvous, especially for the transfer of goods or information; from German *Treff* meeting (-place); compare German *Treffpunkt* rendezvous ■ W. Garner: Make a list . . . of all the drops, pick-ups and treffs. (1983)

To equip with a hidden microphone

bug (1935) Orig US; from earlier sense, equip with a burglar alarm ■ J. D. MacDonald: We bugged both suites. (1958). Hence **bug** a hidden microphone (1946) ■ Agatha Christie: Perhaps you have some idea that this office of mine might have a bug in it? (1961)

spike (1974) Used especially to denote equipping with a *spike microphone*, one which can be driven into a wall to monitor an inner room ■ D. Gethin: Quittenden's plumbers . . . were the crack team who could spike a high security building in under an hour. (1983)

Reconnaissance

sausage balloon (1916) Dated services' slang; applied to an observation balloon; from earlier sense, elongated air-balloon ■ Sapper: A row of sausage balloons like a barber's rash adorned the sky. (1917)

obbo, obo (1925) Dated services' slang; applied to an observation balloon; from *ob(servation + -o*

Assassination

wet (1972) Denoting an activity of intelligence organizations, especially the KGB, involving assassination ■ J. Gardner: He had seen men killed: and killed them himself: he had directed 'wet operations', as they used to be called. (1980)

24. Religion

An (over)enthusiastically religious person

creeping Jesus (*c*1818) Applied to a hypocritically pious person

Bible-banger, -basher (1885) Mainly Australian & New Zealand; a synonym of *Bible-pounder*

Bible-pounder, -puncher, -thumper (1889) Applied to someone, especially a clergyman, who expounds or follows the Bible in a vigorous and aggressive way ■ A. L. Rowse: It's always the Bible-thumpers who are the greatest hypocrites. (1942). Hence **Bible-pounding, -punching, -thumping** (1951)

holy Joe (1889), holy Willie (1916) *holy Joe* from earlier sense, clergyman ■ J. A. Lee: The Holy Willies would throw a party. 'Come to our Sunday School?'

(1934) ■ J. D. Salinger: They all have these Holy Joe voices when they start giving their sermons. (1951)

Christer (1921) US; applied to an over-pious or sanctimonious person; from *Christ + -er* ■ Judson Philips: I'm a Christer and a do-gooder. . . . I wasn't welcome. (1966)

God-botherer (1937) British, orig services' slang; applied to a parson or chaplain, or more generally to anyone who vigorously promotes Christian ideals ■ Kingsley Amis: 'What do you think of the padre, Max?' . . . 'Not a bad chap for a God-botherer.' (1966)

God squad (1965) Orig US colleges' slang; used as a disparaging collective term for (the members of) a religious organization, especially an evangelical Christian group ■ *Observer*: BBC executives . . . said: 'Beware the unexpected—and keep tabs on the God squad.' (1983)

fundi, **fundie**, **fundy** (1982) Applied to a believer in the literal truth of Scripture; short for *fundamentalist*

Excessively religious

pi (1981) Dated; short for *pious*; recorded as a noun ('pious person') around 1870

A member of a particular religion

Prot (1725) Applied derogatorily to a Protestant; compare *Prod*

spike (1902) British; applied derogatorily to an Anglican who advocates or practises Anglo-Catholic ritual and observances; probably from the pointed decoration of Gothic churches
■ A. N. Wilson: There were several other effigies of famous spikes, including the legendary Father Tooth. (1980). So **spiky** (1893) and **spike up** to make more High Church (1923) ■ Barbara Pym: He had been a server at the spikiest Anglo-Catholic church. (1977)

tyke, **tike** (1902) Australian & New Zealand; applied derogatorily to a Roman Catholic; probably an alteration of *Taig* Roman Catholic, influenced by *tike* churlish fellow
■ D. Whitington: Too many bloody tykes in the Labor Party. (1957)

Pape (1935) Scottish/Ulster; applied derogatorily to a Roman Catholic; from *Pope*, or a shortening of *papist* ■ John Braine: Adam's a good Catholic. . . . It's smart to be a Pape now. (1968)

Doolan, **doolan** (1940) New Zealand; applied to an (Irish) Roman Catholic; probably from the Irish surname *Doolan* ■ D. M. Davin: She'll have me a doolan yet, Father. (1947)

Metho (1940) Australian; applied to a Methodist ■ Patrick White: Arch and me are Methoes, except we don't go; life is too short. (1961)

Roman Candle (1941) Applied jocularly to a Roman Catholic ■ P. Haines: She said: 'I've noticed you lots—you're a Roman Candle, aren't you?' 'What?' . . . 'R.C., silly.' (1974)

Prod (1942), **Proddy** (1954), **Proddy-dog**, **Proddy-hopper**, **Proddy-woddy** (1954) Anglo-Irish; applied derogatorily to a Protestant; compare *Prot* ■ Philip Carter: Most of the kids were in tough Prod gangs, like the Tartans. . . . They always seemed to . . . tell if you were as hard-line Prod as they were. (1977)

left-footer (1944) Applied derogatorily to a Roman Catholic ■ J. H. Fullarton: 'What about the R.C.s?' 'Oh, yes. Leave the left-footers behind as gun-picquets.' (1944)

Tim (1958) Scottish; used by Protestants as a nickname for a Roman Catholic; diminutive form of the male personal name *Timothy*

Taig, **Teague** (1971) Anglo-Irish; applied derogatorily to a Roman Catholic; anglicized spelling of the Irish name *Tadhg*, a nickname for an Irish person ■ *Observer*: This week a new slogan appeared along the Shankill Road, the backbone of Protestant West Belfast. It read: 'All Taigs are targets.' (1982)

A priest or clergyman

holy Joe (1874) Orig nautical

sky pilot (1883) Applied especially to a military or naval chaplain ■ B. Broadfoot: At the missions you would get a sermon, say 15 minutes of religion from a sky pilot. (1973)

josser (1887) Australian; from *joss* (as in *joss-man*) + *-er* ■ G. Rose: The old josser, all black robe and beard and upside-down hat and silver cross, addressed himself to me. (1973)

padre (1898) Orig services' slang; from Italian, Spanish and Portuguese *padre*, from Latin *pater* father ■ *Daily News*: The 'fighting padre' is by no means an unknown figure in British wars. (1898)

sin-shifter (*a*1912) Dated; perhaps influenced by *scene-shifter*

joss-man (1913) From *joss* Chinese idol, perhaps from Portuguese *deos* god ■ *Navy News*: I was watch aboard and tried to get a sub, but no joy. I asked the Jossman if I could go ashore, and he told me to go. (1964)

sin bosun (1948) Naval; applied to a ship's chaplain ■ *Navy News*: Well, at least the Sin Bosun doesn't seem too old. (1964)

A church

God-box (1917) Used derogatorily ■ *New Statesman*: A ring-a-ding God-box that will go over big with the flat-bottomed latitudinarians. (1962)

The Salvation Army

Salvo (1891) Australian; also applied in the plural to members of the Salvation Army; from *Sally* + the Australian colloquial suffix *-o*
■ R. McKie: When workers everywhere got their notices and the slump showed every sign of lasting, the Salvos decided to open a doss house. (1978)

Sally (**Army**) (1915), **Sally Ann(e)** (1927) Also applied to a Salvation Army hostel and (*Sally*) in the plural to members of the Salvation Army; alteration of *Salvation* ■ D'Arcy Niland: The woman that runs it, she used to be some sort of high-up with the Sallies down in Sydney. (1957) ■ W. A. Hagelund: Now you go see the Major at the Johnson Street Sally Anne about some meal tickets and beds. (1961) ■ *New Statesman*: Julie Felix sang against the Salvation Army—and we were miles away from the sad Sally where the meth-drinkers are deloused. (1966)

God

Gawd, **gawd**, **gaw** (1877) British; representing a vulgar pronunciation of *God*; mainly used in exclamations (see at **Imprecations** (pp. 341–3))

The Devil

Old Nick (*a*1643) *Nick* perhaps a shortening of *iniquity*, assimilated to the abbreviated form of the name *Nicholas*

Old Scratch (1740) Compare earlier *scratch* hermaphrodite, related to Old Norse *skrat(t)i* goblin, Old High German *scrato* sprite

See also **God slot** at **Entertainment** (p. 344).

Animals

Birds

birdie (1792) An affectionate or child's term for any (small) bird; from *bird* + *-ie*

chook, chookie, -y, chuckie, -y (1855) Australian & New Zealand; applied to a chicken or other domestic fowl; compare British dialect *chuck* chicken ■ *Coast to Coast 1967-68*: His had been wild-eyed, scraggy long-legged chooks, few in number, sneaking into the kitchen after scraps. (1969)

gump (1899) US, vagrants' slang; applied to a chicken; perhaps the same word as *gump* fool, from the notion of chickens being stupid ■ *American Ballads & Folk Songs*: Not even a shack to beg for a lump, Or a hen-house to frisk for a single gump. (1960)

maggie, maggy (1901) Australian; applied to a magpie; probably from earlier British dialect use ■ T. Winton: He could . . . see the scabby trunk above bearing all the open-mouthed maggies that chased them to and from school. (1982)

Jacko (1907) Australian; applied to a kookaburra; from *Jack* kookaburra (short for *laughing jackass* kookaburra) + *-o*

budgie (1936) From *budg(erigar)* + *-ie* ■ Anthony Gilbert: We've got a budgie . . . that Maureen's teaching to talk. (1959)

spag (1951) Australian; applied to a sparrow; from British dialect *spag* house-sparrow ■ *Bulletin* (Sydney): I had found a spag's nest in the letterbox. (1960)

Camels

oont, unt (1862) Indian & Australian; from Hindi & Urdu *ūnṭ* camel ■ *Bulletin* (Sydney): Hell! what a lot of calculation had to go into piloting a couple of smelly oonts! (1933)

hunchy (1919) Australian ■ Lawson & Brereton: I went out west to the Camel Country . . . where turbaned Abdul Mahommed steers his ungainly lopsided 'hunchies' through the glittering sands. (1931)

hump (1935) Australian ■ D. Stuart: I see old Dotty Stanley once . . . with a pair o' camels; it was the first time he'd ever had humps, an' he wasn't too sure of 'em. (1978)

Cats

puss (a1530) Used especially as a calling name; probably from Middle Low German *pūs* (also *pūskatte*) or Dutch *poes*; perhaps ultimately a call to attract a cat

kitty (1719) Used especially as a pet name or calling name; from *kit* shortened form of *kitten* + *-y*

pussy (1726) From *puss* + *-y* ■ Jerome K. Jerome: He strokes the cat quite gently, and calls it 'poor pussy'. (1889)

moggie, moggy (1911) British; compare earlier dialect senses, cow, calf, untidy woman; perhaps a variant of *Maggie* pet form of the female personal name *Margaret* ■ *People's Journal*: Oh, and before I leave this topic of pussies, my neighbour across the lane also had a good laugh from the moggie next door to her. (1973)

mog (1927) British; shortened form of *moggie* ■ Philip Heseltine: Such lovely mogs you can't imagine—including the best cat in the world, surely. (1934)

Cattle

mickey, micky (1876) Australian; applied to a young wild bull; from the male personal name *Mick(e)y* ■ H. G. Lamond: Mickeys roamed through the camping cattle. (1954)

horny, horney (1901) Australian; applied to a bullock; from Scottish dialect *horny* cow ■ C. D. Mills: Nugget gave me a spell after smoke—oh, and I went to the crush to deal with the 'hornies'. (1976)

Chimpanzees

chimp (1877) Abbreviation ■ *Times*: Chimps, picture cards and many diverse forms of advertising bring our teas before . . . buyers. (1957)

Crocodilians

'gator, gator, gater (1844) Orig US; abbreviation of *alligator*

croc (1884) Abbreviation of *crocodile* ■ P. M. Clark: Leaving the corpses of many crocs lying about behind us. (1936)

freshy, freshie (1964) Australian; applied to a freshwater crocodile ■ *Age* (Melbourne): There are no recorded attacks by 'freshies' on humans. (1985)

Dogs

tyke (c1400) Dated; usually used contemptuously or dismissively; from Old Norse *tík* female dog ■ John Brown: Toby was the most utterly shabby, vulgar, mean-looking cur I ever beheld—in one word, a tyke. (1861)

bow-wow (1785) Used as an affectionate or child's term; from earlier use as a representation of a dog's bark ■ Roy Campbell: All the bow-wows, poodles, tykes and curs. (1931)

doggy, doggie (1825) Used as an affectionate or child's term; from *dog* + *-y* ■ Bob Merrill: How much is that doggie in the window? (1953)

ki-yi (1895) US; from earlier sense, howl or yelp of a dog ■ *Buffalo* (New York) *Express*: A butcher in

Brussels made sausage of the carcass of a zoo elephant which had been killed. Doubtless the Brussels kiyis yelped for joy. (1904)

dawg (1898) Representing a colloquial or dialectal pronunciation ■ **Osbert Lancaster:** Beaten copper reminders that a man's best friend is his dawg (beloved of the golf-playing classes). (1939)

mong (1903) Australian; abbreviation of *mongrel* ■ **J. Wright:** Gor'on, ya bloody mong. Git ta buggery. Ya probably lousy with fleas. (1980)

mutt (1906) Orig US; usually applied, contemptuously, to a mongrel; from earlier sense, stupid person ■ **Saturday Evening Post:** That cat! That mutt! they fight it out And back and forth they shuttle. (1949)

pooch (1924) Orig US; origin unknown ■ **Guardian:** It holds the world record for exclamation mark abuse: 'Little Ernest Talbot killed his beloved pooch Sparky— with an ear-splitting high-C note on his violin!' (1992)

goorie, goory, goori (1937) New Zealand; usually applied, contemptuously, to a mongrel; alteration of Maori *kuri*

sausage dog (1938) Jocular; applied to a dachshund; from its cylindrical shape and German connections ■ **Lawrence Durrell:** The door . . . opened and a dispirited-looking sausage-dog waddled into the room. (1958)

Donkeys, mules, etc.

moke (1848) British; applied to a donkey; origin unknown

donk (1916) Abbreviation of *donkey* ■ **Richmal Crompton:** Look out for the donk, you ole ass. (1922)

hard tail (1917) US; applied to a mule, especially an old one; from the imperviousness of their rear ends to the driver's whip

skin (1925) Applied to a mule; compare earlier sense, horse

Fish

tiddler (1885) Applied to any small fish, often specifically the minnow or stickleback; probably related to *tiddly* little ■ **Courier-Mail** (Brisbane): Pastime anglers would not be allowed to keep 'tiddlers'. (1976)

Noah's Ark, Noah (1945) Australian; rhyming slang for *shark* ■ **Bulletin** (Sydney): 'I'll tell you what's worse than the Noahs,' said Edgar. 'What about those bloody dragon-flies?' (1982)

Hippopotamuses

hippo (1872) Abbreviation

Horses

nag (1336) Originally a standard usage, referring to a small riding horse; the slang usage, often with specific reference to an old, slow, or broken down horse, or jocularly to a racehorse, appears to be a 20th-century development; ultimate origin unknown ■ **Thomas Wolfe:** They . . . heard . . .

the two back wheels . . . of an ancient buggy, the lifting hooves of an old boneyard nag, that slowly turned away from the road's centre. (1935) ■ **Countryside:** A nag with a nasty habit of finishing 'out of the money' can prove the odds makers wrong. (1992)

prad (1798) Now Australian; by metathesis from Dutch *paard* ■ **Courier-Mail** (Brisbane): It would surely be more appropriate for the riding [for democracy] to be done on some business man rather than on a prad. (1977)

screw (1821) Dated; applied to an inferior or unsound horse; perhaps from the notion of a jockey *screwing* a horse, forcing it to the front of the field by hard riding ■ **G. T. Chesney:** Lionel was mounted on an obvious screw, but in good going condition. (1893)

plug (1860) Mainly US; applied to an inferior or worn-out horse

moke (1863) Australian; applied especially to an inferior horse; from earlier British sense, donkey ■ **C. D. Mills:** 'How's my horse?' . . . 'Your old moke's alright,' laughed the Boss. (1976)

neddy (1887) Applied especially to a racehorse; from the earlier sense, donkey ■ **Bulletin** (Sydney): Needing extra money for the neddies, he'd let it be known that guests were expected to cough up. (1981)

skinner (1891) Australian; applied to a horse that wins a race at very long odds; from earlier sense, swindler ■ **A. Wright:** Although he had gone up in the weights considerably, his owner decreed that he should win the Rosehill handicap, and give the 'shop' another 'skinner'. (1907)

bronc (1893) Orig and mainly US; abbreviation of *bronco*

skate (1894) Mainly US; applied to a worn-out decrepit horse; origin unknown ■ **Ernest Tidyman:** The man was a gambler. . . . A pony player. Used to bet thousands on the worst-looking skates you've ever seen. (1978)

mudder (1903) Orig and mainly US; applied to a racehorse which runs well on a wet or muddy course; from *mud + -er* ■ **New Yorker:** In my book, Stardust Mel is the best mudder in California. Early last month Mrs. Marjorie Lindheimer Everett's rangy gray gelding splattered through the rain and murk to win. (1975)

tomato sauce (1905) Australian; rhyming slang ■ **J. Alard:** 'Nice weak tomato sauce ta be puttin' money on,' said the Wrecker. (1968)

pony (1907) Applied to a racehorse; usually used in the plural ■ **Dallas Morning News:** Rep. Berry, an ex-gambler from San Antonio, got elected on his advocacy of betting on the ponies. (1961)

mudlark (1909) Applied to a racehorse which runs well on a wet or muddy course ■ **Sunday Telegraph** (Sydney): Born Star a Mudlark. Born Star, a two-year-old, yesterday outclassed the field at Sandown in his first start on a rain-affected track. (1975)

squib (1915) Australian; applied to a racehorse lacking stamina ■ **Sun-Herald** (Sydney): It has to be said . . . that the Golden Slipper is a race for speedy squibs. (1984)

hay burner (1920) US & Australian, jocular; from the notion of hay as the horse's 'fuel'

rosin-back (1923) Circus slang; applied to a horse used by a bareback rider or acrobat; from *rosin* resin, with which the horse's back was rubbed for a firmer seat ■ C. B. Cochrane: A 'rosin-back' is a ring-horse used by bareback riders. . . . Rosin is rubbed into the horse's back to help the rider to get a firm footing as he jumps from the ring on to the horse. (1945)

skin (1923) Dated ■ Ernest Hemingway: They take the first batch of skins out to gallop. (1923)

stickout (1937) US; applied to a racehorse that seems a certain winner ■ *Sun* (Baltimore): A 'stickout' on paper, Nokomis was in front most of the way along the six-furlong route. (1949)

geegee (1941) Applied to a racehorse; often used in the plural, and somewhat euphemistically in the context of betting; from earlier children's use, horse, reduplicated from *gee* a command to a horse to go faster ■ Cleese & Booth: Had a little bit of luck on the gee-gees. (1979)

dog (1944) Applied to a horse that is slow, difficult to handle, etc. ■ Terence Rattigan: Is it going to be dry at Newbury? . . . Walled Garden's a dog on heavy going. (1955)

Insects and the like

live stock (1785) Often jocular; applied to fleas, body lice, etc.

skeeter (1839) US & Australian; applied to a mosquito; abbreviation of regional pronunciation of *mosquito* ■ J. B. Hilton: If a slave broke loose, he would sometimes make a go of it in Florida—if he could survive the 'gators and the skeeters. (1982)

greyback (1840) US; applied to a body louse

roach (1848) Mainly US; abbreviation of *cockroach* ■ Elliot Paul: Her failure to get results kept her hopping like a roach in a skillet. (1942)

creepy-crawly (1858) Applied to any insect or similar small creeping creature considered as disagreeable or frightening ■ *Woman*: Mice, spiders, moths and other creepy-crawlies. (1960)

crumb (1863) US; applied to a body louse ■ J. H. Mullin: If there is crumbs hoppin' around me, I don't want to encourage 'em too much. (1925)

mahogany flat (1864) Applied to a bed-bug; *mahogany* from the bed-bug's colour, *flat* from the shape of its abdomen when empty ■ B. J. Banfill: Until two months ago we had only a log shanty. Somehow the Mahogany Flats took over and we had to burn it. (1967)

seam-squirrel (1899) US, mainly military slang, dated; applied to a body louse ■ C. J. Post: There is the gray-back, or seam-squirrel, from the days of our Civil War. (a1956)

cootie (1917) Applied to a body louse; perhaps from Malay *kutu* biting parasitic insect ■ R. Buckminster Fuller: The Publicitor's cheap brand of lacquer Only stuck to some cooties and fleas. (1962)

pants rabbit (1918) US, mainly military slang, dated; applied to a body louse ■ John Steinbeck: What the hell kind of bed you giving us, anyways? We don't want no pants rabbits. (1937)

toto (1918) Military slang, dated; applied to a body louse; from French military slang *toto* ■ *Radiator*: Dr. Kent Hagler . . . saw no evidence of flea or toto. (1918)

mossie, mozzie (1936) Orig Australian; applied to a mosquito; from *mos(quito* + -ie* ■ *Shooting Times & Country Magazine*: If it *has* chosen unwisely, then the newly-hatched mossies rise triumphantly from the surface only to hit their heads on the caterpillars' safety net and fall back into the liquid. (1973)

wog (1938) Australian; applied to any insect, especially a predatory or disagreeable one; origin unknown ■ *Northern Territory News* (Darwin): Mr Wilson of the City Council was present also and answered questions on the treatment of grubs and 'wogs' on foliage. (1960)

An entomologist

bug-hunter (1889) Jocular ■ A. Wise: Was she one of them? I thought—a passionate bughunter? (1962)

Kangaroos

boomer (1830) Australian; applied to a very large kangaroo; from earlier British dialect sense, anything very large of its kind

roo (1898) Australian; abbreviation ■ *Caravan World* (Australia): The river had brought emus and 'roos close to the road. (1977)

kanga (1917) Australian; abbreviation ■ R. H. Conquest: That kanga's our white hope. Call the dog off! (1965)

Octopuses

ocky (1968) Australian; from *oc(topus* + -y* ■ *Canberra Chronicle*: Watch out for the ockies that roam all over the sand flats. (1984)

Pigs

mudlark (1785) Dated; from the notion that pigs like wallowing about in mud

piggy, piggie (1799) An affectionate or child's term; from *pig* + -y* ■ *Guardian*: Over-dressed pies with pastry piggies on the lid. (1992)

piggy-wiggy, piggy-wig (1862) An affectionate or child's term; a playful rhyming extension of *piggy*

Racoons

coon (1742) Mainly US; abbreviation

Rhinoceroses

rhino (1884) Abbreviation

Sheep

jumbuck (1824) Australian; originally Australian pidgin, but its ultimate source is unknown ■ *Bulletin* (Sydney): With a board of 16 shearers a jumbuck-barbering firm this season cut out 105,000 sheep. (1926)

placer (1921) Australian & New Zealand; applied to a sheep which remains in one place ■ S. J. Baker: *Placers* are often lambs whose mothers have died and who have transferred their affection to some object, such as a bush or stone. (1941)

Snakes

rattler (1827) Orig US; applied to a rattlesnake ■ Paul Theroux: I was moving round the room, hunched like a cowboy that hears a rattler. (1978)

Joe Blake (1905) Australian; rhyming slang for *snake* ■ *Sunday Mail Magazine*: We've camped . . . with the Joe Blakes, the goannas, the flies, and 4000 skinny jumbucks. (1970)

wriggler (1927) Australian ■ W. Watkins: 'Let's go in here and get the wriggler.' 'The men will be home soon.' 'Bugger the men. . . . The snake will have gone by then.' (1972)

A large animal

lunker (1912) North American; applied to an animal, especially a fish, which is an exceptionally large example of its species; origin unknown ■ *Sports Afield*: A bronzed lunker came out of the shadowy depths and smashed the pigskin. (1947)

A scraggy animal

hat-rack (1935) From the resemblance of the protruding ribs and other bones to the pegs of a hat-rack ■ Roy Campbell: One trick is to deprive a hatrack of an old horse of water, and let him have a good lick of salt. (1957)

Sustenance and Intoxication

1. Foodstuffs

Food

grub (1659) Perhaps from the notion of grubs (larvae) as birds' food ■ Elizabeth Taylor: We're here, madam. Grub up! (1957)

eats (1841) Plural of earlier obsolete *eat* food, from the verb *eat* ■ J. P. Donleavy: On the table were eats the like of which I'm sure have never been seen on this isle. (1955)

scoff (1846) Orig South African; from Afrikaans *skof*, from Dutch *schoft* quarter of a day, each of the four meals of a day ■ *Guardian*: Ah! Scoff ahoy! I spy Florida Cocktail and Gammon Steak Hawaii! (1981)

tucker (1850) Australian & New Zealand; from earlier obsolete sense, a meal, from the verb *tuck* consume (as in *to tuck away, to tuck in*) ■ S. Locke Elliott: We've all been off our tucker with the worry. (1977)

chow (1856) Short for *chow-chow* a medley or assortment, from Pidgin English (Indian and Chinese); popularly (but probably erroneously) associated with the use of the chow ('the edible dog of China') as food by poor Chinese ■ *Landfall*: That night at chow time, Rankin called along to Tiny. (1958)

tuck (1857) Schools' slang, dated; from earlier obsolete sense, a hearty meal, from the verb *tuck* consume (as *tucker*) ■ Thomas Hughes: The Slogger looks rather sodden, as if he didn't take much exercise and ate too much tuck. (1857)

pound and pint (1865) British naval slang, dated; applied to a sailor's ration (according to Board of Trade regulations)

jock (1879) Orig dialect; origin unknown ■ Peter Wright: Food becomes . . . *jock* . . . and contrasts oddly with officialese. (1974)

mungaree, munjari (1889) Dated; from Italian *mangiare* to eat ■ Charles Barrett: Chameleons are insectivorous and get their own mungaree (food). (1942)

stodge (1890) Dated; from earlier sense, stuffing oneself with food; compare later independent sense, heavy food ■ 'Taffrail': Cream, jam, mineral waters and all other sorts of 'stodge'. (1917)

poke-out (1894) Applied to a bag of food given to a beggar

munga, manga, munger, mungey, mungy (1907) Australian, New Zealand, and services' slang; abbreviation of *mungaree* ■ Sydney Morning Herald: There were odd complaints about the food . . . from mouths that nonetheless wrapped themselves gleefully around the free munga and booze. (1982)

lump (1912) US; applied to a parcel of food given to a tramp ■ Kenneth Allsop: I met a husky burly taking of his rest And he flagged me with a big lump and a can. (1967)

gut-rot (1916) Applied to unpalatable or unwholesome food (and liquor)

scran (1916) Naval slang; applied to service rations; from earlier general sense, food, provisions; ultimate origin unknown ■ T. E. Lawrence: 'Scran up!' he called in his sailor's belling tone against my ear. (1935)

scarf (1932) US; variant of *scoff* ■ L. Snelling: How's for a bit of scarf, my tummy's anguished. (1973)

slush (1941) Applied especially to food of a watery consistency ■ Jack Thomas: It was years since he had tasted anything but jail slush. (1955)

mush, moosh (1945) Australian; applied to prison food, especially porridge ■ L. Newcombe: 'What's mush?' I asked. . . . 'Breakfast, kid,' said George. 'A dixie full of lumpy gluey, wevilled wheat.' (1979)

munchie (1959) From the verb *munch* + *-ie*

stodge (1963) Applied to heavy, usually fattening food; from earlier sense, semi-solid, usually farinaceous food; compare independent dated slang sense, food ■ *Milton Keynes Express*: Remember that no exercise programme will work if not backed by sensible eating patterns, and cut out stodge from today. (1976)

nosh (1964) From Yiddish; compare German *naschen* to nibble, eat on the sly ■ Charles Drummond: Burglars go for plain, healthy English nosh. (1972)

munchies (1971) US; applied to a snack taken to relieve the 'munchies', hunger caused by taking marijuana

Bread

toke (1843) Dated; applied to (a slice of) bread; origin unknown ■ M. Kendon: Dripping . . . spread on 'tokes' was eaten for eleven o'clock lunch by schoolgirls for well nigh forty years. (1963)

needle and thread (1859) Dated; rhyming slang

slinger (1882) Mainly services' slang; applied to bread soaked in tea; usually used in the plural

rooty (1883) Military slang; from Urdu, Hindi *roṭi*

door-step (1885) British; applied to a thick slice of bread ■ *Listener*: Won't you slice me a doorstep please? (1969)

punk (1891) Dated; from earlier sense, tinder made from wood ■ **Joseph Gores**: 'Punk and plaster?' 'You bet.' The waiter picked up his tray. . . . 'What's punk and plaster?' 'Bread and butter. Con talk.' (1975)

dodger (1897) Australian and services' slang; from US *dodger* hard-baked corn-cake; compare Northern England dialect *dodge* lump ■ **Nino Culotta**: Smack us in the eye with another hunk o' dodger. (1957)

Sandwiches

butty, buttie (1855) Orig Northern England dialect; from *butt(er + -y* ■ *Oxford Mail*: The biggest jam butty in the world. (1965)

wad (1919) British, orig services' slang; also applied to a bun, cake, etc. ■ **Gerald Kersh**: I'm in a caff, getting a tea 'n' a wad. (1942)

dodger (1925) Services', dated; from earlier sense, bread

sanger, sango (1943) Australian; from alteration of *san(dwich + -er, -o* ■ *Sunday Mail* (Brisbane): A colleague went to order a chicken 'sanger' and decided to ask the serving lady why they seemed 'a little thin of late'. (1980)

BLT (1952) Orig US; abbreviation of *bacon, lettuce and tomato*; applied to a sandwich with this filling ■ *US Air*: He eats at his desk every day, sometimes dining on such delicacies as a hot dog or a BLT. (1989)

sarnie (1961) From colloquial and northern pronunciation of *sandwich* ■ *Times*: Questions like the protein content of bacon butties . . . and the vitamin rating of corned beef sarnies. (1980)

sambie, sammie (1976) Australian & New Zealand; from *sam-*, representing the pronunciation of *sand(wich)* + -ie ■ **Barry Humphries**: Some exciting sambies . . . an increasingly popular diminutive for 'sandwiches'. (1976)

sambo (1984) Australian; from *sambie* + -o ■ *Sydney Morning Herald*: The last sprig of parsley disappeared from the final platter of sambos. (1984)

Meat

salt horse (1836) Naval slang; applied to salted beef

red horse (1864) Orig military slang, dated; applied to corned beef

Fanny Adams (1889) British, naval slang; applied to tinned meat, and subsequently (1962) to meat stew; from the name of a young woman murdered *c*1867

tinned dog (1895) Applied to tinned meat ■ **R. Ellis**: Another frugal meal of 'tinned dog', a couple of flats to mend, and straight into our swags. (1982)

Harriet Lane (1896) Mainly nautical, dated; applied to preserved meat, especially Australian tinned meat; from the name of a famous murder victim ■ **W. E. Dexter**: On Sunday we were allowed 1 lb. of preserved meat, known as 'Harriet Lane'. (1939)

Maconochie (1901) British, services' slang, dated; applied to meat stewed with vegetables and tinned, especially as supplied to soldiers on active service; from the name of the makers of the tinned stew, *Maconochie* Brothers, of London ■ *Gun Buster*: He manages to scrape together two tins of Maconochie (stew), a tin of cold potatoes, . . . and some 'issue biscuits'. (1940)

baby's head (1905) Applied to a steak (and kidney) pudding; perhaps from the round shape and pallid appearance of the pudding in its basin ■ **Kenneth Giles**: He went to the counter and ordered kidney soup and a baby's head and chips. (1967)

Kate and Sidney (1914) British; rhyming slang (and partial spoonerism) for *steak and kidney* ■ **Marguerite Steen**: Beefsteak pudding? Phew! A pity Johnny's not here, Ma! Remember how he used to go for your Kate and Sidney? (1949)

schooner on the rocks (1916) Naval slang; applied to a joint of meat roasted on potatoes (or in batter)

underground mutton (1919) Australian; applied to rabbit meat

Sausages

bags of mystery (1864) From the uncertain nature of the ingredients ■ *John o' London's*: The bags of mystery or links of love are sausages. (1962)

winny (1867) US; variant of *wienie* ■ **Thomas Wolfe**: Fortune out of winnies. They're hot, they're hot. (1929)

red-hot (1892) US; applied to a frankfurter or hot dog ■ **Bernard Malamud**: I got this redhot with mustard on it. (1971)

weeny, weeney, weenie (1906) US; anglicized spelling of *wienie* ■ **Paul Theroux**: Father said, '. . . I've got other weenies to roast.' And he went back to his maps. (1981)

wienie (1911) North American; applied to a type of smoked pork or beef sausage; from *wiener* such a sausage (short for *wienerwurst*, from German *Wienerwurst* Viennese sausage) + -ie

banger (1919) Probably from the explosive noises made by frying sausages ■ **Monica Dickens**: The chap had bought him tea and bangers and mash. (1949)

frank (1925) Orig US; short for *frankfurter* ■ *Washington Post*: Safeway Skinless All Meat Franks. 2 lb. pkg. 99c. (1968)

sav (1936) Short for *saveloy* ■ **Charles Drummond**: Some home-made savs—not the shop kind. (1969)

snag (1941) Australian; probably from British dialect *snag* morsel ■ *Bulletin* (Sydney): I make my own snags, my own pies and pasties. (1980)

starver (1941) Australian, dated; applied to a saveloy; apparently from their use as cheap food by the hungry and destitute during the Depression ■ **D'Arcy Niland**: I know what the things I eat cost me. Starvers, crumpets, stale cakes, speckled fruit, pies. (1959)

tube steak (1963) US, euphemistic; applied to a hot dog or frankfurter ■ *Boston Globe*: The food isn't bad which is mainly tube steaks (hot dogs). (1978)

Fish

whales (1890) School and university slang, dated; applied to anchovies on toast ■ M. Cox: They were held at 9.45–10p.m. on Saturdays at the rooms of the readers of the papers, who provided coffee, a cup, and *whales*. (1983)

Spithead pheasant (1948) British nautical, dated; applied to a kipper or bloater; *Spithead* from the name of a British naval anchorage off Portsmouth

Sauces

gippo, gippy, gyp(p)o, gypoo (1914) Mainly services' slang, dated; applied to any greasy gravy or sauce; variant of dialect *jipper* gravy, dripping, stew

red lead (1918) Naval slang, dated; applied to tomato ketchup

red-eye (1927) US; applied to tomato ketchup

mayo (1960) US; abbreviation of *mayonnaise* ■ Lilian Hellman: Run down to the corner and get me a ham and cheese on rye and tell them to hold the mayo. (1969)

Soup

slum (1847) Equivalent to *slumgullion*, and apparently an abbreviation of it

shackles (1886) Applied to any broth, soup or stew; probably from *shackle-bone* knuckle-bone ■ *Telegraph* (Brisbane): Mr. Coppard records how one night he stumbled on a field kitchen and enjoyed a wonderful meal of shackles, a soup made up from leftovers. (1969)

slumgullion (1902) Mainly US; applied to a watery stew or hash; probably a fanciful formation ■ T. Walker: For want of a better word we call it slumgullion. (1976)

hoosh (1905) Dated; applied to a kind of thick soup; origin unknown

Eggs

hen-fruit (1854) Mainly US, dated

googie, also googie egg, googy (egg) (1904) Australian; from Scottish dialect *goggie* child's word for an egg ■ B. Dickins: Two holy eggcups . . . that once supported my daddy's googy egg when he was a tin-lid. (1981)

goog (1941) Australian; abbreviation of *googie* ■ P. Barton: We half filled the tub with water, chucked in a handful of soap powder, and gingerly tipped in about 120 googs. (1981)

Cheese

mousetrap (1947) Applied to inferior or unpalatable cheese; from the use of such cheese to bait mousetraps ■ *Observer*: Although often dismissed as 'mousetrap', Cheddar is much the most popular cheese in Britain. (1975)

Butter and margarine

spread (1812) Dated; applied to butter ■ John Hotten: *Spread*, butter, a term with workmen and schoolboys. (1865)

marge, marg (1922) Abbreviation of *margarine* ■ John Betjeman: In quieter tones we asked in Hall that night Neighbours to pass the marge. (1960)

Maggie Ann, Maggy Anne, also maggy (1933) From the female personal names *Maggie* (familiar form of *Margaret*) and *Ann*, from their phonetic similarity to *margarine* (older pronunciation /maːgəriːn/) ■ Dan Lees: Sam never paid him enough to put maggy on his bread. (1971)

Vegetables

veg (1918) Abbreviation ■ *Economist*: Treasury officials paying for their meat and two veg are rightly suspicious. (1984)

Potatoes

tater, tatie, tato, tator, tattie, tatur, taty (1759) Originally dialectal variants of *potato* ■ Flora Thompson: Mother spent hours boiling up the 'little taturs'. (1939)

murphy (1811) From the Irish surname *Murphy*; from the former prominence of the potato in the Irish diet

spud (1845) From earlier sense, small narrow spade ■ Keith Weatherly: Some sugar, tea and a few spuds and onions formed the rest of their supplies. (1968)

Beans and peas

bullets (1929) ■ *Daily Mail*: He [a schoolboy] calls peas 'bullets'. (1963)

Salad

rabbit food, rabbit's food (1936) Applied disparagingly to lettuce or other green salad vegetables; from their prominence in the diet of pet rabbits ■ Anthony Price: You can both come back with me and eat pounds of rabbit food. (1972)

Tomatoes

tom (1920) Abbreviation ■ *Coventry Evening Telegraph*: Summer of the giant toms. (1976)

Gooseberries

goosegog (1823) Alteration of *gooseberry*; -*gog* is an alteration of *gob* lump ■ Bernard Kops: Redcurrants and black-currants and golden goosegogs. (1959)

Cakes

pufterlooner (1853) Australian; applied to a type of scone made of dough and fried in fat; from the way it 'puffs' up during cooking

sinker (1880) Orig US, dated; applied to a doughnut or dumpling; perhaps from their sinking into the fat or liquid when cooking ■ Edna Ferber: The coffee was hot, strong, revivifying; the sinkers crisp and fresh. (1926)

tabnab (1933) Nautical; applied to a cake, bun, or pastry, or to a savoury snack; origin unknown ■ Kyril Bonfiglioli: My favourite 'tabnab' was . . . a little fried potato-cake with a morsel of kari'd mutton inside. (1978)

Biscuits

squashed fly (biscuit) (1900) Applied to a garibaldi biscuit; from the appearance of the currants in the biscuits ■ C. Lithgow: In 'the break', they grappled for their milk and bun, or 'squashed-fly' biscuit. (1931)

Puddings

pud (1914) Abbreviation; applied to savoury as well as sweet puddings ■ *Southern Evening Echo*: Nostalgic and happy memories of our traditional Christmas 'Pud'. (1976)

frog-spawn (1959) British; applied disparagingly by children to tapioca or sago pudding

Sweets

sucker (1823) Orig dialectal; applied to a sweet consumed by sucking, often specifically a lollipop ■ *Islander* (Victoria, British Columbia): The small children eagerly hunted suckers that had been hidden in a large hay wagon. (1971)

choc (1874) Abbreviation of *chocolate* ■ Andrew York: He comes up to me one day when I was getting after the chocs and says, 'Rhoda, it's me or them chocolates. Take your pick.' (1966)

pogey bait (1918) US; applied to sweets or more broadly to any snack; perhaps from *pogy* a North American herring

chewy, chewie (1924) Australian; applied to chewing gum ■ McDonald & Harding: The easiest to prepare, cheap as mud to buy, and the slowest to eat, is a couple of pieces of chewy. (1976)

gob-stopper (1928) British; applied to a very large, hard, usually spherical sweet; from *gob* mouth, from its speech-inhibiting size

chutty, chuddy (1941) Australian & New Zealand; applied to chewing gum; origin unknown ■ Noel Hilliard: 'Better have some chuddy,' said Tom. (1960)

nutty (1947) Naval slang; applied to chocolates and other sweets ■ John Hale: Their Christmas presents and their nutty and cigarette rations. (1964)

Miscellaneous

parson's nose (1839) Applied to the fatty extremity of a fowl's rump; formerly also known as the *pope's nose* (1796)

slider (1915) Applied to a portion of ice-cream served between two wafers

train smash (1941) Nautical; applied to cooked tinned tomatoes, usually with bacon

spag (1948) Abbreviation of *spaghetti* ■ *Southerly*: I'll shout you a plate of steak and spag. (1969)

spaggers, spadgers (1960) British; from *spag* (*hetti* + *-ers* ■ Iris Murdoch: 'You said you were tired of spaghetti and potatoes—' 'Spuds and spadgers fill you up at least.' (1980)

sac, sacch (1961) Abbreviation of *saccharine* ■ Elleston Trevor: Sacchs. You couldn't get them down there. (1968)

za (1968) US; abbreviation of *pizza* ■ *Verbatim*: One of the boys called up and asked the parlor to *bag the za* (meaning 'cancel the pizza'). (1983)

spag bol (1970) Abbreviation of *spaghetti Bolognese*

Beverages

skilly (1927) Applied to an insipid beverage, especially coffee or tea; from earlier sense, thin porridge or soup; abbreviation of obsolete slang *skilligalee* thin porridge or soup, probably a fanciful formation ■ John Masefield: A cup of skilly completed the repast. (1953)

Tea

split pea (1857) Dated; rhyming slang ■ Sheila Kaye-Smith: I'll make you a nice cup of split pea. (1931)

gun-fire (1912) Army slang, dated; applied to an early-morning cup of tea served to troops before going on first parade; from the firing of the morning gun at the start of the day ■ *Gun Buster*: 'Dawn just breaking, sir,' he affirmed, shoving into my hands a mug of hot 'gunfire'. (1940)

char, cha (1919) British; from Chinese *cha* ■ Howard Spring: I thought of the thousands of cups o' char that batmen had produced at moments like this. (1955)

Rosy (Lee), Rosie (Lee), and with small *r* (and *l*) **(1925)** British; rhyming slang ■ Allan Prior: This is the best cup of rosy I get all day, Janey. (1964)

sergeant-major, sergeant-major's (1925) British, military slang; applied to strong sweet tea, or to tea with rum; usually used attributively, designating this; from the notion that such tea is the prerogative of sergeant-majors; compare the earlier obsolete US military slang sense, coffee with cream or milk and sugar ■ John Wainwright: This tea . . . it damn near dissolved the spoon. A real 'sergeant-major' brew. The way tea *should* be made. (1981)

cuppa (1934) British; representing a colloquial pronunciation of *cup of*, used elliptically for *cup of tea* ■ Germaine Greer: Barbara Castle dealt with [it] by the disgusting expedient of having a cuppa with the women and talking it over heart to heart. (1970)

splash (1960) British; presumably from the sound of tea being poured noisily ■ Celia Dale: Look, I gotta get to work. . . . Give 'er a cup of splash. (1964)

Coffee

mud (1925) ■ Nino Culotta: Got another cuppa mud, Joe? (1957)

joe (1941) North American; origin unknown ■ **Ed McBain:** 'Would you like some coffee?' Carella asked. 'Is there some?' 'Sure. . . . Can we get two cups of joe?' (1963)

java (1945) From earlier sense, Javan coffee ■ **Herbert Gold:** Lots a guys come in for chatter and java, friend. (1956)

Cocoa, drinking chocolate

kye (1943) Nautical; origin unknown ■ *Times:* Kye, as the service names drinking chocolate, is to end. (1968)

Soft drinks

pop (1812) Applied to an effervescing drink; from the sound made when the stopper is removed

2. Eating & Drinking

To consume

neck (1514) Dated; applied especially to drinking; from the notion of pouring something down one's neck ■ **John Masefield:** I do wish . . . you'd chuck necking Scotch the way you do. (1929)

guzzle (1579) Used to suggest greedy eating or drinking; perhaps from Old French *gosillier* chatter, from (Old) French *gosier* throat, from late Latin *geusiae* cheeks ■ **Benjamin Disraeli:** Guzzling his venison pasties. (1826)

stuff oneself (1585) Used to suggest eating to repletion ■ **G. H. Lorimer:** [He] stuffed himself till his hide was stretched as tight as a sausage skin. (1903)

eat like a horse (1707) Used to suggest ravenous eating

snack (1807) Used to denote the eating of small amounts between or instead of meals; from the noun *snack* ■ *Radio Times:* There are three meals a day, 'more or less regular, with no snacking in between'. (1978)

tuck in, tuck into (1810) Used to suggest heartily beginning to eat or drink ■ **Edna Lyall:** Always in at dinner-time and to be found at odd hours tucking in. (1887) ■ *Guardian:* Less extravagant diners can tuck into a bowl of Steamed Rat with Rice for under 50p. (1991)

scoff (1846) Partly variant of *scaff* eat, of unknown origin; partly from the noun *scoff* food ■ **Joyce Porter:** In the dining room the reporters . . . were . . . noisily scoffing down everything that was put in front of them. (1973)

tuck away (1861) ■ *Guardian:* Many people would have come to grief, notably marathon swimmers, many of whom tuck away high carbohydrate meals before taking the plunge. (1992)

polish off (1873) Used to suggest the complete eating or drinking up of something; from the earlier more general sense, finish ■ *Guardian:* I was only prevented from polishing off the whole bottle at supper by my wife who begged the last glass. (1992)

put on the nose-bag (1874) Jocular; from the feeding bag hung over the head of a draught

from the bottle ■ **Archie Hill:** We sat in the stern drinking the pop, trying to count the bubbles as they rose behind our noses. (1976)

Polly (1852) Abbreviation of *Apollinaris*, an effervescent mineral water from Apollinarisburg in the Rhineland ■ **D. Kyle:** 'Soda? Apollinaris?' 'Whisky and Polly . . . I haven't had one in years.' 'It becomes increasingly difficult to come by.' (1973)

fizz (1889) Applied to an effervescing drink ■ **Gillian Freeman:** I'll 'ave a coke. . . . No I won't, I'll 'ave a raspberry fizz. (1955)

spider (1941) Australian; applied to a soft drink with ice-cream floating on it; compare earlier sense, brandy mixed with lemonade

horse ■ **P. G. Wodehouse:** I must rush. I'm putting on the nosebag with a popsy. (1973)

put away (1878) ■ **Graham Greene:** Between us we can probably put away half a bottle of vodka. (1969)

go (c1882) Used especially in the phrase *I, you,* etc. *could go* (a particular drink or food) ■ **David Ballantyne:** I could go a good feed of eels just now. (1948)

get outside (of) (1886) ■ **D. Campbell:** It takes me half an hour to get outside the mixed grill and the ice-cream and coffee. (1967)

shift (1896) ■ **Willie Russell:** Although his speech is not slurred, we should recognize the voice of a man who shifts a lot of booze. (1981)

mug up (1897) Mainly Canadian and nautical; denoting eating a large meal, or having a snack, a meal, or a hot drink ■ **Lyn Hancock:** We . . . mugged up on boiled eggs, toast, jam, and coffee. (1972)

guts (1903) Used to suggest greedy eating or gormandizing ■ **Kylie Tennant:** 'Gutsing again, Briscoe?' she reproved. (1943)

dig in (1912) Used to suggest heartily beginning to eat or drink; from earlier sense, set to work energetically ■ **A. Baron:** Sit down and dig in. Your grub's getting cold. (1952)

hoe in, hoe into (1935) Used to suggest heartily beginning to eat or drink; from earlier sense, set to work energetically ■ **I. L. Idriess:** The local cow . . . took a lick; fancied the salty taste and hoed in for breakfast. (1939)

feed (or stuff) one's face (1939) Used to suggest excessive or impolite eating ■ **Louise Erdrich:** I had a desperate hungry craving. I kept pouring it in and feeding my face fast as I could. (1984) ■ *Time Out:* You already know that thinking about food makes you hungry; tonight you can find out why even as you stuff your face. (1995)

woof (1943) Orig airforce slang; used to denote ravenous swallowing; perhaps an alteration of *wolf* ■ **C. H. D. Todd:** In every case the six dogs at once 'woofed' the tripe. (1961)

nosh (1957) Applied to eating, and often (*US*) specifically to eating between meals; from Yiddish; compare German *naschen* to nibble, eat on the sly ■ *Time*: The politician, equipped with a trowel and the Fixed Smile, gobs mortar on a cornerstone, or noshes his way along the campaign trail. (1970) ■ Charles Drummond: The Sergeant . . . morosely noshed the veal-and-ham pie. (1972)

scarf (1960) US; used to denote eating greedily; variant of *scoff* ■ *Richard Condon*: Let's . . . scarf up some of that osso bucco. (1976)

pig out (1978) Orig and mainly US; used to denote overindulgence by eating and drinking ■ *Jane Fonda*: Troy and Vanessa . . . pig out for days on leftover Halloween candy. (1981)

To drink

slurp (1648) Used to denote drinking noisily; from Dutch *slurpen* ■ *Richmond* (Virginia) *Times-Dispatch*: The stars just whirl in . . . , slurp a cup of coffee and zoom out again. (1947)

swig (c1654) Used to denote drinking deeply; from the noun *swig* drink, draught, of unknown origin

An eater

nosher (1957) From the verb *nosh* eat ■ *Sunday Times*: Gourmet foods to salivate the palates of jaded British noshers. (1974)

An overeater

gannet (1929) Orig naval slang; from the name of the sea-bird, renowned as a great eater ■ *Paul Tempest*: The bet may be on how many plates of porridge one 'gannet' can put away at a sitting. (1950)

pig (1942) Often in the phrase *make a pig of oneself* eat gluttonously ■ *Guardian*: We had made pigs of ourselves on the bread. (1979)

dustbin (1959) Used to denote a greedy and indiscriminate eater ■ Nina Bawden: It's all his own fault. He's been stuffing his face ever since he left London. Greedy pig. Dustbin. (1973)

guzzle-guts (1959) British

Dietary preferences

veggie, veggy (1975) Shortened form of *vegetarian*; sometimes derogatory ■ *City Limits*: Built on a solid base of traditional veggie dishes like nut roasts . . . it doesn't seem to be living up to its reputation. (1986)

Meals

elevenses (1887) Applied to light refreshment taken at about 11 a.m.; from *eleven* + *-ses*; compare earlier obsolete *elevens* and *elevener* in the same sense ■ *Liliput*: On the desk in front of him was a cup of coffee and some sandwiches. 'Elevenses,' he said. (1951)

brekker (1889) British, orig university slang; from *break* (*fast* + *-er* ■ John Paddy Carstairs: I complained of an undesirable brekker kipper. (1965)

bite (1899) Applied to a small meal or a snack; from earlier sense, food to eat ■ C. Carnac: I . . . had a bite with my friend at the fish and chips stall. (1959)

soupy, soupie (1899) US, military slang; applied to a meal or to a summons to a meal; from *soup* + *-y* ■ *Stars & Stripes*: I say 'Yum yum' when 'soupie' blows. (1918)

hash-up (1902) Applied to a hastily cooked meal; from previous sense, a reworking

brekkie, brekky (1904) British; orig children's slang; from *break* (*fast* + *-y* ■ *Private Eye*: I don't reckon I feel like brekkie! (1969)

sit-down (1919) North American, tramps' slang, dated; applied to a free sit-down meal

mug-up (1933) Mainly Canadian and nautical; applied to a snack, a meal, or a drink; from the verb *mug up* have a meal, etc. ■ R. Price: Occasionally they stopped for mug-up. (1970)

fry-up (1967) Applied to a quickly made dish or meal prepared by frying, often of cold cooked food ■ John Wainwright: Then lunch. More often than not a 'fry-up'—I became a dab hand with a frying pan. (1969)

Chinkey, Chinkie, Chinky (1985) Applied to a meal in or from a Chinese restaurant; probably from earlier sense, Chinese restaurant

A large or over-large meal

blow-out (1821) From the notion of being expanded or 'blown out' by a large amount of food ■ Rosamund Lehmann: Have a nice blowout and a good sleep afterwards. (1930)

spread (1822) From the notion of food generously 'spread' out on a table ■ Henry Vizetelly: He . . . was a constant attendant at these little spreads. (1893)

tuck-in (1886) From the verb *tuck in* eat heartily; compare earlier obsolete *tuck-out* in the same sense

beano (1888) Printers' abbreviation of *beanfeast*, which originally denoted an annual dinner given to employees by their employer (at which beans and bacon used to be regarded as an indispensable dish)

slap-up (1889) British; used to denote a large and splendid meal; from earlier more general sense, first-class ■ *Lancashire Life*: There was a slap-up tea at the institute. (1977)

nosh-up (1979) British; from the verb *nosh* eat ■ Alfred Draper: Like most birds she didn't want to lose out on a nosh-up. (1970)

pig-out (1979) Orig US; applied to a bout of excessive eating; from the verb *pig out* ■ *Chicago Tribune*: Favorite pigout food: Turkey. In fact, I love the whole Thanksgiving dinner. (1989)

Food distribution, preparation, cooking, and serving

whip up (1849) Used to denote the speedy preparation of a dish or meal; from *whip* thicken a liquid by beating ■ *Washington Post*: They are . . . as blasé about it as world-class chefs whipping up peanut butter and jelly sandwiches. (1993)

rabbit-o, rabbit-oh (1902) Australian; applied to a travelling seller of rabbit-meat ■ Kylie Tennant: Mrs. Drew knew all about her neighbours from the butcher and the grocer and the rabbit-o. (1945)

irons (1905) Mainly services' slang; applied to eating utensils

sling hash (1906) US; used to denote waiting at tables; back-formation from *hash-slinger* waiter ■ *Life*: She . . . slung hash for a couple of weeks. (1949)

afters (1909) British; applied to the course of a meal that comes after the main course ■ Nevil Shute: 'What's he got for afters?' 'Plummy duff.' (1940)

slum-gun (1917) Military slang; applied to a mobile army kitchen; from *slum* watery stew + *gun* ■ Damon Runyon: Our slum-gun busted down. (1947)

soup gun (1918) US military slang, dated; applied to a mobile army kitchen

me-and-you (1932) Jocular; applied to a menu; adaptation of colloquial pronunciation /miːnjuː/ of *menu* ■ Ngaio Marsh: Come on, Beautiful! Let's have a slant at the me-and-you. (1943)

set-up (1934) US; applied to a place-setting at a restaurant ■ J. D. Macdonald: He led us to a corner booth set up for four, whipped away the extra setups. (1978)

shackle-up (1935) Dated; applied to an act of preparing food in a pot; origin uncertain; compare *shackles* soup or stew ■ James Curtis: A spare shirt and a couple o' tins in case they want to have a shackle up. (1936)

eighty-six (1936) US; used in restaurants and bars to indicate that the supply of an item has run out, or that a customer is not to be served; also applied to a customer to be refused service; probably rhyming slang for *nix*, used to denote refusal ■ G. Fowler: There was a bar in the Belasco building, . . . but Barrymore was known in that cubby as an 'eighty-six'. (1944)

spud-bashing (1940) British, orig services' slang; applied to (a lengthy spell of) peeling potatoes ■ *Times*: Between dashing home from the office . . . and having a bath, there is not much time for spud bashing. (1980)

barbie (1976) Orig Australian; abbreviation of *barbecue* ■ *Age* (Melbourne): On-site tucker . . . ranges from barbecued chicken to 'spaget marinara' ('suitable for the barbie on the building site'). (1983)

nuke (1987) Mainly US; used to denote the cooking or heating of food in a microwave oven ■ M. Muller: After microwaving a couple of burritos (or 'nuking' them, as my nephew calls it), I left the house. (1989)

Dutching (1989) British; applied to the practice of sending food destined for the UK market for irradiation abroad (usually in the Netherlands), to mask any bacterial contamination before it is put on sale; from *Dutch* + *-ing*

to go (1946) US; used of cooked food sold in a restaurant or shop, to denote that it is to be taken away and eaten elsewhere ■ A. Beattie: Can I have a bagel and a coffee to go? (1980)

A second helping of food

seconds (1792) ■ Peter Gzowski: This dish has been served to hundreds of people over the years and requests for seconds (or even thirds) are usual. (1974)

gash (1943) Australian; probably short for *gashion* extras, which may be related to English dialect *gaishen* skeleton, silly-looking person, obstacle ■ W. Watkins: He didn't have to beg the cook for left over scran—gash, the crew called it. (1972)

Preparation and serving of drinks

brew up (1916) Used to denote the making of tea ■ A. Clifford: I thought we might brew up. (1943). Hence **brew-up** (a pause for) the making of tea (1944) ■ *Times*: The . . . petrol tins which the Desert Rats found equally handy for washing in or for a 'brew-up'. (1963)

drum up (1923) Used to denote the making of tea in a billy-can, etc., and also the preparation of a makeshift meal; from *drum* can used for this ■ George Orwell: After getting to Bromley they had 'drummed up' on a horrible, paper-littered refuse dump. (1935). Hence **drum-up** the making of tea or the preparation of a meal (1919)

set-up (1930) US; applied to the glass, ice, soda, etc. required for mixing a drink, which is served to customers, who supply their own spirits, in unlicensed premises ■ W. McCarthy: He looked over to the sideboard and saw a complete assortment of liquors, rums and set-ups. (1973)

drum (1931) Applied to a tin or can in which tea is made

on the rocks (1949) Orig US; used to indicate that a drink is served with ice ■ Robert Ludlum: That was scotch on the rocks, wasn't it? (1978)

Cooks

cooky, cookie, cookey, cookee (1776) From *cook* + -y, etc.

doctor (1821) Applied to a ship's cook and also (US & Australian) to a cook in a camp ■ R. S. Close: Hey doctor! How about something to eat? (1945)

slushy, slushey, slushie (1859) Applied to a ship's cook, especially as a nickname, and also more generally to any cook, or to any unskilled kitchen or domestic help; probably from *slush* food (although not recorded until much later) + -y ■ Kenneth Giles: A grey-headed woman was crying in a corner—'The part-time slushy,' said Porterman. (1970)

poisoner (1905) Australian & New Zealand, jocular; applied especially to a cook on a sheep (cattle, etc.) station ■ Lyndall Hadow: 'I'm not much good at cooking but I'll try.' 'Never you mind about that. Up north we've got the best poisoners in the country.' (1969)

babbling brook, babbler (1919) Australian & New Zealand; applied especially to a cook who

works on a sheep station, army camp, etc.;
babbling brook rhyming slang for *cook; babbler*
short for *babbling brook* ■ *Weekly News* (Auckland):
We worked it out that the old babbler made 112,000 rock cakes
during those four months. (1963) ■ *Sunday Mail* (Brisbane):
Local good cooks asked for the recipe, but minds boggled at
the quantities the army's babbling-brook recited for their
benefit. (1981)

slum burner (1930) Military slang; applied to
an army cook; from *slum* watery stew + *burner*
■ M. Hargrove: Oscar of the Waldorf, in the Army, would still
be . . . a *slum burner*. (1943)

spud barber (1935) Jocular; applied to a potato
peeler ■ G. Foulser: The galley-boy [was] just a spudbarber
after all. (1961)

bab (1936) Australian & New Zealand; short for
babbling brook cook ■ *Bulletin* (Sydney): The bab's
present rate for cooking for more than seven is £14 4s. 11d.
(1959)

Waiting and kitchen staff

hash-slinger (1868) US; applied to a waiter or
waitress; from *hash* food ■ *American Speech*: The
cooks and 'hashslingers' of former years went off to war or to
the shipyards. (1946)

biscuit-shooter (1893) US; applied to a waitress
or sometimes to a waiter

pearl diver (1913) Orig US; applied to someone
who works as a dishwasher in a café or
restaurant

hasher (1916) US; applied to a waiter or waitress;
from *hash* food + *-er* ■ *Listener*: When it came to
making an impression on the 'hashers' in the railroad
'beaneries', the boomers really let themselves go. (1960)

Nippy (1925) British, dated; applied originally to
a waitress in any of the restaurants of J. Lyons &
Co. Ltd. in London, and hence to any waitress;
from *nippy* quick ■ G. V. Galwey: His hands stuck out in
front of him like a Nippy carrying a tray. (1948)

cookie-pusher (1936) US; applied to a waitress

Eating places and food shops

beanery (1887) US; applied to a cheap
restaurant, originally one where beans were
served ■ Ernest Hemingway: Inside the door of the
beanery Scripps O'Neil looked around him. (1933)

hash-joint (1895) US; applied to a cheap eating
place, boarding house, etc.; from *hash* dish of
recooked meat ■ John Dos Passos: Passing the same
Chink hashjoint for the third time. (1930)

eatery (1901) Orig US; from *eat* + *-ery* ■ *Times*: His
inability to make contact with a really good hunk of beefsteak
in the eateries of Germany, Italy and France. (1959)

one-arm joint (1915) US; applied to a cheap
restaurant in which customers support their
plates on a widened chair-arm; based on earlier
one-arm lunch room

nosh, also **nosh bar**, **nosh-house (1917)**
From Yiddish; compare German *naschen* to

nibble, eat on the sly ■ Colin Macinnes: After a quick
bite at a Nosh, and two strong black coffees, I felt up to the
ordeal. (1959)

greasy spoon (1918) Orig US; applied to a
cheap and inferior eating place ■ *Time*: They [sc.
the Marx brothers] . . . ate in coffee pots and greasy
spoons. (1951)

caff (1931) British; colloquial anglicization of *café*
■ *Sunday Times Magazine*: In 1979 . . . the *Sunday Times
Magazine* ran a fearful article predicting the demise of the
working man's caff. (1991)

pull-in (1938) Applied to a roadside café or
refreshment stand at which vehicles can 'pull
in' ■ John Wainwright: A blue and white sign warned five
miles to the next service area. . . . 'They'll be at the next pull-
in.' (1973)

deli (*c*1954) Orig & mainly US; abbreviation of
delicatessen ■ *Guardian*: The deli on the corner may serve
delicious tagliatelle, but is not trying to serve it to millions of
people. (1991)

chippy, **chippie (1961)** British; applied to a fish-
and-chip shop; from *chip* + *-y* ■ *Listener*: In the
industrial towns the housewife . . . found that time, labour, and
money were saved by the chippie. (1965)

noshery (1963) Applied to a restaurant or snack-
bar; from *nosh* eat + *-ery* ■ Kenneth O'Hara: The place
I'm thinking of for lunch . . . has the reputation of a very
superior noshery. (1972)

tratt, **trat (1969)** Abbreviation of *trattoria*
■ *Guardian*: Mostly I mean the white-tiled tratts of SW1, 3
and 7. (1970)

Chinkey, **Chinkie**, **Chinky (1985)** Probably
orig Scottish; applied to a Chinese restaurant;
first recorded in 1985, but in use since at least
the late 1960s; from earlier sense, Chinese
person ■ Irvine Welsh: Three guys stagger oot ay a pub
and intae a Chinky. (1993)

Hungry

peckish (1785) From the notion of being
disposed to 'peck' at food ■ Jerome K. Jerome:
You're a bit peckish too, I expect. (1898)

starving (1882) ■ James Kelman: It was grub as well
right enough he was starving, totally starving. Plus there was
fuck all in the house bar a box of weetabix. (1994)

could eat a horse (1936) ■ C. George: 'Shall I put
the pasta on now?' 'Please do!' He leaned against the door-
jamb, his hair brushing the lintel. 'I could eat a horse, Madame
Chef.' (1991)

Thirsty

dry (*c*1536) Originally in standard use, but
considered colloquial since the late 19th
century

spit chips (1901) Australian; denoting extreme
thirst; from the notion of having dry wood in
one's mouth and throat ■ Alan Marshall: I was
spitting chips. God, I was dry! (1946)

3. Alcohol

Alcoholic drink

booze (c1325) From the verb *booze* drink alcohol
■ T. S. Eliot: We're gona sit here and drink this booze. (1932)

tipple (1581) In modern usage mainly used to denote a particular person's habitual alcoholic drink; from the verb *tipple* drink alcohol ■ *Daily Mail*: He presented her with a picture showing her with a gin and tonic, her favourite tipple. The Queen burst out laughing. (1991)

grog (1804) Often applied specifically to beer; from earlier sense, drink of rum (or other spirits) and water; ultimately perhaps from *Old Grog*, a nickname (from his habit of wearing a grogram (= type of coarse cloth) cloak) of Admiral Edward Vernon (1684–1757), who in 1740 ordered the introduction of such a drink in the Royal Navy in place of neat spirit
■ *Centralian Advocate* (Alice Springs): Mr Forrester agreed that the main 'grog problem' on the town camps was caused by the licensed stores. (1986)

poison (1805) Jocular, orig US; mainly in the phrases *name one's poison* and *What's your poison?* used to ask someone what they would like to drink ■ Mark Twain: In Washoe, when you are . . . invited to take 'your regular poison', etiquette admonishes you to touch glasses. (1866)

juice (1828) Mainly US ■ R. Russell: 'Nuthin' at all like juice, either,' Hassan said. 'No hangover.' (1961)

alky, alchy, alki(e) (1844) Orig and mainly US; often applied specifically to illicit liquor or to whisky; from *alc(ohol + -y* ■ R. & J. Paterson: All they [*sc.* bootleggers] need is a shack and a can of alky. (1970)

tiddly, tiddley (1859) Dated; origin uncertain; compare obsolete rhyming slang *tiddlywink* drink ■ E. V. Lucas: It wasn't oysters that she really wanted, but . . . tiddly. (1930)

neck-oil (1860) Jocular; often applied specifically to beer ■ *Private Eye*: A chance encounter . . . leads Barry to consume a lot of nice neck-oil. (1970)

turps (1865) Australian; applied especially to beer; used mainly in the phrase *on the turps*; from earlier sense, turpentine ■ S. Thorne: Dan was a good bloke, but a terror on the turps. Once he started on rum—look out! (1980)

nose paint (1880) Jocular; from the reddening effect on the nose ■ *American Speech*: He [*sc.* the cowman] drinks . . . nose paint instead of 'whiskey'. (1968)

rabbit (1895) Dated, Australian; mainly in the phrase *run the rabbit* take drink (illegally) from a public house, especially after hours

stagger juice (1896) Jocular, orig Australian ■ J. Wynnum: 'These two bowls of punch look exciting.' . . . 'Well now, that one . . . is our customary Stagger Juice.' (1962)

shicker, shiker, shikker (1901) Australian & New Zealand; often in the phrase *on the shicker*; from the adjective *shicker* drunk ■ *Kings Cross*

Whisper (Sydney): Surfers Paradise beer garden, where everyone got on the shicker. (1966)

shick (1907) Australian & New Zealand; shortening of *shicker*

skimish (1908) From Shelta *škimis* to drink, *škimišk* drunk ■ James Curtis: He had been drinking all that skimish without having had a bite to eat. (1936)

white line (1914) Dated US ■ *Flynn's*: All we could glom was a shot of white line. (1926)

jollop (1920) Probably from *jollop* medicine (not recorded until later) ■ Colin Willock: 'Tell 'em up at the house to bring out the jollop.' The keeper uttered this in a tone that made it quite clear that he considered serving refreshment something completely outside his duties. (1961)

giggle-water (1926), giggle-juice (1939) Jocular, orig US; often applied specifically to champagne ■ Gilbert Hackforth-Jones: Drop o' gin'll go down nicely on top of that giggle-water [*sc.* champagne cocktails]. (1946)

sting (1927) Australian ■ J. de Hoog: You can share a bottle of sting (methylated spirits) down a lane. (1972)

panther juice, panther('s) piss, panther sweat (1929) Mainly US; applied especially to spirits distilled illicitly or locally ■ William Gaddis: Yeah? Well did you ever drink panther piss? the liquid fuel out of torpedoes? (1955)

River Ouse, River Ooze (1931) Rhyming slang for *booze* ■ Robin Cook: The place still bulging with smoke and river ooze. (1962)

wallop (1933) Mainly applied to beer; perhaps from earlier sense, bubbling of boiling liquid ■ Lynton Lamb: Mrs Tyler could do nothing to improve the wallop she served at the Hurdlemakers [Inn]. (1972)

sauce (1940) Orig US ■ William Trevor: 'You often get loonies in joints like that,' he remarked on the street. 'They drink the sauce and it softens their brains for them.' (1976)

jungle juice (1942) Jocular, orig Australian ■ G. Dutton: The Americans had two bottles of bourbon and one of jungle juice made from fermented coconut milk and surgical alcohol. (1968)

smash (1959) North American; applied especially to wine ■ *American Speech*: Let's get in the wind and belt some smash. (1975)

joy-juice (1960) US ■ *Black World*: He could hear the others as in a dream, laughing, telling dirty jokes, playing cards and swizzling joy-juice. (1974)

electric soup (1992) ■ *Observer*: Private Eye's 'Dear Bill' letters purportedly written by Denis to Bill Deedes, golfer, electric soup-drinking chum and former editor of the Daily Telegraph. (1996)

A drink

wet (1719)

slug (1762) Now mainly US; applied to a drink of spirits ■ Louis Heren: Their simple niceness was almost as good as a slug of scotch and a cigarette which I . . . could not enjoy in their company. (1978)

nobbler (1842) Australian; applied to a drink or glass of spirits; from *nobble* drug a racehorse or obsolete *nobble* hit + *-er* ■ *Walkabout*: Whisky costs around 300 rupiahs, or some 75 cents, for a generous nobbler. (1971)

snifter (1844) Orig US; applied usually to a small drink of spirits; from dialect *snift* sniff + *-er* ■ P. G. Wodehouse: And now, old horse, you may lead me across the street to the Coal Hole for a short snifter. (1924)

pony (1849) Applied to a small glass or measure of alcohol ■ G. Hamilton: Os pulled a beer each for me and Tommy, and a pony for himself. He always drank small beers. (1959)

peg (1864) Mainly Anglo-Indian; often applied specifically to a drink of brandy and soda; from the pegs or markers in a drinking-vessel ■ F. M. Crawford: Trial . . . who could absorb the most 'pegs'—those vile concoctions of spirits, ice, and sodawater. (1883)

stiffener (1864) Orig Australian; from its reviving effects ■ Gladys Mitchell: I'll buy you a stiffener in the bar. (1973)

nip (1869) Applied to a small drink of spirits; from earlier obsolete sense, half-pint of beer; ultimately probably short for obsolete *nipperkin* small measure for liquors, of unknown origin

spot (1885) Applied to a small alcoholic drink ■ P. G. Wodehouse: May I offer you a spot? . . . I can recommend the Scotch. (1936)

half (1888) Applied to a half-pint of beer

bevvy, bevie, bevy (1889) British; usually applied specifically to a drink of beer; from *bev(erage* + *-y* ■ Philip Allingham: 'I think this calls for a bevvy,' I said, and we walked off to the nearest pub together. (1934)

gargle (1889) ■ *Guardian*: 'Copy of the Boss's Wit and Wisdom, old boy,' he said, presenting a neatly typed replica of the non-election address. 'Come and have a gargle.' (1987)

snort (1889) Orig US; applied to a small drink of spirits ■ M. E. Atkins: We'll have another snort. . . . C'mon, drink up, I'll fill your glass. (1981)

sherbet (1890) Compare earlier use, cooling drink of Eastern origin ■ F. Archer: He had a strident voice and with a few sherbets under his belt you knew he was about. (1974)

chaser (1897) Orig US; applied to a drink taken after another—originally a weak drink after spirits, but latterly also spirits after a weak drink; from the notion of the later drink pursuing the earlier ■ *Guardian*: They sat around . . . drinking brandy with beer chasers. (1991) ■ *Super Bike*: It was time for some replenishing of Margaritas with piss-beer and Maker's Mark bourbon chasers. (1993)

jolt (1904) Mainly US; applied to a drink of spirits ■ Ross Thomas: She took two green plastic glasses. . . . I poured a generous jolt into both of them. (1973)

sundowner (1909) Orig African English; applied to an alcoholic drink taken at sunset ■ Graham

Greene: He sits there on a hot evening swilling his sundowners without a care in the world. (1978)

tincture (1914) Usually applied to a small drink of spirits ■ Richard Ingrams & John Wells: Rough diamond, especially after a tincture or two. (1980)

shicker, shiker, shikker (1919) Australian & New Zealand; from earlier sense, alcoholic drink ■ A. Wright: I've had a few shikkers, I can't deny it, but it ain't every day a man has a fortune sprung on him. (1919)

taste (1919) US ■ *New Yorker*: He said, 'Take me for a taste.' We went into a bar, and I thought he'd settle down for a few, but he only had two shots. (1976)

the other half (1922) Orig naval slang; applied to a second or return drink; from the notion of a second half-pint of beer ■ Roderick Jeffries: You'll have the other half, Inspector? Two whiskies under the belt are better than one. (1965)

jar (1925) Applied to a glass of beer ■ *Observer*: The painter, Raymond Piper, took us for a jar at his local. (1972)

speedball (1926) US; applied to a glass of wine, specifically one strengthened with additional alcohol

quick one (1928) Applied to a drink intended to be taken quickly ■ Gwen Moffat: Ken Maynard came into the cocktail lounge. . . . 'Just in time for a quick one. . . . Two lagers, please.' (1976)

refill (1929) Applied to a second or further drink ■ *Rolling Stone*: She lets go with a loud, decidedly unsentimental laugh that startles a room-service waiter trying to set down refills on a coffee table hopelessly cluttered with empty glasses and Heineken bottles. (1977)

shorty, shortie (1931) Orig US; applied to a small drink of spirits ■ *Freedomways*: Yarborough . . . yelled, 'Bartender. Give the professor another shorty of gin there.' (1963)

rosiner (1932) Irish & Australian; applied to a stiff drink of spirits; from *rosin* type of resin + *-er* ■ H. D. Brockman: I've not had a solitary spot since four. I need a rosiner. (1947)

tank (1936) Applied to the amount held by a drinking glass, and hence loosely to a drink, especially of beer; probably an abbreviation of *tankard*, but compare *tank up* get drunk and *tanked* drunk ■ *Spectator*: Their carousals over a few friendly tanks at the neighbouring Whitehall milk bar. (1958)

one for the road (1943) Applied to a drink taken before leaving ■ J. Blackburn: 'What about giving me one for the road, my dear.' He gulped down the remains of the sherry. (1972)

sippers (1944) British, naval slang; applied to a sip of rum, especially taken from another's tot, as a reward for some service or in celebration; from *sip* + *-ers* ■ H. Tunstall-Behrens: A bottle appeared with enough in it to give us all 'sippers'. (1956)

middy (1945) Australian; applied to a medium-sized measure of beer, or a similar quantity of another drink; from *mid* middle + *-y* ■ K. Cook: 'Middy of rum, Mick,' said the youth. . . . Ten ounces of rum sold over the bar cost four dollars. (1974)

the office copy (1946) Naval slang, jocular; applied to a second or return drink

shant (1960) From earlier sense, a (quart) pot of drink; ultimate origin uncertain; compare Australian & New Zealand *shanty* (unlicensed) pub ■ *News Chronicle*: We did not want to roll anybody but we had a few shants and I always get a bit garritty then. (1960)

pen and ink (1963) Australian & New Zealand; rhyming slang ■ J. Alard: Are ya gonna have a pen an' ink? (1968)

shooter (1971) US; applied to a measure or drink of spirits, especially whisky ■ Wilson McCarthy: Let's have a shooter and a beer. (1973)

A drink taken to instil courage

Dutch courage (1826) From earlier sense, (false) courage produced by drinking alcohol; from the Dutch origins of gin as drunk to steady the nerves ■ D. Clement & I. la Frenais: The bride . . . groomed and cosseted herself and fandried her hair. The groom gulped Dutch courage with a couple of lorry driving mates. (1978)

Poor-quality drink

rot-gut (1633) ■ Eugene O'Neill: That isn't Phil's rotgut. That's real, honest-to-God bonded Bourbon. (1952)

firewater (1826) Applied to any strong spirit; originally attributed to North American Indians; latterly used jocularly ■ Paul Ablema: I am not a teetotaller but I always use the firewater cautiously. (1991)

popskull (1867) North American ■ *American Speech*: Distillers never refer to a still coil as a 'worm', as did the bootleggers who manufactured popskull and rotgut during Prohibition. (1946)

snake juice (1890) Mainly Australian; applied especially to inferior whisky ■ *Southerly*: Ironbark . . . went into the poison shop. Old Nick handed him a glass of snake juice. (1962)

hooch, hootch (1897) Orig and mainly North American; applied mainly to illicitly distilled whisky or other spirits; abbreviation of Alaskan *Hoochinoo* name of a liquor-making tribe ■ *New Yorker*: The people of the city were prepared to swallow any old hootch under the rule of some wild thirst. (1969)

shypoo, shipoo (1897) Australian; applied especially to inferior beer; origin unknown ■ N. Bartlett: You could get drunk, at Cossack's other pub, on Colonial ale or 'shypoo' at sixpence the quart. (1954)

pink-eye (1900) Mainly Australian & Canadian; probably an alteration of *pinky* inferior wine, but also with some allusion to the drink's effect on the drinker ■ *Coast to Coast*: Better put that bottle away. . . . If the trooper comes round somebody'll be getting into trouble for selling Charley pinkeye again. (1941)

screech (1902) North American

gut-rot (1916) ■ Samuel Beckett: The customer . . . was paying for his gutrot ten times what it cost to produce. (1938)

lunatic soup (1933) Australian & New Zealand ■ *Transair*: They went about destroying themselves with the lunatic soup crippling their larynx as surely as if they'd downed an economy size tin of paint stripper. (1986)

scrap iron (1942) US ■ *Washington Post*: A trio of investigators warned the drinking public yesterday to beware of a new bootleg concoction, 'scrap iron', noted more for its voltage than vintage. (1958)

King Kong (1946) US dated; from the name of the ape-like monster featured in the film *King Kong* (1933)

Sneaky Pete (1949) Orig and mainly US; often applied specifically to illicit liquor ■ J. H. Jones: He walked around an unconscious Sneaky Pete drinker. (1971)

gnat's piss, gnats' piss (1959) Often applied specifically to weak or insipid beer ■ B. S. Johnson: Where'd you get this gnatspiss from, Maurie? . . . I can get you gnatspiss as good as this gnatspiss for sixteen bob a bottle. (1963)

Illicitly distilled or irregularly concocted liquor

sly grog (1825) Australian; applied to alcoholic drink sold by an unlicensed vendor ■ W. Dick: We were on our way to the sly grog joint to buy a dozen bottles. (1969)

moon (1928) US; short for *moonshine* ■ *Saturday Evening Post*: I would buy a couple of pints of moon. (1950)

smoke (1940) US; applied to a cheap drink based on raw alcohol, methylated spirit, solvent, etc.; from earlier sense, cheap whisky ■ *Washington Post*: It was the smoke that made Heaton a loner and junk peddler in the demolition jungles of the Southwest area. (1959)

steam (1941) Australian & New Zealand; applied to cheap wine laced with methylated spirit ■ T. A. G. Hungerford: I've got a bottle of steam in my room—I think I'll have a snort and turn in. (1953)

torp (1945) Short for *torpedo juice* ■ J. Bryan: Someone brought a pint of torp. (1945)

torpedo juice (1946) Applied to intoxicating drink extracted from torpedo fuel, and hence to any strong home-made alcoholic liquor

See also **hooch** (p. 144), **panther juice** (p. 142), **Sneaky Pete** (p. 144).

Types of alcoholic drink: Beer

swipes, swypes (1796) Dated; originally applied to weak inferior beer, and hence to beer in general; perhaps from the verb *swipe* in the obsolete sense 'swig' ■ George Meredith: You may get as royally intoxicated on swipes as on choice wine. (1895)

heavy wet (1821), heavy (1823) *heavy* now applied in Scotland to a particular type of bitter beer ■ *Independent*: Bob Sutherland swigs his fifth pint of 'heavy', knocks it back with a rum chaser. (1991)

she-oak (1848) Australian, dated; applied to Australian-brewed beer; origin uncertain; presumably connected with *she-oak* type of casuarina, but the reason is unclear (a late 19th-century source claims that there was at one time a brewery on She Oak Hill in Hobart,

Tasmania) ■ T. C. Wollaston: Each would take a pull from the jug of 'sheoak' between them. (1914)

pig's ear (1880) Rhyming slang ■ James Curtis: But the most of the fiver would go in the old pig's ear. (1936)

slop (1904) US & Australian; usually used in the plural with the same meaning ■ *Australasian Post*: Bung me and me mate over a droppa slops, will yer love? (1963)

suds (1904) Orig and mainly US ■ C. L. Sonnichsen: The bear . . . was still consuming his free bottle of suds. (1943)

hop (1929) Mainly Australian & New Zealand; usually used in the plural with the same meaning; from earlier sense, climbing plant used for flavouring beer ■ J. Hibberd: I was in a sad state . . . all psychological . . . the hops were having their desired effect. (1972)

amber fluid, amber liquid, amber nectar (1959) Australian ■ *Northern Territory News* (Darwin): There'll be 360 meat pies and 30 kilos of snags [= sausages] to demolish, washed down with 40 cartons of amber fluid. (1980)

coldie (1953) Australian; applied to a glass, bottle, or can of cold beer; from *cold + -ie* ■ *Overland*: Bet they're both downin' a few coldies. (1976)

See also **wallop** (p. 142).

Brandy

O.D.V. (1839) Dated; jocular alteration of *eau de vie*

jackass brandy (1920) US, dated; applied to home-made brandy

Champagne

the widow (1781) In later use associated with *Veuve* (= widow) *Clicquot* name of a brand of champagne ■ G. Boothby: A good luncheon and a pint of the Widow to wash it down. (1899)

fizz (1864) From its effervescence ■ V. M. Cottrell: A bottle of 'fizz' each. (1942)

(the) boy (1882) Dated; origin unknown ■ *Melody Maker*: Lord Delamere came up to them with a foaming magnum of champagne and said, 'Well, boys! you've given us a glorious time! What do you say to a beaker of "the boy"?' (1929)

bubbly (1920) Short for earlier obsolete slang *bubbly water* (1910) ■ *Blackwood's Magazine*: [He] had finished up at dinner with some capital oysters and a bottle of bubbly. (1927)

champers (1955) British; from *champ(agne + -ers* ■ Milo Ainsworth: Champers or something with gin in it? (1959)

shampoo (1957) Arbitrary alteration ■ A. Sinclair: The waiter brings a bottle of champagne. . . . Shampoo, Sheila dear? (1959)

Bolly (1982) British; short for *Bollinger* name of a brand of champagne ■ *Standard*: A special bottle of bolly. (1982)

Gin

lightning (1781) Mainly US; also applied more broadly to any strong, often low-quality alcoholic spirit ■ Laurens van der Post: The fiery Cape brandy known to us children as 'Blitz' or Lightning. (1958)

mother's ruin (1937) Jocular ■ P. Jones: I have been to a party, darling. . . . What would you like? 'Mother's Ruin'? (1955)

needle and pin (1937) Rhyming slang

Methylated spirit

jake (1932) Orig US; from earlier sense, alcoholic drink made from Jamaica ginger; abbreviated form of *Jamaica* ■ John Steinbeck: He would drink jake or whisky until he was a shaken paralytic. (1939)

metho (1933) Australian & New Zealand; from *meth(ylated spirit + -o* ■ B. Dixon: Old Jimmy Taylor had gone a little bit in the mind, from drinking too much beer and metho. (1984)

white lady (1935) Australian; compare earlier sense, cocktail made of gin, orange liqueur and lemon juice

goom (1967) Australian; origin uncertain; possibly from Aboriginal (Jagara and neighbouring languages) *guŋ* fresh water ■ *Meanjin*: Goom! What a name for methylated spirits. (1982)

Pink gin

pinkers (1961) British, mainly naval slang; from *pink (gin) + -ers* ■ D. Clark: 'It was well known that Middleton was the only one who drank pink gin.' . . . 'Rubbish. There were two newcomers. . . . Who knew they didn't drink pinkers?' (1978)

Rum

Tom Thumb (1905) Orig Australian; rhyming slang; from the name of a legendary diminutive character

Whisky

red-eye (1819) US; applied to rough, strong whisky; from its effect on the drinker ■ A. Hynd: Barrow put down a slug of red eye and walked up to her. (1949)

pine-top (1858) US, dated; applied to cheap or illicit whisky

tarantula-juice (1861) US; applied to inferior whisky

forty-rod whisky, forty rod (1863) Orig US; applied to cheap fiery whisky; probably from obsolete *forty-rod lightning* in same sense, supposedly from a jocular reputation for being lethal at forty rods (about 200 metres) ■ *Daily Oklahoman* (Oklahoma City): The mere possession of a few gills of forty rod is not counted as an ample offset to planned assassination. (1948)

white mule (1889) US; applied to illicit or inferior whisky

snake poison (1890) US & Australian ■ Kylie Tennant: If Bee-Bonnet ever again wants me to sample his snake poison, I'll pour it on him and set it alight. (1947)

screech (1902) North American; applied to illicit or inferior whisky ■ W. H. Pugsley: [The rating] gets hold of some bootleg scotch—'high life', they call it on the West Coast, and 'screech' in Newfie—and then he's away to . . . Cells or Detention. (1945)

smoke (1904) US; applied to illicit or inferior whisky ■ *Daily Telegraph*: Twelve additional deaths today are attributed to week-end 'jags', which have been traced to 'speak-easies' in the New York east-end, where the liquor is known as 'smoke'. (1928)

scat (1914) US, dated; origin unknown ■ *Publications of the American Dialect Society*: Peter men don't punch much guff as a rule, but sometimes the scat will loosen them up for some good yarns. (1955)

white lightning (1921) Orig US; applied to illicit or inferior whisky

skee (1959) Australian & New Zealand; shortened from *whisky* ■ G. Jenkin: And for this here quid and a bottle of skee I'm betting at ten to one. (1967)

Wine

pinky, pinkie (1897) Mainly Australian; applied to cheap or inferior (fortified) wine

dago red (1906) US; applied to cheap red wine, especially of Italian origin ■ John Dos Passos: As we poured down the dago red he would become mischievous. (1966)

red ink (1919) Mainly US; applied to cheap red wine ■ Eugene O'Neill: You'd lie awake . . . with . . . the wine of passion poets blab about, a sour aftertaste in your mouth of Dago red ink! (1952)

vino, veeno (1919) Often applied to inferior wine; from Spanish and Italian *vino* wine ■ Lawrence Durrell: I bear up very well under the stacks of local vino I am forced to consume. (1935)

red biddy (1928) Applied to cheap red wine, and also to a drink made from this and methylated spirit ■ Colin Willock: Any idea where we could get any of the hard stuff? This flipping red biddy's burning a hole in my stomach. (1961)

plonk (1930) Orig Australian; applied to cheap or inferior wine; probably from *blanc* in French *vin blanc* white wine, though *plonk* is perhaps more commonly applied now to red wine ■ Nevil Shute: He asked me if I would drink tea or beer or plonk. 'Plonk?' I asked. 'Red wine,' he said. (1950)

Lizzie (1934) Dated; applied to wine from Lisbon ■ M. Ellison: She drinks 'Lizzie' and methylated spirit. (1934)

nelly, nellie, Nelly's death (1935) Australian; applied to cheap wine ■ *Kings Cross Whisper* (Sydney): You've got to get up very early in the morning to catch them sober and then you can't always be sure on account of their habit of keeping a flagon of nellie by the bed. (1973)

Red Ned (1941) Australian & New Zealand; applied to cheap wine or other similar drink ■ Ian Hamilton: Jo clutched the glass of Red Ned that I thrust at him. (1972)

bombo (1942) Australian; applied to cheap wine, often fortified; probably from *bomb* something of explosive effect + -o, but compare obsolete *bumbo* drink concocted from rum, sugar, water, and nutmeg ■ Stuart Gore: He done in the whole issue on sheilas and bombo. (1968)

plink (1943) Australian; applied to very low-quality wine; a jocular alteration of *plonk* cheap wine ■ Hepworth & Hindle: Plink is defined as being cheap plonk. (1980)

fourpenny dark (1955) Australian; applied to cheap wine (originally as served in a miniature mug with a handle); from its price and colour ■ Dorothy Hewett: You better watch your step with that fourpenny dark. It'll get you before you know it. (1976)

A container for drink

long-sleever (1879) Australian; applied to a tall glass, and also to a drink contained in this ■ Xavier Herbert: The priest got out the whisky bottle. Sims had a long-sleever. (1975)

set-up (1930) US; applied to the glass, ice, soda, etc. required for mixing a drink, as served to customers, who supply their own spirits, in unlicensed premises ■ Wilson McCarthy: He looked over to the sideboard and saw a complete assortment of liquors, rums and set-ups. (1973)

stubby, stubbie (1957) Australian; applied to a dumpy beer bottle ■ G. Morley: Phil opened the freezer and pulled out four stubbies. (1972)

tinny, tinnie (1964) Australian; applied to a can of beer ■ *Truck & Bus Transportation*: We doubt if the driver would have enough room on board to stow his lunch box or a couple of tinnies. (1980)

An empty container

marine, dead marine (1831) Dated

old soldier (1909) US, dated

dead soldier (1917) Orig US ■ Raymond Chandler: I held up the dead soldier and shook it. Then I . . . reached for the pint of bonded bourbon. (1940)

A place where alcohol is sold or drunk

crib (1823) Mainly US; applied to a disreputable drinking saloon; from earlier sense, house

drum (1859) Mainly US; applied to a disreputable drinking saloon; from earlier sense, place, house

dive (1871) Orig US; applied to a disreputable nightclub or drinking-den ■ *Spectator*: The degenerate dives of Berlin. (1958)

speakeasy (1889) Orig and mainly US; applied to an illicit liquor store or drinking club, especially during Prohibition; from the verb *speak* + *easy* easily; from the notion of speaking 'easily' or quietly when ordering illicit goods

■ Sinclair Traill: Every cheap speakeasy had its resident piano player. (1958)

boozer (1895) British, Australian & Irish; applied to a pub; from *booze* drink alcohol + *-er* ■ Peter Moloney: The boozer on the corner. (1966)

rubbity-dub, rubbitty-dub, rubbedy-dub, etc. **(1898)** Australian & New Zealand; rhyming slang for *pub*

rubbity, rubbetty, rubbedy, rubberdy, rupperty (1898) Australian & New Zealand; shortening of *rubbity-dub* ■ D'Arcy Niland: How about a gargle? Down to the rubberdy, come on. (1957)

the nineteenth hole (1901) Jocular, orig US; applied to the bar-room in a golf club-house; from its use by golfers after playing the eighteen holes of the course ■ S. Hope: Most golf clubs have a share of 'ear-bashers' as the Aussies call the type who verbally replay their strokes *ad nauseum* [sic] at the 'nineteenth'. (1956)

shypoo, shipoo, shypoo house, shypoo joint, shypoo shop, etc. **(1903)** Australian; applied to a pub that sells inferior drink; from *shypoo* inferior drink ■ H. Drake-Brockman: How about managing that shipoo for me? (1936)

peg-house (1922) Applied to a pub; compare *peg* alcoholic drink

rub-a-dub(-dub) (1926) Australian & New Zealand; applied to a pub; alteration of *rubbity-dub*

speak (1930) US; short for *speakeasy* ■ Eugene O'Neill: There'll be a speak open, and some drunk laughing. (1952)

speako (1931) US; from *speak* + *-o* ■ J. M. Cain: Making the grand tour of all the speako's he knows. (1941)

local (1934) British; applied to a pub serving the immediate neighbourhood ■ Germaine Greer: Women don't nip down to the local. (1970)

beer-off (1939) British; applied to an off-licence ■ Alan Sillitoe: Bill . . . had called at the beer-off by the street-end. (1958)

watering hole (1975) From earlier sense, place where animals drink ■ *Gainesville* (Florida) *Sun*: In a simpler time, players and fans mingled at local watering holes, drinking beers together and becoming friends. (1984)

An employee in such a place

B-girl (1936) US; applied to a woman employed to encourage customers to buy drinks in a bar; abbreviation of *bar-girl* ■ F. Archer: If I stand here, I'm a waitress, see? If I sit down, I'm a B-girl, and this joint doesn't pay for that kind of protection. (1964)

sitter (1938) US, dated; applied to someone employed to sit in a bar and encourage other patrons to buy drinks

The serving of drink

happy hour (1961) Orig US; applied to a period, usually in the early evening, during which

drinks are sold at reduced prices ■ *Times*: Most restaurants and bars have been forced to forget about 'happy hour' where drinks are cheaper. (1985)

To provide or serve with drink

mug (1830) British; used to denote buying a drink for someone; from *mug* drinking vessel ■ Peter Moloney: If ye say to them 'scouse, Mug us dem on de house,' Yer! make Birty and Girty all shirty. (1966)

shout (1850) Australian & New Zealand; used to denote buying a round of drinks; or buying a drink for (someone) ■ *National Times* (Australia): The tightwad . . . wouldn't shout if a shark bit him. (1981) ■ *Caravan World* (Australia): On meeting an old friend a miner would shout him, not a drink as in other places, but a bath. (1977). Hence the noun **shout** (British, Australian & New Zealand) denoting (a turn to pay for) a round of drinks (1854) ■ Desmond Bagley: Honnister addressed the landlord. 'Hi, Monte: a large scotch and a pint of Director's.' 'My shout,' I said. (1977)

top someone **up (1969)** Used to denote replenishing someone's glass with drink ■ J. I. M. Stewart: I tried to teach him how to translate Tacitus, but had more success in topping him up with madeira. (1976)

A drinking spree

drunk (1779) ■ Miles Tripp: 'I went on a seven-day drunk.' 'Like muck you did.' (1952)

bender (1845) Orig US; mainly in the phrase *on a bender*; perhaps from obsolete Scottish *bend* have a bout of hard drinking ■ *Bulletin* (Sydney): Being on a strenuous bender, he had forgotten to sign a cheque. (1933)

bat (1848) Orig US; origin uncertain; compare *on the batter* on a drinking spree ■ Evelyn Waugh: Why don't you switch to rum? It's much better for you. . . . When did you start on this bat? (1942)

booze (1850) Mainly in the phrase *on the booze*; from the verb *booze* drink alcohol ■ Joyce Cary: If I didn't you'd go on the booze and say it was all my fault. (1959)

binge (1854) From the British dialect verb *binge* soak (a wooden vessel) ■ *Guardian*: Some of his colleagues . . . regarded japes such as giving Peter the Great a ride in a wheelbarrow after a drunken binge as unbecoming to a philosopher. (1992)

jag (1891) From earlier sense, as much drink as one can take, from original sense, load for one horse; ultimate origin unknown ■ *Listener*: Sid Chaplin's *Saturday Saga*, the account of two miners on a memorable jag. (1966)

booze-up (1897) ■ John Braine: The traditional lunchtime booze-up. (1957)

souse (1903) US ■ Eugene O'Neill: Bejees, we'll go on a grand old souse together. (1946)

pub crawl (1915) Applied to a slow progress from one pub to another, drinking at each one ■ *Observer*: Heads of the dress firms will take the 100 expected buyers on individual 'pub-crawls'. (1959). Hence the verb **pub-crawl (1937)** ■ *Canadian Magazine*

(Toronto): Across Canada, kids aren't packing the discothèques; instead, they're pub-crawling. (1974)

pub-crawler (1910) ■ J. R. L. Anderson: You're turning me into quite a pub-crawler. (1976)

scoot (1916) Australian & New Zealand; especially in the phrase *on the scoot*; from earlier sense, act of going hastily ■ S. Gore: Make mine a glass this time, seein' I have to go on the scoot with you booze artists to-night. (1962)

blind (1917) British; especially in the phrase *on a blind*; from the notion of being *blind* drunk ■ J. B. Priestley: I'm not off on a blind, if that's what you're worrying about. (1943)

beer-up (1919) Applied to a beer-drinking session ■ Elizabeth Taylor: Does you good to have a bit of a beer-up now and then. (1945)

brannigan (1927) North American; from earlier sense, drunken state

boozeroo (1943) New Zealand; from *booze* + *-eroo* ■ *Landfall*: The Saturday night boozeroo in the Sydenham side-street with the keg in the kitchen-sink. (1952)

sesh (1943) Orig services' slang; shortened from *session* ■ G. Netherwood: Empty lager bottles . . . signified that Hans and Fritz also knew the joys of a desert 'sesh'. (1944)

session (1943) Mainly Australian ■ D'Arcy Niland: I don't want to make a session of it. . . . I'd just like a drink to pick me up. (1955)

swill (1945) Australian & New Zealand; applied to the rapid consumption of alcohol in a pub just before closing time (formerly six p.m.); especially in the phrase *six o'clock swill* ■ G. Cotterell: You ought to see the swill hour in New Zealand, five o'clock to six o'clock. (1958)

piss-up (1952) ■ Roderic Jeffries: How about a piss-up? Anne was only saying yesterday I'd been sober for so long was I declining into my old age? (1965)

liquid lunch (1970) Often jocular; applied to a midday meal at which more alcoholic drink than food is consumed ■ B. Everitt: He . . . refused all offers of liquid lunches and bore me off . . . for a great deal of solid pasta. (1972)

On a drinking spree

on the batter (1839) Origin uncertain; compare *bat* drinking spree ■ John Osborne: Have you been on the batter, you old gubbins! (1957)

on the skite (1869) Scottish; compare earlier *skite* sudden stroke or blow ■ N. Smythe: I was a bit too fond of the old jar, Went on the skite once too often. (1972)

on the (or a) bend (1887) ■ L. A. G. Strong: Been on the bend, 'aven't you? (1936)

on a whizzer (1910) North American, dated

on the bash (1919) Scottish & New Zealand ■ *Kelso Chronicle*: The village tailor . . . had an unfortunate weakness for getting terribly 'on the bash' perhaps twice a year. (1924)

on the piss (1942) ■ *Observer*: And I don't binge. If I'd gone on the piss every time I missed a cut [*sc.* failed to qualify in a golf tournament] I'd be a raging alcoholic by now. (1974)

To drink alcohol (to excess)

booze (c1325) From Middle Dutch *būsen* drink to excess

wet one's whistle (c1386) From the jocular comparison of the mouth or throat with a whistle

tipple (1560) Back-formation from *tippler* drinker of alcohol ■ R. Davies: There was plenty of brandy, for . . . Lind loved to tipple. (1988)

drink like a fish (1640) ■ P. G. Wodehouse: He drank like a fish and was always chasing girls. (1964)

soak (1687) ■ *19th Century*: The shambling and scrofulous shirk whom you may find any night soaking at the pothouse. (1883)

bend (or lift) the (or one's) elbow (1823) ■ *Coast to Coast 1965–6*: He's not much cop. Too fond of bending the elbow. (1967)

binge (1854) Probably from the noun *binge* drinking spree ■ Hilaire Belloc: It is plainly evident that they know how to binge. (1910)

hit the booze (or bottle, jug, pot) (1889) Orig US ■ *Landfall*: Everyone knew he'd turn out a flop. . . . Hit the booze and got T.B. (1957)

slop up (1899) US, dated ■ Jack Black: No use takin' a bunch of thirsty bums along and stealin' money for them to slop up in some saloon the next day. (1926)

tank up (1902) ■ I. Hunter: Behan arrived for the interview 'somewhat full' and proceeded to tank up further in the BBC hospitality room. (1980)

shicker, shiker, shikker (1908) Australian & New Zealand; from the noun *shicker* alcoholic drink ■ Cusack & James: He'd gamble his shirt off on any damn thing that's got a leg to run on, but he doesn't shicker. (1951)

drink (put, see, etc.) someone under the table (1921) Used to denote remaining sober while one's drinking companions collapse into insensibility ■ V. W. Brooks: He was far from sober, or would have been if two tumblers of brandy had been enough to put him under the table. (1936)

souse (1921) ■ M. Watts: Just as they're middling honest and don't souse. (1923)

down (1922) Used especially to denote consuming an alcoholic drink rapidly ■ Wole Soyinka: [He] downs the rest of his beer and calls for more. (1967)

stop (1924) Australian; especially in the phrase *stop one* have an alcoholic drink ■ L. Mann: But if he should recognise any one, he could scarcely avoid asking: 'Could you stop a pint?' (1942)

knock something back (1931) Used especially to denote consuming an alcoholic drink rapidly ■ Mordecai Richler: Hod was knocking back large snifters of brandy. (1968)

sink (1932) Used especially to denote consuming an alcoholic drink rapidly ■ Airey Neave: Each man spoke of what he would do first on arrival in England. 'I shall sink three pints of mild and bitter,' said one. (1953)

bevvy, bevie, bevy (1934) British; from the noun *bevvy* alcoholic drink ■ Frank Shaw *et al.*: Ard cases who could bevvy by the jug. (1966)

chugalug (c1936), chug (1958) Used to denote drinking a glass of beer, etc. at a single swallow; imitative; *chug* by shortening from *chugalug*

sozzle (1937) Back-formation from *sozzled* drunk ■ N. Fitzgerald: We can sit here and sozzle gently and enjoy ourselves. (1953)

be on it (1938) Australian ■ Patrick White: 'It is him,' she said finally. 'It is that bastard. He is on it again.' (1955)

get a spark up (1939) New Zealand; used to denote raising one's spirits by drinking alcohol

be on the bottle (1967) ■ *Daily Mirror*: Watch that daily tipple, ladies. You could end up on the bottle. (1976)

Drunk

merry (1575) Euphemistic ■ N. Hinton: They'd finished the champagne and started on the wine so they were all a bit merry. (1987)

tipsy (1577) Used to suggest mild drunkenness; from *tip* overturn +—*sy*, from the notion of liability to fall over ■ Clare Harkness: Euphorically tipsy on ale, the vicar mistook his way to the . . . lavatories.

overshot (1605) From the notion of being carried to excess

disguised (1607) Dated, euphemistic ■ Walter Besant: He was not 'disguised', his speech was clear. (1884)

mellow (1611) Euphemistic ■ W. S. Maugham: Bartolomeo . . . was, if not drunk, at least mellow. (1946)

high (1627) Now especially in the phrase *as high as a kite* ■ Margery Allingham: He . . . gave them a champagne lunch in a marquee . . . and held a sale. By then everyone was as high as a kite. (a1966)

blind (1630) Short for *blind* (= very) *drunk* ■ W. S. Maugham: On the night he arrived in London he would get blind, he hadn't been drunk for twenty years. (1930)

top-heavy (1687) Dated, euphemistic

boozed (1737) Sometimes followed by *up*

cocked (1737) US

cock-eyed (1737) Orig US; from earlier sense, squint-eyed ■ Eric Linklater: You wouldn't have asked me to marry you if you hadn't been cock-eyed at the time. (1934)

jagged (1737) Dated, mainly US; from *jag* as much drink as one can take + -*ed*

moon-eyed (1737) US ■ *American Speech*: Sid gits moon-eyed every Saturday night. (1940)

oiled (1737) Usually in the phrase *well oiled* ■ Edgar Wallace: He'll come out in a minute, oiled to the world. (1926)

soaked (1737) Often as the second element of a compound ■ Eugene O'Neill: Like a rum-soaked trooper, brawling before a brothel on a Saturday night. (a1953)

stewed (1737) Also in the phrases *stewed to the ears, eyebrows, gills*, etc. ■ Peter de Vries: A casual

observer not familiar with him would have thought he was stewed to the gills as he rose and wobbled over to join me. (1958)

stiff (1737) US ■ G. V. Higgins: I always got stiff on the Fourth because it was the only way I could listen to all that crap. (1975)

happy (1770) Euphemistic; used to suggest mild drunkenness

corned (1785) Dated; from the use of grain in making beer and spirits

slewed (1801) From the past participle of *slew* turn round ■ David Lodge: I was somewhat slewed by this time and kept calling him Sparrow. (1975)

lumpy (1810) Dated ■ *Punch*: For 'boosey' we might substitute 'lumpy' to suit modern parlance. (1845)

swipey (1821) Dated; from *swipe(s)* beer + -*y* ■ Charles Dickens: 'He ain't ill. He's only a little swipey you know.' Mr. Bailey reeled in his boots, to express intoxication. (1844)

ripe (1823) Dated

snuffy (1823) Dated; from earlier sense, affected by snuff ■ *Newcastle Evening Chronicle*: He considered, if a member got 'snuffy', he should go home, and not come there to annoy the meeting. (1891)

mortal (1824) Scottish & Northern English; short for *mortal* (= extremely) *drunk* ■ J. M. Barrie: He doesna strike me except when he's mortal. (1891)

tight (1830) Also in the phrase *as tight as a tick* ■ David Lodge: Among the other guests was Mrs Zapp, extremely tight, and in a highly aggressive mood. (1975)

muzzed (1836) Dated; from the past participle of *muzz* make muzzy, fuddle

half-shot (1838) Orig US; used to suggest moderate drunkenness ■ J. M. Cain: Stuff for guys in college to gag about when they were half shot with beer. (1948)

pickled (1842) ■ Dylan Thomas: On Sundays, and when pickled, he sang high tenor, and had won many cups. (a1953)

swizzled (1843) From *swizzle* any of various frothy alcoholic drinks; ultimate origin unknown ■ *American Spectator*: The editors of *The American Spectator* got somewhat swizzled one night last week and didn't feel so good the next day. (1934)

squizzed (1845) US; origin unknown ■ *Saturday Review of Literature*: A judge of good whiskey, who is, for the purpose of this narrative, slightly squizzed. (1941)

full (c1848) Australian & New Zealand; also in the phrases *as full as a tick, boot, bull, egg, fart, goog*, etc. ■ C. Lee: We were all pretty well full when the van rolled into Mittagong. (1980) ■ D. M. Davin: Wasn't he in here this afternoon and as full as a tick? (1949)

pixilated (1848) Orig US dialect; used to denote mild intoxication; from earlier sense, confused, slightly mad ■ C. Nesbitt: We were both ever so slightly inebriated, no not even that, pixilated, to use the lovely movie euphemism. (1975)

squiffy (1855) Mainly British; origin unknown ■ Dennis Potter: 'There's another bottle,' said Helen. 'Good! I feel like getting a bit squiffy.' (1988)

buffy (1858) Dated; origin unknown ■ Aldous Huxley: She did like boasting about the amount of champagne she could put away without getting buffy. (1924)

elephant('s) trunk, elephants (1859) British, dated; rhyming slang for *drunk* ■ *Evening Standard*: He came home and he found the artful dodger elephant trunk in the bread and butter (He found the lodger drunk in the gutter). (1931)

scammered (1859) Dated; origin uncertain; perhaps related to dialect *scammed* injured or Somerset dialect *scammish* rough, awkward, untidy ■ Michael Sadleir: He's badly scammered, and out for women. (1940)

rotten (1864) Australian ■ J. Famechon: A reporter from one of the Sydney papers—he was the last to leave, rotten. (1971)

shot (1864) Mainly US, Australian, & New Zealand ■ D. R. Stuart: Ah well, I got shot, real staggery . . . but that arrack, hell, it's great stuff. (1979)

boiled (1884) Sometimes in the phrase *as drunk as a boiled owl* ■ Hugh Pentecost: He's boiled to the ears. (1940)

sozzled (1886) Past participle of dialect *sozzle* mix sloppily, probably imitative ■ Ngaio Marsh: 'She'm sozzled,' said Wally, and indeed, it was so. (1963)

stinking (1887) ■ Evelyn Waugh: 'Tight that night?' 'Stinking.' (1934)

loaded (1890) Orig and mainly US ■ *Voice* (New York): A Democrat who stood on the sidewalk made this uncharitable exclamation as S. stepped into a carriage: 'He's loaded'. (1892)

ploughed, plowed (1890) Mainly US ■ G. V. Higgins: I did not get drunk. . . . You and Frank did. You got absolutely plowed. (1985)

squiffed (1890) Variant of *squiffy* ■ Brian Garfield: I'm already a little squiffed. Ought to go on the wagon. (1977)

half-cut (1893) British; used to suggest moderate drunkenness ■ *Radio Times*: Inebriation . . . is the sport of all ranks. How many executives can work reasonably effectively unless they are half-cut? (1971)

tanked (1893) Mainly British; often followed by *up* ■ H. Simpson: Dawlish wrote poetry, and caused acute discomfort by reciting it aloud on starry nights when he was tanked up. (1932)

up the pole (1897) Dated ■ *Daily Chronicle*: Alec went on to football smoker. Came home up the pole at one a.m. . . . 'Up the pole,' Mrs. Norman said, was one of her husband's slang terms for a person under the influence of drink. (1905)

inked (1898) Australian; apparently from an equation of ink with alcoholic liquor; compare *red ink* cheap red wine ■ P. Adam Smith: Driver found well and truly inked and lying down to it. (1969)

shicker, shiker, shikker (1898), shickered, shikkered (1898) Australian & New Zealand; from Yiddish *shiker* drunk ■ *New Zealand Listener*: After midnight, Jerry got so shicker that he was quarrelling with everyone. (1970) ■ Patrick White: 'I'm gunna get out of this!' he announced at last. 'I'm gunna get shickered stiff!' (1961)

soused (1902) From earlier sense, thoroughly wetted ■ Martin Russell: Ralph's a pro. He's soused every night, and I don't recall an edition going astray yet. (1976)

pie-eyed (1904) Orig US; compare *pied* jumbled, confused, and hence unable to focus correctly ■ *Daily Express*: Personally I didn't care if the whole band was pie-eyed, I wanted them to be busy playing good dance music. (1937)

rosy (1905) Used to denote mild drunkenness; from the effect on the complexion ■ Desmond Bagley: Sure, there was drinking. Some of the boys . . . got pretty smashed. . . . I was a bit rosy myself. (1975)

tiddly, tiddley (1905) Used to suggest mild drunkenness; probably from *tiddly* alcoholic drink ■ Beverley Nichols: No more wine, George, thank you. I shall be quite tiddly. (1958)

spiflicated, spifflicated (1906) US; past participle of *spiflicate* overwhelm, crush, destroy, probably a fanciful formation ■ H. A. Smith: I do not believe . . . that I was spifflicated last night. (1971)

tin hats (1909) British nautical, dated ■ W. Lang: If you do come off tin 'ats (i.e. inebriated), go quietly below to the Mess Deck. (1919)

blithered (1911) Australian; from *blither* talk nonsense ■ *Bulletin* (Sydney): A Mildura settler was making home in the dusk one night slightly blithered. (1944)

pipped (1911) Dated; perhaps from *pip* defeat, forestall ■ Mazo de la Roche: Lilly, here, can't see the strings. He's pipped, aren't you, Lilly? (1929)

tonicked (1911) Australian; from *tonic* invigorating drink ■ F. Leechman: But the wicked old lout had been 'tonic'd' as they call it and had wandered about bushed for twenty-four hours. (1961)

piped (1912) US, dated

plastered (1912) ■ Ngaio Marsh: He's overdone it to-night. Flat out in the old bar parlour . . . he was plastered. (1964)

polluted (1912) Orig US ■ P. G. Wodehouse: I was helping a pal to celebrate the happy conclusion of love's young dream, and it may be that I became a mite polluted. (1974)

stung (1913) Australian ■ T. A. G. Hungerford: Jerry's nice and stung today—the third in a row. (1953)

canned (1914) ■ J. J. Connington: Being rather canned, he sticks the candle on the table, and forgets all about it. (1926)

lit (1914) Often followed by *up* ■ Edward Hyams: Some of the lads a bit lit, eh? Who's this in the hedge? (1949)

binged (1916) From the past participle of *binge* drink alcohol ■ *Sunday at Home*: One man was so binged in drink and so enchained by the craving for it. (1925)

molo, mowlow (1916) Australian; origin unknown ■ D. R. Stuart: By the time he ran us down to the wharf to catch the boat back, we were nicely molo. (1979)

blotto (1917) Obscurely from *blot* ■ P. G. Wodehouse: Did you ever see a blotto butler before? (1951)

crocked (1917) Orig US; perhaps from the past participle of *crock* collapse, disable ■ *Guardian*: The curtain fell and the audience retired to get crocked. (1970)

zig-zag (1918) Dated, mainly US; from the uncertain course typically taken by drunks ■ E. Paul: He groped and floundered . . . not completely 'zigzag'. (1923)

stunned (1919) Australian & New Zealand, dated ■ P. Cadey: I'm afraid I got a bit stunned. . . . I had one over the odd. (1933)

paralytic (1921) ■ *Daily Express*: Woman at the Thames Court: I was not drunk. I was suffering from paralysis. Mr. Cairns: I have heard being drunk called being paralytic. (1927)

shellacked (1922) US, dated ■ J. T. Farrell: You know, when I first found out about how you'd get shellacked, I thought it was pretty terrible. (1935)

fried (1923) ■ Noel Coward: After a gay reunion party . . . I retired to be slightly fried, blissfully happy. (1954)

potted (1924) North American ■ *Sun* (Baltimore): Awful calamity at the Park bird bath . . . when somebody discovered the birds were potted due to some members of the Mint Julep Association having emptied their julep glasses in the fountain. (1943)

stonkered (1924) Mainly Australian & New Zealand; from earlier sense, exhausted ■ *Southerly*: 'Tastes absolutely bonzer. . . .' 'I'm out to get stonkered good and proper.' (1946)

gassed (1925) British ■ *Daily Mail*: When I'm with people I laugh so much . . . they figure I'm 'gassed'. But I'm not. I don't drink. (1960)

pinko (1925) Dated; applied especially to someone drunk on methylated spirit

bottled (1927) ■ Aldous Huxley: Bottled as she was . . . Lenina did not forget to take all the contraceptive precautions prescribed by the regulations. (1932)

lubricated (1927) Compare earlier *lubricate* (ply with) drink

paralysed (1927) Mainly US

stinko (1927), (jocular) **stinko paralytico (1942)** From *stink*(ing drunk + -o ■ Diana Ramsay: Jessie's a lush. Stinko most of her waking time. (1974) ■ Evelyn Waugh: 'Darling, she was plastered.' 'Are you sure?' 'My dear, stinko paralytico.' (1942)

well away (1927) Euphemistic ■ Angela Carter: The Colonel . . . overcomes his resistance to vodka to such an extent he is soon well away and sings songs of Old Kentucky. (1984)

whiffled (1927) Origin unknown ■ J. D. Carr: Helen . . . was much too clear-headed . . . ever to let herself get whiffled. (1956)

blasted (1928) Mainly US ■ James Carroll: Den O'Coole forced his way to the bar. . . . He was already blasted. (1978)

pissed (1929) Sometimes followed by *up* ■ Kingsley Amis: An uncle of mine went there a year or two ago and was pissed all the time on about ten bob a day. (1958)

steamed (1929) Usually followed by *up* ■ *Landfall*: Little Spike is six foot two and has a reputation for being a hard case when he is steamed-up. (1950)

as drunk as a piss-ant (1930) Mainly US; *piss-ant* literally 'ant', but influenced by *piss* urine and *pissed* drunk

swacked (1932) US; from past participle of Scottish *swack* gulp, swill, of imitative origin ■ H. Kane: I'm slightly swacked on champagne. (1965)

looped (1934) Mainly US ■ Ross Macdonald: The message . . . didn't come through too clear. She talked as if she was slightly looped. (1973)

kaylied, kailed, kalied (1937) Origin unknown ■ J. Gash: He offered to brew up but my stomach turned. That left him free to slosh out a gill of gin. Dandy was permanently kaylied. (1978)

stocious, stotious (1937) Mainly Anglo-Irish; origin unknown ■ Julia O'Faolain: 'Coming home stocious five nights a week,' said Doris. (1980)

whistled (1938) Origin uncertain; compare 'He was indeed, according to the vulgar Phrase, whistled drunk,' Henry Fielding, *Tom Jones* (1749) ■ *Private Eye*: We all sidled off to a very nice little snug at the Golden Goose, where . . . all of us got faintly whistled. (1979)

liquefied (1939)

plonked (1943) From *plonk* cheap wine + -*ed* ■ *Life*: A few badly plonked soldiers blearily unaware of just where they were. (1943)

juiced (1946) Often followed by *up* ■ Stephen Ransome: He was sitting at the bar brooding over a drink— not making any trouble, not getting juiced up. (1971)

sloshed (1946) British; from the past participle of *slosh* splash, pour liquid ■ Robert Ludlum: They drank a great deal. . . . They appeared quite sloshed. (1978)

stoned (1952) Orig US ■ Jack Kerouac: I had finished the wine . . . and I was proper stoned. (1957)

schnockered (1955) US; jocular alteration of *snockered* ■ Brian Garfield: Bradleigh took the empty glass. 'That's probably enough. You don't want to get schnockered.' (1977)

bombed (1956) Orig US; often used with *out*

tiddled (1956) Variant of *tiddly* ■ Gerald Durrell: 'I've got the most splitting headache.' 'I'm not surprised; you were as tiddled as an owl last night.' (1956)

as pissed as a newt (1957) ■ Richard Mason: Christ, I'm pissed. I'm pissed as a newt. (1957)

honkers (1957) British; origin unknown ■ Christopher Wood: Roll on Wednesday week and we'll all get honkers on champers. (1970)

zonked (1959) Often followed by *out*; from the past participle of *zonk* overwhelm, defeat ■ Joseph Wambaugh: We sat . . . drinking *arak* and wine, and then beer, and we all got pretty zonked. (1972)

bevvied (1960) British; from the past participle of *bevvy* drink alcohol ■ *Linacre Lane*: The Scouser's favourite excuse for an act of hooliganism is *I wuz bevvied*. (1966)

snockered (1961) Perhaps an arbitrary alteration of *snookered* stymied ■ *Globe & Mail* (Toronto): I'll get a bottle of Jack Daniel's for cocktails. Get them snockered on bourbon and they won't know the difference. (1980)

plotzed (1962) Apparently from *plotz* sit down wearily, slouch ■ *M. Allen*: Mimi got drunk that night . . . but something more than liquor knocked her off base. . . . She was so loaded I had to put her to bed, and I know from my own experience that when I am plotzed I go out for the night. (1974)

smashed (1962) Orig US ■ *D. Laing*: He would get smashed on two and a half pints of Worthington E from the wood, and fall about misquoting the poetry of the beat generation. (1973)

out of it (1963) US

molly the monk (1966) Australian; rhyming slang for *drunk* ■ *Kings Cross Whisper* (Sydney): Ophelia was more than a little bit Molly the Monk after Parkinson had been loosening her up a bit with three bottles of Quelltaler hock. (1973)

wiped (1966) Mainly US; usually followed by *out*

wasted (1968) Orig US

wrecked (1968) US

legless (1976) From the notion of being too drunk to stand up ■ *Daily Telegraph*: I must have had well over half a bottle. . . . In the end I was legless and couldn't talk. (1986)

wired (1977) Mainly US; sometimes followed by *up*

Adrian Quist, Adrian (1978) Australian; rhyming slang for *pissed*; from the name of an Australian tennis player (b. 1913) ■ *Sydney Morning Herald*: They didn't look particularly decorous . . . collapsed, Adrian Quist, as the racing men say, under the hedge. (1982)

Brahms and Liszt, Brahms (1978) British; rhyming slang for *pissed*; arbitrary use of the name of two composers, Johannes *Brahms* (1833–97) and Franz *Liszt* (1811–86) ■ *P.S.*: Do you remember the first time you got . . . a bit Brahms? . . . My five cousins took me out round the pubs and I got ill on Pernod and blackcurrant. (1989)

Mozart and Liszt (1979) British; rhyming slang for *pissed*; arbitrary use of the name of two composers, Wolfgang Amadeus *Mozart* (1756–91) and Franz *Liszt* (1811–86) ■ *Ronnie Barker*: Everybody thought I was *Mozart and Liszt*, falling flat on my *Khyber Pass* like that. (1979)

drunk as a skunk (1981) ■ *T3*: It's also got lots of little pointers to work out tack angles and stuff like that— essential for when you're walking home drunk as a skunk. (1997)

tired and emotional (1981) British, euphemistic ■ *Daily Telegraph*: Sensing that Penrose's

efforts might have left him tired and emotional, the four Eye men called at the Mirror building. (1986)

trashed (1981)

ratted (1983) British; probably from *rat-arsed* ■ *Daily Telegraph*: He zipped up his anorak and went out to get ratted with the rest of the ice hockey team. (1987)

rat-arsed (1984) British; compare earlier *as drunk as a rat* ■ *Guardian*: Guillaume Appollinaire talks of distillation, of reality cyphered through shimmery experience. Not a mention of being a rat-arsed French git. (1990)

bladdered (1992) British; from the notion of a full bladder ■ *Observer*: Friends say she and 'Hooky' enjoy hitting the clubs together, getting 'bladdered', and generally acting like soppy teenagers in each other's company. (1995)

A large amount of alcohol drunk

load (1598) Especially in the phrase *get* (or *have*) *a load on* ■ *V. Palmer*: We're not to blame if men get a load on and begin to fight. (1948)

skinful (1788) Used to denote as much alcohol as one can drink ■ *Guardian*: One night, after closing time, a man who'd had a skinful produced a wad from his pocket. (1992)

snootful (1918) From *snoot* nose + *-ful* ■ *Kurt Vonnegut*: Billy didn't usually drink much . . . but he certainly had a snootful now. (1969)

The state of being drunk

brannigan (1892) North American, dated; origin uncertain; perhaps from the surname *Brannigan* ■ *George Ade*: Those who would enjoy the wolfish Satisfaction of shoveling it in each Morning must forego the simple Delights of acquiring a Brannigan the Night before. (1918)

edge (1897) US; often in the phrase *have an edge on* rather drunk ■ *Ernest Hemingway*: 'How do you feel?' . . . 'Swell. I've just got a good edge on.' (1925)

bun (1901) Dated; especially in the phrase *get* (or *have*, *tie*) *a bun on* get drunk; origin unknown ■ *J. van Druten*: We'll celebrate tonight, if you do. And if you don't, well, then we'll tie a bun on anyway, just to forget it all. (1954)

heat (1912) US; especially in the phrase *have a heat on* be drunk

To drink to excess; become drunk

(have had) one over the eight (1925) From the (fanciful) notion that eight pints of beer represents the maximum intake consistent with sobriety ■ *Daily Express*: Luton magistrate: What does he mean by 'one over the eight'? ('A glass too many'?) (1928)

(have had) one too many (1941) ■ *Jimmy Sangster*: Didn't mean to be crude. Must have had one too many. (1968)

feel no pain (1947) Used to imply drunken insensibility ■ *Bickham Sweet-Escott*: There were a great many Anglo-Russian parties, a vast quantity of vodka was drunk, and twice I saw senior Russian officers being carried out of the room evidently feeling no pain. (1965)

tie one on (1951) Mainly US ■ A. Mather: He had . . . tied one on, if you know what I mean. (1982)

A drinker of alcohol; a drunkard

tippler (1580) Applied to a relatively restrained drinker of alcohol; from earlier sense, tavern-keeper

soaker (1593) From *soak* drink alcohol + *-er* ■ G. M. Trevelyan: The upper class got drunk . . . on ale and . . . on wine. It is hard to say whether men of fashion or the rural gentry were the worst soakers. (1946)

boozer (1606) From *booze* drink alcohol + *-er* ■ *Daily Mail*: On its second day, which became known as Black Wednesday, presenter Michael Barratt announced: 'Now let's meet Britain's biggest boozer.' The cameras swung to the Chief Constable of Essex, lined up for a discussion of police procedure. (1991)

soak (1820) From the verb *soak* drink alcohol ■ James Fenton: Old soaks from farmers poets' pubs And after-hours drinking clubs. (1982)

rummy (1851) Mainly US; from *rum* used as a derogatory term for intoxicating liquor in general + *-y* ■ J. H. Chase: Johnnie was a rummy. . . . Drink had rotted him, and he was only two jumps ahead of the nut-factory. (1939)

lush (1890) Mainly US; from earlier sense, alcoholic drink; perhaps a jocular use of *lush* luxuriant ■ David Delman: He's a drunk, ain't he? . . . He's a lush. And a lush is a lousy security risk. (1972)

Jimmy Woodser, Jimmy Wood(s) (1892) Australian & New Zealand; applied to a solitary drinker; from *Jimmy Wood*, the name of a character in a poem of that name (1892) by B. H. Boake, and perhaps the name of an actual person ■ *N.Z.E.F. Times*: You'll find me lonesome in a Naafi, a-drinkin' to me sins, A-sippin' like a Jimmy Woodser. (1942)

shicker, shiker, shikker (1906) Australian & New Zealand; from earlier sense, alcoholic drink ■ Xavier Herbert: He's the biggest shikker in Town. Now nick off, you old sponge. (1938)

stiff (1907) From the adjective *stiff* drunk ■ Newton Thornburg: It had taken a good part of the day just to locate the poor stiff. (1976)

white line (1908) US dated

Jack ashore (1909) From the notion of a *Jack* (= sailor) getting drunk on shore-leave ■ Edmund McGirr: Jack Ashore does not check bills. (1970)

souse (1915) Orig US; from earlier sense, drunken spree ■ Raymond Chandler: Sylvia is not a souse. When she does get over the edge it's pretty drastic. (1953)

wino (1915) Orig US; applied to a habitual excessive drinker of cheap wine or other alcohol, especially one who is destitute; from *wine* + *-o* ■ M. Leitch: He saw the winos watching him out

of bleary eyes as they huddled on their benches passing their brown bottles to and fro. (1981)

rum-hound (1918) Dated; applied to any heavy drinker ■ E. Paul: What he resented was the insinuation that he was a chronic rumhound. (1951)

alky, alchy, alki(e) (1929) Applied to a drunkard or alcoholic; from *alc(oholic* + *-y* ■ *City Limits*: Nazi sympathizers, alkies, junkies and the unemployed. (1986)

rum-pot (1930) North American; applied to any heavy drinker ■ T. H. Raddall: I had him moved in there as soon as that rumpot of a doctor was off tae the toon. (1966)

tanker (1932) From *tank (up)* get drunk + *-er* ■ John O'Hara: But the rest of them! God, what a gang of tankers they were. (1935)

metho (1933) Australian & New Zealand; applied to a methylated spirit addict; from *meth(ylated spirit* + *-o* ■ J. Alard: The old metho snored on. (1968)

wine dot (1940) Australian; applied to a habitual drinker of cheap wine; pun on *Wyandotte* name of a breed of chicken ■ T. A. G. Hungerford: 'Is he a wine-dot?' 'Is he hell! . . . He's never off it.' (1953)

hophead (1942) Australian & New Zealand; from *hop(s)* beer + *-head* addict ■ David Ballantyne: It's Betty that can't hold the liquor. . . . She's a real lily of a hophead. (1948)

lushy, lushie (1944) US; from obsolete *lushy* drunk, from *lush* drunkard + *-y* ■ Mezzrow & Wolfe: The lushies didn't even play good music. (1946)

two-pot screamer (1959) Australian; applied to someone who easily becomes drunk ■ J. de Hoog: It says experienced and sober, ya bloody two-pot screamer. (1972)

piss-head (1961) ■ *Landfall*: My old man was a piss-head too. (1968)

plonko (1963) Australian; applied to someone with a taste for cheap or inferior wine; from *plonk* such wine + *-o* ■ W. Dick: We could go and see if there's any plonkos under Martin's Bridge and chuck rocks at 'em. (1965)

juicer (1967) US; applied to an alcoholic; from *juice* alcoholic drink + *-er*

goomy, goomee (1973) Australian; applied to a drinker of methylated spirit; from *goom* methylated spirit + *-y*

piss artist (1977) Associated with *pissed* drunk; compare slightly earlier sense, loud-mouthed fool ■ *Custom Car*: I refer to the auto/driver self-destruct mechanism know as 'booze'. A piss artist behind the wheel of a 1935 Austin Seven was a killer. (1977)

lager lout (1988) British; applied to a youth (usually one of a group) who typically drinks large amounts of lager or beer, and behaves in an offensive boorish way ■ *Private Eye*: It's a clever wheeze dreamed up by a bunch of lager louts with a GCSE in Spanish. (1989)

A cell for an arrested drunk

drunk tank (1947) North American; applied to a large cell for accommodating several drunks

The effects of drinking (too much) alcohol

grog blossom (1796) Applied to redness of the nose caused by excessive drinking

D.T.'s, D.T. (1858) Abbreviation of *delirium tremens* ■ Kessel & Walton: Delirium tremens—DTs— generally begins two to five days after stopping very heavy drinking. (1969)

nose paint (1880) Jocular; applied to redness of the nose caused by excessive drinking

the jim-jams (1885) Jocular; applied to delirium tremens; a fanciful reduplication

the jimmies (1900) Jocular; applied to delirium tremens; a reduced form of *jim-jams* ■ A. Mason: Riley, . . . you drank too much Scotch last night; be careful that you don't get the Jimmies and jump overboard. (1921)

pink rat(s) (1914) Jocular, dated; = *pink elephants*

pink elephants (1940) Jocular; applied to an apparition supposedly seen by a drunken person ■ E. W. Hildick: It's like pink elephants. Folk 'ud think you'd been drinking if you went round saying you'd seen white mice running about wild! (1960)

beer belly (1942), beer gut (1976) Applied to a paunch developed by drinking too much beer ■ *Rolling Stone*: Woods pauses to tuck his shirt between a beer belly and a silver belt buckle. (1969) ■ *Los Angeles Times*: Fregosi took to wearing the jacket . . . when he began to develop a beer gut while trying to play for the Mets. (1986)

strawberry (1949) Jocular; applied to a red nose caused by excessive drinking ■ C. Smith: His nose . . . had turned . . . to the characteristic boozer's strawberry. (1980)

brewer's goitre (1953) Australian; applied to a paunch developed by drinking too much beer; transferred use of *goitre* swelling of the neck resulting from enlargement of the thyroid gland ■ M. Powell: The condition is known as 'brewers goitre', and it eventually leads to 'brewers droop'. Well, I knew Australia had a small population, but surely not for this reason. (1976)

brewer's droop (1970) Orig Australian; applied to temporary impotence as a result of drinking excessive amounts of alcohol, especially beer ■ M. Knopfler: I'm not surprised to see you here—you've got smoker's cough from smoking, brewer's droop from drinking beer. (1982)

Suffering from the effects of drinking alcohol

hung-over (1950) After *hang-over* ■ Irwin Shaw: He awoke late, feeling headachy and hung-over from the liquor of the night before. (1960)

hung (1958) Probably short for *hung-over* ■ H. Slesar: I know you're hung, Mr. Drew. (1963)

overhung (1964) ■ Ian Fleming: He was considerably overhung. The hard blue eyes were veined with blood. (1964)

A hang-over cure

a hair of the dog (that bit you) (1546) Applied to an alcoholic drink taken to allay the effects of drinking too much alcohol; in allusion to the former belief that one could be cured of a mad dog's bite by one of its hairs ■ N. Fitzgerald: What you need, Frank, is a good stiff hair of the dog. (1967)

corpse reviver (1865) Jocular, orig US; applied to a strong (mixed) drink intended to cure a hang-over ■ Anne Blaisdell: Corpse Reviver Number Three. . . . You take a jigger of Pernod and add some lemon juice and ice cubes and fill the glass with champagne. (1966)

To adulterate a drink

spike (1889) Orig US; used to denote lacing a drink with alcohol, a drug, etc. ■ G. Thompson: She made tea, which he spiked with bourbon. (1980). Hence the noun **spike** (US) denoting a quantity of alcohol, especially spirits, added to a drink (1906) ■ *Times-Picayune* (New Orleans): It's like chips without dips, or punch without the spike. (1974)

needle (1929) US, dated; used to denote the injection of alcohol or ether into a drink, especially beer, to make it more powerful; from the use of a needle to add the alcohol, etc. ■ *American Mercury*: This beer knocks you for a loop. It's needled with ether. (1930)

Adulterated drink

needle beer (1928) US, dated; used to denote beer with added alcohol or ether; compare the verb *needle*

Accompaniments to an alcoholic drink

splash (1922) Applied to a small quantity of liquid, especially soda water, to dilute spirits ■ Graham Greene: The atmosphere of . . . the week-end jaunt, the whisky and the splash. (1935)

rock (1946) Applied to ice or an ice-cube for use in a drink; especially in the phrase *on the rocks* (of spirits) served with ice ■ Nancy Spain: I . . . went in and fixed myself a Scotch on rocks, neat. (1952)

Toasts

here's how (1896) ■ J. B. Priestley: 'Well,' said Mr. Hull, holding up his glass, . . . 'here's how!' (1951)

chin chin (1909) From earlier use as a general salutation to Chinese people; from Chinese *ts'ing ts'ing* ■ Philip Jones: Two glasses appeared, with ice tinkling in the Scotch. Paul raised his, smiling. 'Chin chin.' (1967)

bottoms up (1917) From the notion of draining a glass, so that its bottom is raised ■ Lewis Nkosi: I say bottoms up both to women and to glasses! [He raises his glass.] (1964)

cheerio (1919) British; use of the farewell *cheerio* as a substitute for the standard English toast *cheers* ■ P. G. Wodehouse: Much as the wounded soldier would have felt if Sir Philip Sidney, instead of offering him the cup of water, had placed it to his own lips and drained it with a careless 'Cheerio!'. (1921)

bung-ho (1925) ■ Dorothy Sayers: 'Dry Martini,' said Wimsey. . . . 'Bung-ho!' (1928)

(here's) mud in your eye (1927) ■ Julian Symons: Here's mud in your eye, Eileen. (1956)

down the hatch (1931)

Absence of alcohol

dry (1888) Orig US; applied to someone who opposes the sale and consumption of alcohol; from the earlier adjectival sense, opposed to or free from the sale of alcohol ■ P. G. Wodehouse:

The woman who runs the school is a rabid Dry and won't let her staff so much as look at a snifter. (1965)

on the wagon (1906) Applied to someone who is teetotal; from the earlier phrase *on the water-wagon* ■ Len Deighton: They dug him out of a bar . . . , stoned out of his mind. . . . He stayed on the wagon for years. (1976)

dry out (1908) Orig US; used to denote an alcoholic undergoing treatment to cure addiction ■ Ernest Tidyman: By eight, she had undergone . . . the drying-out procedure in private institutions. (1970)

4. Tobacco

weed (1606) ■ *Daily News*: She had been addicted to the use of the weed, in the specific shape of 'black boy', for over forty years. (1898)

bacco (1792) Dated; shortening of *tobacco* ■ Elizabeth Gaskell: But the 'bacco, and the other things—'. (1853)

baccy, backy, backey, bakky (1821) Shortening of *tobacco* + *-y* ■ George Orwell: Dere's sixpennorth o' good baccy here! (1933)

bacca, baccah, baccer, backa, backer (1823) Dated; shortening of *tobacco* ■ D. H. Lawrence: They'll give you plenty to eat . . . and a bit of bacca. (1920)

snout (1885) British, prisoners' slang; origin unknown ■ *Economist*: The 'snout barons'—prisoners who make a profit from the shortage of tobacco within prisons. (1964)

old rope (1943) Services' slang, dated; applied to strong, evil-smelling tobacco

Cigarettes

fag (1888) Mainly British; from earlier obsolete senses, cigarette end, cheap cigarette; abbreviation of *fag-end* ■ Charles Barrett: Cobbers of the men in detention had hit upon an ingenious method of smuggling fags to them. (1942)

coffin-nail (1888) Orig US; from the fatal effects of cigarette-smoking, perhaps reinforced by the vaguely nail-like shape of cigarettes ■ P. G. Wodehouse: Most of these birds [*sc.* invalids in a sanatorium] would give their soul for a coffin-nail. (1928)

cig (a1889) Abbreviation; also applied to cigars ■ James Fraser: Greens on the slate, never beer. Never cigs, either. (1969)

stinker (1907) Applied especially to a cheap or foul-smelling cigarette or cigar ■ P. G. Wodehouse: Have you such a thing as a stinker? . . . And a match? (1935)

gasper (1914) British, dated; applied especially to a cheap or inferior cigarette; from the effect on the smoker ■ *Listener*: 'Gasper' commercials are with us still at every peak viewing hour. (1965)

pill (1914) From earlier sense, pellet of opium for smoking ■ Dashiel Hammett: Those pills you smoke are terrible. (1927)

ciggy, ciggie (1915) From *cig(arette* + *-y* ■ *Scottish Daily Mail*: What had been 'fags' became 'ciggies' because The Beatles always talked of ciggies. (1968)

scag, skag (1915) Orig US, dated; origin unknown

stick (1919) Also applied to cigars

gippy, gyppie, gyppy (1920) Applied to an Egyptian cigarette; from earlier sense, Egyptian ■ Somerset Maugham: When you once get the taste for them, you prefer them to gippies. (1926)

cigger (1922) Australian; shortened form ■ R. Hall: Last night as we enjoyed a quiet cigger, The stars reflecting open life outback. (1973)

virgin (1923) Dated; applied to a cigarette made from Virginia tobacco; abbreviation of *Virginia*, assimilated to *virgin* person who has not had sex, perhaps in allusion to the mildness of Virginia tobacco ■ C. Brooks: You gave me a virgin; I hadn't smoked one for nearly a fortnight. (1935)

tailor-made (1924) Orig US; applied to a ready-made (as opposed to hand-rolled) cigarette ■ Nicolas Freeling: Martin stayed quiet after distributing his last tailormades. (1962)

tickler (1929) Nautical; applied to a hand-rolled cigarette, and also to the tobacco from which it is made ■ John Hale: Brooks rolls and lights a tickler. (1964)

quirley (1932) US and Australian, dated; applied especially to a hand-rolled cigarette; from the verb *querl* twist or coil

tab (1934) Orig Northern dialect ■ C. Ross: 'Tab?' Duncan looked blank. 'Cigarette?' he said. Duncan accepted. (1980)

doofer, doofah, doovah, doover (1937) British; applied to half a cigarette; probably alteration of *do for* in such phrases as *that will do for now*

durry (1941) Australian; origin unknown ■ N. Manning: ■ *Steve*: (stubbing out his cigarette) Waste of a good durry! (1977)

drag (1942) From earlier sense, an act of smoking, an inhalation

tube (1946) ■ *High Times*: Filter tipped tubes give a smoother smoke to the very end. (1975)

snout (1950) British, mainly prisoners' slang; from earlier sense, tobacco ■ Peter Moloney: Goin down the city fer a booze an a snout. (1966)

roll-up (1950) Orig prisoners' slang; applied to a hand-rolled cigarette

straight (1959) Applied especially to a cigarette containing tobacco as opposed to marijuana

cancer stick (1958)

square (1970) US, mainly Black English; applied to a cigarette containing tobacco (as opposed to marijuana) ■ *Black World*: Light me up a square, baby. (1974)

Cigars

twofer, too-, -fah, -for, -fur (a1911) US; applied to a cigar sold at two for a quarter, and hence to any cheap cigar; from *two* + (representation of) *for* ■ P. G. Wodehouse: I found him . . . lying on the bed with his feet on the rail, smoking a toofah. (1923)

rope (1934) US ■ Herman Wouk: Carter Aster was smoking a long brown Havana tonight. That meant his spirits were high; otherwise he consumed vile gray Philippine ropes. (1978)

la-di-da, la-di-dah (1977) British; rhyming slang ■ *Sunday Times Magazine*: Nerves take over, so a puff or two on a Lusitania cigar. Being too poor to bet or have women, . . . a la-di-dah is my one luxury. (1996)

Cigarette ends

old soldier (1834) US, dated; applied to the discarded butt of a cigar, and also to a quid of chewed tobacco

fag-end (1853) British; from earlier sense, final unused portion of something; *fag* perhaps ultimately from obsolete *fag* droop, hang loose, perhaps an alteration of the verb *flag* ■ Alan Hollinghurst: The flames showed up the hundreds of fag-ends that had unthinkingly been thrown in. (1988)

bumper (1899) Australian & New Zealand; apparently a blend of *butt* and *stump* + *-er*

5. Drugs

An (illegal) drug

dope (1889) Applied to a narcotic drug; perhaps related to earlier sense, stupid person, from the notion of being stupefied with drugs ■ *Trucking International*: Police drugs squad . . . arrested the gang and seized 64 boxes of the 'best' Lebanese dope. (1987)

peter (1899) US; applied to a knock-out drug; origin unknown

■ *Southerly*: He patted the bare mattress . . . where a bumper had burned a hole sometime in the past. (1967)

scag, skag (1915) Orig US, dated; origin unknown

dog-end (1935) British ■ Peter Wildeblood: The ensuing 'dog-ends' are unpicked, re-rolled and smoked again. (1955)

stompie (1947) South African; also applied to a partially smoked cigarette, especially one stubbed out and kept for relighting later; from Afrikaans, diminutive of *stomp* stump ■ J. Meiring: She pulled a stompie out of her pocket and lighted it. (1959)

Cigarette paper

skin (1969) Orig US; applied especially to paper used for rolling marijuana cigarettes

An act of smoking; a smoke

drag (1904) ■ *Coast to Coast 1961–2*: We stopped beside a little trickle of water for ten minutes' break and a drag. (1962)

burn (1941) ■ A. Thorne: Rolling cigarettes for 'a quiet burn'. (1956)

A stoppage of work for a smoke

smoke-ho, smoke-oh, smoke-o, smoko (1865) Australian & New Zealand; also applied to a party at which smoking is allowed; from *smoke* period of smoking + *-o* ■ *Sydney Morning Herald*: Restrictive work practices—from heavily subsidised housing to the provision of pink salmon and oysters for workers' 'smoko' breaks. (1986)

To light a cigarette, etc.

light up (1861) ■ J. B. Priestley: Blandford opened . . . a very fine silver cigarette-box, and both men lit up and were then silent. (1943)

To smoke a cigarette, etc.

drag (1919) Orig US; followed by *at* or *on* ■ Honoria Croome: He lit one cigarette from the butt of another and dragged at it nervously. (1957)

burn (1929) ■ Frank Norman: The more [tobacco] we got the more we used to burn. (1958)

speedball (1909) Orig US; applied to a mixture of cocaine with heroin or morphine ■ William Burroughs: A shot of morphine would be nice later when I was ready to sleep, or, better, a speedball, half cocaine, half morphine. (1953)

junk (1925) Orig US; applied to a narcotic drug, often specifically heroin; origin uncertain, but probably connected with *junk* discarded or waste material ■ John Brown: You do anything for junk. . . . Cheat. Lie. Steal. (1972)

stuff (1929) Orig US; especially in the phrase *on the stuff* on drugs ■ Lilian Hellman: Years before she had told me her son was on the stuff. (1973)

Mickey Finn, Mickey Flynn, Mickey (1931), **Michael** (1942) Orig US; applied to a narcotic used to adulterate an (alcoholic) drink in order to make someone unconscious; from earlier sense, the drink so adulterated ■ Desmond Bagley: Meyrick was probably knocked out by a Mickey Finn in his nightly Ovaltine. (1973) ■ B. Buckingham: He only pretended to trust me and just slipped me a Michael in my drink. I passed out in the car a few minutes after leaving the bar. (1957)

schmeck (1932) Mainly US; applied to a narcotic drug; from Yiddish *schmeck* sniff

mojo (1935) US; applied to a narcotic drug; origin uncertain; perhaps from Spanish *mojar* celebrate by drinking

sugar (1935) Orig US; applied to a narcotic drug

smack (1942) Orig US; probably an alteration of *schmeck* narcotic drug

sting (1949) Australian; often applied specifically to a drug injected into a racehorse ■ F. Hardy: The 'smarties' soon found stings that didn't show on a swab. (1958)

narco (1955) US; abbreviation of *narcotic(s* ■ Dell Shannon: The pedigrees varied from burglary to narco dealing to rape. (1971)

juice (1957) Applied to a drug or drugs; compare earlier sense, alcoholic liquor ■ H. C. Rae: I wasn't interested in him. I mean, when you shoot juice, you lose the other thing. (1972)

tab (1961) Applied to a tablet or pill containing an illegal drug, often specifically LSD; probably short for *tablet* ■ M. Walker: An order for two tabs of acid. (1978)

French blue (1964) Applied to a mixture of amphetamine and a barbiturate ■ Dorothy Halliday: They're all lying around in there wearing beads and stoned out of their skulls on French Blues. (1971)

mellow yellow (1967) US; applied to banana peel used as an intoxicant

minstrel (1967) Applied to a capsule containing an amphetamine and a sedative; from its black and white colour, with reference to the *Black and White Minstrels*, a troupe of British variety entertainers of the 1960s and '70s

torpedo (1971) Applied to a capsule or tablet of a narcotic drug ■ Martin Russell: The phial . . . contained more tablets. . . . He tried to estimate how long . . . it took a couple of the torpedoes to send him off. (1978)

Relating to drugs or drug-users

hoppy (1942) US; from *hop* opium + -*y* ■ Mezzrow & Wolfe: Detroit is really a hoppy town—people must order their opium along with their groceries. (1946)

druggy (1959) Compare earlier sense, of medicinal drugs ■ *Times*: I was enmeshed in a very druggy crowd at the time. (1984)

A stimulant drug

pep-pill (1937) Orig US; from *pep* vigour ■ Eric Ambler: As for that movie star, how do you know he isn't on pep pills? (1974)

uppie (1966) Applied especially to an amphetamine; from *up* raise + -*ie* ■ J. F. Burke: There's nothing in the box but a few uppies. I haven't got a regular prescription. (1975)

upper (1968) Applied especially to an amphetamine; from *up* raise + -*er* ■ Dell Shannon: I want all your pills, man, all the uppers and downers you got. (1981)

up (1969) Applied especially to an amphetamine ■ P. G. Winslow: 'She did take pills, ups, if you get me.' Capricorn understood her to mean amphetamines. (1978)

wake-up pill, wake-up (1969)

A tranquillizing drug

happy pill (1956) Applied to a tranquillizer ■ Isaac Asimov: You've got that tranquillizer gleam in your eye, doctor. I don't need any happy pills. (1966)

downer (1965) Orig US; applied especially to a barbiturate ■ *Daily Telegraph*: Those that shoot dope are soon stoned and on the habit, junkies liable to write their own scripts and thieve your downers and perhaps your chinky. (1983)

downie (1966) Orig US; applied especially to a barbiturate

down (1967) Orig US; applied especially to a barbiturate; often used in the plural; shortened from *downer* ■ M. Kaye: Tom needed money for drugs . . . pot, acid, speed, ups, downs. (1972)

trank, tranq (1967) Abbreviation of *tranquillizer* ■ A. Skinner: We'll have to go back to slipping tranks into his coffee. (1980). Hence **tranked** drugged by tranquillizers (1972) ■ *Observer*: Lulling drugs are prescribed; tots shamble eerily about, tranked. (1974)

Amphetamine

benny, bennie (1949) Orig US; mainly applied to a benzedrine tablet; abbreviation ■ Adam Diment: The benny was starting to wear out and I was hot, thirsty and exhausted. (1967)

dexie, dexy (1951), **dex** (1961) Orig US; applied to (a tablet of) dexamphetamine sulphate; short for *Dexedrine* proprietary name of this ■ Lawrence Sanders: I think he's on something. I'd guess Dexies. (1969) ■ *Harper's*: Pops a dex or a bennie occasionally, especially during exam week. (1971)

goof ball, goof pill (1952) Orig US; applied to a pill containing an amphetamine, or more broadly any stimulant drug; from earlier sense, barbiturate tablet

purple heart (1961), **purple** (1968) Applied to a tablet of the stimulant drug Drinamyl, an amphetamine; from its shape and colour; presumably inspired by the earlier *Purple Heart* name of a US decoration awarded to someone wounded in action ■ Nicholas Stacey: They became more responsible, they took more interest in life, they stopped taking purple hearts and they settled down in their homes, their schools and their jobs. (1971) ■ Charles Drummond: I heard her on at the Doc . . . about some Purples to key them up but he hit the ceiling. (1968)

sweets (1961) US; applied to amphetamine tablets

black bomber (1963) Applied to an amphetamine tablet

pill (1963) Applied to an amphetamine tablet
■ *Guardian*: It's impossible to discover how many adolescents use the more common illicit soft drugs—cannabis, LSD, 'pills' (amphetamines, barbiturates or mixtures of both). (1972)

meth (1967) Orig US; applied to (a tablet of) methamphetamine; abbreviation of *methamphetamine* or of *Methedrine* proprietary name of methamphetamine ■ Joseph Wambaugh: She's a meth head and an ex-con. (1972)

speed (1967) Orig US; applied to an amphetamine drug, especially methamphetamine, often taken intravenously; from its stimulant effect ■ Julian Symons: 'What was he on?' . . . 'Speed mostly. Sometimes acid.' (1975)

white (1967) Applied to an amphetamine tablet
■ H. C. Rae: He had anticipated a rash of arrests for possession of brown drugs and amphetamines—but not this, not a straight leap into the lethal whites. (1972)

crank (1969) US; applied to an amphetamine drug, especially methamphetamine

splash (1969) US; applied collectively to amphetamines

ice (1989) Applied to a crystalline form of methamphetamine, inhaled or smoked as a stimulant; from the drug's colourless, crystalline appearance (like crushed ice) during the manufacturing process ■ *Courier-Mail* (Brisbane): Once ice was something one simply dropped into drinks. Now it could be the latest and most dangerous designer drug being smoked in salons from Beverly Hills to Bronx ghettoes. (1989)

whizz (1993) ■ *Daily Telegraph*: None of the kids a bit older than us ever seem to get a job. They just hang around taking drugs like ecstasy, draw and whizz. It's everywhere. (1996)

Amyl nitrate

popper (1967) Orig US; applied to a capsule of amyl nitrate (or of (iso)butyl nitrate) taken as a stimulant drug; from the fact that the capsule is typically crushed or 'popped', and the drug taken by inhalation ■ R. Silverberg: She closed the door behind him and looked about for something to offer him, a drink, a popper, anything to calm him. (1985)

Barbiturates

goof ball, goof pill (1939) Orig US; applied to a barbiturate tablet or drug ■ Jack Kerouac: She took tea, goofballs, benny. (1957)

bomber (1950) Applied to a capsule containing barbiturates ■ Kate Nicholson: I was planning to go back on bombers today. (1966)

nembie, nebbie, nemish, nemmie, nimby (1950) US; applied to a capsule of Nembutal; from *Nembutal* + a range of suffixes ■ William Burroughs: Next day I was worse and could not get out of bed. So I stayed in bed taking nembies at intervals. (1953)

yellow jacket (1953) US; applied to a pentobarbitone tablet

pill (1963) Applied to a barbiturate tablet

red, red devil (1967), red bird (1969) Applied to (a red-coloured tablet of) the barbiturate Seconal ■ Joseph Wambaugh: What've you got, boy? Bennies or reds? Or maybe you're an acid freak? (1972)

pink lady (1970) Applied to barbiturate or a barbiturate tablet; compare earlier sense, cocktail of gin, grenadine, egg white, etc.

rainbow (1970) Orig US; applied to a capsule of the barbiturates Amytral and Seconal, of which one end is blue and the other red ■ Margaret Millar: Getting their kicks by mixing drinks and drugs, like . . . the high school kid carrying a flask of vodka to wash down the rainbows. (1976)

Bromide

bromo (1916) Applied to (a dose of) a sedative drug containing a bromide mixture; short for *Bromo-seltzer* proprietary name of such a drug
■ *Encounter*: For God's sake a Bromo! (1961)

Cannabis

ganja, ganga (1800) From Hindi *gāñjhā*
■ *Guardian*: The telltale smell of ganja assails your nostrils as soon as you enter. (1992)

Mary Ann (1925) Fanciful alteration of *marijuana*

muggles (1926) Orig US; also used in the singular to denote a marijuana cigarette (1969); origin unknown ■ Mezzrow & Wilson: 'Ever smoke any muggles?' he asked. (1946) ■ A. Arent: Offer our guest a muggle. (1969)

Mary Jane, Mary J, maryjane (1928) Also applied to a marijuana cigarette; fanciful alteration of *marijuana* ■ Dell Shannon: 'What did they buy?' asked Mendoza. 'Oh, Mary Jane. Twenty reefers,' said Callaghan. (1970)

weed (1929) Applied to marijuana or a marijuana cigarette; compare earlier sense, tobacco ■ Jack Kerouac: You could smell tea, weed, I mean marijuana, floating in the air. (1955)

reefer (1931) Orig US; mainly applied to a marijuana cigarette, but also to marijuana itself; from earlier sense, something rolled (from naval use), or perhaps from Mexican Spanish *grifo* marijuana ■ *Chicago Defender*: The humble 'reefer', 'the weed', the marijuana, or what have you by way of a name for a doped cigarette has moved to Park Ave. from Harlem. (1933)

mootah, mooter, moota, mootie, mota, muta, etc. **(1933)** US; origin unknown ■ Ed McBain: One of the guys was on mootah. So he got a little high. (1956)

loco weed (1935) From earlier sense, type of plant that causes brain disease in cattle eating it, from Spanish *loco* mad ■ *Sunday Sun* (Brisbane): Detectives from the CIB Drug Squad in Brisbane are becoming quite familiar now with words like . . . rope and locoweed. (1972)

tea (1935) Orig US; often applied specifically to marijuana brewed in hot water to make a drink; from earlier sense, spiritous or intoxicating drink ■ *San Francisco Chronicle*: A couple of years ago she started blowing tea. (1950)

spliff, splif (1936) Orig West Indian; applied to a marijuana cigarette; origin unknown ■ *High Times*: Like Marley, he's a spliff-toking Rastafarian. (1975)

grass (1938) Orig US ■ Adam Diment: Pure Grass cigarettes, at two dollars a pack and none of your watering down with tobacco. (1968)

jive (1938) Orig US; also applied to a marijuana cigarette ■ *New York Times*: So Diane smoked jive, pod, and tea. (1952)

Mary Warner (1938) Fanciful alteration of *marijuana*

mezz (1938) From the name of *Mezz* Mezzrow (1890–1972), US jazz clarinettist and drug addict

pot (1938) Orig US; probably from Mexican Spanish *potiguaya* marijuana leaves ■ Thomas Pynchon: 'But we don't repeat what we hear,' said another girl. 'None of us smoke Beaconsfields anyway. We're all on pot.' (1966)

stick, stick of tea, stick of weed (1938) Applied to a marijuana cigarette; *stick* from earlier sense, cigarette, cigar ■ Colin MacInnes: 'I'll roll you a stick.' . . . I lit up. . . . 'Good stuff. And what do they make you pay for a stick here?' (1957)

Indian hay (1939) US

ju-ju (1940) Applied to a marijuana cigarette; reduplication of *mari)ju(ana* ■ Nicholas Freeling: 'He had juju cigarettes too; like Russians, with a big mouth piece and pretty loose. . . .' 'The jujus are—you feel very clever.' (1963)

charge (1941) US; from earlier sense, a dose of a narcotic drug ■ *Melody Maker*: Club promoters are worried that hippies could close them down by smoking charge on the premises. (1969)

goof (1941) US; from the effect on the user

rope (1944) Mainly US; compare earlier sense, cigar

shit (1950) Orig US ■ *Daily Telegraph*: Acid (LSD) and 'shit' (cannabis), were on open sale, and . . . a notice was pinned to a tent stating: 'Anybody with some black shit for sale, ask for Irish Mick.' (1972)

bomb (1951) US; applied to a (large) marijuana cigarette ■ E. Wymark: First they simply smoke marijuana. . . . They refer to the smokes as sticks or bombs, depending on their size. (1967)

bomber (1952) US; applied to a (large) marijuana cigarette ■ Jack Kerouac: Victor proceeded to roll the biggest bomber anybody ever saw. (1957)

joint (1952) Applied to a marijuana cigarette ■ *Daily Telegraph*: The making of the joint seemed to be as much a part of the ritual as smoking it. (1972)

pod (1952) Compare *pot* marijuana ■ William Burroughs: A square wants to come on hip. . . . Talks about 'pod', and smokes it now and then. (1959)

roach (1953) Orig US; applied to (the butt of) a marijuana cigarette; from earlier more general sense, cigarette-end ■ M. J. Bosse: I . . . took out my pot pouch and cigarette paper. . . . I . . . rolled myself a joint. . . . I had finished the roach down to my fingernails. (1972)

green (1957) Orig US; applied to marijuana of poor quality; from the colour of uncured marijuana

boo (1959) Orig US; origin unknown ■ *Playboy*: Where's the fun in . . . inhaling carbon-monoxide fumes, when you could be toking refreshing essence of boo smoke. (1985)

hash (1959) Abbreviation of *hashish* ■ Peter Dickinson: 'It's morphine she's been on?' said Pibble. But Tony shook her head. 'Just grass. Hash.' (1972)

Acapulco gold, Acapulco (1965) Applied to a high grade of marijuana, typically brownish- or greenish-gold in colour, originally grown around Acapulco, a seaside resort on the west coast of Mexico

doobie (1967) US; applied to marijuana or to a marijuana cigarette; origin unknown

puff (1989) Applied to marijuana for smoking ■ *Guardian*: In George's book, a drink, a few lines, a bit of puff is okay but those E's and stuff like acid turns people into wrong uns. (1992)

Cocaine

coke (*c*1903) Orig US; abbreviation ■ P. Capon: He started introducing her to drugs. . . . Reefers at first, and then, under the influence of reefers, coke. (1959)

white stuff (1908) Mainly US

snow (1914) Orig US; from its white powdery appearance ■ Adam Hall: Pangsapa was a narcotics contrabandist and would therefore know people . . . prepared to kill for a fix of snow. (1966)

happy dust (1922) From its powdery form and its supposed effect on the user ■ E. St. V. Millay: Your head's So full of dope, so full of happy-dust . . . you're just a drug Addict. (1937)

Charlie (1935) Orig US; from the male personal name, probably because of the shared initial letter ■ *Guardian*: The Loafer was rather surprised to be served champagne. Not a whiff of Charlie, though. (1996)

nose candy (1935) Orig US; applied to cocaine taken by inhaling

blow (1971) Orig US; applied especially to cocaine for inhaling

toot (1978) US; from earlier sense, 'snort' of cocaine

freebase (1980) Orig US; applied to cocaine that has been purified by heating with ether, and is taken by inhaling the fumes or smoking the residue; short for the technical term *freebase cocaine*

crack (1985) Orig US; applied to a hard crystalline form of cocaine broken into small pieces and inhaled or smoked; probably from the cracking sound it makes when smoked or from the fact that it is cracked into small pieces ■ *U.S. News & World Report*: Crack . . . has rocketed from near obscurity to national villainy in the past six months. (1986)

Heroin

dynamite (1924) Orig US; from the drug's effect ■ M. Culpan: 'A little bit of horse? Some dynamite?' Horse was heroin; so was dynamite. (1967)

H (1926) Abbreviation ■ Kenneth Orvis: Suppose I . . . ask you where to connect for H? (1962)

horse (1950) Orig US; perhaps from the shared initial and the horse's power ■ *Daily Telegraph*: He had seen the effects of an overdose of 'horse' before. The skin becomes greenish and there was frothing at the mouth. (1969)

shit (1950) ■ S. Wilson: 'Hope it's good shit,' I whispered as he swabbed my arm. (1980)

the white stuff (1953) Orig US ■ Norman Lucas: Luckier still not to have graduated from pep pills to . . . 'The White Stuff' . . . heroin. (1967)

sugar (1956) Orig US; from earlier more general sense, a drug ■ *Observer*: Detectives call them the 'sugar people' and they are young, rich and blue-blooded. They are also heroin addicts. It is in an ironic double reference to the 'sugar daddy' parents and to the expensive white powder they inject or sniff. (1979)

duji, **dujie** (1959) US; origin unknown

smack (1960) Orig US; from earlier more general sense, a drug ■ *Oz*: In the paper today it said that Jimmy Hendrix got busted for smack. (1969)

schmeck (1966) Mainly US; from earlier more general sense, a drug ■ M. Calpan: 'He was always wild. . . . Anything for kicks. . . . In the end it was schmeck.' 'Heroin?' 'Yes. Hooked.' (1967)

jack (1967) Applied to a tablet of heroin ■ Roger Busby: He's been cranking up on horse. His last jack is wearing off, and he's grovelling on the floor for another pill. (1971)

scag, **skag** (1967) Origin unknown; compare earlier sense, cigarette (stub) ■ N. Adam: I'm no junkie myself, never touched the scag, never even used the White Dragon Pearl. (1977)

scat (1970) From earlier sense, dung, (pl.) animal droppings, from Greek *skat-*, *skōr* dung ■ D. E. Westlake: You're dealing in machismo, man, just like I'm dealing in scat. (1972)

brown sugar (1974) Applied to a drug consisting of heroin diluted with caffeine and strychnine ■ Donald MacKenzie: No more Hong Kong brown sugar. We'll be out of business. (1978)

black tar (1986) Applied to an exceptionally pure form of heroin originating in Mexico

See also **junk** at An (illegal) drug (p. 156).

LSD

acid (1965) Orig US; short for *lysergic acid diethylamide* ■ John Lennon: I was influenced by acid and got psychedelic, like the whole generation, but really, I like rock and roll and I express myself best in rock. (1970)

purple haze (1967), **purple** (1968) Also applied to LSD mixed with methedrine ■ Jimmi Hendrix: Purple haze is in my brain lately things don't seem the same. (1967)

sugar (1967) Applied to LSD taken on a lump of sugar

white lightning (1972) ■ *Village Voice*: Ellen . . . unfolded some tinfoil which she said contained three tabs of Owsley's original 'white lightning', the Mouton-Rothschild of LSD. (1972)

Methadone

phy (1971) British; abbreviation of *Physeptone* a proprietary name of methadone hydrochloride ■ *Times*: She said to him: 'Do you want some phy (Physeptone)?' and made it quite clear that she meant the drug. (1973)

Methylene dioxymethamphetamine (MDMA)

Adam (1985) Probably a reversal and partial respelling of the chemical name *MDMA*, perhaps influenced by the first Adam's connections with Paradise ■ *Observer*: 'Ecstasy'—also known as 'MDMA' or 'Adam'—has been reported on sale in Bath, Bristol and Cardiff. (1988)

ecstasy (1985) Orig US; from its euphoric effect on the user ■ *Sunday Times*: Acid House (the music) and Ecstasy (the drug) became inextricably bound together and the fans turned to it. (1988)

E (1989) Abbreviation of *ecstasy* ■ *New Musical Express*: 'People will dance to anything now,' muses Mal. 'I blame the E meself!' (1990)

Morphine

white stuff (1908), **white** (1914) Mainly US ■ N. Adam: By 1965 they were growing poppies for half the world's white. (1977)

morph (1912) US; abbreviation ■ Herbert Gold: No morph, no! I had really kicked that one, and would do my own traveling from now on. (1956)

mojo (1955) US; from earlier more general sense, a narcotic drug

Opium

hop (1887) US, dated; from earlier sense, plant used for flavouring beer ■ *US Senate Hearings*: Opium in the underworld is referred to [as] . . . 'hop'. (1955)

pill (1887) Dated; applied to a pellet of opium for smoking

twang (1898) Australian, dated; probably a back-formation from *Twankay* variety of green tea ■ T. Ronan: The honest Chinese limits himself to his one pipe of 'Twang' per night. (1945)

mud (1922) US ■ *Flynn's*: Some stiffs uses mud but coke don't need any jabbin', cookin', or flops. You can hit an' go. (1926)

yen (1926) US; probably from Chinese (Cantonese) *yīn* opium, or (Mandarin) *yān* opium

poppy (1935) A revival of an earlier non-slang use

tar (1935) US, dated

gee (1936) Orig US; also applied to other similar drugs; perhaps from *ghee* semifluid Indian butter

Phencyclidine

angel dust (1970) Orig US ■ Joseph Wambaugh: My nephew was arrested because he was holding this angel dust for somebody else. (1978)

rocket fuel (1977) Orig US ■ *Sunday Times*: PCP or 'angel dust', a strong anaesthetic which came after LSD in 1960s drug fashions . . . has recently emerged anew. Now they call it 'rocket fuel' in Chicago and mix it with peanut butter. (1985)

Sodium pentothal

soap (1975) Applied in espionage slang to the truth drug sodium pentothal, or a mixture of this and amphetamines; from the initial letters of *sodium pentothal*, humorously respelled after *soap* cleaning agent ■ J. Gardner: *Soap*—as the Service called it—would sometimes produce spectacular results. (1980)

A quantity, portion, or dose of a drug

deck (1916) US; applied to a package containing narcotic drugs; from earlier sense, pack of playing cards ■ Chester Himes: When it's analysed, they'll find five or six half-chewed decks of heroin. (1966)

jolt (1916) Mainly US; applied to a quantity of a drug in the form of a cigarette, tablet, etc.; from earlier sense, drink of liquor ■ Kim Platt: Her LSD cap would cost about two dollars and fifty cents for the jolt. (1970)

bindle (1921) Applied to a package containing narcotic drugs; from earlier more general sense, package ■ *Dialect Notes*: *Bindle*, a package containing either morphine or cocaine. 'Give me a bindle of snow.' (1923)

bang (1922) US; applied to an injection or inhalation of cocaine, morphine, or heroin ■ Kenneth Orvis: He . . . talked me into sampling a bang. (1962)

charge (1925) US; applied to a dose or injection of a narcotic

snifter (1930) Orig US; applied to a small quantity of cocaine inhaled through the nose ■ John Wainwright: A snifter when the pain's bad. . . . It ain't for kicks. You're no junkie. (1974)

fix-up (1934), **fix (1936)** Orig US; applied to a dose of a narcotic ■ *Oxford Mail*: A weird scene where the dope peddlers gather to beat up Johnny, who gets more into debt with each 'fix'. (1958)

piece (1935) US; applied to an ounce of a drug, especially morphine or heroin

pop (1935) Applied to an injection of a narcotic drug ■ Ngaio Marsh: I'm not hooked. Just the odd pop. Only a fun thing. (1970)

twister (1938) US; applied to an intravenous injection of a mixture of drugs

hit (1951) Orig US; applied to a dose of a narcotic, or to the act of obtaining or giving such a dose ■ *Southerly*: Somebody hands me a joint and I take a hit and hand it to Marlene who takes a hit. (1972)

spike (1953) Orig US; applied to an injection, or the drug injected ■ John Wainwright: It was a mounting yearning. A craving. . . . He needed a spike—badly! (1974)

snort (1951) Orig US; applied to an inhaled dose of cocaine, heroin, etc. ■ Gore Vidal: 'Want a snort?' Bruce produced a cocaine snifter. (1978)

O.D. (1960) Orig US; applied to a (fatal) overdose of drugs; abbreviation of *overdose* ■ *Black World*: A truly brilliant Black filmmaker goes into his grave at 24 . . . an O.D. takes him, he loses a battle of several years—the 'stuff' wins. (1971)

lid (1967) Applied to an ounce of marijuana ■ J. D. MacDonald: We had almost two lids of Acapulco Gold. (1968)

nickel (1967) US; applied to five dollars' worth of marijuana; from *nickel note* five-dollar bill

nickel bag (1967) US; applied to a bag containing, or a measure of, five dollars' worth of a drug, especially heroin or marijuana ■ *Black World*: If . . . he gets high and blurts it out to a stranger in some bar that he got his nickel bag from Joe, the pusher, then Joe's livelihood is endangered. (1973)

trey, tray (1967) US; applied to a three-dollar bag of a narcotic drug; from earlier sense, set of three ■ James Mills: She wants to buy two treys, $3 bags of heroin. He says he has treys, but wants $3.50 for them. (1972)

key (1968) US; applied to a kilogram of a drug; respelling of *ki-* in *kilo* ■ Joseph Wambaugh: On her coffee table she had at least half a key and that's a pound of pot and that's trouble. (1972)

toke (1968) US; applied to a drag on a cigarette or pipe containing marijuana or other narcotic substance; from the verb *toke* smoke a marijuana cigarette

mike (1970) Applied to a microgram of LSD; abbreviation of *microgram* ■ James Wood: They wanted me to tell where I got the mikes. . . . The acid, see? (1973)

weight (1971) Applied to a measure of an illegal drug ■ S. Wilson: Neil was taking colossal risks, there'd be up to thirty weights sitting in the flat at one time. (1978)

toot (1977) US; applied to a 'snort' of cocaine; from the verb *toot* inhale cocaine ■ *Maclean's Magazine*: They slink into some of the finer furnished bathrooms of the city for a quick toot. (1977)

line (1980) Orig US; applied to a dose of cocaine or other powdered drug taken by inhalation; from the arranging of the drug in a long narrow strip for sniffing ■ William Safire: The familiar 'to go on a toot', or to drink heavily and thereby lose a weekend, has been replaced by 'to blow a toot', or to inhale a 'line' of cocaine. (1981)

A drug-taker or addict

fiend (1881) Applied especially to someone addicted to opium or an opiate drug ■ R. H. Davis: With the desperation of a dope fiend clutching his last pill of cocaine. (1914)

dope (1899) US; suggested by earlier senses, idiot and stupefying drug

hypo (1904) Orig US; applied to a drug-addict; abbreviation of *hypodermic* ■ Jack Black: 'Vag these two hypos', said the cop to the desk man. (1926)

head (1911) Orig US; applied to someone addicted to a (usually specified) drug ■ Lee Duncan: I saw the more advanced narcotic addicts . . . , laudanum fiends, and last but not least, the veronal heads. (1936)

hophead (1911) US; applied to a drug-addict ■ Helen Nielsen: I'll mail the letter to that hophead lawyer. (1973)

snow-bird (1914) US; applied to someone who sniffs cocaine, and more broadly to any drug-addict; from *snow* cocaine

cokie, cokey (1916) Orig US; applied to a cocaine-addict; from *coke* cocaine + *-ie* ■ J. G. Brandon: His first glance at the shivering, stricken-looking creature . . . told him that the man was a 'cokey'. (1934)

sniffer (1920) Orig US; applied to someone who inhales drugs or toxic substances ■ *Daily Telegraph*: A glue sniffer is under the influence of a drug for the purposes of the 1972 Road Traffic Act, magistrates decided yesterday when a self-confessed 'sniffer' denied being unfit to drive through drink or drugs while in charge of a motorcycle. (1981)

doper (1922), dopester (1938) Applied to someone who uses or is addicted to drugs; compare earlier sense, one who collects and provides information ■ J. Rice: A dopester seldom drinks and most drinkers have not yet taken to dope. (1938)

hoppy (1922) US; applied to an opium addict; from *hop* opium + *-y* ■ Ben Hecht: A lush, a prosty, a hoppy, and a pain in the neck, say the police. (1941)

junker (1922) US; applied to a drug-addict ■ C. R. Shaw: Next to me in the hospital was Herbie, a junker, who was taking the cure. (1930)

junkie (1923) Orig US; applied to a drug-addict ■ John Brown: Lacerated hands, the hands of junkies, scarred where needles had searched for veins. (1972)

hype, hyp (1924) Orig US; applied to a drug-addict; abbreviation of *hypodermic* ■ Joseph Wambaugh: They were dumb strung-out hypes. (1972)

needle man (1925) US; applied to a drug-addict, especially one who is addicted to injecting drugs

snifter (1925) US; applied to a cocaine addict; from its consumption by inhalation ■ *Detective Fiction Weekly*: A certain cocaine addict, known as Snifter Selton. (1929)

user (1935) Applied to a regular drug-taker ■ *Easyriders*: Harley man, 29 . . . seeks lady 5'7" or under for friend, lover, and partner. . . . No boozers or heavy users. (1983)

joy-popper (1936) Orig US; applied to an occasional taker of illegal drugs ■ John Brown: The weekend ravers and joy-poppers . . . for whom smoke and amphetamines alone were not enough. (1972)

popper (1936) Orig US; applied especially to someone who takes drugs in pill form

student (1936) Orig US; applied to an inexperienced user of illegal drugs, especially one who takes small or occasional doses ■ Nelson Algren: You're not a student any more. . . . Junkie—you're *hooked*. (1949)

muggler (1938) Applied to a marijuana addict; from *muggle(s* marijuana + *-er*

teaman (1938) US; applied to a smoker of marijuana

drugger (1941) Applied to a drug-addict; compare earlier sense, druggist ■ H. R. F. Keating: Your precious Peacock . . . was nothing but a low-down little drugger. I may smoke because I need it for my work, but she just drugged to make herself lower than she was. (1968)

weed-head (1952) Mainly US; applied to a habitual user of marijuana

schmecker, shmecker (1953) US; applied to a drug-addict, especially one who takes heroin; from *schmeck* drug ■ William Burroughs: He went on talking about some old acquaintances who got their start in junk and later turned respectable. 'Now they say, "Don't have anything to do with Sol. He's a *schmecker*".' (1953)

tea-head (1953) Orig US; applied to a habitual user of marijuana

weekender (1955) Orig US; applied to someone who indulges in occasional drug-taking, especially at weekends ■ *Times*: 'Weekenders' . . . who needed 'speed' to get through school and personal crises. (1970)

pipe (1959) Applied to an opium-addict; from earlier sense, pipe used for smoking opium ■ Murtagh & Harris: You can recognize 'pipes', opium addicts, by the odour which clings to them. (1959)

pot-head (1959) Orig US; applied to someone addicted to smoking marijuana ■ *Times Literary Supplement*: A girl . . . herself something of a pothead, who introduces Evans to the joys of the weed. (1974)

pill-head (1961) Applied to a drug-addict ■ Newton Thornburg: Oh, she was a pillhead, yeah. And maybe the world's worst housekeeper too. (1976)

acid head (1966) Orig US; applied to a habitual taker of LSD

druggy, druggie (1966) Orig US; applied to a drug-addict ■ *Washington Post*: Sherlock Holmes fans . . . remember his portrayal as an angstridden druggie a few years back. (1979)

freak (1967) Orig US; applied to someone addicted to a (usually specified) drug ■ *Atavar* (Boston): The life expectancy of the average speed-freak . . . is less than five years. (1967)

crackhead (1986) Orig US; applied to a habitual taker of crack cocaine ■ *Observer*: Charlie and two fellow 'crackheads' took me to a vast housing estate in south London where crack is on sale for between £20 and £25 a deal. (1988)

A non-addict

straight (1967) Orig US; from more general sense, conventional person ■ Kenneth Royce: 'I'm not having the stink of pot in this place.' . . . 'You straights are all the same.' (1974)

Addiction

yen-yen (1886) US, dated; applied to opium addiction or a craving for opium; probably from Chinese (Cantonese) *yīnyīn* craving for opium, from *yǎn* opium + *yǎn* craving ■ Jack Black: He [*sc.* an old Chinese person] was shaking with the 'yen yen', the hop habit. (1926)

monkey (1942) Orig US; especially in the phrase *have a monkey on one's back* be a drug-addict ■ E. R. Johnson: An addict's greatest worry would not be his, since Vito would feed his monkey. (1970)

the needle (1955) Orig US; applied to addiction to injected drugs; especially in the phrase *on the needle* addicted to injecting drugs ■ *Listener*: Middle Britain thinks . . . one puff on the joint leads to the needle. (1973)

jones, Jones (1968) US; applied to a drug-addict's habit; probably from the surname *Jones* ■ *Black World*: I don't have a long jones. I ain't been on it too long. (1971)

To take drugs

dope (1909) ■ M. Hong Kingston: I don't dope anymore. I've seen all there is to see on dope; the trips have been repeating themselves. (1989)

shoot (1914) Orig US; denoting injecting oneself with a drug; often followed by *up* ■ *Oz*: They were using those needles man, they were shooting up. (1971)

sleigh-ride (1915) US; denoting taking a narcotic drug; from the association with *snow* cocaine. Hence **sleigh-rider** (1915)

coke (1924) Orig US; denoting taking cocaine; often followed by *up*; from *coke* cocaine ■ Nicholas Blake: They let him coke himself up for the occasion. (1954)

peter (1925) Denoting taking a stupefying drug; from *peter* knock-out drug

sniff (1925) Denoting inhaling cocaine, the fumes of glue or solvents, etc. through the nose ■ Edgar Wallace: Red, you're . . . a hop-head. . . . We got no room in this outfit for guys who sniff. (1931)

main-line (1934) Orig US; denoting injecting a drug; from *main line* large vein (into which drugs are injected) ■ Michael Pereira: He made himself a fix . . . and he mainlined it. (1972). Hence **main-liner** (1934)

snort (1935) Orig US; denoting inhaling cocaine, heroin, etc. ■ *Daily Telegraph*: Mrs Pulitzer's lawyers claim that she started snorting cocaine after being sucked into the vortex of the 'Palm Beach lifestyle'. (1982)

spike (1935) Orig US; denoting injecting (with) a drug; from *spike* hypodermic needle ■ *Guardian*: The addicts . . . 'll sometime try and spike you, try and get you mainlining too. (1974)

fix (1936) Orig US; denoting injecting oneself with a narcotic drug ■ M. M. Glatt: At first I 'fixed' only once a week, then more often, and after about six months I was addicted. (1967)

blast (1943) Orig & mainly US; denoting smoking marijuana; compare earlier Scottish dialect *blast* smoke tobacco

goof (1944) From the notion of being made *goofy* ■ *Guardian*: Thousands of youths openly . . . 'goofed' amphetamines. (1970)

toke (1952) US; denoting smoking a marijuana cigarette; origin unknown ■ Norman Mailer: He had been over at a friend of his selling drugs, a little crystal, some speed, toked a couple, got blasted. (1979)

skin, skin-pop (1953) Denoting injecting oneself with a drug; from the notion of subcutaneous injection (often as directly contrasted with intravenous injection) ■ *Daily Telegraph*: She had also 'skin-popped' (injected drugs just below the surface of the skin) and taken a vast assortment of pills. (1970) ■ John Brown: The bastard, he mained me. I said to skin it, but he mained it. First time. (1972). Hence **skin-popper** (1953) ■ Hilary Waugh: No marks. She must be a skin-popper. (1970)

use (1953) Used intransitively to denote taking drugs; compare *user* regular drug-taker ■ Kenneth Orvis: Almost twenty-four hours . . . since I've had a fix. . . . Are you the only one? . . . You forget I use, too. (1962)

pop (1956) Denoting taking a narcotic drug, and also injecting a drug into (a blood vessel) ■ Martin Woodhouse: For him the day . . . started when he swallowed the first pill or popped the first vein. (1968)

chase the dragon (1961) Denoting taking heroin by inhalation; from the resemblance between the movements of the smoke from the burning heroin and the undulations of a dragon's tail ■ R. Lewis: There's this myth among the kids that if they inhale the burned skag it isn't going to hurt them. Chasing the dragon, they call it. (1985)

drop (1963) Orig US; often in the phrase *drop acid* ■ Saul Bellow: Some kids are dropping acid, stealing cars. (1984)

do (1967) Orig US ■ *New Yorker:* Their lives . . . involve . . . smoking (tobacco, marijuana, cloves), drinking (everything), and doing drugs—mainly cocaine. (1985)

main (1970) US; short for *main-line* ■ *Time:* All my friends were on heroin. I snorted a couple of times, skinned a lot, and after that I mained it. (1970)

crank (1971) Denoting injecting oneself with an illegal drug; compare *crank* amphetamine drug ■ *Daily Telegraph:* If . . . I continue to crank I will be dead within 18 months. (1972)

speed (1973) Orig US; denoting taking the drug 'speed' ■ S. George: 'You speeding?' He shrugged. 'Yes. Cancels the alcohol.' (1978)

toot (1975) US; denoting inhaling cocaine; from earlier sense, go on a drunken spree ■ *High Times:* You'll feel better knowing that what you toot is cut with the original Italian Mannite Conoscenti. (1979)

freebase (1980) Orig US; denoting inhaling freebase cocaine ■ *Time:* The Los Angeles police say Pryor told them that the accident occurred while he was 'free-basing' cocaine. (1980)

Taking drugs

on (1938) US ■ William Gaddis: She's high right now, can't you see it? She's been on for three days. (1955)

Equipment for taking drugs

hop toy (1881) US, dated; applied to a container used for smoking opium

pipe (1886) Orig US; applied to an opium pipe

gun (1899) US; applied to a hypodermic syringe

hypo (1904) Orig US; applied to a hypodermic needle; abbreviation of *hypodermic* ■ John Wainwright: The night medic . . . held the loaded hypo. (1973)

gonger (1914) US; applied to an opium pipe; probably from *gong* opium

gongerine (1914) US, dated; applied to an opium pipe; from *gonger* + diminutive suffix *-ine*

suey pow, sueypow, sui pow (1914) US, dated; applied to a sponge or rag used for cleaning or cooling an opium bowl; origin unknown

gong (1915) US; applied to an opium pipe; apparently short for *gonger*

stem (1925) US; applied to a pipe for smoking opium or crack ■ *Village Voice:* Now the johns drive up, they don't even say hello. They just go, 'Hey, you got a stem on you?' (1990)

hype, hyp (1929) Orig US; applied to a hypodermic needle; abbreviation of *hypodermic*

needle (1929) Orig US; applied to a hypodermic needle

spike (1934) Orig US; applied to a hypodermic needle ■ Peter Driscoll: This punk kid, shooting amphetamines, can't find enough spikes. (1979)

toy (1934) US; applied to a small tin or jar containing opium

works (1934) US; applied to the apparatus with which a drug-addict takes drugs ■ William Burroughs: I went into the bathroom to get my works. Needle, dropper, and a piece of cotton. (1953)

joint (1935) Dated; applied to hypodermic equipment used by drug-addicts

outfit (1951) Applied to the apparatus with which a drug-addict takes drugs ■ William Burroughs: She keeps outfits in glasses of alcohol so the junkies can fix in the joint and walk out clean. (1953)

skin (1969) Orig US; applied to a paper used for rolling marijuana cigarettes

To give a drug to

dope (1875) Denoting especially the drugging of a racing animal to affect its performance ■ *Times:* He had heard of greyhounds being doped, but not to make them run faster. (1955)

hypo (1925) Orig US; denoting administering a hypodermic injection (to); from *hypo* hypodermic needle ■ *Time:* Because of continuing hypo-ing, his arms and legs become abscessed. (1960)

snow (1927) US; from *snow* cocaine or other drug ■ Raymond Chandler: She looked snowed, weaved around funny. (1934)

hit (1953) Orig US ■ *New York Times:* How did he become an addict? 'You mean, who hit me first? My friend, Johnny.' (1970)

A drugged state

heat (1912) US; applied to a drug-induced state of intoxication; especially in the phrase *have a heat on*

sleigh-ride (1925) US; applied to (the euphoria resulting from) the taking of a narcotic drug, especially cocaine; especially in the phrase *take (or go on) a sleigh-ride* ■ Dell Shannon: It was just some dope out on a sleigh-ride. (1963)

wingding (1927) US; applied to a drug-addict's real or feigned seizure; especially in the phrase *throw a wingding* ■ P. Tamony: It assigned . . . Winifred Sweet . . . to throw a wing-ding . . . in Market Street. (1965)

nod (1942) Applied to a state of drowsiness induced by narcotic drugs; especially in the phrase *on the nod* ■ Kenneth Orvis: While I was on the nod. (1962)

flash (1946) Orig US; applied to the brief pleasurable sensation obtained by injecting a narcotic drug ■ *Oz:* More & more people started shooting it to get the flash all the real hip suckers were talking about. (1971)

high (1953) Applied to a drug-induced euphoria ■ *Times:* The two cigarettes smoked by each subject were intended to produce a 'normal social cannabis high'. (1969)

trip (1959) Orig US; applied to a hallucinatory experience induced by a drug, especially LSD ■ *Scientific American:* One of the volunteers had a bad trip, entering a panicky and nearly psychotic state. (1971). Hence the adjective **trippy** (1969) ■ *New Age:* Trippy music for meditation, massage, free-form movement, tantric loving, and a relaxing environment. (1980)

bummer (1966) Orig and mainly US; applied to an unpleasant experience induced by a hallucinogenic drug; from *bum* bad (as in *bum trip*) + *-er* ■ Timothy Leary: The Western world has been on a bad trip, a 400-year bummer. (1968)

acid trip (1967) Applied to a hallucinatory experience induced by taking LSD

turn-on (1969) Applied to a drug-taker's state of intoxication

munchies (1971) US; applied to hunger caused by taking marijuana; from earlier *munchie* food

In a drugged state

loaded (1923) US; from earlier sense, drunk ■ William Burroughs: He was loaded on H and goof-balls. (1953)

hopped-up, **hopped** (1924) US; from *hop* a narcotic drug ■ *Guardian*: Chuck Berry don't drink either but he gets hopped. (1973)

piped (1924) US; from earlier sense, drunk

teaed, **tea-d** (1928) US; applied to someone in a marijuana-induced euphoria; often followed by *up*; from *tea* marijuana

high (1932) From earlier sense, drunk ■ *New Scientist*: It is far safer to drive a car when high on marihuana than when drunk. (1969)

geed-up (1938) From *gee* opium or other drug

jagged (1938) Sometimes followed by *up*; compare earlier sense, drunk ■ Boyd & Parkes: Solange is—was—God help her, a heroin addict. When we first met, she was all jagged up. She was a reject on the junk heap. (1973)

polluted (1938) Orig US; from earlier sense, drunk

straight (1946) US ■ *Life*: Once the addict has had his shot and is 'straight' he may become admirably, though briefly, industrious. (1965)

stoned (1953) Orig US; from earlier sense, drunk ■ Dorothy Halliday: They're all lying around in there wearing beads and stoned out of their skulls on French Blues. (1971)

strung out (1959) Orig & mainly US ■ *Guardian Weekly*: Young people get strung out on heroin. (1977)

zonked (1959) Often followed by *out*; from *zonk* hit, overwhelm ■ *Daily Telegraph*: A . . . Caucasian woman obviously zonked out . . . and a tracery of leaves resembling cannabis. (1979)

potted (1960) Orig US; applied to someone under the influence of 'pot' or marijuana ■ Busby & Holtham: The Jamaicans . . . didn't appear to be potted. (1968)

out of it (1963) Orig US

bombed (1965) Often followed by *out*; from earlier sense, drunk ■ Olivia Manning: 'Poor little brat! They'll take her off on the heroin trail and she'll die

between here and the Philippines.' 'They're bombed out. Where do they get the stuff?' (1974)

wiped (1966) Orig & mainly US; usually followed by *out*; from earlier sense, tired

smashed (1968) Orig US; from earlier sense, drunk ■ *New Society*: If you're smashed out of your skull all the time on peyote, then even the bizarre patronage of Marlon Brando must seem tolerable. (1977)

spaced (1968) Orig US; denoting drug-induced euphoria, distraction, or disorientation; usually followed by *out* ■ J. Mandelkau: I remember being really spaced out and someone handing me a ladybird—telling me how nice they tasted. (1971)

spacey, **spacy** (1968) Mainly US; denoting drug-induced euphoria, distraction, or disorientation ■ J. A. Carver: His head felt large, and a little spacey, and he felt a heightened sense of geometry, of perspective. (1980)

wasted (1968) Orig US

wrecked (1968) US

blasted (1969) Mainly US; from earlier sense, drunk ■ S. Booth: He seemed as fog-bound as I was, a sweet-tempered English boy staying blasted on grass and coke. (1985)

ripped (1971) Orig US ■ Clive James: On he gabbled as if ripped on Speed. (1975)

tripped-out (1973) Orig US; applied especially to someone under the influence of LSD ■ H. Ferguson: Everyone was gathered round talking about the arrangements they would make for their 'excursion' the following day. They cared so little for my tripped-out state that they turned out the light and left me in the darkened room. (1976)

whacked out (1975) US; from earlier sense, crazy

wired (1977) Mainly US; often followed by *up*; from earlier sense, tense, edgy ■ *Fortune*: From a cocaine-abusing denizen of Wall Street: 'I worked on both Chrysler refinancings, and by the second one, I was wired most of the time.' (1985)

To (cause to) experience the effect of a drug

stone (1952) Orig US; usually followed by *out* ■ G. Mandel: I'd rather stay with the tea. It's great pod. I don't want to stone out. (1952) ■ John Brown: You smoke Egyptian Black, that will stone you out of your head. (1972)

turn on (1953) Orig US; from earlier sense, excite, stimulate ■ Rona Jaffe: She walked in while I was turning on so I offered her some [marijuana]. (1979)

blow someone's **mind** (1965) Orig US; denoting the inducing of hallucinatory experiences in someone by means of drugs, especially LSD ■ J. D. MacDonald: They had some new short acid from the Coast that never gives you a down trip and blows your mind for an hour only. (1968)

freak (1965) Orig US; denoting (causing someone) to have hallucinatory experiences from the use of narcotic drugs; usually followed by *out* ■ *Life*: When my husband and I want to take a trip together . . . I just put a little acid in the kids' orange juice . . . and let them spend the day freaking out in the woods. (1966)

trip (1966) Orig US; denoting experiencing drug-induced hallucinations; sometimes followed by *out* ■ J. Scott: Some of the people here were tripping already. Seemed a pity not to bust 'em. (1980). Hence **tripper** one who experiences hallucinatory effects of a drug (1966) ■ Bernard Malamud: One of the swamis there, a secret acid tripper, got on my nerves. (1979)

string out (1967) US; denoting being under the influence of a drug ■ *Sunday Telegraph*: How long did you string out? (1970)

space out (1968) US; denoting going into a drug-induced euphoria ■ *New York*: Karenga . . . looks like he's going crazy or spacing out on dope. (1970)

get off (1969) Orig US; usually followed by *on* ■ A. Kukla: Did you get off on that acid you took last night? (1980)

O.D. (1969) Orig US; denoting taking an overdose of a drug; abbreviation of *overdose* ■ S. O'Callaghan: Diana has O.D.'d and she's dead. (1970)

mellow out (1974) US; denoting becoming relaxed under the influence of a drug ■ Cyra McFadden: How about we all smoke a little dope and mellow out, okay? (1977)

Physical effects of drug-taking

tracks (1964) Applied to the lines on the skin made by repeated injections of an addictive drug ■ James Mills: Whaddya mean, lemme see your tracks? I'm a pros, man, I shoot up in my thighs. (1972)

Detoxification

dry out (1908) Orig US; applied a drug-addict undergoing treatment to cure addiction ■ *Guardian*: They are not only making firmer contact with the addicts . . . but also giving some of those they have 'dried out' a purpose. (1967)

cold turkey (1921) Orig US; applied to the sudden complete giving up of an addictive drug, especially as a method of withdrawal; from the notion of the simple abruptness of the withdrawal, with reference to a simple dish of cold turkey, without garnish ■ S. George: She took a cold turkey, no methedrine, no sedatives, nothing, just off. (1976)

kick (1936) Orig US; applied to giving up a drug-taking habit ■ Billie Holiday: Along about the end of the war I went to Joe Glaser's office and told him I wanted to kick and I'd need help. (1956)

twister (1936) US; applied to a spasm experienced by a drug-taker as a withdrawal symptom

sick (1951) US; applied to someone suffering drug withdrawal symptoms ■ William Burroughs: The usual routine is to grab someone with junk on him, and let him stew in jail until he is good and sick. (1953)

clean (1953) Applied to someone free from or cured of addiction to drugs ■ *Times*: Only one-tenth of heroin addicts are ever completely 'clean' again. (1970)

To buy or sell drugs

hold (1935) US; denoting being in possession of drugs for sale ■ R. Russell: He was holding, just as Red had said. Santa had the sweets. (1961)

score (1935) Orig US; denoting obtaining an illegal drug ■ William Burroughs: Junk wins by default. I tried it as a matter of curiosity. I drifted along taking shots when I could score. (1953)

connect (1938) US; denoting meeting someone in order to obtain drugs ■ Kenneth Orvis: If you're connecting from Frankie, he should have told you. (1962)

push (1938) Denoting peddling illegal drugs

deal (1958) Used intransitively to denote peddling illegal drugs

A supplier of drugs

connection, connexion (1927) Orig US ■ Jack Kerouac: A couple of Negro characters whispered in my ear about tea. . . . The connection came in and motioned me to the cellar toilet. (1957)

junker (1930) US; compare earlier sense, drug-addict ■ J. Evans: No slim-waisted junker with a snapbrim hat and a deck of nose candy for sale to the right guy. (1949)

mule (1935) Orig US; applied to someone employed as a courier to smuggle illegal drugs into a country and often to pass them on to a buyer; from the role of the mule as a beast of burden ■ Ed McBain: I bought from him a coupla times. He was a mule, Dad. That means he pushed to other kids. (1959)

pusher (1935) Orig US; probably from *push* peddle illegal drugs (although not recorded until a few years later) + *-er* ■ *Howard Journal*: Western loathing for temptation is vented . . . upon the scapegoats of the junkie and the pusher. (1976)

teaman (1950) US; applied to a seller of marijuana; compare earlier sense, marijuana-addict

swing man (1972) ■ John Wainwright: Tell us about all the dope he pushed. . . . He was taking from his swingman. (1973)

superfly (1973) US; from *Super Fly* name of a cocaine dealer in a 1972 US film of the same name

A supply of drugs or place where drugs are available

tea pad (1938) US; applied to a place where one can buy and smoke marijuana

tea party (1944) US; applied to a gathering at which marijuana is smoked ■ Julian Symons: Used to give tea parties—marihuana. (1956)

script (1951) Orig US; applied to a prescription for narcotic drugs; short for *prescription* ■ John Brown: You're just like a bloody junkie I know. Gets his script at mid-day every day, then works his fixes out. (1972)

shooting gallery (1951) US; applied to a place where illegal drugs can be obtained and injected; compare *shoot (up)* inject oneself with a drug

Articles and Substances

1. Things

A thing of a particular type

animal (1922) Often in the phrase *there is no such animal* ■ *Guardian*: There never has been such an animal as the American symphony. (1992)

job (1928) Orig US ■ Brickhill & Norton: A rather imposing moustache. It was one of those bushy black jobs. (1946)

sucker (1978) Orig & mainly US; compare earlier sense, gullible person ■ *Sports Illustrated*: One day David said, 'Never fear, I'll shut that sucker off.' And he grabbed it and gave it a huge twist. (1982)

An unnamed or unspecified thing

thingummy (1796) From obsolete *thingum* in same sense (from *thing* + a fanciful suffix) + -y ■ *Economist*: When the last gets used up, the card is returned to the thingummy supplier. (1987)

thingumajig, thingamajig, thingummyjig (1824) From obsolete *thingum* or *thingummy* + the fanciful element *jig* ■ Elizabeth Banks: I would drive through Hyde Park in a victoria, . . . and everybody would say, 'There goes the editress of the Thingymygig Magazine!' (1902)

thingumabob, thingumebob (1832) Alteration of earlier obsolete *thingumbob* (1751), from *thingum* + the fanciful element *bob* ■ Mary Bridgman: We're going to try him for thingamobob—bigamy. (1870)

you know what (*a*1845) Usually euphemistic; compare earlier obsolete *you wot what* in same sense ■ *New Yorker*: She gives me a pain in my you-know-what. (1976)

jigger (1874) US; usually applied specifically to a device or gadget; origin unknown

dingus (1876) US, dated; from Dutch *ding* thing ■ Dashiell Hammett: Then you think the dingus is worth two million? (1929)

whatsit (*a*1882) Representing a casual pronunciation of *what is it* ■ Pamela Frankau: I couldn't even walk along the passage to the whatsit. (1954)

doodad (1905) Orig & mainly US; often applied specifically to a superfluous ornament; origin unknown ■ D. Enefer: An open lacquered box with hair clips and other doodads. (1966)

hickey, hickie (1909) Now mainly US; usually applied specifically to a device or gadget; origin unknown ■ *Atlantic Monthly*: We have little hickeys beside our seats to regulate the amount of air admitted through a slot in each window. (1932)

doohickey, dohickey, doohicky (1914) Orig & mainly US; perhaps from *doo*(*dad* + *hickey*) thing, gadget ■ Alison Lurie: Just unhitch that dohickey there with a wrench. (1967)

oojah, oojar, and in various comical extensions such as **oojah-ka-piv, oojah-ma-flip (1917)** British, dated; origin unknown ■ B. W. Aldiss: I've seen blokes in hot countries go clean round the oojar because of the perverted practices of native women. (1971)

oojiboo (1918) British services' slang, dated; origin unknown

dingbat (1923) US; compare earlier senses, money, tramp; this meaning perhaps influenced by *dingus* ■ James Thurber: It is sitting on a strange and almost indescribable sort of iron dingbat. (1931)

doodah, dooda, do-da (1924) Compare earlier use in the phrase *all of a doodah* in a state of confusion ■ Honoria Croome: They make little plastic doodahs to use in electrical machinery. (1957)

doojigger, dojigger (1927) US; perhaps from *doo*(*dad* + *jigger*) thing, gadget ■ Thomas Pynchon: The extra little doojigger sort of coming out of the bell. (1966)

whangdoodle, whangydoodle (1931) North American; compare earlier sense, imaginary creature ■ *Globe & Mail* (Toronto): A new company sprang to the fore in Quebec. . . . PQ Productions claimed to have invented the whangdoodle. (1979)

whassit (1931) US; representing a casual pronunciation of *whatsit*

thingy, thingie (1933) From *thing* + -y ■ *Spare Rib*: Then there are those women who make men wear things on their thingies. (1977)

thingummytight, thingummytite (1937) British, dated; from *thingummy* + the fanciful element *tight, tite* ■ Dirk Bogarde: Nothing in the taps of course because the terrorists had buggered up the hydroelectric thingummytites. (1980)

doover, doovah (1941) Australian; origin uncertain; possibly representing a Yiddish pronunciation of Hebrew *davar* word, thing ■ S. Gore: They was humpin' along all these other doovers as well as the tucker. (1968)

gismo, gizmo (1942) Orig & mainly US; often applied specifically to a device or gadget; origin unknown ■ *New Yorker*: Every gismo that made use of a clothes hanger will be demonstrated by its inventor. (1970)

whatchamacallit (1942) Representing a pronunciation of *what you may call it* ■ R. B. Parker: A pet whatchamacallit. . . . Guinea pig. (1974)

gubbins (1944) British; often applied specifically to a device or gadget; from earlier sense, unspecified things, paraphernalia ■ Ivor Brown: You can save more petrol by how you drive than with the gubbinses now floating around. (1958)

doofer, doofah (1945) British; compare earlier sense, half a cigarette (1937); probably ultimately the same word as *doover* (1941) ■ Peter Dickinson: This is a very fancy doofer indeed. . . . It transmits along one wavelength and receives along another. (1970)

whifflow (1961) Fanciful formation ■ Anthony Burgess: The cabin was still a mess of smashed and battered whifflows. (1971)

whatnot (1964) From earlier sense, anything whatever ■ M. Riley: She said . . . tapping the Cellophane-covered éclairs, 'I don't know about you but these always put me in mind of nignogs' whatnots.' (1977)

bizzo (1969) Australian; from *bus(iness + -o* ■ G. Morley: Sheilas sitting down against the wall, legs up in the air, showing their bizzos. (1972)

frobnitz, frob (1983) US, computer slang; probably a fanciful coinage

doobry (1990) British; reportedly current since the 1950s. Probably modelled on similar words beginning *do(o)-*

Unspecified things, paraphernalia

and (I don't know) what all (1702) Denoting various other (unknown or unspecified) things ■ Alison Lurie: That old Mr Higginson. . . . Got his house full of bird dirt and what-all. (1962)

clobber (1890) British; from earlier sense, clothes ■ Lancet: Every cellar stockroom . . . is packed tight with fantastic collections of clobber and junk. (1965)

doings (1919) Usually applied to things needed ■ Graham Greene: Her skirt drawn up above her knees she waited for him with luxurious docility. . . . 'You've got the doings, haven't you?' (1938)

gubbins (1925) British; compare earlier sense, fool ■ New Scientist: Behind that again is the engine and propeller, the fuel tank and various bits of 'gubbins'. (1968)

An object collected from refuse

tot (1873) British; origin unknown

2. Clothing & Accessories

Clothing

duds (1307) Origin uncertain ■ W. Kennedy: Put her in new duds, high heels and silk stockin's. (1979)

best bib and tucker (1747) Denoting someone's smartest clothes; from *bib* upper part of an apron and *tucker* lace frill worn round the neck

togs (1779) From the plural of former vagabonds' slang *tog* coat, apparently a shortening of *togeman(s), togman* cloak or loose coat, from French *toge* or Latin *toga* toga + cant suffix *-man(s)* ■ Daily Telegraph: It's a strange combination: Redgrave, in glamorous togs; a studio audience; a chat-show set. (1992)

rig-out (1823) Applied to a set of clothes, especially an unusual one ■ Robertson Davies: The young Canada during the whole of the nineteenth century wore a strange rig-out that we might imagine as a pair of pants cut down from Uncle Sam's very long legs, and the Union Jack waistcoat of John Bull. (1977)

cits (1829) US, services' slang; applied to civilian clothes; from *cit* civilian ■ Chicago Tribune: They were in full dress uniform. Later they were joined by Maj. Judson of the engineers in 'cits'. (1907)

rig (1843) Applied to a set of clothes ■ Guardian: Brummell's rig was essentially riding gear. (1991)

Sunday best (1846) Denoting one's smartest clothes, originally as worn on a Sunday ■ Frank Sargeson: He was all dressed up in his Sunday best . . . but his hair was any old how. (1949)

get-up (1847) Applied to a set of clothes, especially an unusual one ■ Rachel Praed: Dressed in a well-made tweed suit, that contrasted with the careless get-up of the bushmen round. (1889)

drag (1870) Applied to women's clothes worn by men, and hence (1959) to clothing in general; from the (unaccustomed) length and weight of women's clothes ■ John Osborne: You would never have the fag Of dressing up in drag You'd be a woman at the weekend. (1959) ■ Listener: Laurence Olivier, doing his Othello voice and attired painstakingly in Arab drag. (1966)

clobber (1879) British; origin unknown ■ Observer: To pay for the kiddies' clobber. (1959)

civvies, civies (1889) Services' slang; applied to civilian clothes; from civ(ilian + -ies ■ Daily Telegraph: Young men exchange their uniforms for 'civvies'. (1946)

rig-up (1896) Applied to a set of clothes, especially an unusual one ■ Kathleen Caffyn: Either she's mad or in a peck of trouble, to come . . . in this rig-up. (1896)

dog-robbers (1898) British, naval slang; applied to civilian clothes worn by a naval officer on shore leave; compare earlier *dog-robber* scrounger, officer's orderly ■ Monica Dickens: Then he . . . changed into dog robbers and went into the town to get drunk. (1958)

glad rags (1899) Orig US; applied to one's smartest clothes, and often specifically to formal evening dress ■ H. B. Hermon-Hodge: We all turned out in our glad rags to join in the procession. (1922)

threads (1926) Orig & mainly US ■ John Gardner: Load it and get in on under that set of executive threads. (1978)

drape (1938) Orig US jazz slang; applied to a garment or, in the plural, to clothes, often specifically a zoot suit; from earlier sense, cloth, drapery ■ *Michael Swan:* He was a ... man of thirty-two, wearing gaberdine drapes and a bow-tie. (1957)

mocker, mokker (1947) Australian & New Zealand; origin unknown ■ *Australian Short Stories:* Just wear ordinary mokker. (1984)

schmutter, shmuter, shmutter (1959) Mainly US; from Yiddish *schmatte* rag, from Polish *szmata* ■ *Bookseller:* Several dresses (at trade terms) were bought for Mrs. Wolfe ... from small shmutter merchants. (1972)

vines (1959) US; from *vine* suit of clothes ■ *American Speech:* Without your vines you're nothing but FBI [*sc.* Fat, Black, and Ignorant]. (1975)

kit (1985) Mainly British; often used in the context of undressing; from earlier sense, set of matching garments worn for a sporting or military activity ■ *Sunday Times:* Fiona Pitt-Kethley has agreed to get her kit off to appear on Channel 4's forthcoming Naked Chat Show. (1993)

A garment

number (1894) ■ *Marguerite Steen:* Petula Wimbleby's solution turned out to be an exquisite but throat-high 'little number' redeemed by lumps of jade. (1953)

woolly (1899) Applied to a garment (especially a sweater) knitted from wool ■ *Guardian:* The weather's been wonderful, but it changes. I hope you brought a woolly. (1992)

schmatte, shmatte, schmottah, etc. **(1970)** US; applied especially to a ragged garment; Yiddish, from Polish *szmata* rag ■ *J. Marks:* I ran away from home in San Bernardino when I was fifteen. ... All I took was this *schmottah* I wore Halloween. (1973)

A pocket

pit (1811) ■ *D. W. Maurer:* The most important pocket in the coat from the pickpocket's point of view is the *coat pit*, or the inside breast pocket. ... This is often shortened to *pit*. (1955)

kick (1851) ■ *Sunday Truth* (Brisbane): One of Luke's jobs was to see that the money was banked every week. Luke put it in his own kick. (1968)

sky-rocket (1879) Rhyming slang ■ *Berkeley Mather:* Ten trouble-free runs ... and you're back in England with five thousand quid in your skyrocket. (1973)

sky (1890) Short for *sky-rocket* ■ *P. Hill:* Said 'ee found it [*sc.* a gun] on the rattler. Put it in 'is sky when 'ee got off at Leicester Square. (1979)

side-kicker (1903), sidekick (1916) US criminals' slang, dated; applied to a side-pocket; compare *kick* pocket

slide (1932) US; applied to a trouser pocket ■ *I. Slim:* How would you like a half a 'G' in your 'slide'? (1967)

A hole in a garment

potato (1885) Applied to a hole in a sock or stocking through which the skin shows

■ *Country Gentlemen's Estate Magazine:* Gumboots ... will hole a 'potato' like a cannon-ball in the heels of a new pair of socks in an afternoon. (1973)

spud (1960) Applied to a hole in a sock or stocking through which the skin shows; from earlier sense, potato ■ *M. de Larrabeiti:* There were huge spuds in the heels of their socks. (1978)

A hat

tile (1813) Dated ■ *P. Fitzgerald:* Willis ... had not been able to lay hands on his 'waterproof tile', but made do with a deep-crowned felt hat. (1979)

topper (1820) Applied to a top hat ■ *H. A. Vachell:* The 'topper' you wear on Sunday. (1905)

skimmer (1830) Mainly US; applied to a broad-brimmed boater ■ *Peter de Vries:* The thoroughly incompatible straw hat. ... The brightly banded boater, or 'skimmer' or 'katy'. (1974)

lid (1896) Often applied specifically to a soldier's steel helmet or a motorcyclist's crash-helmet ■ *P. G. Wodehouse:* It is almost as foul as Uncle Tom's Sherlock Holmes deerstalker, which has frightened more crows than any other lid in Worcestershire. (1960)

tin hat (1903) Applied to a military steel helmet

kelly (1915) Mainly US; applied to a man's hat, especially a derby; perhaps suggested by *derby kelly* belly ■ *Lait & Mortimer:* Some of the larger clubs reap up to $50,000 a year for the privilege of checking your kellys. (1948)

gorblimey, gaw-, -blime, -blimy (1919) British, dated; applied to a soft service cap; from the exclamation *gorblimey*

titfer, titfa, titfor (1930) British; short for *tit for tat*, rhyming slang ■ *U. Holden:* The old lady made a show. ... Lil Pratt forgot to fill her mouth. ... She'd not seen a titfer like that since the film of mountain people in the Dardanelles, made after World War One. (1976)

blocker (1934) British; applied to a bowler hat ■ *Frank Shaw:* Foremen traditionally wore bowler-hats, or 'blockers'. (1966)

God forbid, Gawd forbid (1936) British; rhyming slang for *lid* hat ■ *James Curtis:* Why don't you take off your gawd-forbid? We're passing the Cenotaph. (1936)

skid-lid (1958) Applied to a motorcyclist's crash-helmet ■ *C. Watson:* This bird in motor-cycle get-up ... with that great skid-lid hiding half her face. (1977)

Smokey Bear, Smoky Bear (1969) US; applied to a type of wide-brimmed hat; from the name of an animal character used in US fire-prevention advertising ■ *Ian Kemp:* Sergeants Sullivant, McKane and Rothweiller ... wore the round, soft-brimmed hats known by Americans as 'Smokey Bear'—similar to those of the Royal Canadian Mounted Police. (1969)

A garment for the upper body

dicky dirt (1925) British; applied to a shirt; rhyming slang, perhaps suggested by *dicky* false shirt-front (1811)

thousand-miler (1929) Nautical; applied to a dark shirt that does not show the dirt; from its only needing to be washed after a thousand miles of voyaging

Jacky Howe, Jackie Howe (1930) Australian & New Zealand; applied to a sleeveless vest worn especially by sheep-shearers and other rural workers; from the name of *John* Robert *Howe* (?1861–1920), a noted Queensland sheep-shearer

cardy, cardie (1968) Abbreviation of *cardigan* ■ J. Milne: He wore his yellow cardy with the leather buttons. (1986)

boob-tube (1978) Applied to a woman's close-fitting strapless top; from *boob* breast + *tube*, probably inspired by earlier *boob-tube* television ■ My Weekly: Now the rush around to find . . . a variety of tops from waterproofs to 'boob-tubes'. (1986)

A coat

benny, ben (1812) US; applied to an overcoat; apparently a shortening of obsolete *benjamin* overcoat, perhaps from the name of a tailor

mack, mac (1901) Applied to a raincoat; short for *mackintosh* ■ Arthur Behrend: Richardson slipped on his mack and went round to India buildings. (1973)

pussy (1937) Criminals' slang; applied to a fur coat; compare earlier sense, cat ■ John Wainwright: The coat. . . . Ten to one, a fur coat, and there was always somebody ready to lift a pussy. (1972)

mog (1950) Applied to a fur coat; compare earlier sense, cat ■ Eric Partridge: Annuvver 'orse comes up, an' it's . . . a new mog fer the missus. (1950)

A jacket

bum-freezer, (dated) bum-perisher, -shaver, -starver (1889) Mainly British; applied to a short jacket (thought of as) not covering the buttocks ■ Howard Spring: A nice little Eton suit—what Greg inevitably called my bum-freezer. (1955)

tux (1922) US; applied to a dinner jacket; short for *tuxedo* ■ Kate Millett: Daddy doing his tux. First the black tie. Next the studs. (1974)

D.J. (1967) Abbreviation of *dinner jacket* ■ Evening Standard: Curly will look magnificent in his DJ. (1992)

Trousers

bags (1853) British, dated; from the garment's loose fit ■ Dorothy Sayers: Just brush my bags down, will you, old man? (1927)

round-the-houses (1857) Rhyming slang ■ Edward Dyson: No man that wore 'ome-made round-th'-'ouses ever done wonders in this world. (1906)

strides (1889) Now mainly Australian ■ Anthony Burgess: He handed a crumpled bundle to Edwin, saying: 'You'll 'ave to take my strides.' . . . The trousers, Edwin found, were too short. (1960)

rammies (1906) Australian & South African; shortened form of *round-the-houses* trousers ■ Bulletin (Sydney): Old Bill watched the youngest jackeroo disrobing. . . . 'If I was you, young feller,' he said, 'I'd leave them rammies on.' (1933)

loons, loon pants, loon trousers (1971) Dated; applied to casual trousers widely flared from the knees to the ankles; from *loon* pass the time pleasurably, probably reinforced by *pantaloons*

petrol bowsers, petrols (1971) Australian; rhyming slang, from *petrol bowser* petrol pump, petrol tanker

stubbies (1973) Australian; a proprietary name for a brand of shorts

A suit

soup and fish (1918) Applied to a formal dress suit for evening wear ■ Hugh McLeave: Get him to take off his soup-and-fish and show us his scar. (1970)

fiddle and flute (1919), fiddle (1943) US; rhyming slang for *suit*

monkey suit (1920) Orig US; applied to a formal dress suit for evening wear ■ Anthony Fowles: He could . . . hire one of those monkey-suits from Moss Bros. (1974)

whistle and flute (1931), whistle (1941) British; rhyming slang for *suit* ■ Observer: What you ate and where you ate: it mattered as much as your Beemer and the Armani whistle. (1996)

vine (1932) US; from the notion of clothes clinging to the body ■ L. Hairston: I . . . laid out my vine, a clean shirt and things on my bed. (1964)

zoot suit (1942), zoot (1965) Orig US; applied to a man's suit with a long loose jacket and high-waisted tapering trousers, popular especially in the 1940s (originally worn by US blacks); reduplicated rhyming formation on *suit* ■ Thomas Pynchon: Where'd you get that zoot you're wearing, there? (1973)

penguin suit (1967) Applied to a formal dress suit for evening wear; from the black-and-white appearance ■ Observer: Steak Diane was only served in red-plush restaurants, where the staff wore penguin suits and could barely speak a word of English. (1996)

A collar

dog collar (1861) Usually jocular; applied to a clerical collar ■ Joyce Porter: His dog collar gleamed whitely in the darkness of the hall. (1965)

A tie

Peckham rye (1925) British; rhyming slang, from the name of an open space in Peckham, SE London

dicky bow, dickie bow, dickey bow (1977) Applied to a bow tie ■ Observer: The odds, however, would be completely revised if, as rumoured, Robin Day takes off his dickey-bow and leaps into the fray. (1979)

A handkerchief

snot-rag (1886) From *snot* nasal mucus + *rag* ■ Norman Mailer: One of them said he was going to take my shirt and use it for a snotrag, and they all laughed. (1959)

hanky, hankie (1895) From *handk(erchief* + *-y*
■ Nicolas Freeling: Janine was snuffling in a silly little hanky. (1967)

penwiper (1902) Dated

Swimwear

cossie, cozzie (1926) Australian; applied to a swimsuit or pair of swimming trunks; diminutive of *costume* ■ *Times*: A girl in a cozzie with a dead animal draped over her shoulders is a powerful image. (1981)

Nightwear

nightie, nighty (1871) Applied to a night-dress; from *night(-dress* + *-ie* ■ Gavin Black: The hospital nighty . . . felt slightly scratchy. (1972)

jim-jams (1994) Applied to pyjamas; reduplicated formation based on the second syllable of *pyjamas* ■ *Independent on Sunday*: Dr Clements made as strong a case as I've heard for attempting a cross-legged Harrier take-off in your jimjams. (1944)

Protective clothing

pinny (1851) Applied to a pinafore; from *pin(afore* + *-y* ■ John Braine: 'Get me a bloody pinny,' I said, 'and you can go out to work.' (1962)

teddy bear (1917) US; applied to a fur-lined high-altitude flying suit ■ C. Codman: We issue forth . . . clad in fur-lined Teddy Bears and fleece-lined overshoes. (1937)

penguin suit (1971) Applied to a type of tight-fitting suit worn by astronauts

steamer (1982) Applied to a type of wetsuit worn by surfers and wind-surfers, with minimally permeable rubber; probably from its warming effect on the wearer

See also **skid-lid** and **tin hat** at A hat (p. 170).

Underwear

undies (1906) Applied to girls' or womens' underwear; from *und(erwear* + *-ies* ■ Nicolas Freeling: Arlette . . . knows I'm not just belting off for the afternoon because of the black undies. (1967)

underfug (1924) British public schools' slang; applied to an undervest, and also to underpants; from *under-* + *fug* stuffy atmosphere ■ Bruce Marshall: The matron kept everybody's spare shirts, underfugs and towels and dished clean ones out once a week. (1946)

winter woollies (1926) Applied to warm underwear (not necessarily made of wool) ■ *Nature*: The dinosaurs' unsatisfied need was not so much for laxatives as for winter woollies! (1974)

skivvy, scivvy, skivie, skivvie (1932) North American, orig nautical; applied to a vest or undershirt or, in the plural, to underwear (1945); origin unknown ■ Saul Bellow: We had to brush our teeth with salt . . . and sleeping in skivvies, was outlawed; we had to wear pajamas. (1953)

trollies, trolleys (1934) British, mainly schoolgirls' slang; applied to women's underpants; perhaps from *trolly* type of lace ■ Barbara Pym: I bought a peach coloured vest and trollies to match. (1934)

gay deceivers (1942) Dated; applied to a padded bra or to breast-pads; compare earlier *gay deceiver* deceitful rake or dissolute person

falsies (1943) Orig US; applied to a padded bra or to breast-pads; from *false* + *-ie* ■ Monica Dickens: The secretary slouched in . . . her falsies pushing out her sweater like cardboard cones. (1958)

long johns (1943) Applied to underpants with long legs ■ J. Gardner: Boysie picked up the clothes. . . . A suit of woollen long johns, a pair of heavy calf-length stockings. (1969)

passion-killers (1943) Applied to sturdy, practical, and unromantic ladies' knickers, originally those issued to female service personnel

smalls (1943) British; applied to underwear; compare earlier sense, breeches ■ *Guardian*: Not many Americans . . . can have a clear idea of what to use the bidet for, apart from soaking the smalls. (1973)

jock (1952) North American; abbreviation of *jock-strap* ■ Wilson McCarthy: He found the Beretta . . . as well as the jock strap. He quickly took off his trousers, put on the jock. (1973)

pasties (1961) Applied to coverings worn over the nipples of a showgirl's or topless dancer's breasts, especially to comply with legal requirements for entertainers; from *paste* apply (with paste) + *-ies* ■ *Sunday Truth* (Brisbane): Stripper Sharon was promoting a Valley nightclub, wearing nothing on top but a couple of pasties to keep her modest. (1969)

A loincloth

cockrag (1964) Australian; applied mainly to a loincloth worn by an aboriginal; from *cock* penis + *rag* ■ Ngabidj & Shaw: Wallambain threw away his woomera and cock rag and jumped in. (1981)

Gloves

turtle-dove (1857) British; rhyming slang

turtle (1893) British; short for *turtle-dove* ■ James Curtis: Got any turtles? The Gilt Kid, having no gloves, answered: 'No, but I'll buy a pair.' (1936)

Shoes

clodhopper (1836) Applied to a large heavy shoe; compare earlier sense, boorish or clumsy person ■ *Times*: These high-technology developments are far removed from the customised clodhoppers which are the ancestors of today's lightweight sports shoes. (1991)

daisy roots (1859) British; rhyming slang for *boots* ■ *Gen*: Your toes is poking out of your daisy-roots. (1943)

beetle-crusher, beetle-squasher (1860) Jocular; applied to a boot, especially a large or heavy one ■ Rhoda Broughton: What howible boots! Whoever could have had the atwocity to fwame such beetle-cwushers? (1870)

stomper (1899) Orig US; usually applied specifically to a large heavy shoe ■ Kate Millett: The Left wears its jeans and stompers. (1974)

creeper (1904) Mainly British; applied to a soft-soled shoe ■ Edward Blishen: He pointed to my shoes, which were new and crape-soled. 'They're creepers. . . . Real up-to-the-minute yobo's thick-soled creepers.' (1955)

kicks (1904) Orig US ■ *Black World*: My terrible blue-and-white kicks. (1973)

laughing-sides (1937) Australian; a jocular term (supposedly an Aboriginal malapropism) for elastic-sided boots

brothel-creeper (1954) British; applied to a suede or soft-soled shoe ■ Godfrey Smith: 'Poncing about the place in those brothel-creepers of his!'. . . He always wore plush suede shoes. (1954)

welly, **wellie**, **welly-boot (1961)** British; applied to a wellington boot; from *well(ington* + *-y* ■ S. Radley: Perhaps it wasn't done for a parson to wear welly boots under his cassock. (1982)

bovver boot (1969) British; applied to a heavy boot with toe-cap and laces, of a kind characteristically worn by skinheads; from *bovver* disturbance, fighting, from the notion of the boot being used to kick opponents

waffle stomper (1974) US; applied to a boot or shoe with a heavy, ridged sole

DMs (1993) British; abbreviation of *Doctor Marten's*, name of a brand of boot ■ Irvine Welsh: Skinhead haircut, green bomber-jaykit, nine-inch DMs. A stereotypical twat. (1993)

Claire Rayners (1997) British rhyming slang for *trainers*. From the name of the British journalist and agony aunt Claire Rayner

An umbrella

gamp (1864) British, dated; applied especially to an umbrella tied in a loose untidy way; from the name of Sarah Gamp, a nurse in Dickens's *Martin Chuzzlewit* (1844), who owned such an umbrella

brolly (1874) British; abbreviation and alteration of *umbrella*

Jewellery and similar personal items

hoop (1507) Applied to a ring; originally standard English ■ Jack Black: I go in her joint and drop a hoop to one of her frowsy little brums for nine dollars. (1926)

sparkler (1822) Applied to a diamond or other precious stone ■ *Listener*: Two of her safes contained vast quantities of sparklers and folding stuff. (1984)

slag (1857) Criminals' slang, dated; applied to a watch-chain or other decorative chain; probably from obsolete slang *slang* watch-chain, perhaps from Dutch *slang* snake ■ *Clues*: Then we'll take the hot hoops and slags up to the block dealers. (1926)

spark-prop (1879) Criminals' slang, dated; applied to a diamond pin or tie-pin

shiner (1884) Applied to a diamond or other precious stone; usually used in the plural ■ Dorothy Sayers: I never had those shiners. (1934)

kettle (1889) Dated, mainly criminals' slang; applied to a watch ■ James Curtis: Next buckshee kettle that comes my way I'll just stick to it. (1936)

stone (1904) Criminals' slang; applied to a diamond

ice (1906) Orig US; usually applied specifically to diamonds ■ Hartley Howard: Prager caught sight of five hundred grand in cracked ice. (1972)

rock (1908) Orig US; applied to a diamond or other precious stone ■ Ivor Drummond: 'We will see some of the most beautiful jewellery in the world. . . . The emeralds.' . . . 'Personally,' said Jenny, 'I call it vulgar, having all those rocks on a yacht.' (1973)

prop (1914) Criminals' slang; applied to a diamond or valuable piece of jewellery; from earlier obsolete slang sense, scarf pin; compare Dutch *prop* skewer ■ W. F. Brown: 'Did he get any sparkle?' George. 'Yes, a couple of kettles, . . . a lovely groin and a prop.' (1931)

slum (1914) North American; applied to cheap or imitation jewellery; compare earlier obsolete sense, nonsense, blarney ■ Kenneth Orvis: Jewellery. . . . Top stuff. No slum. (1962)

Simple Simon (1928) US, dated; rhyming slang for *diamond* ■ Damon Runyon: I do not see any Simple Simon on your lean and linger [= finger].

groin (1931) Dated, mainly criminals' slang; applied to a ring; probably from the curve of an architectural groin ■ James Curtis: There was one [woman] with three groins on her fingers. (1936)

tomfoolery (1931) British; rhyming slang for *jewellery*

tom (1955) British; applied to jewellery; short for *tomfoolery* ■ G. F. Newman: What d'you do with the tom and money you had out of Manor Gardens this afternoon? (1970)

Bags, luggage

peter (1668) Orig criminals' slang, and latterly taxi-drivers' slang; applied to a portmanteau or trunk, or to any bundle or piece of luggage; from the male forename *Peter*, perhaps in allusion to the keys that are the symbols of Saint Peter ■ Anthony Armstrong: 'Peters' are pieces of luggage,—a threepenny extra for the driver. (1930)

pogue (1812) Criminals' slang; applied to a bag or purse, or to a wallet; perhaps related to obsolete *pough* bag; compare *poke* purse, wallet ■ Michael Crichton: It was the stickman's job to take the pogue once Teddy had snaffled it, thus leaving Teddy clean, should . . . a constable stop him. (1975)

poke (1859) North American; applied to a purse or wallet; from earlier sense, bag or small sack, as in *buy a pig in a poke*

keister, **keester**, **keyster (1882)** US; applied to a suitcase or satchel, a handbag, a burglar's tool-case, a salesman's sample-case, etc.; perhaps from German *Kiste* box, chest ■ **H. E. Goldin:** Ditch that keister. It draws heat (attracts police attention). (1950)

To dress (oneself)

tog out (1793), tog up (1894) Usually denoting dressing in smart clothes; usually in the phrase *togged out, togged up*; from *togs* clothes ■ **J. A. Riis:** Mrs. Cleveland when he was Governor, togged out his staff in the most gorgeous clothes. (1904)

get up (1858) Often denoting someone dressed in unusual clothing; usually in the phrase *got up*; from earlier sense, produce ■ *Guardian:* Not everyone will fork out a small fortune to look as if they are got up in someone else's hand-me-downs. (1991)

do up (1882) Often denoting someone dressed in unusual or particularly stylish clothing; usually in the phrase *done up*; from earlier sense, wrap up, tie up ■ **Lauchmonen:** Brother Polo . . . was done up in flowing white cotton gown like the Jordanite sect wear. (1965)

dude up (1899) Orig US; denoting dressing oneself in one's smartest or most impressive clothes; usually in the phrase *duded up*; from *dude* dandy ■ *Guardian:* The two men, shaved and rested and all duded up. (1960)

doll up (1906) Denoting dressing oneself in one's smartest or most impressive clothes; usually in the phrase *dolled up*; from *doll* small human figure as a toy ■ **Nevil Shute:** She could put on her Number Ones and doll herself up smartly. (1955)

toff up (1914) British; denoting dressing oneself like a toff; from *toff* upper-class person ■ *East End Star:* Notice the perfect stillness when the 'lovely lidy all toffed up' sings. (1928)

poon up (1943) Australian; denoting dressing oneself in stylish or flashy clothes; origin unknown ■ **Dal Stevens:** Some of 'em were young lairs, all pooned up to kill. (1951)

gussy up (1952) Denoting dressing oneself in one's smartest clothes; origin uncertain; compare obsolete Australian slang *gussie* effeminate man, from the diminutive form of the female forename *Augusta*, and obsolete British public school slang *gussy* overdressed ■ **M. G. Eberhart:** 'You're really all gussied up. . . . Coast slang for dressed up,' she explained. (1970)

spiv up (1959) British; denoting dressing oneself in stylish or flashy clothes; from *spiv* (flashily dressed) racketeer ■ **B. W. Aldiss:** We spivved ourselves up, put on clean shirts, and strolled out of camp. (1971)

Dressed

dressed up to the nines (1859) Applied to someone dressed up in their smartest clothes; specific use of obsolete *to the nines* to the highest degree, of uncertain origin ■ *Listener:* So there they are, whenever a concert is given by their own orchestra, dressed up to the nines and bursting with pride. (1965)

lairy, lary, leary, leery (1898) Australian; applied to someone flashily or vulgarly dressed; from earlier sense, knowing, conceited ■ **B. Martyn:** He was a stout fleshy chap wearing a dazzling tie and fancy waistcoat. He was popularly described as a 'bit lairy'. (1979)

dressed up (got up, etc.) like a dog's dinner (1934) Applied to someone dressed up smartly or flashily ■ **James Curtis:** The geezer . . . was dolled up like a dog's dinner with a white tie and all. (1936)

mockered up, mokkered up (1938) Australian & New Zealand; applied to someone dressed up in their smartest clothes; from *mocker* clothes ■ **Caddie:** I won't be likely ter be gettin' mokkered up before Saturday, so I'll pop me clobber termorrer ter raise the wind. (1953)

dressed up (got up, etc.) like a pox doctor's clerk (1949) British; applied derisively to someone smartly dressed ■ **E. Lambert:** They was all dressed like they was at Buckingham Palace and Foran was done up like a pox doctor's clerk. (1965)

sprauncy, sprauntsy, sproncy (1957) British; applied to someone smartly or showily dressed; origin uncertain; perhaps related to dialect *sprouncey* cheerful ■ *Guardian:* The 'sprauntsy' (showy) antique dealers. (1969)

To undress

peel (1785) Denoting taking one's clothes off; now usually followed by *off* ■ *Variety:* The gals are peelin' in 23 clubs through Los Angeles County. (1950)

debag (1914) British; denoting removing someone's trousers, especially as a joke; from *de-* + *bag(s* trousers ■ **Beverley Nichols:** A number of us chased Sir Robert down the moonlit High Street in an endeavour to debag him. (1958)

The clothing business

the rag trade (1890) Applied to the business of manufacturing and selling ladies' garments ■ **J. Coates:** I know that line. It's going to be fashionable. . . . Forgive the digression but I'm in the rag trade. (1957)

Cosmetics

slap (1860) Applied originally to theatrical make-up, such as rouge or grease-paint, and hence more generally to any cosmetic make-up, especially applied thickly or carelessly; from the notion of make-up *slapped* on to the face ■ **J. R. Ackerley:** She was all dolled up, her face thick with slap. (1960)

war paint (1869) Jocular ■ *Landfall:* 'In a moment,' Sylvia said, clicking open her purse. 'Just a daub of warpaint.' (1957)

lippy, lippie (1940) Australian; applied to lipstick; from *lip(stick* + -*y* ■ **D. Hewett:** Just a wee dab of lippy, dear. Look at that, a picture no artist could paint. (1976)

Coiffure

hair-do (1932) Orig US; applied to a style or process of arranging a woman's hair

suicide blonde (1942) Jocular; applied to a woman with hair dyed blonde, especially rather inexpertly or garishly ■ Alan Sillitoe: The snow-white hair of a suicide-blonde flashed around: 'Hey up, Margaret!' (1973)

D.A. (1951) Abbreviation of *duck's arse* ■ Monica Dickens: His hair, which was swept back in the popular D.A. hair-cut into a little drake's tail at the back. (1961)

duck's arse, duck-arse, duck's ass, duck's anatomy, duck's behind (1951), duck-tail (1955) Applied to a hair-style with the hair on the back of the head shaped like a duck's tail, favoured by Teddy boys ■ Nik Cohn: He looked like another sub-Elvis, smooth flesh and duck-ass hair. (1969)

flat-top (1956) Applied to a man's short flat haircut; compare earlier sense, aircraft-carrier

fro, 'fro (1970) US; applied to an Afro haircut; abbreviation of *Afro* ■ Washington Post: He . . . goes through countless hairstyles (from Beatles straightened mop top to angry 'fro). (1993)

natty (1974) Denoting hair that is knotty or matted, as in Rastafarian dreadlocks; from the Jamaican pronunciation of *knotty*

big hair (1988) Orig US; applied to long hair teased and lacquered into a large bouffant ■ *Sunday Times*: Big hair, make-up, shiny pink leotards with contrasting tights are out. (1993)

To straighten curly hair

conk, konk (1944) Orig US, Black English; from *congolene*, the name of a chemical application for straightening hair ■ *New Yorker*: He conked his hair to a sleek russet straightness. (1992)

fry (1968) US, Black English

A wig

divot (1934) US, dated; from earlier sense, portion of turf removed

rug (1940) US ■ *Telegraph* (Brisbane): 'Now, in fact, I do wear a hairpiece in the film I'm making.' . . . The film for which he has donned a 'rug' as they are called, is Meteor. (1978)

toup (1959) Abbreviation of *toupee* ■ Peter Bull: 'Say, Padre, is that a toup?' he naïvely enquires. (1959)

syrup of figs, syrup (1981) Rhyming slang

Irish jig, Irish (1983) Rhyming slang

Uniform

See at **Military, Maritime, & Airforce** (p. 124).

3. **Tools, Implements, & Containers**

An axe

Douglas (1905) Australian; mainly in the phrase *swing Douglas*; formerly a proprietary name in the US for axes, hatchets, etc., produced by the Douglas Axe Manufacturing Co., East Douglas, Mass. ■ James Hackston: Sometimes on a Sunday morning exhibitions of axemanship . . . were given; right and wrong way to swing Douglas. (1966)

kelly (1909) Australian; from a proprietary name for a type of axe ■ Stuart Gore: A man'd better be reckoning on a bit of shut-eye, if he's going to be any good on the kelly in the morning. (1968)

A shovel

idiot stick (1942) US

A pickaxe

mad mick (1919) Orig Australian; rhyming slang for *pick* ■ Frank Huelin: Well, I won't buy drinks f'r any bloody ganger, just f'r a chance to swing a mad mick. (1973)

A jemmy, crowbar

stick (1879) Criminals' slang ■ P. Savage: It's a fair cop. I'll go quiet, and here's my stick (jemmy). (1934)

iron (1941) Criminals' slang ■ *John o' London's*: Tools for breaking into other people's premises are *irons*. (1962)

A key

twister (1940) US

A waste-paper basket

wagger, wagger-pagger, wagger-pagger-bagger (1903) Orig Oxford University slang; addition of the arbitrary jocular suffix *-agger* to the initial letters of *waste*(- *paper basket*)

4. **Weapons**

See also under Armaments at **Military, Maritime, & Airforce** (pp. 124 –5).

equalizer (1899) Orig US; applied to a range of weapons, especially revolvers and clubs; from the notion that a powerful weapon reduces all its actual or potential victims to the same level ■ Ian Jefferies: He just thought anybody running about with a nasty look and an equalizer was a foreigner. (1961)

tool (1938) Criminals' slang ■ J. Mandelkau: We grabbed our tools and by then the Mods were at the bottom of the street. (1971)

Guns

Betsy, Bessy, Betsey, and with lower-case initial **(1832)** Orig US; often applied to one's favourite gun, especially in the phrase *old Betsy*; *Betsy* variant of *Betty*, diminutive of *Bet*, abbreviation of *Elizabeth* ■ J. P. Carstairs: 'You've noticed I'm toting a Betsy?' 'Betsy?' 'Equalizer, rod, gat, iron.' (1965)

iron (1836) Applied to a pistol ■ Rolf Boldrewood: Put down your irons . . . or . . . we'll drop ye where ye stand. (1889)

shooter (1840) Applied especially to a revolver ■ G. F. Newman: Why did you pull the shooter on the two detectives? (1970)

smoke-wagon (1891), smoke-stick (1927), smoke-pole (1929) Orig & mainly US ■ *New Zealand Listener*: A long time since he'd fired the old smoke-pole, anyway. (1970)

gat, gatt (1897) Dated, orig US; applied to a revolver or pistol; short for *Gatling* (gun), a type of automatic machine-gun invented by R. J. Gatling (1818–1903) ■ P. G. Wodehouse: He produced the gat . . . and poised it in an unsteady but resolute grasp. 'Hands up!' he said. (1931)

ironmonger (1902) Applied to firearms collectively ■ John Wainwright: Shove it. You are only here for the ride. If you hadn't been so damned handy with the ironmongery—. (1973)

rod (1903) Mainly US ■ James Carroll: I ain't getting my ass blown off because you're stupid. You won't get near Zorelli with a rod anyways. (1978)

roscoe (1914), John Roscoe (1938) US; *roscoe* from the surname *Roscoe* ■ Edwin Newman: 'You'll shoot me if I don't sell?' . . . His hand went to the bulge again. 'Is that what they call a "roscoe"?' (1979) ■ A. S. Neill: The USA . . . , where anyone can carry a gun, or, to be more topical, should I say a Betsy or a John Roscoe? (1973)

hipe (1917) Army slang; applied to a rifle; representing a pronunciation of *arms* in military commands such as 'Slope arms!' ■ Nevil Shute: It was full of muckin' Jerries. All loosing off their hipes at Bert and me. (1942)

heat, heater (1929) Orig US ■ Raymond Chandler: Then he leaned back . . . and held the Colt on his knee. 'Don't kid yourself I won't use this heat, if I have to.' (1939) ■ P. G. Wodehouse: And Dolly, drop the heater and leave that jewel case where it is, I don't want any unpleasantness. (1972)

Saturday night special, Saturday night pistol (1929) Applied to a cheap handgun of the type used by petty criminals

piece (1930) Mainly US; common in standard use from the 16th century ■ Lawrence Sanders: You're a good shot. . . . But you've never carried a piece on a job. (1970)

A machine-gun

woodpecker (1898) US & Australian, military slang; from the tapping sound of its firing

■ *Yank*: The Japs opened up with what sounded like dual-purpose 75s, 20mm pompoms and woodpeckers. (1945)

typewriter (1915) From the sound of its rapid and often irregular firing ■ Philip Evans: Al Capone['s] . . . torpedoes . . . were mean with a Thompson 'type-writer'. (1973)

chopper (1929) US ■ Ian Fleming: There was a mixture of single shots and bursts from the chopper. (1962)

snubby, snubbie (1981) US; applied to a small short-barrelled pistol; from *snub-nosed* designating such a gun + *-y* ■ Elmore Leonard: You want a snubbie. This one, .38 Special, two-inch barrel. (1983)

plinker (1982) Applied to an airgun or other cheap low-calibre firearm; from *plink* make a high-pitched sound + *-er* ■ *Survival Weaponry*: Lightweight back garden 'plinker'. (1985)

The barrel of a gun

spout (1943) Mainly in the phrase *up the spout* (of a bullet or cartridge) loaded and ready for firing ■ Michael Gilbert: I can count six here in the clip. . . . There's probably one up the spout. (1969)

Knives and other cutting weapons

chiv, chive (1673) Criminals' slang; from Romany *chiv* blade ■ *New Monthly Magazine*: The dreadful clasp-knife called a chiv is exposed and used if necessary. (1834)

toad-sticker (1858), toad-stabber (1885) Mainly US; applied to a large knife ■ J. S. Pennell: I must have picked up this old toadsticker. (1944)

pig-sticker (1890) Applied to a bayonet, knife, or other sharp weapon ■ A. Melville-Ross: Trelawney crossed to the far wall, yanked the knife from it. . . . 'You'll hand over that pig-sticker and come home with uncle.' (1978)

winkle-pin (1924) Military slang; applied to a bayonet

Clubs

sap (1899) US; applied to a club or short staff; from earlier sense, sapwood, soft wood between the heart and the bark ■ Raymond Chandler: He had the sap out this time, a nice little tool about five inches long, covered with woven brown leather. (1940)

nigger-stick (1971) US, offensive; applied to a baton carried by policemen, prison warders, etc. ■ *Black Panther*: They were attacked and brutally beaten by 50 to 60 guards armed with tear gas, plexiglass shields and four-foot long 'nigger sticks'. (1973)

Stones

Irish confetti (1935) Applied to stones, bricks, etc. used as weapons ■ *Observer*: An American friend in Amsterdam, describing last week's riots there, said: 'There's just a lot of Irish confetti around.' (1966)

Other weapons

nigger shooter (1876) US, dated, now offensive; applied to a catapult

moley (1950) British; applied to a gangland weapon consisting of a potato with razor-blades inserted into it; origin unknown ∎ *Spectator*: I suppose if I go on criticising him I shall end up by having the boys with the moleys call on me one dark night. (1959)

To arm oneself

rod up (1929) US; used to denote arming oneself with a gun; from the noun *rod* gun ∎ *Harper's Magazine*: They do not rod up, or arm themselves. (1950)

tool up (1959) From the noun *tool* weapon ∎ J. Mandelkau: We tooled up with pieces of wood and iron bars and hiked over towards their main camp. (1971)

To be armed with (a weapon)

pack (1902) From earlier sense, carry with one ∎ Raymond Chandler: Don't you pack no rod? (1940)

Armed

heeled (1866) Orig US; from the obsolete US slang verb *heel* provide, arm ∎ Ed McBain: 'Were you heeled when they pulled you in?' . . . 'We didn't even have a water pistol between us.' (1956)

tooled up (1959) ∎ J. Barnett: Smith brandished the shotgun . . . to let the minder know he was tooled up. (1982)

5. Explosives

soup (1902) Orig US; applied to nitroglycerine or gelignite, especially as used for safe-breaking ∎ Dorothy Sayers: Sam put the soup in at the 'inges and blowed the 'ole front clean off. (1930)

puff (1904) Orig US, dated; applied to gunpowder or other explosives used for safe-breaking

pete (1931) Applied to nitroglycerine as used for safe-breaking; from earlier sense, a safe

nitro (1935) Abbreviation of *nitroglycerine* ∎ J. Godey: They had an old-time safe. . . . I hit it with a fat charge of nitro. (1972)

jelly, gelly (1941) Used to denote gelignite; shortening of the pronunciation of *gelignite*, influenced by the substance's jelly-like appearance ∎ *Guardian*: Stolen 'gelly' found. (1971)

6. Dirt & Cleanliness

Dirt; dirty material; filth

toe-jam (1934) Applied to dirt that accumulates between the toes ∎ *Black World*: If you miss nose Picking time Then you collect Three and one half milograms Of toejam And give it to barbara's cat. (1973)

gunk (1938) Orig US; applied especially to unpleasant sticky or viscous matter; from the proprietary name of a detergent, registered in 1932 ∎ C. Henry: Too much eye gunk and lipstick—that sort of girl. (1966)

crud (1948) Orig US; recorded once in this sense in Scottish English at the beginning of the 16th century, as a variant of Middle English *curd(e* coagulated material, curd, but in modern use apparently a back-formation from *cruddy* dirty

yuck, yuk (1966) Applied to messy or disgusting material; from the interjection *yuck* indicating distaste ∎ *New Statesman*: Rotting wodges of chilly yuck which once were apples and pears. (1966)

grunge (1968) From earlier sense, someone or something unpleasant ∎ *American Speech*: There's grunge in the bottom of my Dr. Pepper bottle! (1977)

schmutz, shmutz (1968) Mainly US; from Yiddish or German *schmutz* ∎ *Last Whole Earth Catalog*: It delights them to watch us rummaging around in the schmutz. (1972)

gunge (1969) British; applied especially to unpleasant sticky or viscous matter; back-formation from *gungy* sticky, messy ∎ *Listener*:

Adam and Eve emerge from a transportable saucer of murky gunge. (1985)

ook (1969) Applied mainly to slimy or viscous material; apparently a back-formation from *ooky* slimy ∎ Disch & Sladek: She had been . . . glad . . . to be here, to be anywhere so long as it marked an end, so long as she could . . . take a shower to wash off all this brown ook. (1969)

grot (1971) British; back-formation from *grotty* unpleasant ∎ John Wain: This place, the tawdriness, the awful mound of grot it all is, stands between me and feeling anything. (1982)

scunge (1975) Probably a blend of *scum* and *grunge*, but compare *scrungy* dirty ∎ John Wain: God, the scunge of this place. (1982)

Dirtiness

raunch (1967) Orig US; back-formation from *raunchy* dirty ∎ *Time*: Calvin Coolidge High is an actual Manhattan school building, its rust and raunch unretouched for the camera. (1967)

(Disgustingly) dirty, filthy

cruddy (1877) Variant of *curdy* curdlike, apparently of Irish English origin

shitty (1935) Denoting something dirty with excrement ∎ Colleen McCullough: If I catch you flaming little twerps touching that doll again I'll brand your shitty little arses! (1977)

scroungy (1949) Orig & mainly US; from *scrounge* sponge, cadge + *-y* ■ Ed McBain: I'll continue commuting to a scroungy squadroom in perhaps the world's worst neighborhood. (1959)

gungy, gungey (1962) British; applied to something sticky or messy; origin uncertain ■ *Spectator*: If you're in the mood for something gungey, there's certainly something here for you: chicken stuffed with lamb served with a port sauce. (1985)

ooky (1964) Applied to something slimy or viscous; origin unknown ■ Disch & Sladek: The milk was so warm and ooky it was like yogurt. (1969)

grungy (1965) Orig & mainly US; apparently an arbitrary formation, after *grubby, dingy*, etc. ■ *Dirt Bike*: I would like to know who made those blasted white pants so popular—mine are splattered with oil specks and other grungy stains. (1985)

raunchy (1965) Orig US; from earlier sense, incompetent, sloppy ■ *Daily Colonist* (Victoria, British Columbia): I'll bet . . . the girls would boycott guys with dirty, tangled hair, filthy jeans, raunchy sweat shirts and bare feet. (1971)

scuzzy (1969) Orig & mainly North American; perhaps an alteration of *disgusting* ■ *Road & Track*: Let's change the color from the current scuzzy metallic brown to white. (1990)

manky, mankey (1971) British; from earlier sense, inferior, defective ■ *Radio Times*: 'I'm going to have to change my wig, this one's much too manky,' he announces after an extensive session of tonsure teasing. Danny is having a bad hair day. (1996)

scrungy (1974) Mainly US; applied to something or someone grimy or shabby; probably related to *scroungy* shabby, dirty; compare *grungy* dirty ■ *Rolling Stone*: As the scrungy taxi passenger, he has driver De Niro stop the cab and look at his wife's lurid silhouette up against a window. (1977)

yucky, yukky (1975) Applied to something messy or gooey; from earlier sense, unpleasant ■ J. Wilson: Let's get these yucky things off and get you washed. (1977)

Untidy; untidily

topsy-turvy (1528) Denoting a disordered condition; from earlier sense, upside down; ultimately probably from *top* + obsolete *tervy* overturn (probably from unattested Old English *tierfan* roll) ■ *Wall Street Journal*: The topsy-turvy, ever-changing plot makes 'Nightshade' an interesting interplanetary romp. (1989)

higgledy-piggledy (1598) Rhyming jingle probably based on *pig*, with reference to pigs herding together ■ *Economist*: It was thrown together higgledy-piggledy with no overall unity or sense of identity. (1988)

ratty (1856) US; applied to something untidy and in poor condition ■ R. M. Pirsig: John always kept his BMW spic and span. It really did look nice, while mine's always a little ratty, it seems. (1974)

tacky (1862) Orig US; applied to something dowdy or shabby; origin uncertain ■ Hart & Kaufman: An extremely tacky-looking evening wrap. (1937)

any old how (1933) ■ Frank Sargeson: He was all dressed up in his Sunday best . . . but his hair was any old how. (1949)

tatty (1933) Applied to something untidy and in poor condition; from *tat* rag, junk + *-y* ■ *Times*: Nineteenth-century-style songs, played by a jaunty orchestra before tatty red-plush curtains and even tattier scenery, accompany the high jinks. (1963)

slobby (1961) From *slob* slovenly person + *-y* ■ William Burroughs: Vicki told me that I looked like a slobby bum. (1970)

To make dirty

gunge (1976) British; denoting clogging with dirty viscous material; usually followed by *up*; from the noun *gunge* viscous material ■ *Sounds*: A few academic 'experts' know something about the short-term effects of sniffing, but aren't too sure about exactly how it gunges up the body. (1977)

A dirty or untidy place

pigsty (1820) From earlier sense, enclosure for pigs ■ *Woman*: 'The place is usually a pigsty,' confesses Nick. 'I definitely don't do my share of the jobs but then neither does Rachel—we wait until one of our mums come round.' (1992)

tip (1983) Applied especially to a room; from earlier sense, place where waste is tipped for disposal ■ P. Barker: She was anything but pleased: the living-room was a tip (1984)

A dirty, slovenly, or untidy person

slob (1861) Often also implying fatness; from earlier (mainly Irish) sense, mud, muddy land ■ Ed McBain: There are people . . . who always look like slobs. . . . The tendency toward sloppiness first exhibits itself when the subject is still a child. (1960)

rag-bag (1888) Applied to a sloppily-dressed person, especially a woman; from earlier sense, motley collection

slump (1906) Applied to a fat slovenly person; from earlier sense, sudden decline ■ Jeffrey Ashford: D'you reckon we'd waste good bees and honey on a slump like you for nothing? (1960)

litter lout (1927) British; applied to someone who scatters litter antisocially ■ *Guardian*: The packaging industry had been made a scapegoat for the actions of the litter lout. (1972)

something the cat (has) brought in (1928) Applied to someone bedraggled

warb, waub, worb (1933) Australian; applied to a disreputable or slovenly person; probably from *warble* maggot of a warble-fly ■ Kylie Tennant: But it's a no-hoper's jail—a lot of old warbs and kids mixed up with coves like Amos the Cannibal and chaps that razors bounce off. (1967)

tat, tatt (1936) Applied to a shabby person; from earlier sense, rag; ultimate origin uncertain
■ Ngaio Marsh: Do they think it's any catch living in a mausoleum with a couple of old tats? (1947)

litterbug (1947) Orig and mainly US; applied to someone who scatters litter antisocially
■ *Guardian*: He picks up any litter he can find . . . and he is apt to give litter-bugs a severe dressing-down. (1971)

scruffo (1959) Applied to an untidy person; from *scruffy* + *-o* ■ Colin MacInnes: One of the scruffos turned and looked at his choice companions. (1959)

scruff (1960) Applied to an untidy person; partly from earlier collective sense, untidy people, partly a new back-formation from *scruffy* ■ *Daily Mail*: Dome-headed lollipop-lover Theo is promoted to inspector and so minus the scruffs he calls colleagues. (1993)

Clean

squeaky clean (1976) Applied to something washed and rinsed so clean as to squeak ■ Len

Deighton: His . . . long dark hair was wavy and squeaky clean. (1981)

To clean

do out (1728) Applied to cleaning a room
■ Joanna Cannan: 'E's not arriving till . . . this afternoon but I did the room out yesterday. (1955)

sand and canvas (1912) Dated, orig naval slang; applied to cleaning something thoroughly ■ P. A. Eaddy: The Mate was anxious to get on with the 'sand and canvasing' of the bright work. (1933)

bogy, bogey (1960) Australian; applied to taking a bath; from earlier sense, swim ■ *Smoke Signal* (Palm Island): 'Bogey' with plenty of soap and water every day. (1974)

A neat person

neatnik (1959) Mainly US; originally used in contrasting neat people with beatniks; from *neat* + *-nik* as in *beatnik* ■ *Sears Catalog*: A new look in Rally-back Jeans that can be worn by Neatniks of any age. (1969)

Money, Commerce, and Employment

1. **Money**

Money

gelt (*a*1529) From German, Dutch *geld* money; in early use often with reference to the pay of a (German) army; in more general use from the 19th century, reinforced by Yiddish *gelt* money ■ **Charles Drummond**: 'The gelt?' said Reed. . . . 'Four thousand dollars,' said Miss Pocket. (1968)

brass (1597) In early use, applied specifically to bronze or copper coins ■ **B. T. Bradford**: She was obviously a relation of the Bells who were local gentry, posh folk with pots and pots of brass. (1986)

dust (1607) Now mainly US, Black English

ready, reddy (1688) Applied to cash; short for *ready money* ■ **Robin Cook**: Not enough reddy in it in my case. (1962)

rhino (1688) Dated; origin unknown ■ **Henry Mayhew**: You shall have it cheap, for me and my mate are both short of rhino. (1851)

shiners (1760) Dated; applied to money in coin, especially sovereigns or guineas; from the shininess of the coins ■ **Charles Dickens**: Is it worth fifty shiners extra, if it's safely done from the outside? (1838)

the stuff (1775) Dated ■ **P. G. Wodehouse**: I presumed Uncle Tom would brass up if given the green light, he having the stuff in heaping sackfuls. (1971)

iron (1785) ■ **C. Rougvie**: He was earning a bit of iron. (1966)

dibs (1807) Dated; probably from *dibs*, *dib-stones* pebbles for a game

rag (1817) Applied to paper money, and also to an individual note or bill ■ **D. W. Maurer**: That working stiff had over two C's in rag on him. (1955)

hoot, hootoo, hout, hutu (1820) New Zealand; applied especially to money paid in recompense; from Maori *utu* recompense ■ **Kenneth Giles**: I got the idea of starting a chain of those places . . . for blokes without much hoot and wanting a clean bed. (1967)

tin (1836) ■ **Vladimir Nabokov**: He could always let me have as much cash as I might require—I think he used the word 'tin', though I am not sure. (1941)

rivets (1846) Dated; from the appearance of coins ■ **James Curtis**: 'So you got a bit of rivets to speculate?' 'I ain't said so. All I said as I could put up a bit.' (1937)

dough (1851) Orig US ■ **Times**: I'm going back to business and make myself a little dough. (1955)

dosh (1854) Orig US; in recent British use a revival; origin unknown ■ **Michael Kenyon**: 'America! The money's in America!' . . . ''Tis true. The Yankees have the dosh all right.' (1970)

dinero (1856) Orig US; from Spanish *dinero* penny, coin, money ■ **Colin MacInnes**: You need a bit dinero? Five pounds do? (1959)

spondulicks, -ics, -ix, spondoolicks, -iks, -ix (1857) Orig US; a fanciful coinage ■ *Private Eye*: No one seemed very anxious to come up with the spondulicks. (1980)

soap (1860) US; latterly applied especially to money used in bribery ■ *Nation*: This, combined with more or less 'soap', was undoubtedly instrumental in causing his defeat. (1892)

dingbats (1861) US, dated; also used in the singular to denote a coin; origin uncertain; perhaps from *ding* knock + *bat* club; compare *dingus* thingummy

sugar (1862) Dated ■ *Punch*: Political Picnics mean sugar to them as is fly to wot's wot. (1884)

scales, scale (1872) US, dated ■ *American Speech*: The waitress received much scale at the hotel. (1929)

shekels (1883) Often in the phrase *rake in the shekels* make money rapidly; from plural of *shekel* ancient Hebrew coin, from Hebrew *sheqel* ■ **Laurence Olivier**: We extended for another four weeks— not so much to rake in the shekels as because I couldn't bear to say farewell to the part I loved doing so much. (1982)

boodle (1884) Orig US; often applied specifically to money illegally acquired; from earlier sense, booty, loot; ultimately from Dutch *boedel* estate, property ■ **James Joyce**: Ready to decamp with whatever boodle they could. (1922)

oof (1885), **ooftish** (1882) Dated; from Yiddish *ooftisch*, from German *auf dem Tische* on the table (of gambling debts) ■ **Rider Haggard**: Living like a fighting-cock and rolling in 'oof'. (1888)

jack (1890) Orig US ■ **Allan Prior**: I asked him . . . to think of the new suits he could get . . . when the jack came in. (1960)

bees and honey (1892) British; rhyming slang ■ **Jeffrey Ashford**: D'you reckon we'd waste good bees and honey on a slump like you for nothing? (1960)

bottle (1893) British ■ **J. B. Priestley**: Knocker brought out some money. . . . 'Not much bottle. A nicker, half a bar.' (1939)

splosh (1893) From earlier sense, splashing sound ■ P. G. Wodehouse: The jolliness of having all that splosh in the old sock. (1950)

long green (1896) US; from the shape and colour of dollar bills ■ S. Newton: We'll be there tomorrow afternoon with Napoleon and the long green. (1946)

stiff (1897) Dated ■ Hilaire Belloc: He wrang his hands, exclaiming, 'If I only had a bit of Stiff How different would be my life!' (1930)

green (1898) Orig US; from the colour of dollar bills ■ Robert Crawford: When finally we did lay our mitts on a nice pile of green, Arthur simply knuckled under to luxury. (1971)

gonce, gons (1899) Australian, dated; origin uncertain; possibly from German *Ganze* whole, entirety ■ J. S. Litchfield: Old dad can't spare any time for frills; but he's got the gonce all right. He's worth more than most of the first-class travellers on this boat. (1930)

cabbage (1903) Mainly North American; often applied specifically to paper money; from the notion of being green and crisp, like a dollar bill ■ *Observer*: The white, crinkle, cabbage, poppy, lolly, in other words cash. (1960)

oil (1903) US; applied especially to money used for bribery and corruption ■ *Detective Fiction Weekly*: She didn't take care of her protection directly, that is, she didn't slip the oil to the cops herself. (1935)

greens (1904) Orig US; compare *green* ■ *Scottish Daily Mail*: What had been 'dough' in the 20's and became 'readies' and 'greens' in the 50's turned up again as 'bread'. (1968)

mazuma, mazume (1904) US; Yiddish ■ *Times Literary Supplement*: Likewise piling up its mazuma by legerdemain. (1972)

jingle (1906) Australian, dated; applied to money in small coins; from the sound of coins jingling ■ *Bulletin* (Sydney): If he is a youngish man, his pockets are lined with coin, oof, dough, sugar or hay. If he is getting on in years his pockets will hold jingle. (1958)

doubloons (1908) Jocular; from *doubloon* Spanish gold coin ■ Peter Bull: I . . . was anxious to lay my hands on anything that brought in the doubloons. (1959)

kale (1912) North American, dated; from the crinkly green leaves' resemblance to dollar bills ■ *Flynn's*: The kale is cut up an th' biggest corner goes to th' brains. (1926)

scratch (1914) Orig US; compare the verb *scratch* forge banknotes ■ *Private Eye*: This state-funded legal nonsense—which is . . . putting even more scratch into the bulging wallets of the lawyers. (1980)

oscar, Oscar (1917), **Oscar Asche** (1905) Australian & New Zealand; rhyming slang for *cash*, from the name of the Australian actor Oscar Asche (1871–1936) ■ D'Arcy Niland: If you'd been fighting all those blokes in the ring you'd have more oscar in your kick now than the Prime Minister himself. (1959)

snow (1925) Applied especially to money in silver coins ■ James Curtis: Count up that snow while I go through the other drawers. (1936)

poke (1926) From earlier sense, purse, wallet ■ *Evening News* (Edinburgh): Colgan asked him: 'Have you got your poke?' obviously referring to the money. (1974)

lettuce (1929) Orig US; from the crinkliness and greenish-white colour of dollar bills ■ John Wainwright: 'They spend money, in Beirut. . . .' 'Phoenicia Street,' murmured Gantley. 'Anything. . . . Any out-of-this-world luxury. Any service. Anything! You have the lettuce. . . . Phoenicia Street can oblige.' (1974)

dropsy (1930) Often applied specifically to money paid as a tip or bribe; jocular extension of *dropsy* excess of fluids in body tissue, from the notion of 'dropping' money into someone's hand ■ Peter Wildeblood: A nice bit of dropsy to a copper usually does the trick. (1955)

potatoes (1931) US ■ *National Observer* (US): Usually he [*sc.* a horse] runs with a price tag of about $3,500. With those kind of potatoes, it can be hard to get respect. (1976)

bread (1935) Orig US; inspired by *dough* money ■ *Down Beat*: If I had bread (Dizzy's basic synonym for loot) I'd certainly start a big band again. (1952)

readies, reddies (1937) Usually applied to bank notes; from *ready* cash ■ Dick Francis: He sort of winks at me and gives me a thousand quid in readies. (1974)

funny money (1938) Orig US; applied to money which is not what it seems to be, especially counterfeit currency or assets amassed unscrupulously ■ T. Barling: Sadler's got a name for asset-stripping. . . . It's been whispered Tommy Troy's pulled himself a funny-money man. (1976)

ackers, akkas, akkers (1939) British, services' slang; sometimes singular; from *acker* (Egyptian) piastre; ultimately probably from Arabic *fakka* small change, coins; apparently first used among British and Allied troops in Egypt ■ H. R. F. Keating: I can't offer a great deal in the way of ackers. Though you'd get your ten per cent, old man. (1965)

moola, moolah (1939) Orig US; origin unknown ■ Julian Symons: Then the only thing to be settled is the lolly, the moolah. (1975)

lolly (1943) British; from earlier sense, lollipop, apparently with reference to the notion of the Government giving away money 'like lollipops' ■ Gwen Moffat: There's only one person bringing in the lolly in that house. (1973)

loot (1943) From earlier sense, booty; ultimately from Hindi *lūṭ* spoils, plunder ■ Jimmy Sangster: When you've got his sort of loot I don't suppose it matters. (1968)

poppy (1943) ■ *Autocar*: A good many British families which run their own cars must spend at least 13 per cent of the family poppy on that. (1963)

moo (1945) Abbreviation of *moola* ■ Dennis Bloodworth: Most of my nurses . . . don't work for moo. . . . But local stuff I pay. (1975)

white (1960) From earlier slang sense, silver coin ■ *Observer*: The white, crinkle, cabbage, poppy, lolly, in other words cash. (1960)

wonga (1982) British; origin unknown
■ *Observer*: The Leader of Her Majesty's Opposition has shown he isn't averse to spunking off a lot of wonga on pretentious public dining himself. (1996)

Monetary resources

slush fund (1874) Orig US; applied to a reserve fund used especially for political bribery; from earlier naval slang sense, money collected from the sale of *slush* (fat or grease obtained from boiling meat) and used to buy luxuries for the crew ■ *Guardian*: Eisenhower's running mate was accused of being the beneficiary of a 'slush fund' subscribed by wealthy backers. (1962)

pork (1879) US; applied to federal funds obtained through political influence ■ *Marshfield* (Wisconsin) *News-Herald*: That difference of more than $54,000,000 includes a lot of pork for individual senators. (1949)

fall money (1893) Dated; applied to money put aside by a criminal for use if he should be arrested; from *fall* be arrested ■ C. G. Gordon: We had often discussed the matter of 'fall money'. (1929)

kitty (1903) From earlier sense, sum contributed by players in a game and taken by the winner ■ *Listener*: In 1949, the authorities at the hall had enough money in the kitty to install a new aluminium roof. (1969)

pork barrel (1909) Orig and mainly US; applied to the state's funds available for regional expenditure, especially as disbursed subject to political influence; from earlier sense, barrel in which pork is preserved, viewed as a source of one's livelihood ■ *Economist*: It [*sc.* the Macmillan government] has treated some nationalised industries almost as if they were its positive enemies, while a quite considerable pork-barrel has been opened up for a growing number of private firms. (1960)

mad money (1922) Applied to money for use in an emergency, especially money taken by a woman on a date in case her escort abandons her and she has to make her own way home ■ Dell Shannon: I haven't even a dime of mad money with me, hope I don't need it. (1970)

A coin; coins

copper (1788) Applied to a coin (originally) made of copper, such as a penny or US cent ■ *Daily Telegraph*: J Sainsbury shares showed no sign of slackening and the price ended another 4 better at 375p, only a few coppers below the high. (1991)

smash (1821) Applied to loose change ■ Kylie Tennant: Giving her his smash on pay-night so's she can blow it. (1953)

mick (1918) Australian; applied to the reverse side or tail of a coin; origin unknown ■ T. A. G. Hungerford: 'Ten bob he tails 'em!' he intoned, . . . 'I got ten bob to say he tails 'em—ten bob the micks!' (1953)

clod (1925) British; applied to a copper coin; usually used in the plural; from earlier sense, lump ■ Anthony Burgess: He began to search for coppers. 'Lend us a couple of clods,' he said to his twin. (1960)

tiddler (1966) British; applied to a small coin, such as a silver threepenny piece or a 1/2p coin; from earlier sense, something small ■ *Daily Mail*: They will scrap the 1/2p coin—the 'tiddler'—when they change to decimals. (1971)

An amount of money

roll (1846) US & Australian; applied to a collection of bills or notes rolled together, and hence more generally to one's money ■ Jack Black: No Missouri dip would take his roll, extract two fifty-dollar bills, and put the rest back in his pocket. (1926)

wedge (1977) British, orig criminals' slang; applied to a wad of banknotes, and hence more generally to (a significant amount of) money; from the notion of a thick pile of banknotes; compare *wodge* and obsolete slang *wedge* silver plate, silver money ■ *Melody Maker*: Don't part with your hard earned wedge until you've seen it. (1987)

top (or full) whack (1978) British; applied to a very high (especially the highest) price or rate ■ *Money Observer*: Payments then rise by 5.0 per cent a year, so you pay the full whack after eight or nine years. (1989)

A particular multiple of monetary units

pony (1797) Applied to £25; perhaps because (like a pony to a horse) it is small compared to £50, etc. ■ Jimmy O'Connor: 'Bet you the next three guys that come by do that,' he said. 'Make it a pony (£25),' said Charlie. (1976)

monkey (1832) Applied to £500 or $500; origin unknown ■ *Times*: It looks like you are going to be roped into that theft from the pub but it will be all right. It will cost you a monkey (£500). (1973)

rouf, roaf, rofe, roof (1851) Applied to four shillings or four pounds; backslang for *four* ■ Kenneth Royce: From under a pottery sugar jar . . . protruded two jacks. . . . I found a roof under them. (1972)

century (1859) US; applied to $100 or £100 ■ Raymond Chandler: He . . . arranged five century notes like a tight poker hand. (1964)

thou (1869) Applied to £1000 or $1000; from earlier more general sense, thousand ■ *New Yorker*: The gesture cost me a cool ten thou, but I didn't begrudge it. (1965)

grand (1915) Orig US; applied to $1000 or £1000 ■ *Sunday Telegraph*: One 26-year-old [criminal] . . . insisted that he picked up a regular £1,000 a week working with a professional gang. 'Honest, a grand or a couple of grand isn't really big stakes in my game.' (1967)

yard (1926) US; applied to $100 or $1000 ■ V. Patrick: You throw a hundred to the guy who makes the loan. . . . He writes the loan for thirteen hundred, you take twelve, and a yard goes south to him. (1979)

G (1928) US; applied to $1000; abbreviation of *grand* ■ A. Curry: He'd probably drop me a few G's for the names of the guys in London. (1971)

score (1929) Applied to $20 or £20 ■ Kyril Bonfiglioli: You'll have to give me a score to buy an old throwaway shooter. (1979)

half (1931) British, dated; applied to the sum of ten shillings (50p); from ten shillings being half of one pound sterling ■ Graham Greene: She's just a buer [= (loose) woman]—he gave her a half. (1938)

gee (1936) US; applied to $1000; from the pronunciation of the initial letter of *grand* ■ M. Taylor: There's a hundred gees at stake. (1946)

ton (1946) Applied to £100; from earlier more general sense, hundred ■ P. Turnbull: The old man would charge three ton for this but me and the boys will do it for half-price. (1981)

K, k (1968) Applied to £1000 or $1000; used especially with reference to salaries offered in job advertisements; from its use in computing to represent 1000; originally from its use as an abbreviation of *kilo-* ■ Guardian: Who should become unit manager of Guy's itself, at 50K plus expenses? (1991)

A large amount of money

a mint (1655) From earlier sense, an amount of money coined ■ C. H. Spurgeon: Our John Knox would be worth a mint at this hour, but where is he? (1874)

a pot (1856), **pots** (1871) ■ Ouida: You'll make a pot by it, as Barnum did. (1897) ■ *Sports Quarterly*: Some old women with pots of money are up to all the tricks and keep tabs on everything themselves. (1992)

a small fortune (1874) ■ D. Mayo: It's one of the least known islands in the group, and Doreen pays a small fortune to keep it that way. (1962)

big money (1880) Orig US ■ Ring Lardner: It'll be pretty soft for you, because they got the pennant cinched and they'll cut you in on the big money. (1924) ■ Jack Dempsey: My five big-money bouts. (1950)

shirt (1892) In the phrases *bet one's shirt, put one's shirt on* bet all one's money on (especially a horse in a race), *lose one's shirt* lose all one's possessions, especially by gambling or speculation ■ E. B. Mann: He hit the market . . . about the time the bottom dropped out of it. He lost his shirt! (1935)

a bundle (1903) Orig US; from earlier sense, roll of banknotes ■ Guardian: This is not the world's fastest dish, since it requires home-made stock. Nor is it the cheapest, since porcini cost a bundle. (1992)

a poultice (1904) Australian; applied especially to money used as a bribe ■ Nino Culotta: 'Reckon 'e pulled 'im?' 'That's wot I reckon.' . . . 'Yer can't prove ut.' 'Somebody slung in a poultice, I bet.' 'They're all crooked.' (1957) ■ *Sun-Herald*: A bloke who made a poultice in recent weeks when he sold Rupert a quarter of a million Channel Ten shares. (1979)

a packet (1922) ■ P. G. Wodehouse: 'Get in on the short end,' said Aurelia earnestly, 'and you'll make a packet.' (1928)

heavy sugar (1926) US, dated ■ Flynn's: Johns with heavy sugar. (1928)

a motser, a motsa, a motza, a motzer (1943) Australian; often applied specifically to a large amount won in gambling; probably from Yiddish *matse* bread ■ Bulletin (Sydney): Canberra might have cost a motza but it's worth every cent. (1985)

a roll Jack Rice couldn't jump over (1945) Australian

megabucks (1946) Orig US; originally as *megabuck* a million dollars ■ *Cosmopolitan*: Having earned megabucks as Ian Fleming in *Goldeneye*, Charles Dance can afford to help a debt-laden theatre company once in a while. (1989)

a bomb (1958) British ■ A. E. Lindop: Can I have that instead of the five pounds? I might flog it for a bomb in me old age. (1969)

big bucks (1970) Orig US ■ Forbes: They could afford big bucks for advertising and theater rentals and still come out way ahead. (1975)

Large in amount

cool (1728) Used to emphasize the largeness of the amount; perhaps from an original sense, deliberately or calmly counted, reckoned, or told, and hence, all told, entire, whole ■ *Daily Mail*: The deal he negotiated means that the trio are likely to pool a cool $100 million . . . between them. (1991)

A small amount of money

shoestring (1904) Orig US; mainly in the phrase *on a shoestring* at very small expense ■ Colleen McCullough: Australians in England, youth-hosteling on a shoestring. (1977)

peanuts (1936) Orig US; applied especially to inadequate payment; from earlier sense, something small or trivial ■ Scotsman: A salary of £3000 a year is peanuts for a man at the top of his profession. (1973)

chicken-feed (1937) Orig US; from earlier sense, poultry food ■ New Review: In peacetime, officers in the British Army were men of independent means to whom their Army pay was chicken-feed. (1941)

British and other sterling-based currency

Unless another variety of English is specified, the terms in this section are British and refer to British currency.

quid (1688) Applied to a pound; probably from *quid* the nature of something, from Latin *quid* what ■ W. P. Ridge: Milton received only ten quid for the first edition of 'Paradise Lost'. (1929)

kick (*c*1700) Dated; applied to a sixpence; mainly used to denote sixpence as an element in a sum of money (e.g. *two and a kick* two shillings and sixpence); rhyming slang for *six*

mag, meg (1781) Dated; applied to a halfpenny; origin unknown ■ Charles Dickens: It can't be worth a mag to him. (1852)

bob (1789) Applied to a shilling, and latterly used in non-specific references to amounts of money; origin unknown; compare Old French *bobe* coin of low value ■ Guardian: Shergar . . . is alive and well . . . according to the latest person trying to extract a few bob from Lloyds underwriters. (1991)

tizzy, tizzey, tissey (1804) Dated; applied to a sixpenny piece; origin unknown ■ Longman's

Magazine: A man reads, at a 'tizzy', what he had not read when priced at twelve times the humble tanner. (1901)

tanner (1811) Dated; applied to sixpence or a sixpenny piece; origin uncertain; suggested sources include Romany *tawno* young (hence, small) and Latin *tener* young ■ *Bowlers' World*: We'd gone round at nine for a tanner, and as it was Friday night and we were developing a thirst, we decided to play the 'penny end' then call it a do. (1992)

brown (1812) Applied to a penny; long obsolete in British English, but used in Australian until the mid 20th century; from its colour ■ *Sun* (Sydney): Everybody's jumping abut like a double-headed brown had been found at a swy game. (1946)

sov (1829) Applied to a pound; abbreviation of *sovereign* pound ■ T. Barling: There's more to life than bashing pimps and publicans for a handful of sovs. (1988)

deaner, deener, dener, diener (1839) Dated, mainly Australian & New Zealand; applied to a shilling; probably an alteration of *denier* former small French coin, hence small amount of money ■ Frank Sargeson: Could you give me the lend of a bob? . . . I'm on the beach myself, I said, but I can make it a deener. (1946)

finnip, fin(n), finny, fin(n)if(f), finnup, finuf (1839) Applied to a five-pound note; said to represent a Yiddish pronunciation of German *fünf* five ■ Rex Stout: I . . . got out my wallet and extracted a finif. (1966)

fiver (1843) Applied to five pounds or a five-pound note; from *five* + *-er* ■ *Daily Telegraph*: In St Tropez they have ways of taking your money, if not your life: a coke may cost you a fiver and a gin and tonic twice that. (1991)

tenner (1845) Applied to ten pounds or a ten-pound note; from *ten* + *-er* ■ *Independent*: I once went to a tattooist. He said 'Yeah. I'll take em off, only a tenner.' I thought, oo-er, I'll have some of that. (1991)

dollar (1848) Dated, orig British; applied to five shillings; mainly in the phrase *half a dollar* two shillings and sixpence; probably from the former exchange rate of five shillings to one US dollar, but there may be some connection with the use in Britain of Spanish dollar notes overstamped four shillings and nine pence in 1804 ■ Allan Prior: 'You can give me three blacks for a tush,' he said. 'Two blacks for a half a dollar,' was Mr. Thistlethwaite's reply. (1964)

thick 'un, thick one (1848) Dated; applied to a gold sovereign, and also to a crown or five-shilling piece ■ Sapper: Done with you, your Graces; a thick 'un it is. (1926)

rogue and villain (1859) Dated; rhyming slang for *shilling*

tosheroon, tusheroon (1859) Dated; applied to a half-crown; origin unknown ■ *Daily Mirror*: All sorts of things, places and creatures we believed were everlasting have vanished, like trams, tosheroons and Constantinople. (1978)

caser (1860) Dated; applied to a crown (a five-shilling coin); from Yiddish *keser* name of various coins issued in German-speaking states, from earlier application to one of two ornamental crowns placed on a Scroll of the Law, from Hebrew *keter-tora* crown of the Pentateuch ■ J. B. Priestley: Knocker brought some money and examined it. . . . 'A nicker, half a bar, a caser an' a hole.' (1939)

thrum (1865) Dated; applied to a threepenny piece; back-formation from *thrums* threepence, representing a casual pronunciation of *threepence* ■ *Bulletin* (Sydney): I haven't encountered a crook thrum yet. (1933)

flim (1870) Dated; applied to a five-pound note; short for obsolete slang *flimsy* banknote, from the thin paper formerly used for such notes ■ Nicholas Blake: They . . . offer Bert . . . a flim for his boat. (1954)

Jimmy O'Goblin, jimmy o'goblin, jimmy, Jemmy O'Goblin (1889) Applied to a pound; rhyming slang for *sovereign* ■ A. E. W. Mason: I want one thousand jimmies per annum. (1899) ■ *Times*: He . . . had made a profit of some six million jimmy-o-goblins. (1973)

jim (1889) Australian, dated; applied to a pound; short for *Jimmy O'Goblin* ■ A. E. Yarra: The racehorse they have just bought in Bourke for fifty jim. (1930)

oner (1889) Applied to one pound, and also to one hundred pounds; compare earlier sense, something or someone unique or remarkable ■ Parker & Allerton: A one-er for the Guv'nor, and fifty each for me and George here, that's cut price. Two hundred all told, how's that? (1962) ■ H. R. F. Keating: You'd pay me five sovereign? . . . Five golden oners? (1974)

red 'un (1890) Dated; applied to a sovereign ■ A. Hewins: I don't think much o' that stone you got. I'll give you a nice red un for it. (1981)

scrum (1891), scrummy (1894) Australian, dated; applied to a threepenny piece; *scrum* apparently a rhyming form based on *thrum* threepenny piece ■ *Byron Bay Record* (New South Wales): Notify the public that they must bring along their scrummies (the fee for using the dressing sheds is reported 3d. for adults, 1d. children). (1915)

spinnaker (1898) Australian, dated; applied to five pounds or a five-pound note; from earlier sense, large sail ■ N. Pulliam: I'll bet the first Aussie taker a couple of spinnakers the Snowy Mountains dream comes true. (1955)

thrummer (1898) Australian, dated; applied to a threepenny piece; from *thrum* threepenny piece + *-er* ■ *Bulletin* (Sydney): Mac stopped dead, the thrummer half out of his pocket. (1944)

zac, zack, zak (1898) Australian, dated; applied to a sixpence; probably from Scottish dialect *saxpence*

frogskin (1907) Australian, dated; applied to a pound (note); from US *frogskin* dollar ■ *Australian New Writing*: You come back here tomorrow night . . . and it's two frogskins for you and drinks all round! (1944)

trey, tray, trey-bit (1907) Dated, latterly mainly Australian; applied to a threepenny piece; from *trey* (set of) three ■ *National Time* (Australia): Service of the kind just described is as rare these days as finding a trey in the Christmas pudding. (1977)

o'goblin (1909) Dated; applied to a pound; short for *Jimmy O'Goblin* ■ P. G. Wodehouse: Five hundred o'goblins a year. (1925)

nicker (1910) Applied to a pound; origin unknown ■ Julian Symons: Who said there'd be trouble? Anyway, it's a hundred nicker. (1975)

bar (1911) Dated; applied to a pound; usually in the phrase *half a bar* ten shillings; probably from earlier sense, ingot (of gold, etc.)

tosh, tush (1912) Dated; applied to a half-crown or florin; abbreviation of *tosheroon* ■ Julian Maclaren-Ross: Here's a tosh to buy yourself some beer. (1961)

Bradbury (1917) Dated; applied to a one-pound note; from the name of John Swanwick *Bradbury*, Permanent Secretary to the Treasury 1913–19 ■ Gilbert Frankau: Cynthia had decided to 'risk a couple of Bradbury's each way'. (1926)

Fisher (1922) Dated; applied to a one-pound note or other currency note; from the name of Sir Warren *Fisher*, Permanent Secretary to the Treasury 1919–39 ■ *Motor Cycling*: The Bench mulcted him of a couple of Fishers and warned him as to his future behaviour. (1923)

smacker (1924) Applied to a pound; from earlier sense, dollar ■ Lionel Black: 'Gone at twelve thousand pounds.' . . . Twelve thousand smackers for a tray of old coins. Whew! (1979)

oncer (1931) Applied to a one-pound note; compare earlier senses, something that happens only once, a person who only achieves something once ■ Michael Kenyon: They gave you an 'undred quid in oncers to see things their way. (1978)

sprazer, spraser, sprasy, sprazey, etc. **(1931)** Dated; applied to sixpence or a sixpenny piece; from Shelta *sprazi* ■ J. B. Priestley: See if we can't take another spraser or two from the punters. (1939)

sprowsie, sprouse, sprowser (1931) Dated; applied to sixpence or a sixpenny piece; probably a variant of *sprazer* ■ Allan Prior: I walked across to the record player and took some silver out of my pocket. . . . 'Half-Nelson, do me a favour and put a sprouse in there for me. . . . I've got no change.' (1960)

berry (1934) Dated; applied to a pound; usually used in the plural; from earlier US sense, dollar

hole (1935) Dated; applied to a shilling

Joey, joey (1936) Applied to a former twelve-sided British coin of nickel-brass worth three old pence—a threepenny bit; from the male personal name *Joey*; compare earlier sense, fourpenny piece

ogg, og (1937) Australian & New Zealand, dated; applied to a shilling; from older slang *hog*

shilling, (US) dime ■ *Penguin New Writing*: Three quid and seven og. (1946)

Oxford scholar, Oxford (1937) Rhyming slang for *dollar*: applied to a dollar in Australian & New Zealand English and to the sum of five shillings or 25 pence in British English; reported in use in SW England in the 1870s ■ Anthony Burgess: 'We'll say a quid deposit, returnable on return of the hat, and a straight charge of an Oxford for the loan. Right?' 'Right.' The young man handed over his Oxford scholar. (1960)

potatoes (1939) Dated; applied to pounds; from earlier sense, dollars ■ P. G. Wodehouse: Was it conceivable . . . that any man, even to oblige a future brother-in-law, would cough up the colossal sum of two hundred potatoes? (1939)

fiddley-did, fiddley (1941) Australian, dated; applied to a pound; rhyming slang for *quid* ■ R. Bielby: He would 'like to be home right now, putting a couple of fiddleydids on a little horse'. (1977)

spin (1941) Australian, dated; applied to a pound; abbreviation of *spinnaker* ■ S. Gore: Backed Sweet Friday for a spin. . . . But it never run a drum. (1962)

swy, swey, swi, zwei (1941) Australian, dated; applied to a two-shilling piece; compare earlier sense, game of two-up ■ J. Duffy: 'Here's a swy,' he said, ringing it down on the table. 'Buy yourself one on me.' (1963)

trizzie, trizzy (1941) Australian, dated; applied to a threepenny piece; probably an alteration of *trey* ■ *Sunday Truth* (Brisbane): When you peppered the Christmas pud. with trey-bits this year we hope you remembered they will be scarcer next Yuletide and unless you hoard some there will be no trizzies at all for . . . the 1968 plum-duff. . . . A trey-bit or a trizzy is Aussie slang for a three-penny-bit. (1966)

saucepan lid (1951) Applied to a pound; rhyming slang for *quid*

jack, jacks, jax (1958) Applied to five pounds; short for *Jack's alive* obsolete rhyming slang for *five* ■ *Guardian*: 'That one,' says the dealer from Islington, 'that one we know she died in; so it'll cost you a jax.' . . . Five quid for a shroud; cheap at the price. (1968)

sheet (1958) Applied to a one-pound note or a pound; from earlier sense, dollar bill ■ *Hot Car*: Maserati air horns [have] . . . a howling, double high-pitched, screaming note. . . . This cacophony can be yours, whatever car you drive, for less than ten sheets. (1978)

iron man (1959) Orig Australian; applied to a pound or a one-pound note; from earlier US sense, dollar ■ John Wainwright: Ten thousand iron men. . . . We're talking bank-notes. (1974)

smackeroo (1961) Applied to a pound; from earlier sense, dollar

sob (1970) Applied to a pound; probably an alteration of *sov* ■ Kenneth Royce: Norman could have back his fifty sobs; when I failed I didn't want compensation. (1973)

US currency

rock (1840) Applied to a dollar ■ *Cavalier Daily* (University of Virginia): They got a campaign goin' around here to try to stick us students six rocks just to go . . . and listen to some old bag yell her fool head off. (1949)

fiver (1843) Applied to a five-dollar bill; from earlier sense, five-pound note

caser (1849) Dated; applied to a dollar; from earlier (but recorded later) British sense, five-shilling coin

double sawbuck, double saw (1850) Applied to twenty dollars or a twenty-dollar bill ■ *Time*: Any tout or hustler around the track can usually work Eddie for a 'double sawbuck'. (1948)

sawbuck (1850) Applied to ten dollars or a ten-dollar bill; from the x-shaped end (Roman X = 10) of a sawyer's horse or 'buck' ■ Joseph Wambaugh: I gave him a ten, which was just like folding up a sawbuck and sticking it in his arm. He'd be in the same shape twelve hours from now. (1973)

buck (1856) Applied to a dollar; origin uncertain; possibly an abbreviation of *sawbuck* ten dollars ■ Alexander Baron: 'What did you do before the war?' . . . 'Anythin' fer a buck.' (1953)

finif, finnif (1859), fin (1916) Applied to five dollars or a five-dollar bill; from British slang *finnip, finnif* five pounds ■ W. R. Burnett: Costs a fin just to check your hat. (1953)

William, william (1865) Dated; applied to a dollar bill; from punning association of *bill* banknote and *Bill* familiar form of the male personal name *William* ■ C. A. Siringo: Mr. Myers wrote me . . . to buy a suit of clothes with the twenty-dollar 'william'. (1927)

greenback (1870) Applied to a dollar bill; from a name originally applied to a non-convertible US currency note first issued in 1862, during the Civil War, which had a green design on its back ■ *New Yorker*: We observe him on his way to Mexico with a suitcase full of green-backs. (1966)

bit (1873) Applied to a unit of value equal to an eighth of a dollar; now used only in even multiples, especially *two bits*; from earlier application in the Americas to a small silver coin forming a fraction of the Spanish dollar ■ John Steinbeck: If you wanta pull in here an' camp it'll cost you four bits. (1939)

clam (1886) Applied to a dollar; origin uncertain ■ John O'Hara: I hit a crap game for about 80 clams. (1939)

plunk (1891) Dated; applied to a dollar; origin unknown ■ P. G. Wodehouse: Dere's a loidy here . . . dat's got a necklace of jools what's worth a hundred t'ousand plunks. (1929)

tenner (1893) Applied to a ten-dollar bill; from earlier sense, ten-pound note

simoleon, samoleon (1896) Applied to a dollar; origin uncertain; perhaps modelled on *napoleon* French coin ■ D. Anthony: I bet the limit, five thousand simoleons. (1977)

ace (1898) Applied to a dollar or a dollar bill; from earlier sense, (number) one ■ D. W. Maurer: He comes up with a bundle of scratch as big as your fist, but it's a mish—all aces. (1955)

frogskin (1902) Applied to a banknote, and usually specifically a dollar bill; from the colour ■ *Miami Vice*: A deal somewhere in the neighborhood of two hundred million frogskins. (1987)

jitney (1903) Applied to a five-cent piece or nickel; origin unknown ■ William Saroyan: Call that money? A jitney? A nickel? (1947)

iron man (1908) Applied to a dollar ■ E. R. Johnson: An ounce should bring a street pusher about two thousand iron men. (1970)

toadskin (1912) Applied to a banknote, and usually specifically a dollar bill; compare earlier obsolete sense, postage stamp, and also earlier *frogskin* dollar ■ *Flynn's*: Still I can flash a toad-skin now and then, and have a few iron men planted where th' berries grow. (1926)

berry (1916) Applied to a dollar; usually used in the plural ■ John Dos Passos: He had what was left of the three hundred berries Hedwig coughed up. (1936)

fish (1917) Applied to a dollar; from earlier sense, counter used in gambling; ultimately from French *fiche* peg, counter ■ Nelson Algren: Used to get fifteen fish for an exhibition of six-no-count. (1949)

smacker (1920) Applied to a dollar; from *smack* + *-er* ■ *Chicago Herald & Examiner*: Along comes Earl Gray and knocks off the U.S. treasury for 13,000,000 smackers. (1920)

nickel note (1926) Applied to a five-dollar bill; from US *nickel* five-cent coin

skin (1930) Applied to a dollar ■ R. B. Parker: I got a buyer with about a hundred thousand dollars . . . a hundred thousand skins. (1976)

potatoes (1932) Applied to dollars; from earlier sense, money ■ *Sun* (Baltimore): Nobody gives fifteen thousand 'potatoes' to a party committee without wanting something. (1933)

big one (1935) Applied to a thousand dollars or a thousand-dollar bill; from earlier more general sense, a large-denomination bill ■ M. Torgov: 'If you're reluctant to put the house up for sale, well, maybe you should consider just keeping it for yourself, and paying me for my half.' 'That means I'd have to cough up two hundred and fifty big ones, right? I haven't got that kind of bread lying around.' (1990)

pound (1935) Applied to five dollars or a five-dollar bill; from the approximate UK/US exchange rate in the 1930s

fish-skin (1936) Dated; applied to a dollar bill

single (1936) Applied to a one-dollar bill ■ Howard Fast: He . . . took out a wad of bills, peeling off two fives and two singles. (1977)

sheet (1937) Applied to a dollar bill or a dollar

meter (1940) Orig Black English; applied to twenty-five cents or a quarter; from the use of a twenty-five cent coin to operate gas meters

smackeroo (1940) Applied to a dollar; blend of *smacker* and *-eroo* ■ E. V. Cunningham: The price is eight thousand pounds, and the pound was five dollars then, so that makes it forty thousand smackeroos. (1977)

Rich

flush (1603) From earlier sense, plentifully supplied ■ Mortimer Collins: Tom . . . is always very flush or very hard up. (1871)

rolling (in money, it, etc.) **(1782)** ■ *Sun*: Paul Hogan must be rolling in it—he's just turned down a £5 million movie deal to make Crocodile Dundee III for Paramount. (1992)

made of money (1849) Mainly used in negatives and questions ■ Clive Egleton: Book him into a hotel . . . but nothing fancy, we're not made of money. (1975)

heeled (1880) Orig US; now usually preceded by *well*; from earlier sense, equipped ■ *Daily Telegraph*: Though the million and a quarter left by his grandfather has been spread among a large family he is still well-heeled enough. (1968)

oofy (1896) Dated; from *oof* money + *-y*

financial (1899) Australian & New Zealand; applied to someone who is financially solvent or has money ■ Patrick White: 'Shall I tell you, Alf,' he called, 'how us girls got to be financial?' (1961)

in the money (1902) Originally used to denote being among the prize-winners in a competition, show, etc. ■ Tony Parker: She said we could stay there rent free until I was in the money again. (1969)

stakey, staky (1919) Mainly Canadian ■ B. Broadfoot: Why, we was making 15 cents a glass. . . . Both of us were getting stakey as hell. (1973)

A rich person

plute, ploot (1908) Derogatory, mainly US; abbreviation of *plutocrat* ■ *Daily Mail*: 'The plutes', as he [*sc*. Henry Ford] humorously nicknames the financial and industrial interests of the country, would never permit his nomination. (1923)

butter-and-egg man (1924) US; applied to a wealthy unsophisticated man who spends money freely ■ *Antioch Review*: The 'butter-and-egg' man who startles the foreign lecturer with blunt questions. (1948)

fat cat (1928) Orig and mainly US; applied derogatorily to someone who is privileged because of their wealth, and often specifically to one who backs a political party or campaign; latterly in Britain applied specifically to business executives who are unjustifiably highly remunerated ■ *Flying*: Those who view the business jet as a smoke-belching, profit-eating chariot of the fatcat. (1971)

zillionaire (1946) Applied to a multi-millionaire, and hence to an extremely rich person; from *zillion* unmeasurably large number + *-aire*, after *millionaire*, etc. ■ Ian Fleming: He's a zillionaire himself. . . . He's crawling with money. (1959)

richie, richy (1966) Orig & mainly US; from *rich* + *-ie* ■ *Cambridge* (Massachussetts) *Chronicle*: Her only

chance of going to the prom is her budding relationship with Blaine . . ., a 'richie'. (1986)

squillionaire (1979) Applied to a multi-millionaire, and hence to an extremely rich person; from *squillion* unmeasurably large number + *-aire*, after *millionaire*, etc. ■ *Private Eye*: Several of the squillionaires at the back shouting abusive remarks about the morality of queue-barging. (1989)

noove, noov (1984) British, derogatory; applied to a member of the *nouveaux riches*; shortened from *nouveau riche* ■ *Times*: The pupils: 45 per cent sons of Old Etonians. . . . Also largish element of noovs to keep up academic standards and/or provide useful business contacts. (1986)

To be rich

stink of (or with) money (1877) Derogatory ■ I. Brown: We must do our best. He stinks of money. Will you fix up about rooms and for God's sake let's have a decent dinner.

To become rich

make one's (or a) pile (1854) Orig US ■ *Times*: This is tough talk from a man who first made his pile as an investment banker. (1973)

marry money (1858) Used to denote marrying a rich spouse ■ Joan Fleming: You're the answer to a maiden's prayer dear heart. No need for you to do a stroke of work, you can marry money and live the life of a gentleman. (1957)

strike it rich (1884) Orig US; from earlier sense, discover a profitable seam when prospecting ■ *Guardian*: His father was a rolling stone who struck it rich in the oil business. (1991)

Having no money

broke (1716) From an obsolete form of *broken*, past participle of *break* ■ Jack Black: [The landlady] wanted the rent. I told her I was broke. (1926)

hard up (1821) ■ Jerome K. Jerome: You don't feel nearly so hard up with elevenpence in your pocket as you do with a shilling. (1886)

flat (1833) US; short for *flat broke* ■ *Times Literary Supplement*: Satisfying his desires freely when he can, starving when he is 'flat'. (1930)

strapped (1857) Orig US; used to denote a severe shortage of cash; usually followed by *for* ■ Maria Franklin: Also she was strapped for ready money. (1936) ■ *Time*: By the spring of 1974, the whipsaw effect of recession and rising costs—particularly for oil which fuels 80% of Con Ed's generating capacity—left the company strapped. (1977)

stony, stoney (1886) Short for *stony-broke* ■ Eric Gill: The Guild is very hard up, and Hilary is at the very bottom of his fortunes & Joseph . . . is stony as can be too. (1923)

stony-broke, stone-broke (1886) ■ O. Bernier: Naples wasn't exactly short of nobility. . . . Some were stone broke. (1981)

(down) on one's uppers (1895) From the notion of destitute people who have worn out the soles of their shoes, leaving only the uppers ■ David Williams: My guess is the swine's on his uppers. . . . He's going for the ten thousand a year. (1985)

bust (1913) From *bust*, a past participle of *bust* break ■ *Observer*: Companies do go bust. (1964)

motherless (1916) Australian; short for *motherless broke* completely broke ■ B. Bennett: He let half-a-dozen others out at the same time. The motherless hooer. (1976)

skint (1925) British; variant of *skinned* ■ *Times*: Are the British really as skint as we tend to make out? (1981)

skinned (1935) Sometimes followed by *out* ■ *Observer*: I'm skinned, I know I can always count on someone helpin' me. (1958)

a skinner (1943) New Zealand ■ *New Writing*: So I paid for the pair of us, which left me practically a skinner. (1943)

boracic (1959) British; short for *boracic lint*, rhyming slang for *skint* ■ D. Raymond: 'He's boracic,' said someone. 'He's out grafting.' (1984)

uptight (1967) ■ *Esquire*: The expression 'uptight', which meant being in financial straits, appeared on the soul scene in the general vicinity of 1953. (1968)

wiped out (1977) ■ J. Blume: I am almost wiped out financially, but maybe I can pick up a babysitting job over the holidays. (1981)

No money

nuppence (1886) British, dated; blend of *no* and *tuppence* ■ *Observer*: Living on nuppence. (1964)

Any money; a trivial amount of money

brass farthing (1642) British ■ *Guardian*: Off course they do not contribute a brass farthing. The punter pays the levy and no amount of BOLA smokescreen can hide that. (1991)

red cent (1839) Orig US; from the copper of which cents were made ■ Tom Sharpe: 'I'll alimony you for all the money you've got.' 'Fat chance. You won't get a red cent.' (1976)

bean (1893) From earlier applications to a coin and various specific coins ■ Dorothy Sayers: None of the Fentimans ever had a bean, as I believe one says nowadays. (1928)

razoo, brass razoo (1919) Australian & New Zealand; origin unknown ■ Richard Clapperton: He isn't rolling in the stuff—he hasn't got two brass razoos to rub together. (1968)

sponduli(c)k, spondoolick (1923) US; from *spondulicks* money ■ E. P. Oppenheim: 'Do I understand that the young man . . . has dissipated the whole of his patrimony, in twelve months?' he inquired. 'Every bean,' Harold assented. 'Not a spondulik left.' (1923)

cracker (1934) Australian & New Zealand ■ Noel Hilliard: I've got nothing, Harry: not a cracker. (1960)

zac, zack, zak (1953) Australian; from earlier sense, sixpence ■ *National Times* (Sydney): No wonder Paul Keating has angrily refused to give the ABC another zac. (1986)

A penniless person

stumer, stumor, stoomer (1898) Australian, dated; from earlier sense, dud cheque

schlepper, shlepper (1949) Mainly US; applied especially to a poor person regarded as a parasite; from *schlep* drag, toil + *-er* ■ Groucho Marx: The paupers, or schlepper crowd, still hang on to their portable radios, but unfortunately they're not the ones who buy Chryslers. (1950)

To deprive of money

clean out (1812) ■ *Big Comic Fortnightly*: Oh no! There's been a bank raid! I've been cleaned out! (1989)

To lose one's money

come a stumer (or stoomer) (1900) Australian, dated

To have little money

feel the pinch (1861) Applied to someone feeling the effects of having insufficient money ■ *World of Cricket Monthly*: Otago are really feeling the pinch. (1977)

To make payment

shell out (1801) From the notion of taking seeds out of their pod or shell ■ *New Scientist*: The other nations may agree to place them at ESA's satellite operations centre just outside Frankfurt—if the Germans agree to shell out more cash. (1983)

dub in, dub up (1823) Origin unknown ■ Edmund Blunden: Five or six boys 'dub in' for a pot of strawberry jam or treacle. (1923)

fork out, fork up (1831) ■ Hart Crane: The family will just have to fork up a loan or something for me. (1932)

stump up (1833) ■ Grant Allen: The governor . . . fishes out his purse—stumps up liberally. (1893)

blow someone to something (1889) US; denoting paying for someone to have something ■ Arthur Miller: Tell Dad, we want to blow him to a good meal. (1949)

cough up (1894) ■ George Moore: Now, then, old girl, cough up! I must have a few halfpence. (1920)

brass up (1898) From *brass* money ■ P. G. Wodehouse: What did he soak him? Five quid? . . . And Gussie brassed up and was free? (1949)

spring (1906) Australian & US ■ Milton Machlin: We'll spring for the booze. (1976)

kick in (1908) Used to denote paying one's share ■ *Fortune*: Hillard Elkins, producer of *Oh! Calcutta!*, asked him to help back his productions of two Ibsen plays; Lufkin kicked in $10,000. (1972)

go Dutch (1914) Orig US; denoting each person paying for their own food, drink, etc. in a joint undertaking; from *Dutch treat* outing in which expenses are shared equally among participants ■ *Economist*: To suggest a free trade area to any of them in such circumstances looks rather like proposing to a teetotaller that you and he go dutch on daily rounds of drinks. (1957)

pick up the bill (or **check**, **tab**, etc.) **(1945)** Orig US; used to denote bearing the cost of something ■ *Daily Telegraph*: Ratepayers would have to pick up the bill if important jobs were transferred from the county councils to some of the larger districts. (1978)

pop (1959) ■ L. J. Braun: Hell. I didn't buy you anything, but I'll pop for lunch. (1968)

To fail to pay

skunk (1851) US

(Of payments) in advance

up front (1972) Orig US ■ S. Wilson: 'How much cash did you have in mind?' 'Five thousand, up front.' 'I beg your pardon?' 'In advance.' (1982)

Expenses

exes, **ex's**, **exs (1864)** Abbreviation of *expenses* ■ Kenneth Giles: Their ten thousand bucks per year plus exes. (1970)

To spend money recklessly; squander

lash out (1513) ■ *Daily Telegraph*: The poor who lash out on slow horses and unsuitable food might sometimes be more colourful and more fun to be with than the millionaire breakfasting on crispbread and orange juice. (1991)

knock down (1845) Australian & New Zealand; applied to spending all one's money on a spree or drinking bout ■ J. H. Travers: After they made payment, they would book up another three months' supply, and then knock the balance down at the local pub. (1976)

blue (1846) Perhaps a variant of *blow* ■ Walter de la Mare: She had taken a holiday and just blued some of her savings. (1930)

blow (1874) ■ *Economist*: He will probably feel able to blow with a clear conscience the £2,000. (1957)

blow in (1886) Mainly US ■ Frank Sargeson: Then he'd go to town and blow his money in, usually at the races. (1946)

do (1889) Mainly Australian & New Zealand; usually followed by *in* ■ *Bulletin* (Sydney): Now he's done his money in. (1930)

splash (1934) Often followed by *out* ■ Samuel Beckett: He thought for a second of splashing the fourpence. (1938) ■ *Morecambe Guardian*: Splash out on something new to wear; the result will be worthwhile. (1978)

splurge (1934) Orig US; from earlier sense, behave ostentatiously ■ *High Times*: If you really get into omelettes, you should splurge and procure a good copper or stainless steel omelette pan. (1975)

push the boat out (1937) Orig naval slang; used to denote being more than usually open-handed, especially in buying drinks for others ■ John Le Carré: 'Fielding's giving another dinner party tonight.' 'He's pushing the boat out these days.' (1962)

To borrow money, etc.

touch (1760) Often followed by *for* ■ Graham Greene: 'If you would lend me a pound.' . . . Had she 'touched' Henry once too often? (1951)

tap (1840) ■ *Essex Weekly News*: The first gentleman who was tapped for a subscription generously promised £30. (1901)

bite someone's ear (1879) ■ P. G. Wodehouse: His principal source of income . . . was derived from biting the ear of a rich uncle. (1925)

mooch (1899) Also applied more generally to cadging; from earlier senses, loiter, steal ■ D. Morrell: First thing I know, a bunch of your friends will show up, mooching food, maybe stealing, maybe pushing drugs. (1972)

pole (1906) Australian; also applied more generally to cadging or sponging; usually followed by *on* ■ Kylie Tennant: Only his own obstinacy kept him working, but Launce was as independent as any other man in Lost Haven. He wasn't going to pole on Alec. (1945)

hum (1913) Australian; also applied more generally to cadging or sponging; short for *humbug* ■ Xavier Herbert: Gertch—you old blowbag! You're only humming for a drink. Nick off home. (1938)

put the bee on (1914) Dated, mainly US; compare earlier sense, put an end to ■ James Curtis: If a bloke had come up and put the bee on him all the handout would have been . . . a lousy tanner. (1936)

put the nips in (or **into**) **(1917)** Australian & New Zealand ■ F. Huelin: Parsons, priests, doctors, lawyers and professional people generally were legitimate prey, and we had no scruples about 'putting the nips' into them. (1973)

bite (1919) Australian ■ L. Glassop: Can I bite you for a few quid, Lucky? (1949)

nip (1919) Mainly Australian; also applied more generally to cadging ■ H. C. Baker: No chance of nippin' the bricky for a smoke—he don't smoke. (1978)

put the sleeve on (1931) US; compare earlier sense, arrest ■ H. N. Rose: Wait'll I put the sleeve on Joe fer some chewin'. (1934)

put the bite on (1933) Orig and mainly US ■ P. G. Wodehouse: For years and years I have been trying to lend him of my plenty, but he has always steadfastly refused to put the bite on me. (1934)

bot (1934) Australian; also applied more generally to cadging or sponging; from the noun *bot* scrounger

ponce on (or **off**) **(1937)** Usually applied more generally to cadging or scrounging; from earlier sense, live off a prostitute's earnings ■ *Guardian*: Let's face it, New Zealand has been poncing on us for years. (1971)

bludge (1944) Australian & New Zealand; also applied more generally to cadging or scrounging; from earlier sense, shirk ■ Ian Hamilton: He bludged three cigarettes off me. (1967)

Borrowing, cadging

on the tap (1932) From the verb *tap* borrow ■ P. Carter: She was a real moaner and always on the tap, borrowing sugar and milk. (1977)

A borrower or cadger

moocher (1857) From *mooch* borrow + *-er*
■ Kenneth Orvis: You moocher, you—don't you respect a lady's natural curiosity? Be nice to me. After all, I'm paying for this party. (1962)

ear-biter (1899) Dated, orig Australian; from *bite someone's ear* borrow ■ P. G. Wodehouse: Two things which rendered Oofy Prosser a difficult proposition for the ear-biter. (1940)

bludger (1900) Australian & New Zealand; applied to a parasitical person; from earlier sense, prostitute's pimp ■ *Courier-Mail* (Brisbane): Surely if one is willing to give a good day's work for a good day's pay one should be given a chance to earn. I'm no bludger. (1969)

mooch (1914) From the verb *mooch* borrow
■ William Burroughs: Cash was a junk mooch on wheels. He made it difficult to refuse. (1953)

hum (1915) Australian; short for *humbug* ■ White & Halliwell: Two professional hums . . . took an oath at Bendigo no more work they would do. (1983)

bot (1916) Australian & New Zealand; from the parasitic habits of the bot-fly ■ J. H. Fingleton: One of . . . the officials was berating Pressmen . . . as a 'lot of bots who wanted everything for nothing'. (1960)

tapper (1930) From *tap* borrow, cadge + *-er*

poler (1938) Australian; from *pole* cadge + *-er*

A loan

rub (1914) Naval slang ■ W. Lang: 'Innyone as hasn't had a letter can have a rub of mines,' says Moriarty, the big Irishman, generously. (1919)

A mortgage

poultice (1932) Australian; from earlier sense, (large) sum of money ■ *Coast to Coast 1957–1958*: When the farm was free of its 'poultice', her father had promised to hand over to Sam. (1958)

A money-lender

Shylock, shylock (1786) Derogatory & offensive; applied to a hard-hearted money-lender; from the name of the Jewish money-lender in Shakespeare's *Merchant of Venice*
■ Turkus & Feder: 'Sometimes it's as good as 3,000 per cent,' one of the shylocks . . . explained. (1951)

ikey, ike, iky (1864) Derogatory & offensive; applied especially to a Jewish money-lender; from earlier sense, Jew

Borrowed money

O.P.M. (1901) US; abbreviation of *other people's money* ■ Josiah Flynt: It cost me nothing to play the game, because I played it with O.P.M. (1901)

An advance

sub (1866) British; often applied specifically to an advance payment of wages or salary; short for *subsist* *(payment)*, itself short for *subsistence*

(payment). Hence the verb **sub** pay someone a sub (1874)

To beg

See also at **Vagrancy** (pp. 115–16)

schnorr, shnoor (1892) US; see *schnorrer* beggar

panhandle (1903) Mainly US; back-formation from *panhandler* beggar

spear (1912) US

pling (1913) US, dated; origin unknown

tap (1935) From earlier sense, borrow money, cadge ■ George Orwell: They were begging . . . 'tapping' at every . . . likely-looking cottage. (1935)

A beggar

schnorrer, shnorrer (1892) US; from Yiddish, from German *Schnurrer* (from *schnurren* go begging)

panhandler (1897) Orig US; humorously alluding to the beggar's bowl ■ Ed McBain: Don't . . . start screaming if a panhandler taps you on the shoulder. He may only want a quarter for a drink. (1973)

plinger (1913) US, dated; from *pling* beg + *-er*

dummy (1918) Applied to a beggar who pretends to be deaf and dumb; from earlier sense, deaf-mute

tapper (1930) From *tap* beg + *-er* ■ J. Worby: I didn't have time to light a cigarette before I was accosted by a tapper. (1939)

(An act of) begging

stemming (1924), stem (1929) US; from *stem* street frequented by beggars

Wages

stake (1853) From earlier sense, amount won at gambling

screw (1858) ■ T. S. Eliot: He's offered me the job With a jolly good screw, and some pickings in commissions. (1959)

Irishman's rise (1889) Applied to a reduction in pay ■ *Times*: For many low-paid workers with children, an extra £2 a week may be no more than an 'Irishman's rise'. (1972)

greengages (1931) Rhyming slang ■ *Guardian*: The money? Greengages we call it, greengages—wages. You'll be surprised. In a lot of places it's a fiver a night. (1964)

rock of ages (1937) Rhyming slang

gravy (1967) Applied to a gratuity or tip; from earlier sense, unearned or unexpected money ■ *Sun*: When there is a mix-up at the table and two diners leave separate tips, it becomes double gravy. (1967)

toke (1971) North American; applied to a gratuity or tip; origin uncertain; perhaps an abbreviation of *token* ■ *Miami Herald*: They have just gone in and hassled people on tips and tokes. (1981)

To earn as wages

pull in (1529) ■ *Scotsman*: The Archbishop of York . . . pulls in £6000 a year. (1973)

knock out (1871) ■ *Bulletin* (Sydney): What about the school-teacher, the young computer programmer or plumber knocking out about $200 a week? (1975)

Profit

bunce (1719) Origin uncertain; perhaps an alteration of *bonus* ■ Charles Drummond: They take the place for a fee and pocket any bunce. (1968)

clean-up (1878) Orig US; from *clean up* make a profit ■ Kylie Tennant: He was now a hundred pounds in debt; but that, for Alec, was practically no debt at all; one good clean-up . . . and he would be clear. (1946)

velvet (1901) ■ Elliot Paul: A good French mechanic . . . would have to work two and one half days to earn 2,430 francs, which on account of taxes . . . would not be all velvet. (1951)

melon (1908) Applied to large profits to be shared between a number of people; especially in the phrase *cut the melon* ■ *Aurora* (Illinois) *Beacon News*: This year, a record number of your friends and neighbors will split a record 'melon' in our 1948 savings clubs. (1948)

gravy (1910) Applied to unearned or unexpected money; from the notion of gravy as a pleasing addition (to meat) ■ *Globe & Mail* (Toronto): In the past 10 years, the Manitoba Government has reaped about $8-million from the Downs (more than $1-million last year). This revenue is almost pure gravy. (1968)

vigorish, viggerish (1912) US; applied to the percentage deducted by the organizers of a game from the winnings of a gambler, and hence to the rate of interest on a usurious loan; probably from Yiddish, from Russian *vyigrysh* gain, winnings ■ Ed McBain: 'Was he taking a house vigorish?' 'Nope.' 'What do you mean? He wasn't taking a cut? . . . Then why'd he risk having the game in his basement?' (1964)

fast buck (1949), quick buck (1960) Orig US; applied to a quick profit; from *buck* dollar ■ *Zigzag*: It will attract talentless dorks out for a taste of notoriety or a fast buck. (1977) ■ Robert Barnard: Dreaming of luxury, of the quick buck dubiously acquired. (1980)

Something profitable

gravy train (1914), gravy boat (1943) Orig US; applied to a source of easy and often undeserved profit; compare *gravy* unearned or unexpected money ■ Mary McCarthy: There was a moment in the spring when the whole Jocelyn sideshow seemed to be boarding the gravy train, on to fatter triumphs of platitude and mediocrity. (1952)

earner (1970) British; especially in the phrase *a nice little earner* a means of making easy and often illicit profits ■ *Sunday Telegraph*: The family letting rooms on the quiet, or the person who has a 'nice little earner' on the side. (1987)

To make a profit

rake in (1583) Especially in the phrases *rake it in* and *rake in the shekels* ■ *Observer*: He's raking it in already. Writes 'think pieces' for *Honey* magazine. (1969)

clean up (1831) Orig and mainly US ■ Budd Schulberg: I mean profit. That show must be cleaning up. (1941) ■ *20th Century*: A concerted drive to ensure that this 25-year-old veteran cleans up another £16 million. (1960)

coin money, coin it (1863) ■ *Economist*: Restaurateurs and hoteliers in Portsmouth were coining it this week as 2,000 honest Social Democrats and several hundred expense-account journalists ate, drank and slept their way through the SDP wake. (1987)

laugh all the way to the bank (1969) Used to denote a relishing of one's profits; alteration of an original (ironic) *cry all the way to the bank* deplore one's undeserved profits, attributed to the pianist Liberace: ■ *Daily Mirror*: On the occasion in New York at a concert in Madison Square Garden when he had the greatest reception of his life and the critics slayed him mercilessly, Liberace said: 'The take was terrific but the critics killed me. My brother George cried all the way to the bank.' (1956) ■ *National Trust*: The taxpayer may be called in to 'save' it [*sc.* a great house] for the nation. Then the owner laughs all the way to the bank, and the devil can take his conscience. (1985)

To save money

salt away, salt down (1849) Often denoting storing money secretly in order to conceal profits; from the notion of preserving food in salt ■ *Kansas City* (Missouri) *Star*: It is a well known fact that all gamblers salt away their ill-gotten gains and die inordinately rich. (1931)

Money saved

stake (1853) North American; from earlier sense, amount won at gambling ■ John Updike: I worked in that oil town in the Rift . . . and when I had a little stake I hitched back to Istiqlal. (1978)

In debt; in financial difficulty

up King Street (1864) Australian, dated; from the name of a street in Sydney, site of the Supreme Court where bankruptcy cases were heard ■ C. Stead: They don't sweat their guts out for a chap who buys . . . himself a new car when he's up King Street. (1934)

in hock (1926) Compare earlier senses, in prison, in pawn ■ *Collier's*: My cash was gone, and I was in hock for the next three years. (1929)

in the red (1926) From the use of red ink to show debit items and balances in accounts ■ *Times*: The British Transport Commission is already in the red to the tune of at least £30m. (1960)

in Queer Street (1952) British; from *Queer Street* name of an imaginary street inhabited by those in trouble ■ Angus Wilson: He enjoys a little flutter . . . and if he finds himself in Queer Street now and again, I'm sure no one would grudge him his bit of fun. (1952)

An IOU

marker (1887) US ■ *Damon Runyon:* He is willing to take Charley's marker for a million if necessary to get Charley out. (1931)

Cheap

for a song (1601) ■ *Charles Dickens:* I assure you, the things were going for a song. (1865)

dirt cheap (1821) Applied to something very cheap ■ *Economist:* Development costs for the S-Cargo were roughly ¥200m—dirt cheap for a new car. (1988)

on the cheap (1859) ■ *George Orwell:* Anything from theosophy to cat's-cradle, provided you can do it on the cheap. (1939)

cheapie (1898), cheapo (1967) Applied especially to something cheap and of low quality; from *cheap + -ie, -o* ■ *Barr & York:* Cheapo fun dangly earrings. (1982)

el cheapo (1967) Orig US; applied especially to something cheap and of low quality; jocular pseudo-Spanish ■ *80 Microcomputing:* You could get away with an el cheapo cassette recorder for storage. (1983)

Something cheap

cheapie, cheapy (1898), cheapo (1972) Applied especially to something cheap and of low quality; from *cheap + -ie, -o* ■ *Guardian:* It identified insurance shares as a cheapy a couple of years back. (1983) ■ *Listener:* They want to see if you're wearing a Timex cheapo or a Rolex that's worth stealing. (1985)

snip (1926) British; from earlier sense, something easily obtained ■ *Times:* At a time when Beaujolais prices are soaring it is a snip at £1.90. (1977)

steal (1944) Orig US; from earlier sense, act of theft ■ *New York Herald-Tribune:* The asking price is $45,000, but I'm pretty sure you could get it for 43,000, and at that price it's a *steal*. (1951)

special (1966) US; applied to an item for sale at a low price for a limited period ■ *Redbook:* Before you go to the supermarket, check your newspaper for sales. Watch for patterns: 'specials' usually occur toward the beginning of the month, when supplies are highest. (1980)

el cheapo (1977) Orig US; applied especially to something cheap and of low quality; from the adjective *el cheapo* ■ *Washington Post:* An auto repairman who charges high rates may be able to claim that he does better work than el cheapo down the street. (1977)

To sell cheaply

give away (a1899) ■ *Daily Mail:* 'We're giving it away,' said managing director Michael Prendergast as he looked out over the queen of resort's South Bay. 'A full-board budget room Saturday and Sunday for £20 a night, including all entertainment. In our premier suites, the bedspreads alone cost £188.' (1991)

Free of charge

buckshee (1916) British; alteration of *baksheesh*, ultimately of Persian origin ■ *Charles Barrett:* The Chief of Staff . . . snapped, 'Want a buckshee trip, eh?' (1942)

freebie, freebee, freeby (1942) US; from *freebie* something free ■ *Mezzrow & Wolfe:* It's the brakeman who throws freebie passengers off. (1946)

Something free

freebie, freebee, freeby (1928) Orig US; arbitrarily from *free* ■ *Ed Lacy:* She'll write 'free' on the slip. . . . They come in for the freebie and end up buying more copies. (1962)

Expensive

stiff (1824) Applied mainly to a price ■ *A. C. P. Haggard:* He naturally thought 3s. an hour pretty stiff boat hire. (1903)

steep (1856) Applied mainly to a price ■ *Munsey's Magazine:* Forty thousand marks . . . is a pretty steep price even for a royal motor carriage. (1901)

pricey, pricy (1932) From *price + -y* ■ *SLR Camera:* It can . . . be fitted with a motor drive unit, but not with the wide variety of viewing heads and viewing screens available for the more pricy sisters in the catalogue. (1978)

To be expensive

break the bank (1612) From the notion of ruining a bank financially; in earliest use used to denote becoming bankrupt ■ *Guardian:* Yes, by £3bn to £4bn; in a £600bn economy that won't break the bank. (1992)

cost (1895) ■ *F. Scott Fitzgerald:* I like them but my God they cost. (1938)

set back (1900) ■ *Dan Lees:* He was carrying an over-and-under that must have set him back the thick end of a thousand quid, and, behind that much gun, even plus-fours . . . couldn't make him look silly. (1973)

knock back (1946) ■ *Guardian:* The complete CD edition occupies eight feet of shelf space, runs 200 hours, and will knock you back £1,400. (1991)

The (high) cost of something

the damage (1755) Now especially in the phrase *what's the damage?* how much is there to pay? ■ *Barbara Pym:* You must let me know the damage and I'll settle with you. (1977)

nut (1912) US; applied to the cost of a venture ■ *Publishers Weekly:* He submitted a strong script that led Fox to substitute color film and wide screen for black-and-white and the conventional small-screen ratio, and to raise the nut to $400,000. (1972)

the earth (1924) ■ *Agatha Christie:* Would it be terribly expensive? . . . She'd heard they charged the earth. (1961)

an arm and a leg (1956) ■ *Daily Mirror:* She needed half a million dollars to help pay palimony to Judy Nelson. Her lesbian affair has cost an arm and a leg. (1992)

To pay a high price

pay through the nose (1672) ■ *Guardian:* You pay through the nose for the 'show', often menus give no choice, and you are taken to the cleaners for wine and 'extras'. (1992)

A bank

jug (1845) ■ *Observer*: If a villain had seriously suggested screwing a jug (breaking into a bank). (1960)

A cheque

stumer, stumor (1890) Applied to a dud cheque; from earlier sense, something worthless ■ F. M. Ford: Two [were] awaiting court-martial for giving stumer cheques. (1926)

kite (1927) Applied especially to a blank, dud, or forged cheque; from earlier sense, fraudulent bill of exchange, from the phrase *fly a kite* issue such a bill, from the notion of a toy kite as something insubstantial that floats in the air temporarily ■ Tony Parker: He's in for what they call 'kites', dud cheques, you know. (1969)

A safe

peter (1859) Also applied to a cash-box or cash register; from earlier sense, case, trunk ■ G. F. Newman: There was s'posed to be some dough in the Peter. (1970)

box (1904) Orig US

pete, pete-box (1911) Abbreviation of *peter* safe ■ Damon Runyon: This is a very soft pete. It is old-fashioned, and you can open it with a toothpick. (1938)

keister, keester, keyster (1913) US; from earlier sense, suitcase, bag ■ H. E. Goldin: Easy on the soup (crude nitro-glycerine) with that keister or she'll jam. (1950)

A container for money

skin (a1790) Criminals' slang, dated; applied to a purse or wallet ■ James Curtis: Proper jobs I mean. Not nicking skins from blokes what are lit up. (1936)

2. Bribery

A bribe

hush-money (1709) Applied to money paid to prevent disclosure or exposure, or to hush up a crime or discreditable transaction ■ Henry Miller: The cops will be sitting on our necks. . . . The natural thing, under the circumstances, would be to put something aside for hush money. (1953)

sweetener (1847) ■ G. Hammond: Everybody gives 'sweeteners' of some kind or another, even if it's only a bottle at Christmas. (1979)

boodle (1884) Orig US; applied to money acquired or spent in connection with the obtaining or holding of public offices, the material means or gains of bribery and corruption; from earlier senses, counterfeit money, money in general

graft (1901) Orig US; applied to money acquired or spent in connection with the obtaining or

pogue (1812) Applied to a bag, purse, or wallet; perhaps related to obsolete *pough* bag, and compare *poke* purse ■ Michael Crichton: It was the stickman's job to take the pogue once Teddy had snaffled it, thus leaving Teddy clean, should . . . a constable stop him. (1975)

poke (1859) North American; applied to a purse or wallet; from earlier sense, bag or small sack (as in *buy a pig in a poke*)

grouch-bag (1908) US; applied to a hidden pocket or a (draw-string) purse carried in a concealed place, for keeping one's money safe; from *grouch* grumbling ■ *Telegraph* (Brisbane): Groucho . . . earned his nickname in poker games because he always carried his money in a 'grouch bag'. (1969)

Credit cards

plastic money (1974), plastic (1980) Orig US ■ *Which?*: To use your plastic in a cash machine, you need a personal identification number (PIN). (1988)

Welfare

susso (1941) Australian, dated; applied to unemployment benefit (often in the phrase *on (the) susso*) and also to someone paid such benefit; from *sus(tenance + -o* ■ F. Hardy: The very thought . . . of the contempt the respectable held for the sussos changed his mood to defiance. (1963)

baby bonus (1945) Canadian; applied to the family allowance ■ *Globe & Mail* (Toronto): Extra tax on rich to be eliminated; baby bonus to rise. (1976)

pogey, pogy (1960) North American; applied to welfare payment for the needy; from earlier senses, hostel for the poor, welfare office ■ H. T. Barker: During the winter we lived on turnips, potatoes, canned clams and the pogy, and Mother and I would hook rugs for the tourist trade. (1964)

holding of public offices, the material means or gains of bribery and corruption; also applied to the practice of bribery and corruption; from earlier sense, (illegal) profit ■ *Daily Telegraph*: Victims in a wave of graft, corruption and fear were making regular payments for protection. (1970)

oil (1903) US; applied to money used for bribery and corruption ■ *Detective Fiction Weekly*: She didn't take care of her protection directly, that is, she didn't slip the oil to the cops herself. (1935)

dropsy (1930) Jocular extension of *dropsy* excess of fluids in body tissue, from the notion of 'dropping' money into someone's hand ■ Peter Wildeblood: A nice bit of dropsy to a copper usually does the trick. (1955)

pay-off (1930) Orig and mainly US ■ *National Observer* (US): Tanaka is one of several Japanese officials accused of receiving $12 million in pay-offs from Lockheed for promotion of the company's sales in Japan. (1976)

drop (1931) ■ George Orwell: A half-penny's the usual drop (gift). (1933)

payola (1938) Orig US; applied to a bribe or other secret payment to induce someone to use their influence to promote a commercial product, especially one made to a disc-jockey for plugging a record; *-ola* commercial suffix, after *pianola*, etc., used in *Victrola* and other products ■ Thomas Pynchon: They got the contracts. All drawn up in most kosher fashion, Manfred. If there was payola in there, I doubt it got written down. (1966)

squeeze-pidgin (1946) ■ Berkeley Mather: 'What's a squeeze-pidgin?' . . . 'A bribe. . . . Something you *squeeze* out of somebody.' (1970)

sling, sling back (1948) Australian; from the verb *sling* pay a bribe ■ *Canberra Times*: To have a house . . . given to you is, to put it colloquially, a sling of major proportions. (1982)

bung (1958) British; from the verb *bung* bribe ■ Jeffrey Ashford: What's the matter? Not being offered enough bung? (1966)

kickback (1958) Orig US; applied to money paid (illegally) to someone who has made it possible for you to do something; from earlier sense, refund, rebate ■ *Daily Telegraph*: The promoter claims that another member of the committee approached him demanding a kick-back on the profits and, after he had refused this proposal, the permit was somehow no longer forthcoming. (1972)

backhander (1960) Applied to a secret payment; from the notion of concealing payment by making it with the hand reversed; compare earlier sense, blow with the back of the hand, and *back-handed* indirect, ambiguous, devious (as in 'a back-handed compliment') ■ *Listener*: A bit of a backhander and, boy, you're in. (1968)

schmeer, schmear, schmere, shmear, shmeer, shmir (1961) North American; from the verb *schmeer* bribe ■ Ed Lacy: Our lad didn't want the shmear to start with, so he ain't greedy. (1962)

See also **soap** under Money at **Money** (p. 180).

To bribe

palm (1747) Dated; from the notion of putting money into the palm of someone's hand ■ C. G. Harper: Votes which would in other days have been acquired by palming the men and kissing all the babies. (1899)

grease someone's **palm (1807)** Compare earlier obsolete *grease someone's hand* (1526) ■ *Economist*: The property and construction interests, which lavishly grease the palm of the biggest faction in the ruling party. (1987)

square (1859) Denoting conciliation by bribery ■ Elizabeth Bowen: 'What's poor Willy going to think of us?' 'I'll square Willy.' (1969)

oil the knocker (1870) British, dated; applied to bribing a doorman

boodle (1890) Orig US; from the noun *boodle* money for or from bribery ■ W. H. Smith: If you're going to boodle you've got to do it on a party basis. If I wanted to boodle an Illinois legislature, [etc.]. (1904)

reach (1906) US ■ L. Katcher: It is impossible . . . to open a big, notorious gambling operation without buying off public officials. . . . This does not necessarily mean a sheriff or a District Attorney or a chief of police is being reached. (1967)

sling (c1907) Australian; denoting the paying of a bribe ■ F. Hardy: On first name terms with every shire President so long as they didn't forget to sling when backhanders came in. (1971)

get to (1927) US ■ E. D. Sullivan: Gangsters can't operate on a satisfactory scale anywhere until they have 'got to someone'. (1930)

lubricate (1928) ■ *Daily Express*: He made specific charges. One was that taxicab proprietors have to 'lubricate' Scotland-yard before their taxicabs are passed for licensing. (1928)

schmeer, schmear, schmere, shmear, shmeer, shmir (1945) North American; from earlier sense, flatter ■ Leo Rosten: Do the officials expect to be *shmeered* there? (1968)

bung (1950) British; origin unknown ■ John Burke: Don't forget the solicitors. . . . They'll want bunging. (1967)

Acceptance of bribes; corruption

mumping (1970) British; applied to the acceptance by the police of small gifts or bribes from tradespeople; from obsolete *mump* beg

Taking bribes

on the take (1930) Orig US ■ *Boston Sunday Globe*: In an unguarded public moment [he] . . . said, 'Half the people in Philadelphia are on the take.' (1967)

See also *on the pad* at **pad** (below).

An establishment that pays bribes

pad (1970) US; applied to a gambling saloon or similar place which provides police with regular pay-offs; also in the phrase *on the pad* receiving such bribes ■ *Guardian*: [He] was thrilled with becoming a plainclothesman because . . . 'he was now on the pad'. The pad is the regular sum paid to officers for ignoring illegal activities. (1971)

3. **Work**

Work

graft (1853) Applied especially to hard work; perhaps a transferred use of obsolete *graft* depth of earth lifted by a spade, in its original sense 'digging' ■ *Times*: This view is that salvation . . . is to be won by long, hard graft by industrial management. (1968)

yakka, yacca, yacka, yacker, yakker (1888) Australian; applied mainly to hard work; often in the phrase *hard yakka*; from the dated Australian verb *yakker* work, from Aboriginal (Jagara) *yaga* ■ *National Times* (Sydney): Child care remains women's responsibility. . . . There's no evidence that men are taking part in the hard yakka. (1986)

leg work (1891) Applied to work characterized by running of errands, going from place to place in search of information, etc. ■ *Daily Telegraph*: 1,700 men . . . do the surveying leg-work needed for keeping local maps up to date. (1972)

bashing (1940) British, services' slang; applied to arduous work, especially of the specified sort ■ Gerald Kersh: Poor old Gerald done fourteen drills that week, plus a nice basinful of spud-bashing. (1946)

schlep, schlepp, shlep (1964) Mainly US; applied to hard work; from the verb *schlep* work hard ■ *National Observer* (US): Anybody who has ever tried to make even a small amount of a classic brown sauce from scratch would probably agree with Liederman's assessment that 'it's the ultimate schlep'. (1976)

shitwork (1968) Mainly a feminist use; applied to menial or routine work, especially housework

grunt work (1970) US; applied to unskilled or manual work; from *grunt* unskilled worker ■ *Los Angeles Times*: The Hollywood Park chef . . . did much of the grunt work in construction of the cake base. (1989)

To work

graft (1859) Applied especially to working hard; from *graft* hard work ■ Allan Prior: The great mass of mugs were law-abiding . . . doing as they were told, working, grafting. (1966)

schlep, schlepp, shlep ((1963) Mainly US; applied to working hard; from earlier sense, drag ■ Saul Bellow: Why should I *schlepp* out my guts? (1964)

A worker

wallah, walla, wala (1785) Orig Anglo-Indian; applied to someone concerned with or in charge of a usually specified thing, business, etc.; from the Hindi suffix *-wālā* -er ■ J. I. M. Stewart: It's marvellous what these ambulance wallas can do at a pinch. (1977)

grafter (1900) Applied especially to a hard worker; from *graft* work (hard) + *-er* ■ *Times*: He is a grafter rather than a fluent striker, with little back-lift, plenty of concentration, and a willingness to use his feet. (1959)

basher (1940) British, orig services' slang; applied to someone with the stated duties, occupation, etc.; from the notion of using, repairing, etc. a particular implement in a robust or careless way ■ *Gen*: One of the cookhouse bashers that came off at five. (1945)

workaholic (1968) Orig US; applied to someone who works excessively hard; from *work*, after *alcoholic* ■ *Guardian*: They're concerned about the pressures of their jobs, which demand that they become workaholics. (1984)

Working hard

nose to the grindstone (1828) From earlier use denoting oppression or repression ■ *Guardian*: He liked the idea of working with mature students who would not call him a swot if he kept his nose to the grindstone. (1992)

A product of work

foreigner (1943) British, orig military slang; applied to something done or made at work by an employee for personal benefit, or to a piece of work not declared to the relevant authorities; mainly in the phrase *do a foreigner* ■ Alan Bleasdale: We're both gettin' followed, for all we know, we're both goin' t'get prosecuted f'doin' a foreigner while we're on the dole. (1983)

A job or occupation

berth (1778) Applied to (an appointment to) a job; from earlier more specific sense, a situation or job on board a ship ■ *South China Morning Post*: Lord Wilson expressed surprise at the appointment but it is seen as an acceptable berth for the former governor. (1992)

hat (1869) Used to denote an office or occupation symbolized (as if) by the wearing of a hat ■ *Evening Standard*: Wearing his new 'economic overlord' hat the Prime Minister summoned three key figures to Downing Street today. (1967)

lurk (1916) Australian & New Zealand; from earlier sense, scheme, dodge ■ R. Stow: 'What's your lurk, mate?' 'Me? Stockman on a mission.' (1958)

site (1930) US, nautical ■ *New Yorker*: Joe, who generally keeps his own counsel, tells me that he is hoping to get a site—a job—on the Sniktaw. (1977)

number (1948) ■ *Listener*: Transferred to what was described as a 'cushy number' with the Commandos. (1968)

bag (1964) Orig US; applied to the work or other activity that a person prefers to do; from earlier sense, category (of jazz) ■ *Sunday Times*: His bag is paper sculpture. (1966)

To have more than one job

moonlight (1957) Orig US; from the notion of having an evening job in addition to one's usual day job ■ *Times Literary Supplement*: He . . . —naturally for one who moonlights as the *Financial Times*'s gardening correspondent when not otherwise engaged as a Fellow of Magdalen—never misses a turn on botanical or horticultural matters. (1974). Hence **moonlighter** (1957) ■ Clive Egleton: I employ a lot of moonlighters, blokes who take a second job at nights. (1973)

Bar staff

See at **Alcohol** (p. 147).

A bookmaker

bookie, booky (1885) From *book(maker + -ie* ■ *Times:* One of his thirties-style bookie check suits. (1968)

A building-trade worker

Chips (1785) Mainly naval slang; applied to a carpenter, often as a nickname

brickie, bricky (1880) Applied to a bricklayer; from *brick + -ie* ■ *Sunday Times* (headline): Minimum wage hits Germany's British brickies. (1997)

chippy, chippie (1916) Orig naval slang; from *chip + -y* ■ Arnold Wesker: I'll work as a chippy on the Colonel's farm. (1960)

putty (1946) Naval slang, dated; applied to a ship's painter

A butcher

pig-sticker (1886) Dated; applied to a pork butcher

A cook

See at **Eating & Drinking** (pp. 140–1).

A delivery worker

postie, posty (1871) Applied to a postman; from *post(man + -ie* ■ *South Wales Guardian:* He was missed by the upper valley residents on his transfer down to Ammanford, where he has been a 'postie' for the past 13 years. (1977)

milky, milkie (1886) Applied to a milkman; from *milk + -y* ■ *Evening News:* He appeared his normal easy-going self and all he said to me was, 'Hullo milkie.' (1975)

milko, milk-oh (1907) Orig Australian; applied to a milkman; from the call *milk O!* used by milkmen ■ *Canberra Chronicle:* He has spent quite a fair bit of time in banking and an oil company business, but also doubled as a pretty good milko. (1985)

An electrician

sparks (1914) ■ *Listener:* Lord Sneaker tells his sparks to wrap up the lights. (1975)

juicer (1928) From *juice* electricity + *-er* ■ V. J. Kehoe: He directs the . . . juicers to place the lights in the most effective positions. (1957)

A farmer

cockatoo (1845) Australian & New Zealand; applied to a small farmer; probably from earlier sense, a convict serving a sentence on Cockatoo Island in Sydney Harbour ■ O. Duff: The most they [*sc.* sheepfarmers] can hope for is an uneasy truce with dairymen . . . or an alliance with Labour to control the 'cockatoos'. (1941)

tiger (1865) Australian; applied to a sheep shearer ■ F. B. Vickers: Those tigers (he meant the shearers) will make you dance. (1956)

cocky (1872) Australian & New Zealand; applied to a small farmer; from *cock(atoo + -y* ■ Barry Crump: The cocky had a sheep-run in the foothills of the Coromandel Ranges. (1960)

pen-mate (1895) Australian & New Zealand; applied to a shearer who catches sheep out of the same pen as another shearer

drummer (1897) Australian & New Zealand, dated; applied to the worst or slowest sheep-shearer in a team; perhaps a jocular use of obsolete *drummer* commercial traveller ■ H. P. Tritton: It's not every man that is drummer in four sheds running. (1959)

waddy, waddie (1897) US; applied to a cattle rustler, and also to a cowboy, especially a temporary cowhand; origin unknown ■ J. Lomax: He rides a fancy horse, he's a favorite man, Can get more credit than a common waddie can. (1927)

leather-neck (1898) Australian, dated; applied to an unskilled farm-labourer, especially on a sheep station

cow-spanker (1906) Australian & New Zealand; applied to a dairy farmer or stockman ■ *Weekly News* (Auckland): The good old New Zealand cowspanker. (1963)

backyarder (1922) British, dated; applied to someone who keeps chickens in their backyard ■ *Gen:* Backyarders keep fifteen million hens according to Agriculture Ministry census. (1942)

jingling Johnny (1934) Australian & New Zealand; applied to someone who shears sheep by hand

swede-basher (1943) Jocular, derogatory; applied to a farm worker, and hence to any rustic ■ Joyce Grenfell: I tried to sing a song appropriate for the swede-bashers from Lincolnshire, the Cockneys, Scots . . . , and so on. (1976)

stubble-jumper (1961) Mainly Canadian; applied to a prairie farmer ■ *Islander* (Victoria, British Columbia): An authentic stubble-jumper from the prairies was looked upon as being at the very bottom rung of the social and employment ladder. (1973)

A general worker

tiger (1865) Australian; applied to a menial labourer

lobby-gow (1906) US; applied to an errand-boy, messenger, or hanger-on; origin unknown ■ T. Betts: He flung away fortunes in grubstakes to bums, heels, and lobby-gows. (1956)

dogsbody (1922) Orig nautical; applied to a junior person, especially one to whom a variety of menial tasks is given; compare earlier nautical slang sense, dried peas boiled in a cloth ■ *Listener*: I was a sort of general dogsbody to begin with— assistant stage-manager, and what have you. (1967)

ground-hog (1926) US; applied to a worker who operates at ground level; from earlier sense, American marmot

grunt (1926) Orig and mainly US; applied originally to a ground worker in the construction of power lines, and hence to any unskilled worker or labourer ■ *Daily Telegraph*: Better by far not to attempt to be over-smart . . . by using new words like . . . 'grunt' for a guy who does the dirty work. (1986)

wood-and-water joey (1926) Australian; applied to an odd-job man; from *wood-and-water*, in allusion to 'hewers of wood and drawers of water' (*Joshua* xi.21) + obsolete Australian *joey* recent arrival on a goldfield, inexperienced miner ■ *D. Stuart*: You might consider taking a job here with me, wood-and-water joey, general rouseabout. (1978)

working stiff (1930) US; applied to an ordinary working man ■ *Guardian Weekly*: The idea of two young working stiffs [*sc.* Woodward and Bernstein] carrying off the prize is irresistible to youngsters with their careers before them. (1977)

temp (1932) Orig US; applied to a temporary employee, especially a temporary secretary; abbreviation of *temporary* ■ *Economist*: Overstaffing is not solely the result of the unwillingness to use temps. (1967). Hence the verb **temp** work as a temp (1973) ■ *Times*: Most of the students had given as their explanation for deciding to temp: 'To gain office experience before taking up a permanent job.' (1978)

yardbird (1963) US; applied to a worker in a yard ■ *Thomas Pynchon*: 'Yardbirds are the same all over,' Pappy said. . . . The dock workers fled by, jostling them. (1963)

gofer, gopher (1967) Orig and mainly US; applied to someone who runs errands, especially on a film set or in an office; from the verbal phrase *go for*, because the person goes and fetches things; influenced by *gopher* small mammal ■ *Listener*: Burt Lancaster plays Lou, an ex-bodyguard and gofer for the mob, still running the bedraggled tail of the numbers racket. (1981)

A groom

swipe (1929) US; applied to a groom or stableboy; perhaps originally a variant of *sweep* ■ *William Faulkner*: He hasn't got any money. . . . What little there might have been, that cockney swipe threw away long ago on whores and whisky. (1959)

A hairdresser

crimper (1968) British; from *crimp* curl + *-er* ■ *Elleston Trevor*: He'd opened up as a crimper . . . decorating the salon and supervising the work himself. (1968)

A mechanic

grease monkey (1928) ■ *Times Literary Supplement*: In Australia he was impressed by the 'grease-monkey' at Broken Hill who could afford to run a racing stable. (1959)

mech (1951) Abbreviation ■ Alan Hunter: Hanson called over a mech. The mech started it for us and drove it out. (1973)

An office worker

steno (1906) Orig and mainly US; applied to a (female) shorthand-typist; abbreviation of *stenographer* ■ *Motion Picture*: Frances Dee . . . skyrockets to new importance with an amazingly fine performance as a small town steno who wins a five-thousand-dollar lottery. (1935)

pen-pusher (1911) Usually derogatory; applied to someone engaged in writing or desk work ■ John Braine: I saw myself, compared with him, as the Town Hall Clerk, the subordinate pen-pusher, halfway to being a zombie, and I tasted the sourness of envy. (1957)

cookie-pusher (1943) US, derogatory; applied to a diplomat devoting more attention to protocol or social engagements than to work; from earlier sense, man leading a futile social life ■ *Economist*: The popular image of the cookie-pusher in Foggy Bottom [i.e. the US State Department]. (1962)

wallah, walla (1965) Derogatory; applied to a bureaucrat or someone doing a routine administrative job; from earlier sense, person with a particular task ■ *Courier-Mail* (Brisbane): Some wallahs in Canberra are sitting in air-conditioned offices telling us what has been flooded and what hasn't. (1974)

pink button (1973) British, Stock Exchange slang; applied to a jobber's clerk

suit (1979) Derogatory, orig US; applied to a business executive, or to anyone who wears a business suit at work ■ *TV Week* (Melbourne): A kid . . . eager to propel himself out of the mail-room, where he has a menial job, into the executive ranks . . . of those who are called 'suits'. (1987)

sysop (1983) Orig US; someone responsible for (assisting in) the day-to-day running of a computer system; abbreviation of *system operator* ■ *Telelink*: Operational initially for 20 hours a day . . . the board will eventually feature up to 16 sub-boards, each run by separate sysops. (1986)

Office work

admin (1942) Applied to administrative functions or duties, and also to the department of an organization that deals with these; short for *administration* ■ W. Buchan: A mass of practical details—sheer 'admin'. (1961)

An oil-rig worker

rough neck (1917) Orig US; applied especially to a labourer on the rig-floor; compare earlier sense, rough or quarrelsome person ■ *Time*: The centre of the rig's activities is the mud-slicked drill floor, where half a dozen roughnecks struggle day and night with heavy chains and power-driven winches to shove 90-ft.-long pieces of drill pipe into the narrow hole. (1977)

roustabout (1948) Orig US; from earlier sense, general labourer ■ *Offshore Engineer*: The clothing was tested on the rig Sedco 700, operating close to the 62nd parallel, by supervisors and roustabouts on the nightshift. (1975)

A photographer

See at **Entertainment** (p. 345)

A police officer

See at **The Police** (p. 107).

A publicist

adman (1909) Orig US; applied to an advertising copywriter or executive ■ *Observer*: That side of modern life . . . which bears the finger-smears of the ad. man. (1957)

flack (1939) Mainly US; applied to a publicity agent; origin uncertain; said to be derived from the name of Gene *Flack*, a publicity agent in the US film industry ■ Charles Drummond: They were booked to do ten matches in Mexico City; Bull, their flack, had lined up the opposition. (1968). Hence the verb **flack** act as a publicity agent (for) (1963)

A refuse collector

totter (1891) British; applied to a rag-and-bone collector; from the verb *tot* + *-er*

bottle-o, bottle-oh (1898) Australian & New Zealand; applied to a collector of empty bottles ■ Dick Whittington: 'What do you do for a living?' . . . 'I'm the local bottle-O'. (1967)

garbo (1953) Australian; from *garb(age* + the Australian colloquial suffix *-o* ■ *Guardian*: Australian garbos probably could not compete with English dustmen in the length and scale of their strikes. (1971)

sanno (man), sano (man) (1959) Australian; applied to someone who collects excrement from unsewered areas; from *san(itary* + the Australian colloquial suffix *-o* ■ L. Fox: Mother sympathised with the Sanno man's job; she always greeted him. (1977)

binman (c1966) ■ *Daily Telegraph*: Another common request was for . . . a waste-disposal system that would eliminate the need for bin men. (1986)

To collect refuse

tot (1884) British; applied to collecting saleable items from refuse as an occupation; from the noun *tot* such an item ■ Martin Russell: I could earn as much, totting for the corporation. (1976)

A sales representative

rep (1938) From earlier more general use of *rep* as an abbreviation of *representative* ■ Eric Ambler: No travellers seen except on Tuesdays and Thursdays. . . . Reps . . . , Tuesdays and Thursdays. (1938)

A scientist

backroom boy (1943) Applied to someone engaged on (secret) research; from the notion of a secluded room at the rear of premises where secret work is carried out; compare Lord

Beaverbrook in *Listener*: Now who is responsible for this work of development on which so much depends? To whom must the praise be given? To the boys in the back rooms. They do not sit in the limelight. But they are the men who do the work. (1941) ■ *Times*: The man most responsible for the development of the rocket projectile . . . is Group Captain John D'Arcy Bakercarr, . . . whose 'backroom boys' at the Ministry of Aircraft Production have worked unremittingly with him. (1944)

boffin (1945) Applied to someone engaged on (secret) research; apparently originally Royal Air Force slang for a scientist working on radar; compare earlier obsolete application to an elderly naval officer; ultimate origin unknown ■ *Economist*: The unexpected success of the boffins' conference at Geneva . . . ending in agreement on the feasibility of controlling a nuclear test suspension. (1958)

A servant

tweeny, tweeney, tweenie (1888) Dated; applied to a maid-servant assisting both the cook and the housemaid; from 'tween, a reduced form of *between* (from the notion of being 'between' the two posts) + *-y* ■ *Daily News*: A certain useful section of the servant class, who . . . were known as 'tweenies'. (1904)

skivvy, skivey, scivey (1902) Mainly derogatory; applied to a female domestic servant, especially a maid-of-all-work; origin unknown ■ *Times*: This represents a change in the nurses' attitude. No longer will you be the skivvies of the health service. (1974)

tiger (1929) Nautical; applied to a captain's personal steward ■ Richard Gordon: In the old days, you could have swapped the Captain's tiger for the butler in any stately home in the kingdom, and no one would have been the wiser. (1961)

daily (1933) Applied to a domestic cleaner or other servant who does not live on the premises; from the notion of coming to a house every day ■ Laurence Meynell: Most 'dailies' I have known have been disastrous. They come late; charge exorbitantly; drop ash all over the place. (1967)

To do the work of a servant (for)

do for (1844) ■ Bram Stoker: He . . . got . . . the name of an old woman who would probably undertake to 'do' for him. (1914)

skivvy, skivey, scivey (1931) From the noun *skivvy* ■ June Thomson: It wasn't no skivvying job. . . . Mrs King treated me like a friend. (1973)

A shop worker

counter-jumper (1829) Dated, derogatory; applied to a shop assistant or shopkeeper; from the notion of jumping over a counter to go from one part of a shop to another ■ John Braine: You'll not waste your time with bloody consumptive counter-jumpers! (1959)

shoppy, shoppie (1909) Dated; applied to a shop assistant; from *shop* + *-y* ■ H. A. Vachell: Her sparkling eyes, her fine figure, were gifts rarely bestowed upon urban 'shoppies'. (1934)

A tailor

Jew (1916), Jewing-bloke (1945) Nautical; applied to a ship's tailor ■ **Tackline:** The 'Jewing-bloke' had a rather ancient Singer sewing machine, bought when ashore at Alexandria with . . . pay in his pocket. (1945)

A teacher

See at **Education** (p. 315).

A transport worker

cabby, cabbie (1859) Applied to a taxi-driver; from *cab* taxi + *-y* ■ *Sunday Times:* November 5 ('bombfire night', as a cockney cabby has it). (1993)

swamper (1870) Orig US; applied to the assistant to the driver of horses, mules, or bullocks, and hence (1929) to the assistant to the driver of a lorry ■ E. Iglauer: We don't have swampers, a second man on the truck, the way the oil-field men have. (1975)

shack, shacks (1899) North American; applied to a brakeman or guard on a train; origin unknown ■ **Dean Stiff:** A great many hobo writers . . . are full ready to tell the novice how to outwit the brakemen, or shacks. (1931)

jumper (1900) British, dated; applied to a ticket-inspector; from the notion of 'jumping' on to or boarding a bus, tram, etc. to inspect tickets ■ *Daily Express:* If you use a second [class carriage] with a 'third' ticket, watch for the 'jumpers', ready to pounce and demand excess. (1937)

river hog (1902), river pip (1921) North American; applied to someone who guides logs downstream

rounder (1908) US; applied to a transient railway worker ■ *Listener:* His was a six-pipe job whose moans sent every coloured 'rounder' from Chicago to New Orleans into ecstasies. (1961)

wharfie (1911) Australian & New Zealand; applied to a stevedore, docker or other wharf-worker; from *wharf* + *-ie* ■ *National Times* (Australia): A lazy wharfie would be known as 'the Judge' because he was always sitting on a case, and another 'the London Fog' because he would never lift. (1981)

tallow pot (1914) US & Australian, dated; applied to a fireman on a locomotive

gandy dancer (1923) Orig US; applied to a railway maintenance worker or section-hand; origin uncertain; perhaps from a tool called a *gandy* used for tamping down gravel round the rail, and operated by pushing with the foot ■ F. McKenna: Footplatemen have a great regard for gandy dancers, the men who keep the rail safe for the train to run over. (1970)

sea-gull (c1926) New Zealand; applied to a casual, non-union dock labourer ■ Gordon Slatter: Ended up as a sea-gull on the Wellington wharves loading up the Home boats. (1959)

snake (1929) US & Australian; applied to any of various categories of railway worker

winger (1929) British, nautical; applied to a steward; compare earlier sense, cask stored in the wing of a ship's hold ■ *Harper's Bazaar:* Stewards will help you. . . . Behind your back they will call you a 'blood'— . . . they themselves being 'wingers'—and wonder how much 'rent' you will pay them at the end of the voyage. (1962)

hackie, hacky (1937) US; applied to a taxi-driver; from *hack* hackney carriage + *-ie* ■ Margot Neville: And now . . . unearth some other blasted hacky that drove me there. (1959)

snake charmer (1937) Australian; applied to a railway maintenance worker

snapper (1938) British; applied to a ticket inspector; from the clipping of tickets ■ Nino Culotta: 'E doesn't want yer ticket. The snapper's got yer ticket. (1957)

clippie, clippy (1941) British; applied to a bus-conductress; from *clip* (referring to the clipping of tickets) + *-ie* ■ G. Usher: An ex-clippie on a local bus. (1959)

hostie (1960) Australian; applied to a female flight attendant; from *air*) *host(ess* + *-ie* ■ *Sydney Morning Herald:* The hosties . . . are not concerned about Qantas picking up passengers here and there. (1981)

stew (1970) US; applied to a female flight attendant; abbreviation of *stewardess* ■ S. Barlay: I'm Mara. I used to be a stew myself. (1979)

A waiter

See at **Eating & Drinking** (p. 141).

A window-cleaner

shiner (1958) British ■ *Centuryan* (Office Cleaning Services): There we were, shiners and cleaning ladies, surrounding Fred and Dora on the float by the London Wall. (1977)

A work period

hitch (1835) Mainly US; applied to a period of service (e.g. in the armed forces) ■ *Washington Post:* In his work in intelligence, Pounder had many assignments, including a hitch as part of the White House security detail during President John F. Kennedy's Ireland trip. (1973)

lick (1868) US, dated ■ *Putnam's Magazine:* The father . . . did an occasional 'lick of work' for some well-to-do neighbor. (1868)

shop (1885) Theatrical slang; applied to a period of employment or an engagement ■ G. Mitchell: He was an out-of-work actor and was very anxious to get a shop, as he called it. (1978)

dogwatch (1901) Mainly US; applied to a night shift, especially in a newspaper office, or to any late or early period of duty, or the staff employed on this; from the earlier nautical sense, either of two short watches (4–6 or 6–8 p.m.) ■ *Truckin' Life*: Alan and Sue are the hosts and Neville looks after the shop on the dogwatch shift. (1983)

stag (1931) Applied to a spell of duty ■ R. Storey: There's seven stags in the hours o' darkness and only five of you to do 'em. Somebody has to do two. (1958)

trick (1942) US; applied to a term of service on a ship or in the forces; from earlier sense, period of duty at the helm of a ship ■ *Sun* (Baltimore): He reenlisted as a corporal, a rank he held at the end of his former trick. (1942)

Lack or absence of work

See also **Laziness** (pp. 293–5).

A break from work

vac (1709) Mainly applied to a university vacation; abbreviation of *vacation* ■ *Catholic Weekly*: Others lectured to working men in the vacs. (1906)

smoke-ho, smoke-oh, smoke-o, smoko (1865) Australian & New Zealand; applied to a stoppage of work for a rest and a smoke, or to a tea break; from *smoke* period of smoking tobacco + the Australian colloquial suffix -o ■ *Sydney Morning Herald*: Restrictive work practices—from heavily subsidised housing to the provision of pink salmon and oysters for workers' 'smoko' breaks. (1986)

rope-yarn (1886) Mainly naval slang; applied to a day given as a (half-)holiday; from the notion that at such times there are no drills, inspections, etc. and the crew are free to get on with ship's work, such as splicing ropes ■ E. N. Rogers: Rope-yarn Sunday is the seaman's Monday. Actually, it is a half day off and comes on a Wednesday afternoon. (1956)

hols (1905) Abbreviation of *holidays* ■ *Sunday Times*: July and August tends to be the party season (our university hols and the Aussie winter). (1993)

swing (1917) US; applied to a worker's rest period or to a shift system which incorporates such breaks, and also more broadly to time off work ■ James Mills: I went on my swing after that. (1972)

To have no work

sign on (1885) British; denoting registering at the Department of Employment (formerly Labour or Employment Exchange) in order to obtain unemployment benefit, and hence applied to being out of work ■ *Independent*: 3,500 people were prosecuted, along with 15 employers who paid their staff low wages but encouraged them to sign on. (1991)

Unemployment benefit

buroo, brew, broo, b'roo (1934) Dated, mainly Scottish; applied originally to the Employment Exchange, and hence to unemployment benefit; mainly in the phrase *on the buroo* receiving such benefit; representing a regional (mainly Scottish) pronunciation of *bureau*, in 'Labour Bureau'

the pineapple (1937) ■ *Observer*: 'There were just too many people on the pineapple.' The 'pineapple' is slang for the dole. (1971)

compo (1941) Australian & New Zealand; applied to compensation, especially as paid for an injury received while working; from *comp(ensation* + the Australian colloquial suffix -o ■ Patrick White: You got a bad hand. You see the doc. . . . You'll get compo of course. (1961)

To go on strike

hit the bricks (1946) US ■ *Time*: The United Auto Workers hit the bricks against giant General Motors. (1964)

A strike-breaker, blackleg

scab (1777) From earlier more general use as a term of contempt for a person ■ *Socialist Worker*: 180 women walked out. But 70 stayed in. . . . The scabs soon found out what it was like to be hated. (1974). Hence the verb **scab** act as a scab (1806) ■ *Times*: Frantic calls to friends . . . summoned . . . a driver who was prepared to scab as a special favour. (1969)

A retrained person

retread (1941) Mainly US, Australian & New Zealand; originally applied to a retired soldier recalled to service, and hence to a worker undergoing retraining; from earlier sense, renovated tyre ■ David Beaty: A diplomat with thirty years experience . . . not the re-tread given a job with other unwanted Civil Servants. (1977). Hence the verb **retread** to retrain, especially after a period of unemployment (1963) ■ *Wall Street Journal*: To 'retread' many retired nurses and other skilled professionals through refresher courses. (1966)

Equal opportunities

twofer, too-, -fah, -for, -fur (1977) US; applied to a black woman appointed to a post, the appointment being seen as evidence of both racial and sexual equality of opportunity; compare various earlier applications based on the general notion of 'two for one' ■ *Daily Telegraph*: Personnel departments [in the United States] are told always to try and hire a 'toofer'. (1979)

4. Business & Commerce

Salesmanship, selling: A seller

scalper (1869) Orig US; applied to someone who sells tickets, etc., especially below or (now) above the official rates ■ **Gore Vidal:** One-third of the tickets for the rally . . . are now in the hands of scalpers who are selling the most desirable seats . . . for as high as one thousand dollars a-piece! (1978)

shillaber (1913) Mainly North American, dated; applied to someone posing as an enthusiastic or successful customer to encourage other buyers, gamblers, etc.; origin unknown

shill (1916) Mainly North American; applied to someone posing as an enthusiastic or successful customer to encourage other buyers, gamblers, etc.; probably short for *shillaber* ■ **Mario Puzo:** As a shill she played with casino money. . . . She was subject not to fate but to the fixed weekly salary she received from the casino. (1978)

stick (1926) US; applied to someone posing as an enthusiastic or successful customer to encourage other buyers, gamblers, etc. ■ **Godfrey Irwin:** The cash the 'stick' wins is handed back to the operator of the game. .and the stick never has enough of his employer's money to make it worth his while to decamp. (1931)

shoddy dropper (1937) Australian & New Zealand; applied to a pedlar of cheap or falsely described clothing; from *shoddy* woollen yarn + *dropper* one who delivers goods

rep (1938) Applied to a sales representative; abbreviation of *representative* ■ **T. Lloyd:** I am the only member of this club who isn't a farmer's son . . . or a rep. (1969)

ampster, amster (1941) Australian; applied to the accomplice of a showman or trickster, 'planted' in the audience to start the buying of tickets, goods, etc.; perhaps short for *Amsterdam*, rhyming slang for *ram* criminal's accomplice or decoy ■ **H. Porter:** A shady Soho club patronised by dips, amsters, off-duty prostitutes. (1975)

To sell

knock down (1760) Denoting selling something to a bidder at an auction; from the notion of the auctioneer's hammer banging at the conclusion of bidding ■ **Daily Mail:** Although I was the underbidder at £1,100, the wily auctioneer . . . suddenly produced another one and knocked it down to me. (1991)

knock out (1876) British; originally applied to the reselling of items acquired by an auction ring; latterly applied to the selling of stolen items to a fence and to the selling of items by a market stall-holder or similar trader ■ **Observer:** Last week, our local market was knocking out Kiwis at 10 for a quid. (1996)

scalp (1886) Orig US; denoting selling stock, tickets, etc. at below or (now) above the official rates ■ **Sun** (Baltimore): The Stadium attendants told me

they are the same men . . . who scalp at other games, . . . selling 60-cent tickets for $1. (1948)

hustle (1887) North American; denoting selling or serving goods, especially in an aggressive, pushing manner ■ **Black World:** He hustled the watch to a barber for 35 bills. (1973)

shill (1914) Mainly North American; denoting posing as an enthusiastic or successful customer to encourage other buyers, gamblers, etc.; probably short for *shillaber* ■ **Herbert Gold:** It's how to get the audience. . . . I shilled for my wife. (1965)

flog (1919) British, orig services' slang ■ **Margaret Drabble:** Let's go . . . and look at the ghastly thing that Martin flogged us. (1967)

gazump (1971) British; denoting raising the price of a property after having accepted an offer by an intending buyer; from earlier, more general sense, swindle

shift (1976) Usually denoting selling something in large quantities ■ **Church Times:** He was also hopeful that some £40,000-worth of unsold books would eventually be shifted. (1990)

sug (1980) British; denoting selling or attempting to sell someone a product under the guise of market research; acronym from *sell under guise* ■ **Which?:** If someone tries to 'sug' you, write to the Market Research Society. (1988)

To bargain

jew down (1848) Derogatory & offensive; denoting beating someone down in price; from the stereotype of the Jew as a hard bargainer ■ **Harper's Magazine:** Jew the fruitman down for his last Christmas tree. (1972)

wheel and deal (1961) Orig US; denoting shrewd bargaining; from *wheel* person of high rank or importance + *deal* do business ■ **Publishers Weekly:** Lads who . . . wheeled and dealed with megacorporations. (1974)

A bargainer

wheeler-dealer (1960) Orig US; from *wheel and deal* + *-er* ■ **Louis Heren:** He [*sc.* Lyndon Johnson] was a shop-soiled old politico, a wheeler dealer, and past master of consensus politics. (1978)

To buy

gazunder (1988) British; denoting lowering the offer made to the seller of a property, especially just before the exchange of contracts, so putting pressure on the seller to lower the price or risk losing the deal; a blend of *gazump* and *under* ■ **Independent:** Gazumping, gazundering and all manner of noxious debilitations are blamed on slothful solicitors. (1990)

Mail-order

wish book (1933) North American; applied to a mail-order catalogue

Mortgages

Fannie Mae (1948) US; a nickname for the Federal National Mortgage Association, established by the US Government in 1938, and since 1970 a private corporation, which assists banks, trust companies, etc. in the distribution of funds for home mortgages and guarantees mortgage-backed securities; an acronym elaborated from the name of the association, after the female personal names *Fannie* and *Mae*

Deferred payment, credit

tick (1642) Usually in the phrase *on tick*; probably an abbreviation of *ticket*, in the phrase *on the ticket* ■ John Wainwright: Three of the others are already inside, anyway . . . and they were damn near living on tick. (1976)

jaw-bone (1862) North American (orig Canadian) ■ *New Yorker*: A young Canadian . . . started this film on a small grant . . . and apparently finished it on jawbone and by deferring processing costs. (1970)

the never-never (1926) British; applied to hire purchase; from the notion of the indefinite postponement of full payment; compare earlier Australian *on the never* at no cost to oneself ■ Jacqueline Wilson: They've still not paid off their mortgage, you know, and I wouldn't mind betting that Rover of theirs is on the never-never. (1973)

cred (1979) Abbreviation ■ *2000AD*: Special talent for turning any object (cred card, drink cup) into lethal weapon in his hands. (1990)

Prompt payment

on the nail (1600) From earlier, more general meaning, straightaway; origin uncertain, although other languages have parallel phrases meaning 'precisely, exactly' (e.g. French *sur l'ongle*, German *auf den Nagel*) ■ *Observer*: He always paid cash, on the nail. In the terms of the Belgrade mob, he was an honest guy. (1991)

Pawning: In pawn

up the spout (1812) Dated

in pop (1866) British; from the verb *pop* pawn

in hock (1883) Compare earlier sense, in prison ■ *Guardian*: If the goods are still in hock at the end of this time the pawnbroker has to remind the client that the contract has expired. (1991)

A pawnshop

pop-shop (1772) British; from the verb *pop* pawn ■ P. G. Wodehouse: This makes me feel like a pawnbroker. . . . As if you had brought it in to the old pop shop and were asking me what I could spring on it. (1942)

hock-shop (1871) From *in hock* in pawn (not recorded until later) ■ C. Irving: He had previously pawned one of the Matisse oils . . . to the Mont de Piété, the French national hockshop. (1969)

moscow (1910) Australian; latterly mainly in the phrases *in Moscow, gone to Moscow* in pawn; from the verb *moscow* pawn ■ 'Caddie': Me clobber's already in Moscow, an' so is me tan shoes. . . . There don't seem nuthin' a man can raise a deaner on. (1953)

A pawnbroker

uncle (1756) In early usage, usually preceded by a possessive adjective ■ *Times*: 'Uncle' is changing his image. His clients may still be in dire financial straits, but they are no longer the traditional working class. (1988)

To pawn

pop (1731) British ■ J. M. Barrie: It was plain for what she had popped her watch. (1902)

hock (1878) Orig US; from *in hock* in pawn (not recorded until later) ■ C. F. Burke: Then he went and he took everything he had—his automobile—and he hocked them. (1969)

soak (1882) British, dated

moscow (1910) Australian; alteration (presumably influenced by *Moscow* capital city of Russia) of obsolete British slang *moskeneer* pawn an article for more than it is worth, of Yiddish origin, from modern Hebrew *mashkōn* a pledge ■ C. Drew: Do you know where a man can 'moscow' a couple of snakes? (1917)

Price

steal (1942) Orig US; applied to a bargain ■ *News Chronicle*: At £30,000 it was a steal. I think it's worth £75,000. (1960)

daylight robbery (1949) Applied to the charging of an exorbitant price ■ *Guardian*: UB's £335 million payment was certainly seen at the time as what grocers like to call a 'premium price'. But now it seems more like daylight robbery. (1991)

To increase a price

slap something **on (1922)** ■ *Economist*: He slapped on an income-tax surcharge of 7.5%. (1987)

Profit

clean-up (1867) Orig US ■ P. G. Wodehouse: It was the man's intention to make what I might term a quick clean-up immediately after dinner and escape on the nine-fifty-seven. (1929)

push money (1939) US, dated; applied to commission on items sold

A dividend

divvy, divi (1872) Abbreviation ■ Graham Chapman *et al.*: If you'll wait till Saturday I'm expecting a divvy from the Harpenden Building Society. (1970)

Something profitable

skinner (1891) Australian; applied to a betting coup; from earlier sense, swindler, from *skin* to fleece, swindle ■ *Sydney Morning Herald*: Skinner for bookmakers. (1974)

money-spinner (1952) From earlier sense, person who makes large profits; the original meaning (1756) was 'a spider which supposedly brings prosperity to the person it alights on' ■ *Angus Wilson*: If he publishes anything it'll have every chance of being a money spinner. (1958)

earner (1970) Applied to a lucrative job or enterprise; especially in the phrase *a nice little earner* a means of making easy and often illicit profits ■ *Sunday Telegraph*: The family letting rooms on the quiet, or the person who has a 'nice little earner' on the side. (1987)

In profit

quids in (1919) From *quid* one pound ■ *News of the World*: And to make sure you are quids in anyway, we'll give you as well the starting price odds to £10 each way on whichever horse does win. (1976)

To make (as) a profit

clean up (1831) Mainly US; used transitively and intransitively ■ *20th Century*: A concerted drive to ensure that this 25-year-old veteran cleans up another £16 million. (1960) ■ *John Steinbeck*: It's the fastest-selling novelty I've ever handled. Little Wonder is cleaning up with it. (1947)

Loss

downer (1976) Applied to a downward trend in business or the economy ■ *Business Week*: The general market swoon could fall still more during the usual late-December sell-off, when investors are converting their downers to tax losses. (1977)

A customer

regular (a1852) Applied to a regular customer, especially in a pub ■ *Stella Gibbons*: Mr. Waite was not a regular at The Peal of Bells. (1949)

up (1942) US; applied to a prospective customer; perhaps from the sales assistant having to stand 'up' to go and serve a customer ■ *New York Times*: The hottest salesman who ever turned a looker into an up. (1949)

punter (1965) Often used dismissively; from earlier sense, person who bets ■ *Drive*: The more confused you are, the more likely you are to accept his offer. Because you are the punter. (1977)

Investment

spec (1794) Orig US; applied to a commercial speculation or venture, or more broadly to a prospect of future success or gain; abbreviation of *speculation* ■ *John Fowles*: I was rich, a good spec as a husband now. (1963)

piece (1929) Applied to a financial interest in a business, etc.; often in the phrase *a piece of the action*

An investor

angel (1891) Orig US; applied to a financial backer of an enterprise, especially one who supports a theatrical production; from earlier sense, someone imposed on for favours ■ *P. G. Wodehouse*: Ike hasn't any of his own money in the thing. . . . The angel is the long fellow you see jumping around. (1921)

arb (1977) Orig US; short for *arbitrageur* person who trades in securities, commodities, etc., hoping to profit from price differentials in various markets

white knight (1981) Stock Exchange slang; applied to a company that comes to the aid of another facing an unwelcome take-over bid; from earlier sense, a hero or champion

Stocks and shares

churning (1953) Orig US; applied to the practice or result of buying and selling a client's investment, etc. simply to generate additional profit for the broker ■ *Bond Buyer*: The churning of corporate bank accounts on or near tax dates typically pushes the funds rate higher. (1983)

warehousing (1971) Applied to the buying of shares as a nominee of another trader, with a view to a take-over

the Big Bang (1983) Applied to the deregulation of the London Stock Exchange on 27 October 1986, when a number of complex changes in trading practices were put into effect simultaneously; from earlier senses, creation of the universe in one cataclysmic explosion, hence any sudden forceful beginning

Advertisement

ad (1841) Abbreviation ■ *Mary McCarthy*: He was the Average Thinking Man . . . that . . . ad-writers try to frighten. (1942)

Organization

admin (1942) Abbreviation of *administration* ■ *W. Buchan*: A mass of practical details—sheer 'admin'. (1961)

A type of business

racket (1891) From earlier sense, a swindle ■ *John Updike*: I am in the insurance racket. I am a claims adjuster. (1978)

An agreement, a deal

a go (1878) Dated; mainly in the phrase *it's a go* ■ *P. G. Wodehouse*: 'Then say no more,' I said. 'It's a go.' (1936)

5. **Dismissal**

Dismissal

the sack (1825) Often in the phrases *give/get the sack* dismiss/be dismissed; usually applied to dismissal from employment; equivalent phrases recorded in French, Dutch, etc., although the precise derivation is not clear: perhaps the bag of tools returned to an apprentice on dismissal ■ *Cosmopolitan*: They will soon get the sack for revealing themselves as nothing but lazy slobs. (1990)

walking papers (1825) US; usually in such phrases as *get one's walking papers/give someone their walking papers* be dismissed/dismiss someone ■ L. Pryor: Hassan gave me my walking papers last night. (1978)

the bullet (1841) ■ *Crescendo*: It was only the boss's inherent good nature that saved me from the bullet. (1967)

the boot (1881) In the phrases *give/get the boot* dismiss/be dismissed; usually applied to dismissal from employment; from the notion of kicking someone out ■ *Wall Street Journal*: Mr. Kohl's aides say that the chief reason he got the boot was because the chancellor didn't trust him anymore. (1989)

the chuck (1892) Usually in the phrase *give the chuck* dismiss ■ *Argosy*: When they gave me the chuck, you married me out of hand. (1930)

the spear (1897) Australian; in the phrase *get the spear* be dismissed from employment ■ D. McLean: Danny got the spear from the job. (1962)

the push (1899) Usually in the phrases *give/get the push* dismiss/be dismissed; applied especially to dismissal from employment ■ Stan Barstow: 'Hedley Graham has started a month's notice.' 'You don't mean he's . . . ?' 'Got the push? No. He gave Maurice Kendall his resignation on Friday.' (1976)

the shove (1899) Usually in the phrases *give/get the shove* dismiss/be dismissed ■ John Le Carré: They should never have given old Connie Sachs the shove. (1977)

the air (1900) US; in the phrases *give/get the air* dismiss/be dismissed ■ P. G. Wodehouse: Surely you don't intend to give the poor blighter the permanent air on account of a trifling lovers' tiff? (1934)

the gate (1901) Mainly US; usually in the phrases *give/get the gate* dismiss/be dismissed ■ *Saturday Evening Post*: There's no reason why he should be fired . . . or given the gate. (1951)

the bum's rush (1910) Orig US; first applied to forcibly ejecting someone from a place, and hence more generally to dismissing someone; usually in the phrase *give the bum's rush* dismiss; from the notion of hurrying a *bum* (= vagrant) out of a bar or similar place ■ Eric Linklater: I told him I'd give him the bum's rush if he tried to pull that stuff on me. (1931)

the raspberry (1920) Dated; usually in the phrases *give/get the raspberry* dismiss/be dismissed; from earlier sense, derisive sound

the bird (1924) Usually in the phrases *give/get the bird* dismiss/be dismissed; from earlier sense, hissing and booing as a sign of audience disapproval ■ Peter Kemp: She gave him the bird— finally and for good. So he came to Spain to forget his broken heart. (1957)

cards (1929) Usually in the phrases *get one's cards/give someone their cards* be dismissed/dismiss someone; from the notion of the documents (e.g. national-insurance card) returned to an employee when employment ceases ■ Anthony Gilbert: Wouldn't surprise me to know he'd helped himself from the till, and that's why they gave him his cards. (1958)

marching orders (1937) British; usually in such phrases as *get one's marching orders/give someone their marching orders* be dismissed/dismiss someone; from earlier literal military sense, order to march (i.e. to leave by marching) ■ S. Chaplin: He was never any good to you. It makes no difference to me if you give him his marching orders . . . and hitch up with the Lodger. (1961)

the heave-ho (1944) Orig US; usually in the phrases *give/get the heave-ho* dismiss/be dismissed; from earlier sense, sailors' cry when raising the anchor ■ *New Yorker*: Do we keep him on or give him the heave-ho? (1966)

the chop (1945) British; also applied to sudden curtailment or cancellation; often in the phrase *get the chop* be dismissed or stopped ■ *Ink*: The Anglo-Italian tournament . . . must be due for the chop. (1971)

the arse (1955) Australian; in the phrases *give/get the arse* dismiss/be dismissed; probably from the notion of kicking someone out by kicking them in the buttocks ■ John Powers: I'm not worth a day's pay a week. I'm lucky Tarzan doesn't give me the arse out of the place. (1974)

the shaft (1959) Mainly US; usually in the phrases *give/get the shaft* dismiss/be dismissed ■ *American Speech*: She gave him the shaft after he broke their date last weekend. (1977)

the elbow (1971) British; usually in the phrases *give/get the elbow* dismiss/be dismissed; from the notion of elbowing someone aside ■ *Tucker's Luck Annual 1984*: You really think I should give her the elbow?. . . Tough, innit? She'll get over it, they always do! (1983)

the big E (1982) British; usually in the phrases *give/get the big E* dismiss/be dismissed; E from the first letter of *elbow* dismissal

To dismiss, get rid of

be (or get) shut of (1575) ■ Stan Barstow: 'I haven't *got* her.' 'You're well shut, from all I hear.' (1976)

send someone packing (1594) Denoting summary dismissal ■ T. E. Lawrence: As both example and guilt were blatant, the others went packing into the far room while their chiefs forthwith executed sentence. (1926)

show someone **the door** (1778) ■ George Bernard Shaw: 'Does Christine ever lecture them?' . . . 'Catch her at it!' said Krogstad. . . . 'They would soon show her the door.' (1890)

be (or **get**) **shot of** (1802) ■ *Daily Telegraph*: Advising its members to make haste to get shot of unsuitable employees. (1976)

kick upstairs (1821) Denoting removing someone from a post by promoting them ■ William Cooper: The plot was devastatingly simple— Dibdin was to be kicked upstairs and Albert was to take his place. (1952)

sack (1841) Usually denoting dismissing someone from employment; from *the sack* dismissal ■ *Daily Mail*: Jealous boss Terence Hancock blew his top when he discovered that the woman who had spurned his advances was seeing someone else. He sacked her on the spot. (1991)

chuck out (1869) ■ *Engineering*: Chuck out the conventional concepts. (1958)

boot out (1880) ■ Rebecca West: Were not the Turks booted out of here in 1878? (1941)

turf out, turf off (1888) ■ J. I. M. Stewart: These people have become my colleagues. If you use that sort of language about them I'll have to turf you out myself. (1976) ■ O. Jacks: The plane's loaded. . . . I can't turf off passengers. (1977)

spear (1911) Australian; usually denoting dismissing someone from employment; from *the spear* dismissal ■ A. B. Paterson: Didn't he spear (dismiss) you for cutting a plateful of meat off one of them stud rams? (1936)

bust (1918) Often applied specifically to demotion in the armed services ■ *Wall Street Journal*: A branch office manager recalls a friend, also a branch manager, who was busted down to a simple loan-officer status for failing to achieve quotas. (1989)

tie a can to (or **on**) (1926) ■ P. G. Wodehouse: I'm warning you to kiss her goodbye and tie a can to her. Never marry anyone who makes conditions. (1972)

kiss off (1935) US ■ M. & G. Gordon: The same FBI agents . . . getting tough. Well, kiss them off. (1973)

tramp (1941) Australian; denoting dismissing someone from employment; from earlier sense, *stamp on* ■ M. Wattone: I went to the surface and immediately was tramped (sacked). (1982)

wipe (1941) Australian & New Zealand ■ Patrick White: Suspended once—but they didn't wipe me. (1983)

bowler-hat (1953) British; denoting retiring someone compulsorily, especially demobilizing an officer; from the earlier phrase *be given one's bowler hat*, from the bowler hat formerly worn by many British male civilians

eighty-six (1958) US; denoting ejection or debarment from a premises, or more generally rejection or abandonment; from the expression *eighty-six* used in bars and restaurants, indicating that a particular customer is not to be served ■ *New York Times*: On the evening of July 22, Mr. Mailer was filming a dream sequence at the house of Alfonso Ossorio in East Hampton, when Mr. Smith came into the house. 'He told me, "You're 86'd",' Mr. Smith recalled yesterday. (1968)

sling out (1959) ■ W. Marshall: He was so bloody stupid we slung him out. (1977)

To dispose of

bin (1991) British; from the notion of putting something in a rubbish bin ■ *Guardian*: When first screened, it was judged so bad by the domestic audience in Mexico that the series was 'binned'. (1992)

To be dismissed

flunk out (1920) Orig and mainly US; denoting being dismissed from college, etc. after failing an examination; from *flunk* fail an examination ■ *Reader's Digest*: He flunked out of various high schools, not because he was too stupid. (1951)

Behaviour, Attitudes, and Emotions

1. Behaviour

To behave well or satisfactorily

keep one's nose clean (1887) Often implying avoidance of involvement in criminal activity
■ Angus Ross: Denis Fitzgerald . . . a known associate of villains, but managed to keep his own nose clean. (1974)

shape up (1938) ■ *National Observer* (US): After that [*sc.* adolescence] one is expected to shape up, get a job, get married. (1976)

To behave in an unacceptable way

carry on (1828) Denoting someone who behaves, and especially speaks, strangely or over-excitedly
■ R. L. Stevenson: There was Adams in the middle, gone luny again, and carrying on about copra like a born fool. (1892)

muck about (or **around**) **(1856)** Denoting foolish, aimless, or time-wasting behaviour; from *muck* dirt ■ Kylie Tennant: We been mucking about and mucking about, and got nowhere. (1946)

monkey about (or **around**) **(1889)** Denoting mischievous or aimless behaviour; from monkeys' reputation for mischievousness
■ Kipling & Balestier: I don't see how you fellows have the time to monkey around here. (1891)

fart about (or **around**) **(1900)** Denoting foolish, aimless, or time-wasting behaviour; from *fart* break wind ■ John Wainwright: Look! It's important. Stop farting around. (1969)

act up (1903) Denoting abnormal behaviour, often affected in order to impress ■ John Hearne: 'I'm sorry,' he said, 'I'm acting up a bit. I feel pretty tight inside.' (1956)

crap around (1935) US; denoting foolish, aimless, or time-wasting behaviour; from *crap* defecate ■ Stanley Kauffmann: Let's not crap around. Let's get to the business in hand. (1952)

piss about (1961) Denoting foolish, aimless, or time-wasting behaviour; from *piss* urinate
■ T. Lewis: Are you coming in? Or do we piss about all day? (1970)

play silly buggers (or **bleeders, b-s**) **(1961)** Denoting foolish, aimless, or time-wasting behaviour ■ *Guardian*: We don't want people jeopardising our position by playing silly bs. (1979)

Unacceptable in behaviour

out of order (1979) British; from earlier sense, contravening the rules of procedure
■ *Cambridge International Dictionary of English*: His behaviour in the meeting was well out of order. (1995)

To behave like

come (1837) ■ Colin Watson: I never thought he'd come the old green-eyed monster. (1962)

go . . . on someone **(1963)** Denoting adopting a particular mode of behaviour towards someone ■ *New Society* (headline): Amis goes serious on us. (1966)

A period of indulgence in a particular type of behaviour

jag (1913) Orig US; from earlier sense, drinking spree ■ *New Yorker*: A neurotic habit . . . may be overt, like a temper tantrum or a crying jag. (1972)

One's preferred mode of behaviour

thing (1841) Especially in the phrase *do one's own thing* follow one's own inclinations ■ Ed Bullins: Anything that anybody wants to do is groovy with me. . . . Go ahead and do your thing, champ. (1970)

Affected behaviour or speech

gyver, givo, givor, guiver, guyver (1864) Mainly Australian & New Zealand; especially in the phrase *put on the gyver*; origin unknown
■ D. M. Davin: I wouldn't want you to get stuck-up and start putting on the gyver and forgetting your own. (1970)

A person noted for their behaviour

a one (1880) Applied to someone who behaves outrageously or impudently ■ Edward Dyson: 'Oh, Mr. Ellis, you are a one!' she said. (1906)

operator (1951) Applied to someone who behaves in a particular way (often with an implication of underhandedness or unscrupulousness); from earlier sense, one who carries on financial operations ■ *Times*: One almost expects him to say, with J. K. Galbraith, that modesty is a much over-rated virtue, but he is far too smooth an operator to be trapped into such an admission. (1974)

2. **Favour & Disfavour**

In favour

in someone's **good books (1839)** ▪ John
Masefield: You'd ought to be careful with the judy. It's best to
keep in her good books. (1938)

Out of favour

on the shelf (1839) Applied to a woman (or
occasionally a man) with no prospect of
marrying; from earlier sense, put to one side
▪ *Daily Mail:* It is the spare men who will be left on the shelf.
(1991)

in Dutch (1851) Orig US ▪ John Dos Passos: While I
plodded around . . . trying to explain my position and getting
myself deeper in Dutch every time I opened my face, I saw
marvellous scenes. (1968)

in someone's **bad books (1861)** ▪ *Economist:* Mr
Bresser is already in the bad books of some of his colleagues
for his plan to trim Brazil's budget deficit . . . to 2% in 1988.
(1987)

in bad (1907) Orig US ▪ Kingsley Amis: This ought to
put me nicely in bad with the Neddies. (1953)

in the dog-house (1926) Orig US ▪ P. H.
Johnson: He'd been getting bad grades, he was in the dog-
house as it was. (1963)

on the outer (1928) Australian; from *outer* part
of a racecourse outside the enclosure ▪ T. A. G.
Hungerford: And you're on the outer for sticking up for him?
(1953)

(A) favourite

fave (1938) Orig US; used especially in show
business; abbreviation ▪ *Washington Post:* Art
Laffer, the Reaganauts' fave moneyman, threw his curve at the
American Meat Institute just recently. (1982) ▪ *Face:* These
new recruits may have allied themselves to Smithdom's cause
because their former faves, Echo & The Bunnymen for instance,
haven't delivered. (1987)

fave rave (1967) Orig US; applied to a special
favourite piece of music, film, musician, etc.
▪ *Melody Maker:* Smith's quartet version with Stan Getz was
one of the fave rave records of the period. (1967) ▪ *Times:*
The American fan magazine market, always at the ready to
replace a current fave rave. (1973)

That which one favours or prefers

cup of tea (1932) ▪ Muriel Spark: Freddy had stood in
the doorway of the dark Orthodox chapel and, regarding the
heavy-laden altar and the exotic clusters of coloured lamps
hung round it, said, 'It's not really my cup of tea, you know.'
(1965)

bag (1964) Orig US, Black English; from earlier
sense, category or style of jazz ▪ *Sunday Times:* His
bag is paper sculpture. (1966)

scene (1966) ▪ David Lodge: Washing up was more his
scene than body language. (1975)

Someone regarded favourably

fair-haired boy (1909) US, derogatory ▪ *Wall
Street Journal:* Mr. Hessler, an engaging man, was the fair-
haired boy at Unisys. (1989)

blue-eyed boy (1924) British, derogatory
▪ *Times:* During this period, farmers were 'blue-eyed boys'.
(1963)

Favourable opinion or comment

rave (1926) Orig US; applied to an
enthusiastically favourable review ▪ *Listener:* I
yield to none in my admiration for this pianist, whose first
London notice I had the honour to write long before the war (a
'rave' in case you think I am always wrong). (1958)

Brownie point (1944) Orig US; applied to
favour in the eyes of another, especially as
gained by sycophantic or servile behaviour; in
allusion to the points system used for
advancement by the *Brownies* (= junior members)
of the Girl Scouts of America, reinforced by
brown-nose curry favour, flatter ▪ *Times
Educational Supplement:* The clause would not be used to
'punish' teachers. Those who took part in extra activities would
get a Brownie point, he said, but classroom effectiveness
would be the prime test of a teacher's success. (1986)

To regard favourably, like, enjoy, approve of

swear by (*c***1815)** Denoting full confidence in
something ▪ *Washington Post:* My wife swears by the
Palmer House . . . , a restaurant down next to the old Lexington
Market. (1993)

go on (1824) Orig US; usually negative, in the
phrase *not go much on* ▪ *Nevil Shute:* Jo says she
wants to live in Tahiti, but I don't go much on that, myself.
(1960)

lap something **up (1890)** Denoting receiving
something with obvious liking or approval
▪ *Times:* Americans have lapped the book up, already getting
through Dell's first order of 100,000. (1972)

have a soft spot for (1902) Often denoting
sexual fondness ▪ *New Scientist:* He won a scholarship
advertised in New Scientist and has had a soft spot for the
magazine ever since. (1971)

have tickets on (1908) Australian; denoting
having a high opinion of someone or something
▪ Robin Hyde: You must have tickets on her, Starkie. (1938)

have time for (1911) Often used in negative
contexts ▪ *Bulletin* (Sydney): The bulk of the Nashos—
how the Army loathes that term—have little time for the
'protests'. (1966) ▪ M. Allen: 'Yes, I've got a lot of time for
Lester,' the Vicar continued. . . . 'He'll always lend a hand at a
fête or whatever.' (1979)

have a thing about (1936) Often implying an
irrational or obsessive interest or attraction
▪ *Guardian:* What is your favourite piece of clothing? Well,
it's not one specific thing. I love jackets short, long, colourful,
plain. I have a thing about handbags, too. (1991)

dig (1939) Orig US; compare earlier sense, understand, appreciate ■ *Guardian*: He doesn't plan ahead. He doesn't analyse himself or his music. He 'doesn't really dig the music business overall'. (1992)

go a (or (dated) **the**) **bundle on (1942)** Often used in negative contexts; from earlier sense, bet much money on ■ **Adam Diment**: I don't go a bundle on being told I'm a pro. (1968)

get off on (1973) From earlier sense, achieve sexual satisfaction from ■ *Time*: I really get off on dancing. It's a high. (1977)

To express enthusiastic approval (of)

rave (a1704) Usually followed by *about* ■ **John Updike**: So you're the young man my daughter has been raving about. (1978)

be all over someone **(1912)** Denoting an (excessively) great show of favour or affection ■ **Agatha Christie**: 'Were they friendly?' 'The lady was . . . All over him, as you might say.' (1931)

drool (1924) Denoting excessive or sycophantic approval; often followed by *over*; from earlier sense, run with saliva, dribble ■ *Observer*: It wasn't so much the spectacle of a distinguished ex-Prime Minister reduced to the role of a Princess Michael of Kent having to drool over some Happy Eater that she was opening. ('Oh, how very very very good,' she trolled as she was being shown around the ship's bar.) (1991)

go overboard (1931) Orig US ■ *New Zealand Listener*: I cannot admire 'abstract' interpretations any more than I can go overboard about sculpture rigged up out of bicycle parts. (1960)

Showing enthusiastic approval or liking

wow (1921) Orig US; from the interjection *wow* expressing surprise, admiration, etc. ■ *John o' London's*: A chorus of wow reviews from international critics. (1962)

rave (1951) From the noun *rave* enthusiastically favourable review ■ *Tucson Magazine*: These three-day bus tours . . . have received rave notices from all who have gone along. (1979)

Someone who favours or enjoys something; an enthusiast

bug (1841) Orig US; probably from *bug* insect ■ *Daily Colonist* (Victoria, British Columbia): There are no more critical people than what are generally classified as baseball 'bugs'. (1911)

fiend (1884) Orig US; from earlier sense, addict ■ **Ngaio Marsh**: I'm a bit of a camera-fiend myself. (1962)

freak (1895) Orig US; in early use derogatory; from earlier sense, odd or eccentric person ■ **P. Booth**: Boy, are you exercise freaks into punishment. (1986)

buff (1931) Orig US; from earlier sense, someone who is enthusiastic about going to see fires, associating with firemen, etc., from the buff-coloured uniforms of New York City firemen ■ *Globe & Mail* (Toronto): Sports buffs will enjoy many

diversions, with bicycling and camping . . . heading the list. (1968)

nut (1934) Orig US; from earlier sense, mad person ■ **L. Gould**: If you're such a health nut, how come you take all those pills? (1974)

sucker (1957) Orig North American; applied to someone particularly susceptible to the stated thing; followed by *for*; from earlier sense, gullible person ■ *Sunday Times*: I'm a bit of a sucker for celebrity-owned restaurants. (1993)

Liking; fond of; enthusiastic about

mad about (1744) Often implying sexual infatuation ■ *Sunday Mirror*: Gender Bender boys are mad about make-up and adore dressing up. . . . Gender Benders are anything but gay. They make up and dress up out of a sense of fashion. (1984)

nuts about, **nuts on (1785)** Often implying sexual infatuation ■ *New Yorker*: You're nuts about me, right? (1975)

hot on (1865) ■ **T. E. Lawrence**: The Squadron Leader is hot on punishment. (1925)

big on (1867) Orig & mainly US ■ **Cyra McFadden**: He said he'd had amazing results just acting out his anger with his patients. He was also big on video feedback . . . , role-playing . . . and Japanese hot tubs. (1977)

wild about (1868) ■ **Mrs. L. B. Johnson**: I was wild about the sack races! (1967)

keen on (1889) Often implying sexual infatuation ■ **Clifford Bax**: Maxine urged Guinivere to take Buster Graham more seriously. 'He's frightfully keen,' she said, 'on *you*.' (1943)

crazy about (1904) Often implying sexual infatuation ■ **P. G. Wodehouse**: And the unfortunate part of it all is, Bertie, that I'm crazier about him than ever. (1949)

hipped on (1920) Orig US; from *hip* inform ■ *Spectator*: Betjeman is absolutely hipped on his subject. (1962)

potty about (1923) Often implying sexual infatuation ■ *Reveille*: Women are potty about pans—they can't resist buying them. (1975)

sold on (1928) Orig US ■ **Anthony Price**: I've never been absolutely sold on the classics. (1978)

high on (1942) US; from *high* under the influence of drugs ■ *Guardian*: 'I am not high on the Thieu brand of Government,' he [*sc.* McGovern] said, noting that 40,000 people had been executed . . . by it. (1972)

mad keen on (1949) ■ **Lynton Lamb**: Derek Boots was not exactly the type to join us here. . . . I was not so mad keen on him. (1974)

stoked on (1963) Orig & mainly surfing slang; from *stoke* thrill, elate ■ *Sunday Mail* (Brisbane): I'm stoked on Chinese food. (1969)

into (1969) ■ *Listener*: Margaret is 'into' astrology, and consults the *I-Ching* each morning. (1973)

In love with

soft on (1840) ■ **Theodore Dreiser**: He's kinda soft on me, you know. (1925)

gone on (1885) ■ Saul Bellow: I was gone on her and . . . gave her a real embrace. (1978)

To regard with disfavour

have a down on (1828), have (or **get**) **a downer on (1915)** Orig Australian; *down* from obsolete British criminals' slang *down* suspicion, alarm, discovery ■ Somerset Maugham: She had a down on Lady Kastellan and didn't care what she said about her. (1947) ■ Siegfried Sassoon: He asserted that I'd got 'a downer' on some N.C.O. (1936)

have a derry on (1883) Australian & New Zealand; *derry* probably shortened from the refrain *derry down*, used jocularly for *down*, as in *have a down on* ■ Donald Stuart: And warfare, that's another thing Peter has a derry on. (1974)

have a thing about (1936) Implying an irrational or obsessive dislike ■ Nancy Mitford: I nearly fainted. I can't bear knees, I've got a thing about them. (1940)

To disapprove of

take a dim view of (1941) ■ *Daily News* (Perth, Australia): Bukovsky said he took a dim view of the way the West was pursuing detente. (1977)

3. Wanting & Getting

Wanting

itch (a1225) Usually followed by *for* or *to* and an infinitive ■ Charles Kingsley: The men's fingers are itching for a fight. (1853) ■ George Eliot: He had an itch for authorship. (1863)

gasp (c1586) Usually followed by *for* ■ John McVicar: He is gasping for money and I'm his lifesaver for the weekend. (1992)

fancy (1598) ■ *Midwest Living*: Whether you fancy a big flower garden . . . or favor container gardening, you're sure to find a just-right variety or two to enjoy from spring well into fall. (1995)

die (1709) Usually followed by *for* or *to* and an infinitive ■ Grant Allen: The pretty American's dying to see you. (1893)

after (1775) Used to denote something which someone wants to obtain ■ *Daily Mail*: In his McTaggart Lecture tonight, Elstein will categorically deny that he is after the job, modestly assuring delegates that the only job he covets is the one he holds at present. (1991)

vote (1814) Used for suggesting what one wants ■ Janice Galloway: Culture fatigue, she says. I vote we go back to the room and look at each other. (1994)

want (1844) Orig & mainly US and Scottish; used with an adverb to denote where one wants to go; originally used with a range of adverbs, now mainly *out* (denoting withdrawal) and *in* (denoting inclusion) ■ Arthur Hailey: Well, I'm not afraid, or proud, or anything any more. I just want out. (1979)

To dislike strongly

not stick (1899) ■ George Orwell: I can't stick my bloody office . . . signing one chit after another. (1934)

hate someone's **guts (1918)** ■ Noel Coward: You know perfectly well I hate Freda's guts. (1936)

To begin to dislike

go off (1934) ■ Muriel Spark: I simply don't feel anything for him any more. In fact, I've gone off him. (1965)

Antipathetic

allergic (1937) Usually jocular ■ *Punch*: Colonels have a curious effect on me. Quite frankly, I am allergic to them. (1942)

Exclamations of dislike or distaste

ick (1948) Orig US; back-formation from *icky* nasty, disgusting ■ John Irving: Blood, people leaking stuff out of their bodies—ick. (1985)

yuck, yuk (1966) Imitative ■ D. Simpson: It was the way he talked about her. . . . 'You know what older women are, wink, wink.' . . . Yuk! (1983)

yech, yecch, yeck (1969) US; imitative ■ Arthur Hailey: As for the food there—yech! (1979)

make a play for (1905) Orig US; denoting trying to get something; from *play* manoeuvre in a team game ■ P. Field: It's the second time War Ax has made a play for that money. (1961)

yen (1906) From earlier sense, craving for opium; usually followed by *for* or *to* and an infinitive ■ *Listener*: You write your music because you have a real yen to write it. (1983) ■ *Times*: The need for new educational certainties . . . cannot be met by yenning for the relative simplicities of the old 'elementary' education. (1977)

could murder (1935) ■ *Guardian*: Alec McCowen as the . . . Englishman who contains reserves of hidden passion behind statements like 'I could murder a cup of tea'. (1992)

could use (1956) ■ Rumer Godden: 'I could use a gin,' said Bella. (1961)

Wanting something in vain

whistle for something **(1605)** ■ *Guardian*: A remarkable point about the report was the number of women who were prepared to give Tuohy phials of their blood. I mean, I've nothing against the man but he can whistle for mine. (1992)

chance would be a fine thing (1912) ■ *Daily Telegraph*: A speech . . . warning of the dangers of sunbathing has mystified inhabitants of Tasmania. . . . 'Chance would be a fine thing,' snorts one ex-pat. 'Tasmania is rainier than Leeds and cloudier than Morecambe.' (1989)

A person who cannot resist a particular thing

sucker for something **(1960)** From earlier sense, gullible person ■ P. Goodman: Our present poor are absolute sheep and suckers for the popular culture which they cannot afford, the movies, sharp clothes, and up to Cadillacs. (1960)

That which is wanted or needed

the ticket (1838) Perhaps from earlier sense, list of election candidates, or from the notion of the winning ticket in a lottery ■ Graham Swift: But sweetness and innocence were never really the ticket, were they? (1988)

the job (1943) In the phrase *just the job* ■ Harold Pinter: Just the job. We should have used it before. (1960)

the shot (1953) Australian ■ C. Wallace-Crabbe: 'Beer, Bob?' Sandstone asked. . . . 'Just the shot, thanks.' Bob was thirsty now. (1979)

Acquisitiveness

the gimmes (1918), gimme (1927) Orig US; contraction of *give me* ■ C. Morris: One could only write him off as a victim of our acquisitive, thrusting philosophy of get and 'gimme'. (1963)

Acquisitive

on the make (1869) Orig US; applied to someone intent on profit ■ W. M. Duncan: Riordan was on the make. He'd found out something he could use. (1973)

To seize for oneself; to grab; to obtain

bag (1818) From the notion of adding something to one's 'bag' (= orig, amount of game killed and put in a bag) ■ Wall Street Journal: In his absence, Easy Goer bagged the winner's check. (1989)

snaffle (1902) From earlier sense, arrest ■ *Economist*: Its genetically engineered *Rhizobium melioti*—a microbe that lives on the roots of alfalfa plants—snaffles up to 17% more nitrogen from the air than ordinary *Rhizobia*. (1988)

glom (1911) US; usually followed by *on to* in intransitive use; from earlier sense, steal ■ Charlotte Armstrong: Trust Lily Eden, though, to glom on to a customer. (1969)

4. Ambition

An ambitious person

climber (1833) ■ George Bernard Shaw: Do ambitious politicians love the climbers who take the front seats from them? (1924)

go-getter (1910) Orig US ■ Marten Cumberland: He was a go-getter, an *arriviste*, . . . a bull charging at competitive life. (1959)

wannabe, wannabee (1988) Orig US; applied to someone who wants to emulate someone else; a respelling of *want to be* ■ Australasian Post: Scores of Samantha Fox and Linda Lusardi wannabees raided British lingerie shops for skimpy lace and satin undies recently. (1988)

A person on whom, or thing on which, hopes are based

white hope (1911) Orig US; from earlier sense, a white boxer who might beat Jack Johnson, the first black boxer to be world heavyweight champion (1908–15) ■ Lord Berners: He was a composer: the white hope (thus a critic had described him) of English music. (1941)

Ambitious

go-getting (1921) Orig US; from *go-getter* ■ Punch: My future as a go-getting reporter was bleak indeed. (1959)

pushy (1936) Orig US; applied to someone who is unpleasantly self-assertive in getting their way; from *push* + *-y* ■ Thomas Griffith: The more talented . . . can be counted on to disqualify themselves further by seeming too pushy. (1959)

To be too ambitious

bite off more than one can chew (1878) Orig US

5. Indifference

To be indifferent to something; not care

not give (or care) twopence (or tuppence) (a1744) ■ G. W. Appleton: He asked me if you really cared twopence for Kate. (1894)

not give (or care) a damn (1760) ■ Joyce Cary: It was obvious, as one angry young woman remarked, that he didn't give a damn—and so they were enraged. (1959)

not give (or care) a tinker's cuss (or curse, damn), not give a tinker's (1824) *tinker's cuss* from the former reputation of tinkers for profanity ■ Julian Symons: I don't give a tinker's, if you'll forgive the old fashioned way of putting it, who killed Ira Wolfdale. (1983)

not give (or care) a rap (1834) *rap* from earlier *rap* small coin; ultimately a contraction of Irish *ropaire* robber, counterfeit coin ■ Andrew Dobson: Sartre asserts its importance—in contrast to Genet who 'cares not a rap about history' (Sartre, 1963, p. 51). (1993)

not give (or care) a hang (1861) *hang* a euphemistic substitution for *damn* ■ Ouida: She don't care a hang what anybody says of her. (1876)

not give (or care) a toss (1876) ■ Time Out: I don't give a toss whether he's black, white or purple. (1973)

not give (or **care**) **a twopenny** (or **tuppenny**) **damn** (or **hang**) (1897) British ■ D. K. Cameron: It was rich in its lairds, men who . . . gave not a tuppeny damn . . . for anybody. (1980)

not give (or **care**) **a bugger** (1922) British ■ Frederick Raphael: It'd be a wonderful thing to have a magazine that just didn't give a bugger what it said about anyone. (1960)

not give a shit (or **shite**) (1922) ■ B. W. Aldiss: Do you think Churchill gives a shite for the Fourteenth Army? (1971) ■ Kingsley Amis: An interviewer . . . being very rude to a politician . . . and the politician not giving a shit. (1978)

not give (or **care**) **a hoot** (or **two hoots**) (1925) *hoot* probably from *hoot* loud cry, although compare earlier US slang *hooter* anything at all ■ Kylie Tennant: I don't see that it matters two hoots in hell if you don't function. (1943) ■ *Listener*: Winston Churchill was idiosyncratic in that he did not care a hoot about being thought a gentleman. (1966)

not give (or **care**) **a fuck** (1929) ■ *Ink*: We don't give a fuck if we have to stand around all day doing nothing. (1971)

couldn't care less (1946) ■ *Daily Mail*: They live in a world of their own and couldn't care less who knows they are having a whale of a time. (1991)

not give (or **care**) **a frig** (1955) *frig* a euphemistic substitution for *fuck* ■ Mary McCarthy: I don't give a frig about Sinnott's heredity. (1955)

not give (or **care**) **a monkey's** (**fuck**, etc.) (1960) British ■ John Wainwright: 'Not,' snarled Sugden, 'that I give a solitary monkey's toss what you wear.' (1975)

not give (or **care**) **a sod** (1961) British ■ David Storey: I don't give a sod for any of them, Phil. (1973)

could care less (1966) US ■ James Carroll: 'I hate sneaking past your servants in the morning.' 'They know,

anyway. They could care less. Thornton mistreats them horribly.' (1978)

not give (or **care**) **a stuff** (1974) Mainly Australian & New Zealand; from *stuff* have sex with ■ *Bulletin* (Sydney): The list goes on and on and on and as it grows so does the feeling amongst the blokes in the bush that no one gives a stuff. (1977)

not be fussed (1988) British ■ *Independent*: In a recession men don't mind about the holes in their underpants. Their womenfolk, who make almost as many menswear purchases as men, aren't much fussed either and prefer to spend on their children or themselves. (1991)

Indifferent, insouciant

flip (1847) Orig dialect; denoting a non-serious attitude; from *flip* move lightly or nimbly ■ *Times*: The word 'schizophrenia' is flung about today with flip facility. (1970)

couldn't-care-less (1947) ■ *Times Literary Supplement*: The couldn't-care-less attitude of people with little to lose. (1965)

what-the-hell (1968) ■ *Time*: The only real stumbling block is fear of failure. In cooking you've got to have a what-the-hell attitude. (1977)

It doesn't matter; It makes no difference

it's as broad as it's long (1687) ■ Charles Kingsley: The sharper the famine, the higher are prices, and the higher I sell, the more I can spend . . . and so it's as broad as it's long. (1848)

what the hell? (1872) ■ Rosamond Lehmann: As if she'd decided to say at last, 'Oh, what the hell! Let them rip.' (1936)

san fairy ann(e) (1919) Humorous alteration of French *ça ne fait rien* it doesn't matter ■ L. Brain: 'I wish you'd thought of my ulcer before you—' he began, and then broke off. 'Oh, san fairy anne!' (1965)

what the fuck? (1951)

6. **Excellence, Remarkableness**

Excellent

tip-top (1755) From earlier senses, topmost, pre-eminent ■ *Me*: Both actors are back on tiptop form, while Jack Nicholson . . . looks a dead cert for an Oscar nomination. (1993)

dandy (1794) Orig & mainly US; often in the phrase *fine and dandy*; from the noun sense, something very fine ■ Ogden Nash: Candy is dandy But liquor is quicker. (1940)

topping (1822) Dated; from earlier sense, superior, pre-eminent ■ Kurt Vonnegut: That was a really fine performance . . . really topping, really first rate. (1987)

cracking (1833) ■ *Independent*: A pitch that had both pace and bounce, a cracking cricket wicket. (1991)

A1 (1837) From the designation applied in Lloyd's Register to ships in first-class condition

splendiferous (1843) Jocular, orig US; fanciful formation from *splendid*; compare earlier obsolete use (c1460–1546) in the sense 'full of splendour', from medieval Latin **splendifer*

ripping (1858) Dated ■ Rosamond Lehmann: This is a ripping place, and they're being jolly decent to us. (1944)

hunky (1861), **hunky-dory**, **hunky-dorey** (1866) Orig & mainly US; *hunky* from US *hunk* safe, all right + *-y*; *hunky-dory* with unknown second element ■ *Bulletin*: I'll be all hunky. Nurse Dainton tends me like I was made of glass. (1926) ■ John Gardner: Everythink's 'unkey dorey 'ere. No problem. (1969)

spiffing (1872) Dated; from earlier sense, smart ■ **Cleese & Booth**: Oh, spiffing! Absolutely spiffing. Well done! Two dead, twenty-five to go. (1979)

daisy (1879) US, dated; compare earlier *daisy* excellent thing ■ **Edgar Wallace**: I'll introduce you to the daisiest night club in town. (1927)

tipping (1887) British, dated; from *tip* form the tip of something, probably after *topping* and *ripping*

ryebuck, ribuck, etc. **(1892)** Dated, mainly Australian; from earlier sense, genuine ■ **W. S. Ramson**: The *Australian Pocket Oxford* . . . is a real *beaut*, a *ryebuck* dictionary. (1977)

outasight (1893) Orig US; modification of *out-of-sight* (not recorded until later) ■ *Black World*: This Sistuh here sho give some out-a-sight sets. (1973)

corking (1895) Dated; compare *corker* excellent person or thing ■ **Anthony Hope**: It turns out to be a perfectly corking house—a jewel of a house, Stephen! (1911)

super (1895) From earlier cloth-trade slang sense, of the highest quality; ultimately an abbreviation of *superfine* ■ *Evening Post* (Nottingham): His wife Lee, said: 'Isn't it super? We can't get over it.' (1976)

out-of-sight (1896) Orig US ■ **J. D. Corrothers**: 'Out o' sight!' yelled a dozen voices as the poem was concluded. (1902)

bad (1897) Orig US, Black English; from earlier Black English sense, pugnacious, formidable, formidably skilled ■ *Time*: Adds longtime Fan Carolyn Collins: 'Oh man, I don't think he's changed. He got quiet for a while but he's still cool-blooded. He's still bad.' Bad as the best and as cool as they come, Smokey is remarkably low key for a soul master. (1980)

swell (1897) Orig & mainly US; often used as exclamation of approval or satisfaction; from earlier sense, stylish, of high social position ■ **Dashiell Hammett**: 'She's full of gas and ready to go.' 'Swell.' (1930) ■ **Judith Krantz**: All in all, a swell arrangement, and Spider learned a great deal during the year he was Levy's assistant. (1978)

crackerjack (1899) Orig US; from the noun *crackerjack* excellent person or thing ■ *Punch*: These seventy-odd pieces of crackerjack journalism begin with Walter Lippmann's putting Mr. Rockefeller in the witness stand sometime in 1915. (1966)

aces (1901) US; used predicatively; from the plural of *ace* card valued one ■ *American Speech*: That broad (female) is aces with me. (1943)

doozy (1903) Orig & mainly North American; perhaps an alteration of *daisy* excellent, possibly influenced by the name of the celebrated Italian actress Eleonora *Duse* (1859–1924) ■ *Courier-Mail* (Brisbane): Swingers Saturday Night was doozy. (1975)

bonzer, bonze, bonser, etc. **(1904)** Australian, dated; perhaps formed in word play on French *bon* good, influenced by *bonanza* ■ **Vance Palmer**: 'A bonzer night!' she said with drowsy enthusiasm. (1934)

bosker (1905) Australian & New Zealand, dated; origin unknown ■ **Frank Sargeson**: It turned out a bosker day. (1943)

smashing (a1911) Mainly British ■ *Chemistry in Britain*: This is a smashing book for anyone interested in surface chemistry and physics to have available on his bookshelf. (1977)

keen (1914) Orig US ■ *New Yorker*: 'My mother's going to buy me four new dresses.' . . . 'That's keen.' (1940)

snodger (1917) Australian & New Zealand; origin uncertain; compare British dialect *snod* sleek, neat ■ **C. J. Dennis**: It was a snodger day! . . . The apple trees was white with bloom. All things seemed good to me. (1924)

bottling (1919) Australian & New Zealand; compare earlier *bottler* excellent person or thing ■ **Ray Lawler**: They made Dowdie ganger in his place, and what a bottling job he done. (1957)

mean (1920) Orig US ■ *Observer*: Does a mean goulash, taught him by his grandmother and perfected in Hungary. (1973)

wicked (1920) Orig US ■ *Western Mail*: He could, as I say, sidestep off either foot, but what sped him on was a wicked acceleration over 20 yards. (1977)

wizard (1922) Mainly British ■ *Times*: 'How wizard!' they said. . . . 'How absolutely super!' (1974)

peachy (1929) Compare earlier sense, sexually attractive ■ **David Westheimer**: How about it, fellows? . . . Isn't it a peachy idea? (1973)

ace (1930) Orig US; from *ace* card valued one, which outscores others, from the notion of being pre-eminent above all others; originally only in attributive use ■ *Guardian*: It used to be an ace café with a museum attached, but that was in the old days when it was trying to lose its stuffy image. (1991)

cool (1933) Orig US, Black English ■ *Time*: The latest Tin Pan Alley argot, where 'cool' means good, 'crazy' means wonderful. (1953)

plenty (1933) Mainly US ■ **R. P. Smith**: When they want to say a man's good, they say he plays plenty sax or plenty drums. (1941)

solid (1935) US jazz slang ■ *New York Times*: There has been some solid trumpet players who can really send. (1943)

corker (1937) New Zealand; attributive use of the noun *corker* excellent person or thing ■ **D. W. Ballantyne**: The kids told Syd what a corker sixer it had been. (1948)

too much (1937) Orig US ■ **G. Lea**: I want to make it to the City. . . . Man, like the City is too much—and that's where I want to be. (1958)

ready (1938) US; originally and usually applied to music or musicians ■ **Cab Calloway**: That fried chicken was ready. (1944)

socko (1939) Orig & mainly US; compare earlier noun sense, a success, a hit ■ *Underground Grammarian*: Their latest brochure starts right off with this absolutely socko bit of dialog: 'What is cooperative education? In it's simplist [sic] definition, it is learning by doing.' (1981)

curl- (or **kurl-**) **the-mo, curl-a-mo,** etc. **(1941)** Australian; from *curl the mo* succeed brilliantly ■ *Coast to Coast 1967-68:* He . . . lifts one of the brimming pilsener glasses: 'Come an' get it! It's curl-a-mo chico. Lead in the old pencil.' (1969)

dodger (1941) Australian; perhaps from *dodger* bread, but compare *snodger* excellent ■ **Dal Stivens:** Instead of having to risk a knock on the Pearly Gates everything was dodger. (1953)

groovy (1941) Orig US; from earlier sense, playing jazz with fluent inspiration ■ *Observer.* To-morrow I'll tell him to go to hell, and what's so groovy is, he will. (1959)

grouse (1941) Australian & New Zealand; origin unknown ■ **D. R. Stuart:** She's a grouse sort of a joint, this bloody Ceylon, do me. (1979)

rumpty (1941) Australian & New Zealand, dated; origin unknown

in there (1944) US; applied especially to a jazz musician's performance

righteous (1944) US, mainly Black English

gone (1946) Orig US jazz slang; often in the phrase *real gone* ■ **L. J. Brown:** This is a real gone pad . . . it's what the clients expect. (1967)

crazy (1948) Orig US jazz slang ■ **James Baldwin:** She laughed. 'Black Label [Scotch]?' 'Crazy.' (1962)

whizzo, wizzo (1948) Compare earlier w(h)*izzo* an exclamation of delight ■ **Margery Allingham:** I wanted to look at some wizzo lettering on . . . the Tomb. (1955)

jolly d (1949) British, dated; *d* abbreviation of *decent* ■ **N. Fairbrother:** I say. Jolly d. It's *exactly* what I want. (1960)

gear (1951) Orig & mainly British, dated; from the phrase *that's the gear,* an expression of approval ■ **John Burke:** Once we even all sat down and wrote those letters saying how gear she was and all that rubbish. (1964)

beaut (1952) Mainly Australian & New Zealand; compare earlier noun *beaut* excellent person or thing ■ **Nevil Shute:** It's been a beaut evening. (1957)

tremendous (1952) From earlier sense, very great ■ *Guardian:* If Norma hadn't been so supportive none of this would ever have happened. She has been absolutely tremendous. (1991)

end (c1953) US jazz slang; used attributively; from *the end* the best ■ *Nugget.* I was blowing some jazz in the student lounge on this end Steinway. (1963)

far-out (1954) Orig US jazz slang, applied to playing that is daringly creative; often used interjectionally to denote enthusiastic commendation ■ *New Scientist.* 'How does it feel to be alive again after all this time?' 'Far out!' she replied with gusto. (1983)

magic (1956) ■ *Guardian:* Finally we ate in a pizza parlour. 'What's this pisser?' asked Jimmy. 'It's magic,' Gordon told him. (1975)

fab (1957) Abbreviation of *fabulous* ■ *Meet the Beatles:* Most of the Merseyside groups produce sounds which are pretty fab. (1963)

fantabulous (1958) Blend of *fantastic* and *fabulous* ■ *Sunday Express* (Johannesburg): Since the bust up of the fantabulous group, it's been George who's been doing most of the slogging. (1971)

fabulous (1959) From earlier sense, astonishing, incredible; first recorded in 1959, but the evidence of *fab* and *fantabulous* indicates earlier use ■ *Radio Times:* I think it's [sc. Salford] a fabulous place. (1962)

ridiculous (1959) Orig jazz slang ■ *Scottish Daily Mail:* Superlatives . . . gradually increased with the years into 'out-of-sight', 'ridiculous' and 'unbelievable'. (1968)

peachy-keen (1960) US ■ **Nik Cohn:** We dig America. We think it's really peachy-keen. (1969)

boss (1961) Orig & mainly US; from earlier attributive use of *boss* master, chief ■ **Martin Amis:** I have to tell you right off that Martina Twain is a real boss chick by anyone's standards. (1984)

shit-hot (1961) ■ *Sounds:* Chuck Leavell's pretty damn good all the time, and the rhythm section's still shit-hot. (1976)

storming (1961) ■ *Daily Mail:* Everyday People . . . is the mainstream pop disco hit, and . . . certainly deserves to be: it's a storming groove, glitteringly produced. (1991)

uptight (1962) Orig US ■ *Courier-Mail* (Brisbane): Disc jockeys . . . talk in a kind of sub-English . . . as in 'All right baby sock-it-to-me it's allright uptight yeah.' (1969)

knock-out (1966) ■ *Listener.* The wit and repartee of the DJ. . . . 'Hi there—it's great to be with you and welcome to another knock-out show.' (1968)

together (1968) From earlier sense, fashionable, up-to-date ■ *Jamaican Weekly Gleaner.* I read in the Miami Herald that conditions in the women's jails [are] not so together. (1971)

stud (1969) Mainly US; apparently from earlier sense, displaying a masculine sexual character

brilliant (1971) ■ **Sue Townsend:** I allowed Pandora to visit me in my darkened bedroom. We had a brilliant kissing session. (1984)

awesome (1975) Orig & mainly North American; trivialization of earlier sense, staggering, remarkable, prodigious ■ *Making Music:* I just know it'd be an awesome band. (1986)

primo (1975) Orig & mainly US; from Italian *primo* first ■ *American Film:* The Taylor murder had all the elements of a primo Hollywood thriller. (1986)

def (1979) Orig US, rap musicians' slang; often said to be an abbreviation of *definite* or *definitive,* but perhaps better explained as an alteration of *death,* used in Jamaican English as a general intensifier ■ *Smash Hits:* Like all good 'def' and 'baaaaad' rappers do, Sandra and 'Tim' really love their mum. (1988)

killer (1979) Orig US; attributive use of *killer* someone or something excellent ■ *City Limits:* Sometimes James Brown's albums stank, but there was always one killer track. (1986)

brill (1981) British; abbreviation of *brilliant*
■ *Guardian*: It may have been an awful night . . . but the meat and potato pies were brill. (1983)

rad (1982) Orig US surfers' slang; abbreviation of *radical* in same sense ■ *BMX Plus!*: This was just the start of the raddest one-week vacation a freestyler has ever had. (1987)

tubular (1982) Orig & mainly US; often in the phrase *totally tubular*; from earlier surfing slang sense, (of a wave) hollow and well-curved, and so excellent for riding ■ *Herbeck & Ross*: Donatello was at a loss. His brothers continued to top each other: 'Tubular!' 'Radical!' 'Dynamite!' (1990)

radical (1983) Orig US surfers' slang; from earlier sense, at the limits of control and safety ■ *Independent*: 'Radical' . . . no longer has rebellious or left-wing connotations but means . . . wonderful or remarkable. (1988)

fresh (1984) Orig US, rap musicians' slang ■ T. Kidder: Bro, that was fresh! (1989)

mondo (1986) Orig & mainly US; from earlier use as an intensifier, suggesting great extent or size

crucial (1987) British; from earlier sense, essential ■ *Looks*: Yazz's crucial new video *Yazz—The Only Way Is Up* is a must for your Chrissie list, with all her best tracks. (1989)

Excellently

a treat (1898) ■ *New Yorker*: I knew this floor had life left in it. . . . It's come up a treat. (1984)

An excellent person or thing

dinger (1809) Orig & mainly US; from dialect *ding* hit + *-er* ■ John Steinbeck: See how good the corn come along until the dust got up. Been a dinger of a crop. (1939)

clinker (1836) British, orig sporting slang, dated ■ Winifred Holtby: By God she could ride. A clinker across country. (1936)

ripper (1838) Now mainly Australian; compare *ripping* excellent ■ *Courier-Mail* (Brisbane): Nagle has a fine ear for Australian dialect. The book's a 'ripper', as his characters might say. (1976)

bottler (1855) Australian & New Zealand; origin unknown ■ Gordon Slatter: Congratulations boy, a glorious try, a real bottler, you won the game. (1959)

peach (1863) Compare earlier sense, sexually attractive woman ■ *Derbyshire Times*: 1972 Peugeot 504, white, 34,000, a real peach, £1,395. (1976)

bobby-dazzler (1866) Orig dialect; unknown first element + *dazzler*, from the notion of dazzling someone with excellence ■ John Braine: By God, you're what my old Nanny used to call a bobby-dazzler in that dress. (1959)

corker (1882) From earlier sense, something that closes a discussion, from the notion of 'putting a cork in it' ■ P. G. Wodehouse: 'You really enjoy watching fights?' 'I know what you mean,' I said. 'Nine times out of ten they're absolute washouts, of course. But this one was a corker.' (1936)

honey (1888) Orig US ■ *Globe & Mail* (Toronto): A real honey, automatic power steering, power brakes, radio. (1968)

whizzer (1888) From earlier sense, something that whizzes ■ *Zigzag*: 'She's long' features Bill's best guitar solo (despite many other whizzers). (1976)

knock-out (1892) From the notion of being knocked out by excellence ■ Angus Cameron: I've got a version of *Paradise Lost* that is a knock-out. (1970)

smasher (1894) Compare earlier obsolete sense, something unusually large

crackerjack (1895) Orig US; a fanciful formation on *cracker* or the verb *crack* ■ John Buchan: I've got a crackerjack of an editor. (1933)

pippin (1897) From the name of the type of apple ■ John Dos Pasos: He . . . got a book from a man at the hotel. Gosh it was a pippin. (1930)

beaut (1899) Mainly US, Australian, & New Zealand; from earlier sense, beautiful person or thing ■ Keith Weatherly: The bushie grabbed a plate and headed for the camp oven. 'You beaut,' he said. 'Coffee 'll do.' (1968)

peacherino, peacherine, peacheroo (1900) Mainly US; playful extension of *peach* excellent person or thing ■ S. E. White: Plant has a drag with Chairman Gay; don't know what it is, but it's a good one, a peacherino. (1910) ■ Martin Woodhouse: 'She [*sc.* an aeroplane] 's a peach,' he said. 'A real peacheroo.' (1966)

humdinger (1905) Orig US; probably from *hum* sing with closed lips + *dinger* excellent person or thing ■ *Times*: The last set was a humdinger, to use a transatlantic expression. (1958)

hummer (1907) Mainly US; from *hum*(*dinger*) + *-er* ■ N. Scanlan: When the new car was swung out on to the wharf, Mike walked round it and touched it lovingly. 'She's a hummer, Dad.' (1934)

whizz (1908) Perhaps from *whizz* whizzing sound; compare *whizzer* excellent person or thing ■ *Times*: Here are some of the gifts I have given to children in recent years: a massive iron key that could surely unlock the deepest dungeon in Nottingham Castle and makes a whizz of a paper-weight. (1959)

cracker (1914) British; perhaps short for *crackerjack* ■ *Shoot!*: I've played in a few crackers in my time but it's hard to think of a more exciting tussle than the one we had at Anfield in 1985. (1988)

the berries (1917) US, dated ■ H. L. Foster: You think you're the berries, don't you? Well, you might have been once, but you're a flat-tire these days! (1925)

the cat's (1919) US; probably elliptical for *the cat's meow*, etc., though these phrases are not recorded until later

the cat's meow (1921), the cat's pyjamas (1922), the cat's whiskers (1923), the cat's nuts (1928), the cat's balls (1962), the cat's ass (1967) Orig US ■ Sinclair Lewis: This kid used to think Pa Gottlieb was the cat's pyjamas. (1925)

the bee's knees (1923) Orig US, dated; a *bee's knee* was formerly the type of anything small or insignificant, though this sense appears to be a separate development ■ Dennis Potter: As you'd all know, we get a lot of blokes from round here nowadays as do reach Universities. And they think they be the bee's knees. (1967)

pip (1928) Orig & mainly US; from *pip* seed of an apple, etc. ■ *New Yorker*: He has written a pip of a meeting between Jerry and the therapist in the empty house. (1987)

the nuts (1932) US; from *nuts* testicles (compare *the cat's nuts* excellent person or thing) ■ William Gaddis: Get a little cross with mirrors in it, that would be the nuts if you want to suffer your way. (1955)

killer (1937) Orig US; from *kill* amuse, delight, etc. greatly + *-er* ■ *Melody Maker*: George Khan has a solo on the up-tempo passage of the same track which is an absolute killer. (1970)

killer-diller (1938) Orig US; rhyming reduplication of *killer*, probably influenced by *dilly* remarkable person or thing ■ W. C. Handy: My old friend Wilbur Sweatman—a killer-diller and jazz pioneer. (1957)

murder (1940) US, dated ■ Max Shulman: We got on the dance floor just as a Benny Goodman record started to play. 'Oh, B.G.!' cried Noblesse.... 'Man, he's murder, Jack.' (1943)

ruby-dazzler (1941) Australian & New Zealand; apparently from *ruby* red gem + *(bobby)-dazzler* ■ W. S. Ramson: The *Australian Pocket Oxford* . . . is . . . a gem amongst dictionaries if not a *rubydazzler*. (1977)

rumpty (1941) Australian & New Zealand, dated; from the adjective *rumpty* excellent ■ E. G. Webber: What a rumpty. (1946)

snozzler (1941) New Zealand; origin unknown

pipperoo (1942) US; from *pip* excellent thing + fanciful suffix *-eroo* ■ *Washington Post*: Of his beloved Nats, Bass recalls 'some real pipperoos'. (1985)

piss-cutter (1942) North American ■ E. R. Buckler: Gus Jordan's got a new rowboat. It's a real pisscutter! (1968)

a hard (or tough) act to follow (1975) Orig US; applied to someone or something difficult to rival; from the notion of a performer coming next on a variety bill ■ P. F. Boller: It was not easy being the second President of the United States; George Washington was a hard act to follow. (1981)

the dog's bollocks (1989) British; perhaps from the notion of being outstanding, from the prominence of the testicles in the male of certain breeds of dog, but compare earlier *the cat's nuts*, *the cat's balls* ■ *Times*: Before Tony Blair's speech, a chap near me growled: ''E thinks 'e's the dog's bollocks.' Well, he's entitled to. It was a commanding speech: a real dog's bollocks of an oration. (1995)

An excellent or admirable person

goody (1873) Orig US; now mainly used, usually in the plural, to denote one of those on the side of right in a film, book, etc. ■ *Times Literary*

Supplement: The Communists are goodies and John L. Lewis is a baddy. (1958)

sport (1881) Applied to someone who reacts generously or pleasantly even in untoward situations ■ R. H. Davis: All that was asked of the stranded Americans was to keep cool and, like true sports, suffer inconvenience. (1915)

goody-goody (1889) Applied to an excessively or ostentatiously good person; reduplication of *goody*

toff (1898) British; from earlier sense, upper-class person ■ *Daily Chronicle*: One of the witnesses . . . spoke of a generous employer as 'a regular toff'. 'Toff' is perhaps the highest compliment, or the bitterest sneer, according to the tone, that a man who does not make any pretence to magnificence can aim at a man who does. (1906)

white hat (1975) Orig US; from the white hats traditionally worn by the 'goodies' in Hollywood westerns ■ *Guardian Weekly*: His judgments of the men he dealt with. . . . The white hats are Truman [etc.]. A prime villain is Britain's postwar foreign secretary. (1978)

gent (1987) Applied to an admirable man; not recorded in print before 1987, but almost certainly in use well before then; from earlier, neutral sense, gentleman ■ K. Dunn: McGurk was such a gent that nobody who went tap-tapping at his windshield in the dark after the midway was closed ever went screeching in fear or pain or shame through the camp before dawn. (1989)

diamond (1990) British, mainly London slang; applied especially to a stalwart or reliable person

An excellent thing

daisy (1757) Mainly US ■ *Boston Journal*: In a new book upon 'Americanisms,' some of the less familiar are . . . daisy, for anything first-rate. (1889)

dandy (1784) Mainly US; from earlier sense, fop ■ D. Helwig: We . . . sat . . . waiting for Barrow Man to light his fire. At nine-fifteen he did it. It was a dandy. (1968)

splitter (1843) Hunting slang; applied to an excellent hunt ■ *Shooting Times & Country Magazine*: There was more than a holding scent and . . . we were in for a splitter. (1976)

lallapaloosa, lala-, lolla-, -palooser, -paloozer (1904) US; fanciful formation ■ S. J. Perelman: All agreed that Luba Pneumatiç was a lollapaloosa, the Eighth Wonder of the World. (1970)

purler, pearler (1935) Mainly Australian; from *purler* knock-down blow; *pearler* is now the commoner spelling ■ *Weekend Australian*: Flo's 35-minute speech was a pearler. (1980)

blinder (1950) British; applied especially to an excellent performance in a sport; from the notion of being 'dazzlingly' good ■ David Storey: You played a blinder. . . . It was the best game I ever saw. (1960)

zinger (1955) US; from *zing* make a sharp ringing sound + *-er* ■ Richard Adams: My private collection was becoming what an American friend . . . described as a 'zinger'. (1980)

To do (something) excellently

max (1837) US; used transitively and intransitively, denoting doing something to the maximum degree of excellence; from the noun *max*, a colloquial shortening of *maximum* ■ *Washington Post*: Scott has just finished maxing the push-up test at 68, where he was ordered to stop. (1982)

wail (1955) US, orig & mainly jazz slang; denoting performing excellently ■ Shapiro & Hentoff: I revered the amazing Fats Waller, who had lately made a splash wailing on organ at the Lincoln. (1955)

Surpassing (all) others

a cut above (1818) Often denoting (slightly) superior status ■ W. H. Auden: In New England Protestants of Anglo-Scotch stock consider themselves a cut above Roman Catholics and those of a Latin race. (1963)

streets ahead (1898) ■ *Economist*: France is now streets ahead of anyone, with 50% of its local exchanges . . . now running digitally. (1987)

top-notch (1900) ■ *American Speech*: Some successful criminals escape getting a monicker, for they, especially top-notch con men and syndicate members, think it adds 'class' to be without one. (1928)

stickout (1948) US; from the noun *stickout* outstanding sportsman or -woman ■ *Washington Post*: Kramer's only hope for a stickout newcomer would be Australia's Mal Anderson against Gonzales. (1958)

Best

bestest (1868) Used as an emphatic or nursery form of *best*; from *best* + the superlative suffix *-est*; orig dialectal ■ *Times*: The Duchess of York will remain 'the bestest of friends' with the Duke, she announced yesterday. (1996)

Someone or something outstanding or surpassing all others

the daddy of (1865) Orig US; from earlier sense, father ■ William Garner: You graduate from taking little chances to taking big ones. This one was the daddy of 'em all. (1969)

the father and mother of (1892) ■ *Punch*: The stage is set for the father and mother of a row. (1960)

the grand-daddy (or granddaddy) of (1907) Orig US; usually followed by *of*; from earlier sense, grandfather ■ Muriel Beadle: The granddaddy of all electrical storms dumped a cloudburst. (1961)

great (1912) Applied to someone particularly distinguished in their field; usually used in the plural; in use in this sense from the 15th to the 17th centuries, but the current usage appears to be a new formation on the adjective *great* ■ J. Walsh: Statues and paintings of the greats of French science and literature. (1963)

the father of (1930) Mainly Australian & New Zealand ■ D. W. Ballantyne: The local side got the father of a hiding. (1948)

stickout (1942) US; applied to an outstanding sportsman or -woman; from earlier sense, horse considered certain to win a race ■ *Washington Post*: As for third base, ball players and fans alike have no range of choice. Frank Malzone of the Red Sox is a stickout. (1958)

The best

(the) tops (1935) Orig US ■ *Punch*: Cooney's Cassocks stand the test, Choosy Churchmen say they're best. Sure-fire sermons, never flops; Cooney's Cassocks are the tops. (1958)

the end (1948) US, mainly jazz slang; from earlier, negative sense, the limit of endurability ■ *Neurotica*: Senor this shit [*sc.* narcotic] is the end! (1950)

the most (1953) Orig US ■ *Listener*: I would infinitely prefer to listen to the Kenny Everett programme—'the show that's the most with your tea and toast', as that masterly dj himself puts it. (1968)

endsville, endville (1957) US jazz slang, dated; from *the end* the best + *-s-* + *-ville* ■ *Esquire*: Endsville, the greatest. (1959)

To surpass all others

beat the Dutch (1775) Dated; often used in expressions of surprise ■ M. E. W. Freeman: Well, you women do beat the Dutch. (1906)

beat the bugs (c1833) US; often used in expressions of surprise

beat the Jews (1845) US, offensive; often used in expressions of surprise

beat the band (1897) Often used in expressions of surprise ■ Agatha Christie: Well, if that doesn't beat the band! (1923)

To be better than, surpass

knock spots off (1856) Orig US ■ A. L. Rowse: They [*sc.* the Nazis] . . . have at any rate been intelligent, and knocked spots off those public-school gentlemen. (1943)

To be surpassed by

have nothing on (1906) Orig US ■ *Listener*: For a picture of sheer bloodcurdling hatred and human degradation, our playwrights have nothing on this 60-year-old music-drama inspired by Sophocles' play. (1967)

Delightful, pleasing

darling (1805) Applied affectedly to something sweetly pretty or charming; from earlier use as a term of endearment ■ *New Yorker*: Isn't it going to be darling! (1970)

ducky (1897) British; from earlier use as a term of endearment ■ *Punch*: You can wear one of those ducky little lace caps. (1927)

deevy, deevie (1900) Dated, mainly British; affected alteration of *divvy*, from the first syllable of *divine* + *-y* ■ Vita Sackville-West: Tommy, you're going, aren't you? How too deevy! (1930)

217 Behaviour, Attitudes, and Emotions
loverly (1907) Representing a Cockney pronunciation of *lovely* ■ John Wainwright: He 'ad the ackers—believe me—wiv a car like that. . . . A loverly job, it was. (1968)

dreamy (1926) Orig US; applied to something wonderful or delightful ■ Stanley Kauffmann: 'Let us find a cool and lovely garden restaurant and have a slow, exquisite dinner. . . .' 'O.K., Russ. . . . Sounds dreamy.' (1952)

out of this world (1928) Orig US jazz slang ■ John Rossiter: She gave me the skinned fruit. . . . With Cointreau poured on, mine tasted out of this world. (1972)

neat (1934) Mainly US ■ David Westheimer: 'I could drive you on into Idyllwild if you want. . . .' 'That would be neat.' (1972)

mellow (1942) US ■ Dan Burley: The whole town's copping the mellow jive. (1944)

neato (1968) Mainly US; from *neat* delightful + *-o* ■ More (New Zealand): Those were the days when Beaver used to . . . have what she calls 'a neato free time'. (1986)

Delicious

scrumptious (1881) From earlier, more general sense, stylish, handsome, delightful; ultimate origin unknown ■ A. L. Rowse: The scrumptious meal she cooked, Cornish duck and Californian avocado stuffed with shrimp, our own cream from the farm with the delicious sweet. (1976)

yummy (1899) Often used interjectionally; from *yum* an exclamation of pleasurable anticipation, especially at the prospect of food + *-y* ■ J. P. Donleavy: Sitting, facing one another across the white table. Bacon and eggs, tea, bread and butter. Yummy. (1955)

scrummy (1915) From *scrum(ptious)* + *-y*, or a blend of *scrumptious* and *yummy* ■ Good Food Guide 1997: A man who ate . . . 'scrummy' chocolate marquise was a well-satisfied customer. (1996)

nummy (1989) US; probably imitative of the sound of contented eating, after *yummy*

Remarkable, exceptional

some (1808) Orig US ■ Winston Churchill: When I warned them [*sc.* the French Government] that Britain would fight on alone whatever they did, their Generals told their Prime Minister and his divided Cabinet: 'In three weeks England will have her neck wrung like a chicken.' Some chicken! Some neck! (1941)

and a half (1832) ■ M. M. Kaye: Roaring Rory must have been a hell-raiser and a half in his day. (1959)

bodacious (1843) US; perhaps a variant of British dialect *boldacious*, a blend of *bold* and *audacious* ■ Wall Street Journal: My return on investment in the area of poker alone . . . has been most impressive, showing bodacious annual expansion. (1989)

stunning (1849) ■ Daily Mail: The Leeds goalkeeper made a series of stunning saves in Tuesday's 1–0 victory over Nottingham Forest. (1991)

hellacious (1934) US; from *hell* (probably as in *hell of a . . .*) + *-acious*, perhaps after *bodacious* ■ American Banker: 'There was a hellacious turnout,' recalled Mr. Ford of the election, 'and that's what really killed us.' (1981)

unreal (1965) Orig & mainly US; used both positively, to denote something incredibly good, and negatively, to denote something unbelieveably difficult or awful ■ Truckin' Life: I reckon your magazine is unreal. I've never missed an issue for the past four years. (1986) ■ New Yorker: In the summer the dust and the flies are unreal. (1986)

A remarkable or exceptional person or thing

rip-snorter (1842) Orig US ■ Last Whole Earth Catalog: This is Gurney Norman the author speaking, bringing you the end of this folk tale, and it's a rip-snorter. (1972)

stunner (1855) Mainly British ■ E. A. Collard: Next comes a stunner—a skeleton sleigh, red as fire, drawn by a trotter black as coal. (1955)

lulu (1886) Orig US; often used ironically; perhaps from *Lulu*, pet form of the female personal name *Louise* ■ Evening News (Edinburgh): There are some parts of a new book on spying that aren't fit to be printed. . . . This one is a lulu. As long as two years ago, legal proceedings were initiated. (1974)

hot stuff (1900) Orig US; compare earlier, more specific sense, extremely sexually attractive person ■ Warwick Deeping: I'm getting my new M.-B. next week. Hot stuff. She'll do eighty. (1931)

dynamite (1904) Orig US ■ Washington Post: Even detractors will concede that Chung is just dynamite on the air. She's magnetic and compelling. (1993)

dilly (1908) Orig US; from obsolete *dilly* wonderful, from the first syllable of *delightful* or *delicious* ■ Raymond Chandler: You're the most impossible man I ever met. And I've met some dillies. (1958)

phenom (1950) US; applied especially to an unusually gifted person; shortened from *phenomenon* ■ New Yorker: He has a series of run-ins with a militant black rookie phenom. (1986)

A remarkable or exceptional thing

snorter (1859) Applied especially to something remarkable for its size, power, severity, etc.; compare earlier sense, one that snorts ■ J. H. Fingleton: May . . . now hit another 'snorter' through the covers. (1954)

scorcher (1900) Applied in sport to an extremely hard shot or hit ■ Belfast Telegraph: He . . . diverted a scorcher from Pat Spence later in the game. (1977)

something else (1909) Orig North American ■ O.D.: Oh, wow, these guides are . . . something else man! (1977)

doozy, doozie (1916) Orig & mainly North American; often used ironically; from the adjective *doozy* excellent ■ Times: Mr Bentsen was . . . sharply questioned about his short-lived proposal. . . . He admitted the scheme was 'a real doozy'. (1988)

doozer (1930) North American; origin uncertain; probably related to *doozy*, but perhaps a variant of obsolete *douser* heavy blow ■ New Yorker: You know about our crosswinds, I've seen some doozers here too. (1985)

sockeroo (1942) Orig US; applied to something with an exceptional impact; from *sock* strong impact + the fanciful suffix *-eroo* ■ *Spectator*. This latest box-office sockeroo also provides a modest example of the industry's throat-cutting activities. (1964)

something (1958) Usually in such phrases as *quite something, really something* ■ Beverley Nichols: The Ritz Bar, in those days, really was something. (1958)

stormer (1978) British; applied to something of exceptional size, vigour, or excellence
■ *Autosport*. Baird made an absolute stormer of a start to get away in the lead from the green. (1988)

Satisfactory

all is gas and gaiters (1839) Dated ■ Agatha Christie: I've only got to get hold of dear old Stylptitch's Reminiscences . . . and all will be gas and gaiters. (1925)

O.K., OK, ok, okay, okey (1839) Orig US; abbreviation of *orl korrect*, used in 1839 by the Boston smart set (see A. W. Read in *American Speech* (1963) and subsequent discussions). The term was picked up or developed independently as a political slogan (1840) by the supporters of 'Old Kinderhook', Martin van Buren, born at Kinderhook, NY ■ D. H. Lawrence: At first Joe thought the job O.K. (1922)

not (or none) so dusty (1856) British ■ J. B. Priestley: 'You're a swell tonight all right!' . . . 'Not so dusty, Mar,' said Leonard. (1929)

more like (it) (1888) Denoting improvement to a satisfactory standard ■ Angus Wilson: Shopping in the Town Centre provided something more like, and she ambled around, taking her time. (1964)

(all) Sir Garnet (1894) British, dated; from the name of *Sir Garnet* Wolseley (1833–1913), British field-marshal and commander-in-chief of the British Army 1895–99, who was famous for having led several successful military expeditions in the Sudan and elsewhere
■ Anthony Gilbert: She'd been knocked out . . . and her heart not being quite Sir Garnet did the rest. (1958)

right as rain (1894) ■ G. B. Shaw: *Proteus*. How did you get on with the King? *Boanerges*. Right as rain, Joe. You leave the king to me. (1930)

sweet (1898) Australian; often in the phrase *she's sweet* everything is satisfactory ■ Kylie Tennant: 'Everything O.K.?' 'Yep,' said the scrawny man beneath us. 'She's sweet.' (1964)

up to par (1899) From *par* average standard
■ *Washington Post*. How can they feel that their money is secure when the upkeep of the branch they bank with is not up to par? (1993)

jake (1914) Orig US, now Australian & New Zealand; often in the phrase *she's jake* everything is satisfactory; origin unknown ■ *New Zealand Listener*. Long as there's plenty of beer, she'll be jake. (1970)

copacetic, copasetic (1919) US; origin unknown ■ *Down Beat*. We hear two city cops chatting. 'Well, everything seems copacetic,' says one. 'Yeah, we might as well move on,' the other agrees. (1969)

jakeloo, jakealoo, jakerloo (1919) Australian & New Zealand; from *jake* satisfactory + fanciful suffix *-(a)loo* ■ S. Gore: The least you could do now is give some sorta guarantee that me and me Mum and Dad'll be jakeloo, when the invasion starts. (1968)

kayo (1923) Reversal of the pronunciation of *O.K.* under the influence of *K.O.* knock out ■ P. G. Wodehouse: If you think it's kayo, then it's all right by me. (1928)

hotsy-totsy (1926) Orig US; apparently coined by Billie De Beck, US cartoonist ■ Jessica Mann: What the law allows me, is mine. . . . So that's all hotsy totsy. (1973)

oke (1929) Orig US; from *O.K.* ■ Dylan Thomas: Laleham arrangement, though in the air, is oke by me, and if there is any one expression worse than 'sez you' this is it. (1933)

patsy (1930) US, dated; origin unknown

up to snuff (1931) Compare earlier sense, not easily deceived ■ E. B. White: The Central Park piece . . . is up to snuff or better. (1943)

okey-doke, okey-dokey (1932) Orig US; reduplicated form based on *okay, okey* satisfactory ■ Marghanita Laski: Things are okey-doke for a lot of people now. (1944)

tickety-boo, ticketty-boo, tiggity-boo, etc. (1939) British, dated; origin uncertain; perhaps from Hindi *ṭhík hai* all right ■ Salman Rushdie: Everything's in fine fettle, don't you agree? Tickety-boo, we used to say. (1981)

apples (1943) Australian & New Zealand; often in the phrase *she's apples* everything is satisfactory; short for *apples and rice* (or *spice*), rhyming slang for *nice* ■ T. A. G. Hungerford: How's it going, Wally? Everything apples? (1952)

all-right (1953) Used attributively; from the phrase *all right* satisfactory ■ Maurice Procter: He seemed an all-right bloke to me. (1962)

useful (1955) Often somewhat euphemistic
■ Nicholas Stacey: I had been a useful school sportsman and got into the first eleven at most sports at Dartmouth. (1971)

A-OK (1961) Mainly US, orig astronauts' slang; abbreviation of *all (systems) OK* ■ *Daily Telegraph*. The blood sample proved A-OK, but a following ultrasound scan showed a discrepancy in the size of the foetus. (1978)

Something satisfactory

a (little) bit of all right (1898) ■ Victor Canning: You might be on to a bit of all right here. Yes. . . . Sweet and easy as kiss your hand. (1973)

Adequate

not to be sneezed (or sniffed) at (1813)
■ Nat Gould: A thousand pounds . . . was not a thing to be sneezed at. (1891)

better than a poke in the eye (with a burnt stick, etc.) (1852) ■ George Eliot: 'Then,' he said . . . 'Here are those "Letters from Ireland" which I hope will be something better than a *poke in the eye*. (1852)

7. Beauty & Ugliness

Beautiful

easy on the eye (1938) Orig US; applied to something or someone delightful to look at ■ D. E. Stevenson: Miss Walters was certainly easy on the eye. (1943)

A beautiful person or thing

a picture (1815) ■ *Guardian*: The bride was, as they say, 'a picture'. (1961)

beaut, bute (1866) Mainly US, Australian, & New Zealand; abbreviation of *beauty* in the same sense ■ T. H. Thompson: Well, I guess she ain't a bute. (1909)

See also A sexually attractive person at **Sex** (pp. 68–9).

To beautify

glam (1937) Originally intransitive, but now mainly used transitively with *up*; abbreviation of *glamorize* ■ John Osborne: Get yourself glammed up, and we'll hit the town. (1957)

Ugly, unattractive

not much to look at (1861) ■ M. Deane: 'She is just a little fool,' said Roger—'a skittery little fool, with no sense, and not much to look at'. (1905)

drack, drac (1953) Australian; applied especially to a woman; origin uncertain; sometimes said to derive from the name of the US film *Dracula's Daughter* (1936); compare earlier sense, dull, dismal ■ *Sydney Morning Herald*: Mr Hardy said he would put aside his memories . . . of meeting Raquel Welch ('A drac sort—not nearly as good looking in the flesh as you would expect'). (1972)

like the back (end) of a bus (1959) ■ *Options*: Self-confidence has a lot to do with it too—until three years ago, I thought I looked like the back of a bus. (1993)

stop a clock (1994) In such phrases as *a face that would stop a clock* and *ugly enough to stop a clock*; not recorded in print until 1994, but in use before then ■ J. F. Garner: They were differently visaged enough to stop a clock. (1994)

An ugly person or thing

heap (1806) Applied to a slovenly or unattractive woman ■ James Joyce: The fat heap he married is a nice old phenomenon with a back on her like a ball-eye. (1922)

fright (1832) From earlier sense, something scaring ■ Sylvia Plath: Betsy looked a fright. (1963)

Mother Bunch (1847) Applied to an unattractive or untidy fat woman; from the name of a noted fat woman of Elizabethan times ■ *Guardian*: She no more looks like a Mother Bunch

than sounds like one . . . a fairly plump but elegant, well-dressed woman. (1964)

dogface (1849) US

haybag (1851) Applied to an unattractive woman ■ *Spectator*: The weary certainty that one more stranger has paused to inspect her casually and to depart calling her a haybag. (1967)

crow (1866) Orig US; applied to an unattractive (old) woman; often in the phrase *old crow* ■ Damon Runyon: She is by no means a crow. In fact, she is rather nice-looking. (1938)

rag-bag (1888) Applied to a sloppily-dressed person, especially a woman; from earlier sense, motley collection ■ P. Cave: She was neither attractive nor plain; not a raver or a ragbag. (1976)

trout (1897) Applied to an unattractive (old) woman; usually in the phrase *old trout*; probably from the name of the fish, but compare *trot* old woman ■ David Beatty: There were some funny old trouts and some spritely young ones, but no raving beauties. (1914)

plain Jane (1912) Applied to an unattractive woman; from the female personal name *Jane* ■ *Newsweek*: Takarazuka girl players, living like priestesses, are virtually adored by their plain-Jane sisters throughout Japan. (1953)

bag (1922) Orig US; applied to an unattractive (old) woman; often in the phrase *old bag*; probably from earlier obsolete slang sense, vagina ■ Monica Dickens: I've never really known a pretty girl like you. At the training college they were all bags. (1961)

no oil painting (1930) Euphemistic ■ *Listener*: Mr Tillett was no oil painting, but he was a gentlemanly sort of man. (1973)

roach (1930) US; applied to an unattractive woman; compare earlier sense, cockroach

old boot (1958) Applied to an unattractive and typically intransigent (old) woman ■ *Guardian*: Can this really be the same Julia Smith, the producer known as the toughest of tough old boots currently working in British television? (1992)

drack, drac (1960) Australian; applied especially to an unattractive woman; from earlier adjectival sense, unattractive ■ B. Beaver: I thought she was going to kiss it [*sc.* my hand] or bite it like another silly drack I knew once did. (1966)

boiler (1965) Orig Australian; applied to an unattractive (old) woman; often in the phrase *old boiler*; from the notion of a boiling fowl being older and tougher than a young chicken ■ *i-D*: You get a lot of dodgy boilers fronting acts, but here was a woman who didn't need to wear mini-skirts to attract attention. (1993)

8. Bad Quality

Of low quality; bad; inferior; unsatisfactory

lousy (1596) From earlier senses, dirty, contemptible ■ Keith Weatherly: You're not a bad bastard, Hunter, . . . in spite of your lousy cooking. (1968)

not able to hold a candle to (1640) Applied to one who is of lower quality than another; from the notion of not even being worthy to hold a candle for someone else to work by (i.e. take a subordinate role) ■ Guardian: As border guards, these men were supposed to be the elite of the Warsaw Pact's elite, but most of them couldn't hold a candle to us. (1991)

rubbishy (1824) ■ Guardian: The awful truth may be that, like Mr Gummer, we love rubbishy sausages. (1991)

not (what it is) **cracked up to be (1836)** Applied to something of lower quality than it is said to be; from dated crack up praise; compare earlier not (. . .) cracked up for (1829) ■ Enid Bagnold: The emotions have been found by then to be not all they are cracked up to be. (1951)

not much chop (1847) Australian & New Zealand; from Anglo-Indian first (second) chop first (or other) rank or quality, from Hindi chhāp impression, print, stamp, brand, etc. ■ Coast to Coast 1967-68: The street is not much chop, but not seedy, rather claustrophobic from the eight-feet walls of grey concrete on each side. (1969)

bum (1859) Orig US; compare bum lazy person, tramp ■ Anthony Powell: This is a bum party. (1931)

crummy, crumby (1859) From obsolete slang crumb body-louse + -y ■ I. & P. Opie: The game has been taken up by the physical training instructors under such crummy names as 'Poison Circle Tag'. (1969)

not a patch on (1860) Applied to one who is of lower quality than another ■ Guardian: There's Coppola's Godfather III which, though not a patch on I and II, is at least a much better than average movie. (1991)

cheesy, cheesey (1863) Orig US ■ Rose Macaulay: Hare and rabbit fur are just utterly revolting and cheesey. (1930)

rotten (1880) Often in such phrases as rotten luck, rotten shame, etc. ■ Westminster Gazette: Outside the competition they were, comparatively speaking, a rotten team. (1895)

snide (1887), snidey, sniddy, snidy (1890) Dated; from earlier sense, counterfeit ■ Edward Dyson: 'Tain't ther liquor wot's snide, it's ther dead hookity hides what it gets chuted into. (1906)

mouldy (1896) ■ F. M. Hueffer: I slogged like that for Nancy. . . . We could have got along on a major's pay, out there. Just got along! And then the blasted girl goes and gets rotten titles and mouldy houses to her back on the day the bottom drops out of me. (1912)

crook (1900) Australian & New Zealand; from earlier sense, dishonest ■ J. O'Grady: When the mulga starts to die things are crook all rght. (1968)

not much (or **no**) **cop (1902)** British ■ Kenneth Giles: The house . . . has never been much cop. People don't like living opposite a church or a graveyard. (1970)

N.B.G., n.b.g. (1903) Abbreviation of no bloody good ■ Gladys Mitchell: Bang goes our reason for coming here. . . . She said it was N.B.G. and that seems to be just about right. (1973)

chronic (1904) From earlier senses, continuous, persistent ■ Scotsman: 'The weather is chronic,' says a Seaforth Highlander. (1915)

schlock, shlock (1915), schlocky, shlocky (1968) Mainly North American; applied especially to inferior art or entertainment; Yiddish, apparently from slogn strike ■ Publishers Weekly: Shlock fiction with all the necessary ingredients, the result is mindlessly entertaining, if rather tasteless. (1972) ■ Spectator: The concentration on Sinatra arises out of the suspicion that the Reagan entourage of friends and hangers-on is loaded with shabby, shady, schlocky, smarmy, shyster millionaires. (1975)

crappy (1928) Orig US; from earlier sense, made dirty with excrement ■ Weekly Guardian: Rents as high as £52 a month 'for crappy quarters'. (1970)

half-arsed, half-ass, half-assed (1932) Orig US ■ William Gaddis: A half-assed critic . . . thinks he has to make you unhappy before you'll take him seriously. (1955)

kaffir, Kaffir (1934) South African, offensive; from the noun Kaffir used disparagingly of a black South African ■ Spectator: 'That was a real Kaffir shot.' (1961)

ribby (1936) Applied especially to something shabby ■ P. Alexander: She lived at the ribby end of Maida Vale. (1976)

under the arm (1937) British ■ Frank Norman: I read no matter how bad the book and some are right under the arm, stand on me. (1958)

nowhere (1940) Applied to something insignificant or dreary ■ Melody Maker: We all thought it was the most nowhere record we'd made. (1966)

ropy, ropey (1942) Perhaps from earlier sense, sticky and stringy ■ Daily Mail: It is, of course, very difficult to get waiters on New Year's Eve. If you hire them outside, you may get a few ropey types. (1957)

(strictly) for the birds (1944) Orig and mainly US; applied to something worthless or no good, especially appealing only to gullible people ■ Listener: Our answer, at that age, would have been that Stanley Matthews was for the birds. Football was just not mobile enough. (1963)

bodger (1945) Australian; from bodge patch or mend clumsily

piss-poor (1946) ■ Nation Review (Melbourne): I think privately that they look in pisspoor condition; but the spirited bidding rockets the price up to $2.50 in no time. (1973)

poxy (1950) From earlier sense, infected with pox ■ Jimmy O'Connor: The first tray . . . was full of poxy rings worth two or three quid. (1976)

duff (1956) From earlier sense, spurious ■ Crescendo: A duff piano player will still sound duff on a Bosendorffer Grand. (1967)

diabolical (1958) ■ Sue Townsend: Asked our postman about communications between Tunisia and England. He said they were 'diabolical'. (1982)

manky, **mankey (1958)** British; from obsolete *mank* defective (from Old French *manc, manque*, from Latin *mancus* maimed) + *-y*; perhaps influenced by French *manqué* ■ B. W. Aldiss: Have you chucked out that dirty manky beer you poisoned me with last time I came? (1971)

naff (1969) Mainly British; origin unknown; compare northern England dialect *naffhead, naffin, naffy* idiot; *niffy-naffy* stupid; Scottish *nyaff* unpleasant person ■ Record Mirror: A really naff song that wouldn't get anywhere without Ringo's name on it. (1977)

pissy (1972) From earlier sense, of or like urine ■ P. Cave: It makes you realise what a pissy little island we live on, don't it? (1974)

wanky (1972) From *wank* + *-y* ■ Zigzag: We loved that, 'cos it's such a wanky plastic paper and they thought by slagging us early they'd be in first. (1977)

Something of inferior quality

garbage (1592) From earlier sense, refuse, filth ■ Washington Post: The kiwano tasted as if a passion fruit had met a cucumber and gone wrong; the mushy pepino tasted like a cucumber that had lost an argument with a honeydew. They were the most expensive garbage I've ever put out on the street. (1993)

rubbish (1601) From earlier sense, unwanted material, refuse ■ Jonathon Gash: Don't misunderstand—I've sold some rubbish in my time. (1977)

hash-up (1895) Applied to something of low quality concocted afresh from existing material; from the verb *hash up* make a dish of recooked meat, rework ■ Times: A style perilously close to certain Colour Supplement hash-ups and clearly aligned for Overground consumption. (1970)

tripe (1902) ■ W. H. Canaway: The group of girls who were watching some tripe on television. (1973)

slum (1914) US; applied to cheap or imitation jewellery, and also (1929) to cheap prizes at a fair, carnival, etc.; compare the earlier obsolete sense, nonsense, blarney ■ Kenneth Orvis: Jewellery.... Top stuff. No slum. (1962)

crap (1916) Orig US; from earlier sense, excrement ■ Guardian: 'Crap' was the word used by Gerald Ratner to describe his very own jewellery and it's a word that pretty much sums up the state of the high street jewellery market as a whole. (1992)

stinker (1917), stinkeroo (1934) ■ Listener: Stylistically, the Royal Victoria Hospital is indeed a stinker. (1967) ■ J. B. Priestley: They've sunk two-and-a-half million dollars in this new stinkeroo that opens tonight. (1951)

turkey (1927) US; applied to an inferior or unsuccessful film or theatrical production, and hence to anything disappointing or of inferior value ■ Howard Fast: 'Have you ever thought of selling the place?' Jake asked.... 'Oh? And who the hell would buy this turkey?' (1977)

shit, **shite (1930)** From earlier sense, excrement ■ Rolling Stone: I enjoyed Simmons' logic that Shakespeare is 'shit' simply because he can't understand it. (1977)

dog (1938) US; from earlier jazz slang sense, an inferior piece of music ■ New Yorker: Audiences are in a mess.... They don't know what they want.... So many movies are dogs. (1970)

toe-cover (1948) Applied to a cheap and useless present ■ Listener: Gifts are given, not only the completely useless trivia or 'toe-covers' which litter the surgery, but more substantial gifts, such as briefcases. (1983)

tat, **tatt (1951)** Compare earlier sense, shabby person ■ Times Literary Supplement: New ways of getting the johns to spend their money on previously unsellable old tat. (1981)

shocker (1958) From earlier sense, something which shocks ■ Horse & Hound: Lucky Sovereign ran a shocker, presumably either unable or unwilling to give his true running on this firm ground and/or the Epsom course. (1977)

scrubber (1974) Australian & New Zealand; applied in sport to a second-rate player or competitor; compare earlier sense, inferior horse ■ New Zealand Herald: The three winners . . . have rather enjoyed their reputation as 'scrubbers' since they unexpectedly won their club title. (1977)

Bad advice

bum steer (1924) ■ W. H. Whyte: The muddy-headed way so many of us do [sc. talk] gives young men a bum steer. (1957)

Indifferent

so so (1530) Compare German *so so*, Dutch *zoo zoo*, West Frisian *sa sa* in similar use ■ New York Times Magazine: Even though I'm pushing 30, moisturizer plus cream foundation equals the sweats. Not a pretty sight. Possibility of replication: So-so. (1990)

no great shakes (1819) Perhaps in allusion to the shaking of dice ■ Daily Mirror: Sir Richard may not have been particularly great shakes. But he was never given much chance to show his paces. (1976)

nothing to write (or worth writing) home about (1914) ■ Victor Canning: He has a small place in the country.... Don't run away with the idea of anything worth writing home about when I say 'place'. It's a crumby little cottage. (1967)

half-pie (c1926) New Zealand; perhaps from Maori *pai* good ■ Roderick Finlayson: A few straggling houses and a half-pie store. (1938)

To deteriorate in quality

be slipping (1914) ■ Helen MacInnes: The journalist was the first to know he was slipping; next his editors; and then the public. End of a career. (1976)

Notification of bad quality

smoke-up (1927) US; applied to an official notice that a student's work is not up to the required standard ■ Indiana Daily Student: Sikes say 56 p.c. of Frosh probably had one Smoke-up. (1960)

9. Unpleasantness

Unpleasant; deplorable

mangy (1538) From earlier sense, affected with mange ■ Roy Campbell: The poet wags his mangy stump of rhyme. (1930)

hellish (1569) From earlier sense, of hell ■ *Guardian*: The new 1916 album was, as ever, a hellish din. (1991)

beastly (1603) From earlier sense, beastlike ■ Rhoda Broughton: That beastly hole, London. (1878)

snotty (1681) From earlier sense, dirty with nasal mucus ■ J. C. Herold: Albertine had slapped the Crown Prince and called him a snotty brat. (1958)

shocking (1842)

filthy (1875) Often applied specifically to bad weather ■ *Guardian*: On a filthy Thursday night at the National Sports Centre at Crystal Palace when the rain is not falling, a soaking mist hovers. (1991)

Godawful (1878) Orig US ■ Philip McCutchan: I heard the most God-awful racket above my head. (1959)

ungodly (1887) From earlier sense, wicked ■ *Guardian*: Most of the Brighton central front is like Cromwell's definition of English land law: an ungodly jumble. (1992)

like thirty cents (1896) US, dated ■ T. Tobin: Feeling 'like thirty cents' and 'the cold gray dawn of the morning after' became part of the American idiom. (1973)

septic (1914) From earlier sense, putrefying ■ G. Mitchell: Mummy and Daddy have had a row. Isn't it septic of them? (1974)

onkus (1918) Australian; origin unknown ■ D. McLean: All this yabber about Danny is onkus. (1962)

over the fence (1918) Australian & New Zealand; used to stress the unacceptability of something found objectionable ■ *Sydney Morning Herald*: Some publications which unduly emphasise sex were 'entirely over the fence', the Chief Secretary, Mr C. A. Kelly, said yesterday. (1964)

upter, upta (1918) Australian; from the phrase *up to putty* in a mess ■ 'Caddie': Dadda made some derogatory remark about the tucker. 'If it's upter why don't you 'ave a go?' (1953)

white-arsed (1922) ■ *Daily Colonist* (Victoria, British Columbia): Delegates . . . sat in shocked silence when an Indian leader accused them of being 'white-arsed Liberals'. (1975)

shitty (1924) From *shit* + *-y* ■ *Spare Rib*: All the shitty jobs that most women . . . do every day of their lives. (1977)

bloody (1934) From earlier use as a derogatory intensifier ■ R. W. Chambers: 'It's bloody,' I said. 'To call it bloody,' Ker replied, slowly and sadly, 'is fulsome flattery.' (1939)

umpty (1948) Apparently from obsolete military slang *umpty iddy* unwell, from *umpty* and *iddy*, fanciful verbal representations of respectively

the dash and the dot in Morse code ■ Celia Fremlin: This rather umpty friend of his. (1980)

scroungy (1949) Orig and mainly US; from the verb *scrounge* + *-y*; compare **scunge** and **scrungy** at **Dirt & Cleanliness** (pp. 177–8)

poxy (1950) From earlier sense, infected with pox ■ *Guardian*: No well-meaning bearded weirdos trying to set up a community garden in a poxy suburban backwater. (1992)

horrendous (1952) From earlier sense, terrifying ■ *Guardian*: Not that Scotland's rampaging back-row forwards really need any encouragement to give Wales, England or anyone else a horrendous afternoon. (1991)

uncool (1953) From the jazz sense, not 'cool' ■ *It*: The whole place [*sc.* Turkey] . . . is very very uncool. The Turks seem to be ready to turn with a malicious vengeance on young Europeans for the least (often no) provocation. (1968)

grotty (1964) Shortened form of *grotesque* + *-y* ■ *Guardian*: The capacity has increased to 830 now, with 40 staff seats in boxes like grotty cubbyholes under the roof. (1992)

unreal (1966) US; compare earlier sense, remarkable ■ *New Yorker*: In the summer the dust and the flies are unreal. (1986)

shitting (1967) ■ L. Cooper: That shitting girl looks at me as if I was dirt. (1980)

grungy (1972) Mainly US; from earlier senses, dirty, disgusting ■ *New York Times Magazine*: Boyle . . . taught high-school English at his alma mater to avoid the Vietnam draft, drifting into a weekend smack habit and a grungy life outwitting police searches. (1990)

punk-ass (1972) US; applied to a person ■ *Zigzag*: This period of court harassment . . . went on until July 25th, when I was locked up for good by punk-ass Colombo in Detroit. (1977)

shithouse (1972) From earlier noun sense, lavatory ■ *Zigzag*: If you're banned in town A and then banned in town B, well then town C has just got to ban you or it's, 'well what kind of shithouse place are you running there, councillor?' (1977)

hellacious (1976) US; from earlier sense, terrific, tremendous ■ *Daily Telegraph*: During the heaviest ground fighting of the war so far, described by one American commander as 'hellacious', at least 12 American Marines were killed and two injured when two light armoured vehicles were hit. (1991)

wack (1986) US; used especially with reference to (use of) the drug 'crack'; probably shortened from *wacky* or *wacko*, the implication being that it is crazy to get involved in drug-taking ■ *Atlantic*: Crack is wack. You use crack today, tomorrow you be bumming. (1989)

Unpleasantly early

unearthly (1865) Compare earlier senses, sublime, supernatural

ungodly (1889) From earlier sense, unpleasant, deplorable ■ *Guardian*: You know that the Lib-Dems are keen to get their retaliation in first during the campaign, calling a daily news conference at an ungodly 7.15am. (1992)

Disgusting

icky, ikky (1939) From earlier sense, sickly sentimental ■ Herbert Hunter: She wears the most *fright*-ful cardigans. Always some sort of *ikky* colour—to go with everything, I suppose. (1967)

gross (1959) Orig and mainly US; from earlier sense, (of behaviour, etc.) coarse, unrefined ■ Joseph Hyams: 'She really thinks he's gross, huh?' . . . 'The pits,' said Freda. (1978)

scroungy (1959) Orig and mainly US; from earlier senses, unpleasant, dirty, shabby ■ G. Winokur: I was fascinated with the scroungy, low life diseases . . . in that clinic. (1981)

grotty (1964) Shortened form of *grotesque* + *-y* ■ *Times*: 'I don't like the grotty old pub,' says Miss McCormick. (1970)

grody, groady, groddy, groaty, etc. **(1965)** US; often in the phrase *grody to the max*; from *grod-, groat-* (altered forms of *grot(esque)* + *-y*; compare grotty ■ *Los Angeles Times*: Moon Zappa calls her toenails '*Grody* to the *max*', which means disgusting beyond belief. (1982)

grungy (1965) Mainly US; perhaps inspired by *scroungy* ■ *Sunday Times*: In 1973, 47th Street Photo moved one block east to its current location, a grungy walk-up at 67 West 47th Street. (1983)

scuzzy (1968) Orig and mainly North American; from the noun *scuzz* + *-y* ■ *New Musical Express*: Zeppelin were really dumb: visibly hanging out . . . with the scuzziest groupies in town. (1987)

yechy, yecchy (1969) US; from the interjection *yech* + *-y*

yucky, yukky (1970) From the interjection *yuck* + *-y* ■ Mildred Gordon: It's only bats, I say. . . . 'They're weird,' says Linda. 'Yucky.' (1981)

Someone or something unpleasant or unendurable

the end (1938) ■ Gillian Freeman: Donald, you really are the absolute end. (1959)

the pits (1953) Orig US ■ *Observer*: I've never been fined for saying something obscene. It's always been for saying 'You're the pits,' or something.—John McEnroe. (1981) ■ J. Fuller: Hey, give me a little comfort here. This weather is the pits. (1985)

endsville (a1962) US

An unpleasant or despicable person

pig (1546) ■ P. G. Winslow: I had some beautiful birds in London, but I had to stay on the good side of that pig, or she might have noticed more than was good for her. (1977)

beast (1772) From earlier stronger sense, bestial person

blister (1806) Dated British; from earlier sense, swelling on the skin ■ P. G. Wodehouse: Women are a wash-out. I see no future for the sex, Bertie. Blisters, all of them. (1930)

nark (1846) Mainly Australian & New Zealand ■ Vance Palmer: 'Oh, don't be a nark, Miss Byrne,' he coaxes her. (1928)

cunt (1860) From earlier sense, female genitals ■ Samuel Beckett: They think they can confuse me. . . . Proper cunts whoever they are. (1956)

pill (1871) ■ Brian Garfield: 'Do you love your wife?'. . . 'You're a pill. Yes, I love her.' (1977)

rotter (1894) British; from the verb *rot* + *-er* ■ G. Swift: He liked his mother and sisters . .: all other women he classed as 'rotters'. (1900)

so-and-so (1897) Euphemistic ■ Keith Weatherly: It's not much good you staying out if some other so-and-so is going to work it, is there? (1968)

Noah's Ark (1898) Orig Australian; rhyming slang for *nark* ■ J. Alard: Ya knows Bill, yer gettin' to be a real Noah's Ark. (1968)

wowser (1899) Australian & New Zealand, dated; origin uncertain; perhaps from British dialect *wow* howl, grumble; claimed by John Norton (c1858–1916), editor of the Sydney *Truth*, as his coinage

scroucher, scrousher, scrowcher (1901) Australian; origin uncertain; perhaps connected with dialect *scrouch* crouch, bend ■ D'Arcy Niland: Ah, I could puke. That scrousher, that rough-house annie, what's she got to get uppety about? (1966)

whore (1906) From earlier senses, female prostitute, promiscuous woman ■ E. Gaines: 'You hear me whore?' 'I might be a whore, but I'm not a merciless killer,' he said. (1968)

scunge (1912) Orig Scottish; from earlier sense, sly fellow; ultimate origin unknown ■ *Comment* (New Zealand): He obviously thought I must be a bit of a scunge asking political questions. (1967)

crumb (1918) Orig US; probably a back-formation from *crumby, crummy* lousy, dirty, distasteful, of low quality, itself from *crumb* in the obsolete slang sense, body-louse ■ *Women Speaking*: If a man doesn't like a girl's looks or personality, she's a . . . crumb. (1970)

roach (1930) US; from earlier sense, cockroach

face-ache (1937) British; often applied specifically to a mournful-looking person; compare earlier sense, neuralgia ■ Galton & Simpson: On a train . . . a carriageful of the most miserable-looking bunch of face-aches. (1961)

bad news (1946) Applied especially to someone best avoided; from earlier sense, something unpleasant ■ Dulcie Gray: Milly these days was plain bad news. Her fascination had evaporated. (1974)

An unpleasant or despicable male person

Many of the words in this section do not positively denote a male person, but are in practice almost exclusively applied to males rather than females.

shit, shite (1508) From earlier sense, excrement
■ John Irving: Oh, I never knew what *shits* men were until I became a woman. (1978)

scab (1590) From earlier sense, incrustation formed over a wound

rat (1594) ■ *Guardian*: Hope told his star-studded audience: 'In my life a lot of people have called me a rat, so it's good to be one officially.' (1991)

louse (1633) ■ T. Morrison: What a louse Valerian was. (1981)

son of a bitch, son-of-a-bitch, sonofabitch, sonuvabitch, etc. *pl.* **sons of bitches (1707)** Now mainly US ■ J. D. Salinger: Boy, I can't stand that sonuvabitch. (1951)

bugger (1719) From earlier sense, one who practises anal intercourse ■ *Listener*: Come and sit on my other side. Otherwise they will put me beside that bugger Oparin. (1969)

booger (1770) US; from a dialectal pronunciation of *bugger* ■ *Longman Dictionary of Contemporary English*: You wouldn't want to meet him in a dark alley—he's a mean-looking booger. (1995)

sod (1818) Abbreviation of *sodomite* ■ John Braine: It's time he was dead. . . . If you want to destroy the sod, Frank, I'll give you absolutely all the dirt. (1968)

bastard (1830) From earlier sense, one born out of wedlock ■ H. G. Wells: Serve the cocky little bastard right. (1940)

skunk (1841) From earlier sense, smelly animal of the weasel family ■ Pierre Berton: It called Edwards a 'ruffian', a 'moral leper', and a 'skunk . . . whose literary fulminations cannot but create the impression that he was born in a brothel and bred on a dungpile.' (1973)

swine (1842) From earlier more specific sense, sensual, degraded or coarse person ■ *Guardian*: Mr Skinner suddenly found his output being jammed from the Tory benches. 'You swine!' Dame Elaine Kellett-Bowman began to shriek at an ear-splitting high-frequency. (1991)

shicer, schicer, shiser (1846) From German *Scheisser* shitter

b, B (1851) Euphemistic; abbreviation of *bugger* or *bastard* ■ Noel Streatfield: Can't 'elp bein' sorry for the poor old B. (1952)

stink-pot (1854) ■ David Ballantyne: They can call me miserable old stinkpot. (1948)

stiff (1882) Orig US ■ *New York Times*: And if a black man did buy a house, hey, we knocked on his door and said hello. If he was a nice guy, great. If he was a stiff, well, I know lots of white stiffs, too. (1975)

bleeder (1887) ■ James Curtis: Give me the damn groin, you robbing bleeder. (1936)

fucker (*a*1890) From earlier sense, one who copulates ■ Angus Wilson: 'We'll get you, you fucker!' Barley was shouting. (1961)

ratbag (1890) Orig Australian & New Zealand ■ Barry Crump: This'd be the best scrapper among you bunch of ratbags, wouldn't it? (1961)

fink (1894) US; applied especially to a disloyal person; perhaps from German *Fink* person not belonging to the students' association, or from German *Schmierfink* despicable person ■ Raymond Chandler: Now he's looking for the fink that turned him up eight years ago. (1940) ■ Charles Williams: Except for being a rat, a fink, a scab, a thug, and a goon, he's one of the sweetest guys you'll ever meet. (1959)

blighter (1896) British; from *blight* + *-er* ■ J. I. M. Stewart: 'What we have to contrive,' he said, 'is fair shares—or something near it—for each of the little blighters.' (1957)

cheap skate (1896) Dated US

skate (1896) Mainly US; compare earlier sense, worn-out horse ■ Harold Pinter: *Aston*: I saw him have a go at you. *Davies*: . . . The filthy skate, an old man like me. (1960)

stinker (1898) ■ *Daily Mail*: A gang of 'real stinkers' have raided a top wartime air ace and stolen his most prized souvenir—a 6ft. German propellor. (1975)

toe-rag (1912) British; from earlier sense, tramp, vagrant, from the rag wound round a tramp's foot in place of a sock ■ Henry Calvin: Move, ya useless big toerag! (1971)

cocksucker (1918) From earlier sense, one who performs fellatio ■ James Baldwin: If it wasn't for the spooks wouldn't a damn one of you white cock suckers ever get laid. (1962)

S.O.B., s.o.b. (1918) Mainly US; abbreviation of *son of a bitch*, also of silly old bastard, etc. ■ C. Stead: That s.o.b. Montagu got me the job 'ere, you know. (1934)

jelly bean (1919) Orig US; from earlier sense, jelly-like bean-shaped sweet ■ William Faulkner: Are you hiding out in the woods with one of those damn slick-headed jellybeans? (1929)

four-letter man (1923) British, euphemistic; probably from the four letters of the word *shit* ■ Iris Murdoch: Felix regarded Randall as a four-letter man of the first order. (1962)

crut (1925) US; a variant of *crud* ■ Ernest Hemingway: You miserable little crut. (1937)

oik, oick (1925) British; originally applied derisively by schoolboys to members of another school or to unpopular school-fellows, and hence used generally to denote any obnoxious or uncultured male; origin uncertain, though possibly from the verb (h)*oick* spit ■ Nicholas Blake: Smithers is such an oick. (1935)

creep (1926) Orig US ■ *Punch*: 'Maurice Thew School of Body-building'? That'll be that phoney creep upstairs. (1966)

swipe (1929) Probably a variant of obsolete slang *sweep* disreputable or mischievous person ■ R. Park: His tormentors leapt off him. . . . 'Bloody little swipes!' said Mr Mate Solivich. (1951)

twat, twot(t (1929) From earlier sense, female genitals ■ *Guardian*: Miss Currie (who called her teacher a twat) can in part be excused. Her mother has 10 entries in Honourable Insults, a compilation of political invective. (1992)

crud (1930) Orig US; from earlier sense, dirty disgusting material ■ K. A. Saddler: Can't stand the man. A real crud. (1966)

lug (1931) Mainly North American ■ Berkeley Mather: Any other names you can come up with?... You don't owe these lugs anything. (1973)

heel (1932) Orig US; from earlier sense, double-crosser ■ Times Literary Supplement: John Augustus Grimshawe was a heel about money and women. (1958)

arsehole, (US) asshole (1933) Orig US; from earlier sense, anus ■ Blitz: I was on the Farringdon Road, and some arsehole decided to cut across. (1989)

jerk (1935) Orig US; perhaps influenced by the US adjective jerkwater insignificant, inferior, from jerkwater train train on a branch line, from the notion of taking on water by bucket from streams along the track ■ Listener: If... the sponsors get eight letters saying that their comedian is an idiot, or a foul-mouthed jerk, they're terrified. (1958)

basket (1936) Euphemistic alteration of bastard ■ J. Gillespie: He's a nice old basket really. (1958)

turd (1936) From earlier sense, piece of excrement ■ Howard & West: A purple-faced steward walked up to a scrawny, pale heckler and yelled, 'Shut up, you ignorant turd!' (1965)

shitface (1937) Mainly a term of abusive address ■ Martin Amis: 'Why,' I wondered, 'did old shitface come round? What was he after?' (1973)

get (1940) British; from earlier Scottish and Northern English sense, (illegitimate) offspring; compare git ■ Henry Calvin: Put something on him, the stupid get! (1967)

schweinhund, schweinehund, schwine-, etc. (1941) German, from Schwein pig and Hund dog

peasant (1943) Applied especially to someone considered ignorant, stupid or awkward ■ Gavin Lyall: Of course I'm not alone, you—you peasant. D' you think I drive myself? (1964)

slag (1943) Compare earlier senses, coward, thug ■ Daily Telegraph: As sentence was announced, the dead boy's father... shouted: 'I hope you rot in it, you slag.' (1981)

no-goodnik (1944) US; from no-good useless, valueless + -nik ■ New York Times: Lew Archer's job is to find a 17-year-old girl who has run off with a 19-year-old no-goodnik. (1968)

sewer (1945) British ■ Nancy Mitford: Who is that sewer with Linda? (1945)

git (1946) British; variant of get ■ Observer: The girl scarcely turned her head: 'Shutup yerself yer senseless git!' (1967)

ponce (1953) From earlier senses, pimp, male homosexual ■ Peter Wright: An infuriated spectator may shout at a plump, sleek referee, 'You nasty little ponce!' (1974)

mamzer, momser, momza, momzer, pl. mamzerim (1955) US; from earlier sense, illegitimate person ■ R. L. Pike: Johnny Rossi? The

west-coast hood?... And we're keeping momsers like that alive, now? (1963)

mother (1955) US; short for mother-fucker ■ New York Times: 'You mothers! I ain't been out five minutes and I just got outta the pen this morning!' Her name is Judy, and although she is white, she talks black jive. (1975)

peckerhead (1955) US; from pecker penis + head ■ Elmore Leonard: Them peckerheads'd never make it. (1977)

mother-fucker, muthafucka (1956), mother-raper (1966) Orig and mainly US ■ Black Panther: We will kill any motherfucker that stands in the way of our freedom. (1973)

shite-hawk (1958) From earlier Indian English sense, a kite, said to have been in British Army use ■ J. B. Hilton: I liked the man.... And yet he was a shite-hawk. He was a journalist. (1981)

erk, irk (1959) British; from earlier sense, serviceman of low rank

goorie, goory, goori (1959) New Zealand; from earlier sense, (mongrel) dog, from Maori kuri ■ New Zealand Listener: 'Are you going to marry her?' I said. 'Why should I? Let go of me, you goorie,' he said. (1970)

chickenshit (1961) US; from earlier sense, coward

shit-bag (1961) ■ James Patrick: They must be mental. ... Shit-bags the lot o' them. (1973)

shithead (1961) ■ Peter Niesewand: You lying shithead! (1979)

salaud (1962) French, from sale dirty ■ Doris Lessing: Jules said he would only pay me three hundred dollars for it. Salaud! (1962)

rat fink (1964) Mainly US; often applied specifically to an informer or traitor ■ New Yorker: The hairy little hipster Go Go, a ratfink wearing a cross and a yarmulke. (1977)

suck-hole (1966) Canadian & Australian; from the verb suck-hole curry favour ■ Globe Magazine (Toronto): No matter how strong I could become there was still someone in this city of 470,000 who thought I was a suckhole. (1970)

jerk-off (1968) From jerk off masturbate, influenced by the noun jerk ■ W. Sheed: You know perfectly well that the jerk-offs do all the talking at meetings. (1973)

scuzz, scuz (1968) Orig and mainly North American; probably an abbreviation of disgusting, but compare scum and fuzz ■ Joseph Wambaugh: One white, bearded scuz in a dirty buckskin vest and yellow headband. (1972)

grot (1970) Back-formation from grotty unpleasant, disgusting ■ Courier-Mail (Brisbane): If you look like a grot, you'll never get a flat. (1980)

wank (1970) British; from the verb wank masturbate ■ Peter Laurie: Fred's counsel is a fat wank. (1970)

scumbag (1971) Mainly US; from earlier sense, condom ■ Zigzag: What little scumbag would say something like that? (1977)

shag (1971) From the notion of one who *shags* (= copulates with) another ■ Kingsley Amis: The moustached shag and the flat-chested bint . . . had moved away from the bar with their drinks. (1978)

wanker (1972) British; from earlier sense, masturbator ■ U. Holden: Her kiddies . . . rarely spoke except to mutter 'Wanker' or something crude. (1976)

suck (1974) Canadian; from the verb *suck* be contemptible, or abbreviation of *suck-hole* ■ *Citizen* (Ottawa): A neighbor described Rob as 'a quiet guy who was always getting put down a lot. Lots of people used to call him a suck. . . . He didn't do much socially or in the way of sports.' (1975)

piss-artist (1975) British; from the probable earlier sense, drunkard ■ *Sounds*: I am appealing to anybody who knows John and Murdoch of Erkshire Scotland. You know, those piss-artists, protozoans who wrote that letter about a rock band classification. (1977)

sumbitch (1975) US; contraction of *son of a bitch* ■ P. Mallory: The sumbitch has sure got him a way with the womenfolk. (1981)

scrote (1977) British; probably shortened from *scrotum* sac enclosing the testicles ■ Clive Dawson: Who'd be crooked enough to employ an evil little scrote like you, Thomas? (1997)

tosser (1977) Probably from *toss* (*off* masturbate + *-er* ■ *Guardian*: 'Gerrem forrad ovver't half-way line, Machin, yer chuffin' tosser,' bawled one sage, clearly disturbed by Barnsley's initial caution. (1991)

scuzzbag, scuzzball, scuzzbucket (1983) Orig and mainly North American ■ *Newsday*: Her cheating husband, Ernie, a crotch-grabber who brings new meaning to the word 'scuzzbucket'. (1989)

gobshite (1984) Compare earlier US slang sense, spitted-out wad of chewing tobacco; ultimately from *gob* mouth + *shite* excrement ■ *Guardian*: 'Trust me,' I say. 'You know I'm a regular guy. Whenever have I tried to schmooze you? Haven't I always come across?' 'Gobshite,' she says over her shoulder, and is gone. (1992)

An unpleasant or despicable female person

The majority of opprobrious epithets applied to women contain, or can contain, some suggestion of immorality, particularly sexual promiscuity. For them, see under A promiscuous woman at **Sex** (pp. 67–8).

mare (1303) From earlier sense, female horse ■ C. W. Ogle: Forgot her keys! Bah! These mares give me the creeps. (1953)

bitch (1400) In early use often applied specifically to a prostitute, and latterly often applied specifically to a malicious or spiteful woman; from earlier sense, female dog ■ Evelyn Waugh: Mrs Cecil Chesterton was a bitch and a liar. I think you inoffensively make that clear. (1962)

cow (1696) ■ Doris Lessing: It's just that stupid cow her mother. (1960)

madam (1802) Mainly applied specifically to a disrespectful young woman or girl ■ John

Wainwright: 'She was a little madam. *I* couldn't handle her.' And, always, the fault wasn't hers. (1983)

bat (1906) Often in the phrase *old bat* ■ *Sunday Times*: If Riva is to be believed . . . the old bat was even more fearsome than the rest of us ever suspected. When Yul Brynner developed cancer, some years after breaking off a passionate affair with Dietrich, her sole comment was 'goody, goody'. (1993)

moo (1967) British; often in the phrase *silly moo*; from earlier sense, cow, in allusion to *cow* unpleasant woman ■ *Funny Fortnightly*: It was rustling you heard all right—I'm a rustler! And I've rustled *you*, silly moo! Hey! Gerroff! (1989)

Something unpleasant or undesirable

bitch (1814) ■ T. E. Lawrence: 'She' says the incarnate sailor, stroking the gangway of the *Iron Duke*, 'can be a perfect bitch in a cross-sea.' (1931)

beast (1862) From earlier sense, unpleasant person ■ H. C. Bunner: I've got to stay and finish my grind. It's a beast. (1891)

cow (1864) Australian & New Zealand ■ F. D. Davison: Looking for work's a cow of a game! (1940)

bugger (1915) From earlier sense, unpleasant man ■ *Penguin New Writing*: Drilling before breakfast's a bugger, believe me. (1942)

bad news (1917) ■ Hugh Miller: Any kind of witness would be bad news on a job with such a tight specification. (1973)

bastard (1938) From earlier sense, unpleasant person ■ Julian Maclaren-Ross: This bastard of a bump on the back of my head. (1961)

bummer (1966) Orig and mainly US; from earlier sense, bad experience caused by drugs ■ Norman Mailer: It was a bummer. Hitchhiking over to the nuthouse, the whole day got lost. (1979)

An unpleasant experience

purgatory (1807) From earlier sense, place in which souls are purified ■ *Independent*: 'It's purgatory for me,' Higgins ranted on, 'just being involved in the qualifying rounds at Stoke for two months, then this kind of thing happens.' (1991)

nightmare (1927) From earlier sense, frightening or oppressive dream ■ Ritchie Perry: The daily nightmare that many Paulistas called travelling home from work. (1976)

something nasty in the woodshed (1959) Applied to a traumatic experience or concealed unpleasantness in a person's background; from the passage 'When you were very small . . . you had seen something nasty in the woodshed' in Stella Gibbons's *Cold Comfort Farm* (1932)

Something disgusting

gross-out (a1968) US; from *gross out* repel ■ *New Yorker*: Heads splatter and drip. . . . It's just a gross-out. (1984)

turn-off (1975) From *turn off* repel ■ *New York Times*: Patrons dined on cervelle Grenobloise. 'Sounds better in French,' said the chef. . . . 'Brains is a turn-off.' (1975)

Disgusting material

crud (a1508) Recorded once in the early 16th century, but not in regular use until the mid 20th century; variant of *curd* ■ *Guardian*: Dust off the hibachi, scrape the crud off your tongs and fork, buy some charcoal to replace the bag you left out in the rain last summer. (1992)

goo (1900) Orig US; applied mainly to viscous material; origin uncertain; perhaps a shortening of *burgoo* type of stew ■ Stella Gibbons: He . . . began to measure and mince vegetable scraps and scoop out grey, gritty, oily goo from a large tin. (1949)

dreck, drek (1922) From Yiddish *drek* filth, dregs, dung ■ O. Hesky: Meat better than the usual *drek* we get. (1967)

gunk (1938) Orig US; applied mainly to viscous material; from the proprietary name of a detergent, registered in 1932 ■ C. Henry: Too much eye gunk and lipstick—that sort of girl. (1966)

glop (1945) US; applied to a sticky or liquid mess, especially inedible food; coined in 1933 by the US cartoonist Elzie Segar as a meaningless sound uttered by the baby Swee'pea in the comic strip 'Popeye'; compare obsolete *glop* swallow greedily ■ Jean Potts: A cheap, soiled cosmetic case crammed with little bottles of glop. (1962)

gunge (1965) Mainly British; origin uncertain ■ *Listener*: Adam and Eve emerge from a transportable saucer of murky gunge. (1985)

grunge (1968) Probably back-formation from *grungy* ■ *American Speech*: There's grunge in the bottom of my Dr. Pepper bottle! (1977)

grot (1971) Back-formation from *grotty* ■ John Wain: This place, the tawdriness, the awful mound of grot it all is, stands between me and feeling anything. (1982)

scuzz, scuz (1988) Orig and mainly North American; from earlier sense, unpleasant or disgusting person ■ Margaret Atwood: In the larger picture, we're just a little green scuzz on the surface. (1988)

An unpleasant place

hell-hole (1866) From earlier sense, the pit of hell ■ J. B. Priestley: Go and drudge in some hell-hole of an office. (1945)

hole (1876) From earlier sense, cramped and unpleasant lodging ■ *Guardian*: Yesterday they were fighting again, but it's quiet today. I'm ready to go back, bombs and all. It's better than this hole. (1991)

dump (1915) Orig US; from earlier sense, cheap lodging-house ■ *Daily Express*: A uniformed cop patrolled the bar. . . . I didn't think that mattered much at a dump like this. (1942)

flea-bag (1941) From earlier sense, verminous lodging-house ■ Elaine Dundy: God, how I hated Paris! Paris was one big flea-bag. (1958)

arsehole of the universe (1950) ■ Dylan Thomas: This arsehole of the universe . . . this . . . fond sad Wales. (1950)

the armpit of . . . (1968) Orig US ■ *Washington Post*: Your alma mater is still the armpit of the universe. (1986)

shit-hole (1969) From earlier sense, anus ■ *Zigzag*: John went to a Catholic school in Caledonian Road—'a right shit-hole'. (1977)

piss-hole (1973) ■ R. Gadney: Let's get out of this pisshole. (1974)

To be unpleasant

stink (1934) ■ C. D. Simak: 'How did you know that?' 'Just a guess,' I said. 'This whole thing stinks to heaven.' (1963)

suck (1971) Probably from earlier sense, practise fellatio or cunnilingus ■ M. Gordon: All the hotels have the same pictures. The last one, the food sucked. (1978)

To repel

gross out (1965) Orig and mainly US; from *gross* disgusting ■ Cyra McFadden: I can dig it. They're grossing me out too, you know? (1977)

turn off (1965) ■ *Daily Telegraph*: [He] is kinky for short-back-and-sides and turned off by long-haired television performers. (1972)

10. Contemptibleness

A contemptible person

trash (1604) Originally applied to a worthless or contemptible person, but in modern use usually applied collectively to such people; from earlier sense, refuse, rubbish ■ *Independent*: $10 was pocket money to jeans-wearing, Biro-owning Western trash. (1991)

tick (1631) From earlier sense, parasitic insect-like creature ■ Roger Fulford: How often in those early days did I hear those ominous words 'that awful little tick Waugh'. (1973)

snot (1809) From earlier sense, nasal mucus ■ Jennie Melville: We've let the boy go home on bail. . . . Miserable little snot, but no real harm in him. (1981)

squit (a1825) British; applied to a small or insignificant person; perhaps related to the obsolete dialectal verb *squit* squirt ■ E. E. Coxhead: It's impossible, darling. That—that little squit—and Peggy Jacques! (1947)

soor (1848) Anglo-Indian, dated; from Hindi *suār* pig ■ Frank Richards: You black soor, when I order you to do a thing I expect it to be done at once. (1936)

squirt (1848) Orig US; applied to someone insignificant but presumptuous ■ Nicholas Blake: It's about time that squirt Wemyss was suppressed. (1935)

scut, scutt, skut (1873) Perhaps ultimately from *scout* mock, deride, of Scandinavian origin ■ J. B. Cooper: The likes of them skuts to find fault with my cookin'—'deed it's more than O'Callaghan himself would dare do. (1916)

wart (1896) From earlier sense, excrescence on the skin ■ *New York Times Book Review*: What! . . . . is the old wart going to go on some more about reading? (1984)

piss-ant (1903) Now mainly US; from earlier sense, ant, influenced by *piss* urinate ■ F. van W. Mason: You stole my skelp, you no-'count piss-ant. (1972)

tinhorn sport (1906) US ■ Robertson Davies: Swifty Dealer, the village tin-horn sport. (1975)

pipsqueak (1910) From *pip* high-pitched sound + *squeak* ■ Hartley Howard: For a little pip-squeak you make a big noise. (1973)

zob (1911) US, dated; origin unknown ■ Sinclair Lewis: I don't know how you fellows feel about prohibition, but the way it strikes me is that it's a mighty beneficial thing for the poor zob that hasn't got any will-power but for fellows like us, it's an infringement of personal liberty. (1922)

tripe-hound (1923) ■ Ngaio Marsh: You damned little tripe-hound. (1937)

kye (1928) Nautical, dated; origin unknown, but compare British dialect *kyish* dirty

slug (1931) From earlier sense, shell-less mollusc ■ G. & S. Lorimer: 'He didn't love me and I felt pretty bad about it!' 'The complete and utter slug!' (1940)

snurge (1933) Origin unknown ■ Michael Gilbert: He's such a little snurge. . . . He's so bogus. (1955)

zombie (1936) Applied to a dull or apathetic person; from earlier sense, re-animated corpse ■ *Guardian*: Mr. Dawson describes the committee as a parliament of zombies. (1984)

douche-bag (1942) US; from earlier sense, apparatus used for douching ■ *Punch*: 'Send them away!' she hissed. 'If they are found here, those douche-bags will incriminate us all.' (1968)

sad sack (1943) Mainly US; originally applied to a blundering serviceman; from a cartoon character created by the US cartoonist G. Baker ■ Marshall McLuhan: Model mother saddled with a sad sack and a dope. (1951)

yuck (1943) Orig US; origin unknown ■ John Wainwright: Three no-good yucks had felt like playing footsie with the law. (1979)

snotnose (1949) Compare earlier sense, inexperienced person ■ Ed McBain: He was not enjoying this little snotnose . . . and the college girl talk. (1963)

kvetch, kvetsch (1964) US; from Yiddish *kvetsh* from German *Quetsche* crusher, presser

schmegeggy, schmegegge, etc. (1964) US; origin unknown ■ *Observer*: He says he's a schlemiel which is . . better than being a schmagogy . . . Schlemiels . . . drop things and . . . they drop on schmagogys. (1971)

weeny (1964) US; compare earlier senses, child, girl, effeminate man

wonk (1967) Australian; from earlier sense, effeminate or homosexual man ■ R. Donaldson: 'Good on y', y' fat-gutted wonk.' 'An you, Elephant-belly.' (1967)

dweeb (1968) US; origin uncertain; perhaps influenced by *dwarf* and *weed* feeble person ■ *Chicago Tribune*: Any community that can knowingly elect a dweeb like Edwin Eisendrath as alderman obviously has a precious sense of fun. (1990)

snot-rag (1973) From earlier sense, handkerchief ■ John Wainwright: You are a self-opinionated idiot. You, and every snivelling little snot-rag like you. (1973)

Contemptible

sad-ass, sad-assed (1971) North American; *ass* = *arse* ■ *Black World*: How is Philadelphia? . . . Thats one sad-ass city . . . bout to sink into the ground. (1971) ■ D. Sears: A few general comments on sad-assed, puritanical sons-of-bitches individually and collectively. (1974)

11. Ineffectualness, Incompetence

Ineffectual, incompetent

useless (1593) ■ *Sunday Telegraph*: After the hurricane of 1987, Greaves was on TV the next morning calling weather forecasters 'useless ginks'. (1991)

jack-leg (1850) US; applied to someone without skill or training; from the male personal name *Jack* + *-leg* (as in *blackleg*) ■ P. Paxton: These men were 'jack-leg' carpenters. (1853)

chinless (1881) Orig US; applied to someone of weak character; now (British) often in the phrase *chinless wonder* (1962), applied to an ineffectual (young) upper-class man; from the notion that the lack of a prominent chin is a sign of a weak character ■ John Burke: We don't need a lot of chinless wonders sitting up in the House of Lords. (1967) ■ Peregrine Worsthorne: I had made a thing about having my bacon sliced at No 4, which Kingsley maintained was an affectation fit only for chinless twits. (1991)

wet (1916) British ■ Elizabeth Bowen: Cecil is so wet! Coming early like that, then sticking round like that. (1938)

hopeless (1922) From earlier sense, despaired of ■ Olive Norton: 'I'm *hopeless*,' she went on. 'I made a teapot once. It looked dinky. Only it wouldn't *pour*, don't you see.' (1967)

Harry Tate (1925) British, dated; applied to something incompetent or disorderly; from the stage-name of R. M. Hutchison (1872–1940), British music-hall comedian ■ *British Journal of*

Psychology. Native courts have been established [in Uganda]. . . . Their methods have been described as 'Harry Tate' procedure; but they are generally successful in arriving at the facts. (1935)

wimpish (1925) Orig US; from *wimp* ineffectual person + *-ish* ■ *Times*: The Duke of Edinburgh had adopted a new 'limp' handshake. . . . Expecting something flabby and wimpish, the men got royal bonecrushers. (1985)

half-arsed, half-ass, half-assed (1932) ■ Anthony West: You don't know what it is to worry about what half-arsed thing your own son is going to pull on you next. (1961)

pathetic (1937) From earlier sense, evoking pity ■ *Liverpool Echo*: The standard of refereeing in English soccer is pathetic. There is no consistency. (1974)

ham (1941) Partly from *ham* incompetent performer, partly from *ham-fisted, -handed* ■ *Times Literary Supplement*: Nothing he hated more than 'ham' writing and 'prefabricated' characters. (1963)

lame (1942) US; denoting social ineptness ■ *Washington Post*: Posers are really lame. (1986)

drippy (1947) Orig US; from *drip* ineffectual person + *-y* ■ Olive Norton: Men get so drippy when they're over-civilized, don't they? (1967)

Mickey Mouse (1951) Applied to something small and ineffectual; from the name of a mouse-like cartoon character created by Walt Disney (1901–66), US cartoonist ■ *Globe & Mail* (Toronto): The titles kept the press and broadcast media from thinking 'it was such a Mickey Mouse operation'. (1974)

poopy (1957) Mainly US; from *poop* ineffectual person + *-y* ■ *Washington Post*: My first serve is hard when it goes in, but my second one is so poopy Granny could return it. (1980)

nebbich, nebbish, nebbishe, nebbisher, nebish (1960) From *nebbich* ineffectual or incompetent person ■ *Atlantic Monthly*: Paranoid psychopaths who, after nebbish lives, suddenly feel themselves invulnerable in the certain wooing of sweet death. (1969)

wimpy (1967) Orig US; from *wimp* ineffectual person + *-y* ■ *Nutshell* (US): I was this little wimpy kid in elementary school and high school. (1984)

untogether (1969) Applied to someone who is poorly co-ordinated or not in control of their faculties ■ Jilly Cooper: She felt staggeringly untogether. . . . She had a blinding headache. (1976)

drooby (1972) Australian; from *droob* ineffectual person + *-y* ■ *Sunday Mail* (Brisbane): The party was rotten—drooby creeps, spooks, twits, bores etc. (1981)

nerdy (1978) Orig US; from *nerd* ineffectual person + *-y* ■ *Guardian*: She goes for a really tubular type of dude, the kind of hot babe with a cute butt who isn't all hairy and gross but isn't any nerdy zod either. (1982)

spastic (1981) From earlier sense, affected by spastic paralysis ■ *Sunday Telegraph*: They never hear folk music, and it takes an exceptional child not to dismiss the classics as 'boring' and 'spastic'. (1985)

Ineffectually, incompetently

not for toffee (1914) Used to denote incompetence, especially after *can* ■ Margaret Kennedy: Those dreary girls you get in every Drama School who can't act for toffee. (1951)

An ineffectual or incompetent person

duffer (c1730) Perhaps from Scots *doofart* stupid person, from *douf* spiritless ■ G. Smith: While the truly great . . . go unknighted there is no shortage of such accolades for the second-rate: duffers like Henry Newbolt and John Squire. (1984)

plug (1848) Mainly US; perhaps from earlier sense, poor or worn-out horse (although this is not recorded until later) ■ *Redbook Magazine*: You—you broken reed! You doormat! Old steady, unimaginative, dumb *plug*! (1948)

scissor-bill, scissors-bill (1871) Mainly US; from earlier sense, type of bird (the skimmer or shearwater) ■ R. P. Hobson: The hell you did, you big scissorbill, you stepped on my bum leg and my hand both. (1961)

geek (1876) Orig British, dialect; variant of earlier *geck* in same sense, apparently from Low German *geck* ■ Barr & Poppy: When I looked in the mirror, I saw a fuzzy-haired geek with a silly smile. (1987)

ham (1882) Applied to an incompetent performer, especially an actor who overacts; probably short for obsolete US slang *hamfatter* ineffective performer ■ *Times*: 'He thought I was an old ham,' says Miss Seyler indulgently. (1958)

stiff (1882) Orig US; compare earlier sense, corpse ■ *Sun*: A bad customer . . . a stiff who orders the table d'hôte and nothing to drink. (1967)

dub (1887) Orig & mainly US; perhaps related to obsolete slang *dub* beat flat, *dubbed* blunted, pointless ■ Ogden Nash: The unassuming dub Trying to pick up a Saturday game In the locker room of the club. (1949)

ham (1888) US; applied to an incompetent boxer or fighter; partly from *ham* incompetent performer, partly from *ham-fisted, -handed* ■ *Saturday Evening Post*: They want me to slug with this big ham. (1929)

mush-head (1890) US; from *mush* soft matter + *head* ■ *Screenland*: She has married the poor little mush-head that had been wished upon her. (1932)

passenger (1892) Applied to someone who does not or cannot contribute to the joint efforts made by colleagues; from earlier, more specific sense, member of the crew of a racing-boat who adds to the weight without contributing his share to the work ■ John Masters: I'd want to do my share of work. I don't want to be a passenger. (1964)

schlemiel (1892) Mainly US; Yiddish, perhaps from Hebrew *Shelumiel* character in the Bible ■ Budd Schulberg: Don't talk like a schlemiel, you schlemiel. Sounds like you're letting them push you around. (1941)

prune (1895) Orig US; also used in R.A.F. slang for a personification of stupidity and incompetence, especially as *P.O. Prune*; from earlier sense, dried plum ■ Nevil Shute: He wished . . . that he knew what it was that worried her, whether it was some prune that she had left at her last station. (1944)

gazook (1901) Dated, orig US; origin unknown, but compare *gazabo* fellow, guy and *gazob* fool ■ B. Penton: Look at that poor gazook, Sambo. He'd call your old man God Almighty even if he starved him to death. (1936)

rabbit (1904) Applied to an unskilful player of a game ■ Agatha Christie: He could get no fun out of playing [golf] with a rabbit like me. (*a*1976)

feeb (1911) US; short for *feeble-minded* ■ Elizabeth Fenwick: 'He really is the sweetest guy,' Georgia said wistfully. 'Sometimes I envy that pretty little feeb of his. Suppose if I played dumber I could get one too.' (1968)

Gawd-help-us, Gawdelpus (1912) Mainly jocular; from the ironically deprecatory exclamation *God* (or *Gawd*) *help us* ■ P. G. Wodehouse: A potbellied baggy-trousered Gawd-help-us. (1961)

poop (1915) Perhaps short for *nincompoop* ■ Robert Dentry: Those stupid bloody Yankee poops blew the panic whistle and the whole shebang went sky-high. (1971)

punk (1917) Mainly US; compare earlier sense, passive male homosexual, tramp's young companion ■ Ernest Hemingway: This fellow was just a punk . . . a nobody. (1933)

wimp (1920) Orig US; often applied specifically to a weak ineffectual man; origin uncertain; perhaps from *whimper* make weak cries ■ She: Masseur! Huh! He sounds a right little wimp. (1985)

palooka (1925) Mainly US; origin unknown ■ *New Yorker*: A romantic fable about a Philadelphia palooka who gains his manhood. (1977)

prick (1929) Applied to an ineffectual or incompetent man; from earlier sense, penis ■ Elleston Trevor: We don't like bein' pushed around by an incompetent prick of a commanding officer. (1967)

poop-stick (1930) Dated; probably from *poop* excrement + *stick*, but compare *poop* ineffectual person ■ Philip MacDonald: 'You make me sick!' he said. 'Let a little poop-stick like that walk all over you!' (1932)

drip (1932) From the notion of being 'wet' (= ineffectual) ■ Joanna Cannan: Of all the wet drips! (1951)

droop (1932) US ■ *American Speech*: Don't be a droop. (1940)

stumblebum (1932) Orig & mainly US; from the verb *stumble* + *bum* lazy person, loafer ■ Arthur La Bern: These stumble-bums may have stumbled across the real culprit. (1966)

droob, drube (1933) Australian; probably from *droop* ineffectual person ■ J. Jost: You're not normal boy. . . . You're a mug, a droob, a weak mess of shit! (1974)

mess (1936) ■ Muriel Spark: These were lapsed Jews, lapsed Arabs, lapsed citizens, runaway Englishmen, dancing prostitutes, international messes. (1965)

droopy-drawers (1939) Jocular; from earlier sense, someone whose drawers (= underpants)

are too large or long, giving an impression of slovenliness or incompetence ■ Anthony Gilbert: The neighbours round about thought what bad luck on that charming Mr. Duncan having a droopy-drawers for a wife. (1966)

pisher (1942) US; from earlier sense, bed-wetter; ultimately from Yiddish *pisher* one who urinates, from Middle High German *pissen* urinate ■ Ernest Tidyman: Then the marriage. Now that was *really* smart! Who could call him pisher now, with the Jewish princess on his arm? (1978)

shower (1942) British; applied collectively to a group of ineffectual or incompetent people, and hence (1949) to a single such person ■ *Observer*: Some of the people who go out with the hounds these days are a shower. . . . We can't have people turning up as if they have been wearing the same pyjamas for a month. (1973)

no-hoper (1944) Orig Australian; from earlier sense, racehorse with no chance of winning ■ R. Hall: That no-hoper! . . . If you turn out like him I shan't go on lettin you buy me a beer. (1982)

wet fish (1944) ■ Agatha Christie: Audrey marry that wet fish? She's a lot too good for that. (1944)

turkey (1951) US; from earlier sense, something inferior or unsuccessful ■ *Time*: 'Come on, you turkeys! Let's speed this show up!' cries an irreverent observer. (1978)

nerd, nurd (1957) Mainly US; often applied specifically to someone studious but socially inept; origin uncertain; sometimes taken as a euphemistic alteration of *turd*, though perhaps simply derived from the name of a character in the children's book *If I Ran the Zoo* (1950) by 'Dr. Seuss' ■ M. Howard: He feels . . . like a total nerd in his gentleman's coat with the velvet collar. (1986)

lame (1959) US, mainly Black English; applied to a socially unsophisticated person, one who does not fit in with a particular social group; from *lame* socially inept ■ Joseph Wambaugh: They're a couple of lames trying to groove with the Kids. They're nothing. (1972)

nebbich, nebbish, nebbishe, nebbisher, nebish (1960) From Yiddish *nebech* poor thing ■ *Jewish Chronicle*: The kings [in this Jewish chess-set] are dead, long live the nebbishes (the deprived, signifying the decline of royal power). (1973)

spaz, spas (1965) Abbreviation of *spastic* (not recorded in this sense until later) ■ *Guardian*: Come onnnnn—bag your face, you geek, you grody totally shanky spaz. (1982)

nerk (1966) British; origin uncertain; probably a blend of *nerd* and *jerk* ■ Allan Prior: 'Slow it down, you nerk, the girl has to get in,' he yelled. (1966)

pogo (1972) Australian; applied to an ineffectual or incompetent man; short for *pogo stick*, rhyming slang for *prick* ■ J. J. Coe: 'We're on road clearing again. . . .' 'What about bloody 7 section doing it . . . ?' 'Yeah, bloody pogos.' (1982)

spastic (1981) From earlier sense, person affected by spastic paralysis

big girl's blouse, great girl's blouse (1983) British; applied to an ineffectual male, often with a suggestion of effeminacy ■ *Outdoor Walking*: I was, I explained, a bit of a big girl's blouse when it came to crumbling ledges, sheer drops, being underwater for unreasonable lengths of time and squeezing into jam jar sized spaces. (1992)

wuss (1990) Orig & mainly US; origin unknown ■ *Sunday Times*: Last seen here as George Wallace's presidential running-mate, he manages to make the far-right Wallace seem a pinko wuss. (1996)

anorak (1991) British; applied to someone obsessively involved with something (e.g. a hobby) that is generally regarded as boring or unfashionable; from the stereotypical wearing of anoraks by certain types of hobbyist (e.g. train-spotters) ■ *Empire*: Any schoolboy or classics anorak will tell you that the old sheet-wearer was around a good 400 years before boring old monotheism. (1993)

Physically ineffectual; clumsy, awkward

butter-fingered (1615) Denoting a propensity for dropping things; from the notion of having greasy fingers from which things easily slip ■ *Harpers & Queen*: Quarry-tiled kitchen floors [are] lethal if one is butter-fingered with china. (1992)

flat-footed (1912) Denoting an inability to move quickly or adroitly; from earlier sense, having flat feet ■ *Sunday Times*: With the Rovers' defence flat-footed, Cox shot home from six yards. (1993)

ham-handed (1918), **ham-fisted** (1928) From the notion of having large clumsy hands, like hams ■ C. Dixon: The pilot with sensitive hands is a better pilot than one with non~sensitive hands. The latter are bluntly called 'ham~handed'. (1930) ■ C. S. Forester: God damn and blast all you hamfisted yokels. (1938)

mutton-fisted (1918) ■ Dick Francis: I worked in a slovenly fashion and rode . . . like a mutton-fisted clod. (1965)

12. **Sentimentality**

Excessively sentimental

mushy (1870) From earlier sense, soft ■ G. S. Porter: They formed a circle around Sally and Peter and as mushy as ever they could they sang, 'As sure as the grass grows around the stump, You are my darling sugar lump,' while they danced. (1913)

sloppy (1883) Orig US; from earlier sense, wet ■ Rosamond Lehmann: Kate said with a funny look, as if she were saying something a tiny bit embarrassing, on the sloppy side. (1936)

slushy (1889) Orig US; from earlier sense, soft and wet ■ *Sunday Times*: At the album's other extreme, slushy ballads, such as Heal The World, were plainly aimed at white suburban mums and children. (1993)

soppy (1918) From earlier sense, wet ■ *Daily Telegraph*: Lord Parker, Lord Chief Justice, said yesterday he deplored the tendency towards 'soppy and sentimental' treatment of children in juvenile courts. (1961)

A clumsy or awkward person

clod-hopper (1824) Applied to someone who moves clumsily or without skill; from earlier sense, ploughman ■ *Washington Post*: I hear it said all the time . . . that B. J. Armstrong is average, that John Paxson can't play defense or get his own shot, and that the rest of the bench is a bunch of clodhoppers. (1993)

butter-fingers (1837) Applied to someone liable to drop things, often specifically catches at cricket; from earlier *butter-fingered* liable to drop things ■ *Guardian*: The stumblers and butterfingers among us will acquire the grace and elegance of the most accomplished actors, gymnasts and dancers. (1992)

To be clumsy or awkward in movement

have two left feet (1915) ■ Diana Ramsay: Clumsy . . . you've got two left feet. (1975)

Something ineffectual

kludge, kluge (1962) Orig US; applied to an ill-assorted collection of poorly matching parts, and hence more specifically (1972) to a computer system or program that has been improvised or badly put together; coined by J. W. Granholm with ironic reference to German *klug* clever ■ *Which Micro?*: The QL is at last available . . . and without 'kludges' tacked on to make it work. (1984). Hence the verb **kludge, kluge** to improvise with a kludge (1962) ■ *QL User*: Its history was most unfortunate to start with: production delays, 'kludged' machines, extra ROMs hanging off the back. (1984)

To expend effort ineffectually or futilely

flog a dead horse (1872) Compare earlier *mount on a dead horse* in same sense ■ *Cabinet Maker & Retail Furnisher*: If this is the case, we are flogging a dead horse in still trying to promote the scheme. (1971)

gooey (1935) From earlier sense, sticky ■ Ronald Knox: What you mean by a dance is the wireless in the hall playing revolting stuff and you lounging round in pairs and feeling all gooey. (1948)

schmaltzy (1935) Orig US; from *schmaltz* excessive sentiment + *-y* ■ T. P. Whitney: Yuri painted for nothing schmaltzy pictures such as *Nero's Feast* and the *Chorus of Elves* and the like for the German officers on the commandant's staff. (1974)

icky, ikky (1939) Origin uncertain; perhaps a baby-talk alteration of *sticky* or *sickly* ■ Charlie Chaplin: He must hide his blindness. . . . His stumblings and bumpings into things make the little girl laugh joyously. But that was too 'icky'. (1964)

twee (1956) From earlier, appreciative sense, sweet, charming; ultimately from *tweet*, representing a child's pronunciation of *sweet* ■ *Listener*: Mike Nichols's thriller-fantasy about dolphins should be as nauseatingly twee as the worst Disney—but it isn't. (1983)

yechy, **yecchy** (1969) US; from the exclamation *yech* expressing disgust + -*y*

yucky, **yukky** (1970) From the exclamation *yuck* expressing disgust + -*y* ■ *Oxford Times*: The sweetness is fused with enough real feeling to avoid being sugary, except for the rather yucky spoken introduction to 'Meadows of Springtime'. (1977)

Excessive sentiment

gush (1866) From earlier sense, an effusion ■ *Independent*: Most of the interviews elicit embarrassing gush or non-committal plaudits (Spielberg on Jones: 'Quincy is just, like, a spraygun of love'). (1991)

schmaltz, **shmaltz** (1935) Orig US; from German and Yiddish *schmalz* fat, dripping, also used in English (1931–) in the sense 'melted chicken fat' ■ *Spare Rib*: She . . . is saying with appalling schmaltz that 'Josh's warm, funny smile was where I lived now'. (1977)

slush (1937) From earlier sense, rubbishy writing, nonsense, influenced by the notion of 'wetness' ■ *Observer*: The ending is purest slush, and there are some cheap dramatics in the camera work. (1961)

goo (1951) From earlier sense, sticky substance ■ *Times Literary Supplement*: He writes about subjects which, in less skilled hands, have so often and so embarrassingly degenerated into a mess of gush and goo. (1959)

13. **Fairness & Unfairness**

See also Equally or fairly shared at **Sharing, Distribution** (p. 431).

A fair chance, fair treatment

a fair (or **even**, **good**) **shake** (1830) US ■ Studs Terkel: I'd like to see an America where so much power was not in the hands of the few. Where everybody'd get a fair shake. (1980)

fair do's (1859) Orig dialect; plural of *do* action, nominalized form of the verb *do* ■ Andrew Garve: There's no 'nobs' there; it's fair do's for everybody. (1951)

fair dinkum (1890) Australian, dated; from British dialect *dinkum* work, due share of work; compare later sense, genuine ■ J. Harper: Then Gallant Captain Albert With a love for what is right, Jumped in to see fair dinkum And to try and stop the fight. (1924)

a (**fair**) **go** (1904) Australian & New Zealand ■ *Advertiser* (Adelaide): Stop whingeing and give a bloke a go, mates. (1969)

a fair crack of the whip (1924) Orig Australian ■ Lawson Glassop: I am sorry to have to tell you that the Lord's had a fair crack of the whip and He's missed the bus. (1944)

To sentimentalize

schmaltz, **shmaltz** (1936) Orig US; often followed by *up*; from *schmaltz* excessive sentiment ■ Audrey Laski: He . . . tried to lighten his touch; no use giving this visitor the notion that they schmaltzed it up. (1969)

An excessively sentimental person

softy, **softie** (1886) Compare earlier sense, weak-minded person ■ Dorothy Halliday: You didn't know Daddy like I did. He was an awful old softie inside. (1970)

sob sister (1912) Orig US; originally applied specifically to a female journalist writing sentimental articles ■ *Sun* (Baltimore): Forecasting opposition to his plan by 'sob-sisters' Goodwin said 'it wouldn't do any harm to give these sob-sisters a couple of wallops too'. (1939)

A self-pitying person

wet leg (1922) ■ *Times Literary Supplement*: We know how much Auden hated wet-legs, how constantly he repeated his many litanies of his own good fortune. (1981)

(A) sentimental narrative

sob story (1913) Applied to an account intended to evoke a sympathetic response ■ *Guardian*: Any Russian will fall for a sob story if treated right. (1992)

sob stuff (1918) ■ Ngaio Marsh: He puts on a bit of an act like a guide doing his sob-stuff over Mary Queen of Scots in Edinburgh Castle. (1978)

Unfair, unreasonable

not cricket (1851) From the notion that cricket is always played fairly ■ Van Dine: It didn't seem cricket to leave the poor devil there. (1930)

below the belt (1890) From the notion of punching an opponent below the waist (and particularly in the area of the testicles), which is against the rules in boxing ■ *Guardian*: Labour published figures last week showing that the Tory government have closed more grammar schools in the last 20 years than Labour has. Now that was below the belt. (1992)

red-hot (1896) Australian ■ Arthur Wright: 'It's red 'ot,' put in Dave, 'th'way these 'ere owners makes er pore man give 'em a lump in th' sweep.' (1907)

tough (1929) Often followed by *on* ■ P. G. Wodehouse: 'I suppose it's because I'm rather an out-size and modelled on the lines of Cleopatra.' 'Tough!' 'You bet it's tough. A girl can't help her appearance.' (1929)

Something disappointingly unfair

swizzle (1913) British, mainly schoolchildren's slang; probably an alteration of *swindle* ■ Anthony Buckeridge: It was a rotten swizzle, sir, because we flew through low cloud and we couldn't see a thing. (1950)

swizz, swiz (1915) British, mainly
schoolchildren's slang; shortened from *swizzle*
■ **Roy Fuller:** He's given him not out. What a sodding swiz.
(1959)

Unfair treatment

**a raw deal (1912), a rough deal (1931), a
bad deal (1938)** ■ **E. C. Bentley:** The Opposition were
quite content with this situation. If it was what is known
nowadays as a raw deal, they did not mind. (1940)

14. **Pleasure, Enjoyment**

Happy, pleased

chirpy (1837) Applied to someone who is
cheerful or merry; from *chirp* make the sound of
a bird + *-y* ■ *Daily Mail:* The boy was then put on a return
train to rejoin his worried parents. 'He was chirpy, not at all
upset.' said a BR worker. (1991)

as happy as Larry (1905) Orig Australian;
denoting extreme or complete happiness

bucked (1907) British, dated; from *buck* (*up* cheer
up + *-ed* ■ *Punch:* I am so bucked that you have asked me
what to wear when you are accompanying at the concert next
month. (1928)

**tickled, tickled pink, tickled to death
(1907)** ■ **P. G. Wodehouse:** Your view, then, is that he is
tickled pink to be freed from his obligations? (1950) ■ **Elmore
Leonard:** 'I'm tickled to death I'm talking to you,' Mr. Perez
said . . . smiling into the telephone. (1977)

over the moon (1936) Compare earlier *jump
over the moon* be delighted ■ **John Brown:** He goes
back there. She's over the moon, of course, and off they go to
parties. (1972)

up (1942) Denoting a feeling of elation or
euphoria ■ *Gossip:* He was very up about his job (in the
CBS studio mailroom) and people in general. (1981)

on cloud seven (1956), on cloud nine (1959)
on cloud seven US; denoting extreme or complete
happiness; compare non-slang *seventh heaven*
state of utter happiness ■ *Sunday Times:* 'The prime
minister was on cloud nine,' said a member of the British team.
'Everything went according to plan and better.' (1993)

chuffed (1957) British, orig services' slang;
probably from British dialect *chuff* pleased
■ *Crescendo:* I cannot express too much just how 'chuffed' I
am with the drums. (1967)

Euphorically happy, elated, ecstatic

sent (1940) Dated; applied to someone
completely enthralled or entranced, especially
by rhythmic music, drugs, etc.; from the past
participle of *send* delight ■ *Spectator:* The girls wore
thick eye-makeup and 'sent' expressions. (1958)

gone (1946) Orig US, jazz slang; applied to
someone completely enthralled or entranced,
especially by rhythmic music, drugs, etc.
■ *News Chronicle:* The jazz-loving 'hep-cat' who claims that
the music 'sends' him until he is 'gone'. (1959)

To treat unfairly

do the dirty on (1914) ■ **J. B. Priestley:** Anyhow
they did the dirty on yer. (1929)

shaft (1959) Orig & mainly North American;
from the notion of inserting a pointed object
into someone ■ *Official Report of Debates, Canadian
Senate:* As I have told my constituents in Hamilton, Ontario,
which seems to have been continually shafted by this
government. (1970)

A happy person

ray of sunshine (1915) Often applied to one
whose happiness cheers others; often in the
phrase *little ray of sunshine* ■ **Celia Fremlin:** Milly
rather fancied herself in the rôle of little ray of sunshine to
brighten his declining years. (1972)

Pleasure, enjoyment, fun

yum-yum (1885) Often applied specifically to
love-making; reduplication of the interjection
yum expressing pleasurable anticipation
■ **Aldous Huxley:** Enjoying what she called 'a bit of yum-
yum'. (1939)

whoopee (1930) From *make whoopee* have fun
■ **Mary Soames:** The evening broke up about midnight, in a
general atmosphere of whoopee and goodwill. (1945)

jollies (1957) Mainly in the phrase *get one's jollies*
■ *Surfer Magazine:* The announcer acted like this is where
all of the surfers go after dark to get their jollies. (1968)

crack (a1966) Anglo-Irish; often in the phrase *for
the crack* for fun ■ *Sunday Times:* They came to
Lisdoonvarna only for 'the crack'. . . . 'Crack' has several
ingredients, of which two are merriment and mischief, but the
word is really defiant of precise definition. (1982)

A life of pleasure

the life of Riley (or Reilly) (1919) Applied to
an enjoyable carefree existence; from the
common Irish surname: the phrase is said to
come from one of a number of late 19th-century
songs, but was popularized by H. Pease's *My
Name is Kelly* (1919) ■ **J. B. Priestley:** The life of Reilly,
which some people imagine me to lead, has been further away
than a fading dream. (1949)

A euphoric state

high (1953) Applied especially to such a state
induced by drugs ■ *Mail on Sunday:* Another driver on
a high was Britain's Martin Brundle. His Brabham Yamaha was
a splendid 10th—his best of the season. (1991)

A good time; a spree; a party

do (a1824) British; applied to a party or similar
social occasion; from earlier sense, something
done ■ **M. Kerr:** Her family has a 'do' every year on the
anniversary of the day her mother's father died. (1958)

fling (1827) Applied to a brief period of self-indulgence or pleasure, often with the implication of a sexual liaison ■ *Guardian*: 'You should see his girlfriend. She's a cracker.' 'Well, if you feel the slightest desire for a little fling, don't hold back on my account.' (1991)

tea-fight (1849) Jocular, dated; applied to a tea-party ■ *Scotsman*: The good people . . . organise a splendid weekly tea-fight and concert for our behoof. (1901)

a high old time (1858) Applied to a very enjoyable time ■ Jean Potts: You probably had a high old time chasing blondes. (1955)

tear (1869) Applied to a spree, especially a drinking spree; mainly in the phrase *on a tear* ■ *Harper's Magazine*: Got me off on a tear somehow, and by the time I was sober again the money was 'most all gone. (1896)

shindig (1871) Orig US; applied to a lively or noisy party; apparently from earlier sense, blow on the shins, from the notion of clumsy dancing at a party ■ *New Statesman*: The competition among the 'old nobility' to attend what they termed 'Aspers' little shindig' was so fierce that five private detectives were hired to keep out the unwelcome. (1959)

junket (1886) Orig US; applied to a trip, ostensibly undertaken for business or other serious purposes and paid for by an employer, government, etc., which is characterized by the self-indulgent pursuit of pleasure; from earlier non-slang sense, pleasure outing marked by eating and drinking ■ *Telegraph* (Brisbane): United States delegates to the Inter-Parliamentary Union conference in Canberra are upset that their trip has been described as a junket. (1966)

beanfeast (1897) British; applied to a festive meal or other entertainment (in modern use usually with the implication of indulgence at others' expense); from earlier sense, annual dinner given to employees by their employer, at which beans and bacon used to be regarded as an indispensible dish ■ *Guardian*: To follow revelations about a curious friendship with a rich Texan playboy with a sponsored beanfeast in Florida was to ignore the basic tenets of PR. (1992)

jolly (1905), **jolly-up** (1927) *jolly* short for *jollification* ■ Evelyn Waugh: Why can't the silly mutt go off home and leave us to have a jolly up. (1932) ■ William Haggard: It would be a splendid wedding, the sort of big jolly Charles Russell enjoyed. (1971)

jollo (1907) Australian; often applied specifically to a party at which liquor is drunk; from *joll(ity* or *joll(ification* + the Australian suffix *-o* ■ N. Pulliam: My mother used to ask some of the chappies in for a little week-end jollo—like a touch of home, you know. (1955)

a whale of a time (1913) Orig US; applied to a very enjoyable time ■ Barbara Castle: They regaled us with drinks and a superb buffet and we had a whale of a time. (1980)

whoop-up (1913) Mainly North American; applied to a noisy celebration or party; from

whoop it up have a noisy good time ■ Dorris Heffron: I thought it quite . . . sensible of Big Point to have one great annual public whoop-up in which to give a little exercise to the witch and devil of one's soul. (1976)

beano (1914) British; applied to a festive entertainment often ending in rowdyism; abbreviation (originally among printers) of *beanfeast* festive occasion ■ *Listener*: Dear-heart, I fear we will have to make a token appearance at the beano those thrusting young String-Along's are giving tonight. (1967)

bun-fight (1928) Jocular; applied to a tea-party; compare earlier obsolete bun-struggle and *bun-worry* in same sense

whoopee (1929) Dated; applied to a lively or rowdy party; from *make whoopee* have fun ■ Evelyn Waugh: Noel and Audrey are having a little whoopee on Saturday evening. (1930)

ding-dong (1936) Applied to a wild party or gathering; compare earlier sense, heated quarrel ■ Ashley Smith: The sons and daughters . . . coming up for a ding-dong which went on till far into the night. (1961)

rort (1941) Australian; applied to a wild party; ultimately from *rorty* fine, jolly, boisterous, noisy ■ George Johnston: I am not, strictly, a true devotee of the wild Australian 'rort' and always remorseful in my hangovers. (1969)

percolator (1946) US; often applied specifically to a rent party ■ Stephen Longstreet: You could always . . . get together . . . and charge a few coins and have . . . a percolator. (1956)

shake (1946) US; often applied specifically to a rent party ■ *American Speech*: There's a shake at Jim's house. (1977)

skiffle (1946) US, Black English; applied to a rent party; perhaps the original sense, from which 'popular music based on jazz and folk music' developed (although this is recorded earlier); ultimate origin unknown

bash (1948) Orig US ■ *Sunday Times*: He and Lloyd Webber go for the truly mega-bash, with 1,000–1,500 guests, sometimes a sit-down dinner, vast decorated venues and an upmarket guest list. (1991)

wingding (1949) Orig & mainly US; applied to a party or celebration, especially a wild one; compare earlier sense, drug addict's seizure ■ Arthur Hailey: How are you, Nim? Don't see you often at these Jewish wingdings. (1979)

ding (1956) Australian; applied to a party or celebration, especially a wild one; perhaps from *ding-dong* wild party or *wingding* wild party ■ Frank Hardy: It appears that he had drunk fifteen of them there drinking horns of beer at a Commemoration Day ding. (1967)

thrash (1957) Applied to a party, especially a lavish one ■ Kingsley Amis: No quiet family party at all, it had turned out, but a twenty-cover thrash. (1968)

blast (1959) Applied to a party, especially one that is very noisy or wild ■ William Murray: Man, they're throwing a monster blast over on the East Latego later. . . . Everybody's going. (1967)

rave (1960), rave-up (1967) Applied to a lively party or rowdy gathering ■ George Melly: We . . . organized all-night raves. (1965) ■ Hugh Miller: Phyllis McBain is invited to an old-style rave-up, knickers and husbands optional. (1973)

knees-up (1963) British; applied to a wild party or similar gathering, typically featuring energetic dancing; from the title of the Weston & Lee song *Knees up, Mother Brown!* (1939) ■ Len Deighton: As indigenous to London as a Saturday-night knees-up in the boozer. (1967)

smash (1963) North American; applied especially to a wild party ■ *New Yorker*: Every spring the Thrales gave a party. . . . They called this decorous event 'our smash'. (1977)

rage (1980) Australian & New Zealand; from *rage* have a good time ■ *Skyline* (Australia): Have a rage at our Castaway BBQ where the order of dress is strictly Castaway style! (1985)

A drinking spree

See under **Alcohol** (pp. 147–8).

An invitation to a party or similar event

stiffy (1980) British; applied to a formal invitation card; from the thick cardboard of which it is made ■ *Daily Telegraph*: Nigel [Lawson] had in hand a gilt-edged stiffy for a banquet at the Stock Exchange. (1987)

On a spree

on the tiles (1887) From the nocturnal activities of cats ■ Colleen McCullough: They all went out on the tiles. . . . It was some night. (1977)

on the razzle (1908) *razzle* short for *razzle-dazzle* excitement, bustle ■ John Le Carré: Your wife was in England, and you went on the razzle with Leo. (1968)

Someone on a spree

heller (1895) US; from *hell* (*around* + *-er* ■ *Listener*: Jack Harrick, the old hillbilly satyr or 'heller'. (1959)

raver (1959) Applied to someone who has a wild time, especially sexually ■ *Sunday Mail* (Brisbane): I have never analysed why, but many pop musicians are ravers—people who like to live it up—with a strong self-destructive streak. (1978)

rager (1972) Australian & New Zealand; from *rage* have a good time + *-er* ■ *Sunday Mail* (Brisbane): Downstairs on the boom-boom floor, the pretty ragers purred and boogied their youth into another dawn. (1988)

To please, delight

turn someone **on (1903)** Orig US; implying the arousing of someone's approving (often sexual) interest ■ *News of the World*: Dinner jacket, wing collar, and bow tie may not sound the sort of gear to turn on a teeny bopper. (1976)

make someone's **day (1909)** ■ P. G. Wodehouse: That . . . will be great. That will just make my day. (1935)

grab (*a*1915) Orig US ■ *Post* (Cape edition): Elton John is big but if his music doesn't grab you then it just doesn't grab you. (1971)

panic (1927) US ■ Fred Astaire: After a while they were saying 'Oompah-Oompah-Oompah' with the music. . . . Adele absolutely panicked 'em. (1960)

slay (1927) Denoting overwhelming someone with delight, and often specifically convulsing them with laughter ■ Dick Francis: 'Oh God, Dolly, you slay me,' said Chico, laughing warmly. (1965)

send (1932) Orig US, dated; applied especially to pop music ■ Naomi Mitchison: So much modern poetry is ironic or deliberately held on a low note; that may be artistically admirable, but it doesn't send the reader. (1975)

kill (1938) Orig US; denoting overwhelming someone with delight, and often specifically convulsing them with laughter ■ J. D. Salinger: She killed Allie, too. I mean he liked her, too. (1951)

gas (1941) Orig US, jazz slang; probably from *gas* fun ■ *Crescendo*: A . . . cadenza at the end of 'Watermelon man' which really gassed me. (1967)

knock someone **out (1942)** Orig US ■ *Melody Maker*: I only heard half an hour of Ornette but I wasn't knocked out at all. (1966)

groove (1952) Orig US, jazz slang; compare earlier sense, enjoy oneself ■ *Esquire*: Her singing grooved me. (1959)

flip (1956) US, jazz slang; compare earlier sense, become suddenly very excited, angry, etc. ■ Billie Holiday: Meade Lux Lewis knocked them out; Ammons and Johnson flipped them; Joe Turner killed them; Newton's band sent them. (1956)

One that pleases or delights; something enjoyable

sender (1935) Orig & mainly US, dated; applied especially to a pop musician; from *send* delight, enthral + *-er* ■ *Spectator*: Fabian, the teenagers' sender, indistinguishable from Cliff Richards [*sic*]. (1960)

gasser (1944) Orig US, jazz slang; from *gas* please, delight, thrill + *-er* ■ *Sunday Truth* (Brisbane): Ron's Friday night show was a gasser. (1970)

groove (1946) Orig US, jazz slang; probably from *in the groove* performing well ■ *Melody Maker*: This is what makes the Indian one such a groove for me. (1967)

gas (*c*1953) Orig US, jazz slang; from *gas* please, delight, thrill ■ *Frendz*: The Stones . . . were a screaming, speeding, sexy gas. (1971)

turn-on (1969) From *turn on* excite someone's approving interest ■ David Hockney: A medieval city is unstimulating to me, whereas to others it might be a great turn-on. (1982)

Enjoyable

jolly (1549) Orig in standard use, but now colloquial ■ *Independent*: For her, Swan is going to be more than just a jolly night out. (1991)

fun (1950) Orig US ■ Adam Diment: I was remembering Marianne and the fun times we have had. (1968)

To enjoy oneself, have a good time, have fun; to go on a spree

lark about, **lark around** (1857) Denoting enjoying oneself doing silly or mischievous things; from earlier *lark* play tricks, frolic; ultimate origin uncertain; perhaps a modification of dialect *laik* play ■ Harrington O'Reilly: I was always larking about and playing pranks on my schoolfellows. (1889)

paint the town red (1884) Orig US; denoting going on a boisterous spree ■ J. Stern: This settlement . . . is descended on by four lumberjacks from Alaska, looking for somewhere to paint the town red with their savings. (1994)

hell around (1897) Denoting living a life of disreputable pleasure ■ Emma Lathen: 'If he did any helling around, it wasn't here,' the janitor continued. (1969)

party (1922) Orig and mainly US; from the noun *party* ■ Time: Outgoing Democratic National Committee Chairman Robert Strauss partied along with singer Helen Reddy and actor Alan Alda. (1977)

horse about, **horse around** (1928) Orig US ■ Joseph Heller: They were having a whale of a good time as they helped each other set up their cots. They were horsing around. (1961)

make whoopee (1928) Orig US; from *whoopee* exclamation of delight ■ Quentin Crisp: 'It often happens that when we think we're making whoopee we're only making a whoops! instead,' I replied. (1984)

beat it up (1933) Denoting having rowdy fun, typically resulting in breakages ■ Daily Telegraph: What sort of noise did the neighbours complain about? Did the Purdoms and their friends beat it up a little in the evenings? (1958)

whoop it up (1935) Orig US; compare earlier, obsolete sense, create a disturbance ■ Listener: The broadcasting moguls and their groupies whooped it up in Edinburgh and other select watering holes. (1983)

have a ball (1938) Orig US; from the noun *ball* dance ■ Colin MacInnes: My poor old battered parent was really having a tremendous ball. (1959)

ball (1942), **ball it up** (c1953) North American, orig Black English; from the noun *ball* dance, with reference to the phrase *have a ball* ■ Kenneth Orvis: A so-called friend invites you . . . to a coloured joint—to ball it up for a night. (1962)

get one's rocks off (1948) Orig US; often applied specifically to achieving sexual satisfaction; from *rocks* testicles ■ John Irving: I don't get my rocks off by humiliating myself, you know. (1978)

groove (1950) Orig US, jazz slang; sometimes in the phrase *groove it*; from earlier sense, play jazz with a swing ■ Guardian: I had the white Courreges boots, the minis, a huge beehive. I had more hair pieces than Elizabeth Taylor and I was really grooving. (1992)

live it up (1951) Orig US ■ Neil Armstrong: Those who lived it up in the cocktail lounges that night were also emotionally moved. (1970)

swing (1957) Orig US ■ Wall Street Journal: He has to really swing: Motor-cycle racing, free-fall parachuting, [etc.]. (1967)

rave (1961) Compare earlier *rave* lively party ■ Sunday Times: He started out by raving at weekends to Bridlington. (1965)

loon (1966) Denoting passing time in pleasurable activities; origin unknown ■ It: Children and the younger adults alike looning about in wonderful costumes. (1971)

bliss out (1973) US; denoting reaching a state of ecstasy ■ New Yorker: Long-haired Westerners . . . blissing out or freaking out in the streets. (1986)

let one's hair down (1974) Denoting uninhibited activity after a period of restraint; from earlier *let one's (back) hair down* speak frankly ■ Guardian: We are concerned with antiquarianism and gender politics and like to let our hair down with a little shamanic (native American) chanting and drumming. (1992)

rage (1979) Australian & New Zealand ■ Sun (Sydney): 'Over Christmas, I'll probably be drinking too much and raging too much,' said the . . . breakfast Bimbo. (1986)

To cheer up

perk up (a1656) Used both intransitively and transitively ■ Sunday Times: As 1992 fades from view we are invited to perk up. Ignore last year's calamities . . . Instead, watch the busy high streets, note the rising car sales, listen to the upbeat estate agents. . . . Happy days are here again! (1993)

buck up (1844) Dated; used both intransitively and transitively; from *buck* man of spirit ■ B. von Hutten: Don't spoil it all by being weepy. . . . Come, buck up, like a dear, and wish me joy. (1906) ■ James Hackston: As if to buck us up after our recent loss, he promised us poultry on the table. (1966)

To relax, take it easy

cool it (1953) Orig US ■ Crescendo: Cool it will you? I said once a *week*, there's no need to go stark raving mad. (1968)

let it all hang out (1970) Orig US

mellow out (1974) US; usually applied to relaxing under the influence of a drug ■ Cyra McFadden: How about we all smoke a little dope and mellow out, okay? (1977)

chill out (1980) Mainly US ■ Ski: The fat one whistles, waves madly and rudely ignores my fatherly admonitions to chill out. (1989)

Exclamations of delight or exultation

goody, **goodee**, **goody goody** (1796) ■ Henry Miller: I see Halvah and Baklava too. Goody goody! (1953)

whoopee (1862) From *whoop*, an exclamation of excitement + *-ee* ■ Listener: You take your second MB . . . and once you've passed this—whoopee! You're virtually guaranteed to qualify. (1974)

yum, **yum yum** (1878), **yummy** (1899) Expressing delight (as if) at something delicious to eat; imitative of the sound of contented eating ■ Sara Paretsky: 'Lotty talked her into . . . making homemade enchiladas, yum-yum.' 'Yum-yum,' the two little girls chorused. (1982)

quaiss kitir (1898) British services' slang, dated; from Egyptian Arabic, literally 'very nice' ■ W. H. Canaway: 'They'll take us off to Germany and make us have nowt but sausages and beer.' Sergeant Entwistle said, 'Sausages and beer, kwais ketir, I wish I had some now instead of this muck.' (1967)

good egg (1903) British, dated; expressing pleasure, satisfaction, or enthusiastic approval ■ H. E. Bates: 'It seems there's a bar.' 'Good egg,' Pop said. 'That's something.' (1959)

whizzo, wizzo (1905) From *whizz* whizzing sound + *-o* ■ Delano Ames: 'It's really a little surprise for the kiddies.' 'Whizzo!' cried Anna, grabbing it. (1954)

hot dog (1906) US ■ Terence Rattigan: Hot dog! There's some Scotch. (1944)

yippee, yip-ee (1920) Orig US; perhaps connected with the exclamation *hip*, used to introduce a united cheer ■ A. Cornelisen: It's a boy! A boy! Yippee! (1980)

hot diggety dog, hot diggety, hot ziggety (or **ziggedy, ziggetty, ziggity**) **(dog)** (1924) US; from *hot dog*; *diggety, ziggety* probably a fanciful formation ■ M. R. Rinehart: Hot diggety dog! Ain't that something? (1952) ■ *New Yorker*: Mr. Deforest entered with his face bright, his hands folded behind him. 'Well, hot ziggetty, a holiday for me. What have we got going here?' (1984)

right on (1925) Orig US

good-o, good-oh (1926) Orig Australian & New Zealand ■ Frank Sargeson: Yes, good-oh, I said, and thanks very much. (1946)

good show (1940) ■ *Washington Post*: Many of your fellow Washingtonians assume that a young adult like you cares only about herself. You've shown us all how false that is. Good show! (1993)

Geronimo (1941) Orig US; originally used as a shout by trainee US paratroops when jumping out of an aircraft, subsequently as a general battle-cry, and hence as an exclamation of exultation; in allusion to a leap made by a character in the film *Geronimo* (1939)

whacko, wacko (1941) Mainly Australian; from *whack* a blow + *-o* ■ Lionel Davidson: After all it was only two days to—whacko!—Monday. (1978)

hubba-hubba, haba-haba (1944) US; origin unknown

cowabunga (1954) Orig & mainly US; used as an exclamation of exhilaration, delight, or satisfaction, especially in surfing, as the surfer climbs or rides a wave; apparently coined by Eddie Kean, writer of the US television programme 'The Howdy Doody Show' (1947–60); most recently adopted as a rallying-cry by the Teenage Mutant Ninja Turtles ■ *Time*: Shouting . . . 'cowabunga!' they climb a 12-ft. wall of water and 'take the drop' off its shoulder. (1963)

goody gumdrops (1959) British ■ Nicolas Freeling: Buttered toast, and cherry cake, as well as Marmite. Goody, goody gumdrops. (1967)

yay (1963) Origin uncertain; perhaps from *yeah* yes ■ *New Wave Magazine*: The Slits won the argument (Yay!) but we didn't get the interview (Boo!). (1977)

Someone who spoils others' enjoyment

See **party pooper, wet blanket**, and **wet smack** under Spoilsport at **Spoiling, Ruination** (p. 417).

15. Laughter & Amusement

To laugh

split one's sides (1704) Implying hearty laughter

yock, yok (1938) Theatrical slang, mainly US; compare English dialect *yocha* laugh ■ *New Yorker*: There'd be Don, yockin' it up like crazy, . . . he's so hysterical with loyalty laughter. (1951)

crack up (1942) Orig US; implying uncontrollable laughter ■ *Guardian*: When the Rev Flasher (Sid James again) says 'I would like to get my organ in use again' we're unlikely to crack up without Kenneth Williams's eyebrows shooting up his forehead and his mouth forming a perfect 'O' in shocked disbelief. (1992)

laugh like a drain (1948) Implying loud, guffawing and often scornful laughter ■ Kate Nicholson: Old Hester would laugh like a drain if she could see us singing hymns over her. (1966)

piss oneself (1951) From the notion of laughing so much that one urinates

involuntarily ■ *Crisis*: He's yellin' for help, but we were legless an' pissin' ourselves laughin'. (1989)

kill oneself (1956) ■ *Impact*: I don't know if I'd want to do it on my own. Ed and I are sympatico. We kill ourselves laughing. (1994)

fall about (1967) Implying uncontrollable laughter ■ *Times*: The thought of producing a book in that time is enough to make us fall about. (1973)

wet oneself (1970) From the notion of laughing so much that one urinates involuntarily ■ *Guardian*: It's entirely possible that laughter is very good for you, but the language we use to describe its effects has more to do with death and damage than health and vitality: 'I split my sides' . . . 'this will kill you' . . . 'I wet myself'. (1992)

yuck, yuk (1974) Mainly North American; perhaps related to *yock* laugh ■ *Time Out*: Pryor has them yukking at whitey one moment and at themselves the next. (1975)

crease up (1977) Implying uncontrollable laughter; from the notion of laughing so much that one bends over ■ *Guardian*: The 12 contestants . . . are all but crying with laughter. So are the producer, the researchers and the cameramen. . . . Bowen plays it the same every day for two weeks and every day they crease up. (1992)

To cause to laugh

kill (1856) Implying convulsive laughter ■ **Celia Dale**: He kills me sometimes, the things he says. (1960)

break someone **up (1895)** Orig and mainly US, orig theatrical slang; compare earlier sense, upset ■ **M. Wolff**: It . . . breaks me up. I can't help but laugh. (1956)

slay (1927) Implying convulsive laughter ■ **D. O'Sullivan**: They're fun. . . . They'll slay you! (1975)

fracture (1946) US, orig theatrical slang; implying convulsive laughter, or more generally, great amusement ■ **Max Shulman**: We're a riot, hey. We play all kinds of funny stuff. We fracture the people. (1951)

crack someone **up (1966)** Orig and mainly US ■ *Guardian*: Positively the last Things They Never Said . . . 'The Sun and the Mirror please' (Bobby Robson); . . . 'It cracked me up' (Graham Kelly). (1991)

crease (1977) Implying uncontrollable laughter; often followed by *up*; from the notion of laughing so much that one bends over ■ *Today*: On the set of Family Business he had the cast and crew creased up with laughter with his impersonations. (1990)

Laughing

in fits (1856) ■ **P. G. Winslow**: There's one that likes a joke. Times I've had her in fits. (1980)

in stitches (1935) Implying uproarious laughter; often in the phrase *have someone in stitches* make them laugh in this way; from *stitch* sudden sharp pain in the side ■ **D. M. Thomas**: She had them in stitches with her absurd—but true— anecdotes. (1981)

rolling in the aisles (1940) Applied originally to an audience's uncontrollable laughter; usually in the phrase *have people rolling in the aisles* ■ *New Scientist*: 'Chi-Lung?' 'A Chinese philosopher who apparently had the mandarins rolling in the aisles with his quips a couple of thousand years ago.' (1991)

A laugh

belly-laugh (1921) Applied to a deep reverberant laugh ■ *Guardian*: I think Chris Patten is a bit of a spoilsport. . . . He has denied the British electorate and his erstwhile chums one last really good belly laugh. To see Chris Patten making a complete prat of himself with feathers and sword—it's quite something to miss. (1992)

yock, yok (1938) Theatrical slang, mainly US; probably from the verb *yock* laugh ■ *New Yorker*: A chuckle or even a short, muted yock is acceptable from time to time. (1965)

boff (1945), boffo (1992) US; origin unknown

yuck, yuk (1971) Mainly North American; probably from *yuck it up* fool around ■ *National*

Observer: The biggest yuck of the night was when Mr. T. called Mrs. Llewelyn 'Mrs. Rreweryn'. (1976)

Very funny or amusing

rich (1760) Now usually used ironically, to suggest unreasonableness ■ **John Anderson**: 'You have experienced a spontaneous demonstration of disapproval . . . at your last recital.' 'Spontaneous! That's rich.' (1977)

killing (1844) From the notion of 'dying' with laughter ■ **Muriel Spark**: 'That's exactly what I expected you to say,' Marlene said. 'I think you're killing.' (1960)

priceless (1907) From earlier sense, invaluable ■ **Shiva Naipaul**: The European . . . burst out laughing. . . . 'Can you imagine how they must have . . . rolled their eyes? Absolutely priceless.' (1978)

ripe (1923) Usually used ironically, to suggest unreasonableness ■ **James Fraser**: 'What the bloody hell are you playing at?' 'That's ripe considering you just near broke my arm!' (1969)

hysterical (1969) From earlier application to convulsive laughter ■ **G. B. Trudeau**: 'I'm afraid that's no joke, Miss.' 'It's not? But I was told it was hysterical.' (1980)

Fun, amusement

gas (1914) Anglo-Irish ■ **Edna O'Brien**: 'Let's do it for gas,' Baba said. (1962)

Something or someone very funny or amusing

screamer (1831) Dated; applied to a tale, etc. that raises screams of laughter

a scream (1888) From the notion of screaming with laughter ■ *Guardian*: Like the bearded lady, Lorna has curiosity value. . . . 'Yes, isn't it a scream?' she says. (1974)

a riot (1909) Orig theatrical slang; applied to a very amusing performance, situation or person ■ **John Snow**: His rendering of 'Barnacle Bill the Sailor' was a riot and became his party piece. (1976)

a yell (1926) From the notion of yelling with laughter ■ **E. E. Coxhead**: All these doctors and their ecologists—what a yell. (1949)

a laugh (1930) Often used ironically ■ **John Wain**: 'Your friends paid for it.' That was a laugh. My friends . . . were a one-way valve for drinks, cigarettes and loans. (1960) ■ **D. Devine**: She fell for Dr Kendall and he chucked her too. It's a laugh when you think of it. (1972)

a hoot (1942) Orig US; from the notion of hooting with laughter ■ *Punch*: All the chaps chuck their clubs in a heap, and the wives have to pick a club and go off with the owner; it's going to be an absolute hoot! (1969)

laugher (1973) US ■ *Washington Post*: The voice belongs to . . . the engineer-producer for this laugher of a recording session. (1977)

An amusing person

card (1905) British, dated; from earlier sense, person of the stated sort ■ **W. B. Johnson**: That old Witch-Hammer was really quite a card. (1942)

16. Gratitude

Thank you

ta (1772) British; baby-talk alteration of *thank you*
■ D. Clark: 'You know your way, don't you?' 'Ta, love.' (1981)

thanks awfully (1890) British ■ P. G. Wodehouse: The 'Oh, thanks awfully' which betrayed the other's English origin. (1965)

thanks ever so, ta ever so (1914) British
■ Joyce Porter: Well, ta ever so! Be seeing you! (1970)
■ Jessica Mann: 'Thanks ever so,' he said, his voice an octave higher than usual. (1972)

thanks a million (1936) Orig US ■ Harold Nicholson: 'Spend it on Pam.' 'Shall I? Thanks a million.' (1966)

ta muchly (1970)

cheers (1976) British; from earlier use, expressing good wishes before drinking alcohol ■ R. Buckle: Do any small favour for a young Englishman these days and he will thank you by saying 'cheers'. (1978)

thanks a bunch, thanks a bundle (1981) Often used ironically ■ I. Pattison: *Jamesie walks over to suitcase, lifts the lid, takes out a saucepan with an unopened tin it it.* JAMESIE. Rab, lookit! NESBITT. And we went to all the bother of getting yeez firewood! MARY. (*Pointing to fireplace.*) Aye, thanks a bunch! (1992)

17. Depression

Depressed

down (1610) ■ *Daily Mail:* My favourite song is the Liverpool anthem: You'll Never Walk Alone by Gerry and The Pacemakers. If you're feeling really down, it can be very uplifting. (1991)

blue (1821) From earlier senses, anxious, perturbed, disappointed ■ *Wall Street Journal:* David, dear boy, . . . I haven't felt this blue since the fall of France. (1989)

weepy (1863) Denoting tearfulness ■ *Washington Post:* If I were the weepy type, she would have brought tears to my eyes. (1993)

mouldy (1876) Dated ■ Aldous Huxley: One feels a bit low and mouldy after those bouts of flu. (1956)

fed up (1914) From earlier sense, satiated, bored ■ *Daily Mail:* I have been pretty low and fed-up at times and I am, frankly, still in the position of wondering whether I'm ever going to make it. (1991)

gutted (1981) British; from earlier sense, having the guts removed ■ *Sun:* I've heard nothing for four months. I'm gutted because I still love him. (1991)

Depression

the dumps (1714) Often in the phrase (*down*) *in the dumps*; from obsolete *dump* fit of melancholy or depression; probably ultimately of Low German or Dutch origin and a figurative use of Middle Dutch *domp* exhalation, mist, related to English *damp* ■ *Wall Street Journal:* Discouragement feeds on itself. 'The problem is, if people get down in the dumps, they stop selling.' (1989)

the blues (1741) From earlier *blue devils* in same sense ■ *New Statesman:* The post-election blues are beginning. (1960)

the uglies (1846) ■ N. Last: A gloom seems over us all. I've shaken off my fit of the uglies, but I felt I'd just like to crawl into a hole. (1939)

the hump (1873) British ■ T. S. Eliot: You seem to be wanting to give us all the hump. I must say, this isn't cheerful for Amy's birthday. (1939)

the joes (1910) Australian; origin unknown
■ V. Palmer: What I saw in the sugar country gave me the joes. (1957)

the woofits (1918) Origin unknown ■ Nevil Shute: Getting the woofits now, because I don't sleep so good. (1958)

the sterks, the sturks (1941) Australian; perhaps from *stercoraceous* of excrement
■ N. Miles: 'Wouldn't it give you the sturks?' complained Bill. (1972)

blahs (1968) Orig & mainly US; usually *the blahs*; from *blah* dull, perhaps influenced by *blues*
■ *Fortune:* The town's 4,800 first-class casino-hotel rooms are a long way from the 10,000 needed to attract the big conventions that would cure the off-season blahs. (1982)

To depress

get down (1930) ■ Nevil Shute: It's just being cooped up in the office gets you down a bit. (1953)

Depressing, gloomy

down-beat (1952) Orig US ■ *New York Herald-Tribune:* That pictorially memorable march up the twilit hill of a dusty Southern town has an inexplicably plodding and down-beat air about it. (1955)

Something depressing

damper (1748) Mainly in the phrase *put a damper on* have a depressing effect on ■ *Guardian:* Ted will get number and number until he is . . . utterly numb and void. This put a bit of a damper on the wedding. (1992)

bummer (1966) Orig US; often applied specifically to a depressing experience induced by a hallucinogenic drug; from *bum* of low quality + *-er* ■ D. A. Dye: I ain't no sooner off the chopper than I get a letter from my wife sayin' she wants a fucking divorce. What a bummer, man! (1986)

downer (1967) Compare earlier sense, depressant drug ■ *Oz:* When I was in gaol they cut my hair, and that really was a downer. For four or five days I couldn't eat or sleep. I couldn't do nothing. (1971)

Someone depressing

See **party pooper**, **wet blanket**, and **wet smack** under Spoilsport at **Spoiling**, **Ruination** (p. 417).

A dreary(-looking) person

dreary (1925) From the adjective *dreary* ■ H. G. Wells: The parade of donnish and scholastic drearies. (1936)

face-ache (1937) Compare earlier sense, neuralgia ■ Simpson & Galton: Every time I travel on a

train I get lumbered with a carriageful of the most miserable-looking bunch of face-aches you've ever seen in your life. (1961)

drear (1958) Back-formation from the adjective *dreary* ■ J. B. Priestley: He was just a miserable little drear. (1966)

Weeping

waterworks (1647) Often in the phrase *turn on the waterworks* start to cry ■ D. W. Smith: Course I was tactful. Didn't stop the waterworks being turned on, though. (1986)

18. **Hopelessness**

not a leg to stand on (1594) ■ Muriel Spark: She hasn't a leg to stand on in the case. He's divorcing her, she's not divorcing him. (1960)

not a cat (in hell)'s chance (1796) ■ *Guardian*: One seaman said the union had not 'a cat in hell's chance' of beating the Government as well as the shipowners. (1966)

no chance, not a chance (1888)

Buckley's (1895) Australian & New Zealand; in full *Buckley's chance, hope*, etc.; used to denote a forlorn hope; origin obscure; perhaps from the name of William Buckley, a celebrated 19th-century Australian convict known as the 'wild white man' ■ D'Arcy Niland: You reckon I haven't got Buckley's. (1955)

no earthly, not an earthly (1899) ■ *Hockey*: The poor goal-keeper had not an 'earthly'. (1907)

what a hope (1899) ■ Cecil Day Lewis: 'Well, you'd better start giving back the money . . . ,' jeered Tuppy. 'What a hope!' (1948)

on a hiding to nothing (1905) Orig horse-racing slang, denoting that a horse is expected to win easily, so that it gains no credit from victory, and is disgraced by defeat; from *hiding* punishment by beating; based on a commonly used formula (*ten to one*, etc.) for giving racing odds ■ *Times*: Derby know they are on a hiding to nothing

at Fourth Division Colchester, who have a reputation as giant-killers. (1977)

you can't win (1926)

not a snowball's chance (in hell) (1931) ■ Arthur Hailey: 'Told 'em there wasn't a snowball's chance,' a woman assistant dispatcher called over. (1979)

no hope, not a hope (in hell) (1933) ■ Stella Gibbons: Not a hope . . . not a single bloody ghost of a hope in hell. (1959)

some hope(s) (1940) ■ Fred Hoyle: I'd given them the idea I might come up with some explanation. . . . Some hopes. (1966)

not have a prayer (1941) ■ Alan Ross: He went for me. . . . He was a big lad, but he didn't have a prayer. An amateur up against a professional almost never does. (1973)

One who is beyond hope

dead duck (1829) Orig US ■ *Guardian*: It is not difficult to see Ron Dixon forsaking the Tories as a 'dead duck' in Liverpool and plumping for the Liberal Democrats. (1992)

gone goose, gone gosling (1830) Orig US ■ J. & W. Hawkins: If my luck won't hold . . . I'm a gone goose anyway. (1958)

goner (1847) From the adjective *gone* + *-er* ■ Ernest Bramah: If it failed it was—if one may be permitted the word in the excitement of the moment—a 'goner'. (1930)

19. **Confusion**

Confused, bewildered

at sixes and sevens (1670) Also denoting disorganization or disorder; from the earlier phrase *set on six and seven* leave to chance, possibly a fanciful alteration of *set on cinque and sice* (= five and six), a gambling term denoting hazarding everything on throwing a five and a six at dice ■ *Sunday Times*: So what if the government's legal experts are at sixes and sevens about the Maastricht bill? (1993)

(all) at sea (1768) ■ M. A. Noble: Gregory . . . was all at sea to Larwood, whom he flicked three times dangerously through the slips. (1927)

mixed up (1884) Orig US ■ John Bingham: Poor damned old mixed-up queer. (1966)

moggadored, mogodored (1936) Dated; origin uncertain; perhaps connected with Irish *magadh* mock, jeer ■ B. Naughton: He got some of these blokes moggadored: didn't know what to think, or do. (1945)

hung up (1945) Perhaps from *hang up* delay, detain ■ Bernard Malamud: He was more than a little hung up, stupid from lack of sleep, worried about his work. (1971)

To confuse, bewilder

bamboozle (1712) From earlier sense, deceive, trick; ultimately probably of cant origin; compare obsolete *bam* hoax ■ Elizabeth Gaskell: He fairly bamboozles me. He is two chaps. (1854)

flummox (1837) Origin unknown ■ *Economist*: In Australia such information is made available by law without flummoxing everybody between Brisbane and Fremantle. (1987)

discombobberate (1838) US, dated; probably a jocular alteration of *discompose* or *discomfit*

throw (1844) Orig US; compare earlier *throw someone out* disturb someone's self-possession ■ L. Kaufman: I knew my way around in a restaurant and a

bill of fare. Sometimes, even those French dishes didn't throw me. (1950)

discombobulate (1916) Orig and mainly US; variant of *discombobberate* ■ Ellery Queen: I don't want you people to be in any way discombobulated. (1970)

A scene of confusion

madhouse (1919) From earlier sense, mental hospital ■ *Radio Times*: They [sc. chefs] roast and stew and bake in a kind of madhouse of shouted commands, cancelled orders and frayed tempers. (1973)

A moment of confusion

brainstorm (1907) British; applied to a brief mental aberration which causes one to do a foolish or untypical thing; from earlier sense, sudden violent mental disturbance ■ *Independent on Sunday*: When he was at last introduced, Tufnell's very first ball induced a brainstorm in Lambert, who holed out to cover. (1991)

20. Trouble

Trouble, harm, misfortune

merry hell (a1911) Applied to great trouble, upheaval, or disturbance; often in the phrase *raise (play, give, etc.) merry hell* ■ Bernard Fergusson: The Special Boat Squadron ... was to play merry hell in the Eastern Mediterranean during the next two years. (1961)

a packet (1925) Usually in the phrase *cop (catch, etc.) a packet* suffer trouble or misfortune; from earlier sense, (a wound from) a bullet ■ Anthony Price: We've been disbanded. . . . The same thing's happening to the 2nd Northants, they've caught a packet too. (1978)

grief (1929) Often in the phrase *give (make, have, etc.) grief*; from earlier sense, deep sorrow ■ *Face*: Marm has had grief from snobby film critics and from the censorship lobby. (1989)

unshirted hell (1932) US ■ Henry Kissinger: I've been catching unshirted hell every half-hour from the President who says we're not tough enough. (1979)

shtook, schtook, shtuck, schtuck, etc. **(1936)** Usually in the phrase *in (dead) shtook* in (serious) trouble; origin unknown (apparently not a Yiddish word) ■ John Gardner: You know I'm in schtuck with my bosses. (1978)

A setback

knock (1649) Often in the phrase *take a knock* suffer a setback ■ *Encounter*: Like other institutions of the Establishment, it has taken a knock or two in recent years. (1959)

Temporary trouble

hiccup (1965) Orig US; applied to a temporary small problem or delay; from earlier sense, brief breathing spasm ■ *Business*: We look at anomalies in past financial performance—to see whether, for example, there has been a hiccup in gross margins. (1990)

blip (1975) Orig applied specifically to a temporary unwelcome statistical movement; from earlier sense, trace on a radar screen, from the notion of a rise or fall on a graph looking like the rise or fall of a blip on a radar screen ■ *Listener*: Nigel Lawson's dilemma is the Conservative Party's also. Is the first tremor on its happy political landscape merely a 'blip', as the Chancellor has called the storm that has gradually engulfed him? (1989)

(When) trouble occurs

the fat is in the fire (1797) From earlier, obsolete use, denoting the failure of a plan

when the balloon goes up (1943) British; denoting the beginning of expected trouble; from earlier more general use, referring to the start of something ■ *Punch*: The international rules of war [are] apt to be waived when the balloon goes up. (1959)

(when) the shit hits the fan (or the shit flies) (1966) Denoting the moment when a crisis occurs and its repercussions begin to be felt ■ Howard Fast: It's been too quiet. Tomorrow, the shit hits the fan. (1977)

What's the trouble with . . . ?, what's the matter with . . . ?

what's with . . . ? (1940) Orig US; literal translation of Yiddish *voz iz mit ...?* ■ Howard Fast: There are ways to find out what's with Jake. (1977)

Pain

gyp, gip (1910) Usually in the phrase *give someone gyp*; from earlier *give someone gyp* scold someone ■ Ian Jefferies: I should think his tum is giving him gip. (1966)

merry hell (1963) Applied to severe pain; from earlier sense, trouble ■ M. Duggan: Watching mum with a shoehorn wedging nines into sevens and suffering merry hell. (1963)

In trouble

in a pickle (a1620) ■ *Jersey Evening Post*: Don't leave jobs unfinished in order to start on something new, or you'll end up in a right old pickle. (1977)

in a hole (1762) ■ P. G. Wodehouse: 'Mr Bickersteth is in a hole, Jeeves, . . . and wants you to rally round.' 'Very good, sir.' (1925)

in hot water (1765) ■ *Daily Mail*: Another luxury hotel in Moscow has landed itself in hot water. (1991)

in Queer Street (1811) ■ John Wainwright: If Patsold talks, Webb's in queer street. (1980)

up a stump (1829) Orig & mainly US, dated ■ John Galsworthy: Look here, Uncle Soames, I'm up a stump. (1924)

up the spout (1829) From earlier sense, in pawn

in a fix (1834) Orig US; from obsolete *fix* condition, state ■ *Kansas City Times*: What a fix this old world might have been in if our boys had not made it safe for democracy. (1931)

in for (1835) Denoting that one is about to experience something unpleasant; sometimes in the phrase *in for it* about to experience something unpleasant ■ *Guardian*: If he goes outside Woolf and pushes for privatisation and contracting out, we are in for a long period of turmoil. (1991)

in Dutch (1851) Orig US ■ John Dos Passos: While I plodded around . . . trying to explain my position and getting myself deeper in Dutch every time I opened my face, I saw marvellous scenes. (1968)

in the cart (1889) British ■ J. B. Hobbs: We made 238, which was enough practically to put South Africa hopelessly in the cart. (1924)

in the soup (1889) Orig US ■ *Listener*: You find you may want to move a group of pictures . . . to a different part of the building, and if the rooms over there are designed for quite a different kind of picture, you're rather in the soup. (1968)

up against it (1896) Orig North American ■ *Chambers's Journal*: In Canadian phraseology, we were 'up against it' with a vengeance! (1910)

up the (or a) pole (1896) ■ Richard Beilby: We'd 'a' been up the pole without him, that's why we didn't send him on his way. (1970)

for it (1909) Orig services' slang; applied to someone in danger of getting into trouble, and often specifically of being punished ■ *War Illustrated*: Then it is that he realises so acutely that if anything happens to his pilot he is 'for it', as the current flying phrase has it. (1915)

in a jam (1914) Orig US ■ *New Statesman*: He knew instinctively that in a jam it was not done to let down one's own side. (1958)

up the creek (without a paddle) (1918) ■ Ian Kemp: 'You okay?' asked Donovan. . . . 'I thought you were properly up the creek.' (1969)

for the high jump (1919) British; applied to someone in danger of being severely punished; in early use often applied to someone likely to be hanged ■ Eric Ambler: If we fall down on this job . . . it's me for the high jump. (1936)

on the ropes (1924) Implying that someone or something is in serious trouble and near defeat; from the notion of a boxer so weakened that he has to lean on the rope surrounding the ring ■ *Tablet*: There is talk that the Kennedy campaign is not just 'on the ropes', but that it is plain dead. (1980)

up a gum-tree (1926) Compare earlier Australian *up a gum-tree* in another place and US *up a tree* trapped, in difficulties ■ *Encounter*: Until somebody solves the problem of an English idiom we're going to be up a gum-tree. (1959)

in a spot (1929) ■ Erle Stanley Gardner: He was afraid his father would find out. He was in a spot. So he turned to the troubleshooter. (1967)

in the shit (1937) Also in the phrase *in deep shit* in serious trouble ■ B. W. Aldiss: We were all in the shit together and it was madness to try and escape it. (1971) ■ William Gibson: And he's in deep shit with these guys, these heavies from the Sprawl? (1986)

up shit creek (1937) ■ *Private Eye*: If they'd followed her this far up shit creek it's a long way to walk back. (1981)

in the pooh, in the poo (1961) A euphemistic substitute for *in the shit*; from *pooh* excrement ■ James McClure: 'But what . . . if someone . . . gave him the money and support he needed?' 'We might be right in the poo.' (1976)

in lumber (1965) British; compare earlier sense, in prison ■ L. Henderson: I've got to keep at it. Break my bloody leg or something stupid like that and I'm in lumber. (1972)

in deep doo-doo (1989) Orig & mainly US; denoting in serious trouble; a euphemistic substitute for *in deep shit*, given currency in a speech by US President-elect George Bush in 1989; from *doo-doo* excrement ■ *Guardian*: If something goes wrong, however, you're in deep doodoo. (1992)

In financial trouble

in Queer Street (1886) From earlier, more general sense, in trouble ■ Angus Wilson: He enjoys a little flutter . . . and if he finds himself in Queer Street now and again, I'm sure no one would grudge him his bit of fun. (1952)

on the rocks (1889) ■ *Economist*: When ICL was on the rocks, its partner, Fujitsu, suggested that ICL's customers might have more confidence if, say, the 200 most important ones flew to Japan to see how stable ICL's Japanese partner was. (1988)

Lost

slewed (1879) Australian & New Zealand; applied to someone who is lost in the bush ■ Teece & Pike: That is where I must have got 'slewed' for . . . the sun came out and I could see we were heading into the sun instead of having sundown at our backs. (1978)

To be in trouble

catch it, catch it in the neck (1835)
Denoting getting into trouble, usually with the
implication of punishment ■ John Welcome: I'll
catch it if Firmian finds me coffee-housing here. (1961)

get it, get it hot, get it in the neck (1872)
Denoting getting into trouble, usually with the
implication of punishment ■ H. G. Wells: They'll
get it in the neck in real earnest one of these days, if they ain't
precious careful. (1908)

cop it (1909) British; denoting getting into
trouble, usually with the implication of
punishment ■ *Daily Chronicle*: When arrested he
remarked, 'I suppose I shall "cop" it for this.' (1909)

have one's ass in a sling (1960) US; *ass = arse*
■ S. F. X. Dean: Gonna get my ass in some sling if I miss that
plane. (1982)

To cause trouble or harm to someone or something

do someone **a mischief (***c***1385)** ■ Kyril
Bonfiglioli: 'Lost my temper. . . Bloody roadhog.' 'He might
easily have done us a mischief,' I agreed. (1972)

play (merry) hell with (1803) ■ *Listener*: Wingate
and his Chindits would play hell with the Japanese
communications. (1959)

soup (1895) Usually used in the passive; from *in
the soup* in trouble ■ *Daily Telegraph*: Admitting that
he earned £3,000 a year, Lord Taylor said that if he accepted a
junior Ministry he would be 'souped'. (1964)

give someone **the** (or **a**) **run-around (1924)**
Orig US ■ Erle Stanley Gardner: A small-town dentist
. . . , and you think that fits you to give me a run-around in a
murder case. (1934)

bugger someone **about** (or **around**) **(1957)**
British; denoting causing difficulties for
someone ■ Colin Watson: In this trade you get used to
being buggered about a bit by head office. (1972)

hassle (1959) From the noun *hassle* something
troublesome ■ *Guardian*: Police intervention is common.
'They hassle us unnecessarily,' mutters Miranda. 'They move
us on for the sake of it.' (1991)

fuck someone **about** (or **around**) **(1960)**
■ *Independent on Sunday*: 'We did it because we just got
fucked around all the time,' Slash explains. 'Everyone's taken
pot-shots at us and made up stories.' (1991)

drop someone **in it (1991)** ■ *Just Seventeen*: Your
mate reveals she's really dropped you in it with your folks
today, but she's just winding you up. Had you going for a
minute though. (1996)

To upset, distress

turn someone **over (1865)** ■ *New Society*: Escalope
I had, though what they do to those calves turns me over.
(1972)

To have been harmed

have been in the wars (1850) ■ *Guardian*: Sigh
at this criminal omission and hastily endow him with painfully
bilious attack. 'Dear me,' says Aunt E, 'you have all been in the
wars!' (1991)

To make trouble

rock the boat (1931) ■ *Punch*: The trouble with these
people who nail their colours to the mast—they always rock
the boat. (1958)

make waves (1962) Orig US ■ *Publishers' Weekly*:
Dr. Wilkins . . . had just been fired from Willowbrook for
allegedly making waves about conditions. (1972)

stir (1969) Perhaps a back-formation from *stirrer*
trouble-maker ■ B. Bennett: More interested in stirring
than they are in abo poets. (1976)

set (put, etc.) **the cat among the pigeons**
(1976) ■ J. M. Brownjohn: You're putting a petit bourgeois
cat among the pigeons. (1976)

A trouble-maker

mixer (1938) Perhaps from *mix it* quarrel ■ A. E.
Lindop: I knew what a mixer she was, and I knew she was not
capable of keeping a secret. (1966)

bolshie, bolshy (1940) British; applied to an
uncooperative person; from earlier sense,
Bolshevik

stirrer (1963) From the notion of 'stirring' up
trouble ■ *Observer*: Jessica Mitford is what Australians
call a stirrer, meaning a person with a talent for causing
trouble. (1982)

Something or someone very troublesome or annoying

pest (1609) In modern use usually applied to a
person ■ *Daily Telegraph*: The lad went on to be a 12-
year-old pest at shareholder meetings and next month becomes
Taube's personal assistant. (1991)

pebble (1829) Australian, dated; applied to a
troublesome person or animal

hell on wheels (1843) ■ Sinclair Lewis: Looks just
like a sweet little ivory statue, but is she hell on wheels! (1943)

terror (1883) Applied especially to a troublesome
child; often in the phrase *holy terror*
■ A. McCowen: At school I was known as a terror and went
looking for fights. (1979)

handful (1887) Applied to someone or
something difficult to cope with; from earlier
sense, as much as one can hold in one hand
■ *Daily Mail*: I found her a bit of a handful, I suppose, but I
never thought we wouldn't end up friends. (1991)

peb (1903) Australian; applied to a troublesome
person or animal; short for *pebble* in same sense
■ C. J. Dennis: They wus pebs, they wus norks, they wus reel
naughty boys. (1916)

murder (1924) Applied to a very irksome
experience ■ Malcolm Bradbury: Private life was simple
enough, but the communal centres were murder. (1965)

a bind (1930) Mainly British ■ Nevil Shute: But it's
an awful bind for you, at such a time as this. (1953)

a pain (1933) ■ *New Yorker*: She is a pain, and, unconsciously, the source of many of the troubles that follow. (1975)

a menace (1936) From earlier sense, something threatening ■ J. H. Fullarton: That B.S.M.'s a bloody menace. (1944)

a pain in the neck (1941) ■ *Times*: Anthony Quinn . . . plays a wise, noble, feckless, life-loving Greek dispenser of advice, lay preacher and general pain in the neck. (1970)

a pisser (1943) Orig US; compare earlier sense, one who urinates ■ *Melchior's Sleeper Agent*: We could both do with a little liquid cheer. It's been a pisser of a day. (1975)

hassle (1945) Applied to trouble or annoyance caused by having to do something difficult; origin uncertain; perhaps a blend of *haggle* and

tussle ■ Anthony Blond: To write a book without having the hassle of having to sell it too. (1985)

schlep, schlepp (1964) Mainly US; applied to a troublesome business or a piece of hard work; probably from the verb *schlep* drag, toil ■ *National Observer* (US): Anybody who has ever tried to make even a small amount of a classic brown sauce from scratch would probably agree with Liederman's assessment that 'it's the ultimate schlep'. (1976)

a pain in the arse (or **ass**) **(1972)** ■ Ed McBain: Homicide cops . . . were pains in the ass to detectives actually . . . trying to solve murder cases. (1973)

A place of trouble

hot spot (1941) ■ G. Beare: You're putting yourself on the hot-spot, Sammy. (1973)

21. Excitement

Excited

all of a doodah (or **do-da, dooda**) **(1915)** Applied to someone in a state of agitated or dithering excitement; from the refrain *doo-da(h)* of the plantation song 'Camptown Races' ■ P. G. Wodehouse: Poor old Clarence was patently all of a doodah. (1952)

Exciting

wow (1921) North American; from *wow* exclamation of delight ■ *Daily Colonist* (Victoria, British Columbia): Two-foot-high letters inviting you to buy Vitamin E capsules, often at wow potencies, plaster the fronts of drug stores. (1972)

wild (1955) Orig & mainly US ■ *Hot Car*: Naugahyde . . . has long been the favourite amongst Stateside rodders because of its stretchy qualities, amazing range of colours (including some wild marble-like effects). (1978)

(A state or feeling of) excitement; a thrill

a drive (1921) US; applied especially to exhilaration resulting from the use of narcotics; often in the phrase *get a drive out of* ■ Nelson Algren: *Sure* I like to see it hit. Heroin got the drive awright— but there's not a tingle to a ton. (1949)

a kick (1928) Often in the phrase *get a kick out of*, and also in *for kicks* for the sake of excitement or pleasure; from earlier sense, strong stimulant effect ■ *R.A.F. Journal*: We get a great kick out of wearing it. (1942) ■ *Listener*: Antisocial, sexually ruthless, stealing cars for kicks. (1963)

a bang (1929) US; often in the phrase *get a bang out of*; from earlier sense, dose of a drug ■ J. D. Salinger: I hate the movies like poison, but I get a bang imitating them. (1951)

a buzz (1937) Orig US; often in the phrase *get a buzz out of* ■ *Times*: Some players get a 'buzz' from the game [of Space Invaders] and that might explain why they become addicted. (1983)

a charge (1950) Orig US; often in the phrase *get a charge out of*; from earlier sense, dose of a drug ■ *New York Times Magazine*: It seems to me that people get a bigger charge out of their grandchildren than they did from their own offspring. (1963)

thrills and spills (1983) Widely used well before its first recorded date; *spills* probably from *spill* a fall, especially from a horse or vehicle, but compare the rhyming conceit in *Merry Drollery*: The sword doth . . . nimbly come to the point . . . , Thrilling, and drilling, And killing, and spilling (1661) ■ *Air Gunner*: Brocock's fabulous revolvers offer all the thrills and spills of full-bore hand gunning—without the smoke! (1993)

To excite; cause to lose composure; overwhelm emotionally

wow (1924) Orig US; from *wow* exclamation of delight ■ *Daily Telegraph*: Mr Macdonald, who supplied the off-screen commentary for this year's Channel 4 coverage of the SDP conference, had the bright notion of training up a novice speaker who would wow them at Buxton. (1984)

psych (1957) Mainly US; denoting psychological stimulation, especially in order to get into a state of mental preparedness; often followed by *up*; from *psych*, short for *psychology, psychiatry*, etc. ■ *New Yorker*: He's never tried to psych us, or insult us with a pep talk. (1968)

stoke (1963) Mainly surfing slang ■ *South African Surfer*: Your magazine stoked me out of my mind. (1965)

freak out, freak (1964) Orig US; from *freak* (*out*) undergo drug-induced hallucinations ■ *Gandalf's Garden*: He was the first guy I had ever met who used his music to influence people, to turn them on, or freak them out. (1969)

zap (1967) Orig US; compare earlier sense, kill ■ *Theology*: A well-known evangelist invited the undergraduates of Oxford to allow themselves to be 'zapped by the Holy Spirit'. (1983)

To give way to heightened emotion; lose one's composure

tear it (or **things**) **up (1932)** US, mainly jazz slang; denoting performing, behaving, etc. with unrestrained excitement ■ *Listener*: The trumpeter Wild Bill Davison, who 'tore it up' with admirable primitivity and sensuality. (1963)

flip one's wig (1934), **flip one's lid (1941)**, **flip (1950)** Orig US ■ Barry Crump: As he spoke one of the dogs sank his teeth into a tender part and the bull flipped his lid completely. (1960) ■ Ross Macdonald: She's a phoney blonde. . . . I can't understand why he would flip over her. (1969)

freak out (1966), **freak (1967)** Orig US; from earlier sense, undergo drug-induced hallucinations ■ *Nature*: One question asked the respondents how often they had seen other people 'freak out', that is, have intense, transient emotional upsets. (1970)

plotz (1967) US; from Yiddish *platsen*, from Middle High German *platzen* burst ■ Judith Krantz: She came back to pick them up today and *plotzed* for joy all over the studio. (1978)

wet oneself, **wet one's pants (1970)** From the notion of urinating involuntarily when over-excited ■ Michael Underwood: There are quite a few people who'll wet their pants if I get sent down. (1979)

See also To behave frenziedly at **Nervousness, Agitation** (p. 266).

Someone who has lost composure

headless chicken (1993) From such phrases as *rush around like a headless chicken*, from the notion of a decapitated chicken running around aimlessly without a brain to control its movements ■ *Sun*: The players saw the tough side of Taylor as he let fly, accusing them of being headless chickens, of forgetting everything they had worked for and conceding a Sunday parks goal. (1993)

See also A nervous or agitated person at **Nervousness, Agitation** (p. 267).

Exclamations of excitement

pow (1881) Imitative of the sound of a blow, shot, etc. ■ Germaine Greer: Perhaps they will not fall in love all at once but feel a tenderness growing until one day *pow*! that amazing kiss. (1970)

shazam (1940) An invented word, originally used in 'Captain Marvel' adventure stories

22. **Eagerness, Enthusiasm**

Eager, enthusiastic

gung ho (1955) Orig US; from earlier services' slang sense, dedicated to teamwork and effort; originally adopted as a slogan during World War II by the United States Marines under Lt. Col. Evans F. Carlson, from Chinese *kung-ho* Industrial Co-operatives, mistakenly taken in its literal meaning 'work together', from *kung* work and *ho* peace, harmony ■ Ian Kemp: He . . . was one of the most 'gung-ho' (exceptionally keen to be personally involved in combat) characters I ever met. (1969)

Enthusiastic support

sky-rocket (1867) US, dated; applied to an enthusiastic cheer, raised especially by college students

rah rah (1911) Orig US; used as a shout of support or encouragement for a college sports team

To be eager or enthusiastic

champ at the bit (c1645) Denoting eagerness or impatience to start; from the notion of a horse chewing its bit in impatience ■ *Washington Post*: If Bill Clinton thought like a chess player, Republican Kay Bailey Hutchison would not today be a United States senator-elect for Texas, champing at the bit to cast a vote against his economic program. (1993)

fall over oneself (1904) Orig US ■ *Maclean's Magazine*: And last year mink breeders from Scandinavia to California were falling over themselves to buy a piece of the action. (1966)

strain at the leash (1910) Denoting eagerness or impatience to start; from the notion of a dog pulling at its lead in impatience ■ *Independent on Sunday*: We are told that . . . General Schwarzkopf['s] . . . 'soldiers were straining at the leash'. (1991)

An eager or enthusiastic person

eager beaver (1943) Orig US ■ *Observer*: The British pack were like a set of eager beavers. (1959)

An enthusiast

See Someone who favours or enjoys something under **Favour & Disfavour** (p. 208).

An enthusiast for the stated thing

culture vulture (1947) Derogatory, orig US; applied to someone eager to acquire culture; compare Ogden Nash, 'There is a woman—/ There is a vulture / Who circles above / The carcass of culture' (1931) ■ Dylan Thomas: See the garrulous others, also, gabbing and garlanded from one nest of culture-vultures to another. (a1953)

sun-worshipper (1966) Jocular; applied to a devotee of sun-bathing; from earlier sense, one who worships the sun as a god ■ B. H. Deal: Her red bathing suit [was] brilliant against her white skin. Evidently she wasn't the sun worshiper the others were. (1966)

An enthusiasm

bee in one's bonnet (1845) Applied to an obsession with something ■ *Independent*: Fiona

Weir, air pollution campaigner, said: 'Max has strong views and has got a bee in his bonnet over this issue'. (1991)

fever (1885) Applied to enthusiastic or excited interest ■ *Daily Telegraph*: A disparate group of characters, from the local machine knitting society to Admiral's Cup sponsors, whose sole aim is to cash in on Cowes Week fever. (1991)

bug (1902) Orig US; applied to an obsessive enthusiasm or craze; often in the phrases *be bitten by the bug, have got the bug*; compare earlier *bug* person with an obsessive interest in or enthusiasm for something ■ *Which?*: A boy bitten by the railway bug. (1959)

-itis (1903) Jocular; denoting an excessive or obsessive interest in something; from the use

23. **Effort**

To make one's maximum effort

put oneself out (1861) Used to denote an effort that involves some inconvenience to oneself

knuckle down (1864) From previous sense, to admit defeat

sweat one's guts out (1890) ■ Roderic Jeffries: You sweated your guts out for months and finished your book, then the public looked the other way. (1961)

go some (1911) US ■ H. Lieberman: He'd known the girl for two months; for Daughtry that was going some. (1982)

sweat blood (1911) ■ Josephine Tey: I expect he sweats blood over his writing. He has no imagination. (1950)

lean (or bend) over backwards (1925) Orig US; orig with the implication of doing something disadvantageous or distasteful to oneself ■ Joyce Cary: I had provoked in him that conscience, those scruples of justice and right, which might cause him actually to favour my enemy—to, as our transatlantic friends say, lean over backwards in obliging him. (1953)

go to town (1933) Used to denote an effort made with great energy or without restraint ■ *Times Literary Supplement*: Professor MacAndrew goes to town on this novel, deciphering the code which she believes Henry James to have set up. (1980)

pull (or take, get) one's finger out (1941) Used mainly to demand effort of a lazy person; from the notion of idleness characterized by having one's finger inserted in a bodily orifice ■ *Times* (Duke of Edinburgh): I think it is about time we pulled our fingers out. (1961)

beaver away (1946) From the notion of the beaver as an industrious animal; compare *work like a beaver* to work hard (1741) ■ *Spectator*: The Germans beaver away at their scheme for 'entry by stages'. (1967)

go for the doctor (1949) Australian; from the notion of seeking medical help in an emergency

of *-itis* as a suffix in words denoting a disease ■ Winston Churchill: It was impossible to go on in a state of 'electionitis' all through the summer and autumn. (1945)

kick (1946) Often in the phrase *on the—kick* doing, or enthusiastic about, the stated thing ■ *Times Literary Supplement*: Somewhere behind the cumulative high, the peace-kick, the good vibes, efficient entrepreneurs . . . were smiling their mean smiles all the way to the bank. (1971)

Obsessed

hung up (1957) Followed by *on* ■ *New Scientist*: Roszak is very hung up on the power that science grants. (1971)

■ Dal Stivens: There were three of the bastards and they went for the doctor. But I had time to get on my guard. (1951)

go for broke (1951) Orig US; from the notion of staking all one's money in a gambling game, so that if one loses one will be broke ■ *Guardian*: The enemy is 'going all out— . . . he is going for broke'. (1968)

pull out all the stops (1974) From the notion of deploying all the stops on an organ ■ Philip McCutchan: We'll be doing our best, all stops out. (1978)

To make the slightest effort

lift (or stir, move) a finger (1833) Used in the negative to denote unwillingness to make an effort ■ David Garnett: Could anyone honestly say that we should have allowed Paris to be occupied and France defeated without lifting a finger? (1955)

To require a great effort

take some (or a bit of, a lot of) doing (1936) ■ *Time*: His long-suffering wife . . . and their six kids put up with him, which takes some doing. (1969)

A sudden great effort made

blitz (1960) From earlier sense, sudden concerted attack ■ *Guardian*: The women did only the bare essentials of housework during the week, with a 'blitz' at weekends. (1960)

Something requiring great effort

sweat (1923) Compare earlier sense, hard work (a1300) ■ Prince Charles (quoted in *Observer*): Actually sitting down and thinking is a sweat. (1980)

Something requiring little effort

money for jam (1919), money for old rope (1936) Orig services' slang ■ Evelyn Waugh: At the moment there were no mortars and he was given instead a light and easily manageable counterfeit of wood which was slung on the back of his haversack, relieving him of a rifle. At present it was money for old rope. (1942)

An attempt

go (1835) Especially in such phrases as *have a go* (*at*) and (orig Australian & New Zealand) *give it a go* ■ *Punch*: Whether my voice would work the charm, Frankly, I didn't know, But as it couldn't do much harm I thought I'd have a go. (1933) ■ *Times*: Had England been left to score 300 hundred or more at something like 70 an hour as was possible and 'given it a go', the odds would have been heavily against them. (1963)

crack (1836) Orig US; especially in the phrases *have* (or *take*) *a crack* (*at*) ■ **Macdonald Hastings**: We'd like to have a crack at climbing the peak. (1959)

shot (1878) Especially in the phrases *have* (or *take*) *a shot* (*at*) ■ *Throne*: Pinks is going to have a shot at the Wingfield Sculls. (1912)

whirl (1884) Orig US; in such phrases as *give it a whirl* ■ *Times*: John Syer came to me and said he could help. . . . So I thought I would give it a whirl. (1985)

whack (1891) Orig US; especially in the phrases *have* (or *take*) *a whack* (*at*) ■ *Washington Post*: That in itself is reason enough to take another whack at refining the statute on interstate banking. (1993)

lash (1894) Australian & New Zealand; especially in the phrase *have a lash* (*at*) ■ **Kylie Tennant**: If things get any tougher, I guess I'll have a lash at it. (1953)

stab (1895) Orig US; especially in the phrases *have* (or *make*) *a stab at* ■ **William Maxwell**: She may have made a stab at being a mother to my older brother and me. (1980)

burl, birl (1917) Australian & New Zealand; especially in the phrase *give it a burl*; from earlier Scottish sense, spin, whirl ■ **D. M. Davin**: I thought I'd give it a burl. And I made it, got clean away. (1947)

bash (1948) Mainly British; especially in the phrase *have a bash* (*at*) ■ **Iris Murdoch**: Come on . . . have a bash. You can translate the first word anyway. (1957)

24. **Surprise**

To surprise

flabbergast (1772) Usually used in the passive, quasi-adjectivally; origin uncertain; perhaps from *flabby* + *aghast* ■ *Daily Telegraph*: 'I was flabbergasted because I thought we had a contract,' Miss Buggins told the hearing in Chelsea. (1991)

faze (1830) Orig US; denoting discomposure caused by something unexpected; variant of dialect *feeze* frighten, from Old English *fēsian* drive ■ *Coast to Coast 1959-60*: Perrot became an anodized schoolmaster, a disciplinarian no boy could faze. (1961)

knock someone **sideways (1925)** Denoting astounding someone, with either pleasure or shock ■ **Richard Mason**: Their attitude is basically commercial. . . . But my guess is that this stuff will knock them sideways. (1957)

knock someone **out (1942)** Orig US; denoting something that has an overwhelming effect on someone's mind ■ *Melody Maker*: I only heard half an hour of Ornette but I wasn't knocked out at all. (1966)

knock someone **for six (1949)** British; denoting astounding someone, with either pleasure or shock; from *six* a hit over the boundary in cricket

blow someone **away (1975)** Orig & mainly US; denoting something that has an overwhelming effect on someone's mind; compare earlier sense, make drunk or high

To be surprised

eat one's hat (1837) Used to say that one will be surprised if a particular thing does not happen ■ **W. N. Harben**: Ef I don't whack it to you this pop, old hoss, I'll eat my hat. (1904)

can't get over something **(1899)** Denoting inability to recover from a surprise or shock

■ *Evening Post* (Nottingham): His wife Lee, said: 'Isn't it super? We can't get over it.' (1976)

not (or **never**) **know what hit one, wonder what hit one (1923)** Denoting something that takes someone by surprise ■ *Observer*: They must have wondered what hit them in Paris last week, for almost every female member of the British Press made a dead set for the hosiery counter at Galeries Lafayette. (1963) ■ *More!*: If you've got a hot date but you want something more adventurous than a little black Lycra dress, try one of these outfits for size. . . . He won't know what's hit him. (1992)

the mind (or **the imagination**) **boggles (1971)** *boggle* also used transitively, in the phrase *boggle the* (or *someone's*) *mind*; probably a back-formation from *mind-boggling* ■ **L. Sante**: The mind boggles at the spectacle of garrote artists weeping at song about shame . . . ear-chewers remembering their white-haired mothers. (1991)

To take by surprise

spring something **on** someone **(1876)** ■ **D. Eden**: She's a bit upset. I did rather spring it on her. (1979)

To appear suddenly and surprisingly

pop up (1660) ■ **Constant Lambert**: He [*sc.* Glinka] was more than a gifted amateur who happened to pop up at the right time. (1934)

spring from (1853) Used in phrases such as *where did you spring from?* when someone appears unexpectedly ■ **P. G. Wodehouse**: 'Wherever,' she inquired, 'did you spring from, Ed?' (1924)

Surprising, astonishing

mind-boggling (1964), **mind-blowing (1967)** Applied to something that has an overwhelming effect on the mind (in early use often describing the effects of psychedelic drugs) ■ Chris Bonnington: A monstrous bergschrund, a huge, mind-boggling chasm about fifteen feet across. (1973) ■ Helen McCloy: A mind-blowing mustard yellow for the woodwork and on the walls a psychedelic splash of magenta and orchid and lime. (1974)

Surprised, astonished

gob-smacked (1985) British; from *gob* mouth + *smacked* hit, struck; perhaps from the shock effect of being hit in the face or from the theatrical gesture of clapping a hand over the mouth as a gesture of extreme surprise ■ *Observer*. NoW staff described themselves as 'gob-smacked' by the shock news (this is the tabloid way of saying 'very surprised'). (1988)

gob-struck (1988) British; from *gob* mouth + *struck* hit ■ *Guardian*: 'I looked in the mirror and saw this emu.' 'How fast were you going?' 'About 50 mph. . . . I was gobstruck.' (1990)

Something surprising

bombshell (1860) ■ M. Sutherland: Do you think it was kind to let her think she had plenty and then drop down on her like this? It's a regular bomb-shell. (1926)

turn-up (1873) Orig horseracing slang, denoting an unexpected piece of good luck, and hence applied to any unexpected turn of events; often in the phrase *a turn-up for the book(s)* ■ Peter Bull: I reported my findings to Mr Huth, who said . . . perhaps I would like to write the script. Now this was quite a turn-up for the book, as very few people . . . are allowed to say what they write. (1959) ■ *Guardian*: The opening Philip Cornes Novices Hurdle Qualifier has attracted 25 runners, which could be a recipe for a turn-up. (1991)

zinger (1973) US; applied to a surprise question, or an unexpected turn of events (e.g. in a plot); compare earlier senses, wisecrack, punch-line ■ *Publishers Weekly*. There's a zinger toward the end, in which the nominal hit man gets hit, but it doesn't really compensate for the tedium the reader's gone through. (1976)

A shock caused by something unexpected

turn (1846) ■ Walter Besant: It was only a dream. . . . But it gave me a terrible turn. (1886)

Exclamations of surprise or astonishment

bless us (1646), bless me (1709), bless my soul (1851) Dated ■ R. D. Paine: Bless my soul, what sort of a condemned rumshop have I stumbled into? (1923)

strike me blind (dead, pink), (Australian & New Zealand) **strike (me) (1696)** ■ D'Arcy Niland: Strike me pink, Mac, you're not leaving? (1955) ■ Barry Crump: Strike, he went crook! Who the hell was responsible? Had we been blasting fish? (1960)

you could have knocked me down with a feather (1741) First recorded in the form *you might have beat me down with a feather*; the modern form is first recorded in 1853 ■ Somerset Maugham: When I . . . saw Rosie standing there, you could 've knocked me down with a feather. (1930)

Christ (1748) ■ Eugene O'Neill: Christ, what a dump! (1933)

gosh (1757) Orig in *by gosh*, as a euphemistic alteration of *by God* ■ John Dos Passos: 'Gosh,' he was saying at the back of his head, 'maybe I could lay Elsie Finnegan.' (1936)

lawk, lawks, lawk-a-mercy, -mussy (1768) Dated; alteration of *Lord* (*have mercy*) ■ B. L. K. Henderson: Lawkamercy, lad, what's that? (1927)

golly (1775) Euphemistic alteration of *God* ■ *Strand Magazine*: Golly! He took a toss and a half! (1917)

you don't say so (1779) Dated ■ Richard Whiteing: You don't say so; why, I'm going to a meeting at his mother's house. (1899)

by gum, my gum (*c*1815) *gum* a euphemistic alteration of *god* ■ *Private Eye*: By gum, it must be visiting day up at hall. (1970)

blow me tight (1819) ■ Philip MacDonald: 'Blow me *tight*!' said Sergeant Guilfoil. For things were certainly happening in Farnley. (1933)

say (1830) Orig & mainly US ■ William Faulkner: Well, say. Can you tie that. (1932)

lor, lor' (1835) British; alteration of *lord*

crikey (1838) British; alteration of *Christ* ■ John Rae: Crikey, I thought, he's tough. (1960)

begorra, begarra, begorrah (1839) Anglo-Irish; alteration of *by God*

sapristi (1839) Mainly used to suggest Frenchness or a French context; from French, alteration of *sacristi* ■ Agatha Christie: And the card— *my* card! Ah! *Sapristi*—she has a nerve! (1932)

did you ever? (1840) Dated; contracted form of such phrases as *did you ever see such a thing?* ■ John Masefield: Fifty pou-und. Fifty pou-und. Did you ever. (1909)

well I never, well I never did (1848) Contracted form of such phrases as *well I never saw* (or *did see*) *such a thing* ■ David Storey: They tell me. . . . Well, I never. Didn't see that, did he? (1970)

geewhillikins, ge-, je-, -whil(l)iken(s), -whit(t)aker(s) (1851) Orig & mainly US; perhaps a fanciful substitute for *Jerusalem* ■ C. S. Forester: 'Geewhillikins, sir,' said Hubbard; the dark mobile face lengthened in surprise. (1941)

holy Moses (1855) *Moses* probably a euphemistic substitute for *Mary* ■ B. Mason: And Holy Moses, *what* a snafu! Why foul up poor, harmless, gormless Glad? (1980)

my sainted aunt, my (holy, sacred, etc.) aunt (1869) Dated; compare earlier obsolete *my sainted mother* ■ *Boy's Own Paper*: 'My aunt!' exclaimed Guy, with a start. (1888)

sacré bleu (1869) Mainly used to suggest Frenchness or a French context; from French, literally 'sacred blue', dated euphemistic substitute for *sacré Dieu* sacred God ■ Kenneth Benton: But *sacre bleu*! you can't depend on that. (1974)

man (1874) Mainly US ■ *Oxford Advanced Learner's Dictionary*: Man! That's huge! (1995)

gee whiz(z), gee whitz, gee wiz (1876) Orig US; probably an alteration of *geewhillikins* or a euphemistic substitute for *Jesus* ■ Richmal Crompton: 'Gee whiz!' breathed William in ecstasy. (1940)

I'm jiggered, I'll be jiggered (1886) *jiggered* perhaps a euphemistic alteration of *buggered* ■ *Independent*: 'Well, I'll be jiggered,' said Applejack. (1991)

blimey, bli' me, blime (1889) British; contraction of (*God*) *blind me* ■ Richmal Crompton: 'Blimey!' said Charlemagne. 'Pardon him, dear,' said Miss Milton in a shaking voice. 'He doesn't often use bad language.' (1954)

bejabers, bejabbers (1890) Mainly Anglo-Irish; variant of earlier *be jappers*, alteration of *by Jesus*

I say (1890) ■ Graham Chapman et al.: *He opens it, gets out some paper, then drops briefcase before the amazed owner, and ambles back to his chair, neatly grabbing a pen from a passer-by's inside pocket. Policeman* I'll have that! *Man* I say! *The policeman sits down again and starts to draw, talking the while.* (1974)

holy smoke (1892) ■ Ian Cross: 'Holy smoke,' he gasped, 'That's a funny face.' (1960)

strewth, streuth, 'strewth, 'strooth, 'struth, struth (1892) Short for *God's truth* ■ *Sunday Sun* (Brisbane): Struth! What next? says Sam. (1977)

wow (1892) From earlier Scottish use as a general exclamation ■ R. B. Dominic: 'Wow!' Mike Isham whistled reverently. 'No wonder she was willing to murder.' (1980)

boy (1894) Orig US ■ M. Hodge: Boy! They don't wear a damned thing! (1934)

gee (1895) Mainly US; probably short for *Jesus* ■ *Saturday Evening Post*: Gee, that's a long shot. Boloney! That's not the ball—it's the divot. (1928)

gorblimey, gaw-, -blime, -blimy (1896) British; alteration of *God blind me* ■ W. J. Locke: 'Gorblime!' said Chipmunk, 'that's the first I 'eard of it.' (1918)

lumme, lummy (1898) British; alteration of (*Lord*) *love me* ■ *Times*: A pitch which has evoked from Trueman the classic comment: 'Lumme! A green dusty.' (1963)

holy mackerel (1899) *mackerel* probably a euphemistic substitution for *Mary* ■ Terence Rattigan: Holy mackerel! A Duke! (1944)

bejesus, (mainly Anglo-Irish) bejasus (1908) Alteration of *by Jesus*

cripes (1910) Alteration of *Christ* ■ A. F. Grimble: The captain goggled at me for a second, 'Cripes!' he said. (1952)

starve the rats (1908) Australian & New Zealand

coo, coo-er (1911) ■ *Times*: Coo, is that really the time? (1963)

you don't say (1912) Orig US; often used ironically or sarcastically; compare earlier *you*

don't say so ■ Ngaio Marsh: 'The Scorpion's not here, George.' 'You don't say,' Mr. Copper bitterly rejoined. (1962)

zowie (*c*1913) Perhaps a blend of *zap* and *pow* + *-ie* ■ P. G. Wodehouse: He gets out and *zowie* a gang of thugs come jumping out of the bushes, and next thing you know they're off with your jewel case. (1972)

what do you know? (1914) Mainly US ■ Anthony Gilbert: 'Well,' marvelled Frankie, 'what do you know?' (1968)

starve the crows (1918) Australian & New Zealand ■ F. B. Vickers: 'Well, starve the bloody crows,' he exclaimed, stopping to eye me off. (1977)

wowee (1921) From *wow* + arbitrary suffix *-ee*; orig spelt *wowey* ■ *Mad Magazine*: Boy! Wow-wee! That's quite an exciting evening line-up! (1963)

crumbs (1922) British; from earlier *by crum(s)*, a euphemistic substitute for *by Christ* ■ Stella Gibbons: Nothing like that. Crumbs! I should say not. (1956)

Jesus, Jesus (H.) Christ (1922) ■ *Independent*: Each cost £20,000. 'Jesus!' said the man in a pony tail. (1991)

Jeez(e), Geez(e), Jese, Jez (1923) Orig US; shortening of *Jesus* ■ *Private Eye*: Jeez, that's nice of you to say so. (1970)

holy cow (1924) *cow* perhaps a euphemistic substitute for *Christ* ■ *Guardian*: There's a huge red rose explosion lighting up the sky. Holy cow, that was a huge outburst. (1991)

I'm damned, I'll be damned (1925) ■ Henry Miller: Those things never happen to me. So you peddled candies in the Café Royal? I'll be damned. (1953)

starve the lizards (1927) Australian ■ Eric Lambert: 'Starve the bloody lizards!' breathed Clancy. 'Now I've seen the lot!' (1965)

stone the crows (1927) Orig Australian ■ *Guardian*: Not on your nelly, squire. Cor, stone the crows. (1992)

blow me down (1928) ■ R. Byrom: 'Well, blow me down!' I chose a phrase that seemed suitably Old Boy. (1959)

jeepers, jeepers-creepers (1929) Orig US; *jeepers* alteration of *Jesus* ■ Colin MacInnes: I put my head around the door, and jeepers-creepers, nearly had a fit. (1959)

cor (1931) British; often in the phrase *cor blimey*; alteration of *god* ■ *Independent on Sunday*: One youth near me, climbing on to a mate's shoulders, yelled, 'Cor, innee fat!' which seemed to come as a surprise. (1991)

hush my mouth (1931) Southern US

stiffen the crows (1932) Australian & New Zealand

strike a light (1936) British, Australian, & New Zealand ■ Ian Cross: 'Strike a light,' he hissed. . . . 'Get over here, quick,' he said. 'Have a bloody look, man.' (1960)

starve the bardies (1941) Mainly Western Australian; apparently never widely current, but often quoted as a colourful Australianism; based on *starve the crows* (lizards, etc.); *bardie* type of edible wood grub, from Aboriginal (Nyungar) *bardi*

you wouldn't read about it (1950)
Australian & New Zealand; usually implying an
element of incredulity or disgust ■ H. Williams:
You wouldn't read about it. A bloke his missus reckons was a
doctor of philosophy, whatever that was, and just about the
biggest dill you could meet. (1973)

surprise, surprise (1953) Often used ironically
or sarcastically ■ *Times*: The plum Monday spot finally
went—surprise, surprise—to our old friend *Naked City*. (1962)

stiffen the lizards (1959) Australian
■ M. Raymond: Stone the crows and stiffen the lizards.
(1959)

stroll on (1959) British ■ *Beezer*: Stroll on! You're
bald—how did that happen? (1990)

stone me (1961) Probably an adaptation of *stone
the crows* ■ John Wainwright: Stone me!—next thing I
know I have a . . . hand-grenade here in my pocket. (1979)

I'm buggered, I'll be buggered (1966) First
recorded in this sense in 1966, but probably in
use much earlier ■ Arthur La Bern: Well I'll be
buggered. Excuse my French. (1966)

yikes (1971) Origin unknown, but compare *yoicks*
a call used by huntsmen ■ *Detroit Free Press*:
Yikes! Even Paul Newman loses the woman in this new breed
of movies. (1978)

holy shit (1982) Orig US ■ Michael Crichton: Over
the radio, they heard Gennaro say, 'Holy shit, how much more?'
(1991)

Gordon Bennett (1984) British; alteration of
gorblimey, presumably after the name of James
Gordon Bennett (1841–1918), after whom several
motor and aeronautical events were named, or
his father James (1795–1872), a celebrated
newspaper editor and publisher

I'll go to the foot of our stairs (1992)
British, Northern dialect; first recorded in 1992,
but in use earlier ■ *Guardian*: When we watch
Coronation Street at home, we greet each twist of the plot
with a chorus of . . . 'Well, I'll go to the foot of our stairs!' This
is to show that we are sophisticated. (1992)

See also **beat the band, Dutch**, etc. under To surpass
all others at **Excellence, Remarkableness** (p. 216).

25. **Boredom & Disenchantment**

Something or someone boring or tiresome

fag (1780) British; applied to a boring task; from
the verb *fag* tire ■ *Sunday Times*: A review editor will
pay you good money to do that in a 1,200-word piece, so why
go to all the fag of filling up 300 pages? (1993)

grind (1851) British, orig university slang;
applied to a long and boring task ■ *Independent*:
Graham had anticipated that the match would be 'a real grind'
and so it proved, the evening's entertainment taking time to
unravel as both sides seemed to be suffering from
apprehension after the weekend's results. (1991)

drag (1857) ■ Colin MacInnes: The whole thing was
becoming something of a drag. (1959)

bind (1930) British dated, mainly services' slang;
from the verb *bind* bore ■ T. E. Lawrence: Letter
writing is what the R.A.F. call a 'bind'. (1930)

binder (1930) British dated, mainly services'
slang; from the verb *bind* bore + -*er*

dullsville, Dullsville (1960) Orig US; denoting
an imaginary town that is extremely dull or
boring, and hence a condition or environment
of extreme dullness; from *dull* + -*s*- + -*ville*
imaginary place ■ *Oxford Times*: January and February
are traditionally 'dullsville' months in restaurants and pubs and
clubs. (1978)

yawn (1974) From the effect on the bored person
■ *Mail on Sunday*: It took a radio veteran to treat the BBC's
nostalgia mania for the mega-yawn it has become. (1991)

To bore

bind (1929) British dated, mainly services' slang
■ C. H. Ward-Jackson: 'Smith's got his tapes: I suppose he'll

be binding everyone now'. . . . *Binds you rigid, binds you stiff,
bores you completely*. (1943)

feed (1933) British, dated; perhaps a back-
formation from *fed-up* ■ Georgette Heyer: Anyone can
have the super motor boat as far as I'm concerned. Joan, too.
She bars it completely, which feeds Brother Basil stiff. (1933)

bore the pants off (1934) ■ P. G. Wodehouse:
They were . . . creeps of the first water and would bore the
pants off me. (1954)

Boring, dull, tedious

draggy (1860) Orig US; from *drag* something
boring + -*y* ■ *Listener*: I know it's draggy having the au
pair feeding with us; but one has to be madly democratic if one
wants to keep them. (1967)

blah (1922) Orig US ■ H. Roth: You must . . . have come
to realize how blank and blah he made himself. (1955)

feeding (1940) British, dated; from the verb *feed*
bore ■ Morris Marples: 'It's *feeding*, isn't it?' (i.e.
calculated to make one *fed-up*). (1940)

drack, drac (1945) Australian; origin
uncertain; sometimes said to derive from the
name of the US film *Dracula's Daughter* (1936)
■ G. Dutton: You blokes get on to some bloody drack subjects.
(1968)

ho-hum (1969) From *ho-hum* an exclamation of
boredom ■ *Independent*: When you watch Bambi, there's
bite: it tells you something about the world. But The Fox and
the Hound was ho-hum—baby fodder, pabulum. (1991)

Bored, fed-up

sick (1597) Followed by *of*; also in the phrases *sick
and tired of* (1783) and *sick to death of* (1890)

■ *Milton Keynes Express*: I believe people are sick and tired of half-truths and evasions. (1976)

jack (1889) Australian; usually followed by *of*; probably from *jack up* give up ■ *Australian Geographic*: 'The missus might get jack of it and clear out for the city,' observed one miner, 'but most of them come back.' (1986)

browned off (1938) British ■ *Observer*: Medical boards were always being begged by browned-off invalids to pass them fit for active service. (1958)

brassed off (1941) British, orig services' slang ■ Brennan, Hesselyn, & Bateson: Nothing happened, & we came back very brassed off, not having seen a sausage. (1943)

cheesed off, cheesed (1941) British; origin unknown ■ Alexander Baron: Whenever I'm cheesed off I just open it and start reading. (1948) ■ Ian Jefferies: I got cheesed and overtook. (1959)

chocker, chocka, chokker (1942) British, orig naval slang; short for *chock-a-block* full up ■ Frank Norman: I'm a little chocker of this place [*sc*. prison]. (1958)

To become less interested

switch off (1921) ■ *Times*: Does he seriously maintain that in a class of 24 boys, where 23 are working keenly and well, it is invariably the master who is to blame because No. 24 always 'switches off'? (1955)

26. **Composure**

Composure

cool (1953) Orig US, Black English; usually used with a possessive ■ *Listener*: Professor Marcus consistently keeps his cool when sex is being discussed; all the four-letter words are used without blanching. (1967)

Composed, relaxed

slap-happy (1937) Applied to someone who is excessively relaxed or casual; compare earlier sense, punch-drunk

loose (1968) Orig US; especially in the phrase *hang* (or *stay*) *loose* ■ Cyra McFadden: 'And remember,' he told him, waving, 'stay loose'. (1977)

laid-back (1969) ■ *New Society*: It's all cheerfully grotty and relaxed in the usual laid-back Montreal style. (1974)

together (1969) Orig US ■ Alison Lurie: I forgot you, and me, and where I was—I felt very calm, very together. (1974)

To keep one's composure, remain relaxed

keep one's shirt on (1854) Orig US ■ Paul Theroux: 'Keep your shirt on,' Father shouted. (1981)

keep one's hair on (1883) ■ Jonathon Gash: 'Have you seen my car keys?' 'Have I hell!' she screamed, rummaging under the divan for her shoes. 'Keep your hair on.' (1977)

play it cool (1942) ■ Chris Bonnington: John Edwards dived for cover, but Jonathan Lane, the camera-man, played it cool, pausing to switch on the camera before getting out of the way. (1971)

To calm down

simmer down (1871) Orig US ■ D. H. Lawrence: 'Nay, wait a bit! Let me simmer down,' he said. That amused her. (1928)

cool down (1882) ■ *Times*: This game showed that it would be worth while trying the ice-hockey system of on-the-spot discipline with a 'sin-bin' to allow players to cool down. (1973)

cool off (1887) ■ *Smart Set*: He rose suddenly and went upstairs with his anger. . . . He sat there cooling off by the window. (1908)

cool it (1953) Orig US ■ *Crescendo*: Cool it will you? I said once a week, there's no need to go stark raving mad. (1968)

chill out, chill (1979) Mainly US; denoting becoming less tense or relaxing ■ *Ski*: The fat one whistles, waves madly and rudely ignores my fatherly admonitions to chill out. (1989)

See also To lose one's composure at **Excitement** (p. 245).

Impassive

poker-faced (1923) From the inscrutable or expressionless face characteristic of a poker player

po-faced (1934) Probably from *po* chamber-pot, influenced by *poker-faced*

To remain impassive

not bat an eyelid (or **eye**) **(1904)** Orig US ■ *News Chronicle*: [Japan] slipped from . . . past to . . . present without, you might say, batting an eyelid. (1959)

27. A Fuss

to-do (1570) From the verb phrase *to do*, used to denote that which it is necessary to do

brouhaha (1890) From French *brouhaha* ■ Brahms & Simon: I shall never forget the brou-ha-ha . . . when Cousin Geraldine married into Trade. (1946)

carry-on (1890) From the verb *carry on* behave excitedly (see at **Behaviour** (p. 206)) ■ Peter Bull: We were all engaged for a radio version of Hamlet. . . . I had never realized the incredible carry-on connected with these productions. (1959)

palaver (1892) Applied to annoying or troublesome complexities; often in the phrase *fuss and palaver*; from earlier sense, unnecessary, profuse, or idle talk ■ *Radio Times*: As if saying goodbye to all that money isn't enough, you'd have the palaver of writing out the cheques, trudging down to the post office to get the stamps, before finally sending the bloomin' things off. (1992)

song and dance (1895) Orig US ■ Elaine Dundy: If only he hadn't felt obliged to make such a song and dance about it. (1958)

ballyhoo (1928) Orig US; applied to excessive noise, fuss, publicity, etc.; from earlier application to a fairground showman's touting speech; ultimate origin unknown ■ *Economist*: The event was surrounded by the sort of ballyhoo you might expect if Toyota had taken over GM itself. (1988)

whoop-de-do, whoop-de-doo (1929) US; a fanciful extension of the verb *whoop* or the interjection *whoops* ■ *Verbatim*: There was many an angry powwow and much whoop-de-do, but in the end, of course, the bigwigs won. (1981)

hoo-ha, hoo-hah, hou-ha (1931) Origin unknown ■ *Country Life*: Some of these lovely irises may . . . be grown . . . successfully without much hoo-ha. (1971)

performance (1936) ■ Julian Symons: For Christ's sake don't let's make a performance out of it. (1964)

kerfuffle, kafuffle, kufuffle (1946) Variant of Scottish *curfuffle* disorder, agitation, from the verb *curfuffle* put in disorder, from *cur-* (perhaps from Gaelic *car* twist, bend) + *fuffle* put in disorder (perhaps onomatopoeic) ■ Kingsley Amis: A lot of our readers are going to think all this kerfuffle over an old skeleton being snatched is . . . a bit of a joke. (1973)

hoop-la (1948) From the earlier exclamation *houp-la*, *hoop-la*, used to accompany a quick or sudden movement, from French *houp-là* ■ *Guardian*: There is sometimes so much surrounding hoop-la that you lose sight of the various tactics. (1973)

bobsy-die (1952) New Zealand; usually in the phrase *kick up bobsy-die*; from earlier *Bob's-a-dying* fuss, commotion ■ Terence McLean: By generally kicking up bobsy-die. (1960)

To make a fuss (about)

make a thing of (or about) (1934) Denoting over-exaggerating the importance of something; usually used in the negative ■ Edward Grierson: Steady on, Laura. . . . Don't let's make a thing of it. (1952)

28. Anger

(A fit of) anger

mad (1834) US; from *mad* angry ■ M. & G. Gordon: Well, thanks a lot! I go through hell for you and you take your mad out on me. (1973)

wax (1854) Dated; origin uncertain; perhaps from *wax wroth*, angry, etc., become angry ■ B. Duffy: Giggling and swallowing his hiccups, acting the part of Caliban, that professional guest and sporadic author Lytton Strachey called back, Oh, O. Don't be in such a wax now. (1987)

bate, bait (1857) Dated; from *bait* harass, persecute ■ *Observer*: 'Lenny Henry will be back at half time,' the voice on the Tannoy assures us, as the 'funny' man stalks off the pitch in something of a bate. (1996)

the hump (1873) British; mainly in the phrases *get* (or *give*) *the hump* become (or make) angry; compare obsolete *hump the back* show annoyance or sulkiness ■ *Guardian*: One of them . . . flashed a camera right in the face of Paco the other day. And Paco, the star camel, understandably got the hump and gave Ernest a bump and three cracked ribs. (1991)

the needle (1874) Mainly in the phrases *have* (got) *the needle* be angry and *get the needle* become angry; compare the verb *needle* annoy ■ G. F. Newman: He's got the needle with you. You've got to go very careful. (1970)

the spike (1890) Mainly in the phrases *have* (got) *the spike* be angry and *get the spike* become angry; variation on *the needle* ■ Noel Hilliard: But you don't have to get the spike with me just for that. (1960)

the allovers (1893) US, dated; from earlier sense, disquiet

snit (1939) Orig and mainly US; origin unknown ■ C. Boothe: 'I declare, Mrs. Rand, I cried myself into a snit.' 'A snit?' 'I do deplore it, but when I'm in a snit I'm prone to bull the object of my wrath plumb in the tummy.' (1939)

the pricker (1945) Australian & New Zealand; mainly in the phrase *have* (got) *the pricker* be angry; variation on *the needle* ■ D'Arcy Niland: You've got the pricker properly, eh? You'll knock him into next week, will ya? (1955)

wobbler (1942) Orig US; mainly in the phrase *throw a wobbler* fly into a fit of anger ■ *Sunday Times*: Vikki said the camera shots were all wrong, her manager objected to 'the thin sound', and the backing group . . . threw a complete wobbler. (1985)

wobbly (1977) From the adjective *wobbly* unstable; mainly in the phrase *throw a wobbly* fly into a fit of anger ■ *Radio Times*: The debriefing . . . seemed to take an inordinately long time. . . . 'By lunch,' he [*sc.* Simeon Harris] says, 'I was getting a bit fed up, so I threw a wobbly.' (1981)

Angry

mad (a1300) Standard in early use, but now colloquial and mainly US ■ M. Duggan: Are you mad at me? Simpson asked. (1956)

hopping mad (1675) Orig dialect & US; from the notion of being so angry that one is jumping about ■ *Guardian*: Would-be [telephone] subscribers get hopping mad. (1960)

shirty (1846) Compare *get someone's shirt out* annoy someone, and *keep one's shirt on* remain calm ■ John Rae: All right; all right; there's no need to get shirty about it. (1960)

waxy (1853) British, dated; from *wax* anger + *-y* ■ *Punch*: It's no good being waxy about it. (1872)

scotty (1872) Orig & mainly Australian; from the supposed irritability of the Scots ■ N. Keesing: Getting a bit wild was called getting 'scotty'. . . . 'Be good now. I'm a bit scotty with you.' (1982)

ropeable (1874) Australian & New Zealand; from earlier sense, (of an animal) needing to be roped, intractable ■ J. Cantwell: She was going to have my kid, but she dropped it when another bloke put the acid on. I got ropeable and did her. (1963)

on the warpath (1880) Used to imply that someone is angry and seeking a target to vent their anger on; from earlier sense, (of Native Americans) seeking a foe in war

fit to be tied (1894) Compare *ropeable* ■ Clifford Simak: It threw the place into a tizzy. . . . The boss is fit to be tied. When he gets hold of you. . . . (1956)

snaky (1894) Australian & New Zealand ■ *Courier-Mail* (Brisbane): They remain very snaky indeed about allegedly non-impartial treatment from players and umpires in Perth. (1981)

hot under the collar (1895) ■ *Nursing Times*: Erin Pizzey is always hot under the collar about the lack of help a battered wife can get. (1973)

wet (1898) Australian; often in the phrase *get wet* ■ B. Scott: Naturally, Grandad was wet as hell. Pushing a pumper home eleven miles on a Friday night didn't make him too happy. (1977)

snake-headed (1900) Australian ■ M. Franklin: Everybody is snake-headed about your blooming old book. (1946)

up in the air (1906) Orig US ■ Edgar Wallace: Abiboo, who is a strict Mussulman, got up in the air because Bones suggested he might have been once a guinea-pig. (1928)

ratty (1909) From earlier sense, characteristic of rats ■ Tim Heald: I'd simply have asked her what the hell she was so ratty about. (1976)

crook (1910) Australian & New Zealand; mainly in the phrases *go crook (at, on)*, *be crook on*; compare earlier senses, dishonest, inferior, ill ■ *Listener*: I cut off his boot to stop the foot swelling. I remember he went crook on me: he said they were new, and I'd darn well have to buy him a new pair. (1959)

livid (1912) From earlier sense, ashen, pallid, from the notion of being pale with rage ■ Dell Shannon: Mr. MacFarlane would be livid to have it [*sc.* whisky] impounded as evidence. (1973)

batey, baity (1921) British, dated; from *bate* fit of anger + *-y* ■ P. H. Johnson: I'd better roll the damned thing in or Mater will be batey. (1954)

steamed up (1923) Used to suggest angry agitation ■ Dirk Bogarde: The General insists it is sent to all the Brigades. He's getting very steamed up about the bloody little thing. (1980)

off one's block (1925) From *block* head; compare *lose one's block* become angry

ringy (1932) North American ■ M. C. Boatright: He's a good-natured bird and don't git ringy about it. (1934)

ravers (1938) Dated; from *raving* (mad angry + *-ers* ■ Ngaio Marsh: Jeremy . . . will probably go stark ravers if they're sold out of the country. (1967)

butcher's (1941) Australian & New Zealand; often in the phrase *go butcher's* become angry; short for *butcher's hook*, rhyming slang for *crook* angry

lemony (1941) Australian & New Zealand; mainly in the phrase *go lemony at* (or *on*); perhaps from the sourness of lemons ■ S. Gore: Oh, blimey, they went real lemony on 'im. (1968)

crooked (1942) Australian; in the phrase *crooked on* (or *about*); from *crook* angry ■ A. Seymour: Now, if Alf was you he'd have a reason to be crooked on the world. (1962)

salty (1944) US; compare earlier naval sense, aggressive; see also *jump salty* become angry ■ P. G. Winslow: He was furious when I said I didn't have any [money] and got very salty. (1975)

up the wall (1951) Often in the phrases *go* (or *climb, run*) *up the wall* become angry and *drive* (or *send*) *up the wall* infuriate ■ *Observer*: When they found out he was a Catholic, they were up the wall. (1959) ■ *New Yorker*: Success or failure hardly entered into the picture. It was this kind of argument that drove some . . . executives up the wall. (1970)

torqued (1967) US; often followed by *up* ■ Margaret Millar: Can't I even ask a question without you getting all torqued up? (1979)

Annoyed and disappointed

miffed (1811) From past participle of *miff* annoy ■ *Economist*: Howls of fury greeted the Argentine rescheduling. . . . The howls came . . . from the Philippines' finance minister, Mr Jaime Ongpin, who was miffed that Argentina had managed to obtain the same interest rate as Mexico. (1987)

sick (1853) ■ Kazuo Ishiguro: It's just the way you do things. . . . It makes me sick. (1982)

hacked (1892) Orig US; now usually in the phrase *hacked off*; from the past participle of *hack* cut roughly ■ *Rolling Stone*: The big word down there is *commercial*. . . . I wouldn't be so hacked off about it if I didn't love country music. (1969)

pipped (1914) Dated; from *the pip* annoyance ■ A. M. N. Lyons: 'How's Leverton?' 'Rather pipped, thank you,' replied Miss Disney. 'Poor old Ma was raw-beefing him when I left.' (1914)

pissed off (1946), pissed (1971) ■ Barbara Wright: I'm beginning to get pissed off with your rotten little questions. (1967) ■ *Rolling Stone*: Hamilton . . . says half the Cabinet is pissed at him because things are moving so slow. (1977)

choked (1950) ■ *Oz*: My governor is going to be choked when I take the day off. He's going to be double choked if I enjoy myself. (1969)

teed off (1955) Orig and mainly North American; probably a euphemistic substitute for *peed off* (= *pissed off*) ■ G. V. Higgins: He is kind of teed off. . . . I mean, this man is angry. (1981)

chuffed (1960) British, orig services' slang; perhaps from British dialect *chuff* surly ■ Celia Dale: Don't let on they're after you, see, or she'll be dead chuffed, see? She don' like the law. (1964)

sick as a parrot (1979) British ■ *Private Eye*: The Moggatollah admitted frankly that he was 'sick as a parrot' at the way events had been unfolding. (1979)

To be or get angry

raise Cain (1840) Used to denote making an angry scene; perhaps from the equation of Cain (who killed his brother Abel) with the Devil ■ J. B. Priestley: If we stand here talking another minute the mistress'll be raising Cain the way she'll say she's destroyed with the draught. (1930)

fly off the handle (1843) Orig US; orig in the more general sense, lose self-control, from the notion of an axe-head detaching itself from its handle ■ *Times*: Montgomery flew off the handle and told the Minister of Defence . . . that he must find out whether Bevin still stood by what he said. (1958)

go to market (1870) Australian & New Zealand ■ F. J. Hardy: I have me instructions, so it's no use going to market on me. (1950)

blow up (1871) ■ Norman Mailer: At this point, Gary blew up, 'Those sons of bitches, those sons of bitches,' he kept saying. (1979)

have a fit, have forty fits (1877) ■ *Daily Telegraph*: Elgar would have had a fit at the thought of 'designer stubble'. (1991)

boil over (1879) ■ *Guardian*: It was an afternoon to make a manager boil over. (1991)

see red (1901) ■ *Times*: 'The village was incensed when a woman was left to die in her bath because an ambulance man on a go-slow refused to come out,' he said. 'We saw red and said we would form an action group to drive ambulances and cars.' (1974)

lose (or do (in)) one's block (1907) Mainly Australian & New Zealand; compare *off one's block* angry

get one's rag out (1914) ■ Leonard Cooper: Roger was definitely shirty about that. . . . He really got his rag out. (1960)

hit the ceiling (1914) Orig US ■ Elaine Dundy: Larry hit the ceiling and said he had to come along, that he'd spoil everything if he didn't. (1958)

create (1919) British; used to denote making an angry scene ■ Macdonald Hastings: What does he do but come aboard and start creating about the loss of time! (1959)

do one's nut (1919) From *nut* head ■ John Brown: I thought what Grace would say, that she'd do her nut maybe. But she didn't blink an eyelid. (1972)

go (in) off the deep end (1921) Used to denote giving way to anger; from the notion of diving into the deepest part of a swimming pool ■ Tony Parker: I'm not going to do what I've done before, go off the deep end, nothing like that. (1963)

hit the roof (1925) ■ Victor Canning: The P.M. and his cabinet . . . would hit the roof if they knew half of the things that went on. (1971)

blow one's top (1928) ■ *Economist*: This was not just a newly retired officer blowing his top after years of enforced silence. (1958)

have (or get) a cob on (1937) British; origin unknown ■ Richard Gordon: 'Don't you blokes go without me,' he added threateningly. 'I'll get a cob on if you don't wait.' (1953)

blow a fuse (1938) ■ *Rolling Stone*: It was Mercury who would blow a fuse if the lights were out of sync or the PA system malfunctioned. (1977)

jump salty (1938) US; compare *salty* angry ■ *Partisan Review*: That man jumped salty on me. (1958)

get off one's bike (1939) Australian & New Zealand; usually in negative contexts

blow one's stack (1941) Orig US ■ W. H. Canaway: I ain't whingeing, honest. . . . I'm sorry I blew me stack. (1979)

do one's scone (1942) New Zealand; from *scone* head

do one's bun (1944) New Zealand

blow a gasket (1946) From the notion of a gasket (= a joint seal in an engine) bursting ■ *Guardian*: The planning department would have blown a gasket if they were slipped back into the schedule the moment a ceasefire was reached. (1991)

spit chips (1947) Australian ■ I. Southall: Not when I saw Mr Fairhall last. He was spittin' chips because Peter had gone away. (1965)

wig out (1955) Compare *wiggy* mad, crazy ■ Joseph Gores: Kearney was going to wig out when the expense voucher for $100 worth of cocaine came in. (1978)

go spare (1958) British ■ J. N. Smith: The train had just gone. His lordship nearly went spare. (1969)

go through the roof (1958) ■ Julian Symons:
The company are simply wild. They have gone through the roof.
(1975)

lose one's rag (1959) ■ Hill & Thomas: Allison lost
his rag with me over two goals by Leicester's Mike
Stringfellow, both of which he considered were offside. (1975)

spit blood (1963) ■ Linacre Lane: When I think of it I
could spit blood. (1966)

do (or **lose**) **one's nana** (1966) Mainly
Australian; *nana* perhaps from *banana*
■ *Telegraph* (Brisbane): The baby started crying again. I did
my nana and I hit him. (1974)

To become angrily agitated or upset

piss oneself (1969) From earlier sense, urinate
involuntarily

wet oneself, wet one's pants (1970) From
earlier sense, urinate involuntarily ■ Michael
Underwood: There are quite a few people who'll wet their
pants if I get sent down. (1979)

get one's knickers in a twist (1971) British,
jocular ■ *Brand New York*: There is no reason to get one's
knickers in a twist and believe the revolution is nigh. (1982)

To annoy or infuriate

miff (1811) From earlier sense, take offence
■ *Economist*: It is Mr Burnley's manner more than his policies
that miffs several senators. (1987)

rile (1836) From earlier sense, stir up; variant of
earlier *roil* in same sense, of unknown origin
■ *New Scientist*: So much did his lecturing rile Khrushchev,
that the Russian leader bade farewell to the company with the
immortal remark, 'Comrades, and Party Leader Gaitskell, if I
lived in Britain I would vote Conservative!' (1983)

make someone's **blood boil** (1848) ■ *Daily
Mirror*: Sometimes it can make your blood boil to watch it. But
why does it keep on happening? (1992)

get someone's **shirt out** (1859)

rub someone **up the wrong way** (1862)

get (1867) Orig US ■ W. H. Smith: I wish to the Lord he
hadn't been so quick about it. That's what gets me. (1904)

needle (1881) Used to denote deliberately and
persistently annoying someone ■ Dougal Haston:
Once again we'd needled each other into a state of open
warfare. (1972)

nark (1888) Usually passive ■ *Daily Telegraph*: If you
feel especially narked about something, you can turn it into a
theory of human behaviour. (1973)

peeve (1908) Orig US; back-formation from
peevish ■ Rose Macaulay: I suppose he'd peeved me in
some way. (1934)

get someone's **goat** (1910) ■ Buster Keaton: What
got my goat was that when I finally did get knocked off . . . it
was due to an accident outside the theatre. (1960)

give someone **the pip** (1913) From earlier
sense, make someone ill or depressed ■ J. B.
Priestley: A proper old Jonah you're turning into! You give me
the pip, Dad, honestly you do. (1930)

get someone's **nanny-goat, get** someone's
nanny (1914) ■ J. Minifie: Take it easy, old boy. . . .
Don't let them get your nanny. (1972)

get across someone (1926) ■ Mary Stewart: He's
got across that damned Greek. (1960)

burn someone **up** (1931) US ■ Sinclair Lewis: What
burns me up is the fact that . . . 7 per cent of all the families in
the country earned $500 a year or less. (1935)

get on someone's **quince** (1941) Australian
■ A. E. Farrell: These bloody trees are getting on me quince!
(1963)

rip (1941) Australian; mainly in the phrase
wouldn't it rip you, used to express exasperation
■ Lawson Glassop: I had the idea that if you joined the A.I.F.
you had to fight in the front line. I know now how many men it
takes to keep one in those trenches. Do you know our divisions
have even got a mobile laundry, decontamination unit and
mobile bath unit? Wouldn't it rip you? (1944)

get on someone's **tits** (1945) ■ J. Wilson: This
Sherlock Holmes act of yours gets right on my tits. (1977)

get on someone's **wick** (1945) British; said to
be from (*Hampton*) Wick (name of a locality in SW
London), rhyming slang for *prick* penis
■ Kenneth Benton: The way you talk about Pat gets on my
wick. (1977)

piss someone **off** (1946) ■ *Rolling Stone*: She may
not want to be called 'Queen', but only because she considers
herself too young, because she is not out to piss off Aretha
Franklin any more than she already has. (1977)

bug (1949) Orig and mainly US ■ *Times*: The heroine
. . . inquires picturesquely of the hero 'What's bugging you?'
and he replies, succinctly, 'Life.' (1959)

get up someone's **nose** (1951) ■ *Daily Mail*: The
implication that granny was a little winning knockout with a
system that couldn't be bettered . . . does, I'm afraid, get rather
up my nose. (1975)

tick someone **off** (1959) US; compare earlier
sense, reprimand ■ R. L. Simon: Shit, it ticks me off I
spent all the money on this tour and look what happens. (1979)

get to someone (1961) Orig US ■ *New Yorker*: You
can't excuse yourself that way, any more than you can let
drunks and such get to you. (1968)

tee someone **off** (1961) Orig and mainly North
American; compare earlier *teed off* annoyed
■ *New Yorker*: Frankly, it just tees me off. I consider them to
be a god-damned curse. (1977)

Annoyed, upset

sore (*a*1694) Formerly standard usage; now
mainly North American ■ *American Notes &
Queries*: Jonson is likely to have been sore about Shakespeare
. . . styling himself gentle. (1980)

miffed (1824) From past participle of *miff* annoy
■ *Daily Telegraph*: He told us a slightly improper story. The
girls were not shocked but were rather miffed at his thinking
they would not be. (1973)

cut up (1844) ■ *Guardian*: But if Portsmouth were cut up
about the penalty, it was nothing compared with the state of
the pitch. (1991)

peeved (1908) From past participle of *peeve* annoy ■ *Daily Mail*: The agency won't talk about the work; its executives are rather peeved that the news has got out. (1975)

Annoying

pesky (1775) Orig and mainly US; origin uncertain; perhaps an alteration of an unrecorded *pesty*, from *pest* plague + *-y* ■ David Karp: Just stay away from reporters. And if you can't—you have no comment. If they get real pesky, tell them to talk to me. (1956)

balls-aching (1912) ■ R. M. Wilson: I don't quite know why I bother with all this ballsaching fire and semi-satire. (1989). Hence **balls-achingly** (1972)

Something annoying

nark (1923) Applied to an annoying thing; from earlier sense, unpleasant person ■ *Book* (Christchurch, New Zealand): 'It's a nark, isn't it,' she said. 'I thought you'd get by without the op.' (1947)

chizz, chiz (1953) British; applied to an annoying circumstance; from the verb *chisel* cheat ■ Eric Partridge: 'What a chizz!' What a nuisance. (1961)

aggro, agro (1969) Applied to a source of annoyance or inconvenience; abbreviation of *aggr(ravation* + *-o*

A bad temper or fit of sulking

the sulks (1818) From the verb *sulk* ■ W. E. Norris: When you are tired of being in the sulks, let me know. (1894)

the grumps (1844) From obsolete *grump* a slight, snub ■ Louisa May Alcott: Hannah had the grumps, for being up late didn't suit her. (1869)

paddy (1894), paddywhack, paddywack (1899) Apparently the same word as *Paddy(whack* Irish person ■ Osmington Mills: It was my awful temper. I used to get into the biggest paddies when I was a kiddie. (1959) ■ Rudyard Kipling: He's a libellous old rip, an' he'll be in a ravin' paddy-wack. (1899)

moody (1969) British; also in the phrase *pull the moody* to sulk ■ T. Barling: I love you Ollie, so lay off the moodies. (1986)

snit (1971) US; from earlier sense, fit of rage ■ *Daily Progress* (Charlottesville, Virginia): If New York solves its problems through gambling, every state in the union is going to follow suit except Nevada, which will probably secede from the nation in a snit. (1971)

Bad-tempered

crabby (1776) From *crab* small sour apple + *-y* ■ *Ageing and Society*: The 'change of life' makes women crabby. (1993)

grumpy (1778) From obsolete *grump* a slight, snub + *-y* ■ *Daily Mail*: Like a grumpy Father Christmas determined to withhold any presents, James Randi last night continued his sceptical scrutiny of all things occult. (1991)

crotchety (1825) From obsolete *crotchet* whimsical fancy + *-y* ■ *Washington Post*: Joe went to the Banking chairman and his political patron, Henry Gonzalez, a crotchety 77-year-old populist. (1993)

ornery (1887) Now mainly US; applied to a person or animal that is moody and unco-operative; from earlier sense, commonplace; ultimately a dialectal variant of *ordinary* ■ J. Faulkner: Mules is the orneriest critters. (1941)

prickly (1894) Applied to a person who is touchy; from earlier sense, armed with prickles ■ T. Morgan: Janet Vale of the *Morning Telegraph* found him prickly. (1980)

grouchy (1895) Orig US; from *grouch* (to) grumble + *-y* ■ Elliot Paul: Maggie, the unspeakable terrier beloved by the grouchy Madame Marie at the Caveau, took every advantage of her mistress's indulgence. (1942)

narky (1895) From *nark* an annoyance + *-y* ■ *Irish Times*: My husband is narky in the house. If I was to bring heaven down it would not satisfy him. (1973)

spiky (1930) From earlier sense, armed with spikes ■ N. J. Crisp: He seemed more relaxed . . . not as spiky and difficult as he had been. (1981)

stroppy (1951) British; perhaps an alteration of *obstreperous* with altered stem-vowel ■ Adam Diment: Should the shit hit the fan and the Swedes come over stroppy, he could say . . . 'weren't nothing to do with us, son!' (1968)

snitty (1978) Orig and mainly US; from *snit* bad temper + *-y* ■ *People*: A sixteen-year-old orphan, the child of an affair, who lives with her half-brother . . . and his snooty, snitty wife. (1987)

A bad-tempered or discontented person

sore-head (1848) Mainly North American ■ Thomas Wolfe: We thought he was a man, but he turns out to be just a little sore-head. (1939)

grouch (1900) From the verb *grouch* grumble ■ *Listener*: I am probably a humourless old grouch. (1957)

grump (1900) Probably a back-formation from *grumpy* ■ Thomas Griffith: I called on an affectionate grump known throughout the journalism department as 'Pa' Kennedy. (1959)

An angry scene

fireworks (1889) ■ *Economist*: The Labour party has threatened fireworks when the government tries to unload Rolls-Royce. (1987)

ructions (1890) From earlier singular *ruction* disturbance, riot; ultimate origin unknown ■ *Economist*: Such a proposal would cause great ructions within the Labour party. (1987)

Exclamations of annoyance

damn, damn it (1589) ■ Nigel Balchin: I shall have to let go of the other wrench. Damn and blast. (1943)

hell (1678) Often in such phrases as *bloody hell*, *fucking hell* ■ R. P. Bissell: 'Time to get up, Mister Duke.' 'Oh, hell,' I thought. 'Here we go again.' (1954) ■ James

Grant: 'Christ, mate, she's on the game.' 'Bloody hell, Lew, what has that got to do with it?' (1980)

hang it (1703), hang it all (1889) From *hang* execute by suspension, used in various imprecations ■ D. H. Lawrence: Hang it all, one did one's bit! Was one to be let down *absolutely*? (1928)

Christ (1748) ■ Eugene O'Neill: Christ, what a dump! (1933)

darn, darn it (1781) Orig US; expressing (mild) annoyance; euphemistic alteration of *damn* ■ Sinclair Lewis: Darn it, I thought you'd quit this darn smoking! (1922)

tarnation (1790) Mainly US; alteration of *damnation*, apparently influenced by obsolete US slang *tarnal* damned, an alteration of *eternal* ■ C. MacLeod: Tarnation! Here comes another o' them mobile camera units. (1983)

drat (1815) Expressing (mild) annoyance; from archaic 'od rot, euphemistic alteration of *God rot*

bother (1840), bother it (1877) Expressing mild annoyance ■ Virginia Woolf: 'I move,' said Helen, 'that no one be allowed to talk of chastity and unchastity save those who are in love.' 'Oh bother,' said Judith . . . , 'I'm not in love and I'm longing to explain my measures for dispensing with prostitutes and fertilising virgins by Act of Parliament.' (1935)

blow, blow it (1871) From the verb *blow* curse, used in various imprecations ■ Frederic Hamilton: Oh, blow! And I go back to school in ten days. (1922)

rats (1886) Orig US ■ National Observer (US): About a day later another letter from the company turned up in my mailbox. Rats, I thought, they have discovered their mistake and are going to take all the fun out of my life. (1976)

heck (1887) Expressing mild annoyance; euphemistic alteration of *hell* ■ Passing Show: Oh Heck, tell some photographer I can't be photographed. The very sight of a camera nowadays gives me the jitters. (1933)

sugar (1905) A euphemistic substitute for *shit* ■ English Today: We find that the over-50s (especially women) tend to favour 'ersatz' swear-words like . . . *oh sugar!* (1995)

hell's bells (1912) ■ Dorothy Sayers: Hell's bells. Here's somebody at the door. (1927)

blast, blast it (1916) From the verb *blast* curse, used in various imprecations ■ Ngaio Marsh: 'Damnation, blast and bloody hell!' Alleyn said. (1955)

29. Argument, Quarrelling

(An) argument, row

tiff (1754) Applied to a minor quarrel between friends or lovers; from earlier obsolete sense, fit of temper; perhaps ultimately onomatopoeic

breeze (1785) Dated ■ Saturday Review: 'Don't be angry, we've had our breeze. Shake hands.' (1865)

spat (1804) Orig US; applied to a small or unimportant quarrel; probably imitative ■ Daily

shit, shite, shee-y-it, she-it (1920) From earlier sense, excrement ■ Time: Aw, she-it, as the street kids say. (1977)

Jesus, Jesus wept (1922), Jesus Christ (1923), Jesus H. Christ (1924) Presumably in use before the 20th century, but not recorded in print until then ■ Iris Murdoch: He's so spineless. . . . He just wants to be let off and I let him off. Jesus wept! (1974)

bugger (1923), bugger it (1943) From earlier sense, sodomize ■ Guardian: I collected this useful glossary of racing terms. 'That's racing!' (I lost.) 'You win some, you lose some.' (You lost.) 'Can't grumble.' (Oh, bugger.) (1992)

fuck (1929), fuck it (1933) From earlier sense, copulate ■ Sara Paretsky: I heard him whisper 'Oh, fuck' under his breath, but he didn't say anything else. (1992)

shoot (1934) US; partially a euphemistic substitute for *shit* ■ Ruth Moore: 'Oh shoot,' she told Jen, when Jen suggested they'd better write the next batch of boarders not to come. (1950)

wouldn't it (1940) Australian & New Zealand; short for such catchphrases as *wouldn't it rock you?, wouldn't it root you?*, etc. ■ Cusack & James: 'Wouldn't it!' she muttered furiously, 'wouldn't it!' (1951)

sod it (1953) ■ Paul Scott: At seven-fifteen they had to go out to dinner. Sod it. (1953)

son of a bitch, sonofabitch, sonuvabitch, etc. (1953) US; from earlier sense, despicable man ■ Margaret Millar: Sonuvabitch, I don't get it. What's the matter? What did *I* do? (1957)

fucking ada (1962) British; *ada* perhaps arbitrarily from the female personal name *Ada*

hell's teeth (1968) ■ A. MacLeod: 'Hell's teeth!' he swore furiously. (1968)

knickers (1971) British ■ TV Times: When things go wrong then I'll say: 'Knickers. I'll have another go.' (1971)

sod (fuck, etc.) this for a game of soldiers (1979) Expressing irritation or exasperation at a situation or (especially time-wasting) activity ■ R. M. Wilson: Fuck this for a game of soldiers, you conclude. You've got to move before you die. (1989)

flip (1989) British; expressing mild annoyance; first recorded in 1989, but certainly in use before then; probably a back-formation from the intensifier *flipping*, and used partially as a euphemistic substitute for *fuck* ■ Viz: Blinking flip! He didn't buy me my action man space suit. The miserable old twister! Damn him to hell! (1991)

Mail: The £1.3 billion British snack industry has its origins in a 19th century spat between a Red Indian chef and a fastidious customer. (1991)

set-to (1829) From earlier sense, fight ■ Nichols & Armstrong: I like nothing better than a good set-to with a good shop steward. (1976)

Donnybrook, donnybrook (1852) Dated; applied to a heated argument involving many participants; from the name of *Donnybrook*, a suburb of Dublin, Ireland, once famous for its annual fair ■ *Economist*: Imagine the Donnybrook there would be in France or Italy. (1966)

barney (1858) British, Australian, & New Zealand; origin unknown ■ *Encounter*: There was a right barney at the other end of the shop. (1958)

bull and cow (1859) British; rhyming slang for *row* ■ Anthony Gilbert: The murder might have been the result of a private bull-and-cow. (1962)

argy-bargy (1887) Orig Scottish; alteration of earlier *argle-bargle* argument, a reduplication probably formed on *argue* (perhaps influenced by *haggle*) ■ J. B. Priestley: 'Avin' a proper argy-bargy in 'ere, aren't you? Losing your tempers too. (1948)

dust-up (1897) Probably from obsolete slang *dust* row, disturbance + *up* ■ Nevil Shute: He had a bit of a dust up with one of his girl friends. (1944)

bust-up (1899) Compare earlier sense, explosion ■ A. L. Rowse: They were having a tremendous bust-up with the railway porters about their belongings. (1945)

run-in (1905) Orig US; usually in the phrase *have a run-in (with)* ■ Arthur Hailey: I hear you had a run-in with Nancy Molineaux. (1979)

cag, kagg (1916) Nautical; compare obsolete British dialect *caggy* ill-natured ■ Charles Morgan: He was one with . . . a passion for argument on remote unprofessional subjects. He would sit down to what he called a 'cag' as eagerly and patiently as a dog before a rabbit bone. (1932)

ding-dong (1922) Applied to a heated quarrel; from earlier sense, sound of bells ■ John Wyndham: You can't have a proper ding-dong with those quiet ones. (1956)

up-and-downer, up-and-a-downer, upper and downer (1927) Applied to a violent quarrel; from obsolete *up-and-down* applied to violent brawling fights + *-er* ■ Philip MacDonald: I 'appened to hear them in a proper up-and-downer. (1932)

yike (1941) Australian; origin unknown ■ *Business Review Weekly* (Sydney): We have had a

couple of small yikes, mainly on things like contract prices. (1984)

blue (1943) Australian & New Zealand ■ *Sydney Morning Herald*: Priest versus politician. It could be quite a blue. (1981)

rhubarb (1943) US; applied to a noisy dispute or row, especially an argument on the field of play in baseball; perhaps from earlier use representing the murmur of conversation ■ *Times*: 'Rhubarbs', the name used for noisy arguments that break out on the field, started when a Yankee batter, after missing a Perry special, yelled 'spitter' at him. (1973)

ruck (1958) Perhaps from *ruction* or *ruckus* violent commotion or disturbance ■ P. B. Yuill: 'I heard him and her having a ruck about Nicholas, that's all.' 'What kind of a row?' (1976)

See also Fighting at **Violence** (pp. 258–9).

To argue

barney (1876) British, Australian, & New Zealand; from *barney* argument ■ Vance Palmer: No more barneying with pannikin bosses about the length of a smoko or whether the sheep's wet or dry. (1947)

argy-bargy (1888) From *argy-bargy* argument ■ *Blackwood's Magazine*: Do not argy-bargy with such scoundrels. (1922)

part brass-rags (1898) Orig nautical; supposedly from the notion of close comrades sharing each other's polishing rags, and ceasing to do so when they fall out ■ *Economist*: He seems to have finally parted brass rags with the Arab nationalists and President Nasser. (1959)

cag, kagg (1919) Nautical; from *cag* argument

tangle (1953) Orig US; from earlier sense, fight ■ *Times*: The mood of the House was sombre, and he had no desire to tangle with the Secretary of State. (1982)

Argumentative, touchy

feisty (1896) Orig & mainly US; from *feist* fist, small dog + *-y* ■ Dell Shannon: Luther gets a little feisty after a few drinks, and he began to argue with him. (1965)

30. Violence

Fighting; a fight, brawl

set-to (1816) From earlier sense, boxing match

scrap (1846) Perhaps a variant of *scrape* scuffle ■ Jon Cleary: My chaps . . . [are] itching for a scrap, y'know. (1977)

rough house (1887) ■ Bruce Graeme: He's smaller and lighter than me; not nearly so useful in a rough house. (1973)

ruckus, rukus (1890) Mainly US; applied to a violent commotion or disturbance; probably from *ruction* and *rumpus* ■ *Times Literary Supplement*: World Team Tennis . . . now actively encourages

. . . 'audience participation', a polite phrase that covers barracking, beer-cans, and the kind of ruckus that England normally only sees after a Cup Final. (1977)

ram-sammy (1891) Orig dialect; applied to a fight or to a family quarrel; origin unknown

stoush, stouch (1893) Australian & New Zealand; applied to fighting or a brawl; probably from British dialect *stashie* uproar, quarrel ■ *Bulletin* (Sydney): Hayden . . . is prepared to take risks, even a stoush with the left if necessary. (1986)

rough-up (1896) ■ K. S. Prichard: There'd 've been a rough-up in no time, and only half a dozen of us with Paddy against forty or fifty men. (1950)

shemozzle, schemozzle, s(c)hi-, s(c)hlemozzle, etc. **(1916)** Applied to a brawl or commotion; from earlier sense, muddle
■ Peter: In the ensuing shemmozle Samuel got laid out with the butt-end of a rifle. (1916)

rux (1918) Naval slang, dated; applied to a disturbance or uproar; compare *ruckus* commotion and *ruck* row, quarrel ■ Rudyard Kipling: The nastiest rux I ever saw, when a boy, began with 'All hands to skylark.' I don't hold with it. (1931)

up-and-downer, up-and-a-downer, upper and downer (1927) From obsolete *up-and-down* applied to violent brawling fights + *-er*

hey Rube (1935) Orig North American; applied to a fight, originally between circus workers and the general public; from a cry used by circus people; *Rube* short for the male personal name *Reuben*, often applied in North America to a country bumpkin

rammy (1935) Scottish; applied especially to a fight between gangs; perhaps from Scottish dialect *rammle* row, uproar ■ *Evening Standard* (Glasgow): Gallaher had the body, he was Irish, he laid out two slops in the last rammy. (1938)

sort-out (1937) From *sort out* deal forcefully with ■ *Telegraph* (Brisbane): He was the most cantankerous character I have met. I had only been here two days when we had our first sort-out. (1972)

brannigan (1940) North American; applied to a brawl or violent argument; from earlier sense, drunken spree ■ *Toronto Star*: It hadn't exactly been a brawl to rank with the most homeric barroom brannigans in which Simon had ever participated. (1955)

rumble (1946) Mainly US; usually applied specifically to a gang-fight ■ Carl Burke: By the time they got the drink there was a big rumble brewin'. (1969)

punch-up (1958) British ■ *Daily Mirror*: He was fired after an alleged punch-up with another worker. (1976)

tear-up (1964) Orig US; applied to a period of violent destructive behaviour; compare earlier jazz sense, period of wild playing ■ *New Society*: We've had a tear-up with the police. (1982)

thump-up (1967) British; modelled on *punch-up* ■ *Maledicta*: Teacher: 'What would you have if you had 10 apples, and the boy next to you took 6 apples from you?' Boy: 'A thump-up (fight), Miss.' (1978)

aggro, agro (1969) British; applied to aggressive or violent behaviour (especially formerly by skinhead gangs); abbreviation of *aggr(avation* or *aggr(ession* + *-o* ■ Maggie Gee: He had to stop the titters with a bit of aggro, over the next few weeks, a bit of knuckles and a bit of razor. (1981)

bovver (1969) British; applied to disturbance or fighting (especially as caused formerly by skinhead gangs); representing a Cockney pronunciation of *bother* ■ Daniel & McGuire: Around the Collinwood there was about twenty on average but with bovver there was sometimes more than that. (1972)

See also **Argument, Quarrelling** (pp. 257–8).

To fight

square up to someone **(1827)** Denoting preparing to fight with someone ■ F. C. Selous: He squared up to his adversary and . . . struck him a heavy blow. (1893)

scrap (1874) From the noun *scrap* fight ■ *Economist*: The new health secretary, Mr Kenneth Clarke, has shown in the past that he enjoys scrapping with doctors. (1988)

mix it (1900) ■ Dan Lees: These lads don't want to fight for nothing. If they can get away without mixing it they will. (1973)

rough house (1900) Orig US; from the noun *rough house* fight ■ E. L. Rice: Rough-housing with your kid brother. (1929)

stoush, stouch (1909) Australian & New Zealand; from earlier sense, hit ■ J. E. MacDonnell: He was in a position to stoush with the local larrikins. (1954)

mix in (1912) Applied to starting or joining in a fight ■ P. G. Wodehouse: If you see any more gnats headed in her direction, hold their coats and wish them luck, but restrain the impulse to mix in. (1971)

tangle (1928) Orig US ■ Brendan Behan: I don't like tangling with anyone, but Ickey Summers was the sort of little bastard that would pick a fight with you until he lost and the best thing to do with him was to make sure that he lost the first time. (1958)

dish it out (1930) Orig US; denoting very forceful hitting

slug it out (1943) Denoting fighting relentlessly ■ *Black World*: I saw the two shadows boxing on the side of the brick building. . . . It was Bernie and Bennie Speakes, twins about 10, slugging it out in the alley. (1973)

go the knuckle (1944) Australian ■ *Northern Territory News* (Darwin): Katherine went the knuckle against Banks in the NT Football Association—and paid the price. (1984)

rumble (1959) Mainly US; denoting especially taking part in a gang-fight; from the noun *rumble* fight ■ Sam Greenlee: The teenage gangs . . . haven't been rumbling and so they have a lot of latent hostility to get rid of. (1969)

steam in (1961) British; applied to starting or joining in a fight ■ *New Statesman*: As the underworld put it, 'he steamed in like a slag and roughed them up as he topped them.' (1961)

To hit

clout (*c*1314) Originally standard English ■ Martin Braune: She goes around with a mop and clouts people with it. (1985)

sock (*a*1700) Origin unknown ■ Bruce Chatwin: The porter had socked him on the jaw, and he now lay, face down on the paving. (1982)

mill (*c*1700) Dated; from the notion of pulverizing something in a mill

whack (1721) Probably imitative; sometimes applied to corporal punishment ■ *Joseph Conrad*: He whacked the old nigger mercilessly, while a big crowd of his people watched him, thunderstruck. (1902)

crown (1746) Denoting hitting someone on the head ■ *Osmington Mills*: 'Someone crowned me, I take it?' The sergeant nodded. 'With the poker from our own hearth.' (1959)

fan (1785) ■ *Lincoln Steffens*: You wonder why we fan these damned bums, crooks, and strikers with the stick. (1931)

nail (1785) Used mainly in boxing to denote success in hitting someone ■ *Jack Dempsey*: He . . . is in a position to be nailed on the chin. (1950)

bash (1790) Ultimately imitative; perhaps a blend of *bang* and the ending of *dash*, *smash*, etc. ■ *Independent*: I landed him, scrambled up the bank and bashed him on the head five times. (1991)

pop (c1817) Probably imitative; recorded in the 14th and 15th centuries, but there is no evidence of continuity of use between then and the 19th century ■ *Ryan & Jenkins*: When our oldest son, Reid, was pitching in high school, one night the guys on the other bench were razzing him pretty good. 'Jose Conseco's gonna hit a grand slam off your old man!' they said, and other stuff like that. Ruth was ready to come out of the stands and pop every one of them. (1992)

conk (1821) Now mainly US; originally denoting hitting someone on the nose (from *conk* nose), latterly applied to hitting someone on the head (from *conk* head)

slog (1824) Dated, except with reference to hitting the ball hard and wildly in cricket; origin unknown; compare *slug*

wallop (1825) Sometimes applied to corporal punishment; compare earlier sense, move clumsily ■ *R. L. Stevenson*: I have a rope's end of my own to wallop 'em. (1886)

chunk (1835) US; denoting hitting someone or something with something thrown; from the noun *chunk* piece ■ *J. D. MacDonald*: He chunked the four that were turned on to the biggest high, chunked them cold, and he chunked the record player, busted it all to hell. (1968)

belt (1838) Sometimes used with reference to corporal punishment; from earlier sense, hit with a belt ■ *Sports Quarterly*: Being hit by the bandleader was the final straw for the man with the bloody nose and he belted Curtis squarely in the mouth. (1992)

swipe (1851) From earlier sense, make a circular movement with the arms ■ *Mail on Sunday*: In the beginning Massimo patrolled the nightclubs on a souped-up scooter. He was kicked, sworn at and swiped but never sued. (1991)

clip (1855) From the notion of a sharp cutting movement ■ *New Statesman*: After hearing of the incidents in which his boy had been concerned he had 'clipped him round the earhole'. (1961)

slug (1862) Now mainly US; origin unknown; compare *slog* ■ *John Steinbeck*: Cop slugged me from behind, right in the back of the neck. . . . I was rumdum for a long time. (1936)

fetch (1865) Denoting striking a blow against someone, with the person struck as the indirect object ■ *Punch*: Fetch 'im [a donkey] a good whack 'ith your rumbereller! (1865)

plug (1875) Compare earlier sense, shoot ■ *P. G. Wodehouse*: Sidcup got a black eye. Somebody plugged him with a potato. (1971)

sock it to someone **(1877)** Orig & mainly US

biff (1888) Imitative ■ *Alexander Baron*: Where'd you get that bruise on your forehead? Girl friend been biffing you with the old rolling pin? (1950)

slosh (1890) British; from earlier senses, splash, pour liquid ■ *J. Gash*: I've sloshed her . . . sometimes when she'd got me mad. (1977)

stoush, stouch (1893) Australian & New Zealand; from the noun *stoush* fight(ing), punch ■ *E. Lambert*: Get out of that bloody car while I stoush yer! (1965)

dot (1895) British; especially in the phrase *dot a person one* ■ *J. B. Priestley*: Any monkey tricks an' I'll dot yer one. (1951)

soak (1896) US, dated; perhaps influenced by *sock* hit ■ *H. L. Wilson*: If he gets fancy with you, soak him again. You done it once. (1915)

knock someone's **block off (1902)** Denoting hitting someone (especially punching them on the jaw) very hard; often used as a threat; from *block* head ■ *H. G. Wells*: Many suggestions were made, from 'Knock his little block off', to 'Give him more love'. (1939)

hang one on someone **(1908)** ■ *Punch*: There are moments when most of us have felt the keenest desire to hang one on the boss's chin and walk out. (1966)

bean (1910) Mainly US; denoting hitting someone on the head; from *bean* head ■ *P. G. Wodehouse*: Why did you not bean him with a shoe before he could make his getaway? (1924)

dong (1916) Australian & New Zealand ■ *Patrick White*: 'I will dong you one,' shouted Hannah, 'before you tear this bloody fur.' (1961)

sap (1926) US; denoting hitting someone with a club; sometimes followed by *up*, and also used intransitively with *up on*; from the noun *sap* club ■ *Jack Black*: The posse fell upon the convention and 'sapped up' on those therein assembled and ran them . . . out of town. (1926)

bop (1928) Orig US; compare *pop* hit and dialect *bop* throw down with a resounding noise ■ *Cecil Day Lewis*: I can use it [*sc.* a football] to bop them on the head. (1948)

clock (1932) Originally denoting punching someone in the face (from *clock* face), hence more generally hitting someone ■ *P. H. Johnson*: I should have clocked Dorothy, as the saying goes, more times than I care to count. (1959)

nut (1937) Applied to head-butting someone or hitting someone on the head; from *nut* head ■ *J. Mandelkau*: He took it off and as I was getting out of mine he nutted me in the head. (1971)

bonk (1938) Probably imitative of the sound of a blow ■ *New York Times*: This snake came out. My grandfather pulled this wrench out of the plower and he bonked it on the head. (1984)

tag (1940) US; used in boxing; from earlier sense, touch or hit, as in the game of tag ■ *Ring*: If I tag him the way I tagged Shufford, he'll go down. (1986)

cream (1942) Orig & mainly US; from earlier sense, defeat heavily, thrash

pan (1942) Perhaps from *pan* face, from the notion of hitting someone in the face ■ *New Society*: 'To pan' is to punch just once. (1963)

clonk (1943) From earlier sense, make the sound of a hard blow ■ *Spectator*: I have never been able to pick up a hammer without clonking myself one. (1960)

skull (1945) Denoting hitting someone on the head ■ Andrew Berman: My waking came in drugged stages. . . . I had been skulled. (1975)

zonk (1950) Imitative ■ Ian Cross: She zonked me again on the head with this hairbrush. (1960)

king-hit (1959) Australian; denoting punching someone suddenly and hard, and often unfairly; from *king-hit* knock-out punch ■ *Northern Territory News* (Darwin): Nikoletos was reported by goal umpire Peter Hardy after 'king-hitting' McPhee in the first term of the grand final. (1985)

stick one (or **it**) **on** someone **(1960)** ■ *Making Music*: I could have fallen through the floor—I thought he was there to stick one on me. (1986)

To hit repeatedly; assault by hitting

baste (1533) Dated; sometimes used with reference to corporal punishment; perhaps from *baste* moisten cooking meat with melted fat ■ Richard Barham: Would now and then seize . . . A stick . . . And baste her lord and master most confoundedly. (1847)

leather (*a*1625) Originally denoting hitting someone with a leather strap, and hence more generally beating or thrashing someone; often used with reference to corporal punishment ■ Alfred Tennyson: I'd like to leather 'im black and blue. (1882)

towel (1705) Dated; compare obsolete slang (*oaken*) *towel* club, cudgel ■ M. G. Gerard: He caught him by the collar and towelled him down with a cutting whip. (1903)

lather (1797) Dated; usually denoting beating someone with a whip, cane, etc., sometimes as a form of corporal punishment

dust (1803) Sometimes used with reference to corporal punishment; sometimes followed by *off*; perhaps from the notion of knocking someone to the ground (the 'dust') ■ *Time*: [Miners] dusted one of [the district leader's] lieutenants with an old shoe for trying to talk them back to work. (1950)

larrup (1823) Applied to thrashing or flogging someone; often used with reference to corporal punishment; origin unknown ■ P. Dickinson: Mr. Fasting . . . had larruped Jamie. . . . Mother had wanted to send for the Cruelty Man. (1970)

scrag (1835) From earlier sense, hang (on a gallows) or garotte, from the noun *scrag* lean animal, hence (by 1829) the neck ■ I. & P. Opie: The first one to get off, gets scragged by the other lads. (1969)

lay into someone **(1838)** ■ G. R. Sims: She would lay into Master John with her stick. (1887)

paste (1846) ■ Arthur Morrison: 'Is ribs is goin' black where father pasted 'em. (1896)

tan (1862) Dated; usually denoting beating someone with a whip, cane, etc. as a form of corporal punishment; from the earlier phrase *tan someone's hide* beat someone (*c*1670) ■ *Spectator*: Midshipmen, who are boys, are 'tanned', but not Lieutenants of twenty-five. (1903)

do someone **over (1866)** ■ Arthur Upfield: 'Done over properly, wasn't he?' 'From appearances, yes. Mitford must be a rough place.' (1953)

set about someone **(1879)** ■ John Horsley: This got to my father's ears; when I went home he set about me with a strap until he was tired. (1879)

beat (**knock**, etc.) **the tar out of** someone **(1884)** US

do (1888) ■ *Encounter*: I . . . told him . . . I'd do him if I ever saw his face again. (1959)

wade into someone **(1893)** Orig US

roust (1904) North American; earlier senses (stir, etc.) suggest derivation from *rouse* ■ Newton Thornburg: He ran into Sergeant Verdugo, one of the detectives who had rousted him the night of the murder. (1976)

beat (**the**) **bejesus** (or **bejasus**) **out of (1908)** *bejesus* originally an Anglo-Irish expletive, an alteration of *by Jesus* ■ Josephine Tey: I know men who'd beat bejesus out of you for that. (1949)

take to someone **(1911)** New Zealand; applied especially to attacking someone with the fists ■ Noel Hilliard: When we got home he really took to me. That was when I lost a lot of my teeth. (1960)

knock someone **about (1926)** ■ *Guardian*: Why does it matter whether Jeanne Triplehorn enjoys being knocked about by Michael Douglas unless you assume that her behaviour will be seen as typical of women in general? (1992)

work someone **over (1927)** ■ R. Perry: Alan held me and Bernard worked me over. (1978)

tan someone's **arse** (or **backside**, **behind**, **bottom**) **(1938)** Usually denoting beating someone with a whip, cane, etc. as a form of corporal punishment; from the earlier phrase *tan someone's hide* beat someone (*c*1670) ■ Roddy Doyle: I'm warnin' yis, he said.—If one o' yis laughs I'll tan your arses for yis. (1991)

rough someone **up (1942)** ■ M. Braithwaite: They began to rough us up and we kicked and pulled and yelled about what our dads would do if they didn't leave us alone. (1970)

clobber (1946) From earlier sense, attack with severity ■ Osmington Mills: He must have seen me clobber Leeming when he dived for the brief-case. (1959)

fill someone **in (1948)** British ■ *Times*: A naval rating accused of murdering . . . an antique dealer . . . was alleged to have . . . said: 'I filled in a chap and took his money.' (1959)

break someone's **ass (1949)** US ■ Harold Robbins: 'Come on, kid,' he said. 'Let's break their asses!' And then he was running zig-zag across the field. (1949)

bash someone **up (1954)** British ■ *Daily Telegraph*: Discussing intimidation, the lawyer says: 'How would you advise a wretched statutory tenant who is threatened he will be "bashed up" by a rough-looking individual on the staircase one night?' (1963)

duff someone **up (1961)** British ■ R. Lait: They had been duffed up at the police station. (1968)

beat (**knock**, etc.) **the shit out of** someone **(1966)** ■ B. W. Aldiss: The Japs . . . were meek and respectful. . . . The shit had been knocked out of them. (1971)

bust someone's **ass (1980)** US

To knock down

deck (1945) Orig US; from *the deck* the ground ■ *Sunday Times*: I shouldn't have sworn at Arianna. I should have decked her, and if she had been a man, maybe I would have. (1996)

To knock out

out (1896) Orig boxing slang ■ Eugene Corri: Lewis . . . promptly hit him a terrific punch on the point. 'Outed' by bluff! (1915)

wooden (1904) Australian & New Zealand; from the adjective *wooden*, perhaps after *stiffen* kill ■ Arthur Upfield: Got woodened with something wot wasn't a bike chain. (1959)

kayo (1923), K.O., k.o. (1927) (Representation of an) abbreviation of *knock out* ■ *Cleveland* (Ohio) *Plain Dealer*: Rademacher, who was kayoed by Patterson in the sixth round in 1957, won a gold medal in the 1956 Olympic Games for boxing. (1975)

A blow

clout (a1400) Originally standard English; from the verb *clout* hit ■ Walter Besant: The gunner . . . found time to fetch me a clout on the head. (1887)

sock (a1700) Origin unknown

whack (1737) Probably imitative ■ *Guardian*: Give them a whack with a cleaver. (1992)

bash (1805) From the verb *bash* hit ■ *Listener*: A weak, wan lad . . . escaped with no worse than a bash and a hang-over. (1959)

swipe (a1807) Applied to a heavy swinging blow; from the verb *swipe* ■ Michael Crichton: They can break a tyrannosaur's neck with a swipe of their tail. (1991)

wallop (1823) From earlier sense, clumsy or violent movement of the body

pop (1825) Used especially in the phrase *take a pop at*; from the verb *pop* hit; recorded in the 15th century, but there is no evidence of continuity of use between then and the 19th century ■ Jayne Miller: I wouldn't go out and start on anybody, but you do get people who think, 'Look, he's a skinhead, he thinks he's hard, I'll go and have a pop at him.' (1995)

clip (1830) Often used in the phrase *clip (a)round the ear*; from the verb *clip* hit ■ *Guardian*: Scotland is a very macho society: a clip round the ear is considered good for your wife. (1992)

slug (1830) Now mainly US; from the verb *slug* hit

biff (1889) Orig US; compare Scottish dialect *baff* blow ■ W. H. Smith: What an idiot a man can be when he gets a biff that takes his wind. (1904)

paddywhack (1898) Probably a fanciful alteration of *whack* blow, based on earlier *paddywhack* Irish person ■ Frank Sargeson: 'Of course Michael is not going to be unsociable,' she announced. 'I'll have to give him a paddy-whack if he is.' (1965)

woodener (1899) Australian & New Zealand; applied to a staggering or knock-out blow; from the verb *wooden* hit

dinnyhayser, dinnyhazer (1907) Australian; applied to a knock-out blow; reputedly from the name of a boxer, Dinny Hayes ■ W. W. Ammon: Sometimes he let his dinnyhazer go with such viciousness that Stevie shook his head. (1984)

wham (1924) Imitative ■ Chris Bonnington: Have another try. . . . This time the peg held, another half-dozen whams of the hammer, and it was in to the hilt. (1973)

dong (1932) Australian & New Zealand; from the verb *dong* hit

bop (1932) Orig US; from the verb *bop* hit ■ *Guardian*: His tenderly worded advances being repaid with a haymaker bop in the chops from ungrateful, unappreciative women. (1992)

fourpenny one (1936) British ■ Nicolas Freeling: I think he got mad because he gave her a real four-penny one. I bet she has a real black eye. (1964)

slosh (1936) British; from the verb *slosh* hit ■ *Daily Mirror*: I'll give you such a slosh when I get up from here. (1977)

bonk (1970) From the verb *bonk* hit; compare earlier noun use, denoting the sound of a blow

A punch

poke (1796) Often in the phrase *take a poke at* ■ Billie Holiday: She tried to get at me. I took a poke at her, and down the stairs she went. (1956)

bunch of fives (1891) From earlier sense, fist ■ B. W. Aldiss: My regret was that I had not given Wally a bunch of fives in the mush while I had the chance. (1971)

swing (1910) Applied to a punch delivered with a sweep of the arm; especially in the phrase *take a swing at* attempt to punch in such a way ■ W. Winward: If I stand here much longer I'm going to be tempted to take a swing at you. (1983)

haymaker (1912) Applied to a swinging punch; from the resemblance to the swinging action of someone wielding a haymaking fork ■ Emma Lathen: Rising from a collision, he had thrown off his glove and landed a haymaker. (1972)

king-hit (1912) Australian; applied to a knock-out punch, especially an unfair one

stoush, stouch (1919) Australian & New Zealand; from earlier sense, fighting, brawl

roundhouse (1920) Orig US; applied to a heavy blow delivered with a wide sweep of the arm ■ Jack Kerouac: Damion's girl suddenly socked Damion on the jaw with a roundhouse right. (1958)

Sunday punch (1929) US; applied to a knock-out punch; probably from the notion that the victim does not come round until Sunday (or 'the middle of next week')

clock (1959) Often applied specifically to a punch in the face; from the verb *clock* hit ■ Julian Maclaren-Ross: It was my turn to administer the anaesthetic—by a final clock in the jaw. (1961)

knuckle sandwich (1973) Applied to a punch in the mouth ■ A. Buzo: He tried to hang one on me at Leichhardt Oval once, so I administered a knuckle sandwich to him. (1973)

An act of hitting; a beating-up

Jesse, jesse, jessie, jessy (1839) US, dated; in the phrases *give* (someone), *catch*, or *get Jesse*; perhaps from a jocular interpretation of 'There shall come a rod out of the stem of Jesse' (Isaiah xi.1)

pasting (1851) ■ J. D. MacDonald: Fictional heroes . . . can bounce back from a pasting that should have put them in hospital beds. (1950)

doing (1880) ■ Bill Turner: 'For God's sake, man! You'd get three years if you give him a doing,' she exclaimed. (1968)

going-over (1942) Orig US; compare earlier sense, scolding ■ Angus Ross: 'Got a going over, did you?' 'Not much, I got a going over. Want to see the bruises?' (1970)

To kick

boot (1877) ■ Stevenson & Osbourne: I saw a big hulking beast of a Dutchman booting the ship's boy. (1892)

root (1890) Mainly schools' slang; denoting especially kicking someone in the buttocks

put the boot in (1916) Denoting a brutal kicking ■ *Guardian*: When he's lying there some cow in the front row puts the boot in. (1964)

welly, wellie (1966) British; from *welly* wellington boot

A kick

root (1900) Mainly schools' slang; from the verb *root* kick ■ N. Scanlan: Matt gave him 'a root in the gear' and told him not to talk like a stable boy. (1934)

boot (1942) From the verb *boot* kick ■ *Guardian*: The Jockey Club may be seen by some as in need . . . of a boot up the backside. (1991)

welly, wellie (1977) British; from the verb *welly* kick ■ *Guardian*: The first goal began as a misplaced pass by Hirst straight to Fensome, whose long welly into the right corner panicked King into a straight back-pass. (1991)

To attack with a sharp instrument; to stab

chiv, chive (1725) From the noun *chiv(e)* knife ■ *Times*: Three of Heaton's pals threatened to 'chiv' him. (1955)

carve (1897) Orig US; usually followed by *up* ■ Graham Greene: They just meant to carve him up, but a razor slipped. (1938)

chivvy, chivey (1959) British; from *chiv(e)* to knife + -*y* ■ K. Hopkins: He got chivvied at Brighton races. (1960)

To shoot

plug (1870) ■ Graham Greene: Don't say a word or I'll plug you. . . . I don't care a damn if I plug one of you. (1936)

ventilate (1875) From the hole made by the bullet ■ Clive Egleton: You'd just better pray he doesn't kill somebody . . . because he's talking about ventilating people. (1979)

plunk (1888) Orig US; compare earlier senses, pluck (a stringed instrument), propel suddenly ■ D. & H. Teilhet: I wish you'd killed Jeff instead of plunking him in the leg. (1937)

smoke (1926) US ■ *Detective Fiction*: You chiseling rat. You didn't figure Tommy and those heels could hold me, did you? I smoked them just like I'm gonna smoke you, Bugs. (1942)

To attack or worry an animal

sool (1849) Australian & New Zealand; applied to a dog; variant of British dialect *sowl* seize roughly ■ A. Marshall: Urged the dog: 'Sool 'im, Bluey! Get hold of him!' (1946)

A violent person; a thug; a ruffian

rough neck (1836) Orig US; applied to a quarrelsome or uncultivated person ■ Dougal Haston: Jimmy was twenty-eight, and already a qualified architect; we were seventeen-year-old roughnecks. Basically I think . . . he was at heart a roughneck himself. (1972)

rough (1837) From the adjective *rough* ■ Thomas Hardy: Gents with terriers and facetious pipes, roughs with sticks and stones. (1891)

plug-ugly (1856) Orig US; perhaps from *plug* hit + *ugly* ■ *Punch*: Readers who have led sheltered lives will think of plug-uglies, and I hope the cleaner kinds of plug-ugly will think of baths. (1935)

tough (1866) Orig US; from the adjective *tough* ■ I. Hamilton: He graduated to the status of school tough via a series of spectacular playground victories. (1982)

mug (1890) US

roughie (1905) ■ Peter Driscoll: I know a roughie when I see one. . . . He's just one of those blokes who can't stay away from trouble. (1971)

bruiser (1907) From earlier sense, (rough or violent) boxer ■ J. T. Farrell: Two of the bruisers were drawing close to him. He started to run. (1934)

caveman (1926) From earlier sense, prehistoric cave-dweller ■ Aldous Huxley: 'That passionateness of his, that violence—.' Philip laughed. 'Quite the irresistible cave-man.' (1928)

yob (1927) British; applied to a lout or hooligan; from earlier sense, boy; ultimately back-slang for *boy* ■ *Times*: I would not want anybody looking at me to think this man is a thick, stupid, illiterate yob. (1984). Hence the adjectives **yobby** (1955), **yobbish** (1972) ■ *Sunday Telegraph*: The loony Left should not be confused with that other Left which has been described as the Left of the yobbish tendency. (1984)

enforcer (1929) Orig US; applied to a strong-arm man, especially in an underworld gang ■ *Times*: An east London wholesaler was cleared at the Central Criminal Court yesterday of the gangland execution of an underworld 'enforcer'. (1983)

muscle man (1929) Orig US; applied to a muscular man employed to intimidate others with (threats of) violence ■ Paul Oliver: With the considerable returns accruing from operating policy wheels the racket came under the control of syndicates with muscle-men and hired gunmen ensuring that their 'rights' were protected. (1968)

trigger man (1930) Mainly US; applied to a gunman or a hired thug or bodyguard

heavy (1936) Applied to a strongly built man employed to intimidate others with (threats of) violence; from the adjective *heavy* ■ *Times*: Prostitutes were threatened with 'heavies' working for a man named Kenny Lynch. (1973)

goon (1938) Orig US; applied to someone hired by racketeers, etc. to terrorize political or industrial opponents; from earlier sense, stupid person ■ *It*: Heath orders Habershon of Barnet CID to 'turn London over'. And he does exactly that . . . with 500 goons and a score of specially trained dogs. (1971)

hoon (1938) Australian; origin unknown ■ *Sunday Truth* (Brisbane): Two louts . . . walked up behind him. The biggest hoon ruffled up his hair and tried to put his half-smoked cigarette in the young man's hair. (1967)

yobbo, yobo (1938) British; from *yob* + *-o* ■ *News Chronicle*: The local Teddies and yobbos swing their dubious weight behind the strike. (1960)

muscle (1942) Orig US; applied to a muscular man employed to intimidate others with (threats of) violence; often used as a collective plural ■ Helen Nielsen: The muscle on the trucks . . . were free-lancers. (1973)

trog (1956) British; abbreviation of *troglodyte* cave-dweller ■ *Granta*: The scowling vandals, bus-stop boogies, and soccer trogs malevolently lining the streets. (1983)

31. Caution

Cautious, wary

cagey, cagy (1893) Orig US; often also implying uncommunicativeness; origin unknown ■ James Barbican: We hoped they would come out and pick us off, but they were too cagey for that. (1927)

leery (1896) Orig US; from earlier sense, knowing, sly ■ *New Yorker*: Many tennis authorities have been a little leery about placing her on a level with Lenglen. (1970)

ned (1959) Scottish; perhaps from *Ned*, familiar abbreviation of the male personal name *Edward* ■ Peter Malloch: He was a ned. You could always spot them. There was something about them that no trained policeman would ever miss. (1973)

droog (1962) Applied to a young ruffian or to an accomplice or henchman of a gang-leader; an adaptation of Russian *drug* friend, introduced by Anthony Burgess in *A Clockwork Orange* ■ *Times Literary Supplement*: How long ago it seems since the *New York Times* referred to the spray-can droogs of the subways as 'little Picassos'. (1984)

frightener (1962) Applied to a member of a criminal gang employed to intimidate the gang's potential victims ■ *Daily Telegraph*: Soho 'frighteners'—gangsters who try to extort money from club owners—were told . . . at the Old Bailey . . . that they faced severe punishment. (1962)

bovver boy (1970) British; applied to a hooligan, often specifically a member of a gang of skinhead youths ■ *Listener*: Mr Hanna is the nearest thing *Newsnight* has to a bovver boy, but that is not to say that he is a vulgar or crude person. (1983)

clogger (1970) British; applied to a soccer player who tackles heavily, usually fouling opponents; probably from the notion of kicking with clogs

To intimidate

get at (1871) Usually used in the passive ■ *Times Literary Supplement*: We resent, as the Victorians did not, being 'got at' by the social or religious moralist. (1958)

put the frighteners on (1958) ■ Allan Prior: His job had been to put the frighteners on various shopkeepers. (1966)

mau-mau (1970) US; from *Mau Mau*, the name of a secret society fighting for Kenyan independence, from Kikuyu; the verbal usage was apparently coined by the US writer Tom Wolfe (1931–) ■ *Harper's*: His [*sc.* Norman Mailer's] demonstration of the inadequacies and distortions of Kate Millett's Sexual Politics is convincing and indicates that the English Department of Columbia University had been mau-maued by that termagant of Women's Lib. (1971)

A black eye

shiner (1904) ■ G. F. Fiennes: Out shot a telescopic left, and I had the shiner of all time for weeks. (1967)

To be careful (of)

watch (1837) ■ William Haggard: Rex said deliberately: 'I have to watch champagne.' 'Really? But this one won't damage you.' (1963)

mind out (1886) British; often used as an exclamation ■ *American Speech*: English children whizzing around on bicycles . . . will warn each other to keep out of the way by shouting 'Mind out!' (1946)

pussyfoot (1903) Denoting acting (too) warily; from earlier *pussyfoot* person who moves stealthily, like a cat ■ *Observer*: While most papers are still 'pussy-footing' on the Presidency they called their editors together and afterwards announced a unanimous decision. (1928)

watch it (1916) Often used as an exclamation ■ Dennis Bloodworth: We really do have to watch it a bit. Thank God we're officially engaged. (1978)

32. **Nervousness, Agitation**

A state of nervousness or unease

the shakes (1837) ■ Benjamin Bova: The sliding glass doors . . . were locked. . . . So I sat around and waited, trying not to get the shakes. (1976)

the all-overs (1870) Mainly US; from the notion of a feeling affecting the whole body ■ L. Craig: It gives me the all-overs to have a gun pointed in my ribs. (1951)

the jim-jams (1896) From earlier sense, delirium tremens ■ D. Johnson: We're both . . . drained by constant fear, the unrelieved jimjams. (1986)

the willies (1896) Orig US; especially in the phrase *give* someone (or *get*) *the willies*; origin unknown ■ Gerald Kersh: It *can* give you the willies when, in broad daylight, you hear a rifle go off. (1942)

the jimmies (1900) Alteration of *jim-jams* ■ Patrick White: She was not accustomed to see the grey light sprawling on an empty bed; it gave her the jimmies. (1961)

the wind (1916) In the phrases *get the wind up* become nervous and *put the wind up* make nervous ■ C. Alington: I tell you you've absolutely put the wind up Uncle Bob and Peter! They're scared to death of your finding them out. (1922)

the wind-up (1917) From the phrase *get the wind up* ■ Anthony Price: Bit of nerves . . . the old wind-up. (1980)

the heebie-jeebies, the heeby-jeebies, the heebies, etc. **(1923)** Orig US; origin unknown ■ Joan Fleming: You've given me the heeby jeebies. . . . It'll be the end of me. (1959)

the jitters (1929) Origin unknown ■ B. W. Aldiss: The signal came, the machine-gun fire stopped. . . . Geordie was next to me, not showing a sign of his earlier jitters. (1971)

butterflies (1940) Applied to a feeling of internal queasiness at the prospect of a difficult or frightening undertaking; usually in the phrase *butterflies* (earlier *a butterfly* (1908)) *in the stomach* (tummy, etc.) ■ *Sunday Times*: 'I always have butterflies when I open Parliament,' she [*sc.* Queen Elizabeth II] remarked. (1959)

the habdabs, the abdabs (1946) Especially in the phrase *give* someone *the screaming habdabs*; origin unknown ■ *Spectator*: *Treasure Island* gives pleasure and excitement to some and the screaming habdabs to others. (1962)

Take care!

steady (1825) Used to advocate caution and/or restraint; often in such phrases as *steady on*, (dated) *steady there*, (British dated) *steady the Buffs* (from the nickname given to the East Kent Regiment, from the colour of the facings on their uniforms); originally a nautical command to continue steering the present course ■ John Verney: Here, steady on with the sugar, greedy guts. (1959)

the screamers (1948) Dated; from *scream(ing habdabs* + *-ers* ■ Miles Tripp: 'Cut it out, you two,' said Bergen, 'you give me the screamers.' (1952)

the collywobbles (1959) Applied to a feeling of internal queasiness at the prospect of a difficult or frightening undertaking; from earlier sense, stomach cramps

Nervous, ill at ease

funky (1837) From *funk* fear + *-y*

nervy (1891) Compare earlier senses, vigorous, courageous ■ Julie Burrows: Greta was grey as paper and peevish and nervy. (1973)

windy (1916) From *wind* (compare *get the wind up* become nervous) + *-y* ■ Douglas Clark: 'Are you feeling windy?' 'Do I look as if I am?' (1985)

To make nervous or anxious

rattle (1869) Orig US ■ Peter Fleming: But I had the empty satisfaction of seeing that I had (slightly) rattled Pai. (1936)

eat (1893) Orig US; especially in the phrase *what's eating* someone ■ Ian Cross: 'What's eating you?' asked Joe. 'Nothing,' I said. (1957)

To be nervous or anxious

sweat on the top line (1919) Orig services' slang; from the notion of waiting for a number to be called at bingo that will complete the top line of one's card

sweat (1973) ■ D. Devine: No point in being early. Let him sweat. (1978)

To await nervously

sweat on (1917) ■ *Guardian*: What did he do? 'I sweated on it. I waited a day at least.' (1992)

A state of agitation or restlessness

twitter (1678) Now mainly in the phrase *all of a twitter*; from the verb *twitter* make the sound of a bird ■ *Guardian*: Jacqueline Bouvier, a journalist of sorts, is off to London all of a twitter. 'I am going to cover the coronation of Queen Elizabeth the Second.' (1992)

stew (1806) Often in the phrase *in a stew* ■ *Economist*: These two schools have recently got into a stew over the amount of practical money-making experience provided in class. (1987)

state (1837) Often in the phrase *in a state* ■ Violet Jacob: Don't you remember when she went away, what a state you were in and how you raged? (1902)

lather (1839) Often in the phrase *in a lather* ■ Erle Stanley Gardner: You're standing there in a lather of indecision. (1945)

flap (1916) Often in the phrase *in a flap* ■ *Cambridge Review*: It is quite untrue to say that emotionally vulnerable patients who 'get into a flap' over exams will subsequently panic when a real situation threatens them in later life. (1960)

Harry Tate (1932) British, dated; from the stage-name of R. M. Hutchison (1872–1940), British music-hall comedian, used as rhyming slang for *state*

stuma, stumer (1932) Usually in the phrase *in a stuma*; origin unknown ■ W. H. Auden: Poor old Ma in a perfect stuma. (1932)

tizzy (1935) Orig US; origin unknown ■ *Daily Telegraph*: He hopes this mass production of original art may throw 'into a state of total tizzy' an art world where 'more and more money is being made by less and less people'. (1983)

two and eight (1938) British; rhyming slang for *state* ■ M. Cecil: Poor old Clinker! Bet she's in a proper two-and-eight! (1960)

tizz, tiz (1954) Shortening of *tizzy* ■ *Illustrated London News*: The people of Morecambe were thrown into a tizz by this idea of a barrage [across Morecambe Bay]. (1978)

tiswas, tizz-wozz (1960) Perhaps a fanciful enlargement of *tiz(z)* ■ *Observer*: A young man rang up in quite a 'tis-was. (1974)

Agitated, restless

antsy (1838) Orig & mainly US; recorded once in 1838, but the modern usage (first recorded in 1950) appears to be a recoinage, presumably based on the phrase *have ants in one's pants* ■ W. A. Nolen: Her husband got antsy and asked me to have Tom Lewis see her in consultation. (1972)

twitchy (1874) From earlier sense, tending to twitch ■ *Daily Telegraph*: On Tuesday night there had been fighting with neighbouring Croats. People were twitchy. No one smiled. (1991)

jumpy (1879) ■ G. Markstein: She was jumpy about the blackout too. . . . She *is* on edge, he decided. (1974)

toey (1930) Mainly Australian; perhaps from the notion of a restless animal pawing the ground with its toes ■ *National Times* (Australia): Dallas Jongs . . . had a hotel bouncer friend who could get as toey as a Roman sandal. (1981)

jittery (1931) From *jitter(s* + *-y* ■ Alan Ross: Barrington made 33, in his more jittery manner, before flicking at an outswinger and being caught at slip. (1963)

twitched (1959) Compare earlier *twitchy* ■ S. Jackman: The C.O.'s in there and he's a bit twitched. (1981)

To be or become agitated

flap (1912) ■ John Verney: Mummy . . . burst into tears. I put my arm round her waist. 'Please don't flap.' (1959)

have ants in one's pants (1931) Orig US ■ *Washington Post*: Uncle Milton has ants in his pants. (1986)

Tense

edgy (1837) ■ *Times Literary Supplement*: An American family of harassed father, edgy mother and irritated crop-headed boys. (1958)

on edge (1870) ■ J. B. Priestley: Laura had in fact worked much too hard, and now she was altogether too fine-drawn and too much on edge. (1951)

up-tight (1934) Orig US ■ C. Young: He looked worried. Really worried. As the kids say, he was up-tight. (1969)

wired (1982) Orig & mainly US; often followed by *up* ■ Erin Pizzey: He's really wired up. It's fun to see him do the jumping for a change. (1983)

Trembling

the yips (1963) Applied to nervous trembling which causes a golfer to miss an easy putt; origin unknown ■ *Telegraph* (Brisbane): Nevertheless, Jones got a dose of what golfers call 'the yips'. (1972)

the pearlies (1974) Applied to an uncontrollable nervous shaking of the bowing arm sometimes experienced by violinists, etc. before a performance; perhaps shortened from an unrecorded *pearly whites* rhyming slang for *frights*

Frenzy

panic stations (1961) ■ J. Prescot: Someone has been into Greenwood's again . . . and got away with another three hundred. . . . The police seem to be at panic stations about it. (1963)

To behave frenziedly

tear one's hair (out) (1606) ■ *Guardian*: The chef may have been tearing his hair, but I was slopping down his handiwork with some gusto. (1992)

have a fit (or forty fits) (1877) ■ *Daily Telegraph*: Elgar would have had a fit at the thought of 'designer stubble'. (1991)

have kittens (1900) Orig US ■ Anthony Gilbert: Gertrude was going to have kittens when she discovered that extravagance. (1959)

go ape (1955) Orig US; from the frenzied, panic-stricken behaviour (including defecation) of monkeys and apes when captured and caged ■ Tobias Wells: I'm just keeping busy. I've been going ape with nothing to do. (1966)

get one's knickers in a twist (1971) British, jocular ■ *Brand New York*: There is no reason to get one's knickers in a twist and believe the revolution is nigh. (1982)

See also To give way to heightened emotion; lose one's composure at **Excitement** (p. 245).

Frenzied, having lost one's composure

het up (1902) From earlier literal sense, heated ■ *Listener*: One thing that I think endears him to the normal young intellectual, is that he can get tremendously het-up about a cause. (1967)

hot and bothered (1921) ■ James Barlow: Most of the teachers . . . urged silence in hot-and-bothered threats. (1961)

A nervous or agitated person

jitterbug (1934) Dated; from *jitter* move agitatedly + *bug* person with an obsession ■ E. H.

33. Fear

Fear

funk (1743) Orig apparently Oxford University slang; perhaps from obsolete *funk* tobacco smoke ■ J. I. M. Stewart: One oughtn't to let funk be catching. Tony was admitting funk—but perhaps not as much as he had actually been feeling. (1974)

blue funk (1861)

the creeps (1879) Applied especially to a feeling of horror caused by something uncanny; from earlier sense, physical sensation of something crawling over the skin ■ *Guardian*: Hitler's signature never fails to give me the creeps, like the trench signs . . . from the Great War. (1992)

cold feet (1896) Orig US; used to denote fear of doing something risky or dangerous ■ Ian Hay: It seems that the enemy have evacuated Fosse Alley again. Nobody quite knows why: a sudden attack of cold feet, probably. (1915)

wind-up (1917) From *get the wind up* be afraid ■ Anthony Price: Bit of nerves . . . the old wind-up. (1980)

the Jimmy Britts, the jimmies, the Britts (1945) Australian; in such phrases as *have the jimmies, have the Britts up* be afraid; *(Jimmy) Britts* rhyming slang for *shits*, from the name of Jimmy Britt (1879–1940), American boxer; *jimmies* influenced by earlier *jimmies* delirium tremens

the shits (1967) From earlier sense, diarrhoea

Alarm

panic stations (1961) Applied to alarm leading to confused action; modelled jocularly on the military term *action stations* ■ J. Prescot: Someone has been into Greenwood's again . . . and got away with another three hundred. . . . The police seem to be at panic stations about it. (1963)

Afraid

scary (1827) Orig and mainly North American; from *scare* + *-y* ■ L. Craig: He'd been right smart proudified of your not being scary. (1951)

Jones: Sir Samuel Hoare denounced the 'jitterbugs' who feared war. . . . Five days after . . . German troops moved unresisted into Czechoslovakia. (1966)

See also Someone who has lost composure at **Excitement** (p. 245).

A person who worries

worry-guts (1932) ■ Olive Norton: He laughed. 'Worryguts!' 'I wasn't worried. I was just trying to be efficient.' (1966)

worry-wart (1956) Mainly US ■ Joseph Heller: 'Don't be such a worry wart.' 'Don't use that phrase. It makes my skin prickle.' (1974)

funky (1837) From *funk* fear + *-y* ■ George Meredith: If he did not give up to you like a funky traveller to a highwayman. (1871)

windy (1916) From *wind* + *-y*; compare *get the wind up* be afraid ■ D. Clark: 'Are you feeling windy?' 'Do I look as if I am?' (1985)

shitless (1936) Used especially in the phrase *scared shitless*; from the supposed laxative effects of fear ■ *New Musical Express*: The self-appointed guardians of public morality who campaign against pornography because they're simply scared shitless by it. (1976)

spooked (1937) US; past participle of the verb *spook* frighten ■ Elmore Leonard: He was running for town, spooked good now, in a panic. (1977)

Charlie (1954) ■ Frank Norman: I was dead charlie and little fairies were having a right game in my guts. (1958)

shit-scared (1958) Compare *shitless* ■ *Rolling Stone*: Stewart was 'shit scared' about opening night. (1977)

poopy (1963) From *poop* excrement + *-y*; compare *shit-scared* ■ Athol Fugard: Come on. Confess. You were scared, hey! A little bit poopy. (1963)

To be afraid (of)

funk (1813) From earlier sense, flinch ■ Albert Smith: 'I rather funk the governor' replied, in turn, Mr. Spooner. (1849)

shake in one's shoes (1818) From the notion of trembling with fear ■ *Punch*: It had set the whole Liberal party 'shaking in its shoes'. (1873)

shit oneself (1914) From earlier sense, make oneself dirty by defecating; from the supposed laxative effects of fear ■ *Spare Rib*: I was shitting myself before I came, looking for all kinds of excuses. (1977)

get the wind up (1916) From the notion of flatulence as a symptom of fear

sweat blood (1924) ■ W. M. Duncan: I was sitting there sweating blood when those damned cops arrived. (1977)

get the breeze up (1925) Compare *get the wind up* ■ David Ballantyne: She was only making out she hadn't seen you so's you wouldn't get the breeze up. (1948)

run a mile (from) (1949) ■ Alastair Heron: Were a woman to whom he exposed himself to respond sexually, the average exhibitionist would run a mile. (1963)

spook (1957) From earlier sense, (of an animal) to take fright ■ R. M. Pirsig: I spook very easily these days.... *He* never spooked at anything. (1974)

shit a brick or **bricks (1961)** ■ H. Ferguson: By the time I got back to the hospital they were all shitting bricks. (1976)

spit blood (1963) Used to refer to a spy fearing exposure ■ Len Deighton: A man tailed or suspected is said to be 'spitting blood'. (1966)

Frightening

scary (1582) From *scare* + *-y* ■ *Listener*. The threat ... is pretty scary. (1981)

spooky (1854) Applied especially to something eerie and supernatural; from *spook* ghost + *-y* ■ Thomas Wolfe: Don't start that ... spooky stuff! It makes my flesh crawl. (1929)

creepy (1883) Applied to something that produces an uncanny feeling of horror or repugnance; from earlier sense, having a creeping feeling on the skin ■ *Spectator*. A really effective romance of the creepy order. (1892)

windy (1919) Services' slang, dated; compare earlier sense, afraid ■ T. E. Lawrence: Such performances require a manner to carry them off.... A windy business. (1928)

hairy (1966) Perhaps from *hair-raising* ■ *Times*: Lord Snowdon said during a break for an orange juice: 'I was a bit frightened. Some bends are a bit hairy.' (1972)

spooky (1966) Surfers' slang; applied to a dangerous or frightening wave; from earlier sense, eerie

white-knuckle (1988) From the blanching of the knuckles caused by gripping tightly when tensely anxious ■ *Wall Street Journal*. The collapse of the EUA issue shows just how quickly white-knuckle time can arrive in the junk-bond market. (1988)

To frighten

funk (1819) From earlier sense, flinch ■ *Saturday Review*. The jury, 'funked' by the Anarchists, returned extenuating circumstances in the miscreant's case. (1892)

34. **Courage & Cowardice**

Courage

spunk (1773) Compare earlier sense, spark, fire ■ D. H. Lawrence: Oh, I like it! Shows the girl's got spunk. (1928)

pluck (1785) Apparently originally boxing slang; from earlier sense, heart, liver, and lungs of an animal, as removed for use as food ■ *Independent*. Now Russians have proved that they may not be genetically

buffalo (1891) US; denoting frightening or intimidating someone, especially by bluff; from the noun *buffalo* ■ *New York Evening Post*. All the rest [of the newspapers] were what we used to term in the Southwest 'buffaloed' by the McKinley myth—that is, silenced by the fear of incurring the resentment of a people taught to regard McKinley as a saint. (1904)

put the fear of God into (1905) Used to denote terrifying someone ■ Arnold Bennett: When she's my wife I'll put the fear of God into her. (1930)

put the wind up (1916) From the notion of flatulence as a symptom of fear ■ C. Alington: I can tell you you've absolutely put the wind up Uncle Bob and Peter! They're scared to death of your finding them out! (1922)

put the breeze up (1925) Compare *put the wind up*

scare, frighten, etc. **the (living) daylights out of (1951)** ■ *Illustrated London News*: I might have chuckled throughout 'The Suitor' if its chief actor did not happen to scare the living daylights out of me, as the current saying goes. (1964)

spook (1959) From earlier sense, alarm a wild animal ■ M. Gordon: You always act like you're waiting for something.... It spooks me. (1980)

scare the shit out of (1961) ■ *Guardian*. They're fierce. It scares the shit out of me. (1991)

A timorous person

fraid cat, fraidy cat (c1910) Used mainly by children; from *fraid* (reduced form of *afraid*) (+ *-y*) + *cat* ■ Michael Crichton: 'You okay with the fence, Tim?' 'Sure.' 'Want some help?' 'Tim's a fraidy-cat,' Lex called. (1991)

scaredy-cat, scaredy (1933) Used mainly by children; from *scared* + *-y* + *cat* ■ David Ballantyne: Sydney called them scaredy-cats because they wouldn't run like he had. (1948)

Exclamations of fear or alarm

oo-er, ooo-er (1912) ■ Compton Mackenzie: 'Oo-er!' cried Jenny. 'We aren't going to sleep in the dark?' (1912)

yikes (1971) Origin unknown, but compare *yoicks*, a cry used by huntsmen ■ *Detroit Free Press*. Yikes! Even Paul Newman loses the woman in this new breed of movies. (1978)

incapable of enjoying freedom—indeed they have shown some pluck in defending it. (1991)

stiff upper lip (1815) Orig US; applied to courage or resolution in the face of fear or danger; from the notion of a trembling upper lip as a sign of perturbation

Dutch courage (1815) Applied to false courage induced by drinking alcohol; probably from the drinking of gin, regarded as a Dutch drink

balls (*a*1890) Orig US; from earlier sense, testicles (in allusion to 'virile' courage) ■ **Martin Amis:** Just keeping a handhold and staying where you are, . . . even that takes tons of balls. (1984)

guts (1891) From earlier sense, intestines ■ **John Cooper Powys:** I think, if you haven't the guts to act like a man in the matter, you ought to leave this girl alone. (1933)

gimp (1893) Origin unknown ■ **Jean Potts:** She didn't even have the gimp to make the break herself. (1962)

moxie (1930) US; from the name of an American soft drink ■ *Daily Colonist* (Victoria, British Columbia): I was very impressed with his all-round moxie. He could snap back at any of them, news reporters, police, and me. (1975)

cojones (1932) Orig US; from Spanish, plural of *cojón* testicle (in allusion to 'virile' courage) ■ *Guardian:* You have the cojones to ask me if I still got confidence in Britain? (1966)

ticker (1935) US & Australian; from earlier sense, heart ■ *Sunday Sun* (Brisbane): The lady has ticker. . . . She didn't opt for the soft life. (1979)

bottle (1958) British; probably from obsolete slang *no bottle* no good, useless, but often popularly associated with rhyming slang *bottle and glass* arse, and other similar expressions, perhaps with the connotation (in the phrase 'lose one's bottle') of the temporary incontinence associated with extreme fear ■ **S. Dyer:** The government is losing its bottle and is using 'concern for the environment' as something of an excuse to renege on promises and punish the motorist. (1991)

Brave

spunky (1786) From *spunk* courage + *-y* ■ **Roberta Krueger:** These steadfast or spunky heroines invite the audience's admiration. (1993)

plucky (1842) From *pluck* courage + *-y* ■ **J. S. Winter:** You are the pluckiest little woman I ever knew. (1889)

gutsy (1893) Orig US; from *guts* courage + *-y* ■ **Sean O'Faolain:** *Kit Brandon* is the life-story of a woman gangster, a regular tornado, a passionate, lawless 'gutsy' young girl from the mountains. (1937)

tight (1928) US; applied to someone who is tough and unyielding ■ **L. Buckley:** He was a hard, tight, tough Cat. (1960)

ballsy (1935) Orig and mainly US; from *balls* courage + *-y* ■ **Elmore Leonard:** The old man was showing off . . . he knew his way around. Ballsy little eighty-year-old guy. (1983)

game as a piss-ant (1945) Applied to the emboldening effects of alcohol ■ **R. Tullipan:** The old white lady makes you as game as a pissant. (1962)

To retain one's courage

keep one's pecker up (1853) British; *pecker* probably = beak ■ **A. Merritt:** I was talkin' loud to keep my pecker up. (1928)

keep one's chin up (1938) ■ **Irene Baird:** Keep your chin up honey. (1939)

A coward

funk (1860) Dated; from earlier sense, fear

dingo (1869) Australian; from the dingo's reputation as a cowardly animal

funkstick (1889) Dated, originally hunting slang; from earlier sense, huntsman who baulks at difficult fences, from *funk* be afraid of + *sticks* fence ■ **A. E. W. Mason:** She thought of William Mardyke and his timidities. 'He'll never do that. What did you call him?' 'A funkstick.' (1930)

yellow-belly (1930) Orig US; from *yellow* cowardly + *belly* ■ **John Steinbeck:** I'm a cowardly yellow-belly. (1952)

sook (1933) Australian & New Zealand; perhaps from British dialect *suck* duffer ■ *Courier-Mail* (Brisbane): The tough specimen might appear as somewhat of a myth by fearing to be different from his mates in case they might think him a bit of a sook. (1975)

chicken (1936) In literary use in the 17th and 18th centuries, but moribund until revived in US slang in the early 20th century ■ **E. W. Hildick:** 'Speak for yourself—chicken!' he jeered. (1960)

pleep (1942) Military slang, dated; applied to an enemy pilot who refuses aerial combat; perhaps onomatopoeic—'echoic of a timorous young bird', Eric Partridge, *Dictionary of Forces' Slang* 1948

squib (1945) Australian; from earlier sense, small or insignificant person ■ **J. Alard:** 'I'm no squib,' he thought, 'I'll show them.' (1968)

chicken-shit (1947) Orig US; from earlier sense, contemptible person

Cowardly

funky (1837) From *funk* fear + *-y*

yellow (1856) Orig US ■ **O. Jacks:** You're yellow scum. You'll fight when the odds are with you. (1977)

gutless (1900) Orig US; from *guts* courage + *-less* ■ **L. A. G. Strong:** Now you see what a gutless poor worm I am. (1941)

yellow-bellied (1924) Orig US; compare *yellow-belly* coward ■ **M. Hebden:** I'm . . . a yellow-bellied, lily-livered coward. (1979)

chicken (1933) Orig US; adjectival use of *chicken* coward ■ **Stanley Ellin:** You'd just holler for the cops? Why, man, you're chicken. (1952)

milky (1936) From *milk* + *-y*; from the association of milk with mildness or weakness ■ **Heron Carvic:** 'Getting milky?' scoffed Doris. (1969)

chicken-shit (1945) US; adjectival use of *chicken-shit* coward ■ *It:* American groups are not so chickenshit about getting into underground work. (1970)

To lose one's nerve, withdraw pusillanimously

funk (1857) Used transitively; from earlier sense, be afraid of ■ *Times:* Mrs Margaret Thatcher is said to be as firmly committed as ever . . . , despite accusations . . . yesterday that she would 'funk it'. (1985)

squib (1918) Australian; also used transitively; compare *squib* coward ■ **D'Arcy Niland:** The rough-and-tumble doesn't worry me. I'm not squibbing the issue. (1955) ■ *Sydney Morning Herald:* The Treasury-types' eternal search for 'a politician with some guts' is futile. Mr Fraser looked tough enough at the time, but he squibbed. (1984)

punk out (1920) US ■ **H. E. Salisbury:** The Chimp, unfortunately, has a tendency to 'punk out' when the fighting gets tough. (1959)

chicken (1934) Orig US; usually followed by *out*; from *chicken* coward ■ *Economist:* Nobody can trust the others not to chicken out if they take the first plunge. (1965)

dingo (1935) Australian; also used transitively; from *dingo* coward ■ **E. Lambert:** 'Where is Allison?' 'He dingoed at the last minute.' (1952) ■ **Jon Cleary:** You ain't dingoing it, are you? You can't toss in the towel now. (1952)

bottle out (1979) British; from *bottle* courage ■ *Times:* Why did Ken Livingstone 'bottle out' and vote to set a legal GLC rate? (1985)

wimp out (1981) Orig US; from *wimp* feeble or ineffectual person ■ *New England Monthly:* One of the women suggested the night had already been very full and rewarding and she wasn't sure she needed to continue it. 'Hey, are you wimping out?' Patti asked. (1990)

A place to which one withdraws out of fear

funk-hole (1900) From *funk* fear ■ **J. D. Clark:** Deep, dark caves were never occupied except very occasionally as refuges or 'funk holes'. (1959)

35. Perseverance

Perseverance

stick-to-it-iveness (1867) Orig & mainly US ■ *New York Review of Books:* This man who made his million apparently more by stick-to-itiveness than brilliance. (1979)

stickability (1888) Orig US ■ *Daily Telegraph:* All too many lack any degree of 'stickability' and flit from job to job like butterflies. (1962)

To persevere (with)

peg away (1818) Mainly British; denoting persistent laborious work ■ **Len Deighton:** How I envied you doing Greats, while I pegged away at my Civil Law. (1978)

tough it out (1852) Orig US; denoting enduring something unpleasant ■ **Thomas Raddall:** She was a great ol' lady. . . . Just kep' her chin up and . . . toughed it out to the end. (1956)

sweat it out (1876) Orig US; denoting enduring something unpleasant ■ **L. Lewis:** I haven't much time . . . but I'll sweat it out awhile. (1945)

stick something **out (1882)** Usually in the phrase *stick it out* endure something unpleasant ■ **P. P. Read:** He stuck it out for a week and then shinnied down a drainpipe. (1981)

stick with (1915) ■ **Milton Machlin:** 'I've known all along it was a Goddamn fool plan.' . . . 'Then why have you stuck with it so long?' (1976)

plug away (1947) Denoting persistent laborious work ■ *World of Cricket Monthly:* Australia's bowlers plugged away, with Max Walker breaking through when Surrey were 2 wickets down for 147, and snaring 3 quick wickets for only 6 runs. (1977)

hang in (1969) Mainly US; usually used in the imperative in the phrase *hang in there* ■ **Jeffrey Archer:** 'No, no,' said Simon. 'I'll hang in there now that I've waited this long.' (1984)

keep on trucking (1972) US ■ *New Yorker:* Feels like I frosted the ends of my toes a bit, but they're far from my heart, so I'll keep on truckin. (1977)

To remain in a place

stay put (1843) Orig US; from the notion of remaining where placed ■ *Globe & Mail* (Toronto): Fire Chief Dawson told him to stay put until the car could be pulled away safely. (1978)

sit tight (1890) ■ **V. Hunt:** 'Sit tight!' she exclaimed, pinching my arm violently. She always talks slang when she is excited. (1897)

stick around (1912) Orig North American ■ **A. Fox:** You'll be asked to come over here next week . . . and you'll have to stick around for a day or two. (1979)

To recover from a setback

bounce back (1950) ■ **J. D. MacDonald:** Fictional heroes . . . can bounce back from a pasting that should have put them in hospital beds. (1950)

Someone who perseveres; a resolute person

sticker (1824) From *stick* remain + *-er* ■ **Celia Fremlin:** Daphne did not believe in dropping things; she was, as she would have told you, a Sticker. (1967)

pebble (1829) Australian, dated; often in the phrase *as game as a pebble*

36. Conceit, Boastfulness, Ostentation

Conceit

high horse (1782) Orig in such phrases as *on the high horse* and *mount* or *ride the high horse*, now mainly in *on one's high horse* behaving as if one thinks oneself superior to others and *get on* (or *off*) *one's high horse* start (or stop) behaving in this way, and in variations on this theme ■ Dick Clement & Ian la Frenais: 'Now, don't get on your high horse, dad,' suggested Ingrid with a touch of asperity. (1978) ■ *Cosmopolitan:* A good co-worker leaves her high horse parked at the kerb. Be aware of your rights as an employee by all means, but show willing sometimes . . . to do a little more than you have been told to do. (1990)

big head (1850) Orig US ■ *Economist:* The brutal assessment . . . was that Mr Hawke came a cropper because 'the little man with the big head is grossly out of touch with what average Australians now think.' (1988)

side (1878) British; often in the phrase *put on side* give oneself airs ■ B. Mason: But they soon warmed to his lively personality and the sanctifying remark—'He's a good sort; no side about him', was heard three days after he arrived. (1980)

jam (1882) Australian; especially in the phrase *lay* (or *put*) *on jam* give oneself airs; from the notion of jam being a luxury foodstuff ■ Dal Stivens: Sadie put a bit of jam on when she talked, but not too much. (1951)

swelled head (1891), swollen head (1899)

Conceited

hoity-toity (1713) Denoting haughtiness; compare earlier obsolete sense, frolicsome; ultimately a reduplication of obsolete *hoit* behave boisterously (of unknown origin); under the influence of *high* and *height* the now obsolete variant *highty-tighty* evolved (1844) ■ *Sunday Times:* She [sc. Anne Diamond] wasn't the least bit hoity-toity. She was always having me back to her place for a bit of cheese on toast. (1993)

cocky (1768) From *cock* male chicken + *-y*, probably influenced by *cocksure* ■ *Observer:* She's confident without being cocky, and comes across as a genuinely lovely person. (1991)

stuck-up (1829) Applied to someone who has a superior attitude towards others ■ Monica Dickens: I hate these Housemen—stuck-up little boys, they think they know everything. (1942)

jumped-up (1835) British; applied to a self-important person ■ L. A. G. Strong: The better class despise me as a jumped-up chap with too good a conceit of himself. (1942)

too big for one's breeches (1835), too big for one's boots (1879) ■ Marghanita Laski: A young man who was getting too big for his boots. (1952)

highfalutin (1839) Applied to someone or something absurdly pompous or pretentious; from the earlier noun sense, pompous speech, writing, etc.; perhaps ultimately from *high* + *fluting*, present participle of *flute* ■ *New Statesman:* This is . . . a pleasing unsententious compilation, not really a lecture at all. Sir Compton is never highfalutin. (1962)

lairy, lary (1846) Cockney slang; applied to a knowing person, aware of their own cleverness; alteration of *leery* wary ■ B. Naughton: We'll have to keep an eye on him. Spivs are lary perishers. Anything goes wrong they'll never risk their own skin. (1945)

snotty (1870) Compare earlier sense, contemptible ■ *Globe & Mail Magazine* (Toronto): Francois is not always snotty, thank heaven. (1968)

ikey, iky (1887) Dated; apparently from the noun *ikey* Jew ■ T. Prentis: Sez as I'm as ikey as the Dook of Boocle-oo. (1927)

snifty (1889) Orig & mainly US; from dialect *snift* sniff (perhaps of Scandinavian origin) + *-y* ■ H. G. Wells: 'Snifty beast!' . . . That governess made things impossible. (1909)

sidy, sidey (1898) British; from *side* conceit, swagger + *-y* ■ Bruce Marshall: He couldn't very well put himself in first because people might think it rather sidey. (1946)

chesty (1899) US; applied to an arrogant person; from the notion of sticking out one's chest with pride ■ Alan Lomax: George was a little bit chesty, because all the girls around were making eyes at him. (1950)

dicty (1923) US, Black English; origin unknown

hincty, hinkty (1924) US; origin uncertain; perhaps from a clipped form of *handkerchief-head* an Uncle Tom black ■ Chester Himes: All those hincty bitches fell on those whitey-babies like they was sugar candy. (1969)

toffee-nosed (1925) Mainly British; applied to someone who is snobbish or pretentious; *toffee* perhaps punningly after *toffy* resembling a toff (1901) ■ T. E. Lawrence: A premature 'life' will do more to disgust the select and superior people (the R.A.F. call them the 'toffee-nosed') than anything. (1928)

swollen-headed (1928) From *swollen head* conceit ■ *Historical Journal:* Walter Hope was out of work because he was 'too swollen-headed to go back to his old job'. (1993)

pound-noteish (1936) Dated ■ W. H. Auden: When we get pound-noteish . . . send us some deflating image. (1966)

stiff-arsed, (US) stiff-assed (1937) Applied to someone supercilious or stand-offish

big-headed (1942) From *big head* conceit ■ John Braine: The selfish big-headed, hard-hearted young lover. (1959)

smart-arse, smart-arsed, (US) smart-ass, smart-assed (1960) Applied to someone smugly clever ■ *Globe & Mail* (Toronto): It is tempting to be smart-assed when reviewing a Richard Rohmer novel. (1979)

ditsy, **ditzy** (1979) US; origin uncertain; perhaps an alteration of *dicty* ■ *New York Times*: She also has a big repertory of comic voices, ranging from . . . a maternal croon to a ditsy English matron's stiff-upper-register. (1985)

A conceited person

stuffed shirt (1913) Orig US; applied to a pompous person ■ *Islander* (Victoria, British Columbia): He had no time at all for the 'stuffed-shirt' types which were beginning to show in the north [of Canada]. (1969)

big-head (1932) From *big head* conceit ■ Edward Blishen: Saying . . . 'This man was a bighead,' in baffled parody of Shakespeare's funeral speeches. (1955)

toffee-nose (1943) Mainly British; applied to someone who is snobbish or pretentious; back-formation from *toffee-nosed* ■ *Woman*: People thought I was a bit of a toffee-nose for the first few months because I didn't speak to them. (1958)

smart-arse, (US) **smart-ass** (1965) Applied to someone smugly clever ■ J. Barnett: He had indulged in reckless speculation. . . . He was just as much a smart-arse as the Farnham D.I. (1981)

A self-important person

his (or **her**) **nibs** (1821) Used as a mock title for a self-important person; origin unknown; compare earlier *nabs* with same meaning ■ Alan Hunter: Since when were you on first-name terms with His Nibs? (1973)

high-muck-a-muck, high-you-muck-a-muck (1856) North American; apparently from Chinook Jargon *hiu* plenty + *mucka-muck* food ■ *Time*: Not all the Liberal high muckamucks were as warmly defended as Favreau. (1965)

I am (1926) From earlier sense, the Lord Jehovah, from Exodus iii. 14: And God said unto Moses, I am that I am: And he said, Thus shalt thou say unto the children of Israel, I AM hath sent me unto you ■ Nubar Gulbenkian: Cyril Radcliffe . . . did not take the short-cut favoured by so many of his colleagues who say . . . 'I am the great I am, Queen's Counsel'. (1965)

Lord Muck (1937), **Lady Muck** (1957) Applied to a pompous self-opinionated condescending man or woman ■ Jack Thomas: Hey, Lord Muck! May we have the honour of introducing ourselves! (1955) ■ Ian Cross: She sat there, sipping away at her tea like Lady Muck. (1957)

Jack Strop (1945) Nautical; applied to a bumptious or opinionated man

mucky-muck (1968) North American; alteration of *muck-a-muck*, short for *high-muck-a-muck* ■ *Globe & Mail* (Toronto): Orpen was always let out at the members' enclosure, but he never sat with the mucky-mucks. (1968)

A swaggering, showy, or boastful person

swanker (*a*1846), **swank** (1913) From *swank* swagger, behave boastfully (+ *-er*) ■ Richmal Crompton: He was a pariah, outside the pale, one of the 'swanks' who lived in big houses and talked soft. (1923)

tinhorn (1887) US; applied to a pretentious or flashy person; compare earlier *tinhorn gambler* cheap gambler ■ Sinclair Lewis: I'll bet I make a whole lot more money than some of those tin-horns that spend all they got on dress-suits. (1922)

skite (1897) Australian & New Zealand; applied to a boastful person; from the verb *skite* boast ■ A. B. Facey: Charlie was a terrific skite and he told everyone about the incident. (1981)

bucko (1899) Nautical; applied to a swaggering or domineering fellow; from *buck* male animal + *-o* ■ *Blackwood's Magazine*: A great big bucko of a man. (1927)

hot dog (1900) North American; applied to a highly skilled person who is boastful or flashy ■ *Hockey News* (Montreal): Critics label him a 'hot dog' and a 'show-off' and several unprintable things. (1974)

frippet (1908) Applied to a frivolous or showy young woman; origin unknown ■ Elizabeth Taylor: 'Mistress!' he thought. . . . It was like the swine of a man to use such a word for what he and Edwards would have called a bit of a frippet. (1945)

swankpot (1914) British; from *swank* boastful behaviour + *pot*, as in *fusspot*, etc. ■ I. & P. Opie: If a boy is under the necessity of coming to school in a new suit his fellows greet him with, . . . 'Swank pot'. (1959)

drug-store cowboy (1923) US; originally applied to idle young swaggerers who hung around drug-store soda fountains trying to impress girls ■ Pat Frank: She married . . . a marijuana-smoking drugstore cowboy. (1957)

lair, **lare** (1923) Australian; applied to a youth or man who dresses flashily or shows off; back-formation from *lairy* flashily dressed ■ T. A. G. Hungerford: He used to wear gold cuff-links in the coat sleeves of his blue serge suit: I suppose he was what we used to call a lair. (1983)

fancy Dan (1927) US; often applied specifically to a showy but ineffective worker or sportsman ■ Jack Dempsey: The amateur and professional ranks today are cluttered with . . . 'fancy Dans'. (1950)

trombenik, **trombenick** (1931) US; applied to a boaster or braggart; from Yiddish, from *tromba* trumpet, horn + *-nik* suffix denoting a person associated with a specified thing or quality ■ Joseph Heller: The gaudy militarism of the portly trombenik was more Germanic than Jewish. (1979)

fancy pants (1934) Orig US; applied to a showily dressed, conceited person, especially a man ■ Matthew Hunter: Some puffed-up fancy pants . . . said something which made the barmaid laugh. (1967)

God's gift (1938) British, mainly ironic; applied to a man irresistible to women ■ Hugh Clevely: It may do him a bit of good to find out he isn't God's gift to women walking the earth. (1953)

glitterati (1940) Orig US; applied collectively to the fashionable set of literary or show-business people; punningly from *glitter* + the plural suffix *-ati*, as in *literati* ■ *Times*: One member of the glitterati . . . offered to send her own hairdresser to Billie's hotel. (1984)

showboat (1953) Orig & mainly US; applied to an attention-seeker or show-off; from *showboat* show off

teddy bear (1953) Australian; rhyming slang for *lair*

Flash Harry (1960) British; applied to an ostentatious, loudly dressed, and typically bad-mannered man ■ *Times*: Her flash-Harry boy-friend. (1962)

signifier (1962) US, mainly Black English; from *signify* boast, brag + -*er* ■ Herbert Gold: When he bragged like any carnie signifier, then I wondered where and why I was going. (1965)

Wheneye, Whennie (1982) Applied to someone, especially a visitor or foreigner, who exasperates listeners by continually recounting tales of his or her former exploits; respelling of the phrase 'When I (was . . .)' ■ *Daily Mirror*: The islanders now call members of HM Forces 'Whennies'. The reason for this? 'When I stormed Goose Green', 'When I took Tumbledown', 'When I entered Stanley' . . . And so on. (1983)

A suave person

smoothie (1929) Orig US; from *smooth* + -*ie* ■ Hugh Jenkins: I have nothing but contempt for the international art market. It is a racket none the better for being operated by cultivated smoothies. (1979)

To be conceited

have tickets on oneself (1918) Australian ■ Jack Hibberd: You're the bastard that's always been smug and had tickets on himself. (1970)

fancy oneself British ■ *New York Daily News*: 'He was a bit of a Jack-the-lad if you know what I mean.' 'Tell me.' 'Well, he was bright enough, fancied himself, not settled or anything like that.' (1989)

To boast, behave boastfully, self-importantly, or ostentatiously

swank (1809) Origin unknown ■ *Sport*: Lest I may appear to be swanking, let me hasten to add that all of the credit went to someone else. (1950)

skite (1857) Australian & New Zealand; perhaps from earlier *skite* shoot, dart, leave quickly, perhaps from Old Norse *skýt-*, umlauted stem of *skóta* shoot ■ Rodney Hall: That's skiting, if you want to hear me skite. We'd beat the lot of youse, him and me. (1982)

put on the dog (1865) Orig US; denoting putting on airs ■ J. T. Farrell: They were all trying to put on the dog, show that they were lace-curtain Irish, and lived in steam-heat. (1934)

put (or **pile**) **on lugs** (1889) US, dated; denoting putting on airs ■ Sinclair Lewis: Oh, the lugs he puts on—belted coat, and piqué collar. (1920)

shoot one's mouth off, shoot off one's mouth (1896) Orig US; compare earlier sense, talk indiscreetly

lair, lare (1928) Australian; denoting behaving or dressing like a lair; often followed by *up*; from

lair flashily dressed or vulgar man ■ A. F. Howells: Earning something in the vicinity of three pounds ten shillings a week . . . I could still afford to lair up a bit, get on the scoot occasionally with my mates. (1983)

signify (1935) US, mainly Black English ■ Z. N. Hurston: 'Aw, woman, quit tryin' to signify.' 'Ah kin signify all Ah please, Mr. Nappy-chin.' (1935)

shoot a line (1941), **line-shoot** (1942) British ■ Guy Gibson: These things were happening every night, so there was nothing to shoot a line about. (1946) ■ Val Gielgud: He believed Tom to have been line-shooting as far as his swimming prowess was concerned. (1960)

kvell (1967) US; from Yiddish *kveln*, from German *quellen* gush, well up ■ L. M. Feinsilver: You've got reason to kvell. (1970)

See also To talk (of) exaggeratedly at **Communication** (p. 320).

Boastful talk; behaviour intended to impress

swank (1854) From the verb *swank* behave boastfully ■ *Daily Chronicle*: What he said is quite true, barring the whisky—that is all swank. (1905)

skite (1860) Australian & New Zealand; from the verb *skite* boast ■ S. T. Ollivier: 'Alister Bridgeman says it's mostly skite,' Sarah said breezily. (1965)

buck, bukh (1895) Dated; often in the phrase *old buck*; from Hindustani *bak*, Hindi *buk buk* ■ *Penguin New Writing*: Nah then, none o' yer ol' buck, Ernie. (1941)

piss and wind (1922) Applied to boastful but empty talk; often in the phrase *be all piss and wind* be full of empty bravado ■ *Guardian*: Mr Eric Lubbock, the Liberal MP for Orpington . . . said: ' . . . I have heard nothing but piss and wind.' (1969)

(all) gas and gaiters (1923) Applied to pompous but empty talk ■ G. B. Shaw: Its [*sc.* the Bible's] one great love poem is the only one that can satisfy a man who is really in love. Shelley's Epipsychidion is, in comparison, literary gas and gaiters. (1932)

mouth (1935) Orig US; applied to boastful but empty talk; often in the phrase *be all mouth* be full of empty bravado ■ G. F. Newman: The youth . . . for all his mouth and supposed cleverness was easily tricked. (1970)

line-shoot (1943) British, dated; from *shoot a line* talk boastfully ■ Terence Rattigan: Funny thing about gongs. . . . They don't mean a damn thing in war—except as a line-shoot, but in peace time they're quite useful. (1952)

A boastful talker

bullshitter (1933) Applied to someone who talks exaggeratedly in order to impress; from *bullshit* talk nonsense + -*er* ■ John Lennon: He is a bullshitter. But he made us credible with intellectuals. (1970)

line-shooter (1942) British; from *shoot a line* talk boastfully ■ *Listener*: [He] was an awful line-shooter. He claimed to have been at Oxford, but . . . he hadn't been at Oxford. (1973)

Boastful

See **mouthy** under Loquacious at **Communication** (p. 318).

To show off

strut one's stuff (1926) Orig US; denoting displaying one's ability ▪ *Sun* (Baltimore): Rain today made the prospect for off-going for the first card, thus giving the 'mudders' an opportunity to strut their stuff. (1941)

37. Audacity & Rudeness

Audacity, effrontery

face (1537) Now mainly in the phrase *have the face to* do something ▪ H. Rosovsky: When seeking an interview or a hearing it is most important to arrive with or be preceded by such a document, whenever possible composed by someone possessing a lot of 'face'. (1990)

brass (1682) Orig standard English, but latterly colloquial; from the notion of brass being hard and insensible (i.e. to shame) (compare *brazen*) ▪ *Washington Post*: He wants to keep high the capital gains tax rate. . . . And yet he has the brass to say H.R. 820 is 'wise', presumably because venture capital formation is inadequate. (1993)

cheek (1852) From earlier sense, insolence in speaking to someone ▪ *Guardian*: Some journalists have had the cheek to say to me, 'Do you work?' (1991)

chutzpah, chutzpa, chutzbah (1853) Yiddish; common among non-Jews only since the 1960s ▪ O. Hesky: The sheer *chutzpa*—the impudence—of defecting . . . right in front of his own eyes. (1967)

nerve (1887) Mainly in the phrases *have a nerve* and *have the nerve to* do something ▪ S. Brett: Joanne Menzies looked at him coolly. 'You've got a nerve.' (1975)

neck (1893) ▪ L. A. G. Strong: And then you have the sheer neck, the bloody effrontery to say you think there's more in life than I do. (1942)

crust (1900) From the notion of an insensitive outer covering ▪ P. G. Wodehouse: Actually having the crust to come barging in here! (1954)

rind (1903) From the notion of an insensitive outer covering ▪ *Times Literary Supplement*: The *Björn Borg Story* (I'm glad they didn't have the rind to use the word 'Life'). (1977)

brass neck (1984) ▪ *Guardian*: You can only marvel at the brass neck of Rupert Murdoch's *Sun*. Yesterday it launched its Politicians' Complaints Commission, a watchdog—well the *Sun* is nothing if not barking—to scrutinise the performance of MPs and others. (1992)

Impudent talk

lip (1821) ▪ Clement & La Frenais: Cheeky this one, Nutly. Lot of lip. (1978)

sass, sas (1835) US; alteration of *sauce* ▪ P. Welles: Is this what we get? Sass? No gratitude. (1967)

showboat (1951) US ▪ Roger Busby: The Europeans are enough of a handful without DEA prima donnas showboating all over the place. (1987)

Given to showing off

split-arse, split-ass (1917) Dated; services' slang, orig air force ▪ Arthur La Bern: The Royal Air Force and the Fleet Air Arm used to describe certain flyers as 'split-arse types'. This coarse expression was reserved for outstandingly reckless airmen. (1966)

sauce (1835) Probably from the piquancy of sauce; compare obsolete *have eaten sauce* be abusive ▪ C. Morley: My husban' wouldn't take none of his sauce. (1897)

cheek (1840) Dated; mainly in the phrase *give cheek* speak insolently ▪ George Moore: If he gives me any of his cheek I'll knock him down. (1884)

jaw (1846) Dated; from earlier more general sense, talk

back-chat (1901) Apparently orig military slang; applied to impertinent replies, especially to a superior ▪ *New Scientist*: They used to have loudspeakers on the back of their machines that bawled out backchat and delivery instructions to everyone within a radius of a hundred yards. (1983)

Audacious

as bold as brass (1789) Used adjectivally or adverbially; from the notion of brass being hard and insensible (i.e. to shame) (compare *brazen*) ▪ Stanley Weyman: Seeing as he hung back I up to him bold as brass. (1922)

Impudent

sassy (1833) Orig & mainly US; alteration of *saucy* impudent ▪ *Arizona Daily Star*: She plays a leading character, Persona Non Grata, a hip, wise, slightly sassy new friend of Alic. (1979)

fresh (1845) Orig US; perhaps influenced by German *frech* saucy, impudent ▪ Harold Nicholson: 'Those Britishers,' mumbled the President eventually, having taken a large gulp of iced water, 'are getting fresh.' (1932)

lippy (1875) From *lip* impudent talk + *-y* ▪ Ross Thomas: It might learn them not to be so goddamned lippy. (1971)

See also **mouthy** under Loquacious at **Communication** (p. 318).

Embarrassingly frank

near the knuckle (1909), **near the bone** (1941) ▪ A. L. Rowse: Charging him . . . with having 'two harlots begotten with child in his own house'. . . . This was getting pretty near the bone. (1941)

Truculent temperament or demeanour

attitude (1962) Orig US; from the use of the earlier sense, (demeanour arising from) a set of opinions, with negative connotations (as in 'I don't like your attitude') ■ *Washington Post*: Customers with an attitude, and who needs them? (1993)

To speak rudely (to)

cheek (1840) Used transitively; from *cheek* insolent talk ■ *Sunday Telegraph*: She has met the most legendary quiz champion of all, the Australian Barry Jones, who cheeked his questioners and was never once defeated. (1991)

sass (1856) US; alteration of *sauce* ■ William Faulkner: Don't you sass me, nigger boy. (1929)

38. Contempt

schm-, shm- (1929) Added to or replacing the beginning of a word, which then follows the original word, to form a doublet indicating contempt, derision, etc. (e.g. 'Oedipus, Schmoedipus'); in imitation of the many Yiddish words beginning with this letter-sequence ■ I. Goller: 'I know he made Davy go to the Palace to-day with the idea of hastening on the crisis in his illness.' . . . 'Crisis-schmisis!' mocked Barnett disparagingly. (1929)

To regard or treat with contempt

turn up one's nose (1818) ■ Bayard Taylor: What learning there was in those days . . . turned up its nose at the strains of the native minstrels. (1879)

give someone the finger (1890) Orig US; denoting making an obscene gesture with the middle finger raised as a sign of contempt, and hence showing contempt for someone ■ J. Mills: Wayne drove past us slowly, grinning and giving us the finger. We waved back and gave him the finger but it was all very cheerful. (1978)

thumb one's nose (1903) Orig US ■ John Wainwright: They are already thumbing their snotty, aristocratic noses at us. (1973)

look down one's nose (1921) ■ Angus Wilson: When you were all little babies, I used to sing and dance all day. The English neighbours would say 'That young Mrs Middleton's quite mad', and look down their noses—so! (1956)

razz (1921) Orig US; denoting hissing or deriding someone or making fun of them; from *razz* raspberry ■ *TV Times* (Australia): My kids will get razzed about it at school the next day. No one knows more about my mistakes than I do. (1977)

snoot (1928) US; from *snoot* nose (a dialectal variant of *snout*), from the idea of 'looking down one's nose' at someone, perhaps also reinforced by the similarity of *cock a snook* treat someone contemptuously or derisively ■ *Time*: Cinderella (Gemma Craven) gets snooted by her Stepsisters and gazes sorrowfully into the flames of the scullery fire. (1977)

put someone down (1958) Orig US; denoting humiliating treatment; from earlier sense,

sauce (1862) Used transitively; from *sauce* insolent talk ■ B. Potter: He puts on wrong postage . . . and will sauce anybody who is unprovided with small change; he wants reporting. (1892)

lip (1898) Used transitively; from *lip* insolent talk ■ Alfred Draper: If anyone lips you, just swallow it. (1972)

An impudent person

saucebox (1588) ■ F. Parrish: 'I likes a peach.' 'You *are* a peach,' said Dan gallantly. 'Sauce-box,' she said, delighted. 'Ta-ta, then,' said Dan. (1977)

madam (1802) Applied to an impudent (young) woman ■ John Wainwright: She was a little madam. I couldn't handle her. (1983)

snub, silence ■ David Delman: So why did you put him down that way, in front of me? (1972)

rank (1958) US, Black English; denoting insulting or putting down someone, especially within one's social group ■ C. Mitchell-Kernan: 'Barbara was trying to rank Mary', to put her down by typing her. (1971)

blank (1977) British; denoting deliberately ignoring someone; probably from the notion of giving someone a blank stare ■ *Select*: As Alex wanders inside to bid the local support band a polite hello he is blanked outrageously. (1991)

diss, dis (1986) Orig US, Black English; denoting putting someone down, usually verbally; shortened from *disrespect* ■ *Sky Magazine*: What is a Gas Face? That's the kind of face you pull if you're trying to kick it with some girl and she disses you! (1990)

A sign of contempt

snook, snooks (1791) Usually in the phrase *cock a snook* treat someone or something contemptuously or derisively; origin unknown ■ *Times*: East German craft last spring embarked upon a new ploy . . . to net a Danish torpedo, . . . cocking a snook at Nato's Baltic muscle. (1980)

raspberry, (US) razzberry (1890) Applied to a sound or gesture expressing contempt, specifically the continuous noise made by forcing air out of the mouth with the tongue held limply behind the lower lip; abbreviation of earlier *raspberry tart*, rhyming slang for *fart* ■ *South Wales Echo*: The only answer to that kind of nonsense is a long-drawn-out vintage raspberry. (1975)

razoo (1890) North American, dated; from *raz(zberry* + arbitrary suffix -oo ■ Raymond Chandler: My information is Apartment 301, but all I get there is the big razzoo. (1939)

razz (1919) Orig US; abbreviation of *razzberry* ■ *Spectator*: He selects one of them for punishment . . . , delivers a sonorous 'razz' and pretends to cane him. (1961)

Harvey Smith (1973) British; applied to a V-sign or other gesture of contempt; from the name of

Robert *Harvey Smith* (b. 1938), British show-jumper, with reference to a gesture he made during a televised event in 1971 (explained by Harvey Smith as a Victory sign) ■ *Telegraph & Argus* (Bradford): Centuries from now, people may still refer to a two-fingered gesture as a 'Harvey Smith'. (1985)

See also **give the finger** at To regard or treat with contempt (p. 275).

Contemptuous, scornful

sniffy (1871) From the verb *sniff* + *-y* ■ *Journal of the Royal Society of Arts*: Sniffy comments of a patronizing nature about Victorian buildings so regrettably sprinkled throughout earlier books in *The Buildings of England* are carefully avoided. (1979)

Exclamations of contempt or derision

kiss my arse (or **ass**) **(1705)** ■ *Fairbanks* (Alaska) *Daily News-Miner*: McGovern had told an airport antagonist to 'kiss my a . . .'. (1972)

garn (1886) Representing a Cockney pronunciation of *go on!* ■ Anne Holden: 'Garn,' called out someone, 'tell us somefing we don't know!' (1968)

pigs (1906) Australian; often in the phrase *pigs to you* ■ Les Ryan: 'Ar, pigs to you!' 'In your dinger, too!' (1975)

sucks (1913) Used especially by children; usually in the phrases *sucks to you* and *yah boo sucks* ■ *Listener*: The council treated the urbane Mr Cook to the politician's equivalent of 'Yah, boo, sucks'. (1983)

yah boo, **ya(a) boo (1921)** Used especially by children ■ Agatha Christie: Two small boys arrived . . . preparing as usual to say, 'Yah. Boo. Shan't go.' (*a*1976)

nuts (1931) From *nuts* testicles ■ Dick Francis: 'I'll give you a hundred.' 'Nuts.' 'A hundred and fifty.' (1974)

nerts (1932) US; representing a colloquial or euphemistic pronunciation of *nuts* ■ B. Howard: Heaven knows that no little word of mine can possibly be heard above the deepening hosannas, but all the same, I shall say it, and it is Nerts. Nerts to everybody, all round, except the authoress. (1937)

take a running jump (at oneself) (1933) ■ *Landfall*: If you think I'm subsidizing you . . . you can take a running jump at yourself. (1968)

drop dead (1934) Orig US ■ I. & P. Opie: The well-worn sentiments. . . . 'Do me a favour—drop dead.' (1959)

shove it (1941) From the notion of inserting something into the anus ■ L. Stewart: If he doesn't like it he can shove it, but don't worry—he won't. (1978)

upya, upyer (1941) Mainly Australian; alteration of *up you* (not recorded until later) ■ D'Arcy Niland: No, he said, I won't truckle to you. Upya for the rent. (1955)

big deal (1951) Orig US; used ironically to indicate that one is not impressed ■ Simon Harvester: So, I can charge an evening's entertainment to business expenses. Oh, big deal. Carry on. (1966)

get stuffed (1952) British; from *stuff* dispose of as unwanted (as in *stuff it!*) or *stuff* have sex with ■ Ruth Rendell: Who're you giving orders to? You can get stuffed. (1979)

up your arse (or **ass**), **up yours, up you (1956)** ■ Norman Mailer: 'Ain't you got any consideration?' he asked. 'Up your ass, friend.' (1965) ■ Julian Symons: She made a V sign at the audience, said distinctly 'Up yours'. (1975)

get knotted (1963) British; from *knot* tie in a knot ■ M. Forster: 'You are to behave properly.' 'Get knotted,' said Natalie, deliberately. (1965)

knickers (1971) ■ *Pacifist*: This is where the revolution's happening, man, and knickers to the metropolis! (1974)

39. **Meanness**

Mean, ungenerous

tight (1805) ■ J. Gaskell: When I was on the cabs . . . who'd give you a grand-hearted tip, never tight, but all the brass? (1969)

cheap (1904) US ■ Charles Grant: She took some time off. She went West someplace, to see friends, I think. She's too cheap to send me a postcard. (1994)

mingy (1911) Perhaps from *m(ean* + *st(ingy*, or a blend of *mangy* and *stingy* ■ E. V. Lucas: It's dear, but we are not going to be mingy. (1930)

A mean person

Jew (1606) Offensive ■ T. R. G. Lyell: Why waste your time asking him for a subscription? He's a perfect Jew where money's concerned. (1931)

skinflint (*a*1700) From the phrase *skin a flint* go to extreme lengths to save money ■ Cecil Roberts: Which sum the captain, who was a regular skinflint, said was far too much. (1891)

cheapskate (1903) Mainly US; from *cheap* mean + *skate* mean or contemptible person; compare

earlier *cheap skate* contemptible person ■ *Car*: The neighbours would suss it instantly, label you a cheapskate. (1990)

skate (1904) Mainly US; from earlier sense, contemptible person

tightwad (1906) Orig and mainly US; from *tight* + *wad* bundle of banknotes ■ *Sunday Telegraph*: Bleeding tightwad! You'd think with all that cash he'd take a taxi. (1977)

nickel nurser (1926) US, dated; from *nickel* five-cent coin

meany, meanie (1927) From *mean* + *-y* ■ J. B. Priestley: He was at heart, she felt, a cunning old meanie. (1951)

cheap Charlie (1965) US, mainly military slang

Meanness

one-way pockets (1926) Jocular ■ P. G. Wodehouse: His one-way pockets are a by word all over England. (1961)

40. **Honesty**

(See also **Genuineness & Spuriousness** pp. 424–5)

Honest

straight (1864) ■ John Wainwright: Inky was straight. . . . Ten years ago, Inky had walked away from prison . . . and, since that day, he hadn't put a foot wrong. (1977)

on the level (1872) Orig US ■ Robert Graves: He also prefers pools to premium-bond gambling—in which a bloke can't choose his own combination of numbers, so how does one know that it's on the level? (1958)

on the straight (1900)

legit (1908) Abbreviation of *legitimate* ■ Hartley Howard: This dough isn't strictly legit. (1973)

kosher (1924) From earlier sense, genuine ■ L. Gribble: 'No financial irregularities?' 'Strictly kosher. . . . It's so good it stinks.' (1961)

clean (1926) Often applied specifically to someone not carrying incriminating material, such as drugs or weapons ■ Mario Puzo: They'll frisk me when I meet them so I'll have to be clean then, but figure out a way you can get a weapon to me. (1969)

on the legit (1931)

straight-up (1936) Often used adverbially to denote that one is speaking truthfully ■ R. Hill: You looked honest to me . . . and you sounded like a straight-up guy. (1982) ■ W. J. Burley: I don't know where he is, Mr Gill, straight up. (1973)

upfront (1967)

An honest person

straight goods (1903) US, dated; from earlier sense, the truth

clean-skin (1907) Australian; applied to a person with a clean police record; from earlier sense, unbranded animal ■ *Sun-Herald* (Sydney): Cameron's death was . . . ordered because the drug gang had no further use for the former 'clean skin' they had recruited and it was feared he would give evidence against them. (1984)

straight shooter (1928) Mainly US

straight arrow (1969) North American ■ Cyra McFadden: I keep trying to tell you, I'm really a straight arrow. (1977)

Mr. Clean (1973) Applied to an honourable or incorruptible politician ■ *Guardian*: Mr Shultz himself has never been touched by Watergate. . . . His reputation as a 'Mr Clean' . . . has led him . . . to voice a growing sense of unease. (1974)

A reliable person

brick (1840) From the strength and solidity of a brick ■ *Guardian*: I must say she has been an absolute brick and . . . both my parents will really miss her. (1992)

pistol (1984) US ■ J. Phillips: What a pistol she was— still working at the dress shop then, hard as nails and took no truck from anyone. (1984)

To be, remain, or become honest

keep one's nose clean (1887) Orig US ■ Angus Ross: Denis Fitzgerald . . . a known associate of villains, but managed to keep his own nose clean. (1974)

straighten up (1907)

go straight (1940) ■ Roger Simons: I'm goin' straight. Last time I was done was two years ago, and I ain't been tapped on the shoulder since. (1968)

An honest way of life

the straight and narrow (1930) Short for *the straight and narrow path* a course of conventionally moral and law-abiding behaviour; from the action of making the sign of the strait is the gate, and narrow is the way which leadeth unto life, and few there be that find it ■ Fay Weldon: It's only the fear of pregnancy which keeps girls on the straight and narrow. (1978)

The truth

gospel (a.1250) From earlier sense, holy scriptures ■ G. R. Sims: It's gospel every word. (1887)

the straight (1866) US; especially in the phrases *get (at)* or *hear the straight* ■ Lesley Egan: Tell you something. I never heard the straight of that anyway. (1977)

straight goods (1892) US, dated ■ Eugene O'Neill: Is all dat straight goods? (1922)

dinkum oil, dinkum (1915) Australian & New Zealand ■ J. H. Fullarton: Anyway there's no dinkum oil. Only latrinograms . . . it may all be hooey. (1944)

the strong of (1915) Australian; used to refer to the truth about something or the point or meaning of something ■ B. Dawe: H-hey fellers. . . . What's the strong of this—empty glasses? C'mon, it's my shout. (1983)

where it's at (1965) Orig US; used to refer to the true state of affairs

To tell the truth

cross my heart (and hope to die) (1908) Used as an assertion that one is telling the truth; from the action of making the sign of the cross over one's heart as a pledge of sincerity ■ Rose Macaulay: 'Let's both swear.' 'Cross my heart and hope to die. Now what about bed?' (1926)

come clean (1919) Orig US; usually suggesting confession of wrongdoing ■ Joyce Cary: I was wasting my time, because you kept dodging. You never come clean. (1959)

level with (1920) Orig US ■ Len Deighton: I'd better level with you, son. . . . From now on, control is through me. (1974)

swear blind (1937) Used to make a strong assertion that one is telling the truth (but often with the implication that one is not) ■ *Byte*: You can swear blind it's solving a partial differential equation and they would be hard put to prove it is not. (1985)

shoot the works (1946) Orig US; denoting candid speaking

tell it like it is (1964) Orig US, Black English ■ L. Lokos: The crowd responded fervently with 'Amen, amen,' and 'Tell it like it is.' (1969)

let it all hang out (1970) Orig US; denoting candid speaking ■ *Village Voice*: No names, of course, will be used; he doesn't expect everyone will be as willing as he is to let it all hang out. (1972)

41. **Sincerity & Insincerity**

Obsequious behaviour; toadying

arse-licking (1912) ■ Paul Scott: I can't go up and ask Were you my brother's C.O.? . . . it'd look like arse-licking. (1958)

ass-kissing (1942) Mainly US ■ *Rolling Stone*: Glossy fringe publishing, T-shirt peddling and political ass kissing. (1977)

bum-sucking (1949) British ■ Compton Mackenzie: Being accused of sucking up, or even of bum-sucking. (1963)

To behave obsequiously (towards)

kiss someone's **arse** (or **ass**) **(1749)** ■ Henry Miller: If it weren't that I had learned to kiss the boss's ass, I would have been fired. (1934)

suck up (1860) Usually followed by *to* ■ Margaret Mitchell: We hear how you suck up to the Yankees . . . to get money out of them. (1936)

crawl (1881) Orig Australian ■ William Dick: I didn't crawl to him. . . . I wouldn't crawl to no bastard for nothing. (1969)

bum-suck (1930) British; back-formation from *bum-sucker* sycophant ■ Leonard Cooper: He bumsucked to all the rich men. (1960)

suck around (1931) Orig and mainly US; applied to someone who goes about behaving obsequiously ■ George Ade: As for the Landis party on July 10th I have had no invitation but maybe I could suck around and get one. (1934)

brown-nose (1938) Orig US military slang; from the noun *brown-nose* sycophant ■ Julian Symons: If you don't . . . get cracking on a few little jobs for this paper instead of spending your time brown-nosing Mr. Fairfield, you [etc.]. (1960)

lick (someone's) **arse** (or **ass**) **(1959)** ■ *Select*: Even the most outrageous band licks arse to get radio play and press. (1995)

ass-kiss (1961) Mainly US; back-formation from *ass-kissing* ■ Saul Bellow: If it could have been done by ass-kissing his patrons and patronesses, B. B. would have dried away a good many tears. (1984)

suck-hole (1961) Orig and mainly Canadian ■ J. Metcalf: Can't even fix yourself a sandwich without suckholing round that man. (1972)

See also To speak revealingly under **Communication** (pp. 319–20).

Without concealment of the (unattractive) truth

warts and all (1930) Applied originally to candid portraiture; said to be from Oliver Cromwell's request to Peter Lely to paint him without concealing the warts on his face ■ Kenneth Giles: In fact you want a run down on Stanisgate, warts and all. Huh? (1966)

piss in someone's **pocket (1967)** Australian; denoting ingratiation

arse-lick (1968) Back-formation from *arse-licking*

An obsequious person; a toady, sycophant

ass-kisser (1766) Mainly US

creeping Jesus (c1818) Applied to a sycophantic or servile person or one who is hypocritically pious ■ Roy Campbell: The Zulus naturally despise the creeping Jesus type who sucks up to them. (1934)

bum-sucker (1877) British; from *bum* buttocks ■ George Orwell: The lords of property and their hired liars and bumsuckers. (1943)

crawler (1892) Orig Australian ■ John Beede: You've got to be a crawler to get the odd gongs that are going. (1965)

greaser (1900) ■ *Spectator*: The dismissive contempt the little greaser had so richly earned. (1958)

suck (1900) Applied especially to a schoolchild who curries favour with teachers ■ William Gaddis: The shade of the boy whom he had not seen since they were boys together (Martin was Father Joseph's 'suck') lived on the air as though they had parted only minutes before. (1955)

apple-polisher (1927) Orig and mainly US; from the practice of American schoolchildren presenting their teacher with a shiny apple, in order to gain favour ■ E. A. McCourt: The apple-polishers in the front row laughed with forced heartiness. (1947)

arse-licker (1938) ■ *Frendz*: Maybe we should have been talking with Henry Ford rather than this professional arse-licker. (1971)

brown-nose (1938), **brown-noser (1950)** Orig US military slang; from the equation of servility with licking, etc. someone's anus ■ Marshall Pugh: It was part of the tradition to hate a Highland laird or be a brown-nose.

To flatter; to deceive with insincere or flattering talk

blarney (1803) From the noun *blarney* flattery

gammon (1812) British, dated; from *gammon* insincere or flattering talk ■ Georgette Heyer: He added, as a clincher, that Mr. Christopher need not try to gammon him into believing that he wasn't in the habit of wearing full evening-dress. (1963)

butter up (1819) From earlier *butter* in the same sense ■ E. M. Forster: 'This is a great relief to us, it is very good of you to call, Doctor Sahib,' said Hamidullah, buttering him up a bit. (1924)

sawder (1834), soft-sawder (1843) Dated; from the noun (*soft*) *sawder* flattery ■ *Manchester Examiner*: When the Irish electors were to be soft-sawdered. (1883)

soft-soap (1840) From the noun *soft soap* flattery ■ A. K. Green: I am not a clumsy fellow at softsoaping a girl. (1883)

soap (1853) Dated ■ Charles Dickens: These Dear Jacks soap the people shameful, but we Cheap Jacks don't. (1865)

bull (1907) US; from earlier sense, talk emptily

crap (1930) US; from *crap* nonsense ■ Stanley Ellin: I don't want you to crap me. . . . I want your honest opinion. (1958)

schmeer, schmere, shmeer (1930) North American; from Yiddish *schmirn* smear, grease, flatter

sweet-talk (1936) Orig and mainly US; from *sweet talk* flattery ■ Tennessee Williams: I'd say a peculiar slew-footer that sweet talks you while he's got his hand in the cashbox. (1955)

bullshit (1937) Orig US; from the noun *bullshit* exaggeration, flattery ■ Philip Roth: Please, let us not bullshit one another about 'love' and its duration. (1969)

flannel (1941) British; from the noun *flannel* exaggerated or flattering talk ■ John Braine: I managed to flannel him into the belief that I approved of his particular brand of efficiency. (1957)

snow (1945), snow-job (1962) Orig and mainly US; *snow-job* from the noun *snow job* flattery, deception ■ Hillary Waugh: Roger'd be alone in a corner with some girl and . . . looked like he was really snowing them. (1966)

sweetmouth (1948) Mainly US, Black English ■ J. Jones: He went on sweetmouthing me, with his slippery mean eyes. (1973)

Insincere or exaggerated talk intended to flatter or deceive; humbug or flattery

See also **Nonsense** (pp. 334–5).

blarney (1796) From *Blarney* name of a village near Cork, Ireland. In the castle there is an inscribed stone in a position difficult of access. The popular saying is that any one who kisses this 'Blarney stone' will ever after have 'a cajoling tongue and the art of flattery or of telling lies with unblushing effrontery' (Lewis, *Topographical Dictionary of Ireland*) ■ *Times*: You do not want to come here every day to listen to a lot of blarney. (1955)

gammon (1805) British, dated; probably from the 18th- and 19th-century thieves' slang

expressions *give someone gammon, keep someone in gammon* distract someone's attention while an accomplice robs him, which may be an application of the backgammon term *gammon* complete victory achieved before one's opponent has removed any of his pieces

soft soap (1830) Orig US ■ *Sun* (Baltimore): Assailing Governor Lehman for his 'soft soap' manner of campaign, the park commissioner . . . renewed his assault on the Lehman banking family. (1934)

soft sawder (1836), sawder (1854) Dated; apparently a use of *sawder* solder ■ D. G. Rossetti: MacCrac . . . offers £50 for the water-colour, with all manner of soap and sawder into the bargain. (1854)

borak, borac, borack, borax (1845) Australian & New Zealand; from Aboriginal (Wathawurung) *burag* ■ Tom Ronan: The chief steward was full of borack. . . . He wasn't a very good liar, this steward. (1961)

soap (1854) ■ William Faulkner: 'The pattern,' Uncle Gavin said. 'First the soap, then the threat, then the bribe.' (1957)

gush (1863) Applied to effusive flattery

grease (1877) ■ Norman Mailer: You should have seen the grease job I gave to Carter. I'm dumb, but man, he's dumber. (1959)

taffy (1878) North American; from earlier sense, toffee ■ *Daily Colonist* (Victoria, British Columbia): A little 'taffy' doesn't hurt anybody and it makes the world sweeter. (1926)

eyewash (1884) Applied to something that conceals the reality of a situation; from earlier sense, soothing lotion for the eyes ■ *Aeroplane*: Well as this may do as 'eye wash', it is not the real thing. (1913)

bull con (1896) US; applied to a concerted attempt at flattery, deception, or persuasion

B.S. (1900) Mainly North American; abbreviation of *bullshit* ■ J. Goulet: Shit, . . . you can't be around a project like this for two years without picking up some of that B.S. (1975)

bull (1902) Orig US; from earlier sense, ludicrously contradictory statement ■ Guy Gibson: I have never heard such a line of bull in all my life. (1946)

bushwa, booshwa(h), bushwha, bushwah (1906) North American; apparently a euphemistic alteration of *bullshit* ■ J. R. Macdonald: If you're a detective, what was all that bushwa about Hollywood and Sunset Boulevard? (1959)

kidstakes, kidsteaks (1912) Australian & New Zealand; probably from *kid* nonsense, kidding, as in *no kid* ■ A. Kimmins: This isn't kid-stakes. . . . This is deadly serious. (1960)

bullshit (1914) Orig US ■ *Guardian*: Blessedly free of RSC bullshit, his talk would be as much about life as about the play. (1992)

oil (1917) ■ P. G. Wodehouse: Coo to him, and give him the old oil. (1940)

blah, bla, blaa, blah-blah, etc. **(1918)** Orig US; imitative ■ *Observer*: England isn't fooling anyone with so much 'blah' about the world's greatest tournament. (1927)

jazz (1918) Orig US; probably from earlier musical sense ■ Bernard Malamud: I read all about that formalism jazz in the library and it's bullshit. (1971)

applesauce (1919) US; often used as an interjection to deflate or reject flattery; compare earlier theatrical slang sense, silly comedy

drip (1919) Orig US

flannel (1927) British ■ *Penguin New Writing*: The ship's company know what is coming. Jimmy the One is going to give us a pep talk. Tons of flannel. (1945)

madam (1927) ■ John Wainwright: It was not the sort of place conducive to putting over a spot of old madam. The normally glib flannel tended to stick in his throat and the guff and eye-wash hadn't enough elbow-room to . . . sound . . . feasible. (1973)

jive (1928) Orig US; origin unknown ■ *Black World*: Everything that we do must be aimed toward the total liberation, unification and empowerment of Afrika. . . . Anything short of that is jive. (1973)

malarkey, malaky, malarky, mullarkey (1929) Orig US; origin unknown ■ *Observer*: Tall stories . . . of rattlesnakes bringing up a nestful of baby robins, . . . or some such malarkey. (1973)

spinach (1929) US, dated; perhaps from the phrase *gammon and spinach*, part of the refrain of the song 'A frog he would a-wooing go', in allusion to *gammon* specious talk, humbug; popularized by a cartoon caption in the *New Yorker* (1928): 'It's broccoli dear.' 'I say it's spinach, and I say the hell with it.' ■ Alexander Woollcott: This . . . reticence . . . will . . . be described by certain temperaments as . . . good taste. . . . I say it's spinach. (1934)

ackamarackus, ackamaracka (1933) Orig US; mainly in the phrase *the old ackamarackus*; a fanciful pseudo-Latin coinage

bull's wool, bullswool (1933) Australian & New Zealand; euphemistic alteration of *bullshit* ■ Ian Cross: That last bit was bulls-wool of course, but I had to be careful. (1957)

moody (1934) British; probably from the adjective *moody*, but some connection has been suggested with *Moody and Sankey* rhyming slang for *hanky-panky* (from the names of two US hymn writers, Dwight L. Moody (1837–99) and Ira D. Sankey (1840–1908) ■ Roger Busby: The same old moody he'd heard a thousand times before. (1970)

bull dust (1943) Orig US, now Australian; euphemistic alteration of *bullshit*, based on earlier *bull dust* fine powdery dirt or dust ■ J. Hamilton: I'm not in the mood for any of your bulldust. Where have you been all night? (1967)

snow job (1943) Orig US; applied to a concerted attempt at flattery, deception, or persuasion ■ Kylie Tennant: He . . . made a bee-line for the red-head. 'Now for the snow job,' Geechi murmured. (1953)

crock of shit (1945) US ■ Susan Faludi: A male editor assigned reporter Marilyn Goldstein a story on the women's movement with these instructions: 'Get out there and find an authority who'll say this is all a crock of shit'. (1992)

sweet talk (1945) Orig US

schmeer, schmere, shmeer (1961) US; from the verb *schmeer* flatter

A flatterer; an exaggerated talker

flannel-mouth (1881) US

bull artist (1918), bullshitter (1933), bullshit artist (1942) Orig US

snow-man (1967) US; applied to someone who flatters or deceives with plausible words; from *snow* deceive or charm with flattery

Outward show, empty display

razzmatazz, razzamatazz (1958) Applied to noisy, showy publicity or display; from earlier sense, old-fashioned or sentimental jazz ■ John Wain: The enormous selling bonanza that was going on about him, in its astonishing flood of genuine goodwill, even a grain here and there of genuine piety, with unscrupulous salesman's razzmatazz, heightened his sense of living in a dream. (1959)

glitz (1977) Orig US; applied to extravagant but superficial display or show-business glamour; back-formation from *glitzy* ■ *Toronto Life*: There was too much Third-World esoterica and not enough Hollywood glitz. (1985)

Characterized by outward show; flashy

flash (1785) From obsolete *flash* superficial brilliancy ■ *Guardian*: He fetches me from my Miami hotel in a distinctly flash red convertible ('a regular cocaine-dealer type car' he says). (1991)

zazzy (1961) Mainly US; origin uncertain; perhaps from *piz(zazz* + *-y*, but compare also *jazzy, sassy* and *snazzy*

glitzy (1966) Orig US; applied to something glamorous but tawdry; perhaps a blend of *glitter* and *ritzy*, but compare German *glitzerig* glittering ■ *Listener*: The Oscars are the high point of the Western film industry's year—a glitzy, vulgar affirmation that they're getting things right. (1985)

Insincere in manner, ingratiating

slimy (1602) ■ *Guardian*: Coogan creates a student-bashing drunkard and a slimy sports commentator. (1992)

greasy (1848) ■ *Guardian*: Similar lily-white hero, greasy villain, leggy villainess. (1992)

soapy (1854) From *soap* flattery + *-y* ■ Robert Bolt: *Steward* (*to audience, soapy*): Lady Margaret, my master's daughter, lovely; really lovely. (1960)

smarmy, smalmy (1924) From earlier sense, smooth and sleek ■ Simon Raven: He's a smarmy, ingratiating swine. (1962)

An ingratiating person

smoothie, smoothy (1939) Orig US; usually applied to a man; from earlier (positive) sense, suave or stylish person ■ H. Jenkins: I have nothing but contempt for the international art market. It is a racket none the better for being operated by cultivated smoothies. (1979)

To ingratiate oneself

make (or **keep**) **one's marble** (or **alley**) **good** **(1909)** Australian & New Zealand ■ Don Crick: Take my tip, if you wanter make your marble good: say nothing. (1963)

An instance of insincere behaviour

act (1934) Mainly in the phrase *put on an act* act insincerely ■ Monica Dickens: This girl's not naturally like that. She's putting on an act. (1946)

Pretentious

hokey, hokie, hoky (1945) Orig US; applied to something sentimentally or melodramatically artificial; from *hok(um* sentimental or melodramatic material in a play or film + *-ey* ■ *Rolling Stone*: A closing piece [on a record], 'Sometimes', is embarrassingly hokey. (1971)

pseudo (1945) Adjectival use of the prefix *pseudo-* ■ *Times*: The whole conception was 'pseudo'. (1958)

pseud (1962) From the Greek stem *pseud-* false, or a shortening of *pseudo* pretentious ■ *Listener*: A dreamy piano solo, recalling both Beiderbecke's 'In a Mist' and (I know this sounds pseud) early Schoenberg. (1977)

arty-farty, artsy-fartsy (1967) Applied to someone or something pretentiously artistic; modelled on *arty-crafty* ■ Miles Kington: The North is . . . trying to impose their bluff . . . values on our arty-farty-Dartington, southern way of life. (1982)

pseudy (1989) From *pseud* pretentious person + *-y* ■ *Sunday Times*: Your work has been puffed by Rushdie and A S Byatt. McKay has included you in a list of 'pseudy little twerps'. (1993)

A pretentious person

pseudo (1959) From the adjective *pseudo* ■ *Observer*: The undiscriminating, arty chat of a campus pseudo. (1967)

pseud (1964) From the adjective *pseud*, popularized by the *Private Eye* column 'Pseuds Corner' ■ *Jazz Monthly*: As well as being the creator of an avant-garde film on human buttocks, Miss Ono has a long list of other achievements which must put her in the running for the title of Pseud of the Century. (1968)

To render something insincere or artificial

hoke (1935) Orig US; denoting playing a part in a sentimentally or melodramatically artificial manner; usually followed by *up*; back-formation from *hokum* sentimental or melodramatic material in a play or film ■ Marian Babson: Just *try* it straight . . . it's a mistake to hoke it up. (1971)

A person of integrity

mensch, mensh (1953) Orig and mainly US; Yiddish, from German *Mensch* person ■ *New Statesman*: Mr Nixon is seen as an essentially decent man, . . . but not as a *mensch* on the scale of Roosevelt, Eisenhower, Kennedy. (1970)

To be in earnest

mean business (1857) ■ Jerome Weidman: We've decided to show these guys that we mean business. No crapping around. (1937)

Sincerely

honest Injun (1876) Orig US; used as an assertion that what one has said, one believes to be true; perhaps from an assurance of good faith extracted from Native Americans; *Injun* representing a casual pronunciation of *Indian* ■ L. A. G. Strong: 'You've invented him.' 'Which I never, sir, . . .' 'Honest Injun?' (1950)

no kidding, I kid you not (1914) ■ Josephine Tey: 'I'm a policeman.' 'No kidding!' (1952) ■ *Daily Mail*: I kid you not: if seven million schoolchildren had to learn their national curriculum in my bathroom, heads would roll. (1991)

no stuff (1946) US, dated

42. Lying

A lie

fib (1611) Applied to a small or trivial lie; perhaps short for obsolete *fible-fable*, a reduplicated form of *fable* ■ *Listener*: An extraordinarily powerful old bureaucratic nanny . . . goes stalking up and down the United States, pouncing on people who are telling commercial fibs. (1959)

thumper (1677) Dated; from earlier sense, something large

story (a1697) Used especially in the phrase *tell stories* ■ Mrs. Lynn Linton: Now, Eva, . . . I know all about you, so do not begin to deny and tell stories. (1880)

a likely tale (1749), a likely story (1865) Applied to a statement greeted with incredulity

■ Miles Kington: Or so he told Mother, 'A likely story!' she would snort. (1982)

whopper (1791) From earlier sense, something large ■ A. R. Hope: He thinks it's . . . better to get a licking than to tell a whopper. (1870)

good one, good 'un (1813)

whacker (1825) Dated; from earlier sense, something large ■ Thomas Hughes: Oh, there's a whacker! . . . We haven't been within a hundred yards of his barn. (1857)

yarn (1835) Usually in the phrase *spin a yarn* tell lies; from earlier sense, story

tall story, tall tale (1846) From *tall* exaggerated

weasel word (1900) Orig US; applied to a word that is used in a deliberately misleading way

pork pie, **porkie**, **porky** (1984) British; rhyming slang ■ *Observer*: The word 'porkie' was deemed unparliamentary last week, and thus no longer a proper word to be used in the Commons. (1992)

To lie

fib (1690) From the noun *fib* ■ Alexander Smith: Could I have fibbed. . . . Could I have betrayed a comrade? (1863)

spruce (1917) British, orig services' slang; applied especially to lying in order to evade a

duty; origin unknown ■ G. M. Wilson: Dr. Meunier's no fool, he'd have known if she was sprucing. . . . Malingering. Faking tummy trouble. (1967)

A liar

story (1869) Orig mainly children's; now only Black English ■ W. S. Gilbert: Oh, you shocking story! (1893)

To expose a lie

nail (1785) ■ *Daily Mirror*: Jailed gangland killer Reggie Kray has sent an amazing message to the Daily Mirror to nail the lie that he's having a gay affair with a young robber. (1996)

43. **Deception, Cheating**

Deception, swindling, fraud

dodge (1638) Applied to a deceitful trick or clever stratagem, especially one designed to evade something; from earlier sense, act of giving someone the slip ■ *New Scientist*: That would have shown the object to be far older than it really was, if the dodge had not been detected. (1983)

ramp (1812) Applied especially to a swindle or racket involving charging exorbitant prices; from the verb *ramp* swindle ■ W. G. Kerr: On their arrival in Dallas, Wellesley and Renshaw discovered that some serious 'ramps', or swindles, had been going on there. (1977)

put-up job (1838) British; applied to something pre-arranged in an underhanded way ■ Nicolas Freeling: There's going to be a lot saying it's a put-up job. (1974)

sell (1838) Applied especially to a deception that leaves the victim feeling disappointed

slanter, **schleinter**, **schlenter**, **shlanter**, **shlinter**, **slinter** (1864) Australian & New Zealand; applied to a trick or fraudulent stratagem; from Dutch *slenter* trick, probably via Afrikaans and South African English (see **schlenter** under Counterfeit money, cheques, etc. at **Crime** (p. 97)) ■ F. J. Hardy: One rider was prepared to make a sworn statement that the race had been rigged. . . . Cycling enthusiasts became convinced that the Austral had been 'a slanter'. (1950)

skin game (1868) US; from *skin* to swindle + *game* ■ Edmund McGirr: As a very small [antiques] dealer, I was no opposition. . . . His business is rather a skin game. (1973)

try-on (1874) British; applied to an attempt to deceive; from *try it on* ■ P. Townend: It was only a try-on, to see if I would react. (1959)

fiddle (1874) Orig US, now mainly British; often in the phrase *on the fiddle* engaged in swindling or deception; from the verb *fiddle* swindle ■ *Spectator*: I know you'll think this is one of my fiddles. At my last parish we raffled a horse and trap, . . . a clothes horse and a mousetrap. (1959) ■ *New Statesman*: As it was day-

time, everyone in the coffee bar was a sciver, on the dole or on the fiddle or just plain hopeful. (1961)

con game (1899) Orig US; *con* short for *confidence* ■ *Observer*: Various petty fiddles and con games to which Christmas trading lent itself. (1960)

con (1901) Orig US; short for *con trick*, an abbreviated form of *confidence trick* ■ *Listener*: The intellectual theoreticians of visual pop culture have succeeded . . . in pulling a con. (1967)

spiel (1901) Applied to a swindle or a dishonest line of business; from German *Spiel* game ■ T. A. G. Hungerford: This isn't a spiel, Colonel. . . . I know this bloke, and he's on the level. (1954)

bunco, **bunko** (1904) US; from earlier sense, dishonest gambling game played with dice ■ *Spectator*: The bunco-artists from the lunatic fringe of the Democratic party. (1963)

lemon-game, **lemon** (1908) US; applied to a type of confidence trick which involves defrauding a gullible player in a game of pool; from *lemon* gullible person

gyp (1914) Orig US; applied to a trick or swindle; from the verb *gyp* swindle ■ *Boston Sunday Globe*: Some are good, but gyps abound. Authorities report . . . phony practices. (1967)

pay-off (1915) Applied to a type of confidence trick in which the victim loses a large sum of money trying to follow the apparent good luck of the trickster ■ P. J. Smith: It is to his genius that the successful swindle known as the 'Pay Off' was attributed. (1938)

wangle (1915) Applied to an act of obtaining deceitfully; from the verb *wangle* ■ Peter Dickinson: I worked a wangle. I got a line on the Minister of Tourism. (1977)

fast one (1923) Orig US; applied to a deceptive trick; usually in the phrase *pull a fast one* play such a trick ■ Anthony Gilbert: Mad to think they can pull a fast one . . . over the whole community. (1958)

flanker (1923) British, orig services' slang; applied to a trick or swindle; probably from the notion of slipping past the side or 'flank' of someone ■ **Bill Knox**: This bloke wasn't content wi' just fiddling the h.p. He'd been workin' another flanker. (1962)

swindle sheet (1923) Mainly US, jocular; applied to a document making fraudulent claims, especially on an expense account ■ **H. L. Lawrence**: The fare's ten bob. . . . Put it on the swindle sheet. (1960)

ready-up (1924) Australian; applied to a swindle or fraud ■ **H. R. F. Keating**: I don't accept all the pretences and ready-ups you people put out. (1924)

tweedle (1925) Applied to a swindle or confidence trick, especially one involving counterfeit goods (originally a ring); from earlier sense, such a ring ■ **F. D. Sharpe**: One of the oldest methods of crime is the Tweedle. . . . The Tweedler spots a ring worth a lot of money in a jeweller's shop and goes . . . to have an exact . . . replica made. He goes in . . . and when the assistant isn't looking very carefully substitutes the fake for the real thing. (1938)

hype (1926) Orig US; originally applied specifically to the deliberate giving of short change, and hence to any cheating or trickery; from the verb *hype* short-change, deceive ■ **Lawrence Sanders**: He's been on the con or hustling his ass or pulling paper hypes. (1970)

rort (1926) Australian; applied to a fraudulent practice; from *rort* engage in corrupt practices ■ **Jean Devanny**: The cockies are supposed to pay this retention money into the bank . . . but normally they don't pay it in. . . . It's the greatest rort ever. (1936)

have-on (1931) Applied to a (playful) deception; from *have on* deceive ■ **Listener**: Puns, tropes, polyglot have-ons, batty new coinings. (1967)

gazump, gasumph, gazoomph, gazumph, gezumph (1932) British; from the verb *gazump* swindle ■ **Youngman Carter**: I've never known an offer from you that wasn't a *gezumph*. (1969)

short con (1932) US; applied to a small-scale confidence racket

carve-up (1935) British; often implying an unfair distribution; from *carve up* swindle, cheat ■ **Times**: Is the selection of justices of the peace in Britain . . . a 'political carve-up', as alleged by some of the more vociferous of the system's opponents? (1963)

pigeon-drop (1937) US; applied to a confidence trick, especially one which starts with a wallet dropped in front of the victim or 'pigeon' ■ **Harney & Cross**: Sometimes it was the 'pigeon-drop'. A purse or billfold containing a considerable amount of money was dropped. The 'sucker' was allowed to find it right along with a member of the mob. (1961)

trickeration (1940) US, Black English; applied to a trick or stratagem; from *tricker(y* + *-ation* ■ **L. Hughes**: I believe my old lady's pregnant again! Fate must have some kind of trickeration to populate the cullud nation! (1951)

con job (1942) Orig US; *con* short for *confidence* ■ **Wall Street Journal**: Meredith, . . . who in 1962 became the first black to enroll at the University of Mississippi, recently called integration a 'con job'. (1989)

swiftie, swifty (1945) Australian; applied to a deceptive trick; usually in the phrase *pull a swiftie* play such a trick; from *swift* fast + *-ie* ■ **Northern Territory News** (Darwin): Not many opportunities for pulling a swifty you'd think. (1962)

Murphy game, Murphy (1959) US; applied to a type of confidence trick in which the victim is duped by unfulfilled promises of money, sex, etc.; from the surname *Murphy* ■ **New York Times**: Everybody should have a car. . . . How are you going to get it? . . . You know, you can get it playing the Murphy. (1966)

hustle (1963) Orig US; applied to a swindle or racket ■ **Malcolm X**: Each of the military services had their civilian-dress eyes and ears picking up anything of interest to them, such as hustles being used to avoid the draft . . . or hustles that were being worked on servicemen. (1965)

scam (1963) Orig US; applied to a swindle or racket, often specifically a fraudulent bankruptcy; origin unknown ■ **Mario Puzo**: The bribe-taking scam had been going on for nearly two years without any kind of hitch. (1978)

prop game (1966) British; applied to a fraud racket by which householders are coaxed into paying heavily for unnecessary repairs; *prop* abbreviation of *property* ■ **Norman Lucas**: The 'prop game' . . . was a method by which men obtained money from old people by posing as officials. (1967)

shucking and jiving (1966) US, Black English; denoting not speaking or behaving seriously, in an attempt to mislead; from *shuck* deceive and *jive* deceive ■ **H. L. Foster**: For many blacks, shuckin' and jivin' is a survival technique to avoid and stay out of trouble. (1974)

rip-off (1970) From *rip off* swindle ■ **Times**: Britain's 41 motorway service areas . . . have attracted such accolades as 'poor', 'appalling' and 'a rip-off'. (1980)

stroke (1970) British; applied to an underhanded trick; especially in the phrase *pull a stroke* play such a trick ■ **John McVicar**: It would be wrong to let Charles go. . . . He's pulled too many strokes. (1974)

See also **leg-pull** and **wind-up** under An instance of mocking at **Ridicule** (p. 331) and **sting** under Stealing, theft at **Crime** (p. 92).

To deceive, dupe

have (1805) ■ **New Yorker**: You've just been had, dummy. (1987)

try it on (1811) Denoting trying to outwit or deceive someone ■ **Mandy**: Huh! Thought you'd try it on, eh? Beat it, the pair of you—I've seen that trick before. (1989)

string (1812) Now mainly US ■ **H. Engel**: I guess I don't have any reason to believe they'd string me. (1982)

pull the wool over someone's **eyes (1842)** Orig US; denoting especially deceiving someone by hiding one's intentions ■ **Guardian**: You can't pull the wool over my eyes. My days of listening to your baloney are over. (1992)

sell (1849) Dated ■ **Charles Leland**: Nor was I 'selling' him, for I certainly had read the works. (1893)

have someone **on (1867)** Denoting deceiving someone playfully ■ L. P. Hartley: 'Of course,' said Dickie, when the boy had gone off with his *mancia*, whistling, 'he's having us on.' (1951)

shanghai (1871) Orig US; denoting putting someone into an awkward situation by trickery; from earlier sense, force into service on a ship ■ J. Gibson: Most of my guests get shanghaied into giving a general knowledge talk to the boys. (1976)

con (1892) Orig US; from *con trick*, *con man*, etc. ■ *Listener*: This mild tale of a shy boy conned into giving a girl a fortune. (1962)

make a monkey (out) of someone **(1900)** Orig US ■ Michael Innes: The plain fact was that Bulkington had . . . made a monkey of her. It was all very mortifying. (1973)

put something **over on someone (1912)** Often in the phrase *put one over on someone* ■ *Church Times*: She may have been fleeced in Florence, robbed in Ravenna, grossly overcharged in Ostia . . .; but *Baedeker* at least has not tried to put one over on her. (1976)

slip something **over (on)** someone **(1912)** ■ B. McCorquodale: It was something he really wanted to know and was trying to slip it over on her unexpectedly. (1960)

spruce (1919) Compare earlier sense, lie; ultimate origin unknown ■ *Daily Telegraph*: A kipper . . . by inference, should cost more than the untreated fish. Who is sprucing whom? (1978)

two-time (1924) Orig US; denoting deceiving or being unfaithful to someone, especially a partner or lover ■ *Sunday Times*: Judith Exner . . . two-timed the late President John Kennedy with a leader of organised crime. (1981)

take someone **for a ride (1925)** Orig US ■ Angus Wilson: But for Vin, there were winks and the tongue stuck in the cheek, the wide boy who wasn't to be taken for a ride by anyone. (1956)

hype (1926) Orig US; denoting originally short-changing or overcharging, and in more recent use deceiving or conning; origin unknown ■ James Baldwin: He doesn't seem to be trying to hype me, not even when he talked about his wife and kids. (1962)

jive (1928) Orig US; from *jive* pretentious or misleading talk ■ W. Thurman: But I jived her along, so she ditched him, and gave me her address. (1929)

take someone **for a sleigh-ride (1931)** US ■ *Sun* (Baltimore): House Republicans, charging that the taxpayers are being taken for a 'bureaucratic sleighride'. (1950)

shit (1934) Denoting teasing or attempting to deceive ■ C. Kilian: Didja see the wave comin' across the Shelf? . . . There was a wave. I'm not shittin' you. (1979)

sucker (1939) Orig & mainly US; from *sucker* gullible person ■ Joseph Gores: Delaney suckered us into making a payment which he now claims is an admission of guilt because we made it. (1978)

come the raw prawn (over, with, etc.) **(1942)** Australian; denoting trying to deceive someone; supposedly from the notion of a raw prawn as something difficult to swallow (i.e.

believe) ■ Rodney Milgate: Don't come the raw prawn . . . you know there's no such thing. Things don't happen just like that. (1968)

shuck (1959) US; from *shuck* something spurious, sham ■ Carolyn Weston: You shucking me, man, I didn't get rid of nobody! (1976)

Murphy (1965) US; denoting deceiving or duping someone by means of the Murphy game ■ James Mills: I thought he was a complainant . . . some school kid who'd been Murpheyed. (1972)

See also **pull someone's leg, pull someone's pisser**, and **wind someone up** under To make fun of someone or something at **Ridicule** (pp. 330–1).

To swindle, cheat

rook (1590) Applied especially to overcharging; from obsolete *rook* swindler, from earlier sense, crow-like bird ■ *Capital Times* (Madison, Wisconsin): The Federal Trade Commission thinks that a lot of people have been rooked by these buying clubs. (1977)

fiddle (1604) Probably from the quick finger movement involved in playing a fiddle (= violin) ■ *Sunday Times*: The unemployed . . . respond in kind, with . . . a frequent willingness to beat or fiddle the system. (1993)

do (1641) ■ *Times*: The disgruntled 'unchurched' . . . seem to think they are being 'done' by rigourists. (1990)

fleece (1772) Applied especially to overcharging; from earlier, more general sense, deprive of (all) money; ultimately from the notion of depriving a sheep of its fleece ■ *Independent on Sunday*: It goes without saying that all three hospitals were intending to fleece me equally. (1991)

diddle (1806) Mainly British; usually denoting petty cheating; origin unknown ■ *News of the World*: The cheeky madame claimed she was diddled out of her fee when . . . our reporter made an excuse and left after she offered sex. (1992)

burn (1808) ■ *Sunday Truth* (Brisbane): I figured I'd burn the guy for a thousand. (1969)

chisel (1808) Dated; presumably related to *chisel* cutting tool, but the reason for the application is not clear ■ Ouida: I never can stand quiet and see people trying to chisel me. (1863)

clean (1812) Denoting fraudulently depriving someone of all or most of their money; usually followed by *out*

put someone **in the hole (1812)** Dated; denoting defrauding someone ■ Jack Black: I thought you put me in the hole for some coin, but I found out that the people lost just what you both said. (1926)

ramp (1812) Dated; probably from earlier sense, snatch, pluck ■ *Chambers's Journal*: The neighbour who's ramped the man that trusted him. (1892)

skin (1819) Often implying depriving someone of all their money by unfair methods; from the notion of removing the skin ■ P. G. Wodehouse: The only thing to do seems to be to get back to the course and skin a bookie or two. (1930)

do someone **out of** something **(1825)** Denoting depriving someone of something by fraud or unfair means ■ M. K. Joseph: The chiefy who done him out of his stripes. (1957)

come it over (or **with**) someone **(1827)** Denoting trying to get the better of someone by trickery ■ Aldous Huxley: When he saw . . . that no attempt was being made to come it over him, he had begun to take an interest. (1939)

hornswoggle (1829) Orig US; origin unknown ■ Sunday Times: The Americans look for value; you can't . . . hornswoggle them. (1970)

sew someone **up (1838)**

beat (1849) US; often in the phrase *beat someone out of something* ■ Columbus Evening Dispatch: The . . . people who try to beat the street car conductors out of their fare. (1904)

whip-saw (1873) US; denoting cheating or being cheated in two ways at once or by the joint action of two others ■ Desmond Bagley: 'Okay, so you've whipsawed me,' said Follet sourly. (1969)

bunco, **bunko (1875)** US, dated; originally denoting cheating someone at bunco; from *bunco* dishonest gambling game played with dice

gyp (1880) Orig US; perhaps from *gyp* college servant at Cambridge or Durham, itself perhaps from obsolete *gippo* scullion, originally a man's short tunic, from obsolete French *jupeau*; or perhaps shortened from *gipsy* ■ Punch: If he . . . thinks the conductor is trying to gyp him . . . he . . . need only look at the fares table. (1962)

rush (1887) British; applied to overcharging ■ N. W. Schur: 'How much did they rush you for that sherry?' To rush is to charge, with the distinct implication that the price was too high. (1973)

wangle (1888) Orig printers' slang; denoting obtaining something by deceitful or devious means; origin unknown ■ Percy Wyndham Lewis: In the last war like yourself I joined the army, instead of wangling myself into some safe job in London. (1942)

skunk (1890) From earlier sense, fail to pay a bill ■ Elizabeth Fenwick: I'm beginning to think we skunked you over the price. (1971)

screw (1900) Mainly North American; compare earlier sense, copulate with ■ Harry Kemelman: In the business dealings between Hirsh and Goralsky, it wasn't Goralsky that got screwed. It was the other way around. (1966)

sell someone **a pup (1901)** British; denoting especially selling someone something worthless ■ Scottish Daily Mail: The Basset is the aircraft the RAF did not want in the first place. They were sold a pup, in more ways than one. (1968)

gold-brick (1902) Orig & mainly US; from *gold brick* something spurious (see under Someone or something spurious at **Genuineness & Spuriousness** p. 425) ■ Munsey's Magazine: Well, look out they don't gold-brick you, sonny. (1914)

gaff (1903) Mainly gamblers' slang; from earlier sense, gamble, toss up ■ Herbert Gold: I want to play you straight fifty-fifty, not gaff you for fifty-fifty. (1965)

scale (1904) Australian & New Zealand; often denoting failure to pay what is owed; origin unknown ■ S. J. Baker: When we are taken down financially we are *scaled*. (1941)

sting (1905) Denoting swindling, especially by overcharging ■ London Magazine: I've no idea how much her son pays her. . . . I like to think she's really stinging her son. (1981)

take (or **send**) someone **to the cleaners (1907)** Denoting fraudulently depriving someone of all or most of their money ■ Guardian: Many a gilded youth . . . has been 'taken to the cleaners' once too often at midnight parties. (1961)

ream (1914) US, dated; compare earlier sense, enlarge a hole with an implement ■ Stanley Kauffmann: Yeah, I smell the rat. Joe Bass's new relatives. Well, palsy, they're liable to ream you yet. (1952)

paper (1925) Denoting defrauding someone by passing a forged cheque

tweedle (1925) Denoting swindling people or playing confidence tricks; from *tweedle* confidence trick ■ P. G. Winslow: 'Tweedling'—small con jobs, mostly against the old and weak. (1975)

clip (1927) Orig US; applied especially to swindling by overcharging; from earlier sense, rob ■ Observer: A commination against London taxi drivers, delivered with the fervour of a guy who'd really been clipped. (1958)

finagle (1927) US; denoting manipulating, altering, or obtaining by fraudulent or underhanded means; from earlier intransitive sense, scheme, intrigue; ultimately from an alteration of British dialect *fainaigue* cheat (of unknown origin) + *-le* ■ Wall Street Journal: The young president . . . already has finagled a $2 billion loan from the Japanese government. (1989)

gazump, **gasumph**, **gazoomph**, **gazumph**, **gezumph (1928)** British; origin unknown ■ Daily Mail: M.P.s had admitted that they had been 'gazoomphed' by fast-talking racketeers. (1961)

yentz (1930) US; Yiddish, from *yentzen* copulate ■ Judith Krantz: 'I don't *yentz* them,' Maggie explained, Coca-Cola-colored eyes all innocence, 'they just yentz themselves and I try not to run out of tape.' (1978)

ikey, **iky**, **ike (1932)** US, offensive; from *ikey* Jew, Jewish moneylender ■ American Speech: He ikied me out of my turn. (1932)

carve someone **up (1933)** British ■ Harold Pinter: Then after that, you know what they did? They carved me up. Carved me up. It was all arranged, it was all worked out. (1959)

pin (1934) Australian, dated

rim (1945) North American; probably a variant of *ream* ■ D. Hughes: Ten bucks? For that old thing? I'd be rimming you, Charles. (1973)

stiff (1950) Orig & mainly US; denoting cheating or defrauding someone, especially by failing to pay them ■ *Washington Post*: What is McCarthy doing when he refuses to tip a waiter who has given good service? . . . He may be cursed by the waiter he stiffs. (1982)

two-time (1959) From earlier sense, be unfaithful to ■ M. M. Kaye: You can't go two-timing the police and skipping out of the country on a stolen passport. (1959)

scam (1963) Orig US; from the noun *scam* swindle ■ *New Yorker*: Local citizens . . . try to avoid being scammed by the familiar tergiversations of city politicians. (1977)

rip someone **off (1971)** Applied especially to overcharging; compare earlier sense, steal ■ *Observer*: Many women think all garages consider they can 'rip off' women drivers. (1976)

stitch someone **up (1977)** British; denoting swindling, especially by overcharging; from earlier sense, incriminate ■ *Woman*: After shelling out £1.50 for a fold-up version [of an umbrella] she found that she'd been stitched up. . . . Two spokes were broken. (1977)

sug (1980) British; denoting selling someone a product under the pretence of conducting market research; acronym from *sell under guise* ■ *Which?*: If someone tries to 'sug' you, write to the Market Research Society. (1988)

A swindler

shark (1599) Originally perhaps from German *Schurke* worthless rogue, influenced by *shark* rapacious fish

sharper (1681) In modern use often applied specifically to a fraudulent card player or other gambler ■ John Maskelyne: [He] falls an easy prey to the sharper. (1894)

sharp (1797) In modern use often applied specifically to a fraudulent card player or other gambler; from *sharper*, probably influenced by *shark* ■ John Maskelyne: The successful sharp . . . must have unbounded self-confidence if his wiles are to be of any avail. (1894)

magsman (1838) Orig British, now Australian; applied to a confidence trickster; from *mag* chatter + *man* ■ *Bulletin* (Sydney): My mate was a top-shelf magsman on the phone and could mimic the tone of gruff arrogance so characteristic of the cop in my day. (1975)

forty (1876) Australian, dated; applied especially to a fraudulent gambler; originally applied to the members of a Sydney gang, perhaps with reference to the tale of Ali Baba and the Forty Thieves ■ M. M. Bennett: Their numbers swelled with rowdies and 'forties'—gambling sharpers who travelled from shed to shed making five pounds by cheating for every five shillings they earned. (1927)

con man (1886) Orig US; *con* short for *confidence* ■ John Wain: I could forgive Even the worst, the con. men who harangue Their fellow artists. (1961)

spieler (1886) Mainly Australian & New Zealand; applied to a swindler, and especially to a fraudulent gambler; from earlier sense, gambler; ultimately from German *Spieler* player ■ W. W. Ammon: I wouldn't even risk cashing her with you mob of spielers around. (1984)

high-binder (1890) US; applied especially to a fraudulent politician; compare earlier senses, rowdy person, member of a secret Chinese gang ■ *Chicago Daily News*: Central characters of both plays are engaging highbinders and sharpies who are not exactly thieves, but more than slightly overoptimistic in their use of . . . other people's money. (1944)

tug (1896) Australian, dated; often applied specifically to a fraudulent card player or other gambler; origin uncertain; perhaps related to *tug* pull or remove by pulling ■ A. Reid: So that chaps could know why a top-notch tug Can work 'his' ramps in a card-room snug. (1933)

con (1897) Orig US; short for *con man*

twister (1897) British; applied to a swindler or deceitful person ■ *Milton Keynes Express*: He was said to have called two women teachers 'cheats and twisters' and had refused to apologise for his remarks. (1976)

gee, gee-man (1898) Applied to a swindler's accomplice planted in a crowd (e.g. to start bidding); origin unknown; compare *gee* guy, bloke ■ *News Chronicle*: Strategically placed in the crowd, the 'gee men' started the bidding going. (1959)

slicker (1900) Orig & mainly US; applied to a plausible person who deceives others ■ *Morecambe Guardian*: He becomes a sort of Midnight Cowboy, lost and confused by the slickers around him. (1978)

four-flusher (1904) US; applied to someone who imposes on others by bluffing; from *four flush* flush in poker containing only four (instead of five) cards and so almost worthless, hence something not genuine ■ L. A. G. Strong: You shouldn't let these four-flushers come it over you. (1944)

take-down (1905) Australian; applied to a deceiver or cheat

heel (1914) Orig US, dated; applied to a double-crosser; probably from *heel* back part of the foot

sprucer (1917) Applied to someone who deceives others, usually playfully; from *spruce* deceive + -*er* ■ *Listener*: I suspect Peter Eckersley was pulling Cutforth's leg. He was a good 'sprucer', as they used to say in Swadlincote. (1968)

chiseller (1918) From *chisel* defraud, cheat + -*er* ■ Edward Hyams: Harry was easy with all men because they were all equal as chisellers. (1949)

snide, snyde (1919) Applied to a cheat or swindler; from earlier, more general sense, contemptible person ■ Auden & Isherwood: Young Waters is playing too. He's no snyde at the game. (1935)

scaler (1924) Australian & New Zealand; from *scale* defraud, cheat + -*er*

twicer (1924) Applied to a cheat or a deceitful or cunning person; from earlier sense, one who does something twice; perhaps from the notion of duplicity ■ E. Wingfield-Stratford: The recent dismissal . . . of that elderly twicer, Sir Harry Vane. (1949)

tweedler (1925) Applied to a swindler or confidence trickster; from *tweedle* swindle + -*er*

■ J. Gosling: The tweedler will flog you sawdust cigarettes or dummy diamond rings. (1959)

two-timer (1927) Orig US; applied to someone who double-crosses or is unfaithful; from *two-time* deceive + *-er* ■ Geoffrey Jenkins: I'd written him off as a two-timer who'd run away to save his own skin. (1974)

rick (1928) Applied to a swindler's accomplice planted in a crowd (e.g. to start bidding); origin unknown ■ *Sunday Telegraph*: If you are standing near a bookie's joint, undecided, and a merchant dashes in and places a bet, such as 'Seventy pounds to forty. On top', don't take a blind bit of notice. It's a rick bet. . . . It don't even go in the book. Its sole object is to push or goad you into making your bet. (1967)

T.B., t.b. (1930) US; applied to a confidence trickster; from the notion of the common element *con*—in *consumption* (= tuberculosis or T.B.) and *confidence* ■ Chester Himes: Men . . . of all stages of deterioration—drifters and hopheads and tb's and beggars and bums and bindle-stiffs and big sisters. (1942)

con artist (1937) Orig US; *con* short for *confidence* ■ *Sunday Telegraph*: Among the hundreds of thousands passing by each day are customers for prostitutes and drug dealers, mugs for con artists—an old, old New York tradition—and victims for street robbers. (1991)

sharpie (1942) Orig US ■ Saul Bellow: He had chosen to be dreamy . . . and the sharpies cleaned him out. (1964)

take (1945) Australian & New Zealand; applied to a swindler or confidence trickster ■ Noel Hilliard: Only the shrewd-heads go for that hard stuff: the shysters, the takes. (1960)

slick (1959) US; applied to a plausible person who deceives others ■ R. D. Abrahams: These stories commonly turn on some way in which the 'slick' manages to trick the white storekeeper 'Mr. Charlie' into giving him respect and service. (1970)

pigeon-dropper (1961) US; applied to a confidence trickster who uses the pigeon-drop ■ Joseph Wambaugh: Pigeon droppers, pursepicks, muggers. Don't walk the Boulevard at night. (1977)

con merchant (1963) Orig US; *con* short for *confidence*

jive-ass (1964) US; from *jive* pretentious or misleading talk + *ass* (= *arse*) ■ C. Brown: 'You jiveass nigger,' Reb said, laughing. 'No, I'm telling the truth.' (1969)

slickster (1965) US; applied to a swindler ■ C. Brown: All the Muslims now felt as though 125th Street was theirs. It used to belong to the hustlers and the slicksters. (1965)

prop man (1966) British; applied to a fraudster operating the prop game ■ *Guardian*: Gangs operating from Leeds are known as 'the prop men' because the racket began in Leeds when so-called property repairers made exorbitant charges after the gales of February, 1961. (1966)

shonky (1979), shonk (1981) Australian; applied to someone who engages in sharp practice; from *shonky* dishonest ■ *Daily Mirror* (Sydney): 'Shonks' cause building blues. (1988)

scammer, skammer (1980) Orig US; compare earlier sense, small-time criminal ■ Leonard Sanders: 'You're good,' he said, ' but not *that* good. Never try to scam a scammer.' (1980)

Inclined to swindle or cheat; deceitful, underhanded

tricksy (1766) From earlier sense, playful, mischievous ■ *Guardian*: Mutual mistrust and incomprehension just about sums it up: the consumers think the manufacturers are tricksy and evasive; the manufacturers suspect the consumers of triviality. (1992)

sneaky (1833) Applied to something underhanded or secretive; from *sneak* go or act furtively + *-y* ■ *Guardian*: This is a Treasury-driven move which has not been thought through and it has been handled in a sneaky way. (1991)

An establishment where one is swindled

clip-joint (1932) Orig US; applied to a bar, club, etc. charging exorbitant prices ■ *Daily Telegraph*: The 'clip joints' specialise in luring customers inside, by means of attractive showcards and insistent 'hostesses', and then fleecing them. (1964)

44. Betrayal

To betray

rat (1812) Applied to deserting one's own side, especially in politics; usually followed by *on*; from the rat's reputation for treacherousness ■ *Listener*: One's feeling for the Chamberlain government was one of such utter contempt that one felt they might very well rat once again. (1969) ■ D. W. S. Hunt: As I heard him say over the lunch table once, 'to rat is difficult; to re-rat . . . ' and he broke off as though to show that to find a description of a second change of party was beyond even his eloquence. (1975)

pool (1907) Australian; often implying incrimination; apparently from earlier sense, share ■ Kylie Tennant: A man thought he'd do the decent thing and tide a girl over a patch of trouble, and she pools him every time. You can't prove it isn't your kid. (1967)

do the dirty on (1914) British ■ D. O. Barnett: I hope our friends the 133rd will . . . do the dirty on their Prussian friends. (1915)

stab in the back (1916) Implying harming someone in a treacherous way ■ F. Olbrich: All these years with me he's been completely honest and now he stabs me in the back. (1979) Hence the noun **stab in the back** such a betrayal (1922) ■ *Economist*: Trade unionists . . . denounced the Lafontaine proposal as a stab in the back. (1988)

two-time (1924) Orig US; denoting deceiving especially a partner or lover ■ *Sunday Times*:

Judith Exner . . . two-timed the late President John Kennedy with a leader of organised crime. (1981)

fink (1925) US; denoting being disloyal to one's associates; often implying incrimination; usually followed by *on*; from the noun *fink* disloyal person ■ *Rolling Stone*: The gang tries to sell their smack to a black hippie pusher who finks on them. (1969)

sell down the river (1927) Orig US; from earlier sense, deliver over to slavery, from the notion of selling a troublesome slave to the owner of a sugar-cane plantation on the lower Mississippi, where conditions were harsher than in the northern slave states ■ Hayward & Harari: It's my considered opinion, Yurochka, we've been sold down the river. (1958)

blow the whistle on (1934) Implying a revelation of what others had wanted kept secret ■ S. Wilson: So Arnie and Alfie blew the whistle on you all. What are you going to do about it? (1978)

dob in (1955) Australian; often implying incrimination; figurative use of British dialect *dob* put down, throw down ■ *Punch*: Those Canberra wowsers have really dobbed us in this time. (1964)

To betray an associate to the police or other authority; to inform (on); to incriminate

See also **dob in, fink, pool** above.

tell (1539) Usually followed by *on* ■ *Age* (Melbourne): Ooh Aah! I'm going to tell on you: I will inform the authorities. (1974)

squeak (1690) Denoting turning informer ■ E. Amadi: All I want you to do is swear to secrecy. I have assured them that you will not sqeak when once you promise. (1986)

split (1795) Often followed by *on* ■ L. Cody: If I tell you, and you ever split on me, I'll make you very sorry. (1982)

snitch (1801) Often followed by *on*; from *snitch* informer ■ Budd Schulberg: I felt a little guilty about snitching on my neighbor. (1941)

nose (1811) From *nose* police informant ■ Edgar Wallace: You come down 'ere an' expect us to 'nose' for you, and everybody in the court knows we're 'nosing'. (1930)

point the (or one's) **finger at (1833)** Denoting identifying someone or something as being responsible for wrongdoing ■ Isobel Lambot: No one is going to point the finger at us. Neither of us has ever stepped out of line. (1987)

stag (1839) Dated; usually followed by *against*; from *stag* informer

squeal (1846) Denoting turning informer; often followed by *on* ■ T. Tryon: Initiation into the club required a scared oath, sworn in blood . . . never to squeal on a fellow member, and never to break the code of silence. (1989)

nark (1859) British, dated; from *nark* police informer ■ Arthur Morrison: It was the sole commandment that ran there: 'Thou shalt not nark'. (1896)

squawk (1872) US; denoting turning informer ■ *Times Literary Supplement*: The thief who 'squawks' is

expelled as professionally infamous; his occupation's gone. (1937)

sneak (1897) British; orig school slang, applied to a child who tells a teacher about the wrongdoings of another pupil; often followed by *on*; from earlier sense, go or behave furtively ■ *Guardian*: Mr Morton was a member of the ratpack, his life devoted to persuading Royal employees and policemen to sneak on their bosses for money. (1992)

shop (1899) Mainly British; from earlier sense, imprison, from obsolete slang *shop* prison ■ S. Knight: One of the men who is thinking very seriously of 'shopping' Tearle, Oates and the reat of the crew told me, 'One word from me and they go down for a long, long while.' (1984)

scream (1903) Denoting turning informer ■ John Morgan: He never got paid . . . and my information is he's ready to scream. (1967)

peep (1911) From earlier sense, speak in a small voice ■ H. E. Goldin: *Peep*, to betray associates; to give information to the police. (1950)`

pot (1911) Australian; probably from *put the pot on* spoil someone's prospects, perhaps influenced by *pot* outdo, outwit ■ Caddie: What dirty swine has potted me? (1953)

snout (1923) Often followed by *on*; from *snout* police informant ■ Edgar Wallace: Dr. Marford knows, but he's not the feller that goes snouting on his patients. (1930)

put the finger on (1924) Orig US; from the notion of pointing out with the finger ■ *Daily Telegraph*: I have not heard of anyone who wants to put the finger on me. (1971)

talk (1924) ■ William Golding: 'I won't talk. I know nothing.' 'Talk. Yes, that is the word. At some point, Mr. Mountjoy, you will talk.' (1959)

turn someone **in (1926)** Denoting giving someone up to the police ■ M. Sokolinsky: If she'd gone to bed with you, she would have enjoyed it—and then she'd have turned you in. (1977)

have the pencil put on one (1929) US, dated; denoting being reported to the police

sing (1929) Now mainly US; denoting turning informer; often in the phrase *sing like a canary* ■ Peter Niesewand: You don't think they'd sing like canaries? . . . They'll sing, Claud. . . . If they thought it would help them, they'd tell on their mothers. (1981)

finger (1930) Orig US; compare earlier *put the finger on* ■ Raymond Chandler: She's on her way back . . . with . . . the pocket money she got . . . for fingering her brother. (1949)

rat (1932) Usually followed by *on*; from *rat* informer, and compare earlier verb sense, desert one's own side ■ *Sun* (Baltimore): Misunas . . . has 'turned State's evidence'—'ratted' in gangland parlance. (1934)

grass (1936) Orig British; used both transitively, often followed by *up* in recent use, and intransitively, often followed by *on*; from *grass* police informer ■ Joyce Porter: It won't come out! Not unless you start grassing. (1965) ■ *Guardian*: On one level is the prison cell where his sister's boyfriend is banged up, having presumably been grassed up. (1992)

shelf (1936) Australian; apparently from *shelf* informer ■ Vince Kelly: 'Is he all right?' . . . 'Of course he's all right. Pat never shelfed a man in his life. The court records show that.' (1975)

See also To speak revealingly at **Communication** (pp. 319–20).

An instance of informing on someone

rumble (1911) Dated ■ *Life*: The boys slip into town. You wouldn't think they would be noticed. But some busybody catches on and puts in a rumble. (1957)

To fail to keep an appointment with

stand up (1902) Orig US ■ Leslie Thomas: 'What about the other agent, the lady?'. . . 'Stood you up, I shouldn't wonder,' laughed Charles. (1978)

A traitor; one who is disloyal to associates

dog (1846) US & Australian; often in the phrase *turn dog on* betray; sometimes implying a police informer ■ Kylie Tennant: Old Sharkey turned dog on us, didn't he, Bet? Said he'd get me for abduction. (1941)

fink (1902) US; from earlier more general sense, despicable person

rat fink (1964) Mainly US ■ Carl Burke: His name was Judas and he was a rat fink. So this dirty rat fink he says to the pres of the gang, Caiaphas, 'What's in it for me if I put the finger on him?' (1969)

One who betrays associates to the police or other authorities; an informer

See also **dog** above.

stag (1725) Dated; often in the phrase *turn stag*; probably from *stag* male deer, but the reason for the use is not known ■ Harrison Ainsworth: As to clapping him in quod, he might prattle—might turn stag. (1834)

snitch (1785) From earlier sense, nose ■ S. Rifkin: Lopez was an informant . . . a paragon among snitches. (1979)

nose (1789) Originally applied mainly to one who informs against fellow criminals, but in more recent usage denoting any police informant; probably from the notion of the nose as a symbol of inquisitiveness; compare the similar semantic development of *snitch* and *snout* ■ R. Edwards: He knew that CID men are allowed to drink on duty because much of their time is spent with 'noses' or informants. (1974)

split (1812) Dated; from *split* inform on someone

stool-pigeon (1845) Orig US; from earlier senses, pigeon fastened to a stool as a decoy, person employed as a decoy ■ June Thomson: A stool pigeon planted in a local Gestapo prison to eavesdrop on the detainees. (1974)

pigeon (1849) Short for *stool-pigeon* ■ Dell Shannon: A lot of our pigeons offer the info to the other side too. (1971)

nark (1860) British; from Romany *nāk* nose ■ *Times*: If it was thought we were coppers' narks it could endanger the lives of our film crews. (1975)

squealer (1865) From *squeal* turn informer + *-er* ■ John Wainwright: The vengeance of the Clan against squealers . . . would be both hard and painful. (1976)

pimp (*a*1885) Australian & New Zealand; compare earlier sense, manager of prostitutes ■ Xavier Herbert: 'I'm not a pimp.' 'What you mean pimp?' 'I'm not a police-informer.' (1938)

fizgig, phizgig (1895) Australian; compare earlier sense, silly or flirtatious young woman ■ *Sun-Herald* (Sydney): We described him as rather a big crim and also a 'fiz gig'—an interesting word that means a grass, an informer. (1984)

sarbut, sarbot (1897) Birmingham dialect; apparently a proper name ■ Roger Busby: Your sarbut's story wasn't good enough. . . . We were fooled. (1969)

rat (1902) Compare earlier sense, contemptible person ■ George Jackson: You see every time a rat does get put away, the prison authorities always release a different reason for the attack, never that he was an informant. (1970)

screamer (1903) From *scream* turn informer + *-er* ■ *John o' London's*: An informer . . . is now more often referred to . . . as a *singer* or a *screamer*. (1961)

squeaker (1903) From *squeak* turn informer + *-er* ■ Alan Hunter: Dutt had been brooding over the tip-off mystery. . . . The squeaker must have been Rampant. (1973)

stool (1906) US; short for *stool-pigeon* ■ B. Cobb: He said he wasn't a stool, he wasn't giving anybody away. (1962)

snout (1910) Orig British; applied to a police informant; from earlier sense, nose ■ *Observer*: You may have been 'grassed' . . . by a 'snout'. (1982)

finger (1914) From the notion of pointing out with the finger

shelf, shelfer (1916) Australian; probably from the phrase *on the shelf* out of the way ■ W. Moxham: 'Who's going to split? His word wouldn't carry much weight.' 'I'm no shelf.' (1969)

stoolie (1924) US; from *stool* informer + *-ie* ■ Ed McBain: The policeman trusted the stoolie's information. . . . The stoolie trusted the policeman. . . . Cops were averse to working with pigeons they did not know and trust. (1958)

lemon (1931) US; applied especially to a criminal who turns State's evidence ■ George Ingram: 'You think you got the low-down on me: well, see me put it on you!' 'You talk like a "lemon"!' (1935)

grass (1932) Orig British; perhaps short for *grasshopper*, rhyming slang for *shopper* (compare *shop* betray to the police) or for *copper* (= police officer) ■ James Curtis: Tell you the details and then you'll do the gaff on your jack . . . or else turn grass. (1936)

narker (1932) British; from *nark* act as an informer + *-er*

singer (1935) Dated; from *sing* turn informer + *-er*

top-off, top-off man, top-off merchant (1941) Australian; probably an alteration of *tip-*

off ■ H. C. Baker: 'Don't have much to say to that bloke,' he advised, 'he's a top-off.' (1978)

fizzer, **fizz** (1943), **phizzer** (1974) Australian; from fiz(gig + -er ■ *Australian Short Stories*: 'See any drugs over there? . . . We catch twenty a week over there,' he lied. 'Mostly through fizzers.' (1985)

grasser (1950) British; from *grass* inform on someone + -er ■ Roderic Jeffries: 'How reliable was the original information?' 'As reliable as any information is from a grasser.' (1968)

Moreton Bay (1953) Australian; short for *Moreton Bay fig*, rhyming slang for *fizgig* informer ■ *Bulletin* (Sydney): Fifty percent of the Drug Squad's arrests are based on information received and woebetide a user, supplier or anyone else who becomes a dog, a gig or, as the police term it, a Moreton Bay. (1984)

supergrass (1978) British; applied to an informer who tells the police about the activities of a large number of criminals ■ *Listener*: Following information from a supergrass, dozens of people alleged to be members of it had been arrested. (1983)

gig (1984) Australian; short for *fizgig* informer; compare earlier *gig* busybody

(Something) that gives one away

tell-tale (*a*1577) ■ *Wall Street Journal*: Hoses sometimes snake across streets—telltale signs that neighbors are borrowing water from each other again. (1989)

give-away (1882) Orig US; also applied to an (inadvertent) revelation of the facts; often in the phrase *dead give-away* ■ Patrick Quentin: Her expression was a dead give-away. (1959)

45. **Exploitation**

To behave or obtain exploitatively

sponge (1673) Denoting obtaining something from someone exploitatively or living parasitically on another; often followed by *on* or *off*; from the notion of a sponge sucking things up ■ *Guardian*: The Government goes on about people sponging off the state. (1992)

tap (1901) Denoting obtaining something from someone exploitatively; often followed by *for* ■ *Tucson* (Arizona) *Magazine*: Many of the big plush resorts that tap you for $80 to $100 a day. (1979)

gold-dig (1923) Orig US; applied to a woman who marries or forms a sexual relationship with a man solely for the sake of financial gain; back-formation from *gold-digger* ■ John Steinbeck: I'll bet she just gold-dug Eddie. (1947)

promote (1930) Dated, orig US; denoting obtaining exploitatively ■ Z. N. Hurston: You skillets is trying to promote a meal on me. (1942)

lig (1981) British; denoting freeloading, especially by gatecrashing; compare earlier sense, loaf about ■ *Radio Times*: [I] suddenly twigged what ligging was all about when I got my first job as a researcher on *Aquarius*. I found . . . I could get free tickets for everything, everywhere. (1985)

An exploiter

shark (1599) Applied to someone who unscrupulously exploits or swindles others; originally perhaps from German *Schurke* worthless rogue, influenced by *shark* rapacious fish

sponger (1677) Applied to someone who lives at another's expense; from *sponge* obtain things

exploitatively + -er ■ *North Lindsey Star*: Those spongers on the nation's earnings are quite happy without work. (1890)

gold-digger (1915) Orig US; applied to a woman who marries or forms a sexual relationship with a man solely for the sake of financial gain; from earlier sense, one who digs for gold ■ John Braine: It was expensive; that appealed to Lois. Not that she was a gold-digger; but once he started going around with her there were more withdrawals than deposits in his Post Office savings book. (1959)

ligger (1977) British; applied to someone who gatecrashes parties, a freeloader; from *lig* freeload + -er ■ *Observer*: The UK [Snooker] Championship is that sporting anachronism, a ligger-free zone. (1996)

Something that exploits people

tourist trap (1939) Applied to a thing or now usually place that attracts tourists to buy but is overpriced ■ Oswald Wynd: The village . . . [was] now a tourist trap almost entirely given over to eating houses and souvenir shops. (1967)

One that is exploited

doormat (1861) Applied contemptuously to someone who accepts bad treatment without complaint; from the notion of 'wiping one's shoes on' someone ■ *Observer*: She is not such a nullity and 'doormat' as Miss Byron. (1930)

meal ticket (1899) Orig US; applied to someone or something regarded solely as a source of income or livelihood; from earlier sense, ticket entitling a person to a meal ■ Hartley Howard: He was her meal-ticket. Why should she want him sent to the pen? (1972)

46. **Slyness, Artfulness**

Sly, artful

no flies on someone **(1848)** Orig Australian or US; probably from the notion of cattle so active that flies do not settle on them ■ *Observer*: There are no flies on Benaud. If England start bowling their overs slowly, no one will have to draw his attention to it. (1961)

carney, carny (1881) From the obsolete dialect verb *carn(e)y* wheedle ■ **Edward Blishen**: Macbeth was pretty carney in the way he handled Banquo. (1955)

ikey (1889) Derogatory & offensive, dated; compare earlier sense, conceited; ultimately from *ikey* Jew ■ **Farmer & Henley**: Artful little ikey little ways. (1892)

crazy like a fox (1908) Orig US; popularized by its use as a title by the US humorist S. J. Perelman (1944) ■ **Maurice Procter**: 'Crazy,' Martineau mused. 'Crazy like a fox. And as hard to catch.' (1967)

A sly person

fox (*a*1000) ■ **Mayne Reid**: I could not help reflecting on the strange stratagem by which the old fox had saved himself. (1851)

sly-boots (*a*1700) Mainly jocular ■ **Stanley Elkin**: 'Cunning,' Hartshine said, 'absolutely cunning! Wasn't *he* the old slyboots?' (1992)

shrewd-head (1916) Australian & New Zealand ■ **Noel Hilliard**: Only the shrewd-heads go for that hard stuff: the shysters the takes. (1960)

47. **Secrecy, Confidentiality, Concealment**

See also **Communication** (p. 316)

Done or kept in secret

q.t. (1884) Usually in the phrase (*strictly*) *on the q.t.* secretly; abbreviation of *quiet* ■ **Arnold Bennett**: Mind you this is strictly q.t.! Nobody knows a word about it, nobody! (1910) ■ **New Yorker**: This is strictly on the q.t., Senator. (1972)

on the side (1893) Orig US; often used with reference to extramarital sexual affairs ■ **R. L. Hudson**: What would some of you say if I told you that I, as a married man, have had three women on the side? (1968)

hush-hush (1916) Reduplicated form of the interjection *hush* be quiet ■ **Private Eye**: A hush hush top-level inquiry. (1970)

under wraps (1939) ■ *Dumfries Courier*: Show visitors will see numerous others which are still under wraps until nearer the Show. (1978)

Told in confidence

mum's the word (*a*1704) Used as an injunction not to reveal a secret; from the obsolete interjection *mum* hush, be quiet

between you (and) me and the gate-post (1871) Variant of earlier *between you (and) me and the bed-post* (1830–82), *between you (and) me and the post* (1838–73) ■ **P. H. Johnson**: Strictly between you and me and the gate-post, Colonel, I don't care for them. (1959)

To conceal or be concealed

stash (1797) Orig criminals' slang; origin unknown ■ **Damon Runyon**: She must have some scratch of her own stashed away somewhere. (1937)

hole up (1875) From earlier sense, go into a hole or hibernation or shelter ■ **Nicholas Blake**: I bet you Elmer's holed up in Harwich, or somewhere near it. (1954)

lie low (1880) Denoting going into hiding or behaving so as not to attract attention ■ *Wall Street Journal*: How much easier it is to lie low and not engage the enemy if nobody can see you. (1989)

lie (stay, etc.) doggo (1893) Denoting remaining hidden or motionless so as not to be noticed; *doggo* probably from *dog* ■ **Fitzroy Maclean**: Lying doggo with an expression of angelic innocence when he came to see if she was in bed and asleep. (1955)

tuck away (1912) Denoting placement in a concealed or secluded place ■ *Daily Telegraph*: The gardens and backyards of houses tucked away in the town's tortuous streets. (1991)

A hiding place

lurk (1906) Applied to a place where one can meet others in secrecy; from the verb *lurk* stay hidden ■ **J. Gardner**: I met her in a servant's lurk. (1974)

stash (1927) From *stash* conceal ■ **R. Chapman**: If we were on a bank job in a strange city the stash would be in a room we had rented several weeks in advance. In a small town, though, you don't have any stash, because an hour after you moved in everybody in the burg would be checking in. (1930)

trap (1930) US, mainly criminals' slang ■ *Time*: Other mobsters keep their escape money in bank safe-deposit boxes or hiding places called 'traps'. (1977)

Something hidden

stash (1914) From *stash* conceal ■ *Daily Telegraph*: Chief Insp. Newark said he was satisfied Barnes had no stashes of money hidden away. (1979)

In or into hiding

in(to) smoke (1908) Mainly Australian ■ **K. S. Prichard**: Meanwhile Tony's got to be kept in smoke? (1967)

48. Energy, Vigour

Energy, vigour, vitality

get-up (1841), get-up-and-get (1870), get-up-and-go (1907) Orig US ■ P. G. Wodehouse: He'll make a name for himself one of these days. He's got get-up in him. (1915) ■ *Punch*: Tortoises are not easy to race because they are devoid of get-up-and-go. (1962) ■ **Lady Bird Johnson**: Lyndon went to church. . . . I am sorry I did not have the get-up-and-get to go with him. (1964)

jism, chism, gism, jizz (1842) Origin unknown ■ Samuel Beckett: A week will be ample, a week in spring, that puts the jizz in you. (1967)

vim (1843) Orig US; probably from Latin *vim*, accusative singular of *vis* strength, vigour ■ *Independent*: His neo-pop collages are bursting with mental vim and vigour. (1991)

go (1864) From earlier application, with regard to horses, to power of going, mettle ■ **George Leslie**: Physically, he is a wonderful man . . . very wiry, and full of energy and go. (1892)

razzle-dazzle (1889) Rhyming formation on *dazzle* ■ *New York*: It [*sc*. a musical] has pizzazz and razzle-dazzle, bursts of energy and invention, music and laughter. (1978)

zip (1900) From earlier use representing the sound of rapid movement ■ *Independent*: The new blood has put some zip in the team. (1991)

punch (1911) Orig US; from earlier sense, blow with the fist ■ *Oadby & Wigston Advertiser*: Chances were created but there was just no punch up front. (1976)

pep (1912) Abbreviation of *pepper* ■ P. G. Wodehouse: That seems to be all the poor fish is able to do, dash it. He can chafe all right, but there he stops. He's lost his pep. He's got no dash. (1923)

zing (1918) Orig US; from earlier sense, high-pitched sound ■ *Spectator*: While death has not lost its sting, sex has undoubtedly lost its zing. (1985)

stingo (1927) Dated; from earlier sense, strong beer ■ *Observer*: Some shanties, sung by Raymond Newell and a chorus, are full of stingo. (1928)

sock (1936) US; from the verb *sock* hit ■ *Arizona Daily Star*: I figure we have enough speed and sock in our lineup to score runs. (1979)

oomph (1937) Orig US; imitative ■ *Church Times*: This prayer may take the form of thanks—for the fact that I am alive with enough energy and oomph to my personality to hate and lust. (1977)

pizzazz (1937) Orig US; origin unknown ■ G. V. Higgins: Maybe some guy that could recruit more troops and out-fund us gets himself involved in a bloodletting with another guy who has some pizzazz, and . . . they knock each other off. (1975)

piss and vinegar (1942) ■ Roger Busby: Jacko's not such a bad bloke. Full of piss and vinegar and ready to jump for any bugger with braid on his hat. (1978)

zizz (1942) Compare earlier sense, buzzing sound ■ *Times*: The Queensgate centre lacks, perhaps, finesse and a touch of zizz. (1983)

moxie (1943) US; compare earlier sense, courage ■ *Vanity Fair*: She was enrapturing, she was just captivating, she had the same moxie she has today. (1992)

zap (1968) Orig US; from the verb *zap* hit forcefully ■ *New Yorker*: He gives the film a manic zap. (1984)

To instil with vigour, liven up

pep up (1925) From *pep* energy ■ Winifred Holtby: Keep it vivid. Pep it up with a bit o' farce. (1931)

juice up (1964) ■ James Mills: The departmental surgeon asked Jackson if he wanted him to give Lockley a shot of something, he meant juice him up a little, keep him from passing out. (1972)

zap (1979) Orig US; often followed by *up*; from *zap* liveliness, energy ■ *Family Circle*: How to find shoes, hats, accessories that zap last year's clothes to look like new. (1986)

To be lively

hum (1887) Orig US; from earlier sense, be filled with the sound of many voices ■ *Washington Post*: But back at the Insect Club, Englert's most profitable venture, business is humming. (1993)

hot up (1936) British; denoting increasing in vigour, liveliness, or excitement

jump (c1938) Orig US; denoting being full of liveliness and excitement; often in the phrase *the joint is jumping* ■ Jimmy Sangster: The place was really jumping. It took me three minutes to locate the bar through the smoke haze. (1968)

swing (1957) ■ David Lodge: Jane Austen and the Theory of Fiction. Professor Morris J. Zapp. . . . 'He makes Austen swing,' was one comment. (1975)

Energetic, vigorous, lively

rambunctious, rumbunctious (1830) Orig & mainly US; denoting boisterousness; origin unknown; compare earlier *rumbustious* ■ *Time*: Brezhnev inherited many problems from his rambunctious, buccaneering predecessor, Nikita Khrushchev. (1976)

riproarious, riprorious (1830) Orig US; denoting vigour or boisterousness; from *rip* tear, after *uproarious* ■ R. W. Chapman: The *Dictionary of American English* . . . stopped at 1900, before the trickle of that rip-roarious idiom became a flood. (1948)

rip-roaring (1834), rip-snorting (1846) Orig US; denoting vigour or boisterousness ■ *Daily Mail*: It's a rip-roaring, red-blooded yarn that no man or woman will be able to read unmoved. (1923) ■ *Topeka* (Kansas) *Capital*: It is now stated that Bryan will make a rip-snorting speech at the St. Louis convention. (1904)

full of beans (1854) Originally from the notion of a horse fed on beans ■ *Economist*: Lord Cockfield, though 71 years old, is still full of beans. (1988)

rorty (1882) Applied to someone or something boisterous or noisy, coarse or earthy, or crudely comic, and also used as a more general adjective of approval; origin unknown ■ W. Tute: The rorty brigadier must have a taste for lean stringy meat, though of course she had been a baronet's daughter and that made up for a lot. (1969)

sparky (1883) From earlier sense, emitting sparks ■ *Daily Mail*: Would the gratuitously brutal simulated rape he is allowed to perpetrate on Sheila Reid's sparky, larky Irish Nurse have been countenanced when Dame Edith Evans essayed this role? (1991)

hopped up (1923) US; denoting someone full of vigour and enthusiasm; from *hop* narcotic drug ■ Ivor Drummond: A hopped-up son with anarchist-pacifist connections. (1973)

punchy (1926) From *punch* vigour + *-y* ■ *Time*: More gregarious than Woodcock, a punchier speaker, a hair more liberal, Fraser signals a change in style rather than substance. (1977)

bubbly (1939) Denoting vivaciousness; from earlier sense, full of bubbles ■ Barr & York: Tudors are bubbly girls, man-chasers, 'always talking about boys' according to other schools. (1982)

hyper (1942) Orig & mainly US; applied to someone who is extraordinarily active, energetic, or highly strung; short for *hyperactive* ■ *Dirt Bike*: Andre Malherbe never hopped from sponsor to sponsor like a hyper bumblebee in search of a bit more honey. (1985)

jivey, **jivy** (1944) Mainly US; probably from *jive* lively dancing + *-y*

hyped up (1946) Orig US; applied to someone who is over-excited or highly strung; from the notion of the effects of an injection with a hypodermic needle ■ V. Johnston: If some hyped-up character goes past at seventy miles an hour, we'll take out after him. (1970)

zingy (1948) From *zing* vigour, liveliness + *-y* ■ *Guardian*: A zingy collection . . . that every with-it girl is going to adore. (1962)

swinging (1958) Dated ■ Harold Wilson: The press publicized what they called the new swinging style of the Downing Street receptions. (1971)

zizzy (1966) From *zizz* vitality + *-y* ■ *Guardian Weekly*: Zizzy little TV charts. (1983)

zappy (1969) Orig US; from *zap* energy + *-y* ■ *Listener*: The company felt the need for a zappier profile. (1984)

An energetic or lively person

stem-winder (1892) US; applied especially to someone who makes vigorous rabble-rousing speeches; compare earlier sense, keyless watch ■ J. F. Dobie: He's a stemwinder and go-getter. (1926)

go-getter (1921) Orig US; applied to an enterprising person ■ Frank Swinnerton: The go-getter despises the non-go-getter; but never as much as the non-go-getter despises the go-getter. (1926)

tear-arse, (US) **tear-ass** (1923) Applied to a very active, busy person ■ James Fraser: You'll need to settle down. You can't be a teararse all your life. (1976)

dynamo (1938) Often in the phrase *human dynamo*; from earlier sense, machine producing electricity ■ David Ogilvy: I have to rely on . . . empirical techniques for spotting creative dynamos. (1963)

ball of fire (1953) ■ Nancy Mitford: Yes, I know her. Not a ball of fire, is she? (1960)

Energetic activity

go (1965) Especially in the phrase *it's all go* ■ *New Statesman*: Believe me, it's all go with these tycoons, mate. Life's just one frenetic whirl of soigné secretaries and sex-mad air 'ostesses. (1965)

To lose energy

run out of steam (1961) ■ Dick Francis: When I'd run out of steam, they would begin to nod while they listened. (1973)

49. Laziness

A lazy person; a shirker

lazy-bones (1592) ■ J. & M. Stern: Most pop-culture beatniks were silly sorts of characters played for laughs, foremost among them the amiable bongo-patting lazybones Maynard G. Krebs. (1992)

loafer (1830) Applied to someone who spends their time idly; perhaps from German *Landläufer* tramp, from *Land* land + *laufen* (dialect *lofen*) run ■ Virginia Woolf: Half a dozen good-natured loafers offer their services. (1931)

soldier (1840) Nautical, orig and mainly US; mainly in the phrase *old soldier* ■ Bruce Hamilton: He's a bit of an old soldier, but a first-rate seaman, and a hundred per cent reliable at sea. (1958)

mooner (1848) Dated; applied to someone who goes about listlessly; from *moon* move listlessly + *-er* ■ *Punch*: The ancient grey Bridge is delightful to moon on, For ne'er such a spot for the mooner was made. (1884)

passenger (1852) Orig British university slang, applied to a member of a rowing crew who does not pull his weight, and hence to a member of a group who does not contribute any effort and so has to be supported by the others ■ Angus Wilson: If you haven't any appreciation at all for serious research work, then the sooner you get out . . . the better. We're carrying enough passengers already. (1961)

bummer (1855) US; applied to an idler or loafer; perhaps after German *Bummler* one who wanders around idly ■ William Black: A system of local government controlled by 30,000 bummers, loafers, and dead-beats. (1878)

bum (1864) Applied to a lazy shiftless person or a habitual loafer; probably short for *bummer* idler, loafer ■ New Scientist: Then my neighbours start screaming, 'Galileo, you lazy bum, get into bed. You got to go look for work tomorrow.' (1983)

piker (1889) Orig US; compare earlier senses, cautious gambler, sponger ■ H. W. Tilman: He is definitely no piker and although only 22 is one of the old school and believes in discipline. (1971)

scrimshanker, scrimshank (1890) Orig and mainly services' slang; applied to a malingerer or one who avoids duty; from the verb *scrimshank* malinger (+ -er) ■ Evelyn Waugh: Brigade expects us to clean up the house for them. I should have thought some of those half-shaven scrim-shankers I see lounging round Headquarters might have saved us the trouble. (1945)

bench-warmer (1892) US; applied originally to someone who sits idly on a bench, especially a substitute in a sports team, and hence more broadly to any lazy or ineffectual person ■ Los Angeles Times: He thought about leaving after the 1984 season, his third straight year as a bench-warmer. (1986)

sooner (1892) Australian; applied to an idler or shirker; said to be from *sooner* rather, from the notion that such a person would sooner be idle than work ■ Vance Palmer: 'The dirty sooners!' he burst out. 'They don't know a man when they find one, those heads down south.' (1948)

slacker (1898) Applied to someone who avoids work or exertion; from *slack* be lazy + -er ■ Robin Maugham: 'You're a slacker and you're a shirker,' he said. 'You're a little runt in many ways. But you're the best of the lot of them.' (1969)

bludger (1900) Australian; applied to a loafer or someone who avoids his duties; from earlier sense, prostitute's pimp ■ Sydney Morning Herald: The only people who would benefit from full pay on workers' compensation would be 'genuine loafers, shirkers or bludgers,' the Chief Secretary, Mr Willis, said in the Legislative Assembly yesterday. (1971)

clock-watcher (1911) Applied to someone who does no more work than is strictly necessary; from the notion of repeatedly looking at a work-place clock to see if it is time to stop ■ Dorothy Sayers: Mr. Tallboy had left promptly at 5.30. Mr. Copley had seen him go. Clock-watchers, the whole lot of them. (1933)

gold-brick (1914), **gold-bricker** (1919) US; applied to a lazy person or a shirker; from earlier sense, worthless thing, sham ■ John Steinbeck: In the ranks, billeted with the stinking, cheating, foul-mouthed goldbricks, there were true heroes. (1958)

lead-swinger (1918) British; applied to a malingerer or shirker; from the phrase *swing the*

lead malinger ■ Daily Telegraph: 'It would soon put a stop to lead-swingers who take a few days off to paint the house or watch cricket,' the doctor added. (1973)

layabout (1932), **lie-about** (1937) ■ New Scientist: Those of us gifted by nature with inertia but maligned by society as layabouts. (1962) ■ Guardian: This former lie-about has got himself married. (1961)

poler (1938) Australian; applied to a shirker; from *pole* impose or sponge on someone + -er

skiver, skyver (1941) Orig services' slang; from *skive* shirk + -er ■ Daily Telegraph: A Labour-controlled council is to crack down on 'skivers' following a report which alleges large scale absenteeism and sick leave among its manual workers. (1977)

spine-basher (1945) Australian; applied to a loafer; from *spine-bash* rest, loaf about + -er

beach bum (1962) Applied to someone, especially a youth, who hangs about on beaches ■ Observer: He is the reverse of the popular image of a 'surfie' as a beach bum. (1963)

sack rat (1978) US; from *sack* bed ■ Herman Wouk: A perfect solution, you young sack rat. (1978)

couch potato (1979) Orig US; applied to someone who spends leisure time as passively as possible (especially watching TV or videos), eats junk food, and takes little or no exercise; from the notion of reclining like a vegetable on a *couch*; the use of *potato* apparently derives from the original Couch Potato club, founded by cartoonist Robert Armstrong, who represented the typical *boob-tuber* (see at **Entertainment** p. 347) as a vegetable 'tuber', the potato; the expression is said to have been coined by Tom Iacino ■ New Musical Express: [She] gave up opportunities in the world of modelling and in Tinseltown LA in order to stop her kids becoming couch potato video generation trash brains. (1987)

To be lazy; avoid work

loaf (1838) Denoting spending one's time idly; probably a back-formation from *loafer* idle person ■ Economist: At worst he spends Sunday loafing around the cinemas or public houses. (1987)

moon (1848) Denoting behaving or moving about listlessly and unproductively; usually followed by *about* or *around*; from the notion of being moonstruck, distracted or dazed as if by the influence of the moon ■ Jerome K. Jerome: I . . . did nothing whatever, except moon about the house and gardens. (1886)

mike (1859) British; applied to hanging around idly or shirking work; origin unknown; compare British dialect *mitch* skulk, play truant, apparently from Old French *muchier, mucier* hide, lurk ■ P. Evett: [He would] spy on us as we worked, and then . . . thunder at any one he thought was miking. (1974)

lallygag, lollygag (1862) US; applied to dawdling or idling around; origin unknown ■ Springfield (Mass.) Union: The Dow Jones average of 30 industrials, which lollygagged most of the day, gained strongly in afternoon trading. (1973)

scrimshank (1890) Orig and mainly services' slang; applied to malingering or shirking one's duty; origin unknown ■ Iris Murdoch: I was just telling Hilary we saw him skrimshanking yesterday. (1975)

slack (1904) Probably from *slack* lacking rigour, lax, lazy, although previously recorded as a verb in standard use with the meaning 'be idle' in the 16th century ■ *Guardian*: Bond's own attacking partners, Morley and McAvennie, were not exactly slacking but failed to make use of some neat and imaginative approach work. (1991)

dog it (1905) Orig US; applied to acting lazily or half-heartedly, or to shirking or avoiding responsibility, risk, etc.; from the notion of the dog as an idle creature ■ Al Alvarez: Most guys playing for that kind of money will dog it, but Doyle's got no fear. (1983)

spruce (1917) British, orig services' slang; applied to malingering or shirking one's duty; origin unknown ■ G. M. Wilson: Dr. Meunier's no fool, he'd have known if she was sprucing. . . . Malingering. Faking tummy trouble. (1967)

swing the lead (1917) British, orig army slang; applied to malingering or shirking one's duty; apparently from the notion of someone taking depth soundings from a ship with a plumb line (with a lead weight on the end) who sits idly rather than engaging in duties involving exertion ■ *Daily Express*: He said he . . . had been 'swinging the lead' for the purpose of getting a permanent pension. (1927)

bludge (1919) Australian; applied to avoiding effort, especially by relying on others' exertions; from earlier sense (not recorded until later), live on the earnings of a prostitute ■ J. H. Fullarton: You were one of the 95 per cent who bludged at base in Enzed or England or Yankee-land. (1944)

dodge the column (1919) Orig services' slang; applied to someone shirking their duty or avoiding work ■ Howard Spring: My father, so great an expert in dodging any column he didn't see the point of joining. (1955)

skive, skyve (1919) Orig services' slang; applied to someone shirking their duty or avoiding work; often followed by *off*; perhaps from French *esquiver* dodge, slink away, but compare earlier English dialect *skive* move quickly, dart ■ Jessica Mann: The girls who dig are always glad of an excuse to skive off and have a rest. (1973)

gold-brick (1926) Orig and mainly US; denoting having an easy time or shirking; from *gold-brick* shirker ■ Mary McCarthy: Students with applied art or science majors tended to gold-brick on their reading courses. (1952)

goof (1932) Mainly US; applied to idling or wasting time, and also to shirking one's duties; often followed by *off*; from earlier sense, fool about ■ *New Yorker*: If you ever feel like goofing off sometime, I'll be glad to keep the old ball game going and fill in for you here. (1968)

plotz (1941) US; denoting originally sitting down wearily, and hence slouching or lounging around lazily; from Yiddish *platsen*, from Middle High German *platzen* burst, influenced by German *Platz* seat ■ J. Kirkwood: He just kind of plotzed around waiting to fall into some sort of a cushy job. (1960)

spine-bash (1941) Australian; denoting resting or loafing about; from the notion of lying on one's back ■ Roland Robinson: They would rather have stayed in the camp to spine-bash or go down to the swy game. (1958)

skate (1945) US; denoting avoiding obligations or shirking; compare earlier sense, leave quickly ■ *Observer*: I'm not a woman's libber but I don't want to skate (shirk). (1979)

do a never (1946) Nautical, dated; applied to shirking or loafing

lig (1960) Denoting loafing about; from a dialectal variant of *lie* repose ■ *It*: It's a time for ligging in the streets and doing your thing, man. (1969)

piss about (1961) Applied to spending one's time unproductively or futilely ■ T. Lewis: Are you coming in? Or do we piss about all day? (1970)

veg, vedge (1980) Orig and mainly US; denoting passing the time in mindless or vacuous inactivity, especially by watching TV; usually followed by *out*; from *veg* abbreviation of *vegetable*, from the notion of vegetating ■ *Independent*: Cold rubbery pizzas for paralytic lager louts vegging out in front of the late-night movie. (1988)

Laziness; avoidance of work

Maori P.T. (1961) New Zealand; from the Maoris' alleged relaxed attitude to life

A period of lazy inactivity

mike (1825) British; applied to a period of idleness or shirking; compare *mike* hang around idly ■ *Times*: The day of the cheerful veteran forward, gratefully relying upon opportunities for a mild 'mike', may be coming to an end. (1958)

lie-in (1916), lie (1930) Mainly British; applied to staying in bed longer than usual in the morning ■ Gillian Freeman: I'm going to 'ave a bit of a lie in . . . seeing I'm on 'oliday. (1959) ■ Daphne du Maurier: Have a good long lie tomorrow morning. Don't attempt to get up. (1938)

bludge (1943) Australian; also applied to a job needing no effort; from the verb *bludge* avoid effort ■ Jon Cleary: He was happy in his job, it was a good bludge. (1949) ■ *West Australian*: Prime Minister Gorton . . . quoted . . . as saying . . . he was coming to . . . the Commonwealth Prime Ministers' conference 'on a bit of a bludge'. (1969)

Lazy

bone lazy (*a*1825), bone idle (1836) From the notion of being lazy 'to the bone', through and through ■ W. D. Pereira: You should see 'is eldest kid. . . . Bone idle. Goes to one of them ritzy schools, but it won't 'elp 'im none. (1959)

Thought and Communication

1. Belief & Disbelief

To believe

Adam-and-Eve (1925) Rhyming slang ■ E. A. Thorne: A *baby*! Would you Adam-and-Eve it! (1956)

buy (1926) Orig US ■ Mary McCarthy: It doesn't seem likely to me that they cooked it up between them. . . . More likely she half guessed and he told her. I'm willing to buy that for what it's worth. (1952)

To be believable

wash (1849) ■ *Spectator*: He was not to be taken in by plausibilities that 'wouldn't wash'. (1911)

Believe me!

stand on me (1933) British ■ G. F. Newman: You'll be all right, stand on me. (1970)

I don't believe it!

stuff and nonsense (1749) ■ George Eliot: Stuff and nonsense! I don't believe a word of it. It's all a got-up story. (1871)

tell it (or that) to the marines (1806) Apparently from marines' reputation among sailors for being credulous ■ Dick Francis: 'When this is over you can sleep for a fortnight.' 'Yeah?' he said sarcastically. 'Tell it to the marines.' (1967)

my eye (1842) ■ William Faulkner: 'How about Bigelow's Mill . . . that's a factory.' 'Factory my eye.' (1929)

get away (1848) ■ Desmond Cory: 'Do you speak Spanish?' 'Of course I do. I *am* Spanish.' 'Get away.' 'I am. I can prove it.' (1969)

go on (1886) ■ Harold Pinter: *Ben*. The lorry started and ran over him. *Gus*. Go on! *Ben*. That's what it says here. *Gus*. Get away. (1960)

garn (1886) British; representing a Cockney pronunciation of *go on!*

dicken, dickin, dickon (1894) Australian; probably a variant of the exclamation *dickens* or the personal name *Dickens*

come off it (1912) ■ *Listener*: On which side was the preponderance of wealth, as of men and armaments? Do come off it, Mr. Mansfield. (1969)

tell me another (one) (1914) ■ Alistair Campbell: 'I've always looked on you as a friend—perhaps the only true friend I have.' 'Come of it,' I snorted. 'Tell me another one. I'd sooner be friends with a snake.' (1991)

tie that bull outside (or to another ashcan) (1921) US ■ Eugene O'Neill: Aw say, you fresh kid, tie that bull outside! (1933)

my foot (1923) ■ H. E. Bates: 'But it's a serious matter for you.' 'Serious my foot. Why should I worry?' (1961)

hell (1925) Used in expressions like *like hell* and *will I hell* to indicate strong disagreement ■ H. MacInnes: 'I've quite enjoyed it here.' Like hell I have, she added under her breath. (1941)

phooey, phooie (1929) Orig US; from *phoo* expressing disbelief + -*y*

sez you (1931) *sez* a jocular representation of a colloquial pronunciation of *says* ■ B. Graeme: 'He's . . . not nearly so useful in a rough house.' 'Sez you!' Sanders growled. (1973)

my arse (1933) ■ Wilcox & Rantzen: 'I think we should both be pleased that she's made this friendly gesture—even if it is a little eccentric.' 'Eccentric my arse,' he said, shocking me into silence. (1981)

gertcha, gercha, gertcher (1937) British; alteration of *get away* (or *along*) *with you* ■ G. Carr: 'Gertcha!' The orator . . . elbowed him away. (1963)

Aunt Fanny (1945) Especially in the phrase *my Aunt Fanny* ■ G. Carr: 'Agree my Aunt Fanny,' retorted the other loudly. (1954)

get off (1958)

stroll on (1959) British ■ Peter Tinniswood: 'Excuse me, but do you by any chance suffer from hay fever?' 'No,' said Brenda Woodhead. 'Why?' 'Well, your eyes are all puffy and you've got a red nose.'—Bloody rotate, Carter. Bloody stroll on. (1985)

do me (or us) a favour (1963) ■ *Guardian*: Was she hoping to get engaged during the year of the tour? 'Good God, no, do us a favour.' (1969)

pull the other one, (it's got bells on) (1966) Orig as a response to the notion that someone is trying to *pull one's leg* (= make one believe an untruth) ■ Desmond Bagley: 'She doesn't hold the mineral rights.' 'Pull the other one,' scoffed Eric. (1975)

bollocks (1969) British; from earlier sense, nonsense ■ *Guardian*: 'But are we out to get a pound note or are we pulling tarts?' 'The one with high heels fancies you.' 'Bollocks.' 'I'm telling you.' (1992)

2. Understanding

To understand or realize the meaning of something

savvy, **savee**, **savey** (**1785**) Used especially in a question (e.g. 'Do you savvy?'), following an explanation especially to a foreigner or someone thought slow-witted; from Black or pidgin English, after Spanish *sabe usted* you know ■ Malcolm Lowry: Let's have two starboard lights. Savee starboard lights? (1933)

twig (**1815**) From earlier sense, catch sight of ■ 'Tivoli': Make a howler or two, or else he'll twig you've cribbed. (1897)

drop (**down**) **to** (or **on** (**to**)) (**1819**) ■ Russell Braddon: It was the only place we *could* live—without being caught that is. Surprises me you never dropped to it, Mr Prime Minister, sir. (1964).

read someone **like a book** (**1844**) Used to denote easy understanding of a person's thoughts, motives, etc. ■ P. G. Wodehouse: That terrible old woman saw through my subterfuge last night. She read me like a book. (1933)

tumble (**1846**) Used to denote grasping the meaning or hidden implications of an idea, circumstance, etc.; often followed by *to, that* ■ *New Statesman*: By the time you tumble that your drum has been turned over, we're miles away. (1962)

get (or **take**, **have**) someone's **number** (**1853**) Used to denote understanding of a person's real motives, character, etc. ■ *Times Literary Supplement*: Field-Marshal Lord Montgomery . . . had [Augustus] John's number right away. 'Who is this chap?' he demanded to know. 'He drinks, he's dirty, and I know there are women in the background!' (1975)

take a tumble (**to oneself**) (**1877**) Orig US; used to denote realization of the facts of one's situation ■ M. Gee: After a while I give up, and I take a tumble to what's happening. I'm getting the rush. (1959)

catch on (**to**) (**1884**) Orig US ■ Leslie Charteris: He's dumb enough to think that Lucy won't catch on to the extracurricular functions of that busty secretary. (1949)

rumble (**1886**) Used to denote a grasping or recognition of something intentionally concealed ■ Edwin Newman: 'Have you any influence with him?' 'He'd rumble that. He'd think I was your agent.' (1979)

jerry (**to**) (**1894**) Mainly Australian & New Zealand; origin unknown ■ *Bulletin* (Sydney): I should've jerried when the guy gave me the tug. (1975)

get (or **be**) **next** (**to** or **on**) (**1896**) US ■ *Black World*: If he can't get next to what we're about, we'll just have to school him. (1973)

get wise (**to**) (**1896**) Orig US ■ F. H. Kitchen: There would be the very devil to pay if Crutchley . . . got wise to their existence. (1923)

get (**1907**) ■ Iris Bromige: Fiona broke into peals of laughter and became quite helpless for a few moments. 'Don't get it,' said Julian. (1956)

be (or **get**) **jerry** (**on**, **on to**, **to**) (**1908**) US, dated; origin unknown ■ *Flynn's*: I know that th' fly was jerry because he gave me th' once over as I was comin' out. (1926)

have something or someone **taped** (**1914**) Used to denote complete understanding of something or someone; probably either from the notion of tying something up with tape so as to have complete control over it or from the notion of measuring something with a tape ■ *Athenaeum*: 'I got you taped,' an N.C.O. may say to a man, meaning 'I know what you are up to.' (1919)

take a jerry (**to**) (**1919**) Australian & New Zealand; compare *jerry to* in same sense

wise up (**to**) (**1919**) Orig & mainly US ■ *Wall Street Journal*: Antique dealers are wising up to the growing demand for old radios. (1971)

cotton on (**to**) (**1929**) From earlier sense, develop a fondness for ■ Nevil Shute: 'How long have they been doing this?' 'God knows. We've only just cottoned on to it.' (1940) ■ *Observer*: I can see how to put things over. I cotton on quick. (1959)

dig (**1934**) Orig US; perhaps from earlier sense, study hard at a subject, from the notion of strenuous digging ■ *New Yorker*: I just don't dig any of these guys. I don't understand their scenes. (1969)

get the picture (**1938**) Used to denote the grasping of a situation ■ Nicholas Luard: I explained all this. . . . He seems to get the picture. (1975)

know the score (**1938**) Used to denote grasping the essentials of the present situation ■ J. D. Salinger: You've been around schools long enough to know the score. (1962)

click (**1939**) Used to denote that something suddenly becomes clear or understood ■ Anthony Burgess: Then the name clicked, because somebody in the town had talked about Everett. (1960)

get it in one (**1942**) Used to denote immediate comprehension or grasping of a situation ■ Catherine Aird: 'What we are checking on is whether someone tried to kill him. . . .' 'Got it in one, Sloan.' (1975)

the penny drops (**1951**) Used to denote sudden realization or recognition; from the notion of a penny dropped into a slot machine and activating the mechanism ■ *Times*: The penny had begun to drop even before the present fuel crisis. (1973)

latch on (**to**) (**1962**) From earlier sense, grasp or grab something ■ John Wain: It was a long time before I could latch on to what was happening. Then I got it. (1962)

get the message (**1964**) Used to denote the grasping of the import of something said ■ Dan Lees: They don't seem able to make up their minds whether to warn me off or knock me off but I do get the message loud and clear and . . . I'm going. (1972)

gotcha, **gotcher** (**1966**) Used to say that one has understood; representing a casual or

non-standard pronunciaton of (*I have*) *got you*
■ Hillary Waugh: 'Give her background a once-over on your way to Springfield. . . . You might try for a record of her blood type first. She claims it's O but she doesn't carry any card.' Wilks sighed. 'I gotcha.' (1966)

suss (out), **sus (out)** (1966) British; from earlier sense, suspect ■ *Daily Telegraph*: 'If ever my members sussed out that I can't read, I'd be a gonner,' he said. (1975)

get a handle on something (1972) Orig US; used to denote acquiring the means of understanding or of forming an opinion about something ■ *Miami Herald*: I'm still trying to get a handle on our offense. (1984)

3. **Knowledge & Ignorance**

Intelligence

brains (1763) ■ *Daily Mail*: Her 23-year-old co-presenter, who is a trained ballet dancer, has also proved she has brains as well as beauty. (1991)

the upper storey (1885) Used in referring to someone's level of intelligence ■ I. & P. Opie: A person who is 'wanting in the upper storey' is . . . daffy. (1959)

up top (1961) Used in referring to someone's level of intelligence ■ Francis Warner: Mousey little creature, bless her, not much up top if y'know what I mean. (1972)

grey matter (1965) From earlier technical sense, darker tissues of the brain ■ P. G. Wodehouse: I've never been a brainy sort of guy, and what I want is a wife with about the same amount of grey matter I have, and that's how Vee stacks up. (1965)

smarts, **smart** (1970) US; from *smart* clever ■ *Guardian Weekly*: They complain that the level of intelligence is low and that the soldiers have neither the smarts nor the education to work the complicated weapons of modern warfare. (1981)

Good sense

gumption (1719) Orig Scottish; applied to practical good sense or initiative; origin unknown

savvy, **savee**, **savey** (1785) From *savvy* know (see at **Understanding** p. 297) ■ W. R. Titterton: Which idea . . . Armstrong actively disliked because, having more savvy than I had, he saw it meant death to his doctrine. (1936)

horse sense (1832) Orig US; applied to practical good sense and shrewdness ■ I. Wallach: Summoning up his best horse sense (and trying to forget that the horse is an uncommonly stupid animal), Andrew said, 'I agree with Mr. Clifton.' (1960)

common (1906) British; short for *common sense* ■ Harold Pinter: You mutt. . . . Have a bit of common. They got departments for everything. (1960)

Something unintelligible

(all) Greek to (1600) From the notion of ancient Greek as an unintelligible language ■ *Nation* (New York): Schubert clothed his melodies in wondrous harmonies, which were 'Greek' to his contemporaries. (1892)

To defeat someone's understanding

beat (1882) Mainly in the phrase *beats me* ■ Walter de la Mare: Why you should have taken so much trouble about it simply beats me. (1930)

lose (1962) Mainly in the phrase *you('ve) lost me* I don't understand what you've said ■ H. Van Siller: Frazer . . . looked up, frowning. 'You've lost me. What do you mean, exactly?' (1967)

Knowledgeable, clever

cute (1731) Now mainly US, often derogatory; alteration of *acute* ■ *Wall Street Journal*: Shorting big stocks to play little stocks sounds like a cute strategy. But it may be too clever by half. (1989)

fly (1811) British, dated; applied to someone who is very knowing or wide-awake; origin uncertain; perhaps from the verb *fly* ■ Charles Dickens: 'I am fly', says Jo. (1852)

up to snuff (1811) British, dated; applied to someone who is knowing or not easily deceived; apparently from the notion of being old or experienced enough to take snuff

brainy (1845) From *brain* + *-y* ■ Monica Dickens: Betty's fiancé was an undersized but brainy boy. (1956)

savvy (1905) From *savvy* good sense, probably with the ending re-interpreted as the adjectival suffix *-y* ■ *Economist*: A savvy tenant putting a deposit on his house gains a 12-month option to buy at the price ruling when he made the deposit. (1980)

smart-arsed, **smart-arse**, (US) **smart-assed**, **smart-ass** (1960) Derogatory; applied to someone or something ostentatiously or smugly clever ■ *Globe & Mail* (Toronto): It is tempting to be smart-assed when reviewing a Richard Rohmer novel. (1979)

wise-assed (1967), **wise-ass** (1972) US, derogatory; applied to someone or something ostentatiously or smugly clever; probably modelled on *smart-ass(ed)* ■ J. Poyer: Listen to what I have to say, then you can make all the wise-ass remarks you want. (1972)

pointy-headed (1972) US, derogatory ■ *New York Times*: Let the dust gather on the pointy-headed bureaucrats and all the other props from yesteryear. (1975)

A knowledgeable or clever person

clever Dick, **clever-boots** (1847), **clever-clogs** (1866) Applied to a smart or knowing person; mainly used ironically or sarcastically;

Dick from the male personal name ■ I. & P. Opie: There is bound to be some clever-dick who has hidden in a coal-hole and refuses to show himself. (1969) ■ *Listener:* On each double-spread billing page it is three columns to the populars and eight for the clever-clogs. (1983)

smart alec, smart aleck, smart alick (1865) Derogatory, orig US; applied to a know-all; often with capital initial(s); *alec* from the male personal name, a diminutive of *Alexander* ■ Charles Barrett: One smart Alick came to . . . offer his services in return for a large tin of pineapple slices. (1942)

wise guy (1896) Derogatory, orig US; applied to a know-all ■ Budd Schulberg: Listen, wise guy, . . . if you found something wrong . . . why didn't you come and tell me? (1941)

wisenheimer, weisenheimer, wiseheimer (1904) US, derogatory; applied to a know-all; from *wise* + *-enheimer*, as in German names such as *Oppenheimer* ■ *Washington Post:* Then some wisenheimer from the agency decided we needed a trailer. (1959)

egghead (1907) Orig US, usually derogatory; applied to an intellectual ■ *Scientific American:* I fear that, while publicly unspoken, anti-intellectualism and suspicion of 'eggheads' may have been a factor. (1955)

brain (1914) ■ Edgar Wallace: I felt like a fourth form boy listening to a 'brain', and found myself being respectful! (1923)

long-hair (1920) Orig US, usually derogatory; applied to an intellectual; from the stereotypical view of intellectuals as having long hair

brains (1925) Used in the phrase *the brains of* (or *behind*) to denote the cleverest person in a group or the master-mind of a scheme ■ *American Speech:* Big man, the brains behind a dope ring; the one who seldom takes the rap. (1936) ■ *Times:* Admiral Sir William Wynter, 'the brains' of the victory. (1958)

smarty-pants (1941) Orig US; applied to a know-all ■ Monica Dickens: He jumped right in with his slick talk. . . . That smarty pants. (1953)

sharpie (1949) Orig US; compare earlier sense, swindler, cheat

clever-sticks, clever stick (1959) Applied to a clever, smart, or knowing person; often used ironically or sarcastically ■ Compton Mackenzie: Some cleversticks had climbed up a plane-tree to get a better view. (1964)

smarty-boots, smartie-boots (1962) Applied to a know-all ■ Joyce Porter: He was grateful that smartie-boots MacGregor had overlooked the obvious, too. (1965)

smart-arse, (US) smart-ass (1965) Derogatory; applied to a know-all ■ J. Barnett: He had indulged in reckless speculation. . . . He was just as much a smart-arse as the Farnham D.I. (1981)

wise-ass (1971) US, derogatory; applied to a know-all; perhaps a combination of *wise guy* and *smart-ass* ■ John Irving: Benny Potter from New York—a *born* wise-ass. (1978)

pointy-head (1972) US; applied disparagingly to an intellectual or expert; probably a back-formation from *pointy-headed* ■ *Times:* Mr Wallace . . . dismissed it quickly at the end of his address as 'the most callous, asinine, stupid thing that was ever conceived by some pointy-head in Washington DC'. (1972)

bright spark (1974) Usually used ironically or sarcastically ■ *New Scientist:* Some bright spark thought Windsor Castle was on fire and called the fire brigade! (1983)

To be knowledgeable

know what's what (a1553) Denoting a general competence or worldly-wisdom

know a thing or two (1792) Denoting either general competence or a thorough knowledge of one's subject ■ P. G. Wodehouse: The serfs and vassals now know a thing or two and prefer to make their living elsewhere. (1973)

know how many beans make five (1830) Often implying that someone is not easily fooled ■ Anthony Gilbert: Mr. Crook knew how many beans make five. (1958)

know beans (1833) US; mainly used in the negative, denoting ignorance ■ *Independent:* We have this very amusing scene in which George Cole as Root will call you a fool and suggest that you don't know beans about your business. (1991)

know the time of day (1897) Denoting a general competence or worldly-wisdom ■ Ouida: 'She knows the time o' day', said the other. (1897)

know what one is talking about (1921) Often used in the negative, denoting speaking in ignorance ■ *Sun* (Baltimore): The dealer 'popped off without knowing what he was talking about'. (1943)

know one's onions (1922) Denoting either general competence or a thorough knowledge of one's subject ■ Joanna Cannan: Shakespeare knew his onions, didn't he? (1958)

know one's stuff (1927) Orig US; denoting a thorough knowledge of one's subject ■ Agatha Christie: 'He gave me a lot of knowledge about planting things.' 'Yes, he knew his stuff, as you might say.' (1973)

know all the answers (1933) Often used disparagingly, implying smug knowledgeability ■ A. L. Rowse: The positive old lady in the garden, who knew all the answers and could not be told anything, had not ceased to be a marvellous politician. (1955)

To behave in a smugly clever way (towards)

smart-ass (1970) ■ J. Ross: 'I guess it's something to do with the generation gap, sir.' 'Don't smart-ass me!' (1978)

To be very familiar with something

know something **backwards (1904)** ■ *Financial Times:* An eclectic collector . . . , he knows the showrooms backwards. (1983)

know something **inside out (1921)** ■ Nicolas Freeling: A restaurant—that's a simpler affair, and Marguerite knows it inside out. (1967)

know something **like the back of one's hand (1943)** ■ Mary Stewart: I know the district like the back of my hand. (1956)

To lack knowledge

not know someone **from Adam (1784)** Denoting ignorance of someone's identity ■ *Washington Post*: They didn't know me from Adam. They just liked the fact that I was professional and that I had a strong art background. (1993)

dunno, dunna(w), etc. **(1842)** Representing a casual pronunciation of (I) *don't know* ■ Peter Moloney: A sed 'Wharar thee wack?' 'A dunno,' she said back. (1966)

search me (1901) Orig North American; used, mainly in response to a question, to indicate that the speaker does not know the answer or has no idea what to do ■ Dick Francis: 'Where did he go for the summer?' I asked. . . . 'Search me.' (1965)

ask me another (1910) Used to indicate that one does not know the answer to a question ■ Ivy Compton-Burnett: 'Devoted?' said Josephine, raising her brows. 'Ask me another. I am not in a position to give you an account of their feelings.' (1933)

not (have) the foggiest (1917) Used, mainly in response to a question, to indicate that the speaker does not know the answer or has no idea what to do; shortened from *not have the foggiest idea, notion*, etc. ■ J. B. Priestley: 'Is that a good idea?' asked Laura. 'My dear, I haven't the foggiest.' (1951) ■ P. McGerr: 'Then you've no idea what his play's about?' 'Not the foggiest,' she said cheerfully. (1967)

not have a clue (1948) ■ Edward Hyams: 'Sorry, old boy,' he said. 'I haven't a clue.' (1951)

To be ignorant

not know one's arse from one's elbow (1930) ■ Linacre Lane: Don't know 'is arse from 'is elbow. (1966)

not know shit from Shinola (*c*1930) US; *Shinola* from the proprietary name of a brand of shoe polish ■ *Fortune*: We'll package them together for people who don't know s- from Shinola. (1987)

(not) know from nothing (1936) US ■ F. Feikema: Them San dietitians, they don't know from nuthin'. (1945)

Ignorant

pig-ignorant (1972) Denoting crass ignorance ■ Tim Heald: Those press johnnies . . . would never twig. Too gullible and too pig ignorant. (1976)

4. Skill

A skilled person

wizard (1620) From earlier sense, man with magic powers ■ *Times*: Judge Kennet . . . noted that Mr Tzour had been noted as a financial wizard. (1975)

dab (1691), dab hand (1828) Origin unknown ■ *Economist*: Mrs Holladay has provided a beautiful room and, being a dab hand at fund-raising, lots of money. (1987)

ringer (1848) Australian & New Zealand; often applied specifically to the fastest shearer in a shed (1871); from British dialect *ringer* something supremely good ■ Thomas Wood: He can shear a hundred a day: a hundred and twenty, a hundred and fifty; two hundred—even three hundred and twenty, at times, if he is a Ringer—that is the quickest of the team. (1934)

no slouch (1879) Orig US; used to suggest that someone is skilled at a particular activity; from the earlier phrase *no slouch of a* . . . *quite a good* . . . , from *slouch* lazy or incompetent person ■ R. Holles: He was making his pile. . . . He's certainly no slouch in the business world. (1978)

mivvy (1906) Compare the earlier obsolete senses (perhaps not the same word) a marble, (*derogatory*) a woman; ultimate origin unknown ■ Osmington Mills: He's a mivvy with anything like that. (1959)

whizz, whiz, wiz (1914) Orig US; perhaps from *whizz* buzzing sound, via the intermediate sense, something remarkable, but in this sense regarded as short for *wizard* skilled person (whence the spelling *wiz*) ■ *Financial Times*: He has since become a whizz at ping pong. (1982)

hot-shot (1933) Orig US; often used attributively ■ *Guardian*: He was one tenth of a second quicker in practice than the current grand prix hotshot, John Kocinski. (1991) ■ John Wainwright: These hot-shot scientists. They love the limelight. (1973)

whizzo (1977) From *whizz* + *-o* ■ *Sydney Mirror*: Electronics whizzo Dick Smith . . . aims to become the taxman's friend in another way. (1981)

Highly skilled or capable

great (1784) Now followed by *at* ■ *Guardian*: Scotland have shown that they are great at counter-attacking and forcing mistakes. (1991)

nifty (1907) Orig US; from earlier sense, smart, splendid ■ *Observer*: Duncan was nifty on occasions, indeed scored an immaculate goal, but was at other times rather daintily ineffective. (1975)

hot (1914) ■ *Surf '70* (New Zealand): Walsh is not the only hot surfer in New Plymouth. (1970)

mustard (1925) ■ *Daily Express*: Britain is particularly hot on calculus. The Russians and the East Germans are mustard on the theory of numbers and on solid geometry. (1972)

pie (1941) New Zealand; usually used with *on*; from Maori *pai* good

shit-hot (1961) ■ Martin Amis: They've elected a new guy. . . . I don't know anything about him. Except that he's shit-hot. (1973)

bionic (1976) From earlier sense, having electromechanical body parts ■ *Washington Post*: No one in the emergency room seemed to speak English. . . . After two hours, the woman who is frequently described as 'unflappable' and 'bionic' did the appropriate thing. She sat down and cried. (1984)

Skill

green fingers (1934) Applied to exceptional skill at growing plants. Hence **green-fingered** (1946) ■ *Lancet*: Trees like this . . . would soon be produced by hybridisation and plant-hormones under the green-fingered genius of him and his helpers. (1966)

green thumb (1943) Mainly US; = *green fingers* ■ *Listener*: Every kind of briar, of bush rose, of rare bulb, and flowering tree flourished under her green thumb. (1962)

To be skilled at something

have something **down to a fine art (1919)** ■ *Guardian*: I spoke to some stylish regular travellers who had got living out of a suitcase down to a fine, and lightweight, art. (1992)

A skill-less person

rabbit (1904) Applied to an inferior or novice player ■ Agatha Christie: He could get no fun out of playing [golf] with a rabbit like me. (*a*1976)

5. Sanity

Sanity

buttons (1860) Dated ■ N. H. Kennard: They said . . . he had not 'got all his buttons', meaning that he was not 'all there'. (1893)

marbles (1927) Orig North American ■ *Ottawa Journal*: 'I still have most of my marbles,' he said cheerfully. (1973)

The head as the repository of sanity

upstairs (1932) ■ G. W. Brace: He just ain't right upstairs. (1952)

the upper storey (1959) ■ I. & P. Opie: A person who is 'wanting in the upper storey' is . . . daffy. (1959)

Failing sanity

white ants (1908) Australian; especially in the phrase *have white ants* be eccentric or dotty; from the destructiveness of termites or white ants ■ I. L. Idriess: A hardened old nor'-wester can develop a few white 'ants', as well as the veriest new-chum. (1937)

Sane

The terms in this category are often used in negative contexts, implying 'insane'.

compos mentis (1616), compos (1809) Latin, in control of the mind; originally standard English, but latterly (especially in the abbreviated form *compos*) colloquial or jocular; see also **non compos** under Mad (p. 301) ■ Bruce Hamilton: Honestly, is he quite *compos*? (1958)

right (1662) Euphemistic; often in such phrases as *right in the* (or *one's*) *head* ■ J. Hocking: We've got an old aunt of mine in the carriage who isn't exactly right. (1896) ■ M. L. Roby: He ain't right in the head. Got a few marbles missing. (1967)

all there (1864) ■ Edward Hyams: I've never known a really good cow-hand quite all there. (1949)

with it (1961) ■ W. J. Burley: There's an old man, living in a home. . . . He's quite with it—I mean he's mentally alert. (1985)

To be sane

have one's head screwed on (the right way) (1821) Applied to a sensible or level-headed person ■ *Daily News*: Elizabeth has, to use a slang phrase, 'her head very well screwed on'. (1900)

Mad

There is a continuum of usage between 'mad' in the clinical sense, at one extreme, and 'eccentrically foolish or strange' at the other. For convenience, the continuum is divided into two here, 'Mad' and 'Crazy, eccentric', and words are assigned to the one to which they most typically belong. But many are capable of being used in both senses, and with several gradations of connotation in between.

non compos (1628) Originally standard English, but latterly colloquial or jocular; short for *non compos mentis*, Latin, not in control of the mind; compare **compos mentis** at Sane (p. 301)

out of one's head (1825), off one's head (*a*1845) ■ Laurence Meynell: That old woman's a Tartar. No wonder the Duke's gone off his head. (1981)

nuts (1846) Probably from earlier sense, wildly enthusiastic *about* (1785), but compare *nut head*, *off one's nut* mad, and *nut* mad person ■ Nevil Shute: 'Gee,' said Wing Commander Dewar, 'this thing'll drive me nuts.' (1953)

off one's nut (1860) From *nut* head ■ W. R. Burnett: If you think you can muscle into this joint you're off your nut. (1929)

off one's chump (1864) From *chump* head ■ Angus Wilson: This chap Beard seems to be off his chump. He's evacuated all the wallabies. (1961)

loco (1887) Orig US; from Spanish *loco* mad ■ Dick Francis: He'd been quietly going loco and making hopeless decisions. (1965)

off one's onion (1890) From *onion* head ■ H. G. Wells: He come home one day saying Tono-Bungay till I thought he was clean off his onion. (1909)

off one's pannikin (1895) Mainly Australian; from *pannikin* head (from earlier sense, metal drinking vessel) ■ C. J. Dennis: Per'aps I'm orf me pannikin wiv' sittin' in the sun. (1916)

off one's trolley (1896) ■ N. R. Nash: If you suspect Patty, you're off your trolley! (1949)

off one's rocker (1897) From *rocker* curved bar on which something rocks ■ Evelyn Waugh: It's going to be awkward for us if the Emperor goes off his rocker. (1932)

stir-crazy, stir-nuts, stir-simple (1908) Mainly US; applied to someone mentally deranged (as if) from long imprisonment; from *stir* prison ■ Washington Post: A Democratic President would go 'stir crazy' without a depression or war to occupy his time. (1960)

magnoon, macnoon, magnune, mangoon (1917) Australian, orig services' slang; from Arabic ■ Richard Beilby: She could be a bit magnoon in the head. Women are funny like that. (1970)

poggle, puggle, poggled, puggled (1923) British, mainly services' slang; from earlier obsolete slang *poggle, puggle, puggly* mad person, idiot, from Hindustani *pāgal, paglā* mad person ■ B. W. Aldiss: A woman in this bloody dump? You're going puggle, Page, that's your trouble! Too much tropical sun. (1971)

blah (1924) Dated ■ Telegraph & Telephone Journal: The third class is hopeless. . . It consists of the people who, in New York slang, have gone 'blah'. (1924)

doolally, doolally tap (1925) British, orig services' slang; representing a spoken form of *Deolali* (Marashtra, India), site of a British army camp + obsolete *tap* malaria, from Persian *tap* fever, heat ■ James Curtis: What's the matter with that bloke? Doolally? (1936)

off one's rocket (1925) Dated; *rocket* probably replacing *rocker*

off one's conk (1926) From *conk* head ■ Harold Pinter: Why are you getting on everybody's wick? Why are you driving that old lady off her conk? (1959)

mental (1927) ■ James Patrick: They must be mental. . . . Shit-bags the lot o' them. (1973)

round (or around) the bend (1929) ■ J. I. M. Stewart: Right round the bend . . . I mean . . . as mad as a hatter. (1955)

lakes (1934) Shortened from *Lakes of Killarney*, rhyming slang for *barmy* ■ Margery Allingham: Which is not like a bloke who's done a killing unless he's lakes. (1955)

ravers (1938) British, dated; from *raving* (mad) + *-ers* ■ Edward Hyams: 'You said you wanted to meet Sylvester Green. Well, here I am.' . . . 'Stark ravers. I served for

two years with Green. This man isn't even much like him.' (1951)

certifiable (1939) From earlier technical sense, so deranged as to be officially certified insane ■ *Observer*: That I should bet money on the hated adversaries caused even close friends and colleagues to ask which side Wales had been on in the war, and forced a Chilean journalist called Niden Iconomow to consider me certifiable. (1991)

troppo (1941) Australian; applied to someone mentally unhinged (as if) from exposure to a tropical climate; often in the phrase *go troppo*; from *trop(ic* or *trop(ical) + -o* ■ Barry Humphries: Am I going troppo? Mum's gettin' hitched again? (1979)

yarra (1943) Australian; from the name of a mental hospital at *Yarra* Bend, Victoria ■ *Sydney Morning Herald*: Kingston Town is a good horse . . . but in my opinion he would not have lived with Phar Lap. I know a lot of people will say I'm 'Yarra'; but that's my belief. (1980)

rock-happy (1946) US services' slang, dated; applied to someone mentally unhinged from serving too long on a (Pacific) island

bananas (1957) Orig US; perhaps from *banana oil* nonsense ■ Judith Krantz: Jesus, thought Lester, his first movie star and she turns out to be a bit bananas. (1978)

bonkers (1957) Orig British; origin uncertain; recorded earlier (1948) in the sense 'slightly drunk' ■ Simpson & Galton: By half-past three he'll be raving bonkers. (1961)

round the twist (1960) British; based on *round the bend* ■ Desmond Bagley: I swear Ogilvie thought I was going round the twist. (1977)

off one's gourd (1961), out of one's gourd (1963) US; from *gourd* head

starkers (1962) British; from *stark (raving mad) + -ers* ■ L. P. Davies: You belted out of that room. . . . They thought you were starkers. (1972)

out of one's tree (1966) US ■ Newton Thornburg: 'We is duh [= the] loanees.' 'You're out of your tree.' (1976)

barking mad, barking (1968) British; from the notion of barking like a mad or uncontrollable dog ■ Richard Ingrams: It was considered perfectly in order for a man who was clearly barking mad to sit for many years dispensing justice to his fellow citizens. (1984) ■ *Sunday Telegraph*: The fact that she comes across as slightly batty is a cause of great annoyance to the Member for Billericay. ('Barking' is how a journalist who interviewed her for the Spectator put it.) (1991)

out of one's skull (1968) ■ Gore Vidal: I thought that Kalki was out of his skull. (1978)

whacked out (1969) US; compare *wacky* crazy, eccentric

off one's nana (1975) Compare earlier *do one's nana* lose one's temper ■ *Australian*: 'We've all learned to laugh at ourselves and our predicament,' Trevor England said. 'If we hadn't we'd all be off our nanas.' (1975)

A mad person

crazy (1867) Orig US; rare before the late 1960s; noun use of the adjective *crazy* ■ *Guardian*: There's no leadership at all. All this is being done by the street crazies. (1969)

loony, looney (1884) From the adjective *loony* crazy ■ L. Cody: The man was clearly a loony and she wondered how Mr Brierly would deal with him. (1982)

mental (1913) Often applied specifically to a mental patient ■ F. De Felitta: 'What's to prevent him from going?' 'He is a mental.' (1973)

psycho (1942) Abbreviation of *psychopath* ■ Colin MacInnes: Wiz has for all oldies . . . the same kind of hatred psychos have for Jews or foreigners or coloureds. (1959)

nutter (1958) British; often applied to a violently deranged person; from *nut* crazy person + *-er* ■ Andrew Garve: I reckon Chris was right, Rosie—King's a nutter. I reckon he'll go on killin' till there ain't no one left. (1963)

retard (1970) Orig US; applied to a mentally retarded person ■ New Yorker: The younger son, self-described as 'a hard-core retard', dreams of escaping to the wilds of Oregon to gambol with the bears and squirrels. (1971)

head case (1971) Mainly British; applied to a mentally deranged person, and hence to someone whose behaviour is violent and unpredictable ■ James Kelman: Wee Danny could pot a ball with a headcase at his back all ready to set about his skull with a hatchet if he missed. (1983)

sickie, sicky (1973), sicko (1977) North American; applied to someone who is mentally ill or perverted; from *sick* + *-ie, -o* ■ Peter De Vries: 'Shall I . . . make it clear . . . I'm a sickie?' 'No! . . . this— ailment of yours . . . it's an expression of some deep-seated conflict.' (1974) ■ *Chicago Sun-Times*: Is it asking too much for these sickos to stop bothering decent women? (1982)

Someone with a particular mental illness

schizo (1945), schiz (1955) *schiz* mainly North American; abbreviations of *schizophrenic* ■ J. I. M. Stewart: He might have been a schizo . . . for all the tie-up there seemed to be between the Phil of this rational conversation and the Phil who wanted Jean Canaway. (1961) ■ Alison Lurie: How can you tell what a schiz like her is going to do? (1967)

klepto (1958) Abbreviation of *kleptomaniac* ■ E. V. Cunningham: You got it . . . right out of Helen Sarbine's purse. . . . What are you—some kind of nut or klepto? (1964)

pyro (1977) Abbreviation of *pyromaniac* ■ M. Bringle: A pyro grateful for rain. . . . Now I've heard everything. (1987)

To be or become mad

have a screw loose (1833) ■ *Lancashire Life*: An endearing little chap with a screw loose. (1977)

have (or get) a rat (or rats) (1894) Australian & New Zealand, dated ■ Mixer: 'Lend us a quid!' 'Lend you a what! Blime, have you got a rat?' (*c*1926)

psych out (1970) Compare earlier transitive sense, gain a psychological advantage over

Crazy, eccentric

queer (1508) Perhaps from German *quer* oblique, perverse

crack-brained (1634) Dated

cracked (1692) ■ Listener: I suppose all writers of children's classics have been cracked, or at least extremely weird. (1968)

loony, looney (1872) Shortened form of *lunatic* + *-y* ■ Wilcox & Rantzen: She had lost her place in the television 'record book' of loony pets. (1981)

daffy (1884) Applied to something or someone silly or amusingly eccentric; from dialect *daff* simpleton + *-y* ■ Guardian: One of those charming fusions of the daffy benevolence of youth with the guilelessness of middle aged PROs. (1968)

dotty (1885) Often applied to someone harmlessly eccentric, especially due to old age; from earlier obsolete sense, having an unsteady gait; ultimately perhaps from obsolete *dote* feeble-minded person (apparently based on Middle Dutch *dote* folly) (compare obsolete *dottypoll* fool) or related to Scottish *dotter* move unsteadily ■ Rosamond Lehmann: Quite wrapped up in herself—with something pretty rum staring out of her eyes. A bit dotty, perhaps. (1948)

screwy (1887) Orig US ■ R. H. Rimmer: Sheila was Tom's date and I had Tom's sister, Ruth, for a date. Sound screwy? (1966)

barmy, balmy (1891) From earlier sense, flighty; ultimately from *barm* froth + *-y*; the spelling *balmy* (used especially in the US) results from confusion with *balmy* pleasantly mild ■ *Daily Mail*: Teachers' unions called the idea 'barmy' even though European pupils often extend their school week to include Saturday morning. (1991)

barmy (or balmy) on (or in) the crumpet (1891) Dated; from *crumpet* head ■ H. G. Wells: I heard my aunt admit that one of the Stuart Durgan ladies did look a bit 'balmy on the crumpet'. (1909)

meshuga, meshugga(h) meshuger, mash-, mish-, etc.; also, when preceding a noun, **meshugener, meshugenah,** etc. **(1892)** From Yiddish *meshuge*, from Hebrew *mĕshuggā*, participle of *shāgag* go astray, wander ■ Jewish Chronicle: The kids at school call me meshugga. That means crazy. (1973)

touched (1893) From the notion of having been marked out as abnormal by the hand of God ■ Sunday Telegraph: Gordon was known locally to be a bit touched. That was why he was called 'Psyches'. (1991)

nutty (1898) Often in the phrase *nutty as a fruitcake*; from *nut* mad person + *-y* ■ Author: Yeats was a great poet and a fascinating critic, but if he had been hired to give a year's course of lectures on the development of English poetry his performance would have been extremely nutty. (1974)

bats in the belfry (1899) Also in the phrase *have bats in the belfry* be crazy ■ Blackwood's Magazine: The sahib had bats in his belfry, and must be humoured. (1928)

dippy (1899) Origin unknown ■ Times Review of Industry: In past days the senile and the slightly dippy were clapped into institutions. (1967)

batty (1903) From *bats in the belfry* ■ *British Weekly:* He's a bit batty every now and anon. (1926)

up the pole (1904) Compare earlier senses, in error, drunk ■ Gwen Moffat: 'Do you really suspect that Pilgrim—*Pilgrim!*—killed the girl?. . .' 'You're up the pole,' Mrs Kent said to Page. (1974)

cuckoo (1906), **cuckooed** (1918) Orig US; from *cuckoo* silly person ■ Michael Gilbert: Never asked for references?. . . She must be cuckoo. (1955)

dingbats (1911) Australian & New Zealand; also in the phrase *have the dingbats* be crazy; compare earlier US *dingbat* crazy or eccentric person ■ *Landfall:* Your mother's dingbats. (1949)

bats (1919) Short for *bats in the belfry* ■ Elizabeth Bowen: You're completely bats. (1938)

potty (1920) Compare earlier senses, trivial, simple ■ *Daily Mirror:* He played the joyously potty day-dreamer. (1977)

loopy (1925) ■ Ian Cross: Honestly, the pair of them were looking at me as though I was loopy. (1957)

crackers (1928) Orig British; compare *cracked* crazy and earlier obsolete services' slang *get the crackers* go mad (1925) ■ *Daily Telegraph:* Liberal Party is 'crackers', says Ld. Morrison of Lambeth. (1959)

fruity (1929) US; probably suggested by the phrase *nutty as a fruitcake*; compare *fruitcake* crazy person

crackpot (1934) Often applied to something crazily impractical; from *crackpot* crazy person ■ Geoffrey Jenkins: The High Command still thought it a crackpot idea, fraught with all kinds of difficulties and dangers. (1959)

wacky, **whacky** (1935) Orig US; from earlier dialect sense, left-handed ■ *Observer:* She plays the wacky mother of Debra Winger. (1984)

screwball (1936) Mainly US; from *screwball* eccentric person

nutsy, **nutsey** (*a*1941) Orig & mainly US; from *nuts* mad + *-y* ■ *Guardian:* Gee, it was nutsy. (1962)

off the beam (1941) Orig US; from the notion of deviating from the course indicated by a radio beam

(. . .) short of a . . . (1941) From the notion of not having the full complement (of mental faculties) (compare next); the earliest recorded formulation is *short of a sheet* (US & Australian), but more recent examples (since the mid 1980s) usually identify individual elements which go to make up the whole—the commonest are *two* (etc.) *bricks short of a load* and a *few* (etc.) *sandwiches short of a picnic*, but the variations are almost infinite ■ Jack Hodgins: You try to do the right thing by hiring local girls and you discover they can be as thick as fenceposts. There's one in there that's two bricks short of a load, I swear it. (1987) ■ Susan Johnson: I'm afraid he's a few sandwiches short of a picnic. Still, he's harmless. (1990) ■ *Post* (Denver): This guy was weird. . . . He was a few pickles short of a barrel. (1994)

not the full quid (1944) Australian & New Zealand; from a comparison between an amount of money falling short of a pound and someone's mental faculties falling short of those of a normal person

out to lunch (1955) Orig US; applied to someone or something out of touch with reality ■ *Toronto Daily Star:* A girl who would be attracted to Bud's mean streak and bad temper must be a little out to lunch. (1966)

oddball (1957) Orig US; from *oddball* eccentric person ■ *Peace News:* It's always been very much an odd ball way of doing it. (1974)

flaky, **flakey** (1959) Orig US; perhaps from the notion of 'flaking out' through exhaustion, the influence of drugs, etc. ■ *New Yorker:* People can choose their own words to describe Qaddafi's mental state—President Reagan called him 'flaky', and later denied that he considered Qaddafi mentally unbalanced. (1986)

kooky, **kookie** (1959) From *kook* crazy person + *-y* ■ *Nation Review* (Melbourne): 'No Sex Please, We're British!' The funniest, kookiest night of your life. (1973)

weirdo (1962) From earlier *weirdo* bizarrely eccentric person ■ *M. Moore:* The lady I'm looking after is a dear old duck, completely weirdo, but she's got a terrible sense of humour, and I like her. (1974)

wiggy (1963) US; from *wig out* freak out + *-y* ■ *Last Whole Earth Catalog:* Traditionally considerations such as his—economics, organizations, the future—turn a prophet's soul terrible and dark or at least partially wiggy. (1972)

off the wall (1968) Orig US ■ *National Review* (US): Brian knows how to startle the over-interviewed with off-the-wall questions that get surprising answers: Ever see a ghost? (1974)

nutso (1975) Mainly US; from *nuts* mad + *-o* ■ *Time:* He swore off meat about this time and took up vegetarianism 'in my typically nutso way'. (1983)

wacko, **whacko** (1977) Orig & mainly US; from *wack(y* + *-o* ■ D. Uhnak: She's gone slightly wacko politically. (1981)

tonto (1982) Orig US; from Spanish *tonto* silly, foolish ■ *Times Literary Supplement:* You compile a dossier on the habits and rituals of those around you. This is all much more interesting than going tonto at home. (1988)

A crazy or eccentric person

dag (1875) Australian & New Zealand; from British dialect *dag* dare, challenge ■ D. M. Davin: Gerald seemed to have become a bit of a dag since the old days. (1970)

dingbat (1879) US & Australian; compare earlier US *dingbat* coin, projectile; perhaps from *ding* beat + *bat* hitting implement, or from *ding* sound of a bell + *bat* flying animal, with jocular reference to *bats in the belfry* ■ *New York Times:* Miss Sternhagen's mother increases in giddiness, even to wearing what appears to be a feather in her hair. She is, in fact, a certifiable dingbat. (1985)

crackpot (1883) ■ Joyce Cary: The public is used to grievance-mongers and despises 'em—they'll put him down for a crack-pot. (1959)

loon (1885) Dated; often applied to a simpleton; from earlier sense, type of water bird, influenced by *lunatic* and *loony* ■ *Coast to Coast 1944*: There we were, bottled up in camp because the loon in charge couldn't get the order signed for the trucks to leave. (1945)

weirdie, weirdy (1894) From *weird* + *-ie* ■ *Daily Telegraph*: There was not an unwashed bearded weirdie in sight! (1966)

nut (1903) Orig US; often applied to a crank; probably back-formation from *nutty* crazy ■ *Nation Review* (Melbourne): The Worker Student Alliance, a bunch of nuts in Melbourne. (1973)

screwball (1933) Mainly US; from earlier sense, baseball pitched with reverse spin against the natural curve ■ P. G. Wodehouse: You are going to Blandings Castle now, no doubt, to inspect some well-connected screwball? (1939)

ding-a-ling (1935) North American; from the notion of crazy people hearing imaginary bells ■ James Carroll: Hell, Pius—that dingaling—would never of given me my hat. Thank God for Pope John. (1978)

wack, whack (1938) Orig US; probably a back-formation from *wacky* crazy, eccentric ■ G. F. Newman: The cop shrugged. 'Some wack with a grudge.' (1982)

fruitcake (1945) Orig US; from the phrase *nutty as a fruitcake* ■ *Observer*: To be considered as a candidate you must first get onto the Panel, which is a sort of index designed mainly to exclude fruitcakes. (1982)

oddball (1948) Orig US ■ Margaret Truman: Earlier in 1946 an oddball broke into the National Gallery and cut a hole in Dad's portrait. (1973)

flip (1952) Probably from *flip* or *flip one's lid* lose one's composure ■ I. Ross: 'She's a flip. . . . Nuts,' he translated, 'Loony. Off her rocker.' (1961)

weirdo (1955) From *weird* + *-o* ■ *Melody Maker*: This record is for the real weirdos. (1984)

flake (1959) Mainly US; back-formation from *flaky* crazy, eccentric ■ *Easyriders*: Gotta git rid of that flake Bobby Joe. He's just too gutless for the big time. (1983)

fruit (1959) US; shortened from *fruitcake*

nut-case (1959) ■ Boyd & Parkes: They were all shams. . . . She was a nutcase really. (1973)

kook (1960) US; probably from *cuckoo* ■ *Publishers Weekly*: A bona fide kook who is never quite able to get in gear till he finally dies paddling his canoe across the Atlantic. (1973)

tonto (1973) Orig US; from Spanish *tonto* foolish person

nutso (1975) Mainly US; often as a derisive form of address; from *nuts* crazy + *-o* ■ *New York Times*: Hey, nutso, you're not gonna do that, are you? Bug off! (1986)

wacko, whacko (1977) Orig & mainly US; from *wack(y* crazy, eccentric + *-o* ■ Robert Ludlum: 'They

catch a whack-o now and then.' 'Whack-o?' 'Someone who's crossed over the mental line, thinks he's someone he's not.' (1982)

head-banger (1983) From the notion of shaking or banging the head, as associated with mental disorder ■ *Observer*: In the European Parliament, they sit alone with a few Spanish and Danish head-bangers, while the main conservative grouping excludes them. (1989)

A mental hospital

crazy house (1887) US

booby-hatch (1896) Orig & mainly US; compare earlier sense, police station, gaol ■ P. G. Wodehouse: What, tell people you're me and I'm you. Sure we could, if you don't mind being put in the booby-hatch. (1936)

bughouse (1899) US; compare earlier sense, verminous lodging house, and *bug* person obsessed with an idea ■ Ngaio Marsh: You're bigger bloody fools than anybody outside a bughouse. (1940)

rat house (1900) Australian & New Zealand ■ Vance Palmer: Hadn't it been plain all along that there was a streak of madness in the old boy?. . . He had done a spell in the rat-house and was only out on sufferance. (1948)

funny house (1906) US

nut factory (1915) US ■ J. H. Chase: Johnnie was a rummy. . . . Drink had rotted him, and he was only two jumps ahead of the nut-factory. (1939)

giggle-house (1919) Australian & New Zealand ■ *Weekend Australian Magazine*: The classic story of that beautiful poet, John Clare, who had himself locked up in the giggle-house for nearly a quarter of a century. (1982)

loony bin (1919) ■ J. Symonds: Yes, Aunt Marion. She's locked up, you know, in the looney bin. (1962)

nut-house (1929) ■ *Radio Times*: Clothing for the Government, prisons and nut-'ouses—what is it they call 'em now? (1974)

cuckoo house (1930) US

nut college (1931) US

nuttery (1931) From *nut* mad person + *-ery* ■ Dean Stiff: Should the sociotechnic social worker be convinced that you are not normal she will have you bound for a nuttery before sunset. (1931)

the bin (1938) Short for *loony bin* ■ L. A. G. Strong: The chaps who certified you and popped you in the bin. (1942)

snake-pit (1947) From the title of a novel by M. J. Ward ■ Audrey Laski: They had visited him in the snake-pit. (1968)

funny farm (1959) Orig US ■ Eric Ambler: *Intercom* was described as 'the Batman of the funny-farm set' and its editor as 'the Lone Ranger of the lunatic fringe'. (1969)

cuckoo's nest (1962) US; from *cuckoo* crazy (person); popularized by the title of the novel *One Flew Over the Cuckoo's Nest* (1962) by Ken Kesey

cracker factory (1981) US; compare *crackers* crazy

A psychiatrist

loony-doctor (1925) ■ P. G. Wodehouse: She's browsing with Sir Roderick Glossop, the loony-doctor. (1960)

trick cyclist (1930) Jocular alteration of *psychiatrist* ■ *Listener*: Is neurotic, inadequate, unhappy . . . is up in Harley Street being sorted out by a trick cyclist. (1977)

head-shrinker (1950) Orig US ■ *New Scientist*: Dr. Louis West . . . may eventually be taking the caviare out of headshrinkers' mouths with his development of the robot psychiatrist. (1968)

wig-picker (1961) US ■ Mary McCarthy: Was I afraid of what a wig-picker might say? (1971)

shrink (1966), shrinker (1967) Shortening of *head-shrinker* ■ *Times Literary Supplement*: It does not take a shrink to see that a man so humanly flawed and artistically inept has got to be a loser. (1980) ■ J. B. Hilton: It

had to be the clinic for her. Maybe they'd left it too late, or maybe she was too clever for the shrinkers. (1980)

witch-doctor (1966) Services' slang ■ D. Anthony: That sounds like one of your witch doctors at the Retreat. (1979)

To psychoanalyse

psych (1917) Abbreviation ■ *Daily Express*: While for some patients being 'psyched' may be a step towards being cured, to others it may amount to being infected. (1928)

To have (or need) psychiatric treatment

have one's head examined, need one's head examining (1949) Used jocularly to suggest that someone is crazy ■ *New York Times*: Anyone who votes for Nixon ought to have his head examined. (1972)

6. Foolishness

Foolish: Slow-witted, unintelligent, stupid

half-witted (1712) Compare earlier sense, lacking sense, irrational ■ *Guardian*: Anything you get out of an egg is either half-witted or liable to take your leg off at the knee. I draw the line at an alligator. (1992)

gormless (c1746) British; orig *gaumless, gawmless*, from *gaum*, dialectal variant of *gome* notice, understanding (from Old Norse *gaumr* care, heed) + *-less* ■ Louis Golding: She just went on pulling the [beer] handle and in a moment . . . the floor was swilling. 'Mother!' cried little Nellie sharply. 'You *are* gormless!' (1932)

mutton-headed (1768) ■ P. G. Wodehouse: She had caused all the trouble by her mutton-headed behaviour in saying 'Yes' instead of 'No'. (1934)

thick (a1800) Often in the phrase *as thick as two (short) planks* (or *as a plank*) ■ Gordon Honeycombe: 'He must be as thick as two planks,' said Nick. (1974) ■ J. I. M. Stewart: You might expect to become P.M. if you hadn't been so thick as to accept your idiotic life peerage. (1976)

dumb (1823) From earlier sense, unable to speak, probably reinforced by German *dumm* and Dutch *dom* stupid ■ Elizabeth Bowen: One has got to see just how dumb Mr. Quayne was. He had not got a mind that joins one thing and another up. (1938)

mullet-headed (1857) US; from *mullet-head* slow-witted person ■ Mark Twain: They're so confiding and mullet-headed they don't take notice of nothing at all. (1884)

dim (1892) From earlier sense, deficient in light ■ W. Fabian: The sexperts, which is a combination of sex and expert: I glued it together myself. Not so dim; yes? (1924)

bone-headed (1903) Orig US ■ B. M. Bower: 'I'm willing to be just a boneheaded cow-puncher.' 'Accent on the bone,' Pink murmured. 'Them's my sentiments, old socks.' (1940)

dopey, dopy (1903) Orig US; from earlier sense, affected with a drug, sluggish, drowsy ■ Harry

Garner: Step began to laugh. 'That dopey foreman. He didn't bother to check with me.' (1963)

bird-brained (1922) ■ *Guardian*: It became the ultimate bluffer's music, leaving bird-brained pop way behind and rivalling classical music in its scope for cerebral arcana. (1992)

dozy, dozey (1924) British; from earlier sense, sleepy, drowsy ■ Julian Maclaren-Ross: What's funny, you dozey berk? (1961)

lame-brained (1929) Mainly US ■ Kenneth Orvis: Not like the usual lame-brained addict. (1962)

dim-witted (1940) ■ Edmund Crispin: They say he's got 'a madman's cunning', which is their excuse for being too dim-witted to catch him. (1948)

clueless (1943) From *not have a clue* not know ■ John Braine: Their two sons, . . . noisy and clumsy and clueless. (1957)

meat-headed (1949) Mainly US; from *meat-head* slow-witted person + *-ed* ■ W. R. Burnett: Some meat-headed tart. (1949)

pea-brained (1950) ■ R. Guy: That thickheaded pea-brained two-faced thug. (1987)

dumb-assed (1957) US

Out of touch with reality, empty-headed, daft, silly, irresponsible

dizzy (1878) From earlier sense, light-headed, giddy ■ *Penguin New Writing*: A dizzy blonde all dressed up like a dog's dinner. (1945)

dilly (1905) Mainly Australian; perhaps a blend of *daft* and *silly*; compare obsolete British dialect *dilly* cranky, queer ■ J. K. Ewers: Cripes, it'd drive a bloke dilly! (1949)

goofy (1919) Orig US; from *goof* fool + *-y* ■ *Observer*: Commercial television has brought a boom in animation, with comic men and goofy animals bouncing out from everywhere. (1958)

goopy (1926) Orig US; from *goop* fool + *-y*

cockamamie, -mamy, -manie, many (1950)
US; from earlier sense, foolish or ridiculous
person ■ Ed McBain: You marched into the precinct with a
tight dress and a cockamamie bunch of alibis. (1962)

bubble-headed (1952) Orig US ■ *Washington
Post*: Leon Wieseltier . . . dismissed the Hollywood crowd as
'insulated and bubble-headed people' who have no business
meddling in politics. (1993)

ditsy, ditzy (1973) Orig US; applied mainly to
women; perhaps an alteration of *dizzy*
■ *Washington Post*: Willie Scott . . . is a ditsy blond who
sings at a Shanghai nightclub. (1984)

divvy, divy (1975) British (Midland & Northern
dialect); origin unknown

See also Crazy, eccentric at **Sanity** (pp. 303–4).

A foolish person

blockhead (1549) Dated; applied to a slow-
witted person; from the notion of having a
wooden block for a head ■ Samuel Johnson: No
man but a blockhead ever wrote, except for money. (1776)

ass (1578) From the reputation of the ass for
stupidity ■ J. D. Carr: That's not a jack-knife, you ass. . . .
A jack-knife dive is where you bend double and touch your toes
in mid-air, and then straighten out before you hit the water.
(1942)

nit (1588) British; from earlier sense, egg of a
body-louse, and latterly probably influenced by
nitwit fool ■ Philip Cleife: If you think . . . I would be
willing to allow you . . . to board my aircraft . . . then you must
be a nit. (1972)

ninny (1593) Origin uncertain; perhaps from
innocent with prefixed *n* (as in *an innocent*)
■ *Cosmopolitan*: If women are made to look like ninnies by
agencies, why do magazines like *Cosmo* run the ads? (1992)

booby (1599) Dated; probably from Spanish *bobo*
fool, from Latin *balbus* stammering, stuttering
■ Evelyn Waugh: 'Poor simple monk,' I thought, 'poor booby.'
(1945)

clodpoll, clodpole (1601) British; from *clod*
lump + *poll* head ■ *Times Literary Supplement*: The
former editor of the *Far Eastern Economic Review* is worried . . .
that his book will fall into the hands of clodpoles. (1986)

clod (1605) Applied to a slow-witted person; from
earlier sense, lump ■ *Wall Street Journal*: Clod
though he may otherwise be, Edwin Meese is a man of honor.
(1989)

nincompoop (1676) Origin uncertain; perhaps
from the male forename *Nicholas* or *Nicodemus*
(compare French *nicodème* simpleton) with *-n-*
due to association with *ninny* fool + obsolete
poop deceive, cheat, befool ■ Virginia Woolf: Never
could she understand how he cared. But those Indian women
did presumably—silly, pretty, flimsy nincompoops. (1925)

sawney (1700) Perhaps a variant of the male
forename *Sandy*, as in the earlier *sawney*
Scotsman

gump, gumph (1722) Now US; origin unknown
■ Anthony Gilbert: She might do her best to attract
attention—any girl who wasn't a complete gumph would.
(1945)

buffer (1749) British; applied to a foolish old
person; often in the phrase *old buffer*; probably
from the obsolete verb *buff*, imitative of the
sound of a soft body being struck, or from the
obsolete verb *buff* stutter ■ Peter Dickinson: You can
make the correct noises while all the old buffers are woffling
on. (1982)

noodle (1753) Dated; origin unknown ■ Arthur
Helps: I say he is a noodle if he has not previously determined
how and when to leave off. (1875)

half-wit (1755) ■ F. Scott Fitzgerald: We are setting it
aside till we think of a way of half-witting halfwit Hayes and
his Legion of Decency. (1938)

stupe (1762) Shortened from *stupid* ■ Tobias
Wells: His assistant, a big stupe called Jersey Eng. (1967)

dummy (1796) Probably from *dumb* foolish (not
recorded until later) + *-y*; compare earlier sense,
dumb person ■ *Sunday Express Magazine*: The
emphasis at the school was all on rugby and the classics. Art
was for dummies. (1986)

mutton-head (1803) Orig US; applied to a slow-
witted person ■ J. & E. Bonett: Bone-heads, that's what
you are. Mutton-heads. Idiots. (1972)

dummkopf, dumkopf, dumbkopf (1809)
Orig US; from German *Dummkopf* idiot, from
dumm foolish + *Kopf* head ■ *Listener*: They may turn
out, after all, to have been fall guys, dumbkopfs, dupes of their
own chicanery. (1968)

sap (1815) Short for earlier *sapskull* simpleton
■ *Globe & Mail* (Toronto): Bobby Mull . . ., is a sap if he
accepts less than $100,000 from the tight-fisted . . .
management. (1968)

jackass (1823) From earlier sense, male ass
■ *Economist*: He cares little for the sensitivities of his fellow
politicians ('jackasses' is a common epithet). (1988)

silly billy (1834) British; from *Billy*, familiar
form of the male forename *William*; originally
used specifically as a nickname of William
Frederick, Duke of Gloucester (1776–1834), and
of William IV (1765–1837) ■ *Wordpower*: Mr Healey
is a Silly Billy to have waited so long before doing so little of
what everyone knew was necessary. (1977)

fat-head (1842) ■ *Guardian*: When they [*sc.* MPs]
behave like fatheads, people are apt to notice. (1991)

dope (1851) Origin uncertain; perhaps the same
word as earlier *dope* sauce, gravy (from Dutch
doop sauce), or perhaps an alteration of *dupe*
■ P. Capon: Silly dope, he can't go on dodging the Court for
ever. (1959)

muggins (1855) Perhaps from the personal
name *Muggins*, with allusion to *mug* gullible
person ■ *Daily Telegraph*: The letter bomb was not meant
for me personally. I was just the muggins who opened it. (1973)

mullet-head (1857) US; applied to a slow-witted
person; compare earlier use as the name of a

type of freshwater fish, and compare also British dialect *mull-head* fool ■ Z. N. Hurston: Hey, you mullet heads! Get out de way. (1935)

thick (1857) Orig schoolchildren's slang; from *thick* foolish, slow-witted ■ G. Lord: Some of those thicks in Earls Court would do it just for the kicks. (1970)

flat-head (1862) ■ *New Statesman*: Gobbledygook is the defence of the American intellectual aware of the hostile mockery of the surrounding flatheads. (1966)

galoot (1866) Orig US; compare earlier sense, inept or stupid soldier or marine; ultimate origin unknown ■ D. McClean: I've just thought of something that will interest Ian. What a galoot I am not to think of it sooner. (1960)

lunk (1867), lunkhead (1884) Orig US; applied to a slow-witted person; *lunk* perhaps an alteration of *lump*; *lunkhead* was probably the original form, and *lunk* shortened from it ■ *Punch*: The poor lunkhead's concerns soon get lost under all the modelling and backlighting. (1966) ■ *New Yorker*: He looks incredulous, as if he couldn't figure out how he got turned into such a lunk. (1975)

gooney (1872) Now US; a variant of obsolete dialect *gony*, *goney* fool, of unknown origin

twerp, twirp (1874) Origin unknown; the suggestion that it is from the name of T. W. Earp, an early 20th-century Oxford undergraduate, is refuted by evidence of its late 19th-century use ■ Stan Barstow: If she turns me down I'll look more of a twerp than ever. (1960)

juggins (1882) British, dated; perhaps from the surname *Juggins*, or alternatively a fanciful derivative of *mug* fool (compare *muggins*) ■ Iris Murdoch: You are a juggins, you shouldn't walk in those high-heeled shoes. (1985)

chump (1883) From earlier sense, lump of wood ■ *Sunday Times*: Phil Tufnell is a chump. Here in Vishakhapatnam, he was in trouble again, his aberrant ways forcing [the] England management team . . . to impose a £500 fine for ungentlemanly conduct. (1993)

josser (1886) British, dated; origin uncertain; compare Australian *josser* priest

dumbhead (1887) Mainly US; from *dumb* foolish + *head*, after German *Dummkopf*, Dutch *domkop* ■ C. E. Mulford: Have I got to do all the thinking for this crowd of dumbheads? (1921)

schmuck, shmuck (1892) Mainly US; from Yiddish *shmok* penis ■ Groucho Marx: He doesn't know I can write, in fact, he thinks I'm a complete schmuck. (1945)

prawn (1893) Mainly Australian ■ A. O'Toole: The prawn has talked this little sheila into wanting to sell our horse. (1969)

goop (1900) Orig US; coined by Gelett Burgess to denote a mischievous childlike creature ■ David Jacobs: I am very jealous of my position as chairman of *Juke Box Jury*, . . . and I don't believe one can be a placid smiling goop all the time. (1966)

mutt (1901) Orig US; applied to a slow-witted person; abbreviation of *mutton-head* ■ Derwent May: The poor mutt must have driven it along the bank. (1973)

oaf (1902) Applied to a large, slow-witted, clumsy person; from earlier senses, child stolen by the fairies, idiot child; variant of obsolete *auf*, from Old Norse *álfr* elf ■ William Golding: Running in panic lest I should be grabbed by some enormous oaf from the scrum. (1984)

simp (1903) US; abbreviation of obsolete *simple* fool, or of *simpleton* ■ *Publishers Weekly*: The book's assumption is that single men are simps who don't know the difference between a pepper mill and a can opener. (1976)

cluck (1906) US; especially in the phrase *dumb cluck*; from earlier sense, sound made by a hen ■ Stephen Ransome: Showing ourselves up as a fine pair of clucks. (1950) ■ Olivia Manning: For the last half-hour I've been telling these dumb clucks to find me a bloke who can speak English. (1960)

gazob (1906) Australian, dated; perhaps from *gazabo* fellow ■ C. J. Dennis: Ar! but 'e makes me sick! A fair gazob! (1915)

boob (1907) Shortened from *booby* ■ George Bernard Shaw: You gave it away, like the boobs you are, to the Pentland Forth Syndicate. (1930)

bone-head (1908) Orig US; applied to a slow-witted person ■ Arthur Conan Doyle: James was a bonehead—I give you that. (1917)

lemon (1908) ■ Adam Hall: They'd sent me down to show me something and they knew I couldn't see it and I felt a bit of a lemon. (1973)

gorm, gawm (1912) Perhaps a back-formation from *gormless* ■ Heron Carvic: 'It's all finished and it's all wunners.' She smiled with pride. 'Isn't it, you great gorm?' (1969)

rummy (1912) US, dated; compare earlier sense, drunkard

date (1914) British, mainly jocular; mainly in the phrase *soppy date*; from *date* fruit ■ George Ingram: A kid like that ought not to talk about love at her age, the soppy little date. (1935)

poop (1915) Perhaps shortened from *nincompoop* ■ Robert Dentry: Those stupid bloody Yankee poops blew the panic whistle and the whole shebang went sky-high. (1971)

blob (1916) Mainly Australian ■ Bernard Cronin: Maybe they're all right, but it on't do to run risks. Tell some of them blobs they'll need to walk to Green Valley next time they get a thirst up, if they don't act reasonable. (1920)

bozo (1916) Orig & mainly US; perhaps from Spanish *bozal* simple, stupid or from Italian *bozzo* cuckold, bastard, or perhaps a reduplicated form of US *bo* fellow ■ *Encounter*: Frank, the grey bozo behind the counter. (1961)

goat (1916) ■ Kylie Tennant: 'Don't be a goat.' Silly young fools, all three of them. (1947)

goof (1916) Perhaps from obsolete dialect *goff*, *guff* fool, from French *goffe* awkward, stupid, from Italian *goffo*, from Medieval Latin *gufus* coarse ■ Hay & King-Hall: Have you stopped to think what is happening to that poor old goof in the day-cabin, right now? (1930)

gubbins (1916) British; probably the same word as *gubbins* equipment, gadget ■ John Osborne: Have you been on the batter, you old gubbins! (1957)

goofus (1917) US; from *goof* fool + arbitrary suffix -*us* (perhaps after *dingus* thingummy)

Mutt and Jeff (1917) Applied to a pair of slow-witted men, especially one tall and one short; from the names of two characters called *Mutt* (compare *mutt* fool) and *Jeff*, one tall and the other short, in a popular cartoon series by H. C. Fisher (1884–1954), American cartoonist

dumb-bell (1918) Orig US; after *dumb* stupid; compare earlier sense, weighted bar used for exercise ■ *Punch*: A dumb-bell being the kind of person who writes to the manufacturer asking him to replace a gadget that has been lost, and then adds a postscript telling him not to bother as the missing gadget has just been found. (1936)

dumb bunny (1921) Orig US

goon (1921) Orig US; perhaps from *gooney* fool, reputedly as a coinage of F. L. Allen; subsequently influenced by the subhuman cartoon character called Alice the *Goon* created by E. C. Segar in 1933, and in general use from the late 1930s ■ S. Clark: There, you goon. You'll bump into them if you don't watch out. (1959)

dimwit (1922) Orig US; applied to a slow-witted person ■ John Wyndham: He had an uncomfortable awareness of how many ways there were for even a dimwit to contrive a fatal accident. (1956)

Dumb Dora (1922) Applied to a foolish woman or girl; from *dumb* foolish + *Dora* female forename ■ Graham McInnes: They [*sc.* hens] would then wait expectantly, heads cocked on one side with a sort of dumb-Dora inquisitive chuckle. (1965)

nitwit (1922) Perhaps from *nit* egg of a body-louse (compare *nit* fool) + *wit* ■ June Drummond: For God's sake, Beryl, don't be such a nitwit. (1975)

pie-face (1922) US; back-formation from *pie-faced*; from the notion of someone with a round expressionless face, like a pie

dingleberry (1924) Orig US; probably from earlier sense (not recorded until later), piece of dried faecal matter attached to the hair round the anus ■ *Righting Words*: Tell that dingleberry I'm not here. (1990)

BF, B.F., bee eff (1925) Orig British services' slang; abbreviation of *bloody fool* ■ Cecil Day Lewis: You really are a B.F., Arthur. (1939) ■ M. Cecil: 'Your mother's relations,' he muttered, 'bee effs, every one of 'em.' (1960)

ding-dong (1929) US; probably from earlier use, representing the sound of a bell

lame-brain (1929) Mainly US; applied to a slow-witted person ■ *Times Literary Supplement*: We have finished feeling indulgent towards the disaffected lamebrains who turn this kind of stuff out. (1972)

loogan (1929) US, dated; origin unknown ■ P. Cain: There's Rose, with his syndicate behind him, and all the loogans he's imported from back East. (1933)

sparrow-brain (1930) Applied to a slow-witted person ■ Vita Sackville-West: I don't suppose it satisfies anyone, except perhaps a sparrow-brain like mother. (1930)

dumbo (1932) Orig US; from *dumb* foolish + -*o* ■ Sue Townsend: I am sharing a book with three dumbos who take half an hour to read one page. (1984)

bird-brain (1933) Applied to a slow-witted person ■ *Gen*: There are more birdbrains and dim-wits outside the boxing ring . . . as ever stepped around in it. (1943)

twit (1934) Mainly British; perhaps from the verb *twit* reproach, taunt ■ N. Fleming: No one but a prize twit or Captain Oates would have ventured out in this weather. (1970)

berk, birk, burk(e) (1936) Mainly British; abbreviation of *Berkeley Hunt* or *Berkshire Hunt* ■ John Osborne: The Tories were burglars, berks and bloodlusters. (1959) ■ *Sunday Express*: All my mates thought I was a burk to try to break away: now they know they were the burks. (1963)

cockamamie, -mamy, -manie, many (1936) US; applied to a foolish or ridiculous person; origin unknown

Berkeley Hunt, Berkeley (1937) British; rhyming slang for *cunt*; from the name of a celebrated hunt in Gloucestershire; now largely replaced by *berk* ■ A. Bracey: Lane's face cleared. 'Tell us, chum.' 'And spoil the nice surprise! Not bloody likely!' 'You always was a berkeley,' said Lane cheerfully. 'Well, I can wait.' (1940)

dum-dum, dumb-dumb (1937) Orig North American; reduplication of *dumb* foolish ■ *Calgary Herald*: Better they should employ some dumb-dumb. (1970)

oonchook, oonshik, etc. (1937) Irish & Newfoundland; from Irish *óinseach* foolish woman, clown; earlier, in Newfoundland, a man masquerading as a woman in a mummers' parade ■ Flann O'Brien: The divil himself is in the hearts of that Corporation ownshucks. (1961)

galah (1938) Australian; from earlier sense, rose-breasted cockatoo; from Aboriginal (Yuwaalaraay and related languages) *gilaa* ■ H. L. Hendry: These bloody galahs going round now are bowling feet wide of the stumps and being hailed as good bowlers. (1981)

schlep, schlepp, shlep (1939) Mainly US; probably short for *schlepper* fool, although not recorded in this sense till later ■ *New Yorker*: My teacher can just zero in on one phrase, and it's immediately obvious that what I've done is so immature it makes me feel like an absolute schlepp. (1977)

poon (1940) Mainly Australian; origin unknown ■ D. Williamson: What possessed Keren to shack up with a poon like you? (1974)

dill (1941) Australian & New Zealand; probably a back-formation from *dilly* foolish ■ *Telegraph*

(Brisbane): At the start he felt a bit of a dill in a wig and robes. (1969)

drongo (1941) Australian & New Zealand; compare earlier sense, bird of the family Dicruridae found in India, Africa and Australia, from Malagasy *drongo*; perhaps suggested by the use of the word as the name of an Australian racehorse of the 1920s that often finished last ■ *Advertiser* (Adelaide): You Aussie coves are just a bunch of drongoes. (1969)

nana (1941) Orig Australian; perhaps from *banana*; compare *bananas* crazy ■ *Times*: A frank admission that he had made a nana of himself. (1974)

tonk (1941) Mainly Australian; origin unknown ■ Richard Beilby: You're a good bloke, Turk, but sometimes you talk like a tonk. (1970)

clot (1942) British; from earlier sense, lump ■ Penelope Mortimer: Jolly bad luck, what a clot she is. (1958)

klunk, clunk (1942) US; origin unknown ■ *New York Herald-Tribune*: Mr. Wagner has been a remarkably good mayor, and the klunks who don't realize this, they add, understand neither the Mayor himself nor the nature of his responsibilities. (1964)

alec, aleck (1944) Australian; short for *smart alec* know-all ■ Alan Seymour: He looked such a big aleck, marching along as though he'd won both wars single-handed. (1962)

goof ball (1944) From earlier sense, pill containing a drug, influenced by *goof* fool ■ *Washington Post*: You want to know why Michael Jordan may finish his career as the greatest player of all time? Because he's won two championships with this soft goofball as his sidekick. (1993)

knucklehead (1944) Orig & mainly US; applied to a slow-witted person ■ Roger Parkes: What I'm trying to get across to you knuckleheads is that it was not murder! (1971)

nong, nong-nong (1944) Australian; compare *ning-nong* fool ■ *Bulletin* (Sydney): Rod Cavalier has ... turned himself into a ridiculous nong. (1986)

schmendrik, shmendrik (1944) US; from the name of a character in an operetta by Abraham Goldfaden (1840–1908)

boofhead (1945) Australian; perhaps from obsolete *bufflehead* fool; popularized by a comic-strip character of that name created by R. B. Clark in 1939 and running in the Sydney *Daily Mirror* 1941–70 ■ *Australian*: Mr Hayden ... described the former ALP secretary as a boofhead. (1983)

meat-head (1945) Mainly US; applied to a slow-witted person ■ *Newsweek*: Archie Bunker, the middle American hero of 'All in the Family' ... sees himself menaced by a rising tide of spades, ... meatheads, ... fags and four-eyes. (1971)

Charlie, Charley (1946) Mainly British; especially in the phrase *a proper* (or *right*) *Charlie*; from the male forename, a familiar form of *Charles* ■ Alan Simpson & Ray Galton: I felt a right Charlie coming through the customs in this lot. (1961)

tit (1947) Origin uncertain; perhaps from *tit* breast ■ S. Wilson: We always took a gun, and it kept me quite alert, not wishing to make a tit of myself in front of the laird. (1978)

schlump, schloomp, shlump (1948) Orig & mainly US; probably from Yiddish; compare Yiddish *shlumperdick* dowdy, German *Schlumpe* slattern ■ Joseph Heller: Kissinger would not be recalled in history as a Bismarck ... but as an odious *shlump* who made war gladly. (1979)

schmo, shmo (1948) Mainly US; shortened from *schmuck* ■ Dick Francis: 'Who,' he said crossly, 'is going to give that schmo a thousand quid for breaking his ankle?' (1970)

dumbfuck (1949) US; from *dumb* foolish + *fuck*

barmpot (1951) British, orig & mainly northern dialect; from earlier sense, pot for storing barm or yeast, probably influenced by *barmy* slightly mad, foolish ■ T. & P. Morris: Thus a harmless schizophrenic will be classified by the staff as a 'barmpot' and by the prisoners as a 'nutter'. (1963)

bubblehead (1952) Orig US; applied to an empty-headed person (in early use apparently often specifically to Henry A. Wallace, US Vice-President 1941–45); compare *airhead* ■ *Time*: But Jack is not a Hollywood bubblehead.... He sometimes thinks before he says his lines. Or anyway, he thinks he thinks, which for an actor amounts to the same thing. (1988)

nig-nog (1953) British; compare *ning-nong* fool and obsolete *nigmenog* fool ■ Arnold Wesker: A straight line, you heaving nig-nogs, a straight line. (1962)

sawn (1953) Australian; abbreviation of *sawney* fool ■ Kylie Tennant: I'm always getting into trouble through sawns. (1953)

schlepper, shlepper (1954) Mainly US; from earlier sense, poor person ■ *Rolling Stone*: I've got a message for the Penelopes of this world. It's high time they say to their Ulysseses, 'Okay Schlepper, you've been around the world, your turn to keep the home fires burning, I'm splitting on my own trip for a while.' (1977)

ning-nong (1957) Australian; from obsolete British dialect *ning-nang* fool; compare *nig-nog* fool and *nong*(*-nong*) fool ■ *Telegraph* (Brisbane): Even ning-nongs can win prizes on Channel O's daily quiz show. (1973)

dumb-ass (1958) US

oafo (1959) Applied to a large, slow-witted, clumsy person, or to a lout; from *oaf* + *-o* ■ Robin Cook: The middle classes ... the working classes ... not to mention the oafos. (1962)

pea-brain (1959) Applied to an empty-headed person; apparently a back-formation from *pea-brained* ■ Howard Jacobson: The intellectual pogromists and pea-brains, with their scream-squads of love-mongering mystics who have taken over our educational institutions. (1986)

pronk (1959) Origin uncertain; compare Dutch *pronker* fop ■ L. Henderson: Whoever this pronk Durant was he had a lot to learn. (1972)

herbert, Herbert (1960) British; applied to a foolish or ridiculous man; arbitrary use of the male forename ■ T. Barling: A dozen baby-brained herberts looking to face me off just to say they squared up to Kosher Kramer before the cobbles came up a bit smartish. (1986)

dumbshit (1961) US ■ William Gibson: 'Sorry, gentlemen, but this is official warlord biz,' this dumbshit says. (1986)

dipshit (1962) US; compare *dippy* foolish ■ William Gibson: He got up from his chair, walked to the door, and gently edged one of the curtains aside. 'What the fuck are those dipshits doing out there?' (1986)

dipstick (1963) Orig US; perhaps a euphemistic partial substitution for *dipshit*; compare *dippy* foolish ■ R. Blount: If I'd told the truth to that dipstick who played me, I would have just said, 'Sugar'. (1990)

dizz, diz (1963) US; back-formation from *dizzy* foolish

dick-head (1964) From *dick* penis + *head* ■ Alan Bleasdale: But I lost that job, it was alright, I deserved to lose it, I was a dickhead—but haven't we all been at one time or another—haven't we all woken up the next mornin' an' gone 'oh Jesus, did I do that'? (1983)

putz (1964) Mainly US; from earlier sense, penis ■ E. V. Cunningham: 'What are you telling me? That you fell for her—love at first sight?' 'Don't be a putz. I run a gambling house. I don't fall in love.' (1966)

schlub, shlub (1964) US; Yiddish, perhaps from Polish *żłób* fool ■ D. E. Westlake: When a man . . . doesn't know the facts and nobody will tell him . . . and people keep throwing apples and unkind remarks at him, he has no choice but to look like a *shlub.* (1969)

stiffy (1965) US; compare earlier *stiff* objectionable person ■ C. Keil: Negro artists who find their way into white concert halls still find it necessary to 'hip' those 'stiffies' in the audience who insist on clapping their hands in a martial manner. (1966)

gobdaw (a1966) Anglo-Irish; probably from *gob* mouth + *daw* foolish or lazy person; compare Irish *gabhdán* container, gullible person ■ Maeve Binchy: All kinds of old gobdaws much worse-looking than you, look terrific when they're dolled up. (1982)

plonker (1966) British; compare *plonker* penis ■ Smash Hits: I look at a dress and think because it's fashionable it'll look good and then I go out with it on and realise what a plonker I look. (1988)

dork (1967) Mainly US; from earlier sense, penis ■ Zigzag: It will attract talentless dorks out for a taste of notoriety or a fast buck. (1977)

pillock (1967) British; usually applied to a male; from obsolete *pillcock* penis ■ J. Gash: The pillock mistook my astonishment for awe. (1978)

arse (1968) Mainly British; probably in use well before 1968, but its written usage perhaps disguised by the euphemistic spelling *ass* ■ C. Phillips: I got two eyes in me head which is more than I can say for the arse who umpired the game last year. (1985)

klutz, klotz, kluhtz (1968) US; from Yiddish, from German *Klotz* wooden block ■ E.-J. Bahr: Janet is an utter klotz. (1973)

prat (1968) British; from earlier sense, buttocks ■ Car: To max this thing you have to drive like an arrogant prat, running at lights-ablaze 120mph and waiting for a clear space in your lane. (1991)

thickie (1968) From *thick* foolish, slow-witted + *-ie* ■ Times: Teachers still think that engineering is a subject for 'thickies'. (1983)

fuckwit (1969) Orig Australian; perhaps a blend of *fuck* and *nitwit* ■ Christopher Morris: Aren't we a bunch of fuckwits? An elephant could no more get its trunk up its arse than we could lick our balls. (1997)

wally (1969) British; origin uncertain; perhaps a use of the male forename *Wally* (compare *Charlie* fool, *Herbert* fool), a familiar form of *Walter*, but compare also *wallydrag, wallydraigle* feeble or worthless person ■ Daily Telegraph: 'They looked a right load of wallies,' said an eye-witness. (1984)

yo-yo (1970) US; from earlier sense, toy that goes up and down ■ V. Bugliosi: I've got enough problems without some punk yo-yo threatening me. (1978)

airhead (1972) Orig & mainly US; from the notion of having air inside the head rather than a brain ■ Daily Telegraph: One can imagine the media barons when they saw that these entertainment-world 'airheads' (the currently preferred term) . . . had concocted an irresponsibly tendentious account from these very Press reports. (1984)

ditz, dits (1973) US; applied to an empty-headed person, especially a woman; back-formation from *ditzy* empty-headed ■ Guardian: Meryl Streep is serious, Suzanne Somers isn't. That's the way they're seen. . . . I don't think Miss Somers does ditsy tap dances when she gets home. I've been both. I used to be a ditz. Now I'm talented. (1985)

dumb-butt (1973) US; from *dumb* foolish + *butt* buttocks

nully (1973) Perhaps from *null* of no value + *-y*; compare Scottish *nullion* stupid fellow ■ Roger Parkes: He's a sick, junked-up, pathetic old nully. (1973)

thicko (1976) From *thick* foolish, slow-witted + *-o* ■ Paul Theroux: Where's the camp store, thicko? (1981)

gonzo (1977) Orig & mainly US; from *gonzo* bizarre, crazy ■ Custom Car: To make sure I wouldn't make too big a gonzo of myself, . . . I was connected by intercom to the commander who was perched up in the turret. (1977)

wazzock (1983) British; origin uncertain; perhaps dialectal ■ Independent: A plot . . . which boasted that hilarious device in which the hero says 'I need to find a right wazzock'. (1991)

woodentop (1983) British; applied to a slow-witted person; from the notion of having a wooden head; compare earlier sense, uniformed policeman ■ Antony Beevor: They've even got the bleeding Army out. . . . Bunch of woodentops from Chelsea barracks. (1983)

divvy, **divy (1989)** British (Midland & Northern dialect); from *divvy* foolish ■ *Box*: It was an automatic which we shouldn't have used because you can't get the wheel spins and loads of the criminals around Liverpool were saying 'yah divvy ya shoulda used a turbo'. (1989)

To behave foolishly, and especially in a time-wasting way

piddle about, **piddle around (1545)** Perhaps an alteration of *peddle* sell small wares, busy oneself with trifling matters, by association with Low German *piddeln*; in modern use identified with *piddle* urinate (compare *piss about*), which may not historically be the same word ■ *Sounds*: He returned to New York and 'piddled around' doing Public Relations. (1977)

arse about, **arse around**, (US) **ass about**, **ass around (1664)** British & Australian ■ Arnold Wesker: Don't arse around Ronnie, the men want their tea. (1960)

muck about, **muck around (1856)** ■ P. Mansfield: Why don't you haul him in instead of mucking around asking me bloody silly questions? (1957)

faff about, **faff around (1874)** British, orig dialect; compare obsolete *faffle* in same sense, originally meaning 'stutter', of imitative origin ■ Noel Coward: The Welfare Officers appeared, . . . faffed about, used either too much initiative or too little, and retired in due course. (1954)

fart about, **fart around (1900)** From *fart* break wind ■ John Wainwright: Look! It's important. Stop farting around. (1969)

fuck about, **fuck around (1922)** ■ *Guardian*: 'Don't fuck about with the artform,' counters Cressswell. 'It's been working since Max Miller.' (1992)

bugger about, **bugger around (1929)** British & Australian ■ John Wainwright: Let's not bugger around being polite. (1968)

futz around (1929) US; probably an alteration of Yiddish *arumfartzen* fart around; often treated as a euphemistic substitute for *fuck around*

■ Nathaniel Benchley: It's bad for your blood pressure to futz around like this. (1968)

goof around, **goof (1929)** Mainly US; from *goof* fool ■ James Baldwin: I used to like to just . . . go to the movies by myself or just read or just goof. (1962) ■ *Guardian*: It was really just a lot of goofing around and listening to a lot of music that we hadn't taken the time to listen to before. There was nothing heavy going on. (1992)

goof off (1943) Mainly US; often implying loafing about when one should be working; from *goof* fool ■ *Time*: Though U.S. workers have been regularly chided at home for goofing off on the job, they are veritable Stakhanovites compared with some of their European counterparts. (1977)

piss about, **piss around (1961)** British & Australian ■ T. Lewis: Are you coming in? Or do we piss about all day? (1970)

play silly buggers (or **bleeders**, **b's**) **(1961)** British ■ Kenneth Royce: I have to pin something on him to stop him playing silly b's. (1972) ■ Keith Waterhouse: I'm sure none of this had anything to do with the supposed threat to our privacy. It was our God-given right to play silly buggers that was threatened, and the nation responded magnificently. (1976)

prat about (1961) British; from *prat* fool ■ Hugh Miller: Sit down and stop pratting about. (1973)

yuck it up, **yuk it up (1964)** Mainly North American; compare later *yu(c)k* (to) laugh, probably imitative

fanny about, **fanny around (1971)** British; from *fanny* glib talk or *fanny* female genitals ■ *Sunday Times*: 'I don't want you bringing the ball out and fannying around with it the way you do at Arsenal,' Jack Charlton once snapped at him. (1993)

Foolish behaviour

monkey tricks (1653) ■ J. B. Priestley: Any monkey tricks an' I'll dot yer one. (1951)

monkey-shines (c1832) US ■ F. R. Stockton: Most of them played and cut up monkey-shines on the hay. (1894)

7. Gullibility

A gullible person

pigeon (1593) ■ Billie Holiday: So they handed me a white paper to sign. . . . I signed. . . . The rest was up to them. I was just a pigeon. (1956)

sucker (1838) Orig North American; from earlier sense, young animal not yet weaned ■ Arthur Conan Doyle: I'll see this sucker and fill him up with a false confession. (1927)

mark (1845) Often in the phrases *soft mark* and *easy mark* ■ Edmund McGirr: In the twenties it was the Yanks who were the suckers, but now . . . it's us who are the marks. (1973)

mug (1859) British; perhaps a use of *mug* face ■ L. Griffiths: I see mugs all around me. I see opportunities, possibilities, expectations and bargains and deals. (1985)

fly-flat (1864) Criminals' slang, dated; applied to a gullible person who thinks him- or herself clever; from *fly* clever + obsolete slang *flat* gullible person ■ Joyce Cary: 'I don't see why we should consider the speculators.' 'A lot of fly-flats who thought they could beat us at the game.' (1938)

fruit (1894) Orig US, dated; compare earlier sense, pleasant person ■ *Punch*: It was a flaw in the new play that its mugs were such 'easy fruit'. (1913)

patsy (1903) Orig US; perhaps from Italian *pazzo* fool

fall guy (1906) Orig US ■ Saul Bellow: Perhaps he was foolish and unlucky, a fall guy, a dupe, a sucker. (1956)

lemon (1908) ■ P. G. Wodehouse: I don't know why it is, rich men's sons are always the worst lemons in creation. (1931)

rummy (1912) US, dated; from earlier sense, drunkard

steamer (1932) Abbreviation and alteration of *steam tug*, rhyming slang for *mug* ■ Mario Puzo: The third player at the table was a 'steamer', a bad gambler who chased losing bets. (1978)

soft touch, **easy touch (1940)** Applied especially to someone easily induced to part with money ■ H. Kurnitz: Dorsey's appetite for easy money . . . was honed to a razor edge. . . . He sensed a vast soft touch. (1955)

Joe Soap (1943) ■ John Brown: Who do you think I am, moosh? Joe Soap? (1972)

pushover (1944) Orig US; from earlier sense, one who is easily pushed or knocked to the ground ■ *New Yorker*: This department, always an old pushover for a picture horse, picks Foolish Pleasure. (1975)

schnook, **shnook (1948)** US; apparently Yiddish (compare Yiddish *shnut* snout or German *Schnucke* small sheep) ■ Norman Mailer: I'd be making a stinking seven hundred and fifty a week now like all those poor exploited schnooks. (1955)

imbo (1953) Australian; applied especially to the victim of a criminal; from *imb(ecile + -o*

muggins (1973) Used to refer self-deprecatingly to oneself as someone easily fooled or imposed on; from earlier sense, fool ■ Elizabeth Lemarchand: 'In a nutshell,' Michael said, '. . . Muggins [*i.e.* himself] has agreed to be in charge.' (1973)

To accept gullibly

swallow (1594) ■ Richard Littledale: Over-readiness to swallow marvels . . . is credulity. (1880)

fall for (1903) Orig US ■ J. J. Farjeon: I held out my pocket-case, and said I'd found it on the floor of the hotel. 'Is it yours?' I asked. To my surprise, he fell for it beautifully. (1929)

take a wooden nickel (or **wooden money**) **(1915)** US; denoting being swindled; from *wooden nickel* counterfeit coin ■ M. Torrie: Having advised her . . . not to accept any wooden nickels, [he] drove back. (1971)

8. Education

Learning

get the hang of (1845) Orig US; denotes that someone has learnt how to do or cope with something; orig applied to the handling of tools

sleeping dictionary (1928) Applied to a foreign woman with whom a man has a sexual relationship and from whom he learns the rudiments of her language

sit next to (or **by**, **with**) **Nellie (1963)** Denotes learning how to do a job by watching others do it ■ *Listener*: Journalists are the casual labourers of the intellectual world. . . . Most training still consists of sitting next to Nellie. (1972)

Intensive study

swot, **swat (1850)** British, dated; applied to work or study at school or college, originally specifically mathematics; a dialectal variant of *sweat* ■ H. A. Vachell: Our object is . . . to get through the 'swat' with as little squandering of valuable time as possible. (1905)

groise, **groize (1913)** British public schools' slang; perhaps an alteration of *grease*

To study hard

cram (1810) Orig university slang; used to denote intensive teaching or study in preparation for an exam; from the notion of forcing knowledge into someone ■ *Daily News*: Their boys had not been crammed, but had diligently studied their subjects. (1879) ■ E. J. Worboise: She can cram for an examination. (1881)

swot, **swat (1860)** British; denoting intensive studying, especially in preparation for an exam; often followed by *up*; from the noun *swot* hard work or study ■ *Times*: Mr. Forester must have 'swotted up' the subject of wartime Atlantic convoys just as he 'swotted up' the subject of the Navy in Nelson's time. (1955)

mug up, **mug up on (1848)** Used to denote learning a subject by concentrated study; origin unknown ■ Ezra Pound: Chiyeou didn't do it on readin'. Nor by muggin' up history. (1940)

bone up (1887) Orig US; used to denote learning more about a topic by diligent study; usually followed by *on* ■ *Daily Telegraph*: Mr Robert Powell, . . . who is on the set as technical adviser but who wastes no opportunity to bone up on his hobby—Romanesque architecture. (1968)

groise, **groize (1913)** British public schools' slang; from the noun *groise* hard work(er) ■ Arnold Lunn: We all have to groise a lot harder than we used. (1913)

Cribs

pony (1827) Orig US; applied esp. to a crib used for classical translation; perhaps from the notion of the student being helped by 'riding' on the crib ■ William Faulkner: She kept the dates written down in her Latin 'pony'. (1931)

trot (1891) US ■ *Times Literary Supplement*: The translations are rarely better than lame trots. (1984)

Teaching

leccer, lecker, lekker (1899) British, dated; alteration of *lecture* ■ *Daily Express*: A dilapidated basket filled with gay-coloured 'lekker' notebooks. (1928)

private business (1900) Eton College; applied to extra tuition ■ D. Newsome: Half-an-hour's preparation for his Private Business lecture on Napoleon. (1979)

Schools and other educational establishments

school (1767) US; applied to a college or university ■ Irwin Shaw: The proms at which he played the trumpet in the band, to help pay his way through school. (1977)

poly (1858) Abbreviation of *polytechnic* ■ Iris Murdoch: When he left school he went into the poly, you know, the polytechnic. . . . He had a student grant. (1978)

heifer paddock (1885) Australian; applied to a girls' school; from the notion of female cattle ■ N. Pulliam: Basketball here is mainly an indoor game. Mostly its just played in the heifer paddocks—oh, pardon me, I mean in the girls' schools. (1955)

the shop (1889) Australian; applied to the University of Melbourne

uni (1898) Mainly Australian and New Zealand; abbreviation of 'university' ■ *Australian* (Sydney): Unis look to industry for more funds. (1984)

tech (1906) Orig US; abbreviation of 'technical college' ■ Robert McCrum: Rosie's pride would not let her admit that she . . . had been to the local Tech. (1980)

puppy-hole (1922) Eton College, dated; applied to a pupil-room, in which pupils work with their tutors

cram-shop (1926), crammer (1931) Applied to a school or other institution that prepares pupils for exams by intensive study; from *cram* to prepare pupils in this way ■ Joyce Cary: The young man . . . made Ella promise to play [the piano] with him every afternoon when he could escape from what he called his cram-shop. (1946) ■ *Daily Telegraph*: The spectre of January retakes at some smart London crammer. (1986)

kinder (1955) Australian; abbreviation of *kindergarten* ■ Morris Lurie: Little Norbert and little Hermione and little all the rest of them, are all tucked nicely away in their kinders and creches and day-care centres. (1983)

prepper (1956) British; used for a preparatory school; from *prep* (*school* + *-er* ■ Richard Gordon: 'Actually, I'm a stinks beak in a prepper,' he confessed. (1962)

kindy, kindie (1959) Australian & New Zealand; applied to a kindergarten; from *kind*(*ergarten*) + *-y* ■ *Daily News* (Perth): Lorrelle Holman (5), of Mt Pleasant, is learning pots about the animal kingdom, thanks to her local kindy. (1980)

Relating to schools

preppy (1900) US; used to denote students in a preparatory school or their characteristics, esp. immaturity; from *prep*(*aratory* + *-y* ■ Mary

McCarthy: When he finally did ask, . . . it was in a casual preppy voice. (1971)

shoe (1962) US; used to denote conformity to the dress, behaviour, or attitudes of students at exclusive schools and colleges; origin unknown ■ *New York Times*: Perhaps it is significant that one favourite mode of protest in the fifties was satire. We—a lot of us—were cool, ironic, 'shoe'. (1973)

Pupils and students

tug (1864) Applied at Eton College to a student on the foundation, a colleger as opposed to an oppidan; in wider use, applied to a studious or academic pupil, a swot; origin uncertain

fresher (1882) British; applied to a first-year university student; from *fresh*(*man* + *-er* ■ Sara Duncan: According to the pure usage of Oxonian English, he was a 'Fresher'. (1891)

co-ed (1893) Orig US; applied to a female student at a co-educational institution; from earlier sense, co-educational institution ■ *Daily Telegraph*: Undergraduates and co-eds sought more violent or dramatic ways of expressing their feelings. (1970)

frat (1895) US, college; applied to (a member of) a college fraternity; abbreviation of 'fraternity' ■ *Punch*: The only Frank Lloyd Wright building on my campus was a frat. house. (1967)

pledge (1901) US; applied to a student who has pledged to join a fraternity (or sorority)

bug (1909) British, schoolboys'; applied to a schoolboy, esp. of the stated sort; from earlier sense, insect ■ John Rae: You're new, Curlew, and new bugs should be seen and not heard. (1960)

Tab (1914) British, university, dated; applied to a member of Cambridge University; short for *Cantab*.

frosh (1915) North American; applied to a college freshman or a member of a freshman sports team, and also to freshmen collectively; modified shortening of *freshman*, perhaps influenced by German *Frosch* frog, (*dialect*) grammar-school pupil ■ *University of Waterloo* (Ontario) *Gazette*: 'A university is a very special kind of place,' Wright told the 2,000 frosh. (1985)

rushee (1916) US, colleges'; applied to someone 'rushed' or entertained to assess their suitability for membership of a fraternity or sorority ■ *American Speech*: The girl rushee who does not have 'tights- omania' will be blackballed in short order. (1960)

upper (1929) British, public schools'; applied to a pupil of the upper school; from the adjective *upper*

preppy, preppie (1970) US; applied to a pupil at a preparatory school ■ *New York*: His first year as a preppie had left Junius feeling like a pound of plaster of Paris. (1970)

sweat-hog (1976) US; applied to a difficult student singled out in school or college for special instruction ■ *Senior Scholastic*: John Travolta

... [is] back in the classroom ... as the leader of the sweathogs in ABC's *Welcome Back, Kotter.* (1976)

A hard-working pupil

swot, swat (1850) British, derogatory; from earlier sense, hard study ■ *Economist*: Mr Augstein ... still looks like a frail sixth-form swot, peering critically through his spectacles at an imperfect world. (1987)

grind (a1889) US college, dated; often in the phrase *greasy grind* ■ Sinclair Lewis: He told himself that, with this conceited grind, there was no merit in even a boarding-house courtesy. (1951)

groise, groize (1913), groiser, groizer (1936) British public schools'; from *groise* hard study ■ Morris Marples: A corps groize is one who tries to gain favour by his efficiency in the O.T.C. (1940)

wonk (1962) US; compare earlier senses, cadet, effeminate man ■ *New York Times Magazine*: At Harvard the excessively studious student is derided as a 'wonk', which Amy Berman, Harvard '79, fancifully suggests may be 'know' spelled backward. (1980)

Teachers

prof (1838) Orig US; abbreviation of *professor*; originally spelt *proff* ■ H. L. Wilson: I bet Wilbur thinks the prof is awful old-fashioned, playing with his fingers that way. (1916)

beak (1888) British, schoolboys', dated; from earlier sense, magistrate ■ John Betjeman: Comparing bruises, other boys could show Far worse ones that the beaks and prefects made. (1960)

schoolie, schooley (1889) Australian and northern English; from *school*(*teacher* + *-ie*; also applied in British naval slang to a classroom instructor ■ *Bulletin* (Sydney): The few local kids grew up until, except for the schoolie's tribe, there was on'y my youngest at the school. (1944) ■ John Hale: The schoolies began to ... brace themselves for another day of ramming drill and P.T. ... into the minds and bodies of eight divisions of apprentices. (1964)

chalkie, chalky (1945) Australian; from *chalk* + *-ie*; from teachers' use of chalk for writing on blackboards ■ L. Clancy: After I was taken on as a staff member I used to drink with a group of 'chalkies', as they like to call themselves. (1979)

teach (1958) Abbreviation ■ Archie Hill: 'I always suspected it, Hill,' Teach had called across the classroom. (1976)

Academics

acca, acker (1977) Australian ■ *Sun* (Melbourne): Ackers up from the university, who read Saturday's 'Sydney Morning Herald' (it used to be the 'Guardian') at half time. (1984)

School subjects

stinks (1869) British; applied to chemistry, from the unpleasant smells produced in the course of its study ■ Angus Wilson: Eventually ... the laboratory work will be on a scale that will make this place look like a school stinks room. (1961)

Examination and assessment

viva (1891) Short for *viva (voce examination*; also used as a verb, in the sense 'to examine aurally' ■ *Westminster Gazette*: If a man has done his paperwork either very well or very badly, the 'viva' is almost entirely formal. (1897)

practical (1934) Short for *practical examination* ■ F. Olbrich: He would get through this damned exam if it was the last thing he did. ... There would still be the practicals, of course. (1979)

smoke-up (1927) US; applied to an official notice that a student's work is not up to the required standard ■ *Indiana Daily Student*: Sikes say 56 p.c. of Frosh probably had one Smoke-up. (1960)

To fail in an examination

pluck (1713) British university slang, dated; possibly from the former convention that one could veto a candidate for a degree at Oxford by tugging the sleeve of a procter's gown during the degree ceremony ■ George Sala: If you had to pass an examination for the post ... in all probability be plucked. (1894)

flunk (1837) Orig and mainly US; often used with *out* when intransitive; from earlier sense, fail, give in ■ *Word Study*: For if English teachers had always based their grades in English on the moral probity of their students' private lives, they would have had to flunk such naughty boys as Christopher Marlowe ... and ... Edgar Allan Poe. (1966) ■ *Times*: I was utterly, deeply, completely depressed and flunked my A levels. (1970)

plough (1853) British university slang, dated; reportedly a conscious substitution for the earlier *pluck* ■ *Times*: My young friend was undeservedly ploughed. (1883)

pill (1908) Dated; from earlier sense, to blackball

zap (1961) ■ *National Observer* (US): A graduate student whose 'scholarly potential' is not overwhelmingly lauded 'is going to get zapped'. (1976)

Discipline and punishment

poena (1842) Schoolchildren's, dated; applied to an exercise given as punishment; from Latin *poena* punishment ■ L. A. G. Strong: If you were in disgrace he ... helped you with your poena and shooed you out of the empty classroom. (1941)

prog, proggins (1890) British; jocular alteration of *proctor*, official responsible for discipline at Oxford and Cambridge universities; *prog* also used as a verb, in the sense 'subject to the proctor's authority' ■ G. B. Grundy: He did not care a — for all the — proggins in the kingdom. (1945) ■ *Guardian*: This evening may be the last ... on which undergraduates can be progged. (1965)

impot (1899) Dated school slang, mainly British; applied to a task assigned as a punishment; abbreviation of *imposition* ■ Raymond Massey: Mr Luce succeeded in ruining our handwriting. He used to hand out 'impositions' by handfuls. These 'impots' were enormous multiplication sums, ten figures by ten figures, or fifty or a hundred lines. They would be done after school hours. (1976)

Corporal punishment

cuts (1915) Australian & New Zealand ■ D. Adsett: If anyone was careless enough to use the wrong peg, their coat, hat and bag could be thrown to the floor without fear of getting the cuts. (1963)

sixer (1927) Applied to six strokes of the cane; from *six* + *-er* ■ Colleen McCullough: They all got sixers, but Meggie was terribly upset because she thought she ought to have been the only one punished. (1977)

To play truant

wag, wag it (1841) Compare *hop the wag* ■ W. S. Walker: They had 'wagged it' from school, as they termed it, which . . . meant truancy in all its forms. (1901)

play hookey, play hooky (1848) Orig US; compare *hook it* and *sling one's hook* make a hurried departure ■ *Globe & Mail* (Toronto): Youngsters who play hooky are . . . merely afraid of their classrooms. (1965)

hop the wag, (dated) **play the wag (1861)** *wag* probably from earlier sense, mischievous boy ■ M. Todd: The two of them had 'hopped the wag' from school one afternoon. (1964) ■ Jerome K. Jerome: He had caught it . . . by that unaccountable luck that appears always to wait upon a boy when he plays the wag from school, and goes out fishing on a sunny afternoon. (1889)

9. Communication

The voice

Hobson's choice, Hobson's (1937) British; rhyming slang ■ *New Statesman*: The landlady, Queenie Watts, throws her Hobsons . . . so hard that on a clear night you could hear it in Canning Town. (1961)

To speak (to)

jaw (1748) Usually derogatory, and often implying tedious or overlong speech ■ *Winston Churchill*: To jaw-jaw is always better than to war-war. (1954)

spit out (1855) Used to denote openly stating or revealing something; usually in the phrase *spit it out* ■ Anthony Price: 'Well—spit it out, man! Don't just stand there,' Willis exhorted him. (1981)

pipe up (1889) Used to denote someone boldly starting to speak ■ *Daily Mail*: When the congregation was asked for any reason why the couple shouldn't be married, her 13-year-old brother piped up: 'Yes. She can't cook.' (1991)

word (1905) Australian ■ K. S. Pritchard: Ted worded a mate of his on the *Western Star*. (1967)

mensh, mench (1937) Mainly in the phrase *don't mensh* don't mention it; also used as a noun; abbreviation of *mention* ■ Frederick Nolan: 'Thanks, Lucky.' 'Don't mensh, don't mensh,' Luciano said. (1974)

bunk off (1877) British; from the noun *bunk* hurried departure ■ *Time Out*: A lot of kids here bunk off, as all kids do. The rate here is about 18%. (1973)

hook Jack (1877) US; compare *play hookey* ■ J. C. Lincoln: The boy 'hooked Jack' for a whole day. (1905)

bag school, bag it (1892) US ■ *Philadelphia Bulletin*: Threatening him with castor oil, when he seemed set to bag school, never did any good. (1948)

sag (1959) Merseyside slang; from earlier sense, sink or hang down (with intermediate naval sense, drift off course) ■ *Woman*: I re-visit childhood haunts in Liverpool, meet the next generation in the Cathedral grounds where we used to 'sag'—that is, play truant. (1965)

Expulsion

super (1902) British, dated; used to denote the removal of a pupil from a form or school because of age; short for *superannuate* ■ Terence Rattigan: He was super'd from Eton. (1945)

flunk out (1920) Orig and mainly US; used to denote expulsion from a college, etc. for failing an examination; from *flunk* fail an examination ■ *Reader's Digest*: He flunked out of various high schools, not because he was too stupid. (1951)

Holiday

vac (1709) British; short for *vacation* ■ *Catholic Weekly*: Others lectured to working men in the vacs. (1906)

give (1956) Used in the imperative ■ Polly Hobson: 'Come on. Give.' 'That ruddy policeman went digging things up and he found out I'd written my own testimonials.' (1968)

To repeat what one has said

come again (1884) Orig US; used to ask someone to repeat what they have said ■ Anthony Gilbert: Nurse Alexander startled them all by saying suddenly, 'No scones.' Crook turned. 'Come again, sugar?' (1956)

To reply

come back (1896) Orig US ■ F. N. Hart: Just as I was thinking of something really bright to come back with, a nice soft little voice in the back of the hall said [etc.]. (1928)

Something said

peep (1903) Usually used in negative contexts; from earlier sense, cheep, squeak ■ *Picture Post*: 'One more peep out of you, Mister, and I'll get the boys to push you and your b— stall in the oggin', which was a nearby canal. (1954)

mouthful (1922) Orig US; applied to something important or noteworthy said ■ P. G. Wodehouse: 'Nice nurse?' 'Ah, there you have said a mouthful, Pickering. I have a Grade A nurse.' (1973)

dicky-bird, dickey-bird (1932) British; rhyming slang for *word*; usually used in negative contexts ■ *Alfred Draper*: George didn't say a dicky bird when I ambled in. (1970)

To converse

yarn (1857) From the noun *yarn* chat, conversation ■ *Colleen McCullough*: Their parents yarned over cups of tea, swapped tall stories and books. (1977)

chew the fat (or **rag**) **(1885)** Usually implying lengthy discussion ■ *Josephine Tey*: We had that paper in the pantry last Friday and chewed the rag over it for hours! (1948)

schmooze, schmoos(e) (1897) Orig US; used to denote lengthy gossipy conversation; from Yiddish *shmuesn* ■ *William Safire*: A 'stoop', from the Dutch word for 'step', is a description of the porch and front steps on which Brooklynites sit and schmooze. (1980)

chin-wag (1920) From the noun *chin-wag* conversation ■ *Alexander Baron*: Didn't he send her down to the village to chinwag with the Indian chiefs? (1954)

rap (1929) Mainly US ■ *Tucson* (Arizona) *Citizen*: Obviously relishing the opportunity to rap with what Jordan called the 'press biggies from out of town'. (1979)

shoot the breeze (1941) US ■ *R. K. Smith*: There were other negative signs, too. No one had come by to shoot the breeze, to have a cup of coffee. (1971)

natter (1943) From obsolete dialect *gnatter* talk grumblingly ■ *Sunday Times*: They . . . nattered away for an hour about nothing. (1958)

(A) conversation, talk

chit-chat (1605) Often applied to gossipy conversation; reduplication of *chat* with alteration of vowel ■ *N. Frye*: The literary chit-chat which makes the reputations of poets boom and crash in an imaginary stock exchange is pseudo-criticism. (1951)

jaw (1748) ■ *J. R. Ackerley*: He invited the two of us into the billiard-room of Grafton House . . . for a 'jaw'. (1968) ■ *Times Literary Supplement*: Without these things, committee work is just endless jaw and empty substitute. (1972)

mag, meg (1778) Dated; from the verb *mag* chatter ■ *E. C. Sharland*: You go away for a while, my dear, and let me have a little mag with Emma. (1885)

yarn (1857) Mainly Australian & New Zealand; from earlier sense, narrative, story ■ *Times*: I still see some of the Roman Catholics in the street . . . and we have a yarn. (1984)

chin (1877) Orig and mainly US; often applied specifically to insolent talk ■ *New Yorker*: We'd like to have a little chin with you right now. (1952)

chin-wag (1879) ■ *Private Eye*: Anyway, he sloped in for a chinwag with the Boss. (1980)

rag-chewing (1885) Mainly US; from *chew the rag* converse

buck, bukh (1895) Dated; often applied specifically to boastful talk or insolence; especially in the phrase *old buck*; from Hindustani *bak*, Hindi *buk buk* ■ *Penguin New Writing*: Nah then, none o' yer ol' buck, Ernie. (1941)

gabfest (1897) Orig and mainly US; applied to a gathering for talk or a lengthy conversation; from *gab* talk + *fest* meeting for a particular purpose, from German *Fest* celebration ■ *Spectator*: A shambles as big as the Labour gabfest. (1960)

bull session (1920) Orig and mainly US; applied especially to a conversation among a group of males ■ *Guardian*: The kind of college 'bull session' that is common among English students. (1960)

yap (1930) Applied to a conversation or chat; from earlier sense, loquacious talk ■ *R. Lawler*: Real ear-basher he is, always on for a yap. (1957)

rhubarb (1934) Theatrical slang; a word repeated to give the impression of the murmur of conversation ■ *John Betjeman*: And in the next-door room is heard the tramp And 'rhubarb, rhubarb' as the crowd rehearse A one-act play in verse. (1960)

schmooze, schmoos(e) (1939) Orig US; applied to a lengthy gossipy conversation; from Yiddish *shmues*, from Hebrew *shĕmū'ah* rumour ■ *Billie Holiday*: [Lena Horne] insisted on taking me out with her and bought me lunch, and we had a wonderful schmooze about the old days in Hollywood. (1956)

rabbit, rabbit and pork (1941) *rabbit and pork* rhyming slang for *talk* ■ *Frank Norman*: We still had quite a heated rabbit about it. (1958)

natter (1943) From the verb *natter* ■ *News Chronicle*: From the swarm he singled out one bird. . . . 'That's Joey, . . . he usually comes for a natter when there's nothing else doing.' (1951)

skull session (1959) US ■ *David Jordan*: Joe was ready for the skull session. (1973)

visit (1988) US; from earlier sense, instance of going to see someone ■ *Oxford Advanced Learner's Dictionary*: We had a nice visit on the phone. (1995)

To say

sez (1844) Jocular representation of the pronunciation of *says* ■ *John Stroud*: If I make a movement, he sez: 'Oh, don't be disgusting!' he sez. (1960)

go (1967) Orig US; used mainly in the historic present, in direct speech; from earlier sense, make the characteristic noise of an animal ■ *M. Rosen*: So I go, 'Time for the cream, Eddie.' And he goes, 'No cream.' (1983)

To discuss

kick around (1939) Orig US ■ *G. Douglas*: They kicked the details around for a few more minutes and then left them to stew. (1971)

A discussion

confab (1701) Abbreviation of *confabulation* ■ *South China Morning Post*: After a confab with our Lai See colleague, we find this to be the most expensive bottle of water yet reported in Hongkong. (1992)

powwow (1812) From earlier sense, Native American conference ■ *Manchester Guardian Weekly*: The associated lobbies that oppose the [St. Lawrence] seaway, the railroads, coal-owners, and Eastern port authorities, went into a round of emergency pow-wows. (1954)

huddle (1929) Applied to a close or secret discussion; especially in the phrase *go into a huddle*; from earlier sense, small close group ■ James Bertram: He went into a huddle with one of his minions. (1947)

Loquacity

big mouth (1890) Orig and mainly US; compare earlier sense, loquacious person ■ M. K. Rawlings: Now mister impudent big-mouth. (1938)

yackety, yackity, yaketty, yakkety, yakkity (1953) Used to express the sound of incessant chatter; usually reduplicated or followed by *ya(c)k*; imitative ■ Desmond Bagley: The Sergeant . . . only talks when he has something to say. Everybody else goes yacketty-yack all the time. (1982)

Loquacious

mouthy (1589) Often also implying boastfulness or impudence; from *mouth* + *-y* ■ *Guardian*: His mouthy confidence has no limits. Sure of his place in the England side for years to come, Catt was outspoken on the subject of payments to the lads. (1997)

To talk loquaciously

blabber (c1375) Imitative ■ *Guardian*: But would they like me to come down and settle up with it now? And so I blabber on. (1992)

blether, blather (1524) From Old Norse *blaðra* talk stupidly ■ *Guardian*: So what the devil is Norman Fowler blethering on about? (1992)

spout (1780) ■ *Times Literary Supplement*: The seedy group of coffee-bar philosophers . . . spouting their sad rehash of dated Fascist clichés. (1957)

gab (1786) Apparently onomatopoeic; compare *gabble* ■ *Wall Street Journal*: She often discovers that she has been gabbing long after her call has been cut off. (1989)

talk the hind leg off a donkey (horse, etc.) **(1808)** ■ G. H. D. & M. Cole: You can talk the 'ind leg off any donkey. (1942)

witter, whitter (1808) Orig Scottish; used to denote annoyingly inconsequential or rambling talk; often followed by *on*; perhaps a variant of Scottish *whitter* twitter ■ Osmington Mills: You might . . . try making the tea, instead of wittering on about Cordon Bleu methods. (1966)

mag, meg (1810) Dated; from the female personal name *Mag* (short for *Margaret*), perhaps inspired by obsolete *Mag's tales* nonsense, trifling ■ James Runciman: I'll snap your backbone across my knee if you meg half a second more. (1885)

go on (a1822) Often followed by *about* or *at* ■ *Listener*: How much of what I have been so tediously going on about here is reflected in the programme itself? (1969)

yatter (1825) Orig Scottish dialect; imitative, perhaps after *yammer* + *chatter* ■ J. N. Harris: This dear old Betty was yattering at me on Sunday morning when I was hung over to the eyeballs. (1963)

gas (1852) Orig US; from the noun *gas* lengthy but empty talk ■ Rudyard Kipling: I'm 'fraid I've been gassing awf'ly, sir. (1893)

shoot one's mouth off, shoot off one's mouth (1864) Orig US ■ *Rocky Mountain News* (Denver, Colorado): A Dutch married woman . . . was taxed $17.80 for 'shooting off her mouth' against the virtue and morality of a neighbouring maiden. (1864)

yap (1886) From earlier sense, bark sharply ■ *Daily Telegraph*: A lot of women who are happy to yap away normally, became tongue-tied when they had to talk and drive. (1975)

waffle, woffle (1900) Used to denote inconsequential or rambling talk; from earlier sense, yelp ■ Peter Dickinson: You can make the correct noises while all the old buffers are woffling on. (1982)

run off at the mouth (1909) US ■ *National Observer*: The man they simply ran off at the mouth about here, Jimmy Carter. (1976)

talk someone's ear off (1935) US ■ *National Observer*: Heck! I could talk your ear off. But let me just say that in all my 40 years of organizing and escorting tours, I haven't found a better one than this one. (1976)

run one's mouth (1940) US, mainly Black English ■ *Time*: All there is to real estate is running your mouth a bit, knocking on doors and asking people if they want to sell their house. (1977)

bend someone's ear (1942) ■ *Observer*: What have getting drunk, getting laid and swearing a lot got to do with green-tinted issues? Not a lot, although the concerned chattering classes who bend my ear think otherwise. (1991)

ear-bash (1944) Mainly Australian; probably a back-formation from *ear-basher* loquacious talker ■ S. Gore: Just like you hear 'em ear-bashin' each other in Parliament to this day. (1968)

rabbit (1950) From the noun *rabbit* talk ■ *Guardian Weekly*: A girl reporter from Rolling Stone rabbits on idiotically about the Maharishi. (1977)

yack, yak (1950) Imitative ■ J. Trenhaile: Those two will yak all day. (1981)

yackety-yack, yackety-yacket(y) (1953) ■ Monica Dickens: Our laundry's full of yackety-yacketing women this morning. (1953)

yacket (1958) Back-formation from *yackety* ■ *New Yorker*: We warn them, we yacket away night and day . . . but they never learn. (1969)

bang on (1959) Used to denote insistent or repetitious talk about a particular subject ■ *Car*: So if you bang on now about how wonderful these cars were, don't be surprised by the odd hollow laugh from your more mature patrons. (1990)

yacker, yakker (1961) From the noun *yacker* ■ *Financial Times*: 'Yellow Polka-Dot Bikini'—one of the scratchy 78s . . . —yackers melodiously while the characters gallivant through daytime Calcutta. (1982)

bash someone's ear (1962) ■ *Daily Telegraph*: Mr Wigg bashes the ear as once he bashed the square. (1962)

bang someone's ear (1965) US

fat-mouth (1970) US, mainly Black English; from the noun *fat-mouth* loquacious talker

keep on (1977) Often followed by *about* or *at* ■ *Transatlantic Review:* One will keep on about 'the slicks' he wants to write for. (1977)

Loquacious talk

gab (1790) From the verb *gab* ■ R. L. Stevenson: There's no fair way to stop your gab. (1893)

gas (1847) ■ Cecil Day Lewis: The sisters would sit on the tiny patch of lawn at the back of the house, shelling peas and having a great old gas. (1960). Hence **gassy** (1863) ■ Lord Rosebery: The last development of the Irish question was a gassy meeting in St. James's Hall the previous night. (1892)

yacker, yakker (1882) Australian; imitative ■ Patrick White: Couldn't get on with me work—not with all the yakker that was goin' on in 'ere. (1973)

yap (1907) From the verb *yap* ■ Keith Weatherly: Never mind that yap. Where's the tucker? (1968)

waffle, woffle (1937) From the verb *waffle* ■ *Spectator:* There is a special relationship between Britain and the United States, a special relationship more serious than the waffle we get at banquets. (1965)

yack, yak, yak-yak (1958) From the verb *yack* ■ Nicolas Freeling: The sudden head-down butt jabbed into someone's face, is a highly effective way of putting a stop to his yack. (1983)

yackety-yack, yackety-yacket(y) (1958) From the verb *yackety-yack* ■ *Woman:* For once the place will be free of giggles and girlish yakitty-yak. (1959)

stem-winder (1973) US; applied to a vigorous rabble-rousing speech; from earlier sense, impassioned public speaker ■ *Time:* The 1,008 cadres and 24 fraternal foreign delegations ... endured no fewer than 55 speeches, including an eight-hour stem-winder by Le Duan. (1977)

A loquacious talker

blatherskite, bletherskate (c1650) Orig Scottish dialect, now mainly US; applied to a noisy talkative person, especially one who talks utter rubbish; from *blather, blether* foolish chatter + *skite*, alteration of *skate* the fish (in Scots used contemptuously)

windbag (1827) ■ *Atlantic City:* You'll be stopped dead by a posse of venomous old windbags. (1991)

big mouth (1889) Orig and mainly US; often also implying boastfulness or lack of discretion ■ E. E. Coxhead: He was such a big mouth. He picked up strangers ... and told them the story of his life. (1951)

gas-bag (1889) ■ *Economist:* The gunmen retort by openly despising their political leaders, even 'that gasbag Ian Paisley'. (1988)

fat-mouth (1926) US, mainly Black English; often implying exaggerated claims ■ Joseph Heller: Okay, fatmouth, out of the car. (1961)

loud-mouth (1934) ■ *Daily Mail:* These 625 vain, devious loud-mouths ... are our elected representatives. (1959)

ear-basher (1941) Mainly Australian; from *bash someone's ear*

stem-winder (1942) US; applied to an enthusiastic talker or impassioned public speaker; from earlier sense, forceful person

yacker, yakker (1959) From *yack* talk loquaciously + *-er* ■ *New York Times:* She just brought the parrot along for the ride. ... He was quite a yakker. (1984)

motor mouth (1971) Orig US ■ *National Observer:* The increasing number of 'motor mouths' posing as sports broadcasters,. . . statisticians and whatever. (1977)

rapper (1971) Orig US; from *rap* talk loquaciously + *-er* ■ Christina & Richard Milner: He is recognized as among the best talkers or 'rappers' in the hustling world. (1973)

To speak frankly

talk turkey (1903) Orig North American; in early use also as *talk cold turkey* ■ Agatha Chrisite: Send for a high powered lawyer and tell him you're willing to talk turkey. Then he fixes ... the amount of alimony. (1967)

lay it on the line (1954) Orig US ■ E. E. Sumner: I'll lay it on the line for you, if you like. Are you thinking of asking my girl to marry you? (1967)

To speak revealingly

blow (1575) Used to denote giving away secret information ■ Edgar Wallace: This officer 'blew' the raid to Tommy. (1925)

blab (1583) From earlier sense, chatter ■ *Evening Standard:* The fact that Princess Diana seems to have blabbed to the tabloids has confused her many supporters. (1992)

let on (1725) Orig dialectal and US ■ Kylie Tennant: Maybe Orry didn't like to let on he'd made a mistake in the first place. (1946)

blow the gaff (1812) Used to denote giving away secret information; origin uncertain ■ Bryan Forbes: It's my hunch you were primarily responsible for blowing the whole gaff. (1986)

shoot one's mouth off, shoot off one's mouth (1864) Orig US ■ W. J. Burley: With Matthew Eva shooting his mouth off about Peters it could turn ugly. (1973)

cough (1901) Orig US; usually used to denote confessing ■ W. J. Burley: Once he realized we had it on him he was ready to cough fast enough. (1970)

get something off one's chest (1902) Used to denote relieving one's mind by making a statement or confession ■ Anthony Powell: I wanted to see you to get some things off my chest. I've got to tell them to somebody. (1939)

spill (1917) Orig US ■ Irwin Shaw: He picked up the phone to call the Colonel, spill everything. (1977)

tip one's hand(s) (or mitt) (1917) Orig and mainly US; applied to inadvertently disclosing one's intentions ■ *Economist:* Mr Hunt will not tip his hand on the price at which he will buy more bullion. (1979)

spill the beans (1919) Orig US ■ *Sun* (Baltimore): A Government publication in this country spilled the beans concerning our urgent interest in experiments with uranium. (1945)

open up (1921) Used to denote speaking openly or frankly, ceasing to be secretive
■ M. Braithwaite: Although he never answered—or perhaps because of it—I opened up to him completely, telling him things I'd never told anyone. (1970)

talk (1924) ■ *Times Literary Supplement*: He is, as they say, not talking, and refused to be interviewed by the authors of this book. (1976)

spill one's guts (out) (1927) Mainly US; applied to divulging or confessing as much as one can ■ Arthur Hailey: The kid—he was eighteen, by the way, and not long out of trade school—broke down and spilled his guts. (1979)

See also To betray an associate to the police or other authority under **Betrayal** (pp. 287–90) and To tell the truth under **Honesty** (pp. 277–8).

A revealing speaker

blabber (1557) From *blab* + *-er*

blabbermouth (1936) Orig US ■ David Karp: No, Burney isn't a blabbermouth. He tells you a lot less than he knows. (1956)

Pretentious or misleading talk

hot air (1873) Orig US ■ Angus Wilson: Gerald in his new mood thought only he shouldn't have poll-parroted his life away in humbug and hot air. (1956)

mumbo jumbo (1896) From earlier sense, object of unintelligent veneration; perhaps ultimately from Mande *mama dyumbo* ■ *Times*: Labour's elected representatives . . . mouth the mumbo-jumbo of capitalism: 'The pound must be kept strong', 'We must all buy British'. (1975)

blah, bla, blaa (1918) Orig US; often reduplicated; imitative ■ E. H. Clements: A good deal of blah about waste of public money. (1958)

jazz (1918) ■ Bernard Malamud: I read all about that formalism jazz in the library and it's bullshit. (1971)

jive (1928) Orig US; origin unknown; compare later sense, type of popular dance ■ *Black World*: Everything that we do must be aimed toward the total liberation, unification and empowerment of Afrika. . . . Anything short of that is jive. (1973)

moody (1934) British; probably from the adjective *moody*, but some connection has been suggested with *Moody and Sankey* rhyming slang for *hanky-panky* (from the names of two US hymn writers, Dwight L. Moody (1837–99) and Ira D. Sankey (1840–1908)) ■ Roger Busby: The same old moody he'd heard a thousand times before. (1970)

gobbledygook, gobbledegook (1944) Orig US; applied to pretentious jargon; probably representing a turkey's gobble ■ Meyer Dolinsky: I had been subjected to too much psychiatric gobbledygook. (1959)

To talk (to) pretentiously or ostentatiously

speechify (1723) Denoting the making of pompous speeches, or talking as if one were doing this; from *speech* + *-ify*

blah, blah-blah (1924) From the noun *blah*
■ George Orwell: The tactless utterances of Americans who for years have been blahing about 'Indian freedom' and British imperialism. (1942)

woof (1934) US, Black English; from earlier sense, bark gruffly ■ Joseph Wambaugh: He was woofing me, because he winked at the blond kid. (1972)

To talk (of) exaggeratedly

lay it on (1600) Often in the phrases *lay it on thick* and *lay it on with a trowel* ■ *Times*: If we are laying it on a bit thick it's only because we want you to volunteer out of a mature realisation of what the Army can be like. (1976)

pile it on (1852) ■ J. B. Priestley: I fancy you're piling it on too much. There are lots of things you can enjoy, if you set about it properly. (1943)

strong it (1964) British ■ G. F. Newman: Don't you think that's stronging it? (1970)

See also To boast at **Conceit, Boastfulness, Ostentation** (p. 273).

Insolent talk

lip (1821) ■ Mark Twain: 'Don't you give me none o' your lip,' says he. (1884)

mouth (1935) Orig US

To talk insolently to

lip (1898) ■ Alfred Draper: If anyone lips you, just swallow it. (1972)

smart-mouth (1976) US; from the noun *smart mouth* ■ J. L. Hensley: He . . . beat up three kids . . . when one of them smart-mouthed him. (1978)

An insolent talker

smart mouth (1968) US; also applied to someone who is good at repartee ■ *Sun Magazine* (Baltimore): I was a smart mouth, a troublemaker in school. (1968)

Glib or persuasive talk

spiel (1896) Applied especially to a salesman's patter; from German *Spiel* game, play ■ *Listener*: A long spiel . . . from a tart about how much horrider Soho has become. (1980). Hence **spieler** a glib talker (1894)

fanny (1933) ■ Gerald Kersh: A Guardsman comes to Bill with some Fanny about needing some cash. (1942)

To talk to glibly, persuasively or cajolingly

See also at **Sincerity & Insincerity** (pp. 278–81)

jolly along (1890), jolly up (1893) Orig US; denoting trying to put someone into a good mood ■ Helen McCloy: He protested, he argued, he even tried to jolly them along. They only became bolder. (1973)

fanny (1949) From the noun *fanny* glib talk ■ Allan Prior: They could not fanny Norris into thinking they believed he might have been out to a woman. (1965)

fat-mouth (1971) US; compare earlier sense, talk excessively ■ Bernard Malamud: I ain't asking you to fatmouth me, just as I am not interested in getting into any argument with you. (1971)

To shout

holler (1699) Mainly US; a variant of *hollo* cry out, and related to *hallo* ■ Times: When Colonel Aldrin jumped off the last step of the moon ladder . . . everyone in the Aldrin home was whooping and hollering. (1969)

cry (shout, yell, etc.) **blue murder (1859)** Applied to shouting desperately, as if being attacked ■ Anthony Gilbert: Corpses don't yell blue murder. (1959)

rort (1931) Often applied specifically to shouting abuse or complaints; back-formation from *rorty* jolly, noisy ■ M. Harrison: It isn't you . . . that I'm rorting at. (1935)

To swear

cuss (1815) Orig US; euphemistic alteration of *curse* ■ Washington Post: He didn't do a lot of drinking. And in all the years I knew him, I never heard him cuss. (1993)

blind (1943) Mainly in the phrase *eff and blind*; from the use of *blind* in imprecations such as *blind me!*

eff (1943) Implying the use of the word *fuck*; usually used more broadly, especially in the phrase *eff and blind* swear strongly or continuously; from the use of *eff* as a written euphemistic representation of the first letter of *fuck* ■ Arnold Wesker: He started effing and blinding and threw their books on the floor. (1959) ■ J. Gaskell: He would argue and eff in an intellectual ecstasy all afternoon. (1965)

Amatory talk

sweet nothings (1900) ■ Martin Amis: Half the guests, including DeForest (after a minute of sweet-nuthins with Rachel), had wisely got the hell out as soon as dinner was over. (1973)

To talk amorously

chat (up) (1898) See under To flirt, woo, court at **Sex** (pp. 65–6)

Misunderstanding

crossed wires, crossed lines (1932) From the notion of an incorrect telephone connection ■ Listener: This crossing of the political wires had many repercussions in politics. (1958)

To be, become or remain silent

shut one's face (or **head, mouth, trap**) **(1809), shut it (1886)** ■ Best Short Stories: 'Shut your daft grinning face,' growled Arthur. (1939) ■ John Hale: What you'll do is shut your trap and get back to your reasty [= rancid] pit. (1964) ■ George Millar: 'Enough,' cried Boulaya. 'Shut it, Frisé. . . . You know nothing.' (1945)

button (up) one's lip (or **face, nose**) **(1836), button it (1980)** Orig US ■ Harpers and Queen: I laugh involuntarily, and am met with an impatient glare. I hastily button my lip. (1992)

shut up (1840) ■ Anthony Masters: 'Shut up, Arthur.' 'I beg your pardon, Terence.' (1983)

dry up (1853) ■ F. Scott Fitzgerald: 'Oh, dry up!' retorted Basil. (1928)

cut the cackle (1889) Orig in the phrase *cut the cackle and come to the horses*, implying a cutting short of prevaricatory talk ■ Percy Wyndham Lewis: Cut the cackle Arthur—I'm pressed for time! (1930)

shurrup (1893) Representing a casual pronunciation of *shut up* ■ Cyril Ray: You shurrup, shurrup; I've just about had enough of you. (1960)

pipe down (1900) ■ Evelyn Waugh: Groans of protest rose from the other cells where various tramps and pickpockets were trying to get some sleep: 'Aw, pipe down!' (1945)

chuck it (1901) British; from earlier sense, stop it ■ E. W. Walters: 'Chuck it!' snapped the ill-nourished boy. (1908)

clam (1916) Mainly US; usually followed by *up* or *up on*; from the notion of the clam taciturnly but firmly closing its shell ■ M. M. Kaye: I didn't mean to pry, but there's no need . . . to clam up on me. (1959)

put a sock in it (1919) British ■ Nevil Shute: 'For Christ's sake put a sock in it,' he had said . . . 'and tell them I want an ambulance down here.' (1944)

dummy up (1925) US ■ Raymond Chandler: You can't dummy up on a murder case. (1942)

give something **a rest (1931)** Orig US; denoting stopping talking about something; often in the phrase *give it a rest* ■ Ruth Rendell: 'All right Mother,' said Vera. 'Let's give it a rest, shall we?' (1971)

nark it (1936) British; from earlier sense, stop doing something annoying ■ R.A.F. Journal: Nark it, Flight, . . . you sound like a penny uplift. (1943)

shuddup (1940) Representing a casual pronunciation of *shut up* ■ Frederic Mullally: 'Shuddup,' Macdonald snorted. (1978)

wrap up (1943) ■ Osmington Mills: 'Geoff, wrap up about the jigsaws,' Charles entreated him. (1959)

turn it up (1945) British; from earlier sense, stop doing something ■ J. B. Priestley: 'Are you sure you can trust her?' 'Yes, Joe. So turn it up.' (1961)

belt up (1949) British ■ Listener: May we hope that Hamilton will do a service to art by belting up and going back to school? (1969)

shtoom up, shtoom it (1958) From *shtoom* silent ■ J. Gash: Shtum it. Sounds carry in this. (1982)

nitto (1959) Criminals' slang; also used to mean 'stop, desist'; compare obsolete *nit* used as a warning of someone's approach ■ D. Warner: You guys better nitto. The Sparrow's got a line to your run-in. (1962)

shaddup (1959) Representing a casual pronunciation of *shut up* ■ Daily Mirror: 'Snooker isn't a trifle!' 'Aw, Shaddup!!' (1977)

kiss off (1967) From earlier sense, stop doing something annoying ■ Wilson McCarthy: 'I thought you had stopped smoking.' 'Kiss off, I just started again.' (1973)

leave it out (1969) British; from earlier sense, stop doing something annoying ■ Paul Theroux: No—leave it out! He had been wrong. (1986)

To force to be silent

shut someone **up (1814)** ■ Poor Nellie: Looks at you and shuts you up just like Snorker, my old form master. (1887)

Saying nothing; silent

mum (1521) Often in the phrase keep mum; imitative of closed lips ■ Economist: Most British 'brand' companies keep mum about their most important assets. (1988)

mum's the word (a1704) Used as an injunction to say nothing; from the obsolete interjection mum hush, be quiet

nuff said, nuf(f) ced, nuf(f) sed, abbreviations **N.C., N.S. (1840)** Orig US; used as an indication that nothing more need be said on a particular topic; nuff abbreviation and alteration of enough ■ John Aiken: 'He and Steinherz knew one another at university before they were here.' 'Nuff said, I suppose.' (1971)

oyster (1910) Australian; from the proverbial uncommunicativeness of the oyster ■ H. Anderson: The boy was dragged off to the police station where he remained 'oyster'. (1971)

buttoned up (1936) Often implying a general reservedness or uncommunicativeness ■ Monica Dickens: Why is she so quiet and buttoned up? (1946)

shtoom, schtoom, shtum(m), stumm, etc. **(1958)** Yiddish, from German stumm silent, mute ■ G. Markstein: Keep stumm about how you heard. . . . You can always say you picked up a rumour. (1981)

Information

the goods (1877) Orig US; applied especially to information giving one an advantage or hold over another; usually in the phrase have (or get) the goods on ■ Mary McCarthy: He had a sudden inkling that they would have liked to get the goods on Mulcahy. (1952)

griffin (1891) British, dated; applied to a tip (in racing, etc.); from earlier sense, signal ■ A. M. N. Lyons: 'This is the Straight Griffin, Fred,' said Mr. Cozenza: 'the absolute straight Tip.' (1912)

griff (1891) British; applied to a tip or piece of news or reliable information; short for griffin ■ John Wainwright: The informant was saying: 'It's griff, guv. The real thing.' (1968)

dope (1899) Orig horse-racing slang; apparently from the notion of a drug (dope) administered to a racehorse to affect its performance ■ Agatha Christie: I shouldn't dream of . . . denying it. You've obviously cabled to America and got all the dope. (1945)

tip-off (1901) Orig US; applied especially to information about criminal activity; from the verb tip off ■ Observer: There was a tip-off available

about when it [sc. a bank] was going to be stacked up with cash. (1960)

a line (1903) Orig US; in the phrases get a line on acquire information about, have a line on, and give someone a line on ■ P. G. Wodehouse: If you want to get a line on how she feels, she gave me a letter to give you. . . . Here it is. (1935)

info (1913) Abbreviation of information ■ New Scientist: Generating info for schools. (1971)

drum (1915) Australian; applied to a piece of reliable information, especially a racing tip ■ D. O'Grady: Gave us the drum on where to get hold of the particular rifles we had our eyes on. (1968)

the low-down (1915) Orig US; denoting the relevant information or the inside story; often followed by on ■ M. Mackintosh: One of his minions will . . . give me the official low-down on Fisher. Possible police record, etc. (1973)

oil (1915) Australian & New Zealand; applied to information or news; from the notion of information being essential as oil is to machinery ■ F. B. Vickers: 'That's if all goes well, mate,' said the man who was giving me the oil. (1977)

good oil (1916) Australian; applied to reliable information; compare oil information, news ■ Australian Roadsports & Drag Racing News: This week's good oil . . . on what is being built is . . . a new Chevy-powered Datsun. (1979)

reader (1920) US, criminals' slang, dated; applied to a circular notifying police officers of a suspected criminal to be arrested

ikey, ike, iky (1936) Possibly from an unattested use of ikeymo Jew as rhyming slang for info information ■ J. G. Brandon: 'E passed the ike, that there was somethink on there. (1936)

gen (1940) British, orig services' slang; perhaps an abbreviation of general in the official phrase 'for the general information of all ranks', or possibly from part of the words genuine or intelligence ■ Daily Telegraph: A vast amount of 'gen' is included, and this will be invaluable for settling arguments. (1970)

poop (1941) Orig and mainly US; origin unknown ■ Roy Hayes: How did you get the poop on Kovács? (1973)

poop sheet (1941) Orig and mainly US; applied to a written notice, report, etc. containing information ■ M. Allen: He sends in a report—straight facts, no frills, and a minimum use of adjectives. What he says is included in the mimeographed poop sheet the organization sends out every month. (1974)

rundown (1945) Orig US; applied to a catalogue of information, facts, etc., or a brief description; from earlier horse-racing slang sense, list of entries and betting odds ■ Thomas Pynchon: John Nefastis . . . brought out his Machine. . . . 'You know how this works?' 'Stanley gave me a kind of rundown.' (1966)

spec (1956) Applied to a detailed working description of something; short for specification

■ **James Carroll**: The 707 spec sheets she had memorised
. . . at the Black September training camp. (1976)

scam (1964) Orig US; compare earlier sense, a
trick, swindle ■ *New Musical Express*: No, still no
scam on Donny and Marie. (1976)

To give information

tip someone **the wink (1676)** Denoting giving
someone private information, especially
discreetly ■ **Anthony Gilbert**: When I'm in the market for
trouble of that kind I'll tip you the wink. (1955)

tip someone **off (1891)** Orig US ■ **Ted Allbeury**:
Was there any mileage in tipping them off? Experience said
that tippers-off always got their hands caught in the machinery.
(1975)

wise someone **up (1905)** US ■ **P. G. Wodehouse**:
You won't wise him up that I threw a spanner into the
machinery? (1922)

put someone **wise (to) (1913)** Orig US ■ **Graham
Greene**: I met him my first term at school. . . . He was a year
older and knew the ropes. He put me wise to a lot of things.
(1950)

drum (1919) Australian; often followed by *up*;
from *drum* information ■ **D'Arcy Niland**: Jesus, don't
bite me, son. I was only gonna drum you. (1969)

hip (1938) Orig US; from *hip* informed, aware;
often followed by *to* ■ *Black World*: I had just about
decided to find some way to hip her to contraceptives. (1973)

gen (1943) British, orig services' slang; from *gen*
information; almost always followed by *up*
■ **Edward Hyams**: He wanted information; I had it. I was in a
position to, as we said then, gen him up. I genned him up.
(1958)

pull someone's **coat (1946)** US, Black English
■ **Bernard Malamud**: The black . . . said: 'Lesser, I have to
pull your coat about a certain matter.' (1971)

clue (1948) Usually followed by *up* or *in* ■ **Colin
MacInnes**: You meet all kinds of cats . . . who can clue you up
in all kinds of directions. (1959) ■ *Independent*: Main
Chance clued us in on how the police play in 'Just A Friendly
Game Of Baseball'. (1991)

mark someone's **card (1961)** British; denoting
tipping someone off or putting someone right;
from the annotation of someone's racecard with
a tip for the winning horse ■ **G. F. Newman**: The
third was to phone the insurance assessor and mark his card.
(1970)

Giving information

newsy (1832) Often applied to a letter; from *news*
+ *-y* ■ *Guardian*: When I send you a long, newsy letter, what
do I get? A phone call. (1992)

To have information about

have something on someone **(1919)** Orig US;
denoting the possession of incriminating
information against someone ■ **L. J. Vance**: You
haven't got any thing on me. (1923)

Informed, aware

in the know (1883) Denoting the possession of
secret or inside knowledge ■ *Daily Express*: The
surtax was slipped into the Finance Act of 1927 very much as a
'joker' is occasionally insinuated into an American Tariff Act—
that is to say, surreptitiously, without anybody except those in
the know being aware of the significance of what was
happening. (1928)

on (1885) US; applied to someone who is aware of
or alert to something ■ **Rex Stout**: Wolfe, turning and
seeing Saul, was on as quick as I had been. He said . . .
'What?' (1973)

hip (1904) Orig US; often followed by *to*; origin
unknown ■ *Spectator*: Audiences there are hip to the
latest gossip. (1959)

ready (1967) US, Black English; applied to
someone who is aware of or alert to what is
going on

sussed (1984) British; from *suss out* realize ■ *Gay
Times*: I butt in—'Em, em'—in my most sussed manner. (1990)

A person with information

dopester (1907) Orig US; applied to someone
who collects information on, and forecasts the
result of, sporting events, elections, etc.; from
dope information + *-ster* ■ *Economist*: The inside
dopesters, squeezing the latest gossip about intra-party
machinations out of politicians. (1964)

Misleading information, rumour

mulga wire, mulga (1899) Australian; applied
to the bush telegraph; from Australian *mulga*
the outback, from earlier sense, type of acacia
tree, from Aboriginal (Yuwaalaraay) *malga* + *wire*
telegraph ■ **K. S. Prichard**: The troops've had it all by
mulga. They've heard too. (1950)

scuttlebutt (1901) Orig US, naval slang; used as
the name of a miscellany column in the *Smoking
Lamp* (1901–), from the earlier sense, water-butt
on deck (around which sailors would gather to
exchange gossip) ■ *Sun* (Baltimore): Also a cause for
betting was the ultimate destination. In navy slang 'scuttlebutt'
was rife and had the ship bound everywhere from China to
Murmansk. (1943)

furphy (1915) Australian; applied to a false
rumour or absurd story; from the name of a
firm, J. Furphy & Sons Pty. Ltd. of Shepparton,
Victoria, manufacturing water and sanitary
carts used in World War I: the name 'Furphy'
appeared on such carts, whose drivers were
sources of gossip ■ *Sydney Morning Herald*: The
Premier described the rumours of changes to the legislation as
a great furphy that had got out of control. (1986)

latrine rumour, latrine (1918) Services' slang,
dated; applied to a baseless rumour believed to
originate in gossip in the latrines

dirt (1926) Applied to scurrilous information or
gossip ■ **Evelyn Waugh**: Good morning, darling, what's the
dirt today? (1934)

latrinogram (1944) Services' slang; humorous adaptation of *latrine rumour*; from *latrin(e + -o- + -gram* ■ D. M. Davin: According to current latrino-gram we were going to be given a rest. (1947)

scam (1972) From earlier sense, information ■ William McGivern: There's been a security break. . . . He's scheduled a press conference. . . . The scam is he's going to break what we know on Spencer. (1972)

Narrative, story-telling

yarn (1812) Orig nautical; applied to a story, usually a long or incredible one; originally in the phrase *spin a yarn* tell a story

tear-jerker (1921) Orig US; applied to a story (film, song, etc.) calculated to evoke sadness or sympathy ■ Patricia Wentworth: Three copies of the famous *East Lynne*. A notorious tear-jerker. (1953)

whodunit, whodunnit (1930) Applied to a story about the solving of a mystery, especially a murder; representing *who done* (= did) *it?* ■ *Times*: In the whodunnit, we are conditioned to look for not the most obvious but the *least likely* suspect. (1980)

Megillah (1957) Applied to a long, complicated, or tedious story; especially in the phrase *a whole Megillah*; from *Megillah* any of five books of the Old Testament: Song of Solomon, Ruth, Lamentations, Ecclesiastes, and Esther (from Hebrew *megillah* roll, scroll), in allusion to the length of the books; *a whole Megillah* translated from Yiddish *a gantse Megillah* ■ Sidney Sheldon: 'Do you know the most peculiar thing about this whole megillah?' queried Moody thoughtfully. (1970)

A storyteller

magsman (1918) Australian; applied to a raconteur; compare earlier sense, confidence trickster ■ *Telegraph* (Brisbane): Hardy . . . became the official yarn-spinning champion of Australia today. He won the magsman's championship in Darwin. (1967)

A letter

line (1647) Applied to a short letter ■ Jane Carlyle: Dearest,—Just a line to say that all goes well. (1865)

kite (1859) Criminals' slang; usually applied to an illicit or surreptitious letter or note, specifically one smuggled into or out of prison ■ H. Bryan: Having settled on the girl, one [*sc.* a prisoner] would send her a 'kite', or love letter. (1953)

stiff (1889) Dated; applied mainly to a note surreptitiously passed in a prison; compare earlier sense, bill of exchange ■ A. Griffiths: Other 'stiffs'—the prison term for anonymous or clandestine letters—were scattered about. (1904)

mash note (1890) Dated; applied to a love-letter; from obsolete *mash* infatuation, of unknown origin ■ *New Yorker*: A pen that roared through the Twenties and Thirties writing checks, letters, autographs . . . jazz and mash notes. (1970)

stinker (1912) Applied to a strongly worded letter ■ Laurence Durrell: I was afraid . . . that you would write me a stinker calling me a peach fed sod. (1945)

yum-yum (1943) Naval; applied to a love-letter; from earlier sense, love-making ■ *Times*: Would the sin bosun (chaplain) frown, one wonders, at hearing a love-letter described as a 'yum-yum'? (1962)

stiffy, stiffie (1980) British; applied to a formal invitation card (made of thick cardboard) ■ *Daily Telegraph*: Nigel [Lawson] had in hand a gilt-edged stiffy for a banquet at the Stock Exchange. (1987)

bluey (1990) British, services' slang; applied to an airmail letter-form available free of charge to service personnel stationed abroad and to their correspondents at home; from its colour ■ *Times*: Blueys . . . are being distributed to post offices by the defence ministry. (1991)

To write a letter

drop (1769) Perhaps from the notion of dropping a letter into a letter-box ■ *Bristol* (New Hampshire) *Enterprise*: Just drop a card to your county agent. (1945)

Salutations

SWAK (1925) Orig services' slang; abbreviation of *sealed with a kiss* (on envelopes)

SWALK (1948) Orig services' slang; abbreviation of *sealed with a loving kiss* (on envelopes) ■ Dorothy Halliday: I posted him a long letter with SWALK on it to make him laugh. (1973)

NORWICH (1961) Abbreviation of (k)*nickers off ready when I come home* (on envelopes)

BOLTOP (1989) Abbreviation of *better on lips than on paper* (on envelopes or at the bottom of a letter, next to an X for a kiss); first recorded in print in 1989, but in use much earlier ■ *Daily Telegraph*: During the war there were soldiers who marked their letters to wives and sweethearts BOLTOP. (1989)

A typewriter

typer (1892) Dated, orig US ■ *Morning Post*: It is . . . typewritten, for . . . 'we have bagged another German typer'. (1915)

mill (1913) US, dated ■ H. L. Mencken: Writers' cramp was cured . . . on the advent of the *mill*, i.e., the typewriter. (1948)

The telephone

blower (1922) ■ John Wyndham: I'd of said the old girl was always listenin' when there was anyone on the blower. (1957)

dog and bone, dog (1961) British, rhyming slang; compare earlier US rhyming slang *switch and bone* ■ *Minder*, Thames Television: Get on the dog; invite old Arthur down here for an evening on the river. (1983)

To telephone

buzz (1929) ■ Ellery Queen: I wouldn't have buzzed you so early in the morning except that Ritter just phoned. (1929)

give someone **a buzz (1930)** From *buzz* sound made by a telephone ■ G. Usher: Shall I give him a buzz? (1959)

give someone **a tinkle (1938)** From the ringing sound made by a telephone ■ Beryl Bainbridge:

'Next time you're in London,' advised Ashburner, 'give me a tinkle and I'll take you to my Oxfam shop.' (1980)

give someone **a bell (1982)** British ■ G. F. **Newman:** I was going to give you a bell. But I thought it best to give the phone a miss. (1986)

A signal

office (1803) Dated; especially in the phrase *give* (or *take*) *the office* ■ Rolf Boldrewood: Ride about the country till I give you the office. (1890)

griffin (1889) Dated; origin unknown ■ *Cassell's Saturday Journal:* Plank yourself at the corner to give the griffin (signal) if you hear or see owt. (1889)

emma (1891) Military slang; used for the letter *e* in telephone and code messages; see **pip** (below)

peg (1911) Applied to a railway semaphore signal

pip (1913) Military slang; used for the letter *p* in telephone and code messages, especially in *pip emma* = p.m. ■ Colleen McCullough: The second hand was just sweeping up to 9:40 pip-emma. (1977)

red board (1929) US; applied to a railway stop signal

ten-four, **10-4 (1962)** Orig and mainly US; used as a radio code signal signifying 'message received', and hence more broadly to denote affirmation; also used as a verb to denote understanding of a communication; one of a set of code phrases, all beginning with the number ten, used originally in radio communication by the police in the US and later adopted by Citizens' Band radio operators ■ *National Observer:* Judge Floyd Smith, a CB operator himself, went by the 'handle' of 'Marryin' Sam', the bride was 'Little Lulu', and the groom was 'Stanley Steamer'. They didn't say 'I do'; they

said '10-4'. And the judge didn't pronounce them man and wife; he said, 'Put the hammer down.' (1976)

squawk (1975) Applied to an identification signal given out by an aircraft; from the verb *squawk* signal

To signal

squawk (1956) Orig US; applied to an aircraft transmitting an identification signal, enabling its position to be located by radar ■ J. Gardner: His eyes remained on the huge radarscope. . . . The indicator numbers 12—'squawked' by the Boeing's transponder—flicked off and changed. (1982)

Public address

squawk-box (1945) US; applied to a loudspeaker or public-address system, and also to an intercom

Language

lingo (1660) Originally applied to a foreign language, and now also to the jargon of a particular group; probably from Portuguese *lingoa* language ■ *Independent:* 'Chatty-Catty' and friends were era-typical, smart-alecky dolls which . . . talked back at you in up-to-the-minute kid lingo. (1991)

-speak (1949) Used as a suffix to denote a particular variety of language or characteristic mode of speaking; originated by George Orwell in his novel *Nineteen Eighty-Four* in *Newspeak* an artificial language for official communications and *Oldspeak* standard English ■ *Guardian:* 'I am very sorry that I cannot be with you today. . . . I am most grateful and touched that you have decided to name a locomotive after me,' it [*sc.* a telegram] said in classic royalspeak. (1981)

10. Greetings & Farewells

Hello

hi (1862) Orig North American; from earlier use as an exclamation to attract attention ■ P. G. Wodehouse: A musical voice in his left ear said 'Hi'. (1972)

wotcher, **wotcha (1894)** British; alteration of *what cheer?* ■ J. Gash: 'Hello, Lovejoy.' 'Wotcher, love.' (1980)

long time no see (1900) Orig US; a jocular form of broken English, used as a greeting after prolonged separation ■ David Beaty: 'Hello, Clive.' 'Long time no see.' (1959)

how's tricks (1915) Orig US; used as a greeting ■ A. Fraser: 'Well,' he greeted me, 'how's tricks?' (1959)

g'day, **gidday**, **gooday (1928)** Australian; representing a casual pronunciation of *good day* ■ *Overland:* 'G'day,' I said. 'G'day,' the fella answered. 'G'day,' said Benny. (1973)

hiya, **hiyah (1940)** Apparently shortened from *how are you?* and influenced by *hi* ■ *Elizabethan:*

Robin Fawcett turned the grin on Friday and me and said 'Hi-ya'. (1959)

what gives (1940) Orig US; used as a greeting; from earlier use as a general enquiry about what is happening

yo (1966) Orig & mainly US; used as a greeting, originally among young blacks

A handshake or other greeting

the glad hand (1895) Orig US; applied to a cordial handshake or other greeting; often used rather ironically ■ *New Statesman:* Crude economic reasons do not explain why Mikoyan should have been given the glad hand. (1959)

skin (1942) US, Black English; applied to the skin of the palm of the hand, as making contact in shaking or slapping hands in friendship or solidarity; especially in the phrases *give* (*some*) *skin, gimme some skin* ■ H. L. Foster: The viewer of TV sporting events will often observe black athletes, and whites too now, giving skin after a home run, a touch-down, or at the start of a basketball game. (1974)

To greet

glad-hand (1903) Orig US; denoting greeting cordially, especially by shaking hands; from *glad hand* handshake ■ *Economist:* General de Gaulle has stood aloof from the backslapping and glad handing. (1958)

press the flesh (1926) Orig US; denoting greeting by physical contact, especially a handshake ■ *Time:* Aides had to coax him into playing fewer tennis matches with celebrities . . . and spending more time pressing the flesh. (1977)

Goodbye

bye (1709) Shortened from *goodbye* ■ Carolyn Weston: The secretary smiled sweetly. . . . 'I'll do that, Mr. Farr. Get a good night's sleep now. 'Bye.' My office wife, he thought sourly. (1972)

ta-ta (1823) A nursery alteration of *goodbye* ■ Russell Braddon: 'All right, Mr. McLeod, fall out.' . . . 'Ta-ta, Rod—see you in Australia.' (1951)

au reservoir (1853) Dated; jocular substitution for *au revoir* ■ E. F. Benson: 'Must be trotting along,' she said. . . . 'Her Majesty is coming, I believe.' 'Oh, I didn't know she was in Tilling,' said Georgie. 'Is she staying with you?' 'Naughty! I only meant the Queen of Tilling.' 'Oh, I *see*,' said Georgie. '*Au reservoir*.' (1935)

so long (1865) Orig US; compare German *so lange* goodbye ■ Joseph Wambaugh: So long, Puerto Vallarta! With his luck he'd die of Aztec Revenge anyway, first time he had a Bibb lettuce salad. (1978)

hooray (1898) Australian & New Zealand; from earlier use as an exclamation of pleasure ■ *New Zealand Listener:* Best of luck on the lake. Hooray! (1965)

hurroo, hooroo (1906) Australian & New Zealand; alteration of *hooray* ■ *Coast to Coast 1967-68:* The others have, one by one, . . . lurched off— 'Hooroo!' 'Seeya, mate!' (1969)

olive oil (1906) Dated; jocular substitution for *au revoir* ■ Eric Partridge: For 'good-bye', the boys at Dulwich already in 1906 used . . . *olive oil* (au revoir). (1933)

pip-pip (1907) Dated; from the sound of a motor-horn at departure ■ George Sims: The nine-day 'British Week' had ended. . . . Fisherman's Wharf had been buzzing with 'Cheerio, pip pip and smashing' voices. (1973)

toodle-oo, tootle-oo, toodle-pip, tootle-pip (1907) British, dated; *toodle, tootle* perhaps from *toot* short blast on a motor-horn; *toodle-oo, tootle-oo* probably influenced by French *à tout à l'heure* goodbye ■ *Standard* (London): Toodlepip to the poor British Exec. (1983)

cheero (1910) British, dated; from *cheer* take heart + the interjection *o* ■ Siegfried Sassoon: Cheero! I wish they'd killed you in a decent show. (1918)

cheerio, cheerioh (1914) British; alteration of *cheero*, influenced by *cheery* happy ■ B. W. Aldiss: My slit-trench is the first on the right, next to the cookhouse. Cheerio, Ali, you old robber! (1971)

Abyssinia (1934) Jocular, dated; punning use of *Abyssinia*, former name of Ethiopia, based on its supposed resemblance to a casual pronunciation of *I'll be seeing you*, an expression of farewell ■ L. P. Hartley: Good-bye, dear, cheerio, Abyssinia. (1949)

cheerie-bye (1934) British; from *cheeri(o* + *good)bye* ■ T. Girtin: Well, cheeriebye. Be seeing you. (1959)

(I'll) be seeing you (1934) Implied in *Abyssinia*, although not independently recorded before 1937 ■ Joyce Porter: Well, ta ever so! Be seeing you! (1970)

T.T.F.N. (1948) British, dated; abbreviation of *ta-ta for now*, a catch-phrase popularized by the 1940s BBC radio programme *Itma* ■ *Observer:* JY [sc. Jimmy Young] said TTFN to Mr Healey. (1976)

see you later, alligator (1956) Orig US, jocular, dated; the formulaic reply is *in a while, crocodile*; predated by obsolete *dig you later, alligator*; first recorded as the title of a song by R. C. Guidry, which was popularized by Bill Haley and the Comets; *alligator* probably from earlier sense, jazz fan

see you (1962) Shortened from earlier phrases such as *see you around, see you later, see you soon* ■ John Irving: 'See ya,' she called, and drove off. . . . 'See ya,' Garp mumbled after her. (1978)

byee (1964) Alteration of *bye* ■ Martin Braune: 'I hope I haven't made you late. 'Byee!' And with that trailing phrase she was off like the bad fairy. (1985)

tatty-bye (1971) British; from *tatty* (a fanciful alteration of *ta-ta*) + *(good)bye* ■ Marian Babson: I'll say tatty-bye for now then. . . . And we'll see you soon. You know the way, don't you? (1974)

11. **Complaining**

To complain

squawk (1875) Orig US; denoting vociferous affronted complaining; from earlier sense, make a short high-pitched cry ■ *Sun* (Baltimore): When you pass a law and hire somebody to enforce it, you can't squawk if your kids get pinched for violating it. (1948)

belly-ache (a1881) Orig US; from the noun *belly-ache* pain in the stomach ■ Erskine Caldwell: I

reckon there's enough to complain about these days if a fellow wants to belly-ache some. (1933)

chew the rag (or fat) (1885) Dated; from earlier sense, have a discussion ■ *Punch:* I got me woes . . . An' she's got 'ers, the good Lord knows, Although she never chews the fat. (1916)

grouse (1885) Orig military slang; origin uncertain, but probably related to *grouch*

■ *Economist*: Senior West German officers are openly grousing about growing difficulties with money and manpower. (1988)

beef (1888) Orig US; from earlier sense, talk loudly or idly ■ Honoria Croome: Stop beefing, Frank. You'll be seeing her again soon enough. (1957)

crab (1891) From earlier sense, criticize ■ F. Scott Fitzgerald: The thing to do is to forget about the heat. . . . You make it ten times worse by crabbing about it. (1925)

whip the cat (1905) Australian & New Zealand; compare earlier sense, suffer remorse ■ V. Palmer: If there's anything wants doing you've only got to ask Macy Donovan. . . . And he makes light of it, too. No whipping the cat: no setting himself up as a little tin god. (1948)

raise (merry) hell (*a*1911), raise Cain (1930) Orig US; denoting vociferous or violent complaining; both from earlier senses, behave rowdily or violently; *Cain* from the name of the man who according to the Bible (Genesis iv) was the first murderer, therefore held to be the epitome of evil ■ J. B. Priestley: If we stand here talking another minute the mistress'll be raising Cain the way she'll say she's destroyed with the draught. (1930)

grouch (1916) Orig US; variant of *grutch* complain, from Old French *groucier, groucher* murmur, grumble ■ H. L. Foster: The tourists . . . all came back to the train at a painfully slow walk, . . . and grouched all the way home. (1925)

nark (1916) Compare earlier sense, annoy ■ *Times Literary Supplement*: This naturally brings out the worst in their opponents and in the resultant narking and name-calling the 'legitimate contention' is lost sight of. (1958)

bitch (1918) Orig US; perhaps from the notion of insulting someone by calling them a 'bitch' ■ Budd Schulberg: What the hell have you got to bitch about when I'm putting the money in your pocket? (1941)

sound off (1918) Orig US ■ *Washington Post*: Voters may buy into a Republican ticket with themes from the party's last national convention: sounding off against big government, violent crime, abortion and gun control. (1993)

cry (scream, yell, etc.) blue murder (1921) Denoting vociferous or frantic complaining; from *blue murder* a cry of alarm at being attacked (1859) ■ *Economist*: ABC's affiliates screamed blue murder when ESPN grabbed audience share by signing a deal to cable-cast football games. (1988)

moan (*a*1922) Orig services' slang; from earlier senses, make a low mournful sound, lament ■ *Landfall*: He felt through his pockets for a cigarette, found a butt and lit it. Why moan? (1948)

tick (1925) Orig services' slang ■ B. W. Aldiss: Certainly there was always something to tick about. Our manoeuvres were pure hell. (1971)

gripe (1928) Orig US; compare earlier sense, cause pain in the stomach (compare *belly-ache*) ■ *Boston Traveler*: People are always griping about kids hanging around and being at the wrong places at the wrong time. (1967)

bind (1943) British, dated, orig services' slang; compare earlier sense, bore, weary ■ D. Buckingham: Eddy's been binding to Vic about you. (1959)

whinge (1946) Introduced into Australian slang from Irish, Scottish and northern dialect, where the meaning 'complain peevishly' had evolved from earlier 'whine'; ultimately from a northern form of Old English *hwinsian* whine ■ *Sunday Times*: 'What sort of people do Australians hate most?' 'The whingeing Pom. . . . Poms that come over and do nothing but whinge.' (1983)

carry on (1947) From earlier more general sense, talk angrily and at length ■ Nevil Shute: She don't half carry on about the beer I drink. (1947)

kvetch, kvetsch (1965) US; from Yiddish *kvetshn* ■ *Harper's Magazine*: After listening to Kashouk *kvetch* for a couple of hours, Sol Hurok . . . put the question direct. 'Tell me, Kashouk,' Hurok wanted to know. 'If you always lose so much money, why do you stay in business?' (1971)

A complaint; an instance of complaining

stink (1851) Used in the phrase *raise* (or *kick up, make*) *a stink* to denote complaining vigorously; from earlier sense, row, furore ■ Michael Cronin: The first thing he'd do when he got back was see his M.P. and kick up a stink. (1959)

niggle (1886) Compare earlier sense, small cramped handwriting ■ *Times Literary Supplement*: In view . . . of the fact that his book should . . . go into a second edition . . . , one or two minor niggles may conveniently be ventilated. (1974)

crab (1893) From the verb *crab* complain, find fault ■ *Observer*: The only 'crab' we have against this is that cavalry of old effected most of their success by charging infantry. (1927)

beef (1899) Orig US; also applied to a ground for complaint; from the verb *beef* complain ■ *Daily Express*: The beef is, Why should every battle we fight have to be a 'Battle of Britain'? (1945)

squawk (1909) Orig US; applied to a sudden vociferous complaint; from earlier sense, short high-pitched cry ■ Marghanita Laski: They was just told to shut down and shut down they did . . . there wasn't a squawk out of none of them. (1948)

moan (1911) Orig services' slang; in this use probably a nominalization of *moan* complain, grumble (although this is not recorded until later) rather than a slang revival of earlier standard English *moan* complaint, lament ■ *Times*: It's the one moan I have about international rugby. There ought . . . to be referees from neutral countries. (1974)

grouch (1913) Orig US; from earlier sense, (a fit of) ill humour; ultimately a variant of *grutch* complaint, from the verb *grutch* complain ■ George Orwell: Part of his grouch was that he had tried to join the Air Force . . . and always been put off. (1940)

bleat (1916) Applied to a feeble complaint; from earlier sense, sound made by a sheep ■ Nevil

Shute: He had heard nothing . . . in reply to his signal stating Mr. Honey's bleat. (1948)

grouse (1918) From the verb *grouse* complain ■ *Daily Express*: I cannot understand the point of view of the hanging committee. . . . I have no grouse against them. I am not an Academician, but I do not agree with their choice. (1927)

gripe (1929) Orig US; also applied to a ground of complaint; compare earlier sense, pain in the stomach (compare *belly-ache*) ■ *Chemical & Engineering News*: As a standard bearer in the cause of accurate nomenclature, you may be interested in one of my pet gripes. (1954)

bitch (1945) Orig US; also applied to an instance or session of complaining; from the verb *bitch* complain ■ Ben Elton: Everyone develops nervous ticks due to . . . never feeling safe to have a really good bitch. (1991)

drip (1945) Orig naval slang ■ *Guardian*: One of the accused, Able Seaman Edward Kirkbride, said he remembered someone saying: 'I am going to have a drip (complaint).' (1970)

whinge (1947) From the verb *whinge* complain ■ *Times*: In my one-but-last whinge I was going on about the burdensome duties of The Talk. (1985)

A complainer

grouser (1885) From *grouse* complain + *-er* ■ *Wall Street Journal*: The grousers still have a point insofar as order of finish is concerned. (1989)

grouch (1900) Orig US; from earlier sense, (a fit of) ill humour ■ *Listener*: I am probably a humourless old grouch. (1957)

wowser (1900) Australian & New Zealand; applied to an excessively puritanical or prudish person; origin uncertain; perhaps from British dialect *wow* howl, grumble; claimed by John Norton (*c*1858–1916), editor of the Sydney *Truth*, as his coinage ■ *Bulletin* (Sydney): Victoria's publicans seem utterly to have lost their marbles. They have made common cause with the wowsers. (1986)

moaner (1929) From *moan* complain + *-er* ■ Ian Kemp: Burmeister . . . once said to me, 'Limey, you and Goad are the two biggest moaners in my squad.' (1969)

belly-acher (1930) From *belly-ache* complain + *-er* ■ *Listener*: The subordinate who argued about orders was always 'a bellyacher'. (1958)

whinger (1934) From *whinge* complain (but recorded earlier) + *-er* ■ *Guardian*: No true Basildonian can stand a whinger. 'So patients complain of a cold, complain of wanting a sick note, complain of wanting to thank you for resurrecting grandma, and so on'. (1992)

griper (1937) Orig US; from *gripe* complain + *-er*

narker (1937) From *nark* complain + *-er* ■ *Daily Telegraph*: His motto will be to celebrate not denigrate, and I commend this to the legion of glib narkers who tend to monopolise the screen. (1971)

sourpuss (1937) Orig US; applied to a peevish person; from *sour* + *puss* face ■ *Logophile*: He had always been henpecked by his wife, a sourpuss with a waspish temper. (1980)

binder (1944) British, dated, orig services' slang; from *bind* complain + *-er*

misery (1951), **misery guts (1974)** Applied to someone who is always gloomy and complaining ■ *Guardian*: If I hadn't been sitting next to old misery guts, I wouldn't have bothered. (1992)

moaning minnie, moaning Minnie, Moaning Minnie (1962) Applied to someone who is pessimistic and always complaining; compare earlier application to a trench-mortar (from the sound made by the projectile) ■ *New Zealand News*: I don't want to give the impression of being a moaning Minnie but may I . . . make a special plea to the railmen to . . . get back to work. (1972)

kvetch, kvetsch, kvet(s)cher (1968) US; from earlier more general sense, contemptible person

Complaining

on about (1863) In the phrase *be* (or *go, keep*) *on about something* complain (interminably) about something ■ Muriel Spark: Your step-dad's on about young Leslie. (1960)

12. Criticism

Adverse criticism, disapprobation

the bird (1884) Orig theatrical slang, applied specifically to a show of disapproval by an audience, especially in the form of hissing; usually in the phrases *get the bird, give someone the bird*; compare earlier obsolete *the big bird* in same sense, and *goose* express disapproval of by hissing ■ P. G. Wodehouse: Would a Rudge audience have given me the bird a few years ago? (1928)

stick (1956) British; from earlier sense, punishment (as if) by beating with a stick; usually in such phrases as *get some stick, give someone stick* ■ *Daily Telegraph*: I told him that he could expect trouble from the branches. . . . He will come in for some stick over this. (1980)

bad mouth (1960) Orig US; applied to disparaging remarks or maligning; from earlier sense, curse, spell; ultimately a translation of *da na ma* in the Vai language of southern Liberia and Sierra Leone, or of some similar expression in various other African or West Indian languages ■ *Fortune*: The bad-mouth went out over the CB network. Every accident was blamed on the anti-skid brake. (1979)

flak (1968) Orig US; from earlier sense, anti-aircraft fire ■ *Times*: When someone left the office lights on during a power crisis, they . . . got a good deal of flack in the morning. (1981)

licks (1971) US; from *lick* a blow, beating ■ *Time*: Barbara Streisand's A Star is Born does not deserve the licks it has got from Jay Cocks. (1977)

An instance of adverse criticism

rap (1777) Orig US; from earlier sense, a blow ■ *National Observer* (US): 'Mr Fixit' is coming to town, and that is no rap on Jimmy Carter. More than anything else, the American people want government to work. (1977)

slam (1884) US ■ R. L. Duncan: I don't take that description as a slam. I was a great piece of ass. (1980)

crack (1923) Orig US; applied to a sharp (humorous) remark criticizing someone; often in the phrase *make a crack at*; from earlier sense, brisk conversation, news ■ *Listener*: Mr Davis's book . . . is devoid of 'personalities' in the malign sense, except for one snide (and unworthy) crack at Pope Paul VI on page 114. (1967)

side-swipe (1924) Applied to an indirect or passing criticism; from earlier sense, glancing blow ■ *Annual Register*: He allowed himself one side-swipe at the security services, declaring that 'the £60 million spent on these services under the right hon. gentleman's premiership have been less productive . . . than the security services of the *News of the World*.' (1964)

swipe (1932) Usually in such phrases as *take a swipe at*; from earlier sense, a blow ■ *New Scientist*: It only remained . . . for Mr Soper to have a swipe at the conservation intentions of the government, and it was all over. (1983)

hatchet job (1944) Applied to a fierce and unwarranted verbal attack on someone or something, especially in print, and especially one intended to ruin their reputation ■ *Guardian*: One critic . . . was the meanest son of a bitch that ever lived. His criticism was a hatchet job on every book. (1959)

To speak or write critically or disparagingly of; to criticize

roast (1782) ■ P. G. Wodehouse: I've an idea . . . that the critics will roast it. (1920)

slate (1848) From earlier obsolete sense, scold ■ George Saintsbury: You slated this [book], and it has gone through twenty editions. (1890)

get at someone **(1891)** ■ John Osborne: Don't look hurt. I'm not getting at you. I love you very much. (1957)

knock (1892) Orig US ■ Kingsley Amis: I shouldn't like you to get the idea I'm trying to knock Portugal and the Portuguese. (1958)

rap (1906) Orig US, often journalistic; from earlier sense, hit ■ *Boston Globe*: Teachers rapped for failure to understand their pupils. (1967)

pan (1911) Often applied to a film, theatrical or musical performance, etc.; compare earlier sense, cook in a pan ■ Nicholas Blake: The lurid headline, 'Famous Woman Explorer Pans Domesticity.' (1939)

slam (1916) Orig US ■ John Irving: A long, cocky letter, quoting Marcus Aurelius and slamming Franz Grillparzer. (1978)

sandbag (1919) Orig & mainly US; from earlier sense, coerce, bully ■ *Listener*: Mr Heath and Mr Wilson sandbagging each other at televised press conferences. (1974)

soak (1925) US, dated; from earlier senses, punish, hit hard ■ H. L. Foster: I found that we had on board . . . the man whose newspaper soaked my last book. (1925)

bad-mouth (1941) Orig US; see *bad mouth* criticism ■ P. Booth: But now Jo-Anne was a bitter enemy who could be relied on to bad-mouth her at every opportunity. (1986)

blast (1953) Mainly journalistic; perhaps from earlier sense, destroy by explosion ■ *Daily Mail*: House of Commons fitness trainer Vicki Rose has blasted MPs for being one of the unhealthiest groups in Britain. (1991)

rubbish (1953) Orig & mainly Australian & New Zealand; from *rubbish* worthless material; compare *trash* criticize ■ *Observer*: His plight, and that of the cricketers, have both been latched on to as a chance, not to be missed, of rubbishing the Poms. (1975)

clobber (1955) From earlier sense, hit, beat up ■ Wallis & Blair: The Press sure clobbered Roger Law. . . . Don't know why I got off so easy. (1956)

tee off on (1955) US; from *tee off* hit a golf ball off the tee, from the notion of hitting out ■ Harry Kurnitz: I thought you were about to tee off on Ben. . . . Let's both stop making cracks. (1955)

take someone **to the cleaners (1963)** Compare earlier sense, deprive someone of all their money ■ *Listener*: I hoped Mr Carr might round on Mr Cousins and start taking the apprenticeship system to the cleaners. (1963)

dump on (or **all over**) someone **(1966)** Mainly US; denoting unfair criticism; from earlier sense, treat unfairly ■ *Woman's Own*: One minute I'm with a woman who makes me feel like a man, the next I'm with someone who's dumping all over me. (1985)

give someone **a serve (1967)** Australian ■ *Sydney Morning Herald*: One gets fed up to the neck of hearing spokesmen . . . who speak in the proudest Pommy accents roasting Australia and giving Australians a serve. (1983)

slag (1971) Usually followed by *off* ■ Eamon Dunphy: When the game starts, if things start going wrong, everyone blames them. Everyone slags them off. (1976)

bag (1975) Australian ■ *Australian*: It pains me to report that Choice, journal of the Australian Consumers' Association, bags Vegemite for having too much salt in it. (1986)

do a number on someone **(1975)** US

trash (1975) Mainly US; denoting condemning something as worthless; probably from earlier sense, discard as worthless; compare *rubbish* criticize ■ *London Review of Books*: She writes . . . yet another trashing of radical chic. This might be more gripping had she herself not trashed radical chic already. (1981)

have a go at (1977) From earlier sense, attack ■ **Catherine Aird**: Pathologists had hobbyhorses, too, and obesity was . . . Dr. Dabbe's. He was always having a go at Sergeant Gelven . . . about his weight. 'See you soon,' was his favourite form of greeting to the portly detective, 'on my slab.' (1977)

tear someone or something **down (1978)** US ■ **Isaac Bashevis Singer**: The insolence of a writer tearing down a piece before it's been performed! (1978)

have (or **take**) **a pop at** someone **(1992)** British; compare earlier senses, hit someone, shoot at someone ■ **Daily Express**: Tight-head prop Probyn has had a pop at England team boss Geoff Cooke for ditching him from the national side. (1993)

To speak sarcastically; to sneer

sling off (1900) Australian & New Zealand; often followed by *at* ■ **Richard Beilby**: I wasn't slinging off at your religion. (1977)

chuck off (1901) Australian & New Zealand; often followed by *at* ■ **A. E. Manning**: Your friends 'chuck off' at you for being a 'goodie-goodie'. (1958)

To express derision or disapproval (of); to barrack; to tease

goose (1838) Theatrical slang; denoting expressing disapproval of a play, actor, etc. by hissing; from the hissing of geese

chiack, chyack (1853) Australian & New Zealand; see *chi-hike* ■ **K. S. Prichard**: The rowdy bodgie youths kept seats near this group, chiacking the buxom, brassy-haired waitress as she rushed around with a tray-load of dishes and lively back-chat. (1967)

chi-hike, chi-ike (1874) From obsolete *chi-hike* a shout of salutation ■ **Spectator**: Half a dozen chi-iking louts. (1962)

To insult

signify (1932) US, mainly Black English; denoting making insulting remarks or insinuations ■ **C. Mitchell**: I wasn't signifying at her, but . . . if the shoe fits, wear it. (1969)

Insults, abuse

verbal (1973) British; often in the phrase *give*

someone the verbal ■ **Observer**: Each 'ball' consisted of a distinctly lethargic head-high bouncer . . . , followed by a rousing collection of verbals (money will be paid to lip-reading viewers for translation). (1982)

Being criticized

on the pan (1923) US ■ **A. Aylesworth**: Five college professors sitting around a table. . . . A sixth professor who wasn't there because he had snagged a job at a better institution, was on the pan. MacSnuft leaned across at the rest of us and contributed: 'He's an ignoramus!' (1939)

Someone who speaks critically or disparagingly

knocker (1898) Orig US; from *knock* criticize + *-er* ■ **Shooting Times & Country Magazine**: Today the 'knockers' seem to delight in slamming anything British. (1972)

Monday-morning quarterback (1932) US; applied to someone who criticizes something (originally the play in an American football game) only with the benefit of hindsight

nitpicker (1951) Orig US; applied to a pedantic or captious critic; from the notion of searching minutely in hair to pick out the nits ■ **New Statesman**: Some of the . . . modern buildings . . . which provide a real feast for art-historical nit-pickers. (1964)

hatchet man (1952) Applied to someone who criticizes with great severity, especially in order to destroy a reputation; from earlier sense, hired killer ■ **News Chronicle**: The Kennedy family went into action with a commando team of political hatchet-men. (1960)

back-seat driver (1955) Applied to someone who criticizes or attempts to direct without responsibility, or who controls affairs from a subordinate position; from earlier sense, passenger in the rear seat of a car who gives unsolicited directions to the driver ■ **Guardian**: She [Margaret Thatcher] is not so much a backseat driver as an obstacle lying in the road. (1991)

To moderate one's criticism

pull one's punches (1934) Usually used in the negative; from earlier sense, lessen the force of one's blows ■ **Time Out**: The film pulls all its political punches, settling instead for sentimental narrative. (1977)

13. **Ridicule**

To make fun of someone or something; mock, tease

rag (1808) British, dated; compare earlier sense, scold ■ **Times**: The President is now ragged mercilessly on national television, by talk show hosts, by comics, and in cartoons. (1975)

kid (1811) Probably from the noun *kid*, in the sense 'make a goat of' or 'make a child of' ■ **Listener**: Mrs O'Hare has, of course, come in for a lot of kidding and wry jokes. (1969)

josh, joss (1852) Orig US; origin unknown ■ **P. H. Kocher**: When Pippin and Merry are reunited with their comrades . . . Gimli joshes them over and over as 'truants' who had to be rescued. (1972)

pull someone's **leg (1888)** Often denoting making fun of someone by telling them something untrue ■ **Graham Greene**: 'You aren't pulling my leg, are you?' the sergeant said. 'Not this time, sarge.' (1938)

rot (1890) British, dated; compare *rot* nonsense, rubbish ■ **Ian Hay**: We don't do any work: we just rot Duck-face. We simply rag his soul out. (1914)

horse (1901) US, dated ■ **P. Buranelli**: Always playing jokes on each other, they began to 'horse' each other cryptographically. (1928)

razz (1921) Orig US; from the noun *razz* reprimanding ■ **Billie Holiday**: When I came to work the other girls used to razz me, call me 'Duchess' and say, 'Look at her, she thinks she's a lady.' (1956)

rib (1930) Orig US; from the dialect sense, beat someone on the ribs ■ L. P. Hartley: When the chaps rib her she doesn't quite know how to act up. (1955)

take the mickey (or **micky, mike, Michael**) **(out of) (1935)** Mainly British; origin unknown ■ Lionel Davidson: Jesus, did we take the Michael! We used to chat 'em up, these old bats out looking for prospects. (1966) ■ B. W. Aldiss: Geordie looked anxiously at me, in case I thought he was taking the micky too hard. (1971) ■ Berkeley Mather: Watch it. . . . The Swami don't dig taking the mike out of the gods. (1973)

wise off (1943) US; denoting making wisecracks at someone; usually followed by *at* ■ P. Mallory: He's a real meanie. I wouldn't be wising off at him if I were you. (1981)

take the piss (out of) (1945) British ■ R. Hill: When Hope replied 'He's a Hungarian' he thought at first he was taking the piss. Wield seemed prepared to accept this as a serious contribution, however. (1978)

get someone **at it (1958)** ■ Frank Norman: He had half sused that the boggie was getting him at it. (1958)

mickey-take (1959) British; from *take the mickey* ■ *Vogue*: They'd think you were a nutter and laugh and mickey-take. (1959) ■ *Spectator*: One looks forward after reading this brilliant exercise in mickey-taking to Miss Tracy's next novel. (1967)

pull someone's **pisser (1969)** British; *pisser* penis, a jocular substitution for *leg* ■ B. W. Aldiss: He was pulling your pisser, Wal. Malaria's no worse than a cold to the Wogs, is it, Bamber? (1971)

smart-mouth (1976) US; denoting being cheeky to someone or being witty at their expense ■ J. L. Hensley: He . . . beat up three kids . . . when one of them smart-mouthed him. (1978)

wind someone **up (1979)** British; often denoting making fun of someone by telling them something untrue; from the notion of activating something with a winding mechanism ■ *Match*: All he kept saying was 'boss, you're kidding me, boss you're winding me up'. (1987)

Ridicule

razoo, razzoo, razzooh (1890) North American; often in the phrases *give the razoo* to

ridicule, *get the razoo* be ridiculed; probably an alteration of *raspberry, razzberry* reprimand, censure, with arbitrary suffix *-oo*, perhaps after *kazoo* ■ *Washington Post*: Yesterday's hero, Fidel Castro, now gets the lustiest Bronx razzoohs since Adolf Hitler was flipping his wig for the cameras. (1959)

An instance of mocking; send-up

leg-pull (1915) From *pull someone's leg* make fun of someone ■ John Ardagh: His whole operation might be partly a leg-pull at the expense of serious literature. (1970)

mickey-take, micky-take (1968) British; from *take the mickey* mock ■ *Listener*: He parried Kenneth Allsop's micky-take. (1968)

piss-take (1977) British; from *take the piss* mock ■ *Spare Rib*: It's a bit of a pisstake, sending up the whole bi-sexuality thing. (1977)

wind-up (1984) British; from *wind someone up* make fun of someone ■ *Times*: My recollection of this is quite clear. I thought it was a wind-up to be honest with you. (1984)

Someone who mocks or ridicules

kidder (1888) From *kid* mock, tease + *-er* ■ P. G. Wodehouse: 'Mr Winklethorpe told me I was very good with the wooden clubs,' she said defiantly. 'He's a great kidder,' said Ramsden. (1922)

piss-taker (1976) British; from *take the piss* mock ■ *New Society*: 'What's funny about a jeweller? . . . He's a piss taker. (1976)

Mocking

sarky (1912) British; from *sarc(astic* + *-y* ■ *Diary of a Public School Girl*: Made some currant buns. Bob very sarky about them. (1930)

An object of ridicule

fright (1751) Dated ■ Harrison Ainsworth: 'You mustn't marry that ridiculous old fright', she whispered. (1864)

sight (1862) Applied to a ridiculous or shocking spectacle ■ William Faulkner: 'Ain't he a sight now,' Snopes cackled. (1940)

sketch (1917) Dated ■ J. B. Priestley: You do look a sight, Dad. . . . I never saw such a sketch. (1930)

14. Assent & Refusal

Expressions of assent, agreement, or acceptance

OK, ok, okay, okey, okey-doke, okey-dokey, etc. **(1839)** Orig US; from original adjectival sense, satisfactory ■ Dawn Powell: He saw that tiresome red-faced fellow . . . , the man who knew everybody and said 'okie-dokie' to everything. (1936) ■ J. Montgomery: By mid-1929, when sound films had spread across Britain, there was hardly a town or village

without some child who was saying 'O.K.' when previously he would have said 'Yes'. (1957)

yes siree, yes sirree (1846) Mainly US; *siree* probably from obsolete dialect *sirry*, from *sir* ■ Billie Holiday: Yes siree bob, life is just a bowl of cherries. (1956)

I don't mind if I do (c1847) Often used specifically in accepting the offer of a drink

■ Joyce Porter: 'Another cup of tea, Mr Dover?' 'I don't mind if I do,' said Dover, passing his cup. (1967)

you bet, **you bet you (1857)** Orig US ■ S. E. White: 'He's a quick thinker, then,' said Bob. 'You bet you!' (1910)

yah, **ya**, **yar (1863)** Orig a dialectal form, but in recent British use representing the speech of 'Sloane Rangers'; a variant of *yea* or *yes* ■ *Telegraph Sunday Magazine*: 'Can I tempt you with a crouton?' 'Yar, absolutely.' (1986)

yep (1891) Orig US; a variant of *yes* ■ Rona Jaffe: 'Oh? You got a new car?' . . . 'Yep. . . . Look out the window.' (1979)

right-o, **right-oh**, **right-ho (1896)**, **righty-oh**, **righty-ho (1927)** ■ Rudyard Kipling: We'll expect her at nine, then. . . . Righto! (1930) ■ Joyce Porter: 'I should make it now, Prissy.' . . . 'Rightie-ho!' Lady Priscilla set off . . . for the kitchen. (1973)

same here (1896) Denoting agreement, especially as applied to one's own case ■ Harry Kemelman: 'To tell the truth, I think it was the *rebbitzin* that wrote it and he signed it.' 'Same here.' (1972)

sure thing (1896) Orig US ■ Dorothy Sayers: 'Should you care to make one in our next dope-raid?' 'Sure thing. When do you expect it?' (1933)

yeah (1905) Orig US; a variant of *yes* ■ B. Langley: 'The shooting. That was Tony.' 'Tony?' 'Yeah, he done that.' (1977)

yup (1906) Orig US; a variant of *yes* ■ John Irving: 'Is that you, Roger?' 'Yup.' (1978)

too right (1919) Australian & New Zealand ■ *Zigzag*: Something better change—too right mate! (1977)

not half (1920) From earlier adverbial sense, considerably, emphatically ■ James Curtis: 'My God, you got the gaff weighed up good.' 'Not half. A bloke drummed it for me and put me wide.' (1936)

right on (1925) Orig US ■ *Black World*: If Marx were alive he could see his way clear to say to this observation, 'Right on, Brother!' (1973)

fair enough (1926)

■ Agatha Christie: Wilbraham considered. 'Fair enough,' he said at last. 'I agree.' (1934)

not much (1926) Ironically from earlier sense, certainly not ■ Angus Ross: 'Got a going over, did you?' 'Not much, I got a going over. Want to see the bruises?' (970)

you're telling me (1932) Denoting strong concurrence ■ *Times*: When he declares that 'overnutrition has its dangers' . . . the layman is inclined to reply 'You're telling me.' (1954)

I wouldn't (or **won't**) **say no (1939)** Denoting (unenthusiastic) acceptance ■ *Economist*: China . . . wants Saudi investment in China. It would not say no to the sort of cheap loans it has coaxed out of other oil producers like Kuwait. (1987)

natch (1945) Orig US; colloquial abbreviation of *naturally* ■ Peter Wildeblood: 'You don't mean to say,' she whispered tragically, 'that we're going to eat?' 'Why, natch. We're going to have another drink first, though.' (1957)

wilco, **willco (1946)** Orig services' slang; an abbreviation of *will comply*, used to express acceptance of instructions, especially those received by radio or telephone ■ David Beaty: 'Please clear the runway quickly for the President's Starjet!' . . . 'Wilco,' he said. (1977)

ten-four, **10-4 (1962)** Orig & mainly US; originally a radio code phrase signifying 'message received', one of a set of such phrases, all beginning with the number ten, used by the police in the USA and later adopted by Citizens' Band radio operators, and hence used more broadly as a message of affirmation

An endorsement, acceptance, or authorization

OK, **ok**, **okay**, **okey (1841)** Orig US; from original adjectival sense, satisfactory ■ *Review of English Studies*: It is Pound who is to give the O.K. to the gods (not to God). (1956) ■ *Freedomways*: Nothing goes down without his okay. (1973)

say-so (1902) Orig US; compare earlier sense, affirmation, assertion ■ W. Fabian: 'Give 'em to me.' 'Not without Bob's sayso.' (1924)

the all-clear (1936) Denoting authorization to proceed with something; from earlier sense, signal giving information that there is no further danger

the nod (1948) Orig US; in such phrases as *get the nod* and *give the nod*; from the notion of signalling assent by nodding the head

Permission

open slather (1919) Australian & New Zealand; denoting the opportunity to act without restraint; *slather* from the British dialect and US verb *slather* use in large quantities, squander ■ B. Scott: The bloke who finished first was to have open slather with Maria. (1977)

To assent to, authorize, endorse

OK, **ok**, **okay**, **okey (1888)** Orig US; from original adjectival sense, satisfactory] ■ R. S. Woodworth: Not that Freud would OK our account of dreams up to this point. Far from it. (1921)

To accept with reluctance

lump (1833) Usually in the phrase *lump it*; often in the phrase *like it or lump it*; from earlier obsolete sense, sulk ■ *Cosmopolitan*: I am the eccentric Squire of Sayle and I do things in my own eccentric way and if you don't like it you can lump it because I have got the money and you haven't. (1992)

wear (1925) Usually used in the negative; often in the phrase *wear it* ■ P. H. Johnson: The mother said this was very kind but that Peter would never—she was given to girlish slang—'wear it'. (1970)

Expressions of refusal, denial, or rejection

no siree, **no sirree (1848)** Mainly US; *siree* probably from obsolete dialect *sirry*, from *sir* ■ Joseph Di Mona: The senator wouldn't protect him. No siree. (1973)

no sir, nossir (1856) Mainly US ■ Edmund McGirr: Joe Silverman don't like his neck being breathed down. Nossir. (1968) ■ *Listener:* In Texas, do you think they're going to inquire about the hanging of the venison . . . ? No, sir. They wonder if there's any shepherd's pie. (1973)

nothing (1883) Orig US; used to express denial or rejection of what someone has just said ■ T. Barling: 'It just slipped out.' 'Slipped nothing. You couldn't resist.' (1974)

not much (1886) ■ Arnold Bennett: Do you suppose I was going to let you go by that steamer? Not much. (1911)

no fear (1887) ■ Arnold Bennett: I invite him to dinner! And in his own hotel! No fear! (1930)

nope (1888) Orig US; extended form of *no* ■ H. C. Rae: 'Anybody asking for me?' 'Nope.' (1971)

not likely (1893) ■ George Bernard Shaw: Walk! Not bloody likely. . . . I am going in a taxi. (1914) ■ C. E. Montague: The German sentries said, 'Go back, or we shall have to shoot.' The Englishmen said 'Not likely!' advanced to the German wire, and asked again for an officer. (1922)

not on your life (1896) Orig US ■ Harry Carmichael: 'Why not get in touch with your lawyer?' 'Not on your life! . . . It would be a tacit admission of my guilt.' (1972)

nix (1902) Denoting refusal; also used in the phrase *nix on* to signify emphatic rejection; from the noun *nix* nothing ■ Dorothy Sayers: As for getting an experienced actor and giving him a show in the part—nix! (1932) ■ R. D. Paine: Camp Stuart at ten o'clock. Nix on that kid stuff. (1923)

nothing doing (1910) ■ *People:* It was suggested that she should come incognito. Nothing doing. (1947)

nah, na (1920) Representing a colloquial or vulgar pronunciation of *no* ■ *New Society:* The waiter knows better. 'Nah, you don't want herrings, I'm gonna give you the soup.' (1966)

stick (1922) Used in various phrases expressing contemptuous rejection, usually with the underlying idea of inserting an object into the anus ■ Peter Driscoll: If you do earn your thousand pounds you can stick it, d'you hear? Stick it right up where it belongs. I don't want a penny of it. (1971)

no soap (1926) Orig and mainly US ■ Edmund Crispin: 'The police tried to trace the handkerchief, I take it?' 'They did, but no soap.' (1977)

I should cocoa (or coco) (1936) Rhyming slang for 'I should say so'; *cocoa* probably a fanciful use of *cocoa* chocolate drink ■ Olive Norton: What me? . . . I should coco. Sheila'd think I was off my head. (1967)

over my dead body (1936) ■ *Times:* If the number of distinguished gentlemen who cry 'Over my dead body' really

mean what they say, this will be a fairly lethal summer in Whitehall. (1963)

not on your Nelly (1941) *Nelly* short for *Nelly Duff*, rhyming slang for *puff* (breath of) life—i.e. 'not on your life' ■ *Globe & Mail* (Toronto): I appear to be giving away most of the plot? Not on your nelly. That's only the beginning. (1974)

not Pygmalion likely (1949) Euphemism for 'not bloody likely', which occurs in Shaw's *Pygmalion* (1914) and caused a sensation at the time of the play's first London production (see at *not likely*, above) ■ G. Fallon: 'Are you thinking of joining in?' 'Not Pygmalion likely,' Bland returned brusquely. (1967)

stuff (1955) Used in various phrases expressing contemptuous rejection, usually with the underlying idea of inserting an object into the anus ■ Joyce Porter: He should have taken a stronger line. . . . Told old Crouch to stuff it. (1973)

no way (1968) Orig US ■ *New Yorker:* He said he wouldn't start up a gang today—no way. (1975)

Refusing assent

not having any (1902) ■ A. L. Rowse: Lady Mary Hastings was thought of for promotion to the bed of Ivan the Terrible. She was not having any. (1955)

A refusal, rejection, rebuff

thumbs-down (1929) From spectators in Roman amphitheatres signalling that a defeated gladiator should be killed by extending the thumb downwards ■ *Daily Telegraph* (heading): Baldwin statue gets thumbs down from Foot. (1982)

brush-off (1941) Orig US ■ Monica Dickens: The bleakly familiar: 'The post has been filled', or the more courteous brush-off: 'We will keep your letter on record in case a suitable post arises'. (1958)

Something that must not be done

no-no (1942) Reduplication of *no* expressing refusal ■ *Sunday Advocate-News* (Barbados): Plants that require a great deal of moisture are no-noes unless you have your own well. (1975)

To refuse, reject

nix (1903) US; from the noun *nix* nothing ■ *Tucson* (Arizona) *Daily Citizen* (heading): Nude bathing nixed. (1973)

To refuse to give something

hold out on (1907) Orig US; often denoting refusal to give information ■ Gavin Black: If I find out that you've been holding out on me over this identification, I'll come down on you like a pile driver. (1972)

15. Nonsense

rubbish (1612) Often used interjectionally; from earlier sense, worthless stuff, trash ■ *Mail on Sunday*: In the leaflets was rubbish about the 'plot of worldwide Jewry'. (1991)

balderdash (1674) Often used interjectionally; compare earlier sense, froth; ultimate origin unknown ■ *Economist*: In May, the development corporation wrote giving notice that it would end the management agreement, which, it claimed, the council itself had repudiated by conducting its survey. That is balderdash, says the council. (1988)

hogwash (1712) From earlier sense, kitchen swill, etc. for pigs ■ *Spectator*: The whole of the artistic world has been debauched by the hogwash of the do-it-yourself vogue. (1965)

all my eye (and Betty Martin) (1768) Often used interjectionally; origin uncertain; it has been claimed that the whole phrase represents British soldiers' or sailors' attempts to pronounce *O mihi, beate Martine*, an invocation to St Martin, patron saint of innkeepers and reformed drunkards ■ *Walter de la Mare*: You might be suggesting that both shape and scarecrow too were all my eye and Betty Martin. (1930)

twaddle (1782) Alteration of obsolete *twattle* idle talk, itself perhaps an alteration of *tattle* in the same sense ■ *Sir Frederick Treves*: He was guided by personal . . . experience, and not by the twaddle of theorists. (1906)

blatherskite, bletherskite (1825) From earlier sense, person who talks rubbish ■ *Colin Wilson*: For Nietzsche . . . there is no such thing as abstract knowledge; there is only useful knowledge and unprofitable blatherskite. (1956)

rot (1848) Often used interjectionally ■ *Eugene O'Neill*: It's damned rot! I'd like to see anyone influence Edmund more than he wants to be. (*a*1953)

bosh (1850) Often used interjectionally; from Turkish *boş* empty ■ *William Gaddis*: A lot of bosh, of course, . . . but it gives these fool scientists something to do. (1952)

balls (1857) Often used interjectionally; from earlier sense, testicles ■ *Angus Wilson*: 'Look here! this is awful balls,' said John. (1956) ■ *Leonard Cooper*: Fanciful? Balls! It's what happens. (1960)

bunkum (1862) Variant of obsolete *buncombe*, from *Buncombe* County, North Carolina, USA, whose member gave an irrelevant speech in Congress *c*1820 simply to impress his constituents ■ *Wall Street Journal*: 'That's bunkum,' says Terence Meaden, a local meteorologist. 'The idea that there is some intelligence operating is pure fantasy.' (1989)

poppycock (1865) Orig US; from Dutch dialect *pappekak* soft excrement ■ *Punch*: If you still think that harmonisation is so much Brussels poppycock . . . then draw comfort from this statistic. (1977)

punk (1869) From earlier sense, rotten wood ■ *Times*: I don't like the family Stein. There is Gert, there is Ep, there is Ein. Gert's writings are punk, Ep's statues are junk, Nor can anyone understand Ein. (1973)

flapdoodle (1878) Origin unknown; compare earlier sense (1833–66) 'the stuff they feed fools on' Frederick Marryat ■ *Daily Telegraph*: It's the one form of theatre which never calls for explanation or critical flapdoodle. (1987)

guff (1884) Orig US; from earlier sense, puff, whiff ■ *Crescendo*: The sleeve-notes give us a lot of guff about getting with it and so on and tell us nothing constructive. (1966)

tommy-rot (1884) From the male first name *Tommy* ■ *Nicholas Blake*: You know what the other side says— . . . 'Woman's place is in the kitchen'—all the rest of that Neanderthal tommyrot. (1939)

piffle (1890) Often used interjectionally; from the earlier verb *piffle* talk triflingly ■ *Guardian*: Faber used to be a good publisher under Geoffrey Faber and T. S. Eliot, but nowadays it just produces middlebrow, patronising piffle. (1992)

tosh (1892) Origin unknown ■ *J. Morris*: Anna Novochka also denies it: pure tosh, she says. (1985)

squit (1893) British; compare earlier sense, small or insignificant person ■ *Arnold Wesker*: Love? I don't believe in any of that squit—we just got married. (1959)

crap (1898) From earlier sense, excrement ■ *Punch*: And what a load of crap that was. (1964)

bunk (1900) Orig US; abbreviation of *bunkum* ■ *Henry Ford*: History is more or less bunk. (1916)

drool (1900) Orig US; from earlier sense, spittle ■ *Nicolas Freeling*: He switched the radio on—no short wave, and the medium band was filled with drool. (1966)

bilge (1908) From earlier sense, foul matter that collects in the bottom of a ship's hull ■ *P. G. Wodehouse*: She wrote this novel and it was well received by the intelligentsia, who notoriously enjoy the most frightful bilge. (1954)

bullshit (1914) Orig US ■ *Douglas Adams*: 'With half the wealth of the former Galactic Empire stored on it somewhere it can afford to look frumpy.' Bullshit, thought Ford. (1979)

claptrap (1915) From earlier sense, language designed to catch applause ■ *Times*: Cannot our educationists turn away from the pretentious claptrap put about during the past 20 years? (1955)

garbage (1918) From earlier sense, material of low quality ■ *Mail on Sunday*: All this US against Them is a bunch of garbage. (1991)

bollocks, ballocks (1919) Often used interjectionally; from earlier sense, testicles ■ *It*: It's really a load of bollocks. (1969)

drip (1919) Orig US ■ *B. Gray*: 'We'll have nothing of the sort,' interrupted Joy, putting a welcome stop to this drip. (1946)

baloney, boloney (1922) Orig US; often used interjectionally; commonly regarded as from

Bologna (*sausage*), but the connection remains conjectural ■ John Braine: All that baloney about going upstairs to play a harp or downstairs to roast. (1959)

gup (1924) British; from earlier Anglo-Indian sense, gossip; from Hindustani *gup* ■ *Punch*: Need I give the jury any more of this gup? (1927)

hooey (1924) Orig US; often used interjectionally; origin unknown ■ Germaine Greer: The horse between a girl's legs is supposed to be a giant penis. What hooey! (1970)

macaroni (1924) Mainly Australian; rhyming slang for *baloney* ■ Joseph von Sternberg: What is flashed from the projector overhead will be the same old macaroni. (1965)

heifer dust (1927) Dated

horse feathers (1928) US; from the incongruity of the notion of a horse having feathers ■ John Gardner: Mostyn pointed out that . . . they could court-martial him *in camera*. . . . On reflection, Boysie realised that this was all a load of horse feathers. (1967)

eyewash (1930) From earlier sense, specious talk, humbug ■ *Economist*: This does not mean that the proposals . . . are so much eyewash. (1957)

shit (1930) From earlier sense, excrement ■ *Rolling Stone*: I enjoyed Simmons' logic that Shakespeare is 'shit' simply because he can't understand it. (1977)

pills (1935) From *pills* testicles ■ I. Miller: I explained to him about the prayers. . . . 'Awful pills,' I whispered; 'but it can't be helped.' (1935)

tripe (1935) Sometimes used interjectionally; from earlier sense, material of low quality ■ *Church Times*: Bomber Harris, who initially said, 'The idea is tripe,' could be said to have been proved right. (1993)

cock (1937) Mainly British; from earlier sense, fictitious narrative, short for *cock-and-bull story* ■ Louis McIntosh: What he usually improvised was just a load of cock. (1956)

phooey (1946) From *phooey* interjection expressing incredulity, probably influenced by *hooey* nonsense ■ Raymond Chandler: So let's not have any more of that phooey about 'as literature my stuff still stinks'. (1946)

16. Emphatic Language

Very, extremely

as anything (1542) ■ Frederick Raphael: The soft toys were cuddlesome as anything. (1965)

filthy (1616) Now only in the phrases *filthy dirty*, *filthy rich*, and *filthy great* (the last on the analogy of *dirty great*) ■ J. B. Priestley: I organise these parties for her—she's filthy rich. (1954)

deadly (1688) From earlier sense, fatally ■ *Guardian*: Matisse, visiting in 1930, described the town as 'deadly dull'. (1992)

crud (1951) From earlier sense, dirt, filth ■ T. Sturgeon: Would you say that . . . the writer of all this crud, believes . . . in what he writes? (1955)

cobblers (1955) British; often used interjectionally; from earlier sense, testicles ■ *Melody Maker*: Geno Washington says Grapefruit's recent attack on the Maryland Club, Glasgow, was 'a load of cobblers'. They are one of the best audiences in Britain, says Geno. (1968)

horse shit (1955) US; often used interjectionally ■ *It*: 'This is definitely the weekend of the big bust!' 'Horseshit! You've said the same thing for the past six weekends!' (1970)

crut (1958) US; variant of *crud* in same sense

shuck (1958) From earlier sense, something of little value ■ G. Lea: I know about double negative too, but that's a lot of shuck. (1958)

rollocks (1961) Usually used interjectionally; euphemistic alteration of *bollocks* ■ B. Wells: 'Rollocks!' said Maguire and his voice was deliberately gruff to hide his embarrassment. (1961)

cod, cods, cod's (1963) British; abbreviation of *codswallop* ■ Miles Tripp: If you think it's all a load of cod's why the hell waste a pound? (1970)

codswallop (1963) Mainly British; origin unknown, despite popular theories of a Mr Cod and his beer ■ Allan Prior: All that stuff about mutual respect between police and criminal was a load of old codswallop. (1966)

rhubarb (1963) Compare earlier theatrical use to denote the murmur of conversation ■ *Telegraph* (Brisbane): They gave me some rhubarb about violating the firework zone. (1976)

schmegeggy, shmegegge, etc. **(1968)** US; from earlier sense, idiot

Unintelligible language; gibberish

double Dutch (1876) ■ *Daily Mail*: Since, in the popular mind, the Scots are somehow 'out there'—another country, so to speak—the fact that it all sounds like double-Dutch only adds to the impression. (1991)

Insincere or exaggerated talk intended to flatter or deceive; humbug or flattery

See at **Sincerity & Insincerity** (pp. 278–81).

dreadfully (1697) Qualifying words denoting an undesirable state of affairs; from earlier sense, badly ■ *Punch*: Half-a-dozen dreadfully common young bicyclists were commenting on her discomfiture with delighted exclamations of 'Giddy old Kipper', 'Sweet Seventeen', 'Cheero, Maudie—you'll win!' (1907)

whopping (1706) Used with adjectives denoting large size, especially *great* ■ Boot & Thomas: It certainly had more flair than old LBJ taking a table of journalists and staffers into the men's room, there to reduce them to awe and wonderment at the size of his whopping great Texas trouser snake. (1976)

mighty (1715) From earlier sense, greatly ■ *Times*: They left it till mighty near no-side before they got their noses thankfully in front. (1958)

hellish (1768) ■ *Oxford Advanced Learner's Dictionary*: Hellish expensive. (1995)

thundering (1809) Dated ■ *Daily Mail*: Too experienced to let even a thundering smart girl swing it on him as easily as that. (1923)

awful (1818) From the adjective *awful* ■ R. D. Paine: A prairie town called Follansbee that looks awful good to me. (1923)

as sin (1821) In the phrases *(as) ugly as sin*, *(as) miserable as sin* ■ Nevil Shute: I think it looks ugly as sin, and it's starting to ponk a bit. (1944)

real (1827) Orig Scottish & US; from earlier sense, really, genuinely ■ *Daily Mirror*: I'm havin' a rest—I feel real listless. (1976)

rattling (1829) Dated; used especially in the phrase *rattling good* ■ A. G. Hays: This is a rattling good story. (1930)

fearfully (1835) British ■ Dorothy Sayers: I'm really fearfully sorry you copped that packet that was meant for me. (1933)

jolly (1838) British; from earlier standard use as an intensifier, originally in the sense 'pleasantly' ■ S. Thompson: Jolly lucky the C.O. didn't notice it yesterday—he gets 'baity' on these occasions. (1921)

not half (1851) ■ Parker & Allerton: It doesn't half nark them. (1962)

whacking (1853) Used with adjectives denoting large size, especially *great* ■ *Guardian*: It was either a whacking great asteroid crash or a massive slurping of lava in the Deccan plateau in India 65 million years ago. (1992)

awfully (1859) British; from earlier sense, so as to inspire awe ■ John Galsworthy: Thanks, old man, awfully good of you—will you bob in, then? (1924)

veddy (1859) Often jocular; representing a childish, affected, or (US) British pronunciation of *very* ■ *Publishers Weekly*: Note humorous anachronism as Dylan's fish-girl pours him tea from a bone china teapot—veddy British! (1975)

frightfully (1875) British; from earlier sense, to a frightful degree ■ Peter Kemp: I say, you know, it's frightfully nice of you chaps to go on this show. (1958)

madly (1888) ■ Nancy Mitford: It's madly wearing to the optic nerve centres. (1945)

dead (1894) From earlier sense, completely, fully ■ D. G. Phillips: I'll show you the ropes. . . . You'll find the job dead easy. (a1911) ■ *Guardian*: I had this geezer, know what I mean, he was doing dead good saying 'I beg your Lordship's indulgence' in rhyming slang. (1991)

dirty (1894) Now usually used with adjectives denoting size ■ Douglas Clark: Time for a dirty great pint. (1971)

howling (1895) Dated ■ *Saturday Evening Post*: Glad! You're howling right I'm glad. (1928)

cracking (1903) Used in the phrase *cracking good* ■ Ian Cross: Probably turning out to be a cracking-good saint. (1957)

stiff (1905) Used especially after *bore* and *scare* ■ *English*: Billy Temple, who announced in Westminster School Hall that 'the longer poems of Milton bored him stiff'. (1956)

stinkingly (1906), stinking (1926) Denoting excessiveness; mainly in the phrases *stinking(ly) drunk*, *stinking(ly) rich* ■ Margaret Kennedy: He is . . . frightfully good-looking . . . and stinkingly rich. (1951) ■ Ngaio Marsh: She was in affluent circumstances, stinking rich in fact. (1978)

pink (1922) In the phrase *tickled pink* extremely pleased ■ *Scottish Daily Express*: We are tickled pink that we were able to come home to do the concert at Liverpool Philharmonic Hall. (1976)

all (1932) ■ *Daily Telegraph*: You can spoof politics, sports, business—but when it comes to religion, they get all upset. (1991)

plenty (1934) US ■ R. M. Pirsig: This notebook gets plenty grease-smeared and ugly. (1974)

piss- (1940) Used in such compound adjectives as *piss-poor*, *piss-wet*, etc. ■ J. Antoine: 'Here we are,' I said to Joe. 'On a piss-wet cliff and there's no bloody water for a brew!' (1974)

rigid (1943) Used especially after *bore* and *scare*; modelled on *stiff* ■ K. Campbell: It's no tourist place, I assure you. . . . You'd be bored rigid. (1972)

zonking (1958) British; used before adjectives denoting positive quality or large size ■ *Times*: Rather than play these zonking great parts . . . I will try to find some dazzling little cameo roles. (1976)

thumping (1961) Used with adjectives denoting large size, especially *great* ■ *Independent on Sunday*: By then, the fraudster could be on his way to the Bahamas and you could be on your way to a thumping great overdraft. (1991)

mucho (1973) Orig US; from Spanish *mucho* very ■ *Tucson Magazine*: Your magazine is mucho enjoyable. (1978)

mondo (1979) Orig & mainly US; from Italian *mondo* world ■ *New York Press*: When your train finally does arrive—especially if you're taking the mondo weirdo J, M or Z train—you always end up the only humanoid in a car. (1990)

stonking (1980) British; used before adjectives denoting positive quality or large size ■ *Independent*: When they've got their dosh, they go out and have a stonking good time. (1990)

seriously (1981) Orig US; mainly in such phrases as *seriously rich* ■ *Daily Mail*: They could be called the Trumps of Texas—seriously wealthy with a penchant for flaunting that wealth. (1991)

well (1986) ■ *Face*: A city where Walters is 'well sound' and Led Zeppelin are 'a better buzz'. This is Liverpool in 1988. (1989)

way (1988) ■ *New Musical Express*: When we recorded it originally I doubled up the drums and it sounded way Gary Glitter, way Clash. (1990)

Extreme in amount, bigness, badness, difficulty, etc.

thundering (1618) Dated ▪ J. M. Barrie: Such a thundering lie. (1900)

fearful (1634) ▪ *Daily Mail*: We cut instantly to a terrible old boxing film with . . . Lee Marvin getting a fearful thumping. (1991)

frightful (1752) ▪ Ngaio Marsh: You'll think me a frightful silly-billy. (1958)

a (or the) devil of a (1767) ▪ H. Pearson: Devil of a temper you've got, Doyle! By Crums, it's hardly safe to go out with you. (1943)

a (or the, one) hell of a (1776) ▪ *New Yorker*: His forehand is a hell of a weapon. (1969)

ever such (1803) ▪ E. M. Delafield: My Pops says I'm ever such a lucky girl to have such heaps of friends. (1933)

awful (1818) From earlier sense, very bad ▪ Winston Churchill: Please excuse bad writing as I am in an awful hurry. (Many kisses.) xxx WSC. (1894)

almighty (1824) ▪ *Observer*: There was an almighty fuss when Tim Rice, lyricist, was admitted to the Cricket Writers' Club. (1991)

one (1828) Now mainly US; see also *one hell of a, one helluva* ▪ Joseph Di Mona: 'Tell everyone I'm not Cuban,' said Medwick, hoping to get a rise out of the driver. But none came. This was one serious boy. (1973)

and a half (1832) ▪ M. M. Kaye: Roaring Rory must have been a hell-raiser and a half in his day. (1959)

unholy (1842) From earlier sense, impious ▪ *New Scientist*: The bitter pill of generic substitution was leaked to the press, and created a totally unwanted side effect: an unholy row. (1983)

howling (1865) ▪ *Magnet*: 'You howling ass!' shouted Bulstrode. 'I tell you he's busted my two-guinea camera.' (1908)

a (or the, one) helluva (1910) *helluva* representing a casual pronunciation of *hell of a* ▪ *Times*: It's very unfortunate looking like him: he must have a helluva life. (1968)

mucho (1942) Orig US; from Spanish *mucho* much, many ▪ *Making Music*: Warm valve distortion sound, plus mucho volume make this an amp worthy of its chart placing. (1986)

mondo (1979) Orig & mainly US; from Italian *mondo* world ▪ *People*: The freshly painted mural on the side of the Hollywood Plaza apartment building marks the apogee of mondo ego publicity. (1987)

Much, very much

a sight (1836), a damned (or damn) sight (1928) *a sight* from earlier sense, a great quantity ▪ Elizabeth Lemarchand: I'm a damn sight saner than people who spend their lives rat-racing and jabbering their heads off. (1969) ▪ Edmund Crispin: Be a sight cooler there than it is here, I reckon. (1977) ▪ Margaret Hinxman: John realized his inspector was sparking on all cylinders. He looked a damned sight fresher than Waller felt. (1977)

miles (1885) ▪ Nicolas Freeling: This hasn't been done cold-bloodedly for money. . . . Makes it all miles easier. (1974)

way (1941) Orig US ▪ *Rolling Stone*: He was a country & western singer and he drank way too much. (1977).

See also **bags, heaps, loads, lots, no end**, and **a whole lot** under A large amount at **Quantity** (pp. 398–9).

Completely, fully, utterly

plumb, plum (1587) Now mainly US; from earlier sense, exactly ▪ Elizabeth Lemarchand: They must both be plumb crazy. (1973)

dead (1589) From earlier sense, to the point of death ▪ Doris Lessing: 'That's right,' said Charlie, 'you're dead right.' (1963)

perfectly (1790) Dated ▪ Queen Victoria: The pride of giving life to an immortal soul is very fine . . . perfectly furious as I was to be caught [= pregnant]. (1858)

proper (1816) Recorded in standard use in the 15th century ▪ *Northern Echo*: Alan Milburn, Darlington's NHS conscious Labour candidate, has been proper poorly. (1992)

plenty (1842) Followed by an adjective of size and *enough* ▪ M. E. Morgan: Cut the hood . . . making it plenty large enough to slip on easily over Dolly's head. (1908)

good and (1885) Orig US ▪ Bill Knox: [It] can wait until we're good and ready. (1969)

motherless (1898) Australian; mainly in the phrase *motherless broke* ▪ K. S. Prichard: 'But I know what it is to be hard up, don't forget,' he said. 'Stony, motherless broke, like I was in Sydney.' (1946)

Harry (1925) British, mainly nautical; used before adjectives and adverbs suffixed with *-ers*; from the male personal name *Harry* ▪ *Lancet*: Get in there, and strip off Harry Nuders. (1946) ▪ *Guardian*: In the old Imperial Aircraft days . . . the engineer would bring the old kite down harry plonkers on the grass. (1969)

tooting (1932) US; usually used with a preceding adverb ▪ Bernard Malamud: You're plumb tootin' crazy. (1952)

plain (1959) From earlier sense, simply ▪ *Bridgewater Mercury*: Others may have family problems, housing difficulties—or are just plain lonely. (1976)

totally (1972) Orig US; used as a simple intensive before adjectives, especially in such phrases as *totally awesome, totally tubular*, etc.; from earlier non-intensive use ▪ *Washington Post*: Scott Wallace is padded and pumped. . . . Awesome, man, totally awesome. (1981)

Complete, utter

regular (1821) ▪ John Rae: You're becoming a regular creeping Jesus. (1960)

proper (a1825) Recorded in standard usage from the 14th to the 17th centuries ▪ *Listener*: The plebeian engineer was a proper Charlie to let himself be roped in for it. (1957)

pluperfect (1889) Dated; from earlier sense, more than perfect ▪ 'Contact': I fully expect that we of the air service will lead the armies of pursuit and make ourselves a pluperfect nuisance to the armies of retreat. (1917)

pink (1896) Dated; mainly in the phrase *the pink limit* ▪ Bruce Marshall: These rotten new kids really are the pink limit. (1946)

sweet (1958) Used in various phrases meaning 'nothing at all' ■ B. Broadfoot: The government provided sweet bugger all. Absolutely sweet bugger all. (1973)

right (1960) British; from earlier sense, truly so called ■ *Observer*: 'The Government did not know that there was no settlement in writing, and how could an order apply to something which did not exist,' he said. 'The Government made a right mess of it.' (1973)

prize (1976) Probably in use earlier, but not recorded until 1976; from earlier sense, (worthy of) winning a prize ■ Miles Tripp: I've been made a fool, a prize bloody fool. (1978)

Cursed, cursedly

damned (1596) Used as an adjective and adverb; from the earlier adjectival sense, accursed; adverbial use first recorded in 1757 ■ Dorothy Sayers: Some damned thing at the Yard, I suppose. At three ack emma! (1927) ■ Ernest Raymond: Damned jolly little bint, that one, too! (1930)

confounded (1652) Dated; used as an adjective and adverb; from the past participle of *confound*, as used in various imprecations ■ *Broadside*: Dancing the jig, Every fellow with a cig, And a cig of confounded bad tobacco. (a1889) ■ *Beaver*: 'These confounded nitchies,' he was wont to exclaim, 'are lazy, good-for-nothings.' (1947)

bloody (1676) Now mainly British & Australian; used as an adjective and adverb, and also sometimes as an infix; perhaps from earlier sense, bloodthirsty, cruel ■ *Landfall*: You mind your own bloody business. (1950) ■ Elizabeth Taylor: You bloody know you didn't. (1953) ■ Laurence Meynell: Remember the *News Chronicle*? . . . On sale one day. Amalga-bloody-mated the next. (1963)

damn (1775) Used as an adjective and adverb; a clipped form of *damned* ■ Ngaio Marsh: I call it a damn poor show. Leaving us high and dry. (1970)

deuced (1782) Dated; used as an adjective and adverb; from *deuce*, used in a range of imprecations ■ W. J. Locke: I'm panning out about this, because it seems so deuced interesting. (1915)

darn (1789) Orig US; used as an adjective and adverb; euphemistic alteration of *damn* ■ *New Yorker*: We want to make darn sure we get there and back. (1969)

blessed (1806) Used as an adjective and adverb; used as a euphemistic substitute for *cursed* ■ Edward Dyson: Who should come sprintin' upstairs but me nibs, pale's er blessed egg, hair on end—fair dilly. (1906)

darned (1807) Orig US; used as an adjective and adverb; euphemistic alteration of *damned* ■ Sinclair Lewis: Machine looks brand new now—not that it's so darned old, of course; had it less 'n three years. (1922)

all-firedly (1833) Mainly US; used as an adverb; from *all-fired* + *-ly* ■ Hugh de Selincourt: I'm most all-firedly sorry about it. (1924)

concerned, consarned (1834) US, dated; used as an adjective; compare earlier sense, troubled ■ M. E. Wilkins: I've always heard tell that there was two kinds of old maids—old maids an' consarned old maids. (1887)

precious (1836) Used as an adjective; from earlier sense, egregious, arrant ■ Thomas Hughes: It's hard enough to see one's way, a precious sight harder than I thought last night. (1857)

all-fired (1837) Mainly US; used as an adjective and adverb; probably a euphemistic alteration of *hell-fired* ■ M. M. Atwater: Tell him to get all-fired busy on it. (1935)

dad-blasted (1840), dad-blamed (1883), dad-gasted (1892) US; used as an adjective; *dad* euphemistic alteration of *god*

blasted (1843) Used as an adjective and adverb; from earlier sense, accursed ■ *Frontier*: That blasted 'ding bat' of a Ford, as Stub calls it, just naturally stood on its hind legs . . . and turned a flip-flop. (1923)

beastly (1844) British; used as an adjective and adverb; from earlier sense, unpleasant(ly), offensive(ly) ■ George Orwell: It's getting beastly hot, isn't it? . . . Isn't it simply *baking*! (1934) ■ Ngaio Marsh: We'll all have a brood over the beastly thing. (1941)

god-damn, god-damned, god-dam (1844) Mainly US; used as an adjective and adverb; from the imprecation *God damn (me, you,* etc.) ■ W. C. Woods: Now you men knock off the goddam chatter in there and listen up. (1970)

dratted (1845) Dated; used as an adjective; from the past participle of *drat*, used in mild curses ■ Ellen Wood: If that dratted girl had been at her post. (1869)

perishing (1847) Dated, mainly British; used as an adjective and adverb; from earlier sense, deadly ■ Margery Allingham: These perishing crooks, who do they think they are all of a sudden? (1952)

adjective (1851) Euphemistically substituted for an expletive adjective (e.g. *bloody*) ■ *Idler*: To know where the adjective blazes they are going. (1894)

doggone (1851) US; used as an adjective and adverb; from *dog gone on it*, a euphemistic substitute for *God damn it* ■ Erskine Caldwell: When I get a load of it, I'll know dog-gone well my ship has come in. (1933)

goldarn, goldarned, goldurn, goldurned (1856), goldang, goldanged (1877) US; used as an adjective and adverb; euphemistic alteration of *god-damn, god-damned* ■ *Reader's Digest*: Another great story ruined by a goldurned eyewitness. (1948)

bleeding (1858) Mainly British & Australian; used as an adjective and adverb; used as a substitute, originally euphemistic, for *bloody* ■ *Times*: Why don't you bleeding do something about it? (1967)

blooming (1879) Mainly British & Australian; used as an adjective and adverb; used as a euphemistic substitute for *bloody*; from the notion of something being at full bloom, and hence at its extreme point ■ D. H. Lawrence: The upper classes. . . . Such bloomin' fat-arsed dool-owls. (1929)

dashed (1881) Dated, mainly British; used as an adjective and adverb; from the past participle of *dash* strike, used as a euphemistic substitute for *damned* ■ P. G. Wodehouse: I've a dashed good mind to chuck the whole thing. (1932)

bally (1885) Mainly British; used as an adjective and adverb; used as a euphemistic substitute for *bloody*; perhaps from *balls* nonsense + -*y* ■ Hugh Walpole: All the time behind you and them some force was insisting on places being taken, connections being formed. One was simply a bally pawn . . . a bally pawn. (1922)

dang, danged (1886) Mainly US; used as an adjective and adverb; euphemistic alteration of *damn*(*ed*) ■ W. A. Fraser: I was that danged near bushed, toward the last that I was feared I might go right on sleepin'. (1910)

qualified (1886) Dated; used as an adjective; used as a euphemistic substitute for *bloody*, *damned*, etc. ■ E. C. R. Lorac: I . . . knocked my head on those qualified rocks. (1949)

blankety, blankety-blank (1888) Used as an adjective; used as a euphemistic substitute for an expletive; from the notion of leaving a 'blank' where an expletive has been deleted ■ Maud Diver: Colonel Stanham Buckley . . . inquired picturesquely of a passing official when the blank this blankety blank train was supposed to start. (1908)

blithering (1889) Used as an adjective; used mainly before words denoting a fool (especially *idiot*); from the present participle of *blither* talk senselessly ■ Gilbert Frankau: I was a blithering idiot to get in—knowing you as well as I do. (1926)

frigging (*a*1890) Used as an adjective and adverb; from the present participle of *frig* copulate, masturbate, used as a euphemistic substitute for *fucking* ■ Keith Waterhouse: Take your frigging mucky hands off my pullover. (1959)

fucking (*a*1890) Used as an adjective and adverb; from the present participle of *fuck* copulate ■ W. H. Auden: I'm so bored with the whole fucking crowd of you I could scream! (1969)

sanguinary (1890) Used as an adjective; used as a jocular or euphemistic substitute for *bloody*; from earlier sense, relating to blood ■ G. B. Shaw: The inhabitants raise up their voices and call one another sanguinary liars. (1910)

flaming (1895) Used as an adjective and adverb; from earlier sense, burning hot ■ Private Eye: He's saved my life if he only flamin' knew it. (1969)

plurry (1900) Australian & New Zealand; used as an adjective and adverb; Maori alteration of *bloody* ■ R. D. Finlayson: It's all right for Pakeha's to spout about Maori art but it won't help me to get manure for my plurry cow farm. (1938)

adjectival (1910) Euphemistically substituted for an expletive adjective (e.g. *bloody*) ■ Gladys Mitchell: Beresford told him to take his adjectival charity elsewhere. (1959)

flipping (1911) Mainly British; used as an adjective and adverb; a use of the present participle of the verb *flip* as a euphemistic substitute for *fucking* ■ Guardian: They wax indignant about pornography but when it comes to doing anything about it they are bone flipping lazy. (1971)

sodding (1912) British; used as an adjective and adverb; from the present participle of the verb *sod*, as used in imprecations ■ Kingsley Amis: Cuts his own hair now, you see. Too sodding mean to pay out his one-and-six, that is what it is. My God. (1954) ■ Dirk Bogarde: I'll remember this sodding day until the day I die. (1980)

blinking (1914) British; used as an adjective and adverb; used as a euphemistic substitute for a strong expletive ■ Observer: The type of golfer who . . . hurls the bag of clubs after it, accompanied by the remark, 'Go on, have the blinking lot'. (1927)

ruddy (1914) British; used as an adjective and adverb; euphemistic alteration of *bloody* ■ Oxford Times: Most of the groups I heard there and elsewhere played too ruddy loud. (1979)

blerry, blerrie, blirry (1920) South African; alteration of *bloody*; used as an adjective ■ C. Lassalle: Do you boys call this blerry muck breakfast? (1986)

poxy (1922) Used as an adjective; from earlier sense, infected with pox ■ Mervyn Peake: Every poxy sunrise of the year, eh, that you burst out of the decent darkness in that plucked way? (1950)

bee (1926) British; used as an adjective and adverb; a respelling of the letter B, used as a euphemistic substitute for *bloody* ■ John Galsworthy: It's a bee nuisance. (1926)

mucking (1929) Used as an adjective and adverb; a euphemistic alteration of *fucking* ■ Richard Adams: You'd better lend him a hand. . . . We'll be 'alf the mucking night else. (1974)

effing (1931) Used as an adjective and adverb; used as a euphemistic substitute for *fucking*, *eff* representing a spelling of its initial letter ■ Private Eye: The relatives get effing tough. (1969)

hellishing, hellishun (1931) Mainly Australian & New Zealand; used as an adjective and adverb; from *hellish* + -*ing* (as in *fucking*, *sodding*, etc.) ■ Edmund McGirr: I don't know that anybody . . . has any knowledge of how hellishing thorough we are. (1968)

fricking (1936) Used as an adjective and adverb; euphemistic alteration of *frigging* ■ Chicago Tribune: You could see your own skeleton. . . . Your own fricking bones X-rayed. (1987)

Pygmalion (1949) Used quasi-adverbially in the phrase *not Pygmalion likely*, a euphemism for *not bloody likely*; from the use of the phrase *not bloody likely* in G. B. Shaw's *Pygmalion* (1914), which caused a sensation at the time of the play's first London production ■ G. Fallon: 'Are you thinking of joining in?' 'Not Pygmalion likely.' Bland returned brusquely. (1967)

cotton-picking (1952) Orig Southern US; used as an adjective and adverb; compare earlier Southern US *cotton-picker* contemptible person

■ Michael Kenyon: Damn Mickey McQuaid for ever bringing me to this pixilated, cotton-pickin' country. (1970)

mother-fucking (1959), mother-loving (1964), mother-raping (1966) Orig & mainly US; used as an adjective ■ John Morris: Get her out of that mother-lovin' joint an' into the cab. (1969) ■ Stanley Ellin: 'You motherfucking black clown,' Harvey says without heat, 'nothing is changed.' (1974)

naffing (1959) British; used as an adjective and adverb; from the verb *naff (off)*, used as a euphemistic substitute for *fuck* ■ Clement & La Frenais: Stealing your tin of naffing pineapple chunks? Not even my favourite fruit. (1976)

steaming (1962) Used as an adjective ■ A. Garner: Roland! You great steaming chudd! Come back! (1965)

mothering (1968) US; used as an adjective; from *mother* (short for *mother-fucker*) + *-ing* ■ New Yorker: I'm out there cutting that mothering grass all day! (1975)

pissingly (1971), pissing (1974) Used as an adverb ■ Peter Way: 'Pissing awful weather,' said Don. (1979)

Certainly, definitely

bleeding well (1884), jolly well (1898), blooming well (1907), bloody well (1921), fucking well (1922), ruddy well (1933), damn well (1941), sodding well (1962) ■ Evelyn Waugh: I should bleeding well say there was. (1928) ■ N. Fleming: If these jokers want to tail us, they've damn well got to do it properly from behind. Overtake and give them the shake. (1970) ■ William Gibson: You can fucking well buy me some clothes, okay? (1986)

Reinforcement formulae

my (colonial, etc.) oath (1859) Australian & New Zealand ■ John Wainwright: My oath—those couple of hours were some session. (1977)

and how (1865) Orig US ■ Listener: 'Alas,' wrote Harrington, 'all earthly things do fail to mortals in enjoyment.' And how. (1965)

sure 'nuff, sho' 'nuff (1880) US, mainly Black English; *'nuff* shortening of *enough* ■ J. D. Carr: He's sho' nuff in good shape and ought to thank you. (1971)

cross my heart (1908) Used as an assertion of the truth of what one has said or of the sincerity of a promise; often in the phrase *cross my heart and hope to die*; from the notion of making the sign of the cross over one's heart ■ Angus Wilson: Cross her heart, might she die if she sneaked. (1952)

py korry (1938) New Zealand; Maori alteration of *by golly*

no shit (1960) US ■ Spectator (New Canaan High School, Connecticut): I turned to Steve and told him that Cheryl said he looked like a fruit because of his pants. I told him I liked his pants, no shit. (1978)

To the maximum extent

with a vengeance (1568) From earlier sense, with a curse ■ Daily Chronicle: In Kiel, where the revolution started, matters appear to be going 'left' with a vengeance. (1918)

like mad (1653) ■ Daily Mail: Her 1958 Christmas card from John Lennon—on which he had written 'I love you like mad'—fetched £8,000 from a Japanese buyer. (1991)

like anything (1681) ■ Lewis Carroll: They wept like anything to see Such quantities of sand. (1872)

like the devil (1791) Compare French *comme le diable* ■ Sylvia Plath: Each time I moved my feet hurt like the devil. (1963)

and no mistake (1818) Used to emphasize a preceding statement ■ New Zealand Geographer: He was a tough old dag, and no mistake. (1945)

like fun (1825) Dated

like sin (1840) ■ Mark Twain: I have been working like sin all night to get a lecture written. (1868)

the (living) daylights out of (1848) In such phrases as *beat, scare*, etc. *the (living) daylights out of*; from obsolete *daylights* eyes ■ Illustrated London News: I might have chuckled throughout 'The Suitor' if its chief actor did not happen to scare the living daylights out of me, as the current saying goes. (1964)

like hell (1855) ■ D. H. Lawrence: 'And I shall miss thee, Jack.' . . . 'Miss you like hell.' (1922)

talk about (1863) ■ W. M. Duncan: Talk about trouble! Goodness knows what Frank will say. (1973)

until one is blue in the face (1864) From the notion of being livid with effort ■ Observer: I've been looking into . . . cases of dealers' rings . . . until I'm blue in the face. (1968)

like billy-o (1885) ■ Sunday Mail Magazine (Brisbane): There was Amundsen . . . with his dogs going like billyo for the Pole. (1969)

to the wide (1915) In such phrases as *blind, broke, dead, out*, etc. *to the wide* ■ Laurie Lee: Wake up, lamb. . . . He's wacked to the wide. Let's try and carry him up. (1959)

fit to burst (1916) ■ Guardian: The tumultuous foot-soldiers of his self-styled insurgency cheered fit to burst. (1992)

like crazy (1924) Orig US ■ Punch: Here were all those guys consuming like crazy and having to be regularly restocked. (1968)

as they come (1925) ■ P. G. Wodehouse: It's his sister Beulah. She was the one who put him up to it. She's the heavy in the sequence. As tough as they come. (1936)

good and proper (1928) ■ H. E. Bates: I'm in trouble. I'm going to have a baby. . . . I've had it. Good and proper. I'm up the creek. (1961)

in spades (1929) Orig US; from spades being the highest-ranking suit in bridge ■ Richard Nixon: Anybody who gets to the top in the Communist hierarchy and stays at the top has to have a great deal of political ability and a great deal of toughness. All three of the Soviet leaders have this in spades. (1972)

like stink (1929) ■ D. Devine: She wasn't really clever, she just worked like stink. (1972)

seven bells out of (1929) Orig nautical; in such phrases as *knock, scare*, etc. *seven bells out of* ■ Malcolm Lowry: Yis. He's knocked seven bells out of harder cases than you in his time. (1933)

with knobs on (1930) British; indicating ironic or emphatic agreement, or in retort to an insult, etc. ■ Anthony Price: If the A.S. 12 was the answer to Egypt's Russian missile boats, the A.S. 15 was the answer with knobs on. (1970)

the pants off (1933) In such phrases as *bore, scare, talk*, etc. *the pants off* ■ P. G. Wodehouse: They were . . . creeps of the first water and would bore the pants off me. (1954)

like nobody's business (1938) ■ *Times*: Poirot . . . adds . . . 'Never do I pull the leg.' That, alas, is not true. He teased poor Hastings like nobody's business. (1975)

as all get out (1941) US ■ Sara Peretsky: He felt guilty as all get-out when I told him who the doctor was and how bad she'd been hurt. (1992)

one's ass off (1946) Orig & mainly US; in such phrases as *work one's ass off, run one's ass off*, etc., denoting maximum effort; from *ass = arse* ■ *Melody Maker*: You want to . . . retire to your bedroom and practise your ass off for a year till you become competent enough to try it. (1984)

well and truly (1948) From earlier sense, properly, in due form ■ David Potter: As soon as the cup was well and truly won by England. (1971)

like a hole in the head (1951) Mainly in the phrase *need something like a hole in the head* applied to something not wanted at all or something useless; compare Yiddish *ich darf es vi a loch in kop* ■ William Gaddis: I need this drink like I need a hole in the head. (1955)

big-time (1957) Orig US; from the noun *big time* high level of prestigious achievement ■ *Washington Post*: 'Everybody is turning the heat up on our organization big-time,' he told a rally of more than 2,000 people in Louisville. (1993)

out of one's mind (head, skull, etc.) (1967) In such phrases as *bored, scared, pissed out of one's mind* ■ Win: Yeah, I'm scared out of my mind. The thought of prison doesn't exactly excite me. (1968)

Quite, somewhat

on the . . . side (1713) ■ A. J. Cronin: She was on the thin side . . . and her liquid, brownish eyes were too large. (1952)

sort of, sort o', sort a' (1790), sorta, sorter (1839) ■ D. H. Lawrence: You say a man's got no brain, when he's a fool. . . . And when he's got none of that spunky wild bit of a man in him, you say he's got no balls. When he's sort of tame. (1928)

kind of, kind o', kind a' (1804), kinder (1834) ■ J. N. Harris: He was one of these handsome guys with a kind of ugly expression. (1963)

kind of sort of, kinder sorter (1901) ■ Frank Norris: Makes it go down kind of sort of slick. (1901)

17. Imprecations

See also Exclamations of annoyance at **Anger** (pp. 256–7), Exclamations of surprise or astonishment at **Surprise** (pp. 248–50).

hang (13. .) Used in a range of mild oaths usually expressing irritation or impatience; from earlier sense, execute by suspending from a rope ■ F. F. Moore: He said he'd be hanged if he'd go to Madame Darius' squeeze—meaning this joyous entertainment. (1893) ■ A. P. Herbert: I'm fizzy and fiery and fruity and tense, So let's have a sundae and hang the expense! (1927)

for God's sake (c1300) Standard English in early use, but now often as an expletive ■ Joyce Cary: For God's sake, don't talk ballocks, Johnson. (1939)

confound (c1330) Dated; used in a range of oaths expressing irritation, originally denoting 'bring to perdition', but regarded since the early 18th century as relatively mild; from earlier sense, destroy ■ Ford Madox Ford: The doctors won't pass me G.S., confound them. (1918)

for Christ's sake (c1386) Standard English in early use, but now often as an expletive ■ John Masters: For Christ's sake, wake up, you chairborne bastard. (1954)

damn (1589) Used in a range of oaths expressing irritation; from earlier sense, bring to perdition ■ Hart Crane: I am to sail to *Mexico* (damn the gendarmes!)

next Saturday. (1931) ■ L. A. G. Strong: 'Aren't you perhaps afraid the inadequacy may be on your side?' . . . 'Damn you, Walter. You do get under a man's skin.' (1948)

hell (1596) Used in oaths, especially *what (who, why*, etc.) *the* (or *in*) *hell*, usually expressing impatience or irritation; often in such phrases as *bloody hell, fucking hell*, etc. ■ *Landfall*: Why in hell didn't you get John to build it for you? (1968) ■ James Fraser: 'What the bloody hell are you playing at?' 'That's ripe considering you just near broke my arm!' (1969)

dickens (1598) Used in oaths, especially *what (who, why*, etc.) *the* (formerly also *a*) *dickens*, usually expressing astonishment, impatience, or irritation; probably from the surname *Dickens*, used as a euphemistic substitute for *devil* ■ P. G. Wodehouse: I remember . . . wondering how the dickens a female of her slight build and apparently fragile physique could possibly get that wristy follow-through into her shots. (1936)

deuce (1694) Dated; used in oaths, especially *what (who, why*, etc.) *the deuce*, usually expressing impatience or irritation; from Low German *duus*, probably ultimately with the sense 'a throw of two at dice' (the lowest-scoring throw with two dice), and hence denoting the embodiment of bad luck, and used as a euphemistic substitute for *devil* ■ Ezra Pound: And what the deuce of your punctuation? . . . How much deliberate, and therefore to be taken (by me) with studious meticulousness?? (1918) ■ R. D. Paine: He just now cut loose with 'Goodness gracious. . . . I should call this the deuce of a mess'. (1923)

blow (1781) Used in a range of mild oaths expressing irritation, usually with the underlying implication of ignoring or disregarding ■ Frederic Hamilton: I'm absolutely blowed if I know what to do. (1922) ■ *Listener*. It is no longer proper to use as our second national motto in education 'Blow you, Jack, our top five per cent. are absolutely splendid'. (1963)

darn (1781) Orig US; euphemistic alteration of *damn*, used in place of it in a range of mild oaths expressing irritation ■ *Globe & Mail Magazine* (Toronto): 'Play, darn it!' he shouted to the open-mouthed pianist. (1968)

tarnation (1790) Mainly US; used in oaths, usually expressing impatience or irritation; a euphemistic alteration of *damnation*, apparently influenced by obsolete US slang *tarnal* damned, an alteration of *eternal* ■ M. K. Rawlings: Git away, you blasted bacon-thieves! . . . Git to tarnation! (1938)

bugger (1794) Used as the equivalent of *damn* in various oaths and exclamations, usually expressing contempt or exasperation; from earlier sense, sodomize ■ Samuel Beckett: I'll be buggered if I can understand how it could have been anything else. (1953) ■ David Pinner: Bugger me, he thought, looking at the grin on his watch, it's three o'clock! (1967)

blazes (1818) Used as a euphemistic substitute for *hell* in a range of oaths and exclamations, especially *go to blazes* and *what (who, where, etc.) the blazes*; from the notion of the flames of hell ■ Cecil Day Lewis: What the blue blazes is all this? (1948)

jiggered (1837) Used in mild oaths, especially *I'll be jiggered* and *I'm jiggered*, often expressing surprise; perhaps a euphemistic alteration of *buggered*

Sam Hill (1839) North American; used as a euphemistic substitute for *hell*, especially in the phrases *what in (or the) Sam Hill*; origin unknown, except for the substitution of *hill* for *hell* ■ M. E. Freeman: What in Sam Hill made you treat him so durned mean fur? (1918)

bother (1844) Used in a range of mild oaths expressing irritation ■ *Fraser's Magazine*: Bother the parson! (1877)

Godfrey (1853) US; used in mild oaths, as a euphemistic substitute for *God* ■ William Faulkner: They hadn't even cast the dogs yet when Uncle Buck roared, 'Gone away! I godfrey, he broke cover then!' (1942)

drat (1857) Used in mild oaths, as a euphemistic substitute for *damn*; from earlier interjectional use, expressing annoyance ■ Florence Nightingale: 'Drat' hockey and long live the horse! Them's my sentiments. (1900)

tunket, tunkett (1871) US; used as a euphemistic substitute for *hell*, especially in the phrases *who (what, why, etc.) in tunket*; origin unknown ■ E. Graham: 'And why not, in tunket?' she says. (1951)

Gawd (1877) British; used in oaths or as an oath; representing a nonstandard pronunciation of *god*, and often functioning as a euphemistic substitute for it ■ Arthur Morrison: Run, for Gawd's sake, or the woman'll croak! (1896) ■ Louis Stone: Gawd, 'e's stiffened 'im! (1911)

heck (1887) A euphemistic alteration of *hell*, used in a range of oaths and exclamations, especially *what (who, where, etc.) the heck* and *by heck*; compare earlier dialectal *hecky* in same sense ■ *Punch*: He insisted on St. Isinglas because he thought everything here was so well organised. The heck it is. (1933) ■ *80 Microcomputing*: When a large system can't figure out what the heck your program is trying to do, it spits it out as a dump. (1981)

buggery (1898) Used in various oaths, especially *go to buggery* go away, get lost; from earlier sense, sodomy ■ E. Lindall: 'Sah. You sick.' 'Go to buggery,' Minogue snarled. 'Yes, sah,' Basikas said, and stood aside. (1966)

sod (1904) Used as the equivalent of *damn* in various oaths and exclamations, usually expressing contempt or exasperation; from *sod* despicable person, male homosexual, probably on the model of *bugger* ■ Paul Scott: At seven-fifteen they had to go out to dinner. Sod it. (1953) ■ John Wain: 'He'll come out,' said Swarthmore. 'And if he doesn't, we'll sit where we are and you'll get paid for a full day's work, with overtime if necessary, and you won't have to do a stroke.' 'I'd rather be at home,' said the chief cameraman, 'and sod the overtime. I'm definitely sickening for something.' (1967)

frig (1905) Used as a euphemistic substitute for *fuck* in various oaths and exclamations, usually expressing contempt or exasperation; from earlier sense, copulate ■ Laurence Meynell: 'And what about the rent?' 'Frig the rent.' (1970)

rass (c1918) Jamaican; used as a verb and noun in various oaths and exclamations, usually expressing contempt or exasperation; from earlier sense, buttocks; ultimately a metathesized version of *arse* ■ Ian Fleming: 'Rass, man! Ah doan talk wid buckra.' The expression 'rass' is Jamaican for 'shove it'. (1965)

fuck (1922) Used as a verb and noun in various oaths and exclamations, usually expressing contempt or exasperation; from earlier sense, copulate; see also *for fuck's sake* (1966) ■ Francis King: 'Suppose any of the neighbours were to look out and see them.' 'Oh, f- the neighbours!' 'Really, Henry!' (1959) ■ G. Lord: What the fuck do you think you're doing? (1970)

for Pete's sake, for the love of Pete (1924) *Pete* a euphemistic substitute for *pity*, itself used in oaths in place of *God* and *Christ* ■ William Golding: Marry me, Taffy, for Pete's sake marry me. (1959)

bee aitch (1928) Representing the letters *b h*, a euphemistic abbreviation of *bloody hell* ■ John Galsworthy: Mr. Blythe's continual remark: 'What the bee aitch are they all about?' (1928)

Chrisake, Chrissake (1933) Mainly US; usually preceded by *for*; representing a casual pronunciation of *Christ's sake* ■ Maurice Procter: For Chrissake gimme a cigarette. (1954)

shag (1933) Used as the equivalent of *fuck* in various oaths and exclamations, usually expressing contempt or exasperation; from earlier sense, copulate ■ G. Pinsent: 'Then shag you!' I shouted, as he swaggered away. (1973)

screw (1949) Used as the equivalent of *fuck* in various oaths and exclamations, usually expressing contempt or exasperation; from earlier sense, copulate ■ Roald Dahl: 'Don't shout. There might be keepers.' 'Screw the keepers!' he cried. (1960)

for fuck's sake (1966) ■ *Anarchy.* A lad of 13 who has had his hand up for some time trying to attract the chairman's attention says 'Oh, for fuck's sake.' (1968)

A curse

sailor's blessing (1876) Nautical

soldier's farewell (1909) Applied to a parting curse ■ F. D. Sharpe: As you pass through the door, you'll sometimes hear a raspberry. . . . No one wants to accept responsibility for that soldier's farewell. (1938)

sailor's farewell (1937) Applied to a parting curse ■ *Listener.* The sole baker there . . . found himself ruined, and in some anger he gave the village a sailor's farewell and announced that he was off. (1974)

18. Names

moniker, monicker, monniker, monica, monekeer, etc. **(1851)** Also applied to someone's nickname; origin unknown ■ *Times Literary Supplement.* Henry Handel Richardson herself . . . was able to hide behind the male signature on her books (her maiden name wedded to two favourite family monikers). (1959)

handle (1870) Orig US; also applied to someone's nickname; from earlier sense, honorific title ■ C. F. Burke: One night Jesus met a guy named Nicodemus. How's that for a handle? (1969)

tag (1980) Orig US; applied to a nickname or other (often elaborately decorative) identifying mark written as the signature of a graffiti artist ■ *Times.* Gang members . . . used coloured paints and red pencils to deface hundreds of buses in Birmingham with their nicknames, or 'tags'. (1987). Hence the verb **tag** to decorate with a tag (1980) ■ *New Musical Express.* Rap Kids don't drink much and were once inclined to tag previously paint-free walls. (1990)

A signature

John Hancock (1903), John Henry (1914) US; from the name of *John Hancock* (1737–93), the

first signatory of the American Declaration of Independence (1776) ■ *Listener.* Even today an American handing you a contract is apt to say: 'And now if you will just give us your John Hancock.' (1972) ■ T. Barling: Sign your John Henry there. . . . Your name is Balkin. You'd better get used to it. (1974)

A title

handle (1832) Applied to an honorific title or similar distinction attached to a personal name; from the phrase *a handle to one's name* a title attached to one's name ■ *News of the World.* 'I get very angry if people call me Lord David.' David . . . hates the sort of questions people ask once they find out about his 'handle'. (1977)

Pseudonymously

aka (1955) Orig US; abbreviation of *also known as* introducing a pseudonym, nickname, etc. ■ *Times.* He is perhaps a shade too comfortable and not enough of a cad as Johnson, aka Ramirez, the outlaw. (1982)

The Arts, Entertainment, and the Media

1. Entertainment

show biz (1945) Orig US; abbreviation of *show business* ■ *Liverpool Echo*: Blackpool remains . . . the heartland of Northern showbiz. (1976)

Broadcasting; radio and television

sparks (1914) Applied to a radio operator, especially on board ship ■ P. F. Westerman: A burly, jovial-featured man . . . greeted Mostyn as he stepped off the gang-plank. 'Hello, you're our Sparks, aren't you?' (1922)

ham, radio ham (1919) Orig US; applied to someone whose hobby is sending and receiving radio messages; from earlier sense, inexpert performer

shack (1929) US; applied to a room or small building housing radio equipment

tele (1936) Shortening of *television* ■ *Gay News*: Hardly home-loving types, likely to be content with baked beans on toast and the tele. (1977)

wop (1939) Applied in the RAF to a radio operator; acronym from *w(ireless op(erator* ■ R. Barker: Wireless operator/air gunners . . . most of the wop/A.G.s . . . came straight from gunnery school. (1957)

telly (1940) Shortening of *television* ■ G. F. Newman: On the news, on the telly tonight. (1970)

snifter (1944) US; applied to a portable radio direction-finder; from dialect *snift* to sniff + *-er*

the box (1950) Applied to television; from earlier sense, gramophone, radio ■ E. Humphreys: I saw one of your plays, Dicky. On the old box. (1963)

kidvid (1955) Orig US; applied to a television or video programme made for children, and hence to children's broadcasting; from *kid* + *vid(eo-* ■ *Fortune*: She's bringing a new, nonviolent, Disney-created cartoon series to NBC's kidvid schedule. (1985)

pianist (1955) Applied to a radio operator

goggle-box (1959) Orig British; applied to a television set ■ *Times*: Mr. Wilson was . . . so good at television appearances, that he had convinced himself that he, single-handed, could win elections 'with the help of the goggle box'. (1967)

idiot box (1959) Applied derogatorily to a television set ■ P. Flower: I thought you spent all your time with the idiot box. (1972)

the tube (1959) Orig and mainly US; applied to television; from the notion of a television's cathode-ray tube ■ *Sunday News* (New York): She . . . is making a name for herself as a singer on the tube. (1965)

boob tube (1963) Orig and mainly US; applied derogatorily to television; from *boob* fool + *tube* television ■ M. French: I sit and watch the stupid boob tube. (1977)

tranny, trannie (1969) Mainly British; applied to a transistor radio; from abbreviation of *transistor* + *-y* ■ *Listener*: The Controller surely had her tranny in the shed with her. (1976)

God slot (1972) Applied to a period in a broadcasting schedule regularly reserved for religious programmes

prog (1975) Applied to a broadcast radio or television programme; abbreviation of *programme* ■ *Listener*: Nice to have you with us on the prog, we say, don't we, fans? (1975)

boom box (1981) Orig US; applied to a large portable radio, especially as used to play loud pop music ■ *Washington Post*: How about a law against playing 'boom boxes' in public places? (1985)

ghetto-blaster (1981) Orig US; applied to a large portable radio, especially as used to play loud pop music; from its use in the Black quarter of American cities; also termed jocularly *ghetto guitar* and *third-world briefcase* ■ *Christian Science Monitor*: Six feet tall, 16 years old, and carrying a 'ghetto blaster'. (1983).

zapper (1981) Orig US; applied to a remote-control unit for a television or video recorder; from *zap* deal a blow to + *-er* ■ *Los Angeles Times*: Hit the zapper, Maude. Maybe there's some bowling on another channel. (1987). Hence **zap** to fast-forward a video recorder so as to go quickly through the advertisements in a recorded television programme, or to switch through other channels during advertisements when watching programmes off-air (1983)

video nasty (1983) Applied to a horror video film ■ *Listener*: Unless one has seen a video nasty . . . it is difficult to imagine the depths of degradation to which certain producers are willing to sink. (1984)

Films

picture (1896) Applied to a film, and in the plural to the cinema ■ *Home Chat*: The pictures one sees nowadays are . . . in much better taste than those of a few years ago. (1913)

flick, (dated) flicker (1926) Applied to a film, and in the plural to the cinema; from the flickering effect of early cinema films ■ John Braine: Where shall we go this afternoon anyway? Tanbury and tea at the Raynton, then a flick? (1959) ■ Frank Swinnerton: He would take her to the theatre, the ballet, the flicks. (1949) ■ Gish & Pinchot: Mother, guess who we saw acting in 'flickers'? (1969)

pic (1936) Short for *picture* ■ Anne Blaisdell: All of a sudden, Latin romances sort of passé. . . . Everybody doing the big war pics. (1973)

fleas and itches (1967) Australian; rhyming slang for *pictures*, with an allusion to the vermin infesting cheap cinemas ■ D. O'Grady: When not too tired, a man was able to visit . . . the open-air fleas-n' itches. (1968)

Photography

soup (1929) Applied to the chemicals in which film is developed ■ Len Deighton: Any special instructions? Over or under development? Fine grain soup? (1978)

A photograph

snap (1894) Orig US; applied usually to an informal or casually taken photograph; short for *snapshot*, from the notion of taking an instantaneous photograph ■ Time: They even had a prospectus put together for publishers and included some sample snaps. (1977). Also the verb **snap**, denoting taking a photograph (1890) ■ Guardian: We got the job done all the same. And without all those photographers snapping our every move. (1991)

smudge (a1931) Applied especially to a photograph taken by a street or press photographer; perhaps from the blurring of a hastily taken snapshot, but first applied in prison slang to a picture of a fingerprint

pic (1948) Short for *picture*; in use since the 1880s denoting a painting, but evidence is lacking for its application to a photograph before the mid 20th century ■ Sunday Post (Glasgow): I sent £7.22 to photographer in Wembley for two coloured photos of a show jumping event in Warwickshire. When no pics came I wrote. (1976)

piccy, picky (1968) From *pic(ture* + *-y*; in use since the 1880s denoting a painting, but evidence is lacking for its application to a photograph before the 1960s ■ Hot Car: The end result of fitting these packages on your Ford can be, if the piccies are anything to go by, rather on the eye-catching side. (1977)

A photographer

snapper (1910) From *snap* take photographs + *-er* ■ Ripped & Torn: And thanks a lot to all you budding photographers for the offers of photos, just send 'em in you snappers. (1977)

mug-faker (1933) Dated; applied to a street photographer; from *mug* face ■ Margery Allingham: These old photographers—mugfakers we call 'em—in the street. (1952)

shutter-bug (1940) Applied to an enthusiastic (amateur) photographer; from *shutter* device allowing light into a camera + *bug* enthusiast, fan

smudger (1961), smudge (1968) Applied especially to a street or press photographer; compare earlier *smudge* photograph ■ Q: Cole is on his way to a photo-session with acclaimed French smudge Claude Gassian. (1990)

The theatre

rep (1925) Applied to repertory theatre or a repertory company; abbreviation of *repertory* ■ Manchester Guardian: She has returned to 'weekly rep.', producing for a sound but as yet undistinguished company which must perform potboilers for most of the year. (1959)

On stage

fit-up (1864) Applied to a temporary stage set, piece of scenery, etc., and hence (in full *fit-up company*) to a travelling company which carries makeshift scenery and props that can be set up temporarily ■ Daily Telegraph: Today there are some 40 off-Broadway houses. You might add another 40 off-off-Broadway clubs and fit-ups. (1970)

stooge (1913) Orig US; applied to a stage hand; see **stooge** under **Variety** (p. 345)

spot (1920) Short for *spotlight*

greengage (1931) British; rhyming slang for *stage*

nigger (1934) Applied to a screen used in film-making to mask studio lights or create special lighting effects; from earlier sense, black person

on the green (1940) British; used to mean 'on stage'; *green* abbreviation of *greengage* stage ■ Times Literary Supplement: If a modern producer asks a stage-manager to summon down a man from the flies, we might well hear the cry: 'Bill, come down on the green a minute'. (1957)

iron (1951) Applied to a metal safety curtain; short for *iron curtain*

Variety

stooge (1913) Orig US; applied to a stage assistant, especially one who acts as the butt or foil for a leading character or comedian; origin unknown; the possibility has been suggested that it represents an altered form of *student*, students having frequently been employed as stage assistants. Hence **stooge** to act as a stooge (1939) ■ Scientific American: That Strang often stooged for Geller is well established. (1979)

jazzbo, jasbo (1917) US; applied to a vaudeville act featuring low comedy; origin unknown; perhaps an alteration of the personal name *Jasper*

revusical (1931) Orig US; applied to a musical revue; blend of *revue* and *musical* ■ American Speech: Pardon Us Please, 'presenting thirty-five stars in person', advertises itself in newspapers as a *Revusical*. (1941)

tab show (1951) US; applied to a short version of a musical, especially one performed by a travelling company; from *tab(loid* condensed + *show*

second banana (1953) US; applied to a supporting comedian in a burlesque entertainment

top banana (1953) US; applied to the leading comic in a burlesque entertainment ■ *New York Times*: Miss Burnett is a . . . very, very funny woman. She is a superb top banana. (1978)

one-liner (1969) Applied to a short joke or witty remark ■ *Times Literary Supplement*: His dear cousins collapse in mirth at Berry's one-liners and monologues. (1976)

Recording

platter (1931) Mainly US; applied to a gramophone record ■ *Tobias Wells*: I went into Fink Roth's pad and found treasures. Good old platters and stamps. I sold them. Got a good price for the records. The stamps were only so-so. (1967)

wax (1932) Mainly US; applied to a gramophone record; from the 'wax' discs in which the recording stylus cuts its groove. Hence **on wax** on a gramophone record ■ *W. C. Handy*: Recording companies . . . made them available on wax. (1941). Hence **wax** to record for the gramophone (1935) ■ *Daily Times* (Lagos): Another new LP Record waxed by the Celestial Church of Christ Choir. (1976)

plate (1935) US, dated; applied to a gramophone record

side (1936) US; applied to a recording or record ■ *James Baldwin*: 'How about some sides?' . . . Lorenzo put on something . . . by the Modern Jazz Quartet. (1960)

Recorded

canned (1904) Derogatory; mainly applied to music ■ *Independent*: No canned music, no TV. Wonderful sea views, kind, efficient staff, good food, good value. (1991)

Circuses and fairs

barker (1699) Now mainly US; applied to someone who calls out in public to advertise a circus or other show; from earlier sense, noisy assailant ■ *H. A. Franck*: The secretary was a man . . . with the voice of a side-show barker. (1910)

tober, tobur (1890) Applied to the site occupied by a circus, fair, etc.; from Shelta *tobar* road ■ *E. Seago*: How can I walk about the tober without me trousers, I'd be askin' ye? (1933)

razzle-dazzle (1891) Applied to a type of fairground ride; from earlier sense, excitement and bustle ■ *David Braithwaite*: Four years before his death in 1897, Savage patented the 'Razzle Dazzle', otherwise known as 'Whirligig' or 'Aerial Novelty'. (1968)

spruik (1902) Australian & New Zealand; used to denote calling out in public to advertise a circus or other show; origin unknown ■ *N. Bartlett*: Spruiked for a circus in the U.S.A. (1954). Hence **spruiker**, **sprooker** (1902)

razor-back (1904) US; applied to a circus hand, especially one who loads and unloads the wagons; from earlier sense, a scraggy animal ■ *New Yorker*: Some people . . . were watching the roller

coaster. . . . I went up to the razorback who ran the controls. (1975)

rosin-back (1923) Applied to a horse used by a bareback rider or acrobat, and hence to a bareback rider; from *rosin* resin, with which the horse's back was rubbed for a firmer seat ■ *C. B. Cochran*: A 'rosin-back' is a ring-horse used by bareback riders. . . . Rosin is rubbed into the horse's back to help the rider to get a firm footing as he jumps from the ring on to the horse. (1945)

star-back (1931) Applied to an expensive, reserved seat at a circus

Venues

nigger heaven (1878) US dated, now offensive; applied to the top gallery in a theatre

peanut gallery (1888) US; applied to the top gallery in a theatre

nitery, niterie (1934) Orig and mainly US; applied to a night club; from *nite*, arbitrary respelling of *night* + *-ery* ■ *Boston Sunday Herald*: Our story begins in a narrow strip of niteries on 52nd Street. (1967)

nabes (1935) US; applied to local cinemas; from the pronunciation of *neighb(ourhood* ■ *New Yorker*: They picked an aging star, slapped together a moldy script, and sent the results out to the nabes. (1970)

spot (1936) Applied to a place of entertainment; especially in *night spot* night club ■ *F. Usher*: They went to a night spot . . . where they drank champagne. (1959)

flea-pit (1937) British; applied to a shabby and allegedly verminous cinema ■ *Ink*: He went to a fleapit cinema. (1971)

track (1945) US; applied to a ballroom or dance-hall ■ *Malcolm X*: I dig our holding this all-originals scene at the track. (1965)

bughouse (1946) Applied to a tatty or second-rate theatre or cinema; compare earlier sense, lunatic asylum ■ *John Osborne*: If there's nothing else on, I still go . . . to the bug house round the corner. (1957)

ozoner (1948) US; applied to a drive-in cinema; from *ozone* + *-er*, in allusion to the open-air viewing arrangements

skin house (1970) US; applied to an establishment featuring nude shows, pornographic films, etc. ■ *Harper's Magazine*: The skin houses were mostly playing short subjects—a girl taking a bath in a sylvan stream, a volley-ball game in a nudist camp. (1970)

Organizations

indie (1942) Orig US; applied to an independent theatre, film, or record company; abbreviation of *independent*

auntie (1958) Applied in Britain to the BBC and in Australia to the Australian Broadcasting Corporation, thought of as being conservative in style or approach; from the notion of an aunt as a comfortable and conventional figure

■ *Listener*: The BBC needs to be braver and sometimes is. So let there be a faint hurrah as Auntie goes over the top. (1962)

Beeb (1967) Representing an abbreviation of the pronunciation of *BBC* ■ *Times*: The licence fee the 'Beeb' is asking for is a shade less than the 18p a day for a popular newspaper. (1985)

Performers

omee, omie (1859) Applied to an itinerant actor; showman's corruption of Italian *uomo* man ■ Ngaio Marsh: 'A lot of omies the others were then. . . .' 'Ted means they were bad actors doing worse shows in one-eyed towns up and down the provinces.' (1937)

ham (1882) Applied to an inexpert performer, especially an actor who overacts; probably short for obsolete US slang *hamfatter* ineffective performer ■ *Times*: 'He thought I was an old ham,' says Miss Seyler indulgently. (1958)

ham-bone (1893) US; applied to an inferior or amateur actor, especially one who speaks in a spurious Black accent, or to a mediocre musician ■ Buster Keaton: Because I was also a born hambone, I ignored any bumps . . . I may have got at first on hearing audiences gasp. (1960)

vent (1893) Abbreviation of *ventriloquist* ■ *National Observer*: We've got magicians here. . . . We've got jugglers, mentalists, clowns, and vents. (1976)

legit (1897) Applied to a legitimate actor ■ Noel Coward: When she stabs herself—she takes such a time about it—that's legits all over. (1936)

spear-carrier (1960) Applied to an actor with a walk-on part

tummler, toomler, tumeler (1966) Orig and mainly US; applied to someone responsible for entertaining the patrons at a hotel or the like; from earlier sense, someone who plays the fool; ultimately from Yiddish, from German *tummeln* to stir ■ L. M. Feinsilver: Danny Kaye and other entertainers got their starts as tumelers in the Catskills. (1970)

veejay, VJ (1982) Mainly US; applied to someone who presents a programme of (pop music) videos, especially on television; from the pronunciation of the initial letters of *video jockey*, after *DJ* (= disc jockey)

brat pack (1985) Orig US; applied to a group of young Hollywood film stars of the mid-1980s popularly regarded as enjoying a rowdy, fun-loving lifestyle; punningly after *rat-pack*, itself applied earlier to a brash Hollywood set including Frank Sinatra. Hence **brat packer** member of a brat pack (1985)

Audiences

paper (1785) Applied to free admission tickets to the theatre or other entertainment ■ Josephine Tey: Johnny Garson can tell you how much paper there is in the house. (1951). Hence **paper** to fill (a theatre, etc.) by means of free passes (1879)

stage-door Johnny (1912) Mainly US; applied to a (young) man who frequents stage doors for the company of actresses

Aunt Edna (1953) Used of a typical theatre-goer of conservative tastes; coined by Terence Rattigan (1911–77), British playwright ■ N. F. Simpson: The author . . . leans forward . . . to make simultaneous overtures of sumptuous impropriety to every Aunt Edna in the house. (1958)

vidiot (1967) Orig and mainly US; applied to a habitual and undiscriminating watcher of television and videos; blend of *video* and *idiot*; compare **couch potato** at **Laziness** (p. 294) ■ *Washington Times*: They are eyeballing the Federal Communications Commission as carefully as any youthful vidiot ever did the Teenage Mutant Ninja Turtles. (1991)

Genres

panto (1852) Abbreviation of *pantomime* ■ *R.A.F. News*: The organizers ran an 'ad lib' version of the panto 'Cinderella'. (1977)

horse opera (1927) Orig US; applied to a 'Western' film or television series; from the prominent role of horses in such productions

soap (1943) Orig US; short for *soap opera* ■ *American Poetry Review*: If you turn on day-time T.V. you will see most of his actors playing rather similar roles in soaps. (1978)

oater (1951), (dated) **oats opera, oat opera (1942)** Mainly US; applied to a 'Western' film or television series; based on *horse opera*, from the notion of oats as horses' food

starrer (1951) Applied to a film or play with a leading star in a principal role; from *star* + *-er* ■ Mario Puzo: A Kellino starrer would get the studio's two million back. (1978)

shoot-'em-up, shoot-em-up, shootemup (1953) Orig US; applied to a fast-moving story or film, especially a Western, of which gun-play is a dominant feature ■ *New York Times*: The new or free-form Western has several choice entries. . . . 'Oklahoma Crude', a splendid shootemup about a lady wildcatter in the oilfields. (1973)

sitcom (1964) Orig US; abbreviation of *situation comedy* ■ *Globe & Mail* (Toronto): A domestic sitcom about a pair of newlyweds. (1970)

skin-flick (1968) Applied to an explicitly pornographic film

sudser (1968) US; applied to a soap opera; from *suds* + *-er* ■ *Washington Post*: Clooney's autobiography . . . has been turned into another drabby shabby TV sudser. (1982)

Performance

spot (1923) Orig US; applied to a place for an individual item of entertainment in a television, radio or theatre show ■ Gerald Durrell: He appeared on the local television as 'Uncle Ambrose', doing a children's spot in which he always had an animal of some sort to show them and talk to them about. (1972)

gig (1926) Applied to an engagement for a musician or musicians playing jazz, dance-music, etc.; origin unknown ■ L. Hairston: Pa—knockin' hisself out on a mail-handler gig at the Post Office where the pay is so lousy he's gotta work a part-time gig. (1964)

preem (1937) US; applied to the first performance of a play, film, etc.; abbreviation of *premiere* ■ *Variety*: The mother-daughter act . . . has been bought by ABC and set for an Oct. 4 preem. (1948). Hence **preem** to premiere (a play, film, etc.) (1942)

shtick, schtick, schtik, shtik (1961) US; applied to a theatrical routine, gimmick, etc.; from Yiddish, from German *Stück* piece, play ■ *Time*: The former Prime Minister is not at all apologetic about his Yuletide shtik, pointing out that he has chosen to write books and sell records rather than go the David Frost route. (1977)

Acting

mug (1855) Used to denote making faces, especially before an audience, a camera, etc.; from *mug* face ■ *Times*: Grimaces and gestures straight out of silent films, properly deserving the name 'mugging'. (1961)

corpse (1873) Used to denote laughing inadvertently on stage or forgetting one's lines ■ Alan Bennett: *Mrs Brodribb*: When Max -. *Geoff*: Max (*He corpses*). (1972)

super (1889) Denoting appearing in a play or film as an extra; from the noun *super* extra, short for *supernumerary* ■ *New Yorker*: Chance for man to super in new Met production of Aida. (1976)

profesh (1901) Abbreviation of *profession*, applied especially to the theatre ■ E. Pugh: 'Mr. Alexander, . . . being a hartist in his profesh, which there's only one thing as keeps him off the London stage at this present moment, and that is—' 'Eggs!' (1914)

legit (1908) Applied to acting in serious drama, as opposed to revue, musical comedy, etc.; abbreviation of *legitimate* ■ John Osborne: I'd gone legit. for a while . . . and I'd been in 'The Tale of Two Cities'. (1957)

dry (1934) Used to denote forgetting one's lines on stage; from earlier *dry up* stop talking ■ Milton Shulman: 'O.K., Allan,' said the director into his microphone. 'If she fluffs badly or dries we'll go straight to Three.' (1967)

hoke (1935) Orig US; used to denote playing (a part) in a sentimental or melodramatic way; often followed by *up*; back-formation from *hokum* sentimental or melodramatic material in a film or play ■ Marian Babson: Just *try* it straight . . . it's a mistake to hoke it up. (1971)

ham (1942) Applied to an inexpert or over-theatrical acting performance; from earlier sense, inexpert or over-theatrical actor ■ *Listener*: The mummer who thinks that all acting before his

time was 'ham'. (1959). So **hammy (1929)** ■ David Jordan: Condon raised an eyebrow in a hammy attempt to be supercilious. (1973)

hokey, hokie, hoky (1945) Orig US; applied to something sentimental or melodramatic; from *hoke* or *hokum* + *-y* ■ *Rolling Stone*: A closing piece [on a record], 'Sometimesi', is embarrassingly hokey. (1971)

idiot board, idiot card, idiot sheet (1952) Applied to a board displaying a television script to a performer

Rehearsal

stagger, stagger-through (1964) Applied to a preliminary rehearsal or run-through of a play, television programme, etc.

Review

rave (1926) Orig US; applied to a highly enthusiastic review; often used adjectivally ■ *Listener*: I yield to none in my admiration for this pianist, whose first London notice I had the honour to write long before the war (a 'rave' in case you think I am always wrong). (1958)

Finance and administration

ducat, ducket(t) (1871) Applied to a ticket of admission; probably from earlier sense, coin; perhaps influenced by *docket* and *ticket* ■ *Guardian*: My wife and I had a couple of ducketts to see the Marxes' Broadway musical, 'Animal Crackers'. (1970)

angel (1891) Orig US; applied to the financial backer of a theatrical enterprise ■ P. G. Wodehouse: Ike hasn't any of his own money in the thing. . . . The angel is the long fellow you see jumping around. (1921). Hence **angel** to finance (a theatrical production) (1929)

Tin Pan Alley (1908) Orig US; applied to the world of popular-music writing, publishing and administration, and also to an area where there are many song publishing houses, specifically (formerly) in New York in 28th Street and in London around Denmark Street

ice (1927) US; applied to profit from the illegal sale of theatre, cinema, etc. tickets ■ *Economist*: Kick-backs—'ice' as it is called on Broadway—on theatre tickets whose prices are marked up illegally. (1964)

two-fer, -for (1948) Applied to a coupon that entitles someone to buy two tickets for a theatre show for the price of one; from *two* + (a representation of) *for*

roadie (1969) Applied to someone who organizes and supervises a touring pop group, etc., or to an assistant who helps with this; from *road* + *-ie*, from the notion of being *on the road* travelling

2. **Journalism & Newspapers**

gonzo (1971) Orig and mainly US; applied to a type of committed, subjective journalism characterized by factual distortion and exaggerated rhetorical style; introduced by the US journalist Hunter S. Thompson to denote his own style of writing; perhaps ultimately suggested by Italian *gonzo* fool(ish) (perhaps from Italian *Borgonzone* Burgundian) or Spanish *ganso* goose, fool

Newspapers

rag (1734) Derogatory

bladder (1842) Mainly US; probably from German *Blätter* sheets (of paper) ■ *Observer*: The news of your return has caused hardly a ripple in the daily bladders. (1973)

linen-draper (1857) British; rhyming slang

Pink 'Un (1887) A nickname for a newspaper printed on pink paper, especially the *Sporting Times* and the *Financial Times*; = pink one ■ *Guardian*: Today . . . the first Financial Times will hit Wall Street. . . . But for all the . . . computer setting . . . the new international Pink 'un depends very much for its birth on the weather. (1979)

blat, blatt (1932) Orig US; from German *Blatt* sheet, newspaper ■ *Times*: An otherwise bald and unconvincing interview on the telly or column in the blats. (1986)

tab (1939) Applied to a tabloid newspaper; abbreviation ■ Jane Leavy: It's days like this that make me glad I work for a feisty little tab like the *Trib*, which is to say a scummy rag specializing in boobs, bodies, and baseball. (1990)

the heavies (1950) Applied to serious newspapers ■ *Author*: The popular press, thrown off balance and uncertain of its role, lost out to the heavies and the provincials. (1971)

Magazines

mag (1801) Abbreviation

The media

meeja, meejah, meejer (1983) Jocular or derogatory; respelling of *media*, representing a common informal pronunciation of the word ■ J. Neel: We aren't middle-class poor anymore, you know. I am part of the rich *meeja*. (1988)

News, features, etc.

funnies (1852) Orig US; applied to (the section of a newspaper containing) comic strips ■ P. G.

Wodehouse: We've only read the movie section and the funnies. (1936)

obit (1874) Abbreviation of *obituary*; earlier non-slang use in the 15th–17th centuries derived directly from Old French *obit* death

screamer, screamer headline (1926) Applied to a large headline

snap (1937) Applied to a short news report, especially one dispatched or broadcast from the scene ■ Louis Heren: Valentine found a telephone . . . , dictated a couple of snaps, and then . . . removed the microphone from the phone thus making it useless for the opposition. (1978)

Journalists

hack (1810) British; applied especially to a staff newspaper writer; a slight development from the earlier sense, literary scribbler; the term is often applied jocularly by journalists to themselves ■ *Arena*: 'Good story'. The other hacks had seen bodies float by: we were the first to see them being fished out. (1988)

sob sister (1912) Orig US; applied to a female journalist who writes sentimental stories ■ *Sun* (Baltimore): Forecasting opposition to his plan by 'sob-sisters' Goodwin said 'it wouldn't do any harm to give these sob-sisters a couple of wallops too'. (1939)

slot man (1926) US; applied to a newspaper's chief sub-editor or a news editor; from *slot* the middle of a semi-circular desk at which sub-editors work, occupied by the chief sub-editor

tripe-hound (1928) From earlier sense, unpleasant person

scribe (1929) Mainly US; from earlier sense, writer of documents

journo (1967) Orig Australian; from *journ(alist* + *-o* ■ *Times*: Journos who work with the written word are seldom at ease with spoken English. (1985)

hackette (1984) British; applied to a female journalist; from *hack* + *-ette* ■ *Times*: The worlds of newspapers and publishing are unbuttoned, and hackettes can wear pretty well anything. (1987)

A newspaper seller or delivery boy

newsie, newsy (1875) Mainly US and Australian; from *news* + *-ie* ■ *John o' London's*: To be polite the newsie took a couple of swigs of it. (1962)

3. **Music & Dance**

Music

dots (1927) Mainly jazz slang; applied to the notes on sheet music, and hence to written or printed music itself

lick (1932) Mainly jazz slang; applied to a short solo or phrase, usually improvised ■ *Globe & Mail* (Toronto): The blues riff is even better, full of Charlie Parker-like bebop licks. (1970)

rideout (1939) Jazz slang; applied to a final chorus ■ *New Yorker*: 'On the Other Side of the Tracks' . . . has an ebullient and remarkable rideout section. (1977)

screamer (1940) Jazz slang; applied to a passage of music containing shrill notes on a woodwind instrument, and also to a note of this kind

mop (1944) US; applied to a final cadence of three notes at the end of a jazz number

sounds (1955) Orig US; applied to pop music, especially records ■ *Daily Mirror*: Together cats don't buy records, they buy sounds, and they never blow their cool. (1968)

A musical instrument

ivories (1818) Applied to the keys of a piano or other instrument; from the keys being made of ivory ■ *Times*: Its cover portrays the Prime Minister, seated at the organ, tinkling one lot of ivories and flashing the other lot. (1974)

joanna, joana, johanna, etc. **(1846)** Rhyming slang for *piano* ■ *Listener*: The old Jo-anna intrudes its amateurish thumpings. (1972)

bull-fiddle (1880) US; applied to a double bass or cello ■ *Steinbeck & Ricketts*: A deep and yet penetrating tone like the lowest string of an incredible bull-fiddle. (1941)

Strad (1884) Short for *Stradivarius*; applied to a violin, etc. made by Antonio Stradivari ■ *Sunday Times*: 'It was all right for rehearsal, but not quite fair when people turn up with their £200,000 Strads,' mused Gordon, a music teacher and church organist. (1993)

traps (1903) Orig US; applied in a jazz or dance band to percussion instruments or devices (e.g. wood-blocks, whistles) used to produce a variety of special effects, and also to these together with the standard jazz or dance band drum-kit; origin uncertain; probably some slang application of *trap* device for capturing

dog-house (1920) Jazz slang; applied to a double bass; from its supposed resemblance in wooden bulkiness to a dog's kennel ■ *H. T. Webster*: When the bull-fiddler plucks the strings he is slapping the doghouse. (1933)

gob-stick (1923) Jazz slang, dated; applied to a clarinet; from *gob* mouth + *stick*; compare earlier dialect sense, spoon or other eating implement ■ *Dylan Thomas*: The double-bed is a swing-band with coffin, oompah, slush-pump, gob-stick. (1938)

sax (1923) Abbreviation of *saxophone* ■ *Picture-Play Magazine*: How I used to envy Laura playing beautifully mellow notes on her sax. (1926)

kitchen (1931) Applied to the percussion section of an orchestra or band; probably from the fanciful resemblance between the timpani (kettledrums) and other percussion instruments to kitchen implements and vessels ■ *S. R. Nelson*: Next in the rhythm section we will have a look at the 'gentlemen of the kitchen'. (1934)

horn (1935) Jazz slang; applied to a trumpet, or more broadly to any wind instrument ■ *G. Avakian*: Each of these trio cuttings ends with Bix picking up his horn to play the coda. (1959) ■ *Crescendo*: If I'm happy with the horn I've got, the mouthpiece, the set-up, the reed and everything. (1966)

liquorice-stick (1935) Jazz slang; applied to a clarinet; from the instrument's long thin black appearance

peck horn (1936) Jazz slang; applied to a mellophone, saxophone, or other similar instrument; origin unknown ■ *Sunday Times*: Straight band singers were unknown in the Twenties—everyone, even Bing Crosby, had an instrument to hold. 'I had a peckhorn, like a flugel-horn.' (1975)

pretzel (1936) Applied to a French horn; from earlier sense, knot-shaped savoury biscuit; from the French horn's convoluted shape

squeeze-box (1936) Applied to an accordion or concertina; from its being played by pushing the two parts together; compare earlier obsolete nautical sense, ship's harmonium ■ *Chris Bonington*: He was already ensconced in the bar at the Clachaig, his squeeze box out, a dram of whisky at his side and a cigarette in his mouth. (1973)

woodpile (1936) Applied to a xylophone; from its tuned wooden bars ■ *Time*: Red Norvo kept salting his half-hour stands with such tunes as . . . he used to rap out on his 'woodpile' (xylophone) with Paul Whiteman's band 20 years ago. (1951)

slush pump (1937) US; applied to a trombone ■ *John Wainwright*: Get Walt to help on the slushpump try-outs. Walt stays first trombone. (1977)

piccolo (1938) US; applied to a juke-box ■ *New York Amsterdam News*: The Harlem Hamfats grind out the tune on myriad Harlem piccolos. (1938)

skin (1938) Jazz slang; applied to a drum; usually used in the plural

vibes (1940) Abbreviation of *vibraphone* + -*s* ■ *Rolling Stone*: He fell back on his musical training to support the family, playing trumpet and vibes in a succession of third-rate cabaret bands. (1977)

easy rider (1949) Applied to a guitar; probably from a guitar's portability, but compare earlier sense, sexually satisfying lover, perhaps suggesting a link between the guitar's curved outlines and those of a voluptuous woman

axe (1955) Jazz and rock music slang; originally applied to a saxophone, but now usually a guitar; perhaps suggested by *sax* saxophone, or from such expressions as 'Swing that axe, man!' ■ *Rolling Stone*: While Keith bashes madly on the drums, . . . Pete Townsend disposes of his axe with good natured dispatch. (1969)

An instrumentalist

sticks (1909) Naval slang; applied to a drummer

bull-fiddler (1933) Applied to a double-bass player ■ W. C. Handy: As usual the bull-fiddler sawed away in G. (1957)

monkey-hurdler (1936) US; applied to an organist; perhaps from the traditional organ-grinder's monkey ■ W. Morum: Nelson's a monkey hurdler. . . . He plays one of those Wurlitzer organs at the talkies. (1951)

pretzel-bender (1936) Applied to a French-horn player

skin-beater (1936) Dated; applied to a drummer in a jazz or dance band ■ *New York Times Book Review*: Red, the reefer-smitten skin beater. (1953)

tickler (1948) Applied to a pianist; from the phrase *tickle the ivories* play the piano ■ James McClure: I'm the tickler. Pianist. Y'know. (1975)

axeman (1976) Jazz and rock music slang; applied to a guitarist, especially one who plays in a band or group ■ *Washington Post*: He learned guitar from Fats Domino's axeman, Walter (Papoose) Nelson. (1985)

To play music

spiel (1870) US; from German *spielen* play ■ G. S. Perry: Denver's Symphony chooses to spiel only when winter's winds doth blow. (1947)

fake (1926) Jazz slang; applied to improvising ■ *Spotlight*: There was enough good music 'faked' in those days. (1944)

sock (1927) Applied to performing jazz in a swinging manner; often in the phrase *sock it* (*out*) ■ *New Yorker*: From the top—'Watermelon Man'. Let's sock it out and give Mrs. Ritterhouse a chance to really cook. (1976)

ride (1929) Applied to playing jazz with an easy-flowing rhythm ■ John Wainwright: When Ellington opens on an eight-bar piano intro . . . you know that . . . when the full outfit starts leaning back and riding, you are going to be lifted cloud-high. (1977)

tear it (or **things**) **up** (1932) US; applied to performing with unrestrained excitement ■ *Listener*: The trumpeter Wild Bill Davison, who 'tore it up' with admirable primitivity and sensuality. (1963)

get off (1933) US, jazz slang; applied to improvising skilfully ■ Rudolph Blesh: The present-day solo is esteemed modern and full of ideas in direct proportion to the more unrecognizable it makes the melody. Such 'getting off' conceals lack of true invention. (1955)

slap (1933) US; applied to playing the double bass without a bow in jazz style, specifically by pulling the strings so as to let them snap back on to the fingerboard

groove (1935) Orig US; applied to playing jazz or similar music with swing, and also to dancing to or listening to such music with great pleasure; from the *groove* in a gramophone record ■ *Melody Maker*: The rhythm section . . . grooves along in true Basie manner. (1967)

give (1936) Orig US; applied to playing music, especially jazz, excitingly or enthusiastically; often followed by *out* ■ *Woman's Own*: You feel that you're in a real jam session with everybody giving, the joint jumping. (1958)

woodshed (1936) Applied especially to performing or rehearsing in private; from the notion of a woodshed as a secluded place where one can do things unobserved ■ A. Young: Drew's got an alto [horn]. . . . Drew dont hardly touch it, he too busy woodsheddin his drums. (1968)

cook (1943) Orig US; denoting playing with excitement, inspiration, etc. ■ *Crescendo*: The band used to get up on the bandstand and *really* cook. (1968)

run down (1948) US; applied to rehearsing or performing music ■ R. Russell: Bernie struck off a rich chord and began running the tune down in his immaculate post-Teddy Wilson style. (1961)

belt out (1953) Applied to playing or singing with great vigour or volume ■ John Steinbeck: One of the finest jazz combos I ever heard was belting out pure ecstasy. (1959)

wail (1955) US; applied to performing jazz very well, with great feeling, etc. ■ Shapiro & Hentoff: I revered the amazing Fats Waller, who had lately made a splash wailing on organ at the Lincoln. (1955)

Performance

woodshed (1946) Applied to a place where a musician may, or should, practise in private; from the verb *woodshed* play privately ■ *Rolling Stone*: Leavell's playing won't scare many jazz pianists into the woodshed. (1977)

groove (1954) Orig US; applied to a session at which jazz or similar music is played, especially well or with inspiration; from the verb *groove* play with swing ■ *Jive Jungle*: The all night 'grooves' began. (1954)

tear-up (1958) Orig US; applied to a period or passage of wild and inspired jazz playing; from *tear it up* perform enthusiastically ■ *Listener*: The music is not the tear-up associated with jazz at the Phil. (1983)

Playing music

in the (or **a**) **groove** (1932) Orig US; applied to playing jazz or similar music with fluent inspiration; from the *groove* in a gramophone record ■ *Hot News*: The Boswells are not in the hot groove. (1935)

A musician

red-hot momma (1926) Applied to an earthy woman jazz-singer

rideman (1935) US; applied to someone who improvises jazz with a pronounced rhythm; compare *ride* play jazz rhythmically ■ *Band Leaders & Record Review*: Within a horn blast of Hollywood and Vine, the crossroads of Glamour-town, can be found many lairs of the hepcats—haunts of gates and ride men. (1945)

gate (1937) US; applied to a jazz musician; often used as a term of address; perhaps short for *gate-mouth*, a nickname given to the US jazz trumpeter Louis Armstrong, or alternatively a shortening of *alligator* ■ *Collier's*: You've handicapped your tunes with stuff no gate wants to play. (1939)

jitterbug (1937) Applied to a jazz musician; compare earlier sense, nervous person

swingster (1937) Orig US; applied to someone who plays jazz with swing; from *swing + -ster*

muso (1967) Orig Australian; applied especially to a professional musician; from *mus(ician + -o* ■ K. Gilbert: I used to be a muso and a hustler from the city but I'm a tribal man too. (1977)

A music fan

cat (1932) Orig US; applied to an expert in, or someone expertly appreciative of, jazz ■ *Woman's Own*: 'It's got beat and a lot of excitement,' said one teenage 'cat' I talked to. (1958)

alligator (1936) Orig US; applied to a fan of jazz or swing music; perhaps related to earlier obsolete US sense, worthless person ■ *Collier's*: It's this jive, hep-cat, alligator, jitterbug craze—this swing mania! (1939)

icky, ikky (1937) US; applied to someone who is ignorant of true swinging jazz and likes the 'sweet' kind; probably from the sense (not recorded until later) sweet, sickly, sentimental. So **icky, ikky** used as an adjective to denote such a person (1935)

hep-cat (1938), hip-cat (1944) Orig US; applied to an enthusiast for jazz, swing music, etc.; from *hep, hip* fully informed + *cat* fan ■ Colin MacInnes: It was like getting a hip cat into a symphony concert, but I succeeded. (1959) ■ *Times*: Mr. Louis Armstrong and his fellow hepcats. (1961)

hepster (1938), hipster (1956) Orig US; applied to an enthusiast for jazz, swing music, etc.; from *hep, hip* fully informed + *-ster* ■ *Spectator*: Yet although jazz seems to have burst out of the locked treasure casket over which an egghead minority of hepsters crooned for so many years, it still remains a curiously unreal cult. (1958)

jitterbug (1938) Orig US; applied to a jazz fan; compare earlier sense, jazz musician ■ *Times*: I am told that in the U.S.A. there is a class of people who sit listening in hysterical excitement to what is called 'hot-music' and waiting for the final crash. Americans in their forcible language call them the 'Jitter-bugs'. There are many people in Europe to-day who seem to be behaving in much the same way. (1939)

groupie, groupy (1967) Applied to an ardent follower of a touring pop group, especially a girl who tries to have sex with them; from *group + -ie* ■ *Times*: His defence described the sisters as 'groupies', girls who deliberately provoke sexual relations with pop stars. (1970)

head-banger (1979) Applied to a young person shaking violently to the rhythm of pop music, especially heavy metal ■ *Telegraph* (Brisbane): Brisbane headbangers will have a chance to scream and wave their fists when Dio plays at Festival Hall. (1986)

Musical style

razzmatazz, razzamatazz (1894) Orig US; applied to rag-time or early jazz or to old-fashioned 'straight' jazz, and hence to sentimental jazz; origin unknown; perhaps an alteration of *razzle-dazzle* excitement, bustle ■ C. Coben: And while we kiss, kiss, kiss away all our cares, The player piano's playin' razzamatazz, I wanna hear it again. (1950)

gut-bucket (1929) Orig US; applied to a primitive unsophisticated style of jazz; perhaps from a type of improvised double bass used in such music, made from a washtub and a catgut string

ride (1930) Applied in jazz to an easy swinging rhythm or passage; from the verb *ride* play rhythmically ■ John Wainwright: The washboard player tapped the off-beats . . . lifting the rhythm and giving it ride. (1973)

screwball (1936) Mainly US; applied in jazz to fast improvisation or unrestrained swing; compare earlier sense, eccentric person ■ R. P. Dodge: When inspiration leaves the player . . . he becomes what is known as a screw-ball player. I must say that I prefer the jump style to the screw-ball style. (1947)

hotcha (1937) Mainly US; used to denote jazz or swing music that has a strong beat and a high emotional charge; compare earlier use (1932), in combination with the traditional interjection *hey nonny nonny*; originally a fanciful extension of *hot* ■ Cyril Ray: There are hotcha gramophone records. (1960)

ricky-tick (1938) Applied to a simple repetitive rhythm, as in early 'straight' jazz, and hence to rag-time and old-fashioned jazz; imitative ■ *New York Times*: To the ricky-tick of Guy Lombardo's 'I don't want to get well, I'm in love with a beautiful nurse', three maimed Army veterans fumble through a dance routine. (1968). Hence **ricky-tick, ricky-ticky** used as an adjective to denote music or a tempo that is repetitive or dull (1942) ■ *Times Literary Supplement*: Weill's errant and loudly stated bass-line throwing up the odd chord that violently subverts the triteness of the ricky-ticky melody. (1976)

funky (1954) Orig US; applied to jazz or rock music which is earthy or bluesy, with a heavy rhythmical beat; from earlier sense, smelly ■ *Frendz*: Brown Sugar and Bitch are Jagger at his foxy, dirty, funky best. (1971). Hence **funk** such music (1959) ■ *Making Music*: The bass rhythm is an extension of the pattern that dominated funk in the mid seventies. (1987)

rinky-tink (1962) Mainly US; applied to a jazz or ragtime piano on which simple repetitive tunes are played; imitative ■ *News & Courier* (Charleston, S. Carolina): Scott Joplin played his toe-tappers on a rinky-tink piano. (1974)

A musical group

combo (1935) Orig US; applied to a small instrumental band, especially playing jazz; from earlier sense, combination, partnership ■ *New York Times*: The Conspiracy is a chatty three-guitar combo that sings songs and makes jokes. (1970)

ork (1936) Mainly US; applied especially to a jazz or dance band; abbreviation of *orchestra* ■ *Zigzag*: 'Weeping Willow'—recorded in London backed . . . by Georgie Fame, Colin Green and the Norrie Paramour Ork! (1977)

To dance

hoof (1925) Orig US; used intransitively or with *it*; from *hoof* foot ■ Anthony Gilbert: A pretty nifty dancer himself in his young days and still able to hoof it quite neatly. (1958)

juke, jook, jouk (1937) Orig and mainly US; applied especially to dancing at a cheap roadhouse or to the music of a jukebox; from *juke* brothel, cheap roadhouse ■ Tennessee Williams: I'd like to go out jooking with you tonight. . . . That's where you get in a car and drink a little and drive a little and stop and dance a little to a juke box. (1958)

terp (1942) Orig US; compare *terp* dancer ■ *Spartanburg* (S. Carolina) *Herald*: Donna McKechnie is the best dancer in the musical comedy theater (one dance critic tripped over his typewriter when he suggested Donna can't terp). (1974)

bop (1962) Mainly British; applied to dancing to pop music; from earlier sense, play bop music ■ Jilly Cooper: The conference gang, on the other hand, bop until their thatched hair nearly falls off. (1979)

groove (1968) Orig US; applied to dancing to rock music; from earlier senses, play jazz or rock music excitingly, enjoy oneself ■ *Time Out*: Lope down to Bar Rumba and see if there's still room to groove at *That's How It Is*, the essential stop-off for Soho's *jazzamatazz* cognoscenti. (1994)

4. **Sport**

Physical exercise

ekker (1891) British, school and university slang; from the first syllable of *exercise* + -er ■ *Wykehamist*: Whatever the supposed range of activities that qualify as ekker, the demands of the major games . . . usually over-ride all others. (1970)

physical torture (1900) Jocular alteration of *physical training* ■ W. C. Anderson: The physical torture program . . . started promptly at 0630 every morning at Eglin Air Force Base. (1968)

To dance erotically

grind (1928) Denoting dancing while gyrating or rotating the hips ■ Milton Machlin: Deidre began to grind very hard and very close to him. (1976). Hence the noun **grind** such a movement (1938)

bump (1936) Denoting a striptease dancer thrusting forward the abdomen or hips. Hence the noun **bump** such a movement (1938) ■ *Punch*: Sing a song . . . and do a bump-and-grind routine. (1964)

An informal dance party

hop (1731) ■ D. M. Davin: What about coming to the Arts Faculty bob hop on Saturday? (1970)

bop (1970) Mainly British; from earlier sense, dancing to bop music ■ Barr & York: Couples meet at bops or know each other from London. (1982)

A dancer

hoofer (1923) Applied to a (professional) dancer; from *hoof* dance + -er ■ *Sunday Express*: She was impressed by one of the male dancers. . . . The one-time hoofer ended up by working for her for 40 years. (1973)

torso-tosser (1927) Dated; applied to a female erotic dancer ■ F. P. Keyes: Barbara Villiers, a torso-tosser who got to be no less than the Duchess of Cleveland. (1954)

stepper (1934) Orig US ■ *Westindian World*: It's a great steppers tune with a good, hard rhythm all the way through it. (1981)

terp (1937) Orig US; applied to a stage dancer, especially a chorus girl, and also to a ballroom dancer; abbreviation of *terpsichorean* of dancing

rug-cutter (1938) US; applied to an expert or enthusiastic dancer ■ Norman Mailer: He seemed full of strength and merriment. He would clap two geishas to him, and call across . . . to another soldier. 'Hey, Brown,' he would shout, 'ain't this a rug-cutter?' (1959)

A disc jockey

jock (1952) Abbreviation ■ *Blues & Soul*: He may be the top radio jock in the land as far as our music's concerned . . . but he should realise that he's no expert on all manner of other things. (1987)

physical jerks (1919) Jocular ■ Albert Sachs: In the afternoon, I am busy doing physical jerks. (1966)

rec (1929) Abbreviation of *recreation* ■ Emma Lathen: The wedding presents were supposed to go on the Ping-Pong table in the rec room. (1975)

To take exercise

pump iron (1972) Orig US; applied to exercising with weights as a form of fitness training or body-building technique ■ *New York Times*: Arnold

Schwarzenegger . . . , believed by many to have the world's most perfect male body, was pumping iron the other day at the Mid-City Gym. (1976)

Players

skipper (1830) Applied to the captain of a sports team (originally a curling team, later any team); from earlier sense, ship's captain ■ *Daily Mail*: It will be hard for skipper Graham Gooch to discount yesterday's two-and-a-half hour innings from Botham, especially as Hick failed again. (1991). Hence the verb **skipper** act as captain of a team (1950) ■ *Daily Mail*: Trevor Peake will skipper the side. (1991)

champ (1868) Orig US boxing slang; abbreviation of *champion* ■ *Globe & Mail* (Toronto): U.S. Open champ Gay Brewer . . . had a 75 at Spyglass in the first round. (1968)

bench-warmer (1905) US; applied to a substitute in a sports team; from earlier sense, someone who sits idly on a bench ■ *Los Angeles Times*: He thought about leaving after the 1984 season, his third straight year as a bench-warmer. (1986)

frosh (1922) North American; applied to a member of a freshman sports team, and to such a team collectively; from earlier sense, freshman

stickout (1942) US; applied to an outstanding sportsman or -woman; from earlier sense, horse that seems a certain winner ■ *Washington Post*: As for third base, ball players and fans alike have no range of choice. Frank Malzone of the Red Sox is a stickout. (1958)

prepper (1945) US; applied to a member of a preparatory sports team, and also to such a team; from *prep*(*aratory* + *-er* ■ *Anderson* (South Carolina) *Independent*: Audie Mathews, 6-4, of Chicago Heights, Ill., one of the nation's most coveted preppers, is reported to be considering North Carolina State, Illinois, Oregon, Purdue and UCLA. (1974)

jock (1963) North American; applied to a male athlete, especially at university; from the wearing of jock-straps by athletes ■ *Time*: Rocks for jocks, elementary geology course popular among athletes at Pennsylvania. (1972)

swing man (1969) US; applied to a versatile player who can play effectively in different positions

scrubber (1974) Mainly Australian & New Zealand; applied to a second-rate player or competitor, one not of professional standard; compare earlier sense, inferior horse ■ *New Zealand Herald*: The three winners . . . have rather enjoyed their reputation as 'scrubbers' since they unexpectedly won their club titles. (1977)

Instructors

springer (1935) Nautical; applied to a physical-training instructor in the navy ■ *John Hale*: The springers all fancy their chance in the training line. (1964)

Officials

ref (1899) Abbreviation of *referee* ■ *Listener*: Adam is able to make good jokes about Cambridge . . . and there is no ref to blow the whistle on him. (1976). Hence the verb **ref**

act as referee (1929) ■ *Punch*: Who says the game was badly reffed? The sending-off of Nobby Stiles, For nothing, was supremely deft. (1968)

ump, umps (1915) Mainly US, orig baseball slang; abbreviation of *umpire* ■ *New Yorker*: That's why Nick Colosi, National League ump, was a featured attraction at the Auto Show last week. (1975)

Venues

rec (1931) Abbreviation of *recreation* (*area, ground*, etc.) ■ *J. R. Ackerley*: The only open space, besides the Rec., in the neighbourhood. (1960)

the outer (1943) Australian; applied to the uncovered area for non-members at a sports ground; from earlier sense, part of a racecourse outside the enclosure ■ *Alan Ross*: Fine drizzle delayed things for half an hour, then shirts were ripped off again in the Outer, the beer cans were set up, and play proceeded. (1963)

The ball

pill (1908) Used in football, golf, and other sports ■ *P. G. Wodehouse*: 'I don't mind her missing the pill,' said the young man. 'But I think her attitude toward the game is too light-hearted.' (1922)

Baseball

hardball (*a*1883) Applied to baseball, in contrast to softball ■ *Plain Dealer* (Cleveland, Ohio): We both knew Eric Miller from our days at St. Ed. He had expressed an interest in athletics and we knew that he backed a AAA hardball team. (1974)

slugger (1883) Applied to a hard-hitting batter; from earlier, more general sense, hard hitter ■ *Times of Zambia*: The new holder of baseball's all-time Home Run record, Japanese slugger Sadaharu Oh. (1977)

whiff (1913) Denoting a missing of the ball by the batter, and also applied to the pitcher causing the batter to strike out; from earlier sense, blow or puff slightly ■ *Nebraska State Journal*: Hurler whiffs. (1941)

sacker (1914) Applied to a fieldsman who guards a base; usually in *first sacker* (= first baseman), etc. ■ *H. E. West*: Wally Pipp became the Yankee first sacker in 1915, and Lou Gehrig succeeded him ten years later and is still going strong. (1938)

slug-fest (1916) Applied to a hard-hitting encounter; from *slug* hit + *fest* special occasion, festival ■ *Arizona Daily Star*: Powers gave up four runs on seven hits, a contrast from the 33-hit slugfest of Friday night. (1979)

gopher ball (1932) Applied to a pitch that can be scored from, especially one hit for a home run; from the verbal phrase go *for*, because the batter 'goes for' runs, or the ball 'goes for' a homer ■ *R. Coover*: Partridge was throwing gopher balls and his . . . teammates were fielding like a bunch of bush-leaguers. (1970)

shell (1942) Denoting scoring heavily against an opposing player or team; often used in the passive; from earlier sense, bombard with explosive shells ■ *First Base*: Gooden . . . was shelled twice by Boston in the World Series, finishing 0-3 in the post-season. (1987)

Boxing

mill (1810) Denoting fighting as a boxer; from earlier sense, hit ■ *London Daily News*: He was an ageing journeyman boxer who had spent years milling in small halls, and then got a chance to make it big. (1987)

pug (1858) Dated; applied to a boxer or prize-fighter; abbreviation of *pugilist* ■ John Buchan: The man had been in the ring, and not so very long ago. I wondered at Medina's choice, for a pug is not the kind of servant I would choose myself. (1924)

mittens (1883) Dated; applied to boxing gloves; from earlier sense, type of glove ■ James Greenwood: That's their mittens they've got tied up in that hankercher. They're fighting coves. (1883)

ham (1888) US; applied to an incompetent boxer or fighter; from earlier sense, inexpert performer ■ *Saturday Evening Post*: They want me to slug with this big ham. (1929)

dive (1921) Orig US; applied to a feigned knock-out; mainly in the phrase *take a dive*; originally applied to a genuine knock-out. Hence the verb **dive** feign a knock-out (1921)

palooka, palooker, paluka (1925) Mainly US; applied to an unexceptional boxer; origin unknown ■ *New York Times*: Leon Spinks . . . does not rate highly with at least one former heavyweight title holder. 'He is a palooka,' says Ingemar Johansson. (1978)

round heels, round-heeler (1926) Mainly US; applied to a low-quality boxer; from the notion that someone with round heels easily falls over

ring-worm (1929) US, dated; applied to someone who regularly attends boxing matches ■ *Sun* (Baltimore): 'Ring worms', as some are in the habit of referring to fight fans, have a hot one coming up Friday night when Kid Gavilan takes a shot at Bobo Olson and his middleweight title. (1954)

slug-fest (1933) US; applied to a hard-hitting boxing contest; from *slug* hit + *fest* special occasion, festival; compare the earlier application to baseball games ■ Gene Tunney: If Dempsey would gamble with me in a slug-fest I would beat him to the punch every time. (1933)

slug-nutty (1933) US; denoting someone who is punch-drunk; from *slug* hit + *nutty* mad ■ Ernest Hemingway: He's been beat up so much he's slug-nutty. (1950). Hence **slug-nuttiness** punch-drunkenness (1943)

Caving

spelunker (1942) North American; applied to one who explores caves, especially as a hobby; from obsolete *spelunk* cave, from Latin *spelunca*, Old French *spelonque, spelunque* ■ Ed McBain: The cave seemed not in the least bit inviting. He had always considered spelunkers the choicest sorts of maniacs. (1980). Hence **spelunk** explore caves as a hobby (1946)

Chess

patzer (1959) Applied to a weak player; origin uncertain; compare German *patzen* bungle ■ *Daily Telegraph*: So Fischer after beating off a ferocious attack . . . 'played like a patzer', said one American Grandmaster, 'went to sleep on the job', said another. (1972)

Cricket

keeper (1744) Short for *wicketkeeper* ■ *Cricketer*: A tall 'keeper's rise from his crouch is less rapid than a smaller man's. (1975)

peg (1865) Applied to a stump ■ Ray Robinson: Cunis swung one so late and so far that it hit Gandotra's leg peg. (1972)

slog (1869) Denoting hard, wild hitting (at) the ball; from earlier, more general sense, hit hard; ultimate origin uncertain, but probably connected with *slug* hit hard ■ *Cricketer International*: The incredible thing is that he never had to slog once to make his runs. (1980). Hence the nouns **slog** a wild hit (1865) and **slogger** a wild hitter (1850) ■ *Daily Telegraph*: He . . . hit, in all, 17 fours and a six without a single slog. (1991) ■ *Independent on Sunday*: This time, though, we will not be seeing a wayward quickie and tail-end slogger: De Freitas should be travelling as a senior player. (1991)

timbers (1876) Applied to the stumps or wicket; from stumps being made of wood, and falling when hit ■ *Times*: It must have interested elder listeners when they recently heard one of the B.B.C.'s fluent commentators on Test match cricket call the wickets the timbers. (1963)

blob (1889) Applied to a batsman's score of nought ■ Bruce Hamilton: A cricketer . . . may make a string of blobs, and then hit a couple of hundreds. (1958)

Aunt Sally (1898) Dated; applied to a wicketkeeper; from the notion that the bowler 'aims' the ball at the wicketkeeper in the same way as people aim balls at a fairground Aunt Sally, a dummy typically in the shape of an old woman smoking a clay pipe ■ *Observer*: A 'keeper' . . . who combines batsmanship with all the 'Aunt Sally's' excellencies. (1927)

gaper (1903) Applied to an easy catch, especially one that is dropped; probably from the notion that something which 'gapes' open offers easy success; see also **sitter** at **Easiness** (p. 406) ■ *Times*: Certain of the younger members of the side were dropping some regular 'gapers'. (1963)

sticky dog (1925), sticky (1954) Dated; applied to a wicket made difficult to bat on by rain and hot sun ■ A. G. Moyes: Again, the 'sticky' provides plenty of excitement. (1954)

quickie (1934) Applied to a fast bowler; from earlier more general sense, something quick ■ *News of the World*: Their other unknown quickie, Len Pascoe . . . , isn't as fast as Lillee or Thomson. (1977)

agricultural (1937) Used to characterize a stroke as ungraceful or clumsy; from the unsophisticated strokeplay associated with village cricket ■ *Times*: Keith . . . took an agricultural swing at Wardle and was bowled. (1955)

ton (1958) Applied to a century; apparently from earlier darts use ■ *Lancashire Life*: Scoring a century didn't mean a hoot to me then. . . . Now, as an experienced pro, I know I must make a 'ton' and then keep going to get another. (1978)

sledging (1975) Orig Australian; applied to unsportsmanlike attempts by fielders to upset a batsman's concentration by abuse, needling, etc.; from *sledge* large hammer ■ *Guardian*: Geoff Howarth says he intends to complain about the amount of swearing, sledging and unchecked short-pitched bowling New Zealand have faced. (1983)

Croquet

Aunt Emma (1960) Applied to an unenterprising player or unenterprising play ■ *Croquet*: He played too much 'Aunt Emma'. (1967)

Darts

ton (1936) Applied to a score of one hundred; probably from earlier sense, large amount ■ *Atlantic Monthly*: Now he's averaging 60 or more, frequently throws a 'ton'—a round of 100 or more points—and can put a dart into a fifty-cent piece area every time. (1973)

arrow (1946) Applied to a dart ■ *Morecambe Guardian*: Best individual scores: B. Lilly (Royal) 180 in three arrows; B. Norris (Smugglers) 180 in three arrows. (1976)

Football

footer (1863) British, dated; applied to the game of football; from *foot(ball* + *-er* ■ *Evelyn Waugh*: I had to change for *F-f-footer*. (1945)

pigskin (1894) US; applied to a football; from its originally being made of pigskin leather ■ *Anderson* (South Carolina) *Independent*: He carried the pigskin on the end around 11 times for 73 yards, or an average of 6.6 yards per carry. (1974)

footy, footie (1906) Mainly Australian & New Zealand; applied to the game of football; from *foot(ball* + *-ie* ■ *Southerly*: Evans . . . strides off with her to ask race-goers, cinema queues and footy fans to sign peace petitions. (1967)

get a (or the) guernsey (1918) Australian; denoting selection for a football team; from *guernsey* sleeveless shirt worn by Australian Rules footballers, from earlier sense, thick shirt worn by seamen; ultimately from *Guernsey*, name of one of the Channel Islands

goalie (1921) Applied to a goal-keeper (in ice-hockey as well as soccer); from *goal* + *-ie*; in early use spelt *goalee*—the spelling *goalie* is not recorded before 1957 ■ *Jeremy Potter*: Most English goalies were prize examples of British phlegm, but Basil outdid the continental keepers in panache. (1967)

subway alumni (1947) US; applied to city-dwelling supporters of a college football team who, though not graduates of the college, attend games or follow the results

sticks (1950) Applied to soccer goal-posts; especially in the phrase *between the sticks*, usually with reference to the position of the goalkeeper ■ *Wymondham & Attleborough Express*: Wortwell could not produce the form of recent weeks and crashed heavily to their hosts. David Loome took over between the 'sticks'. (1976)

stiff (1950) Applied in soccer to a member of the reserve team; usually used in the plural ■ *Sun*: Gunners sign Metchick for stiffs. (1970)

keeper (1957) Abbreviation of *goal-keeper* ■ *Oxford Mail*: Bicester's Phillip Pratt (10) heads the ball past Thame keeper Micky Taylor for his second goal. (1974)

the box (1960) Applied in soccer to the penalty area; short for *penalty box* ■ *FourFourTwo*: When he wasn't directly involved Yeboah was crouched on the edge of the box, waiting for that Brian Deane knock-down, Gary McAllister through-ball or Rod Wallace cut-back. (1995)

woodwork (1960) Applied to the frame of soccer goalposts ■ *Grimsby Evening Telegraph*: Twice in the first half, Scunthorpe hit the Bradford woodwork. (1977)

aerial ping-pong (1964) Australian, jocular; applied to Australian Rules Football; from the frequent exchange of high kicks in the game ■ *Bulletin* (Sydney): In Europe . . . cycling is about the same mad preoccupation as aerial ping pong is to the Melbourne crowds. (1985)

nutmeg (1968) British; applied in soccer to the act of kicking the ball between the legs of an opposing player (and retaining it afterwards); perhaps from earlier slang *nutmegs* testicles ■ *Times*: Woodcock . . . could include successive 'nutmegs' on Donachie and Booth among his contributions. (1977). Hence the verb **nutmeg** denoting outsmarting an opponent by doing this (1979)

sack (1969) North American; denoting tackling the quarterback behind the line of scrimmage before he can make a pass ■ *Washington Post*: Kilmer . . . was sacked hard early in the second quarter by Bears tackle Ron Rydalch. (1976). Hence the noun **sack** applied to such a tackle (1972) ■ *Detroit Free Press*: Other changes have been made, this year and in recent years, to put juice into the offence, the feeling being that people come to see touchdowns and not quarterback sacks. (1978)

clogger (1970) British; applied to a soccer player who tackles heavily, usually fouling his opponent ■ *Times*: There are cloggers in football and it is more than a healthy reaction to cherish the thought of one day getting one's revenge. (1970)

dive (1984) Applied to an intentional fall taken, usually on being tackled, in order to deceive an opponent or official; from earlier boxing sense, feigned knock-out

Golf

foozle (1888) Orig US; denoting playing an inept shot; from earlier obsolete sense, do something clumsily, fool around; ultimately from German dialect *fuseln* work hurriedly and badly, work slowly ■ *Graham McInnes*: The rest of the eighteen holes were a miserable exhibition of foozling, duffing, [etc.]. (1965)

duff (1897) British; denoting mishitting a shot or a ball; perhaps a back-formation from *duffer* incompetent person ■ *Sunday Express*: The ninth provided Landale's crowning error, for he duffed two mashie shots. (1927)

nineteenth hole (1901) Jocular, orig US; applied to the bar-room in a club-house; from its use by golfers after playing the eighteen holes of the course ■ *Josephine Tey*: A good chap who played a very steady game and occasionally, when it came to the nineteenth, expanded into mild indiscretions. (1948)

whiff (1913) US; denoting missing the ball; also used as a noun, applied to a failure to hit the ball; probably originally a baseball usage ■ *New York Herald Tribune*: On the first tee he took a careful stance and then fanned the air four times. After the fourth whiff he growled, 'This is the hardest course I ever played.' (1952)

shoot (1922) Orig US; denoting recording a particular score for a hole or a round ■ *Saturday Evening Post*: They shot a twelve-under-par score in winning their first match. (1941)

pin-splitter (1926) Applied originally to an excellent golfer, and subsequently (1961) to an accurate shot to the *pin* (the flag marking the hole), or a club used for this ■ *Country Gentlemen's Magazine*: Gents Pinsplitter Golf Clubs. (1973)

gimme (1929) Applied to a short putt conceded to one's opponent; contraction of *give me*, from the notion of being so easy that it can be given

Mulligan (1949) Applied to an extra stroke awarded after a poor shot, not counted on the score card; probably from the surname *Mulligan* ■ *Guardian*: He [*sc*. Bill Clinton] scores between 80 and 90 depending on how many mulligans he gives himself. (1996)

Greyhound racing

the dogs (1927) Applied to greyhound racing or a greyhound race meeting ■ *Economist*: He ... failed his Bar examinations because he preferred horse-racing, the 'dogs' and dancing. (1959)

tin hare (1927) Mainly Australian; applied to the electric hare used in greyhound racing

gracing, greycing (1928) British, dated; blend of *greyhound* and *racing* ■ *E. C. Ash*: Greyhound Racing, or 'Gracing', as it is sometimes termed, started in 1926. (1935)

roughie (1934) Australian; applied to an outsider in a dog race

Horseracing

jock (1826) Abbreviation of *jockey* ■ *National Observer* (US): Yarosh had been getting threats from the male jockeys who said they were going to 'put her through the rail'; on the way to the hospital, Yarosh scribbled a note saying, 'Did the other jocks say he did it on purpose too?' (1976)

nobble (1847) Denoting drugging, laming, etc. a racehorse to prevent its winning; from earlier, obsolete sense, hit; probably the same word as British dialect *knobble*, *knubble* knock, hit, from the noun *knob* ■ *News Chronicle*: Lord Rosebery

confirms today that his horse which was nobbled was Snap. (1951)

stiff one, **stiff 'un** (1871), **stiff** (*a*1890) Orig US; applied to a horse which is unlikely (or not intended) to win; perhaps from *stiff* corpse, in jocular allusion to the horse's sluggish progress ■ *Damon Runyon*: There is also a rumor that Follow You is a stiff in the race. (1935)

pea (1888) Mainly Australian; applied to a horse tipped to win; perhaps from the phrase *this is the pea I choose* in thimble-rigging ■ *F. Hardy*: I've got the tip about it. Old Dapper Dan earwigged at the track. Swordsman is the pea. (1958)

cert (1889) Applied to a horse that is considered certain to win; often in the phrase *dead cert*; abbreviation of *certainty* ■ *Man of the World*: Love-in-Idleness is bound to take the Rous Memorial, and I hear Pioneer is a cert. for the St. James's. (1889)

wrong 'un (1889) Applied to a horse held in check so that it loses the race ■ *Howard Spring*: Hansford had never been known to tip a wrong 'un. (1935)

stipe (1902) Mainly Australian; applied to a stipendiary racing steward; abbreviation of *stipendiary* ■ *Australian*: The racing page screamed Stipes Probe Jockey. (1977)

mudder (1903) Orig and mainly US; applied to a horse which runs well on a wet or muddy racecourse; from *mud* + *-er* ■ *New Yorker*: In my book, Stardust Mel is the best mudder in California. Early last month Mrs. Marjorie Lindheimer Everett's rangy gray gelding splattered through the rain and murk to win. (1975)

hot pot (1904) Australian; applied to a horse strongly fancied or backed to win ■ *Sporting Globe* (Melbourne): A southern 'hot-pot'—Lord Setay—dismally let his supporters down at Albion Park last Saturday night. (1969)

outer (1915) Australian; applied to the part of a racecourse outside the enclosure

roughie (1922) Australian; applied to an outsider in a horserace ■ *Sun-Herald* (Sydney): Punters were reluctant to support him. ... Consequently Pepper Moss went out as a 12-1 'roughie'. (1973)

springer (1922) Applied to a horse on which the odds suddenly shorten ■ *J. Prescot*: Plenty of punters like to know how the market's moving so that they can go for the 'springer', the horse that suddenly shortens in price because someone in the know slaps a lot of money on at the last possible moment. (1961)

red board (1935) US; applied to the board on which the official winners of a horserace are declared

stickout (1937) US; applied to a horse that seems a certain winner ■ *Sun* (Baltimore): A 'stickout' on paper, Nokomis was in front most of the way along the six-furlong route. (1949)

hoop (1941) Australian; applied to a jockey; from the coloured bands on a jockey's shirt ■ *Bulletin* (Sydney): Now Moore and Higgins two of the best hoops in the history of racing. (1984)

no-hoper (1943) Australian; applied to a racehorse with no chance of winning

the nanny-goat (1961) Applied to the Tote; rhyming slang ■ *Daily Mail*: The poor old ailing Tote—the Nanny Goat, as they call it. (1970)

Running

sweat (1916) British, public schools' slang; applied to a long training run ■ *Wilfred Blunt*: Long melancholy 'sweats' (runs) over the downs [at Marlborough]. (1983)

Skiing

snow bunny (1953) North American; applied to an inexperienced skier, usually female, or to a pretty girl who frequents ski slopes ■ *Globe & Mail* (Toronto): 'Watching you for only two runs, I can see you're not just a "snow bunny", Coral!' 'No, I was on the women's ski-team at college.' (1968)

ski bum (1960) North American; applied to a skiing enthusiast who works casually at a resort in order to ski ■ *New York Times*: Ski-bum shortage shakes the resorts. (1978)

Surfing

surf-bum (1958) Applied to a surfing enthusiast who frequents beaches suitable for surfing

gremlin (1961) Applied to a young surfer, and also (1967) to a trouble-maker who frequents the beaches but does not surf; compare earlier sense, mischievous sprite that causes mechanical faults ■ *International Surfing*: There is really a lot of talent running around these days in the form of young gremlins. (1967)

kook (1961) Applied to a novice or inexpert surfer; from earlier sense, crazy person ■ *Surfer*. All most of [these surfers] are is a bunch of loud-mouthed kooks who come down here and clutter up the beach. (1966)

greenie (1962) Applied to a large wave before it breaks

gremmie, gremmy (1962) Short for *gremlin* ■ *Surfer Magazine*: He worked all morning with several beach gremmies piling 12-foot sections of plywood and rocks into a small reef on the wet sand. (1968)

hodad (1962) Applied to a non-surfer who hangs around surfing beaches; origin unknown

outside (1962) Denoting an area out at sea, beyond the breaking waves

soup (1962) Applied to the foam of a breaking wave

surfie, surfy (1962) Orig and mainly Australian; applied to a surfing enthusiast who frequents beaches suitable for surfing, and also to one who frequents surfing beaches but does little or no surfing; from *surf* + *-ie* ■ *Times Literary Supplement*: He agrees to deliver a deal for this scruffy surfie and the plot is primed. (1981)

wipe out (1962) Denoting knocking or being knocked off a surfboard ■ *Surfer*. Frye misjudged one of his turns high in the curl and wiped-out in the white water. (1968). Hence **wipe-out** a fall from a surfboard as a result of a collision with another surfboard or a wave (1962) ■ *People* (Australia): One bad wipeout—at Sunset Beach, Hawaii—earned him broken ribs. (1970)

gun (1963) Applied to a large heavy surfboard used for riding big waves ■ *Surf '70*: While in Hawaii I had two boards. They were an 8 ft 9 in 'hot-dog' and a 9 ft 6 in tracker type gun. (1970)

hot dog (1963) Applied to a type of small surfboard; compare earlier sense, highly skilled (and boastful) person

pipe-line (1963) Applied to (the hollow part of) a large wave, and also to the coastal area where such waves occur ■ *New Zealand Listener*. The achievement by which the champion surfers are judged is their ability to ride the Hawaiian pipeline. . . . The pipeline breaks less than 50 yards from the beach over a coral reef. (1965)

wahine (1963) Applied to a girl surfer; from earlier sense, Maori woman; from Maori, Hawaiian, and other Polynesian languages ■ *Surfer*. There are other things he did on the board, too, especially the full-moon tandem rides with wahines. (1966)

greenback (1965) Applied to a large wave before it breaks

pounder (1967) Applied to a large breaker

mush (1969) Applied to the foam produced when a wave breaks ■ *Surf '70*. If there is any flat mush the board tends to stop and lose its turning ability. (1970)

shred (1977) Denoting cutting rapidly through the water on a surfboard ■ *Surfer*. I love the way they . . . just shred everything in sight—carving, slashing aerials and snapbacks. (1985)

grommet, grommit (1986) Applied to an enthusiastic young surfer or skateboarder; origin uncertain; compare *grummit* ship's boy, ring or wreath of rope (especially in nautical contexts) ■ *Wavelength Surfing*. If you want the city surf life of Sydney, sharing each wave with a hoard [*sic*] of surf-crazed young grommits, then Manly is definitely the place for you. (1986)

Swimming

dip (1843) Applied to a brief swim ■ *Leslie Stephen*: He rode sixty miles from his house to have a dip in the sea. (1874)

bogy, bogey, bogie (1849) Australian; used as a noun and a verb denoting bathing or swimming, and also (taking) a bath; from Aboriginal (Dharuk) *bu-gi* ■ *F. D. Davison*: They went down for a bogey on warm days. (1946)

shark-bait (1920), shark-baiter (1924) Australian; applied to a lone or daring swimmer far out from shore ■ *Australian Encyclopedia*: Solitary bathers are more often attacked than groups, but the 'shark-baiter' farthest off shore is not necessarily the victim. (1965)

belly-flop (1937) Applied to a dive in which one hits the water abdomen-first; from earlier sense, sudden drop to the ground to avoid enemy fire ■ **Robin Hyde:** 'It hurt,' she added. . . . 'So I didn't do any more worshipful belly-flops.' (1937)

Tennis

tramlines (1937) Applied to the two parallel lines marking the edge of the singles court and the doubles court ■ **G. Forbes:** Cliff . . . hit a two-hander down Rodney's tramlines. (1978)

5. Cards & Gambling

Playing-cards

broads (1781) Dated; used especially in the game of three-card monte ■ **F. D. Sharpe:** They . . . were also playing the Broads on the train. (1938)

flats (1812) Dated

paper (1842) US; applied to a playing-card, and also collectively to card-sharpers' marked cards

puppy foot (1907) US; applied to the ace of clubs, or to any club card; from the resemblance of the club symbol to a small paw-print ■ **Daily Progress** (Charlottesville, Virginia): The ace of clubs is often called the puppyfoot. (1932)

A card (to be played)

bullet (1807) Applied to an ace in the game of brag or poker; often in the phrase *two bullets and a bragger* a winning hand

bragger (1807) US; applied to a nine or jack in the game of brag ■ **Herbert Asbury:** In American Brag there were eight 'braggers'—the jacks and nines of each suit. (1938)

ace in the hole (1915) Mainly North American; applied to a high-value card or trump card concealed up one's sleeve

Dice

tats, tatts (1688) Dated; often applied specifically to false or loaded dice; origin unknown

A throw at dice

snake eyes (1929) North American; applied to a throw of two ones with a pair of dice

A gambler

spieler (1859) Orig US, now mainly Australian; from German *Spieler* player, gambler ■ **Detective Fiction Weekly:** Hard on their trail would come all the 'magsmen', the 'spielers', the dips, the 'broadsmen', and the 'pickers up'. (1929)

broadsman (1860) Dated; applied to a card-sharper, especially in the game of three-card monte; from *broads* cards + *-man* ■ **F. D. Sharpe:** Broadsmen, or three card sharpers, kept the Flying Squad busy in its early days. (1938)

punter (1873) Applied originally to someone who backs horses, and hence to someone who stakes money on football pools, lotteries, stocks and shares, etc.; from *punt* gamble + *-er* ■ **Sport:** I know of many punters who have decided to follow one system and then after a short losing spell switched to another system. (1951)

high-roller (1881) Orig US; applied to someone who gambles large sums; probably from the notion of rolling dice ■ **Sunday Mail** (Brisbane): The Hughes places had included some of the chief centres for the big-money gamblers, or 'high-rollers'. (1972)

tinhorn gambler (1885) US; applied to a cheap gambler, especially one who acts showily; perhaps from the use by such gamblers of a small tin container for shaking their dice

piker (1889) Orig US; applied to a cautious gambler; from obsolete US slang *pike* gamble cautiously, of unknown origin ■ **H. L. Wilson:** 'I says to myself the other day: "I'll bet a cookie he'd like to be like me!"' Homer was a piker, even when he made bets with himself. (1919)

mechanic (1909) US & Australian; applied to someone who cheats at gambling games, especially cards ■ **Daily Telegraph:** As croupier . . . always on guard for the sharps—the mechanics. (1966)

ringie (1917) Australian & New Zealand; applied to the ring-keeper in the game of two-up

Gambling games

sweep (1849) Shortened from *sweepstake*

bunco, bunko (1873) US; applied to a type of dishonest gambling game played with dice; from *banco*, variant of Spanish *banca* card-game similar to monte

swy, swey, swi, zwei, swy-up (1913) Australian; applied to the game of two-up; from German *zwei* two ■ **Action Front:** His income from 'Swi' will be a thing of the past. (1941)

chemmy, shemmy (1923) Abbreviation and alteration of *chemin de fer* a card-game ■ **Punch:** How to behave when a . . . bingo-club or a chemmy-party . . . is visited by the police. (1962)

---

tank (1976) Denoting losing deliberately ■ **Guardian:** But it is ironic that Connors, a player generally considered too honest to 'tank' to anyone, should be the one to suffer. (1979)

Wrestling

matman (1923) Applied to a wrestler; from *mat* floor-covering in a wrestling ring ■ **Globe & Mail Magazine** (Toronto): He became one of the best known mat men in Canada. 'Wrestling always fascinated me,' he says now. (1968)

rats and mice (1932) Applied to a game of dice; rhyming slang for *dice* ■ F. D. Sharpe: We used to play dice with them. . . . Rats and Mice the game was called. (1938)

Gambling activity

action (1887) Orig US ■ Damon Runyon: And he is well established as a high player in New Orleans, and Chicago, and Los Angeles, and wherever else there is any action in the way of card-playing, or crap-shooting. (1933)

A gambling establishment

spieler (1931) Orig US; compare earlier sense, gambler ■ Jimmy O'Connor: A well-known boxing referee who used to run a dirty low-down dive of a spieler. (1976)

pad (1970) US; applied to a gambling saloon which provides police with regular pay-offs

To gamble

spiel (1859) From German *spielen* play ■ Wolf Mankowitz: You go to the dog tracks in the evening? Not for me. . . . Horses? No horses, neither. You must spiel something. Poker, shemmy? (1953)

punt (1873) From earlier more specific sense, lay a stake against the bank in card-games such as baccarat and faro; ultimately from French *ponter* in same sense ■ *Observer*: Institutions . . . used the traded options market to punt on stock . . . which would benefit from increased military spending. (1991)

fade (1890) US; denoting betting against the player throwing the dice in the game of craps

roll the bones (1929) US; denoting playing dice ■ Saxon, Dreyer, & Tallant: Today in the colored sections of the city there are always circles of men 'rollin' the bones' playing Indian Dice, which is any game of Craps unsupervised by a syndicate and without a player for the 'house'. (1945)

seven out (1934) US; in the game of craps, denoting throwing a seven and so losing one's bet

sandbag (1940) Orig & mainly US; in poker, denoting holding off from raising at the first opportunity in the hope of raising by a larger amount later ■ D. Anthony: He fondled his stack of blue chips. He was sandbagging me. I gave him the same dose of silence. (1977)

go for the doctor (1949) Australian; denoting betting all one's money, specialized use of the more general sense, make the maximum effort ■ Lawson Glassop: Go for the doctor. Slap a tenner on it. (1949)

An instance of gambling

flutter (1883) British; applied to a small bet; from earlier sense, an attempt, try ■ *Daily Telegraph*: The British are great gamblers, as the success of betting shops, the pools and bingo shows. The human instinct to have a flutter is as strong in Britain as anywhere else. (1991)

punt (1965) From *punt* gamble ■ *Daily Telegraph*: People will still have a punt on Wimbledon. (1976)

Something gambled on

springer (1922) Applied to a racehorse on which the betting odds suddenly shorten

A stake

shirt (1892) In the phrases *bet one's shirt, put one's shirt on* stake all one's money, especially on a horse in a race, and *lose one's shirt* lose all one's stake ■ T. S. Eliot: Marriage is a gamble. But I'm a born gambler. And I've put my shirt—no, not quite the right expression—Lucasta's the most exciting speculation I've ever thought of investing in. (1954)

Winnings

pay-off (1905) Applied to money paid to the winner of a gambling game ■ *Globe & Mail* (Toronto): How about the $800 daily double payoff the track made one day on a bet that never was made. Is that not bookmaking? (1970)

vigorish, viggerish (1912) US; applied to the percentage deducted by the organizers of a game from the winnings of a gambler; probably from Yiddish, from Russian *výigrýsh* gain, winnings ■ Ed McBain: 'Was he taking a house vigorish?' 'Nope.' 'What do you mean? He wasn't taking a cut? . . . Then why'd he risk having the game in his basement?' (1964)

Bookmaking

pick-up man (1944) US; applied to someone who collects (and pays out) money wagered with bookmakers ■ Alan Wykes: These agents are known as 'pickup men' . . . ; they collect and pay out on behalf of the bookmakers, who pay them 10 per cent of their net winnings. (1964)

A tipster

tip-slinger (1915) Australian; applied to a racecourse tipster ■ *Bulletin* (Sydney): By their conversation most of them were tipslingers or urgers. (1934)

urger (1919) Australian; applied to a racecourse tipster ■ A. Kimmins: 'An urger,' explained Lugs patiently, 'is a man who looks around for suckers like you and tips each one a different horse. Someone's *got* to win.' (1960)

A fruit-machine

one-arm(ed) bandit (1938) Orig US; from the single lever at the side by which it is operated ■ Dick Francis: There's more cars parked along the streets down there than one-armed bandits in Nevada. (1972)

pokey, pokie (1965) Australian; applied to a fruit-machine with card symbols; from *pok(er machine)* + *-ey* ■ *Telegraph* (Brisbane): He bought a beer and walked over to the nearest 'pokey' with the change from a £5 ($10) note. He put this through the machine and tripled his money. (1969)

Time and Tide

1. Time

Time

nickel and dime (1935) Dated; rhyming slang

A very long time

a month of Sundays (1832), **a week of Sundays** (1898) Perhaps from the notion of the tedium of the traditional Sunday, but compare the contemporary but obsolete *a week of Saturdays* (1831) in same sense ■ **Douglas Sladen:** He . . . got to know her more intimately in that five minutes than he might otherwise have done in a week of Sundays. (1901) ■ *Chicago Tribune:* This was the first time that a press agent had hit on a truthful first page story in a month of Sundays. (1949)

a dog's age (1836) Orig US ■ **Mazo de la Roche:** She hasn't laid an offering on the altar of Jalna for a dog's age. (1933)

donkey's years, donkeys' years (1916) ■ **J. I. M. Stewart:** It was donkey's years since he had been in an English train. (1955)

yonks (1968) Mainly in the phrase *for yonks*; origin unknown ■ **Anthony Blond:** Nicholas Bagnall and David Holloway have run the *Telegraph's* book pages for yonks. (1985)

light years (1971) From *light year* distance that light travels in one year ■ *Guardian:* By the end of the second half of normal time the first 45 minutes seemed light-years away. (1991)

A very short time

jiffy (1785) Often in the phrase *in a jiffy* in a very short time; origin unknown ■ *Guardian:* If his car had a puncture he wouldn't sit in the back seat until someone put the spare wheel on. He would be out in a jiffy, giving a hand to speed things up. (1992)

tick (1879) Mainly British; from the notion of the time between two ticks of a clock ■ **E. Reveley:** Just wait a tick while I tell George where we'll be, and then we can go down together. (1983)

mo, mo' (1896) Especially in the phrase *half a mo* (wait for) a short time; abbreviation of *moment* ■ **T. S. Eliot:** 'Arf a mo', 'arf a mo'. It's lucky for you two as you've got someone what's done a bit o' lookin' into things to keep you in line. (1934)

jig-time (1916) Mainly US; usually in the phrase *in jig-time* in a very short time ■ **L. W. Robinson:** If I was you, I'd see Gracie Hutchinson. . . . She'd solve your problem in jig time. (1968)

sec (1956) Abbreviation of *second* ■ **Alison Lurie:** I wonder if you could hold the baby for me, Missus Turner, please, just for a sec. (1962)

Temporarily

pro tem (1835) Abbreviation of Latin *pro tempore* for the time ■ **Clement & La Frenais:** 'Night porter?' Fletcher nodded sourly. 'Pro tem, yes.' (1978)

Permanence

fixture (1788) Applied, often derogatorily, to a person or thing permanently in a particular place or situation ■ *Guardian:* Dr Al-Anbari became a fixture at all the Arab social gatherings in New York. (1991)

(have) come to stay, be here to stay (1863) Orig US; denoting a permanent presence ■ **John Wainwright:** 'I don't go for them [*sc.* automatic gears]. They'll kill real driving.' . . . 'They're here to stay, mate, whether you go for 'em, or not.' (1971)

for keeps (1871) Orig US; denoting that something will continue for ever ■ *Guardian:* Economic and Monetary Union . . . means that a Dutch uncle will move into the household for keeps. (1992)

Punctual(ly)

on the dot (1909) ■ **W. R. Burnett:** She's always been very scrupulous about settling her bill on the dot. (1953)

A very long time in the past

the year dot (1895) From the notion of a date so old that it cannot be particularized ■ **Anthony Gilbert:** It's . . . the wife who poisons the husband, not some confederate he met in Cuba in the year dot. (1956)

Until a long time in the future

until the cows come home (1610) ■ *Cosmopolitan:* I could go on lapping up Pimms number one till the cows come home, I'm in that sort of mood. (1992)

until kingdom come (1898) From *kingdom come* heaven, paradise (from the clause *thy kingdom come* in the Lord's Prayer), from the notion of lasting until the end of the world ■ *New Scientist:* If she fancies short, hairy men with bow legs then that's her problem. She could have him till kingdom come as far as I was concerned. (1991)

Dawn

sparrow-fart (1886) Orig dialectal ■ **Hugh McLeave:** It was important enough to bring you out here at sparrow fart. (1974)

crack of dawn (1923) Compare earlier *crack of day* ■ **Somerset Maugham:** He had slipped away at crack of dawn. (1948)

In the morning

ack emma (1898) Orig military slang, now dated; from the former military communications code-names for the letters *a* and *m* ■ *Dorothy Sayers*: Some damned thing at the Yard, I suppose. At three ack emma! (1927)

Afternoon

after (1890) Abbreviation ■ *John Mulgan*: Boss wants us to get the hay in up top this after. (1939)

2. **Beginning**

To begin

See also **Speed** (pp. 380–2).

fire away (1775) Now used mainly in the imperative as a demand or invitation to begin or continue ■ *Guardian*: A multi-coloured God . . . said he would like to discuss a few questions about the meaning of life. Without hesitation Yudhishthira responded with the Hindi equivalent of: 'Fair enough squire; fire away.' (1991)

kick off (1911) From earlier sense, begin a football match by kicking the ball ■ *Frank Sargeson*: To kick off with we'd fool about in the water. (1942)

shoot (1915) Orig US; used mainly in the imperative as a demand or invitation to begin or continue ■ *Herman Wouk*: 'Can I pick your brain on one more point?' 'Shoot.' (1978)

snap (in) to it (1918) Applied to beginning with haste or urgency ■ *Boston Sunday Herald*: The Senator . . . spent half an hour persuading a very reluctant repairman to come. 'Why,' asked a guest, 'didn't you just tell him to snap to it?' (1967)

hoe in (1935) Australian & New Zealand; often applied specifically to starting to eat eagerly ■ *I. L. Idriess*: The local cow . . . took a lick; fancied the salty taste and hoed in for breakfast. (1939)

get cracking (1937) Usually applied to beginning with haste or urgency ■ *New Yorker*: Before Dr. Latham can get cracking with his computer, someone at the Mission Control . . . will flip a switch. (1969)

get stuck in (1941) Orig Australian; usually applied to beginning eagerly or with gusto ■ *Mirage*: Noticed old J. D. was getting stuck into a feed in the Flight kitchen yesterday. (1966)

get weaving (1942) Orig R.A.F. slang; usually applied to beginning with haste or urgency; from *weave* move repeatedly from side to side, in R.A.F. usage, fly a devious course, especially in avoiding or escaping danger ■ *B. W. Aldiss*: Pack your night things in a small pack and get weaving, while I lay on transport. (1971)

get moving (1963) Usually applied to beginning with haste or urgency ■ *Grimsby Evening Telegraph*: 'Like sexism and racism, ageism has had its day,' said Dr. Alex Comfort, a world expert on ageing. Old people had to get moving and be bloody-minded to improve their lot. (1977)

arvo (1927) Australian; representing a voiced pronunciation of *af-* of *afternoon* + the Australian colloquial suffix *-o* ■ *Jon Cleary*: That how you spend your Sunday arvos, Rupe? (1952)

In the afternoon/evening

pip emma (1913) Orig military slang, now dated; from the former military communications code-names for the letters *p* and *m* ■ *Colleen McCullough*: The second hand was just sweeping up to 9:40 pip-emma. (1977)

To use for the first time

christen (1990) First recorded in 1990, but in use earlier; from earlier sense, baptize ■ *Daily Star*: Huddersfield's Lee Makel bought a new pair of boots before this game—and christened them with his first goal at the McAlpine Stadium. (1996)

From the beginning

from the word go (1834) Orig US ■ *Times*: It was wrong from the word 'go' to put in a limitation such as 60. (1963)

on the ground floor (1872) Orig US; orig and mainly applied to joining in an enterprise from its beginning ■ *Anita Loos*: My problem was that, without realizing it, I was in on the ground floor of a sex revolution: the twentieth century's breakdown of romantic love between the sexes. (1966)

from the top (1976) Orig and mainly applied to the starting of a performance from the beginning of a piece; first recorded in the 1970s, but in use before that ■ *New Yorker*: From the top— 'Watermelon Man'. Let's sock it out and give Mrs. Ritterhouse a chance to really cook. (1976)

As a beginning; to start with

as (or for) a starter, for starters (1873) Orig US ■ *New Yorker*: Most of the program was devoted to the lessons in campaign management that could be learned from Presidential races, real and fictional (A scene was shown from the movie 'The Candidate', in which the media adviser said to Robert Redford, 'O.K., now, for starters, we got to cut your hair and eighty-six the sideburns'). (1980)

first off (1880) Orig US ■ *Nation* (New York): Men of science . . . no longer admit first off what simple good sense shows to us. (1915)

for (or as) openers (1967) Orig US ■ *Paul Erdman*: I'd like to ask you a few simple questions . . . for openers, what's with this place here? (1974)

Let's begin!

here goes (1829) Said when one is about to start something exciting, risky, etc. ■ *Washington Post*: Dear Mr. President, At a holiday dinner at the New Year, you challenged those present to do something for you: to tell you if we felt you were making a mistake. . . . So here goes: Mr. President, don't feel so besieged. (1993)

3. **Deferral & Stopping**

To defer, postpone

sleep on something **(1519)** Denoting postponing a decision on something until the next day, with the implication that a night's sleep will facilitate judgment ▪ P. Gregory: Let me think about it, though. I'd like to sleep on it. (1962)

sit on something **(1906)** Denoting failing to deal with something over a long period ▪ Margaret Hinxman: She'd 'sat' on the article . . . until . . . a deadline had galvanized her into putting words on paper. (1983)

let something **ride (1921)** Denoting taking no immediate action about something ▪ J. Wade: I let it ride. I couldn't be bothered to reply. (1961)

take a rain check (1959) Orig & mainly US; denoting reserving the right not to take up a particular offer until convenient; often followed by *on*; from *rain check* ticket given to a spectator at an outdoor event providing for a refund of their entrance money or admission at a later date if the event is interrupted by rain ▪ Len Deighton: 'Let me take a rain-check.' 'On a love affair?' I said. (1976)

In a state of being deferred or postponed

on the back burner (1963) Orig US; from the use of the rearmost ring, hotplate, etc. on a cooking stove for simmering rather than boiling ▪ *Times*: He had misgivings about the GM bid for BL because under its global strategy Britain had been put on the 'backburner' for the last decade. (1986)

To delay, hold back, hesitate, wait

dilly-dally (1741) A fanciful reduplication of *dally* ▪ R. L. Stevenson: There is no time to dilly-dally in our work. (1883)

hold one's horses (1844) Orig US; usually used in the imperative (*hold your horses!*) urging someone not to take precipitate action ▪ N. Fitzgerald: 'I'm going in to the station *now*,' he said. 'Hold your horses,' Marr said. 'The night's young.' (1967)

hang about, hang around (1892) ▪ G. F. Newman: He didn't hang around afterwards. (1970) ▪ *Melody Maker*: In a front room in Shepherds Bush, however, plots are being hatched—and hang about, because I'm not going to bore you with yet another . . . yarn. (1973)

watch this space (1917) Used to indicate that one should wait for further developments to be announced; originally an injunction to look regularly at a particular portion of a newspaper so as not to miss future announcements ▪ Julian Rathbone: Where is he? Watch this space for exciting revelations in the next few days. (1979)

hold it (1926) ▪ Evelyn Berckman: 'Let's go and talk to her quickly, quickly—.' 'Hold it, darling,' she interrupted. (1973)

hang on (1939) ▪ *Woman's Own*: Hang on a minute. . . . I'm coming with you. (1971)

To stop doing something; desist

leave off (c1400) Orig standard English; colloquial mainly when used with a gerund as object and as an order to stop doing something annoying ▪ *Guardian*: When I muttered privately about possible humbuggery not only Attenborough's friends, but also those who reasonably should have been enemies, gave vent to similar cries of 'No, no!' 'Leave off!' 'Shame!' (1992)

give over (1526) Orig standard English; often as an order to stop doing something annoying ▪ Isobel Lambot: 'Elinor,' said Lucton, exhausted, 'for pity's sake, give over.' (1987)

stow (1676) Dated; often in an order to stop doing something annoying; often in the phrase *stow it* ▪ Kingsley Amis: No use telling her to stow it or cheese it or come off it because she really believes it. (1984)

stash, stach (1794) Orig criminals' slang, dated; origin unknown ▪ W. Craig: She is requested to 'stash' tragedy and give them comedy. (1903)

cheese (1812) Orig thieves' slang, dated; often in the phrase *cheese it*; origin unknown ▪ P. G. Wodehouse: He had been clearing away the breakfast things, but at the sound of the young master's voice cheesed it courteously. (1923)

turn something **up (1885)** Often in an order to stop doing something annoying; often in the phrase *turn it up* ▪ *Illustrated Sporting & Dramatic News*: After one disastrous round . . . I intimated to the champion my intention to turn it up. (1893)

chuck (1888) Dated; often in an order to stop doing something annoying; often in the phrase *chuck it*

nark (1889) British; often in an order to stop doing something annoying; usually in the phrase *nark it* ▪ I. & P. Opie: Saying by the one being tortured: "Ere, nark it.' (1959)

chop (1896) US; often in the phrase *chop it*

knock something **off (1902)** Often in an order to stop doing something annoying; often in the phrase *knock it off* ▪ Joseph Heller: 'Hey, knock it off down there,' a voice rang out from the far end of the ward. 'Can't you see we're trying to nap?' (1961)

cut something **out (1903)** Often in an order to stop doing something annoying; often in the phrase *cut it out* ▪ M. Guybon: 'Cut it out!' said Pryanchikov, struggling violently. 'I'm sick of prosecutors and trials.' (1970)

can (1906) Orig US; often in an order to stop talking or making a noise; often in the phrase *can it* ▪ Elizabeth Ferrars: Carver winced at the noise. 'Can that bloody row, can't you?' he grunted. (1953)

lay off (1908) ▪ Dulcie Gray: I'd lay off stirring up trouble for a bit if I were you. (1974)

snap out of something **(1918)** Denoting desisting from an attitude, changing a mood, pattern of behaviour, etc. by sudden effort; often imperative in the phrase *snap out of it!* ■ Rhona Petrie: Oh, snap out of it. You'll pull through on your ownsome. (1967)

call it a day (1919) Denoting stopping or abandoning what one is doing; compare earlier *call it half a day* in same sense (1838) ■ John Braine: We'll call it a day. . . . Don't think badly of me. (1957)

tie a can to (1926) ■ P. G. Wodehouse: Tie a can to the funny stuff, see? If I want to laugh, I'll read the comic strip. (1942)

break something **down (1941)** Australian & New Zealand; often in an order to stop doing something annoying, especially talking or making noise; usually in the phrase *break it down* ■ Hugh Atkinson: The barman was worried about the noise and kept saying uselessly, 'Now, now, blokes, break it down,' and 'Fair go there, fellars.' (1961)

pack something **up (1942)** Orig US; often in an order to stop doing something annoying; often in the phrase *pack it up* ■ Alexander Baron: Pack it up, Joyce. I'm telling you. (1951)

pack something **in (1943)** Often in an order to stop doing something annoying; often in the phrase *pack it in* ■ Daily Mirror: Hey! You! That's my missus—pack it in! (1977)

kiss off (1945) Often in an order to stop doing something annoying

jack something **in (1948)** British; often in an order to stop doing something annoying; often in the phrase *jack it in*

wrap it up (1957) Often in an order to stop doing something annoying; from *wrap up* finish ■ George Sanders: 'Wrap it up,' he would shout. (1960)

get off someone's **back (1961)** Denoting stopping harrassing or annoying someone ■ Joseph Heller: Then stop picking on me, will you? Get off my back, will you? (1961)

leave it out (1969) British; often in an order to stop doing something annoying

See also To be, become or remain silent at **Communication** (pp. 321–2).

Something cancelled

scrub (1952) Applied especially to a flying mission ■ Virgil Grissom: I was prepared for the scrub, and it was not long in coming. (1962)

To give (something) up

shut up shop (1650) Denoting giving up one's former activity; from earlier sense, close one's business ■ George Orwell: Office babus are the real rulers of this country now. . . . Best thing we can do is to shut up shop and let 'em stew in their own juice. (1934)

give something **up as a bad job (1862)** Denoting abandoning something that has no chance of success ■ Listener: Harold and Bernard Cohen were the two foremost British painters during the early 'sixties who were trying to evolve a visual language to correspond to what 'the artist thinks'. Now both seem to have given this up

as a bad job and fallen in line with current reductivist tendencies. (1967)

chuck (1883) ■ D. G. Mackail: He . . . concluded by asking her to chuck it all and marry him. (1929)

pack something **up (1951)** ■ Osmington Mills: I packed up my job last week. (1959)

pack something **in (1953)** ■ Kenneth Clark: He had long ago 'packed it in', and spent his life sitting by the window dozing, with a volume of Pepys' Diary upside down on his knee. (1974)

toss it in (1956) New Zealand ■ New Zealand Listener: In the end they saw some hogsbacks up above the col so they tossed it in and glissaded down back to their bivvy. (1971)

jack something **in (1958)** British; from earlier sense, stop doing something ■ Kenneth Royce: I'm beginning to wonder if it's worth it. . . . Let me jack it in. (1972)

To dispense with

skip it (1934) Orig US; used as an order or exhortation to drop a subject or avoid doing something ■ Mary McCarthy: 'Oh, Dr James,' she sighed. 'Let's skip it this time.' (1943)

scrub round (1943) British, orig services' slang ■ T. White: I was required to do no less than fifteen days' cells. Reason: disobedience. Luckily, the captain had a sense of humour and finally scrubbed round it. (1964)

To put a stop to

choke something **off (1818)** Perhaps originally from the notion of making a dog loosen its hold by choking it ■ Economist: Yet it did not want high rates to choke off economic recovery. (1987)

put the fritz on something, **put** something **on the fritz (1903)** Orig & mainly US; origin unknown ■ R. H. R. Smithies: It's Mother's plan to put the fritz on shoplifting. (1968)

put the tin hat on something **(1919)** Denoting bringing something to a usually unwelcome close or climax ■ C. Dickson: Next . . . came the point that put the tin hat on it. (1943)

wash something **up (1925)** US ■ John O'Hara: They said act of God and fire etc. wash up a contract automatically. (1940)

pull the plug on something **(1961)** Orig from the notion of flushing something down the lavatory, but latterly usually with reference to the disconnecting of a piece of electrical equipment, specifically a life-support system ■ Observer: Any prudent banker would have pulled the plug on Court Line long ago. (1974)

zero (1965) Denoting the elimination or deletion of something; often followed by *out* ■ Tennis: 'Zero Screen 311!' he bellowed. (1990)

zap (1976) Orig US; from earlier sense, kill (with a ray gun) ■ Sunday Sun-Times (Chicago): Atari seeks to zap X-rated video games. (1982)

To turn off

kill (1886) Orig US; applied to a motor, a light, etc. ■ Donald MacKenzie: I moved the hired car into the cobbled courtyard. . . . I killed the motor. (1971)

To squash someone, prevent someone acting; check, snub

sit on someone **(1865)** ■ Noel Streatfield: In the tube going home, Pauline and Petrova pestered Posy for criticism of the production; but the moment she made any, they sat on her, asking her what she thought she knew about it. (1936)

slap someone **down (1938)** ■ Times: The police sergeant who conducted the prosecutions was often slapped down by the clerk of the court for leading his witnesses. (1973)

To finish

wrap something **up (1926)** Denoting completing something, especially satisfactorily ■ Pat Frank: I guess that wraps it up for tonight. . . . I don't know of anything else we can do. (1957)

Something finished

history (1884) Applied to something that is past and no longer relevant or important; often in the phrase *ancient history* ■ P. Spencer: You won't get anywhere by fretting about it. . . . It's ancient history by now, anyway. People do odd things in drink. (1961)

The end

thirty (1895) US, used by journalists, printers, etc.; from the use of the figure 30 to mark the end of a piece of journalist's copy ■ Gore Vidal: 'When we know those two things, it's fat thirty time.' Bruce had obviously been impressed by journalism school. (1978)

curtains (1901) Orig US theatrical slang; from the notion of the closing of the curtain at the end of a theatrical performance ■ D. Lowrie: There ain't much dope here now, an' it's curtains t' get nailed with it. (1912)

the end of the line (1948) Orig US ■ E. Burgess: It looks like the end of the line for Roylake. Unless he can think up something—fast! (1959)

the end of the road (1954) ■ Guardian: The end of the road for Mr. Dubcek's Czechoslovakia may not have been reached after all. (1968)

endsville, Endsville, Endville (1961) US; from *end* (+ *-s-*) + *-ville* ■ Frank Sinatra: You can be the most artistically perfect performer in the world, but the audience is like a broad—if you're indifferent, endsville. (1984)

The game is up

the jig is up (1800) From *jig* game, trifle ■ Nature: The weight of opinion seems to be that the jig is up for the map's supporters. (1974)

4. Experience & Inexperience

An experienced person

old stager (1570) *stager* perhaps originally from Old French *estagier* inhabitant, resident, although later associated with obsolete *stager* actor ■ Observer: He closed quickly on the Kenyan David Kibet and another old-stager, Said Aouita. (1991)

old sweat (1919) Applied to an old soldier

To gain experience

see (get a look at, etc.) the elephant (1835) US; denoting seeing the world, or the bright lights of the big city, or more broadly getting experience of life; from the notion of the elephant as an exotic animal seen only rarely, in zoos and circuses ■ T. V. Olsen: Saturdays some of the boys from the three big outfits come in to see the elephant. (1960)

An inexperienced person; a beginner

greenhorn (1682) Often applied specifically to a novice in a trade; from earlier, obsolete sense, raw recruit in the army (1650); ultimately from the notion of a calf with 'green' or young horns ■ Rider Haggard: I suppose you are not hoaxing us? It is, I know, sometimes thought allowable to take a greenhorn in. (1885)

greenie (1848) US; from *greenhorn* + *-ie*

greener (1875) Probably from *green*(horn + *-er* ■ Israel Zangwill: He was a 'greener' of the greenest order, having landed at the docks only a few hours ago. (1892)

shorthorn (1888) US, dated; from the notion of a calf whose horns have not yet grown long; compare earlier sense, cattle of a breed with short horns, and *greenhorn* inexperienced person ■ A. H. Lewis: Don't let no shorthorn have my room. (1905)

shavetail (1891) Orig US, services' slang; often applied specifically to a newly commissioned officer; from earlier sense, untrained pack animal identified by a shaven tail ■ Len Deighton: I was a shavetail, just out of pilot training. (1976)

rookie, rooky (1892) Mainly North American; applied especially to a raw recruit in the army or the police, or to a novice in a sports team; probably a modified alteration of *recruit* ■ H. A. Franck: From the lieutenant to the newest uniformless 'rookie' every member of the police was swarming in and out of the building. (1913)

rook (1901) US, dated; abbreviation of *rookie*

poop-ornament (1902) Naval slang, dated; applied to a ship's apprentice

boot (1911) US, services' slang; applied to a recruit in basic training, and hence to an (inexperienced) junior officer ■ American Speech: It is taught to the 'boot' before he leaves boot camp. (1963)

green pea (1912) US; compare *green* inexperienced

Hun (1916) British, dated; applied to a flying cadet during World War I; from earlier sense, German soldier, apparently from the cadets' destructive effect on the aircraft in which they were training ■ E. M. Roberts: Every pilot is a Hun until he has received his wings. (1918)

quirk (1916) British, dated; applied to an inexperienced pilot; perhaps from *quirk* eccentricity, oddity, but compare *erk* person of low rank in the R.A.F. ■ C. F. S. Gamble: The pilot, a very harmless, innocent 'quirk', hardly fledged, straight from Chingford. (1928)

wart (1916) Naval slang; applied to a junior midshipman or naval cadet

ninety-day wonder (1917) US; applied to a graduate of a ninety-day officers' training course, and hence any inexperienced, newly commissioned officer; humorously, after *nine-day wonder* ■ W. C. Woods: A pale punk kid to run my company, another ninety day wonder. (1970)

war baby (1917) Applied to a young or inexperienced officer

poodle-faker (1918) British, services' slang; applied derisively to a new young officer; from earlier sense, ladies' man

rocky (1919) British, naval slang; applied to a recruit in the R.N.V.R. or another naval division ■ Kerr & Granville: The active-service men labelled them [*sc.* R.N.V.R. ratings] a 'rocky' lot—'rocky' being an oblique reference to unstable sea-legs and the waved tapes in their blue jean collars. (1957)

wonk (1929) Nautical; applied especially to a cadet or midshipman; perhaps from *wonky* unsteady, unsound

stooge (1930) Applied to a newcomer, especially a new prisoner or first offender

butter-boy (1939) British; applied to a new taxi driver ■ Cyril Ray: [The] owner-driver . . . is called a 'butter-boy' when he first appears on the rank, taking the butter from the older hands' bread, they say. (1960)

snotnose (1941) Derogatory; from the notion of a child with a nose running with mucus

■ Howard Fast: So don't be young snotnose with me. I like serious boys. (1977)

sprog (1941) British, services' slang; applied to a raw recruit or a trainee; perhaps from obsolete *sprag* lively young man ■ J. Hillier: Never mind, Wendy, you sprogs of 'B' flight will learn to fly yet—if you live long enough! (1943)

yardbird (1941) US services' slang; applied to a raw recruit; from *yard* enclosed area + *bird* person ■ *Yank*: Who is it the yardbird sees when he gets red-lined on the payroll for signing his name wrong? (1942)

nozzer (1943) British, nautical; applied to a new recruit or novice sailor; perhaps an alteration of *No, sir*

macker, macca (1944) Australian; applied mainly to a new recruit; origin unknown ■ J. Wynnum: Only a macca in the outfit, too. Only been in half as long as us. (1965)

red-arse (1946) Services' slang, dated; applied to a raw recruit ■ D. M. Davin: You were only a bloody redarse in those days. (1947)

nig-nog (1967) British; probably antedating *nig-nog* fool, but not recorded until later ■ *Times*: 'Nig-nog' was used on the railways and elsewhere long before coloured immigrants appeared. . . . It is usually taken as a mildly contemptuous but good-humoured name for an unskilled man or novice. (1967)

Inexperienced

green (1548) From the notion of unripeness in plants ■ *Times*: Very early in her voyage she encountered a very severe storm, and that with a green crew. (1894)

raggedy-ass, -assed (1930) US, orig services' slang ■ J. A. McPherson: Who taught you the moves when you were just a raggedy-ass waiter? (1969)

wet behind the ears (1931) ■ W. J. Burley: I am not an abortionist but neither am I wet behind the ears. I've been around. (1968)

green-ass (1949) US

white-shoe (1957) Mainly US; applied to an immature person ■ *New York Times*: Covert operations can be stripped from the CIA . . . So can such monkey business as dropping simulated poison canisters in the New York subways—the games of white-shoe boys who never grew up. (1975)

5. Fashionableness, Stylishness

Fashion

fash (1895) Abbreviation of *fashion* ■ *Washington Post*: Two heaps on the floor afforded a primer on kiddie fash ins and outs. (1986)

Fashionable, up-to-date

O.K., okay, okey (1869) Applied to something currently socially or culturally acceptable; from earlier sense, satisfactory ■ Stephen Potter: The

word 'diathesis' . . . is now on the O.K. list for conversationmen. (1950)

hot (1908) Applied to someone or something (originally news) excitingly of the moment ■ *Daily Mail*: Miss Roberts hasn't done badly either. The hottest female star of the moment has already been paid £2 million. (1991)

with it (1931) Orig US ■ *Daily Mail*: Horne made a strong attempt to get with it. Result: the stronger emphasis on fashionwear. (1971)

in (1960) ■ Olive Norton: It *is* the in place. You'd be surprised who you meet there. (1970)

way-in (1960) From the adverb *way* + *in*, after *way-out* eccentric, unconventional ■ *Punch*: There's a real way-in guy looking like how a guy on *The Times Saturday Review* ought to look like. (1967)

trendy (1962) Sometimes used derogatorily; from *trend* + *-y* ■ *Lancet*: Pathobiology (a trendy name for general pathology) seems to be a fashionable subject in the United States. (1972)

switched on (1964) ■ D. Devine: Her mother wasn't switched on, she knew nothing of modern fashion. (1970)

where it's at (1965) Orig US ■ *Melody Maker*: The musicians frequently became frustrated . . . not really believing their own bands were where it was at. (1971)

together (1968) ■ *Daily Mirror*: No finer honour can be bestowed on a man down the King's Road than to be called a together cat. (1968)

funky (1969) Orig US; from earlier sense, (of jazz or rock) earthy, bluesy ■ *Holiday Which?*: Once across Broadway from Washington Square, you're in East Village, which is where funky New York is now found. (1990)

big (1970) ■ *Daily Telegraph*: A bale of soft material, patterned in that modernismus which was so big in the Thirties, and now survives mainly in British Rail. (1970)

fash (1977) Abbreviation of *fashionable* ■ *Hair*: Flash and fash feeling for a successful new season style. (1985)

happening (1977) Orig US ■ *Jackie Pop Special*: Some people must really go trainspotting because they think it's the happening thing to do. (1989)

(Fashionably) stylish or smart

natty (1785) Apparently related to *neat* ■ *Daily Telegraph*: Alex Higgins entered the arena without a tie, attire bottomed off with a natty pair of purple suede shoes. (1991)

dressy (1785) Denoting clothing that is elaborately elegant; from earlier sense, fond of (elaborate) dressing ■ *Daily Mail*: It looked wonderful but, with its full-length overskirt, perhaps just a little 'too dressy', felt Andrea, for a ball that wasn't black tie. (1991)

spiffy (1853) Mainly US; origin unknown; compare obsolete dialect *spiff* smart, obsolete slang *spiff* well-dressed man, swell, and *spiv* ■ Herman Wouk: She's turned into quite the spiffy New York gal. (1978)

spiffing (1861) Dated; compare *spiffy*

nifty (1868) Orig US; origin uncertain; a connection with *magnificent* has been suggested ■ Joanna Cannan: I . . . got the niftiest white overalls. (1958)

swish (1879) Origin uncertain; perhaps from *swish* hissing sound ■ Peter Dickinson: The architects . . . had made their name running up swish hotels in Beirut. (1974)

snappy (1881) Especially in the phrase *snappy dresser* ■ Paul Theroux: A woman waiting for her lover . . . whom she would describe as a snappy dresser, a riot, a real card. (1977)

doggy (1885) Dated; from *dog* (compare *put on (the) dog* behave ostentatiously) + *-y* ■ A. J. Worrall: I like your tie, it is very doggy. (1932)

classy (1891) From *class* + *-y* ■ *Daily Mail*: Bamboo in a glazed pot. Very classy. (1991)

posh (1918) Perhaps related to obsolete *posh* money, a dandy; apparently nothing to do with 'port out, starboard home', of cabins on the sea-passage between Britain and India ■ *Lancashire Life*: The poshest Granada Ghias . . . have electric windows. (1977)

ritzy (1920) Orig US; from the name of César Ritz (1850–1918), Swiss-born proprietor of luxury hotels + *-y* ■ *People*: That glamour gal of British trains, the ritzy, resplendent Golden Arrow. (1947)

dicty (1925) US, Black English; from earlier sense, wealthy, snobbish, conceited

snazzy (1932) Orig US; origin unknown ■ Joan Lock: They've made the plain uniforms look as snazzy as possible with whiter-than-white hat-bands, belts and gaiters. (1968)

sharp (1940) Orig US ■ *Observer*: It's more a desire for things you haven't got but feel you've a right to, because other people have them—a sharp suit, good things, neat things, flashy things. (1962)

swanky (1940) From earlier sense, (of a person) swaggering, pretentiously grand ■ *Spectator*: An English producer and a London critic . . . in the swanky bar of the Excelsior. (1959)

groovy (1941) Orig US; from earlier sense, playing with inspiration ■ *Listener*: There are a lot of guys going round with groovy hair-styles. (1968)

cool (1946) Orig US; from earlier sense, sophisticated ■ *Observer*: They got long, sloppy haircuts and wide knot ties and no-press suits with fat lapels. Very cool. (1959)

zooty (1946) From *zoot* (*suit*) (in allusion to the stylishness of zoot suits) + *-y* ■ Saul Bellow: Her lover, too, with long jaws and zooty sideburns. (1964)

hip (1951) Orig US; from earlier sense, fully informed ■ V. Ferdinand: We sometimes . . . go in for that kind of living thinking it's hip. (1972)

hep (1957) Orig US; variant of *hip* ■ *Guardian*: Not even its bitterest critics could accuse the Labour party of being 'hep'. (1960)

swinging (1958) Applied to something lively and modern ■ *Weekend Telegraph*: Diana Vreeland . . . editor of *Vogue* . . . has said simply 'London is the most swinging city in the world at the moment'. (1965)

go (1962) Orig US, dated; compare *the go* that which is fashionable ■ *Time*: Beatniks, whose heavy black turtleneck sweaters had never looked particularly go with white tennis socks. (1963)

glam (1963) Abbreviation of *glamorous* ■ Celia Dale: She was . . . wearing eye-shadow and a great deal of lipstick. 'You're looking very glam,' he said. (1964)

radical (1971) Orig surfers' slang; from earlier sense, at or exceeding the limits of safety

whizzy (1977) Applied to something admired for its up-to-dateness; from *whizz* + *-y* ■ *Making Music*: A whizzy Roland-style alpha wheel for modifying your sounds. (1986)

preppy (1980) US; applied to clothes, etc. that are fashionably smart, like a student's uniform; compare earlier sense, suitable to a preparatory school, immature ■ *Guardian*: The look is smart but casual, preppy without being prim, sporty without being impractical. (1992)

rad (1982) Orig North American; abbreviation of *radical* ■ *Sunday Mail Magazine* (Brisbane): Your son thinks he's so rad! (1988)

fresh (1984) Orig & mainly US; a slight shift from the standard meaning, associated with the language of rap and hip-hop ■ T. Kidder: Bro, that was fresh! (1989)

piss elegant (1991) Used ironically ■ J. Keenan: 'What's he supposed to be like?' asked one. 'Very piss elegant,' said the young mimic. 'Stuck-up British chintz queen.' (1991)

That which is fashionable

the kick (a1700) Dated ■ E. Lynn Linton: Mrs. West naturally wanted 'the last new kick'. (1894)

(all) the rage (1785) ■ *Daily Express*: Cut-outs are all the rage-cut-outs in wood and in cardboard painted. (1927)

all (or quite) the go (c1787) Dated ■ *Sunday Mail Magazine* (Brisbane): In Brisbane, Aroma's in Savoir Faire in Park Road is all the go, too. That one's a ton of fun, with a clientele to match. (1988)

A fashionable or stylish person

swell (1786) Dated; in later use also applied to someone of high social position ■ *Law Times*: The plaintiff stated that the defendant was one of the greatest swells in the City . . . and had often readily paid £20 or £30. (1892)

slicker (1900) Orig & mainly US; applied to a smart and sophisticated person; especially in the phrase *city slicker* ■ Xan Fielding: The two city-slickers were travelling on business. (1953)

nut (1904) Dated; applied to a fashionable or showy young man of affected elegance ■ Rose Macaulay: He always looked the same, calm, unruffled, tidy, the exquisite nut. (1920)

hipster (1941) Orig US; applied to someone who is in touch with contemporary ideas and fashions; from *hip* fully informed + *-ster* ■ *Partisan Review*: Carrying his language and his new philosophy like concealed weapons, the hipster set out to conquer the world. (1948)

hippie, hippy (1953) US, dated; applied to someone who is in touch with contemporary ideas and fashions; from *hip* fully informed + *ie*; compare later sense, person leading an unconventional life, taking hallucinogenic drugs, etc. (1965) ■ D. Wallop: Man, I really get a bellyful of these would be hippies. (1953)

slick (1959) US; applied to a smart and sophisticated person; apparently a back-formation from *slicker* ■ E. Bullins: Dandy's mother had a civil-service job in the city, and the city slick Dandy was from Philly. (1971)

swinger (1965) ■ Joseph Gores: The Dukum Inn . . . looked . . . like an aging swinger getting up in the morning with his teeth still in the water glass. (1972)

trendy (1968) Often used derogatorily; from the adjective *trendy* ■ *Listener*: The 'trendies" concern for the individual seems to relate more to his place in society than to his soul. (1982)

Something smart or stylish

sharpie (1970) North American; compare *sharp* stylish ■ *Tucson* (Arizona) *Citizen*: Starter home . . . carpeting, drapes and remodeled kitchen. Call . . . to see this little sharpie. (1979)

Something fashionable or popular

crowd puller (1955) ■ *Mail on Sunday*: 'HDTV will be a crowd puller,' claims Dixons' Danny Churchill. (1991)

hot property (1958) ■ *Rolling Stone*: The Hagers, potentially hot property, now have Record One. (1969)

To become or be fashionable

catch on (1887) ■ *Daily Mail*: Fortunately the great British blue overall does not look like it's going to catch on in the United States. (1991)

swing (1957) ■ *Times*: The fashion collections . . . are supposed to have proved . . . that 'London swings again'. (1983)

To make or become more stylish or smart

spiff (1877) Used transitively; usually followed by *up*; back-formation from *spiffing* or *spiffy* ■ *Arizona Daily Star*: The man doing it was an interior decorator, not an art conservator, and he did what he felt was best—he went in and spiffed up the church. (1979)

posh up (1919) Often in the phrase *poshed up*; from *posh* stylish, smart ■ Philip Purser: We . . . had dined at a rotten, poshed-up Thames pub. (1968)

glam (1937) Used transitively and intransitively; denoting making oneself glamorous; usually followed by *up*; abbreviation of *glamour* ■ John Osborne: Get yourself glammed up, and we'll hit the town. (1957)

tart (1938) Mainly British; used transitively and intransitively; usually denoting flashiness or gaudiness; usually followed by *up*; from *tart* promiscuous woman, prostitute ■ Jilly Cooper: They were tarting up in the Ladies. (1976) ■ *Observer*: American dealers would tart up the junk and sell it at suburban auctions at three times the English price. (1978)

spiv (1959) British; used transitively; denoting dressing oneself up flashily; from *spiv* (flashily dressed) small-time criminal ■ **B. W. Aldiss:** We spivved ourselves up, put on clean shirts, and strolled out of camp. (1971)

Unfashionable, unstylish

out (1966) ■ *Daily Telegraph:* They [*sc.* children] want to

6. Old

one foot in the grave (1632) ■ James Payn: He has twenty thousand a year . . . And one foot in his grave. (1886)

the wrong side of (a1663) Denoting an age in excess of the stated age; formerly also *the shady side of* ■ G. F. Newman: Tasting stir, Goldby suddenly realized he was the wrong side of thirty for acquiring the habit. (1970)

Anno Domini (1885) From earlier use, applied to years of the Christian calendar; from the notion of the passing of the years ■ E. V. Lucas: When the time came for A. to take the bat he was unable to do so. *Anno Domini* asserted itself. (1906)

pushing . . . (1974) Used to denote that someone is nearly a particular (advanced) age ■ *Guardian:* In the mid-1930s, when his own work had run dry and he was pushing 70, any normal professional would have retired. (1993)

An old person

oldster (1848) From *old* + *-ster*, after *youngster* ■ *Wall Street Journal:* 'The youngsters are chafing at the bit and aren't willing to wait and see how the civil rights bill shapes up,' he adds, 'and we oldsters can't hold back any longer.' (1964)

oldie, oldy (1874) From *old* + *-ie* ■ John Brown: We've got our rights, haven't we, same as the oldies. (1972)

crock (1876) Applied especially to an old person who is debilitated or an invalid; often in the phrase *old crock*; from earlier meaning, old ewe ■ *Guardian:* Behind him at yesterday's launch . . . were enough old crocks to remind you that Major does come from a new generation. (1992)

wrinkly, wrinklie (1972) From the noun *wrinkle* + *-ie*, with reference to older people's wrinkled skin ■ *Church Times:* I am a wrinkly whose monthly cheque from the Church Commissioners is labelled 'Diocesan Dignitary'. (1983)

crumbly, crumblie (1976) From the adjective *crumbly*, with reference to the physical effects of old age ■ Sue Townsend: At the end of the party Rick Lemon put 'White Christmas' by some old crumblie on the record deck. (1984)

woopie, woopy (1986) Orig North American; applied to a rich old person, able to enjoy an affluent and active lifestyle in retirement; acronym from *well-off old(er) person* + *-ie*, after *yuppie* ■ *Daily Telegraph:* We are in the age of the 'woopy' . . . and it is about time we all recognised that fact, planned for our own future and helped them to enjoy theirs. (1988)

eat savoury things most of all; but there are certain 'in' sweet-stuffs and a very great many 'out' ones. (1966)

naff (1970) Mainly British; from earlier sense, worthless, faulty ■ *Times:* Gaultier had turned everything that fashion most despises, what English youth calls 'naff', into high style. (1985)

An old man

old boy (a1500) ■ *Daily Mail:* But then the old boy, refusing to admit that he's a widower and prone to long, animated conversations with his late wife, does not set great store by reality. (1991)

buffer (1749) British; applied to a silly, incompetent, or reactionary old man; usually in the phrase *old buffer*; probably from the obsolete verb *buff* imitative of the sound of a soft body being struck, or from the obsolete verb *buff* stutter ■ *London Review of Books:* I take my stand among the other old buffers here. (1979)

codger (1756) Applied especially to an old man with strange habits; usually in the phrase *old codger*; perhaps a variant of *cadger* sponger ■ Percy Bysshe Shelley: I . . . sign the agreement for the old codger's house. (1821)

poppa stoppa (1944) US, Black English; applied especially to an elderly man who is smart or effective; rhyming form on *poppa* father

An old woman

trot (1530) Dated, derogatory; usually in the phrase *old trot*; from Anglo-Norman *trote*, of unknown origin ■ E. V. Lucas: Miss Graham got an old trot after a good deal of messing about. (1906)

old girl (1791) ■ *Guardian:* If she felt any real regret over her final farewell, Dame Joan Sutherland never showed it. . . . Besides, she didn't want anyone to start saying 'Why does the old girl go on still?' (1991)

tab (1909) Derogatory; usually in the phrase *old tab*; short for earlier obsolete slang *tabby* (catty) older woman ■ Ruth Rendell: We've got some old tab coming here. . . . Pal of my ma-in-law's. (1971)

biddy (1938) Derogatory; usually in the phrase *old biddy*; from earlier (derogatory) sense, woman ■ *Sunday Times:* Most can look upon La Cicciolina and think only what an entirely unerotic old biddy she is. (1993)

ma (1951) Used as a title or form of address for an older (married) woman; from earlier sense, mother; shortening of *mamma* ■ P. G. Wodehouse: 'Did Ma Purkiss make a speech?' 'Yes, Mrs Purkiss spoke.' (1966)

See also **bag, boiler, crow, old boot**, and **trout** under An ugly person or thing at **Beauty & Ugliness** (p. 219).

An (old) person with old-fashioned or reactionary ideas or habits

has-been (1606) Applied to someone who is no longer as successful, famous, important, etc. as they once were; from *has* 3 present singular of *have* + *been* past participle of *be* ■ Joseph Wambaugh: When I retire I'm just a has-been. (1972)

fogy, fogey (1780) Usually in the phrase *old fogy*; related to obsolete slang *fogram* old-fashioned person, of unknown origin ■ John Rae: Some old fogey they have dragged out of retirement.

fossil (1857) From earlier sense, remains of a living thing preserved in the ground ■ *Guardian*: Today's young bloods, though heirs to the Osborne revolution, mostly regard the man himself as an old fossil. (1992)

moss-back (1878) US; from earlier sense, large old fish so sluggish that it has a growth of algae on its back ■ *Trevanian*: The moss-backs of the National Gallery had pulled off quite a coup in securing the Marini Horse for a one-day exhibition. (1973)

fuddy-duddy (1904) Origin unknown ■ Nevil Shute: People may call the Sheikh of Khulal an old fuddy-duddy, but he's an important man in these parts. (1951)

fud, fudd (1910) Orig and mainly US; usually in the phrase *old fud*; shortened from *fuddy-duddy*, perhaps later reinforced by the name of Elmer Fudd, character in Bugs Bunny cartoons from *c*1939 ■ *New Yorker*: Steve Martin playing straight man to his fud, they're a manic-depression team. (1984)

dug-out (1912) Applied to someone of outdated appearance or ideas, especially a retired officer, etc. recalled to temporary military service; from the notion of digging out something previously disposed of by burying; compare earlier *dug-out* canoe made from a hollowed-out tree trunk, excavated shelter ■ A. J. Toynbee: These 'elder statesmen' are the last people to whom a community can safely commit its destinies in an emergency, since . . . these 'dug-outs' are doubly incapacitated. (1939)

blimp, Blimp, Colonel Blimp (1934) British; from Colonel *Blimp*, the name of a character invented by David Low (1891–1963), cartoonist and caricaturist, pictured as a rotund pompous ex-officer voicing a rooted hatred of new ideas ■ *Daily Telegraph*: His usual comic character of pub pundit or cockney blimp. (1968). Hence **blimpish** (1938), **blimpishness** (1941)

fart (1937) Usually in the phrase *old fart*; from earlier sense, escape of intestinal gas from the anus ■ *Ink*: Marty Feldman said to the judge as he left the witness stand, 'I don't think he even knew I was here, the boring old fart.' (1971) ■ *Radio Times*: He has been critical of some of the more 'right-on' comedians, some of whom he thinks have sold out. 'You get older and turn into more of a fart. That's what everyone does really.' (1994)

Old-fashioned, outdated

mossy (1904) US; applied to someone or something extremely reactionary or conservative; from the notion of moss growing on old things

old hat (1911) ■ Val Gielgud: She . . . had made all jokes on the subject of mothers-in-law not only 'old hat' but . . . meaningless. (1974)

hairy (1950) Orig US; from the notion of something so old that it has grown hairs

Senility

dodder (1819) Used of an old person to denote slow and shaking progress; from earlier sense, tremble ■ Mrs. Humphry Ward: Old Alresford, too, was fast doddering off the stage. (1894). Hence **doddery** (1866) ■ *Chambers's Journal*: The old man . . . seemed to have become very doddery as he descended from the buggy. (1921)

gaga (1917) Applied to dottiness in old age; from French *gaga* senile person, senile ■ Angus Wilson: If Godmanchester was so gaga that he blabbed like this, then our prospects were alarming. (1961). Hence **gaga** used as a noun to denote a senile person (1938) ■ Arthur Koestler: Couldn't understand what he said. . . . Disastrous old gaga. (1941)

An old or worn-out thing

chestnut (1880) Orig US; applied to a too-often-repeated story, and hence to anything stale or trite; origin uncertain, but the following is recorded by W. Dimond *Broken Sword* (1816): Zavior. . . . When suddenly from the thick boughs of a cork tree—*Pablo.* (Jumping up.) A chestnut, Captain, a chestnut. . . . Captain, this is the twenty-seventh time I have heard you relate this story, and you invariably said, a chestnut, till now ■ *Listener*: Souzay's recital [of songs] . . . is a rare and welcome experience—the more so as on this occasion the chestnuts of the repertoire are avoided. (1962)

rinky-dink (1956) US; applied to something worn out or antiquated; from earlier sense, something worthless ■ *New Yorker*: Red Garter . . . eighteen-nineties rinky-dink, complete with fire engine, but the banjo band is above average. (1969)

An old or worn-out vehicle

crock (1903) From earlier sense, debilitated old person ■ H. G. Wells: I understand you want all of these out-of-date crocks of yours . . . to fly again. (1935)

tin Lizzie (1915) Applied to an old or decrepit car; *Lizzie* from the female forename, an abbreviation of *Elizabeth*; originally applied to an early model of Ford car ■ D. M. Davin: The pace they drove their old tin lizzies. (1949)

struggle-buggy (1925) US, dated; applied especially to a battered old motor vehicle

heap (1926) Applied especially to a battered old motor vehicle ■ C. F. Burke: You will be like a guy who paid no attention to his heap and it broke down in the traffic. (1969)

jalopy, jalloppy, jaloppi(e), jollopy (1929) Orig US; applied to a battered old motor vehicle, and also to an old aeroplane; origin unknown ■ M. E. B. Banks: Perhaps a succession of broken down jalopies has impaired my faith in the internal combustion engine. (1955)

oil-burner (1938) Applied to a run-down vehicle which uses too much engine oil

orphan (1942) Applied to a discontinued model of motor vehicle

rust-bucket (1945) Applied (*North American*) to an old rusty ship or (*mainly Australian*) to an old rust-ridden car ■ *Truck & Bus Transportation*: The oldest Volvos . . . are far from being rust buckets. (1984)

banger (1962) British; usually in the phrase *old banger*; from the noise it makes when running ■ *Times*: It is true though that one misses out on one's husband's early years of struggle: the rented flats, . . . the third-hand old bangers, the terrifying overdraft. (1985)

Worn out by long or rough usage or by neglect

moth-eaten (1551) ■ *Daily Telegraph*: Alf Gover's precious but cramped, moth-eaten old cricket school in Wandsworth. (1991)

the worse for wear (1782) ■ T. Berger: The vehicles in view were routine automobiles, two of them the worse for wear, with dents and rust and jagged antenna-stems. (1982)

rusty (1796) Applied to something that has deteriorated through lack of practice; from earlier sense, affected by rust ■ James Payn: To have to admit that her French was a little rusty. (1888)

played out (1863) ■ *Independent on Sunday*: Romania's National Theatre of Craiova . . . had previously seemed to offer no more than redundant allegories on played-out revolutions. (1991)

warby (1923) Australian; compare *warb* disreputable person ■ Robert Conquest: They're old police boots, a bit worn down in the heels and warby in the soles. (1978)

past it (1928) Applied especially to people past their prime ■ John Guthrie: One never dreamed of going to them for advice. The fact was they were past it; they had lived their lives. (1950)

beat-up (1930) Mainly US ■ W. R. Burnett: The girl was sitting once more in the beat-up leather chair. (1953)

shot (1933) Mainly US ■ G. V. Higgins: Your boiler is one of those old things . . . I think it's about shot. (1981)

clapped out (1946) British; from the past participle of *clap* hit ■ *Daily Express*: The clapped-out car handed in for replacement. (1960)

over the hill (1950) Orig US; applied especially to people past their prime ■ *New York Times Book Review*: Must you feel 'over the hill' after 40? (1962)

stove-up (1974) North American; from earlier sense, (of a person) exhausted ■ D. Sears: An elderly man in levis and stove-up range-boots was . . . in the lower bunk. (1974)

To be old or worn out

have (or have grown) whiskers (1935) Applied especially to news, a story, etc. that is no longer novel ■ D. O'Sullivan: 'Did I ever tell you the one about the Scotsman and the octopus?' . . . 'It has whiskers.' (1977)

have had it (1959) From earlier sense, be defeated or killed ■ *New Zealand Listener*: He re-wound the cord and tried again: no spark. 'It's had it, I think.' (1959)

To remove or dismiss because of old age or obsolescence

pension off (1848) From the notion of giving a pension to an old person on retirement ■ *Listener*: The convention system . . . is an old and cunning harridan, as irrelevant as Mayor Daley, and should be pensioned off. (1968)

A place for old people

granny flat (1965) Applied to a flat for an old person, especially in a relative's house

Costa Geriatrica (1977) British, jocular; applied to a coastal area with a large residential population of old and retired people, especially the south coast of England; after *Costa Brava*, etc. from Spanish *costa* coast + mock-Latin *geriatrica* of or for the elderly

7. Weather

(See also under **Temperature** p. 372.)

Hughie (1912) Australian & New Zealand; diminutive of the male personal name *Hugh*; used as the name of the 'god' of the weather, esp. in the phrase *send her down, Hughie!* an appeal for rain

QBI (1938) RAF, dated; abbreviation of 'quite bloody impossible' (flying conditions) ■ *Times*: Instructions . . . as to height and position to be kept when flying in controlled areas during 'Q.B.I.' conditions. (1938)

Rain

spit (1567) Applied to rain (and formerly also

snow) falling in small scattered drops ■ John Service: Feeling that it was spittin' through the win', I quickened my step. (1887)

spot (1849) Orig dialectal; applied to rain falling in scattered drops ■ *Westminster Gazette*: It began to spot with rain. (1909)

send her (or it) down, Davy (also Hughie, etc.) (1919) Australian & New Zealand; used to express a wish for rain to fall ■ K. S. Prichard: Miners and prospectors would turn out and yell to a dull, dirty sky clouded with red dust: 'Send her down! Send her down, Hughie!' (1946)

piss (1950) Denoting rain falling heavily; often used with *down* ■ June Thomson: Tucker wouldn't come . . . not with it pissing down with rain. (1977)

Wind

Irishman's hurricane, **Irish hurricane (1827)** Applied jocularly to a flat calm

cock-eye Bob, **cock-eyed Bob (1894)** Australian; applied to a cyclone, and also to a thunderstorm

twister (1897) Orig US; applied to a whirlwind, originally specifically in the Mississippi

8. Temperature

Cold weather

brass monkey (1857) Used allusively in referring to very cold weather; mainly in the phrase *cold enough to freeze the balls off a brass monkey*; possibly from *brass monkey* plate on a man-of-war's deck on which cannon balls were stacked, which contracted in cold weather and made its load of balls unstable ■ *Guardian*: Brass monkey weather. (1973)

Uncomfortably cold

parky (1895) British; origin unknown ■ Tim Heald: 'Cold isn't it?' 'Pretty parky.' (1975)

Hot weather

scorcher (1874) Applied to a very hot day ■ F. V. Kirby: A heavy mist . . . gave promise of a hot day, and it turned out a scorcher. (1899)

region ■ Jon Cleary: You hear the twister warnings, too? (1977)

Fog

pea-souper (1890) Applied to a dense yellow fog (formerly in London and other cities); from the colour of soup made from dried peas

A weather forecaster

the weatherman (1901) From earlier sense, one who observes the weather ■ *Listener*: We asked the weatherman, Jack Scott, to demonstrate some of those extraordinary regional variations for us. (1983)

sizzler (1901) Orig US; applied to a very hot day or period ■ G. H. Lorimer: Satan may be down in Arizona cooking up a sizzler for the corn belt. (1904)

Comfortably warm

warm as toast (1855) ■ Robert Louis Stevenson: It keeps this end of the valley as warm as a toast. (1883)

(Uncomfortably) hot

roasting (1768) ■ W. C. Baldwin: In the middle of a regular roasting hot day. (1863)

baking (1786) ■ George Orwell: It's getting beastly hot, isn't it? . . . Isn't it simply *baking*! (1934)

boiling (1930) ■ Rosamond Lehmann: He was the sort of boy who would . . . declare on the coldest day that he was boiling. (1930)

scorching (1940) ■ Arnold Wesker: This hut . . . is going to be your home for the next eight scorching weeks. (1962)

Location and Movement

1. Places

A locality

parts (c1400) Often in the phrase *in these/those parts* ■ *Oxford Mail*: When we first saw the man we thought nothing about it. Roadsters are a common sight in these parts. (1970)

way (1573) Used after a place-name to denote a particular locality ■ **Chester Himes**: Then he met a high-yellah gal, a three-quarter keltz, from down Harlem way. (1938)

neck of the woods (1839) Orig US; applied originally to a settlement in wooded country, and hence to any district or neighbourhood, especially one in which a particular person lives ■ *Listener*: Some jerk has applied for a job as the new Cyril Connolly. Perhaps you would look him over, he lives in your neck of the woods. (1967)

possie, pozzy (1915) Orig & mainly Australian & New Zealand; often applied specifically to a military position; from *pos(ition + -ie* ■ *Chronicles of the New Zealand Expeditionary Force*: In the small hours we reached our next 'possie'—a shell-torn gully near Pusieux. (1919)

nabe (1935) US; from the pronunciation of *neighb(ourhood*

turf (1953) Orig and mainly US; applied to the streets controlled by a juvenile street gang and regarded by them as their territory, and hence (1962) to the part of a city or other area in which a criminal, detective, etc. operates ■ **H. E. Salisbury**: These blocks constituted the 'turf' of a well-known street-gang. (1959) ■ **D. Bennett**: Special Branch would not want to be involved in a killing so far from their own turf. (1976)

twenty (1975) Orig and mainly US; used on Citizens' Band radio to denote one's location or position; shortened from *10-20* in the 'ten-code', a police (and subsequently CB) communication code ■ *Citizens' Band*: Thank you Silver Fox for your excellent work in what is a very important area, with . . . all the fender-benders that occur around that twenty. (1985)

Everywhere

all over the shop (1874) Often implying random or disordered scattering ■ **J. I. M. Stewart**: At one of Anthea Gender's [parties] one was substantially although not too obtrusively in the presence of grandees drawn from all over the shop. (1978)

all over the auction (1930) Australian ■ **Nevil Shute**: You'd be surprised at the number of letters that there are—all over the auction. (1960)

Cities and towns

the Smoke, the Big Smoke, the Great Smoke (1848) British & Australian; applied to any large city, especially (*British*) London ■ *Telegraph* (Brisbane): He falls for a beautiful blonde who wants him to stay in the Big Smoke—but city life has no appeal. (1968) ■ *New York Daily News*: 'Casinos . . . ?' echoed Harry. Derek nodded. 'One in Brighton, one up in the Smoke.' (1989)

Birmingham

Brum (1862) Shortening of *Brummagem*, dialect form of *Birmingham*

Boston, Massachusetts

Bean Town (1901) From the inhabitants' legendary liking for beans ■ **Robert Ludlum**: He's what they call a functioning alcoholic, something of a character in Bean Town's shadier districts. (1990)

Chicago

the Windy City (1887) ■ **Kyril Bonfiglioli**: The scent of the Chicago River as it slides greasily under the nine bridges in the centre of the Windy City. (1979)

Chi (1895) Abbreviation; pronounced /ʃaɪ/

Dallas, Texas

Big D (1930) ■ **Norman Mailer**: They found her vagina in North Carolina and part of her gashole in hometown Big D. (1967)

Hollywood

Tinseltown (1975) Often used in allusion to the supposedly glittering world of Hollywood cinema ■ *Economist*: It is sad for Tinseltown that Mr Puttnam could not find out whether his hunch was right. (1987)

New Orleans

the Big Easy (1970) Apparently coined by James Conaway as the title of a novel, and popularized by the 1986 film based on this

New York

the Big Town (1902)

the Big Apple (1909), the Apple (1938), the Big A (1980) Apparently from earlier obsolete US slang *big apple* important person, big shot (compare *top banana* big shot); in early use mainly applied specifically to the top New York City racetracks; adopted into jazz musicians' slang in the 1930s, and often applied specifically to Harlem; revived and popularized in 1971 by Charles Gillett, president of the New York Convention and Visitors Bureau, as part of a publicity campaign for the city ■ *United States 1980/81*: Many Broadway-bound shows play Chicago before heading for the Big Apple. (1979)

Philadelphia

Philly, Phillie (1891) From *Phil(adelphia + -y* ■ *Rogue*: After a while, Kitty murmured something to Cappy, and he held her close, answering, 'We'll just have to wait till we pull into Philly, honey.' (1961)

Portsmouth

Pompey (1899) Applied to the town and dockyards of Portsmouth, and also to Portsmouth Football Club; alteration of *Portsmouth*, perhaps influenced by the name of the Roman general ■ *C. S. Forester*: The grim wife he had in Pompey. (1943)

San Francisco

Bay City (1879) ■ *Raymond Chandler*: They put Dad in charge of the Bureau of Records and Identification, which in Bay City is about the size of a tea-bag. (1940)

Sydney

steak and kidney (1905) Australian; rhyming slang

Ypres

Wipers (1914) Representing the anglicized pronunciation of *Ypres* adopted by Allied servicemen during World War I, when the town was the site of three significant battles involving great loss of life ■ *Nancy Mitford*: We'd like to see old Wipers again. . . . We had the time of our lives in those trenches when we were young. (1960)

A city, place or situation with the stated characteristics

-ville (1843) Orig US; used as a suffix forming the name of fictitious places with reference to a particular (often unpleasant) quality; from French *ville* town, as in many American town names ■ *J. Aitkin*: University? Man, that's just dragsville. (1967)

city (1960) Orig US ■ *Rolling Stone*: All my life I'm taught by my family *to keep it going*, don't get boring at the dinner table. When I learned I could do that by just being honest, whole vistas of trouble opened up. I get on a talk show, I get talking and *whoa!* Trouble city! (1979)

Countries and states: Australia

the other side (1827) Australian & New Zealand; applied to the other side of Australia

Oz (1908) Orig Australian; alteration of initial element of *Australia* ■ *Private Eye*: If they guess I'm from Oz the shit will really hit the fan. (1970)

Aussie (1917) Australian; compare earlier sense, an Australian ■ *Australian*: 'Cheers from A Sunburnt

Country!' the advertisement trumpets. 'Toast your Pommie mates with a gift from good old Aussie.' (1974)

Australasia; the antipodes

down under (1886) Usually applied to Australia or New Zealand or both ■ *Daily Mail*: The steeplechaser Kinlark, a gift to the Prince from 'down under'. (1922)

Britain

the Old Dart (1892) Australian & New Zealand; applied to Britain (or England) as the mother country; *dart* apparently an alteration of *dirt* ■ *Bulletin* (Sydney): He was a forward in the British team of 1904, led by Bedell Sievwright, about the best side from the Old Dart to visit these shores. (1933)

Blighty, blighty (1915) British, army slang, dated; used by soldiers serving abroad; contracted form, originating in the Indian army, of Hindustani *bilāyatī, wilāyatī* foreign, European ■ *J. R. Ackerley*: I was not happy in Blighty. (1968)

Gibraltar

Gib (1869) Abbreviation ■ *Scotsman*: For an imaginatively designed haven of peace amid the bustle of Gib's traffic visit the Almeda Botanical Gardens. (1995)

Hong Kong

Honkers (1987) From *Hong K(ong + -ers*, perhaps subliminally influenced by *honkers* drunk ■ *Guardian*: In describing, not exactly flatteringly, the attitudes of pink-faced young westerners in Hong Kong, he writes as follows. ' . . . They take these Cathay Pacific stewardesses (known in the local argot as LBFMs, little brown fucking machines) to the discotheques. . . .' Word of this broke in Honkers. Cathay Pacific, seething, politely turned the author away at the departure gate. (1992)

Mesopotamia

Mespot, Mess-pot (1917) Dated; abbreviation ■ *John Buchan*: What front were you on—the Western, Palestine, Mespot? (1933)

New South Wales

Ma State, Ma (1906) Australian; from *ma* mother; from the fact that New South Wales was the earliest Australian colony ■ *Bulletin* (Sydney): South Australia . . . missed a great opportunity by not bunging a few million over to the Ma State. (1954)

New Zealand

Pig Island (1917) Australian & New Zealand; from the introduction there by Captain Cook of pigs, which later reverted to a wild state ■ *Frank Sargeson*: 'Young man,' he said, 'it is my advice that you get off back to England. . . . Pig Island is no place for the likes of you.' (1967)

the Shaky Isles, the Shivery Isles (1933) Australian; from the frequency of earthquakes in New Zealand

Queensland

Bananaland (1893) Australian, jocular; from the abundance of bananas grown in the state

Soviet Union

Redland (1942) Dated, orig US; from its association with *reds* communists ■ William Garner: Morton picked up the camera. . . . He said, 'Exacta. Made in Dresden. East Germany. A favourite with Redland agents.' (1969)

Tasmania

Tassie, Tassey, Tassy (1892) From *Tas(mania + -ie* ■ *Herald* (Melbourne): Come to 'Tassie' the Casino State. (1977)

USA

Uncle Sam (1813) Usually applied to the US nation or government; jocular extension of the letters *US* ■ *Economist*: Israel, of course, was helped by having Uncle Sam on its side. (1988)

Stateside, stateside (1943) Used as an adjective and adverb denoting the USA ■ Len Deighton: Fernie fixed the consignment to a ship heading stateside. I notified my contacts in New York. (1963)

the Big PX (1962) US, military slang; applied to the USA as a place of easily available consumer goods and home comforts; from *PX* the name applied to shops on US military bases

the world (1971) US, military slang; used by soldiers serving abroad, originally in Vietnam; mainly in the phrase *go (get, etc.) back to the world* ■ D. A. Dye: You'll kill boo-coo gooks before you go on back to the World. (1987)

U.S. of A. (1973) Abbreviation of *United States of America* ■ A. Melville-Ross: You'll be told . . . that won't be until you're back in the US of A under tight security wraps. (1983)

Vietnam

Nam, 'Nam (1969) US; used especially in the context of the Vietnam War; abbreviation ■ *Publishers Weekly*: Four Americans caught in Vietnam. . . . The GIs become buddies in Germany. . . . Now in 'Nam' they hope their camaraderie will be closer still. (1974)

Buildings and institutions

the Rag (and Famish) (1858) Dated; applied to the Army and Navy Club in London ■ Nevill & Jerningham: The familiar name of the 'Rag', by which it is generally known, was invented by Captain William Duff, of the 23rd Fusiliers. . . . Coming in to supper late one night, the refreshment obtainable appeared so meagre that he nicknamed the club the 'Rag and Famish'. (1908)

the Yard (1888) Short for *Scotland Yard*, the name of the headquarters of the Metropolitan Police ■ *Daily Mail*: The Yard was called in after the collapse of a small engineering company, which had traded successfully with the MoD for more than 25 years. (1991)

Buck House (1922) Jocular alteration of *Buckingham Palace*, the name of the British

sovereign's residence in London ■ George Sims: They said it was like Buck House but it was a right load of old schmutter! You see, everyone's an antique dealer today. (1967)

the 'In' and 'Out' (1925) Applied to the Naval and Military Club in London; from the words 'In' and 'Out' painted on pillars at the entrance to and exit from the club ■ *Guardian*: Two London clubs, the 105-year-old Naval and Military, better known as the 'In and Out', and the 92-year-old Devonshire, may merge. (1967)

Ally Pally (1949) Rhyming abbreviation of *Alexandra Palace*, the name of a building in Muswell Hill, North London, the original headquarters of BBC Television ■ Simon Brett: Back in Ally Pally days . . . you were just a technical boffin with all the sound recording stuff. (1979)

Thiefrow (1973) Applied jocularly to London's Heathrow Airport, after its then reputation for lax security, luggage theft, etc.; alteration of *Heathrow*, after *thief* ■ E. Ward: Jewel couriers are hired for . . . security and insurance. Special air freight is available but London Airport is still called Thief Row. (1981)

Harvey Nicks (1991) Applied to Harvey Nichols, an upmarket department store in West London ■ *Radio Times*: Dame Edna recommended the giving of possums for Christmas. Can one buy them at Harvey Nicks? (1997)

Prisons

the Moor (1869) Applied to Dartmoor Prison in Devon; abbreviation ■ Frank Norman: I'm doing a bleeding neves. I'll be going down the Moor soon that will be the third poxy time. (1958)

the Ville, the 'Ville, the (')ville (1903) Applied to Pentonville Prison in London; abbreviation ■ L. Henderson: Yeah, that's right, he was in the 'Ville. (1972)

the Scrubs (1923) Applied to Wormwood Scrubs Prison in London; abbreviation ■ Allan Prior: He had . . . taken his medicine, which had turned out to be three years in the Scrubs. (1966)

Big Q (1961) Applied to San Quentin Prison in California

Roads

drag (1851) Now mainly US; especially in the phrase *the main drag* ■ J. P. Carstairs: We drove through . . . the main drag of Babaki. (1965)

stem (1914) US; especially in the phrase *the main stem*

the Main Stem (1928), the Big Stem (1934) US; applied to Broadway or the entertainment area around it ■ J. P. McEvoy: The Main Stem hears under cover that 'Get Your Girl' may fold up soon for lack of suitable house. (1928)

The sea

the pond (1641) Now mainly US; mainly applied specifically to the North Atlantic Ocean; often in the phrase *on this (or the other) side of the pond* in Britain, or North America ■ John Motley: I should have been very sorry to have crossed the Atlantic (or the pond, as the sailors call it) without a single storm. (19832)

the herring-pond (1686) Mainly applied specifically to the North Atlantic Ocean

the big pond (1833) Applied to the (North) Atlantic Ocean ■ *Outing* (US): [They] have hardly sustained their reputation on either side of the big pond. (1902)

the ditch (1841) Applied in naval slang to the sea; formerly applied specifically in US slang to the Atlantic Ocean, and in R.A.F. slang to the English Channel ■ *Manual of Seamanship*: A smart seaman would not talk officially of the sea by a favourite slang expression 'the ditch'. (1922)

the drink (1856) Orig US; from earlier sense, any body of water, including a river ■ Laurence Meynell: [He] had fished us out of the drink just, and only just, in time. (1960)

the salt chuck (1868) W Canadian and NW US; Chinook jargon, from *salt* + *chuck* water ■ *Islander* (Victoria, British Columbia): In 1905, most people lived close to the saltchuck and along Rainey Creek. (1975)

the big drink (1882) US; applied to the ocean, often specifically the Atlantic Ocean; compare earlier application to the Mississippi River ■ M. E. Braddon: I was coming across the Big Drink as fast as a Cunard could bring me. (1882)

2. **Habitation, Territory**

A dwelling, a house, a building

drum (1846) Applied especially to someone's home; from earlier sense, street, from Romany *drom* road ■ Louis Southworth: They probably checked at the Probation Office as soon as they left my drum. (1966)

place (1891) Applied to a person's home ■ *Screw*: Young male nude model. Experienced, handsome. . . . Completely versatile and cooperative. Your place or mine. (1972)

pogey (1891) North American, dated; applied to a hostel or poor-house; origin unknown

digs (1893) British; applied to lodgings; short for obsolete *diggings* in same sense, perhaps from the notion of entrenching oneself in a place ■ Anthony Lejeune: His old digs . . . where he lived when he used to work for us. (1959)

hang-out (1893) Applied to a place one lives in or often visits; from *hang out* reside, frequent ■ *Globe & Mail Magazine* (Toronto): It is 3 a.m. in a steam bath known as an after-midnight homosexual hangout. (1968)

semi (1912) British; short for *semi-detached* (*house*) ■ Barbara Pym: That house which, in the estate agents' language, was on its way to becoming a 'twenty thousand semi'. (1977)

the puddle (1889) Mainly applied specifically to the North Atlantic Ocean; often in the phrase *on this* (or *the other*) *side of the puddle* in Britain, or North America ■ *SLR Camera*: For many years the American company . . . have made fine enlarging frames (masking frames this side of the puddle) both for retail distribution and for exclusive use by Simmon-Emega. (1978)

the Big Ditch (1909) US; applied to the North Atlantic Ocean

the oggin (1946) Naval slang; apparently from *hog-wash*, from an earlier contemptuous application of *hog-wash* 'disgusting liquid' to the sea ■ Dan Lees: No one told the two gunners that the sub was about to crash-dive and they had to run like hell to avoid being left behind in the oggin. (1973)

the Med (1948) Applied to the Mediterranean Sea; abbreviation ■ Gillian Freeman: We went all round the Med., Istanbul, Capri, Gib. (1955)

Heavenly bodies: The moon

Oliver, oliver (1781) Dated; possibly from *Oliver* Cromwell (1599–1658), but no convincing reason for the application has ever been suggested ■ *New Review*: 'There's a moon out.' 'The better for us to pick 'em off, Dan,' I returned, laughing at him. 'What—Oliver? damn Oliver!' said Zacchary. 'Let's push forward and come to quarters.' (1895)

The sun

currant bun (1938) Rhyming slang

pad (1914) Applied to a place to sleep, a lodging (from earlier sense, bed), and hence to someone's home

gaff (1932) Applied especially to someone's home; compare earlier senses, fair, cheap place of public entertainment; ultimate origin unknown ■ Julian MacLaren-Ross: I was keeping an eye on the gaff—seen you going in. (1961)

walk-back (1945) US; applied to a rear apartment

stash (1946) Mainly US; from earlier sense, hiding place ■ *Listener*: Susan Sontag went to see Philip Johnson, the New York architect, or rather she 'moseyed along to his stash on Park'. (1965)

hoochie, hoochy, hooch, hootch (1952) Services' slang; applied to a shelter or dwelling, especially one that is insubstantial or temporary; perhaps from Japanese *uchi* dwelling ■ *Fremdsprachen*: A stereo set was blaring in an enlisted men's hootch shortly after midnight. (1971)

condo (1964) Orig & mainly North American; applied to an owner-occupied flat; abbreviation of *condominium*

granny flat (1965) Applied to a flat for an old person, especially in a relative's house ■ Michael

Innes: It seemed wholly amiable in the Mullions to incorporate this not particularly close kinswoman in their household, even if it was on what was coming to be known as the granny-flat principle. (1981)

warehouse (1970) US; applied to a large and impersonal institution providing accommodation for mental patients, old people, or poor people

des res (1986) British, orig estate agents' slang; applied to a house or other dwelling presented as a highly desirable purchase; shortened from *desirable residence* ■ *Times*: The days of the 'des res' that clearly isn't are set to end for estate agents. (1990)

Parts of a dwelling: A door

Rory O'More, rory (1892) Rhyming slang; from the name of a legendary Irish rebel ■ James Curtis: Some lousy berk must have been snooping around the place and found that rory open. (1936)

The floor

Rory O'More, rory (1857) Rhyming slang; from the name of a legendary Irish rebel

Stairs

apples and pears, apples (1857) British; rhyming slang ■ J. G. Bennett: One of the removal men asked him if a sofa was to go 'up the apples'. (1962)

A dweller

slummy, slummie (1934) Applied to a slum-dweller; from *slum* squalid neighbourhood + *-y*

3. **Remoteness & Nearness**

Remote

miles from anywhere, miles from nowhere (1908) ■ *Daily Mail*: The old boat 'conked out' miles from anywhere. (1929)

A remote place

back of (or o') Bourke (1898) Australian; often used adjectivally; from *Bourke*, a town in the extreme west of New South Wales ■ *Canberra Times*: One of the customers whose accent was decidedly back o' Bourke complained that she had mixed up his order. (1981)

the sticks (1905) Orig US ■ Whiteman & McBride: They had all the real New Yorker's prejudice against 'the sticks'. (1926)

tank town (1906) US; originally applied to a small unimportant town at which trains stopped to take on water

boondock (1909) US, orig military slang; usually used in the plural; from Tagalog *bundok* mountain ■ *Spectator*: Those who have been feeling the public pulse out in the boondocks report a good deal of unrest. (1965)

Nar Nar Goon (1918) Australian; used as the name of any small, insignificant, and remote

■ James Patrick: Big Fry . . . tauntingly called out: 'We're the slummies!' (1973)

guinea-pig (1939) British, dated; applied to an evacuee or billetee during World War II; apparently from the fact that the billeting allowance was one guinea (£1 5p)

To reside in or frequent a place

hang out (1811) ■ P. G. Wodehouse: The head of the family has always hung out at the castle. (1936)

Homeless

on the streets (or street) (1852)

An area for which one has responsibility; territory

stamping ground (1821) Applied to a place where someone may generally be found ■ *Independent*: Tom Moody, back on his old stamping ground after joining Worcestershire this season with Warwickshire's blessing, made 91. (1991)

manor (1924) British; applied originally to a police district or similar administrative area, and hence (1959) more generally to someone's own particular territory ■ *Independent on Sunday*: 'The Brindles, the Richardsons and the Frasers used to keep order in this manor,' a garage owner said. (1991)

patch (1963) British; applied to an area for which a police officer has responsibility, and hence more generally to someone's own particular territory ■ D. Devine: Smith was from the south and had never before turned up in Christie's patch. (1969)

town; from the name of a small town southeast of Melbourne ■ *Age* (Melbourne): Television football commentaries generally tend to be about as rewarding as a night game at Nar Nar Goon football ground in a power strike. (1981)

Woop Woop (1918) Australian; used as the name of an imaginary town in the remote outback, supposedly backward; jocular formation, probably influenced by the use of reduplication in Aboriginal languages to indicate plurality or intensity ■ *Sydney Morning Herald*: It was like council night in Woop Woop—Federal Parliament on Tuesday, that is. (1986). Hence **the woop-woops** remote country (1950)

boonie (1956) US; usually used in the plural; from *boon(dock* + *-ie*

the middle of nowhere (1960) ■ Adelaide Lubbock: I got going again pretty quickly as I didn't want to be caught by the storm in the middle of nowhere. (1963)

An (unsophisticated) person from a remote place

hick (1565) Now mainly US; pet-form of the personal name *Richard* ■ J. Hansen: He was killed. . . . They just stopped playing him. As though we was such hicks we didn't know there's such a thing as tapes these days

(1970). Hence **hick** used adjectivally to denote lack of sophistication (1920) ■ *Listener*: Telly was still rather a hick affair back in 1951. (1967)

Reuben (1804) North American, dated; from the male personal name

redneck (1830) US ■ *Dialect Notes*: *Redneck, n.*, An uncouth countryman. 'The hill-billies came from the hills, and the rednecks from the swamps.' (1904)

Hoosier (1846) US; from earlier sense, inhabitant of Indiana

hayseed (1851) US, Australian & New Zealand ■ Frank Sargeson: He might be identified as either peasant or hayseed. (1965)

dude (1887) US; applied to a non-westerner or city-dweller who tours or stays in the west of the US, especially a holiday-maker on a ranch; from earlier sense, fastidiously dressed man, dandy; probably from German dialect *Dude* fool ■ Homer Croy: I'm going to put up the finest cattle barn in the state—that is, belonging to a real dirt farmer, not to one of them city dudes. (1924)

jasper (1896) US; from the male personal name *Jasper*

Reub, Rube, rube (1896) North American; short for *Reuben* ■ Joseph Gores: The rube who wanders into the pool hall and loses a few games. . . . Then the bets get bigger and he . . . starts clearing tables. (1973)

hill-billy (1900) Mainly US; from *hill* + *Billy*, pet-form of the male personal name *William* ■ *Daily Mail*: At 47 the hillbilly who used to scratch a living as a dirt farmer at Greasy Creek in the Ozark Mountains has come a long way. (1957)

woodchuck (1931) US; from earlier sense, species of North American marmot ■ R. Banks:

He could go to weddings or funerals . . . and not look like a hick, a woodchuck. (1989)

ridge-runner (1933) US; applied to a Southern mountain farmer

swede-basher (1943) British, jocular; from earlier sense, agricultural worker ■ Joyce Grenfell: I tried to sing a song appropriate for the swede-bashers from Lincolnshire, the Cockneys, Scots . . . , and so on. (1976)

cornball (1952) Orig US; from earlier sense, sweet made of popped corn—from the notion of making corny remarks ■ *Movie*: An expatriate cornball like Jerry Court. (1962)

culchie (1958) Anglo-Irish; apparently an alteration of *Kilti(magh)*, the name of a country town in Co. Mayo ■ Bob Geldof: We Dublin boys called the country pupils 'culchies', which they hated. (1986)

shit-kicker (1966) US

Near

within (a) cooee/cooey (of) (1836) Australian & New Zealand; from the notion of being within hailing distance; *cooee* from Aboriginal (Dharuk) *guwi* a call used to communicate over distance ■ *Weekly News* (Auckland): But nothing that Roux has achieved on this tour came within coo-ee of the effort of Gainsford. (1965)

Distance

klick, click, klik (1967) North American, orig military slang; applied to a kilometre; origin uncertain; used by US service personnel during the Vietnam War ■ J. Savarin: They're gone sixty miles by now. Nearly a hundred klicks, if you prefer. (1982)

4. Movement

To go, walk

ankle (1926) Dated ■ P. G. Wodehouse: Ankling into the hospital and eating my grapes with that woman's kisses hot upon your lips. (1932)

choof, chuff (1947) Australian; from *chuff* puff as a steam-train does ■ B. Hardy: 'If my presence is going to cause trouble,' I said, 'I'd rather not be here, so I think I'll choof off.' (1979)

To go laboriously

traipse, trapes (1593) Origin unknown ■ R. V. Jones: For days we had to traipse for water down six flights of stairs and hundreds of yards to a stand pipe in the road. (1978)

flog (1925) ■ *Times*: [Lorry drivers] are being encouraged to 'flog on' even in bad weather. (1964)

schlep, schlepp, shlep (1963) Mainly US; from earlier sense, drag, carry ■ D. E. Westlake: We don't both have to hang around. Why don't you shlep back to the station? (1972)

yomp (1982) British, orig military slang; applied to marching with heavy equipment over difficult terrain; brought into prominence when used by the Royal Marines during the Falklands conflict; origin uncertain; compare *yump* (of a rally car or its driver) leave the ground while taking a crest at speed ■ *Sunday Times*: So the sweaty soldier yomping to battle ends up with blisters and a pool of water inside the boot. (1984)

trog (1984) British; origin uncertain; perhaps a fanciful blend (compare *trudge, traipse, trek, slog, jog*, etc.) ■ *Sunday Times*: Saudi newspapers . . . made much of the fact that Charles had trogged all the way out to Gatwick and set a precedent. (1987)

To go aimlessly

mooch, mouch (1851) From earlier sense, skulk, loiter; ultimately probably from Old French *muchier* (Norman dialect *mucher*) hide, skulk ■ *Guardian*: The day before I was mooching through Soho, thoughts of fate and folly uppermost. (1991)

shag (1851) Origin unknown ■ W. H. Canaway:
We'd been shagging around over these mountains for four days
now, and we hadn't seen one single musk deer. (1976)

To go in a particular direction

hang (a) left/right (1966) Orig & mainly US;
denoting making a left/right turn, especially in
driving or skiing ■ *Sunday Telegraph*: Hang a right on
Santa Monica Freeway, hang a left on Harbour and another on
Sixth Street. (1984)

To go casually

toddle (1724) Implying short leisurely steps;
often used familiarly to mean simply 'walk, go';
from earlier sense, (of a very young child) walk
unsteadily ■ *Sunday Times*: So would the MP toddle up
the high street and ask real people what they thought? (1993)

sashay, sasshay, sashy (1865) Mainly US;
from earlier sense, perform a chassé; ultimately
representing an altered pronunciation of *chassé*
gliding dance step ■ James Michener: I see her
sashayin' past in a dress I know she stole from Miss Susan.
(1978)

waltz (1887) Often implying casual boldness or
lack of effort; from earlier sense, dance the
waltz ■ Frederick Nolan: He'll walk any nomination . . .
and waltz into the White House without even having to put up
a fight. (1974)

mosey (1891) Orig US; from earlier sense, go
away quickly ■ Diana Ramsay: I thought I'd mosey on
over to the liquor store. (1974)

breeze (1907) Orig US; usually implying a
cheerful casualness ■ Roy Campbell: My favourite
brother George . . . breezed in to look for me. (1951)

To go forcefully

barge (1904) From earlier sense, bump into
something ■ *Chambers's Journal*: I hadn't barged about
the world then. (1923)

To move with a view to initiating action

up (1831) Followed by *and* and a verb denoting
the action ■ Ogden Nash: One of these days not too
remote I'll probably up and cut your throat. (1961)

To lift or carry with effort

lug (c1400) From earlier sense, pull, tug
■ *Independent*: Often he had to lug his tape recorder into an
impossible corner to try to get broadcast-quality sound. (1991)

hike (1867) Applied to lifting or conveying
something forcibly or laboriously; origin
uncertain; compare earlier sense, walk
(vigorously) ■ *Blackwood's Magazine*: We flitted across
the road like ghosts in the moonlight, hiking our equipage, and
deposited same at the door of a wooden inn. (1927)

hoick, hoik (1898) Perhaps a local variant of *hike*
lift ■ *Country Life*: Is there anything conceivably related to
the art of fly fishing in hoicking out trout that have had no
chance to live a natural life? (1972)

schlep, schlepp, shlep (1922) Mainly US; from
Yiddish *shlepn*, from German *schleppen* drag
■ *Publishers Weekly*: The one thing you would not want to

schlep along on a backpacking trip is this book, which runs to
over 340 pages. (1973)

To pull with sudden vigour

yank (1848) Orig US; origin unknown ■ Francis
Chichester: I kept the seaplane on the surface, planing until I
thought it was going as fast as it could, when I yanked the
stick back hard, to pull her off suddenly. (1964)

To put

shove (1827) Usually implying rough, careless,
or rapid placement; from earlier sense, push
roughly ■ Kylie Tennant: They'll only dock my pay or
shove me in clink. (1946)

bung (1839) Usually implying careless
placement; from earlier sense, throw ■ P. G.
Wodehouse: Telling the butler to bung Mr. Mulliner into the
drawing-room and lock up all the silver. (1933)

chuck (1841) Denoting putting (as if) by
throwing carelessly; from earlier sense, throw
■ *Guardian*: If we are all so afraid of happiness, why do we
spend so much time and money in pursuit of it: chucking
alcoholic drinks down our throats . . . etc. (1992)

park (1908) Denoting placing something or
someone temporarily ■ Graham Greene: The girl was
parking her gum on the back of the telephone directory while
she got down to a long satisfactory conversation. (1978)

plonk (1941) Denoting firm placement on to a
horizontal surface; often followed by *down*;
compare earlier sense, hit with a plonking
sound ■ *Spectator*: A nasty-looking structure will be
plonked down in front of King's Cross, thus ruining its two
magnificent archways. (1967)

sling (1972) Denoting careless placement, often
by means of throwing; from earlier sense, throw
forcefully ■ *Guardian*: It [*sc.* the ignition key] will still
be there, to operate the steering column lock—and give
status-conscious customers something impressive to sling
onto the saloon bar counter. (1992)

To pour carelessly

slosh (1875) From earlier sense, splash about in
mud or wet ■ Eugene O'Neill: He sloshes whiskey from
the decanter into both their glasses. (*a*1953)

To move from side to side or up and down

wiggle (a1225) From or related to (Middle) Low
German *wiggelen*, Middle Dutch *wighelen*,
frequentatives formed from the base *wig-*
(compare obsolete English and Scottish dialect
wig move from side to side) ■ G. S. Porter: Father . . .
pulled his lower lip until his ears almost wiggled. (1913)

waggle (1594) A frequentative form of *wag*
■ *Daily Express*: The Nimrod [aircraft] then waggled its
wings and started back. (1972)

jink (1785) Orig Scottish; often implying darting
evasively with sudden quick changes of
direction; apparently onomatopoeic, expressing
the idea of nimble motion ■ *Daily Telegraph*: I can
see him jinking his way past our mid-field players. (1932)

jiggle (1836) A diminutive or frequentative form
of *jig* ■ *Guardian*: When I refuse, his eyebrows jiggle
alarmingly behind his spectacles. (1992)

5. **Falling**

A fall

mucker (1852) British; from *muck* dung, dirt + *-er*; from the notion of falling into muck ■ John Galsworthy: You're riding for a fall and a godless mucker it'll be. (1914)

cropper (1858) Used especially in the phrase *come (fall, get) a cropper*; perhaps from the phrase *neck and crop* ■ *Times*: I came a proper cropper, dearie, all black and blue I was. (1963)

purler (1869) From *purl* overturn + *-er* ■ *Horse & Hound*: Even Up went a real purler at the last fence on the far side. (1976)

gutser, gutzer (1918) Australian & New Zealand; from *guts* belly + *-er* ■ Norman Lindsay: Snowy . . . threw himself recklessly off it and landed such a gutser that he knocked all the wind out of himself. (1933)

smeller (1923) Used especially in the phrase *come a smeller*; perhaps from the notion of 'smelling' the ground ■ P. G. Wodehouse: A man's brain whizzes along for years exceeding the speed limit, and then something suddenly goes wrong with the steering gear and it comes a smeller in the ditch. (1934)

pratfall (1939) Theatrical slang, mainly North American; applied to a comedy fall (on to the buttocks); from *prat* buttocks + *fall*

wipe-out (1962) Surfing; applied to a fall from one's surfboard as a result of a collision with another surfboard or a wave; from the verb *wipe out*

To fall

keel over (1897) From previous sense, capsize ■ *Daily Mail*: The moment when the hero's uncle keeled over in the lobby of the Ritz Hotel with a fatal heart attack. (1991)

pratfall (1940) Theatrical slang, mainly North American; used to denote falling on the buttocks; from the noun *pratfall*

hit the deck (1954) Often used to denote deliberate falling, usually in taking avoiding action ■ *Independent*: As the gunman sprayed shoppers with bullets, Gregory Read, an Australian Vietnam War veteran, ran through the mall yelling at people to 'hit the deck'. (1991)

wipe out (1962) Surfing slang; used to denote knocking or being knocked off one's surfboard; from previous sense, destroy

6. **Speed**

Rate of speed

bat (1824) From earlier sense, a blow or stroke with a bat, club, etc. ■ John Welcome: We turned on to the main . . . road and started going a hell of a bat across the Cotswolds. (1961)

lick (1847) From earlier sense, a spurt at racing ■ Patrick Ruell: Caroline contrived to be first down the gangway and set off along the quay at a good lick. (1974)

A speed of one hundred miles an hour

ton (1954), ton-up (1961) British; used especially with reference to motor cycles; *ton* used especially in the phrase *do the* (or *a*) *ton*; from earlier sense, score of one hundred in a game ■ *Hansard Lords*: In that case you must have been doing a 'ton', if very few cars passed you. (1973)

Fast

like a shot (1809) ■ W. E. Norris: If I could hear of any chance of employment elsewhere, I'd take it like a shot. (1894)

in two (or three) shakes (of a lamb's tail), in a brace (or couple) of shakes (1816) ■ Elizabeth Lemarchand: I'll knock you up bacon and eggs in a brace of shakes. (1973)

double-quick (1822) Orig military, from the notion of marching at twice the speed of 'quick' time ■ John Braine: If we were married and I made just one mistake in business . . . she'd be off double-quick. (1959)

like a dose of salts (1837) From the sudden effect of aperient salts ■ John Wainwright: If we don't hold 'em they'll go through this city like a dose of salts. (1968)

pronto (1850) Orig US; from Spanish *pronto* fast ■ P. Cave: You tell that bastard to come and see me. . . . Pronto. (1976)

nippy (1853) From earlier sense, inclined to nip, sharp ■ I. M. Banks: It's a limited edition; the go-faster model; even nippier than this beast, once it gets going. (1990)

spanking (1857) Dated; from earlier sense, very big or fine ■ F. T. Bullen: A large canoe . . . was coming off to us at a spanking rate. (1899)

lickety-split, lickerty-, licketty-, -ity-, -oty-, -spit (1859) US; fanciful coinage ■ *Last Whole Earth Catalog*: Just like that. Stopped in here a few minutes, then took off up that creek lickety-split. (1972)

on the double, at the double (1865) From earlier sense, (of marching) at a double rate, twice as fast

PDQ, pdq (1875) Abbreviation of *pretty damn quick* ■ Rudyard Kipling: He went as his instructions advised p.d.q.—which means 'with speed'. (1891)

pacey, pacy (1906) From *pace* + *-y* ■ *Daily Telegraph*: The Celeste's low slung, pacey appearance isn't just for show. The 2 litre model has a top speed of 105 mph. (1977)

off the bat (1907) US; used to imply no delay; from the notion of the ball having just been hit by the baseball bat ■ *New Yorker*: You can tell right off the bat that they're wicked, because they keep eating grapes indolently. (1955)

jildi, jeldi, jildy, juldie, etc. **(1919)** Military, orig Anglo-Indian; from the noun *jildi* haste ■ M. K. Joseph: Hey, Antonio, where's me rooty [= bread]? And make it juldy, see? (1957)

like a bat out of hell (1921) ■ Ian Fleming: The motor cyclist . . . had gone like a bat out of hell towards Baker Street. (1961)

in two ups (1934) Australian ■ J. Morrison: Too close to dark now, Mister, but we'll have you out of that in two ups in the morning. (1967)

like gangbusters (1942) Orig and mainly US; from *gangbuster* aggressively successful policeman

like the clappers (1948) British; from *clapper* tongue of a bell ■ John Wain: Seeing it's you, I'm going to surrender like the clappers. (1958)

sharpish (1952) ■ Ted Allbeury: They shuffled him back to Moscow pretty sharpish. (1975)

like a bomb (1954) Orig US

High speed

toe (1889) Australian & New Zealand ■ *Sun-Herald* (Sydney): In Lawson and Hogg we have two penetrating fast bowlers who have enough 'toe' to keep any batsman honest. (1983)

a rate of knots (1892) Originally in the form (*at*) *the rate of knots* ■ Colin Bateman: His eyes were darting from front to wing mirror and our speed was still picking up. You can do a fair rate of knots in a Saab. (1995)

Haste

jildi, jeldi, jildy, juldie, etc. **(1890)** Dated military, orig Anglo-Indian; used in such phrases as *on the jildi* in a hurry, and *do* or *move a jildi*; from Hindustani *jaldi* quickness

To go fast

whizz, whiz (1591) From earlier sense, make a rushing, buzzing sound ■ Ian Hay: Watching for the motors that whizzed . . . along the straight white road. (1914)

streak (1768) Probably an altered spelling of obsolete *streek* go fast, influenced by such phrases as *like a streak* (*of lightning*) fast ■ Elizabeth Lemarchand: I got out at last, and streaked up to the bungalow. (1973)

nip (1825) From earlier sense, pinch ■ Michael Gilbert: If you nip along now . . . you could catch her before the practice starts. (1955)

scoot (1847) Orig US; apparently a variant of earlier obsolete nautical slang *scout* in the same sense ■ *Saturday Review*: He scoots off like a rabbit in the opposite direction. (1892)

travel (1884) ■ Michael Kenyon: Mercy, the lorry's travelling. Foot down. (1970)

belt (1890) Orig dialect and US ■ *New Statesman*: Cor, we used to belt along that road. (1962)

nick (1896) Australian; used to denote going quickly or unobtrusively; perhaps related to *nip* go quickly ■ *Sydney Morning Herald*: There is no lavatory so the Labor candidate . . . and his helpers nick across the road to use Ansett's. (1981)

swing the gate (1898) Australian & New Zealand; used to refer to the fastest shearer in a shearing shed

scorch (1906) From earlier sense, burn ■ A. C. Clarke: By keeping the torp tail-heavy and nose-up he was able to scorch along on the surface like a speed-boat. (1957)

go some (1912) US; from earlier sense, go well ■ James Hackston: He had the easy movements of the retriever, and for a big dog could go some. (1966)

shift (1922) ■ Michael Kenyon: You'll have time for a bite at Murphy's if you shift. (1970)

blind (1923) From the notion of going blindly or heedlessly ■ *Daily Express*: By recreation I do not mean blinding along the Brighton road at fifty miles an hour. (1928)

ball the jack (*c.*1925) US ■ J. H. Street: They think as soon as you die you go balling-the-jack to God. (1941)

barrel (1930) Orig and mainly US; applied especially to a motor vehicle ■ Quentin Tarantino: An old gas-guzzling, dirty, white 1974 Chevy Nova barrels down a homeless-ridden street in Hollywood. (1994)

highball (1935) US; from earlier sense, to signal a train driver to proceed, from the noun *highball* signal to proceed originally given by hoisting a ball ■ *Saturday Evening Post*: Everyone else had highballed . . . out of there. (1946)

pour (on) the coal (1937) Applied to flying an aircraft or driving a motor vehicle; from earlier sense, cause an aircraft to accelerate

bat (1938) From earlier sense, move, go ■ *Reader's Digest*: A Department Sanitation truck was batting along as fast as it could go. (1938)

burn (1942) Applied especially to a motor vehicle ■ *Sunday Mail* (Brisbane): In burns a police car. . . . Out jumps a senior sergeant. (1972)

beetle (1948) From earlier slang sense, move like a beetle ■ Noel Coward: There was . . . a terrible scene . . . and Freda beetled off to America. (1952)

bomb (1960) Orig US ■ Irvine Welsh: Then it comes back: Swanney and Alison takin us doon the stairs, gittin us intae a taxi n bombin up tae the Infirmary. (1993)

zap (1968) From earlier use, representing the sound of a bullet, laser, etc. ■ *Times*: Several smaller craft zap past. (1985)

A fast person or thing

goer (1613) From earlier sense, one who or that which goes ■ Thomas Hughes: The Tally-ho was a tip-top goer, ten miles an hour including stoppages. (1857)

scooter (1917) Mainly US; applied to a fast vehicle, especially a train or car; from *scoot* go fast + *-er* ■ J. Evans: 'We'll use your scooter, Mac. . . . Where's she parked?' . . . I wondered how they knew I had a car. (1948)

quickie, quickey, quicky (1940) Applied especially to something quickly or briefly done;

from *quick* + *-ie* ■ R. H. Rimmer: Yesterday they were asking some of the girls if they were hookers or 'hos'. Kathy told Mohammed that a tough Irish kid offered her ten dollars for a 'quickie'. (1975)

swiftie, **swifty** (1945) Applied to someone who thinks or acts fast; from *swift* + *-ie*

To accelerate

let rip (1843) From *rip* go unchecked ■ *Dumfries Courier*: The present difficult decision . . . will be thrust into insignificance if inflation lets rip again. (1978)

give her (**it**, etc.) **the gun** (1917) Orig US ■ George Bagby: She slid behind the wheel, gave the hearse the gun, swung it around. (1968)

step on the gas, **step on it** (1920) Orig US; applied to acceleration in a motor vehicle, from the notion of pressing the gas pedal with the foot ■ Graham Greene: 'Step on it, Joe.' They ricocheted down the rough path. (1939)

gun (1930) From the phrase *give her the gun* accelerate a vehicle ■ Paul Durst: He gunned the Volkswagen and fell in behind. (1968)

pour (**on**) **the coal** (1937) Applied to accelerating an aircraft ■ J. M. Foster: He poured the coal to his plane and banked to avoid passing too close. (1961)

Acceleration

welly, **wellie** (1977) British; from earlier sense, forceful kick, from the notion of 'kicking' the accelerator of a motor vehicle ■ D. Gethin: 'When I say go, give it some welly. . . . Go.' . . . Explosions sounded. (1983)

To hurry

stir one's stumps (1559) From the notion of moving one's *stumps* (= legs) quickly

crack on (1837) Orig mainly nautical

get a move on (1888) Orig US ■ C. E. Mulford: Come on! Come on!. . . Get a move on! Will you hurry up! (1911)

buck up (1890) ■ Ian Hay: 'Hallo, you fellows—finished?' 'Yes, buck up!' commanded Rumbold. (1913)

get a hump on (1892) US ■ W. E. Wilson: 'Let's git a hump on, Allen,' Abe said; and the two boys dipped their oars deeper into the brown water. (1940)

get or **put one's skates on** (1895) British, orig military ■ W. J. Burley: I'd better be getting my skates on, I'm catching the night train and I haven't done a thing about getting ready. (1976)

get a wiggle on (1896) Orig US ■ *Newsweek*: If Americans don't get a wiggle on . . . they may forfeit their place in the vanguard of the human future that will be lived outside the cradle of Earth. (1990)

shake a leg (1904) Compare earlier sense, dance ■ P. G. Wodehouse: 'Clean this place up.' . . . 'Yes, sir.' 'And shake a leg.' (1952)

drag ass, **haul ass**, **tear ass** (1918) US ■ L. Erdrich: Well, all I can say is he better drag ass to get here, that Gerry. (1984) ■ 'Dr. Dre' et al.: But you know I never stumble or lag last I'm almost home so I better haul ass. (1990) ■ P. Auster: There was no way I was going to let them catch me again. I tore ass out of there and headed for the woods, running for all I was worth. (1991)

make it snappy, **look snappy** (1926) ■ J. I. M. Stewart: Make it snappy. Taxi's waiting. (1976)

rattle one's dags (1968) Australian & New Zealand; *dag* lump of matted wool and excrement on a sheep's behind ■ S. Thorne: Hurry up! Get down there 'n bleed him! Rattle your dags! (1980)

Be quick!

chop-chop (1834) Pidgin English, from Chinese *k'wâi-k'wâi* ■ *Chinese Repository*: 'More soon, more better; sendee chop-chop,' I told him. (1836)

A direct and speedy route

beeline (1830) Orig US; especially in the phrase *make a beeline for*; from the notion that bees take the most direct route in returning to their hives

Slowness

the slows (1843) Applied to an imaginary disease accounting for slowness ■ Dick Francis: They might as well send him [a racehorse] to the knackers. Got the slows right and proper, that one has. (1970)

A slow person or animal

slowcoach (1837) ■ Jerome K. Jerome: There are plenty of lazy people and plenty of slow-coaches, but a genuine idler is a rarity. (1886)

slowpoke (1848) Mainly US; from *slow* + obsolete US *poke* lazy person ■ Salman Rushdie: Come on, slowpoke, you don't want to be late. (1981)

To go slowly

drag the chain (1912) Australian & New Zealand; often used to denote falling behind the rest ■ Gordon Slatter: Stop dragging the chain and have one with me. (1959)

7. **Arrival**

To arrive

show up (1888) Also used elliptically without *up* (1951) ■ *Guardian*: The unfortunate Princess of Wales was disappointed when both Meryl Streep and Shirley MacLaine failed to show up for the premiere of Postcards From The Edge.

(1991) ■ John le Carré: She didn't show. . . . It was the first time she'd broken a date. (1974)

blow in (1895) Orig US ■ *War Illustrated*: He just blew in out of the black-out and asked if he might use the telephone. (1940)

lob (1911) Australian; usually denoting unceremonious arrival; often followed by *in*; probably from earlier sense, move heavily or clumsily ■ *Age* (Melbourne): The Chinese Noodle Shop Restaurant seemed the logical choice, so three of us lobbed there at 8 o'clock. (1984)

roll up (1920) Orig Australian; from earlier sense, congregate, assemble ■ Martin Woodhouse: They had to wait for me to roll up because I had the D.F. set, which meant I was the only one who could pin it down precisely. (1968)

roll in (1985) ■ *More!*: Toby stayed out till gone three one night and then rolled in absolutely plastered. (1992)

To arrive eventually in the stated place or condition

fetch up (1858) Orig US; from earlier sense, come to a stop ■ *Listener*: I grew used to bummelling around the Bond Street dealers and fetching up for tea at the National Gallery or the Tate. (1971)

wind up (1918) ■ *National Observer* (US): Somebody who wants to get away from it all is likely to wind up in a chalet in a Heidilike village on a mountain. (1976)

To announce one's arrival

make one's number (1942) Also in broader sense, make oneself known ■ Donald Seaman: 'Will you go to the conference site today?' 'Might as well make my number with the R.U.C.' (1974)

To approach

belly up (1907) US; denoting a bold approach; originally applied literally to walking up to something (e.g. a bar) and standing with one's stomach against it; usually followed by *to* ■ *Wall Street Journal*: Only a handful of FDIC-administered institutions have been allowed to belly up to its [*sc.* the Federal Reserve's] window. (1989)

A welcome or reception of the stated sort

mitt (1904) In the phrases *the glad mitt* a friendly welcome, *the frozen* (or *icy*) *mitt* an unfriendly welcome; from earlier sense, hand ■ Allan Prior: She'd have taken it and then handed me the frozen mitt. (1960)

8. **Departure**

To go away

cut and run (1704) Orig nautical; applied to a hurried departure in order to escape; from the notion of escaping by cutting the anchor rope rather than taking the time to haul the anchor up ■ *Hutchinson's Pictorial History of the War*: We anticipated a cut-and-run operation by a force consisting of two or three battleships and a couple of carriers. (1945)

push off (1740) From earlier sense, set a boat going by pushing against the shore ■ Emma Page: She must be quite certain to leave when the girl with the frizzy hair decided to push off. (1973)

mizzle (1781) British; origin uncertain; compare Shelta *misli* go ■ R. Llewellyn: There was a girl with him. . . . He fell behind the table, and she mizzled. (1970)

make oneself scarce (1809) ■ Jilly Cooper: The droppers-in will be so embarrassed that they'll apologise and make themselves scarce. (1969)

toddle (1812) Often followed by *along* or *off*; from earlier sense, go, walk ■ *New Scientist*: Would Ptolemy have seen the error of his ways, instantly recanted and toddled off to join the Copernican revolution? (1983)

clear off (1816) ■ J. Aitken: Here I am, on the spot after the office cleaners have cleared off. (1971)

clear out (1825) ■ G. B. Shaw: The definite intention to clear out of India as soon as the natives are capable of self rule is the most pious of superfluities. (1900)

make a move (1827)

hop the twig (or **stick**) (1828) Compare earlier sense, die ■ P. McCutcheon: You've not asked yourself why he hopped the twig. . . . Did a disappearing act. (1986)

cut dirt (1829) US, dated ■ *Western Scenes*: Now you cut dirt, and don't let me see you here again. (1853)

vamoose (1834) Orig and mainly US; applied to a hurried departure; often used in the imperative; from Spanish *vamos* let us go ■ J. Reeves: 'See anyone?' asked Winston. 'Not a soul. Whoever it was has vamoosed.' (1958)

make tracks (1835) Orig US ■ *Guardian*: 'I've got to make tracks,' I informed the driver in a singsong voice. (1992)

take oneself off (1836) Dated ■ Charles Dickens: He . . . took himself off on tip-toe. (1838)

leg it (1837) From earlier senses, go on foot, walk fast or run ■ *Today*: It was then, on May 4, that Nadir decided to leg it—leaving behind personal debts of £80 million. (1993)

shove (1844) Orig US; usually followed by *off*; from earlier sense, set a boat going by pushing against the shore ■ Nicolas Freeling: I have to ferry you down to the office. . . . Let's shove, shall we? (1975) ■ D. Anthony: My, look at the hour. I'd better shove off. (1979)

scarper (1846) Implying a hasty departure; probably from Italian *scappare* escape, get away, reinforced (at the time of World War I) by rhyming slang *Scapa Flow* go ■ Edmund Crispin: He's downstairs now with the others—and they're keeping a sharp eye on him; he won't have a chance to scarper again. (1977)

scoot (1847) Orig US; implying a hasty departure; from earlier senses, slide, go quickly ■ J. Sweeney: Forster always got wind of the warrant's being drawn out and . . . conveniently scooted. (1904)

hook it (1851) ■ Xavier Herbert: Pack your traps and get ready to hook it first thing mornin' time. (1939)

slide (1859) Dated, orig US; applied to a hurried and secretive departure ■ Edgar Wallace: There's only one word that any sensible man can read in this situation, and that word is—slide! (1932)

slope off (1861) Usually applied to a surreptitious or sheepish departure ■ *Sunday Times*: Outside Brixton Mosque there is much gathering and gossiping. One group of flamboyantly-attired young bloods arrives, hovering by the bus-stop and cackling like drains at a succession of private jokes. Thirty minutes later they slope off without so much as a prayer within. (1993)

skedaddle (1862) Orig US military slang, introduced during the Civil War of 1861–5; applied to a hurried departure; probably a fanciful formation ■ *Guardian*: Once the shooting began, many stars cancelled foreign trips or skedaddled from Israeli/Middle East film location sites. (1991)

get, git (1864) ■ Kenneth Giles: Anybody in a room either gets or pays for another twenty-four hours. (1967)

skip out (1865) Applied to a hurried departure, usually in order to escape obligations ■ June Thomson: Bibby hadn't turned up. He wondered if he had skipped out. (1977)

light out (1866) US; perhaps from the nautical verb *light* lift, haul ■ Josephine Tey: The girl had lit out. . . . She had dressed in a hurry and gone. (1948)

do a bunk (c1870) British; applied to a hurried departure, often in order to escape; origin unknown ■ G. B. Shaw: If my legs would support me I'd just do a bunk straight for the ship. (1921)

hit the road (or (US) trail, (dated) grit) (1873) ■ *Christian Science Monitor*: These two hit the road together, modern pilgrims making very little progress. (1973)

sling one's hook (1874) ■ L. P. Hartley: Anyhow, she's gone, walked out, slung her hook. (1955)

bunk (1877) British; usually applied to leaving or being absent from school without permission; usually followed by *off* ■ *Time Out*: A lot of kids here bunk off, as all kids do. The rate here is about 18%. (1973)

beat it (1878) Orig US ■ John Wyndham: Fedor had not waited once the plane was down. He had switched off the lights, and beat it. (1951)

guy (1879) Origin unknown ■ *Times*: Hurry up, I have had to do a chap, we will have to guy out of here. (1963)

hit (or punch, split, take) the breeze (1883) ■ Damon Runyon: And with this she takes the breeze and I return to the other room. (1931)

lam (1886) US; often followed by *out*; perhaps from *lam* to beat ■ M. Mackintosh: The time of death . . . [was] four days before Fisher lammed out. (1973)

shoot the crow (1887) Scottish; implying a hasty departure or absconding, especially to avoid paying a bill ■ William McIlvanney: There'll only be his mother in the house. His father shot the crow years ago. (1977)

smoke (1893) Australian; usually implying a hurried departure; usually followed by *off*; perhaps from the phrase *like smoke* very quickly ■ Patrick White: Dubbo had gone all right. Had taken his tin box, it seemed, and smoked off. (1961)

blow (1897) Orig US; usually implying a hurried departure ■ Eric Linklater: 'And what's happened to Rocco?' . . . 'He's blown. He's gone up north.' (1937)

do a guy (1897) From the verb *guy* leave ■ Norman Venner: He's just picked me up out of the road with a sprained ankle, or very near it, bandaged me up like a medical student, and brought me home. Then he wants to do a guy at the front door. (1925)

do (or make) a get (1898) Australian & New Zealand; applied to a hurried departure, often in order to escape ■ Arthur Upfield: Musta done a get after bashing up his wife. (1963)

nick off (1901) Australian; usually used to convey contemptuous dismissal; from *nick* go quickly ■ Xavier Herbert: He's the biggest shikker in Town. Now nick off, you old sponge. (1938)

cut along (1902) Often used in the imperative to children and subordinates ■ Michael Innes: 'And now you'd better cut along.' Captain Cox was a great believer in the moral effects of abrupt dismissals on the young. (1949)

get lost (1902) Orig US; now mainly used to convey contemptuous dismissal ■ Henry Calvin: The last time Carabine came in I told him to get lost. (1962)

run along (1902) Often used in the imperative to children and subordinates ■ Graham McInnes: Tell your Mother we're going to the flicks and I'll be back about eleven. Better run along now. (1965)

screw (off) out (1903) Orig US ■ D. Richards: Now if you don't screw off out of here, I'll use the phone. (1974)

shemozzle, schemozzle (1903) Dated; presumably from the noun *shemozzle* commotion ■ W. H. Auden: He was caught by a common cold and condemned to the whiskey mines, But schemozzled back to the Army. (1944)

skidoo (1905) North American; applied to a speedy departure; origin uncertain; perhaps from *skedaddle* ■ Bernard Malamud: 'If you skidoo now . . . you'll get spit.' 'Who's skidooing?' (1963)

get the (or to) hell out (a1911) Applied to a speedy departure ■ P. G. Wodehouse: You ought to be in bed. Get the hell out of here, Bodkin. (1972)

buzz off (1914) Often used to convey contemptuous dismissal; probably a euphemistic substitution for *bugger off* (although that is not recorded until later) ■ *Morecambe Guardian*: When a 79-year-old motorist was asked to move his car he told a police sergeant to 'buzz off'. (1976)

hop it (1914) Often used to convey contemptuous dismissal; perhaps from *hop the twig* ■ T. S. Eliot: The commission bloke on the door looks at us and says: "op it!' (1934)

skate (1915) Implying a hasty departure ■ Gilbert Frankau: When one's happy—well, time simply flies. Me for the hay. Let's get our bill, and skate. (1937)

do (or pull) a fade-out (1918) US

drag (or haul) (one's) ass (or tail) (1918) Mainly US

take a run-out powder (1920), take a powder (1934) Mainly US; applied to a hasty departure or absconding ■ Eugene O'Neill: I stuck it till I was eighteen before I took a run-out powder. (a1953) ■ Nicholas Blake: 'Where's the Yank?' . . . 'Gone. He took a powder.' (1954)

bugger off (1922) Often used to convey contemptuous dismissal ■ *Private Eye*: Let's get up to palace, pick up O.B.E.'s and bugger off 'ome, like. (1969)

go fly a kite (1927) Orig US; used to convey contemptuous dismissal ■ Hugh Pentecost: 'He suggested,' said Bradley, with a sigh, 'that I go fly a kite!' (1942)

see a man about a dog (1927) Orig US; used as a jocular or euphemistic excuse for leaving or being absent, especially when going to the lavatory or going to buy a drink ■ *Private Eye*: I got to see a man about a dog! (1969)

scram (1928) Orig US; implying a hasty departure; often used in the imperative; probably short for *scramble* ■ P. G. Wodehouse: 'Go away, boy!' he boomed. 'You mean "Scram!", don't you, chum?' said George, who liked to get these things right. (1962)

fuck off (1929) Often used to convey contemptuous dismissal ■ Samuel Beckett: She wants to know if you're the one in charge. Fuck off, said Lemuel. (1958)

amscray (1931) Pig Latin for *scram* ■ M. Bishop: I told that . . . daddy bastard to amscray. (1988)

dash (1932) From earlier sense, move quickly ■ *Independent*: Anyway, must dash: I hear there's a free cheese-tasting on at Sainsbury's. (1995)

jack off (1935) ■ George Orwell: Flo and Charlie would probably 'jack off' if they got the chance of a lift. (1935)

run (1935) Implying a speedy or urgent departure ■ Andrew Bergman: 'Helen, we'll be running,' said Wohl. . . . There was a final chorus of good-byes. (1975)

do a mickey (or micky, mick) (1937) *mick* a variant of *mike* period of idleness or shirking, reinterpreted as a personal name ■ S. Chaplin: I laid the ring on the notepaper and did a mickey as soon as I heard the front doorbell go. (1961)

go and have a roll (1941) Usually used to convey contemptuous dismissal

do (or take) a fade (1942) US; *fade* short for *fade-out* ■ Kenneth Orvis: Then, pal, we'll both do a fade. (1962)

go through (1943) Australian; applied to a hurried departure, especially in order to avoid an obligation

eff off (1945) Usually used to convey contemptuous dismissal; *eff* a variant of *ef*, name of the letter F, euphemistically representing the verb *fuck* ■ Laurence Meynell: 'Eff off,' Johnny told Antonio. Antonio effed off to the other end of the bar. (1963)

shoot through (1947) Australian & New Zealand; applied to a hurried departure, especially in order to avoid an obligation ■ *Bulletin* (Sydney): Me wife's shot through. . . . Can't get a bird. . . . Can't pay the rent. (1985)

bug off (1952) US; often used to convey contemptuous dismissal; compare *bugger off* ■ *Guardian*: If you happen to be a worker, a homosexual, a woman, a Hispanic, you can bug off. Bush is playing to ITT, IBM, ATT, Dow Chemical, GM. (1992)

split (1954) Orig US ■ *Sounds*: In the main hall Roger Scott from London's Capital Radio arrived, took one look at the wasteland and split. (1977)

bug out (1955) Mainly US; from earlier military sense, run away, desert; ultimate origin uncertain ■ J. Christopher: There was no sign of movement. . . . 'Give it five minutes. If there's nothing showing by then, either he's bugged out or he's asleep.' (1959)

piss off (1958) Often used to convey contemptuous dismissal ■ B. W. Aldiss: I'll have a drink when I feel like it, and not before. You two piss off if you're so bloody thirsty! (1971)

do a scarper (1958) From the verb *scarper* leave hastily ■ Frank Norman: We had all planned to do a scarper. (1958)

have it on one's toes (1958) Applied to making a quick escape, originally on foot ■ P. B. Yuill: I had it across the road on my toes. (1976)

naff off (1959) British; usually used (as a euphemistic substitute for *fuck off*) to convey contemptuous dismissal; origin of *naff* uncertain; perhaps from *eff*, with the addition of the final -*n* of a preceding word (as in the noun phrase *an eff*); compare also obsolete backslang *naf* = *fan* female genitals ■ *Sunday Times*: Princess Anne . . . lost her temper with persistent photographers and told them to 'naff off'. (1982)

skip it (1959) Applied to a hurried departure ■ Myles na Gopaleen: The son turned out to be a very bad bit of work, sold all the furniture to buy drink and then skipped it to America. (a1966)

take off (1959) ■ Judson Philips: You'd better take off. I've just got to get some sleep. (1972)

sod off (1960) Usually used to convey contemptuous dismissal ■ *Observer*: I am simply waiting for the day when I can say 'sod off' to your institution. (1977)

do a runner (1981) British; applied to a hurried departure, and originally specifically to a quick escape from the police or other authority ■ *More!*: They sense you want something else, but they're so scared of whatever it might be that they do a runner. (1992)

To leave the ground; take off

unstick (1912), get (come, etc.) unstuck (1913) Applied to an aircraft ■ John Gardner: The British Airways Trident unstuck from the cold stressed-concrete. (1977). Hence the noun **unstick** applied to the moment of take-off (1926)

scramble (1940) Applied to a rapid taking off by a group of military aircraft ■ Brennan & Hesselyn: The signal to scramble came at about eleven o'clock. . . . We rushed to our aircraft and in less than two minutes were off the ground. (1942). Hence the noun **scramble** applied to such a take-off (1940)

To leave an aircraft by ejecting

punch out (1970) ■ *Sunday Times*: It never occurred to me to 'punch out' (eject). (1974)

To depart frequently

do a Melba (1971) Australian, jocular; applied to someone who makes several farewell performances or comebacks; from the name of Dame Nellie *Melba* (stage name of Helen Mitchell) (1861–1931), Australian soprano, who was famous for being unable to retire conclusively ■ *Sydney Morning Herald*: It has been intensified by talk from Sir Robert that he is under pressure to stay on, thus giving rise to speculation that he is planning to 'do a Melba'. (1974)

To leave (a place)

vamoose (1847) US, dated; from earlier sense, depart

skip (1884) Orig US ■ *Detroit Free Press*: Cliff won't go along with Molly's scheme to take Olive's $10,000 and skip town. (1977)

stash (1889) Criminals', dated; from earlier sense, desist from, leave off

blow (1902) Orig and mainly US ■ J. Davis: 'Let's blow this joint, Garfield.' 'Hang on!' (1984)

scarper (1937) From earlier sense, depart; mainly in the phrase *scarper the letty* leave one's lodgings without paying the rent

split (1956) Orig US; from earlier sense, depart; often in the phrase *split the scene* leave a particular place ■ *Sunday Sun* (Brisbane): When he split the Brisbane scene he left behind documents that could be incriminating to the drug gangsters. (1971) ■ S. Wilson: He and Miranda split Scotland for good and came down to London. (1978)

Go away!

imshi, imshee, imshy (1916) British & Australian, services' slang; from colloquial (Egyptian) Arabic *imshi* ■ J. Waten: You must leave. Imshee and what not. (1966)

9. Transport

To transport, carry, take

tote (1676) Orig US; probably of dialect origin ■ *Chatelaine* (Canada): I toted a canvas bag over one shoulder. (1979)

cart (1881) Implying taking something heavy or cumbersome over a long distance or with considerable effort; from earlier sense, convey in a cart ■ B. Trapido: I tell him how . . . we carted home a great quantity of accumulated litter from our desks in a plaid blanket which we carried between us down the hill. (1982)

schlep, schlepp, shlep (1922) Mainly US; Yiddish *shlepn*, from German *schleppen* drag

twenty-three skidoo (1926) US, dated; origin unknown; compare *skidoo* leave ■ Desmond Bagley: This elderly, profane woman . . . used an antique American slang. . . . I expected her to come out with 'twenty-three, skidoo'. (1978)

on your bike (1967) British; now often also with the implication that the person addressed should go and look for work; this was popularized by a speech given by Employment Secretary Norman Tebbitt at the 1981 Conservative Party Conference, in which he pointed out that his father had not rioted in the 1930s when unemployed, but 'got on his bike and looked for work' ■ *Times*: 'On your bike, Khomeini', the crowd shouted outside the Iranian Embassy during the siege. (1981)

A departure

moonlight flit (1824), flit (1952), moonlight (1958) Applied to a hurried departure by night, especially to avoid paying a debt ■ *Sunday Truth* (Brisbane): They live on the generosity of the small country storekeeper, then do a flit. (1970) ■ R. Parkes: It's no good him trying to find 'em. . . . Done a moonlight, they did. (1971)

One who departs

fly-by-night (1823) Dated; applied to someone who runs away in order to evade creditors; from such people's nocturnal departure

moonlighter (1903) Applied to someone who does a moonlight flit ■ *Sunday Mail* (Brisbane): Brisbane flat owners . . . estimate that moonlighters—tenants who slip away overnight without paying the rent—are costing them £100,000 a year. (1964)

skip (1915) North American; applied to someone who runs away in order to evade creditors; compare *skip out* depart hurriedly, abscond ■ *Detroit Free Press*: Jean Phelan traces all kinds of hard-to-locate 'skips'—the defaulters who have 'skipped' out. (1978)

To wish to leave

want out (1870) Orig Scottish, Northern Irish, & US ■ *Time Out*: One of the kids who had paid his money . . . wanted out. (1973)

■ *New Yorker*: When her husband, Sidney, was alive he sustained a rupture, and Mrs. Singer says she had to schlepp him in and out of bed several times a day. (1975)

To travel, go on a journey

knock about (1833), knock (a)round (1848) Denoting travelling and living in various places ■ Compton Mackenzie: He had knocked about all over the Pacific and would have been a splendid companion. (1929) ■ *Wall Street Journal*: Dirk de Jong knocked around the Caribbean for 20 years. (1989)

hop (1923) ■ *Sunday Times*: There is this blinding deal in France, son. Hop over there quick and you'll be in. (1993)

jet (1946) Denoting travel by jet aeroplane; used both intransitively and transitively; from *jet* jet aeroplane ■ *Time*: Jetting home to Moscow . . . Krushchev exuded confidence. (1959) ■ *Daily Telegraph*: Clarksons jet you to top resorts like Alpbach, Auffach, [etc.]. (1968)

A journey, trip

hop (1909) Often applied specifically to a stage of a journey ■ Keith Weatherly: They had about three hundred miles to go, and because of the road conditions they decided to do it in two hops. (1968)

jump (1923) Orig US ■ Billie Holiday: We were playing big towns and little towns, proms and fairs. A six-hundred-mile jump overnight was standard. (1956)

A ticket

ducat, ducket(t) (1871) Applied especially to a railway ticket; probably from earlier sense, coin; perhaps influenced by *docket* and *ticket* ■ *Macmillan's Magazine*: So I took a ducat (ticket) for Sutton in Surrey. (1879)

The desire to travel

itchy feet (1943) ■ *Sun*: Most Capricorn goats normally have their feet planted firmly on the ground. Not this week. If anything, you appear to have itchy feet, not to mention the travel bug. (1992)

Driving and road manoeuvres

tailgate (1951) Orig US; denoting driving too close behind another vehicle; from US *tailgate* tail-board on a lorry, etc. ■ *Good Morning*: In the dangerous sphere of motorway driving, for example, they would not tailgate at speeds where if the man in front stopped suddenly they could not . . . help but stop in exactly the same place on the road. (1976)

Mexican overdrive (1961) US, jocular; applied to the putting of the gears of a vehicle, especially a truck, into neutral while coasting downhill

wheelie (1966) Orig US; applied to the stunt of riding a bicycle or motor-cycle for a short distance with the front wheel off the ground; from *wheel* + *-ie* ■ *Daily Mail*: That's the bike seen on TV with crash-hatted kids doing wheelies. (1985)

U-ey, uy, youee (1973) Australian; applied to a U-turn; from *U(-turn* + *-y* ■ *Truckin' Life*: The turning circle is 15.2 m (49.8 ft). Not natural U-ey material but adequate for a six tonner. (1983)

wheelie (1973) Australian; applied to a sharp U-turn made by a motor vehicle, causing skidding of the wheels; compare earlier sense, riding a cycle with the front wheel off the ground ■ J. S. Borthwick: Tom did a wheelie into Route 77. (1982)

A driver

road hog (1891) Applied to an inconsiderate (usually obstructive) driver or cyclist ■ Kyril Bonfiglioli: 'Lost my temper. . . . Bloody road hog.' 'He might easily have done us a mischief,' I agreed. (1972)

cowboy (1928) Orig US; applied to a reckless or inconsiderate driver; from cowboys' reputation for boisterousness ■ *Truckin' Life*: Equipment Manager Lindsay King demands . . . minimum of five years interstate driving . . . and a steady nature and background. . . . 'We have to weed out the cowboys. . . . we need the top professional drivers.' (1984)

hackie, hacky (1937) US; applied to a taxi-driver; from US *hack* taxi + *-ie*, *-y* ■ Margot Neville: And now . . . unearth some other blasted hacky that drove me there. (1959)

gipsy, gypsy (1942) US; applied to the driver of an independently operated truck ■ *Boston Sunday Globe*: The primary violators among truck drivers are the so-called 'gypsies' who operate independently. (1967)

greaser (1964) Orig US; applied to a member of a gang of youths with long hair and riding motor-cycles

bikie (1967) Australian & New Zealand; applied to a motor-cyclist, specifically a member of a gang of motor-cyclists, usually leather-jacketed, with a reputation for violent or rowdy behaviour; from *bike* + *-ie* ■ *Sydney Morning Herald*: The NSW police are still seeking a member of the Bandido bikie gang over the Milperra massacre on September 2. (1984)

See also A transport worker at **Work** (p. 199).

A pilot

George (1931) British; applied to the automatic pilot of an aircraft; from earlier services' slang sense, airman

A passenger

strap-hanger (1905) Applied to a passenger on a bus, train, etc. who has to stand, holding on to an overhead support, because all the seats on the vehicle are taken, and hence more broadly to a commuter on public transport ■ *Times*: Washington . . . commuters . . . are not strap-hangers like New Yorkers, Londoners and Parisians. (1981)

legal (1923) British; applied to a taxi passenger who pays the exact fare without a tip ■ Herbert Hodge: Some 'legals' are simply mean, and give excuses instead of a tip. (1939)

A pedestrian

ped (1863) Now mainly US; abbreviation ■ Dallas Barnes: A ped about three-quarters of a block away. (1973)

Walking

per boot (1895) Australian, jocular ■ *Bulletin* (Sydney): Touring Grippsland per boot, Mat was hailed . . . by a dog-tired cocky. (1941)

Shanks's pony (1898) Applied to going on foot as opposed to being transported; from earlier parallel expressions such as *Shanks's nag* (a1774) and *Shanks's mare* (a1795); *Shanks's* jocularly from *shank* leg

Traffic offences

run (1935) Mainly Australian; denoting driving through a red traffic light

feed the bears (1975) Orig and mainly US; denoting receiving a ticket or paying a fine for a traffic offence; compare *bear* police officer

hotting (1991) British; applied to joyriding in stolen high-performance cars, especially dangerously and for display; from *hot* stolen, perhaps reinforced by *hot-wire* steal a car by bypassing the ignition system ▪ *Observer*: What started as a campaign against 'hotting'—displays of high-speed handbrake turns in stolen cars—has turned into a dispute over territory. (1991) Hence **hotter** one who engages in hotting (1991)

Accidents

pile-up (1929) Applied to a (motor) accident involving a collision, typically a multiple one ▪ *New Scientist*: A recent pile-up on the M1 in Bedfordshire involving 30 cars has apparently moved the Ministry of Transport to do some thinking. (1968)

prang (1942) British, orig R.A.F. slang; applied to a crash or crash-landing of an aircraft, and subsequently to any crash involving vehicles; origin uncertain; perhaps from the sound of a crash ▪ Hunt & Pringle: 'P/O Prune' is the title bestowed upon a pilot who has several 'prangs' on his record. (1943) ▪ *Sunday Times*: The grisly enormities of American stock-car racing, with an hysterical ghoul of a commentator who revelled in every prang. (1959)

a wing and a prayer (1943) Used jocularly for referring to an emergency landing by an aircraft ▪ W. Marshall: The co-pilot brought it in. . . . Wing and a prayer! (1977)

shunt (1959) British; applied to a motor accident, especially a nose-to-tail collision ▪ G. Vaughan: 'Another bloody shunt,' Yardley groaned. The Zagreb trunk was notorious for accidents. (1978)

fender-bender (1961) Mainly US; applied to a usually minor motor accident; from North American *fender* vehicle's wing or mudguard ▪ Platt & Darvi: A fender-bender at a busy intersection. (1981)

shunt-up (1976) British; applied to a multiple motor accident; from *shunt* motor accident, modelled on *pile-up*

To crash

prang (1941) British, orig R.A.F. slang; applied to crashing an aircraft or other vehicle; from the noun *prang* crash ▪ Nevil Shute: After so many operations it was an acute personal grief to him that he had pranged his Wimpey. (1944) ▪ Tom Wisdom: The driver may well have left his 'flasher' on many corners ago and is happily oblivious of the fact until you move off on his signal and 'prang' him. (1966)

wrap something **(a)round** something **(1950)** Denoting crashing a vehicle into a stationary object ▪ *Times*: The men towing the boat from one training venue to another wrapped it round a traffic light. (1984)

total (1954) North American; denoting wrecking a car, etc. completely ▪ *Guardian*: Daddy's BMW which she can drive any time she wants as long as she doesn't total it. (1982)

buy the farm (1955) Orig US services' slang; denoting crashing an aircraft, usually fatally; explained as referring to government compensation paid to a farmer when a jet aircraft crashes on his farm ▪ *Economist*: These demonstrations cost money and lives. A number of commercial test pilots have 'bought the farm' while doing demonstrations. (1988)

Vehicle registration

tag (1935) North American; applied to a vehicle licence plate ▪ *Billings* (Montana) *Gazette*: [They] observed a Thunderbird with Louisiana tags circling the block. (1976)

rego, reggo (1967) Australian; from *reg(istration* + *-o* ▪ R. Hall: If the cops catch us they'll have us cold: no rego, one headlamp, baldy tyres. (1982)

reg (1969) British; abbreviation ▪ *Daily Mail*: At midnight, a businessman and his female companion took a drive to the beach in his H-reg Mercedes. (1991)

Taxis

hack (1704) Now only US; short for *hack(ney carriage*

duck-shoving (1870) Australian & New Zealand; applied to the practice of taxi-drivers not waiting their turn in the rank, but touting for passengers

Jixi, Jixie (1926) British, dated; applied to a two-seater taxi licensed in 1926; from *Jix*, nickname of Sir William Joynson-Hicks (1865–1932), Home Secretary in 1926 + *-i*, after *taxi*

clock (1930) Applied to a taximeter ▪ Anthony Armstrong: Unscrupulous young men . . . who didn't mind paying what was already on the clock and a bribe besides. (1930)

roader (1939) Applied by taxi-drivers to a long-distance fare or journey ▪ *London-Wide Radio Taxis*: Roaders are an everyday event on radio. Put yourselves into the shoes of a director of a company who requires a taxi for a long distance haul. Does he go out into the street and hail a cab or send his secretary to find one? Of course he doesn't. He rings for a cab. (1978)

Railways

gricer (1968) Applied to a railway enthusiast, especially one who assiduously seeks out and photographs unusual trains, and hence more loosely to a train-spotter; origin uncertain: variously associated with grouse-shooting (likened to train-spotting), *Gricer* as a surname, etc. ▪ *New Scientist*: Some of the gricers, earnest fresh-faced young men . . . who had cut their milk teeth on Hornby trains, had booked on this train two years ago. (1981)

See also **gandy dancer, rounder, shack, snake, snake charmer** under A transport worker at **Work** (p. 199).

Flying and air travel

split-arse, split-ass (1917) Services' slang, dated; applied to a pilot given to performing stunts and to an aircraft having good manoeuvrability, and hence used as a verb denoting making a sudden turn in an aircraft and performing stunt flying, and as a noun denoting a flying stunt and an aircraft performing such a stunt ■ *V. M. Yeates:* They were sufficiently splitarse and did all the stunts, but there was nothing like a Camel for lightness of touch. (1934) ■ *V. M. Yeates:* Something fired at him. He splitarsed and nearly hit an SE. (1934)

stooge (1941) R.A.F. slang; denoting flying without any fixed purpose or target; from earlier sense, act compliantly, or as the puppet of another ■ *M. K. Joseph:* Been in 691 Squadron, stooging around the Channel ports all winter. (1958). Hence **stooge** a flight during which one does not expect to meet the enemy (1942) ■ *Miles Tripp:* At one stage we saw a Fortress orbiting slowly, presumably on a stooge with a team of W/Ops jamming enemy frequencies. (1952)

10. **Vehicles**

A vehicle

machine (1687) Usually applied to a wheeled vehicle; in the 18th and early 19th centuries commonly applied to a stage-coach or mail-coach, and in the 20th century reapplied to a mechanized vehicle, such as a car, bicycle, or aeroplane ■ *Saturday Evening Post:* As I neared my own house I slowed the machine. (1919)

A towed vehicle

Queen Mary (1943) British, dated; applied to a long low-loading road trailer; after the Cunard passenger liner, the Queen Mary

pup (1951) US; applied to a four-wheeled trailer drawn by a tractor or other road vehicle

A motor vehicle

motor (1900) British; applied to a car; originally standard English (short for *motor car*), but latterly in slang use ■ *Anthony Masters:* Mr Sprott flashed a warrant card and Arthur's indignation quietened. 'Ever seen one of these before?' 'It's not a Fulham season ticket, is it?' 'In the motor.' 'Hang about!' 'I said—*in* the motor, Daley.' (1984)

runabout (1900) Applied to a small light car ■ *Times:* Whereas the Mini is really a Town runabout, the Metro is conceived as a family car that will be more comfortable for longer runs. (1980)

one-lunger (1908) Applied to a vehicle driven by a single-cylinder engine; from earlier sense, such an engine

flivver (1910) Orig US; applied to an old or cheap car, originally especially a Model A or Model T Ford; origin unknown ■ *Saul Bellow:* He had driven a painted flivver. (1956)

lizzie (1913), tin lizzie (1915) Orig US; applied to an old or dilapidated car, originally especially

grease job (1961), greaser (1972) Applied to a smooth landing; compare the earlier phrase *grease* (a plane) *in* land smoothly ■ *Amateur Photographer:* The undercarriage structure was intact and . . . the plane could make a 'greaser' (1980)

red eye (1968) Applied to aeroplane flights on which passengers are unable to get enough sleep because of differences in time-zones between the place of departure and arrival ■ *National Observer:* Schweiker . . . and Newhall took the red-eye special back to Washington that same night. Newhall just wanted to sleep, but Schweiker was, in Newhall's words, 'euphoric'. (1976)

viff (1972) Applied to an aircraft's ability to change direction abruptly as a result of a change in the direction of thrust of the engine(s), and also used as a verb denoting such a change; from the initial letters of *vectoring in forward flight* ■ *Times Literary Supplement:* The VSTOL Harrier with its swivelable jets and ability to 'viff'. (1983)

an early model of Ford car; from the female personal name *Lizzie,* pet form of *Elizabeth* ■ *D. M. Davin:* The pace they drove their old tin lizzies. (1949)

bus (1921) Dated; applied to a car, especially an old or dilapidated one ■ *Jonathon Gash:* 'Of course. Why not? I gave him a lift to the station.' 'Did he survive?' She's always pulling my leg about my old bus. (1977)

struggle-buggy (1925) US, dated; applied especially to an old or dilapidated car

heap (1926) Applied to an old or dilapidated vehicle ■ *C. F. Burke:* You will be like a guy who paid no attention to his heap and it broke down in the traffic. (1969)

crate (1927) Orig US; applied to an old or dilapidated vehicle ■ *F. E. Baily:* His Rolls 'll give you more respect in the eyes of the reporters than my old crate would. (1937)

jalopy, gillopy, jalapa, jollopy, jallopy, jaloppi(e) (1926) Orig US; applied to a dilapidated old motor vehicle; origin unknown ■ *M. E. B. Banks:* Perhaps a succession of broken down jalopies has impaired my faith in the internal combustion engine. (1955)

ride (1930) US ■ *Christina Milner:* With his unspectacular conservative suits and modest 'ride' (a Toyota station wagon). (1972)

scooter (1930) Mainly US; applied to a (fast) car; from *scoot* go quickly + *-er* ■ *J. Evans:* 'We'll use your scooter, Mac. . . . Where's she parked?' . . . I wondered how they knew I had a car. (1948)

short (1932) US; applied to a car; often in the phrase *hot short* stolen car; perhaps from earlier sense, street-car ■ *Wilson McCarthy:* Everybody brings him hot cars . . . shorts, we get up north, he fixes 'em up and then sells 'em. (1975)

jam jar (1934) British; rhyming slang for *car* ■ Robin Cook: Parking this dreadful great orange-and-cream jamjar . . . slap under a no-parking sign. (1962)

drag (1935) Applied to a car; compare earlier obsolete sense, horse-drawn vehicle ■ *Observer:* A stately great drag . . . with a smart chauffeur at the wheel. (1960)

iron (1935) Orig US; applied to an old motor vehicle ■ Mack Reynolds: Well, it would mean being able to maintain a decent hovercar rather than the . . . four wheel iron he was currently driving. (1967)

oil-burner (1938) Applied to a run-down vehicle which uses too much engine oil ■ Brian Garfield: Even in an old oil-burner he could have gone three times as far in a day's drive if he'd wanted to. (1975)

orphan (1942) Applied to a discontinued model of motor vehicle

hot rod, rod (1945) Orig US; applied to a motor vehicle modified to have extra power and speed

crummy (1946) US; applied to a truck or other vehicle used to transport loggers to and from the woods; from earlier sense, caboose ■ B. Hutchison: Most of these men . . . travel perhaps forty miles to work in a 'crummy'. (1957)

passion wagon (1948) Jocular; applied to an old jalopy suitable for petting, etc. in

bomb (1953) Australian & New Zealand; applied to an old car ■ Frank Sargeson: We had a job shoving her into the bomb. (1967)

rag-top (1955) US; applied to a convertible car with a soft roof ■ *Springfield* (Massachusetts) *Daily News:* The last U.S. built convertible, a Cadillac Eldorado, rolls along the assembly at the General Motors' plant in Detroit Wednesday. It ended an era for ragtops that began 74 years ago. (1976)

wheels (1959) Orig US; applied to a car ■ Gavin Lyall: 'Did you find me some wheels?'. . . 'Yep: a Renault 16TX.' (1982)

woody, woodie (1961) Orig surfers' slang; mainly US; applied to an estate car with timber-framed sides; from *wood + -y*

banger (1962) Applied to an old, dilapidated, and noisy vehicle; usually in the phrase *old banger* ■ *Times:* It is true though that one misses out on one's husband's early years of struggle: the rented flats, . . . the third-hand old bangers, the terrifying overdraft. (1985)

rust-bucket (1965) Mainly Australian; applied to an old rusty car; from earlier sense, old rusty ship

hog (1968) US; applied to a large, often old, car ■ *Black Scholar:* He bought him a 'Hog' with all the accessories on it. Man, this Cadillac had air horns, white-walls, [etc.]. (1971)

limo (1968) Orig US; abbreviation of *limousine* ■ R. Moore: The company should be sending a limo for me. I'd be happy to drop you off. (1973)

sheen (1969) US; applied to a car or van; probably an abbreviation of *machine* ■ *American*

Speech: Hey, look down the street pas' that sheen double-parked. (1975)

pig (1971) British; applied to a type of armoured personnel carrier; from its snout-shaped bonnet ■ *Times:* The Pig, the armoured vehicle most used in Belfast. (1978)

gas guzzler (1973) Orig US; applied to a large car with excessively high fuel consumption; from US *gas* petrol ■ *Washington Post:* The big American family sedan may be a gas-guzzler. But it can also be an insurance bargain. (1985)

pimpmobile (1973) US; applied to a large flashy car used by a pimp ■ *Daily Mail:* The pimpmobiles—the long, long Cadillacs with a Rolls front—no longer cruise everywhere. They are finding it less profitable to keep girls here. (1975)

scoot (1977) Applied to a car; compare earlier sense, motor-cycle and *scooter* fast car ■ *Custom Car:* For this season he's gone over to a radical Volvo-engined scoot. (1977)

stink-pot (1978) Applied to a lorry or other vehicle that gives off foul exhaust fumes; compare earlier application to a ship ■ Desmond Bagley: The truck broke through . . . and it killed them. . . . Lousy stinkpots! Never have liked them except when I'm in a hurry. (1978)

A lorry

red ball (1934) US; applied to a fast goods lorry; from earlier sense, fast goods train

rig (1938) US; compare earlier sense, horse vehicle ■ *Times:* Mr Nixon came on the air . . . to urge the drivers to get their 'big rigs' back on the road. (1974)

six by six, six by (1942) US, services' slang; applied to a six-wheel truck with six-wheel drive

ute (1943) Mainly Australian & New Zealand; applied to a small truck for carrying light loads; abbreviation of *utility*, as in *utility truck* or *vehicle* ■ *NZ Farmer:* Now Nissan has followed it with a tough new 4 x ute, known at this stage just as the 720. (1984)

passion wagon (1948) Applied to a truck taking service personnel on short leave to a town or other place of entertainment

artic (1951) British; short for *articulated lorry* ■ Douglas Rutherford: To see a woman at the wheel of a big artic was surprising. (1977)

gipsy, gypsy (1960) US; applied to an independently operated truck; from earlier sense, driver of such a truck

A bus

short (1914) US, dated; applied to a street-car or tram; apparently from the relatively short duration of tram-rides as compared with those on a train

tub (1929) Mainly criminals' slang; often in the phrase *work the tubs* pick pockets on buses or at bus-stops

scooter (1961) Applied to a single-deck (fast-running) bus; compare earlier sense, (fast) car ■ *New York Times*: Fleets of flag-bedecked scooter-buses. (1972)

A make of car

Merc (1933) British; short for *Mercedes* ■ John Wainwright: There is a pale blue Merc parked not far from the club entrance. (1974)

Jag (1959) Short for *Jaguar* ■ Ted Allbeury: They've bought a car. A Jag—second-hand. (1974)

Roller (1977) British; applied to a Rolls-Royce car; from *Roll(s-Royce* + *-er*, probably influenced by *roller* one that rolls ■ *Observer*: In the new series . . . Jools meets a Martian . . . and takes him on a guided tour of Britain in the Roller. (1989)

A bicycle

bone-shaker (1874) Applied originally to an early type of bicycle with solid tyres (from its effect on the rider), and subsequently jocularly to any (old or dilapidated) bicycle

push-bike (1913) Applied to an ordinary bicycle, as opposed to a motor-cycle ■ Dorothy Halliday: Derek . . . thought of a push-bike. . . . He didn't want to be followed. (1970)

grid (1922) ■ *Coast to Coast 1942*: 'I'll walk and wheel the bike, and if my dad's home he can drive out in the car to meet me.' 'Gosh, no!' you said. 'Here, you go on, on my grid, an' I'll do the walking.' (1943)

chopper (1965) Orig US; applied to a motor-cycle, especially a large powerful one or one with high handlebars ■ *Economist*: An Evel Knievel doll on the notorious chopper motor bike. (1977)

hog (1967) US; applied to a large, often old, motor-cycle

scoot (1968) US; applied to a motor-cycle; abbreviation of *scooter*

A train

loco (1833) Short for *locomotive* ■ A. MacLean: To haul this heavy load with a single loco? . . . Thirty hours, I'd say. (1974)

side-door Pullman (1887) North American, dated; used mainly by tramps; applied to a railway goods wagon with sliding doors in the sides; *Pullman* from the name of a luxurious type of railway carriage; from the use of such wagons by tramps

dog-box (1905) Australian; applied to a compartment in a railway carriage without a corridor; from earlier sense, compartment in a railway van for conveying dogs ■ E. O. Schlunke: We had to get out of our sleepers into dog-boxes and found we still had over a hundred miles to go. (1958)

crummy (1916) US, dated; applied to a caboose or railway car on a goods train used by the train's crew or to transport workmen; from the adjective *crummy*, variant of *crumby* infected with lice, from *crumb* louse

drag (1925) US; applied to a freight train

red ball (1927) US; applied to a fast goods train

locie, loci, lokey, etc. **(1942)** North American & New Zealand; abbreviation of *locomotive* ■ A. P. Gaskell: She often saw wisps of smoke rising against the bush on the hills at the back. . . . Sometimes she heard a lokey puffing. (1947)

Spam can (1967) British; applied to a streamlined steam locomotive formerly used on the Southern Region of British Rail

A ship, boat

tub (a1618) Applied to a slow clumsy ship ■ Hall & Osborne: His old tub of a vessel . . . was known from one end of the Pacific to the other. (1901)

sub (1917) Applied to a submarine; abbreviation ■ Adam Diment: Boris snooping round Holy Loch and the nuclear subs. (1968)

pig boat (1921) US; applied to a submarine ■ *Newsweek*: Presumably Germany will now build up to this by constructing ocean-going pigboats. (1939)

windbag (1924) Applied to a sailing ship or windjammer ■ W. McFee: He had been cook in a windbag and a sailor before the mast. (1946)

tin fish (1928) Dated; applied to a submarine; compare earlier sense, torpedo

crate (1933) Applied to an old or unseaworthy vessel

flat-top (1942) US; applied to an aircraft-carrier ■ C. S. Forester: Escort vessels and destroyers and baby flat-tops were coming off the ways as fast as America and England and Canada could build them. (1955)

rust-bucket (1945) North American; applied to an old rusty ship

skunk (1945) Military; applied to an unidentified surface craft ■ *New York Times Magazine*: The cruiser is . . . useful at times for coastal bombardment or to seek out and destroy enemy 'skunks' (surface craft). (1952)

stink-pot (1972) Applied to a boat that gives off foul exhaust fumes ■ Howard Fast: They're gone now, all of them [sc. fishing-boats with sails]. Nothing but stinkpots—I'm sorry—oil burners. (1977)

fizz-boat (1977) New Zealand; applied to a motor boat or speedboat; from the noise made by the engine ■ *Metro* (Auckland): There are everyman's little fizz-boat to the great petrol guzzling twin 200 horsepower outboard motor driven racing machines. (1984)

Parts of a ship

mud-hook (1827) Dated; applied to an anchor

monkey island, monkey's island (1912) Applied to a small bridge above the pilot-house ■ P. J. Abraham: Up on the monkey island he had realized there would be no power for the lights. (1963)

perisher (1925) Naval; applied to a periscope; jocular re-application of *perisher* annoying person

the sharp end (1948) Applied to the bows ■ Dick Francis: Arne pointed the sharp end back. . . . The dinghy slapped busily through the little waves. (1973)

An aircraft

bus (1910) Dated; applied to an aeroplane, especially an old or dilapidated one ■ John Buchan: Got here last night after a clinkin' journey, with the bus [sc. an aeroplane] behavin' like a lamb. (1924)

penguin (1915) Services' slang, dated; applied to a low-powered machine incapable of flight, used to train aircrew

kite (1917) British, mainly services' slang; applied to an aeroplane ■ Miles Tripp: The Squadron hasn't lost a single kite in the last three raids. (1952)

quirk (1917) British services' slang, dated; applied to a type of slow steady aeroplane, to a plane used to train novice pilots, or to any peculiar plane; compare earlier sense, inexperienced airman

crate (1918) Orig services' slang; applied to an old aeroplane ■ Times: You must travel in an antiquated two-engined crate which goes puttering over Central Asia at about 90 miles an hour. (1957)

flying boxcar (1918) US services' slang; applied to a large cumbersome aeroplane

flivver (1926) US; applied to a small aeroplane; compare earlier sense, old or dilapidated car

ruptured duck (1930) US services' slang, dated; applied to a damaged aeroplane

duck (1931) US; applied to an amphibious aeroplane

bird (1933) Applied to an aeroplane, a guided missile, a rocket, or a space-craft ■ Alan Shepard: I really enjoy looking at a bird that is getting ready to go. (1962)

grasshopper (1941) US; applied to a light military aircraft used for observation, liaison, etc.

puddle-jumper (1944) US; applied to a small, light, manoeuvrable aeroplane ■ Detroit Free Press: Any one . . . can call his plane an air ambulance even if it's just a 'puddle-jumper' without medical equipment. (1978)

squirt (1945) Services' slang, dated; applied to a jet aeroplane ■ L. R. Gribble: To fly the squirts in combat meant the development of a new technique. (1945)

A helicopter

egg-beater (1936) US; from the resemblance of the rotors to those of a mechanical egg-whisk

chopper (1951) Orig US services' slang ■ Listener: A naval helicopter or 'chopper' going about its flights and hoverings. (1958)

whirlybird (1951) Orig US

sky bear (1975) North American; applied to a police helicopter

A type of aircraft

Rumpty (1917) Applied to the Farman training aeroplane, used in World War I; from rump,

after bumpety ■ V. M. Yeates: Tom told them the first time he went up was in a Rumpty, that was to say, a Maurice Farman Shorthorn, a queer sort of bus like an assemblage of birdcages. (1934)

Spit (1941) Abbreviation of Spitfire, name of a British fighter aeroplane used in World War II ■ James McClure: I was flying Spits, Hurricanes, while Bonzo . . . was in Bomber Command. (1980)

Wimpey, Wimpy (1941) Applied to a Wellington, a British bomber aeroplane used in World War II; from J. Wellington Wimpy, name of a character in the 'Popeye' cartoons ■ Nevil Shute: There was a Wimpey running up one engine, somewhere away out in the middle distance of the aerodrome. (1944)

Parts of an aircraft

the office (1917) Applied to an aeroplane's cockpit ■ V. M. Yeates: He put his head in the office and flew by the instruments. (1934)

the pulpit (1933) British services' slang, dated; applied to an aeroplane's cockpit ■ Gen: A fighter pilot climbs into the 'pulpit' of his plane. (1942)

undercart (1934) Applied to an aircraft's undercarriage ■ Nevil Shute: Honey had ruined a Reindeer at Gander by pulling up its under-cart. (1948)

greenhouse (1941) Dated; applied to a cockpit canopy ■ W. H. Auden: 'Why have They killed me?' wondered Bert, our Greenhouse gunner. (1947)

An engine and its parts

rev (1901) Applied to a rotation of an engine; abbreviation of revolution ■ Daily Telegraph: As I got round the bend onto the main road I felt the revs begin to build up. When this happened I changed up a gear. (1972)

one-lunger (1908) Applied to a single-cylinder engine

mill (1918) Applied to the engine of an aircraft or a hot-rod racing car ■ Brian Garfield: This was an old car but it must have had a souped-up mill. (1975)

pot (1941) Mainly services' slang; applied to an aircraft cylinder or carburettor

carb (1942) Abbreviation of carburettor ■ Hot Car: I would like to fit an S.U. carb from a Mini or a Morris 1100 to the Escort. (1977)

percolator (1942) Mainly US; appled to a carburettor

tranny (1970) Orig & mainly US; applied to the transmission of a motor vehicle, especially of a truck or van; from tran(smission + -y ■ Billings (Montana) Gazette: That was $1,500 or $1,700 damage to the tranny and the guy in the coffee pot cost $150. (1976)

cat (1988) British; abbreviation of catalytic converter ■ Performance Car: If I remove the cat, could I use leaded petrol or will it damage the engine? (1989)

Given enhanced engine performance

souped-up (1931) Orig US ■ Brian Garfield: A souped-up car with enormous rear tires growled past him. (1975)

hopped-up (1945) Compare earlier sense, under the influence of drugs ■ *Islander* (Victoria, British Columbia): At the urge of the hopped-up motor in seconds they were tearing up Nanaimo Street. (1971)

Instrumentation

dash (1902) Abbreviation of *dashboard* ■ Martin Woodhouse: I fitted the key into the truck's dash and backed off. (1966)

gyro (1910) Abbreviation of *gyro-compass*

clock (1934) Applied to a speedometer or milometer; from the clock-like dial ■ *Commercial Motor.* Neither vehicle had much mileage on the clock. (1970)

speedo (1934) Abbreviation of *speedometer* ■ Peter Hill: The car [was as] steady as a rock . . . as the speedo reached up towards its limit. (1976)

electrics (1946) Applied to the electric circuits in a vehicle ■ *Sunday Times*: He tried to lower his flaps part way—forgetting, in the anxiety of the moment, that without electrics his flap position indicator would not work. (1963)

Brakes

anchors, anchor (1936) ■ Priestley & Wisdom: There is more to it . . . than just putting on the brakes—or, to use the colourful language of the sporting motorist, 'clapping on the anchors'. (1965)

A tyre

skin (1954) ■ *Hot Car.* The answer is to run at the same pressure as the standard tyres, as by dropping the pressure any more than two pounds, you could cause sidewall failure, even in the big American skins. (1977)

Fuel

juice (1909) Applied to petrol ■ Keith Weatherly: The Rover had him worried. If she ran out of juice . . . he had to walk in. (1968)

A mechanical fault

gremlin (1941) Orig R.A.F. slang; applied to a mischievous sprite imagined as the cause of mechanical faults, originally in aircraft; origin unknown, but probably formed by analogy with *goblin*; a single instance of an earlier sense, junior officer in the R.A.F., is recorded (1929) ■ *Times*: The King said that on his way back from Italy they thought they heard a gremlin in the royal aeroplane. (1944)

A shop selling vehicle accessories and spares

speed shop (1954) Orig US ■ *Hot Car.* You can often pick up reasonable headers off the shelf from a good speed shop. (1977)

Abstract Qualities and States

1. Size

Large

thumping (1576) From the verb *thump* + *-ing*
■ *Guardian*: If the streets were clean, the manufacturing trade deficit a thumping surplus . . . the British would not need the kick . . . which war now gives them. (1991)

hulking (1698) From the noun *hulk* large unwieldy person or mass + *-ing* ■ Benjamin Jowett: A great hulking son ought not to be a burden on his parents. (1875)

whopping (1706) From the verb *whop* hit + *-ing*
■ *Punch*: That's a wopping [*sic*] majority against us. (1869)

great (1715) Used to emphasize other adjectives denoting large size, such as *big, huge, thick* ■ L. P. Hartley: It was a great big thing, the size of a small haystack. (1961)

whacking (1806) From the verb *whack* + *-ing*
■ J. Davis: She looks . . . like a whacking frigate. (1806)

tidy (1838) From earlier sense, fairly good ■ Sir Montagu Gerard: They do swear a tidy bit. (1903)

walloping (1847) From the verb *wallop* + *-ing*
■ Mordecai Richler: Joshua slid behind the bar, which was unattended, and poured himself a walloping cognac. (1980)

hefty (1871) From earlier sense, weighty
■ *Sunday Times*: On top of the hefty basic wage is a bonus system from the pool of tips. (1972)

corking (1895) Compare *corker* large one
■ *Women's Home Journal*: He . . . engaged me, at a corking fee, to come up and take this case. (1926)

astronomical (1899) From the large distances between stars, galaxies, etc. ■ Edward Hyams: The value of stage, film, broadcasting and other rights was astronomical. (1953)

sollicking (1917) Australian; compare *sollicker* large one ■ Kylie Tennant: It was a great big sollicking stitch if ever there was one. (1947)

ginormous (1948) British; from gi(*gantic* + e)*normous* ■ *Sunday Express*: Since Brands Hatch, doors have opened and it's possible to make ginormous money. (1986)

zonking (1958) From the verb *zonk* + *-ing* ■ Peter Bull: She was now technically a 'star' after her zonking success as Claudia. (1959)

humongous, humungous (1970) Orig US; origin uncertain; perhaps based on *huge* and *monstrous* ■ *Sunday Times*: His wife went the whole hog and ordered a 'combo Mexicano' ('for those with a humongous appetite') which consisted of a chicken taco, a beef enchilada and a cheese enchilada. (1992)

mega (1981) From the prefix *mega-* great, as in *megastar, mega-millionaire*, etc. ■ *Investors Chronicle*: The insurance companies helped promote the industry as a whole with their mega launches and promotions. (1988)

Large one

thumper (1660) Dated; from the verb *thump* + *-er* ■ J. Collins: They gave me a Thumper of a Christmas Box. (1804)

monster (1759) From earlier sense, animal of huge size; often used as an adjective ■ Kingsley Martin: Buying from the all-purpose shop bullseyes and, for a penny, 'monsters', which were big bottles of fizzy lemonade. (1966) ■ *Guardian*: Many older housewives . . . find great satisfaction in a monster weekly 'bake'. (1961)

whopper (1785) From the verb *whop* hit + *-er*
■ R. S. Surtees: We killed the fox—my eyes, such a wopper [*sic*]! (1854)

whacker (1828) From the verb *whack* + *-er* ■ J. R. Green: The Dome which ought to be a whacker is a poor wee thing. (1872)

boomer (1843) Australian; from earlier sense, large kangaroo ■ Tom Ronan: Fights you're talking about! Well, I just seen a boomer! (1956)

daddy (1865) Used to denote the most impressively large example; usually followed by *of* ■ William Garner: You graduate from taking little chances to taking big ones. This one was the daddy of 'em all. (1969)

corker (1882) From earlier sense, excellent or astonishing person or thing ■ *Sun*: First he netted a corker of 6lb 12 oz and followed it up an hour later with a 6lb 4oz specimen. (1992)

jumbo (1883) Often used as an adjective; from earlier sense, big clumsy person, probably from the second element of *mumbo-jumbo* (perhaps from Mande *mama dyumbo*); popularized in the late 19th century as the name of an elephant, famous for its size, originally at London Zoo and in 1882 sold to a circus ■ Julian May: There were bracket fungi . . . stiff jumbos . . . capable of bearing a man's weight. (1982) ■ *Sun*: The Prime Minister handled his jumbo Press conference amid the splendour of Lancaster House with poise and style. (1973)

sollicker, soliker (1898) Australian; perhaps from British dialect *sollock* impetus, force
■ Franklin & Cusack: She gave me a sollicker of a dose out of a blue bottle. (1939)

lunker (1912) North American; applied to an animal, especially a fish, which is an exceptionally large example of its species; origin unknown ■ *Sports Afield*: A bronze lunker came out of the shadowy depths and smashed the pigskin. (1947)

doozy (1916) Orig & mainly North American; from earlier sense, excellent or astonishing thing

doozer (1930) North American; compare *doozy* ■ K. M. Wells: A storm was brewing. 'A real doozer,' I mumbled. 'A doozer.' (1956)

blockbuster (1946) Applied to something large in scale or effect; from earlier sense, aerial bomb capable of destroying a whole block of buildings ■ *Guardian*: The main work was a purely orchestral blockbuster, Shostakovich's Leningrad Symphony. (1991)

King Kong (1955) Used as a nickname for anyone of outstanding size or strength; from the name of the ape-like monster featured in the film *King Kong* (1933) ■ *Guardian*: Finn MacCool was a legendary Irish giant, a King Kong with a generous heart. (1974)

grand(d)addy (1956) Used to denote the most impressively large example; usually followed by *of* ■ Muriel Beadle: The granddaddy of all electrical storms dumped a cloudburst. (1961)

Long

as long as one's arm (1846) Used to indicate great length ■ Margery Allingham: Jock has a record as long as your arm. (1938)

A tall person

beanpole (1837) Applied jocularly to a very tall thin person; from earlier sense, stick up which a bean plant is grown

lofty (1933) Used as a nickname for a very tall (or *ironically*, very short) person

Small

tiddy (1781) Origin uncertain; perhaps a baby-form of *little* ■ Mary Kelly: Do you know this Richborough? . . . There's a tiddy railway, power cables, and the castle. (1958)

weeny (1790) Orig dialect; from *wee* small + *ti*) *ny* ■ W. J. Locke: They're little tiny weeny shells. (1922)

itty (1798) Baby-form of *little*; used mainly in addressing or referring to small children and animals ■ *Guardian*: Now, ah reckon Lady Bird an' ah will git ahselves an itty bit o' sleep. (1964)

teeny (1817) Variant of *tiny* ■ *New Yorker*: Their [videodisc] system has a teeny laser beam instead of a needle to get the images onto the TV screen. (1982)

teenty (1844) US; alteration of *teeny* ■ C. F. Woolson: You were six months old—a little teenty baby. (1894)

poky, pokey (1849) Usually used to denote inadequate space; from earlier sense, taken up with petty matters ■ *Daily Telegraph*: A pokey, little, highly rented flat. (1971)

dinky (1858) From earlier sense, neat, dainty; ultimately from obsolete Scottish *dink* neat (of unknown origin) + *-y* ■ K. M. Wells: You will need a stove of sorts, something better than the dinky little two-burner alcohol contraption with which so many so-called cruising ships are fitted. (1960)

ickle (1864) Baby-form of *little* ■ Polly Hobson: She changed her role. Now she was Daddy's ickle girl. (1968)

tiddly (1868) Variant of *tiddy* ■ J. Goodman: The whole bally case for the prosecution is built on tiddly bits of non-evidence. (1978)

teeny-weeny (1894) ■ H. Lawrence: Jewel has a bird brain. You know what a bird brain is? Teeny-weeny. (1948)

teensy, teenzy (1899) Orig US dialect; probably from *teeny* + *-sy* ■ S. Strutt: 'Would you like a drink?' . . . 'Darling, that would be lovely. Perhaps just a teensy one!' (1981)

bitsy (1905) Mainly US; from *bit* or *bitty* + *-sy* ■ William Golding: A bitsy village with reed thatch and wrought-iron work. (1959)

bitty (1905) US; from earlier sense, consisting of little bits ■ Raymond Chandler: That toy. . . . It's just a little bitty gun, a butterfly gun. (1940)

teensy-weensy, teensie-weensie (1906) ■ *Times*: The statement as it stands is . . . just a teensie-weensie bit unfair to my own firm. (1973)

mingy (1911) Used to denote a disappointingly or meanly small amount or size; perhaps from *m(ean + st) ingy*, or a blend of *mangy* and *stingy* ■ Cecil Beaton: A mingy little tray he had picked up from heaven-knows-where. (1926)

itsy-bitsy (1938) Baby-form of *little* + *bitsy* ■ Hartley Howard: If Frankie was here he'd break you into itsy-bitsy pieces. (1972)

itty-bitty (1938) ■ Ludovic Kennedy: I felt, here I am in this itty-bitty tropical village, a tremendous long ways from anywhere. (1969)

pint-size, pint-sized (1938) Applied to a child or small person; from the notion of a pint being a small amount ■ *Guardian*: Long double-breasted riding macs for the pint-sized. (1973)

titchy (1950) British; from *titch*, variant of *tich* small person + *-y* ■ *Spectator*: Towering six foot three inches over a titchy Laertes. (1958)

Small one

shrimp (c1386) Applied to a small or puny person ■ Naryantara Sahgal: At least one could hold up one's head with a distinguished-looking Kashmiri Brahmin Prime Minister, but here was this shrimp who was a Kayasath as well, and filling up the secretariat with Kayasaths. (1985)

squib (1586) Now Australian; applied to a small or insignificant person; from earlier sense, explosive device ■ *Courier-Mail* (Brisbane): We have numerous utility expressions for people such as . . . sparrow, squib, nugget and streak, for men of varying sizes. (1979)

pinky, pinkie (1808) Applied especially to the little finger; partly from obsolete *pink* small,

partly from Dutch *pink* little finger, + *-y* ■ W. H.
Auden: O lift your pin-kie, and touch the win-ter sky. (1962)

tiddler (1927) Applied to a small person or thing,
or to a child; from earlier sense, a stickleback or
other small fish ■ Edward Blishen: A couple of days
with Class 1A and . . . he will know a deuce of a lot . . . about
the little tiddlers. (1980)

peanuts (1934) Orig US; applied especially to an
insignificant amount of money or an
inadequate payment ■ J. B. Priestley: 'How was the
poker game?' 'Peanuts. All I got was about twenty-five dollars
and a headache.' (1946)

tich, titch (1934) Applied to a small person or a
child; from Little *Tich*, stage name of the
diminutive English music-hall comedian Harry
Relph (1868–1928), who was given the nickname
as a child because of a resemblance to the so-
called 'Tichborne claimant' (Arthur Orton
(1834–98), who claimed to be the long-lost Roger

Tichborne, heir to an English baronetcy)
■ Dannie Abse: I vowed to work harder. To make more
money. For you and the titch. (1960)

peanut (1942) Applied to a small or unimportant
person

Short person

short-arse, short-ass (1706) ■ Martin Amis:
'What's her real name?' I implored. 'Jean.' 'Oh, the short-arse?
Yeah, she's all right. Boring dress.' (1973)

shorty, shortie (1888) Often with capital initial
as a derisive or jocular nickname or form of
address ■ Bartimeus: Your middle watch, Shortie? (1914)

To reduce

boil down (1880) ■ *Saturday Review*: It is surprising
to see how much research Mr. S. has sometimes contrived to
boil down into a single line. (1880)

2. Quantity

Nothing

zip (1900) Orig and mainly US; from earlier
sense, light fast sound or movement ■ Judith
Krantz: No launch, no commercials, no nothing. Zip! Finished!
Over! (1980)

bugger-all (1918) Mainly British ■ Ian Jefferies:
'What did they offer to give you?' 'Bugger-all.' (1961)

fuck-all (1918) ■ Alison Lurie: You don't know fuck-all
about life. (1985)

Fanny Adams (1919) British; mainly in the
phrase *sweet Fanny Adams*; from the name of a
young woman murdered *c*1867; sometimes
understood as a euphemism for (*sweet*) *fuck-all* in
the same sense ■ J. R. Cole: What do they do? Sweet
Fanny Adams! (1949)

damn-all (1922) ■ Dorothy Sayers: I'll tell you my story
as shortly as I can, and you'll see I know damn all about it.
(1926)

sweet F. A. (1930) British; abbreviation of *sweet
Fanny Adams* ■ John Gardner: The small industrial
organisation whose own security officers know sweet FA.
(1967)

S.F.A. (1933) British; abbreviation of *sweet Fanny
Adams* ■ *Bulletin* (Sydney): Ask any modern sailor who has
been refused an issue of pay or rations 'What luck?' and he
will be apt to reply 'Sweet Fanny Adams', or just 'S.F.A.',
meaning that he received nothing. (1933)

not a sausage (1938) ■ *Times*: Mr Healey said the
press did not print Labour's actual policies. 'Not a sausage.'
(1981)

wot no . . .? (1945) British; originally a World
War II catchphrase protesting against shortages,
written as the caption accompanying a drawing
of the imaginary character Mr Chad; later also
in extended humorous use; *wot* representing a

casual pronunciation of *what* ■ K. Conlon: Joanna
sent a postcard which said, 'Wot no tulle and confetti?' (1979)

sod-all (1958) ■ Kingsley Amis: There's been sod-all
since. (1958)

zilch (1966) Orig and mainly US; origin unknown
■ *Sounds*: Three further 45s ensued in 1979 and '80, plus an
album which didn't sell. After that, zilch. (1984)

A trivial or insignificant amount or number

Used mainly in negative contexts, to connote
'nothing at all'. For words used in the phrases
not give a — and *not care a* —, expressing
indifference, see To be indifferent to something at
Indifference (p. 210).

twopence, tuppence (1691) In such phrases as
not worth twopence and *not give* (or *care*) *twopence*,
and also *for twopence* with the smallest
encouragement ■ E. M. Forster: I'd jump out of the
window for twopence. (*a*1960)

a damn (1760) In the phrases *not worth a damn*,
not give (or *care*) *a damn* ■ *American Mercury*: Dat
what you shooting ain't worth a damn! (1942)

**a tinker's cuss, a tinker's curse, a
tinker's damn (1824)** In such phrases as *not
worth a tinker's cuss, not matter a tinker's cuss* and
not give (or *care*) *a tinker's cuss*; from the former
reputation of tinkers for profanity ■ Osbert
Sitwell: The human being who is not worth a tinker's cuss,—
or, in a more elegant simile, two hoots—does not exist. (1942)
■ *Jewish Chronicle*: It doesn't matter a tinker's cuss whether
you amend the constitution to call the chairman president.
(1973)

a rap (1834) Mainly in the phrases *not give* (or
care) *a rap, not matter a rap*; from earlier sense,
small coin; ultimately a contraction of Irish
ropaire robber, counterfeit coin ■ *Punch*: It don't
matter a rap whether it's rough or fine. (1875)

a hooter (1839) US, dated; origin unknown
■ E. A. Dix: 'Do you mean that you don't know anything about
the matter at all?' . . . 'Not a hooter.' (1900)

a hill of beans (1863) Orig US ■ D. H. Lawrence:
Saying my say and seeing other people sup it up doesn't
amount to a hill o' beans, as far as I go. (1926)

a hoot (1878), two hoots (1925) Mainly in the
phrases *not give (care, matter) two hoots (a hoot)*;
probably the same word as *hoot* loud cry, but
compare earlier US slang *hooter* anything at all
■ *Listener*: The bonus payments scheme takes into account
not merely the important nutrients in milk (protein, vitamins
and minerals, commonly known as the 'non-fat solids') but also
fat content, which doesn't matter a hoot to anyone who doesn't
want to make butter or cheese. (1969)

**doodly-squat (1934), diddly-squat (1963),
diddly-shit (1964)** US; a fanciful formation
■ *Sunday Times Magazine*: When it was all over, I got a
huge free bag of ginseng. Lucy got diddly-squat. 'You see?' I
told her smugly, as we walked back out on the street.
'Sometimes it pays to be a crybaby.' (1997)

doodly (1939) US; shortened from *doodly-squat*

diddly (1964) US; shortened from *diddly-squat*
■ *New York Times Magazine*: This ballplayer would be
shown fumbling on the guitar, prompting the veteran rock
musician to say, 'Bo, you don't know diddly'. (1990)

squat (1967) US; probably shortened from *doodly-
squat*, or perhaps from *squat* defecate ■ Peter
Benchley: It'll be another forecast-of-Armageddon cover that
won't amount to squat. (1979)

A small amount or number

spot (a1400) ■ D. B. Wyndham Lewis: What about a spot
of lunch? (1924)

skerrick (1825) Now mainly Australian; origin
unknown ■ Frank Clune: These wadless blokes of the
Never-Never have to pay road, car, petrol, State, Federal and
Unemployment Relief taxes, and never get a skerrick in
exchange. (1936)

lick (1841) Now US; often used adverbially in *a
lick* slightly, somewhat, mainly in negative
contexts; from the notion of as much as can be
licked ■ *Black Scholar*: His grandfather was a preacher
and he couldn't read a lick. (1971) ■ M. & G. Gordon: If
you've got a lick of sense, you'll mosey back into the
woodwork. (1973)

**smidgen, smidgin, smidgeon, smitchin,
etc. (1845)** Orig US; origin unknown, perhaps
from *smitch* bit (of unknown origin) + *-en, -in*
representing a dialect pronunciation of *-ing*
■ *People's Journal*: My family would eat mince pies to a
band playing so long as there's at least a smidgeon of rum
butter to wipe over the top crust. (1973)

dribs and drabs (1861) *drib* probably short for
dribble; *drab* probably a fanciful formation based
on *drib*, although compare earlier *drab*
prostitute ■ *Daily News*: It [*sc.* a payment] was received
in dribs and drabs. (1888)

fat lot (1892) Ironical ■ Barbara Wright: Fat lot of use
it was me getting my posterior frozen for a whole night to do
my host a favour. (1967)

tad (1940) Orig and mainly US; often used
adverbially in *a tad* slightly, somewhat; from
earlier sense, small child ■ *Time*: White House
watchers also think they can glimpse a tad of arrogance
showing through the good ole boy pose. (1977) ■ *New York
Times*: The Mayor's pitch is a tad exaggerated both on the
law's certainty and on the roominess of New York's prisons.
(1980)

skosh (1959) US, orig services' slang; mainly
used adverbially in *a skosh* slightly, somewhat;
from Japanese *sukoshi* a little, somewhat,
apparently picked up by US servicemen in the
Korean war ■ *Cycle World*: The GSX-R's seat is more
comfortable than the Yamaha's thinly padded perch, and its
bars are a skosh higher. (1988)

Small in amount

measly (1864) From earlier sense, spotty (as if)
with measles ■ *Sunday Telegraph*: A spineless
exhibition by the early Yorkshire batting—they have mastered
only a measly five batting points all season—put them on the
rack yet again. (1974)

mingy (1926) From earlier sense, mean
■ *Economist*: Trading profit was a mingy ¥11.1 billion, of
which Salomon Brothers . . . accounted for three-fifths.
(1988)

Having less than desirable

shy (1895) Orig US betting slang ■ Rex Stout: I
merely thought some women were a little shy on brains,
present company not excepted. (1975)

short on (1922) ■ Evelyn Waugh: It's just this kind of
influence these children need. . . . They're rather short on
culture at the moment. (1942)

An amount or quantity

gobbet (1553) Now mainly applied to a piece of
food, or to a quantity of something abstract,
such as information or a literary or musical text
■ Dorothy Sayers: Playing the most ghastly tripe,
sandwiched in with snacks of Mendelssohn and torn-off
gobbets of the 'Unfinished'. (1930)

gob (1555) British; applied to a lump of slimy
matter; from earlier more general sense, lump

dose (1607) Applied especially to an amount or
period of something beneficial or unpleasant;
from earlier sense, quantity of medicine taken
■ *Economist*: Military co-operation between France and West
Germany has come in pretty small doses. (1987)

dollop (1812) Applied to a shapeless lump of
something soft; from earlier sense, tuft of
grass

glob (1900) Applied to a lump of slimy matter;
probably a blend of *blob* and *gob* ■ *New Scientist*:
Throughout the long coasting time, the fuel has been free of
the pull of gravity. It is probably floating around the half-empty
fuel tank in globs. (1962)

nibble, nybble (1970) Jocular; applied in
computing to half a byte or four bits; based on
byte

Number

See also at **Money** (p. 180)

One

Kelly's eye (1925) Used in the game of bingo and its forerunners ■ L. A. G. Strong: A game of 'house' was in progress, and a voice monotonously droned the numbers: ' . . . Kelly's eye.' (1933)

Three

trey, **tray (1887)** From earlier sense, the three at dice or cards, from Old French and Anglo-Norman *treis*, *trei* three (modern French *trois*) ■ Dan Burley: A deuce or tray of haircuts ago. (1944)

Four

rouf, **roaf**, **rofe**, **roof (1851)** Dated British backslang, mainly criminals'

Eleven

legs eleven (1919) Used in the game of bingo and its forerunners ■ Evelyn Waugh: Kelly's eye—number one; legs, eleven; and we'll Shake the Bag. (1945)

Sixty six

clickety click (1933) Used mainly in the game of bingo and its forerunners; rhyming slang ■ *Daily Telegraph*: Clickety click, 66; Gates of Heaven, No. 7.

A thousand

thou (1867) Often applied specifically to a thousand pounds, dollars, etc., and also (1902) to a thousandth part; abbreviation ■ *New Yorker*: The gesture cost me a cool ten thou, but I didn't begrudge it. (1965)

K, **k (1968)** Applied especially to a thousand pounds, dollars, etc., often with reference to salaries offered in job advertisements; from its use in computing to represent 1000; orig from its use as an abbreviation of *kilo-*

An unspecified number

umpty (1905) Dated; often used on an analogy with *twenty*, etc.; a fanciful verbal representation of the dash in Morse code ■ W. Faulkner: 'I never got to Heidelberg,' Charles said. 'All I had was Harvard and Stalag umpty-nine.' (1959)

To increase

skyrocket (1895) Orig US; used of prices, statistics, etc. to denote a sudden steep rise ■ John Steinbeck: The incidence of GI dysentery skyrocketed. (1943)

hike (1904) Orig US; from earlier sense, drag, lift ■ *Observer*: The Bank of England hiked its minimum lending rate . . . to 9 per cent. (1973). Hence **hike** an increase (1931) ■ *Economist*: A wave of spending at the end of last year in anticipation of hikes in indirect taxes. (1966)

jack something **up (1904)** Orig US; from earlier sense, raise with a jack ■ *Daily Telegraph*:

Reinvestment would then jack up earnings per share and hence the value of the equity. (1971)

up (1934) Orig US; from earlier more specific sense, raise a bid, stake, etc. at cards; ultimately from the adverb *up* ■ Richard Crossman: I'd talked this over with the Dame before lunch and cautiously suggested that we should make our target 135,000 houses. . . . Harold immediately upped me to 150,000. (*a*1974)

bump something **up (1940)** ■ *Spectator*: It is wise at night to look out for places which bump up the prices without warning. (1958)

zoom (1970) Used to denote a sudden sharp rise, especially in prices, costs, etc.; from earlier sense, (of an aircraft) to climb suddenly ■ *National Observer* (US): By March 1978 . . . the dropout total would zoom to 498,300—50 times the total as of March 1972. (1976)

An increase

bulge (1930) Applied to a temporary increase in volume or quantity ■ *Times*: The school population 'bulge' is moving up toward the 11–15 ages. (1956)

A large amount (of)

heaps (*a*1547) Also used adverbially in the sense 'much' ■ *Guardian*: There was so much demand, we put heaps of pressure on the workmen to get it all done. (1991) ■ Susan Coolidge: I'm glad she did, for I feel heaps better already. (1872)

loads (1606), **a load (1655)** *loads* also used adverbially in the sense 'much' ■ *Guardian*: There have been loads of cancellations, no doubt about it. (1991) ■ *Guardian*: Expect loads more of this sort of thing over the coming months. (1992)

piles (1622) ■ Sylvia Plath: It would be nice, living by the sea with piles of little kids and pigs and chickens. (1963)

no end (1623) Also used adverbially in the sense 'much' ■ R. E. Knowles: You'll have no end of fun with him. (1909) ■ *New Yorker*: Thomas had been impressed no end by the sight of Klüver . . . fixing an art-and-technology malfunction with a pair of pliers. (1970)

more than you can shake a stick at (1808) Orig and mainly US ■ Ed McBain: We get more damn cancellations than you can shake a stick at. (1960)

lots (1812) Also used adverbially in the sense 'much' ■ *Radio Times*: All that time my money's sitting in the bank earning lots of lovely interest. (1992)

swag (1812) Now mainly Australian & New Zealand; from earlier sense, loot ■ *New Journalist* (Australia): It is cheaper to buy a swag of aged situation comedies . . . than to produce even the simplest studio-bound program in Australia. (1973)

lashings (1829) Orig Anglo-Irish ■ *Lancet*: The crusty wholemeal bread . . . eaten with lashings of butter. (1966)

raft (1830) US; often in the phrase *a whole raft of*; variant of *raff* abundance (obsolete except in *riff-raff*), probably influenced by *raft* log-boat ■ *Time*: There were a whole raft of programs in the '60s followed by eight years when there was no attempt to work with any degree of compassion. (1977)

gobs, a gob (1839) US; from earlier more specific sense, a large amount of money ■ *Washington Post*: Jacobs said it would actually gain revenue because it would encourage 'oodles and gobs of compliance'. (1993)

slew, slue (1839) Orig US; from Irish *slua(gh)* crowd, multitude ■ *Radio Times*: Roger Dennhardt had served three years of a 13-year sentence for armed robbery when . . . he offered to give evidence for the Crown against a slew of former associates. (1982)

oceans (1840) ■ Margharita Laski: Poor People's children . . . had oceans of pocket-money because Poor People didn't understand the value of money. (1952)

wodge, wadge (1860) Applied orig to something bulky; perhaps an alteration of *wedge* ■ *Private Eye*: True, there's a wadge of self-opinionated dolts who drive around in head scarves and Range Rovers. (1977)

oodles (1869) Origin unknown ■ *She*: The cover assures me that there are 'oodles of prizes', which indeed there are. (1967)

scads (1869), a scad (1950) Mainly US; from *scad* dollar, hence (in the plural) money; ultimate origin unknown ■ *Washington Post*: In addition to King, scads of other veteran players should contend. (1993)

a stack (1870), stacks (1892) Orig US ■ E. F. Davies: Chesshire had stacks of letters from a girl friend and decided to read one a day for a month. (1952)

bushels (1873) Now mainly US; from earlier sense of *bushel*, unit of capacity equal to eight gallons ■ *Guardian*: The Tracey Ullman Show (BBC 2) . . . has won rave reviews and bushels of Tony Awards. (1991)

steen, 'steen (1886) US; used to denote an indefinite (but fairly large) number; shortened from *sixteen* ■ Sinclair Lewis: 'I've told you lots of times about building a really first-class inn,' said Myron. . . . 'Yes, sure, steen thousand times,' said Effie. (1934)

chunk (a1889) ■ G. Paley: He owes me a chunk of dough. (1985)

masses (1892) ■ Anne Morice: I'm sure you've got masses to do. (1974)

tons (1895) Also used adverbially in the sense 'much' ■ J. M. Barrie: I say! Do you kill many [pirates]?' 'Tons'. (1911) ■ Dorothy Halliday: He was looking tons better, with his ribs done up in cräpe. (1970)

steenth, 'steenth (1899) US; used to denote the latest in an indefinitely long series; from earlier sense, sixteenth ■ B. Reynolds: For the steenth time, you ride in a Chandler car. (1927)

lotta, lotter (1906) Contraction of *lot of* ■ *Black World*: Lotta big talk, but when you get there nothin is happenin. (1971)

a whole lot (1907) Orig US; also used adverbially in the sense 'much' ■ *Punch*: As soon as you join the Land Army you will find . . . that you are in the thick of a whole lot of live stock. (1940) ■ James Curtis: 'Well,' said the Gilt Kid, 'this is a whole lot better than making

scrubbing brushes back in the old Monastery Garden.' 'Yes, and saying to yourself, "Roll on Cocoa".' (1936)

reams (1913) From an earlier, more specific application to a large amount of paper ■ *San Francisco Examiner*: Spacecraft sent there in recent years have dispelled legends and added reams of sound, ordered data, yet the charisma of Mars remains. (1976)

bags (1917) From *bag* quantity of game shot; also used adverbially, in the sense 'much' ■ Arnold Wesker: We 'ad bags o' fun, bags o' it. (1962) ■ J. B. Morton: It's not gay, this life, but it might be bags worse. (1919)

umpteen, umteen (1918) From *ump(ty* indefinite number + *-teen* ■ Kenneth Giles: I leave business to the Estate managers, six of 'em with umpteen clerks and typists. (1973). Hence **umpteenth** (1918)

lotsa (1927) Contraction of *lots of* ■ *It*: The Notting Hill Carnival was lotsa fun for seven days and nights. (1971)

mucho (1942) From Spanish *mucho* much, many ■ *Making Music*: Warm valve distortion sound, plus mucho volume, make this an amp worthy of its chart placing. (1986)

squillion (1943) Used to denote an indeterminably large number of millions; arbitrary alteration of *million, billion*, etc. ■ *Independent*: The Prime Minister intends to fill the gap between the Queen's Christmas broadcast and the Boxing Day walk by reading Sir Frank Layfield's squillion-word report on Sizewell. (1986)

zillion (1944) Mainly US; used to denote an indeterminably large number of millions; from *z* (representing the last in a long sequence) + *m)illion* ■ *Guardian*: The whiff of news managers at work, rather than an urge to hear about British Telecom's zillion-pound share sale from the horse's mouth, took me to BT's big press conference on Friday. (1984). Hence **zillionth** (1972)

loadsa (1988) Contraction of *loads of* ■ *The Sport*: It [Clare Short MP's bill to outlaw certain sorts of pornography] stands no chance and would deprive loadsa people—men and women—of a lot of pleasure. (1988)

Having a large amount

long on (1913) Orig US ■ *Good Food Guide*: Two inspectors describe it [*sc.* a restaurant] as long on gemütlichkeit and short on good cooking. (1973)

Everyone

(all) the world and his wife (1731) ■ *World*: So much has been heard of Hardelot lately . . . that its name must be familiar to all the world and his wife. (1912)

Everything

the whole lot (1805) ■ R. D. Symons: It only takes one ole' mossy-horn to take fright at his own shadder to start the whole lot off. (1973)

the whole boodle (1833), the whole kit and boodle (a1861) US, dated; *boodle* possibly from Dutch *boedel* estate, possession ■ *Newsweek*: It gave the farm and the whole kit and boodle to Stanley. (1946)

the whole boiling (1837) Dated; from *boiling* a quantity boiled at one time ■ *F. P. Verney*: I'd like to hike out the whole boiling o' um. (1870)

the whole caboodle (*a*1848), the whole kit and caboodle (1888) Orig US; *caboodle* an alteration of *boodle* ■ *Listener*: The whole kit and caboodle of us were then investigated by the FBI to see how many subversives there were among us. (1969) ■ *Strand Magazine*: Actually, the whole caboodle, sold, not pawned, produced seventy, not fifty—hundred and twenty in all. (1923)

the lot (1867) ■ *Times*: The death of his father . . . triggers off a crisis for him too, producing a temporary breakdown, dismissal from his job, separation from his wife, the lot. (1970)

shebang, shee-bang, (obsolete) chebang (1869) North American; mainly in the phrase *the whole shebang*; from earlier senses, hut, tavern; ultimate origin unknown ■ *R. E. Megill*: The standard deviation is then calculated by dividing the total number of wells, *N*, into the sum of all the group deviations . . . and then taking the square root of the whole shebang. (1977)

the whole bag of tricks (1874), the whole box of tricks (1964) An allusion to the fable of 'the Fox and the Cat' ■ *Arnold Bennett*: I've had three 3 a.m. midwifery cases this week—forceps, chloroform, and the whole bag of tricks. (1898) ■ *Times*: Abolition would lead to the whole box of tricks based on 'kidology', with gimmicks of every kind and stamps of every colour. (1964)

sub-cheese, sub-cheeze, sub-chiz (1874) Dated military slang, orig Anglo-Indian; also in the phrase *the whole sub-cheese*; from Hindustani *sab* all + *chiz* thing ■ *B. W. Aldiss*: Of course we were lugging our ammo, machine-guns, mortars, and the whole *subcheeze* with us. (1971)

the whole shooting match (1896) Orig US ■ *BP Shield International*: This had the effect of tilting up the whole shooting match. (1974)

the (whole) works (1899) Orig US ■ *L. Kallen*: I have uncovered a sensational story that is crying to be written. . . . Best-seller list, movie, the works. (1979)

everything but (or except) the kitchen sink (1948) Orig services' slang ■ *L. White*: He goes out and buys himself an XKE Jaguar . . . it had everything but the kitchen sink on it. (1967)

the guntz (1958) Perhaps from Yiddish *gants* whole, from German *Ganze* whole, entirety ■ *John Morgan*: You don't want a pay-day, you boys are asking for the guntz. (1967)

the whole bang shoot (1963) ■ *J. N. Harris*: Before Baldwin Ogilvy agrees to locking his client away in the funny farm, he might like to investigate the whole bang shoot. (1963)

the whole schmeer (1969) North American; from *schmeer* bribery, flattery ■ *Harry Kemelman*: Some special kind of prayer maybe where you could ask for the success of our enterprise . . . especially the financing, but I was thinking of the whole *shmeer*. (1972)

the full monte, the full monty (1986) British, of uncertain origin; *monty* perhaps from the abbreviated form of the name *Montague*, as in *Montague Burton*, a British firm of gentlemen's outfitters (the expression is often applied to a full suit of clothes, especially formal wear). First recorded in 1986, although often claimed as earlier ■ *Guardian*: When conducting a funeral he wears the full monty: frock coat, top hat and a Victorian cane with metal tip. (1995)

The maximum amount

the mostest (1885) Orig dialectal; especially in the phrase *the hostess with the mostest* the perfect hostess; from *most* + the superlative suffix *-est* ■ *Daily Herald*: Here's the hostess with the mostest. . . . Her guests all agreed Sophia was pretty good . . . well, pretty, anyway. (1968)

Excess: An excessive amount; as much as one can bear

bellyful (1687) ■ *Sports Quarterly*: I have had a bellyful of trouble over the years, with white cops in particular. (1992)

orgy (1883) From earlier sense, licentious revelry ■ *Guardian*: By the time the present orgy of take-overs has finished, it will be even worse. (1991)

earful (1917) Used to denote as much as one can tolerate hearing ■ *Sewell Ford*: A parlor Bolshevist . . . had started to give me an earful about the downtrodden. (1922)

gutful (1923) ■ *Daily Telegraph*: Lately, we have had a 'gutful' of the permissiveness that seems to tolerate violence against the police. (1970)

basinful (1935) British ■ *News Chronicle*: I've had a basinful of bowler-hat and furled-umbrella parts. (1960)

Having more than is desirable

lousy with (1843) Orig US; *lousy* from earlier sense, infested with lice ■ *Winifred Holtby*: Leckton told me last month they threw in sixteen and a half couple of hounds and couldn't see a dog. Lost in thistles and willow herb—but lousy with foxes. (1936)

awash with (1954) ■ *Times*: Perhaps Britain was awash with voters who wanted Wilson on a free home trial. (1985)

Full

choc-a-block (1889) From earlier nautical sense, (of a tackle) with the two blocks run close together so that they touch each other, and are at the limit of hoisting ■ *W. S. Maugham*: The city's two or three inns were chock-a-block and men were sleeping three, four and five in a bed. (1946)

bursting (or bulging) at the seams (1962) ■ *Economist*: A doctor in one of the orphanages is only too happy to see children leave. 'The orphanages are bursting at the seams,' he says. (1988)

Behaviour, an event, etc. that is more than one can tolerate

a bit thick (1902) From the notion of thickness as being excessive ■ *W. E. Johns*: The way you snaffled my Hun! I call that a bit thick. . . . He was my meat, absolutely, yes by Jingo. (1942)

the limit (1906), the frozen limit (1916), the giddy limit (1952) Orig and (*the frozen limit*) mainly US ■ **Agatha Christie:** This house is the absolute limit!... I don't see why I should have to be burdened with such peculiar parents. (1949) ■ **W. H. L. Watson:** I don't mind their machine-guns, but their Minnenwerfer are the frozen limit! (1917)

over the odds (1922) ■ **Sapper:** I admit ... that to be called a damned Englishman by Pedro Gonsalvez is a bit over the odds. (1930)

a bit much (1939) ■ **Marshall Pugh:** 'I say, that's a bit much,' the military man said. 'Not on.' (1958)

OTT (1982) British; applied to something outrageous; abbreviation of *over the top* ■ *Sun:* The Bill continues to go from strength to strength because all the bobbies are completely O.T.T. (1988)

To produce in excessive quantity

churn something **out (1912)** ■ *Saturday Review:* Nor is there any doubt at all that 'Limelight' is preferable to the vast majority of pictures churned out by Hollywood each year. (1952)

Excessive in quantity

a dime a dozen (1930) North American; applied to something so plentiful as to be worthless ■ **Irwin Shaw:** 'I thought you were too good looking just to be nobody.' 'A dime a dozen,' Wesley said. 'I'm just a seaman at heart.' (1977)

wall-to-wall (1967) Often jocular; applied to something ubiquitous; from earlier sense, (of a carpet) covering the entire floor ■ *New Statesman:* Their sponsors include the IBA ... and the BBC (in whose Reithian corridors the epithet 'wall-to-wall Dallas' was reputedly coined). (1984)

Curbing excess

eighty-six on (1981) US; used to request no more of something; from *eighty-six*, used in restaurants to denote that the supply of an item has run out ■ **William Safire:** Eighty-six on etymologies for 'cocktail'. (1981)

Calculation

tot something **together (1760), tot** something **up (1839)** Used to denote adding up; *tot* from the dated noun *tot* total, short for *total* ■ **Stuart & Park:** A waiter totting up the account as you passed through. (1895)

yay, yea (1960) US; used in estimating quantity or size, especially in the phrases *yay big* and *yay high*; probably from *yea* yes ■ **Thomas Kochman:** Jeff fired on him. He came back and all this was swelled up bout yay big, you know. (1972)

number crunching (1971) Applied to computer calculations involving very large numbers ■ *Nature:* If that mini can also be connected in to a large mainframe computer as a 'front-end machine', then the tasks which can be carried out (particularly 'number crunching') can be that much more sophisticated and complex. (1975)

3. Fate

Something dependent on chance

toss-up (1809) ■ *Wall Street Journal:* Some said it's a toss-up whether oil prices go up or down. (1989)

The perverse workings of fate

(that's) how (or **the way) the cookie crumbles (1956)** Orig US; denoting the way things turn out, as fate decrees, without any possibility of alteration ■ **P. G. Wodehouse:** Oh well, that's the way the cookie crumbles. You can't win 'em all. (1961)

Murphy's law (1958) Orig US; applied to a humorous principle embodying the tendency of things to go wrong; apparently developed from a remark of Captain E. *Murphy* of the Wright Field Aircraft Laboratory in 1949 ■ *New York Times Magazine:* 'If anything can go wrong, it will,' says Murphy's Law. (1974)

Sod's law (1970) Applied to a humorous principle embodying the tendency of things to go wrong; from *sod* despicable person

That which is preordained

one's name (and number) is on something **(1917), one's number is on** something **(1925)** Used with reference to a bullet, shell, etc., with the implication that one is doomed to be killed by it ■ **Dick Francis:** The bomb probably had my name on it in the first place. (1973) ■ **Celia Fremlin:** I'm as safe here as ... any where ... if it's got your number on it, you'll get it, no matter where you are! (1974)

A run of (good or bad) luck

spin (1917) Australian & New Zealand; from the spinning of a coin in the game of two-up ■ **H. P. Tritton:** When I remarked that he'd had a tough spin he grinned, 'Served me right for being such a blanky fool.' (1964)

Bad luck

hard lines (1824) Probably of nautical origin ■ **John Wainwright:** It was hard lines about the Wilture chap. Being shot could not be a pleasant experience. (1985)

hard cheese (1876), hard cheddar (1931) British; often used as an exclamation of commiseration ■ **J. I. M. Stewart:** It was hard cheese on him coming up against another top-class specimen. (1973)

Saltash luck, Saltash chance (1914) Applied to luck resulting in a miserable task that involves getting wet through; supposedly from the lucklessness of the fishermen of Saltash, a port in Cornwall ■ **Bartimeus:** One of the securing chains wants tautening. . . . 'Saltash Luck' for some one! (1914)

rough spin (1924) Australian; applied to a misfortune or piece of bad luck

tough shit (1934) Orig US; often used as an ironic exclamation ■ **James Carroll:** Tough shit, Lady! Morning wears to evening and hearts break. (1978)

T.S. (1944) US, services' slang; abbreviation of *tough shit*

tough titty (1958) Often used as an ironic exclamation ■ **Anthony Burgess:** [I got] robbed and rumpled.—Tough titty she said with little sympathy. (1971)

snake eyes (1972) North American; from earlier sense, a throw of two ones with a pair of dice ■ **Gore Vidal:** Let's just hope it won't be snake eyes for Jim Kelly. (1978)

Unlucky

stiff (1918) Australian & New Zealand ■ **R. Boyd:** I recall . . . a waiter . . . responding to my cirumspect enquiry about the possibility of a glass of wine with the succinct phrase: 'I think you'll be stiff, mate.' (1960)

shit out of luck (1942) ■ **Mario Puzo:** So you see, my dear, you're shit out of luck. (1978)

An unlucky person

schlimazel, shlemazl, etc. **(1948)** Mainly US; applied to someone consistently unlucky or accident-prone; Yiddish, from Middle High German *slim* crooked and Hebrew *mazzāl* luck

■ *Encounter.* If the *schlimazl* went into the hat business, babies would be born without heads. (1960)

Lucky

jammy (1915) Compare earlier sense, excellent ■ **Trevanian:** 'I almost always win. Isn't that odd?' The Sergeant regarded the slim body. . . . 'I'd say you were bloody jammy.' (1973)

tinny (1918) Australian & New Zealand; from *tin* (*back* lucky person + *-y* ■ **Osmar White:** You'll have to be pretty tinny to pin down those blokes. (1978)

tin-arsed (1937) Australian & New Zealand

A lucky person

tin back, tin arse, tin bum (1897) Australian ■ **D'Arcy Niland:** I come up with a stone worth five hundred quid. . . . Tin-bum, they call me. (1955)

A piece of good luck

break (1926) Orig US ■ **Graham Greene:** We had a lucky break. (1938)

To enjoy good luck

luck out (1954) US ■ **Joseph Wambaugh:** I started making inquiries . . . and damned if I didn't luck out and get steered into a good job. (1972)

luck into (1959) Orig US; denoting acquiring something by good fortune ■ **Jean Potts:** The rent was fantastically low; she had lucked into it a couple of years ago through an artist friend. (1970)

4. Possibility, Probability, & Certainty

A negligible prospect

With the exception of *fat chance* and *fat show*, these expressions are used in negative or other non-assertive contexts.

an earthly (1899) Elliptical for *an earthly chance* any chance at all ■ *Listener.* Received standard, like the Liberals, won't stand an earthly. (1965)

a cat's chance, a cat in hell's chance (1902) First recorded in its current form in 1902, but compare 'No more chance than a cat in hell without claws; said of one who enters into a dispute or quarrel with one greatly above his match', Francis Grose *A Classical Dictionary of the Vulgar Tongue* (1796) ■ *Guardian.* One seaman said the union had not 'a cat in hell's chance' of beating the Government as well as the shipowners. (1966)

fat chance (1906) ■ **W. S. Maugham:** Fat chance I've got of going to France now. (1933)

a Chinaman's chance (1911) Mainly US ■ **F. Yerby:** You haven't a Chinaman's chance of raising that money in Boston. (1951)

a hope (or chance) in hell (1923) ■ **Jack Trevor Story:** 'What are the chances of a job here, then?' Albert

asked. 'For you—not a chance in hell.' She spoke matter-of-factly. (1963)

a snowball's chance (in hell) (1931) Orig US ■ **Arthur Hailey:** 'Told 'em there wasn't a snowball's chance,' a woman assistant dispatcher called over. (1979)

fat show (1948) New Zealand ■ **David Ballantyne:** It would be corker if he could go outside with Carole Plowman. . . . Fat show! (1948)

Something unlikely to happen

pie in the sky (1911) Orig US; usually applied to an extravagant claim or promise that is unlikely to be fulfilled ■ *Undercurrents:* To expect the NHS to encompass all sorts of fringe or alternative practices whilst even the level of basic medical care that people want is unobtainable in some areas (abortion) is pie in the sky. (1977)

Something certain

a sure thing (1836) Orig US ■ **Ngaio Marsh:** I appreciate your reluctance to form a theory too soon. . . . But . . . it looks a sure thing to me. (1963)

a moral (1861) Australian; short for *a moral certainty* ■ *Canberra Times.* The senior puisne judge (who is an absolute moral for the Chief Justiceship come February next year) . . . is almost certainly among the ranks of the deeply concerned. (1986)

a cinch (1888) Orig US; often applied specifically to a horse considered certain to win a race; from earlier sense, saddle-girth, hence a firm or secure hold

cert (1889) Often applied specifically to a horse considered certain to win a race; often in the phrase *a dead cert*; abbreviation of *certainty*
■ *Me*: Jack Nicholson—as a menacing colonel who's trying to fix the case—looks a dead cert for an Oscar nomination. (1993)

a monty, a monte (1894) Australian & New Zealand; often applied specifically to a horse considered certain to win a race; probably from US *monte* game of chance played with cards, from Spanish *monte* mountain ■ J. Wynnum: I was given the drum . . . that if I put my name to the dotted line, I'd be a monty to get drafted to the U.S. destroyer. (1965)

a lead-pipe cinch (1898) US ■ *New York Times*: To be sure, speculation in gold is not a lead-pipe cinch; its price can go down as well as up. (1973)

a lay-down (1935) Orig US ■ *Times*: A prize will go to the best-dressed trainer of the meeting. It sounds like a lay-down for Henry Cecil. (1984)

a motser, a motsa, a motza, a motzer (1936) Australian; probably from earlier sense (not recorded until later), a large amount of money ■ Richard Beilby: You better let that bugger get well ahead. . . . The Stuka'll be a motsa to have a go at him. (1970)

stone ginger (1936) From the name of a celebrated New Zealand racehorse

stickout (1937) US; applied to a horse that seems a certain winner ■ *Sun* (Baltimore): A 'stickout' on paper, Nokomis was in front most of the way along the six-furlong route. (1949)

Impossible

no go (1825) Often in the phrase *it's* (or *it was*) *no go* ■ J. R. Lowell: 'You must rise', says the leaven. 'I can't', says the dough; 'Just examine my bumps, and you'll see it's no go'. (1888)

Possible, possibly

on the cards (1849) Perhaps from the notion that any given number on a playing card is equally likely to be turned up, or perhaps from the notion of playing cards being used to foretell the future ■ *Daily Mail*: The Footsie fell 12.1 to 2573.3 on lack of support. A rally could be on the cards today. (1991)

Certain(ly)

as sure as eggs is (or are) eggs (1699) The original recorded form is *as sure as eggs be eggs*

as sure as God made little (green) apples (1874) Mainly US ■ M. Lasswell: I'm gonna learn to read sure as God made little apples. (1942)

in the bag (1922) Orig US; applied to something that is certain to be successfully achieved ■ *Economist*: The message . . . contains a frank warning that independence is not 'in the bag'. (1957)

for sure (1971) In standard use since the 16th century; in modern colloquial use, mainly in the phrase *that's for sure* ■ C. Ross: Well, who's telling? Not me, that's for sure. (1981)

as sure as hell (1976) Orig US ■ *Listener*: Wayne . . . introduces me to Commemorativo Tequilla. 'It doesn't hurt your head, but it may hurt your back, as you sure as hell fall over a lot.' (1976)

To be certain

bet one's life (1852) Orig US ■ P. G. Wodehouse: 'You will order yourself something substantial, marvel-child?' 'Bet your life,' said the son and heir tersely. (1913)

bet one's boots (1856) Orig US ■ Malcolm Lowry: 'You bet your boots,' he replied. (1933)

I bet, I'll bet, bet (1857) ■ *Independent*: I bet Derek Jarman never had as much fun as this. (1991)

bet one's bottom dollar (1866) Orig US; *bottom dollar* = last dollar ■ *Dissent*: And I'd bet my bottom dollar that Negro hipsters, among themselves, often put down the whites. (1958)

betcha, betcher (1922) Representing a colloquial pronunciation of *bet you* or *bet your* (*life*) ■ G. Butler: I collared a kid . . . and asked him if he wanted to earn a shilling. 'You betcha, mister,' he said. (1940)

Uncertain

touch and go (1815) Denoting something that is uncertain as to the result; compare earlier application to something quickly done ■ *Daily Mail*: James is one of two surviving triplets born 12 weeks early, and it was touch and go whether he would make it. (1991)

on spec (1832) British; denoting doing something without the certainty of success; *spec* abbreviation of *speculation* ■ B. Hines: 'Is he expecting you?' 'No, we just came on spec.' (1981)

To cause to be uncertain

keep guessing (1896) Orig US ■ H. Zink: Murphy proceeded with considerable caution, sometimes withdrawing from a position, sometimes forcing it, and altogether keeping his opponents guessing what he would do next. (1930)

5. **Risk**

Risky

dicey (*c*1944) Orig airforce slang; from *dice* (from the risk of gambling with dice) + *-y* ■ P. Capon: The river got a little dicey. I thought we'd wait for the moon. (1959)

A risky or dangerous experience or situation

scrape (1709) Perhaps from the notion of being 'scraped' when going through a narrow passage ■ *Independent*: Mickey Rooney and his friends would go off, they'd get into a scrape and his father . . . would . . . get them out of trouble. (1991)

shaky do (1942) Dated, orig R.A.F. slang ■ Fitzroy Maclean: The earth all round was kicked up by a burst from the plane's tail-gunner. . . . 'This,' said the Australian, 'is going to be a shaky do.' (1949)

To do something risky; take a risk

chance it (1870) ■ Edward Copeland: Genteel novelists almost never make their heroines authors; didactic novelists must have a very pressing moral justification indeed for them to chance it. (1994)

chance one's arm (1889), **chance one's mit** (1919) ■ *Economist*: Mr. Macmillan may have no more by-elections in this Parliament by which to judge when to chance his arm. (1959)

ask for trouble, ask for it (1909) ■ Harold Pinter: I don't know how they live down there. It's asking for trouble. (1960)

push one's luck (*a*1911) From the notion of presuming on the continuation of a run of good luck ■ John Welcome: He had never won the Derby and . . . had . . . announced that he would not die until he did. As he must by now be touching eighty. . ., this was pushing his luck pretty hard. (1959)

lead with one's chin (1949) Denoting behaving or speaking incautiously; from earlier boxing slang sense, leave one's chin unprotected against an opponent's punches ■ *Listener*: I thought it was a good idea to say that I was prejudiced to begin with, to lead with my chin. (1968)

stick one's neck out (1926) Orig US; denoting exposing oneself to danger, criticism, etc. ■ H. Hastings: We've stuck our necks out—we're looking for trouble, see? (1950)

dice with death (1941) Orig motor-racing slang ■ *Guardian*: The President may yet be dicing with political death. (1992)

go for broke (1951) Orig US; denoting risking everything in one determined effort at something ■ *Guardian*: If he were to go for broke on behalf of the Negroes . . . the President would endanger the moral reform cause. (1963)

go (out) for one's tea (1978) Northern Ireland; denoting going out on a dangerous mission ■ F. Burton: A Provo would scoff at the Officials' merely elocutionary skills while they were 'going out for their tea' (that is, going on military operations which might result in their death). (1978)

As a speculation; without certainty of success

on spec (1832) Orig US; *spec* short for *speculation* ■ B. Hines: 'Is he expecting you?' 'No, we just came on spec.' (1981)

6. **Advantage & Disadvantage**

An advantage

plus (1708) ■ *Washington Post*: Radio city is one block from the Hotel Victoria. Other location plusses: Madison Square Garden is two blocks away, so are all subways. (1959)

the bulge (1841) Dated, orig US; especially in the phrase *have the bulge on* have the advantage over ■ P. G. Wodehouse: The Assyrians had the bulge on him. (1963)

grouter (1902) Australian; applied to an unfair advantage; especially in the phrase *come in on the grouter* gain an unfair advantage; often applied specifically, in the game of two-up, to waiting until a long run of heads or tails and then betting on the opposite on the assumption that it must soon come up; origin unknown

ace in the hole (1908) Orig US; applied to an advantage so far held in reserve; from earlier sense, high-value playing card concealed up one's sleeve ■ *New York Times*: In the long haul, . . . AM's ace in the hole may be the $213 million net operating loss carryforward it still has left from its 1981–82 losses. (1984)

the catbird seat (1942) US; especially in the phrase *in the catbird seat* in a superior or advantageous position; from *catbird* an American thrush

mileage (1962) Applied to advantage or benefit to be extracted from a particular situation; from earlier sense, miles travelled ■ Ted Allbeury: They'd enjoy stirring up the Canadians, and the French-Canadians would . . . get a lot of political mileage. (1974)

In an advantageous situation

sitting pretty (1921) ■ *Listener*: At the moment the motor industry is 'sitting pretty'. (1959)

To be in an advantageous situation

have (got) it made (1955) Orig US ■ Adam Diment: She had . . . big, well-proportioned hips. I tell you, if the derrière gets with-it again this bird had it made. (1968)

have (got) it wired (1955) Orig US ▪ *Dirt Bike*: All he had to do was stay on time—maybe even drop a few more points, and he still had it wired. (1985)

The most advantageous course of action

best bet (1941) Orig US ▪ *John o' London's*: The best bet would have been to ship this Mexican funny [*sc.* a film] straight out on circuit. (1961)

To get an advantage over someone; put someone in a disadvantageous situation

get (or **have**) **the dead-wood on (1851)** US; from *dead wood* pin in tenpin bowling that has been knocked down and lies in the alley in front of those remaining ▪ **Erle Stanley Gardner**: Well, they've evidently got the dead-wood on you now, Perry. They know that you took Eva Martell to that rooming-house. (1951)

get (or **have**) **the drop on (1867)** Orig US; from earlier more specific sense, beat someone to the draw with one's firearm ▪ **Nicholas Blake**: He suspects Miss Thistlethwaite . . . of having got the drop on him. (1940)

have someone **by the short hairs (1888)** Compare earlier obsolete *have where the hair is short* (1872); *short hairs* = pubic hair ▪ **Sayers & Eustace**: She's evidently got her husband by the short hairs. (1930)

have someone **on toast (1889)** ▪ E. F. Benson: To think that half an hour ago that little squirt thought he had us on toast. (1916)

catch someone **bending (1910)** From the notion of the vulnerability of someone bending over ▪ **Angus Wilson**: He then goes off singing, 'My word, if I catch you bending, my word, if I catch you bending.' (1967)

have (or **get**) **the jump on (1912)** Orig US ▪ *Real Estate Review*: Each of these new developers hopes to get the jump on the other by adding more square footage to the units and giving more in amenities. (1972)

have the goods on (1913) Denoting having knowledge or information that gives one a hold over someone ▪ **Mary McCarthy**: He had a sudden inkling that they would have liked to get the goods on Mulcahy. (1952)

have the wood on (1926) Australian & New Zealand; perhaps in allusion to the Australian slang verb *wooden* hit, knock unconscious ▪ **Leslie Haylen**: It was another of his occasions of fear: she liked having the wood on you. (1965)

have someone **over a barrel (1939)** Orig US; apparently in allusion to the state of someone placed over a barrel to clear their lungs of water after being rescued from drowning ▪ Letitia McClung: You sure have me over a barrel. You caught me red-handed. (1945)

have someone **by the short and curlies (1948)** *short and curlies* = pubic hair ▪ John Gardner: 'Stalemate?'. . . 'Looks like it. . . . Got us hard by the short and curlies. I wouldn't try arguing.' (1969)

have someone **by the balls (1950)** ▪ *Harper's*: As you can see, I'm one of the fortunate few who has Blue Cross by the balls. (1993)

A disadvantage

minus (1708) ▪ *Economist*: Moreover, London's rivals are still affected by plenty of minuses. Zurich's stamp tax continues to smother the development of Swiss securities trading. . . . (1988)

Someone or something disadvantageous

a liability (1974) ▪ *Lancaster Guardian*: British Rail want to close it because it is a maintenance liability. (1987)

A disadvantageous situation

the short end (1904) Orig US ▪ *Time*: Annie went back to Broadway on the short end of a 6-2 score. (1977)

In a disadvantageous situation

snookered (1915) British; from earlier literal sense, (in snooker) unable to hit the object ball because another ball is between it and the cue ball

behind the eight ball (1932) US; from the disadvantage, in a variety of the game of pool, of having the black ball (numbered 8 and which one is penalized for touching) between the cue ball and the object ball ▪ *New York Herald*: An attempt to describe what makes the drawings funny lands you behind the eight ball. (1944)

with one's pants down (1932), (mainly British) **with one's trousers down (1966)** Orig US; mainly in the phrase *caught with one's pants* (or *trousers*) *down* caught in a state of embarrassing unpreparedness ▪ F. Clifford: By that time the shooting will seem to be as haphazard as can possibly be, as if we'd almost been caught with our trousers down. (1967)

off the pace (1951) Orig US; denoting a position behind the leader in a contest; originally applied in horse-racing to one who is slower than the leading horses, especially in the early part of a race ▪ *Rally Sport*: The best two-wheel drive car was in 20th place, seven seconds per mile off the pace. (1987)

Lack of advantage; a stalemate

Mexican stand-off (1891) Orig and mainly US ▪ Donald MacKenzie: As things stood it was a Mexican standoff. He couldn't go to the law but . . . nor could the Koreans. (1979)

7. **Easiness**

Easy

like/as easy as shelling peas/ (dated) **beans** (a1688)

like/as easy as falling off a log (1839) ■ *Times*: Acting? said Ernest Borgnine. Why, there was nothing to it, really. 'For me,' he said, 'it's as easy as falling off a log.' (1973)

soft (1841) Applied derogatorily to something that is easy and pleasant; current in standard English in the 17th century ■ Kingsley Amis: 'Damon, what's a wanker?'. . . 'These days a waster, a shirker, someone who's fixed himself a soft job or an exalted position by means of an undeserved reputation on which he now coasts.' 'Oh. Nothing to do with tossing off then?' 'Well, connected with it, yes, but more metaphorical than literal.' (1978)

as easy as winking (1907) From earlier obsolete *like winking* (1827) ■ H. Wyndham: She'll . . . make a hundred and fifty a week as easy as winking. (1907)

as easy as ABC (1912)

cushy (1915) Applied to a post, job, etc. that is easy and pleasant; Anglo-Indian, from Hindustani ḳhūsh pleasant ■ Alan Sillitoe: You were always on the lookout for a cushy billet. (1970)

like/as easy as taking candy from a baby/child/ etc. (1926) ■ *Flynn's*: Jack rollin' th' workstiffs was like takin' candy from th' kids. (1926)

Bob's your uncle (1937) British; used to express the ease with which a task can be completed successfully ■ Nicholas Blake: Three curves and a twiddle, label it 'Object', and bob's your uncle. (1949)

no sweat (1955) Orig US; used to emphasize that something can be done easily ■ *Publishers Weekly*: Mrs Wallach complains that she cannot use plastic book jackets on books with maps on the inside covers. No sweat! We paste the book pocket . . . on the next inside page, [etc.]. (1972)

no problem (1963) Orig US; used to emphasize that something can be done easily ■ Martin Amis: Finally, every time I emptied my glass, he took it, put more whisky in it, and gave it back to me, saying 'No problem' again through his nose. (1973)

easy-peasy (1976) Orig children's slang; arbitrary reduplication of *easy* ■ *Fast Forward*: 'Easy-peasy' we hear you cry. 'We'll wait until we hear the chart and then rush a postcard in,' we hear you cheatingly thinking to yourself. (1990)

Something easy to do

child's play (c1386)

gift (1832) ■ *Gramophone*: Even in No. 6 (a gift, I would have thought, for so nimble-fingered a pianist), . . . Kazkevich shows little beyond a token involvement. (1994)

snap (1877) Mainly North American ■ *Technology Week*: Blazing a path to the moon is no snap. Neither is charting a career. (1967)

pudding (1887), **pud** (1938) US; applied especially to an easy college course

pie (1889) Orig US; especially in the phrase *as easy (simple*, etc.) *as pie* ■ P. G. Wodehouse: This kid Mitchell was looked on as a coming champ in those days. . . . I guess I looked pie to him. (1929)

snip (a1890) ■ Nevil Shute: It is a snip; we will get both of them. (1945)

dolly (1895) Applied in cricket to a very easy catch; often used adjectivally ■ *Times*: Lane-Fox . . . failed to get to the pitch of the ball and cocked up a dolly catch. (1955)

sitter (1898) Used especially in sporting contexts; probably from the notion of a game bird that sits and is therefore easy to shoot ■ *Observer*: A series of very bad shots, including a double fault by Borotra, the missing of absolute 'sitters' by both players and the driving of many easy balls into the net well over the baseline. (1927)

duck soup (1902) Orig and mainly US ■ Ogilvy & Anderson: The number 307, comes out, in binary notation, to be 100111001, which would not have the convenience of 307 at the grocery store, but is duck soup for the Computer. (1966)

pipe (1902) US ■ P. G. Wodehouse: This show's a pipe, and any bird that comes in is going to make plenty. (1952)

gaper (1903) Applied in cricket to an easy catch, especially one that is dropped; probably from the notion that something which 'gapes' open offers easy success ■ *Times*: Certain younger members of the side were dropping some regular 'gapers'. (1963)

cinch (1904) Orig US; from earlier sense, a certainty ■ Herbert Quick: The recent progress in bacteriological science . . . seemed to make the diagnosis a cinch. (1911)

pushover (1906) Orig US; from the notion of pushing something over without any effort ■ Peter Malloch: About the security van. . . . It's going to be hard to take. . . . Eight years ago they were a push-over. (1973)

soda (1917) Australian; perhaps from earlier sense, the deal card in the game of faro ■ G. H. Johnston: 'The Middle East was a soda beside this,' one of them told me. (1943)

money for jam (1919), **money for old rope** (1936) Orig services' slang ■ Evelyn Waugh: At the moment there were no mortars and he was given instead a light and easily manageable counterfeit of wood which was slung on the back of his haversack, relieving him of a rifle. At present it was money for old rope. (1942)

breeze (1928) Orig US ■ S. Carpenter: All in all, the test was a breeze. (1962)

kid stuff, kid's stuff, kids' stuff (1929) Orig US

a piece of cake (1936) ■ Terence McLean: They took the field against Canterbury as if the match were a 'piece of cake'. (1960)

doddle (1937) British; perhaps from the verb *doddle* walk unsteadily ■ Martin Woodhouse: If the climb had reached any level of difficulty higher than Moderate, which is the Climbers' Club's polite way of labelling a gumshoe doddle, we'd have died. (1966)

drop-in (1937) US; often applied to money easily acquired from someone; perhaps from the notion of a gullible person 'dropping into' a confidence trick

snack (1941) Australian ■ R. Beilby: 'How could I do that, Harry?' 'Easy. It'll be a snack.' (1970)

turkey shoot (1947) US; applied to a military engagement in which the enemy are easily routed; first recorded in 1947, but brought to prominence in the Gulf War (1991); from the fact that the turkey, a cumbersome bird, often presents a sitting target ■ *New Yorker*: The Administration was . . . coming under substantial fire for engaging in 'overkill': Kuwait had been liberated; tens of thousands of Iraqi soldiers had surrendered; and it was clearly no contest. Even American soldiers were expressing some revulsion at being engaged in a 'turkey shoot'. (1991)

a piece of piss (1949) ■ *Observer*: John Lines, who has a tough fight defending his seat in Bartley Green ward, snorted when asked if his task would be easier under a Labour government and answered bluntly: 'Piece of piss'. (1996)

cushy number (1959) ■ *Listener*: Transferred to what was described as a 'cushy number' with the Commandos. (1968)

8. Difficulty

Difficult

ticklish (1591) Applied to something that is difficult because it requires sensitive handling; from earlier sense, sensitive ■ *New York Daily News*: The older man . . . headed for the Grand Hotel where he was so well-known as to be considered an honorary resident when it came to the ticklish question of late-night drinking. (1989)

hairy (1848) ■ William Cooper: The problem was of the kind that Mike described in his up-to-date slang as 'hairy'. (1966)

no picnic (1888) ■ Bernard Fergusson: It was going to be no picnic co-ordinating land, sea and air forces from so many different points of departure at so many different speeds. (1961)

dodgy (1898) Implying difficulty with an element of risk; from earlier sense, full of dodges, evasive ■ Harold Pinter: It'd be a bit dodgy driving tonight. (1960)

solid (1916) Australian & New Zealand ■ Ruth Park: After all, Auntie Josie's got all them kids to look after. It must be pretty solid for her with Grandma as well. (1948)

no joke (1920) From earlier sense, a serious matter ■ *Daily Telegraph*: It is no joke, day after day seeking to plead a cause which Mother Russia has declared beyond redemption. (1991)

laugher (1964) US; applied to an easily won baseball game

gimme (1986) Orig US; from earlier golfing sense, short putt conceded to one's opponent

In an easy situation

in clover (1710) From the notion of 'clover being extremely delicious and fattening to cattle' (Samuel Johnson) ■ Robert Vaughan: He has been sometimes in clover as a travelling tutor, sometimes he has slept and fared hard. (1856)

on a plate (1935) Applied to something easily acquired ■ Leonard Cooper: That was an easy one— Steyne had handed it to us on a plate. (1960)

To do something easily

romp (1881) Orig horse-racing slang, from the notion of winning in a carefree manner ■ Jimmy Sangster: I romped through the training, passing out eventually with the highest marks anyone could remember. (1968)

do something **(standing) on one's head (1896)** ■ J. M. White: The climb he wanted me to attempt was a simple one. At Cambridge I could have done it standing on my head. (1968)

Easily

a mile off (1970) ■ Joyce Porter: She was on the scrounge. . . . You could spot it a mile off. (1970)

fiddly (1926) Applied to something small and awkward to do or use; from *fiddle* tinker + -*y* ■ *Times*: 'Fiddly things' should be done by automatic machines. (1960)

Something difficult

brute (1876) From earlier sense, unpleasant person

a tall order (1893) Orig US ■ C. A. W. Monckton: I . . . told the police we would make the attempt; clearly they thought we were taking on a devil of a tall order. (1920)

bastard (1915) From earlier sense, unpleasant person ■ Maurice Shadbolt: At first Ned and Nick had to milk in the open, which was a bastard when it rained. (1972)

bugger (1915) From earlier sense, unpleasant person ■ R. Russell: That solo is a bugger to play. (1961)

pig (1925) From earlier sense, unpleasant person ■ *Hot Car*: The car became a pig to start. (1978)

bitch (1928) From earlier sense, something unpleasant ■ *Guardian*: He thinks the script is too long and perfunctory. I thought that was a bitch of a combo to pull off, myself. (1992)

cow (1933) Australian & New Zealand; from earlier sense, something unpleasant ■ Dorothy

Hewett: I starched your petticoat stiff as a board, and it was a cow to iron. (1956)

swine (1933) From earlier sense, unpleasant person ■ Helen MacInnes: This car's . . . a swine to drive at slow speeds. (1976)

honey (1934) US; ironical re-application of earlier sense, someone or something good of its kind

sod (1936) From earlier sense, unpleasant person ■ *Hot Car.* The finish will be a nice satin which is a sod to keep clean. (1977)

ball-breaker (1942), ball-buster (1954) Orig US; applied to a difficult, boring, or exasperating task, problem, or situation; from *balls* testicles

hot potato (1952) Applied to a thing or situation that is difficult or unpleasant to deal with; from the notion of being difficult to hold; compare the earlier phrase *drop something like a hot potato* get rid of something quickly ■ *New Scientist.* The current hot potato in the sociological field is the question of poverty in Britain today. (1969)

tough nut (1977) Often in the phrase *a tough nut to crack* something difficult to do ■ *Independent.* It's difficult to beat the three-year-olds in the King George because of the weight concession. . . . Generous [sc. a horse] will be a tough nut to crack. (1991)

Something difficult to solve; a problem

teaser (1759) ■ Noel Coward: Oh Lord! That's a teaser—arithmetic's never been my long suit. (1959)

poser (1793) From obsolete *pose* puzzle + *-er* ■ *Daily Mail:* Nigel Jemson presented Nottingham Forest manager Brian Clough with a selection poser yesterday. (1991)

brain-teaser (1923) ■ Ogilvy & Anderson: Here are some of the super brain-teasers that Sierpinski asks us to ponder. (1966)

skull buster (1926) US ■ Mezzrow & Wolfe: Most of my skullbusters got solved at The School. (1946)

The most difficult situation

the hot seat (1942) Usually in the phrase *in the hot seat* ■ *Listener.* After fifteen months in this critical hot seat . . . between listeners and the BBC I am saying my farewell. (1966)

the sharp end (1976) Usually in the phrase *at the sharp end*; from earlier nautical slang sense, the bows of a ship ■ Anthony Price: The distant sound of bombing indicated that he was very close to the sharp end of the war. (1980)

To have something difficult to do

have one's work cut out (1862) ■ R. A. Freeman: 'You will have your work cut out,' I remarked, 'to trace that man. The potter's description was pretty vague.' (1927)

9. Precision, Approximation, & Correctness

Precise(ly)

to a T, to a tee (1693) T perhaps short for *tittle* the smallest detail ■ *Listener.* John Hollis had Walter off to a tee. (1966)

bang (1828) Orig US ■ L. A. G. Strong: Bang opposite him . . . hung a . . . blue cylinder. (1931)

on the button (1903) Orig US ■ *New Yorker.* I . . . then strolled jauntily over to Ricky's, at five o'clock on the button. (1952)

straight-up (1910) ■ Arnold Bennett: This new Licensing Act will close every public house . . . at eleven o'clock, and a straight-up eleven at that! (1910)

spot on (1920) ■ *Notes and Queries.* His thesis is provocative, its evidences spot-on, and his conclusions pretty convincing. (1982)

bang on (1936) ■ *Spectator.* As a realistic tale of low life in London, it is bang on. (1958)

on the nose (1937) US ■ Norman Mailer: Malcolm Cowley was right on the nose when he wrote that *The Deer Park* was a far more difficult book to write than *The Naked and the Dead.* (1959)

on the schnozz (1949) US; from *schnozz* nose ■ Ellery Queen: Twenty minutes to twelve on the schnozz. (1967)

slap bang (1963) Compare earlier, obsolete sense, without delay ■ Anthony Smith: That gas was contentedly holding over three-quarters of a ton 1,500 feet above a lake and slap bang in the middle of the sky. (1963)

Approximation

guesstimate (1934) Orig US; applied to an estimate based on both guesswork and reasoning; blend of *guess* and *estimate* ■ *Daily Telegraph.* £1000 tax free clear profit. . . . This is proved performance—not an optimistic guesstimate. (1970)

ballpark (1957) Orig US; used adjectivally to denote that something is approximately but not precisely right, and also in the phrase *in the (right) ballpark*, denoting plausible accuracy; from *ballpark* baseball stadium, from the notion of a broad area ■ *New Yorker.* How many times per week do you have sexual relations? On the average—just a ballpark figure. (1984) ■ *SLR Camera.* This basic filtration, though, has very often saved me a test strip because it's got me into the right ball park filter-wise. (1978)

Correct, right

on the beam (1941) From the notion of being on the course indicated by a radio beam ■ *Observer.* Hugh Burden, as Barnaby, was right on the beam from the start. (1948)

To be correct

cook with gas (or (dated) **electricity**, **radar**) **(1941)** Orig US ■ *Time*: Many a student . . . figured that . . . Thurman Arnold was cooking with gas. (1942)

cook on the front burner (1945) US, dated ■ N. Carter: 'These pens are no good.' . . . 'You're cooking on

the front burner, Mac,' I replied in a kind of English to relieve my feelings. (1965)

To correct, put right

straighten out (1956) Denoting showing someone where they are mistaken ■ William Styron: Look, Sophie, you're confusing me. Straighten me out. Please. (1979)

10. **Mistakes**

bloomer (1889) Orig Australian; from *blooming error* ■ *Economist*: 'The Times' . . . has this week made a bloomer about a president. (1959)

howler (1890) From earlier sense, something glaring or excessive ■ *The Month*: The specimens of schoolboy blunders which, under the head of 'Howlers', are so popular in our journals. (1894)

flub (1900) Orig US; applied especially to a bad shot in golf or other sports; origin unknown ■ John Steinbeck: In my younger days I played tennis. . . . A servant . . . could pick up his masters flubs at doubles. (1952)

blob (1903) British; from earlier sense, score of nought at cricket ■ Leonard Cooper: He'd been in trouble with us before and he knew that another blob would about finish him. (1960)

slip-up (1909) From the verb *slip up* ■ George Orwell: I suppose there *may* be some slip-up, but if not my address . . . will be The Cotswold Sanatorium. (1948)

boner (1912) Orig US; from *bone + -er*; compare *bone-head*; phrase *pull a boner* to make a mistake ■ *Spectator*: This Government has made about every boner possible. (1960)

floater (1913) British ■ Angus Wilson: I've as good as said that we don't want your money. . . . Just the sort of floater I would make, babbling on. (1967)

boob (1934) Mainly British; from earlier sense, fool ■ Peter Moloney: Newspapers have I read in every town And many a boob and misprint I have seen. (1966)

clinker (1934) Orig and mainly US; applied esp. to a film, song, etc. with little or nothing to commend it ■ *Video World*: There are countless Grade Z horror clinkers that provide unintentional amusement because of the ineptitude with which they are made. (1986)

bish (1937) British; origin unknown ■ Barbara Goolden: She suddenly realised she'd made an [*sic*] complete bish. (1956)

fluff (1937) Applied especially to a mistake in speaking lines, playing music, etc. or in a sporting activity; from the verb *fluff* make a mistake (in) ■ *Times*: In addition he achieved four astonishing place kicks, which made his costly fluff against France unbelievable. (1960)

black (1939) Orig services' slang; especially in the phrase *put up a black* make a blunder ■ Nevil Shute: Probably I should have to . . . leave Government service altogether, having put up such a black as that. (1948)

rock (1939) US; used in baseball, esp. in phrase *pull a rock* to make a mistake ■ *Birmingham (Alabama) News*: How does a guy who has been labeled 'the perfect player' feel after pulling his first 'rock' in a long and brilliant baseball career? (1951)

blue (1941) ■ Barry Crump: Trouble with you blokes is you won't admit when you've made a blue. (1961)

blooper (1947) Orig and mainly US; applied especially to a mistake in a radio or television broadcast; from earlier baseball slang sense, a weakly hit ball ■ *Daily Telegraph*: The Administration had made a 'blooper' over the custom of allowing members of Congress to provide constituents with guided tours of the White House. (1961)

clanger (1948) Applied esp. to a mistake that attracts attention; phrase *drop a clanger* to make such a mistake; from *clang + -er* ■ *New Statesman*: Mr Macmillan is the kind of Premier who enjoys covering up for any Cabinet colleague that drops a clanger. (1958) ■ *Daily Mail*: I have boobed dreadfully, old boy. Apparently a carnation with gongs is a terrible clanger. (1959)

whiff (1952) US; applied to a failure to hit the ball in baseball or golf; from earlier verb sense, miss the ball

boo-boo (1954) Orig US; probably a reduplication of *boob* ■ Osmington Mills: My fault, I'm afraid. I've just made what the Yanks call a boo-boo. (1967)

goof, goof-up (1954) From verb sense, make a blunder ■ *Daily Telegraph*: I believe they have made a goof. (1970)

ricket (1958) Orig criminals' slang; origin unknown ■ *Observer*: My fear was that it was Lord Hill, then chairman of the BBC, and that I was going to be hauled over the coals for making some awful ricket. (1996)

clink (1968) US; used mainly in baseball; transferred use of *clink* sharp ringing sound ■ *Washington News*: Ed Brinkman, the shortstop, merely yelled, 'clink'. (1968)

To make a mistake

slip up (1855) Orig US ■ Anne Morice: Somewhere along the line I had slipped up. (1971)

fluff (1884) Denoting especially making a mistake in speaking lines, playing music, etc. ■ Cecil Day Lewis: I had kept fluffing when I practised them [*sc.* songs]. (1960)

duff (1897) Orig golf slang, denoting playing a shot badly, and hence more generally making a mess of something; back-formation from *duffer* incompetent person

drop a brick (1923) ■ Sapper: The stones of Stonehenge are little pebbles compared to the bricks you dropped, but I forgive you. (1928)

boob (1935) Mainly British; from earlier noun sense, mistake ■ Nevil Shute: If I boob on this one it'll mean the finish of the business. (1951)

goof (1941) From earlier sense, behave foolishly ■ *Daily Telegraph*: The Census Bureau has admitted that it 'goofed' when it wrote it off as a ghost town. (1971)

screw up (1942) Orig US ■ Arthur Hailey: But you and your people really screwed up today! (1979)

fuck up (1945) Orig US; compare earlier sense, ruin, spoil ■ *Maledicta*: The RSV translates 'They were well-fed lusty stallions' but the King James [Bible] totally fucked up here and confused Hebrew *maškīm* 'well-balled' (where the -*īm* is the marker of the plural) with Hebrew

maškīm 'rising early in the morning' (where the *īm* is part of the root). (1980)

To make a mistake in understanding

get hold of the wrong end of the stick (1890) ■ George Orwell: Listen, Hilda. You've got hold of the wrong end of the stick about this business. (1939)

get someone **wrong (1927)** Orig US ■ Nicolas Freeling: Don't get me wrong; there's no offence meant. (1974)

Mistaken

all wet (1923) Orig and mainly US; *wet* from earlier sense, ineffectual ■ Alexander Baron: You're all wet if you think I'm giving up that easy. (1951)

off (the) **beam (1941)** From the notion of not being on the course indicated by a radio beam ■ Nicholas Blake: Never heard of him. You're off the beam. (1954)

off base (1947) US ■ *Publishers Weekly*: Off base with his moralizing, an innocent in economics, overshadowed by the Kennedys. (1974)

11. **Success**

See also **Defeat & Victory** (pp. 419–21)

To succeed, achieve success

win through (1644) Implying eventual success after difficulty ■ Edmund Crispin: I won through, though. . . . I survived. (1977)

come off (1864) From earlier sense, happen, turn out ■ Listener: Another fascinating original . . . appeared to be about a man in hell. I am not sure that it entirely came off. (1966)

strike oil (1875) Applied especially to suddenly hitting on a source of rapid profit and wealth ■ Sapper: The general consensus of opinion was that if his cricket was up to the rest of his form, Bob had struck oil. (1930)

work like a charm (1882) Applied to something that achieves its object with perfect success; from the notion of a magic *charm* that brings success; compare earlier *act like a charm*, *work to a charm* ■ F. N. Hart: Bill Stirling gave her one the other night, and she said it worked like a charm. (1934)

arrive (1889) Usually applied specifically to successfully establishing one's position or reputation; after French *arriver* ■ English Studies: The book was Herrick's greatest success. . . . With *Together* Herrick arrived. (1936)

make out (1891) From earlier sense, manage, get along ■ W. G. McAdoo: Without my wife's . . . help I could not have made out at all. (1931)

win out (1896) Orig US; implying eventual success after difficulty ■ Times Educational Supplement: The book has a brisk story and impeccable moral attitudes: gypsies, orphans, teachers and policemen are all good, ordinary people who win out in the end. (1984)

cut the mustard (1902) Mainly US; applied to something that comes up to expectations or meets requirements ■ Citizen (Ottawa): What if it doesn't work out? What if I'm bored with it? What if I'm no good at it? What if I just can't cut the mustard? (1974)

bring home the bacon (1909) From the notion of being the person who supplies his or her household with food, and hence more broadly of providing the means to keep others going ■ Philip Larkin: The College takes a number of fellows like him to keep up the tone . . . but they look to us to bring home t' bacon. (1946)

make the grade (1912) Orig US; implying reaching a required standard ■ Listener: A would-be thief who cannot make the grade. (1958)

make it (1912) ■ Observer: Bombers . . . lurching along the runway like a swarm of crippled insects, until finally they make it into the air. (1970)

get somewhere (1923) ■ E. H. W. Meyerstein: Even when Jews 'get somewhere'—if they marry Englishwomen they are condemned by their wives. (1940)

curl the mo (1941) Australian; probably from *mo* moustache, denoting self-satisfied twirling of the moustache ■ Truth (Sydney): Breasley saw Kintore donkey-lick a field of youngsters in the Federal Stakes, and had salt rubbed into his wound when the Lewis cuddy Valour curled the mo in the Bond Handicap. (1944)

hit the jack-pot (1944) Implying success due to luck; from the notion of winning a large (accumulated) prize in gambling or a lottery ■ South China Morning Post: I don't think that it is possible indefinitely to spend one's weekends working out different sorts of proposals in the hope that, somewhere along the line, one will hit the jackpot. (1992)

pay off (1951) Applied to something which has a successful or profitable outcome ■ *Listener*. There are signs, already, that this policy of patience is paying off. (1959)

strike (it) lucky (1951) Applied to achieving sudden success through luck ■ *Financial Times*. The Bush strikes lucky more often than any fringe theatre has a right to. (1984)

ace it (1955) US; often applied specifically to achieving high marks in an exam ■ *New Yorker*. The flight was over almost before it started. 'Our tradition is "Give us a few seconds and we'll ace it." . . . But this time we had no chance.' (1986)

have (got) it made (1955) Orig US; implying that someone is certain of (easy) success ■ *Times Literary Supplement*. The abstentions of 1972 were due not to this disillusionment but to an overwhelming conviction that Mr Nixon had it made, so why take time . . . to go out and vote? (1974)

go (off) with a bang (1956) ■ Angus Wilson: The discussion, to Professor Clun's discomfort and to Jasper's delight, went with a bang. (1956)

get the (or a) guernsey (1959) Australian; applied to someone who gains recognition or selection; from earlier sense, be selected for a football team, from *guernsey* sleeveless shirt worn by Australian Rules footballers, from earlier sense, thick sweater worn by seamen; ultimately from *Guernsey* name of one of the Channel Islands

To be achieving success

not look back (1893) Used to denote unbroken success since a particular point in time ■ *Radio Times*. Jules Verne . . . wrote *Five Weeks in a Balloon*, scored an immediate success, and never looked back. (1949)

go great guns (1913) Perhaps inspired by the earlier nautical *blow great guns* blow a violent gale, ultimately from obsolete *great gun* cannon, piece of artillery ■ *Times*: Arsenal, going great guns in their functional, efficient way, must see the league title within their sights. (1971)

have one's moments (1926) Implying intermittent success ■ Tucker Coe: Hargerson had his moments; happily this was one of them. (1972)

be laughing (1930) Applied to someone who is in a fortunate or successful position ■ M. Stanier: So long as you're a jump ahead you're laughing. (1975)

go places (1934) Orig US; implying increasing success or rising status in one's career, social life, etc. ■ L. A. G. Strong: They were jealous because she'd made the grade. . . . She was going places. (1944)

cook with gas (or electricity, radar) (1941), cook on the front (or top) burner (1945) From the notion of gas as superior to earlier solid fuels ■ Kenneth Orvis: Those Mounties cook with gas. With gas, brother—they're murder. (1962)

come up roses (1969) Applied to a situation which is developing very favourably or successfully ■ *Time*: Aired over eight consecutive nights, *Roots* came up roses for ABC. (1977)

go (or be, do) gangbusters (1975) US; applied especially to commercial success in the entertainment industry; compare *like gangbusters* successfully ■ *Wall Street Journal*: Although the company's cable operations are going gangbusters, its finances are still shaky. (1989)

Succeeding

on a roll (1976) Orig North American; implying a sequence of successes ■ *New Yorker*. Culpepper was on a roll. . . . He could do no wrong. (1985)

To have been successful

have had a good innings (1870) Applied to someone whose successful turn at something has come to an end, especially someone who has died after a long life ■ *Daily Telegraph*: The resignation has yet to be announced by the council but its director . . . confirms: 'David has informed us of his decision. He's had a good innings and we're looking for a replacement.' (1991)

To succeed in doing or dealing with

crack (1712) Denoting dealing successfully with a difficult or puzzling situation ■ *Guardian*: Some denizen of the deep at the Scottish Office, working on plans for local government reorganisation: 'At last, secretary of state, I think we've cracked it.' (1992)

make a go of (1877) Denoting making an undertaking successful ■ Gillian Freeman: You have to make a go of marriage, you have to work to make a marriage a success. (1959)

pull off (1887) From earlier sense, win (a prize) ■ *Times*: Having succeeded in their earlier experiments, there seems no reason why they should not pull off another major 'first'. (1968)

bring off (1928) ■ Marghanita Laski: They each hoped to goodness Daisy could bring it off. (1952)

hack (1955) Orig US; mainly in the phrase *hack it* ■ *Newsweek*: I had proved to the world during my four years in the Senate . . . that I can hack it. (1972)

To succeed in obtaining

notch (1837) Often followed by *up*; originally applied to obtaining a score in a sport, from the practice of keeping score by cutting notches in a piece of wood ■ *Economist*. Tanzania could probably notch up a growth rate of around 6%. (1987)

land (1854) From the notion of catching or *landing* a fish ■ Eugene O'Neill: I'll bet you tink yuh're goin' out and land a job, too. (1946)

swing (1934) ■ Kenneth Orvis: Phil had gotten himself a white nest-egg. Now how . . . could a half-broke addict-musician have swung that? (1962)

To succeed in catching (a vehicle)

make (1955) ■ Michael Crichton: You be there at five p.m. tomorrow and I'll be waiting for you. . . . Can you and Dr. Sattler make that plane? (1991)

To succeed in providing what is required

deliver (or **come up with**) **the goods (1879), deliver (1942)** Orig US ■ Duke of Devonshire: I am convinced that the Irish Government intend . . . to deliver the goods . . . in the true spirit of the Act. (1922) ■ Fred Astaire: I have a horror of not delivering—making good, so to speak; and I can't stand the thought of letting everybody down—studio and public as well as myself. (1959)

To ensure or bring about success

do the trick (1812) ■ Guardian: Sanctions will do the trick, they contend, or rather must be given time to do the trick. (1991)

turn the trick (1933) US ■ Springfield (Mass.) Daily News: A couple of American college products turned the trick for the Whalers. North Dakota graduate Alan Hangsleben and New Hampshire alumnus Cap Raeder shared the hero's role in the triumph. (1976)

To ensure success in or against

sew up (1904) Often applied specifically to ensuring the favourable outcome of a match ■ News of the World: Charlton appeared to have the game sewn up. (1977)

wrap up (1937) Often applied specifically to ensuring the favourable outcome of a match ■ Billings (Montana) Gazette: Nastase wrapped up Ramirez, 6-2, 9-7, 6-3. (1976)

To improve

look up (1806) ■ Sunday Telegraph: All the evidence around me suggested that for rodents, at least, life ought to be looking up. (1991)

pull one's socks up (1893) British; applied to trying to improve one's performance, work, behaviour, etc. ■ Southern Evening Echo (Southampton): The dismissal was unfair because Mr. Collier had not been given adequate warning and a chance 'to pull his socks up' before dismissal. (1976)

pull (lift, raise, etc.) **oneself (up) by one's (own) boot-straps (1936)** Applied to improving one's position by one's own efforts ■ Listener: A rather naïve faith in humanity's ability to pull itself up by its own bootstraps. (1962)

Success

joy (1945) Mainly in negative and interrogative contexts ■ Scotsman: Parking the car in this bay we started to look for a path and a break in the barbed wire—again with no joy. (1973)

A great success

good thing (1820) Applied to something that will ensure success; often in the phrase on to a good thing ■ J. D. Brayshaw: As luck would have it, I managed to put the old man on to a good thing. (1898)

tear (1869) US; applied in sport to a winning streak; mainly in the phrase on a tear ■ Chicago Tribune: In the fifth, Mitch Webster, who has been on a tear, hustled his second single of the night into a double. (1988)

winner (1913) Applied to something that succeeds or is a potential success; from earlier sense, one that wins ■ Times: The last crop of new ballets commissioned for the Edinburgh International Ballet company includes one winner, a near miss, and a very honourable mention. (1958)

wow (1920) Orig US; from the interjection wow expressing surprise, admiration, etc. ■ V. Connaught: From that moment forward, she was a wow with every Australian in the land. (1962)

smash (1930) Short for smash hit ■ Times: [His] aim . . . has been to expand a truthful little ethnic comedy into a popular smash. (1978)

socko (1937) Orig and mainly US; from earlier use, imitative of the sound of a blow ■ P. G. Wodehouse: Triumph or disaster, socko or flop, he went on forever like one of those permanent officials at the Foreign Office. (1973)

sockeroo (1942) Orig US; from sock hit + -eroo ■ Spectator: This latest box-office sockeroo also provides a modest example of the industry's throat-cutting activities. (1964)

smasheroo (1948) Orig and mainly US; from smash success + -eroo ■ New Yorker: Is one going to make the burning a big Broadway smasheroo of a scene? (1975)

blockbuster (1957) Applied especially to a best-selling book, film, etc.; from earlier sense, very large bomb ■ Church Times: If we really want our children to be Green, our best hope probably lies in persuading Steven Spielberg to feature rampant pelargoniums in his next blockbuster, under the title Botanic Park. (1993)

The highest level of success

the big time (1910) Orig US ■ Crescendo: Scores of drummers who hit the big time play Premier. (1966)

A successful person

comer (1879) Mainly US; applied to someone who shows promise of achieving success ■ Guardian: Congressman John Lindsay . . . has sprung into national notice as the most attractive 'comer' in his party. (1965)

whizz-kid, whiz-kid (1960) Applied to an exceptionally successful or brilliant young person, especially in politics or business ■ Sunday Express: Prime Minister Margaret Thatcher will meet Britain's latest whizz-kid inventor when she hosts a unique gathering of inventors and financiers at Downing Street tomorrow. (1985)

Successful

socko (1939) Applied to something stunningly successful or effective; from the noun socko success ■ T. P. McMahon: The blue of the incense rising to the white gold of the altar . . . the soaring voices of the seventy or so nuns . . . provided a socko finish. (1972)

Successfully

swimmingly (c1622) ■ *Daily Telegraph*: All went swimmingly until he brought in the pudding, soft strawberry meringue on a bed of cream, and stood too close behind his mother. (1991)

like gangbusters (1940) Orig and mainly US; from the notion of forcefulness and energy as exemplified in the opening sound effects of the US radio crime serial *Gangbusters* (1936–57)

like a dream (1949) Implying effortless success ■ *Guardian*: The Piccadilly one-way system . . . worked 'like a dream' throughout the day. (1961)

A prize

pot (1885) Applied to a (silver) cup or other

trophy awarded to a winner ■ *Windsor Magazine*: A few pots won upon playing-fields. (1897)

Congratulations!

bully for you (him, etc.) **(1864)** Often used ironically; from earlier *bully* excellent, capital

congrats (1884) Abbreviation of *congratulations* ■ *Melody Maker*: *Congrats*! Congratulations, Acker Bilk, on your stand about poor amplification. (1962)

congratters (1906) British; from *congrat(ulations* + *-ers* ■ Olive Norton: The Brig lifted his glass. 'Congratters, my dear. Good show.' (1966)

good on you (him, etc.) **(1907)** Mainly Australian & New Zealand ■ *New Zealand Listener*: 'Good on you!' said Dad, smacking my new leg approvingly, 'that's the spirit.' (1959)

12. **Spoiling, Ruination**

To spoil, ruin, botch, make a mess of

dish (1788) From the notion of food being *done*, and *dished* up ■ Tim Heald: This effectively dished Lady Antonia's chances of the same treatment. (1983)

pox (1802) From earlier sense, infect with venereal disease ■ *Saturday Review* (US): Wilmington, Delaware, poxed at that time by 1,200 abandoned one- and two-story homes. (1977)

bitch (1823) ■ R. Daniel: But for a squall bitching his escape route . . . he would be in France. (1960)

make a hash of (1833) From *hash* medley, jumble ■ Laurence Meynell: Frankly I'm terrified I'll make a hash of it. (1981)

bugger (1847) Usually followed by *up* ■ Angus Wilson: No hippos in their natural lovely setting of the Severn or beavers buggering up the Broads. (1961)

ball up (1884) Orig US; ultimately from *ball* spherical object, and perhaps influenced by *balls* nonsense, but the semantic development is not clear ■ June Drummond: These electrical devices are always getting balled up. (1959)

puckeroo, buckeroo, pukeru (1885) New Zealand; from Maori *pakaru* break ■ *New Zealand Listener*: Bad show, fighting. I puckerooed things properly last night. (1970)

boss (1887) Dated; sometimes followed by *up*; compare *boss-shot* unsuccessful attempt ■ Marjoribanks: You're simply bossing up the whole show by philandering with a widow. (1903)

foozle (1888) Mainly golf slang; from earlier, obsolete sense, fool around; ultimately probably from German dialect *fuseln* work hurriedly and badly, work slowly ■ Graham McInnes: The rest of the eighteen holes were a miserable exhibition of foozling, duffing, [etc.]. (1965)

make a balls of (1889) From *balls* nonsense ■ Samuel Beckett: I've made a balls of the fly. (1958)

put a crimp in (or into, on) (1896) US ■ *New Yorker*: Finally, a giant black panther leaps upon me and devours my mind and heart. This puts a terrific crimp in my evening. (1969)

cruel (1899) Australian ■ Ian Hamilton: I've got a good job and I don't want to cruel it while everything's going for me. (1967)

fluff (1902) Applied especially to botching a shot or other action in sport or to wrongly speaking lines, playing music, etc.; from earlier intransitive sense, make a mistake ■ *Times*: Palmer fluffed it because there was a hedge where his backswing should have gone. (1971)

make a muck of (1906) British ■ Nevil Shute: He's made a bloody muck o' things, the way I knew he would. (1947)

rot (1908) Often followed by *up* ■ Ann Bridge: I've got a complex about the whole business, and you know why. Well, that might rot it all up, at any moment. (1932)

flub (1916) Orig US; sometimes followed by *up*; origin unknown; compare earlier noun *flub* mistake ■ Stanley Kauffmann: They'll bring someone else in for the other job if you flub it. (1952)

fuck up (1916) ■ *It*: The . . . neatly planned plot to fuck up their transport scene. (1969)

fritz (1918) US; usually followed by *up* or *out*; from *on the fritz* ruined, defective, out of order

muck up (1922) Mainly British ■ Michael Cronin: 'Lena could muck it all up.' 'I don't think she will, so long as she's scared about herself.' (1959)

jigger (1923) Usually followed by *up*; apparently a back-formation from *jiggered up* tired ■ *Daily Mail*: I've 'jiggered' up my Rolls-Royce. (1923)

louse up (1934) Orig US ■ *Human World*: If . . . he tries to sabotage his actions—he louses up a machine he is purporting to work, for example [etc.]. (1972)

bollix, bollux (1937) Usually followed by *up*; from earlier *bollix* mess, confusion ■ John Steinbeck: He'd made a mess of things. He wondered if he'd bollixed up the breaks. (1952)

piss up (1937) ■ David Craig: Did I let them just unload it because they pissed up a job?. . . This was my money that had been lifted. (1976)

snarl up (1937) From *snarl* make complicated or confused ■ *Economist*: A . . . wish to snarl up the relations between the western governments. (1960)

goof (1938) Orig US; usually followed by *up*; from earlier sense, make a mistake ■ *Life*: Now, it's hard to goof up pictures. (1969)

banjax (1939) Anglo-Irish; origin unknown; perhaps originally Dublin slang ■ Gavin Lyall: The man *is* a twit. I mean, he banjaxed that Zurich trip. (1969)

foul up (1942) Mainly US, orig services' slang ■ Stanley Ellin: You've got fine bone structure, but look at the way you're fouling it up. (1958)

screw up (1943) From *screw* copulate, probably as a semi-euphemistic substitute for *fuck up* ■ Peter Niesewand: Military men usually screw things up . . . and the people are bloody glad to see the back of them. (1981)

snafu (1943) Orig US services' slang; from *snafu* a bungle, a mess ■ G. Markstein: My arrangements seemed snafued. I guess the lines got crossed. (1981)

balls up (1947) British; compare earlier *ball up*, *make a balls of* in same sense, and also the noun *balls-up*, recorded earlier ■ Stanley Price: The public would laugh fit to bust if someone really ballsed-up the Civil Service. (1961)

cock up (1948) British; from slang senses of the noun *cock*, penis, nonsense ■ Graham Swift: I'm sorry I messed up your classes, sir. I'm sorry I cocked things up for you. (1983)

make a pig's ear of (1954) British ■ Douglas Adams: What use is your life to anyone? When I think of what you've made of it the phrase 'pig's ear' comes irresistibly to mind. (1979)

trash (1975) Mainly US; perhaps from earlier sense, vandalize ■ *Time*: The presentation is ignorant, cluttered and coarse, and it trashes the sculpture. Works that need to be walked around . . . can only be seen frontally. (1976)

To put a stop to, thwart

put the kibosh (or kybosh) on (1834) Origin of *kibosh* uncertain; perhaps from obsolete costermongers' slang *kye* eighteen pence (from Yiddish *kye* eighteen) + obsolete slang *bosh* pence, the underlying notion perhaps being a 'derisory sum' ■ *Sunday Post* (Glasgow): She'd been looking forward to some salmon fishing, but the heatwave's put the kibosh on that. (1975)

kibosh, kybosh (1884) From the phrase *put the kibosh on* ■ *Listener*: What a pity that the stipend has not kept pace . . . with the fall in the value of money (and it even comes to you less PAYE, thus kiboshing manoeuvrability in the field of expenses!). (1969)

put the bee on (1908) Dated, mainly US; perhaps suggested by *sting* ■ P. G. Wodehouse: The old boy . . . got the idea that I was off my rocker, and put the bee on the proceedings. (1927)

sprag (1911) Australian, dated; from earlier sense, stop a wheel moving with a bar or chock, from the noun *sprag* such a bar or chock; ultimate origin unknown ■ U. R. Ellis: Attempt to sprag New State Referendum. (1965)

scupper (a1918) From earlier sense, surprise and massacre ■ *Economist*: The suspicion is still alive that there would have been secret rejoicing in Whitehall if the French Assembly had scuppered the common market. (1957)

put paid to (1919) ■ John Braine: I wanted to put paid to Communism once and for all. (1957)

stonker (1941) Australian & New Zealand; from earlier sense, kill ■ R. L. Seddon: Benzine restrictions have stonkered my car. (1945)

put the mockers (or mocker) on (1949) Orig Australian; from earlier *mocker* jinx ■ *Bulletin* (Sydney): The double loss put the mockers on everything. Lake Macquarie is not the place to live without wheels. (1983)

To frustrate someone's purposes

settle someone's hash (1803) Compare earlier *hash* dish of recooked meat ■ R. H. Mottram: He's settled my hash, right enough. (1930)

cook someone's goose (a1851) ■ *Evening Standard*: Far from . . . pouring oil on troubled waters you were very positively using your talents to cook Mr Mudd's goose. (1991)

put the (or someone's) pot on (1864) Australian ■ Vance Palmer: There's an election coming on, and there's a chance I'll be dumped. . . . This afternoon's work has probably put my pot on. (1957)

nark (1891) Australian; from earlier sense, stop ■ Richard Beilby: Ya'd do anything to nark me, anything to put me down, wouldn't ya? (1975)

ditch (1899) Dated, orig US; from earlier sense, throw into a ditch, probably influenced by *dish* ruin ■ *Springfield* (Massachusetts) *Republican*: Its enactment into law would have ditched them in their present reciprocity campaign. (1911)

tear it (1909) British; usually in the phrase *that's torn it* ■ M. Procter: He looked at his watch. 'That's torn it,' he said. (1954)

put the (or a) mock(s) on (1911) Australian ■ Wally Grout: I hope I am not 'putting the mock' on Norm because my feelings are the same as the rest of the Australian Test players: When O'Neill is a doubtful Test starter the job always looks grimmer. (1965)

cramp someone's style (1917) ■ R. C. Guidry: See you lat-er, al-li-ga-tor, Aft-er 'while, croc-o-dile,—Can't you see you're in my way, now, Don't you know you cramp my style? (1957)

put the skids under (1918) Orig US ■ Julian Symons: A plan by one gang to put the skids under another. (1975)

put the moz (or **mozz**) **on (1924)** Australian; *moz(z)* an abbreviation of dated Australian slang *mozzle* luck, from Hebrew *mazzā* luck ■ Keith Stackpole: She felt she put the moz on him. . . . She couldn't bear to go in case she was a jinx. (1974)

queer someone's **pitch (1927)** From earlier sense, interfere with or spoil the business of a salesman or showman ■ Elizabeth Lemarchand: He's a decent lad. . . . He would never have risked queering Wendy's pitch with Eddy. (1973)

rock the boat (1931) Denoting making things awkward for others ■ *Punch*: The trouble with these people who nail their colours to the mast—they always rock the boat. (1958)

moz, mozz (1941) Australian; from the phrase *put the moz on* ■ John Powers: Don't let him mozz you, Monk. You've made it through the first week—that's the hard one. (1973)

root (1944) Australian; often in the phrase *wouldn't it root you!* denoting frustration and exasperation; perhaps from Australian *root* copulate with ■ *Telegraph* (Brisbane): Mr. Whitlam later admitted having said in an aside: 'It is what he put in his guts that rooted him.' (1973)

put the mockers (or **mocker**) **on (1949)** See under To put a stop to, thwart (p. 414).

fix someone's **wagon (1951)** US ■ J. D. Salinger: What ever became of that stalwart bore Fortinbras? Who eventually fixed *his* wagon? (1959)

banjax (1956) From earlier sense, spoil, ruin ■ Terry Wogan: I am out to banjax the bookies. (1979)

To go wrong

snafu (1975) US; from earlier transitive sense, mess up, ruin ■ J. Grady: Every now and then something snafus and there is one hell of a mess. (1975)

An instance of spoiling or ruining something; a bungle, botch, mess

balls-up (1934) Compare *ball up* and *make a balls of* spoil ■ Roy Fuller: Stuart Blackledge made a ballsup of the valuation. (1958)

bollix, bollux (1935) Alteration of *bollocks* testicles, nonsense ■ James Blish: Some kind of intra-departmental bollix. (1957)

muck-up (1939) From *muck up* spoil ■ Evelyn Waugh: You seem to have made a pretty good muck-up. (1942)

foul-up (1943) Orig US services' slang; from *foul up* spoil, bungle ■ *Observer*: He traces the foul-up back to 1953. (1967)

snafu (1943) Orig US services' slang; from the adjective *snafu* ■ B. Mason: And Holy Moses, what a snafu! Why foul up poor, harmless, gormless Glad? (1980)

cock-up (1948) British; from *cock up* spoil ■ Joyce Porter: George turned the local boys on it and you've never seen such a cock-up in your life! (1964)

fuck-up (a1950) From *fuck up* spoil ■ Mordecai Richler: I'm sorry about this fuck-up, Mr Griffin. (1968)

piss-up (1950) From *piss up* spoil ■ R. Esser: Just what a pissy-arsed bugger like you would say. . . . You mean it might be one hell of a piss-up. (1969)

screw-up (1960) Orig US; from *screw up* spoil ■ Laver & Collins: Bad courts were just one more factor in a general screw-up. (1971)

snarl-up (1960) From *snarl up* mess up ■ *Financial Times*: Small organisational snarl-ups, such as failing to get out the Speakers' Handbook in time. (1974)

To be spoiled, ruined, or lost

go to the dogs (1619) From the notion that dogs are worthless recipients, and that anything given to them is effectively thrown away ■ Anthony Price: Gildas . . . was . . . denouncing the rulers of Britain as a bunch of rat-finks who were letting the country go to the dogs. (1975)

go to pot (1699) From earlier sense, be cut up as meat for the cooking pot ■ Sheila Kaye-Smith: If we hung on now, still further crippled by death-duties, the land would simply go to pot. (1923)

bang goes (1868) ■ T. E. Lawrence: I am afraid I have to drive from here to Urfa (Edessa) which is going to cost me about £7: so bang go my proposed purchases in Damascus. (1909)

go to the bow-wows (1893) Jocular substitution of *bow-wows* (nursery word for 'dogs') for *dogs* ■ W. K. Post: Everything was going to the bow-wows. (1893)

go west (1919) From earlier sense, die ■ G. D. H. Cole: Wilson sighed. 'There's valuable evidence gone west', he said. 'It may be hard to pick up the trail now.' (1925)

hit the skids (1920) Orig US; denoting going into a decline ■ *Daily Mirror*: They were only 378p when the £ hit the skids a week ago. (1976)

pfft, pffft (1930) US journalists' slang, dated; denoting especially a relationship that is about to break up; verbal use of *pfft*, US variant of *phut* (as in go phut) ■ *New Yorker*: International Politics, March 29, 1937. 'Adolf and Benito have phffft! The break will be announced soon enough.' (1940)

have had one's (or its) **chips (1959)** British; probably from the notion of relinquishing poker chips after losing ■ *Guardian*: That's why the traditional mainframe . . . has 'had its chips'. (1991)

come (**fall**, etc.) **apart at the seams (1965)** ■ *Times*: My marriage . . . came apart at the seams. (1977)

go down the Swanee (1977) From the name of a river in Georgia and Florida, USA ■ *Observer*: A senior Leyland convener . . . called on the Government to give Leyland 'latitude' in settling its pay problems. Without that, he said, the company 'would go down the Swanee'. (1977)

To become inoperative; go awry

go phut (1888) *phut* imitative of the sound of a dull impact, or from Hindi *phaṭ* crack, sound of a slap (first recorded in English in the writings of Rudyard Kipling, who was born in India)

■ *Daily Telegraph*: The kids had broken a window, and the colour television had gone phut. (1972)

conk, konk (1917) Usually followed by *out*; perhaps from *conk* hit on the head ■ *Daily Mail*: The old boat 'conked out' miles from anywhere. (1929)

go blooey, go blooie (1920) US; from earlier sense, explode; ultimately from *blooey* representing the sound of an explosion ■ Whiteman & McBride: I spilled the salt. It rained. At rehearsal my fiddle went blooey. (1926)

pack up (1928) From the notion of packing up one's equipment after finishing a task, preparatory to leaving ■ J. L. Anderson: None of us had much confidence in it [*sc.* our ancient engine] and it packed up a few days later. (1967)

poop (1931) Orig US; denoting a machine, etc. breaking down; often followed by *out*; origin unknown ■ Bernard Malamud: If it [*sc.* the heating system] pooped out, and it pooped often—the furnace had celebrated its fiftieth birthday—you called the complaint number of Rent and Housing Maintenance. (1971)

In a spoiled or ruined condition; inoperative

up the spout (1829) Compare earlier sense, in pawn ■ L. P. Hartley: Where would the Knightons be if it wasn't for Mrs Knighton? Up the spout, down the drain—anywhere but in the position of influence and honour. (1955)

on the slide (1884) Applied to someone or something on the decline ■ Nik Cohn: He began to flag. By early 1964, he was definitely on the slide. (1969)

bung (1885) Australian & New Zealand; often in the phrase *go bung*; from earlier sense, dead ■ A. Groom: The telephone line's been mostly bung and broke since, but I got through. (1930)

out of whack (1885) Mainly US ■ Martin Amis: Everything is out of whack at Appleseed Rectory; its rooms are without bearing and without certainty. (1975)

puckerood, buckerooed, pukerued (1885), puckeroo, buckeroo, pukeru (1925) New Zealand; from Maori *pakaru* broken; to break ■ S. T. Ollivier: I come to see if you've got a spare shovel. Mine's puckerooed and I got a cow in the drain. (1965)

on the rocks (1889) Often applied specifically to a marriage or other relationship that is on the point of ending ■ Edmund Wilson: [Roberto Rossellini's] headlined romance with Sonali Das Gupta is now reported on the rocks. (1958)

kaput (1895) From German *kaputt*, from French *capot* without tricks in the card-game of piquet ■ Julian Symons: Sherlock Holmes is finished. Finito. Kaput. (1975)

on the blink (1901) Orig US; applied to something, especially a machine, electronic device, etc., that seems about to become inoperative; probably from the notion of a guttering candle ■ Jeffrey Ashford: No good, David. The 'frig. is on the blink again. (1960)

on the fritz (1902) US; usually applied to machinery that is no longer working; origin unknown ■ *Guardian*: It appeared, for an awful moment,

that a cue had failed, that the teleprompter was on the fritz. (1962)

on the toboggan (1910) US; applied to someone or something on the decline; from the notion of a toboggan sliding downhill ■ Jack Dempsey: A veteran of thirty or thirty-one who is on the 'toboggan'. (1950)

spitchered (1920) Orig nautical; from Maltese *spicca* finished, ended, perhaps ultimately from Italian *spezzare* break into pieces ■ Peter Dickinson: That damned gadget might . . . be functioning right as rain in thirty seconds, or it might be spitchered for ever. (1970)

on the skids (1921) Orig US; applied to someone or something on the decline ■ *Irish Press*: The Irish shoe industry, after being on the skids for six years, may be finding its feet again. (1977)

sunk (1922) ■ A. P. Herbert: 'Hell!' thought Mr. Ransom, 'we're sunk!' (1934)

buggered up (1923), buggered (1947)

washed up (1923) Orig & mainly US ■ William Saroyan: We're washed up as a race, we're through, it's all over. (1934)

trashed (1926) Mainly US; often followed by an adverb; probably from the obsolete *trash* treat as trash ■ *Tucson* (Arizona) *Citizen*: 'I've sat through this movie three times.' . . . 'In this trashed-out theater? The picture's that good?' 'It's a lousy picture! I can't get my feet unstuck from the floor!!' (1979) ■ *Dirt Bike*: Track-N-Trail has just come up with a solution to the age-old problems of mud, cold, rain, and trashed knuckles for you offroaders. (1980)

goosed (1928) ■ John Welcome: If I've guessed wrong and Jason has found out right, then we're goosed. (1959)

down the drain (1930) Especially in the phrase *go down the drain* ■ J. H. Chase: We had paid out good money to get those policies, and we couldn't afford to let them go down the drain. (1952)

shot (1933) Mainly US ■ I. Petite: At that point they discovered that the transmission bearings were 'shot'. (1970)

fucked up (1939), fucked (1955) ■ William Gibson: Your lungs are filling up with fluid, your kidneys aren't working, your heart's fucked. (1988)

finito (1945) Applied to something that is finished for the worse; from the past participle of Italian *finire* to finish ■ Armistead Maupin: You tell your friend that she'd better report to me on Friday or she's out on her ass . . . Friday . . . After that, *finito*. (1982)

snafu (1942) Orig US services' slang; acronym of 'situation normal: all fucked (or fouled) up' ■ David Divine: Situation Snafu. . . . Send for the Seabees. (1950)

U/S, U.S. (1942) Usually applied to machinery that is no longer working properly; originally a services' slang abbreviation of *unserviceable* ■ Maureen Duffy: The device seems to have gone U.S. They're dodgy things because they're so small. (1978)

fubar (1944) US, euphemistic, often jocular, orig services' slang; acronym of 'fucked (or fouled) up beyond all recognition', probably inspired by *snafu* ■ *Guardian*: Space jargon. . . . Fubar, all fouled up, i.e. in chaos. (1969)

rooted (1951) Australian; often in *get rooted!* an expression of contempt or annoyance; from *root* ruin, frustrate someone's purposes ■ Dal Stivens: 'It looks as though we're rooted, smacker,' I told Herb. (1951)

blooey, blooie (1961) US; from *go blooey* become inoperative ■ John Updike: A clear image suddenly in the water wavering like a blooey television set. (1961)

down the pan (1961) Especially in the phrase *go down the pan*; from *pan* lavatory bowl ■ *Independent*: He agreed his game had 'gone down the pan' since victory in the US Open last year. (1991)

down the tube(s) (1963) Orig US; especially in the phrase *go down the tube(s)* ■ *Guardian*: Four years' work down the tubes with little to show for it. (1992)

down the gurgler (1981) Australian; especially in the phrase *go down the gurgler*; from *gurgler* plughole, drain ■ *Courier-Mail* (Brisbane): Channel 7 is making a big comeback locally but Channel 0 is going down the proverbial gurgler. (1988)

Something that spoils or ruins

fly in the ointment (1833) After Ecclesiastes 10:1, Dead flies cause the ointment of the apothecary to send forth a stinking savour ■ Aldous Huxley: There is only one fly in the ointment

13. Failure

Something that fails; an unsuccessful person or thing; a fiasco

damp squib (1847) Applied to something anticlimactic ■ *Times*: Possibly because too much was expected of it, the long-range study of Britain's transport needs by a Ministry of Transport group under Sir Robert Hall is something of a damp squib. (1963)

duffer (1855) Australian & New Zealand; applied to an unproductive mine, goldfield, or claim; compare earlier *duff* worthless ■ N. Miles: I haven't had much luck on the last four 'duffers' I've sunk. (1972)

frost (1885) Orig theatrical slang; perhaps from the notion of getting a cool reception ■ R. Lindner: Look, Doc. This analysis is a frost, isn't it? (1955)

stumer, stumor (1886) Origin unknown ■ *Daily Telegraph*: While in the course of a year countless shares will establish new lows only half a dozen will turn out to be real stumers and eventually worthless. (1970)

plug (1889) Applied to a book that sells badly ■ *Publisher's Circular*: Out of the vast number of publications issued, some must, indeed, turn out to be plugs. (1928)

stiff (*a*1890) Orig US; applied to one that is certain to lose, and often specifically to a racehorse which is unlikely (or not intended) to win; compare earlier sense, foolish or useless

offered by commercial propagandists; they want your money. (1936)

nigger in the woodpile (1852) Orig US, offensive, now taboo; applied to an unsuspected or hidden factor that has an adverse effect ■ Anthony Gilbert: The nigger in the woodpile on this occasion being an elderly spinster of decided views. (1958)

spanner in the works (1934) Especially in the phrase *throw a spanner in the works* ■ *News Chronicle*: Mr. Cousins has thrown a spanner into the Labour Party's works. (1959)

A spoilsport

wet blanket (1857) ■ Susan Faludi: The wet-blanket girlfriend of Peter, Rebecca recoils with disgust at their new bundle of joy. (1992)

wowser (1900) Australian & New Zealand; applied to an excessively puritanical person, especially one who tries to stop others having fun; compare earlier sense, unpleasant person ■ *Bulletin* (Sydney): Victoria's publicans seem utterly to have lost their marbles. They have made common cause with the wowsers. (1986)

wet smack (1927) Orig US ■ P. G. Wodehouse: The man is beyond question a flat tyre and a wet smack. (1929)

party pooper (1954) US; applied to someone who throws a pall of gloom over a party or other social engagement

person ■ *Sun* (Baltimore): We either get shut out or find we are on a stiff which won't run. (1944)

wash-out (1902) ■ *Guardian*: The house is divided over Lush's much-anticipated album. Some have detected a wash-out. (1992)

morning-glory (1904) US, dated; applied to something (e.g. a racehorse) which fails to maintain its early promise; compare earlier use as the name of a type of climbing plant

boss-shot (1912), bosh-shot (1939) Applied to an unsuccessful attempt; from earlier sense, badly aimed shot (apparently from the notion of a shot fired by a boss-eyed person); *bosh-shot* altered after *bosh* nonsense ■ George Orwell: The Nazis chop people's heads off . . . and sometimes the executioner makes a bosh shot. (1939)

flivver (1914) US, dated; origin uncertain; compare earlier sense, small or cheap car

dud (1915) Applied to a bomb, shell, firework, etc. that fails to explode or ignite; from earlier sense, worthless or counterfeit item ■ *Public Opinion*: All the torpedoes they carry are duds. (1923)

flop (1919) From the verb *flop* fail ■ *Economist*: As a gesture of defiance Argentina's one-day general strike last week was a flop. (1957)

no soap (1926) Orig & mainly US; used to denote a completely unsuccessful attempt ■ Edmund

Crispin: 'The police tried to trace the handkerchief, I take it?' 'They did, but no soap.' (1977)

turkey (1927) US; applied to an unsuccessful film or theatrical production ■ Groucho Marx: The boys at the studio have lined up another turkey for us. . . . I saw the present one the other day and didn't care much for it. (1939)

no dice (1928) Orig US; used to denote a completely unsuccessful attempt ■ P. G. Wodehouse: I was around at her bank this morning trying to find out what her balance was, but no dice. Fanny won't part. (1952)

flopperoo, floperoo (1931) North American; originally applied specifically to a theatrical venture that fails; from *flop* fail + the jocular suffix *-eroo* ■ Roderic Jeffries: His case was a real flopperoo. (1970)

non-starter (1934) Applied to one with no chance of success, especially due to impracticability; from earlier sense, competitor who does not start ■ Ann Bridge: That's one reason why non-intervention is such a non-starter. (1942)

stiff (1937) Orig US; applied especially to a venture in the entertainment industry that fails; from earlier sense, one that is certain to lose ■ *American Weekly:* Juggy listened to the tune and was disheartened. 'It's a stiff,' he said—meaning that it was no good. (1949)

bomb (1952) US; applied especially to a theatrical venture that fails ■ *New Yorker:* What had once been called a failure became a 'bomb'. (1961)

pratfall (1953) Applied to an embarrassing or humiliating failure; from earlier sense, a fall on to the buttocks ■ *Rolling Stone:* Why has an important investigation so quickly degenerated into a series of pratfalls? (1977)

fizzer (1957) Australian; from earlier sense, firework that fails to go off ■ *Facts on File:* John Howard . . . ridiculed the prime minister's address as the biggest fizzer since Halley's Comet. (1986)

lead balloon (1960) From the notion of something that cannot but fall; often in the phrase *go down like a lead balloon,* punning on *go down* descend and *go down* be received ■ Len Deighton: With this boy it went over like a lead balloon. (1962)

non-event (1962) Applied to something anticlimactic ■ *Wall Street Journal:* Thursday's release of the preliminary report on the U.S. third-quarter gross national product was something of a nonevent. (1989)

flunk-out (1967) US; applied to a student who fails a course

no-no (1972) From earlier sense, something that should not be done ■ *Observer: Nationwide* . . . has my strict instructions never to touch the subject of rock music again: its piece on Bob Dylan was a total no-no. (1972)

A failure of function

bug (1889) Orig US; compare earlier sense, insect ■ *Engineering:* The seven-and-a-half years . . . was not an excessive time to . . . get the 'bugs' out of a new system of that kind. (1958)

glitch (1962) Applied to a sudden brief irregularity or malfunction of equipment, etc., originally especially in a spacecraft; origin unknown ■ *Product Engineering:* It generated digital transients that caused the abort guidance to send false signals. Phillips said it took an inordinately long time to find this glitch. (1969)

See also **gremlin** under A mechanical fault at **Vehicles** (p. 393).

To be unsuccessful

flunk (1837) Orig & mainly US; originally applied specifically to failing an exam; often followed by *out*; from earlier sense, give in, back down ■ *Sunday Times* (Johannesburg): Sinatra himself said: 'I've flunked out with women more often than not. Like most men, I don't understand them.' (1971)

come to grief (1862) Denoting something that proves abortive; from earlier sense, suffer a disaster, especially a fall ■ *Economist:* Several existing projects have come to grief on the rocks of over-ambition and shortsightedness. (1987)

come (or go) a mucker (1869) British; from *mucker* heavy fall ■ Gladys Mitchell: I like old Jimmy boy and I wouldn't want to see him come a mucker. (1974)

come a cropper (1874) From earlier sense, fall heavily ■ Terence Rattigan: We bachelors welcome competition from married men. We so much enjoy watching them come the inevitable cropper. (1951)

duffer (1880) Australian & New Zealand; denoting a mine proving unproductive or becoming exhausted; often followed by *out*; from *duffer* mine that fails ■ C. Simpson: Billy's tin show must have duffered out by now. (1952)

miss the bus (1886), miss the boat (1929) Denoting failure due to losing an opportunity; originally recorded in the form *miss the omnibus* ■ *Manchester Guardian Weekly:* He [*sc.* Neville Chamberlain] . . . boasted that Hitler has 'missed the bus'. (1940) ■ *Times:* Some firms were missing the boat because their managements were not prepared to be adventurous. (1973)

flop (1898) From the notion of collapsing limply ■ Peter Fleming: She published a book on that journey, which flopped. (1936)

crap out (1908) US; from earlier technical use in craps (a game of chance played with dice)

come unstuck (1911) ■ *Listener:* This is where the theory comes unstuck. (1958)

flivver (1912) US, dated; probably from the noun *flivver* failure, but recorded earlier

come a gutser (1918) Australian & New Zealand; from earlier sense, fall heavily ■ *Canberra Times:* 'The Opposition,' raged Mr Dawkins during Wednesday's Question Time in the House of Representatives, 'has come an absolute gutser on this one!' (1983)

get (or go) nowhere, not get anywhere (1925) ■ Willa Cather: Mrs. Rosen felt that she was not getting anywhere. (1932)

fold (1928) Applied to a business, project, etc., or to a theatrical venture; often followed by *up* ■ Noel Coward: In spite of excellent press notices . . . the play folded up at the end of eight weeks. (1937) ■ *Sunday Times*: This generous subsidy could not go on for ever and when it was withdrawn the magazine folded. (1971)

lay an egg (1929) Applied to a performer or performance that fails ■ Leonard Feather: The singer had been laying eggs at the Zanzibar . . . and Shaw was undecided what to do with him. (1949)

not get to first base (1938) US; denoting failing at the very beginning of an undertaking; from the notion of the batter in baseball being thrown out before reaching first base ■ P. G. Wodehouse: She gives you the feeling that you'll never get to first base with her. (1962)

bomb (1953) Orig US; often followed by *out* ■ *TV Times* (Australia): Everyone had expected it to be [good], so when it bombed it was a shock. (1968)

fuck up (1953) Orig US; compare earlier sense, make a mistake, blunder ■ *Rolling Stone*: We fucked up in New York. (1977)

stiff (1988) Applied especially to a venture in the entertainment industry; from the noun *stiff* failure ■ *Washington Post*: 'River Deep, Mountain High' had stiffed on the pop charts here . . . , but in England it went to No. 2. (1993)

To fail at or in
....

fall down on (1899) Orig US ■ *Spectator*: The Congress party is falling down on the job of rallying public confidence in the present policies of the Government of India. (1959)

flunk (1924) Orig & mainly US; denoting failing an exam, course, etc.; compare earlier sense, fail a candidate ■ *Times*: I was utterly, deeply, completely depressed and flunked my A levels. (1970)

fluff (1955) Denoting failing an exam; from earlier sense, do badly, make a mistake in ■ *Daily Telegraph*: Many school-children . . . awaiting their summer exam results have now got this particular worry. Has mother fluffed hers—or has she got through? (1970)

bomb (1962) US; denoting failing an exam

To designate as failing
....

flunk (1843) Orig & mainly US; denoting failing an examination candidate; from earlier intransitive sense, fail ■ *Word Study*: For if English teachers had always based their grades in English on the moral probity of their students' private lives, they would have had to flunk such naughty boys as Christopher Marlowe, James Boswell, Dylan Thomas, and Baltimore's own Edgar Allan Poe. (1966)

plough (1853) Dated, orig university slang; denoting failing an examination candidate ■ *Times*: My young friend was undeservedly ploughed. (1883)

pill (1908) Dated; denoting failing an examination candidate; from earlier sense, blackball ■ Warwick Deeping: Gorringe had a sick face. . . . 'Pilled,' thought Kit, and was not sorry, for Gorringe needed a course of pilling. (1925)

14. Defeat & Victory

To defeat (heavily)
....

whip, (US dialect) **whup (1571)** Now US ■ R. S. Warren Bell: If Eccles uses his weight cleverly, Wardour will be whipped to a cert. (1901) ■ *Punch*: The Matt Dillon urge to 'whup' the Commies. (1968)

thrash (1606) ■ *Westminster Gazette*: It touched land, and a man jumped out waving his hat and exclaiming, 'Hurrah, Wellington has thrashed Boney!' (1903)

pulverize (1631) From earlier sense, crush to dust ■ *Guardian*: And a 'much weaker' opponent must not merely be defeated but pulverized if the central lesson of World Order is to be learned. (1991)

do (1794) ■ L. A. G. Strong: If I do Sid, I'm to have a go at Sailor Berridge. (1948)

lick (1800) ■ John Steinbeck: S'pose Curley jumps a big guy an' licks him. Ever'body says what a game guy Curley is. And s'pose he does the same thing and gets licked. (1937)

smash (1813) ■ *Western Daily Press*: To join in a British expedition to 'smash' the Mahdi. (1884)

walk over (1823) ■ *Guardian*: They thought they could walk all over us. But we have won. (1991)

skunk (1843) US ■ David Delman: She'll skunk Nell Duncan today, and win. (1972)

knock (or **beat**) **the socks off (1845)** US ■ *Arizona Daily Star*: 'Trucks have been beating our socks off,' said . . . a spokesman for the Atchison, Topeka & Santa Fe Railway in Chicago. 'But now we have a chance to get some of the business back.' (1979)

skin (1862) US ■ *Verbatim*: Puns ('Eagles *skin* Washington') . . . offer limitless opportunities to the enterprising sports journalist. (1981)

whitewash (1867) Orig US; applied originally, in baseball and other games, to defeating opponents while preventing them from scoring, and hence to inflicting a heavy defeat ■ *Korean Times*: Husky south Korean girls white-washed Thailand 106-17 . . . in the second game. (1972)

make mincemeat of (1876) From earlier sense, chop into small pieces ■ *Times*: Thames R.C. made mincemeat of all their opponents in the Grand Eights. (1955)

wax (1884) US; origin unknown

wipe the floor with (1887) Orig US; used to denote humiliating defeat ■ G. A. Birmingham: He was so infernally certain that the Emperor would wipe the floor with us. (1918)

donkey-lick, **donkey-wallop (1890)** Australian; applied especially to horse-racing;

lick from *lick* defeat ■ *National Times* (Australia): The Pommies . . . threw in a quartet of speedsters that had been donkey-licked by every cricketing nation around the world. (1981)

run (or **make**) **rings round** (1891) Used to denote comprehensive and humiliating defeat ■ *Sporting Mirror*: The return of Dodds revitalised the Everton attack which ran rings round Sheffield United. (1947)

ring (1894) Australian; applied to defeating other shearers in a shed in a speed contest

wallop (1895) ■ *Sunday Times*: Boro were walloped 5-1 at Villa last weekend. (1993)

walk round (1901) US ■ *Westminster Gazette*: To use a colloquial expression, they 'walked round' Gamble and Davies. (1901)

slaughter (1903) Orig US ■ *C. E. Merriam*: He was hopelessly beaten . . . in the primaries of 1907; and again slaughtered . . . in the primaries of 1915. (1929)

slather (1910) North American; from earlier senses, spill, squander, smear; ultimate origin unknown ■ *Globe & Mail* (Toronto): Canadians can get slathered in Olympic hockey. (1968)

cream (1929) Orig US; applied especially to sporting contests; perhaps from the notion of 'creaming' butter and other foods by vigorous beating ■ *James Carroll*: Brady had pretended, for ambition's sake, to garner less power than Curley, and in the end Curley had creamed him. (1978)

shellac (1930) Orig and mainly US; from earlier sense, varnish with shellac

eat someone **alive** (1939) ■ *Fusion* (US): At first, in solitaire play, most gamers will be eaten alive by the CPU, but once the learning curve is slammed, gamers will be performing tomahawk jams, alley oops and all them other 'phat' moves with elan. (1995)

take (1939) ■ *Publishers Weekly*: They broke their tie with the Giants and went on to take the Tigers in seven wild World Series games. (1976)

massacre (1940) ■ *Independent*: This would have been the worst thing he could have done and he would then have been massacred by Richie Richardson and company. (1991)

take someone **apart** (1942) ■ *Birmingham Post*: League leaders Liverpool were taken apart by the speed, skill and determination of the entire Villa side. (1976)

hammer (1948) ■ *Times*: Challenging the well-entrenched leaders in the United Kingdom car rental industry seems to hold no fears for Crook. He is hoping to hammer them on both quality and price. (1973)

cane (1960) From earlier sense, beat with a cane; compare also earlier slang sense, damage severely ■ *Weekend Times*: We have lived with America's Vietnam memory for more than 20 years. The Americans fought there, and got caned. (1996)

dust someone **off** (1960) From earlier sense, kill ■ *Times*: They have always been dusted off in the inter-zone matches. (1960)

shred (1966) Orig US; applied mainly to a sporting contest ■ *New York Times*: The Celtics shredded the Los Angeles Lakers with a third-quarter explosion. (1966)

zilch (1969) US; from *zilch* zero, nothing, from the notion of preventing one's opponent from scoring

starch (1974) North American; used in boxing to denote defeating one's opponent by a knockout; from the notion of rendering stiff or rigid on the canvas ■ *Los Angeles Times*: A promotional video cassette sent out to the boxing media showing scenes of Pazienza starching inferior opponents. (1990)

To defeat narrowly

pip (1891), **pip at** (or **on**) **the post** (1924) *pip* from earlier sense, blackball, from the noun *pip* small ball ■ *Scottish Daily Express*: As anchorman, Ian Hutcheon did a magnificent job, shooting a final 71 to pip the Japs and tie for the individual section. (1976) ■ *Times*: Shell . . . now have a record eight managing directors; BP . . . have just been pipped at the post—they have only seven. (1969)

nip (1942) US; applied especially to a sporting contest ■ *Anderson* (South Carolina) *Independent*: Danny Ford banged out four hits and knocked in two runs as Augusta College nipped Erskine, 6-5, here Thursday. (1974)

A (heavy) defeat

drubbing (1769) From earlier literal sense, a beating, from *drub* hit, probably ultimately from Arabic *ḍaraba* beat ■ *Times*: The Communists, who are still licking their wounds after the drubbing they got in 1950. (1955)

thrashing (1815) ■ *Liverpool Daily Post*: The county suffered a 'one innings' thrashing [at cricket] at the hands of their antagonists. (1885)

licking (1831) ■ *Wall Street Journal*: When interest rates were rising last autumn, many Wall Streeet firms took a licking on their big bond portfolios. (1989)

whitewash (1867) Orig US; originally applied to a defeat in which the loser fails to score, and hence to any heavy defeat ■ *Times*: Miss Truman who yesterday allowed Mrs. Cawthorn but 23 points in what the players of darts would term a 'whitewash'. (1961)

hammering (1900) ■ *Guardian*: Wales . . . were given a record 34-6 hammering at Twickenham last February. (1991)

shellacking (1931) Orig US ■ *Herman Wouk*: The Japs can't recover from the shellacking they took at Midway. (1978)

massacre (1940) ■ *Guardian*: In the fall-out from last week's massacre at Murrayfield, the columns of Welsh newspapers have been filled with less than polite urgings to return to a set-piece base. (1991)

caning (1976) ■ *Guardian*: Perhaps it is not so surprising to see Oldham . . . taking a 5-1 caning at Oxford United. (1991)

wipe-out (1977) From earlier sense, annihilation ■ *Daily Mirror*: A record 140,000 [motor-cycling] fans have watched the embarrassing wipe-out by 410 points to 379. (1977)

Completely defeated

gone a million (1913) Australian & New Zealand ■ *New Zealand Listener*: We scraped in in that game, only because Elvidge scored his usual try. . . . Otherwise, we were gone a million. (1958)

lurked (1917) Dated; applied to someone beaten in a game of chance; perhaps connected with *lurch* beat in a game of skill, leave in the lurch ■ Charles Morgan: Four straight aces. Good enough? You're lurked, Sandford. (1938)

To admit defeat (and give up)

throw (or **chuck**) **up** (or **in**) **the sponge (1860)** From the throwing of a sponge into the ring as an admission of defeat in boxing ■ David Gervais: The best he can get out of England is to throw in the sponge, return to work at the advertising agency and settle down with Rosemary in suburbia. (1993)

climb down (1889) Used to denote withdrawal from a position previously maintained. Hence the noun **climb-down** (1887) ■ Angus Wilson: The French have sent a tremendous climbdown note. (1961)

drop one's bundle (1897) Australian & New Zealand ■ S. Gore: It started to rain, too. And at this, he really drops his bundle. (1968)

throw (or **chuck, toss**) **in the towel (1915)** From the throwing of a towel into the ring as an admission of defeat in boxing ■ M. Russell: 'Don't give up.' . . . 'Have no fear. . . . I shan't throw in the towel, I promise you.' (1979)

sky the wipe (1916) Australian, dated; used to denote admitting defeat in boxing; from *sky* throw and *wipe* handkerchief (after *throw in the towel*) ■ Bulletin (Sydney): It is generally understood that a boxer must consider himself beaten when his seconds 'sky the wipe'. (1933)

say (**cry, holler**, etc.) **uncle (1918)** North American; *uncle* perhaps from Irish *anacol* deliverance, mercy, assimilated to English *uncle* parent's brother ■ David Delman: 'Stop it, darling, please.' 'Say uncle.' 'Uncle.' (1972)

throw in one's hand (1923) From earlier sense, retire from a card game, especially poker

15. **Power, Influence**

clout (1868) Orig US; applied especially to political or commercial influence; after one isolated 19th-century occurrence, the usage is not recorded again before the 1930s; from earlier sense, heavy blow ■ Ink: France and other countries have large agricultural surpluses and farmers with electoral 'clout'. (1971)

pull (1889) Orig US ■ Judith Krantz: His future in the giant corporation was assured in the long run through family pull, since he had, on his mother's side, as one said in slang, *du piston*. (1978)

drag (1896) Orig US; applied especially to political influence; compare *pull* ■ Ernest Hemingway: We had a big drag with the waiter because my old man drank whisky and it cost five francs, and that meant a good tip. (1923)

■ *Economist*: An international understanding outside Egypt is needed before the board can throw in its hand. (1957)

To lose deliberately

throw (1868) Orig US ■ *Times*: During the Chancellorship of Mr Roy Jenkins, Lord Allen had to 'throw' their occasional [tennis] matches for fear of puncturing the considerable vanity of his political master. (1978)

take a dive (1942) Orig US; from earlier more specific boxing sense, fall over deliberately when hit

A trophy for defeat

wooden spoon (1858) Jocular; applied to a hypothetical trophy awarded to one who finishes last in a competition; from an earlier application to a wooden spoon presented by custom at Cambridge University to the lowest of those taking honours in the mathematical tripos. Hence **wooden spoonist** (1927), **wooden spooner** (1954) a winner of the wooden spoon ■ *Nation Review* (Melbourne): 4BH slips to fourth place in the five station market, with perennial wooden spooners, 4BK, only 2000 listeners behind. (1973)

To win easily

win hands down (1882) Originally applied to a jockey dropping his hands, and so relaxing his hold on the reins, when victory appears certain ■ *Times*: Double this speed, however, and the submarine wins hands down. (1958)

walk (1937) ■ *Times*: I went to the British [championship] thinking I'd walk it. . . . This was a mistake. . . . It was a close shave. (1976)

A victory

result (1973) British; used especially in sport ■ *Mail on Sunday*: Cricket is sport, not war. You work hard to get a result. Somebody wins and somebody loses. (1991)

in (1929) Orig US; usually in the phrase *have an in with* have a means of access to or influence with ■ J. B. Priestley: I have an *in* with a couple of the directors. (1966)

poke (1965) Applied mainly to horsepower ■ *Sunday Mail Magazine* (Brisbane): I expect you'd prefer something with a bit more poke. A Ferrari say, or an Aston Martin. (1979)

To have in one's power

have (or **get**) someone **by the short hairs (1888)** From the notion of seizing someone by the pubic hairs so that they are immobilized; compare earlier obsolete *get someone where the hair is short* ■ Sayers & Eustace: She's evidently got her husband by the short hairs. (1930)

have (or **get**) someone **over a barrel** (1938)
Orig US; apparently in allusion to the state of
someone placed over a barrel to clear their
lungs of water after being rescued from
drowning ■ Letitia McClung: You sure have me over a
barrel. You caught me red-handed. (1945)

have (or **get**) someone **by the short and
curlies** (1948) Orig services' slang ■ Peter Hill:
There is no need for kid gloves now, we've got him by the short
and curlies. (1976)

To assert one's power

throw (**chuck**, etc.) **one's weight about** (or
around) (1917) Usually implying objectionable
officiousness ■ J. P. Marquand: Bill King . . . always
used to say that Bo-jo was a bastard, a big bastard. Perhaps he
meant that Bo-jo sometimes threw his weight around. (1941)

To exert influence

pull wires (1862) Mainly US; usually denoting
private or secret influence; see *pull strings* ■ Lee
Duncan: Us guys . . . pull wires to get jobs as guards, and you
convicts go over the wall whenever you can. (1936)

pull strings (1938) Usually denoting private or
secret influence; from the notion of
controlling the movements of a puppet by
means of strings ■ Graham Greene: Rice is still short,
but I'm certain Aunt Marion can pull strings with the grocer.
(1955)

To be in a position of power

call the shots (1967) Orig & mainly US
■ *Sunday Telegraph*: They felt that an anti-Old Etonian cabal
was calling the shots. (1981)

16. Coercion

Coercion, pressurizing

squeeze play (1916) Mainly US; from earlier
baseball sense, tactic involving bunting or
hitting the ball softly so that the runner at
third base can reach home ■ D. Wecter: You
perhaps mentioned the fact that Hitler was putting the squeeze
play on Hindenburg a few years later. (1944)

heat (1928) Orig US ■ *Listener*: The moment seemed
opportune to 'turn the heat' on Turkey. (1957)

hardball (1973) US; applied to uncompromising
and especially intimidatory methods, especially
in politics; especially in the phrase *play hardball*;
from earlier sense, baseball (as opposed to
softball) ■ *Fortune*: If anyone wants to play hardball, Cub
can operate in the 5% to 6% range and still be profitable,
because its costs are so lean. (1983)

To pressurize

sweat (1764) Denoting interrogating someone
closely, often with (threats of) violence ■ John Le
Carré: Probably Mikhel intercepted and read it. . . . We could
sweat him, but I doubt if it would help. (1979)

crowd (1828) Orig US ■ Sara Paretsky: Sure, I like
him. But don't crowd me into making any other declarations.
(1992)

put the screws on (1834) Orig US; often
denoting the enforcing of a debt repayment;
from *screws* thumbscrew

crowd the mourners (1842) US, dated;
denoting exercising undue or unseemly
pressure

prod (1871) Denoting strong urging or goading
■ *Independent*: The Soviet Union's descent into chaos might
prod the European Community into action. (1991)

press-gang (1882) Denoting making someone
do something against their will; from earlier
sense, force to join the navy or army by means
of a press-gang ■ *Guardian*: You might imagine recruits

to succeed Speaker Weatherill would have had to be
pressganged. Far from it. They're queueing up for the job.
(1992)

hustle (1887) US; denoting selling or obtaining
things by pressurizing people ■ *Black World*: He
hustled the watch to a barber for 35 bills. (1973)

sool (1889) Australian & New Zealand; denoting
strong urging or goading; often followed by *on*;
compare earlier sense, (of a dog) attack or worry
an animal ■ P. Barton: The cooking teacher, sooled on by
half a dozen or so by-now-tearful girls, took to me with a large
wooden spoon. (1981)

jolly someone **along** (1890) Orig US; denoting
using pleasant behaviour as a way of getting
someone to behave as one wants; from the
adjective *jolly* ■ Helen McCloy: He protested, he argued,
he even tried to jolly them along. They only became bolder.
(1970)

put the acid on (1906) Australian; denoting
putting pressure on someone for a loan, a
favour, etc. ■ Patrick White: And a woman like that,
married to such a sawney bastard, she wouldn't wait for 'em to
put the acid on 'er. (1966)

put the bite on (1919) Orig & mainly US;
denoting putting pressure on someone for a
loan, a favour, etc. ■ Stephen Ransome: Everybody
keeps putting the bite on me for money I haven't got. (1950)

be on someone's **wheel** (1922) Mainly
Australian; denoting hounding or pressurizing
someone ■ Osmar White: The inspector's been on my
wheel to trace him. (1969)

muscle (1929) Orig US ■ C. F. Coe: Mebbe it's a new
mob. If they're musclin' Rap, it won't be long before they're
musclin' us too. (1935)

put the lug on (1929) US; denoting putting
pressure on someone for a loan, a favour, etc.
■ Margaret Truman: My father also knew, from his inside
contacts with Missouri Democrats, that the governor . . . was

'putting the lug' (to use Missouri terminology) on state employees to contribute to his campaign fund. (1973)

gee (1932) Denoting urging or encouraging someone to greater activity; usually followed by *up*; from earlier sense, direct a horse by the call of 'gee' ■ R. Fuller: The directors of the company must be gee'd up. (1956)

stand over someone **(1939)** Australian; denoting intimidating or threatening someone, especially in order to extort money ■ Frank Hardy: We'll have to stand over them to get our money. (1958)

put the squeeze on (1941) Orig US ■ S. Brill: Spilotro's army of enforcers . . . put the squeeze on hard-pressed loan-shark victims. (1978)

strong-arm (1941) From earlier sense, manhandle ■ *Observer*: The OAS had financed themselves initially by strong-arming contributions from rich settlers, who usually shared their sympathies. (1977)

railroad (1952) Orig US; from earlier sense, rush someone or something into, through, etc. somewhere ■ Brian Garfield: Take all the time you want. Nobody wants to railroad him. (1975)

twist someone's **arm (1953)** ■ R. V. Beste: I had to twist his arm a bit but he came through. (1969)

lean on (1960) Orig US ■ *New York Times*: 'An Attorney General would resign too if he thought he was being leaned on by the Prime Minister or senior ministers on a pending prosecution,' a former Attorney General said. (1975)

17. **Organization**

Organization, administration, bureaucracy

bumf, bumph (1930) British, derogatory; applied collectively to documents; from earlier sense, toilet-paper ■ M. K. Joseph: Matthews is bringing the bumf. . . . He says be sure and type it on Army Form A2. (1957)

admin (1942) Applied (often derogatorily) to administrative functions or duties, or to the department of an organization that deals with these; short for *administration* ■ W. Buchan: A mass of practical details—sheer 'admin'. (1961)

To organize

jack something **up (1942)** New Zealand ■ *New Zealand Listener*: I'll see you right at a boardin' place until you get jacked up. (1971)

To organize one's affairs efficiently

get one's shit together (1969) US

get one's act together (1973) Orig US
■ *Times*: We need to get our act together. . . . Users have been divided so far and are being picked off by the publishers one by one. (1984)

hardball (1984) US; from the noun *hardball* uncompromising methods ■ *Observer*: She rebelled occasionally, hard-balling O'Neill into attaching to a Bill an Amendment that would help her District, by threatening to kill a million dollar pork-barrel destined for his. (1984)

Someone who intimidates or coerces others

enforcer (1929) US; applied to a criminal gang's strong-arm man ■ Estes Kefauver: Dead beside him was his lieutenant and 'enforcer', Charlie Gargotta. (1951)

muscle man (1929) Orig US; applied to a muscular man employed to intimidate others with (threats of) violence ■ Paul Oliver: With the considerable returns accruing from operating policy wheels the racket came under the control of syndicates with muscle-men and hired gunmen ensuring that their 'rights' were protected. (1968)

standover man, standover merchant (1939) Australian; from *stand over* intimidate ■ Cusack & James: It was Joe's bodyguard, Curly—stand-over man as well, they said. (1951)

muscle (1942) Orig US; applied collectively to people employed to use or threaten violence ■ Helen Nielsen: The muscle on the trucks . . . were free-lancers. (1973)

Inducement

come-on (1902) ■ Monica Dickens: They like the sound of foreign investments. It has that magic, millionaire ring to it, like foreign exchange. Just another come-on. (1958)

get it together (1975) ■ *New Society*: Tez thinks he'll be a rock star . . . tomorrow. Meanwhile he's having trouble getting it together and lives off the SS. (1975)

Disorganization

couldn't organize (run, etc.) **a piss-up in a brewery (1984)** British; denoting incompetence at organization or administration; from the notion of the easy availability of beer for a piss-up (= bout of heavy drinking) in a brewery

too many chiefs and not enough Indians (1988) Denoting (disorganization due to) an excess of managerial staff and not enough ordinary workers ■ *National Trust Magazine*: The way the National Trust has grown, I can't help feeling that there are too many Chiefs and not enough Indians. (1992)

Disorganized

shambolic (1958) British; from *shamb(les* scene of complete disorder + *-olic* ■ *Times*: The average listener is in the position of anybody who encounters an organization at work for the first time. It may appear shambolic but how much is that because he hasn't yet made sense of it. (1975)

18. **Subservience**

hen-pecked (a1680) Applied to a man dominated by a woman, typically his wife; from the notion of the plucking of some of the feathers of the domestic cock by his hens ■ George Bernard Shaw: He may be henpecked: what married man is not? (1939). Hence **hen-peck (1688)** ■ W. M. Thackeray: That my lady was jealous and henpecked my lord. (1852)

play second fiddle (1809)

eat crow (1877) US; used to denote that someone is forced to do something extremely disagreeable and humiliating; formerly also *eat boiled crow*, from the notion of swallowing something unpalatable ■ *New Yorker*: I was going to apologize, eat crow, offer to kiss and make up. (1970)

take a back seat (1881) Orig US ■ *Times*: Those who think that the trade union movement should take a back seat in the Labour movement should think again. (1959)

under the cosh (1958) ■ *Observer*: As for the Criminal Justice Act, it could be very useful to have all the villains under the cosh, as they expressed it. It made it much easier to get information. (1960)

pussy-whipped (1963) Orig and mainly US; applied to a man dominated by a woman; from either *pussy* woman or *pussy* female genitals ■ Judith Krantz: Some men are pussy whipped from the day they are born, some have it happen to them later in life, some never. (1978)

A subservient person

squidge (1907) US; applied to someone who does troublesome duties for another; origin unknown

■ George Ade: When Mr. and Mrs. Al Laflin and I traveled in distant countries, we always hired a 'squidge' the moment we arrived in a new town. His job was to stay with us and accept all the hardships and worries. (1942)

monkey-man (1924) US; applied to a weak and servile husband

stooge (1937) From earlier sense, stage assistant ■ *Detroit Free Press*: Joshua Nkomo and Robert Mugabe . . . branded the moderate African leaders as 'sworn stooges of Premier (Ian) Smith'. (1978)

See also A subservient black person at **Ethnic & National Groups** (pp. 41–2)

To submit

knuckle under (1882) ■ *Times*: He replied that there was no power on earth to make a local party accept a candidate. He was rather sorry they knuckled under to Transport House in this division. (1955)

To put in a subservient position

have someone **on toast (1886)** From the notion of food prepared and ready to be eaten, served on toast ■ E. F. Benson: To think that half an hour ago that little squirt thought he had us on toast. (1916)

get (or **have**) someone **by the short and curlies (1948)** From the subservient condition of someone seized by the pubic hair ■ Peter Hill: There's no need for the kid gloves now, we've got him by the short and curlies. (1976)

19. **Genuineness & Spuriousness**

(See also **Honesty** pp. 277–8)

Genuine

ryebuck, ribuck, etc. **(1859)** Mainly Australian, dated; of uncertain origin; compare German *Reibach* profit ■ R. H. Knyvett: They even knew our slang, for there was 'The "Fair Dinkum" Store' and across the way 'Ribuck Goods'. (1918)

kosher (1896) From earlier sense, in accordance with Jewish law; ultimately from Hebrew *kāshēr* right ■ Colin MacInnes: It's all very well sneering at universities . . . but really and truly, it would be wonderful to have a bit of kosher education

dinkum (1900) Australian & New Zealand; especially in the phrase *fair dinkum*; from the noun *dinkum* (hard) work, of unknown origin ■ S. Gore: 'Well, stone the crows!' say the crew. 'His God musta been dinkum after all.' (1968)

dinky-di(e), dinki-di(e) (1915) Australian & New Zealand ■ *The Australian*: Sinister karate chopping Japanese battling with true-blue dinki-di locals. (1969)

ridge (1938) Australian; from an obsolete word for 'gold' ■ D. Ireland: I convinced her the whole thing was ridge! (1971)

ridgy-didge (1953) Australian; from assumed *ridgy* genuine, from *ridge* genuine + -*y* ■ *Sydney Morning Herald*: The old-timers insist that Kalgoorlie two-up is 'the real game' and that ridgie-didge players will skirt the casino ring. (1986)

for real (1956) Orig US ■ *Black Panther*: This is no 'scare tactic', it is for real. (1973)

actual (1966) British; in the phrase *your actual* ■ *Times*: There won't be any room for your actual horny-handed sons of toil in the TUC; there'll be too many sharp-suited managers. (1976)

Something or someone genuine

McCoy (1883) In the phrase *the real McCoy* (or *Mackay, McKie*); origin uncertain; amongst the suggested derivations are that in its original form, *the real Mackay*, it refers to the true chieftain of the clan Mackay, a much disputed position, and that the variant *the real McCoy* (first recorded in 1922) refers to Kid *McCoy*, the professional name of US boxer Norman Selby (1873–1940), who was nicknamed 'the real McCoy' to distinguish him from other boxers who tried to use his name ■ *Guardian*: Sadler's Wells is playing host to the regal offspring Royal Ballet, and not, please note, a second eleven but the real Macoy [*sic*]. (1972)

the goods (1904) ■ Angus Wilson: He was the most awful old fraud himself, you know. Oh, not as an historian, you always said he was the goods. (1956)

Spurious

snide (1859) Dated; origin unknown

duff (1889) British; from the noun *duff* something spurious ■ G. Netherwood: It was said by the erks that he once sold rock on Blackpool sands. This was just 'duff gen'. (1944)

phoney, phony (1900) Origin unknown ■ *Daily Telegraph*: Like his singing, he is gentlemanly: no long hair, exaggerated clothes, or phony emotionalism. (1970)

bodger (1945) Australian; from the verb *bodge* patch or mend clumsily ■ F. J. Hardy: This entailed the addition of as many more 'bodger' votes as possible. (1950)

moody (1958) Criminals' ■ N. J. Crisp: 'I don't have to tell you,' Kenyon went on, 'how easy it is to plant moody information about a copper.' (1978)

Something or someone spurious

quack (1659) Orig applied to an unqualified person claiming to be a doctor, and hence to any charlatan; abbreviation of *quacksalver*, from early modern Dutch (now *kwakzalver*): first element probably from the stem of *kwakken* prattle, second element from *zalf* salve

duff (1781) British; perhaps from *duff* dough

not (quite) the clean potato (1822) Dated ■ M. Franklin: She was the only great-granddaughter of old Larry Healey of Little River, none so clean a potato, if rumour was correct. (1931)

gold brick (1889) Orig US; applied to something with only a surface appearance of value; especially in the phrase *sell someone a gold brick* swindle someone, especially by passing off a sham as valuable; from the practice of passing off an ingot of base metal as gold ■ *Chicago Daily News*: It used to be the city slicker who sold gold bricks to the hick from the country. (1947)

phoney, phony (1902) From the adjective *phoney* ■ *New Yorker*: This simple test—a way of telling the phonies from the truly committed. (1977)

shuck (1958) From earlier sense, something of little value (original sense, husk, pod) ■ Alvin Toffler: The recently graduated son . . . proclaims the nine-to-five job a degrading sham and a shuck. (1980)

20. Triviality, Insignificance

Trivial, insignificant

piddling (1559) From *piddle* urinate ■ *Maclean's Magazine*: In plain words, I found out what my job was. No piddling assignment either. What it amounted to was saving the country. (1971)

fiddling (1652) ■ Douglas Adams: The Galactibanks refuse to deal in fiddling small change. (1979)

twopenny-halfpenny, tuppeny-ha'penny (1809) British; from the notion of twopence-halfpenny as a trivial sum ■ *Guardian*: Braying over a promised crackdown on tuppeny ha'penny social security scroungers. (1992)

one-horse (1853) Mainly US & Australian; applied to something, especially a town, small and unimportant; from the notion of a carriage small enough to be pulled by one horse ■ *Zigzag*: I've a new song . . . about a girl of sixteen trying to get out of a one horse town. (1977)

jerkwater (1897) US; from earlier application to a train operating on a branch line, from the notion of a locomotive with a small boiler that had to be replenished with water 'jerked' (i.e. pulled up) from track-side streams in a bucket ■ R. Lockridge: It won't be easy for him to get another job if he's fired. . . . Maybe at some jerkwater college at half what he's getting now. (1970)

two-bit (1932) US; from *two bits* twenty-five cents or two eighths of a dollar ■ T. Willis: Some other two-bit General will try shooting us up. (1978)

pissing (1937) Compare *piddling* ■ Nicolas Freeling: 'Fuck it,' said Metcalfe angrily. 'I'm only a pissing sergeant.' (1975)

small-time (1938) Orig US; from earlier application to the minor vaudeville circuit ■ Irwin Shaw: Do you intend to be a small-time tennis pro . . . all your life? (1977)

Something or someone trivial or insignificant

small beer (1777) From earlier sense, weak beer, probably in allusion to the metaphor in Shakespeare's *Othello* 2.i.161: To suckle fools, and chronicle small beer (1604) ■ *Daily Mail*: Delivery of each card costs about £1.30—small beer compared with frauds which can run to £6,000 a card. (1991)

small fry (a1797) Applied collectively to insignificant people or things; from earlier sense, young animals ■ *Observer*: The consensus is that Kearns and Madigan are small fry; they are no gangsters. (1991)

small potatoes (1846) Orig US ■ *Gramophone*: Serenus is small potatoes by CBS or RCA standards but its albums are tastefully produced and carefully annotated. (1976)

putty medal (1898) Applied to an appropriately worthless reward for insignificant service ■ Mary Kelly: 'You know what you'll be given for all this?' . . . 'A putty medal. Sooner have a cheque.' (1958)

pipsqueak (1910) Applied to a small and insignificant person (or thing); from *pip* high-pitched sound + *squeak* ■ G. Macmunn: It does not pay in the East to let pip-squeaks beard the mighty. (1930)

pie-eater, pie-biter (1911) Australian; applied to an insignificant person, especially a petty criminal ■ Kylie Tennant: He's one of those big he-men that go sneaking around the park waiting to snitch some chromo's handbag. Just a pie-eater. (1953)

cog in a (or **the**) **machine (1934)** Orig US; applied to someone with a necessary but insignificant role in a large organization or group ■ Erich Fromm: We have all become cogs in the bureaucratic machine. (1976)

small-timer (1935) Applied to an insignificant person; from *small-time* + *-er* ■ Roger Simons: She was a small timer when I met 'er. . . . Then she got so 'igh and mighty she wouldn't speak to me. (1959)

21. Similarity

the like(s) of (1637) Used to denote other similar people or things ■ *Guardian*: Naturally the likes of Time magazine wanted to find out about the gentle giant's past. (1991)

spit (1885) Used in the phrase *be the (dead) spit of* be an exact likeness or counterpart of; from earlier phrase *the very spit of*, perhaps from the notion of the likeness having been 'spat' out ■ Arthur Upfield: The son's the dead spit of the old man. (1953)

ringer (1891) Orig US; used in the phrase *be a (dead) ringer for* (or *of*), be an exact likeness or counterpart of; from earlier sense, one fraudulently substituted for another ■ *Sun*: I didn't notice the fella at the time, but he really is a dead ringer for Cap'n Bob. (1992)

ring (1899) Australian & New Zealand; used in the phrase *be the dead ring for* (or *of*) be the exact likeness or counterpart of; abbreviation of *ringer* ■ E. Hill: Now you're the dead ring o' that girl, and you speak the same. (1951)

chip off the old block (1929) Used to denote similarity in character to a parent or other older relative; from earlier phrases *chip of the same block, chip of the old block* ■ Somerset Maugham: His heir was a nephew . . . not a bad boy, but not a chip off the old block, no, sir, far from it. (1947)

Boringly similar

samey (1929) British; from *same* + *-y* ■ *Sunday Times*: Many of his pictures of expensive men and women on expensive horses seem samey. (1959)

22. Suitability

Suitable, in accordance with what one wants or likes

up one's alley (1924) Orig US ■ Dale Carnegie: Bridge will be in a cinch for you. It is right up your alley. (1936)

up (or **down**) **one's street (1929)** Compare earlier obsolete *in one's street* in same sense ■ *It*: If you like Miles Davis's 'In a Silent Way' then Don Cherry has a new release which is just up your street. (1977)

See also That which is wanted or needed at **Wanting & Getting** (p. 210)

To be suitable

suit someone's book (1851) Orig bookmakers' slang; from the notion of being an acceptable bet ■ *Economist*: An early election could suit Mr Mulroney's book. (1987)

suit someone down to the ground (1867) ■ R. N. Carey: It is tipping, Chriss, and suits you down to the ground. (1903)

To be suited to (something); have the necessary qualities for (something)

be cut out (1645) Followed by *for* or *to* and an infinitive ■ M. Cost: 'I'm so sorry, Fanchon.' '*N'importe*! You and Albert Augustus were cut out for tight-rope walking from birth.' (1952) ■ D. H. Lawrence: My mother was . . . cut out to play a superior rôle in the god-damn bourgeoisie. (1929)

have (got) what it takes (1929) Orig US ■ Billie Holiday: Sometimes I wonder how we survived. But we did. If we didn't have what it took at the beginning, we picked it up along the way. (1956)

23. **Strangeness**

Strange, odd, eccentric

rum (1774) An application of obsolete *rum* fine, splendid, as in *rum cove* fine fellow ■ George Bernard Shaw: He must have been a rum old bird. . . . Not rum enough to be noticed. (1930)

freaky (1824) From *freak* odd thing or person + *-y* ■ *Guardian*: The orgasmic concerto . . . is typical of the best moments of this extraordinarily freaky film. . . . As anarchic comedies go, it travels a good deal further than most. (1992)

zany (1918) Applied to something or someone amusingly or ridiculously strange; from earlier sense, buffoon-like ■ *House & Garden*: Luncheon-mats of the subtlest as well as the zaniest designs. (1959)

off-beat (1938) Orig US; from earlier musical sense, on an unaccented beat ■ *Observer*: It is the off-beat things, the eccentricities, that help give salerooms their perpetual appeal and surprise. (1959)

way-out (1959) From *way* far + *out* ■ Judson Philips: Vardon thought up a way-out scheme to commit a murder. (1972)

zonky, zonkey (1972) From *zonk*(ed intoxicated + *-y* ■ *Times*: His book is really a study in ideas—or to coin an appropriately zonkey term—*weirdology*. (1980)

creepy (1992) Applied to something uncannily or disturbingly strange; from earlier sense, eerily frightening ■ Sara Paretsky: This is not just curious, it's downright creepy. I think I need to talk to Mr. Mohr. (1992)

A strange or eccentric person or thing

original (1824) Applied to an eccentric or unique individual; from earlier sense, person who acts in an original way ■ *Guardian*: Mr Lowry is an outspoken original, his liberalism unreconstructed. (1988)

card (1853) Applied to a person regarded as a 'character'; from earlier sense, person of a particular type ■ Arnold Bennett: It would be . . . a topic for years, the crown of his reputation as a card. (1905)

oddball (1948) Orig US; from *odd* + *ball*; often used adjectivally ■ D. Sears: The oddest of a family where odd-balls were not the exception. (1974) ■ *Washington Post*: Life aboard a submarine has its oddball moments. (1959)

odd bod (1955) Applied to an eccentric person; *bod* short for *body* ■ J. Roffman: Anyone would, except you who have an inborn bias toward the odd bods in society. (1976)

24. **Severity, Oppressiveness**

Severe, hard, uncompromising

hard-nosed (1927) Orig US; from earlier sense, (of a hunting dog) having little or no sense of smell ■ *Times*: Dolly's hard-nosed business approach to publishers probably did not have universal support. (1973)

heavy (1970) From earlier jazz slang sense, serious, profound ■ *It*: The Bournemouth drug squad (reputed to be one of the heaviest squads in the country). (1971)

hard-assed (1971), hard-ass (1973) Orig & mainly US ■ G. Benford: You Hiruko guys so hard-ass let's see you corner it. (1983) ■ C. S. Murray: Canadian customs are notoriously hard-assed about drugs. (1989)

To deal with severely, harshly, or oppressively

give someone **beans (1835)** Orig US ■ P. G. Wodehouse: He wanted to give me beans, but Florence wouldn't let him. She said 'Father you are not to touch him. It was a pure misunderstanding.' (1946)

give someone **hell (1851)** ■ Ngaio Marsh: Gabriel would give me hell and we would both get rather angry with each other. (1940)

put someone **through it (1872)** Orig US ■ Agatha Christie: Mad as a hatter. . . . My goodness, he must have put you through it now and again! (*a*1976)

give someone **the works (1920)** Orig US

sock (1939) US; denoting imposing something onerous (e.g. a heavy charge) on someone ■ *Detroit Free Press*: The township socked the company with a building permit violation. (1978)

put someone **through the wringer (1942)** Orig US; often applied specifically to uncompromising interrogation; from the notion of wringing out wet clothes ■ *Times*: Not since the controversial Bishop of Durham . . . has an episcopal appointee been put through the wringer in this fashion. (1984)

shaft (1959) Orig & mainly US; often also implying unfair treatment; from *the shaft* harsh treatment ■ *Debates of the Senate of Canada*: As I have told my constituents in Hamilton, Ontario, which seems to have been continually shafted by this government. (1970)

clobber (1969) From earlier sense, hit ■ *Daily Telegraph*: Butlin's is heavily clobbered by the increase in Selective Employment Tax. (1969)

Harsh treatment

the gaff (1896) US; in the phrase *stand* (or *take*, *give*, etc.) *the gaff*; probably from *gaff* steel spur for a fighting cock ■ W. M. Raine: Just because he shuts his mouth and stands the gaff. (1924)

stick (1942) Usually in the phrase *get* (or *give*) *some stick*; often implying harsh criticism; from the notion of striking with a stick ■ *Daily Telegraph*: I told him that he could expect trouble from the branches. . . . He will come in for some stick over this. (1980)

the shaft (1959) Orig & mainly US; usually in the phrase *get* (or *give*) *the shaft*; from the notion of inserting a rod, etc. up someone's rectum ■ *Modern Photography*: I would give more of my business to Minolta but for the company's uncooperative, anti-consumer thinking. Doubtless there are many such as myself who have gotten the shaft. (1979)

A severe, hard, or uncompromising person

hard case (1836) Orig US; applied to someone aggressively difficult to deal with ■ **Rudyard Kipling**: It [*sc.* a school] . . . had been made up . . . by drafts from Haileybury . . . and, I think, a percentage of 'hard cases' from other schools. (*a*1936)

hard nut (1888) ■ **Jonathon Gash**: While he ordered at the bar I glanced at him. This bloke was a hard nut and no mistake. (1981)

tough nut (1892) Orig US ■ *Times*: For the 'tough nut' the youth club as at present constituted offered no fold. (1950)

hard ticket (1903) Orig US

ball-breaker (1942), ball-buster (*c*1944) Orig US; applied to a hard or demanding person, especially a person who sets difficult work or problems or a dominating woman who destroys the self-confidence of a man; from earlier sense, difficult problem ■ **Neil Armstrong** *et al.*: The quality control inspector is a sort of nitpicker. We're the ball breakers, in plain English. We're the most unwanted people. (1970) ■ *Observer*: A meticulously groomed, flint-profiled ball breaker with a taste for leopard-skin prints, Margo is the repository of every known prejudice common among the landless landed gentry. (1975) ■ **Marilyn French**: A woman who blames men or male society for anything, who complains, is seen as a . . . castrator, an Amazon, a ballbuster. (1980)

hard-ass (1978) Orig & mainly US; back-formation from *hard-assed* ■ **J. Welch**: It would have been funny, Hartpence the hardass snitching, if Jack hadn't got stabbed. (1990)

25. Searching

To search a person or place

shake down (1915) Orig and mainly US; applied especially to the police; compare earlier sense, pressurize ■ **Desmond Bagley**: Once Mayberry had been shaken down the guards were taken from Penny and Gillian. (1977). Hence the noun **shake-down** a search of a person or place (1914) ■ *Landfall*: But about nine o'clock, without any warning, there was a shake-down [of prisoners]. (1958)

toss (1939) US, police slang ■ **Ed McBain**: We ought to try for an order to toss his apartment. (1980). Hence the noun **toss** such a search (1970) ■ **James Mills**: You wanta give her a toss, give her a toss, but let's not stand here all night. (1972)

spin (1972) British, police slang; often in the phrase *spin the drum* search the place ■ **J. Barnett**: We iron him to the banisters while we spin the drum from top to bottom. (1982)

To search a person

frisk (1789) From earlier sense, move in a lively way; from the notion of searching rapidly ■ *New Statesman*: Showing his teeth in a vicious snarl as they frisk him and open his jacket to feel under his arm. (1970)

go through (1861)

fan (1927) ■ **Edgar Wallace**: Legally no policeman has the right to 'fan' a prisoner until he gets into the police station. (1927)

To search and rob a person or place

turn over (1859) ■ **Laurence Meynell**: What about that girl's bedroom that got turned over? (1981)

go through (1865) ■ **R. W. Service**: The girls were 'going through' a drunken sailor. (1945)

go over (1889) Dated ■ *Referee*: A few who had . . . gone over the landlord, left him skinned. (1889)

To search for in order to harm

gun for (1888) From the notion of going in search of someone with a gun ■ *New York Times*: Others talked of mysterious influences that had been 'gunning' for financiers of prominence. (1903)

To search an area or place

scout around (or about, round) (1886) ■ **G. V. Higgins**: We're even bigger suckers for a planted story . . . if we really had to scout around for it. (1977)

recce, reccy (1943) Orig military slang; short for *reconnoitre* ■ **Evelyn Waugh**: I'm going out myself with the adjutant to recce training areas. (1945)

recon (1966) US military slang; abbreviation of *reconnoitre* ■ **Ian Kemp**: Our orders are to recon only, and avoid all contact with the enemy whatsoever. (1969)

punt around (1970) British, police slang; applied to patrolling an area; probably from *punt* place a bet

A search of an area

recco (1917) Military slang; abbreviation of *reconnaisance* ■ **W. Simpson**: That was the last 'recco.' flight we made, and for months we had to content ourselves with mock air battles. (1942)

recon (1918) US military slang; often used attributively; abbreviation of *reconnaisance* ■ **Ed McBain**: Our recon patrol found an enemy base camp. (1977)

recce, reccy (1941) Orig military slang; short for *reconnaisance* ■ **Arthur Hailey**: I sometimes think about two guys in Korea, close buddies of mine. We were on a recce patrol near the Yalu river. (1979)

punt (1974) British, police slang; used in the phrase *have a punt around* patrol an area; from the verb *punt* ■ **G. F. Newman**: Thought I'd have a punt around, see who's about. (1974)

To search inquisitively

ferret (1580) From the earlier sense, hunt with ferrets; from the notion of the ferret as a restless and assiduous searcher ■ *Sunday Times*: The referee is supposed to make an instant decision but M Dume decided to wait and ferret around underneath the bodies. (1993)

nose (1648) ■ P. G. Wodehouse: He began to nose about. He pulled out drawer after drawer. (1925) ■ **Rosamond Lehmann**: I thought of her nosing in my room for signs. (1936)

poke (1715) From the notion of poking one's nose into things ■ James Payn: Having a lawyer to poke and pry into his accounts. (1888)

To investigate or assess a person, situation, etc.

suss, sus (1969) Usually followed by *out*; from earlier sense, grasp, realize ■ *Daily Mirror*: It took me about half a day to suss out the industry and realise how easy it would be to move in. (1977)

scope out (1977) US ■ R. B. Parker: I leaned against the front wall . . . and scoped things out. (1986)

To search for different possibilities

shop around (1922) From the notion of comparing the quality and price of a particular item in various shops ■ J. I. M. Stewart: It's usual to shop around a little. To send in a list of three or four colleges. (1976)

To search for information

pump (1656) Applied to persistent questioning to elicit information

pick someone's **brains (1838)** Denoting eliciting information from someone; from the notion of picking (= stealing from) someone's pocket ■ **Laurence Meynell**: The old fool is thinking of writing a book about collecting furniture and she means to pick everybody's brains. (1982)

grill (1894) Applied to persistent questioning to elicit information; from earlier sense, cook on a grill ■ *Radio Times*: Listeners will be able to 'grill' leading public figures over the air when *It's Your Line*, a new-style 'live' current affairs programme begins. (1970)

To find by searching

ferret something **out (1577)** ■ Joseph Conrad: My friend took the trouble to ferret out the complete record of that man for me. (1907)

nose something **out (a1630)** ■ Doris Lessing: What people were trying to do, in their continual moving about and around, nosing out news, taking in information, was to isolate residues of truth in rumour. (1974)

dig something **up (1861)**, **dig** something **out (1864)** ■ O. Henry: Ogden digs up a deck of cards, and we play casino. (1909) ■ P. Williams: It was Carolyn who . . . dug out two old volumes of eighteenth century pictures lying forgotten in a cupboard. (1929)

sniff something **out (1946)** ■ J. Barnett: You should concentrate more on sniffing out the sex fiends than speculating on spies. (1979)

An ability to find things

a nose for (1875) ■ J. Cassells: He was a damned good reporter . . . and he had a nose for a story. (1972)

26. Intrusion

poke (stick, shove, etc.) one's nose in (1611) ■ Mark Pattison: A flourishing Evangelical, who poked his nose into everything. (1883)

stick (shove, get, etc.) one's oar in (1630) ■ J. R. Ackerly: One who preferred to stand outside of life and observe it, not (as he would have phrased it) to 'put one's oar in'. (1968)

butt in (1899) Orig US; from *butt* shove with the head ■ E. Eager: 'I'm sorry,' he said, 'butting in like this, but I've got to tell you something.' (1957)

horn in (1912) Orig US; often followed by *on*; from the notion of an ox pushing in with its horns ■ P. G. Wodehouse: I suppose she felt she owed you something, after horning in on your big scene like that and trying to steal your publicity the way she did. (1936)

mess with (1913) Orig and mainly US; used to denote interfering, especially with someone or something one cannot handle ■ *Guardian*: Then, as if to say 'don't mess with me', Seles let fly. In another 19 minutes it was all over. (1991)

crash (1921) Orig US; used to denote entering without permission ■ Roy Fuller: I hope you'll forgive me crashing your excellent party. (1953)

muscle in (1929) Often followed by *on* ■ John Wainwright: 'The Ponderosa' was his spread, and no cheap, jumped-up, fiddle-foot was gonna muscle in. (1973)

stickybeak (1933) Australian & New Zealand; from the noun *stickybeak* inquisitive person ■ Lawson Glassop: You deny me the right to think as I like. . . . You must prod, and pry, and sticky-beak. (1945)

get into the act, get (or be) in on the act (1947) Orig US; used to denote involving oneself in an activity ■ *Spectator*: President Chamoun got back into the act by announcing that they would not be asked to withdraw from the Lebanon. (1958)

prodnose (1958) From the noun *prodnose* inquisitive person ■ *Daily Telegraph*: It is perhaps high time that the industrial psychologists who are encouraged to prodnose into most things got to work on the Press. (1969)

hack into (1985) Used to denote gaining unauthorized access to a computer system; probably from earlier sense, cut roughly ■ *Times*: The cost of restoring a computer system which is hacked into can run into hundreds and thousands of pounds for investigating and rebuilding the system. (1989)

An intrusive person

buttinsky, buttinski (1902) Orig US; humorously from *butt in* + *-sky, -ski*, final element in many Slavic names ■ P. G. Wodehouse: It is never pleasant for a man of sensibility to find himself regarded as a buttinski. (1960)

An inquisitive person

nosey parker, nosy parker (1907) Mainly British; said to have been applied originally as a nickname of a man who spied on courting couples in Hyde Park, London ■ David Craig: All nosey parkers in this street. (1974)

stickybeak (1920) Australian & New Zealand; probably from the notion of sticking one's 'beak' (= nose) into something ■ R. Hall: Disguised as a mobile heap of blankets in case some stickybeak might be awake and prying. (1982)

prodnose (1934) From the verb *prod* + *nose*; from the notion of sticking one's nose into something ■ D. Robinson: I'll tell you why, you squalid prodnose. (1973)

27. **Involvement**

Involved (in)

mixed up in (1882) ■ M. Hebden: I'll throw this into Pinow's lap. It's German and high-level, and I don't want to be mixed up in it. (1970)

in on (1923) ■ Michael Innes: Don't imagine I have the slightest wish to be in on your muckraking. (1973)

in on the act (1951) Orig US ■ Listener: No one for a moment supposes that Friendly will not be in on the act. (1967)

into (1969) ■ It: He was basically into being a hustler, which he was very, very good at. (1969)

Involvement

a piece (share, etc.) of the action (1957) Orig US; applied to involvement in a (potentially) profitable activity ■ Maclean's Magazine: And last year mink breeders from Scandinavia to California were falling over themselves to buy a piece of the action. (1966)

To be involved

have a finger in the pie (1659) ■ Recruiters' Bulletin: Even though us 'gobs' were on the

A busybody

yenta, yente (1923) US; Yiddish, originally a personal name

An imposter

ringer (1896) US; from earlier sense, one substituted for another ■ Malcolm Bradbury: This is quite a party. I'm going to feel a real ringer. (1965)

Inquisitive

nosey, nosy (1882) From *nose* + *-y*; from the notion of sticking one's nose into something ■ Daily Express: Marylebone man: Being nosey, I goes to 'ave a look. Magistrate: Being what? Clerk: Nosey; meaning curious. (1928)

Non-intrusion

leave someone or something **be (1825)** A colloquial substitution of *leave* for *let* ■ Eugene O'Neill: Leave Hugo be! . . . He's earned his dream! (1946)

'Conny' standing by, Why, we all had a finger in the pie. (1915)

To become involved

get (climb, hop, jump, etc.) on the bandwagon (1899) Orig US; denoting joining what seems likely to be a successful enterprise; from *band-wagon* large wagon capable of carrying the band in a procession, hence one carring a band of successful (political) leaders ■ Hansard Commons: The Tory party are now trying to climb on to the band wagon. (1950)

get into (or in on) the act (1947) Orig US ■ Spectator: President Chamoun got back into the act by announcing that they would not be asked to withdraw from the Lebanon. (1958)

To cause to become involved

let in for (1837) Usually denoting involvement in an unwelcome responsibility; often used reflexively ■ James Curtis: I don't want to say 'O.K.' and then find out that I've let myself in for . . . doing a blag on the crown jewels. (1936)

28. **Sharing, Distribution**

A sharing out

carve-up (1935) Applied to a sharing out of spoils, often dishonestly gained ■ News Chronicle: In practice it is a carve-up among the Big Four. (1959)

A share given or received

slice (1550) ■ Sunday Times: Aided by a slice of luck and their own courage, Waterloo held out. (1993)

whack (1785) ■ Maeve Binchy: They still had to pay a huge whack of the wedding reception cost, and the cake, and the limousines. (1988)

rake-off (1888) Orig US; applied to a share of proceeds ■ Joyce Cary: I didn't say fifty to you. Sorry. But the agency would give me a rake off on reprints. (1959)

split (1889) Applied to a share of proceeds ■ J. T. Farrell: I wasn't working for a long time, and then I got me this job, and now I'm also lined up with a can-house, and get my split on anybody I bring there. (1934)

cut (1918) Orig US ■ *New York*: The net proceeds of a $2 million stock offering after the underwriter had taken his cut. (1970)

chop (1919) Australian & New Zealand; especially in the phrase *be in for one's chop* ■ D. H. Crick: Tell him his quid today'll be worth ten bob tomorrow, so he better get in for his chop. (1966)

To contribute a share to something

chip in (1861) Orig US; from the notion of putting in or staking chips in a gambling game ■ *Commentary*: The help of the Ford Foundation (which chipped in more than $100,000). (1960)

muck in (1952) Denoting equal participation; from earlier sense, share eating arrangements or living accommodation ■ *Times*: The company . . . all muck in, take small or big parts. (1970)

A contribution solicited from a number of people

whip-round (1874) From earlier obsolete *whip* in same sense ■ *Centuryan* (Office Cleaning Services): It appears a whip-round for the drinks was suggested. (1977)

Equally or fairly shared

even Stephen, even Steven (1866) Rhyming phrase based on the male personal forename *Stephen, Steven* ■ Ray Bradbury: It's a fifty-fifty fight. Even Stephen. (1955)

fifty-fifty (1913) Orig US ■ Howard Wadman: It will take much of the sting out of the opposition if the ownership is fifty-fifty. (1949)

Per item

a throw (1898) Orig US ■ *Author*: The cost of research. . . . The BBC Archives charge £2 a throw. (1975)

29. Avoidance

To avoid or evade something

dodge (1680) From earlier sense, move around, change one's position ■ *New Scientist*: While research strives to remove the limit, products which dodge the issue are appearing. (1983)

cut (1791) Dated ■ W. S. Maugham: She was prepared to cut an engagement in London. (1930)

wriggle out (1848) ■ *Economist*: Attempts by Saudi Arabia to wriggle out of its role as OPEC's 'swing' producer . . . look like succeeding. (1987)

duck (1896) Orig US; followed when intransitive by *out of* ■ M. M. Kaye: I should like to duck the whole situation by getting roaring drunk. (1959) ■ *Sunday Times*: He even tried to duck out of asking for the resignation of his own oldest friend, William Rogers, his first secretary of state. (1993)

give something **a miss (1919)** ■ Joanna Cannan: I'm afraid I've given church a miss this morning. (1950)

skive (1919) British, orig military slang; applied to avoiding one's work or duty; often followed by *off*; perhaps from French *esquiver* dodge, slink away, or from earlier *skive* split or cut (leather, rubber, etc.), from Old Norse *skífa* ■ J. Mann: The girls who dig are always glad of an excuse to skive off and have a rest. (1973). Hence the noun **skive (1958)** ■ J. Ditton: He thought the sentry was on the skive. Thought he'd come down . . . for a cup of coffee. (1980)

dodge Pompey (1929) Naval slang; applied to avoiding work on board ship; compare *Pompey* Portsmouth

skip it (1934) Orig US; used as an exhortation to avoid a topic ■ Robert Dentry: At home . . . we cope and never give it a second thought. Out here we—oh, skip it! (1971)

odds (1958) ■ G. F. Newman: I can't odds being mixed up in crime. (1970)

skip (1961) From earlier sense, pass over and move to the next ■ K. H. Cooper: Women suffering from cramps find exercise extremely uncomfortable. Common sense alone tells them to skip exercise during those days. (1970)

weasel out (1962) Applied to avoiding an obligation, especially dishonourably; also used with *one's way* ■ Mario Puzo: A real fucking claim agent weaseling out of his obligations. (1978) ■ *Spectator*: Jilly Cooper was too kind-hearted to name those who weaseled out of the exercise. (1981)

To avoid at all costs

not touch something **with (the end of) a barge-pole (1893)** ■ Mrs Humphrey Ward: If he tries to leave me this funny old place . . . there are two can play at that game. I wouldn't touch it with a barge-pole. (1918)

not touch something **with a forty-foot pole (1903), with a ten-foot pole (1909)** ■ E. O. Schlunke: Attracting a lot of business of the more or less shady sort that our reputable men wouldn't touch with a forty-foot pole. (1958) ■ Paul Erdman: No respectable bank . . . would touch our business with a ten-foot pole. (1974)

avoid like the plague (1936) Compare earlier *avoid as the plague* (1835) ■ Ellis Peters: I will avoid him like the plague. (1979)

A narrow avoidance of danger

touch and go (1815)

squeak (1822) Dated; also used in the phrases *near squeak* and *tight squeak*; see also *narrow squeak* ■ Arthur Ransome: You oughtn't to have waited. It's going to be a squeak getting home across the Wade. (1939)

near go (1827) Dated ■ *Fraser's Magazine*: Which . . . would have been a near go for his neck. (1841)

narrow squeak (1833) ■ Anthony Trollope: 'It was a very narrow squeak,' Mr. Crawley said when his friend congratulated him on his escape. (1867)

close shave (1834) ■ Desmond Varaday: The leopard . . . tumbled in a heap between the crouching Freddie and me. . . . 'A very close shave,' I muttered. (1964)

close call (1881) Orig US ■ Josephine Tey: The exciting things of life—riding, love-making, rescue, close calls. (1949)

narrow shave (1892)

near thing (1894) Compare earlier sense, something barely effected ■ Desmond Varaday: When one moving coil lashed over the crocodile's head, Mulembe snapped at it with spiky-toothed jaws which almost bit through. . . . It was a near thing for the snake. (1964)

30. **Abandonment**

To discard, get rid of

chuck (c1879), chuck up (1864), chuck it (1888), chuck in (1944) From the notion of throwing a towel, sponge, etc. into the boxing ring as an admission of defeat (see at **Defeat** p. 421) ■ G. K. Chesterton: But the souls of Christian peoples. . . . Chuck it, Smith! (1915) ■ Freya Stark: This is my last on official paper, as I chuck this job on Friday week. (1933) ■ J. Tickell: Damn politics. Listen, I'll chuck it up and we'll go and live in Kerry. (1936) ■ *Independent*: The 24-year-old waitress chucked her job in to join the fight for independence. (1991)

sling (1902) Often followed by *in* or *up* ■ Kylie Tennant: We both slung in our jobs . . . and went off after him. (1953)

dump (1919) From earlier sense, deposit on a dump ■ Dal Stivens: Dumping me like this for a couple of dumb sailors. (1946)

ditch (1921) From earlier sense, throw into a ditch ■ Peter Kemp: Davis . . . was struggling to carry the heavy wireless set; I shouted to him to ditch it and save himself. (1958)

kiss goodbye to (1935) Usually implying an involuntary or unwelcome separation from something ■ Val Gielgud: If she chooses one of the Eltham team for a partner, poor George can kiss the trophy goodbye. (1970)

pack up (1942), pack in (1943) ■ *News of the World*: He has been ordered to pack in his job and return for the final four weeks of term. (1976)

dice (1943) Australian; from earlier sense, gamble away by playing dice ■ F. Hardy: No bastard puts my daughter in the family way then dices her . . . and gets away with it. (1963)

To abandon, leave

leave in the lurch (1596) Denoting abandoning someone in adverse circumstances

A person who avoids things

ostrich (1808) Applied to someone who avoids facing up to the reality of a situation; from the myth that ostriches bury their head in the sand when pursued because they cannot tell the difference between seeing and being seen ■ *Economist*: A characteristic of these American manufacturers of more modest means is that they are neither 'visionaries' nor 'ostriches'. (1987)

skiver (1941) Applied to someone who avoids work or duty; from *skive* + *-er* ■ *Daily Telegraph*: A Labour-controlled council is to crack down on 'skivers' following a report which alleges large scale absenteeism and sick leave among its manual workers. (1977)

dodger (1948) From *dodge* + *-er* ■ *Morning Star*: Heavier fines for TV and radio licence dodgers have been called for by the Postmaster General. (1969)

without assistance; from obsolete *lurch* a cheat, swindle, hence a state of discomfiture, apparently from obsolete French *lourche* game resembling backgammon, also in *demeurer lourche* be discomfited (originally in the game) ■ Douglas Adams: 'Left in the lurch by a lift,' muttered Zaphod, who was feeling at his least jaunty. (1979)

run out on (1920) ■ Dorothy Halliday: I decided I was going back to Rome. . . . Johnson, on whom I was running out, listened to me with patience. (1973)

leave holding (or to hold) the baby (1928) Denoting leaving someone else to deal with a difficult responsibility ■ P. G. Wodehouse: That gentle pity which the kind-hearted always feel when they regard the fellow whom Fate has called upon to be the Patsy, the Squidge or, putting it another way, the man who has been left holding the baby. (1953)

walk out on (1937) Originally applied to leaving a theatre before the performance is finished ■ *Daily Mail*: I don't feel you ought to walk out on the person you've lived with for years and years. (1991)

To stop attempting, give up on

give away (1948) Australian ■ P. Barton: It just wouldn't work. . . . The lunch gong sounded and everyone gave it away. (1981)

To weaken by withdrawing support

pull the rug (out) from under (1946) Orig US ■ *Detroit Free Press*: When the rug was pulled out from under me in movies and television I went back to the theater. (1978)

To be abandoned

stew in one's own juice (1885) In phrases implying that one has been left to suffer the (bad) consequences of one's actions; compare earlier obsolete *fry in one's own grease* and French *cuire dans son jus* ■ George Orwell: Office babus are the real rulers of this country now. . . . Best thing we can do is to shut up shop and let 'em stew in their own juice. (1934)

Rid of

shot of (1802) Orig dialectal; usually in the phrases *be shot of* and *get shot of*; perhaps from obsolete Scottish *shoot* avoid, escape ■ Richard Gordon: His love for his old hospital, like one's affection for the youthful homestead, increased steadily with the length of time he had been shot of it. (1952) ■ *Daily Telegraph*: Advising its members to make haste to get shot of unsuitable employees. (1976)

Index

even Stephen, even
  Steven 431
ever such 337
everything but (or
  except) the kitchen
  sink 400
ex 52
ex-con 114
exes, ex's, exs 189
expecting 21
eye 109
eye someone up 14
eyeball 13
eyeful 69
Eyetie, Eyety, Eyetye,
  Eytie, Eyto 34
eyewash 279, 335

F
fab 213
fabulous 213
face 44, 54, 274
face the music 107
face-ache 54, 223, 240
face-fungus 4
factory 110, 111
fade 360
faff about, faff around
  312
fag 81, 155, 250
fag hag 83
fag-end 156
fagged 22
faggot 46, 81
fair crack of the whip
  232
fair dinkum 232
fair do's 232
fair enough 332
fair go 232
fair shake 232
fair-haired boy 207
fairy 81
fake 351
fall 101, 113
fall about 237
fall apart at the seams
  415
fall down on 419
fall for 65, 313
fall guy 99, 313
fall money 182
fall over oneself 245
falsies 172
family jewels 6
fan 260, 428
fancy 209
fancy Dan 272
fancy man 71
fancy oneself 273
fancy pants 272

Fannie Mae 202
fanny 9, 10, 320, 321
fanny about, fanny
  around 312
Fanny Adams 135, 396
fantabulous 213
far out 62
far-out 213
farmer 121
fart 370
fart about (or around)
  206, 312
fash 366, 367
fast buck 191
fast one 282
fat cat 187
fat chance 402
fat is in the fire 241
fat lot 397
fat show 402
fat-head 307
fat-mouth 319, 321
father and mother of
  216
father of 216
fatso 12, 54
fatty 12, 54
fave 207
fave rave 207
faze 247
fearful 337
fearfully 336
Fed 108
fed up 239
feeb 230
feed 250
feed one's face 138
feed the bears 388
feeding 250
feel 73
feel no pain 152
feel someone's collar
  101
feel the pinch 188
feelthy 79
feisty 258
fella, fellah 45
feller 44
femme, fem 47, 83
fence 96
fender-bender 388
ferret 429
ferret something out
  429
fetch 260
fetch up 383
fever 246
fib 281, 282
fiddle 98, 171, 282, 284
fiddle and flute 171
fiddley-did, fiddley 185
fiddling 425

fiddly 407
fiend 162, 208
fifty-fifty 431
filbert 1
fill someone in 262
filth 110
filthy 222, 335
fin 186
finagle 285
financial 187
finger 95, 288, 289
fingers in the till 92
finif, finnif 186
finish 23
finito 416
fink 110, 224, 288, 289
finnip, fin(n), finny,
  fin(n)if(f), finnup,
  finuf 184
fire away 362
firewater 144
fireworks 256
first off 362
fish 42, 125, 186
fish-skin 186
Fisher 185
fist-fuck 78
fit 99
fit as a fiddle 29
fit to be tied 253
fit to burst 340
fit-up 99, 345
five o'clock shadow 4
five-finger discount 92
five-to-two 39
fiver 184, 186
fix 98, 161, 163
fix someone's wagon
  415
fix-up 161
fixture 361
fizgig, phizgig 289
fizz 138, 145
fizz-boat 391
fizzer, fizz 123, 290, 418
flab 12
flabbergast 247
flack 198
fladge, fladj, flage 78
flak 328
flake 305
flake out 28
flaky, flakey 304
flaming 339
flaming onions 125
flanker 282
flannel 279, 280
flannel-mouth 280
flap 266
flapdoodle 334
flapper 4
flash 78, 97, 164, 280

Flash Harry 273
flat 187
flat-foot 108
flat-footed 231
flat-head 308
flat-top 175, 391
flats 359
flatty, flattie 107
flea-bag 25, 227
flea-pit 346
fleas and itches 345
fleece 284
flick, flicker 344
flim 184
fling 234
Flip 36, 211, 235, 245, 257,
  305
flip one's lid 245
flip one's wig 245
flipper 4
flipping 339
flit 82, 386
flivver 389, 392, 417, 418
floater 31, 114, 409
flog 201, 378
flog a dead horse 231
floozie, floosie, floozy
  67
flop 12, 25, 417, 418
flop-house 25
flopperoo, floperoo
  418
flowery 111
flub 409, 413
fluff 409, 413, 419
flummox 241
flunk 315, 418, 419
flunk out 205, 316
flunk-out 418
flush 187
flutter 360
fly 298
fly boy 122
fly in the ointment 417
fly off the handle 254
fly-by-night 386
fly-flat 91, 312
flying boxcar 392
fogy, fogey 370
fold 419
folks 51
fool around 68
footer 356
footie, footy 73
footsie, footsy 73
footy, footie 356
foozle 356, 413
for a song 192
for a starter, for
  starters 362
for Christ's sake 341
for fuck's sake 343

get into 76
get into (or in on) the act 430
get into the act, get 429
get it in one 297
get it together 423
get it, get it hot, get it in the neck 243
get jerry (on, on to, to) 297
get knotted 276
get lost 384
get moving 362
get next (to or on) 297
get nowhere, not get anywhere 418
get off 166, 296, 351
get off on 77, 208
get off one's bike 254
get off someone's back 364
get off with 65
get on someone's quince 255
get on someone's tits 255
get on someone's wick 255
get on the band-wagon 430
get one's act together 423
get one's end away 77
get one's finger out 246
get one's knickers in a twist 255, 266
get one's leg over 77
get one's nuts off 77
get one's oar in 429
get one's rag out 254
get one's rocks off 76, 236
get one's shit together 423
get one's skates on 382
get outside (of) 138
get shot of 205
get shut of 205
get some 76
get some z's 24
get someone at it 331
get someone by the short and curlies 405, 422, 424
get someone by the short hairs 421
get someone over the barrel 422
get someone wrong 410

get someone's goat 255
get someone's nanny-goat, get someone's nanny 255
get someone's number 297
get someone's shirt out 255
get something off one's chest 319
get somewhere 410
get stuck in 362
get stuffed 276
get the breeze up 267
get the dead-wood on 405
get the drop on 405
get the (or a) guernsey 411
get the hang of 313
get the (or to) hell out 384
get the jump on 405
get the message 297
get the picture 297
get the wind up 267
get to 194
get to someone 255
get unstuck 385, 418
get up 174
get up someone's nose 255
get weaving 362
get wise (to) 297
get, git 384
get-up 169, 292
get-up-and-get 292
get-up-and-go 292
ghetto-blaster 344
G.I. can 125
Gib 374
giddy limit 401
gift 406
gig 13, 290, 347
gig-lamps 15
giggle 124
giggle-house 305
giggle-juice 142
giggle-water 142
gimme 210, 357, 407
gimmes 210
gimp 28, 269
ginger-beer, ginger 81
gink 13, 45
ginormous 394
ginzo, guinzo 34
gippo, gippy, gyp(p)o, gypoo 136
gippo, gypo, gyppo 35, 42
gippy, gyppie, gyppy 35, 42, 155

gippy tummy, gyppy tummy 19
gipsy, gypsy 387, 390
girls 47, 53
gism 292
gismo, gizmo 168
git 225
give 105, 316, 351
give away 192, 432
give head 78
give her (it, etc.) the gun 382
give it to someone (hot/hot and strong) 105
give over 363
give someone a bell 325
give someone a buzz 324
give someone a piece of one's mind 105
give someone a pull 66
give someone a serve 329
give someone a tinkle 324
give someone beans 427
give someone curry 105
give someone gyp, or gip 105
give someone hell 427
give someone the finger 275
give someone (or something) the once-over 14
give someone the pip 255
give someone the (or a) run-around 243
give someone the works 427
give something a miss 431
give something a rest 321
give something the up-and-down 14
give something up as a bad job 364
give-away 290
glad eye 64
glad hand 325
glad-hand 326
glad rags 169
glam 70, 219, 367, 368
glamour boy 122
glamour puss 69
glass-house 112
glitch 418
glitterati 272

glitz 280
glitzy 280
glob 397
glom 93, 210
glop 227
gnat's piss, gnats' piss 144
go 16, 138, 203, 247, 292, 293, 317, 367
go (in) off the deep end 254
go (off) with a bang 411
go (or be, do) gangbusters 411
go (out) for one's tea 404
go . . . on someone 206
go a (or dated) the) bundle on 208
go a mucker 418
go all the way (or the whole way) make 76
go and have a roll 385
go ape 266
go blooey, go blooie 416
go down 77, 113
go down the Swanee 415
go Dutch 188
go fly a kite 385
go for a Burton 31
go for broke 246, 404
go for the big spit 20
go for the doctor 246, 360
go great guns 411
go nowhere 418
go off 24, 77, 209
go on 207, 296, 318
go over 428
go overboard 208
go phut 415
go places 411
go poo-poo(s) 18
go some 246, 381
go someone scone-hot 105
go spare 254
go steady 80
go straight 277
go the knuckle 259
go through 93, 385, 428
go through the roof 255
go to market 254
go to pot 415
go to the bow-wows 415
go to the dogs 415
go to town 246
go west 31, 415

go with 80
go-getter 210, 293
go-getting 210
goalie 356
goat 66, 308
gob 3, 21, 121, 397
gob-smacked 248
gob-stick 350
gob-stopper 137
gob-struck 248
gobbet 397
gobbledygook,
  gobbledegook 320
gobby 121
gobdaw 311
gobs, a gob 399
gobshite 226
God forbid, Gawd
  forbid 39, 50, 170
God slot 344
God squad 128
God-botherer 128
God-box 129
god-damn, god-
  damned, god-dam
  338
God's gift 69, 272
Godawful 222
Godfrey 342
goer 66, 381
gofer, gopher 197
goggle 14
goggle-box 344
gogglers 2
goggles 15
going-over 104, 263
gold brick 425
gold-brick 285, 294, 295
gold-bricker 294
gold-dig 290
gold-digger 290
goldang, goldanged
  338
goldarn, goldarned,
  goldurn, goldurned
  338
golly 248
gonce, gons 181
gone 21, 213, 233
gone a million 420
gone goose, gone
  gosling 240
gone on 65, 209
goner 31, 240
gong 110, 124, 164
gonger 164
gongerine 164
gongoozler 14
gonzo 311, 349
goo 227, 232
goo-goo eyes 65
good and 337

good and proper 340
good buddy 63
good egg 237
good oil 322
good on you (him etc.)
  413
good one, good 'un 281
good shake 232
good show 237
good thing 412
good-o, good-oh 237
goods 96, 322, 425
goody 215
goody gumdrops 237
goody, goodee, goody
  goody 236
goody-goody 215
gooey 231
goof, goof-up 159, 163,
  295, 308, 409, 410, 414
goof around, goof 312
goof ball 310
goof ball, goof pill 157,
  158
goof off 312
goofus 309
goofy 306
goog 136
googie, googie egg,
  googy (egg) 136
gook 36, 42
goolies 8
goom 145
goombah, goomba,
  gumbah 62, 90
goomy, goomee 153
goon 114, 264, 309
gooney 308
goop 308
goopy 307
goorie, goory, goori
  131, 225
goose 38, 76, 330
gooseberry 66
goosed 416
goosegog 136
gopher ball 354
gorblimey, gaw-,
  -blime, -blimy 170,
  249
Gordon Bennett 250
gorgeous Gussie 70
gorm, gawm 308
gormless 306
gosh 248
gospel 277
got it made 404, 411
got it wired 405
got what it takes 426
gotcha, gotcher 297
got up like a dog's
  dinner 174

got up like a pox
  doctor's clerk 174
governor, guv'nor 51
grab 235
gracing, greycing 357
graft 88, 118, 193, 195
grafter 89, 195
gramp, gramps 52
gran 52
grand 182
grand(d)addy 395
grand-daddy (or
  granddaddy) of 216
grandad, grand-dad 52
grandaddy, grand-
  daddy 52
grandma 52
grandpa 52
grandpappy 52
grandpop 52
granny 52
granny flat 371, 376
grass 108, 159, 288, 289
grasser 290
grasshopper 108, 392
gravel agitator 120
gravel-crusher 120
gravel-grinder 120
gravy 190, 191
gravy boat 191
gravy train 191
grease 279
grease job 389
grease monkey 197
grease someone's palm
  194
grease-ball 35, 37
greaser 37, 278, 387, 389
greasy 280
greasy spoon 141
great 216, 300, 394
great girl's blouse 231
Great Smoke 373
green 159, 181, 366
green about the gills
  26
green fingers 301
green pea 366
green thumb 301
green-ass 366
greenback 186, 358
greener 365
greengage 345
greengages 190
greenhorn 365
greenhouse 392
greenie 358, 365
greens 73, 181
gremlin 358, 393
gremmie, gremmy 358
grey 40
grey matter 298

greyback 132
gricer 388
grid 391
grief 241
griff 322
griffin 322, 325
grift 88
grifter 89
grill 35, 429
grim 26
grind 250, 315, 353
gringo 39
gripe 327, 328
griper 328
gripes 27
grody, groady, groddy,
  groaty, etc. 223
grog 142
grog blossom 154
groin 173
groise, groize 313, 315
groiser, groizer 315
grommet, grommit 358
groove 66, 235, 236, 351,
  353
groovy 213, 367
grope 72
Groper 38
gross 223
gross out 227
gross-out 226
grot 177, 225, 227
grotty 222, 223
grouch 256, 327, 328
grouch-bag 193
grouchy 256
ground-hog 197
groupie, groupy 58, 68,
  352
grouse 213, 326, 328
grouser 328
grouter 404
grub 134
grumble 71
grump 256
grumps 256
grumpy 256
grunge 177, 227
grungy 178, 222, 223
grunt 121, 197
grunt work 195
gubbins 169, 309
guesstimate 408
guff 334
guinea, ginny, guinny
  35
guinea-pig 377
gump 130
gump, gumph 307
gumption 298
gumshoe 109
gumsucker 37

jakes 19

jalopy, gillopy, jalapa, jollopy, jalloppy, jaloppi(e) 370, 389

jam 271

jam jar 390

jam sandwich 110

jam-rag 21

jammy 402

jane 47

jankers 123

Jap 36, 126

jar 143

jasper 45, 378

jaunty, jaundy, jonty 119

java 138

jaw 274, 316, 317

jaw-bone 202

jazz 74, 76, 320

jazz (1918) 280

jazzbo, jasbo 41, 345

jazzing 74

jeepers, jeepers-creepers 249

Jeez(e), Geez(e), Jese, Jez 249

jeff, Jeff Davis 39

jelly 49, 69

jelly bean 87, 224

jelly roll 9, 74

jelly, gelly 177

jelly-bellied 12

jelly-belly 12

jerk 225

jerk off, jerk-off 79, 225

jerkwater 425

jerry 19, 34

jerry (to) 297

Jesse, jesse, jessie, jessy 263

jessie, jessy 82

Jesus Christ 257

Jesus H. Christ 257

Jesus, Jesus (H.) Christ 249

Jesus, Jesus wept 257

jet 387

Jew 199, 276

Jew boy 38

jew down 201

Jewing-bloke 199

jiffy 361

jig 41

jig is up 365

jig-a-jig, jig-jig 74

jig-time 361

jigaboo, jiggabo, jijjiboo, zigabo, etc. 41

jigger 168, 413

jiggered 342

jiggered up 23

jiggery-pokery 88

jiggle 379

jildi, jeldi, jildy, juldie, etc. 381

jills 44

jim 184

Jim Crow 41

jim-jams 154, 172, 265

jimmies 154, 265

Jimmy 58

Jimmy Britts, the jimmies, the Britts 267

Jimmy Grant, jimmygrant 42

Jimmy O'Goblin, jimmy o'goblin, jimmy, Jemmy O'Goblin 184

Jimmy Riddle, jimmy 17

Jimmy the One 58

Jimmy Woodser, Jimmy Wood(s) 153

jingle 181

jingling Johnny 196

jink 379

jism, chism, gism, jizz 292

jit 41

jitney 186

jitterbug 267, 352

jitters 265

jittery 266

jive 159, 280, 284, 320

jive-ass 287

jivey, jivy 293

Jixi, Jixie 388

joanna, joana, johanna, etc. 350

job 43, 88, 99, 168, 210

jobs for the boys 88

jock 6, 35, 134, 172, 353, 354, 357

jocker 82, 115

Joe 37, 45, 138

Joe Blake 133

Joe Bloggs 46

Joe Blow 45

Joe Doakes, Joe Dokes 45

Joe Public 45

Joe Soap 46, 313

joes 239

Joey, joey 185

John Hancock 343

John Henry 343

John Hop 108

John Law 108

John Roscoe 176

John Thomas 7

John, john 7, 86, 108

john, johnny 19

johndarm 107

johnny 79

Johnny Foreigner 42

Johnny, Johnnie 107

Johnson, Jim Johnson 7

joint 159, 164

joker 44

jollies 233

jollo 234

jollop 29, 142

jolly 122, 234, 235, 336

jolly along 320

jolly d 213

jolly someone along 422

jolly up 320

jolly-up 234

jolly well 340

jolt 113, 143, 161

jones, Jones 163

jonnop 108

josh, joss 330

joss-man 129

josser 45, 129, 308

journo 349

joy 412

joy-house 87

joy-juice 142

joy-popper 162

ju-ju 159

judy 47

jug 111, 193

juggins 308

jugs 5

juice 96, 142, 157, 393

juice up 292

juiced 151

juicer 153, 196

juke, jook, jouk 353

juke, jook, jouk, juke-house, juke-joint 87

Jumble 40

jumbo 394

jumbuck 132

jump 74, 292, 387

jump down someone's throat 105

jump on the band-wagon 430

jump salty 254

jumped-up 271

jumper 199

jumpy 266

jungle 116

jungle bunny 40

jungle juice 142

junk 156

junker 162, 166

junket 234

junkie 162

juvie, juvey 50, 89, 112

K

K 57

K, k 183, 398

kaffir, Kaffir 220

kagg 258

kale 181

kanga 132

kaput 416

kark, cark 31

karzy, carsey, carsy, karsey, karzey 19

Kate and Sidney 135

Kathleen Mavourneen 112

kaylied, kailed, kalied 151

kayo 218, 262

keel over 31, 380

keen 212

keen on 208

keep guessing 403

keep nit 14

keep on 319

keep on trucking 270

keep one's chin up 269

keep one's eyes peeled 14

keep one's eyes skinned 14

keep one's hair on 251

keep one's nose clean 206, 277

keep one's pecker up 269

keep one's shirt on 251

keep tabs on, keep (a) tab on 14

keep yow 14

keeper 355, 356

keister, keester, keyster 10, 173, 193

kelch, kelt, -tch, keltz 39

kelly 5, 170, 175

Kelly's eye 398

kerfuffle, kafuffle, kufuffle 252

kettle 173

key 161

Keystone 108

Khyber Pass, Khyber 10

ki-yi 130

kibosh, kybosh 414

kick 166, 170, 183, 244, 246, 368

kick around 317

kick ass 106

kick in 188

leg art 80
leg it 383
leg work 195
leg-pull 331
legal 387
legit 50, 88, 277, 347, 348
legless 152
legs eleven 398
lemon 1, 282, 289, 308, 313
lemon-game 282
lemony 253
length 75
les, les(s)ie, lessy, lez(z),
   lezzy 83
lesbo, lesbie 83
leso, lezo, lezzo 83
let in for 430
let it all hang out 236,
   278
let on 319
let one's hair down 236
let rip 382
let something ride 363
lettuce 181
letty 25
level with 277
liability 405
lib 118
libber 117
liberate 94
lick 199, 350, 380, 397, 419
lick (someone's) arse
   (or ass) 278
lickety-split, lickerty-,
   licketty-, -ity-, -oty-, -
   spit 380
licking 420
licks 329
lid 161, 170
lie 295
lie doggo 291
lie in 25
lie low 291
lie-about 294
lie-down 24
lie-in 295
life 112
life of Riley (or Reilly)
   233
lifer 113
lifer 57
lift 92
lift a finger 246
lift oneself (up) by
   one's (own)
   bootstraps 412
lift the (or one's) elbow
   148
lig 290, 295
ligger 290
light out 384
light up 156

light years 361
light-fingered 96
lightning 145
like a bat out of hell
   381
like a bomb 381
like a dose of salts 380
like a dream 413
like a hole in the head
   341
like a log 25
like a shag on a rock 63
like a shot 380
like anything 340
like billy-o 340
like crazy 340
like death warmed up
   23, 26
like fun 340
like gangbusters 381,
   413
like hell 340
like mad 340
like nobody's business
   341
like sin 340
like stink 340
like the back (end) of a
   bus 219
like the clappers 381
like the devil 340
like thirty cents 222
like(s) of 426
like falling off a log 406
like shelling
   peas/beans 406
like taking candy from
   a baby/child/ etc. 406
likely story 281
likely tale 281
Limey 33
limit 401
limo 390
line 162, 322, 324
line-shoot 273
line-shooter 273
linen-draper 349
lingo 325
lip 102, 274, 275, 320
lippy 274
lippy, lippie 174
liquefied 151
liquorice-stick 350
listener 2
lit 150
litter lout 178
litterbug 179
(little) bit of all right
   68, 218
(little) man in the boat
   9

littley 50
live it up 236
live stock 132
livid 253
(living) daylights out of
   340
lizzie 81, 83, 146, 389
load 28, 152, 398
loaded 150, 165
loads 398
loadsa 399
loaf 1, 294
loaf o(f) bread 30
loafer 293
lob 383
lobby-gow 196
local 147
locie, loci, lokey, etc.
   391
loco 302, 391
loco weed 159
lofty 395
loid, 'loid 91, 94
loiner 33
lolly 181
loner 64
long green 181
long johns 172
long on 399
long time no see 325
long-hair 299
long-sleever 146
loo 19
looey, looie, louie 58
loogan 309
look down one's nose
   275
look up 412
look-see 13
looker 69
loon 236, 305
loons, loon pants, loon
   trousers 171
loony bin 305
loony, looney 303
loony-doctor 306
looped 151
loopy 304
loose 251
loot 57, 181
lor, lor' 248
Lord Muck 272
lose 298
lose (or do (in)) one's
   block 254
lose one's nana 255
lose one's rag 255
loser 114
lot 54, 400
lots 398
lotsa 399
lotta, lotter 399

loud 16
loud-mouth 319
lounge lizard 67
louse 224
louse up 413
lousy 26, 220
lousy with 400
love juice 21
love-up 73
lover boy, lover man
   67, 72
loverly 217
low-down 322
low-heel 67
lowie, lowey 67
lubricate 194
lubricated 151
luck into 402
luck out 402
lug 2, 225, 379
lughole 2
lulu 217
lumber 73, 96, 101
lumme, lummy 249
lump 116, 134, 332
lumpy 149
lunatic soup 144
lunchbox 6
lunk 308
lunker 133, 394
lunkhead 308
lurgy, lurgi 26
lurk 88, 195, 291
lurked 421
lurkman 89
lush 153
lushy, lushie 153
luv 54

M

ma 51, 53, 369
Ma State, Ma 374
mac, mack 53
macaroni 34, 335
McCoy 424
machine 7, 389
mack, mac 87, 171
macker, macca 366
Maconochie 6, 135
mad 252, 253
mad about 208
mad keen on 208
mad mick 175
mad minute 123, 126
mad money 182
madam 226, 275, 280
made 90
made of money 187
madhouse 241
madly 336
mag 349
mag, meg 183, 317, 318

mog 130, 171

moggadored, mogodored 240

moggie, moggy 130

mojo 157, 160

moke 131

mole 48, 128

moley 177

moll 49, 84, 90, 95

mollock 76

molly the monk 152

molly-dook, molly-dooker, molly-duke 5

molo, mowlow 150

mom 51

momma 51

mommy 51

Monday-morning quarterback 330

mondo 214, 336, 337

money for jam 246, 406

money for old rope 246, 406

money-spinner 203

mong 131

moniker, monicker, monniker, monica, monekeer, etc. 343

monkey 50, 163, 182

monkey about (or around) 206

monkey island, monkey's island 391

monkey man 51

monkey parade, monkey's parade, monkeys' parade 66

monkey suit 171

monkey tricks 312

monkey-hurdler 351

monkey-man 424

monkey-shines 312

monster 394

Montezuma's revenge 19

month of Sundays 361

monty, monte 403

moo 181, 226

mooch 189, 190

mooch, mouch 378

moocher 190

moody 256, 280, 320, 425

mooey, moey, mooe 2, 3

moola, moolah 181

moon 9, 112, 144, 294

moon-eyed 149

mooner 293

moonlight 195, 386

moonlight flit 386

moonlighter 386

Moor 375

moose 36

mootah, mooter, moota, mootie, mota, muta, etc. 159

mop 350

moral 402

more like (it) 218

more than you can shake a stick at 398

Moreton Bay 290

morning-glory 417

morph 160

mortal 149

moscow 202

mosey 379

moss-back 370

mossback, mossy-back 61

mossie, mozzie 132

mossy 370

most 216

mostest 400

mot, mort 46

moth-eaten 371

mother 225

Mother Bunch 12, 219

mother-fucker, muthafucka 225

mother-fucking 340

mother-loving 340

mother-raper 225

mother-raping 340

mother's ruin 145

mothering 340

motherless 188, 337

motor 389

motor mouth 319

motser, motsa, motza, motzer 183, 403

move a finger 246

mouldy 125, 220, 239

mouse 27

mousetrap 136

mouth 273, 320

mouthful 55, 316

mouthpiece 102

mouthy 318

moxie 269, 292

moz, mozz 415

Mozart and Liszt 152

Mr Big 57

Mr Charlie 39

Mr Clean 277

Mrs. 51

mucho 336, 337, 399

muck about, muck around 206, 312

muck in 431

muck up, muck-up 413, 415

mucker 62, 380

mucking 339

mucky-muck 272

mud 137, 161

mud in your eye 155

mud-hook 4, 391

mud-hooks 11

mudder 131, 357

mudlark 131, 132

muff 9, 47, 85

muff-diver 78

mug 2, 90, 93, 147, 263, 312, 348

mug book 101

mug shot 101

mug up 138

mug up, mug up on 313

mug-faker 345

mug-up 139

mugger 95

muggins 307, 313

muggler 162

muggles 158

mule 98, 166

mulga wire, mulga 323

mullet-head 307

mullet-headed 306

Mulligan 357

mulligrubs 28

mum 51, 322

mum's the word 291, 322

mumbo jumbo 320

mummy 51

mumper 115

mumping 88, 194

mums 51

mumsy 51

munchie 134

munchies 134, 165

munga, manga, munger, mungey, mungy 134

mungaree, munjari 134

munt 41

murder 215, 243

murder one 103

murphy 136, 284

Murphy game, Murphy 283

Murphy's law 401

muscle 264, 422, 423

muscle in 429

muscle man 264, 423

mush 4, 73, 358

mush, moosh 2, 3, 53, 111, 134

mush-head 229

mushy 231

muso 352

mustang 119

mustard 300

mutt 131, 308

Mutt and Jeff 15, 124, 309

mutton-fisted 231

mutton-head 307

mutton-headed 306

muzzed 149

my (colonial, etc.) oath 340

my arse 296

my eye 296

my foot 296

my sainted aunt, my (holy, sacred, etc.) aunt 248

mystery 48, 85

N

nab 100, 107

nabe 373

nabes 346

naff 221, 369

naff off 385

naffing 340

Naffy 127

nag 131

nah, na 333

nail 76, 101, 260, 282

nailer 107

Nam, 'Nam 375

nan 52

nan-nan 52

nana 310

nana, nanna 52

nance 81

nancy, nancy-boy 81

nanny-goat 358

nap 25, 116

napoo, na poo, napooh 30, 102

napper 1

Nar Nar Goon 377

narc, nark, narco 109

narco 157

nark 223, 255, 256, 288, 289, 327, 363, 414

nark it 321

narker 289, 328

narks 27

narky 256

narrow shave 432

narrow squeak 432

nasho 122

natch 332

natter 317

natty 175, 367

naughty 74, 76, 79

nav 123

N.B.G., n.b.g. 220

N.C 322

near go 431

near the bone 274

not to be sneezed (or
  sniffed) at 218
not touch something
  with (the end of) a
  barge-pole 431
not touch something
  with a forty-foot pole
  431 notch 411
notch-house 87
nothing 333
nothing doing 333
nothing to write (or
  worth writing) home
  about 221
nowhere 220
nozzer 366
nozzle 3
N.S. 322
nuff said, nuf(f) ced,
  nuf(f) sed 322
nuke 140
nuke, (US) nook 124, 126
nully 311
number 47, 170, 195
number crunching 401
number one 16, 44
number two 18
nummy 217
nuppence 188
nut 1, 103, 192, 208, 260,
  305, 368
nut college 305
nut factory 305
nut-case 305
nut-house 305
nutmeg 356
nuts 8, 215, 276, 301
nuts about, nuts on
  208
nutso 304, 305
nutsy, nutsey 304
nutter 303
nuttery 305
nutty 137, 303
nymphet 70
nympho 67

O

oaf 308
oafo 310
OAO 62, 71
oater 347
oats 74
oats opera, oat opera
  347
obbo, obo 14, 111, 128
obit 349
obs 14
ocean wave 4
oceans 399
ocker, Ocker 38

ocky 132
O.D. 161, 166
odd bod 427
oddball 304, 305, 427
odds 431
odds and sods 120
O.D.V. 145
ofay 39
off 103
off (the) beam 410
off base 410
off colour 26
off it 31
off one's block 253
off one's chump 301
off one's conk 302
off one's gourd 302
off one's head 301
off one's nana 302
off one's nut 301
off one's onion 302
off one's own bat 64
off one's pannikin 302
off one's rocker 302
off one's rocket 302
off one's trolley 302
off the bat 380
off the beam 304
off the hooks 30
off the pace 405
off the wall 304
off-beat 427
office 325, 392
office copy 144
office hours 104
ogg, og 185
oggin 376
o'goblin 185
oik, oick 224
oil 181, 193, 279, 322
oil can 125
oil the knocker 194
oil-burner 371, 390
oiled 149
oily wad 121
oink 60
OK, ok, okay, okey,
  okey-doke, okey-
  dokey, etc. 218, 331,
  332, 366
oke 218
old bean 53
Old Bill 109, 110
old boot 219
old boy 51, 52, 369
old chap 53
old cock 52
Old Dart 374
old fellow 51
old flame 80
old fruit 53
old girl 51, 369

old hat 370
old lady 51
old man 7, 51, 53, 56
Old Nick 129
old pot 51
old rope 155
Old Scratch 129
old ship 121
old soldier 146, 156
Old Sparky 104
old stager 365
old sweat 121, 365
old thing 54
old woman 51
oldie, oldy 369
oldster 369
olive oil 326
Oliver, oliver 376
omee, omie 45, 347
on 164, 323
on a hiding to nothing
  240
on a plate 407
on a roll 411
on a whizzer 148
on about 328
on cloud nine 233
on cloud seven 233
on edge 266
on one's Jack Jones, on
  one's jack 63
on one's ownsome 64
on one's Pat Malone,
  on one's pat 63
on one's tod 64
on one's uppers 187
on spec 403, 404
on the (or a) bend 148
on the back burner 363
on the bash 86, 148
on the batter 148
on the beam 408
on the blink 416
on the button 408
on the cards 403
on the carpet 106
on the cheap 192
on the dot 361
on the double, at the
  double 380
on the fritz 416
on the game 86, 91
on the grass 114
on the green 345
on the ground floor
  362
on the job 77
on the knock 86
on the legit 277
on the level 277
on the make 66, 210
on the mat 106

on the mend 29
on the nail 202
on the nose 16, 408
on the outer 207
on the pan 106, 330
on the peg 106
on the pirate 66
on the piss 148
on the pull 66
on the razzle 235
on the rocks 140, 242,
  416
on the ropes 242
on the schnozz 408
on the shelf 207
on the sick 26
on the side 291
on the . . . side 341
on the skids 416
on the skite 148
on the slide 416
on the straight 277
on the streets (or
  street) 377
on the stump 118
on the take 194
on the tap 189
on the tiles 235
on the toboggan 416
on the turf 86
on the wagon 155
on the warpath 253
on your bike 386
oncer 185
one 206, 337
one foot in the grave
  369
one for the road 143
one of those, one of
  them 81
one of us 81
one-arm joint 141
one-arm(ed) bandit 360
one-horse 425
one-liner 346
one-lunger 389, 392
one-night stand 74
one-pipper 58
one-way pockets 276
one's arse, one's ass 44
one's ass off 341
one's name is on
  something 401
one's number is on
  something 401
one's number is up 31
oner 184
onion 1
onkus 222
oo-er, ooo-er 268
oodles 399
oof 180

ooftish 180
oofy 187
oojah, oojar, oojah-ka-
    piv, oojah-ma-flip 168
oojiboo 168
ook 177
ooky 178
oomph 68, 292
oonchook, oonshik,
    etc. 309
oont 130
op 30, 110, 126
open slather 332
open up 320
operator 206
O.P.M. 190
oppo 62
orderly buff 120
orderly dog 120
orderly pig 120
oreo 42
organ 7
orgy 400
original 427
ork 353
ornery 256
orphan 371, 390
ort 10
orthopod 29
oscar, Oscar 181
Oscar Asche 181
ostrich 432
other 74
other half 143
other side 374
other thing 73
OTT 401
ou 45
out 83, 102, 262, 369
out like a light 28
out of it 152, 165
out of one's gourd 302
out of one's mind
    (head, skull, tree, etc.)
    301, 302, 341
out of order 206
out of this world 217
out of whack 416
out to lunch 304
out-of-sight 212
outasight 212
outer 354, 357
outfit 43, 45, 54, 122, 164
outside 115, 127, 358
outside job 88
oven 6
over my dead body 333
over the fence 222
over the hill 371
over the moon 233
over the odds 401
over the wall 114

overhung 154
overshot 149
owner 57
Oxford scholar, Oxford
    185
oyster 322
Oz 38, 374
ozoner 346
Ozzie 38

P

pa 51
pacey, pacy 380
pack 177
pack in 432
pack something in 364
pack something up 364
pack up 416, 432
package 70, 91
packet 183, 241
pad 194, 360, 376
paddle one's own
    canoe 64
paddlefoot 120
paddy 256
Paddy Doyle 113
paddy wagon 110
Paddy Wester 121
Paddy, paddy 34
paddywhack,
    paddywack 256, 262
padre 129
pain 244
pain in the arse (or ass)
    244
pain in the neck 244
paint the town red 236
Pak 36
Paki 36
pal 52, 62, 63
pal around 63
palaver 252
pale about the gills 26
pale-face 40
pally 63
palm 194
palone, polone, polony
    48, 83
palooka, palooker,
    paluka 230, 355
palsy 63
palsy, palsie 62
palsy-walsy, palsie-
    walsie, palsey-walsey
    62, 63
pan 2, 261, 329
panhandle 190
panhandler 190
panic 235
panic stations 266, 267
pannikin 1
pansy, pansy-boy 82

panther juice,
    panther('s) piss,
    panther sweat 142
panto 347
pants off 341
pants rabbit 132
papa 51, 71
Pape 129
paper 285, 347, 359
paper-hanger 98
pappy 51
para 126
paralysed 151
paralytic 151
park 379
parky 372
parlour pink 117
parlour-house 86
parlour-jumper 95
parson's nose 137
part brass-rags 258
parts 373
party 126, 236
party pooper 417
pash 65
pass 66
pass in one's chips 31
pass in one's dinner
    pail 31
pass in one's marble 31
passenger 229, 293
passer 98
passion wagon 390
passion-killers 172
passman 114
past it 371
paste 261
pasties 172
pasting 263
Pat 34
patch 114, 377
patha patha, phata
    phata 75
pathetic 229
patootie 49, 70, 71
patsy 218, 313
patzer 355
pavement princess 85
paw 4
Pay 119
pay off 411
pay through the nose
    192
pay-off 193, 282, 360
paybob 119
payola 194
P.B.I. 120
PDQ, pdq 380
pea 57, 357
pea-brain 310
pea-brained 306
pea-soup 37

pea-souper 37, 372
peach 68, 214
peacherino,
    peacherine,
    peacheroo 69, 214
peachy 70, 212
peachy-keen 213
peaky 26
peanut 396
peanut gallery 346
peanuts 183, 396
pearl diver 141
pearlies 4, 266
pearly whites 4
peasant 225
peb 243
pebble 243, 270
peck 39, 72
peck horn 350
Peck's bad boy 50
pecker 7
peckerhead 225
peckerwood,
    peckawood 39
Peckham rye 171
peckish 141
peculiar 26
ped 387
pedigree 101
pee 16, 17
pee-wee 16
peel 11, 174
peeler 107
peep 288, 316
peepers 2
peeve 255
peeved 256
peg 3, 143, 325, 355
peg away 270
peg out 31
peg-house 87, 147
peggy 121
pego 7
pegs 11
pen 111
pen and ink, pen 16,
    144
pen-mate 196
pen-pusher 197
pencil 7
penguin 119, 392
penguin suit 171, 172
penman 98
penny drops 297
pennyweighter 95
pension off 371
penwiper 172
peola 41
people 51
pep 292
pep up 292
pep-pill 157

snooze 24
snoozer 45
snore-off 24
snorer 3
snork 50
snort 143, 161, 163
snorter 217
snot 21, 227
snot-rag 171, 228
snotnose 228, 366
snotty 57, 222, 271
snout 155, 156, 288, 289
snow 159, 164, 181, 279
snow bunny 358
snow job 280
snow-bird 36, 162
snow-job 279
snow-man 280
snowball's chance (in hell) 402
snowdrop 122
snozzler 215
snubby, snubbie 176
snuff 103, 104
snuff it 31
snuff out 103
snuff-box 3
snuffles 27
snuffy 149
snuggle-pup, snuggle-pupper, snuggle-puppy 70
snurge 228
so 81
so long 326
so so 221
so-and-so 44, 223
soak 148, 153, 202, 260, 329
soaked 149
soaker 153
soap 161, 180, 279, 347
soapy 280
sob 185
S.O.B., s.o.b. 224
sob sister 232, 349
sob story 232
sob stuff 232
sock 259, 262, 292, 351, 427
sock it to someone 260
sockeroo 218, 412
socko 212, 412
sod 45, 81, 224, 342, 408
sod it 257
sod off 385
sod this for a game of soldiers 257
sod-all 396
Sod's law 401
soda 406
sodding 339
sodding well 340

soft 406
soft on 65, 208
soft sawder 279
soft soap 279
soft touch, easy touch 313
soft-sawder 279
soft-soap 279
softy, softie 232
soixante-neuf 78
sold on 208
soldier 121, 293
soldier's farewell 343
solid 212, 407
solitary 112
sollicker, soliker 394
sollicking 394
some 217
some hope(s) 240
something 218
something else 217
something nasty in the woodshed 226
something the cat (has) brought in 178
son of a bitch, son-of-a-bitch, sonofabitch, sonuvabitch, etc. 45, 224, 257
song and dance 252
sonny boy 53
sonny, sonnie 53
sook 269
sool 263, 422
sooner 294
soor 227
sooty 41
soppy 231
sore 255
sore-head 256
sort 43, 48
sort of, sort o', sort a' 341
sort someone out 106
sort-out 259
sorta, sorter 341
sound off 327
sounds 350
soup 177, 243, 345, 358
soup and fish 171
soup gun 140
soup-strainer 4
souped-up 392
soupy, soupie 139
sourpuss 328
souse 147, 148, 153
soused 150
souvenir 93
sov 184
sozzle 149
sozzled 150
space out 166

spaced 165
spacey, spacy 165
spade 41
spag 34, 130, 137
spag bol 137
spaggers, spadgers 137
spaghetti 34
Spam can 391
Spam medal 124
spanking 380
spanner in the works 417
spare 71
spare tyre 12
spark out 28
spark-prop 173
sparkler 173
sparks 196, 344
sparky 293
sparrow cop 108
sparrow-brain 309
sparrow-fart 361
spastic 229, 230
spat 257
spaz out 27
spaz, spas 230
spazz out 27
-speak 325
speak 147
speakeasy 146
speako 147
spear 190, 204, 205
spear-carrier 57, 347
spec 58, 203, 322
special 30, 192
specimen 43
specky 15
specs, specks 14
speechify 320
speed 158, 164
speed cop 108
speed shop 393
speedball 143, 156
speedo 393
spelunker 355
spend 77
spend a penny 16
spew 20
spic, spick, spig, spik 37
spider 138
spiel 282, 320, 351, 360
spieler 286, 359, 360
spiff 368
spiffing 212, 367
spiffy 367
spiflicated, spifflicated 150
spiggoty, spiggity, spigotti, spigoty 37
spike 25, 128, 129, 154, 161, 163, 164, 252

spike-bozzle, spike-boozle 126
spiky 256
spill 319
spill one's guts (out) 320
spill the beans 319
spin 185, 401, 428
spinach 280
spindly 12
spine-bash 295
spine-basher 294
spinnaker 184
spit 371, 392, 426
spit blood 255, 268
spit chips 141, 254
spit out 316
spitchered 416
Spithead pheasant 136
spiv 88, 89, 368
spiv up 174
splash 137, 154, 158, 189
splendiferous 211
splib 41
splice 52
spliced 52
spliff, splif 159
split 48, 107, 288, 289, 385, 386, 430
split beaver 80
split one's sides 237
split pea 137
split up 80
split-arse, split-ass 274, 388
splitter 215
splosh 181
splurge 189
sponduli(c)k, spondoolick 188
spondulicks, -ics, -ix, spondoolicks, -iks, -ix 180
sponge 290
sponger 290
spook 41, 127, 268
spooked 267
spooky 268
spoon 65, 66
spoons 65
spoons with (or about, on) 65
sport 53, 215
spot 112, 143, 345, 346, 347, 371, 397
spot on 408
spout 176, 318
sprag 414
sprauncy, sprauntsy, sproncy 174
sprazer, spraser, sprasy, sprazey, etc. 185

straight 61, 84, 156, 163, 165, 277
straight and narrow 277
straight arrow 277
straight goods 277
straight leg 120
straight shooter 277
straight-up 277, 408
straighten out 409
straighten up 277
strain at the leash 245
strain the potatoes (or spuds) 17
strap-hanger 387
strapped 187
strawberry 28, 154
streak 12, 13, 381
street cred 55
streetman 89
streets ahead 216
stretch 102, 104, 112
strewth, streuth, 'strewth, 'strooth, 'struth, struth 249
(strictly) for the birds 220
strides 171
strike (it) lucky 411
strike a light 249
strike it rich 187
strike me blind (dead, pink), strike (me) 248
strike oil 410
string 87, 283
string out 166
string up 104
string-bean 13
striper 58
stripes 114
stripey 121
stroke 283
stroll on 250, 296
strong it 320
strong of 277
strong-arm 423
stroppy 256
struggle-buggy 370, 389
strung out 165
strut one's stuff 274
stubbies 171
stubble-jumper 196
stubby, stubbie 146
stuck on 65
stuck-up 59, 271
stud 45, 69, 213
student 162
stuff 76, 157, 180, 333
stuff and nonsense 296
stuff oneself 138
stuff one's face 138

stuffed shirt 272
stuma, stumer 266
stumblebum 230
stumer, stumor 97, 193, 417
stumer, stumor, stoomer 188
stump up 188
stumps 10
stung 150
stunned 151
stunner 68, 217
stunning 70, 217
stupe 307
sturks 239
sub 190, 391
sub-cheese, sub-cheeze, sub-chiz 400
sub-deb 47
subway alumni 356
suck 77, 226, 227, 278
suck around 278
suck up 278
suck-hole 225, 278
sucker 137, 168, 208, 284, 312
sucker for something 209
sucks 276
suds 145
sudser 347
suey pow, sueypow, sui pow 164
sug 201, 286
sugar 157, 160, 180, 257
sugar daddy 86
sugar, sugar-babe, sugar-baby, sugar-pie 54
suicide blonde 175
suit 197
suit someone down to the ground 426
suit someone's book 426
sulks 256
sumbitch 226
sun-worshipper 245
Sunday best 169
Sunday punch 263
sundowner 143
sunk 416
Sunny Jim, Sonny Jim 53
sunshine 53
super 57, 212, 316, 348
superfly 166
supergrass 290
sure 'nuff, sho' 'nuff 340
sure thing 332, 402

surf-bum 358
surface 25
surfie, surfy 358
surprise, surprise 250
sus, suss 99
sus (out), sus (out) 298
suss, sus 99, 429
sussed 323
susso 193
swacked 151
swag 96, 398
SWAK 324
SWALK 324
swallow 128, 313
swamper 115, 199
swank 272, 273
swanker 272
swankpot 272
swanky 367
swear blind 277
swear by 207
sweat 246, 265, 358, 422
sweat blood 246, 267
sweat it out 270
sweat on 265
sweat on the top line 265
sweat one's guts out 246
sweat-hog 314
swede-basher 196, 378
Sweeney, Sweeny 110
sweep 359
sweet 218, 338
sweet F. A. 396
sweet man 72
sweet nothings 321
sweet on 65
sweet talk 280
sweet-talk 279
sweetback, sweetback man 71, 87
sweetener 193
sweetheart 54
sweetie 54
sweetie pie 54
sweetie-pie 69
sweetmouth 279
sweets 158
swell 212, 368
swelled head 271
swiftie, swifty 283, 382
swig 139
swill 148
swimmingly 413
swindle sheet 283
swine 224, 408
swing 68, 104, 200, 236, 262, 292, 368, 411
swing both ways 84
swing man 166, 354
swing the gate 381

swing the lead 295
swinger 66, 368
swinging 293, 367
swingle 66
swingster 352
swipe 8, 93, 197, 224, 260, 262, 329
swipes, swypes 144
swipey 149
swish 82, 107, 367
swishing 106
switch 97
switch off 251
switch-hitter 84
switched on 367
swizz, swiz 233
swizzle 232
swizzled 149
swollen head 271
swollen-headed 271
swot, swat 313, 315
swy, swey, swi, zwei 185
swy, swey, swi, zwei, swy-up 359
syph, siph, siff 28
syphon the python 17
syrup of figs, syrup 175
sysop 197

T

ta 239
ta muchly 239
ta-ta 326
tab 2, 47, 123, 155, 157, 314, 349, 369
tab show 345
tabby 47
tabnab 137
tacky 178
tad 397
Taff 35
Taffia, Tafia 35
Taffy 35, 279
tag 261, 343, 388
Taig, Teague 129
tail 9, 71, 74, 75, 100
tail-end charlie 120
tailgate 387
tailor-made 155
take 76, 93, 96, 287, 420
take a back seat 424
take a dim view of 209
take a dive 421
take a fade 385
take a jerry (to) 297
take a lunar 13
take a powder 385
take a rain check 363
take a run-out powder 385
take a running jump (at oneself) 276

Tim 129
timbers 10, 355
time 112
tin 111, 180
tin back, tin arse, tin
  bum 402
tin ear 2
tin fish 125, 391
tin hare 357
tin hat 170
tin hats 150
tin lid 50
tin Lizzie 370, 389
Tin Pan Alley 348
tin-arsed 402
tincture 143
tinhorn 272
tinhorn gambler 359
tinhorn sport 228
tinker's cuss, a tinker's
  curse, a tinker's
  damn 396
tinkle 17
tinned dog 135
tinny 402
tinny, tinnie 146
Tinseltown 373
tip 178
tip off 103
tip one's hand(s) (or
  mitt) 319
tip someone off 323
tip someone the wink
  323
tip-off 322
tip-slinger 360
tip-top 211
tipping 212
tipple 142, 148
tippler 153
tipsy 149
tired and emotional
  152
tiswas, tizz-wozz 266
tit 46, 310
tit(s) and ass (or arse),
  tits and bums 80
titchy 395
titfer, titfa, titfor 170
tits 5
titter 46
titties 5
tizz, tiz 266
tizzy 266
tizzy, tizzey, tissey 183
to a T, to a tee 408
to go 140
to the wide 340
to-do 252
toad-stabber 176
toad-sticker 176
toadskin 186

tobacco baron 114
tober, tobur 346
toc emma, tock emma,
  toch emma 125
tochus, tochas, tochess,
  tuchus, tuchas,
  tokus, tocus 10
toco, toko 106
toddle 379, 383
todger, tadger 8
toe 381
toe-cover 221
toe-jam 177
toe-rag 224
toe-ragger 115
toey 266
toff 59, 215
toff up 174
toffee-nose 59, 272
toffee-nosed 59, 271
tog out 174
tog up 174
together 213, 251, 367
togs 169
Tojo 36
toke 134, 161, 163, 190
tom 47, 85, 86, 136, 173
Tom Thumb 145
tom, Tom 42
tom-cat 68
tom-tit 18
tomato 70
tomato sauce 131
tomfoolery 173
Tommy 120
tommy-rot 334
ton 183, 356, 380
ton-up 380
tonicked 150
tonk 8, 82, 310
tons 399
tonto 304, 305
too big for one's boots
  271
too big for one's
  breeches 271
too many chiefs and
  not enough Indians
  423
too much 212
too right 332
toodle-oo, tootle-oo,
  toodle-pip, tootle-pip
  326
tool 7, 175
tool up 177
tool-man 95
tooled up 177
toospeg 3
toot 19, 159, 162, 164
toothy-peg 3
tooting 337

toots 48
tootsy, tootsie, tootsy-
  wootsy, tootsie-
  wootsie, etc. 11, 47
top 57, 102
top banana 57, 346
top brass 56
top dog 57
top sergeant, top
  cutter, top kick, top
  kicker, top soldier 57
top someone up 147
top-heavy 149
top-notch 216
top-off, top-off man,
  top-off merchant
  289
top whack 182
topper 58, 170
topping 211
tops 216
topsy-turvy 178
torch 98, 99
torp 125, 144
torpedo 90, 157
torpedo juice 144
torqued 253
torso-tosser 353
tosh 53, 334
tosh, tush 185
tosheroon, tusheroon
  184
toss 428
toss in the towel 421
toss it in 364
toss off 79
toss-up 401
tosser 226
tot 169, 198
tot something together
  401
tot something up 401
total 388
totally 337
tote 386
tothersider 37
toto 132
totter 198
totty 47
touch 189
touch and go 403, 431
touch up 73
touched 303
tough 232, 263
tough act to follow 215
tough it out 270
tough nut 408, 428
tough shit 402
tough titty 402
toup 175
tourist trap 290
towel 261

towelhead 42
town clown 108
toy 164
toy boy 72
track 346
track with 65
tracks 166
trade 82, 85, 86, 128
train smash 137
traipse, trapes 378
tramlines 359
tramp 67, 205
trank, tranq 157
trannie 84
tranny 392
tranny, trannie 344
trap 3, 96, 107, 291
traps 350
trash 227, 329, 414
trashed 152, 416
tratt, trat 141
travel 381
treat 214
treff 128
tremendous 213
trendy 367, 368
trey, tray 112, 161, 398
trey, tray, trey-bit 185
tribe 51
trick 71, 74, 77, 86, 91, 113,
  200
trick cyclist 306
trickeration 283
tricksy 287
trigger man 264
trim 48, 74
trip 164, 166
tripe 221, 335
tripe-hound 228, 349
triple-A 125
tripped-out 165
trizzie, trizzy 185
trog 264, 378
trollies, trolleys 172
trombenik, trombenick
  272
troppo 302
trot 65, 117, 313, 369
trots 19
trouble and strife 51
trout 219
trump 57
try it on 283
try-on 282
T.S. 402
T.T.F.N. 326
tub 390, 391
tubby 12
tube 7, 156, 344
tube steak 136
tubular 214
tuck 134

473

widdle 17
wide 87
wide boy 90
widgie, weegie 61
widow 145
wienie 135
wife 81
wig out 254
wig-picker 306
wigging 104
wiggle 379
wiggy 304
wilco, willco 332
wild 244
wild about 208
wilding 92
William, william 186
willies 265
willy, willie 7
wimp 48, 230
wimp out 270
Wimpey, Wimpy 392
wimpish 229
wimpy 229
win hands down 421
win out 410
win through 410
wind 265
wind someone up 331
wind up 383
wind-up 265, 267, 331
windbag 319, 391
window-pane 15
windy 265, 267, 268
Windy City 373
wine dot 153
wing 4
wing and a prayer 388
wingco, winco, winko 58
wingding 164, 234
winger 62, 199
wingy 28
winkle 8
winkle-pin 176
winner 412
winny 135
wino 153
winter woollies 172
wipe 103, 205
wipe out 358, 380
wipe the floor with 419
wipe-out 103, 380, 420
wiped 23, 152, 165
wiped out 188
Wipers 374
wired 152, 165, 266
wise guy 299
wise off 331
wise someone up 323
wise up (to) 297
wise-ass 298, 299

wise-assed 298
wisenheimer, weisenheimer, wiseheimer 299
wish book 201
witch-doctor 306
with a ten-foot pole 431
with a vengeance 340
with it 301, 366
with knobs on 341
with one's pants down 405
with one's trousers down 405
within (a) cooee/cooey (of) 378
witter, whitter 318
wizard 212, 300
wobbler 252
wobbly 253
wodge, wadge 399
wog 29, 40, 42, 94, 132
wolf 67, 81
wolly, wally 109
wonder what hit one 247
wonga 182
wonk 40, 82, 228, 315, 366
wood-and-water joey 197
Woodbine 33
woodchuck 378
wooden 262
wooden cross 30
wooden kimono 32
wooden nickel, wooden money 97
wooden overcoat 32
wooden spoon 421
wooden suit 32
woodener 262
woodentop 109, 311
woodpecker 176
woodpile 350
woodshed 351
woodwork 356
woody, woodie 390
woof 138, 320
woofits 26, 239
woofter, wooftah 83
woolly 109, 170
woolly bear 125
Woop Woop 377
woopie, woopy 60, 369
woozy, whoosy, whoozy, woozey 27
wop 34, 344
word 106, 316
work like a charm 410
work someone over 261
work the tubs 93

workaholic 195
working girl 85
working stiff 197
works 164
world 375
worry-guts 267
worry-wart 267
worse for wear 371
wot no . . .? 396
wotcher, wotcha 325
wouldn't it 257
wow 208, 244, 249, 412
wowee 249
wowser 223, 328, 417
Wrac 120
Wraf 119
wrap it up 364
wrap something (a)round something 388
wrap something up 365
wrap up 321, 412
wreck 26
wrecked 152, 165
wren 48
Wren, wren 119
Wrennery 127
wriggle out 431
wriggler 133
wrinkly, wrinklie 369
wrong 'un 357
wrong side of 369
wuss 231

Y

yack, yak, yak-yak 318, 319
yacker, yakker 318, 319
yacket 318
yackety, yackity, yaketty, yakkety, yakkity 318
yackety-yack, yackety-yacket(y) 318, 319
yah boo, ya(a) boo 276
yah, ya, yar 332
Yahudi, Yehudi 39
yakka, yacca, yacka, yacker, yakker 195
Yank 36, 379
Yankee, (dated) Yankey, Yanky 36
yap 3, 317, 318, 319
yard 7, 182, 375
yardbird 114, 197, 366
yardie 90
yarn 281, 317, 324
yarra 302
yatter 318
yawn 250

yay 237
yay, yea 401
yeah 332
year dot 361
yech, yecch, yeck 209
yechy, yecchy 223, 232
yekke, Yekke, Yekkie 39
yell 238
yell blue murder 321, 327
yellow 269
yellow jack 28
yellow jacket 158
yellow peril 36
yellow-bellied 269
yellow-belly 269
yen 161, 209
yen-yen 163
yenta, yente 430
yentz 285
yep 332
yes siree, yes sirree 331
Yid 38
yike 258
yikes 250, 268
yippee, yip-ee 237
yips 266
yo 325
yo-yo 311
yob 264
yobbo, yobo 264
yock 237
yock, yok 238
yok 39, 237
yomp 123, 378
yonks 361
you bet, you bet you 332
you can't win 240
you could have knocked me down with a feather 248
you don't say 249
you don't say so 248
you know what 168
you wouldn't read about it 250
you're telling me 332
youee 387
yours truly 44
yuck, yuk 177, 209, 228, 237, 238
yuck it up, yuk it up 312
yucky, yukky 178, 223, 232
yum, yum yum 236
yum-yum 74, 233, 324
yum-yum girl, yum-yum tart 85